The Oxford Bank of New Words

Finalized new entries are deposited with The Oxford Bank of New Words, the database that feeds new editions of all Oxford dictionaries and which, typically, holds over 3,000 properly authenticated entries at any one time.

The British National Corpus

How are the words of our language actually used? What are the most frequently used meanings of common words? To answer such questions accurately Oxford uses The British National Corpus, an unrivalled balanced collection of 100 million words of text representing every kind of writing and speech in English. Using rapid computer search-and-analysis techniques, Oxford lexicographers can answer the most complex language queries.

OWLS The Oxford Word & Language Service

This is a unique word-help centre set up to answer special language-related questions raised by teachers, writers, specialist institutes, and everyday native-speakers of English worldwide.

The Oxford
Minireference
Thesaurus

The Oxford Minireference Thesaurus

Compiled by
ALAN SPOONER

CLARENDON PRESS · OXFORD

Oxford University Press, Great Clarendon Street, Oxford OX2 6DP

Oxford New York

Athens Auckland Bangkok Bogota Bombay
Buenos Aires Calcutta Cape Town Dar es Salaam
Delhi Florence Hong Kong Istanbul Karachi
Kuala Lumpur Madras Madrid Melbourne
Mexico City Nairobi Paris Singapore
Taipei Tokyo Toronto Warsaw

and associated companies in
Berlin Ibadan

Oxford is a trade mark of Oxford University Press

British Library Cataloguing in Publication Data

Data available

Library of Congress Cataloging in Publication Data
Spooner, Alan.
The Oxford minireference thesaurus / compiled by Alan Spooner.
p. cm.
1. English language—Synonyms and antonyms. I. Title.
423'.1—dc20 PE1591.S76 1992 91–44317
ISBN 0-19-860096-8

3 5 7 9 10 8 6 4 2

Printed in Great Britain by
Charles Letts (Scotland) Ltd., Dalkeith, Scotland

Contents

The Oxford Minireference Thesaurus

COMPILER AND EDITOR-IN-CHIEF
Alan Spooner

MANAGING EDITOR
Sara Tulloch
ASSISTANT EDITORS
Anne Knight   Christine Cowley

Preface

A THESAURUS helps you find the words you need to express yourself more effectively and more interestingly. This thesaurus is designed to combine within its small format maximum ease of use with maximum helpfulness. It includes a larger range of synonyms and other information than might be expected in a book of this size. Headwords are arranged in a simple alphabetical sequence, and the organization of each entry is straightforward and largely self-explanatory. Normally, you will find what you want under the headword you look up, though cross-references may be necessary if you need opposites, or if you want a larger range of words to choose from.

A thesaurus should be used with caution. Firstly, no synonym list should be regarded as 'complete'. Many could be extended, some almost indefinitely. Consider, for example, the variety of words we might substitute for (say) *good* or *pleasant*. Secondly, seldom in English are two words completely interchangeable. So-called synonyms may convey distinct nuances of meaning, or belong to different contexts, or carry different signals about the writer or intended reader – and so on. I hope, therefore, that this volume will be a useful resource, but not just as a lifeless repository of 'words to use': my main hope is that a thesaurus – even a small one like this – will prompt us to *think* about language, and enable us to exploit more fully our own knowledge and understanding of its complex processes.

ALAN SPOONER

Nottingham Polytechnic
November 1991

Using the thesaurus

In this thesaurus you will find

Headwords
The words you want to look up are printed in bold and arranged in a single alphabetical sequence. In addition, there may be sub-heads in bold at the end of main entries for derived forms and phrases.

Synonyms
Synonyms are listed alphabetically, except that distinct senses of a headword are numbered and treated separately.

   Under some headwords, in addition to the lists of synonyms given there, a cross-reference printed in SMALL CAPITALS takes you to another entry to provide an extended range of synonyms. These cross-references are marked by the arrowhead symbol ▷.

Related words
Lists of words which are not synonyms but which have a common relationship to the headword (eg, kinds of vehicle listed under *vehicle*) are printed in italic, flagged by the symbol □.

Antonyms
Cross-references printed in SMALL CAPITALS introduce you to lists of opposites. These cross-references are preceded by the abbreviation *Opp*.

Part-of-speech labels
Part-of-speech labels are given throughout. (See list of abbreviations.) Under each headword, uses as *adjective, adverb, noun,* and *verb* are separated by the symbol ●.

Illustrative phrases
Meanings of less obvious senses are indicated by illustrative phrases printed in *italic*.

Usage warnings
Usage markers in *italic* precede words which are normally informal, derogatory, etc. (See list of abbreviations.)

Abbreviations used in this thesaurus

Parts of speech

adj	adjective
adv	adverb
int	interjection
n	noun
prep	preposition
vb	verb

Other abbreviations

derog	normally used in a derogatory, negative, or uncomplimentary sense
fem	feminine
inf	normally used informally
joc	normally jocular or joking
old use	old-fashioned or obsolete
opp	opposites, antonyms
plur	plural
poet	poetic
sl	slang
Amer	word or phrase usually regarded as American usage.
Fr	word or phrase common in English contexts, but still identifiably French.
Ger	ditto German

Gr	ditto Greek
It	ditto Italian
Lat	ditto Latin
Scot	word or phrase usually regarded as Scottish usage.
▷	This symbol shows that you will find relevant information if you go to the word indicated.

A

abandon *vb* 1 evacuate, leave, quit, vacate, withdraw from. 2 break with, desert, *inf* dump, forsake, *inf* give someone the brush-off, jilt, leave behind, *inf* leave in the lurch, maroon, renounce, repudiate, strand, *inf* throw over, *inf* wash your hands of. 3 *abandon a claim.* abdicate, cancel, cede, *sl* chuck in, discard, discontinue, disown, *inf* ditch, drop, finish, forfeit, forgo, give up, postpone, relinquish, resign, scrap, surrender, waive, yield.

abbey *n* cathedral, church, convent, friary, monastery, nunnery, priory.

abbreviate *vb* abridge, compress, condense, curtail, cut, digest, edit, précis, prune, reduce, shorten, summarize, trim, truncate. Opp LENGTHEN.

abdicate *vb* renounce the throne, *inf* step down. ▷ ABANDON, RESIGN.

abduct *vb* carry off, kidnap, *inf* make away with, seize.

abhor *vb* detest, execrate, loathe, recoil from, shudder at. ▷ HATE.

abhorrent *adj* abominable, detestable, disgusting, execrable, horrible, loathsome, nauseating, obnoxious, odious, offensive, repellent, repugnant, repulsive, revolting. ▷ HATEFUL. Opp ATTRACTIVE.

abide *vb* 1 accept, bear, brook, endure, put up with, stand, *inf* stomach, submit to, suffer,

tolerate. 2 ▷ STAY. **abide by** ▷ OBEY.

ability *n* aptitude, bent, brains, capability, capacity, cleverness, competence, expertise, facility, faculty, flair, genius, gift, intelligence, knack, *inf* know-how, knowledge, means, potential, potentiality, power, proficiency, prowess, qualification, resources, scope, skill, strength, talent, training, wit.

ablaze *adj* afire, aflame, aglow, alight, blazing, burning, fiery, flaming, incandescent, lit up, on fire, raging. ▷ BRILLIANT.

able *adj* 1 accomplished, adept, capable, clever, competent, effective, efficient, experienced, expert, gifted, *inf* handy, intelligent, masterly, practised, proficient, qualified, skilful, skilled, strong, talented, trained. Opp INCOMPETENT. 2 allowed, at liberty, authorized, available, eligible, equipped, fit, free, permitted, prepared, ready, willing. Opp UNABLE.

abnormal *adj* aberrant, anomalous, atypical, *inf* bent, bizarre, curious, deformed, deviant, distorted, eccentric, erratic, exceptional, extraordinary, freak, funny, heretical, idiosyncratic, irregular, *inf* kinky, malformed, odd, peculiar, perverse, perverted, queer, singular, strange, uncharacteristic, uncommon, unexpected, unnatural, unorthodox, unrepresentative, untypical,

1

unusual, wayward, weird.
Opp NORMAL.

abolish *vb* abrogate, annul,
cancel, delete, destroy, dispense
with, do away with, eliminate,
end, eradicate, finish, *inf* get rid
of, invalidate, liquidate, nullify,
overturn, put an end to, quash,
repeal, remove, rescind, revoke,
suppress, terminate, withdraw.
Opp CREATE.

abominable *adj* abhorrent,
appalling, atrocious, awful,
base, beastly, brutal, contemptible, cruel, despicable, detestable, disgusting, distasteful,
dreadful, execrable, foul, hateful, heinous, horrible, immoral,
inhuman, inhumane, loath-
some, nasty, nauseating, obnoxious, odious, offensive, repellent, repugnant, repulsive,
revolting, terrible, vile.
▷ UNPLEASANT. *Opp* PLEASANT.

abort *vb* 1 be born prematurely,
die, miscarry. 2 *abort take-off*.
call off, end, halt, nullify, stop,
terminate.

abortion *n* 1 miscarriage,
premature birth, termination of
pregnancy. 2 ▷ MONSTER.

abortive *adj* fruitless, futile,
ineffective, ineffectual, pointless, stillborn, unavailing,
unfruitful, unproductive,
unsuccessful, useless, vain.
Opp SUCCESSFUL.

abound *vb* be plentiful, flourish,
prevail, swarm, teem, thrive.

abrasive *adj* biting, caustic,
galling, grating, harsh, hurtful,
irritating, rough, sharp.
▷ UNKIND. *Opp* KIND.

abridge *vb* abbreviate,
compress, condense, curtail,
cut, digest, edit, précis, prune,
reduce, shorten, summarize,

telescope, truncate.
Opp EXPAND.

abridged *adj* abbreviated, bowd-
lerized, censored, compact,
concise, condensed, cut, edited,
inf potted, shortened, tele-
scoped, truncated.

abrupt *adj* 1 disconnected,
hasty, headlong, hurried,
precipitate, quick, rapid,
sudden, swift, unexpected,
unforeseen, unpredicted. 2 *an
abrupt drop*. precipitous, sharp,
sheer, steep. 3 *an abrupt
manner*. blunt, brisk, brusque,
curt, discourteous, gruff, impolite, rude, snappy, terse, unceremonious, uncivil, ungracious.
Opp GENTLE, GRADUAL.

absent *adj* 1 away, *sl* bunking
off, gone, missing, off, out, playing truant, *inf* skiving.
Opp PRESENT. 2 ▷ ABSENT-
MINDED.

absent-minded *adj* absent,
absorbed, abstracted, careless,
day-dreaming, distracted,
dreamy, far-away, forgetful,
heedless, impractical, inattentive, oblivious, preoccupied,
scatterbrained, thoughtless,
unaware, unheeding, unthinking, vague, withdrawn, wool-
gathering. *Opp* ALERT.

absolute *adj* 1 categorical,
certain, complete, conclusive,
decided, definite, downright,
entire, full, genuine, implicit,
inalienable, indubitable, infallible, *inf* out-and-out, perfect,
positive, pure, sheer, supreme,
sure, thorough, total, unadulterated, unalloyed, unambiguous, unconditional, unequivocal, unmitigated, unmixed,
unqualified, unquestionable,
unreserved, unrestricted, utter.
2 *absolute ruler*. almighty, auto-

absorb vb 1 assimilate, consume, devour, digest, drink in, fill up with, hold, imbibe, incorporate, ingest, mop up, receive, retain, soak up, suck up, take in, utilize. Opp EMIT. 2 absorb a blow. cushion, deaden, lessen, reduce, soften. 3 absorb a person. captivate, engage, engross, enthrall, fascinate, involve, occupy, preoccupy. ▷ INTEREST. **absorbed** ▷ INTERESTED.

absorbent adj absorptive, permeable, pervious, porous, spongy. Opp IMPERVIOUS.

absorbing adj engrossing, fascinating, gripping, riveting, spellbinding. ▷ INTERESTING.

abstain vb abstain from avoid, cease, decline, deny yourself, desist from, eschew, forgo, give up, go without, refrain from, refuse, reject, renounce, resist, shun, withhold from.

abstemious adj ascetic, austere, frugal, moderate, restrained, self-denying, self-disciplined, sober, sparing, teetotal, temperate. Opp SELF-INDULGENT.

abstract adj 1 abstruse, academic, hypothetical, indefinite, intangible, intellectual, metaphysical, notional, philosophical, theoretical, unpractical, unreal, unrealistic. Opp CONCRETE. 2 abstract art. non-pictorial, non-representational, symbolic. ● n digest, outline, précis, résumé, summary, synopsis.

cratic, despotic, dictatorial, omnipotent, sovereign, totalitarian, tyrannical, undemocratic. 3 absolute opposites. inf dead, diametrical, exact, precise.

abstruse adj complex, cryptic, deep, devious, difficult, enigmatic, esoteric, hard, incomprehensible, mysterious, mystical, obscure, perplexing, problematical, profound, puzzling, recherché, recondite, unfathomable. Opp OBVIOUS.

absurd adj anomalous, crazy, daft, eccentric, farcical, foolish, grotesque, idiotic, illogical, incongruous, irrational, laughable, ludicrous, nonsensical, outlandish, paradoxical, preposterous, ridiculous, risible, senseless, silly, stupid, surreal, unreasonable, untenable, zany. ▷ FUNNY, MAD. Opp RATIONAL.

abundant adj ample, bounteous, bountiful, copious, excessive, flourishing, full, generous, lavish, liberal, luxuriant, overflowing, plenteous, plentiful, prodigal, profuse, rampant, rank, rich, well-supplied. Opp SCARCE.

abuse n 1 assault, cruel treatment, ill-treatment, maltreatment, misappropriation, misuse, perversion. 2 verbal abuse. curse, execration, imprecation, insult, invective, obloquy, obscenity, slander, vilification, vituperation. ● vb 1 batter, damage, exploit, harm, hurt, ill-treat, injure, maltreat, manhandle, misemploy, misuse, molest, rape, spoil, treat roughly. 2 abuse verbally. affront, berate, be rude to, inf call names, castigate, criticize, curse, defame, denigrate, disparage, insult, inveigh against, libel, malign, revile, slander, inf slate, inf smear, sneer at, swear at, traduce, upbraid, vilify, vituperate, wrong. ▷ COMPLIMENT.

abusive *adj* acrimonious, angry, censorious, contemptuous, critical, cruel, defamatory, denigrating, derisive, derogatory, disparaging, harsh, hurtful, impolite, injurious, insulting, libellous, obscene, offensive, opprobrious, pejorative, profane, rude, scathing, scornful, scurrilous, slanderous, vituperative. *Opp* KIND, POLITE.

abysmal *adj* 1 bottomless, boundless, deep, extreme, immeasurable, incalculable, infinite, profound, unfathomable, vast. 2 ▷ BAD.

abyss *n inf* bottomless pit, chasm, crater, fissure, gap, gulf, hole, opening, pit, rift, void.

academic *adj* 1 educational, pedagogical, scholastic. 2 bookish, brainy, clever, erudite, highbrow, intelligent, learned, scholarly, studious, well-read. 3 *academic study*. abstract, conjectural, hypothetical, impractical, intellectual, notional, pure, speculative, theoretical, unpractical.
● *n inf* egghead, highbrow, intellectual, scholar, thinker.

accelerate *vb* 1 *inf* do a spurt, *inf* get a move on, go faster, hasten, increase speed, pick up speed, quicken, speed up. 2 bring on, expedite, promote, spur on, step up, stimulate.

accent *n* 1 brogue, cadence, dialect, enunciation, inflection, intonation, pronunciation, sound, speech pattern, tone. 2 accentuation, beat, emphasis, force, prominence, pulse, rhythm, stress.

accept *vb* 1 acquire, get, *inf* jump at, receive, take,

welcome. 2 acknowledge, admit, assume, bear, put up with, reconcile yourself to, resign yourself to, submit to, suffer, tolerate, undertake. 3 *accept an argument*. abide by, accede to, acquiesce in, adopt, agree to, approve, believe in, be reconciled to, consent to, defer to, grant, recognize, *inf* stomach, *inf* swallow, take in, *inf* wear, yield to. *Opp* REJECT.

acceptable *adj* 1 agreeable, appreciated, gratifying, pleasant, pleasing, welcome, worthwhile. 2 adequate, admissible, appropriate, moderate, passable, satisfactory, suitable, tolerable, unexceptionable. *Opp* UNACCEPTABLE.

acceptance *n* acquiescence, agreement, approval, consent, willingness. *Opp* REFUSAL.

accepted *adj* acknowledged, agreed, axiomatic, canonical, common, indisputable, recognized, standard, undeniable, undisputed, universal, unquestioned. *Opp* CONTROVERSIAL.

accessible *adj* approachable, at hand, attainable, available, close, convenient, *inf* get-at-able, *inf* handy, reachable, ready, within reach. *Opp* INACCESSIBLE.

accessory *n* 1 addition, adjunct, appendage, attachment, component, extension, extra, fitting. 2 ▷ ACCOMPLICE.

accident *n* 1 blunder, chance, coincidence, contingency, fate, fluke, fortune, hazard, luck, misadventure, mischance, misfortune, mishap, mistake, *inf* pot luck, serendipity. 2 calamity, catastrophe, collision, *inf* contretemps, crash, derailment, disaster, *inf* pile-up, *sl* shunt, wreck.

accidental *adj* adventitious, arbitrary, casual, chance, coincidental, *inf* fluky, fortuitous, fortunate, haphazard, inadvertent, lucky, random, unconscious, unexpected, unforeseen, unfortunate, unintended, unintentional, unlooked-for, unlucky, unplanned, unpremeditated. *Opp* INTENTIONAL.

acclaim *vb* applaud, celebrate, cheer, clap, commend, exalt, extol, hail, honour, laud, praise, salute, welcome.

accommodate *vb* 1 aid, assist, equip, fit, furnish, help, oblige, provide, serve, suit, supply. 2 *accommodate guests*. billet, board, cater for, entertain, harbour, hold, house, lodge, provide for, *inf* put up, quarter, shelter, take in. 3 *accommodate yourself to new surroundings*. accustom, adapt, reconcile.
accommodating ▷ CONSIDERATE.

accommodation *n* board, home, housing, lodgings, pied-à-terre, premises, shelter. □ *apartment, barracks, inf bedsit, bedsitter, billet, boarding house, inf digs, flat, guest house, hall of residence, hostel, hotel, inn, lodge, married quarters, motel, pension, rooms, self-catering, timeshare, youth hostel.* ▷ HOUSE.

accompany *vb* 1 attend, chaperon, conduct, convoy, escort, follow, go with, guard, guide, look after, partner, squire, *inf* tag along with, travel with, usher. 2 be associated with, be linked with, belong with, coexist with, coincide with,

complement, occur with, supplement.

accompanying *adj* associated, attached, attendant, complementary, concomitant, connected, related.

accomplice *n* abettor, accessory, ally, assistant, associate, collaborator, colleague, confederate, conspirator, helper, *inf* henchman, partner.

accomplish *vb* achieve, attain, *inf* bring off, carry off, carry out, carry through, complete, conclude, consummate, discharge, do successfully, effect, execute, finish, fulfil, perform, realize, succeed in.

accomplished *adj* adept, expert, gifted, polished, proficient, skilful, talented.

accomplishment *n* ability, attainment, expertise, gift, skill, talent.

accord *n* agreement, concord, congruence, harmony, rapport, unanimity, understanding.

account *n* 1 bill, calculation, check, computation, invoice, receipt, reckoning, *inf* score, statement, tally. 2 chronicle, commentary, description, diary, explanation, history, log, memoir, narration, narrative, portrayal, record, report, statement, story, tale, version, *inf* write-up. 3 *no account.* advantage, benefit, concern, consequence, consideration, importance, interest, merit, profit, significance, standing, use, value, worth.
account for ▷ EXPLAIN.

accumulate *vb* accrue, agglomerate, aggregate, amass, assemble, bring together, build up, collect, come together, gather,

grow, heap up, hoard, increase,
mass, multiply, pile up, stack
up, *inf* stash away, stockpile,
store up. Opp DISPERSE.

accumulation *n inf* build-up,
collection, conglomeration,
gathering, growth, heap, hoard,
mass, pile, stock, stockpile,
store, supply.

accurate *adj* authentic, careful,
certain, correct, exact, factual,
faithful, faultless, meticulous,
minute, nice, perfect, precise,
reliable, right, scrupulous,
sound, *inf* spot-on, strict, sure,
true, truthful, unerring, veracious. Opp INACCURATE.

accusation *n* allegation, alleged
offence, charge, citation,
complaint, denunciation,
impeachment, indictment,
summons.

accuse *vb* arraign, attack,
blame, bring charges against,
censure, charge, condemn,
denounce, hold responsible,
impeach, impugn, incriminate,
indict, inform against, make
allegations against, *inf* point
the finger at, prosecute,
summons, tax. Opp DEFEND.

accustomed *adj* common,
conventional, customary, established, expected, familiar,
habitual, normal, ordinary,
prevailing, regular, routine, set,
traditional, usual, wonted. get
accustomed ▷ ADAPT.

ache *n* anguish, discomfort,
distress, hurt, pain, pang,
smart, soreness, suffering,
throbbing, twinge. ● *vb* 1 be
painful, be sore, hurt, pound,
smart, sting, suffer, throb.
2 ▷ DESIRE.

achieve *vb* 1 accomplish, attain,
bring off, carry out, complete,

conclude, consummate,
discharge, do successfully,
effect, engineer, execute, finish,
fulfil, manage, perform, succeed
in. 2 *achieve fame*. acquire,
earn, gain, get, obtain, procure,
reach, score, win.

acid *adj* sharp, sour, stinging,
tangy, tart, vinegary.
Opp BLAND, SWEET.

acknowledge *vb* 1 accede,
accept, acquiesce, admit,
affirm, agree, allow, concede,
confess, confirm, declare,
endorse, grant, own up to,
profess, yield. Opp DENY.
2 *acknowledge a greeting*.
answer, notice, react to, reply
to, respond to, return.
3 *acknowledge a friend*. greet,
hail, recognize, salute, *inf* say
hello to. Opp IGNORE.

acme *n* apex, crown, culmination, height, highest point,
maximum, peak, pinnacle,
summit, top, zenith. Opp NADIR.

acquaint *vb* advise, announce,
apprise, brief, disclose, divulge,
enlighten, inform, make aware,
make familiar, notify, reveal,
tell.

acquaintance *n* 1 awareness,
familiarity, knowledge, understanding. 2 ▷ FRIEND.

acquire *vb* buy, come by, earn,
get, obtain, procure, purchase,
receive, secure.

acquisition *n* accession, addition, *inf* buy, gain, possession,
prize, property, purchase.

acquit *vb* absolve, clear, declare
innocent, discharge, dismiss,
exculpate, excuse, exonerate,
find innocent, free, *inf* let off,
liberate, release, reprieve, set
free, vindicate. Opp CONDEMN.
acquit yourself ▷ BEHAVE.

acrid *adj* bitter, caustic, harsh, pungent, sharp, unpleasant.

acrimonious *adj* abusive, acerbic, angry, bad-tempered, bitter, caustic, censorious, churlish, cutting, hostile, hot-tempered, ill-natured, ill-tempered, irascible, mordant, peevish, petulant, quarrelsome, rancorous, sarcastic, sharp, spiteful, tart, testy, venomous, virulent, waspish. *Opp* PEACEABLE.

act *n* 1 achievement, action, deed, effort, enterprise, exploit, feat, move, operation, proceeding, step, undertaking. 2 *act of parliament*. bill [= *draft act*], decree, edict, law, order, regulation, statute. 3 *a stage act*. item, performance, routine, sketch, turn. ● *vb* 1 behave, carry on, conduct yourself, deport yourself. 2 function, have an effect, operate, serve, take effect, work. 3 *Act now!* do something, get involved, make a move, react, take steps. ▷ BEGIN. 4 *act a role*. appear (as), assume the character of, *derog* camp it up, characterize, dramatize, enact, *derog* ham it up, imitate, impersonate, mime, mimic, *derog* overact, perform, personify, play, portray, pose as, represent, seem to be, simulate. ▷ PRETEND.

acting *adj* deputy, interim, provisional, stand-by, stopgap, substitute, surrogate, temporary, vice-.

action *n* 1 act, deed, effort, endeavour, enterprise, exploit, feat, measure, performance, proceeding, process, step, undertaking, work. 2 activity, drama, energy, enterprise, excitement, exercise, exertion,

initiative, liveliness, motion, movement, vigour, vitality. 3 *action of a play*. events, happenings, incidents, story. 4 *action of a watch*. functioning, mechanism, operation, working, works. 5 *military action*. ▷ BATTLE.

activate *vb* actuate, animate, arouse, energize, excite, fire, galvanize, *inf* get going, initiate, mobilize, motivate, prompt, rouse, set in motion, set off, start, stimulate, stir, trigger.

active *adj* 1 agile, animated, brisk, bustling, busy, dynamic, energetic, enterprising, enthusiastic, functioning, hyperactive, live, lively, militant, moving, nimble, *inf* on the go, restless, spirited, sprightly, strenuous, vigorous, vital, vivacious, working. 2 *active support*. assiduous, committed, dedicated, devoted, diligent, employed, engaged, enthusiastic, hard-working, industrious, involved, occupied, sedulous, staunch, zealous. *Opp* INACTIVE.

activity *n* 1 action, animation, bustle, commotion, energy, excitement, hurly-burly, hustle, industry, life, liveliness, motion, movement, stir. 2 hobby, interest, job, occupation, pastime, project, pursuit, scheme, task, undertaking, venture. ▷ WORK.

actor, actress *n* artist, artiste, lead, leading lady, performer, player, star, supporting actor, trouper, walk-on part. ▷ ENTERTAINER. **actors** cast, company, troupe.

actual *adj* authentic, bona fide, certain, confirmed, corporeal, current, definite, existing, factual, genuine, indisputable, in existence, legitimate, living, material, real, realistic, tangible, true, truthful, unquestionable, verifiable. *Opp* IMAGINARY.

acute *adj* 1 narrow, pointed, sharp. 2 *acute pain*. cutting, excruciating, exquisite, extreme, fierce, intense, keen, piercing, racking, severe, sharp, shooting, sudden, violent. 3 *an acute mind*. alert, analytical, astute, canny, *inf* cute, discerning, incisive, intelligent, keen, observant, penetrating, perceptive, percipient, perspicacious, quick, sharp, shrewd, *inf* smart, subtle. ▷ CLEVER. 4 *an acute problem*. compelling, crucial, decisive, immediate, important, overwhelming, pressing, serious, urgent, vital. 5 *an acute illness*. critical, serious. *Opp* CHRONIC, DULL, STUPID.

adapt *vb* 1 acclimatize, accommodate, accustom, adjust, attune, become conditioned, become hardened, become inured, fit, get accustomed (to), get used (to), habituate, harmonize, orientate, reconcile, suit, tailor, turn. 2 *adapt to a new use*. alter, amend, change, convert, metamorphose, modify, process, rearrange, rebuild, reconstruct, refashion, remake, remodel, reorganize, reshape, transform, vary. ▷ EDIT.

add *vb* annex, append, attach, combine, integrate, join, put together, *inf* tack on, unite. *Opp* DEDUCT. **add to** ▷ INCREASE. **add up (to)** ▷ TOTAL.

addict *n* 1 alcoholic, *sl* dope-fiend, *sl* junkie, *inf* user. 2 *a TV addict*. ▷ ENTHUSIAST.

addiction *n* compulsion, craving, dependence, fixation, habit, obsession.

addition *n* 1 adding up, calculation, computation, reckoning, totalling, *inf* totting up. 2 accession, accessory, accretion, addendum, additive, adjunct, admixture, afterthought, amplification, annexe, appendage, appendix, appurtenance, attachment, continuation, development, enlargement, expansion, extension, extra, increase, increment, postscript, supplement.

additional *adj* added, extra, further, increased, more, new, other, spare, supplementary.

address *n* 1 directions, location, whereabouts. 2 *deliver an address*. discourse, disquisition, harangue, homily, lecture, oration, sermon, speech, talk. • *vb* 1 accost, apostrophize, approach, *inf* buttonhole, engage in conversation, greet, hail, salute, speak to, talk to. 2 *address an audience*. give a speech to, harangue, lecture. **address yourself to** ▷ TACKLE.

adept *adj* accomplished, clever, competent, expert, gifted, practised, proficient. ▷ SKILFUL. *Opp* UNSKILFUL.

adequate *adj* acceptable, all right, average, competent, fair, fitting, good enough, middling, *inf* OK, passable, presentable, respectable, satisfactory, *inf* so-so, sufficient, suitable, tolerable. *Opp* INADEQUATE.

adhere *vb* bind, bond, cement, cling, fuse, glue, gum, paste, stick. ▷ FASTEN.

adherent n aficionado, devotee, disciple, fan, follower, inf hanger-on, supporter.

adhesive adj glued, gluey, gummed, self-adhesive, sticky.

adjoining adj abutting, adjacent, bordering, closest, contiguous, juxtaposed, nearest, neighbouring, next, touching. Opp DISTANT.

adjourn vb break off, defer, discontinue, dissolve, interrupt, postpone, prorogue, put off, suspend.

adjournment n break, delay, interruption, pause, postponement, prorogation, recess, stay, stoppage, suspension.

adjust vb 1 adapt, alter, amend, arrange, balance, change, convert, correct, modify, position, put right, rectify, re-fashion, regulate, remake, remodel, reorganize, reshape, set, set to rights, tailor, temper, tune, vary. 2 acclimatize, accommodate, accustom, conform, fit, habituate, harmonize, reconcile yourself.

administer vb 1 administrate, command, conduct affairs, control, direct, govern, head, lead, manage, organize, oversee, preside over, regulate, rule, run, superintend, supervise. 2 administer justice. apply, carry out, execute, implement, prosecute. 3 administer medicine. deal out, dispense, distribute, dole out, give, hand out, measure out, mete out, provide, supply.

administrator n boss, bureaucrat, civil servant, controller, director, executive, head, manager, managing director, derog mandarin, organizer, superintendent. ▷ CHIEF.

admirable adj awe-inspiring, commendable, creditable, deserving, enjoyable, estimable, excellent, exemplary, fine, great, honourable, laudable, likeable, lovable, marvellous, meritorious, pleasing, praiseworthy, valued, wonderful, worthy. Opp CONTEMPTIBLE.

admiration n appreciation, approval, awe, commendation, esteem, hero-worship, high regard, honour, praise, respect. Opp CONTEMPT.

admire vb applaud, appreciate, approve of, be delighted by, commend, enjoy, esteem, have a high opinion of, hero-worship, honour, idolize, laud, like, look up to, love, marvel at, praise, respect, revere, think highly of, value, venerate, wonder at. ▷ LOVE. Opp HATE. **admiring** ▷ COMPLIMENTARY, RESPECTFUL.

admission n 1 access, admittance, entrance, entrée, entry. 2 acceptance, acknowledgement, affirmation, agreement, avowal, concession, confession, declaration, disclosure, profession, revelation. Opp DENIAL.

admit vb 1 accept, allow in, grant access, let in, provide a place (in), receive, take in. 2 admit guilt. accept, acknowledge, agree, allow, concede, confess, declare, disclose, divulge, grant, own up, profess, recognize, reveal, say reluctantly. Opp DENY.

adolescence n boyhood, girlhood, growing up, puberty, inf your teens, youth.

adolescent adj boyish, girlish, immature, juvenile, pubescent, puerile, teenage, youthful.

• *n* boy, girl, juvenile, minor, *inf* teenager, youngster, youth.

adopt *vb* 1 accept, appropriate, approve, back, champion, choose, embrace, endorse, espouse, follow, *inf* go for, patronize, support, take on, take up. 2 befriend, foster, stand by, take in, *inf* take under your wing.

adore *vb* adulate, dote on, glorify, honour, idolize, love, revere, reverence, venerate, worship. ▷ ADMIRE. *Opp* HATE.

adorn *vb* beautify, decorate, embellish, garnish, grace, ornament, trim.

adrift *adj* 1 afloat, anchorless, drifting, floating. 2 aimless, astray, directionless, lost, purposeless, rootless.

adult *adj* developed, full-grown, full-size, grown-up, marriageable, mature, nubile, of age. *Opp* IMMATURE.

adulterate *vb* alloy, contaminate, corrupt, debase, defile, dilute, *inf* doctor, pollute, taint, thin, water down, weaken.

advance *n* betterment, development, evolution, forward movement, growth, headway, improvement, progress.
• *vb* 1 approach, bear down, come near, forge ahead, gain ground, go forward, make headway, make progress, *inf* make strides, move forward, press ahead, press on, proceed, progress, *inf* push on. *Opp* RETREAT. 2 *science advances*. develop, evolve, grow, improve, increase, prosper, thrive. 3 *advance your career*. accelerate, assist, benefit, boost, expedite, facilitate, further, help the progress of, promote.

Opp HINDER. 4 *advance a theory*. adduce, cite, furnish, give, present, propose, submit, suggest. 5 *advance money*. lend, loan, offer, pay, proffer, provide, supply. *Opp* WITHHOLD.

advanced *adj* 1 latest, modern, sophisticated, ultra-modern, up-to-date. 2 *advanced ideas*. avant-garde, contemporary, experimental, forward-looking, futuristic, imaginative, innovative, inventive, new, novel, original, pioneering, progressive, revolutionary, trend-setting, unconventional, unheard-of, *inf* way-out. 3 *advanced maths*. complex, complicated, difficult, hard, higher. 4 *advanced for her age*. grown-up, mature, precocious, sophisticated, well-developed. *Opp* BACKWARD, BASIC, OLD.

advantage *n* 1 aid, asset, assistance, benefit, boon, convenience, gain, help, profit, service, use, usefulness. 2 *have an advantage*. dominance, edge, *inf* head start, superiority. **take advantage of** ▷ EXPLOIT.

advantageous *adj* beneficial, constructive, favourable, gainful, helpful, invaluable, positive, profitable, salutary, useful, valuable, worthwhile. ▷ GOOD. *Opp* USELESS.

adventure *n* 1 chance, enterprise, escapade, exploit, feat, gamble, incident, occurrence, operation, risk, undertaking, venture. 2 danger, excitement, hazard.

adventurous *adj* 1 audacious, bold, brave, courageous, daredevil, daring, enterprising, *derog* foolhardy, heroic, intrepid, *derog* rash, *derog* reckless, valiant, venture-

some. 2 *an adventurous trip.*
challenging, dangerous, difficult, eventful, exciting, hazardous, perilous, risky.
Opp UNADVENTUROUS.

adversary *n* antagonist,
attacker, enemy, foe, opponent,
rival. *Opp* FRIEND.

adverse *adj* 1 antagonistic,
attacking, censorious, critical,
derogatory, disapproving,
hostile, hurtful, inimical, negative, uncomplimentary, unfavourable, unfriendly, unkind,
unsympathetic. 2 *adverse conditions.* contrary, deleterious,
detrimental, disadvantageous,
harmful, inappropriate, inauspicious, opposing, prejudicial,
uncongenial, unfortunate,
unpropitious. *Opp* FAVOURABLE.

advertise *vb* announce, broadcast, display, flaunt, make
known, market, merchandise,
notify, *inf* plug, proclaim, promote, promulgate, publicize,
inf push, show off, *inf* spotlight,
tout.

advertisement *n inf* advert,
announcement, bill, *inf* blurb,
TV break, circular, commercial, hand-out, leaflet, notice,
placard, *inf* plug, poster, promotion, publicity, *old use* puff,
sign, *inf* small ad.

advice *n* admonition, caution,
counsel, guidance, help, opinion, recommendation, suggestion, tip, view, warning.
▷ NEWS.

advisable *adj* expedient, judicious, politic, prudent, recommended, sensible. ▷ WISE.
Opp SILLY.

advise *vb* 1 admonish, advocate,
caution, counsel, encourage,
enjoin, exhort, guide, instruct,

prescribe, recommend, suggest,
urge, warn. 2 ▷ INFORM.

adviser *n* cicerone, confidant(e),
consultant, counsellor, guide,
mentor.

advocate *n* 1 apologist, backer,
champion, proponent,
supporter. 2 ▷ LAWYER.
● *vb* argue for, back, champion,
endorse, favour, recommend,
speak for, uphold.

aerodrome *n* airfield, airport,
airstrip, landing-strip.

aesthetic *adj* artistic, beautiful,
cultivated, in good taste, sensitive, tasteful. *Opp* UGLY.

affair *n* 1 activity, business,
concern, interest, issue, matter,
operation, project, question,
subject, topic, transaction,
undertaking. 2 circumstance,
episode, event, happening, incident, occasion, occurrence,
proceeding, thing. 3 *love affair.*
affaire, amour, attachment,
intrigue, involvement, liaison,
relationship, romance.

affect *vb* 1 act on, agitate, alter,
attack, change, concern,
disturb, grieve, have an effect
on, have an impact on, *inf* hit,
impinge on, impress, influence,
modify, move, pertain to,
perturb, relate to, stir, touch,
transform, trouble, upset.
2 *affect an accent.* adopt,
assume, feign, *inf* put on.
▷ PRETEND.

affectation *n* artificiality, insincerity, mannerism, posturing,
pretension. ▷ PRETENCE.

affected *adj* 1 artificial,
contrived, insincere, mannered,
inf put on, studied, unnatural.
▷ PRETENTIOUS. 2 *affected by
disease.* afflicted, attacked,
damaged, distressed, hurt,

infected, injured, poisoned, stricken, troubled.

affection n amity, attachment, feeling, fondness, friendliness, friendship, liking, partiality, regard, *inf* soft spot, tenderness, warmth. ▷ LOVE. *Opp* HATRED.

affectionate adj caring, doting, fond, kind, tender, warm. ▷ LOVING. *Opp* ALOOF.

affinity n closeness, compatibility, fondness, kinship, likemindedness, likeness, liking, rapport, relationship, resemblance, similarity, sympathy.

affirm vb assert, attest, aver, avow, confirm, declare, maintain, state, swear, testify.

affirmation n assertion, avowal, confirmation, declaration, oath, promise, pronouncement, statement, testimony.

affirmative adj agreeing, assenting, concurring, confirming, consenting, positive. *Opp* NEGATIVE.

afflict vb affect, annoy, bedevil, beset, bother, burden, cause suffering to, distress, grieve, harass, harm, hurt, oppress, pain, pester, plague, rack, torment, torture, trouble, try, vex, worry, wound.

affluent adj 1 flourishing, *inf* flush, *sl* loaded, moneyed, *usu derog* plutocratic, prosperous, rich, wealthy, *inf* wellheeled, well-off, well-to-do. 2 *affluent life-style*. expensive, gracious, lavish, luxurious, opulent, pampered, self-indulgent, sumptuous. *Opp* POOR.

afford vb 1 be rich enough, find enough, have the means, manage to give, sacrifice, spare, *inf* stand. 2 ▷ PROVIDE.

afloat adj aboard, adrift, at sea, floating, on board ship, under sail.

afraid adj 1 aghast, agitated, alarmed, anxious, apprehensive, *inf* chicken, cowardly, cowed, craven, daunted, diffident, faint-hearted, fearful, frightened, hesitant, horrified, horror-struck, intimidated, jittery, nervous, panicky, panicstricken, pusillanimous, reluctant, scared, terrified, terrorstricken, timid, timorous, trembling, uneasy, unheroic, *inf* windy, *inf* yellow. *Opp* CONFIDENT, FEARLESS. 2 *[inf] I'm afraid I'm late.* apologetic, regretful, sorry, unhappy. **be afraid** ▷ FEAR.

afterthought n addendum, addition, appendix, extra, postscript.

age n 1 advancing years, decrepitude, dotage, old age, senescence, senility. 2 *a bygone age.* days, epoch, era, generation, period, time. 3 *[inf] ages ago.* aeon, lifetime, long time. ● vb decline, degenerate, develop, grow older, look older, mature, mellow, ripen. **aged** ▷ OLD.

agenda n list, plan, programme, schedule, timetable.

agent n broker, delegate, emissary, envoy, executor, *old use* functionary, go-between, intermediary, mediator, middleman, negotiator, proxy, representative, spokesman, spokeswoman, surrogate, trustee.

aggravate vb 1 add to, augment, compound, exacerbate, exaggerate, heighten, increase, inflame, intensify, magnify, make more

serious, make worse, worsen.
Opp ALLEVIATE. **2** [Some think
this use wrong.] ▷ ANNOY.

aggressive *adj* antagonistic,
assertive, attacking, bellicose,
belligerent, bullying, *sl* butch,
contentious, destructive,
hostile, jingoistic, *sl* macho,
militant, offensive, provocative,
pugnacious, pushful, *inf* pushy,
quarrelsome, violent, warlike,
zealous. *Opp* DEFENSIVE, PEACE-
ABLE.

aggressor *n* assailant, attacker,
belligerent, instigator, invader.

agile *adj* acrobatic, active,
adroit, deft, fleet, graceful,
limber, lissom, lithe, lively,
mobile, nimble, quick-moving,
sprightly, spry, supple, swift.
Opp CLUMSY, SLOW.

agitate *vb* **1** beat, churn,
convulse, ferment, froth up,
ruffle, shake, stimulate, stir,
toss, work up. **2** alarm, arouse,
confuse, discomfit, disconcert,
disturb, excite, fluster, incite,
perturb, rouse, shake up, stir
up, trouble, unnerve, unsettle,
upset, worry. *Opp* CALM. **agitated** ▷ EXCITED, NERVOUS.

agitator *n Fr* agent provocateur,
demagogue, firebrand, rabble-
rouser, revolutionary, trouble-
maker.

agonize *vb* be in agony, hurt,
labour, struggle, suffer, worry,
wrestle.

agony *n* anguish, distress,
suffering, torment, torture.
▷ PAIN.

agree *vb* **1** accede, accept,
acknowledge, acquiesce, admit,
allow, assent, be willing,
concede, consent, covenant,
grant, make a contract, pledge
yourself, promise, undertake.

2 accord, be unanimous, be
united, coincide, concur,
conform, correspond, fit, get on,
harmonize, match, *inf* see eye
to eye, suit. *Opp* DISAGREE.
agree on ▷ CHOOSE. **agree
with** ▷ ENDORSE.

agreeable *adj* acceptable,
delightful, enjoyable, nice.
▷ PLEASANT. *Opp* DISAGREE-
ABLE.

agreement *n* **1** accord, affinity,
compatibility, compliance,
concord, conformity, congruence, consensus, consent,
consistency, correspondence,
harmony, similarity, sympathy,
unanimity, unity. **2** acceptance,
alliance, armistice, arrangement, bargain, bond, compact,
concordat, contract, convention, covenant, deal, *Fr* entente,
pact, pledge, protocol, settlement, treaty, truce, understanding. *Opp* DISAGREEMENT.

agricultural *adj* **1** agrarian,
bucolic, pastoral, rural. **2** *agricultural land.* cultivated,
farmed, planted, productive,
tilled.

agriculture *n* agronomy, crofting, cultivation, farming, growing, husbandry, tilling.

aground *adj* beached, grounded,
helpless, high-and-dry,
marooned, shipwrecked, stranded, stuck.

aid *n* advice, assistance, avail,
backing, benefit, collaboration,
contribution, cooperation,
donation, encouragement, funding, grant, guidance, help, loan,
patronage, prop, relief, sponsorship, subsidy, succour, support.
● *vb* abet, assist, back, befriend,
benefit, collaborate with,
contribute to, cooperate with,

encourage, facilitate, forward, help, *inf* lend a hand, profit, promote, prop up, *inf* rally round, relieve, subsidize, succour, support, sustain.

ailing *adj* diseased, feeble, infirm, poorly, sick, suffering, unwell, weak. ▷ ILL.

ailment *n* affliction, disease, disorder, infirmity, malady, sickness. ▷ ILLNESS.

aim *n* ambition, aspiration, cause, design, desire, destination, direction, dream, end, focus, goal, hope, intent, intention, mark, object, objective, plan, purpose, target, wish.
• *vb* 1 address, beam, direct, fire at, focus, level, line up, point, send, sight, take aim, train, turn, zero in on. 2 *aim to win.* aspire, attempt, design, endeavour, essay, intend, mean, plan, propose, resolve, seek, strive, try, want, wish.

aimless *adj* chance, directionless, pointless, purposeless, rambling, random, undisciplined, unfocused, wayward. *Opp* PURPOSEFUL.

air *n* 1 airspace, atmosphere, ether, heavens, sky, *poet* welkin. 2 *fresh air.* breath, breeze, draught, oxygen, waft, wind, *poet* zephyr. 3 *air of authority.* ambience, appearance, aspect, aura, bearing, character, demeanour, effect, feeling, impression, look, manner, mien, mood, quality, style. • *vb* 1 aerate, dry off, freshen, refresh, ventilate. 2 *air opinions.* articulate, disclose, display, exhibit, express, give vent to, make known, make public, put into words, show off, vent, voice.

aircraft *n old use* flying-machine. □ *aeroplane, airliner, airship, balloon, biplane, bomber, delta-wing, dirigible, fighter, flying boat, glider, gunship, hang-glider, helicopter, jet, jumbo, jump-jet, microlight, monoplane, plane, seaplane, turboprop, VTOL (vertical take-off and landing).*

airman *n* aviator, flier, pilot.

airport *n* aerodrome, airfield, air strip, heliport, landing-strip, runway.

airy *adj* blowy, breezy, draughty, fresh, open, spacious, ventilated. *Opp* STUFFY.

aisle *n* corridor, gangway, passage, passageway.

akin *adj* allied, related, similar.

alarm *n* 1 alert, signal, warning. □ *alarm-clock, bell, fire-alarm, gong, siren, tocsin, whistle.* 2 anxiety, apprehension, consternation, dismay, distress, fright, nervousness, panic, trepidation, uneasiness. ▷ FEAR.
• *vb* agitate, daunt, dismay, distress, disturb, panic, *inf* put the wind up, scare, shock, startle, surprise, unnerve, upset, worry. ▷ FRIGHTEN.
Opp REASSURE.

alcohol *n sl* bevvy, *inf* booze, drink, hard stuff, intoxicant, liquor, spirits, wine.

alcoholic *adj* brewed, distilled, fermented, *sl* hard, inebriating, intoxicating, spirituous, *inf* strong. • *n* addict, dipsomaniac, drunkard, inebriate, toper. *Opp* TEETOTALLER.

alert *adj* active, agile, alive (to), attentive, awake, careful, circumspect, eagle-eyed, heedful, lively, observant, on the alert, on the lookout, *inf* on the qui vive, on the watch, on your guard, on your toes, perceptive, quick, ready, responsive, sensitive, sharp-eyed, vigilant, wary, watchful, wide-awake. *Opp* ABSENT-MINDED, INATTENTIVE. ● *vb* advise, alarm, caution, forewarn, give the alarm, inform, make aware, notify, signal, tip off, warn.

alibi *n* excuse, explanation.

alien *adj* exotic, extra-terrestrial, foreign, outlandish, remote, strange, unfamiliar. ● *n* foreigner, newcomer, outsider, stranger.

alight *adj* ablaze, afire, aflame, blazing, bright, burning, fiery, ignited, illuminated, lit up, live, on fire, shining. ● *vb* come down, come to rest, descend, disembark, dismount, get down, get off, land, perch, settle, touch down.

align *vb* 1 arrange in line, line up, place in line, straighten up. 2 *align with the opposition.* affiliate, agree, ally, associate, co-operate, join, side, sympathize.

alike *adj* akin, analogous, close, cognate, comparable, corresponding, equivalent, identical, indistinguishable, like, matching, parallel, related, resembling, similar, the same, twin, uniform. *Opp* DISSIMILAR.

alive *adj* 1 active, animate, breathing, existent, existing, extant, flourishing, in existence, live, living, *old use* quick, surviving. 2 *alive to new ideas.* ▷ ALERT. *Opp* DEAD.

allay *vb* alleviate, assuage, calm, check, compose, diminish, ease, lessen, lull, mitigate, moderate,

mollify, pacify, quell, quench, quiet, quieten, reduce, relieve, slake (*thirst*), soften, soothe, subdue. *Opp* STIMULATE.

allegation *n* accusation, assertion, charge, claim, complaint, declaration, deposition, statement, testimony.

allege *vb* adduce, affirm, assert, asseverate, attest, aver, avow, claim, contend, declare, depose, insist, maintain, make a charge, plead, state.

allegiance *n* devotion, duty, faithfulness, *old use* fealty, fidelity, loyalty, obedience.

allergic *adj* antagonistic, antipathetic, averse, disinclined, hostile, incompatible (with), opposed.

alleviate *vb* abate, allay, ameliorate, assuage, check, diminish, ease, lessen, lighten, make lighter, mitigate, moderate, pacify, palliate, quell, quench, reduce, relieve, slake (*thirst*), soften, soothe, subdue, temper. *Opp* AGGRAVATE.

alliance *n* affiliation, agreement, association, bloc, bond, cartel, coalition, combination, compact, concordat, confederation, connection, consortium, covenant, entente, federation, guild, league, marriage, pact, partnership, relationship, syndicate, treaty, understanding, union.

allot *vb* allocate, allow, apportion, assign, award, deal out, *inf* dish out, dispense, distribute, divide out, *inf* dole out, give out, grant, mete out, provide, ration, set aside, share out.

allow *vb* 1 approve, authorize, bear, consent to, enable, endure, grant permission for, let, license, permit, *inf* put up with, sanction, *inf* stand, suffer, support, tolerate. *Opp* FORBID. **2** acknowledge, admit, concede, grant, own. **3** ▷ ALLOT. *Opp* DENY.

allowance *n* **1** allocation, allotment, amount, measure, portion, quota, ration, share. **2** alimony, annuity, grant, maintenance, payment, pension, pocket money, subsistence. **3** *allowance on the full price.* deduction, discount, rebate, reduction, remittance, subsidy. **make allowances for** ▷ TOLERATE.

alloy *n* admixture, aggregate, amalgam, blend, combination, composite, compound, fusion, mixture.

allude *vb* **allude to** hint at, make an allusion to, mention, refer to, speak of, suggest, touch on.

allure *vb* attract, beguile, bewitch, cajole, charm, coax, decoy, draw, entice, fascinate, inveigle, lead on, lure, magnetize, persuade, seduce, tempt.

allusion *n* hint, mention, reference, suggestion.

ally *n* abettor, accessory, accomplice, associate, backer, collaborator, colleague, companion, comrade, confederate, friend, helper, helpmate, *inf* mate, partner, supporter. *Opp* ENEMY. ● *vb* affiliate, amalgamate, associate, band together, collaborate, combine, confederate, cooperate, form an alliance, fraternize, join, join forces, league, *inf* link up, marry, merge, side, *inf* team up, unite.

almighty *adj* **1** all-powerful, omnipotent, supreme. **2** ▷ BIG.

almost *adv* about, all but, approximately, around, as good as, just about, nearly, not quite, practically, virtually.

alone *adj* apart, by yourself, deserted, desolate, forlorn, friendless, isolated, lonely, lonesome, on your own, separate, single, solitary, solo, unaccompanied, unassisted.

aloof *adj* chilly, cold, cool, detached, disinterested, dispassionate, distant, formal, frigid, haughty, inaccessible, indifferent, remote, reserved, reticent, self-contained, self-possessed, *inf* standoffish, supercilious, unapproachable, unconcerned, undemonstrative, unemotional, unforthcoming, unfriendly, uninvolved, unresponsive, unsociable, unsympathetic. *Opp* FRIENDLY, SOCIABLE.

aloud *adv* audibly, clearly, distinctly, out loud.

also *adv* additionally, besides, furthermore, in addition, moreover, *joc* to boot, too.

alter *vb* adapt, adjust, amend, change, convert, edit, emend, enlarge, modify, reconstruct, reduce, reform, remake, remodel, reorganize, reshape, revise, transform, vary.

alteration *n* adaptation, adjustment, amendment, change, conversion, difference, modification, reorganization, revision, transformation.

alternate *vb* come alternately, follow each other, interchange, oscillate, replace each other, rotate, *inf* see-saw, substitute for each other, take turns.

alternative n 1 choice, option, selection. 2 back-up, replacement, substitute.

altitude n elevation, height.

altogether adv absolutely, completely, entirely, fully, perfectly, quite, thoroughly, totally, utterly, wholly.

always adv consistently, constantly, continually, continuously, endlessly, eternally, everlastingly, evermore, forever, invariably, perpetually, persistently, regularly, repeatedly, unceasingly, unfailingly, unremittingly.

amalgamate vb affiliate, ally, associate, band together, blend, coalesce, combine, come together, compound, confederate, form an alliance, fuse, integrate, join, join forces, league, inf link up, marry, merge, mix, put together, synthesize, inf team up, unite. Opp SPLIT.

amateur adj inexperienced, lay, unpaid, unqualified. ▷ AMATEURISH. • n dabbler, dilettante, enthusiast, layman, non-professional. Opp PROFESSIONAL.

amateurish adj clumsy, crude, inf do-it-yourself, incompetent, inept, inexpert, inf rough-and-ready, second-rate, shoddy, unpolished, unprofessional, unskilful, unskilled, untrained. Opp SKILLED.

amaze vb astonish, astound, awe, bewilder, confound, confuse, daze, disconcert, dumbfound, inf flabbergast, perplex, inf rock, shock, stagger, startle, stun, stupefy, surprise. **amazed** ▷ SURPRISED.

amazing adj astonishing, astounding, awe-inspiring, breathtaking, exceptional, exciting, extraordinary, inf fantastic, incredible, miraculous, notable, phenomenal, prodigious, remarkable, inf sensational, shocking, special, staggering, startling, stunning, stupendous, unusual, inf wonderful. Opp ORDINARY.

ambassador n agent, attaché, Fr chargé d'affaires, consul, diplomat, emissary, envoy, legate, nuncio, plenipotentiary, representative.

ambiguous adj ambivalent, confusing, enigmatic, equivocal, indefinite, indeterminate, puzzling, uncertain, unclear, vague, woolly. ▷ UNCERTAIN. Opp DEFINITE.

ambition n 1 commitment, drive, energy, enterprise, enthusiasm, inf go, initiative, inf push, pushfulness, self-assertion, thrust, zeal. 2 aim, aspiration, desire, dream, goal, hope, ideal, intention, object, objective, target, wish.

ambitious adj 1 assertive, committed, eager, energetic, enterprising, enthusiastic, go-ahead, inf go-getting, hard-working, industrious, keen, inf pushy, zealous. 2 ambitious ideas. inf big, far-reaching, grand, grandiose, large-scale, unrealistic. Opp APATHETIC.

ambivalent adj ambiguous, backhanded (compliment), confusing, doubtful, equivocal, inconclusive, inconsistent, indefinite, self-contradictory, inf two-faced, unclear, uncommitted, unresolved, unsettled. ▷ UNCERTAIN.

ambush n ambuscade, attack, snare, surprise attack, trap. • vb attack, ensnare, entrap, intercept, lie in wait for, pounce on, surprise, swoop on, trap, waylay.

amenable *adj* accommodating, acquiescent, adaptable, agreeable, biddable, complaisant, compliant, cooperative, deferential, docile, open-minded, persuadable, responsive, submissive, tractable, willing. *Opp* OBSTINATE.

amend *vb* adapt, adjust, alter, ameliorate, change, convert, correct, edit, emend, improve, make better, mend, modify, put right, rectify, reform, remedy, reorganize, reshape, revise, transform, vary.

amiable *adj* affable, agreeable, amicable, friendly, genial, good-natured, kind-hearted, kindly, likeable, well-disposed. *Opp* UNFRIENDLY.

ammunition *n* buckshot, bullet, cartridge, grenade, missile, projectile, round, shell, shrapnel.

amoral *adj* lax, loose, unethical, unprincipled, without standards. ▷ IMMORAL. *Opp* MORAL.

amorous *adj* affectionate, ardent, carnal, doting, enamoured, erotic, fond, impassioned, loving, lustful, passionate, *sl* randy, sexual, *inf* sexy. *Opp* COLD.

amount *n* aggregate, bulk, entirety, extent, lot, mass, measure, quantity, quantum, reckoning, size, sum, supply, total, value, volume, whole.
● *vb* **amount to** add up to, aggregate, be equivalent to, come to, equal, make, mean, total.

ample *adj* abundant, bountiful, broad, capacious, commodious, considerable, copious, extensive, fruitful, generous, great, large, lavish, liberal, munificent, plentiful, profuse, roomy, spacious, substantial, unstinting, voluminous. ▷ BIG, PLENTY. *Opp* INSUFFICIENT.

amplify *vb* **1** add to, augment, broaden, develop, dilate upon, elaborate, enlarge, expand, expatiate on, extend, fill out, lengthen, make fuller, make longer, supplement. **2** *amplify sound*. boost, heighten, increase, intensify, magnify, make louder, raise the volume. *Opp* DECREASE.

amputate *vb* chop off, cut off, dock, lop off, poll, pollard, remove, sever, truncate. ▷ CUT.

amuse *vb* absorb, beguile, cheer (up), delight, divert, engross, enliven, entertain, gladden, interest, involve, make laugh, occupy, please, raise a smile, *inf* tickle. *Opp* BORE. **amusing** ▷ ENJOYABLE. FUNNY.

amusement *n* **1** delight, enjoyment, fun, hilarity, laughter, mirth. ▷ MERRIMENT. **2** distraction, diversion, entertainment, game, hobby, interest, joke, leisure activity, pastime, play, pleasure, recreation, sport.

anaemic *adj* bloodless, colourless, feeble, frail, pale, pallid, pasty, sallow, sickly, unhealthy, wan, weak.

analogy *n* comparison, likeness, metaphor, parallel, resemblance, similarity, simile.

analyse *vb* anatomize, assay, break down, criticize, dissect, evaluate, examine, interpret, investigate, scrutinize, separate out, take apart, test.

analysis *n* breakdown, critique, dissection, enquiry, evaluation, examination, interpretation, investigation, *inf* post-mortem, scrutiny, study, test. *Opp* SYNTHESIS.

analytical *adj* analytic, critical, *inf* in-depth, inquiring, investigative, logical, methodical, penetrating, questioning, rational, searching, systematic. *Opp* SUPERFICIAL.

anarchy *n* bedlam, chaos, confusion, disorder, disorganization, insurrection, lawlessness, misgovernment, misrule, mutiny, pandemonium, riot. *Opp* ORDER.

ancestor *n* antecedent, forebear, forefather, forerunner, precursor, predecessor, progenitor.

ancestry *n* blood, derivation, descent, extraction, family, genealogy, heredity, line, lineage, origin, parentage, pedigree, roots, stock, strain.

anchor *vb* berth, make fast, moor, secure, tie up. ▷ FASTEN.

anchorage *n* harbour, haven, marina, moorings, port, refuge, sanctuary, shelter.

ancient *adj* 1 aged, antediluvian, antiquated, antique, archaic, elderly, fossilized, obsolete, old, old-fashioned, outmoded, out-of-date, passé, superannuated, time-worn, venerable. 2 *ancient times.* bygone, earlier, early, former, *poet* immemorial, *inf* olden, past, prehistoric, primeval, primitive, primordial, remote, *old use* of yore. *Opp* MODERN.

angel *n* archangel, cherub, divine messenger, seraph.

angelic *adj* 1 beatific, blessed, celestial, cherubic, divine, ethereal, heavenly, holy, seraphic, spiritual. 2 *angelic behaviour.*

exemplary, innocent, pious, pure, saintly, unworldly, virtuous. ▷ GOOD. *Opp* DEVILISH.

anger *n* angry feelings, annoyance, antagonism, bitterness, choler, displeasure, exasperation, fury, hostility, indignation, ire, irritability, outrage, passion, pique, rage, rancour, resentment, spleen, tantrum, temper, vexation, wrath. ● *inf* aggravate, antagonize, *sl* bug, displease, *inf* drive mad, enrage, exasperate, incense, incite, inflame, infuriate, irritate, madden, make angry, *inf* make someone's blood boil, *inf* needle, outrage, pique, provoke, *inf* rile, vex. ▷ ANNOY. *Opp* PACIFY.

angle *n* 1 bend, corner, crook, nook, point. 2 *a new angle.* approach, outlook, perspective, point of view, position, slant, standpoint, viewpoint. ● *vb* bend, bevel, chamfer, slant, turn, twist.

angry *adj inf* aerated, apoplectic, bad-tempered, bitter, *inf* bristling, *inf* choked, choleric, cross, disgruntled, enraged, exasperated, excited, fiery, fuming, furious, heated, hostile, *inf* hot under the collar, ill-tempered, incensed, indignant, infuriated, *inf* in high dudgeon, irascible, irate, livid, mad, outraged, provoked, raging, *inf* ratty, raving, resentful, riled, seething, smouldering, *inf* sore, splenetic, *sl* steamed up, stormy, tempestuous, vexed, *inf* ugly, *inf* up in arms, wild, wrathful. ▷ ANNOYED. *Opp* CALM. **be angry, become angry** *inf* be in a paddy, *inf* blow up, boil, bridle, bristle, flare up, *inf* fly off the handle,

fulminate, fume, *inf* get
steamed up, lose your temper,
rage, rant, rave, *inf* see red,
seethe, snap, storm. **make
angry** ▷ ANGER.

anguish *n* agony, anxiety,
distress, grief, heartache,
misery, pain, sorrow, suffering,
torment, torture, tribulation,
woe.

angular *adj* bent, crooked,
indented, jagged, sharp-
cornered, zigzag. *Opp* STRAIGHT.

animal *adj* beastly, bestial, brutish, carnal, fleshly, inhuman,
instinctive, physical, savage,
sensual, subhuman, wild.
● *n* beast, being, brute, creature, *plur* fauna, organism,
plur wildlife. □ *amphibian,
arachnid, biped, carnivore,
herbivore, insect, invertebrate,
mammal, marsupial, mollusc,
monster, omnivore, pet, quad-
ruped, reptile, rodent, scavenger,
vertebrate.* ▷ BIRD, FISH, INSECT.
□ *aardvark, antelope, ape,
armadillo, baboon, badger,
bear, beaver, bison, buffalo,
camel, caribou, cat, chamois,
cheetah, chimpanzee, chinchilla,
chipmunk, coypu, deer, dog,
dolphin, donkey, dormouse,
dromedary, elephant, elk,
ermine, ferret, fox, frog, gazelle,
gerbil, gibbon, giraffe, gnu,
goat, gorilla, grizzly bear,
guinea-pig, hamster, hare,
hedgehog, hippopotamus, horse,
hyena, ibex, impala, jackal,
jaguar, jerboa, kangaroo, koala,
lemming, lemur, leopard, lion,
llama, lynx, marmoset, marmot,
marten, mink, mongoose,
monkey, moose, mouse,
musquash, ocelot, octopus, opos-
sum, orang-utan, otter, panda,
panther, pig, platypus, polar
bear, pole-cat, porcupine,
porpoise, rabbit, rat, reindeer,
rhinoceros, roe, salamander,
scorpion, seal, sea-lion, sheep,
shrew, skunk, snake, spider,
squirrel, stoat, tapir, tiger, toad,
vole, wallaby, walrus, weasel,
whale, wildebeest, wolf, wolver-
ine, wombat, yak, zebra.*

animate *adj* alive, breathing,
conscious, feeling, live, living,
sentient. ▷ ANIMATED.
Opp INANIMATE. ● *vb* activate,
arouse, brighten up, *inf* buck
up, cheer up, encourage, energize, enliven, excite, exhilarate,
fire, galvanize, incite, inspire,
invigorate, kindle, liven up,
make lively, move, *inf* pep up,
inf perk up, quicken, rejuvenate, revitalize, revive, rouse,
spark, spur, stimulate, stir,
urge, vitalize.

animated *adj* active, alive,
bright, brisk, bubbling, busy,
cheerful, eager, ebullient, energetic, enthusiastic, excited,
exuberant, gay, impassioned,
lively, passionate, quick, spirited, sprightly, vibrant, vigorous, vivacious, zestful.
Opp LETHARGIC.

animation *n* activity, briskness,
eagerness, ebullience, energy,
enthusiasm, excitement, exhilaration, gaiety, high spirits,
life, liveliness, *inf* pep, sparkle,
spirit, sprightliness, verve,
vigour, vitality, vivacity, zest.
Opp LETHARGIC.

animosity *n* acerbity, acrimony,
animus, antagonism, antipathy,
asperity, aversion, bad blood,
bitterness, dislike, enmity,
grudge, hate, hatred, hostility,
ill will, loathing, malevolence,
malice, malignancy, malignity,
odium, rancour, resentment,

sarcasm, sharpness, sourness, spite, unfriendliness, venom, vindictiveness, virulence. *Opp* FRIENDLINESS.

annex *vb* acquire, appropriate, conquer, occupy, purloin, seize, take over, usurp.

annihilate *vb* abolish, destroy, eliminate, eradicate, erase, exterminate, extinguish, extirpate, *inf* finish off, *inf* kill off, *inf* liquidate, nullify, obliterate, raze, slaughter, wipe out.

annotation *n* comment, commentary, elucidation, explanation, footnote, gloss, interpretation, note.

announce *vb* 1 advertise, broadcast, declare, disclose, divulge, give notice of, intimate, make public, notify, proclaim, promulgate, propound, publicize, publish, put out, report, reveal, state. 2 *announce a speaker*. introduce, lead into, preface, present.

announcement *n* advertisement, bulletin, communiqué, declaration, disclosure, intimation, notification, proclamation, promulgation, publication, report, revelation, statement.

announcer *n* anchorman, anchorwoman, broadcaster, commentator, compère, disc jockey, DJ, *poet* harbinger, herald, master of ceremonies, *inf* MC, messenger, newscaster, newsreader, reporter, town crier.

annoy *vb inf* aggravate, antagonize, *inf* badger, be an annoyance to, bother, *sl* bug, chagrin, displease, distress, drive mad, exasperate, fret, gall, *inf* get at, *inf* get on your nerves, grate,

harass, harry, infuriate, irk, irritate, jar, madden, make cross, molest, *inf* needle, *inf* nettle, offend, peeve, pester, pique, *inf* plague, provoke, put out, rankle, rile, *inf* rub up the wrong way, ruffle, *inf* spite, tease, trouble, try (someone's patience), upset, vex, worry. ▷ ANGER. *Opp* PLEASE.

annoyance *n* 1 chagrin, crossness, displeasure, exasperation, irritation, pique, vexation. ▷ ANGER. 2 *Noise is an annoyance*. *inf* aggravation, bother, harassment, irritant, nuisance, offence, *inf* pain in the neck, pest, provocation, worry.

annoyed *adj* chagrined, cross, displeased, exasperated, *inf* huffy, irritated, jaundiced, *inf* miffed, *inf* needled, *inf* nettled, offended, *inf* peeved, piqued, *inf* put out, *inf* riled, *inf* shirty, *inf* sore, upset, vexed. ▷ ANGRY. *Opp* PLEASED. **be annoyed** *inf* go off in a huff, take offence, *inf* take umbrage.

annoying *adj inf* aggravating, bothersome, displeasing, exasperating, galling, grating, inconvenient, infuriating, irksome, irritating, jarring, maddening, offensive, provocative, provoking, tiresome, troublesome, trying, upsetting, vexatious, vexing, wearisome, worrying.

anoint *vb* 1 embrocate, grease, lubricate, oil, rub, smear. 2 bless, consecrate, dedicate, hallow, sanctify.

anonymous *adj* 1 incognito, nameless, unacknowledged, unidentified, unknown, unnamed, unspecified, unsung. 2 *anonymous letters*. unattributed, unsigned. 3 *anonymous* *style.* characterless, impersonal, nondescript, unidentifiable, unrecognizable, unremarkable.

answer *n* 1 acknowledgement, *inf* comeback, reaction, rejoinder, reply, response, retort, riposte. 2 explanation, outcome, solution. 3 *answer to a charge.* counter-charge, defence, plea, rebuttal, refutation, vindication. ● *vb* 1 acknowledge, give an answer, react, rejoin, reply, respond, retort, return. 2 explain, resolve, solve. 3 *answer a charge.* counter, defend yourself against, disprove, rebut, refute. 4 *answer a need.* correspond to, echo, fit, match up to, meet, satisfy, serve, suffice, suit.
answer back ▷ ARGUE.

antagonism *n* antipathy, dissension, enmity, friction, opposition, rancour, rivalry, strife. ▷ HOSTILITY.

antagonize *vb* alienate, anger, annoy, embitter, estrange, irritate, make an enemy of, offend, provoke, *inf* put off, upset.

anthem *n* canticle, chant, chorale, hymn, introit, paean, psalm.

anthology *n* collection, compendium, compilation, digest, miscellany, selection, treasury.

anticipate *vb* 1 forestall, obviate, preclude, pre-empt, prevent. 2 [Many think this use incorrect.] ▷ FORESEE.

anticlimax *n* bathos, *inf* come-down, *inf* damp squib, disappointment, *inf* let-down.

antics *plur n* buffoonery, capers, clowning, escapades, foolery, fooling, *inf* larking-about,

pranks, *inf* skylarking, tomfoolery, tricks.

antidote *n* antitoxin, corrective, countermeasure, cure, drug, neutralizing agent, remedy.

antiquarian *n* antiquary, antiques expert, collector, dealer.

antiquated *adj* aged, anachronistic, ancient, antediluvian, archaic, dated, medieval, obsolete, old, old-fashioned, *inf* out, out-dated, outmoded, out-of-date, passé, *inf* past it, *inf* prehistoric, *inf* primeval, primitive, quaint, superannuated, unfashionable. ▷ ANTIQUE. *Opp* NEW.

antique *adj* antiquarian, collectible, historic, old-fashioned, traditional, veteran, vintage. ▷ ANTIQUATED. ● *n* collectible, collector's item, curio, curiosity, *Fr* objet d'art, rarity.

antiquity *n* classical times, days gone by, former times, *inf* olden days, the past.

antiseptic *adj* aseptic, clean, disinfectant, disinfected, germ free, germicidal, hygienic, medicated, sanitized, sterile, sterilized, sterilizing, unpolluted.

antisocial *adj* alienated, anarchic, disagreeable, disorderly, disruptive, misanthropic, nasty, obnoxious, offensive, rebellious, rude, troublesome, uncooperative, undisciplined, unruly, unsociable. ▷ UNFRIENDLY. *Opp* SOCIABLE.

anxiety *n* 1 angst, apprehension, concern, disquiet, distress, doubt, dread, fear, foreboding, fretfulness, misgiving, nervousness, qualm, scruple, strain, stress, tension, uncertainty, unease, worry. **2** *anxiety to succeed*. desire, eagerness, enthusiasm, impatience, keenness, longing, solicitude, willingness.

anxious *adj* **1** afraid, agitated, alarmed, apprehensive, concerned, distracted, distraught, distressed, disturbed, edgy, fearful, *inf* fraught, fretful, *inf* jittery, nervous, *inf* nervy, *inf* on edge, overwrought, perturbed, restless, tense, troubled, uneasy, upset, watchful, worried. **2** *anxious to succeed*. avid, careful, desirous, *inf* desperate, *inf* dying, eager, impatient, intent, *inf* itching, keen, longing, solicitous, willing, yearning. **be anxious** ▷ WORRY.

apathetic *adj* casual, cool, dispassionate, dull, emotionless, half-hearted, impassive, inactive, indifferent, indolent, languid, lethargic, listless, passive, phlegmatic, slow, sluggish, tepid, torpid, unambitious, uncommitted, unconcerned, unenterprising, unenthusiastic, unfeeling, uninterested, uninvolved, unmotivated, unresponsive. *Opp* ENTHUSIASTIC.

apathy *n* coolness, inactivity, indifference, lassitude, lethargy, listlessness, passivity, torpor. *Opp* ENTHUSIASM.

apex *n* **1** crest, crown, head, peak, pinnacle, point, summit, tip, top, vertex. **2** *apex of your career*. acme, apogee, climax, consummation, crowning moment, culmination, height, high point, zenith. *Opp* NADIR.

aphrodisiac *adj* arousing, erotic, *inf* sexy, stimulating.

apologetic *adj* ashamed, blushing, conscience-stricken, contrite, penitent, red-faced, regretful, remorseful, repentant, rueful, sorry. *Opp* UNREPENTANT.

apologize *vb* ask pardon, be apologetic, express regret, make an apology, repent, say sorry.

apology *n* acknowledgement, confession, defence, excuse, explanation, justification, plea.

apostle *n* crusader, disciple, evangelist, follower, messenger, missionary, preacher, propagandist, proselytizer, teacher.

appal *vb* alarm, disgust, dismay, distress, harrow, horrify, nauseate, outrage, revolt, shock, sicken, terrify, unnerve. ▷ FRIGHTEN. **appalling** ▷ ATROCIOUS, BAD, FRIGHTENING.

apparatus *n* appliance, *inf* contraption, device, equipment, gadget, *inf* gear, implement, instrument, machine, machinery, mechanism, *inf* setup, system, *inf* tackle, tool, utensil.

apparent *adj* blatant, clear, conspicuous, detectable, discernible, evident, manifest, noticeable, observable, obvious, ostensible, overt, patent, perceptible, recognizable, self-explanatory, unconcealed, unmistakable, visible. *Opp* HIDDEN.

apparition *n* chimera, ghost, hallucination, illusion, manifestation, phantasm, phantom, presence, shade, spectre, spirit, *inf* spook, vision, wraith.

appeal *n* **1** application, call, *Fr* cri de coeur, cry, entreaty, petition, plea, prayer, request,

solicitation, supplication.
2 allure, attractiveness, charisma, charm, *inf* pull, seductiveness. ● *vb* ask earnestly, beg, beseech, call, canvass, cry out, entreat, implore, invoke, petition, plead, pray, request, solicit, supplicate. **appeal to** ▷ ATTRACT.

appear *vb* **1** arise, arrive, attend, begin, be published, be revealed, be seen, *inf* bob up, come, come into view, come out, *inf* crop up, enter, develop, emerge, *inf* heave into sight, loom, materialize, occur, originate, show, *inf* show up, spring up, surface, turn up. **2** *I appear to be wrong.* look, seem, turn out. **3** *appear in a play.* ▷ PERFORM.

appearance *n* **1** arrival, advent, emergence, presence, rise. **2** *a smart appearance.* air, aspect, bearing, demeanour, exterior, impression, likeness, look, mien, semblance.

appease *vb* assuage, calm, conciliate, humour, mollify, pacify, placate, propitiate, quiet, reconcile, satisfy, soothe, *inf* sweeten, tranquillize, win over. *Opp* ANGER.

appendix *n* addendum, addition, annexe, codicil, epilogue, postscript, rider, supplement.

appetite *n* craving, demand, desire, eagerness, fondness, greed, hankering, hunger, keenness, longing, lust, passion, predilection, proclivity, relish, *inf* stomach, taste, thirst, urge, willingness, wish, yearning, *inf* yen, zeal, zest.

appetizing *adj* delicious, *inf* moreish, mouthwatering, tasty, tempting.

applaud *vb* acclaim, approve, *inf* bring the house down, cheer, clap, commend, compliment, congratulate, eulogize, extol, *inf* give someone a hand, give someone an ovation, hail, laud, praise, salute. *Opp* CRITICIZE.

applause *n* acclaim, acclamation, approval, cheering, clapping, éclat, ovation, plaudits. ▷ PRAISE.

appliance *n* apparatus, contraption, device, gadget, implement, instrument, machine, mechanism, tool, utensil.

applicant *n* aspirant, candidate, competitor, entrant, interviewee, participant, postulant.

apply *vb* **1** administer, affix, bring into contact, lay on, put on, rub on, spread, stick. ▷ FASTEN. **2** *rules apply to all.* appertain, be relevant, have a bearing (on), pertain, refer, relate. **3** *apply common sense.* bring into use, employ, exercise, implement, practise, use, utilize, wield. **apply for** ▷ REQUEST. **apply yourself** ▷ CONCENTRATE.

appoint *vb* **1** arrange, authorize, decide on, determine, establish, fix, ordain, prescribe, settle. **2** *appoint you to do a job.* assign, choose, co-opt, delegate, depute, designate, detail, elect, make an appointment, name, nominate, *inf* plump for, select, settle on, vote for.

appointment *n* **1** arrangement, assignation, consultation, date, engagement, fixture, interview, meeting, rendezvous, session, *old use* tryst. **2** choice, choosing, commissioning, election, naming, nomination, selection.

3 job, office, place, position, post, situation.

appreciate *vb* 1 admire, applaud, approve of, be grateful for, be sensitive to, cherish, commend, enjoy, esteem, favour, find worthwhile, like, praise, prize, rate highly, regard highly, respect, sympathize with, treasure, value, welcome. 2 *appreciate the facts.* acknowledge, apprehend, comprehend, know, realize, recognize, see, understand. 3 *value appreciates.* build up, escalate, gain, go up, grow, improve, increase, inflate, mount, rise, soar, strengthen. *Opp* DEPRECIATE, DESPISE, DISREGARD.

apprehensive *adj* afraid, concerned, disturbed, edgy, fearful, *inf* jittery, nervous, *inf* nervy, *inf* on edge, troubled, uneasy, worried. ▷ ANXIOUS. *Opp* FEARLESS.

apprentice *n* beginner, learner, novice, probationer, pupil, starter, tiro, trainee.

approach *n* 1 advance, advent, arrival, coming, movement, nearing. 2 access, doorway, entrance, entry, passage, road, way in. 3 *your approach to work.* attitude, course, manner, means, method, mode, *Lat* modus operandi, procedure, style, system, technique, way. 4 *an approach for help.* appeal, application, invitation, offer, overture, proposal, proposition. ● *vb* 1 advance, bear down, catch up, come near, draw near, gain (on), loom, move towards, near, progress. *Opp* RETREAT. 2 *approach a task.* ▷ BEGIN. 3 *approach someone for help.* ▷ CONTACT.

approachable *adj* accessible, affable, informal, kind, open, relaxed, sympathetic, *inf* unstuffy, well-disposed. ▷ FRIENDLY. *Opp* ALOOF.

appropriate *adj* applicable, apposite, apropos, apt, becoming, befitting, compatible, correct, decorous, deserved, due, felicitous, fit, fitting, germane, happy, just, *old use* meet, opportune, pertinent, proper, relevant, right, seasonable, seemly, suitable, tactful, tasteful, timely, well-judged, well-suited, well-timed. *Opp* INAPPROPRIATE. ● *vb* annex, arrogate, commandeer, confiscate, expropriate, gain control of, *inf* hijack, requisition, seize, take, take over, usurp. ▷ STEAL.

approval *n* 1 acclaim, acclamation, admiration, applause, appreciation, approbation, commendation, esteem, favour, liking, plaudits, praise, regard, respect, support. *Opp* DISAPPROVAL. 2 acceptance, acquiescence, agreement, assent, authorization, *inf* blessing, confirmation, consent, endorsement, *inf* go-ahead, *inf* green light, licence, mandate, *inf* OK, permission, ratification, sanction, seal, stamp, support, *inf* thumbs up, validation. *Opp* REFUSAL.

approve *vb* accede to, accept, affirm, agree to, allow, assent to, authorize, *inf* back, *inf* bless, confirm, consent to, countenance, endorse, *inf* give your blessing to, *inf* go along with, pass, permit, ratify, *inf* rubber-stamp, sanction, sign, subscribe to, support, tolerate, uphold, validate. *Opp* REFUSE, VETO.

approve of ▷ ADMIRE.

approximate *adj* close, estimated, imprecise, inexact, loose, near, rough. *Opp* EXACT.
● *vb* **approximate to** approach, be close to, be similar to, border on, come near to, equal roughly, look like, resemble, simulate, verge on.

approximately *adv* about, approaching, around, *Lat* circa, close to, just about, loosely, more or less, nearly, *inf* nigh on, *inf* pushing, roughly, round about.

aptitude *n* ability, bent, capability, facility, fitness, flair, gift, suitability, talent. ▷ SKILL.

arbitrary *adj* **1** capricious, casual, chance, erratic, fanciful, illogical, indiscriminate, irrational, random, subjective, unplanned, unpredictable, unreasonable, whimsical, wilful. *Opp* METHODICAL. **2** *arbitrary rule*. absolute, autocratic, despotic, dictatorial, high-handed, imperious, summary, tyrannical, tyrannous, uncompromising.

arbitrate *vb* adjudicate, decide the outcome, intercede, judge, make peace, mediate, negotiate, pass judgement, referee, settle, umpire.

arbitration *n* adjudication, *inf* good offices, intercession, judgement, mediation, negotiation, settlement.

arbitrator *n* adjudicator, arbiter, go-between, intermediary, judge, mediator, middleman, negotiator, ombudsman, peacemaker, referee, *inf* troubleshooter, umpire.

arch *n* arc, archway, bridge, vault. ● *vb* arc, bend, bow. ▷ CURVE.

archetype *n* classic, example, ideal, model, original, paradigm, pattern, precursor, prototype, standard.

archives *n* annals, chronicles, documents, history, libraries, memorials, museums, papers, records, registers.

ardent *adj* eager, enthusiastic, fervent, hot, impassioned, intense, keen, passionate, warm, zealous. *Opp* APATHETIC.

arduous *adj* backbreaking, demanding, exhausting, gruelling, heavy, herculean, laborious, onerous, punishing, rigorous, severe, strenuous, taxing, tiring, tough, uphill. ▷ DIFFICULT. *Opp* EASY.

area *n* **1** acreage, breadth, expanse, extent, patch, sheet, size, space, square-footage, stretch, surface, tract, width. **2** district, environment, environs, locality, neighbourhood, part, precinct, province, quarter, region, sector, terrain, territory, vicinity, zone. **3** *an area of study*. field, sphere, subject.

argue *vb* **1** answer back, *inf* bandy words, bargain, bicker, debate, deliberate, demur, differ, disagree, discuss, dispute, dissent, expostulate, fall out, feud, fight, haggle, have an argument, *inf* have words, object, protest, quarrel, remonstrate, *inf* row, spar, squabble, take exception, wrangle. **2** *argue a case*. assert, claim, contend, demonstrate, hold, maintain, make a case, plead, prove, reason, show, suggest.

argument *n* **1** altercation, bickering, clash, conflict, controversy, difference (of opinion), disagreement, dispute, expostulation, feud, fight, protest, quarrel, remonstration, row, *inf* set-to, squabble, *inf* tiff, wrangle. **2** consultation, debate, defence, deliberation, dialectic, discussion, exposition, polemic. **3** *argument of a lecture.* abstract, case, contention, gist, hypothesis, idea, outline, plot, reasoning, summary, synopsis, theme, thesis, view.

arid *adj* **1** barren, desert, dry, fruitless, infertile, lifeless, parched, sterile, torrid, unproductive, waste, waterless. *Opp* FRUITFUL. **2** *arid work.* boring, dreary, dull, pointless, tedious, uninspired, uninteresting, vapid.

arise *vb* come up, crop up, get up, rise. ▷ APPEAR.

aristocrat *n* grandee, lady, lord, noble, nobleman, noblewoman, patrician. ▷ PEER.

aristocratic *adj inf* blueblooded, courtly, élite, gentle, highborn, lordly, noble, patrician, princely, royal, thoroughbred, titled, upper class.

arm *n* appendage, bough, branch, extension, limb, offshoot, projection. ● *vb* equip, fortify, furnish, provide, supply. **arms** ▷ WEAPON(S).

armed services *plur n* force, forces, troops. □ *air force, army, militia, navy.* □ *cavalry, infantry.* □ *battalion, brigade, cohort, company, corps, foreign legion, garrison, legion, patrol, platoon, rearguard, regiment, reinforcements, squad, squadron, task-force, vanguard.*
▷ FIGHTER, RANK, SOLDIER.

armistice *n* agreement, ceasefire, peace, treaty, truce.

armoury *n* ammunition-dump, arsenal, depot, magazine, ordnance depot, stockpile.

aroma *n* bouquet, fragrance, odour, perfume, redolence, savour, scent, smell, whiff.

arouse *vb* awaken, call forth, encourage, foment, foster, kindle, provoke, quicken, stimulate, stir up, *inf* whip up.
▷ CAUSE. *Opp* ALLAY.

arrange *vb* **1** adjust, align, array, categorize, classify, collate, display, dispose, distribute, grade, group, lay out, line up, marshal, order, organize, *inf* pigeon-hole, position, put in order, range, rank, set out, sift, sort (out), space out, systematize, tabulate, tidy up.
2 *arrange a party.* bring about, contrive, coordinate, devise, manage, organize, plan, prepare, see to, settle, set up.
3 *arrange music.* adapt, harmonize, orchestrate, score, set.

arrangement *n* **1** adjustment, alignment, design, disposition, distribution, grouping, layout, marshalling, organization, planning, positioning, setting out, spacing, tabulation. ▷ ARRAY.
2 agreement, bargain, compact, contract, deal, pact, scheme, settlement, terms, understanding. **3** *musical arrangement.* adaptation, harmonization, orchestration, setting, version.

array *n* arrangement, assemblage, collection, demonstration, display, exhibition, formation, *inf* line-up, muster, panoply, parade, presentation, show, spectacle. ● *vb* **1** adorn, apparel, attire, clothe, deck, decorate, dress, equip, fit out, garb, rig out, robe, wrap. 2 ▷ ARRANGE.

arrest n apprehension, capture, detention, seizure. ● vb 1 bar, block, check, delay, end, halt, hinder, impede, inhibit, interrupt, obstruct, prevent, restrain, retard, slow, stem, stop. 2 arrest a suspect. apprehend, inf book, capture, catch, inf collar, detain, have up, hold, inf nab, inf nick, inf pinch, inf run in, seize, take into custody, take prisoner.

arrival n 1 advent, appearance, approach, coming, entrance, homecoming, landing, return, touchdown. 2 new arrivals. caller, newcomer, visitor.

arrive vb 1 appear, come, disembark, drive up, drop in, enter, get in, land, make an entrance, inf roll in, inf roll up, show up, touch down, turn up. 2 ▷ SUCCEED. **arrive at** ▷ REACH.

arrogant adj boastful, brash, brazen, bumptious, cavalier, inf cocky, conceited, condescending, disdainful, egotistical, haughty, inf high and mighty, high-handed, imperious, impudent, insolent, lofty, lordly, overbearing, patronizing, pompous, presumptuous, proud, scornful, self-admiring, self-important, smug, snobbish, inf snooty, inf stuck-up, supercilious, superior, vain. Opp MODEST.

arsonist n fire-raiser, incendiary, pyromaniac.

art n 1 aptitude, artistry, cleverness, craft, craftsmanship, dexterity, expertise, facility, knack, proficiency, skilfulness, skill, talent, technique, touch, trick. 2 artwork, craft, fine art.

□ architecture, batik, carpentry, cloisonné, collage, crochet, drawing, embroidery, enamelling, engraving, etching, fashion design, graphics, handicraft, illustration, jewellery, knitting, linocut, lithography, marquetry, metalwork, modelling, monoprint, needlework, origami, painting, patchwork, photography, pottery, printmaking, sculpture, sewing, sketching, spinning, weaving, woodcut, woodwork.

artful adj astute, canny, clever, crafty, cunning, deceitful, designing, devious, inf fly, inf foxy, ingenious, knowing, scheming, shrewd, skilful, sly, smart, sophisticated, subtle, tricky, wily. Opp NAIVE.

article n 1 item, object, thing. 2 magazine article. ▷ WRITING.

articulate adj clear, coherent, comprehensible, distinct, eloquent, expressive, fluent, derog glib, intelligible, lucid, understandable, vocal. Opp INARTICULATE.

● vb ▷ SPEAK.

articulated adj bending, flexible, hinged, jointed.

artificial adj 1 fabricated, made-up, man-made, manufactured, synthetic, unnatural. 2 artificial style. affected, assumed, bogus, concocted, contrived, counterfeit, factitious, fake, false, feigned, forced, imitation, insincere, laboured, mock, inf phoney, pretended, pseudo, inf put on, sham, simulated, spurious, unreal. Opp NATURAL.

artist n craftsman, craftswoman. □ architect, carpenter, cartoonist, commercial artist, designer, draughtsman, draughtswoman, engraver, goldsmith, graphic *designer, illustrator, mason, painter, photographer, potter, printer, sculptor, silversmith, smith, weaver.* ▷ ENTERTAINER, MUSICIAN, PERFORMER.

artistic *adj* aesthetic, attractive, beautiful, creative, cultured, decorative, *inf* designer, imaginative, ornamental, tasteful. *Opp* UGLY.

ascend *vb* climb, come up, defy gravity, fly, go up, levitate, lift off, make an ascent, mount, move up, rise, scale, slope up, soar, take off. *Opp* DESCEND.

ascent *n* ascension, climb, gradient, hill, incline, ramp, rise, slope. *Opp* DESCENT.

ascertain *vb* confirm, determine, discover, establish, find out, identify, learn, make certain, make sure, settle, verify.

ascetic *adj* abstemious, austere, celibate, chaste, frugal, harsh, hermit-like, plain, puritanical, restrained, rigorous, self-controlled, self-denying, self-disciplined, severe, spartan, strict, temperate. *Opp* SELF-INDULGENT.

ash *n* burnt remains, cinders, clinker, embers.

ashamed *adj* 1 abashed, apologetic, chagrined, chastened, conscience-stricken, contrite, discomfited, distressed, guilty, humbled, humiliated, mortified, penitent, red-faced, remorseful, repentant, rueful, shamefaced, sorry, upset. 2 *ashamed of your nakedness.* bashful, blushing, demure, diffident, embarrassed, modest, prudish, self-conscious, sheepish, shy. *Opp* SHAMELESS.

ask *vb* appeal, apply, badger, beg, beseech, catechize, crave,

demand, enquire, entreat, implore, importune, inquire, interrogate, invite, petition, plead, pose a question, pray, press, query, question, quiz, request, require, seek, solicit, sue, supplicate. **ask for** ▷ ATTRACT.

asleep *adj* comatose, *inf* dead to the world, dormant, dozing, *inf* fast off, hibernating, inactive, inattentive, *inf* in the land of nod, *sl* kipping, napping, *inf* off, *inf* out like a light, resting, sedated, sleeping, slumbering, snoozing, *inf* sound off, unconscious, under sedation. ▷ NUMB. *Opp* AWAKE.

aspect *n* 1 angle, attribute, characteristic, circumstance, detail, element, facet, feature, quality, side, standpoint, viewpoint. 2 air, appearance, attitude, bearing, countenance, demeanour, expression, face, look, manner, mien, visage. 3 *a southern aspect.* direction, orientation, outlook, position, prospect, situation, view.

asperity *n* abrasiveness, acerbity, acidity, acrimony, astringency, bitterness, churlishness, crossness, harshness, hostility, irascibility, irritability, peevishness, rancour, roughness, severity, sharpness, sourness, venom, virulence. *Opp* MILDNESS.

aspiration *n* aim, ambition, craving, desire, dream, goal, hope, longing, objective, purpose, wish, yearning.

aspire *vb* aspire to aim for, crave, desire, dream of, hope for, long for, pursue, seek, set your sights on, strive after, want, wish for, yearn for.

aspiring ▷ POTENTIAL.

assail vb assault, bombard, pelt, set on. ▷ ATTACK.

assault n battery, inf GBH, mugging, rape. ▷ ATTACK.
• vb abuse, assail, inf beat up, inf do over, fall on, fight, fly at, jump on, lash out at, inf lay into, mob, molest, mug, inf pitch into, pounce on, rape, rush at, set about, set on, strike at, violate, inf wade into. ▷ ATTACK.

assemble vb 1 come together, congregate, convene, converge, crowd, flock, gather, group, herd, join up, meet, rally round, swarm, throng round. 2 accumulate, amass, bring together, collect, gather, get together, marshal, mobilize, muster, pile up, rally, round up. 3 build, construct, erect, fabricate, fit together, make, manufacture, piece together, produce, put together. Opp DISMANTLE, DISPERSE.

assembly n assemblage, conclave, conference, congregation, congress, convention, convocation, council, gathering, meeting, parliament, rally, synod. ▷ CROWD.

assent n acceptance, accord, acquiescence, agreement, approbation, approval, compliance, consent, inf go-ahead, permission, sanction, willingness. Opp REFUSAL. • vb accede, accept, acquiesce, agree, approve, be willing, comply, concede, concur, consent, express agreement, give assent, say 'yes', submit, yield. Opp REFUSE.

assert vb affirm, allege, argue, asseverate, attest, claim, contend, declare, emphasize, insist, maintain, proclaim, profess, protest, state, stress, swear, testify. **assert yourself** ▷ INSIST.

assertive adj aggressive, assured, authoritative, bold, inf bossy, certain, confident, decided, decisive, definite, dogmatic, domineering, emphatic, firm, forceful, insistent, peremptory, derog opinionated, positive, derog pushy, self-assured, strong, strong-willed, derog stubborn, uncompromising. Opp SUBMISSIVE.

assess vb appraise, assay (metal), calculate, compute, consider, determine, estimate, evaluate, fix, gauge, judge, price, reckon, review, inf size up, value, weigh up, work out.

asset n advantage, aid, benefit, blessing, boon, inf godsend, good, help, profit, resource, strength, support. **assets** capital, effects, estate, funds, goods, holdings, means, money, possessions, property, resources, savings, securities, valuables, wealth, inf worldly goods.

assign vb 1 allocate, allot, apportion, consign, dispense, distribute, give, hand over, share out. 2 assign to a job. appoint, authorize, delegate, designate, nominate, ordain, prescribe, put down, select, specify, stipulate. 3 assign my success to luck. accredit, ascribe, attribute, credit.

assignment n chore, duty, errand, job, mission, obligation, post, project, responsibility, task. ▷ WORK.

assist vb abet, advance, aid, back, benefit, boost, collaborate, cooperate, facilitate, further, help, *inf* lend a hand, promote, *inf* rally round, reinforce, relieve, second, serve, succour, support, sustain, work with. *Opp* HINDER.

assistance *n* aid, backing, benefit, collaboration, contribution, cooperation, encouragement, help, patronage, reinforcement, relief, sponsorship, subsidy, succour, support. *Opp* HINDRANCE.

assistant *n* abettor, accessory, accomplice, acolyte, aide, ally, associate, auxiliary, backer, collaborator, colleague, companion, comrade, confederate, deputy, helper, helpmate, *derog* minion, partner, *inf* right-hand man, *inf* right-hand woman, second, second-in-command, stand-by, subordinate, supporter.

associate *n* ▷ ASSISTANT, FRIEND. ● *vb* 1 ally yourself, be friends, combine, consort, fraternize, *inf* gang up, *inf* go around (with), *sl* hang out (with), *inf* hob nob (with), join up, keep company, link up, make friends, mingle, mix, side, socialize. *Opp* DISSOCIATE. 2 *associate snow with winter.* bracket together, connect, put together, relate, *inf* tie up.

association *n* affiliation, alliance, amalgamation, body, brotherhood, cartel, clique, club, coalition, combination, company, confederation, consortium, cooperative, corporation, federation, fellowship, group, league, marriage, merger, organization, partnership, party, society, syndicate, trust, union. ▷ FRIENDSHIP.

assorted *adj* different, differing, *old use* divers, diverse, heterogeneous, manifold, miscellaneous, mixed, motley, multifarious, sundry, varied, various.

assortment *n* agglomeration, array, choice, collection, diversity, farrago, jumble, medley, mélange, miscellany, *inf* mishmash, *inf* mixed bag, mixture, pot-pourri, range, selection, variety.

assume *vb* 1 believe, deduce, expect, guess, *inf* have a hunch, have no doubt, imagine, infer, presume, presuppose, suppose, surmise, suspect, take for granted, think, understand. 2 *assume duties.* accept, embrace, take on, undertake. 3 *assume an air of.* acquire, adopt, affect, don, dress up in, fake, feign, pretend, put on, simulate, try on, wear.

assumption *n* belief, conjecture, expectation, guess, hypothesis, premise, premiss, supposition, surmise, theory.

assurance *n* commitment, guarantee, oath, pledge, promise, vow, undertaking, word (of honour).

assure *vb* convince, give a promise, guarantee, make sure, persuade, pledge, promise, reassure, swear, vow. **assured** ▷ CONFIDENT.

astonish *vb* amaze, astound, baffle, bewilder, confound, daze, *inf* dazzle, dumbfound, electrify, *inf* flabbergast, leave speechless, nonplus, shock, stagger, startle, stun, stupefy, surprise, take aback, take by surprise, *inf* take your breath away, *sl* wow. **astonishing** ▷ AMAZING.

astound vb ▷ ASTONISH.

astray adv adrift, amiss, awry, lost, off course, inf off the rails, wide of the mark, wrong.

astute adj acute, adroit, artful, canny, clever, crafty, cunning, discerning, inf fly, inf foxy, guileful, ingenious, intelligent, knowing, observant, perceptive, perspicacious, sagacious, sharp, shrewd, sly, subtle, wily. Opp STUPID.

asylum n cover, haven, refuge, retreat, safety, sanctuary, shelter.

asymmetrical adj awry, crooked, distorted, irregular, lop-sided, unbalanced, uneven, inf wonky. Opp SYMMETRICAL.

atheist n heathen, pagan, sceptic, unbeliever.

athletic adj acrobatic, active, energetic, fit, muscular, powerful, robust, sinewy, inf sporty, inf strapping, strong, sturdy, vigorous, well-built, wiry. Opp WEAK.

athletics n field events, track events. □ cross-country, decathlon, discus, high jump, hurdles, javelin, long jump, marathon, pentathlon, pole-vault, relay, running, shot, sprint, triple jump.

atmosphere n 1 aerospace, air, ether, heavens, ionosphere, sky, stratosphere, troposphere. 2 ambience, aura, character, climate, environment, feeling, mood, spirit, tone, inf vibes, vibrations.

atom n inf bit, crumb, grain, iota, jot, molecule, morsel, particle, scrap, speck, spot, trace.

atone vb answer, be punished, compensate, do penance,

expiate, make amends, make reparation, make up (for), pay the penalty, pay the price, recompense, redeem yourself, redress.

atrocious adj abominable, appalling, barbaric, blood-thirsty, brutal, brutish, callous, cruel, diabolical, dreadful, evil, execrable, fiendish, frightful, grim, gruesome, hateful, heartless, heinous, hideous, horrendous, horrible, horrific, horrifying, inhuman, merciless, monstrous, nauseating, revolting, sadistic, savage, shocking, sickening, terrible, vicious, vile, villainous, wicked.

atrocity n crime, cruelty, enormity, offence, outrage. ▷ EVIL.

attach vb 1 add, affix, anchor, append, bind, combine, connect, couple, fix, join, link, secure, stick, tie, unite, weld. ▷ FASTEN. Opp DETACH. 2 ascribe, assign, associate, attribute, impute, place, relate to. **attached** ▷ LOVING.

attack n 1 aggression, ambush, assault, battery, blitz, bombardment, broadside, cannonade, charge, counter-attack, foray, incursion, invasion, offensive, onset, onslaught, pre-emptive strike, raid, rush, sortie, strike. 2 verbal attack. abuse, censure, criticism, diatribe, impugnment, invective, onslaught, tirade. 3 attack of coughing. bout, convulsion, fit, outbreak, paroxysm, seizure, spasm, stroke, inf turn. ● vb 1 ambush, assail, assault, inf beat up, inf blast, bombard, charge, counterattack, descend on, inf do over, engage, fall on, fight, fly at, invade, jump on, lash out at, inf lay into, mob, mug, *inf* pitch into, pounce on, raid, rush, set about, set on, storm, strike at, *inf* wade into. **2** *attack verbally.* abuse, censure, criticize, denounce, impugn, inveigh against, libel, malign, round on, slander, snipe at, traduce, vilify. *Opp* DEFEND. **3** attack a task. ▷ BEGIN.

attacker *n* aggressor, assailant, critic, detractor, enemy, intruder, invader, mugger, opponent, persecutor, raider, slanderer. ▷ FIGHTER.

attain *vb* accomplish, achieve, acquire, arrive at, complete, earn, fulfil, gain, get, grasp, *inf* make, obtain, procure, *inf* pull off, reach, realize, secure, touch, win.

attempt *n* assault, bid, effort, endeavour, *inf* go, start, try, undertaking. • *vb* aim, aspire, do your best, endeavour, essay, exert yourself, *inf* have a crack, *inf* have a go, make a bid, make an assault, make an effort, put yourself out, seek, strive, *inf* sweat blood, tackle, try, undertake, venture.

attend *vb* **1** appear, be present, go (to), frequent, present yourself, *inf* put in an appearance, visit. **2** accompany, chaperon, conduct, escort, follow, guard, usher. **3** *attend carefully.* concentrate, follow, hear, heed, listen, mark, mind, note, notice, observe, pay attention, think, watch. **attend to** assist, care for, help, look after, mind, minister to, nurse, see to, take care of, tend, wait on.

attendant *n* assistant, escort, helper, usher. ▷ SERVANT.

attention *n* **1** alertness, awareness, care, concentration, concern, diligence, heed, notice, recognition, thought, vigilance. **2** *kind attention.* attentiveness, civility, consideration, courtesy, gallantry, good manners, kindness, politeness, regard, respect, thoughtfulness.

attentive *adj* **1** alert, awake, concentrating, heedful, intent, observant, watchful. *Opp* INATTENTIVE. **2** ▷ POLITE. *Opp* RUDE.

attire *n* accoutrements, apparel, array, clothes, clothing, costume, dress, finery, garb, garments, *inf* gear, *old use* habit, outfit, raiment, wear, *old use* weeds. • *vb* ▷ DRESS.

attitude *n* **1** air, approach, aspect, bearing, behaviour, carriage, demeanour, disposition, frame of mind, manner, mien, mood, posture, stance. **2** *political attitudes.* approach, belief, feeling, opinion, orientation, outlook, position, standpoint, thought, view, viewpoint.

attract *vb* **1** allure, appeal to, beguile, bewitch, bring in, captivate, charm, decoy, enchant, entice, fascinate, *sl* get someone going, interest, inveigle, lure, magnetize, seduce, tempt, *sl* turn someone on. **2** *a magnet attracts iron.* drag, draw, pull, tug at. **3** *attract attention.* ask for, cause, court, encourage, generate, incite, induce, invite, provoke, seek out, *inf* stir up. *Opp* REPEL.

attractive *adj* adorable, alluring, appealing, appetizing, becoming, bewitching, captivating, *inf* catchy (*tune*), charming, *inf* cute, delightful, desirable, disarming, enchanting, endearing, engaging, enticing, enviable, fascinating, fetching, flattering, glamorous, goodlooking, gorgeous, handsome, hypnotic, interesting, inviting, irresistible, lovable, lovely, magnetic, personable, pleasing, prepossessing, pretty, quaint, seductive, sought-after, stunning, *inf* taking, tasteful, tempting, winning, winsome. ▷ BEAUTIFUL. *Opp* REPULSIVE.

attribute *n* characteristic, feature, property, quality, trait. ● *vb* accredit, ascribe, assign, blame, charge, credit, impute, put down, refer, trace back.

audacious *adj* adventurous, courageous, daring, fearless, *derog* foolhardy, intrepid, *derog* rash, *derog* reckless, venturesome. ▷ BOLD. *Opp* TIMID.

audacity *n* boldness, *inf* cheek, effrontery, forwardness, impertinence, impudence, presumptuousness, rashness, *inf* sauce, temerity. ▷ COURAGE.

audible *adj* clear, detectable, distinct, high, loud, noisy, recognizable. *Opp* INAUDIBLE.

audience *n* assembly, congregation, crowd, gathering, house, listeners, meeting, onlookers, *TV* ratings, spectators, *inf* turnout, viewers.

auditorium *n* assembly room, concert-hall, hall, theatre.

augment *vb* add to, amplify, boost, eke out, enlarge, expand, extend, fill out, grow, increase, intensify, magnify, make larger, multiply, raise, reinforce, strengthen, supplement, swell. *Opp* DECREASE.

augur *vb* bode, forebode, foreshadow, forewarn, give an omen, herald, portend, predict, promise, prophesy, signal.

augury *n* forecast, forewarning, omen, portent, prophecy, sign, warning.

auspicious *adj* favourable, *inf* hopeful, lucky, positive, promising, propitious. *Opp* OMINOUS.

austere *adj* 1 abstemious, ascetic, chaste, cold, economical, exacting, forbidding, formal, frugal, grave, hard, harsh, hermit-like, parsimonious, puritanical, restrained, rigorous, self-denying, self-disciplined, serious, severe, sober, spartan, stern, *inf* straitlaced, strict, thrifty, unpampered. 2 *austere dress.* modest, plain, simple, unadorned, unfussy. *Opp* LUXURIOUS, ORNATE.

authentic *adj* accurate, actual, bona fide, certain, dependable, factual, genuine, honest, legitimate, original, real, reliable, true, trustworthy, truthful, undisputed, valid, veracious. ▷ AUTHORITATIVE. *Opp* FALSE.

authenticate *vb* certify, confirm, corroborate, endorse, substantiate, validate, verify.

author *n* 1 composer, dramatist, novelist, playwright, poet, scriptwriter. ▷ WRITER. 2 architect, creator, designer, father, founder, initiator, inventor, maker, mover, organizer, originator, parent, planner, prime mover, producer.

authoritarian *adj* autocratic, *inf* bossy, despotic, dictatorial, dogmatic, domineering, strict, tyrannical.

authoritative *adj* approved, certified, definitive, dependable, official, recognized, sanctioned, scholarly. ▷ AUTHENTIC.

authority *n* **1** approval, authorization, consent, licence, mandate, permission, permit, sanction, warrant. **2** charge, command, control, domination, force, influence, jurisdiction, might, power, prerogative, right, sovereignty, supremacy, sway, weight. **3** *authority on wine*. *inf* boffin, *inf* buff, connoisseur, expert, scholar, specialist. **the authorities** administration, government, management, officialdom, *inf* powers that be.

authorize *vb* accede to, agree to, allow, approve, *inf* back, commission, consent to, empower, endorse, entitle, legalize, license, make official, mandate, *inf* OK, pass, permit, ratify, *inf* rubber-stamp, sanction, sign the order, sign the warrant, validate. **authorized** ▷ OFFICIAL.

automatic *adj* **1** conditioned, habitual, impulsive, instinctive, involuntary, natural, reflex, spontaneous, unconscious, unintentional, unthinking. **2** automated, computerized, electronic, mechanical, programmable, programmed, robotic, self-regulating, unmanned.

autonomous *adj* free, independent, self-determining, self-governing, sovereign.

auxiliary *adj* additional, ancillary, assisting, *inf* back-up, emergency, extra, helping, reserve, secondary, spare, subordinate, subsidiary, substitute, supplementary, supporting, supportive.

available *adj* accessible, at hand, convenient, disposable, free, handy, obtainable, procurable, ready, to hand, uncommitted, unengaged, unused, usable. *Opp* INACCESSIBLE.

avaricious *adj* acquisitive, covetous, grasping, greedy, mercenary, miserly.

avenge *vb* exact punishment, *inf* get your own back, repay, requite, take revenge.

average *adj* common, commonplace, everyday, mediocre, medium, middling, moderate, normal, regular, *inf* run of the mill, typical, unexceptional, usual. ▷ ORDINARY. *Opp* EXCEPTIONAL. • *n* mean, mid-point, norm, standard. • *vb* equalize, even out, normalize, standardize.

averse *adj* antipathetic, disinclined, hostile, opposed, reluctant, resistant, unwilling.

aversion *n* antagonism, antipathy, dislike, distaste, hostility, reluctance, repugnance, unwillingness. ▷ HATRED.

avert *vb* change the course of, deflect, draw off, fend off, parry, prevent, stave off, turn aside, turn away, ward off.

avoid *vb* abstain from, be absent from, *inf* beg the question, *inf* bypass, circumvent, dodge, *inf* duck, elude, escape, eschew, evade, fend off, find a way round, get out of the way of, *inf* get round, *inf* give a wide berth to, help (*can't help it*), ignore, keep away from, keep clear of, refrain from, run away from, shirk, shun, side-step, skirt round, *inf* skive off, steer clear of. *Opp* SEEK.

await vb be ready for, expect, hope for, lie in wait for, look out for, wait for.

awake adj 1 aware, conscious, insomniac, open-eyed, restless, sleepless, inf tossing and turning, wakeful, wide awake. 2 ▷ ALERT. Opp ASLEEP.

awaken vb alert, animate, arouse, awake, call, excite, kindle, revive, rouse, stimulate, stir up, wake, waken.

award n badge, cap, cup, decoration, endowment, grant, medal, prize, reward, scholarship, trophy. ● vb accord, allot, assign, bestow, confer, decorate with, endow, give, grant, hand over, present.

aware adj acquainted, alive (to), appreciative, attentive, cognizant, conscious, conversant, familiar, heedful, informed, knowledgeable, mindful, observant, responsive, sensible, sensitive, versed. Opp IGNORANT, INSENSITIVE.

awe n admiration, amazement, apprehension, dread, fear, respect, reverence, terror, veneration, wonder.

awe-inspiring adj awesome, old use awful, breathtaking, dramatic, grand, imposing, impressive, magnificent, marvellous, overwhelming, solemn, inf stunning, stupendous, sublime, wondrous. ▷ FRIGHTENING, WONDERFUL. Opp INSIGNIFICANT.

awful adj 1 ▷ AWE-INSPIRING. 2 awful weather. ▷ BAD.

awkward adj 1 blundering, bungling, clumsy, gauche, gawky, inf ham-fisted, inelegant, inept, inexpert, maladroit, uncoordinated, ungainly, ungraceful, unskilful, wooden.

2 an awkward load. bulky, cumbersome, inconvenient, unmanageable, unwieldy. 3 an awkward problem. annoying, difficult, perplexing, thorny, inf ticklish, troublesome, trying, vexatious, vexing. 4 an awkward silence. embarrassing, touchy, tricky, uncomfortable, uneasy. 5 awkward children. inf bloody-minded, sl bolshie, defiant, disobedient, disobliging, exasperating, intractable, misbehaving, naughty, obstinate, perverse, inf prickly, rebellious, refractory, rude, stubborn, touchy, uncooperative, undisciplined, unruly, wayward. Opp COOPERATIVE, EASY, NEAT.

awning n canopy, flysheet, screen, shade, shelter, tarpaulin.

axe n battleaxe, chopper, cleaver, hatchet, tomahawk. ● vb cancel, cut, discharge, discontinue, dismiss, eliminate, get rid of, inf give the chop to, make redundant, rationalize, remove, sack, terminate, withdraw.

axle n rod, shaft, spindle.

B

baby n babe, child, infant, newborn, toddler.

babyish adj childish, immature, infantile, juvenile, puerile, simple. Opp MATURE.

back n 1 adj dorsal, end, hind, hinder, hindmost, last, rear, rearmost. ● n 1 end, hind quarters, posterior, rear, stern, tail, tail-end. 2 reverse, verso.

Opp FRONT. ● *vb* 1 back away,
back off, back-pedal, backtrack,
inf beat a retreat, give way, go
backwards, move back, recede,
recoil, retire, retreat, reverse.
Opp ADVANCE. 2 ▷ SUPPORT.
back down ▷ RETREAT. **back
out** ▷ WITHDRAW.

backer *n* advocate, *inf* angel,
benefactor, patron, promoter,
sponsor, supporter.

background *n* 1 circumstances,
context, history, *inf* lead-up,
setting, surroundings. 2 breeding, culture, education, experience, grounding, milieu, tradition, training, upbringing.

backing *n* 1 aid, approval, assistance, encouragement, endorsement, funding, grant, help,
investment, loan, patronage,
sponsorship, subsidy, support.
2 *musical backing.* accompani-
ment, orchestration, scoring.

backward *adj* 1 regressive,
retreating, retrograde, retrogressive, reverse. 2 afraid,
bashful, coy, diffident, hesitant,
inhibited, modest, reluctant,
reserved, reticent, self-effacing,
shy, timid, unassertive,
unforthcoming. 3 *a backward
pupil.* disadvantaged, handicapped, immature, late-starting,
retarded, slow, subnormal,
underdeveloped, undeveloped.
Opp FORWARD.

bad *adj* [*Bad* describes anything
we don't like. Possible synonyms are almost limitless.]
1 *bad men, deeds.* abhorrent,
base, beastly, blameworthy,
corrupt, criminal, cruel, dangerous, delinquent, deplorable,
depraved, detestable, evil,
guilty, immoral, infamous,
malevolent, malicious, malignant, mean, mischievous,

nasty, naughty, offensive,
regrettable, reprehensible,
rotten, shameful, sinful, unworthy, vicious, vile, villainous,
wicked, wrong. 2 *a bad accident.* appalling, awful, calamitous, dire, disastrous, distressing, dreadful, frightful, ghastly,
grave, hair-raising, hideous,
horrible, painful, serious,
severe, shocking, terrible,
unfortunate, unpleasant,
violent. 3 *bad driving, work.*
abominable, abysmal, appalling, atrocious, awful, cheap,
inf chronic, defective, deficient,
diabolical, disgraceful, dreadful, egregious, execrable, faulty,
feeble, *inf* grotty, hopeless,
imperfect, inadequate, incompetent, incorrect, ineffective, inefficient, inferior, *inf* lousy, pitiful, poor, *inf* ropy, shoddy,
inf sorry, substandard,
unsound, unsatisfactory,
useless, weak, worthless. 4 *bad
conditions.* adverse, deleterious,
detrimental, discouraging,
inf frightful, harmful, harsh,
hostile, inappropriate, inauspicious, prejudicial, uncongenial,
unfortunate, unhelpful, unpropitious. 5 *bad smell.* decayed,
decomposing, diseased, foul,
loathsome, mildewed, mouldy,
nauseating, noxious, objectionable, obnoxious, odious, offensive, polluted, putrid, rancid,
repellent, repulsive, revolting,
rotten, sickening, smelly, sour,
spoiled, tainted, vile. 6 *I feel
bad.* ▷ ILL. *Opp* GOOD.

badge *n* chevron, crest, device,
emblem, insignia, logo, mark,
medal, sign, symbol, token.

bad-tempered *adj* acrimonious,
angry, bilious, cantankerous,
churlish, crabbed, cross,

inf crotchety, disgruntled, disobliging, dyspeptic, fretful, gruff, grumbling, grumpy, hostile, hot-tempered, ill-humoured, ill-tempered, irascible, irritable, malevolent, malign, moody, morose, peevish, petulant, quarrelsome, querulous, rude, scowling, short-tempered, shrewish, snappy, *inf* stroppy, sulky, sullen, testy, truculent, unfriendly, unsympathetic. *Opp* GOOD-TEMPERED.

baffle *vb* 1 *inf* bamboozle, bemuse, bewilder, confound, confuse, defeat, *inf* floor, *inf* flummox, foil, frustrate, mystify, perplex, puzzle, *inf* stump, thwart. **baffling** ▷ INEXPLICABLE.

bag *n* basket, carrier, carrier-bag, case, handbag, haversack, holdall, reticule, rucksack, sack, satchel, shopping-bag, shoulder-bag. ▷ BAGGAGE.
• *vb* capture, catch, ensnare, snare.

baggage *n* accoutrements, bags, belongings, *inf* gear, impedimenta, paraphernalia. ▷ LUGGAGE.

bait *n* allurement, attraction, bribe, carrot, decoy, enticement, inducement, lure, temptation. • *vb* annoy, goad, harass, hound, jeer at, *inf* needle, persecute, pester, provoke, tease, torment.

balance *n* 1 scales, weighing-machine. 2 equilibrium, equipoise, poise, stability, steadiness. 3 correspondence, equality, equivalence, evenness, parity, symmetry. 4 *spend a bit & save the balance*. difference, excess, remainder, residue, rest, surplus. • *vb* 1 cancel out, compensate for, counteract,

counterbalance, counterpoise, equalize, even up, level, make steady, match, neutralize, offset, parallel, stabilize, steady. 2 keep balanced, keep in equilibrium, poise, steady, support. **balanced** ▷ EVEN, IMPARTIAL, STABLE.

bald *adj* 1 baldheaded, bare, hairless, smooth, thin on top. 2 *bald truth*. direct, forthright, plain, simple, stark, straightforward, unadorned, uncompromising.

bale *n* bunch, bundle, pack, package, truss. • *vb* **bale out** eject, escape, jump out, parachute down.

ball *n* 1 drop, globe, globule, orb, shot, sphere, spheroid. 2 dance, disco, party, social.

balloon *n* airship, dirigible, hot-air balloon. • *vb* ▷ BILLOW.

ballot *n* election, plebiscite, poll, referendum, vote.

ban *n* boycott, embargo, interdiction, moratorium, prohibition, proscription, taboo, veto. • *vb* banish, bar, debar, disallow, exclude, forbid, interdict, make illegal, ostracize, outlaw, prevent, prohibit, proscribe, put a ban on, restrict, stop, suppress, veto. *Opp* PERMIT.

banal *adj* boring, clichéd, cliché-ridden, commonplace, *inf* corny, dull, hackneyed, humdrum, obvious, *inf* old hat, ordinary, over-used, pedestrian, platitudinous, predictable, stereotyped, trite, unimaginative, uninteresting, unoriginal, vapid. *Opp* INTERESTING.

band *n* 1 belt, border, fillet, hoop, line, loop, ribbon, ring, strip, stripe, swathe. 2 association, body, clique, club, company, crew, flock, gang, herd, horde, party, society, troop. ▷ GROUP. **3** [*music*] ensemble, group, orchestra.

bandage *n* dressing, gauze, lint, plaster.

bandit *n* brigand, buccaneer, desperado, footpad, gangster, gunman, highwayman, hijacker, marauder, outlaw, pirate, robber, thief.

bandy *adj* bandy-legged, bowed, bow-legged. ● *vb bandy words.* exchange, interchange, pass, swap, throw, toss. ▷ ARGUE.

bang *n* **1** blow, *inf* box, bump, collision, cuff, knock, punch, slam, smack, stroke, thump, wallop, whack. ▷ HIT. **2** blast, boom, clap, crash, explosion, pop, report, thud, thump. ▷ SOUND.

banish *vb* **1** deport, drive out, eject, evict, excommunicate, exile, expatriate, expel, ostracize, oust, outlaw, rusticate, send away, ship away, transport. **2** ban, bar, *inf* black, debar, eliminate, exclude, forbid, get rid of, make illegal, prohibit, proscribe, put an embargo on, remove, restrict, stop, suppress, veto.

bank *n* **1** camber, declivity, dike, earthwork, embankment, gradient, incline, mound, ramp, rampart, ridge, rise, slope, tilt. **2** *river bank.* brink, edge, margin, shore, side. **3** *bank of controls.* array, collection, display, file, group, line, panel, rank, row, series. ● *vb* **1** cant, heel, incline, lean, list, pitch, slant, slope, tilt, tip. **2** *bank money.* deposit, save.

bankrupt *adj inf* broke, failed, *sl* gone bust, gone into liquida-

tion, insolvent, ruined, spent up, wound up. ▷ POOR. *Opp* SOLVENT.

banner *n* banderole, colours, ensign, flag, pennant, pennon, standard, streamer.

banquet *n inf* binge, *sl* blow-out, dinner, feast, repast, *inf* spread. ▷ MEAL.

banter *n* badinage, chaffing, joking, persiflage, pleasantry, raillery, repartee, ribbing, ridicule, teasing, word-play.

bar *n* **1** beam, girder, pole, rail, railing, rod, shaft, stake, stick, strut. **2** barricade, barrier, check, deterrent, hindrance, impediment, obstacle, obstruction. **3** band, belt, line, streak, strip, stripe. **4** *bar of soap.* block, cake, chunk, hunk, ingot, lump, nugget, piece, slab, wedge. **5** *drink in a bar.* café, canteen, counter, inn, lounge, pub, public house, saloon, taproom, tavern, wine bar. ● *vb* **1** ban, banish, debar, exclude, forbid, forbid to enter, keep out, ostracize, outlaw, prevent from entering, prohibit, proscribe. **2** *bar the way.* arrest, block, check, deter, halt, hinder, impede, obstruct, prevent, stop, thwart.

barbarian *adj* ▷ BARBARIC. ● *n* boor, churl, heathen, hun, ignoramus, lout, pagan, philistine, savage, vandal, *sl* yob.

barbaric *adj* barbarous, brutal, brutish, crude, inhuman, primitive, rough, savage, uncivil, uncivilized, uncultivated, wild. ▷ CRUEL. *Opp* CIVILIZED.

bare *adj* **1** bald, denuded, , exposed, naked, nude, stark-naked, stripped, unclad, unclothed, uncovered, undressed.

2 *bare moor.* barren, bleak, desolate, featureless, open, treeless, unwooded, windswept. **3** *bare trees.* defoliated, leafless, shorn. **4** *a bare room.* austere, empty, plain, simple, unadorned, undecorated, unfurnished, vacant. **5** *a bare wall.* blank, clean, unmarked. **6** *bare facts.* direct, explicit, hard, honest, literal, open, plain, straightforward, unconcealed, undisguised, unembellished. **7** *the bare minimum.* basic, essential, just adequate, just sufficient, minimal, minimum. ● *vb* betray, bring to light, disclose, expose, lay bare, make known, publish, reveal, show, uncover, undress, unmask, unveil.

bargain *n* **1** agreement, arrangement, compact, contract, covenant, deal, negotiation, pact, pledge, promise, settlement, transaction, treaty, understanding. **2** *bargain in the sales.* *inf* giveaway, good buy, good deal, loss-leader, reduced item, *inf* snip, special offer. ● *vb* argue, barter, discuss terms, do a deal, haggle, negotiate. **bargain for** ▷ EXPECT.

bark *vb* **1** growl, yap. **2** *bark your shin.* abrade, chafe, graze, rub, score, scrape, scratch.

barmaid, barman *ns* attendant, server, steward, stewardess, waiter, waitress.

barracks *n* accommodation, billet, camp, garrison, lodging, quarters.

barrage *n* **1** ▷ BARRIER. **2** *barrage of gunfire.* assault, attack, battery, bombardment, cannonade, fusillade, gunfire, onslaught, salvo, storm, volley.

barrel *n* butt, cask, churn, cistern, drum, hogshead, keg, tank, tub, tun, water-butt.

barren *adj* **1** arid, bare, desert, desolate, dried-up, dry, empty, infertile, lifeless, non-productive, treeless, uncultivated, unproductive, unprofitable, untilled, useless, waste. **2** childless, fruitless, infertile, sterile, sterilized, unfruitful.
Opp FERTILE.

barricade *n* ▷ BARRIER. ● *vb* bar, block off, defend, obstruct.

barrier *n* **1** bar, barrage, barricade, blockade, boom, bulwark, dam, earthwork, embankment, fence, fortification, frontier, hurdle, obstacle, obstruction, palisade, railing, rampart, stockade, wall. **2** *barrier to progress.* check, drawback, handicap, hindrance, impediment, limitation, restriction, stumbling-block.

barter *vb* bargain, deal, exchange, negotiate, swap, trade, traffic.

base *adj* contemptible, cowardly, degrading, depraved, despicable, detestable, dishonourable, evil, ignoble, immoral, inferior, low, mean, scandalous, selfish, shabby, shameful, sordid, undignified, unworthy, vulgar, vile. ▷ WICKED. ● *n* **1** basis, bed, bedrock, bottom, core, essentials, foot, footing, foundation, fundamentals, groundwork, infrastructure, pedestal, plinth, rest, root, stand, substructure, support, underpinning. **2** camp, centre, depot, headquarters, post, starting-point, station. ● *vb* build, construct, establish, found, ground, locate, position, post, secure, set up, station.

basement *n* cellar, crypt, vault.

bashful *adj* abashed, backward, blushing, coy, demure, diffident, embarrassed, faint-hearted, inhibited, meek, modest, nervous, reserved, reticent, retiring, self-conscious, self-effacing, shamefaced, sheepish, shy, timid, timorous, uneasy, unforthcoming. *Opp* ASSERTIVE.

basic *adj* central, chief, crucial, elementary, essential, foremost, fundamental, important, intrinsic, key, main, necessary, primary, principal, radical, underlying, vital. *Opp* UNIMPORTANT.

basin *n* bath, bowl, container, dish, pool, sink, stoup.

basis *n* base, core, footing, foundation, ground, infrastructure, premise, principle, starting-point, support, underpinning.

bask *vb* enjoy, feel pleasure, glory, lie, lounge, luxuriate, relax, sunbathe, wallow.

basket *n* bag, hamper, pannier, punnet, skip, trug.

bastard *n* illegitimate child, *old use* love-child, natural child.

bat *n* club, racket, racquet.

bath *n* douche, jacuzzi, pool, sauna, shower, *inf* soak, *inf* tub, wash.

bathe *vb* **1** clean, cleanse, immerse, moisten, rinse, soak, steep, swill, wash. **2** *bathe in the sea.* go swimming, paddle, plunge, splash about, swim, *inf* take a dip.

bathos *n* anticlimax, *inf* comedown, disappointment, *inf* letdown. *Opp* CLIMAX.

baton *n* cane, club, cudgel, rod, staff, stick, truncheon.

batter *vb* beat, bludgeon, cudgel, keep hitting, pound. ▷ HIT.

battery *n* **1** artillery-unit, emplacement. **2** *electric battery.* accumulator, cell. **3** *assault and battery.* assault, attack, *inf* beating-up, blows, mugging, onslaught, thrashing, violence.

battle *n* action, air-raid, Armageddon, attack, blitz, brush, campaign, clash, combat, conflict, confrontation, contest, crusade, *inf* dogfight, encounter, engagement, fight, fray, hostilities, offensive, pitched battle, pre-emptive strike, quarrel, *inf* shoot-out, siege, skirmish, strife, struggle, war, warfare. ● *vb* ▷ FIGHT.

battlefield *n* arena, battleground, theatre of war.

bawdy *adj* broad, earthy, erotic, lusty, *inf* naughty, racy, *inf* raunchy, ribald, *inf* sexy, *inf* spicy. □ [*derog synonyms*] *inf* blue, coarse, dirty, immoral, improper, indecent, indecorous, indelicate, lascivious, lecherous, lewd, licentious, obscene, pornographic, prurient, risqué, rude, salacious, smutty, suggestive, titillating, vulgar. *Opp* PROPER.

bawl *vb* cry, roar, shout, thunder, wail, yell, yelp.

bay *n* **1** bight, cove, creek, estuary, fjord, gulf, harbour, indentation, inlet, ria, sound. **2** alcove, booth, compartment, niche, nook, opening, recess.

bazaar *n* auction, boot-sale, bring-and-buy, fair, fête, jumble sale, market, sale.

be *vb* **1** be alive, breathe, endure, exist, live. **2** *be here all day.* continue, dwell, inhabit, keep going, last, occupy a position, persist, remain, stay, survive. **3** *the next event will be tomorrow.* arise, befall, come about, happen, occur, take place. **4** *want to be a writer.* become, develop into.

beach *n* bank, coast, coastline, foreshore, littoral, sand, sands, seashore, seaside, shore, *poet* strand.

beacon *n* bonfire, fire, flare, light, lighthouse, pharos, signal.

bead *n* blob, drip, drop, droplet, globule, jewel, pearl.

beaker *n* cup, glass, goblet, jar, mug, tankard, tumbler.

beam *n* **1** bar, board, boom, brace, girder, joist, plank, post, rafter, spar, stanchion, stud, support, timber. **2** *beam of light.* gleam, pencil, ray, shaft, stream. ● *vb* **1** aim, broadcast, direct, emit, radiate, send out, shine, transmit. **2** *beam happily.* grin, laugh, look radiant, radiate happiness, smile.

bear *vb* **1** carry, hold, prop up, shoulder, support, sustain, take. **2** *bear an inscription.* display, exhibit, have, possess, show. **3** *bear gifts.* bring, carry, convey, deliver, fetch, move, take, transfer, transport. **4** *bear pain.* abide, accept, brook, cope with, endure, live with, permit, *inf* put up with, reconcile yourself to, *inf* stand, *inf* stomach, suffer, sustain, tolerate, undergo. **5** *bear children, fruit.* breed, *old use* bring forth, develop, engender, generate, give birth to, produce, spawn, yield. **bear out** ▷ CONFIRM. **bear up** ▷ SURVIVE. **bear witness** ▷ TESTIFY.

bearable *adj* acceptable, endurable, supportable, survivable, sustainable, tolerable.

bearing *n* **1** air, appearance, aspect, attitude, behaviour, carriage, demeanour, deportment, look, manner, mien, poise, posture, presence, stance, style. **2** *evidence had no bearing.* applicability, application, connection, import, pertinence, reference, relation, relationship, relevance, significance.

bearings aim, course, direction, line, location, orientation, path, position, road, sense of direction, tack, track, way, whereabouts.

beast *n* brute, creature, monster, savage. ▷ ANIMAL.

beastly *adj* abominable, barbaric, bestial, brutal, cruel, savage. ▷ VILE.

beat *n* **1** accent, pulse, rhythm, stress, tempo, throb. **2** *policeman's beat.* course, itinerary, journey, path, rounds, route, way. ● *vb* **1** batter, bludgeon, buffet, cane, clout, cudgel, flail, flog, hammer, knock about, lash, *inf* lay into, manhandle, pound, punch, scourge, strike, *inf* tan, thrash, thump, trounce, *inf* wallop, whack, whip. ▷ HIT. **2** *beat eggs.* agitate, blend, froth up, knead, mix, pound, stir, whip, whisk. **3** *heart was beating.* flutter, palpitate, pound, pulsate, race, throb, thump. **5** *beat an opponent.* best, conquer, crush, defeat, excel, get the better of, *inf* lick, master, outclass, outdistance, outdo, outpace, outrun, outwit, overcome, overpower, overthrow, overwhelm, rout, subdue, surpass, *inf* thrash, trounce, vanquish, win against, worst. **beat up** ▷ ATTACK.

beautiful *adj* admirable, aesthetic, alluring, appealing, artistic, attractive, becoming, bewitching, brilliant, captivating, charming, *old use* comely, dainty, decorative, delightful, elegant, enjoyable, exquisite, *old use* fair, fascinating, fetching, fine, good-looking, glamorous, glorious, gorgeous, graceful, handsome, irresistible, lovely, magnificent, neat, picturesque, pleasing, pretty, pulchritudinous, quaint, radiant, ravishing, scenic, seductive, sensuous, sexy, spectacular, splendid, stunning, superb, tasteful, tempting. *Opp* UGLY.

beautify *vb* adorn, bedeck, deck, decorate, embellish, garnish, make beautiful, ornament, prettify, *derog* tart up, *inf* titivate. *Opp* DISFIGURE.

beauty *n* allure, appeal, attractiveness, charm, elegance, fascination, glamour, glory, grace, handsomeness, loveliness, magnificence, picturesqueness, prettiness, pulchritude, radiance, splendour.

becalmed *adj* helpless, idle, motionless, still, unmoving.

beckon *vb* gesture, motion, signal, summon, wave.

become *vb* 1 be transformed into, change into, develop into, grow into, mature into, metamorphose into, turn into. 2 *Red becomes you.* be appropriate to, be becoming to, befit, enhance, fit, flatter, harmonize with, set off, suit. **becoming** ▷ ATTRACTIVE, SUITABLE.

bed *n* 1 resting-place. □ air-bed, berth, bunk, cot, couch, couchette, cradle, crib, divan, four-poster, hammock, pallet, palliasse, truckle bed, water-bed. 2 bed of concrete. base, foundation, groundwork, layer, substratum. 3 *river bed.* bottom, channel, course, watercourse. 4 *flower bed.* border, garden, patch, plot.

bedclothes *plur n* bedding, bed linen. □ bedspread, blanket, bolster, continental quilt, counterpane, coverlet, duvet, eiderdown, electric-blanket, mattress, pillow, pillowcase, pillowslip, quilt, sheet, sleeping-bag.

bedraggled *adj* dirty, dishevelled, drenched, messy, muddy, scruffy, sodden, soiled, stained, unkempt, untidy, wet, wringing. *Opp* SMART.

beer *n* ale, bitter, lager, mild, porter, stout.

befall *vb* be the outcome, *old use* betide, chance, come about, *inf* crop up, eventuate, happen, occur, take place, *inf* transpire.

before *adv* already, earlier, in advance, previously, sooner.

befriend *vb inf* chat up, *inf* gang up with, get to know, make friends with, make the acquaintance of, *inf* pal up with.

beg *vb* 1 *inf* cadge, scrounge, solicit, sponge. 2 *beg a favour.* ask, beseech, cajole, crave, entreat, implore, importune, petition, plead, pray, request, supplicate, wheedle.

beget *vb* breed, bring about, cause, create, engender, father, generate, give rise to, procreate, produce, propagate, result in, sire, spawn.

beggar *n* cadger, destitute person, down-and-out, homeless person, mendicant, pauper, ragamuffin, scrounger, sponger, tramp, vagrant. ▷ POOR.

begin vb 1 activate, approach, attack, be first, broach, commence, conceive, create, embark on, enter into, found, inf get cracking, inf get going, inaugurate, initiate, inspire, instigate, introduce, kindle, launch, lay the foundations, lead off, move into, move off, open, originate, pioneer, precipitate, provoke, set about, set in motion, set off, set out, set up, inf spark off, start, inf take steps, take the initiative, take up, touch off, trigger off, undertake. 2 *Spring begins gradually.* appear, arise, break out, come into existence, crop up, emerge, get going, happen, materialize, originate, spring up. Opp END.

beginner n 1 creator, founder, initiator, inspiration, instigator, originator, pioneer. 2 *only a beginner.* apprentice, fresher, greenhorn, inexperienced person, initiate, learner, novice, recruit, starter, tiro, trainee.

beginning n 1 birth, commencement, conception, creation, dawn, embryo, emergence, establishment, foundation, genesis, germ, inauguration, inception, initiation, instigation, introduction, launch, onset, opening, origin, outset, point of departure, rise, source, start, starting-point, threshold. 2 *beginning of a book.* preface, prelude, prologue. Opp END.

begrudge vb be bitter about, covet, envy, grudge, mind, object to, resent.

behave vb 1 acquit yourself, act, inf carry on, comport yourself,

conduct yourself, function, operate, perform, react, respond, run, work. 2 *told to behave.* act properly, be good, be on best behaviour.

behaviour n actions, attitude, bearing, comportment, conduct, courtesy, dealings, demeanour, deportment, manners, performance, reaction, response, ways.

behead vb decapitate, guillotine.

behold vb descry, discern, espy, look at, note, notice, see, set eyes on, view.

being n 1 actuality, essence, existence, life, living, reality, solidity, substance. 2 animal, creature, individual, person, spirit, soul.

belated adj behindhand, delayed, last-minute, late, overdue, posthumous, tardy, unpunctual.

belch vb 1 inf burp, emit wind. 2 *belch smoke.* discharge, emit, erupt, fume, gush, send out, smoke, spew out, vomit.

belief n 1 acceptance, assent, assurance, certainty, confidence, credence, reliance, security, sureness, trust. 2 *religious belief.* attitude, conviction, creed, doctrine, dogma, ethos, faith, feeling, ideology, morality, notion, opinion, persuasion, principles, religion, standards, tenets, theories, views. Opp SCEPTICISM.

believe vb 1 accept, be certain of, count on, credit, depend on, endorse, have faith in, reckon on, rely on, subscribe to, inf swallow, swear by, trust. Opp DISBELIEVE. 2 assume, consider, inf dare say, feel, gather, guess, hold, imagine,

believer *n* adherent, devotee, disciple, fanatic, follower, proselyte, supporter, upholder, zealot. *Opp* ATHEIST.

belittle *vb* be unimpressed by, criticize, decry, denigrate, deprecate, depreciate, detract from, disparage, minimize, *inf* play down, slight, speak slightingly of, underrate, undervalue. *Opp* EXAGGERATE, FLATTER, PRAISE.

bell *n* alarm, carillon, chime, knell, peal, signal. ▷ RING.

belligerent *adj* aggressive, antagonistic, argumentative, bellicose, bullying, combative, contentious, defiant, disputatious, fierce, hawkish, hostile, jingoistic, martial, militant, militaristic, provocative, pugnacious, quarrelsome, violent, warlike, warmongering, warring. ▷ UNFRIENDLY. *Opp* PEACEABLE.

belong *vb* 1 be owned (by), go (with), pertain (to), relate (to). 2 be at home, feel welcome, have a place. *belong to a club.* be affiliated with, be a member of, be connected with, *inf* be in with.

belongings *n* chattels, effects, *inf* gear, goods, impedimenta, possessions, property, things.

belt *n* 1 band, circle, loop. 2 *belt round the waist.* cincture, cummerbund, girdle, girth, sash, strap, waistband, *old use* zone. 3 *green belt.* area, district, line, stretch, strip, swathe, tract, zone.

bemuse *vb* befuddle, bewilder, confuse, mix up, muddle, perplex, puzzle, stupefy.

bench *n* 1 form, pew, seat, settle. 2 counter, table, work-bench, work-table. 3 *magistrate's bench.* court, courtroom, judge, magistrate, tribunal.

bend *n* angle, arc, bow, corner, crank, crook, curvature, curve, flexure, loop, turn, turning, twist, zigzag. ● *vb* 1 arch, be flexible, bow, buckle, coil, contort, crook, curl, curve, deflect, distort, divert, flex, fold, *inf* give, loop, mould, refract, shape, turn, twist, warp, wind, yield. 2 bow, crouch, curtsy, duck, genuflect, kneel, lean, stoop.

benefactor *n inf* angel, backer, *derog* do-gooder, donor, *inf* fairy godmother, patron, philanthropist, promoter, sponsor, supporter, well-wisher.

beneficial *adj* advantageous, benign, constructive, favourable, fruitful, good, health-giving, healthy, helpful, improving, nourishing, nutritious, positive, productive, profitable, rewarding, salubrious, salutary, supportive, useful, valuable, wholesome. *Opp* HARMFUL.

beneficiary *n* heir, heiress, inheritor, legatee, recipient, successor (*to title*).

benefit *n* 1 advantage, asset, blessing, boon, convenience, gain, good thing, help, privilege, prize, profit, service, use. *Opp* DISADVANTAGE. 2 *unemployment benefit.* aid, allowance, assistance, *inf* dole, *inf* handout, grant, payment, social security, welfare. ● *vb* advance,

judge, know, maintain, postulate, presume, speculate, suppose, take it for granted, think. **make believe** ▷ IMAGINE.

advantage, aid, assist, better, boost, do good to, enhance, further, help, improve, profit, promote, serve.

benevolent *adj* altruistic, beneficent, benign, caring, charitable, compassionate, considerate, friendly, generous, helpful, humane, humanitarian, kindhearted, kindly, liberal, magnanimous, merciful, philanthropic, supportive, sympathetic, unselfish, warmhearted. ▷ KIND. *Opp* UNKIND.

benign *adj* gentle, harmless, kind. ▷ BENEFICIAL, BENEVOLENT.

bent *adj* 1 angled, arched, bowed, buckled, coiled, contorted, crooked, curved, distorted, folded, hunched, looped, twisted, warped. 2 [*inf*] *a bent dealer.* corrupt, criminal, dishonest, illegal, immoral, untrustworthy, wicked. *Opp* HONEST, STRAIGHT. ● *n* ▷ APTITUDE, BIAS.

bequeath *vb* endow, hand down, leave, make over, pass on, settle, will.

bequest *n* endowment, gift, inheritance, legacy, settlement.

bereavement *n* death, loss.

bereft *adj* deprived, destitute, devoid, lacking, robbed, wanting.

berserk *adj inf* beside yourself, crazed, crazy, demented, deranged, frantic, frenetic, frenzied, furious, infuriated, insane, mad, maniacal, rabid, violent, wild. *Opp* CALM. **go berserk** ▷ RAGE, RAMPAGE.

berth *n* 1 bed, bunk, hammock. 2 *berth for ships.* anchorage, dock, harbour, haven, landing-stage, moorings, pier, port,

quay, slipway, wharf.
● *vb* anchor, dock, drop anchor, land, moor, tie up. **give a wide berth to** ▷ AVOID.

beseech *vb* ask, beg, entreat, implore, importune, plead, supplicate.

besiege *vb* beleaguer, beset, blockade, cut off, encircle, encompass, hem in, isolate, pester, plague, siege, surround.

best *adj* choicest, excellent, finest, first-class, foremost, incomparable, leading, matchless, optimum, outstanding, pre-eminent, superlative, supreme, top, unequalled, unrivalled, unsurpassed.

bestial *adj* animal, beast-like, beastly, brutal, brutish, inhuman, subhuman. ▷ SAVAGE.

bestow *vb* award, confer, donate, give, grant, present.

bet *n inf* flutter, gamble, *inf* punt, speculation, stake, wager.
● *vb* bid, chance, do the pools, enter a lottery, gamble, *inf* have a flutter, hazard, lay bets, *inf* punt, risk, speculate, stake, venture, wager.

betray *vb* 1 be a Judas to, be a traitor to, be false to, cheat, conspire against, deceive, denounce, desert, double-cross, give away, *inf* grass on, incriminate, inform against, inform on, jilt, let down, *inf* rat on, report, *inf* sell down the river, sell out, *inf* shop, *inf* tell tales about, *inf* turn Queen's evidence on. 2 *betray secrets.* disclose, divulge, expose, give away, indicate, let out, let slip, manifest, reveal, show, tell.

better *adj* 1 preferable, recommended, superior. 2 convalescent, cured, fitter, healed,

healthier, improved, *inf* on the mend, progressing, recovered, recovering, restored.
● *vb* ▷ IMPROVE, SURPASS.

beware *vb* avoid, be alert, be careful, be cautious, be on your guard, guard (against), heed, keep clear (of), look out, mind, shun, steer away (from), take care, take heed, take precautions, watch out, *inf* watch your step.

bewilder *vb* baffle, *inf* bamboozle, bemuse, confound, confuse, daze, disconcert, disorientate, distract, floor, *inf* flummox, mislead, muddle, mystify, perplex, puzzle, stump.

bewitch *vb* captivate, cast a spell on, charm, enchant, enrapture, fascinate, spellbind.

bias *n* 1 aptitude, bent, inclination, leaning, liking, partiality, penchant, predilection, predisposition, preference, proclivity, proneness, propensity, tendency. 2 [*derog*] bigotry, chauvinism, favouritism, imbalance, injustice, nepotism, one-sidedness, partiality, partisanship, prejudice, racism, sexism, unfairness.
● *vb* ▷ INFLUENCE.

biased *adj* bigoted, blinkered, chauvinistic, distorted, emotive, influenced, interested, jaundiced, loaded, one-sided, partial, partisan, prejudiced, racist, sexist, slanted, tendentious, unfair, unjust, warped. *Opp* UNBIASED.

bicycle *n* *inf* bike, cycle, penny-farthing, *inf* push-bike, racer, tandem, *inf* two-wheeler.

bid *n* 1 offer, price, proposal, proposition, tender. 2 *a bid to win.* attempt, *inf* crack, effort,

endeavour, *inf* go, try, venture.
● *vb* 1 make an offer, offer, proffer, propose, tender. 2 ▷ COMMAND.

big *adj* 1 above average, *inf* almighty, ample, astronomical, bold, broad, Brobdingnagian, bulky, burly, capacious, colossal, commodious, considerable, elephantine, enormous, extensive, fat, formidable, gargantuan, generous, giant, gigantic, grand, great, gross, heavy, hefty, high, huge, *inf* hulking, husky, immeasurable, immense, impressive, *inf* jumbo, *inf* king-sized, large, largish, lofty, long, mammoth, massive, mighty, monstrous, monumental, mountainous, overgrown, oversized, prodigious, roomy, sizeable, spacious, stupendous, substantial, swingeing (*increase*), tall, *inf* terrific, thick, *inf* thumping, tidy (*sum*), titanic, towering, *inf* tremendous, vast, voluminous, weighty, *inf* whacking, *inf* whopping, wide. 2 *a big decision.* grave, important, influential, leading, main, major, momentous, notable, powerful, prime, principal, prominent, serious, significant. 3 *a big number.* ▷ INFINITE. 4 *a big name.* ▷ FAMOUS. 5 *a big noise.* ▷ LOUD. *Opp* SMALL.

bigot *n* chauvinist, fanatic, prejudiced person, racist, sexist, zealot.

bigoted *adj* intolerant, one-sided, partial, prejudiced. ▷ BIASED.

bill *n* 1 account, invoice, receipt, statement, tally. 2 advertisement, broadsheet, bulletin, circular, handbill, handout, leaflet, notice, placard, poster,

sheet. **3** *a Parliamentary bill.*
draft law, proposed law. **4** *a
bird's bill.* beak, mandible.

billow *vb* balloon, belly, bulge,
fill out, heave, puff out, rise,
roll, surge, swell, undulate.

bind *vb* **1** attach, clamp,
combine, connect, fuse, hitch,
hold together, join, lash, link,
rope, secure, strap, tie, truss,
unify, unite, weld. ▷ FASTEN.
2 *bind a wound.* bandage,
cover, dress, encase, swathe,
wrap. **3** *bound to obey.* compel,
constrain, force, necessitate,
oblige, require. **binding**
▷ COMPULSORY, FORMAL.

biography *n* autobiography, life,
life-story, memoirs, recollec-
tions. ▷ WRITING.

bird *n inf* birdie, chick, cock,
joc feathered friend, fledgling,
fowl, hen, nestling. □ *gamebird,
plur* poultry, seabird, wader,
waterfowl, wildfowl. □ albatross, auk, bittern, blackbird,
budgerigar, bullfinch, bunting,
bustard, buzzard, canary,
cassowary, chaffinch, chiff-chaff,
chough, cockatoo, coot, cormo-
rant, corncrake, crane, crow,
cuckoo, curlew, dabchick,
dipper, dove, duck, dunnock,
eagle, egret, emu, falcon, finch,
flamingo, flycatcher, fulmar,
goldcrest, goldfinch, goose,
grebe, greenfinch, grouse, gull,
hawk, heron, hoopoe, hornbill,
humming bird, ibis, jackdaw,
jay, kingfisher, kestrel, kite,
kiwi, kookaburra, lapwing,
lark, linnet, macaw, magpie,
martin, mina bird, moorhen,
nightingale, nightjar, nuthatch,
oriole, osprey, ostrich, ousel,
owl, parakeet, parrot, partridge,
peacock, peewit, pelican,
penguin, peregrine, petrel,

pheasant, pigeon, pipit, plover,
ptarmigan, puffin, quail, raven,
redbreast, redstart, robin, rook,
sandpiper, seagull, shearwater,
shelduck, shrike, skua, skylark,
snipe, sparrow, sparrowhawk,
spoonbill, starling, stonechat,
stork, swallow, swan, swift, teal,
tern, thrush, tit, toucan, turkey,
turtle-dove, vulture, wagtail,
warbler, waxwing, wheatear,
woodcock, woodpecker, wren,
yellowhammer.

birth *n* **1** childbirth, confinement, delivery, labour, nativity,
parturition. **2** ancestry, background, blood, breeding, derivation, descent, extraction,
family, genealogy, line, lineage,
parentage, pedigree, race,
stock, strain. **3** ▷ BEGINNING.
give birth bear, calve, farrow,
foal. ▷ BEGIN.

bisect *vb* cross, cut in half,
divide, halve, intersect.

bit *n* **1** atom, bite, block, chip,
chunk, crumb, division, dollop,
fraction, fragment, gobbet,
grain, helping, hunk, iota,
lump, modicum, morsel, mouthful, part, particle, piece,
portion, sample, scrap, section,
segment, share, slab, slice, snippet, soupçon, speck, spot, taste,
titbit, trace. **2** *Wait a bit.* flash,
instant, *inf* jiffy, minute,
moment, second, *inf* tick, time,
while.

bite *n* **1** nip, pinch, sting. **2** *a bite
to eat.* morsel, mouthful,
nibble, snack, taste. ▷ BIT.
● *vb* **1** champ, chew, crunch, cut
into, gnaw, masticate, munch,
nibble, nip, rend, snap, tear at,
wound. **2** *An insect bit me.*
pierce, sting. **3** *The screw won't
bite.* grip, hold.

bitter *adj* 1 acid, acrid, harsh, sharp, sour, unpleasant. 2 *a bitter experience.* calamitous, dire, distasteful, distressing, galling, hateful, heartbreaking, painful, poignant, sorrowful, unhappy, unwelcome, upsetting. 3 *bitter remarks.* acrimonious, acerbic, angry, cruel, cynical, embittered, envious, hostile, jaundiced, jealous, malicious, rancorous, resentful, savage, sharp, spiteful, stinging, vicious, violent, waspish. 4 *a bitter wind.* biting, cold, fierce, freezing, perishing, piercing, raw. *Opp* KIND, MILD, PLEASANT.

bizarre *adj* curious, eccentric, fantastic, freakish, grotesque, odd, outlandish, outré, surreal, weird. ▷ STRANGE. *Opp* ORDINARY.

black *adj* blackish, coal-black, dark, dusky, ebony, funereal, gloomy, inky, jet, jet-black, moonless, murky, pitch-black, pitch-dark, raven, sable, sooty, starless, unlit. ● *vb* 1 blacken, polish. 2 ▷ BLACKLIST.

blackleg *n sl* scab, strikebreaker, traitor.

blacklist *vb* ban, bar, blackball, boycott, debar, disallow, exclude, ostracize, preclude, proscribe, put an embargo on, refuse to handle, repudiate, snub, veto.

blade *n* dagger, edge, knife, razor, scalpel, vane. ▷ SWORD.

blame *n* accountability, accusation, castigation, censure, charge, complaint, condemnation, criticism, culpability, fault, guilt, imputation, incrimination, liability, onus, *inf* rap, recrimination, reprimand, reproach, reproof, responsibility, *inf* stick, stricture. ● *vb* accuse, admonish, censure, charge, chide, condemn, criticize, denounce, *inf* get at, hold responsible, incriminate, rebuke, reprehend, reprimand, reproach, reprove, round on, scold, tax, upbraid. *Opp* EXCUSE.

blameless *adj* faultless, guiltless, innocent, irreproachable, moral, unimpeachable, upright. *Opp* GUILTY.

bland *adj* affable, amiable, banal, boring, calm, characterless, dull, flat, gentle, insipid, mild, nondescript, smooth, soft, soothing, suave, tasteless, trite, unappetizing, unexciting, uninspiring, uninteresting, vapid, watery, weak, *inf* wishy-washy. *Opp* INTERESTING.

blank *adj* 1 bare, clean, clear, empty, plain, spotless, unadorned, unmarked, unused, void. 2 *a blank look.* apathetic, baffled, baffling, dead, *inf* deadpan, emotionless, expressionless, featureless, glazed, immobile, impassive, inane, inscrutable, lifeless, poker-faced, uncomprehending, unresponsive, vacant, vacuous. ● *n* 1 emptiness, nothingness, vacuity, vacuum, void. 2 *blanks on a form.* box, break, gap, line, space.

blaspheme *vb* curse, execrate, imprecate, profane, swear.

blasphemous *adj* disrespectful, godless, impious, irreligious, irreverent, profane, sacrilegious, sinful, ungodly, wicked. *Opp* REVERENT.

blast *n* 1 gale, gust, wind. 2 blare, din, noise, racket, roar, sound. 3 ▷ EXPLOSION.

• *vb* ▷ ATTACK, EXPLODE. **blast off** ▷ LAUNCH.

blatant *adj* apparent, bare-faced, bold, brazen, conspicuous, evident, flagrant, glaring, obtrusive, obvious, open, overt, shameless, stark, unconcealed, undisguised, unmistakable, visible. *Opp* HIDDEN.

blaze *n* conflagration, fire, flame, flare-up, holocaust, inferno, outburst. • *vb* burn, erupt, flame, flare.

bleach *vb* blanch, discolour, etiolate, fade, lighten, pale, peroxide (*hair*), whiten.

bleak *adj* bare, barren, blasted, cheerless, chilly, cold, comfortless, depressing, desolate, dismal, dreary, exposed, grim, hopeless, joyless, sombre, uncomfortable, unpromising, windswept, wintry. *Opp* COMFORTABLE, WARM.

bleary *adj* blurred, *inf* blurry, cloudy, dim, filmy, fogged, foggy, fuzzy, hazy, indistinct, misty, murky, obscured, smeary, unclear, watery. *Opp* CLEAR.

blemish *n* blot, blotch, chip, crack, defect, deformity, disfigurement, eyesore, fault, flaw, imperfection, mark, mess, smudge, speck, stain, ugliness. □ *birthmark, blackhead, blister, callus, corn, freckle, mole, naevus, pimple, pustule, scar, spot, verruca, wart, whitlow,* sl *zit*. • *vb* deface, disfigure, flaw, mar, mark, scar, spoil, stain, tarnish.

blend *n* alloy, amalgam, amalgamation, combination, composite, compound, concoction, fusion, mélange, mix, mixture, synthesis, union. • *vb* 1 amalgamate, coalesce, combine, commingle, compound, fuse, harmonize, integrate, intermingle, intermix, meld, merge, mingle, synthesize, unite. 2 *blend in a bowl*. beat, mix, stir together, whip, whisk.

bless *vb* 1 anoint, consecrate, dedicate, grace, hallow, make sacred, ordain, sanctify. 2 *bless God's name*. adore, exalt, extol, glorify, magnify, praise. *Opp* CURSE.

blessed *adj* 1 adored, divine, hallowed, holy, revered, sacred, sanctified. 2 ▷ HAPPY.

blessing *n* 1 benediction, consecration, grace, prayer. 2 approbation, approval, backing, concurrence, consent, leave, permission, sanction, support. 3 *Warmth is a blessing*. advantage, asset, benefit, boon, comfort, convenience, *inf* godsend, help. *Opp* CURSE, MISFORTUNE.

blight *n* affliction, ailment, *old use* bane, cancer, canker, curse, decay, disease, evil, illness, infestation, misfortune, *old use* pestilence, plague, pollution, rot, scourge, sickness, trouble. • *vb* ▷ SPOIL.

blind *adj* 1 blinded, eyeless, sightless, unseeing. □ *astigmatic, colour-blind, longsighted, myopic, near-sighted, short-sighted, suffering from cataract, suffering from glaucoma, visually handicapped*. 2 *blind devotion*. blinkered, heedless, ignorant, inattentive, indifferent, indiscriminate, insensible, insensitive, irrational, mindless, oblivious, prejudiced, unaware, unobservant, unreasoning. • *n* awning, cover, curtain, screen, shade, shutters. ● *vb* **1** dazzle, make blind. **2** ▷ DECEIVE.

blink *vb* coruscate, flash, flicker, flutter, gleam, glimmer, shimmer, sparkle, twinkle, wink.

bliss *n* blessedness, delight, ecstasy, euphoria, felicity, gladness, glee, happiness, heaven, joy, paradise, rapture. ▷ PLEASURE. *Opp* MISERY.

bloated *adj* dilated, distended, enlarged, inflated, puffy, swollen.

block *n* **1** bar, brick, cake, chock, chunk, hunk, ingot, lump, mass, piece, slab. **2** ▷ BLOCKAGE. ● *vb* **1** bar, barricade, *inf* bung up, choke, clog, close, congest, constrict, dam, fill, impede, jam, obstruct, plug, stop up. **2** *block a plan.* deter, halt, hamper, hinder, hold back, prevent, prohibit, resist, *inf* scotch, *inf* stonewall, stop, thwart.

blockage *n* barrier, block, bottleneck, congestion, constriction, hindrance, impediment, jam, obstacle, obstruction, resistance, stoppage.

blond, blonde *adj* bleached, fair, flaxen, golden, light, platinum, silvery, yellow.

bloodshed *n* bloodletting, butchery, carnage, killing, massacre, murder, slaughter, slaying, violence.

bloodthirsty *adj* barbaric, brutal, feral, ferocious, fierce, homicidal, inhuman, murderous, pitiless, ruthless, sadistic, sanguinary, savage, vicious, violent, warlike. ▷ CRUEL. *Opp* HUMANE.

bloody *adj* **1** bleeding, bloodstained, raw. **2** *a bloody battle.*

cruel, gory, sanguinary. ▷ BLOODTHIRSTY.

bloom *n* **1** blossom, bud, floret, flower. **2** *bloom of youth.* beauty, blush, flush, glow, prime. ● *vb* be healthy, blossom, *poet* blow, bud, burgeon, *inf* come out, develop, flourish, flower, grow, open, prosper, sprout, thrive. *Opp* FADE.

blot *n* **1** blob, blotch, mark, smear, smirch, smudge, *inf* splodge, spot, stain. **2** *blot on the landscape.* blemish, defect, eyesore, fault, flaw, ugliness. ● *vb* bespatter, blemish, blotch, blur, disfigure, mar, mark, smudge, spoil, spot, stain. **blot out** ▷ OBLITERATE. **blot your copybook** ▷ MISBEHAVE.

blotchy *adj* blemished, brindled, discoloured, inflamed, marked, patchy, smudged, spotty, streaked, uneven.

blow *n* **1** bang, bash, *inf* belt, *inf* biff, box (*ears*), buffet, bump, clip, clout, clump, concussion, hit, jolt, knock, punch, rap, slap, *inf* slash, smack, *inf* sock, stroke, swat, swipe, thump, thwack, wallop, welt, whack, whop. **2** *a sad blow.* affliction, *inf* bombshell, calamity, disappointment, disaster, misfortune, shock, surprise, upset. ● *vb* blast, breathe, exhale, fan, puff, waft, whine, whirl, whistle. **blow up 1** dilate, enlarge, expand, fill, inflate, pump up. **2** exaggerate, magnify, make worse, overstate. **3** blast, bomb, burst, detonate, dynamite, erupt, explode, go off, set off, shatter. **4** [*inf*] erupt, get angry, lose your temper, rage.

blue *adj* 1 aquamarine, azure, cerulean, cobalt, indigo, navy, sapphire, sky-blue, turquoise, ultramarine. 2 ▷ BAWDY. 3 ▷ SAD. ● *vb* ▷ SQUANDER.

blueprint *n* basis, design, draft, model, outline, pattern, pilot, plan, project, proposal, prototype, scheme.

bluff *vb* cozen, deceive, delude, dupe, fool, hoodwink, mislead.

blunder *n inf* boob, *inf* clanger, *sl* cock-up, error, fault, Fr faux pas, gaffe, howler, indiscretion, miscalculation, misjudgement, mistake, slip, slip-up, solecism. ● *vb* be clumsy, *inf* botch up, bumble, bungle, *inf* drop a clanger, err, flounder, *inf* foul up, *sl* goof, go wrong, *inf* make a hash of something, make a mistake, mess up, miscalculate, misjudge, *inf* put your foot in it, slip up, stumble.

blunt *adj* 1 dull, rounded, thick, unpointed, unsharpened, worn. *Opp* SHARP. 2 blunt criticism. abrupt, bluff, brusque, candid, curt, direct, downright, forthright, frank, honest, insensitive, outspoken, plain-spoken, rude, straightforward, tactless, unceremonious, undiplomatic. *Opp* TACTFUL. ● *vb* abate, allay, anaesthetize, dampen, deaden, desensitize, dull, lessen, numb, soften, take the edge off, weaken. *Opp* SHARPEN.

blur *vb* bedim, befog, blear, cloud, conceal, confuse, darken, dim, fog, mask, muddle, obscure, smear, unfocus.

blurred *adj* bleary, blurry, clouded, cloudy, confused, dim, faint, foggy, fuzzy, hazy, ill-defined, indefinite, indistinct, misty, nebulous, out of focus, smoky, unclear, unfocused, vague. *Opp* CLEAR.

blurt *vb* **blurt out** be indiscreet, *inf* blab, burst out with, come out with, cry out, disclose, divulge, exclaim, *inf* give the game away, let out, let slip, reveal, *inf* spill the beans, tell, utter.

blush *vb* be ashamed, colour, flush, glow, go red, redden.

blustering *adj* angry, boasting, boisterous, bragging, bullying, crowing, defiant, domineering, hectoring, noisy, ranting, self-assertive, showing-off, storming, swaggering, threatening, vaunting, violent. *Opp* MODEST.

blustery *adj* gusty, squally, unsettled, windy.

board *n* 1 blockboard, chipboard, clapboard, panel, plank, plywood, scantling, sheet, slab, slat, timber, weatherboard. 2 board of directors. cabinet, committee, council, directorate, jury, panel. ● *vb* 1 accommodate, billet, feed, house, lodge, put up, quarter, stay. 2 board a bus. catch, embark (on), enter, get on, go on board.

boast *vb sl* be all mouth, *inf* blow your own trumpet, bluster, brag, crow, exaggerate, gloat, praise yourself, *sl* shoot a line, show off, *inf* sing your own praises, swagger, *inf* swank, *inf* talk big, vaunt.

boaster *n inf* big-head, *inf* big mouth, braggadocio, braggart, *inf* loudmouth, *inf* poser, show-off, swaggerer, swank.

boastful *adj inf* big-headed, bragging, *inf* cocky, conceited, egotistical, ostentatious, proud, puffed up, swaggering, swanky, swollen-headed, vain, vainglorious. *Opp* MODEST.

boat *n* craft, ship. ▷ VESSEL.

boatman *n* bargee, coxswain, ferryman, gondolier, lighterman, oarsman, rower, waterman, yachtsman. ▷ SAILOR.

bob *vb* be agitated, bounce, dance, hop, jerk, jig about, jolt, jump, leap, move about, nod, oscillate, shake, toss about, twitch. **bob up** ▷ APPEAR.

body *n* 1 anatomy, being, build, figure, form, frame, individual, physique, shape, substance, torso, trunk. 2 cadaver, carcass, corpse, mortal remains, mummy, relics, remains, *sl* stiff. 3 association, band, committee, company, corporation, society. ▷ GROUP. 4 *body of material*. accumulation, agglomeration, collection, corpus, mass.

bodyguard *n* defender, guard, minder, protector.

bog *n* fen, marsh, marshland, mire, morass, mudflats, peat bog, quagmire, quicksands, salt-marsh, *old use* slough, swamp, wetlands. **get bogged down** be hindered, get into difficulties, get stuck, grind to a halt, sink.

bogus *adj* counterfeit, fake, false, fictitious, fraudulent, imitation, *inf* phoney, sham, spurious. *Opp* GENUINE.

Bohemian *adj inf* arty, *old use* beatnik, bizarre, eccentric, hippie, informal, nonconformist, off-beat, unconventional, unorthodox, *inf* way-out, weird.

boil *n* abscess, blister, carbuncle, chilblain, eruption, gathering, gumboil, inflammation, pimple,

pock, pustule, sore, spot, tumour, ulcer, *sl* zit.
● *vb* 1 cook, heat, simmer, stew. 2 bubble, effervesce, foam, seethe, steam. 3 ▷ RAGE.

boisterous *adj* animated, disorderly, exuberant, irrepressible, lively, loud, noisy, obstreperous, riotous, rollicking, rough, rowdy, stormy, tempestuous, tumultuous, undisciplined, unrestrained, unruly, uproarious, wild. *Opp* CALM.

bold *adj* 1 adventurous, audacious, brave, confident, courageous, daredevil, daring, dauntless, enterprising, fearless, *derog* foolhardy, forceful, gallant, hardy, heroic, intrepid, *inf* plucky, *derog* rash, *derog* reckless, resolute, self-confident, unafraid, valiant, valorous, venturesome.
2 [*derog*] *a bold request*. brash, brazen, *inf* cheeky, forward, fresh, impertinent, impudent, insolent, pert, presumptuous, rude, saucy, shameless, unashamed. 3 *bold colours, writing*. big, bright, clear, conspicuous, eye-catching, large, obvious, prominent, pronounced, showy, striking, strong, vivid. *Opp* FAINT, TIMID.

bolster *n* cushion, pillow.
● *vb* ▷ SUPPORT.

bolt *n* 1 arrow, dart, missile, projectile. 2 peg, pin, rivet, rod, screw. 3 *bolt on a door*. bar, catch, fastening, latch, lock.
● *vb* 1 bar, close, fasten, latch, lock, secure. 2 *The animals bolted*. abscond, dart away, dash away, escape, flee, fly, run off, rush off. 3 *bolt food*. ▷ EAT.
bolt from the blue ▷ SURPRISE.

bomb n bombshell, explosive. ▷ WEAPON. • vb ▷ BOMBARD.

bombard vb 1 assail, assault, attack, batter, blast, blitz, bomb, fire at, pelt, pound, shell, shoot at, strafe. 2 badger, beset, harass, importune, pester, plague.

bombardment n attack, barrage, blast, blitz, broadside, burst, cannonade, discharge, fusillade, hail, salvo, volley.

bombastic adj extravagant, grandiloquent, grandiose, high-flown, inflated, magniloquent, pompous, turgid.

bond n 1 chain, cord, fastening, fetters, handcuffs, manacles, restraints, rope, shackles. 2 bond of friendship. affiliation, affinity, attachment, connection, link, relationship, tie, unity. 3 a legal bond. agreement, compact, contract, covenant, guarantee, legal document, pledge, promise, word. • vb ▷ STICK.

bondage n enslavement, serfdom, servitude, slavery, subjection, thraldom, vassalage.

bonus n 1 bounty, commission, dividend, gift, gratuity, hand-out, honorarium, largesse, payment, inf perk, reward, supplement, tip. 2 addition, advantage, benefit, extra, inf plus.

bony adj angular, emaciated, gangling, gawky, lanky, lean, scraggy, scrawny, skinny, thin, ungainly. Opp GRACEFUL, PLUMP.

book n booklet, copy, edition, hardback, paperback, publication, tome, volume, work.
□ album, annual, anthology, atlas, bestiary, old use chap-book, compendium, concordance, diary, dictionary, digest, directory, encyclopaedia, fiction, gazetteer, guidebook, handbook, hymnal, hymn-book, jotter, ledger, lexicon, libretto, manual, manuscript, missal, notebook, omnibus, picture-book, prayer-book, primer, psalter, reading book, reference book, music score, scrap-book, scroll, sketch-book, textbook, thesaurus, vade mecum. ▷ WRITING. • vb 1 book for speeding. arrest, take your name, write down details. 2 book in advance. arrange, buy, engage, order, organize, reserve, sign-up.

booklet n brochure, leaflet, pamphlet, paperback.

boom n 1 bang, blast, crash, explosion, reverberation, roar, rumble. ▷ SOUND. 2 boom in trade. bonanza, boost, expansion, growth, improvement, increase, spurt, upsurge, upturn. ▷ PROSPERITY. 3 boom across a river. ▷ BARRIER. • vb 1 ▷ SOUND. 2 ▷ PROSPER.

boorish adj barbarian, ignorant, ill-bred, ill-mannered, loutish, oafish, philistine, uncultured, vulgar. Opp CULTURED.

boost n aid, encouragement, fillip, impetus, help, lift, push, stimulus. • vb advance, aid, assist, augment, bolster, build up, buoy up, encourage, enhance, enlarge, expand, foster, further, give an impetus to, heighten, help, improve, increase, inspire, lift, promote, push up, raise, support, sustain. Opp DEPRESS.

booth n box, carrel, compartment, cubicle, hut, kiosk, stall, stand.

booty n contraband, gains, haul, loot, pickings, pillage, plunder, spoils, *inf* swag, takings, trophies, winnings.

border n 1 brim, brink, edge, edging, frame, frieze, frill, fringe, hem, margin, perimeter, periphery, rim, surround, verge. 2 borderline, boundary, frontier, limit. 3 *flower border*. bed, herbaceous border.
● vb abut on, adjoin, be adjacent to, be alongside, join, share a border with, touch.

bore vb 1 burrow, drill, mine, penetrate, sink, tunnel. ▷ PIERCE. 2 *bore listeners*. alienate, depress, jade, *inf* leave cold, tire, *inf* turn off, weary. *Opp* INTEREST.

boring adj arid, commonplace, dead, dreary, dry, dull, flat, humdrum, long-winded, monotonous, prolix, repetitious, repetitive, soporific, stale, tedious, tiresome, trite, uneventful, unexciting, uninspiring, uninteresting, vapid, wearisome, wordy. *Opp* INTERESTING.

born adj congenital, genuine, instinctive, natural, untaught.

borrow vb adopt, appropriate, be lent, *inf* cadge, copy, crib, make use of, obtain, pirate, plagiarize, *inf* scrounge, *inf* sponge, take, use, usurp. *Opp* LEND.

boss n employer, head. ▷ CHIEF.

bossy adj aggressive, assertive, authoritarian, autocratic, bullying, despotic, dictatorial, domineering, exacting, hectoring, high-handed, imperious, lordly, magisterial, masterful, officious, oppressive, overbearing, peremptory, *inf* pushy, self-assertive, tyrannical. *Opp* SERVILE.

bother n 1 ado, difficulty, disorder, disturbance, fuss, *inf* hassle, problem, *inf* to-do. 2 annoyance, inconvenience, irritation, nuisance, pest, trouble, worry. ● vb 1 annoy, bewilder, concern, confuse, disconcert, dismay, disturb, exasperate, harass, *inf* hassle, inconvenience, irk, irritate, molest, nag, perturb, pester, plague, trouble, upset, vex, worry. 2 be concerned, be worried, care, mind, take trouble. ▷ TROUBLE.

bottle n flask. □ carafe, carboy, decanter, flagon, jar, jeroboam, magnum, phial, pitcher, vial, wine-bottle. **bottle up** ▷ SUPPRESS.

bottom adj deepest, least, lowest, minimum. ● n 1 base, bed, depth, floor, foot, foundation, lowest point, nadir, pedestal, substructure, underneath, underside. *Opp* TOP. 2 basis, essence, grounds, heart, origin, root, source. 3 *your bottom*. *vulg* arse, backside, behind, *inf* bum, buttocks, *joc* posterior, rear, rump, seat, *inf* sit-upon.

bottomless adj deep, immeasurable, unfathomable, unplumbable.

bounce vb bob, bound, bump, jump, leap, move about, rebound, recoil, ricochet, spring.

bound adj 1 certain, committed, compelled, constrained, destined, doomed, duty-bound, fated, forced, obligated, obliged, pledged, required, sure. 2 *bound with rope*. ▷ BIND.
● vb bob, bounce, caper, frisk, frolic, gambol, hop, hurdle, jump, leap, pounce, romp, skip, spring, vault. **bound for** aimed

at, directed towards, going to, heading for, making for, off to, travelling towards.

boundary n border, borderline, bounds, brink, circumference, confines, demarcation, edge, end, extremity, fringe, frontier, interface, limit, margin, perimeter, threshold, verge.

boundless adj endless, everlasting, immeasurable, incalculable, inexhaustible, infinite, limitless, unbounded, unconfined, unflagging, unlimited, unrestricted, untold. ▷ VAST. Opp FINITE.

bounty n alms, altruism, beneficence, benevolence, charity, generosity, giving, goodness, kindness, largesse, liberality, munificence, philanthropy, unselfishness.

bouquet n 1 arrangement, bunch, buttonhole, corsage, garland, nosegay, posy, spray, wreath. 2 bouquet of wine. ▷ SMELL.

bout n 1 attack, fit, period, run, spell, stint, stretch, time, turn. 2 battle, combat, competition, contest, encounter, engagement, fight, match, round, inf set-to, struggle.

bow vb 1 bend, bob, curtsy, genuflect, incline, kowtow, nod, prostrate yourself, salaam, stoop. 2 ▷ SUBMIT.

bowels n 1 entrails, guts, inf innards, insides, intestines, viscera, vitals. 2 core, depths, heart, inside.

bower n alcove, arbour, bay, gazebo, grotto, hideaway, pavilion, pergola, recess, retreat, sanctuary, shelter, summerhouse.

bowl n basin, bath, casserole, container, dish, pan, pie-dish, tureen. ● vb fling, hurl, lob, pitch, throw, toss.

box n carton, case, chest, container, crate. □ bin, caddy, canister, cartridge, casket, coffer, coffin, pack, package, punnet, tea-chest, tin, trunk. ● vb inf engage in fisticuffs, fight, punch, scrap, spar. ▷ HIT.

boxer n prize-fighter, sparring partner. ● bantamweight, cruiserweight, featherweight, flyweight, heavyweight, lightweight, middleweight, welterweight.

boy n derog brat, inf kid, lad, schoolboy, son, derog stripling, derog urchin, youngster, youth.

boycott n ban, blacklist, embargo, prohibition. ● vb avoid, black, blackball, blacklist, exclude, inf give the cold-shoulder to, ignore, make unwelcome, ostracize, outlaw, prohibit, spurn, stay away from.

bracing adj crisp, exhilarating, health-giving, invigorating, refreshing, restorative, stimulating, tonic.

brag vb crow, gloat, show off. ▷ BOAST.

brain n cerebrum, inf grey matter, intellect, intelligence, mind, inf nous, reason, sense, understanding, wisdom, wit.

brainwash vb condition, indoctrinate, re-educate.

branch n 1 arm, bough, limb, prong, shoot, sprig, stem, twig. 2 department, division, office, offshoot, part, ramification, section, subdivision, wing. ● vb diverge, divide, fork, ramify, split, subdivide. **branch out** ▷ DIVERSIFY.

brand *n* kind, label, line, make, sort, trademark, type, variety. • *vb* 1 burn, identify, label, mark, scar, stamp, tag. 2 censure, characterize, denounce, discredit, stigmatize, vilify.

brash *adj* brazen, bumptious, insolent, rash, reckless, rude, self-assertive. ▷ ARROGANT.

bravado *n* arrogance, bluster, braggadocio, machismo, swagger.

brave *adj* adventurous, audacious, bold, chivalrous, cool, courageous, daring, dauntless, determined, fearless, gallant, game, *sl* gutsy, heroic, indomitable, intrepid, lion-hearted, *derog* macho, noble, *inf* plucky, resolute, spirited, stalwart, stoical, stout-hearted, tough, unafraid, uncomplaining, undaunted, unshrinking, valiant, valorous, venturesome. *Opp* COWARDLY.

bravery *n* audacity, boldness, *sl* bottle, courage, daring, dauntlessness, determination, fearlessness, fibre, firmness, fortitude, gallantry, *inf* grit, *inf* guts, heroism, intrepidity, mettle, *inf* nerve, *inf* pluck, prowess, resolution, spirit, *sl* spunk, stoicism, tenacity, valour, will-power. *Opp* COWARDICE.

brawl *n* affray, altercation, *inf* bust-up, clash, *inf* dust-up, fracas, fray, *inf* free-for-all, mêlée, *inf* punch-up, quarrel, row, scrap, scuffle, *inf* set-to, tussle. • *vb* ▷ FIGHT.

brazen *adj* barefaced, blatant, cheeky, defiant, flagrant, impertinent, impudent, insolent, rude, shameless, unabashed, unashamed. *Opp* SHAMEFACED.

breach *n* 1 aperture, break, chasm, crack, fissure, gap, hole, opening, rent, space, split. 2 alienation, difference, disagreement, divorce, drifting apart, estrangement, quarrel, rift, rupture, schism, separation, split. 3 *breach of law.* contravention, failure, infringement, offence, transgression, violation.

bread *n* □ brioche, cob, croissant, French bread, loaf, roll, stick of bread, toast. ▷ FOOD.

break *n* 1 breach, breakage, burst, chink, cleft, crack, crevice, cut, fissure, fracture, gap, gash, hole, leak, opening, rent, rift, rupture, slit, split, tear. 2 *break from work.* *inf* breather, breathing-space, hiatus, interlude, intermission, interval, *inf* let-up, lull, pause, respite, rest, tea-break. 3 *break in service.* disruption, halt, interruption, lapse, suspension. • *vb* 1 breach, burst, *inf* bust, chip, crack, crumple, crush, damage, demolish, fracture, fragment, knock down, ruin, shatter, shiver, smash, *inf* smash to smithereens, snap, splinter, split, squash, wreck. ▷ DESTROY. 2 *break the law.* contravene, defy, disobey, disregard, fail to observe, flout, go back on, infringe, transgress, violate. 3 *break a record.* beat, better, do more than, exceed, excel, go beyond, outdo, outstrip, pass, surpass. **break down** ▷ ANALYSE, DEMOLISH. **break in** ▷ INTERRUPT, INTRUDE. **break off** ▷ FINISH. **break out** ▷ ESCAPE. **break through** ▷ PENETRATE. **break up** ▷ DISINTEGRATE.

breakdown *n* 1 collapse, destruction, disintegration,

downfall, failure, fault, hitch, malfunction, ruin, stoppage. **2** analysis, classification, detailing, dissection, itemization, *inf* rundown.

breakthrough *n* advance, development, discovery, find, improvement, innovation, invention, leap forward, progress, revolution, success.

breakwater *n* groyne, jetty, mole, pier, sea-defence.

breath *n* breeze, gust, murmur, pant, puff, sigh, stir, waft, whiff, whisper.

breathe *vb* **1** exhale, inhale, pant, puff, respire, suspire. **2** hint, let out, tell, whisper.

breathless *adj* exhausted, gasping, out of breath, panting, *inf* puffed, *inf* puffing and blowing, tired out, wheezy, winded.

breed *n* ancestry, clan, family, kind, line, lineage, nation, pedigree, progeny, race, sort, species, stock, strain, type, variety. ● *vb* **1** bear young ones, beget young ones, increase, multiply, procreate, produce young, propagate (*plants*), raise young ones, reproduce. **2** *breed contempt*. arouse, cause, create, cultivate, develop, engender, foster, generate, induce, nourish, nurture, occasion.

breeze *n* air-current, breath, draught, waft, wind, *poet* zephyr.

breezy *adj* airy, *inf* blowy, draughty, fresh, gusty, windy.

brevity *n* briefness, compactness, compression, conciseness, concision, curtness, economy, incisiveness, pithiness, shortness, succinctness, terseness.

brew *n* blend, compound, concoction, drink, hash, infusion, liquor, mixture, potion, preparation, punch, stew. ● *vb* **1** boil, cook, ferment, infuse, make, simmer, steep, stew. **2** *brew mischief*. concoct, contrive, *inf* cook up, develop, devise, foment, hatch, plan, plot, prepare, scheme, stir up.

bribe *n sl* backhander, bribery, *inf* carrot, enticement, *sl* graft, gratuity, incentive, inducement, *inf* payola, protection money, *inf* sweetener, tip. ● *vb* buy off, corrupt, entice, *inf* grease your palm, influence, offer a bribe, pervert, reward, suborn, tempt, tip.

brick *n* block, breeze-block, cube, set, sett, stone.

bridge *n* arch, connection, crossing, link, span, way over. □ *aqueduct, Bailey bridge, drawbridge, flyover, footbridge, overpass, pontoon bridge, suspension bridge, swing bridge, viaduct.* ● *vb* connect, cross, fill, join, link, pass over, span, straddle, tie together, traverse, unite.

bridle *vb* check, control, curb, restrain.

brief *adj* **1** cursory, ephemeral, evanescent, fast, fleeting, hasty, limited, little, momentary, passing, quick, sharp, short, short-lived, temporary, transient, transitory. **2** *brief comment.* abbreviated, abridged, compact, compendious, compressed, concise, condensed, crisp, curt, curtailed, incisive, laconic, pithy, shortened, succinct, terse, thumbnail, to the point. *Opp* LONG. ● *n* **1** advice, briefing, data, description, directions, information, instructions, orders, outline, plan. **2** *a barrister's brief.* argument, case, defence, dossier, summary.

• *vb* advise, coach, direct, enlighten, *inf* fill someone in, give someone the facts, guide, inform, instruct, prepare, prime, *inf* put someone in the picture.

briefs *n* camiknickers, knickers, panties, pants, shorts, trunks, underpants.

brigand *n* bandit, buccaneer, desperado, footpad, gangster, highwayman, marauder, outlaw, pirate, robber, ruffian, thief.

bright *adj* 1 ablaze, aglow, alight, beaming, blazing, burnished, colourful, dazzling, flashing, *derog* flashy, fresh, *derog* gaudy, glaring, gleaming, glistening, glittering, glossy, glowing, incandescent, lambent, light, luminous, lustrous, pellucid, polished, radiant, refulgent, resplendent, scintillating, shimmering, shining, shiny, showy, sparkling, twinkling, vivid. 2 *bright sky*. clear, cloudless, fair, sunny. 3 *bright prospects*. auspicious, favourable, good, hopeful, optimistic, rosy. 4 *a bright smile*. ▷ CHEERFUL. 5 *bright ideas*. ▷ CLEVER. *Opp* DULL.

brighten *vb* 1 cheer (up), enliven, gladden, illuminate, light up, liven up, *inf* perk up, revitalize, smarten up. 2 *The sky brightened*. become sunny, clear up, lighten.

brilliant *adj* 1 coruscating, dazzling, glaring, glittering, glorious, intense, resplendent, scintillating, shining, showy, sparkling, splendid, vivid. ▷ BRIGHT. *Opp* DULL. 2 [*inf*] *a brilliant game*. ▷ EXCELLENT.

brim *n* brink, circumference, edge, limit, lip, margin, peri-

meter, periphery, rim, top, verge.

bring *vb* 1 bear, carry, convey, deliver, fetch, take, transfer, transport. 2 *bring a friend*. accompany, conduct, escort, guide, lead, usher. 3 *The play brought great applause*. attract, cause, create, draw, earn, engender, generate, get, give rise to, induce, lead to, occasion, produce, prompt, provoke, result in. **bring about** ▷ CREATE. **bring in** ▷ EARN, INTRODUCE. **bring off** ▷ ACHIEVE. **bring on** ▷ ACCELERATE, CAUSE. **bring out** ▷ EMPHASIZE, PRODUCE. **bring up** ▷ EDUCATE, RAISE.

brink *n* bank, border, boundary, brim, circumference, edge, fringe, limit, lip, margin, perimeter, periphery, rim, skirt, threshold, verge.

brisk *adj* 1 active, alert, animated, bright, businesslike, bustling, busy, crisp, decisive, energetic, fast, keen, lively, nimble, quick, rapid, *inf* snappy, *inf* spanking (*pace*), speedy, spirited, sprightly, spry, vigorous. *Opp* LEISURELY. 2 *a brisk wind*. bracing, enlivening, fresh, invigorating, refreshing, stimulating.

bristle *n* barb, hair, prickle, quill, spine, stubble, thorn, whisker, wire. • *vb* become angry, become defensive, become indignant, bridle, flare up.

brittle *adj* breakable, crackly, crisp, crumbling, delicate, easily broken, fragile, frail, frangible, weak. *Opp* FLEXIBLE, RESILIENT.

broad *adj* 1 ample, capacious, expansive, extensive, great, large, open, roomy, spacious, sweeping, vast, wide. 2 *broad daylight*. clear, full, open, plain, undisguised. 3 *broad outline*. general, imprecise, indefinite, inexact, non-specific, sweeping, undetailed, vague. 4 *broad tastes*. all-embracing, catholic, comprehensive, eclectic, encyclopaedic, universal, wide-ranging. 5 *broad humour*. bawdy, *sl* blue, coarse, earthy, improper, impure, indecent, indelicate, racy, ribald, suggestive, vulgar. ▷ BROAD-MINDED. *Opp* FINITE, NARROW.

broadcast *n* programme, relay, show, telecast, transmission.
• *vb* 1 advertise, announce, circulate, disseminate, make known, make public, proclaim, promulgate, publish, relay, report, send out, spread about, televise, transmit. 2 *broadcast seed*. scatter, sow at random.

broadcaster *n* anchor-man, announcer, commentator, compère, disc jockey, DJ, link-man, newsreader, presenter. ▷ ENTERTAINER.

broaden *vb* branch out, build up, develop, diversify, enlarge, expand, extend, increase, open up, spread, widen. *Opp* LIMIT.

broad-minded *adj* all-embracing, balanced, broad, catholic, comprehensive, cosmopolitan, eclectic, enlightened, liberal, open-minded, permissive, tolerant, unbiased, unbigoted, unprejudiced, unshockable. *Opp* NARROW-MINDED.

brochure *n* booklet, broadsheet, catalogue, circular, folder, handbill, leaflet, pamphlet, prospectus, tract.

brooch *n* badge, clasp, clip, fastening.

brood *n* children, clutch (*of eggs*), family, issue, litter, offspring, progeny, young.
• *vb* 1 hatch, incubate, sit on. 2 *brood over mistakes*. agonize, dwell (on), *inf* eat your heart out, fret, mope, sulk, worry. ▷ THINK.

brook *n* beck, burn, channel, *poet* rill, rivulet, runnel, stream, watercourse.
• *vb* ▷ TOLERATE.

browbeat *vb* badger, bully, coerce, cow, hector, intimidate, tyrannize. ▷ FRIGHTEN.

brown *adj* beige, bronze, buff, chestnut, chocolate, dun, fawn, khaki, ochre, russet, sepia, tan, tawny, terracotta, umber.
• *vb* bronze, burn, colour, grill, tan, toast.

browse *vb* 1 crop grass, eat, feed, graze, pasture. 2 *browse in a book*. dip in, flick through, leaf through, look through, peruse, read here and there, scan, skim, thumb through.

bruise *n* black eye, bump, contusion, discoloration, *inf* shiner, welt. • *vb* blacken, crush, damage, discolour, injure, knock, mark. ▷ WOUND.

brush *n* 1 besom, broom. 2 *brush with police*. ▷ CONFLICT. • *vb* 1 comb, groom, scrub, sweep, tidy, whisk. 2 *just brushed the gatepost*. graze, touch. **brush aside** ▷ DISMISS, DISREGARD. **brush-off** ▷ REBUFF. **brush up** ▷ REVISE.

brutal *adj* atrocious, barbaric, barbarous, beastly, bestial, bloodthirsty, bloody, brutish, callous, cold-blooded, cruel, dehumanized, ferocious, hard-hearted, heartless, inhuman, inhumane, merciless, murderous, pitiless, remorseless, ruthless, sadistic, savage, uncivilized, unfeeling, vicious, violent, wild. ▷ UNKIND. *Opp* HUMANE.

brutalize *vb* dehumanize, harden, inure, make brutal.

brute *adj* crude, irrational, mindless, physical, rough, stupid, unfeeling, unthinking. ▷ BRUTISH. ● *n* 1 beast, creature, dumb animal. ▷ ANIMAL. 2 [*inf*] *a cruel brute.* barbarian, bully, devil, lout, monster, ruffian, sadist, savage, swine.

brutish *adj* animal, barbaric, barbarous, beastly, bestial, boorish, brutal, coarse, coldblooded, crude, cruel, *inf* gross, inhuman, insensitive, loutish, mindless, savage, senseless, stupid, subhuman, uncouth, unintelligent, unthinking. *Opp* HUMANE.

bubble *n* air-pocket, blister, hollow, vesicle. ● *vb* boil, effervesce, fizz, fizzle, foam, froth, gurgle, seethe, sparkle. **bubbles** effervescence, fizz, foam, froth, head, lather, suds.

bubbly *adj* carbonated, effervescent, fizzy, foaming, seething, sparkling. ▷ LIVELY.

buccaneer *n* adventurer, bandit, brigand, corsair, marauder, pirate, privateer, robber.

bucket *n* can, pail, scuttle, tub.

buckle *n* catch, clasp, clip, fastener, fastening, hasp. ● *vb* 1 clasp, clip, do up, fasten, hitch up, hook up, secure. 2 bend, bulge, cave in, collapse, contort, crumple, curve, dent, distort, fold, twist, warp.

bud *n* shoot, sprout. ● *vb* begin to grow, burgeon, develop, shoot, sprout. **budding** ▷ POTENTIAL, PROMISING.

budge *vb* 1 change position, give way, move, shift, stir, yield. 2 *can't budge him.* alter, change, dislodge, influence, move, persuade, propel, push, remove, shift, sway.

budget *n* accounts, allocation of funds, allowance, estimate, financial planning, funds, means, resources. ● *vb* allocate money, allot resources, allow (for), estimate expenditure, plan your spending, provide (for), ration your spending.

buff *n* ▷ ENTHUSIAST. ● *vb* burnish, clean, polish, rub, shine, smooth.

buffer *n* bulwark, bumper, cushion, fender, pad, safeguard, screen, shield, shock-absorber.

buffet *n* 1 bar, café, cafeteria, counter, snack-bar. 2 *a stand-up buffet.* ▷ MEAL. ● *vb* ▷ HIT.

bug *n* 1 ▷ INSECT, MICROBE. 2 *bug in a computer program.* breakdown, defect, error, failing, fault, flaw, *inf* gremlin, imperfection, malfunction, mistake, *inf* snarl-up, virus. ● *vb* 1 intercept, interfere with, listen in to, spy on, tap. 2 [*sl*] *Untidiness bugs me.* ▷ ANNOY.

build *vb* assemble, construct, develop, erect, fabricate, form, found, *inf* knock together, make, put together, put up, raise, rear, set up. **build up** ▷ INTENSIFY.

builder *n* bricklayer, construction worker, labourer.

building *n* construction, edifice, erection, piece of architecture, *inf* pile, premises, structure.

□ arcade, barn, barracks, basilica, boat-house, bungalow, cabin, castle, cathedral, chapel, château, church, cinema, college, complex, cottage, dovecote, factory, farmhouse, flats, fort, fortress, garage, gazebo, gymnasium, hall, hangar, hotel, house, inn, library, lighthouse, mansion, mausoleum, mill, monastery, monument, mosque, museum, observatory, outbuilding, outhouse, pagoda, palace, pavilion, pier, power-station, prison, pub, public house, restaurant, school, shed, shop, silo, skyscraper, stable, storehouse, studio, summerhouse, synagogue, temple, theatre, tower, villa, warehouse, windmill.

bulb n 1 corm, tuber. □ amaryllis, bluebell, crocus, daffodil, freesia, hyacinth, lily, narcissus, snowdrop, tulip. 2 electric bulb. lamp, light.

bulbous adj bloated, bulging, convex, distended, ovoid, pear-shaped, pot-bellied, rotund, rounded, spherical, swollen, tuberous.

bulge n bump, distension, hump, knob, lump, projection, protrusion, protuberance, rise, swelling. ● vb belly, billow, dilate, distend, enlarge, expand, project, protrude, stick out, swell.

bulk n 1 amplitude, bigness, body, dimensions, extent, immensity, largeness, magnitude, mass, size, substance, volume, weight. 2 the bulk of the work. inf best part, greater part, majority, preponderance.

bulky adj awkward, chunky, cumbersome, large, unwieldy. ▷ BIG.

bulletin n account, announcement, communication, communiqué, dispatch, message, news-flash, notice, proclamation, report, statement.

bullion n bar, ingot, nugget, solid gold, solid silver.

bull's-eye n bull, centre, mark, middle, target.

bully vb bludgeon, browbeat, coerce, cow, domineer, frighten, harass, hector, intimidate, oppress, persecute, inf pick on, inf push around, terrorize, threaten, torment, tyrannize.

bulwark n defence, earthwork, fortification, parapet, protection, rampart, redoubt, wall. ▷ BARRIER.

bump n 1 bang, blow, buffet, collision, crash, knock, smash, thud, thump. 2 bulge, distension, hump, knob, lump, projection, protrusion, protuberance, rise, swelling, tumescence, welt. ● vb 1 bang, collide with, crash into, jar, knock, ram, slam, smash into, strike, thump, wallop. ▷ HIT. 2 bounce, jerk, jolt, shake. **bump into** ▷ MEET. **bump off** ▷ KILL.

bumptious adj arrogant, inf big-headed, boastful, brash, inf cocky, conceited, egotistic, forward, immodest, officious, overbearing, over-confident, pompous, presumptuous, pretentious, inf pushy, self-assertive, self-important, smug, inf snooty, inf stuck-up, swaggering, vain, vainglorious, vaunting. Opp MODEST.

bumpy adj 1 bouncy, jarring, jerky, jolting. 2 a bumpy road. broken, irregular, jagged, knobbly, lumpy, pitted, rocky, rough, rutted, stony, uneven. Opp SMOOTH.

bunch n 1 batch, bundle, clump, cluster, collection, heap, lot, number, pack, quantity, set, sheaf, tuft. 2 bunch of flowers. bouquet, posy, spray. 3 [inf] bunch of friends. band, crowd, gang, gathering, mob, party, team, troop. ▷ GROUP.
• vb assemble, cluster, congregate, crowd, flock, gather, group, herd, huddle, mass, pack. Opp DISPERSE.

bundle n bag, bale, bunch, carton, collection, pack, package, packet, parcel, sheaf, truss.
• vb bale, bind, enclose, fasten, pack, package, roll, tie, truss, wrap. **bundle out** ▷ EJECT.

bung n cork, plug, stopper.
• vb ▷ THROW.

bungle vb blunder, botch, sl cock up, inf foul up, fluff, inf make a hash of, inf make a mess of, inf mess up, mismanage, inf muck up, inf muff, ruin, inf screw up, spoil.

buoy n beacon, float, marker, mooring buoy, signal.
• vb buoy up ▷ RAISE.

buoyant adj 1 floating, light. 2 a buoyant mood. ▷ CHEERFUL.

burden n 1 cargo, encumbrance, load, weight. 2 burden of guilt. affliction, albatross, anxiety, care, cross, duty, handicap, millstone, obligation, onus, problem, responsibility, sorrow, trial, trouble, worry.
• vb afflict, bother, encumber, hamper, handicap, impose on, load (with), inf lumber (with), oppress, overload (with), inf saddle (with), strain, tax, trouble, weigh down, worry.

burdensome adj bothersome, difficult, exacting, hard, heavy, onerous, oppressive, taxing, tiring, troublesome, trying, wearisome, wearying, weighty, worrying. Opp EASY.

bureau n 1 desk, writing-desk. 2 travel bureau. agency, counter, department, office, service.

bureaucracy n administration, government, officialdom, paperwork, inf red tape, regulations.

burglar n cat-burglar, housebreaker, intruder, robber. ▷ THIEF.

burglary n break-in, forcible entry, house-breaking, larceny, pilfering, robbery, stealing, theft, thieving.

burgle vb break in, pilfer, rob. ▷ STEAL.

burial n entombment, funeral, interment, obsequies.

burlesque n caricature, imitation, mockery, parody, pastiche, satire, inf send-up, spoof, inf take-off, travesty.

burly adj athletic, beefy, brawny, heavy, hefty, hulking, husky, muscular, powerful, stocky, stout, inf strapping, strong, sturdy, thickset, tough, well-built. Opp THIN.

burn n blister, charring.
• vb 1 be alight, blaze, flame, flare, flash, flicker, glow, smoke, smoulder, spark, sparkle. 2 carbonize, consume, cremate, destroy by fire, ignite, incinerate, kindle, light, reduce to ashes, set fire to, set on fire. 3 burn your skin. blister, brand, char, scald, scorch, sear, shrivel, singe, sting, toast. ▷ FIRE. HEAT.

burning adj 1 ablaze, afire, aflame, alight, blazing, flaming, glowing, incandescent, lit up, on fire, raging, smouldering.

2 *burning pain*. biting, blistering, boiling, fiery, hot, inflamed, scalding, scorching, searing, smarting, stinging. **3** *burning chemicals*. acid, caustic, corrosive. **4** *a burning smell*. acrid, pungent, reeking, scorching, smoky. **5** *a burning desire*. acute, ardent, consuming, eager, fervent, flaming, frenzied, heated, impassioned, intense, passionate, red-hot, vehement. **6** *a burning issue*. crucial, important, pertinent, pressing, relevant, urgent, vital.

burrow *n* earth, excavation, hole, retreat, set, shelter, tunnel, warren. ● *vb* delve, dig, excavate, mine, tunnel.

burst *vb* **1** break, crack, disintegrate, erupt, explode, force open, give way, open suddenly, part suddenly, puncture, rupture, shatter, split, tear. **2** ▷ RUSH.

bury *vb* cover, embed, enclose, engulf, entomb, immerse, implant, insert, inter, lay to rest, plant, put away, secrete, sink, submerge. ▷ HIDE.

bus *n old use* charabanc, coach, double-decker, minibus, *old use* omnibus.

bushy *adj* bristling, bristly, dense, fluffy, fuzzy, hairy, luxuriant, rough, shaggy, spreading, sticking out, tangled, thick, thick-growing, unruly, untidy.

business *n* **1** affair, concern, duty, function, issue, matter, obligation, problem, question, responsibility, subject, task, topic. **2** calling, career, craft, employment, industry, job, line of work, occupation, profession, pursuit, trade, vocation, work.

3 buying and selling, commerce, dealings, industry, marketing, merchandising, selling, trade, trading, transactions. **4** company, concern, corporation, enterprise, establishment, firm, organization, *inf* outfit, partnership, practice, *inf* set-up, venture.

businesslike *adj* careful, efficient, hard-headed, logical, methodical, neat, orderly, practical, professional, prompt, systematic, well-organized. *Opp* DISORGANIZED.

businessman, businesswoman *ns* dealer, entrepreneur, executive, financier, industrialist, magnate, manager, merchant, trader, tycoon.

bustle *n* activity, agitation, commotion, excitement, flurry, fuss, haste, hurly-burly, hurry, hustle, movement, restlessness, scurry, stir, *inf* to-do, *inf* toing and froing. ● *vb* dart, dash, fuss, hasten, hurry, hustle, make haste, move busily, rush, scamper, scramble, scurry, scuttle, *inf* tear, whirl.

busy *adj* **1** active, assiduous, bustling about, committed, dedicated, diligent, employed, energetic, engaged, engrossed, *inf* hard at it, immersed, industrious, involved, keen, occupied, *inf* on the go, pottering, preoccupied, slaving, *inf* tied up, tireless, *inf* up to your eyes, working. *Opp* IDLE. **2** *busy shops*. bustling, frantic, full, hectic, lively.

busybody *n* gossip, meddler, *inf* Nosey Parker, scandalmonger, snooper, spy. **be a busybody** ▷ INTERFERE.

butt n 1 haft, handle, shaft, stock. 2 *water butt.* barrel, cask. 3 *cigar butt.* end, remains, remnant, stub. 4 *butt of ridicule.* end, mark, object, subject, target, victim. ● vb buffet, bump, jab, knock, poke, prod, punch, push, ram, shove, strike, thump. ▷ HIT. **butt in** ▷ INTERRUPT.

buttocks n *vulg* arse, backside, behind, bottom, *vulg* bum, *Amer* butt, *Fr* derrière, fundament, haunches, hindquarters, *joc* posterior, rear, rump, seat.

buttress n pier, prop, support. ● vb brace, prop up, reinforce, shore up, strengthen, support.

buxom adj ample, bosomy, *vulg* chesty, full-figured, healthy-looking, plump, robust, rounded, voluptuous. Opp THIN.

buy vb acquire, come by, gain, get, get on hire purchase, *inf* invest in, obtain, pay for, procure, purchase. Opp SELL.

buyer n client, consumer, customer, purchaser, shopper.

bypass vb avoid, circumvent, dodge, evade, find a way round, get out of, go round, ignore, neglect, omit, sidestep, skirt.

by-product n adjunct, complement, consequence, corollary, repercussion, result, side-effect.

bystander n eyewitness, looker-on, observer, onlooker, passer-by, spectator, watcher, witness.

C

cabin n 1 bothy, chalet, cottage, hut, lodge, shack, shanty, shed, shelter. 2 *cabin on a ship.* berth, compartment, deckhouse, quarters.

cable n 1 chain, cord, flex, guy, hawser, lead, line, mooring, rope, wire. 2 *news by cable.* message, telegram, wire.

cacophonous adj atonal, discordant, dissonant, disharmonious, harsh, noisy, unmusical. Opp HARMONIOUS.

cacophony n atonality, caterwauling, din, discord, disharmony, dissonance, harshness, jangle, noise, racket, row, rumpus, tumult. Opp HARMONY.

cadence n accent, beat, inflection, intonation, lilt, metre, pattern, rhythm, rise and fall, sound, stress, tune.

cadet n beginner, learner, recruit, tiro, trainee.

cadge vb ask, beg, scrounge, sponge.

café n bar, bistro, brasserie, buffet, cafeteria, canteen, coffee bar, coffee house, coffee shop, diner, restaurant, snack-bar, take-away, tea-room, tea-shop.

cage n aviary, coop, enclosure, hutch, pen, pound.
● vb ▷ CONFINE.

cajole vb *inf* butter up, coax, flatter, inveigle, persuade, seduce.

cake n 1 bun, gateau. 2 *cake of soap.* bar, block, chunk, cube, loaf, lump, mass, piece, slab.
● vb 1 coat, clog, cover, encrust, make dirty, make muddy. 2 coagulate, congeal, consoli-

date, dry, harden, solidify, thicken.

calamitous adj awful, cataclysmic, catastrophic, deadly, devastating, dire, disastrous, distressful, dreadful, fatal, ghastly, ruinous, serious, terrible, tragic, unfortunate, unlucky, woeful.

calamity n accident, affliction, cataclysm, catastrophe, disaster, misadventure, mischance, misfortune, mishap, tragedy, tribulation.

calculate vb add up, ascertain, assess, compute, count, determine, do sums, enumerate, estimate, evaluate, figure out, find out, gauge, judge, reckon, total, value, weigh, work out. **calculated** ▷ DELIBERATE. **calculating** ▷ CRAFTY.

calibre n 1 bore, diameter, gauge, measure, size. 2 ability, capability, capacity, character, competence, distinction, excellence, genius, gifts, importance, merit, proficiency, quality, skill, stature, talent, worth.

call n 1 bellow, cry, exclamation, roar, scream, shout, yell. 2 bidding, invitation, signal, summons. 3 *social call*. stay, stop, visit. 4 *no call for it*. cause, demand, excuse, justification, need, occasion, request, requirement. • vb 1 bellow, clamour, cry out, exclaim, hail, roar, shout, yell. 2 *call on friends*. drop in, socialize, visit. 3 *called her "Jane"*. baptize, christen, dub, name. 4 *play called "Lear"*. entitle, title. 5 *call me at 7*. arouse, awaken, get someone up, rouse, wake, waken. 6 *call a meeting*. convene, gather, invite, order, summon. 7 *call by phone*.

contact, dial, phone, ring, telephone. **call for** ▷ FETCH, REQUEST. **call off** ▷ CANCEL. **call someone names** ▷ INSULT.

calligraphy n copperplate, handwriting, illumination, lettering, penmanship, script.

calling n business, career, employment, job, line of work, métier, occupation, profession, pursuit, trade, vocation, work.

callous adj apathetic, cold, cold-hearted, cool, dispassionate, hard-bitten, inf hard-boiled, hardened, hard-hearted, inf hard-nosed, heartless, inhuman, insensitive, merciless, pitiless, ruthless, inf thick-skinned, uncaring, unconcerned, unemotional, unfeeling, unsympathetic. ▷ CRUEL. Opp SENSITIVE.

callow adj adolescent, inf born yesterday, inf green, immature, inexperienced, innocent, juvenile, naïve, raw, unsophisticated, inf wet behind the ears, young. Opp MATURE.

calm adj 1 airless, even, flat, glassy, poet halcyon (days), like a millpond, motionless, placid, quiet, slow-moving, smooth, still, unclouded, unwrinkled, windless. 2 collected, derog complacent, composed, controlled, cool, dispassionate, equable, impassive, imperturbable, inf laid-back, level-headed, moderate, pacific, passionless, patient, peaceful, poised, quiet, relaxed, restful, restrained, sedate, self-possessed, sensible, serene, tranquil, undemonstrative, unemotional, unexcitable, inf unflappable, unhurried, unperturbed, unruffled, untroubled. Opp EXCITABLE,

STORMY. • n flat sea, peace, quietness, stillness, tranquillity. ▷ CALMNESS. • vb appease, compose, control, cool, lull, mollify, pacify, placate, quieten, sedate, settle down, smooth, sober down, soothe, tranquillize. Opp DISTURB.

calmness n derog complacency, composure, equability, equanimity, imperturbability, level-headedness, peace of mind, sang-froid, self-possession, serenity, inf unflappability. Opp ANXIETY, EXCITEMENT.

camouflage n blind, cloak, concealment, cover, disguise, façade, front, guise, mask, pretence, protective colouring, screen, veil. • vb cloak, conceal, cover up, disguise, hide, mask, obscure, screen, veil.

camp n bivouac, camping-ground, campsite, encampment, settlement.

campaign n action, battle, crusade, drive, effort, fight, manoeuvre, movement, offensive, operation, push, struggle, war.

campus n grounds, setting, site.

canal n channel, waterway.

cancel vb abandon, abolish, abort, abrogate, annul, call off, countermand, cross out, delete, drop, eliminate, erase, expunge, frank (stamps), give up, invalidate, override, overrule, postpone, quash, repeal, repudiate, rescind, revoke, scrap, inf scrub, wipe out, write off. **cancel out** ▷ NEUTRALIZE.

cancer n canker, carcinoma, growth, malignancy, melanoma, tumour.

candid adj blunt, direct, fair, forthright, frank, honest, ingenuous, just, inf no-nonsense, objective, open, out-spoken, plain, sincere, straight, straightforward, transparent, true, truthful, unbiased, undisguised, unequivocal, unflattering, unprejudiced. Opp INSINCERE.

candidate n applicant, aspirant, competitor, contender, contestant, entrant, nominee, inf possibility, pretender (to throne), runner, suitor.

cane n bamboo, rod, stick. • vb ▷ THRASH.

canoe n dug-out, kayak.

canopy n awning, cover, covering, shade, shelter, umbrella.

canvass vb campaign, census, enquiry, examination, investigation, market research, opinion poll, poll, probe, scrutiny, survey. • vb ask for, campaign, inf drum up support, electioneer, seek, solicit.

canyon n defile, gap, gorge, gulch, pass, ravine, valley.

cap n covering, lid, top. ▷ HAT. • vb ▷ COVER.

capable adj able, accomplished, adept, clever, competent, effective, effectual, efficient, experienced, expert, gifted, inf handy, intelligent, masterly, practised, proficient, qualified, skilful, skilled, talented, trained. Opp INCAPABLE. **capable of** apt to, disposed to, equal to, liable to.

capacity n 1 content, dimensions, magnitude, room, size, volume. 2 ability, acumen, capability, cleverness, competence, intelligence, potential, power, skill, talent, wit. 3 in an official capacity. appointment, duty, function, job, office, place, position, post, province, responsibility, role.

cape *n* **1** cloak, coat, cope, mantle, robe, shawl, wrap. **2** head, headland, peninsula, point, promontory.

caper *vb* bound, cavort, dance, frisk, frolic, gambol, hop, jig about, jump, leap, play, prance, romp, skip, spring.

capital *adj* **1** chief, controlling, first, foremost, important, leading, main, paramount, preeminent, primary, principal. **2** *capital letters.* big, block, initial, large, upper-case. **3** ▷ EXCELLENT. ● *n* **1** chief city, centre of government. **2** assets, cash, finance, funds, investments, money, principal, property, *sl* (the) ready, resources, riches, savings, stock, wealth, *inf* the wherewithal.

capitulate *vb* acquiesce, be defeated, concede, desist, fall, give in, relent, submit, succumb, surrender, *inf* throw in the towel, yield.

capricious *adj* changeable, erratic, fanciful, fickle, fitful, flighty, impulsive, inconstant, mercurial, moody, quirky, uncertain, unpredictable, unreliable, unstable, variable, wayward, whimsical. *Opp* STEADY.

capsize *vb* flip over, invert, keel over, overturn, tip over, turn over, *inf* turn turtle, turn upside down.

capsule *n* lozenge, medicine, pill, tablet.

captain *n* **1** boss, chief, head, leader. **2** commander, master, officer in charge, pilot, skipper.

caption *n* description, explanation, heading, headline, superscription, title.

captivate *vb* attract, beguile, bewitch, charm, delight, enamour, enchant, enrapture, enslave, ensnare, enthral, entrance, fascinate, hypnotize, infatuate, mesmerize, seduce, *inf* steal your heart, *inf* turn your head, win. *Opp* DISGUST.

captive *adj* caged, captured, chained, confined, detained, enslaved, ensnared, fettered, gaoled, imprisoned, incarcerated, jailed, restricted, secure, taken prisoner, *inf* under lock and key. *Opp* FREE. ● *n* convict, detainee, hostage, internee, prisoner, slave.

captivity *n* bondage, confinement, custody, detention, duress, imprisonment, incarceration, internment, protective custody, remand, restraint, servitude, slavery. ▷ PRISON. *Opp* FREEDOM.

capture *n* apprehension, arrest, seizure. ● *vb* apprehend, arrest, *inf* bag, bind, catch, *inf* collar, corner, ensnare, entrap, *inf* get, *inf* nab, net, *inf* nick, overpower, secure, seize, snare, take prisoner, trap. ▷ CONQUER. *Opp* LIBERATE.

car *n* automobile, *inf* banger, *joc* bus, *joc* jalopy, motor, motor car, *sl* wheels. □ cab, convertible, coupé, Dormobile, estate, fastback, hatchback, jeep, Land Rover, limousine, Mini, panda car, patrol car, police car, saloon, shooting brake, sports car, taxi, tourer. ▷ VEHICLE.

carcass *n* **1** body, cadaver, corpse, meat, remains. **2** *carcass of a car.* framework, hulk, remains, shell, skeleton, structure.

card n cardboard, pasteboard.
□ *bank card, birthday card, business card, calling card, credit card, get-well card, greetings card, identity card, invitation, membership card, notelet, picture postcard, playing-card, postcard, union card, Valentine, visiting card.*

care n 1 attention, carefulness, caution, circumspection, concentration, concern, diligence, exactness, forethought, heed, interest, meticulousness, pains, prudence, solicitude, thoroughness, thought, vigilance, watchfulness. 2 anxiety, burden, concern, difficulty, hardship, problem, responsibility, sorrow, stress, tribulation, vexation, woe, worry. ▷ TROUBLE. 3 *left in my care.* charge, control, custody, guardianship, keeping, management, protection, safe-keeping, ward. ● vb be troubled, bother, concern yourself, mind, worry.
care for ▷ LOVE, TEND.

career n business, calling, craft, employment, job, livelihood, living, métier, occupation, profession, trade, vocation, work. ● vb ▷ RUSH.

carefree adj 1 blasé, casual, cheery, contented, debonair, easy, easy-going, happy-go-lucky, indifferent, insouciant, inf laid-back, light-hearted, nonchalant, relaxed, unconcerned, unworried. ▷ HAPPY. 2 *carefree holiday.* leisured, peaceful, quiet, relaxing, restful, trouble-free, untroubled. Opp ANXIOUS.

careful adj 1 alert, attentive, cautious, chary, circumspect, heedful, mindful, observant, prudent, solicitous, thoughtful,

vigilant, wary, watchful. 2 *careful work.* accurate, conscientious, deliberate, diligent, exhaustive, fastidious, derog fussy, judicious, methodical, meticulous, neat, orderly, organized, painstaking, particular, precise, punctilious, responsible, rigorous, scrupulous, systematic, thorough, well-organized. Opp CARELESS.
be careful ▷ BEWARE.

careless adj absent-minded, heedless, ill-considered, imprudent, inattentive, incautious, inconsiderate, irresponsible, negligent, rash, reckless, thoughtless, uncaring, unguarded, unthinking, unwary. 2 *careless work.* casual, confused, cursory, disorganized, hasty, imprecise, inaccurate, jumbled, messy, perfunctory, scatter-brained, shoddy, slapdash, slipshod, inf sloppy, slovenly, thoughtless, untidy. Opp CAREFUL.

carelessness n haste, inattention, irresponsibility, negligence, recklessness, inf sloppiness, slovenliness, thoughtlessness, untidiness. Opp CARE.

caress vb cuddle, embrace, fondle, hug, kiss, make love to, sl neck with, nuzzle, pat, pet, rub against, smooth, stroke, touch.

caretaker n custodian, janitor, keeper, porter, superintendent, warden, watchman.

careworn adj gaunt, grim, haggard. ▷ WEARY.

cargo n consignment, freight, goods, lading (*bill of lading*), load, merchandise, payload, shipment.

69

caricature *n* burlesque, cartoon, parody, satire, *inf* send-up, spoof, *inf* take-off, travesty.
• *vb* burlesque, distort, exaggerate, imitate, lampoon, make fun of, mimic, mock, overact, overdo, parody, ridicule, satirize, *inf* send up, *inf* take off.

caring *n* concern, kindness, nursing, solicitude.

carnage *n* blood-bath, bloodshed, butchery, havoc, holocaust, killing, massacre, pogrom, shambles, slaughter.

carnal *adj* animal, bodily, erotic, fleshly, natural, physical, sensual, sexual. ▷ LUSTFUL. *Opp* SPIRITUAL.

carnival *n* celebration, fair, festival, festivity, fête, fiesta, fun and games, gala, jamboree, merrymaking, pageant, parade, procession, revelry, show, spectacle.

carp *vb* cavil, find fault, *inf* go on, *inf* gripe, grumble, object, pick holes, quibble, *inf* split hairs, whinge. ▷ COMPLAIN.

carpentry *n* joinery, woodwork.

carriage *n* 1 coach. ▷ VEHICLE. 2 bearing, comportment, demeanour, gait, manner, mien, posture, presence, stance.

carrier *n* 1 bearer, conveyor, courier, delivery-man, delivery-woman, dispatch rider, errand-boy, errand-girl, haulier, messenger, porter, postman, runner. 2 *carrier of a disease.* contact, host, transmitter.

carry *vb* 1 bring, *inf* cart, communicate, ferry, fetch, haul, lead, lift, *inf* lug, manhandle, move, relay, remove, ship, shoulder, take, transfer, transmit, transport. ▷ CONVEY. 2 *carry weight.* bear, hold up,

maintain, support. 3 *carry a penalty.* demand, entail, involve, lead to, occasion, require, result in. **carry on** ▷ CONTINUE. **carry out** ▷ DO.

cart *n* barrow, dray, truck, wagon, wheelbarrow.
• *vb* ▷ CARRY.

carton *n* box, cartridge, case, container, pack, package, packet.

cartoon *n* animation, caricature, comic strip, drawing, sketch.

cartridge *n* 1 canister, capsule, case, cassette, container, cylinder, tube. 2 *cartridge for a gun.* magazine, round, shell.

carve *vb* 1 slice. ▷ CUT. 2 *carve stone. inf* chip away at, chisel, engrave, fashion, hew, incise, sculpture, shape.

cascade *n* cataract, deluge, flood, gush, torrent, waterfall.
• *vb* ▷ POUR.

case *n* 1 box, cabinet, carton, casket, chest, container, crate, pack, packaging, suitcase, trunk. ▷ LUGGAGE. 2 *case of mistaken identity.* example, illustration, instance, occurrence, specimen, state of affairs. 3 *rules don't apply in his case.* circumstances, condition, context, plight, predicament, situation, state. 4 *a legal case.* action, argument, cause, dispute, inquiry, investigation, lawsuit, suit.

cash *n* banknotes, bills, change, coins, currency, *inf* dough, funds, hard money, legal tender, money, notes, *inf* (the) ready, *inf* the wherewithal.
• *vb* exchange for cash, realize, sell. **cash in on** ▷ PROFIT.

cashier n accountant, banker, check-out person, clerk, teller, treasurer. • vb ▷ DISMISS.

cask n barrel, butt, hogshead, tub, tun, vat.

cast n 1 ▷ SCULPTURE. 2 *cast of a play.* characters, company, dramatis personae, performers, players, troupe. • vb 1 bowl, chuck, drop, fling, hurl, impel, launch, lob, pelt, pitch, project, scatter, shy, sling, throw, toss. 2 *cast a sculpture.* form, found, mould, shape. ▷ SCULPTURE.

cast off ▷ SHED, UNTIE.

castaway adj abandoned, deserted, exiled, marooned, rejected, shipwrecked, stranded.

caste n class, degree, estate, grade, level, position, rank, standing, station, status, stratum.

castigate vb censure, chasten, chastise, *old use* chide, correct, discipline, lash, punish, rebuke, reprimand, scold, *inf* tell off. ▷ CRITICIZE.

castle n château, citadel, fort, fortress, mansion, palace, stately home, stronghold, tower.

castrate vb emasculate, geld, neuter, spay, sterilize, unsex.

casual adj 1 accidental, chance, erratic, fortuitous, incidental, irregular, promiscuous, random, serendipitous, sporadic, unexpected, unforeseen, unintentional, unplanned, unpremeditated, unstructured, unsystematic. Opp DELIBERATE. 2 *casual attitude.* apathetic, blasé, careless, *inf* couldn't-care-less, easy-going, *inf* free-and-easy, lackadaisical, *inf* laid-back, lax, negligent, nonchalant, offhand, relaxed,

inf slap-happy, *inf* throwaway, unconcerned, unenthusiastic, unimportant, unprofessional. Opp ENTHUSIASTIC. 3 *casual clothes.* comfortable, informal. Opp FORMAL.

casualty n dead person, death, fatality, injured person, injury, loss, victim, wounded person.

cat n kitten, *inf* moggy, *inf* pussy, tabby, tom, tomcat.

catacombs n crypt, sepulchre, tomb, underground passage, vault.

catalogue n brochure, directory, index, inventory, list, record, register, roll, schedule, table. • vb classify, codify, file, index, list, make an inventory of, record, register, tabulate.

catapult vb fire, fling, hurl, launch. ▷ THROW.

cataract n cascade, falls, rapids, torrent, waterfall.

catastrophe n blow, calamity, cataclysm, crushing blow, débâcle, devastation, disaster, fiasco, holocaust, mischance, mishap, ruin, ruination, tragedy, upheaval. ▷ MISFORTUNE.

catch n 1 bag, booty, capture, haul, net, prey, prize, take. 2 *suspected a catch.* difficulty, disadvantage, drawback, obstacle, problem, snag, trap, trick. 3 *catch on a door.* bolt, clasp, clip, fastener, fastening, hasp, hook, latch, lock. • vb 1 clutch, ensnare, entrap, grab, grasp, grip, hang on to, hold, hook, net, seize, snare, snatch, take, tangle, trap. 2 *catch a thief.* apprehend, arrest, capture, *inf* cop, corner, detect, discover, expose, intercept, *inf* nab, *inf* nobble, stop, surprise, take by surprise, unmask. 3 *caught* *me unawares.* come upon, discover, find, sur- prise.

4 *catch a bus.* be in time for, get on. **5** *catch a cold.* become infected by, contract, get. **catch on** ▷ SUCCEED, UNDERSTAND.

catch-phrase ▷ SAYING.

catch-22 ▷ DILEMMA. **catch up** ▷ OVERTAKE.

catching *adj* communicable, contagious, infectious, spreading, transmissible, transmittable.

catchy *adj* attractive, haunting, memorable, popular, singable, tuneful.

categorical *adj* absolute, authoritative, certain, complete, decided, decisive, definite, direct, dogmatic, downright, emphatic, explicit, express, firm, forceful, *inf* out-and-out, positive, strong, total, unambiguous, unconditional, unequivocal, unmitigated, unqualified, unreserved, utter, vigorous. *Opp* TENTATIVE.

category *n* class, classification, division, grade, group, head, heading, kind, order, rank, ranking, section, sector, set, sort, type, variety.

cater *vb* cook, make arrangements, minister, provide, provision, serve, supply.

catholic *adj* all-embracing, all-inclusive, broad, broad-minded, comprehensive, cosmopolitan, eclectic, general, liberal, universal, varied, wide, wide-ranging.

cattle *plur n* beef, bullocks, bulls, calves, cows, heifers, livestock, oxen, steers, stock.

catty *adj inf* bitchy, ill-natured, malevolent, malicious, mean, nasty, rancorous, sly, spiteful,

venomous, vicious. ▷ UNKIND. *Opp* KIND.

cause *n* **1** basis, beginning, genesis, grounds, motivation, motive, occasion, origin, reason, root, source, spring, stimulus. **2** agent, author, *old use* begetter, creator, initiator, inspiration, inventor, originator, producer. **3** *cause of his lateness.* excuse, explanation, pretext, reason. **4** *a good cause.* aim, belief, concern, end, ideal, object, purpose, undertaking. ● *vb* **1** arouse, awaken, begin, bring about, bring on, create, effect, effectuate, engender, foment, generate, give rise to, incite, kindle, lead to, occasion, precipitate, produce, provoke, result in, set off, spark off, stimulate, trigger off, *inf* whip up. **2** compel, force, induce, motivate.

caustic *adj* **1** acid, astringent, burning, corrosive, destructive. **2** *caustic criticism.* acidulous, acrimonious, biting, bitter, critical, cutting, mordant, pungent, sarcastic, scathing, severe, sharp, stinging, trenchant, virulent, waspish. *Opp* MILD.

caution *n* **1** alertness, attentiveness, care, carefulness, circumspection, discretion, forethought, heed, heedfulness, prudence, vigilance, wariness, watchfulness. **2** *let off with a caution.* admonition, caveat, *inf* dressing-down, injunction, reprimand, *inf* talking-to, *inf* ticking-off, warning. ● *vb* **1** advise, alert, counsel, forewarn, inform, *inf* tip off, warn. **2** *cautioned by the police.* admonish, censure, give a warning, reprehend, reprimand, *inf* tell off, *inf* tick off.

cautious *adj* 1 alert, attentive, careful, heedful, prudent, scrupulous, vigilant, watchful. 2 *cautious comments. inf* cagey, calculating, chary, circumspect, deliberate, discreet, gingerly, grudging, guarded, hesitant, judicious, non-committal, restrained, suspicious, tactful, tentative, unadventurous, wary, watchful. Opp RECKLESS.

cavalcade *n* march-past, parade, procession, spectacle, troop.

cave *n* cavern, cavity, den, grotto, hole, pothole, underground chamber. ● *vb* **cave in** ▷ COLLAPSE, SURRENDER.

cavity *n* cave, crater, dent, hole, hollow, pit.

cease *vb* break off, call a halt, conclude, cut off, desist, discontinue, end, finish, halt, *inf* kick (*a habit*), *inf* knock off, *inf* lay off, leave off, *inf* pack in, *inf* pack up, refrain, stop, terminate. Opp BEGIN.

ceaseless *adj* chronic, constant, continual, continuous, endless, everlasting, incessant, interminable, never-ending, non-stop, permanent, perpetual, persistent, relentless, unending, unremitting, untiring. Opp INTERMITTENT, TEMPORARY.

celebrate *vb* 1 be happy, have a celebration, let yourself go, *inf* live it up, make merry, *inf* paint the town red, rejoice, revel, *old use* wassail. 2 *celebrate an anniversary.* commemorate, hold, honour, keep, observe, remember. 3 *celebrate a wedding.* officiate at, solemnize. **celebrated** ▷ FAMOUS.

celebration *n* banquet, binge, carnival, commemoration, feast, festivity, *inf* jamboree,

joc jollification, merry-making, observance, *inf* orgy, party, *inf* rave-up, revelry, *church* service, *inf* shindig, solemnization. □ *anniversary, birthday, festival, fête, gala, jubilee, remembrance, reunion, wedding.*

celebrity *n* 1 ▷ FAME. 2 big name, *inf* bigwig, dignitary, famous person, idol, notability, personality, public figure, star, superstar, VIP, worthy.

celestial *adj* 1 astronomical, cosmic, galactic, interplanetary, interstellar, starry, stellar, universal. 2 *celestial beings.* angelic, blissful, divine, ethereal, godlike, heavenly, seraphic, spiritual, sublime, supernatural, transcendental, visionary.

celibacy *n* bachelorhood, chastity, continence, purity, self-restraint, spinsterhood, virginity.

celibate *adj* abstinent, chaste, continent, immaculate, single, unmarried, unwedded, virgin. ● *n* bachelor, spinster, virgin.

cell *n* cavity, chamber, compartment, cubicle, den, enclosure, living space, prison, room, space, unit.

cellar *n* basement, crypt, vault, wine-cellar.

cemetery *n* burial-ground, churchyard, graveyard, necropolis.

censor *vb* amend, ban, bowdlerize, *inf* clean up, cut, edit, exclude, expurgate, forbid, prohibit, remove.

censorious *adj* fault-finding, *inf* holier-than-thou, judgemental, moralistic, Pharisaical, self-righteous. ▷ CRITICAL.

censure n accusation, admonition, blame, castigation, condemnation, criticism, denunciation, diatribe, disapproval, *inf* dressing-down, harangue, rebuke, reprimand, reproach, reprobation, reproof, *inf* slating, stricture, *inf* talking-to, *inf* telling-off, tirade, verbal attack, vituperation.
• *vb* admonish, berate, blame, *inf* carpet, castigate, caution, chide, condemn, criticize, denounce, lecture, rebuke, reproach, reprove, scold, take to task, *sl* tear (someone) off a strip, *inf* tell off, *inf* tick off, upbraid.

census n count, survey, tally.

central *adj* 1 focal, inner, innermost, interior, medial, middle. 2 *central facts*. chief, crucial, essential, fundamental, important, key, main, major, overriding, pivotal, primary, principal, vital. *Opp* PERIPHERAL.

centralize *vb* amalgamate, bring together, concentrate, rationalize, streamline, unify. *Opp* DISPERSE.

centre n bull's-eye, core, focal point, focus, heart, hub, inside, interior, kernel, middle, midpoint, nucleus, pivot. *Opp* PERIMETER. • *vb* concentrate, converge, focus.

centrifugal *adj* dispersing, diverging, moving outwards, scattering, spreading. *Opp* CENTRIPETAL.

centripetal *adj* converging. *Opp* CENTRIFUGAL.

cereal n corn, grain. □ barley, corn on the cob, maize, millet, oats, rice, rye, sweet corn, wheat.

ceremonial *adj* celebratory, dignified, liturgical, majestic, official, ritual, ritualistic, solemn, stately. ▷ FORMAL. *Opp* INFORMAL.

ceremonious *adj* civil, courteous, courtly, dignified, formal, grand, *derog* pompous, proper, punctilious, *derog* starchy. ▷ POLITE. *Opp* CASUAL.

ceremony n 1 celebration, commemoration, *inf* do, event, formal occasion, function, occasion, parade, reception, rite, ritual, service, solemnity. 2 ceremonial, decorum, etiquette, formality, grandeur, pageantry, pomp, pomp and circumstance, protocol, ritual, spectacle.

certain *adj* 1 adamant, assured, confident, constant, convinced, decided, determined, firm, invariable, positive, resolved, satisfied, settled, stable, steady, sure, undoubting, unshakable, unwavering. 2 *certain proof*. absolute, authenticated, categorical, certified, clear, clear-cut, conclusive, convincing, definite, dependable, established, genuine, guaranteed, incontestable, incontrovertible, indubitable, infallible, irrefutable, known, official, plain, reliable, settled, sure, true, trustworthy, unarguable, undeniable, undisputed, undoubted, unmistakable, unquestionable, valid, verifiable. 3 *certain disaster*. destined, fated, guaranteed, imminent, inescapable, inevitable, inexorable, predestined, predictable, unavoidable. 4 *certain to pay up*. bound, compelled, obliged, required, sure. 5 *certain people*. individual, particular, some, specific, unnamed, unspecified. *Opp* UNCERTAIN. **be certain**

▷ KNOW. **for certain** ▷ DEFINITELY. **make certain** ▷ ENSURE.

certainty n 1 actuality, certain fact, inf foregone conclusion, foreseeable outcome, inevitability, necessity, inf sure thing. 2 assertiveness, assurance, authority, certitude, confidence, conviction, credence, positiveness, proof, sureness, truth, validity. Opp DOUBT.

certificate n authorization, award, credentials, degree, diploma, document, guarantee, licence, pass, permit, qualification, warrant.

certify vb 1 affirm, asseverate, attest, authenticate, aver, avow, bear witness, confirm, declare, endorse, guarantee, notify, sign, swear, testify, verify, vouch, vouchsafe, warrant, witness. 2 certify as competent. authorize, charter, commission, franchise, license, recognize, validate.

chain n 1 bonds, coupling, fetters, handcuffs, irons, links, manacles, shackles. 2 chain of events. column, combination, concatenation, cordon, line, progression, row, sequence, series, set, string, succession, train. • vb bind, clap in irons, fetter, handcuff, link, manacle, shackle, tether, tie. ▷ FASTEN.

chair n armchair, carver, deckchair, dining-chair, easy chair, recliner, rocking-chair, throne. ▷ SEAT. • vb ▷ PRESIDE.

chairperson n chair, chairman, chairwoman, convenor, director, leader, moderator, organizer, president, speaker.

challenge vb 1 accost, confront, inf have a go at, take on, tax. 2 challenge to duel. dare, defy,

old use demand satisfaction, provoke, summon. 3 challenge a decision. argue against, call in doubt, contest, dispute, dissent from, impugn, object to, query, question, take exception to.

challenging adj inspiring, stimulating, testing, thought-provoking, worthwhile. ▷ DIFFICULT. Opp EASY.

chamber n cavity, cell, compartment, niche, nook, space. ▷ ROOM.

champion adj great, leading, record-breaking, supreme, top, unrivalled, victorious, winning, world-beating. • n 1 conqueror, hero, medallist, prize-winner, record-breaker, superman, superwoman, titleholder, victor, winner. 2 champion of the poor. backer, defender, guardian, patron, protector, supporter, upholder, vindicator. 3 [old use] champion in lists. challenger, contender, contestant, fighter, knight, warrior. • vb ▷ SUPPORT.

championship n competition, contest, series, tournament.

chance adj accidental, adventitious, casual, coincidental, inf fluky, fortuitous, fortunate, haphazard, inadvertent, incidental, lucky, random, unexpected, unforeseen, unfortunate, unlooked-for, unplanned, unpremeditated. Opp DELIBERATE. • n 1 accident, coincidence, destiny, fate, fluke, fortune, gamble, hazard, luck, misfortune, serendipity. 2 chance of rain. danger, liability, likelihood, possibility, probability, prospect, risk. 3 occasion, opportunity, time, turn. • vb 1 ▷ RISK. 2 ▷ HAPPEN.

chancy adj dangerous, *inf* dicey, *inf* dodgy, hazardous, *inf* iffy, insecure, precarious, risky, speculative, ticklish, tricky, uncertain, unpredictable, unsafe. Opp SAFE.

change n 1 adaptation, adjustment, alteration, break, conversion, deterioration, development, difference, diversion, improvement, innovation, metamorphosis, modification, modulation, mutation, new look, rearrangement, refinement, reformation, reorganization, revolution, shift, substitution, swing, transfiguration, transformation, transition, translation, transmogrification, transmutation, *inf* turn-about, U-turn, variation, variety, vicissitude. 2 *small change.* ▷ CASH. ● vb 1 acclimatize, accommodate, accustom, adapt, adjust, affect, alter, amend, convert, diversify, influence, modify, process, rearrange, reconstruct, refashion, reform, remodel, reorganize, reshape, restyle, tailor, transfigure, transform, translate, transmogrify, transmute, vary. 2 *opinions change.* alter, be transformed, *inf* chop and change, develop, fluctuate, metamorphose, move on, mutate, shift, vary. 3 *change one thing for another.* alternate, displace, exchange, replace, substitute, switch, swop, transpose. 4 *change money.* barter, convert, trade in. **change into** ▷ BECOME. **change someone's mind** ▷ CONVERT. **change your mind** ▷ RECONSIDER.

changeable adj capricious, chequered (*career*), erratic, fickle, fitful, fluctuating, fluid,

inconsistent, inconstant, irregular, mercurial, mutable, protean, shifting, temperamental, uncertain, unpredictable, unreliable, unsettled, unstable, unsteady, *inf* up and down, vacillating, variable, varying, volatile, wavering. Opp CONSTANT.

channel n 1 aqueduct, canal, conduit, course, dike, ditch, duct, groove, gully, gutter, moat, overflow, pipe, sluice, sound, strait, trench, trough, watercourse, waterway. ▷ STREAM. 2 avenue, means, medium, path, route, way. 3 *TV channel.* *inf* side, station, waveband, wavelength. ● vb conduct, convey, direct, guide, lead, pass on, route, send, transmit.

chant n hymn, plainsong, psalm. ▷ SONG. ● vb intone. ▷ SING.

chaos n anarchy, bedlam, confusion, disorder, disorganization, lawlessness, mayhem, muddle, pandemonium, shambles, tumult, turmoil. Opp ORDER.

chaotic adj anarchic, confused, deranged, disordered, disorderly, disorganized, haphazard, *inf* haywire, *inf* higgledy-piggledy, jumbled, lawless, muddled, rebellious, riotous, *inf* shambolic, *inf* topsy-turvy, tumultuous, uncontrolled, ungovernable, unruly, untidy, *inf* upside-down. Opp ORDERLY.

char vb blacken, brown, burn, carbonize, scorch, sear, singe.

character n 1 distinctiveness, flavour, idiosyncrasy, individuality, integrity, peculiarity, quality, stamp, taste, uniqueness. ▷ CHARACTERISTIC. 2 *a forceful character.* attitude, constitution, disposition, individuality, make-up, manner, nature, personality, reputation, temper, temperament. 3 *a famous character*. figure, human being, individual, person, personality, *inf* type. 4 *She's a character! inf* case, comedian, comic, eccentric, *inf* nut-case, oddity, *derog* weirdo. 5 *character in a play*. part, persona, portrayal, role. 6 *written characters*. cipher, figure, hieroglyphic, ideogram, letter, mark, rune, sign, symbol, type.

characteristic *adj* 1 *[of an individual]* distinctive, distinguishing, essential, idiosyncratic, individual, particular, peculiar, recognizable, singular, special, specific, symptomatic, unique. 2 *[of a kind]* representative, typical. ● *n* attribute, distinguishing feature, feature, hallmark, idiosyncrasy, mark, peculiarity, property, quality, symptom, trait.

characterize *vb* brand, delineate, depict, describe, differentiate, distinguish, draw, identify, individualize, mark, portray, present, recognize, typify.

charade *n* absurdity, deceit, deception, fabrication, farce, make-believe, masquerade, mockery, *inf* play-acting, pose, pretence, *inf* put-up job, sham.

charge *n* 1 cost, expenditure, expense, fare, fee, payment, postage, price, rate, terms, toll, value. 2 *in my charge*. care, command, control, custody, guardianship, jurisdiction, keeping, protection, responsibility, safe-keeping, supervision, trust. 3 *criminal charges*. accusation, allegation, imputa-

tion, indictment. 4 *cavalry charge*. action, assault, attack, drive, incursion, invasion, offensive, onslaught, raid, rush, sally, sortie, strike. ● *vb* 1 ask for, debit, exact, levy, make you pay, require. 2 accuse, blame, impeach, indict, prosecute, tax. 3 *charge with a duty*. burden, commit, empower, entrust, give, impose on. 4 *charged us to do our best*. ask, command, direct, enjoin, exhort, instruct. 5 *charge an enemy*. assail, assault, attack, *inf* fall on, rush, set on, storm, *inf* wade into.

charitable *adj* bountiful, generous, humanitarian, liberal, munificent, open-handed, philanthropic, unsparing. ▷ KIND. *Opp* MEAN.

charity *n* 1 affection, altruism, benevolence, bounty, caring, compassion, consideration, generosity, goodness, helpfulness, humanity, kindness, love, mercy, philanthropy, self-sacrifice, sympathy, tender-heartedness, unselfishness, warm-heartedness. 2 *old use* alms, alms-giving, bounty, donation, financial support, gift, *inf* hand-out, largesse, offering, patronage, poor relief. 3 *good cause*. the needy, the poor.

charm *n* 1 allure, appeal, attractiveness, charisma, fascination, hypnotic power, lovable nature, lure, magic, magnetism, power, pull, seductiveness. ▷ BEAUTY. 2 *magic charm*. curse, enchantment, incantation, magic, mumbo-jumbo, sorcery, spell, witchcraft, wizardry. 3 *charm on a bracelet*. amulet, lucky charm, mascot, ornament, talisman, trinket. ● *vb* allure, attract, beguile, bewitch, cajole, captivate, cast a spell on, decoy, delight, disarm, enchant, enrapture, intrigue, lure, mesmerize, please, seduce, soothe, win over. **charming** ▷ ATTRACTIVE.

chart n diagram, graph, map, plan, sketch-map, table.

charter vb 1 employ, engage, hire, lease, rent. 2 ▷ CERTIFY.

chase vb drive, follow, go after, hound, hunt, pursue, run after, track, trail.

chasm n abyss, canyon, cleft, crater, crevasse, drop, fissure, gap, gulf, hole, hollow, opening, pit, ravine, rift, split, void.

chaste adj 1 abstinent, celibate, inf clean, continent, good, immaculate, inexperienced, innocent, moral, pure, sinless, uncorrupted, undefiled, unmarried, virgin, virginal, virtuous. Opp IMMORAL. 2 chaste dress. austere, becoming, decent, decorous, maidenly, modest, plain, restrained, severe, simple, tasteful, unadorned. Opp INDECENT.

chasten vb 1 restrain, subdue. ▷ HUMILIATE. 2 ▷ CHASTISE.

chastise vb castigate, chasten, correct, discipline, penalize, rebuke, scold. ▷ PUNISH, REPRIMAND.

chastity n abstinence, celibacy, continence, innocence, integrity, maidenhood, morality, purity, restraint, sinlessness, virginity, virtue. Opp LUST.

chat n chatter, inf chin-wag, inf chit-chat, conversation, gossip, inf heart-to-heart. • vb chatter, converse, gossip, inf natter, prattle. ▷ TALK. **chat up** ▷ WOO.

chauvinist n bigot, inf MCP (= male chauvinist pig), patriot, sexist, xenophobe.

cheap adj 1 bargain, budget, cut-price, inf dirt-cheap, discount, economical, economy, fair, inexpensive, inf knock-down, low-priced, reasonable, reduced, inf rock-bottom, sale, under-priced. 2 cheap quality. base, inferior, poor, second-rate, shoddy, inf tatty, tawdry, inf tinny, inf trashy, worthless. 3 a cheap insult. contemptible, crude, despicable, facile, glib, ill-bred, ill-mannered, mean, silly, tasteless, unworthy, vulgar. Opp EXPENSIVE, WORTHY.

cheapen vb belittle, debase, degrade, demean, devalue, discredit, downgrade, lower the tone (of), popularize, prostitute, vulgarize.

cheat n 1 charlatan, cheater, inf con-man, counterfeiter, deceiver, double-crosser, extortioner, forger, fraud, hoaxer, impersonator, impostor, mountebank, inf phoney, inf quack, racketeer, rogue, inf shark, swindler, trickster, inf twister. 2 artifice, bluff, chicanery, inf confidence trick, deceit, deception, sl fiddle, fraud, hoax, imposture, lie, misrepresentation, pretence, inf put-up job, inf racket, inf rip-off, ruse, sham, swindle, inf swizz, treachery, trick. • vb 1 bamboozle, beguile, bilk, inf con, deceive, defraud, sl diddle, inf do, double-cross, dupe, sl fiddle, inf fleece, fool, hoax, hoodwink, outwit, inf rip off, rob, inf short-change, swindle, take in, trick. 2 cheat in an exam. copy, crib, plagiarize.

check adj ▷ CHEQUERED.
● n 1 break, delay, halt, hesitation, hiatus, interruption, pause, stop, stoppage, suspension. 2 medical check. check-up, examination, inf going-over, inspection, investigation, inf once-over, scrutiny, test. ● vb 1 arrest, bar, block, bridle, control, curb, delay, foil, govern, halt, hamper, hinder, hold back, impede, inhibit, keep in check, obstruct, regulate, rein, repress, restrain, retard, slow down, stem, stop, stunt (growth), thwart. 2 check answers. Amer check out, compare, cross-check, examine, inspect, investigate, monitor, research, scrutinize, test, verify.

cheek n audacity, boldness, brazenness, effrontery, impertinence, impudence, insolence, presumptuousness, rudeness, shamelessness, temerity.

cheeky adj arrogant, audacious, bold, brazen, cool, discourteous, disrespectful, flippant, forward, impertinent, impolite, impudent, insolent, insulting, irreverent, mocking, pert, presumptuous, rude, inf saucy, shameless, inf tongue-in-cheek. Opp RESPECTFUL.

cheer n 1 acclamation, applause, cry of approval, encouragement, hurrah, ovation, shout of approval. 2 ▷ HAPPINESS.
● vb 1 acclaim, applaud, clap, encourage, shout, yell. Opp JEER. 2 comfort, console, delight, encourage, exhilarate, gladden, make cheerful, please, solace, uplift. Opp SADDEN. **cheer someone up** ▷ COMFORT, ENTERTAIN. **cheer up** ▷ BRIGHTEN. **Cheer up!**

inf buck up, look happy, inf perk up, smile, sl snap out of it, take heart.

cheerful adj animated, bouncy, bright, buoyant, cheery, inf chirpy, contented, convivial, delighted, elated, festive, gay, genial, glad, gleeful, good-humoured, hearty, hopeful, jaunty, jocund, jolly, jovial, joyful, joyous, jubilant, laughing, light, light-hearted, lively, merry, optimistic, inf perky, pleased, positive, rapturous, sparkling, spirited, sprightly, sunny, warm-hearted. ▷ HAPPY. Opp CHEERLESS, CHEERLESS.

cheerless adj bleak, comfortless, dark, depressing, desolate, dingy, disconsolate, dismal, drab, dreary, dull, forbidding, forlorn, frowning, funereal, gloomy, grim, joyless, lacklustre, melancholy, miserable, mournful, sober, sombre, sullen, sunless, uncongenial, unhappy, uninviting, unpleasant, unpromising, woeful, wretched. ▷ SAD. Opp CHEERFUL.

chemical n compound, element, substance.

chemist n old use apothecary, Amer drug-store, pharmacist, pharmacy.

chequered adj 1 check, criss-cross, in squares, like a chess-board, patchwork, tartan, tessellated. 2 chequered career. ▷ CHANGEABLE.

cherish vb be fond of, care for, cosset, foster, hold dear, keep safe, look after, love, nourish, nurse, nurture, prize, protect, treasure, value.

chest n 1 box, caddy, case, casket, coffer, crate, strongbox, trunk. 2 breast, rib-cage, thorax.

chew *vb* bite, champ, crunch, gnaw, grind, masticate, munch, nibble. ▷ EAT. **chew over** ▷ CONSIDER.

chick *n* fledgling, nestling.

chicken *n* bantam, broiler, cockerel, fowl, hen, pullet, rooster.

chief *adj* 1 arch, best, first, greatest, head, highest, in charge, leading, major, most experienced, most honoured, most important, oldest, outstanding, premier, principal, senior, supreme, top, unequalled, unrivalled. 2 *chief facts*. basic, cardinal, central, dominant, especial, essential, foremost, fundamental, high-priority, indispensable, key, main, necessary, overriding, paramount, predominant, primary, prime, salient, significant, substantial, uppermost, vital, weighty. *Opp* UNIMPORTANT. ● *n* administrator, authority-figure, *inf* bigwig, *inf* boss, captain, chairperson, chieftain, commander, commanding officer, commissioner, controller, director, employer, executive, foreman, forewoman, *inf* gaffer, *Amer inf* godfather, governor, head, king, leader, manager, managing director, master, mistress, *inf* number one, officer, organizer, overseer, owner, president, principal, proprietor, ring-leader, ruler, superintendent, supervisor, *inf* supremo.

chiefly *adv* especially, essentially, generally, in particular, mainly, mostly, particularly, predominantly, primarily, principally, usually.

child *n* 1 adolescent, *inf* babe, baby, *Scot* bairn, *inf* bambino, boy, *derog* brat, girl, *derog* guttersnipe, infant, juvenile, *inf* kid, lad, lass, minor, newborn, *inf* nipper, offspring, *inf* stripling, toddler, *inf* tot, *derog* urchin, youngster, youth. 2 daughter, descendant, heir, issue, offspring, progeny, son.

childhood *n* adolescence, babyhood, boyhood, girlhood, infancy, minority, schooldays, *inf* teens, youth.

childish *adj* babyish, credulous, foolish, immature, infantile, juvenile, puerile. ▷ SILLY. *Opp* MATURE.

childlike *adj* artless, frank, *inf* green, guileless, ingenuous, innocent, naïve, natural, simple, trustful, unaffected, unsophisticated. *Opp* ARTFUL.

chill *n* ▷ COLD. ● *vb* cool, freeze, keep cold, make cold, refrigerate. *Opp* WARM.

chilly *adj* 1 cold, cool, crisp, fresh, frosty, icy, *inf* nippy, *inf* parky, raw, sharp, wintry. 2 *a chilly greeting*. aloof, cool, dispassionate, frigid, hostile, ill-disposed, remote, reserved, *inf* standoffish, unforthcoming, unfriendly, unresponsive, unsympathetic, unwelcoming. *Opp* WARM.

chime *n* carillon, peal, striking, tintinnabulation, tolling. ● *vb* ▷ RING.

chimney *n* flue, funnel, smokestack.

china *n* porcelain. ▷ CROCKERY.

chink *n* 1 cleft, crack, cranny, crevice, cut, fissure, gap, opening, rift, slit, slot, space, split. 2 ▷ SOUND.

chip n 1 bit, flake, fleck, fragment, piece, scrap, shard, shaving, shiver, slice, sliver, splinter, wedge. 2 *a chip in a cup*. crack, damage, flaw, gash, nick, notch, scratch, snick.
• vb break, crack, damage, gash, nick, notch, scratch, splinter. **chip away** ▷ CHISEL.
chip in ▷ CONTRIBUTE, INTERRUPT.

chisel vb carve, *inf* chip away, cut, engrave, fashion, model, sculpture, shape.

chivalrous adj bold, brave, chivalric, courageous, courteous, courtly, gallant, generous, gentlemanly, heroic, honourable, knightly, noble, polite, respectable, true, trustworthy, valiant, valorous, worthy. *Opp* COWARDLY, RUDE.

choice adj ▷ EXCELLENT.
• n 1 alternative, dilemma, need to choose, option. 2 *make your choice*. choosing, decision, election, liking, nomination, pick, preference, say, vote. 3 *a choice of food*. array, assortment, diversity, miscellany, mixture, range, selection, variety.

choke vb 1 asphyxiate, garrotte, smother, stifle, strangle, suffocate, throttle. 2 *choke in smoke*. cough, gag, gasp, retch.
3 *choked with traffic*. block, *inf* bung up, clog, close, congest, constrict, dam, fill, jam, obstruct, smother, stop up. **choke back** ▷ SUPPRESS.

choose vb adopt, agree on, appoint, decide on, determine on, distinguish, draw lots for, elect, establish, fix on, identify, isolate, name, nominate, opt for, pick out, *inf* plump for, prefer, select, settle on, show a

preference for, single out, vote for.

choosy adj dainty, discerning, discriminating, exacting, fastidious, finical, finicky, fussy, *inf* hard to please, nice, particular, pernickety, *inf* picky, selective. *Opp* INDIFFERENT.

chop vb cleave, cut, hack, hew, lop, slash, split. ▷ CUT. **chop and change** ▷ CHANGE.

chopper n axe, cleaver.

choppy adj roughish, ruffled, turbulent, uneven, wavy. *Opp* SMOOTH.

chore n burden, drudgery, duty, errand, job, task, work.

chorus n 1 choir, choral society, vocal ensemble. 2 *join in the chorus*. refrain, response.

christen vb anoint, baptize, call, dub, name.

chronic adj 1 ceaseless, constant, continuing, deeprooted, habitual, incessant, incurable, ineradicable, ingrained, lasting, lifelong, lingering, long-lasting, long-lived, long-standing, never-ending, non-stop, permanent, persistent, unending. *Opp* ACUTE, TEMPORARY. 2 [*inf*] *chronic driving*. ▷ BAD.

chronicle n account, annals, archive, chronology, description, diary, history, journal, narrative, record, register, saga, story.

chronological adj consecutive, in order, sequential.

chronology n 1 almanac, calendar, diary, journal, log, schedule, timetable. 2 *establish the chronology*. dating, order, sequence, timing.

chubby adj buxom, dumpy, plump, podgy, portly, rotund, round, stout, tubby. ▷ FAT. *Opp* THIN.

chunk n bar, block, brick, chuck, *inf* dollop, hunk, lump, mass, piece, portion, slab, wad, wedge, *inf* wodge.

church n abbey, basilica, cathedral, chapel, convent, monastery, nunnery, parish church, priory.

churchyard n burial-ground, cemetery, graveyard.

chute n channel, incline, ramp, rapid, slide, slope.

cinema n films, *old use* flicks, *Amer* motion pictures, *inf* movies, *inf* pictures.

circle n 1 annulus, band, circlet, disc, hoop, ring. 2 circle of friends. association, band, body, clique, club, company, fellowship, fraternity, gang, party, set, society. ▷ GROUP.

● vb 1 circulate, circumnavigate, circumscribe, coil, compass, corkscrew, curl, curve, go round, gyrate, loop, orbit, pirouette, pivot, reel, revolve, rotate, spin, spiral, swirl, swivel, tour, turn, wheel, whirl, wind. 2 *trees circle the lawn*. encircle, enclose, encompass, girdle, hem in, ring, skirt, surround.

circuit n journey round, lap, orbit, revolution, tour.

circuitous adj curving, devious, indirect, labyrinthine, mean-dering, oblique, rambling, roundabout, serpentine, tortuous, twisting, winding, zigzag. *Opp* DIRECT.

circular adj 1 annular, discoid, ringlike, round. 2 *circular conversation*. circumlocutory, cyclic, periphrastic, repeating, repetitive, roundabout, tautologous. ● n advertisement, leaflet, letter, notice, pamphlet.

circulate vb 1 go round, move about, move round, orbit. ▷ CIRCLE. 2 *circulate gossip*. advertise, disseminate, distribute, issue, make known, noise abroad, promulgate, publicize, publish, *inf* put about, send round, spread about.

circulation n 1 flow, movement, pumping, recycling. 2 broadcasting, diffusion, dissemination, distribution, promulgation, publication, spreading, transmission. 3 *newspaper circulation*. distribution, sales-figures.

circumference n border, boundary, circuit, edge, exterior, fringe, limit, margin, outline, outside, perimeter, periphery, rim, verge.

circumstance n affair, event, happening, incident, occasion, occurrence. **circumstances** 1 background, causes, conditions, considerations, context, contingencies, details, factors, facts, influences, particulars, position, situation, state of affairs, surroundings. 2 finances, income, resources.

circumstantial adj conjectural, deduced, inferred, unprovable. *Opp* PROVABLE.

cistern n bath, container, reservoir, tank.

citadel *n* acropolis, bastion, castle, fort, fortification, fortress, garrison, stronghold, tower.

cite *vb* adduce, advance, *inf* bring up, enumerate, mention, name, quote, *inf* reel off, refer to, specify.

citizen *n* burgess, commoner, denizen, dweller, freeman, householder, inhabitant, national, native, passport-holder, ratepayer, resident, subject, taxpayer, voter.

city *n* capital, conurbation, metropolis, town, urban district.

civil *adj* 1 affable, civilized, considerate, courteous, obliging, respectful, urbane, well-bred, well-mannered. ▷ POLITE. *Opp* IMPOLITE. 2 *civil administration*. civilian, domestic, internal, national. *Opp* MILITARY. 3 *civil liberties*. communal, public, social, state. **civil rights** freedom, human rights, legal rights, liberty, political rights. **civil servant** administrator, bureaucrat, *derog* mandarin.

civilization *n* achievements, attainments, culture, customs, mores, organization, refinement, sophistication, urbanity, urbanization.

civilize *vb* cultivate, domesticate, educate, enlighten, humanize, improve, make better, organize, refine, socialize, urbanize.

civilized *adj* advanced, cultivated, cultured, democratic, developed, domesticated, educated, enlightened, humane, orderly, polite, refined, sociable, social, sophisticated,

urbane, urbanized, well-behaved, well-run. *Opp* UN-CIVILIZED.

claim *vb* 1 ask for, collect, command, demand, exact, insist on, request, require, take. 2 affirm, allege, argue, assert, attest, contend, declare, insist, maintain, pretend, profess, state.

clairvoyant *adj* extra-sensory, oracular, prophetic, psychic, telepathic. ● *n* fortune-teller, oracle, prophet, seer, sibyl, soothsayer.

clamber *vb* climb, crawl, move awkwardly, scramble.

clammy *adj* close, damp, dank, humid, moist, muggy, slimy, sticky, sweaty, wet.

clamour *n* babel, commotion, din, hubbub, hullabaloo, noise, outcry, racket, row, screeching, shouting, storm, uproar. ● *vb* call out, cry out, exclaim, shout, yell.

clan *n* family, house, tribe.

clannish *adj derog* cliquish, close, close-knit, insular, isolated, narrow, united.

clap *n* bang, crack, crash, report, smack. ▷ SOUND. ● *vb* 1 applaud, *sl* put your hands together, show approval. 2 *clap on the back*. ▷ HIT.

clarify *vb* 1 clear up, define, elucidate, explain, explicate, gloss, illuminate, make clear, simplify, *inf* spell out, throw light on. *Opp* CONFUSE. 2 *clarify wine*. cleanse, clear, filter, purify, refine. *Opp* CLOUD.

clash *vb* 1 bang, clang, clank, crash, resonate, ring. ▷ SOUND. 2 ▷ CONFLICT. 3 *The events clashed.* ▷ COINCIDE.

clasp n 1 brooch, buckle, catch, clip, fastener, fastening, hasp, hook, pin. 2 cuddle, embrace, grasp, grip, hold, hug.
• vb 1 ▷ FASTEN. 2 cling to, clutch, embrace, enfold, grasp, grip, hold, hug, squeeze. 3 *clasp your hands.* hold together, wring.

class n 1 category, classification, division, domain, genus, genus, grade, group, kind, league, order, quality, rank, set, sort, species, sphere, type. 2 *social class.* caste, degree, descent, extraction, grouping, lineage, pedigree, standing, station, status. □ aristocracy, bourgeoisie, commoners, (the) commons, gentry, lower class, middle class, nobility, proletariat, ruling class, serfs, upper class, upper-middle class, (the) workers, working class. 3 *class in school.* band, form, Amer grade, group, set, stream, year. • vb ▷ CLASSIFY.

classic adj 1 abiding, ageless, deathless, enduring, established, exemplary, flawless, ideal, immortal, lasting, legendary, masterly, memorable, notable, outstanding, perfect, timehonoured, undying, unforgettable, inf vintage. ▷ EXCELLENT. Opp COMMONPLACE, EPHEMERAL. 2 *a classic case.* archetypal, characteristic, copybook, definitive, model, paradigmatic, regular, standard, typical, usual. Opp UNUSUAL. • n masterpiece, masterwork, model.

classical adj 1 ancient, Attic, Greek, Hellenic, Latin, Roman. 2 *classical style.* dignified, elegant, pure, restrained, simple, symmetrical, wellproportioned. 3 *classical music.*
established, harmonious, highbrow, serious.

classification n categorization, codification, ordering, organization, systematization, tabulation, taxonomy. ▷ CLASS.

classify vb arrange, bracket together, catalogue, categorize, class, grade, group, order, organize, inf pigeon-hole, put into sets, sort, systematize, tabulate. **classified** ▷ SECRET.

clause n article, condition, item, paragraph, part, passage, provision, proviso, section, subsection.

claw n nail, talon. • vb graze, injure, lacerate, maul, rip, scrape, scratch, slash, tear.

clean adj 1 decontaminated, dirtfree, disinfected, hygienic, immaculate, laundered, perfect, polished, sanitary, scrubbed, spotless, sterile, sterilized, tidy, unadulterated, unsoiled, unstained, unsullied, washed, wholesome. 2 *clean water.* clarified, clear, distilled, fresh, pure, purified, unpolluted. 3 *clean paper.* blank, new, plain, uncreased, unmarked, untouched, unused. 4 *a clean edge.* neat, regular, smooth, straight, tidy. 5 *a clean fight.* chivalrous, fair, honest, honourable, sporting, sportsmanlike. 6 *clean fun.* chaste, decent, good, innocent, moral, respectable, upright, virtuous. Opp DIRTY. • vb cleanse, clear up, tidy up, wash. □ bath, bathe, brush, buff, decontaminate, deodorize, disinfect, dryclean, dust, filter, flush, groom, hoover, launder, mop, polish, purge, purify, rinse, sand-blast, sanitize, scour, scrape, scrub, shampoo, shower, soap, sponge,

spring-clean, spruce up, sterilize, swab, sweep, swill, vacuum, wipe, wring out.
Opp CONTAMINATE. **make a clean breast of** ▷ CONFESS.

clean-shaven adj beardless, shaved, shaven, shorn, smooth.

clear adj 1 clean, colourless, crystalline, glassy, limpid, pellucid, pure, transparent. **2** *clear weather*. cloudless, fair, fine, sunny, starlit, unclouded. Opp CLOUDY. **3** *clear colours*. bright, lustrous, shining, sparkling, strong, vivid. **4** *clear conscience*. blameless, easy, guiltless, innocent, quiet, satisfied, sinless, undisturbed, untarnished, untroubled, unworried. **5** *clear handwriting*. bold, clean, definite, distinct, explicit, focused, legible, positive, recognizable, sharp, simple, visible, well-defined. **6** *clear sound*. audible, clarion (*call*), distinct, penetrating, sharp. **7** *clear instructions*. clear-cut, coherent, comprehensible, explicit, intelligible, lucid, perspicuous, precise, specific, straightforward, unambiguous, understandable, unequivocal, well-presented. **8** *clear case of cheating*. apparent, blatant, clear-cut, conspicuous, evident, glaring, indisputable, manifest, noticeable, obvious, palpable, perceptible, plain, pronounced, straightforward, unconcealed, undisguised, unmistakable. Opp UNCERTAIN. **9** *clear space*. empty, free, open, passable, uncluttered, uncrowded, unhampered, unhindered, unimpeded, unobstructed.
● vb **1** disappear, evaporate, fade, melt away, vanish.
2 become clear, brighten, clar-

ify, lighten, uncloud. **3** clean, make clean, make transparent, polish, wipe. **4** *clear weeds*. disentangle, eliminate, get rid of, remove, strip. **5** *clear a drain*. clean out, free, loosen, open up, unblock, unclog. **6** *clear of blame*. absolve, acquit, exculpate, excuse, exonerate, free, inf let off, liberate, release, vindicate. **7** *clear a building*. empty, evacuate. **8** *clear a fence*. bound over, jump, leap over, pass over, spring over, vault. **clear away** ▷ REMOVE. **clear off** ▷ DEPART. **clear up** ▷ CLEAN, EXPLAIN.

clearing n gap, glade, opening, space.

cleave vb divide, halve, rive, slit, split. ▷ CUT.

clench vb **1** clamp up, close tightly, double up, grit (*your teeth*), squeeze tightly. **2** clasp, grasp, grip, hold.

clergyman n archbishop, ayatollah, bishop, canon, cardinal, chaplain, churchman, cleric, curate, deacon, fem deaconess, dean, divine, ecclesiastic, evangelist, friar, guru, imam, inf man of the cloth, minister, missionary, monk, padre, parson, pastor, preacher, prebend, prelate, priest, rabbi, rector, vicar. Opp LAYMAN.

clerical adj **1** *clerical and administrative work*. office, secretarial, inf white-collar. **2** *a clerical collar*. canonical, ecclesiastical, episcopal, ministerial, monastic, pastoral, priestly, rabbinical, sacerdotal, spiritual.

clerk n assistant, bookkeeper, computer operator, copyist, filing clerk, office boy, office girl, office worker, inf pen-pusher, receptionist, recorder, scribe, secretary, shorthand-typist, stenographer, typist, word-processor operator.

clever *adj* able, academic, accomplished, acute, adept, adroit, apt, artful, artistic, astute, *inf* brainy, bright, brilliant, canny, capable, *derog* crafty, creative, *derog* cunning, *inf* cute, *inf* deft, dextrous, discerning, expert, *derog* foxy, gifted, guileful, *inf* handy, imaginative, ingenious, intellectual, intelligent, inventive, judicious, keen, knowing, knowledgeable, observant, penetrating, perceptive, percipient, perspicacious, precocious, quick, quick-witted, rational, resourceful, sagacious, sensible, sharp, shrewd, skilful, skilled, slick, *derog* sly, smart, subtle, talented, *derog* wily, wise, witty. *Opp* STUPID, UNSKILFUL. **clever person** *inf* egghead, expert, genius, *derog* know-all, mastermind, prodigy, sage, *derog* smart alec, *derog* smart-arse, virtuoso, wizard.

cleverness *n* ability, acuteness, astuteness, brilliance, *derog* cunning, expertise, ingenuity, intellect, intelligence, mastery, quickness, sagacity, sharpness, shrewdness, skill, subtlety, talent, wisdom, wit. *Opp* STUPIDITY.

cliché *n* banality, *inf* chestnut, commonplace, hackneyed phrase, platitude, stereotype, truism, well-worn phrase.

client *n plur* clientele, consumer, customer, patient, patron, shopper, user.

cliff *n* bluff, crag, escarpment, precipice, rock-face, scar, sheer drop.

climate *n* 1 ▷ WEATHER. 2 *climate of opinion.* ambience, atmosphere, aura, disposition, environment, feeling, mood, spirit, temper, trend.

climax *n* 1 acme, apex, apogee, crisis, culmination, head, highlight, high point, peak, summit, zenith. *Opp* BATHOS. 2 *sexual climax.* orgasm.

climb *n* ascent, grade, gradient, hill, incline, pitch, rise, slope. • *vb* 1 ascend, clamber up, defy gravity, go up, levitate, lift off, mount, move up, scale, shin up, soar, swarm up, take off. 2 incline, rise, slope up. 3 *climb a mountain.* conquer, reach the top of. **climb down** ▷ DESCEND.

clinch *vb* agree, close, complete, conclude, confirm, decide, determine, finalize, make certain of, ratify, secure, settle, shake hands on, sign, verify.

cling *vb* adhere, attach, fasten, fix, hold fast, stick. **cling to** ▷ EMBRACE.

clinic *n* health centre, infirmary, medical centre, sick-bay, surgery.

clip *n* 1 ▷ FASTENER. 2 *clip from a film.* bit, cutting, excerpt, extract, fragment, part, passage, portion, quotation, section, snippet, trailer. • *vb* 1 pin, staple. ▷ FASTEN. 2 crop, dock, prune, shear, snip, trim. ▷ CUT.

cloak *n* 1 cape, cope, mantle, poncho, robe, wrap. ▷ COAT. 2 ▷ COVER. • *vb* cover, disguise, mantle, mask, screen, shroud, veil, wrap. ▷ HIDE.

clock *n* time-piece. □ *alarm-clock, chronometer, dial, digital clock, grandfather clock, hour-*

glass, pendulum clock, sundial, watch.

clog *vb* block, *inf* bung up, choke, close, congest, dam, fill, impede, jam, obstruct, plug, stop up.

close *adj* **1** accessible, adjacent, adjoining, at hand, convenient, handy, near, neighbouring, point-blank. **2** *close friends.* affectionate, attached, dear, devoted, familiar, fond, friendly, intimate, loving, *inf* thick. **3** *close comparison.* alike, analogous, comparable, compatible, corresponding, related, resembling, similar. **4** *a close crowd.* compact, compressed, congested, cramped, crowded, dense, *inf* jam-packed, packed, thick. **5** *close scrutiny.* attentive, careful, concentrated, detailed, minute, painstaking, precise, rigorous, searching, thorough. **6** *close with information.* confidential, private, reserved, reticent, secretive, taciturn. **7** *close with money.* illiberal, mean, *inf* mingy, miserly, niggardly, parsimonious, penurious, stingy, tight, tight-fisted, ungenerous. **8** *close atmosphere.* airless, confined, fuggy, humid, muggy, oppressive, stale, stifling, stuffy, suffocating, sweltering, unventilated, warm. *Opp* DISTANT, OPEN.
● *n* **1** cessation, completion, conclusion, culmination, end, finish, stop, termination. **2** cadence, coda, finale. **3** *close of a play.* denouement, last act.
● *vb* **1** bolt, fasten, lock, make inaccessible, padlock, put out of bounds, seal, secure, shut. **2** *close a road.* bar, barricade, block, make impassable,

obstruct, seal off, stop up. **3** *close proceedings.* complete, conclude, culminate, discontinue, end, finish, stop, terminate, *inf* wind up. **4** *close a gap.* fill, join up, make smaller, reduce, shorten. *Opp* OPEN.

closed *adj* **1** fastened, locked, sealed, shut. **2** completed, concluded, done with, ended, finished, over, resolved, settled, tied up.

clot *n* embolism, lump, mass, thrombosis. ● *vb* coagulate, coalesce, congeal, curdle, make lumps, set, solidify, stiffen, thicken.

cloth *n* fabric, material, stuff, textile. □ astrakhan, bouclé, brocade, broderie anglaise, buckram, calico, cambric, candlewick, canvas, cashmere, cheesecloth, chenille, chiffon, chintz, corduroy, cotton, crepe, cretonne, damask, denim, dimity, drill, drugget, elastic, felt, flannel, flannelette, gabardine, gauze, georgette, gingham, hessian, holland, lace, lamé, lawn, linen, lint, mohair, moiré, moquette, muslin, nankeen, nylon, oilcloth, oilskin, organdie, organza, patchwork, piqué, plaid, plissé, plush, polycotton, polyester, poplin, rayon, sackcloth, sacking, sailcloth, sarsenet, sateen, satin, satinette, seersucker, serge, silk, stockinet, taffeta, tapestry, tartan, terry, ticking, tulle, tussore, tweed, velour, velvet, velveteen, viscose, voile, winceyette, wool, worsted.

clothe *vb* accoutre, apparel, array, attire, cover, deck, drape, dress, fit out, garb, *inf* kit out, outfit, robe, swathe, wrap up. *Opp* STRIP. **clothe yourself in** ▷ WEAR.

clothes *plur n* apparel, attire, *inf* clobber, clothing, costume, dress, ensemble, finery, garb, garments, *inf* gear, *inf* get-up, outfit, *old use* raiment, *inf* rig-out, *sl* togs, trousseau, underclothes, uniform, vestments, wardrobe, wear, weeds. □ *anorak, apron, blazer, blouse, bodice, breeches, caftan, cagoule, cape, cardigan, cassock, chemise, chuddar, cloak, coat, crinoline, culottes, décolletage, doublet, dress, dressing-gown, duffel coat, dungarees, frock, gaiters, gauntlet, glove, gown, greatcoat, gym-slip, habit, housecoat, jacket, jeans, jerkin, jersey, jodhpurs, jumper, kilt, knickers, legwarmers, leotard, livery, loincloth, lounge suit, mackintosh, mantle, miniskirt, muffler, necktie, négligé, night-clothes, nightdress, oilskins, overalls, overcoat, pants, parka, pinafore, poncho, pullover, pyjamas, raincoat, robe, rompers, sari, sarong, scarf, shawl, shirt, shorts, singlet, skirt, slacks, smock, sock, sou'wester, spats, stocking, stole, suit, surplice, sweater, sweatshirt, tail-coat, tie, tights, trousers, trunks, t-shirt, tunic, tutu, uniform, waistcoat, wet-suit, wind-cheater, wrap, yashmak.* ▷ HAT, SHOE, UNDERCLOTHES.

cloud *n* billow, haze, mist, rain cloud, storm cloud. ● *vb* blur, conceal, cover, darken, dull, eclipse, enshroud, hide, mantle, mist up, obfuscate, obscure, screen, shroud, veil.

cloudless *adj* bright, clear, star-lit, sunny, unclouded. *Opp* CLOUDY.

cloudy *adj* 1 dark, dismal, dull, gloomy, grey, leaden, lowering,

overcast, sullen, sunless. *Opp* CLOUDLESS. 2 *cloudy windows.* blurred, blurry, dim, misty, opaque, steamy, unclear. 3 *cloudy liquid.* hazy, milky, muddy, murky. *Opp* CLEAR.

clown *n* buffoon, comedian, comic, fool, funnyman, jester, joker. ▷ IDIOT.

club *n* 1 bat, baton, bludgeon, cosh, cudgel, mace, staff, stick, truncheon. 2 association, brotherhood, circle, company, federation, fellowship, fraternity, group, guild, league, order, organization, party, set, sisterhood, society, sorority, union. ● *vb* ▷ HIT. **club together** ▷ COMBINE.

clue *n* hint, idea, indication, indicator, inkling, key, lead, pointer, sign, suggestion, suspicion, tip, tip-off, trace.

clump *n* bunch, bundle, cluster, collection, mass, shock (*of hair*), thicket, tuft. ▷ GROUP.

clumsy *adj* 1 awkward, blundering, bumbling, bungling, fumbling, gangling, gawky, graceless, *inf* ham-fisted, heavy-handed, hulking, inelegant, lumbering, maladroit, shambling, uncoordinated, ungainly, ungraceful, unskilful. *Opp* SKILFUL. 2 amateurish, badly-made, bulky, cumbersome, heavy, inconvenient, inelegant, large, ponderous, rough, shapeless, unmanageable, unwieldy. *Opp* NEAT. 3 *a clumsy remark.* boorish, gauche, ill-judged, inappropriate, indelicate, indiscreet, inept, insensitive, tactless, uncouth, undiplomatic, unsubtle, unsuitable.

cluster *n* assembly, batch, bunch, clump, collection,

crowd, gathering, knot.
▷ GROUP. ● vb ▷ GATHER.

clutch n clasp, control, evil embrace, grasp, grip, hold, possession, power. ● vb catch, clasp, cling to, to grab, grasp, grip, hang on to, hold on to, seize, snatch, take hold of.

clutter n chaos, confusion, disorder, jumble, junk, litter, lumber, mess, mix-up, muddle, odds and ends, rubbish, tangle, untidiness. ● vb be scattered about, fill, lie about, litter, make untidy, inf mess up, muddle, strew.

coach n 1 bus, carriage, old use charabanc. 2 games coach. instructor, teacher, trainer, tutor. ● vb direct, drill, exercise, guide, instruct, prepare, teach, train, tutor.

coagulate vb clot, congeal, curdle, inf jell, set, solidify, stiffen, thicken.

coarse adj 1 bristly, gritty, hairy, harsh, lumpy, prickly, rough, scratchy, sharp, stony, uneven, unfinished. Opp FINE, SOFT. 2 coarse language. bawdy, blasphemous, boorish, common, crude, earthy, foul, immodest, impolite, improper, impure, indecent, indelicate, offensive, ribald, rude, smutty, uncouth, unrefined, vulgar. Opp REFINED.

coast n beach, coastline, littoral, seaboard, seashore, seaside, shore. ● vb cruise, drift, freewheel, glide, sail, skim, slide, slip.

coastal adj maritime, nautical, naval, seaside.

coat n 1 □ anorak, blazer, cagoule, cardigan, dinnerjacket, doublet, duffel coat, greatcoat, jacket, jerkin, mackintosh, overcoat, raincoat, tailcoat, tunic, tuxedo, waistcoat, wind-cheater. 2 an animal's coat. fleece, fur, hair, hide, pelt, skin. 3 coat of paint. coating, cover, film, finish, glaze, layer, membrane, overlay, patina, sheet, veneer, wash. ▷ COVERING. ● vb ▷ COVER. coat of arms ▷ CREST.

coax vb allure, beguile, cajole, charm, decoy, entice, induce, inveigle, manipulate, persuade, tempt, urge, wheedle.

cobble vb cobble together botch, knock up, make, mend, patch up, put together.

code n 1 etiquette, laws, manners, regulations, rulebook, rules, system. 2 message in code. cipher, secret language, signals, sign-system.

coerce vb bludgeon, browbeat, bully, compel, constrain, dragoon, force, frighten, intimidate, press-gang, pressurize, terrorize.

coercion n browbeating, brute force, bullying, compulsion, conscription, constraint, duress, force, intimidation, physical force, pressure, inf strong-arm tactics, threats.

coffer n box, cabinet, case, casket, chest, crate, trunk.

cog n ratchet, sprocket, tooth.

cogent adj compelling, conclusive, convincing, effective, forceful, forcible, indisputable, irresistible, logical, persuasive, potent, powerful, rational, sound, strong, unanswerable, weighty, well-argued. ▷ COHERENT. Opp IRRATIONAL.

cohere vb bind, cake, cling together, coalesce, combine, consolidate, fuse, hang together, hold together, join, stick together, unite.

coherent adj articulate, cohering, cohesive, connected, consistent, integrated, logical, lucid, orderly, organized, rational, reasonable, reasoned, sound, structured, systematic, unified, united, well-ordered, well-structured. ▷ COGENT. Opp INCOHERENT.

coil n circle, convolution, corkscrew, curl, helix, kink, loop, ring, roll, screw, spiral, twirl, twist, vortex, whirl, whorl.
• vb bend, curl, entwine, loop, roll, snake, spiral, turn, twine, twirl, twist, wind, writhe.

coin n 1 bit, piece. 2 [plur] cash, change, coppers, loose change, silver, small change. ▷ MONEY.
• vb 1 forge, make, mint, mould, stamp. 2 coin a name. conceive, concoct, create, devise, dream up, fabricate, hatch, introduce, invent, make up, originate, produce, think up.

coincide vb accord, agree, be congruent, be identical, be in unison, be the same, clash, coexist, come together, concur, correspond, fall together, happen together, harmonize, line up, match, square, synchronize, tally.

coincidence n 1 accord, agreement, coexistence, concurrence, conformity, congruence, congruity, correspondence, harmony, similarity. 2 meet by coincidence. accident, chance, fluke, luck.

cold adj 1 arctic, biting, bitter, bleak, chill, chilly, cool, crisp, cutting, draughty, freezing, fresh, frosty, glacial, heatless, ice-cold, icy, inclement, keen, inf nippy, numbing, inf parky, penetrating, perishing, piercing, polar, raw, shivery, Siberian, snowy, unheated, wintry. 2 cold hands. blue with cold, chilled, dead, frostbitten, frozen, numbed, shivering, shivery. 3 a cold heart. aloof, apathetic, callous, cold-blooded, cool, cruel, distant, frigid, hard, hard-hearted, heartless, indifferent, inhospitable, inhuman, insensitive, passionless, phlegmatic, reserved, standoffish, stony, uncaring, unconcerned, undemonstrative, unemotional, unenthusiastic, unfeeling, unkind, unresponsive, unsympathetic. ▷ UNFRIENDLY. Opp HOT, KIND. • n 1 chill, coldness, coolness, freshness, iciness, low temperature, wintriness. Opp HEAT. 2 cold in the head. catarrh, inf flu, influenza, inf the sniffles. feel the cold freeze, quiver, shake, shiver, shudder, suffer from hypothermia, tremble.

cold-blooded adj barbaric, brutal, callous, hard-hearted, inhuman, inhumane, merciless, pitiless, ruthless, savage. ▷ CRUEL. Opp HUMANE.

cold-hearted adj apathetic, cool, dispassionate, frigid, heartless, impassive, impersonal, indifferent, insensitive, thick-skinned, uncaring, unemotional, unfeeling, unkind, unresponsive, unsympathetic. ▷ UNFRIENDLY. Opp FRIENDLY.

collaborate vb 1 band together, cooperate, join forces, inf pull together, team up, work together. 2 [derog] collude, connive, conspire, join the opposition, inf rat, turn traitor.

collaboration n 1 association, concerted effort, cooperation, partnership, tandem, teamwork. 2 [derog] collusion, connivance, conspiracy, treachery.

collaborator n 1 accomplice, ally, assistant, associate, co-author, colleague, confederate, fellow-worker, helper, helpmate, partner, joc partner-in-crime, teammate. 2 collaborator with an enemy. blackleg, inf Judas, quisling, inf scab, traitor, turncoat.

collapse n break-down, break-up, cave-in, destruction, downfall, end, fall, ruin, ruination, subsidence, wreck, • vb 1 break down, break up, buckle, cave in, crumble, crumple, deflate, disintegrate, double up, fall apart, fall down, fall in, fold up, give way, inf go west, sink, subside, tumble down. 2 collapse in the heat. become ill, inf bite the dust, black out, inf crack up, faint, founder, inf go under, inf keel over, pass out, old use swoon. 3 sales collapsed. become less, crash, deteriorate, diminish, drop, fail, slump, worsen.

collapsible adj adjustable, folding, retractable, telescopic.

colleague n associate, business partner, fellow-worker. ▷ COLLABORATOR.

collect vb 1 accumulate, agglomerate, aggregate, amass, assemble, bring together, cluster, come together, concentrate, congregate, convene, converge, crowd, forgather, garner, gather, group, harvest, heap, hoard, lay up, muster, pile up, put by, rally, reserve, save, scrape together, stack up, stockpile, store. Opp DISPERSE. 2 collect money for charity. be given, raise, secure, take. 3 collect goods from a shop. acquire, bring, fetch, get, load up, obtain, pick up. **collected** ▷ CALM.

collection n 1 accumulation, array, assemblage, assortment, cluster, conglomeration, heap, hoard, mass, pile, set, stack, store. ▷ GROUP. 2 old use alms-giving, flag-day, free-will offering, offertory, voluntary contributions, inf whip-round.

collective adj combined, common, composite, co-operative, corporate, democratic, group, joint, shared, unified, united. Opp INDIVIDUAL.

college n academy, conservatory, institute, polytechnic, school, university.

collide vb collide with bump into, cannon into, crash into, knock, meet, run into, slam into, smash into, strike, touch. ▷ HIT.

collision n accident, bump, clash, crash, head-on collision, impact, knock, pile-up, scrape, smash, wreck.

colloquial adj chatty, conversational, everyday, informal, slangy, vernacular. Opp FORMAL.

colonist n colonizer, explorer, pioneer, settler. Opp NATIVE.

colonize vb occupy, people, populate, settle in, subjugate.

colony n 1 dependency, dominion, possession, protectorate, province, settlement, territory. 2 ▷ GROUP.

colossal adj Brobdingnagian, elephantine, enormous, gargantuan, giant, gigantic, herculean, huge, immense, *inf* jumbo, mammoth, massive, mighty, monstrous, monumental, prodigious, titanic, towering, vast. ▷ BIG. *Opp* SMALL.

colour *n* **1** coloration, colouring, hue, pigment, pigmentation, shade, tincture, tinge, tint, tone. □ amber, azure, beige, *black*, *blue*, *bronze*, *brown*, *buff*, *carroty*, *cherry*, *chestnut*, *chocolate*, *cobalt*, *cream*, *crimson*, *dun*, *fawn*, *gilt*, *gold*, *golden*, *green*, *grey*, *indigo*, *ivory*, *jet-black*, *khaki*, *lavender*, *maroon*, *mauve*, *navy blue*, *ochre*, *olive*, *orange*, *pink*, *puce*, *purple*, *red*, *rosy*, *russet*, *sandy*, *scarlet*, *silver*, *tan*, *tawny*, *turquoise*, *vermilion*, *violet*, *white*, *yellow*. **2** *colour in your cheeks.* bloom, blush, flush, glow, rosiness, ruddiness. ● *vb* **1** colour-wash, crayon, dye, paint, pigment, shade, stain, tinge, tint. **2** blush, bronze, brown, burn, flush, redden, tan. *Opp* FADE. **3** *coloured by prejudice.* affect, bias, distort, impinge on, influence, pervert, prejudice, slant, sway. **colours** ▷ FLAG.

colourful *adj* **1** bright, brilliant, chromatic, gaudy, iridescent, multicoloured, psychedelic, showy, vibrant. **2** *colourful personality.* dashing, distinctive, dynamic, eccentric, energetic, exciting, flamboyant, flashy, florid, glamorous, unusual, vigorous. **3** *colourful description.* graphic, interesting, lively, picturesque, rich, stimulating, striking, telling, vivid. *Opp* COLOURLESS.

colouring *n* colourant, dye, pigment, pigmentation, stain, tincture. ▷ COLOUR.

colourless *adj* **1** albino, ashen, blanched, faded, grey, monochrome, neutral, pale, pallid, sickly, wan, *inf* washed out, waxen. ▷ WHITE. **2** bland, boring, characterless, dingy, dismal, dowdy, drab, dreary, dull, insipid, lacklustre, lifeless, ordinary, tame, uninspiring, uninteresting, vacuous, vapid. *Opp* COLOURFUL.

column *n* **1** pilaster, pile, pillar, pole, post, prop, shaft, support, upright. **2** *newspaper column.* article, feature, leader, leading article, piece. **3** *column of soldiers.* cavalcade, file, line, procession, queue, rank, row, string, train.

comb *vb* **1** arrange, groom, neaten, smarten up, spruce up, tidy, untangle. **2** *comb the house.* hunt through, ransack, rummage through, scour, search thoroughly.

combat *n* action, battle, bout, clash, conflict, contest, duel, encounter, engagement, fight, skirmish, struggle, war, warfare. ● *vb* battle against, contend against, contest, counter, defy, face up to, grapple with, oppose, resist, stand up to, strive against, struggle against, tackle, withstand. ▷ FIGHT.

combination *n* **1** aggregate, alloy, amalgam, blend, compound, concoction, concurrence, conjunction, fusion, marriage, mix, mixture, synthesis, unification. **2** alliance, coalition, confederacy, confederation, consortium, conspiracy, federation, grouping, link-up, merger, partnership, syndicate, union.

combine vb 1 add together, amalgamate, bind, blend, bring together, compound, fuse, incorporate, integrate, intertwine, interweave, join, link, *inf* lump together, marry, merge, mingle, mix, pool, put together, synthesize, unify, unite. *Opp* DIVIDE. 2 *combine as a team.* ally, associate, band together, club together, coalesce, connect, cooperate, form an alliance, gang together, gang up, join forces, team up. *Opp* DISPERSE.

combustible adj flammable, inflammable. *Opp* INCOMBUSTIBLE.

come vb 1 advance, appear, approach, arrive, draw near, enter, get to, move (towards), near, reach, visit. 2 *take what comes.* happen, materialize, occur, put in an appearance, show up. **come about** ▷ HAPPEN. **come across** ▷ FIND. **come apart** ▷ DISINTEGRATE. **come clean** ▷ CONFESS. **come out with** ▷ SAY. **come round** ▷ RECOVER. **come up** ▷ ARISE. **come upon** ▷ FIND.

comedian n buffoon, clown, comic, fool, humorist, jester, joker, wag. ▷ ENTERTAINER.

comedy n buffoonery, clowning, facetiousness, farce, hilarity, humour, jesting, joking, satire, slapstick, wit.

comfort n 1 aid, cheer, consolation, encouragement, help, moral support, reassurance, relief, solace, succour, sympathy. 2 *living in comfort.* abundance, affluence, contentment, cosiness, ease, luxury, opulence, plenty, relaxation, well-being. *Opp* DISCOMFORT,

POVERTY. ● vb assuage, calm, cheer up, console, ease, encourage, gladden, hearten, help, reassure, relieve, solace, soothe, succour, sympathize with.

comfortable adj 1 *inf* comfy, convenient, cosy, easy, padded, reassuring, relaxing, roomy, snug, soft, upholstered, warm. 2 *comfortable clothes.* informal, loose-fitting, well-fitting, well-made. 3 *a comfortable life.* affluent, agreeable, contented, happy, homely, luxurious, pleasant, prosperous, relaxed, restful, serene, tranquil, untroubled, well-off. *Opp* UNCOMFORTABLE.

comic adj absurd, amusing, comical, diverting, droll, facetious, farcical, funny, hilarious, humorous, hysterical, jocular, joking, laughable, ludicrous, *inf* priceless, *inf* rich, ridiculous, sarcastic, sardonic, satirical, side-splitting, silly, uproarious, waggish, witty. *Opp* SERIOUS. ● n 1 ▷ COMEDIAN. 2 ▷ MAGAZINE.

command n 1 behest, bidding, commandment, decree, directive, edict, injunction, instruction, mandate, order, requirement, ultimatum, writ. 2 authority, charge, control, direction, government, jurisdiction, management, oversight, power, rule, sovereignty, supervision, sway. 3 *command of a language.* grasp, knowledge, mastery. ● vb 1 adjure, *old use* bid, charge, compel, decree, demand, direct, enjoin, instruct, ordain, order, prescribe, request, require. 2 *command a ship.* administer, be in charge of, control, direct, govern, have authority over, head, lead, manage, reign over, rule, supervise.

commandeer vb appropriate, confiscate, hijack, impound, requisition, seize, sequester, take over.

commander n captain, commandant, commanding-officer, general, head, leader, officer-in-charge. ▷ CHIEF.

commemorate vb be a memorial to, be a reminder of, celebrate, honour, immortalize, keep alive the memory of, memorialize, pay your respects to, pay homage to, pay tribute to, remember, salute, solemnize.

commence vb embark on, enter on, inaugurate, initiate, launch, open, set off, set out, set up, start. ▷ BEGIN. *Opp* FINISH.

commend vb acclaim, applaud, approve of, compliment, congratulate, eulogize, extol, praise, recommend. *Opp* CRITICIZE.

commendable adj admirable, creditable, deserving, laudable, meritorious, praiseworthy, worthwhile. ▷ GOOD. *Opp* DEPLORABLE.

comment n animadversion, annotation, clarification, commentary, criticism, elucidation, explanation, footnote, gloss, interjection, interpolation, mention, note, observation, opinion, reaction, reference, remark, statement.
● vb animadvert, criticize, elucidate, explain, interject, interpolate, interpose, mention, note, observe, opine, remark, say, state.

commentary n 1 account, broadcast, description, report.

2 *commentary on a poem.* analysis, criticism, critique, discourse, elucidation, explanation, interpretation, notes, review.

commentator n announcer, broadcaster, journalist, reporter.

commerce n business, buying and selling, dealings, financial transactions, marketing, merchandising, trade, trading, traffic, trafficking.

commercial adj business, economic, financial, mercantile, monetary, money-making, pecuniary, profitable, profit-making, trading. ● n *inf* advert, advertisement, *inf* break, *inf* plug.

commiserate vb be sorry (for), be sympathetic, comfort, condole, console, feel (for), grieve, mourn, show sympathy (for), sympathize.
Opp CONGRATULATE.

commission n 1 appointment, promotion, warrant. 2 *commission to do a job.* booking, order, request. 3 *commission on a sale.* allowance, *inf* cut, fee, percentage, *inf* rake-off, reward. 4 ▷ COMMITTEE.

commit vb 1 be guilty of, carry out, do, enact, execute, perform, perpetrate. 2 *commit to safekeeping.* consign, deliver, deposit, entrust, give, hand over, put away, transfer.
commit yourself ▷ PROMISE.

commitment n 1 assurance, duty, guarantee, liability, pledge, promise, undertaking, vow, word. 2 *commitment to a cause.* adherence, dedication, determination, devotion, involvement, loyalty, zeal.

3 *social commitments*. appointment, arrangement, engagement.

committed adj active, ardent, *inf* card-carrying, dedicated, devoted, earnest, enthusiastic, fervent, firm, keen, passionate, resolute, single-minded, staunch, unwavering, whole-hearted, zealous. *Opp* APATHETIC.

committee n body, council, panel. □ assembly, board, cabinet, caucus, commission, convention, junta, jury, parliament, quango, synod, think-tank, working party. ▷ GROUP, MEETING.

common adj 1 average, *inf* common or garden, conventional, customary, daily, everyday, familiar, frequent, habitual, normal, ordinary, plain, popular, prevalent, regular, routine, *inf* run-of-the-mill, standard, stock, traditional, typical, undistinguished, unexceptional, unsurprising, usual, well-known, widespread, workaday. ▷ COMMONPLACE. 2 *common knowledge*. accepted, collective, communal, general, joint, mutual, open, popular, public, shared, universal. 3 *the common people*. lower class, lowly, plebeian, proletarian. 4 [*inf*] *Don't be common!* boorish, churlish, coarse, crude, disreputable, ill-bred, inferior, loutish, low, rude, uncouth, unrefined, vulgar, *inf* yobbish. *Opp* ARISTOCRATIC, DISTINCTIVE, UNUSUAL. • n heath, park, parkland.

commonplace adj banal, boring, forgettable, hackneyed, humdrum, mediocre, obvious, ordinary, pedestrian, plain,

platitudinous, predictable, prosaic, routine, standard, trite, unexciting, unremarkable. ▷ COMMON. *Opp* MEMORABLE. ● n ▷ PLATITUDE.

commotion n *inf* ado, agitation, *inf* bedlam, bother, brawl, *inf* brouhaha, *inf* bust-up, chaos, clamour, confusion, contretemps, din, disorder, disturbance, excitement, ferment, flurry, fracas, fray, furore, fuss, hubbub, hullabaloo, incident, *inf* kerfuffle, noise, *inf* palaver, pandemonium, *inf* punch-up, quarrel, racket, riot, row, rumpus, sensation, *inf* shemozzle, *inf* stir, *inf* to-do, tumult, turbulence, turmoil, unrest, upheaval, uproar, upset.

communal adj collective, common, general, joint, mutual, open, public, shared. *Opp* PRIVATE.

communicate vb 1 commune, confer, converse, correspond, discuss, get in touch, interrelate, make contact, speak, talk, write (to). 2 *communicate information*. advise, announce, broadcast, convey, declare, disclose, disseminate, divulge, express, get across, impart, indicate, inform, intimate, make known, mention, network, notify, pass on, proclaim, promulgate, publish, put across, put over, relay, report, reveal, say, show, speak, spread, state, transfer, transmit, write. 3 *communicate a disease*. give, infect someone with, pass on, spread, transfer, transmit. 4 *The passage communicates with the kitchen*. be connected, lead (to).

communication n 1 communi-cating, communion, contact, interaction, old use intercourse. □ announcement, bulletin, cable, card, communiqué, conversation, correspondence, dialogue, directive, dispatch, document, fax, gossip, inf grapevine, information, intelligence, intimation, letter, inf memo, memorandum, message, news, note, notice, proclamation, report, rumour, signal, statement, talk, telegram, transmission, wire, word of mouth, writing. □ CB, computer, intercom, radar, telegraph, telephone, teleprinter, walkie-talkie. 2 mass communication. mass media, the media. □ advertising, broadcasting, cable television, magazines, newspapers, the press, radio, satellite, telecommunication, television.

communicative adj articulate, inf chatty, frank, informative, open, out-going, responsive, sociable. ▷ TALKATIVE. Opp SECRETIVE.

community n colony, commonwealth, commune, country, kibbutz, nation, society, state. ▷ GROUP.

commute vb 1 adjust, alter, curtail, decrease, lessen, lighten, mitigate, reduce, shorten. 2 ▷ TRAVEL.

compact adj 1 close-packed, compacted, compressed, consolidated, dense, firm, heavy, packed, solid, tight-packed. Opp LOOSE. 2 handy, neat, portable, small. 3 abbreviated, abridged, brief, compendious, compressed, concentrated, condensed, short, small, succinct, terse. ▷ CONCISE. Opp LARGE. ● n ▷ AGREEMENT.

companion n accomplice, assistant, associate, chaperone, colleague, comrade, confederate, confidant(e), consort, inf crony, escort, fellow, follower, inf henchman, mate, partner, stalwart. ▷ FRIEND, HELPER.

company n 1 companionship, fellowship, friendship, society. 2 [inf] company for tea. callers, guests, visitors. 3 mixed company. assemblage, association, band, body, circle, club, community, coterie, crew, crowd, ensemble, entourage, gang, gathering, society, throng, troop, troupe (of actors). 4 trading company. business, cartel, concern, conglomerate, consortium, corporation, establishment, firm, house, line, organization, partnership, inf set-up, syndicate, union. ▷ GROUP.

comparable adj analogous, cognate, commensurate, compatible, corresponding, equal, equivalent, matching, parallel, proportionate, related, similar, twin. Opp DISSIMILAR.

compare vb check, contrast, correlate, draw parallels (between), equate, juxtapose, liken, make comparisons, make connections (between), measure (against), relate (to), set side by side, weigh (against). **compare with** ▷ EQUAL.

comparison n analogy, comparability, contrast, correlation, difference, distinction, juxta-position, likeness, parallel, relationship, resemblance, similarity.

compartment n alcove, area, bay, berth, booth, cell, chamber, *inf* cubbyhole, cubicle, division, hole, kiosk, locker, niche, nook, partition, pigeonhole, section, slot, space, subdivision.

compatible *adj* 1 harmonious, like-minded, similar, well-matched. ▷ FRIENDLY. 2 *compatible claims*. accordant, congruent, consistent, consonant, matching, reconcilable. *Opp* INCOMPATIBLE.

compel *vb* bind, bully, coerce, constrain, dragoon, drive, exact, force, impel, make, necessitate, oblige, order, press, press-gang, pressurize, require, *inf* shanghai, urge.

compendium *n* abridgement, abstract, anthology, collection, condensation, digest, handbook, summary.

compensate *vb* 1 atone, *inf* cough up, expiate, indemnify, make amends, make good, make reparation, make restitution, make up for, pay back, pay compensation, recompense, redress, reimburse, remunerate, repay, requite. 2 counterbalance, counterpoise, even up, neutralize, offset.

compensation *n* amends, damages, indemnity, recompense, refund, reimbursement, reparation, repayment, restitution.

compère *n* anchor-man, announcer, disc jockey, host, hostess, linkman, Master of Ceremonies, MC, presenter.

compete *vb* 1 be a contestant, enter, participate, perform, take part, take up the challenge. 2 be in competition, conflict, contend, emulate, oppose, rival, strive, struggle, undercut, vie.

▷ FIGHT. *Opp* COOPERATE. **compete with** ▷ RIVAL.

competent *adj* able, acceptable, accomplished, adept, adequate, capable, clever, effective, effectual, efficient, experienced, expert, fit, *inf* handy, practical, proficient, qualified, satisfactory, skilful, skilled, trained, workmanlike, worthwhile. *Opp* INCOMPETENT.

competition *n* 1 competitiveness, conflict, contention, emulation, rivalry, struggle. 2 challenge, championship, contest, event, game, heat, match, quiz, race, rally, series, tournament, trial.

competitive *adj* 1 aggressive, antagonistic, combative, contentious, cut-throat, hard-fought, keen, lively, sporting, well-fought. 2 *competitive prices.* average, comparable with others, fair, moderate, reasonable, similar to others.

competitor *n* adversary, antagonist, candidate, challenger, contender, contestant, entrant, finalist, opponent, participant, rival.

compile *vb* accumulate, amass, arrange, assemble, collate, collect, compose, edit, gather, marshal, organize, put together.

complain *vb inf* beef, *inf* bellyache, *sl* bind, carp, cavil, find fault, fuss, *inf* gripe, groan, *inf* grouch, grouse, grumble, lament, moan, object, protest, wail, whine, *inf* whinge. *Opp* PRAISE. **complain about** ▷ CRITICIZE.

complaint *n* 1 accusation, *inf* beef, charge, condemnation, criticism, grievance *inf* gripe, grouse, grumble, moan, objection, protest, stricture, whine, whinge. **2** *a medical complaint.* affliction, ailment, disease, disorder, infection, malady, malaise, sickness, upset. ▷ ILL-NESS.

complaisant *adj* accommodating, acquiescent, amenable, biddable, compliant, cooperative, deferential, docile, obedient, obliging, pliant, polite, submissive, tractable, willing. *Opp* OBSTINATE.

complement n **1** completion, *inf* finishing touch, perfection. **2** *a full complement.* aggregate, capacity, quota, sum, total. ● *vb* add to, complete, make whole, perfect, round off, top up.

complementary *adj* interdependent, matching, reciprocal, toning, twin.

complete *adj* **1** comprehensive, entire, exhaustive, full, intact, total, unabbreviated, unabridged, uncut, unedited, unexpurgated, whole. **2** accomplished, achieved, completed, concluded, done, ended, finished, over. ▷ PERFECT. **3** *a complete disaster.* absolute, arrant, downright, extreme, *inf* out-and-out, outright, pure, rank, sheer, thorough, thoroughgoing, total, unmitigated, unmixed, unqualified, utter, *inf* wholesale. *Opp* INCOMPLETE. ● *vb* **1** accomplish, achieve, carry out, clinch, close, conclude, crown, do, end, finalize, finish, fulfil, perfect, perform, round off, terminate, *inf* top off, *inf* wind up. **2** *complete forms.* answer, fill in.

complex *adj* complicated, composite, compound, convoluted, elaborate, *inf* fiddly, heterogeneous, intricate, involved, *inf* knotty (*problem*), labyrinthine, manifold, mixed, multifarious, multiple, multiplex, ornate, perplexing, problematical, sophisticated, tortuous, *inf* tricky. *Opp* SIMPLE.

complexion n appearance, colour, colouring, look, pigmentation, skin, texture.

complicate *vb* compound, confound, confuse, elaborate, entangle, make complicated, mix up, muddle, *inf* screw up, *inf* snarl up, tangle, twist. *Opp* SIMPLIFY. **complicated** ▷ COMPLEX.

complication n complexity, confusion, convolution, difficulty, dilemma, intricacy, *inf* mix-up, obstacle, problem, ramification, set-back, snag, tangle.

compliment n accolade, admiration, appreciation, approval, commendation, congratulations, encomium, eulogy, felicitations, flattery, honour, panegyric, plaudits, praise, testimonial, tribute. ● *vb* applaud, commend, congratulate, *inf* crack up, eulogize, extol, felicitate, flatter, give credit, laud, pay homage to, praise, salute, speak highly of. *Opp* INSULT.

complimentary *adj* admiring, appreciative, approving, commendatory, congratulatory, encomiastic, eulogistic, favourable, flattering, *derog* fulsome, generous, laudatory, panegyrical, rapturous, supportive. *Opp* ABUSIVE, CONTEMPTUOUS, CRITICAL.

comply *vb* abide (by), accede, accord, acquiesce, adhere (to), agree, assent, be in accordance, coincide, concur, consent, correspond (to), defer, fall in (with), fit in, follow, fulfil, harmonize, keep (to), match, meet, obey, observe, perform, respect, satisfy, square (with), submit, suit, yield. ▷ CONFORM. *Opp* DEFY.

component *n* bit, constituent, element, essential part, ingredient, item, part, piece, *inf* spare, spare part, unit.

compose *vb* 1 build, compile, constitute, construct, fashion, form, frame, make, put together. 2 *compose music.* arrange, create, devise, imagine, make up, produce, write. 3 *compose yourself.* calm, control, pacify, quieten, soothe, tranquillize. **be composed of** ▷ COMPRISE. **composed** ▷ CALM.

composition *n* 1 assembly, constitution, creation, establishment, formation, formulation, *inf* make-up, setting up. 2 balance, configuration, layout, organization, structure. 3 *a literary composition.* article, essay, story. ▷ WRITING. 4 *a musical composition.* opus, piece, work. ▷ MUSIC.

compound *adj* complex, complicated, composite, intricate, involved, multiple. *Opp* SIMPLE. ● *n* 1 alloy, amalgam, blend, combination, composite, composition, fusion, mixture, synthesis. 2 *compound for cattle.* *Amer* corral, enclosure, pen, run. ● *vb* ▷ COMBINE, COMPLICATE.

comprehend *vb* appreciate, apprehend, conceive, discern, fathom, follow, grasp, know, perceive, realize, see, take in, *inf* twig, understand.

comprehensible *adj* clear, easy, intelligible, lucid, meaningful, plain, self-explanatory, simple, straightforward, understandable. *Opp* INCOMPREHENSIBLE.

comprehensive *adj* all-embracing, broad, catholic, compendious, complete, detailed, encyclopaedic, exhaustive, extensive, far-reaching, full, inclusive, indiscriminate, sweeping, thorough, total, universal, wholesale, wide-ranging. *Opp* SELECTIVE.

compress *vb* abbreviate, abridge, compact, concentrate, condense, constrict, contract, cram, crush, flatten, *inf* jam, précis, press, shorten, squash, squeeze, stuff, summarize, telescope, truncate. *Opp* EXPAND. **compressed** ▷ COMPACT, CONCISE.

comprise *vb* be composed of, comprehend, consist of, contain, cover, embody, embrace, include, incorporate, involve.

compromise *n* bargain, concession, *inf* give-and-take, *inf* halfway house, middle course, middle way, settlement. ● *vb* 1 concede a point, go to arbitration, make concessions, meet halfway, negotiate a settlement, reach a formula, settle, *inf* split the difference, strike a balance. 2 *compromise your reputation.* damage, discredit, disgrace, dishonour, imperil, jeopardize, prejudice, risk, undermine, weaken. **compromising** ▷ SHAMEFUL.

compulsion *n* 1 coercion, duress, force, necessity, restriction, restraint. 2 *compulsion to* *smoke*. addiction, drive, habit, impulse, pressure, urge.

compulsive *adj* 1 besetting, compelling, driving, instinctive, involuntary, irresistible, over-powering, overwhelming, powerful, uncontrollable, urgent. 2 *compulsive drinker*. addicted, habitual, incorrigible, incurable, obsessive, persistent.

compulsory *adj* binding, contractual, *Fr* de rigueur, enforceable, essential, impera-tive, imposed, incumbent, indis-pensable, inescapable, manda-tory, necessary, obligatory, official, prescribed, required, requisite, set, statutory, stipu-lated, unavoidable. *Opp* OPTIONAL.

compunction *n* contrition, hesi-tation, pang of conscience, qualm, regret, remorse, scruple, self-reproach.

compute *vb* add up, ascertain, assess, calculate, count, deter-mine, estimate, evaluate, meas-ure, reckon, total, work out.

computer *n* mainframe, micro, microcomputer, mini-computer, PC, personal computer, robot, word-processor.

comrade *n* associate, colleague, companion. ▷ FRIEND.

conceal *vb* blot out, bury, camouflage, cloak, cover up, disguise, envelop, gloss over, hide, hush up, keep dark, keep quiet, keep secret, mask, obscure, screen, secrete, suppress, veil. *Opp* REVEAL. **concealed** ▷ HIDDEN.

concede *vb* accept, acknowledge, admit, agree, allow, confess, grant, make a concession, own, profess, recognize. **concede defeat** capitulate, *inf* cave in,

cede, give in, resign, submit, surrender, yield.

conceit *n* arrogance, boastful-ness, egotism, self-admiration, self-esteem, self-love, vanity. ▷ PRIDE.

conceited *adj* arrogant, *inf* bigheaded, boastful, bump-tious, *inf* cocksure, *inf* cocky, egocentric, egotistical(al), grand, haughty, *inf* high and mighty, immodest, narcissistic, over-weening, pleased with yourself, proud, self-centred, self-import-ant, self-satisfied, smug, snob-bish, *inf* snooty, *inf* stuck-up, supercilious, *inf* swollen-headed, *inf* toffee-nosed, vain, vainglorious. *Opp* MODEST.

conceive *vb* 1 become pregnant. 2 *conceive a plan*. conjure up, contrive, create, design, devise, *inf* dream up, envisage, evolve, form, formulate, frame, germi-nate, hatch, imagine, initiate, invent, make up, originate, plan, plot, produce, realize, suggest, think up, visualize, work out. ▷ THINK.

concentrate *n* distillation, essence, extract. ● *vb* 1 apply yourself, attend, be absorbed, be attentive, engross yourself, think, work hard. 2 accumu-late, centralize, centre, cluster, collect, congregate, converge, crowd, focus, gather, mass. *Opp* DISPERSE. 3 *concentrate a liquid*. condense, reduce, thicken. *Opp* DILUTE. **concen-trated 1** ▷ INTENSIVE. 2 con-densed, evaporated, reduced, strong, thick, undiluted.

conception *n* 1 begetting, conceiving, fathering, fertiliza-tion, genesis, impregnation, initiation, origin. ▷ BEGINNING. 2 ▷ IDEA.

concern n 1 attention, care, charge, consideration, heed, interest, regard. 2 *no concern of yours.* affair, business, involvement, matter, problem, responsibility, task. 3 *matter for concern.* anxiety, burden, disquiet, distress, fear, malaise, solicitude, worry. 4 *business concern.* business, company, corporation, establishment, enterprise, firm, organization. ● vb affect, be important to, be relevant to, interest, involve, matter to, pertain to, refer to, relate to.

concerned adj 1 *concerned parents.* bothered, caring, distressed, disturbed, fearful, perturbed, solicitous, touched, troubled, uneasy, unhappy, upset, worried. ▷ ANXIOUS. 2 *the people concerned.* connected, implicated, interested, involved, referred to, relevant. ▷ RESPONSIBLE.

concerning prep about, apropos of, germane to, involving, re, regarding, relating to, relevant to, with reference to, with regard to.

concert n performance, programme, show. ▷ ENTERTAINMENT, MUSIC.

concerted adj collaborative, collective, combined, cooperative, joint, mutual, shared, united.

concession n adjustment, allowance, reduction.

concise adj brief, compact, compendious, compressed, concentrated, condensed, epigrammatic, laconic, pithy, short, small, succinct, terse. ▷ ABRIDGED. Opp DIFFUSE.

conclude vb 1 cease, close, complete, culminate, end, finish, round off, stop, terminate. 2 assume, decide, deduce, gather, infer, judge, reckon, suppose, surmise. ▷ THINK.

conclusion n 1 close, completion, culmination, end, epilogue, finale, finish, peroration, rounding-off, termination. 2 answer, belief, decision, deduction, inference, interpretation, judgement, opinion, outcome, resolution, result, solution, upshot, verdict.

conclusive adj certain, convincing, decisive, definite, persuasive, unambiguous, unanswerable, unequivocal, unquestionable. Opp INCONCLUSIVE.

concoct vb contrive, cook up, counterfeit, devise, fabricate, feign, formulate, hatch, invent, make up, plan, prepare, put together, think up.

concord n agreement, euphony, harmony, peace.

concrete adj actual, definite, existing, factual, firm, material, objective, palpable, physical, real, solid, substantial, tactile, tangible, touchable, visible. Opp ABSTRACT.

concur vb accede, accord, agree, assent. ▷ COMPLY.

concurrent adj coexisting, coinciding, concomitant, contemporaneous, contemporary, overlapping, parallel, simultaneous, synchronous.

condemn vb 1 blame, castigate, censure, criticize, damn, decry, denounce, deplore, deprecate, disapprove of, disparage, execrate, rebuke, reprehend, reprove, revile, *inf* slam, *inf* slate, upbraid. Opp COMMEND. 2 convict, find guilty, judge, pass judgement,

prove guilty, punish, sentence.
Opp ACQUIT.

condensation *n* haze, mist,
precipitation, *inf* steam, water-
drops.

condense *vb* 1 abbreviate,
abridge, compress, contract,
curtail, précis, reduce, shorten,
summarize, synopsize.
Opp EXPAND. 2 *condense a
liquid.* concentrate, distil,
reduce, solidify, thicken.
Opp DILUTE.

condescend *vb* deign, demean
yourself, humble yourself,
lower yourself, stoop. **condescending** ▷ HAUGHTY.

condition *n* 1 case, circumstance, *inf* fettle, fitness, form,
health, *inf* nick, order, shape,
situation, state, *inf* trim, working order. 2 limitation, obligation, prerequisite, proviso,
qualification, requirement,
requisite, restriction, stipulation, terms. 3 *medical condition.*
▷ ILLNESS. ● *vb* acclimatize,
accustom, brainwash, educate,
mould, prepare, re-educate,
inf soften up, teach, train.

conditional *adj* dependent,
limited, provisional, qualified,
restricted, safeguarded, *inf* with
strings attached. *Opp* UN-
CONDITIONAL.

condone *vb* allow, connive at,
disregard, endorse, excuse,
forgive, ignore, let someone off,
overlook, pardon, tolerate.

conducive *adj* advantageous,
beneficial, encouraging, favourable, helpful, supportive. **be
conducive to** ▷ ENCOURAGE.

conduct *n* 1 actions, attitude,
bearing, behaviour, comportment, demeanour, deportment,
manners, ways. 2 *conduct of*

affairs. administration, control,
direction, discharge, government, guidance, handling, leading, management, operation,
organization, regulation,
running, supervision.
● *vb* 1 administer, be in charge
of, chair, command, control,
direct, escort, govern, handle,
head, look after, manage,
organize, oversee, preside over,
regulate, rule, run, steer, superintend, supervise, usher.
2 *conduct me home.* accompany,
escort, guide, lead, pilot, take,
usher. 3 *conduct electricity.*
carry, channel, convey, transmit. **conduct yourself**
▷ BEHAVE.

confer *vb* 1 accord, award,
bestow, give, grant, honour
with, impart, invest, present.
2 compare notes, consult,
converse, debate, deliberate,
discourse, discuss, exchange
ideas, *inf* put your heads
together, seek advice. ▷ TALK.

conference *n* colloquium,
congress, consultation, convention, council, deliberation,
discussion, forum, seminar,
symposium. ▷ MEETING.

confess *vb* acknowledge, admit,
be truthful, *inf* come clean,
concede, disclose, divulge,
inf make a clean breast (of),
own up, unbosom yourself,
unburden yourself.

confession *n* acknowledgement,
admission, declaration, disclosure, expression, profession,
revelation.

confide *vb* consult, *inf* spill the
beans, open your heart, speak
confidentially, *inf* tell all, tell
secrets, unbosom yourself,
trust.

confidence n 1 belief, certainty, credence, faith, hope, optimism, positiveness, reliance, trust. 2 aplomb, assurance, boldness, composure, conviction, firmness, nerve, panache, self-assurance, self-confidence, self-possession, self-reliance, spirit, verve. *Opp* DOUBT, HESITATION. **have confidence in** ▷ TRUST.

confident adj 1 certain, convinced, hopeful, optimistic, positive, sanguine, sure, trusting. 2 *a confident person.* assertive, assured, bold, *derog* cocksure, composed, cool, definite, fearless, secure, self-assured, self-confident, self-possessed, self-reliant, unafraid. *Opp* DOUBTFUL.

confidential adj 1 classified, *inf* hush-hush, intimate, *inf* off the record, personal, private, restricted, secret, suppressed, top secret. 2 *confidential secretary.* personal, private, trusted.

confine vb bind, box in, cage, circumscribe, constrain, *inf* coop up, cordon off, cramp, curb, detain, enclose, gaol, hedge in, hem in, *inf* hold down, immure, incarcerate, isolate, keep in, limit, localize, restrain, restrict, rope off, shut in, shut up, surround, wall up. ▷ IMPRISON. *Opp* FREE.

confirm vb 1 authenticate, back up, bear out, corroborate, demonstrate, endorse, establish, fortify, give credence to, justify, lend force to, prove, reinforce, settle, show, strengthen, substantiate, support, underline, witness to, vindicate. 2 *confirm a deal.* authorize, *inf* clinch, formalize, guarantee, make legal, make

official, ratify, sanction, validate, verify.

confiscate vb appropriate, commandeer, expropriate, impound, remove, seize, sequester, sequestrate, take away, take possession of.

conflict n 1 antagonism, antipathy, contention, contradiction, difference, disagreement, discord, dissension, friction, hostility, incompatibility, inconsistency, opposition, strife. 2 altercation, battle, *inf* brush, clash, combat, confrontation, contest, dispute, encounter, engagement, feud, fight, quarrel, row, *inf* set-to, skirmish, struggle, war, warfare, wrangle. • vb be at odds, be at variance, be incompatible, clash, compete, contend, contradict, contrast, *inf* cross swords, differ, disagree, oppose each other. ▷ FIGHT, QUARREL.

conform vb acquiesce, agree, be good, behave conventionally, blend in, *inf* do what you are told, fit in, *inf* keep in step, obey, *inf* see eye to eye, *inf* toe the line. ▷ COMPLY.

conformist n conventional person, traditionalist, yes-man. *Opp* REBEL.

conformity n complaisance, compliance, conventionality, obedience, orthodoxy, submission, uniformity.

confront vb accost, argue with, attack, brave, challenge, defy, encounter, face up to, meet, oppose, resist, stand up to, take on, withstand. *Opp* AVOID.

confuse vb 1 disarrange, disorder, distort, entangle, garble, jumble, *inf* mess up, mingle, mix up, muddle, tangle, *inf* throw into disarray, upset. **2** *rules confuse me.* agitate, baffle, befuddle, bemuse, bewilder, confound, disconcert, disorientate, distract, *inf* flummox, fluster, mislead, mystify, perplex, puzzle, *inf* rattle, *inf* throw. **3** *confuse twins.* fail to distinguish.

confusing ▷ PUZZLING.

confused *adj* **1** chaotic, disordered, disorderly, disorganized, higgledy-piggledy, jumbled, messy, mixed up, muddled, *inf* screwed-up, *sl* shambolic, *inf* topsy-turvy, twisted. **2** *confused ideas.* aimless, contradictory, disconnected, disjointed, garbled, incoherent, inconsistent, irrational, misleading, obscure, rambling, unclear, unsound, unstructured, woolly. **3** *confused mind.* addled, addle-headed, baffled, bewildered, dazed, disorientated, distracted, flustered, fuddled, *inf* in a tizzy, inebriated, muddle-headed, *inf* muzzy, mystified, non-plussed, perplexed, puzzled. ▷ MAD. *Opp* ORDERLY.

confusion *n* **1** *inf* ado, anarchy, bedlam, bother, chaos, clutter, commotion, confusion, din, disorder, disorganization, disturbance, fuss, hubbub, hullabaloo, jumble, maelstrom, *inf* mayhem, mêlée, mess, *inf* mix-up, muddle, pandemonium, racket, riot, rumpus, shambles, tumult, turbulence, turmoil, upheaval, uproar, welter, whirl. **2** *mental confusion.* bemusement, bewilderment, disorientation, distraction, mystification, perplexity, puzzlement. *Opp* ORDER.

congeal *vb* clot, coagulate, coalesce, condense, curdle, freeze, harden, *inf* jell, set, solidify, stiffen, thicken.

congenial *adj* acceptable, agreeable, amicable, companionable, compatible, genial, kindly, suitable, sympathetic, understanding, well-suited. ▷ FRIENDLY. *Opp* UNCONGENIAL.

congenital *adj* hereditary, inborn, inbred, inherent, inherited, innate, natural.

congested *adj* blocked, choked, clogged, crammed, crowded, full, jammed, obstructed, overcrowded, stuffed. *Opp* CLEAR.

congratulate *vb* applaud, compliment, felicitate, praise.

congregate *vb* assemble, cluster, collect, come together, convene, converge, crowd, forgather, gather, get together, mass, meet, muster, rally, rendezvous, swarm, throng. ▷ GROUP.

conjure *vb* bewitch, charm, compel, enchant, invoke, raise, rouse, summon. **conjure up** ▷ PRODUCE.

conjuring *n* illusions, legerdemain, magic, sleight of hand, tricks, wizardry.

connect *vb* **1** attach, combine, couple, engage, fix, interlock, join, link, put on, switch on, tie, turn on, unite. ▷ FASTEN. **2** associate, bracket together, compare, make a connection between, put together, relate, tie up. *Opp* SEPARATE.

connection *n* affinity, association, bond, coherence, contact, correlation, correspondence, interrelationship, link, relationship, relevance, tie, *inf* tie-up, unity. *Opp* SEPARATION.

conquer vb 1 annex, beat, best, capture, checkmate, crush, defeat, get the better of, humble, inf lick, master, occupy, outdo, overcome, overpower, overrun, overthrow, overwhelm, possess, prevail over, quell, rout, seize, silence, subdue, subject, subjugate, succeed against, surmount, take, inf thrash, triumph over, vanquish, worst. ▷ WIN. 2 conquer a mountain. climb, reach the top of.

conquest n annexation, appropriation, capture, defeat, domination, invasion, occupation, overthrow, subjection, subjugation, inf takeover. ▷ VICTORY.

conscience n compunction, ethics, honour, fairness, misgivings, morality, morals, principles, qualms, reservations, scruples, standards.

conscientious adj accurate, attentive, careful, diligent, dutiful, exact, hard-working, high-minded, honest, meticulous, painstaking, particular, punctilious, responsible, rigorous, scrupulous, serious, thorough. Opp CARELESS.

conscious adj 1 alert, awake, aware, compos mentis, sensible. 2 a conscious act. calculated, deliberate, intended, intentional, knowing, planned, premeditated, self-conscious, studied, voluntary, waking, wilful. Opp UNCONSCIOUS.

consecrate vb bless, dedicate, devote, hallow, make sacred, sanctify. Opp DESECRATE.

consecutive adj continuous, following, one after the other, running (3 days running), sequential, succeeding, successive.

consent n acquiescence, agreement, approval, assent, concurrence, imprimatur, permission, seal of approval. ● vb accede, acquiesce, agree, approve, comply, concede, concur, conform, submit, undertake, yield. Opp REFUSE. **consent to** ▷ ALLOW.

consequence n 1 aftermath, by-product, corollary, effect, end, inf follow-up, issue, outcome, repercussion, result, sequel, side-effect, upshot. 2 of no consequence. account, concern, importance, moment, note, significance, value, weight.

consequent adj consequential, ensuing, following, resultant, resulting, subsequent.

conservation n careful management, economy, good husbandry, maintenance, preservation, protection, safeguarding, saving, upkeep. Opp DESTRUCTION.

conservationist n ecologist, environmentalist, inf green, preservationist.

conservative adj 1 conventional, die-hard, hidebound, moderate, narrow-minded, old-fashioned, reactionary, sober, traditional, unadventurous. 2 conservative estimate. cautious, moderate, reasonable, understated, unexaggerated. 3 conservative politics. right-of-centre, right-wing, Tory. Opp PROGRESSIVE. ● n conformist, die-hard, reactionary, right-winger, Tory, traditionalist.

conserve vb be economical with, hold in reserve, keep, look after, maintain, preserve, protect, safeguard, save, store up, use sparingly. Opp DESTROY, WASTE.

consider vb 1 inf chew over, cogitate, contemplate, deliberate, discuss, examine, meditate, mull over, muse, ponder, puzzle over, reflect, ruminate, study, inf turn over, weigh up. ▷ THINK. 2 believe, deem, judge, reckon.

considerable adj appreciable, big, biggish, comfortable, fairly important, fairly large, noteworthy, noticeable, perceptible, reasonable, respectable, significant, sizeable, substantial, inf tidy (amount), tolerable, worthwhile. Opp NEGLIGIBLE.

considerate adj accommodating, altruistic, attentive, caring, charitable, cooperative, friendly, generous, gracious, helpful, kind, kind-hearted, kindly, neighbourly, obliging, polite, sensitive, solicitous, sympathetic, tactful, thoughtful, unselfish. Opp SELFISH.

consign vb commit, convey, deliver, devote, entrust, give, hand over, pass on, relegate, send, ship, transfer.

consignment n batch, cargo, delivery, load, lorry-load, shipment, van-load.

consist vb consist of add up to, amount to, be composed of, be made of, comprise, contain, embody, include, incorporate, involve.

consistent adj 1 constant, dependable, faithful, predictable, regular, reliable, stable, steadfast, steady, unchanging, undeviating, unfailing, uniform, unvarying. 2 The stories are consistent. accordant, compatible, congruous, consonant, in accordance, in agreement, in harmony, of a piece. Opp INCONSISTENT.

console vb calm, cheer, comfort, ease, encourage, hearten, relieve, solace, soothe, succour, sympathize with.

consolidate vb make secure, make strong, reinforce, stabilize, strengthen. Opp WEAKEN.

consort vb consort with accompany, associate with, befriend, be friends with, be seen with, fraternize with, inf gang up with, keep company with, mix with.

conspicuous adj apparent, blatant, clear, discernible, distinguished, dominant, eminent, evident, flagrant, glaring, impressive, manifest, marked, notable, noticeable, obtrusive, obvious, ostentatious, outstanding, patent, perceptible, plain, prominent, pronounced, self-evident, shining (example), showy, striking, unconcealed, unmistakable, visible. Opp INCONSPICUOUS.

conspiracy n cabal, collusion, connivance, inf frame-up, insider dealing, intrigue, machinations, plot, inf racket, scheme, stratagem, treason.

conspirator n plotter, schemer, traitor, inf wheeler-dealer.

conspire vb be in league, collude, combine, connive, cooperate, hatch a plot, have designs, intrigue, plot, scheme.

constant adj 1 ceaseless, chronic, consistent, continual, continuous, endless, eternal, everlasting, fixed, immutable, incessant, invariable, neverending, non-stop, permanent, perpetual, persistent, predictable, regular, relentless, repeated, stable, steady, sustained, unbroken, unchanging, unending, unflagging, uniform, uninterrupted, unremitting, unvarying. 2 a *constant friend.* dedicated, dependable, determined, devoted, faithful, firm, indefatigable, loyal, reliable, resolute, staunch, steadfast, tireless, true, trustworthy, trusty, unswerving, unwavering. *Opp* CHANGEABLE.

constitute *vb* appoint, bring together, compose, comprise, create, establish, form, found, inaugurate, make (up), set up.

construct *vb* assemble, build, create, engineer, erect, fabricate, fashion, fit together, form, *inf* knock together, make, manufacture, pitch (*tent*), produce, put together, put up, set up. *Opp* DESTRUCTIVE.

construction *n* 1 assembly, building, creation, erecting, erection, manufacture, production, putting-up, setting-up. 2 building, edifice, erection, structure.

constructive *adj* advantageous, beneficial, cooperative, creative, helpful, positive, practical, productive, useful, valuable, worthwhile. *Opp* DESTRUCTIVE.

consult *vb* confer, debate, discuss, exchange views, *inf* put your heads together, refer (to), seek advice, speak (to), *inf* talk things over. ▷ QUESTION.

consume *vb* 1 devour, digest, drink, eat, *inf* gobble up, *inf* guzzle, *inf* put away, swallow. 2 *consume energy.* absorb, deplete, drain, eat into, employ,

exhaust, expend, swallow up, use up, utilize.

contact *n* connection, join, junction, touch, union. ▷ COMMUNICATION. ● *vb* apply to, approach, call on, communicate with, correspond with, *inf* drop a line to, get hold of, get in touch with, make overtures to, notify, phone, ring, sound out, speak to, talk to, telephone.

contagious *adj* catching, communicable, infectious, spreading, transmittable.

contain *vb* 1 accommodate, enclose, hold. 2 be composed of, comprise, consist of, embody, embrace, include, incorporate, involve. 3 *contain your anger.* check, control, curb, hold back, keep back, limit, repress, restrain, stifle.

container *n* holder, receptacle, repository, vessel. ▷ BAG, BARREL, BOTTLE, BOWL, BOX, CUP, DISH, GLASS, LUGGAGE, POT.

contaminate *vb* adulterate, befoul, corrupt, debase, defile, dirty, foul, infect, poison, pollute, soil, spoil, stain, sully, taint. *Opp* PURIFY.

contemplate *vb* 1 eye, gaze at, look at, observe, regard, stare at, survey, view, watch. ▷ SEE. 2 cogitate, consider, day-dream, deliberate, examine, meditate, mull over, muse, plan, ponder, reflect, ruminate, study, work out. ▷ THINK. 3 envisage, expect, intend, propose.

contemporary *adj* 1 *contemporary with me at school.* coeval, coexistent, coinciding, concurrent, contemporaneous, simultaneous, synchronous. 2 *contemporary music.* current, fashionable, the latest, modern, newest, novel, present-day, *inf* trendy, topical, up-to-date, *inf* with-it.

contempt *n* abhorrence, contumely, derision, detestation, disdain, disgust, dislike, disrespect, loathing, ridicule, scorn. ▷ HATRED.
Opp ADMIRATION. **feel contempt for** ▷ DESPISE.

contemptible *adj* base, beneath contempt, despicable, detestable, discreditable, disgraceful, dishonourable, disreputable, ignominious, inferior, loathsome, low-down, mean, odious, pitiful, *inf* shabby, shameful, worthless, wretched.
▷ HATEFUL. *Opp* ADMIRABLE.

contemptuous *adj* arrogant, belittling, condescending, derisive, disdainful, dismissive, disrespectful, haughty, *inf* holier-than-thou, imperious, insolent, insulting, jeering, lofty, patronizing, sarcastic, scathing, scornful, sneering, *sl* snide, snobbish, *inf* snooty, *sl* snotty, supercilious, superior, withering. *Opp* RESPECTFUL. **be contemptuous of** ▷ DESPISE.

contend *vb* 1 compete, contest, cope, dispute, grapple, oppose, rival, strive, struggle, vie. ▷ FIGHT, QUARREL. 2 *contend that you're innocent.* affirm, allege, argue, assert, claim, declare, maintain, plead.

content *adj* ▷ CONTENTED.
• *n* 1 constituent, element, ingredient, part. 2 ▷ CONTENTMENT. • *vb* ▷ SATISFY.

contented *adj* cheerful, comfortable, *derog* complacent, content, fulfilled, gratified, peaceful,

pleased, relaxed, satisfied, serene, smiling, smug, uncomplaining, untroubled, well-fed. ▷ HAPPY. *Opp* DISSATISFIED.

contentment *n* comfort, content, contentedness, ease, fulfilment, relaxation, satisfaction, serenity, smugness, tranquillity, well-being. ▷ HAPPINESS. *Opp* DISSATISFACTION.

contest *n* ▷ COMPETITION, FIGHT.
• *vb* 1 compete for, contend for, fight for, *inf* make a bid for, strive for, struggle for, take up the challenge of, vie for. 2 *contest a decision.* argue against, challenge, debate, dispute, doubt, oppose, query, question, refute, resist.

contestant *n* candidate, competitor, contender, entrant, opponent, participant, player, rival.

context *n* background, environment, frame of reference, framework, milieu, position, setting, situation, surroundings.

continual *adj* eternal, everlasting, frequent, limitless, ongoing, perennial, perpetual, recurrent, regular, repeated. ▷ CONTINUOUS. *Opp* OCCASIONAL.

continuation *n* 1 continuance, extension, maintenance, prolongation, protraction, resumption. 2 addition, appendix, postscript, sequel, supplement.

continue *vb* 1 carry on, endure, go on, keep on, last, linger, persevere, persist, proceed, pursue, remain, stay, *inf* stick at, survive, sustain. 2 *continue after lunch.* *inf* pick up the threads, recommence, restart, resume. 3 *continue a series.*

extend, keep going, keep up, lengthen, maintain, prolong.

continuous *adj* ceaseless, constant, continuing, endless, incessant, interminable, lasting, never-ending, non-stop, permanent, persistent, relentless, *inf* round-the-clock, *inf* solid, sustained, unbroken, unceasing, unending, uninterrupted, unremitting.
▷ CHRONIC, CONTINUAL.
Opp INTERMITTENT.

contour *n* curve, form, outline, relief, shape.

contract *n* agreement, bargain, bond, commitment, compact, concordat, covenant, deal, indenture, lease, pact, settlement, treaty, understanding, undertaking. • *vb* 1 become denser, become smaller, close up, condense, decrease, diminish, draw together, dwindle, fall away, lessen, narrow, reduce, shrink, shrivel, slim down, thin out, wither. *Opp* EXPAND.
2 agree, arrange, close a deal, covenant, negotiate a deal, promise, sign an agreement, undertake. 3 *contract a disease*. become infected by, catch, develop, get.

contraction *n* 1 diminution, narrowing, shortening, shrinkage, shrivelling. 2 abbreviation, diminutive, shortened form.

contradict *vb* argue with, challenge, confute, controvert, deny, disagree with, dispute, gainsay, impugn, oppose, speak against.

contradictory *adj* antithetical, conflicting, contrary, different, discrepant, incompatible, inconsistent, irreconcilable, opposed, opposite. *Opp* COMPATIBLE.

contraption *n* apparatus, contrivance, device, gadget, invention, machine, mechanism.

contrary *adj* 1 conflicting, contradictory, converse, different, opposed, opposite, other, reverse. 2 *contrary winds*. adverse, hostile, inimical, opposing, unfavourable. 3 *a contrary child*. awkward, cantankerous, defiant, difficult, disobedient, disobliging, disruptive, intractable, obstinate, perverse, rebellious, *inf* stroppy, stubborn, subversive, uncooperative, unhelpful, wayward, wilful. *Opp* HELPFUL.

contrast *n* antithesis, comparison, difference, differentiation, disparity, dissimilarity, distinction, divergence, foil, opposition. *Opp* SIMILARITY.
• *vb* 1 compare, differentiate, discriminate, distinguish, emphasize differences, make a distinction, set one against the other. 2 be set off (by), clash, conflict, deviate (from), differ (from). **contrasting** ▷ DISSIMILAR.

contribute *vb* add, bestow, *inf* chip in, donate, *inf* fork out, furnish, give, present, provide, put up, subscribe, supply.
contribute to ▷ SUPPORT.

contribution *n* 1 donation, fee, gift, grant, *inf* hand-out, offering, payment, sponsorship, subscription. 2 addition, encouragement, input, support.
▷ HELP.

contributor *n* 1 backer, benefactor, donor, giver, helper, patron, sponsor, subscriber, supporter. 2 ▷ WRITER.

control *n* 1 administration, authority, charge, command, curb, direction, discipline, government, grip, guidance, influence, jurisdiction, leadership, management, mastery, orderliness, organization, oversight, power, regulation, restraint, rule, strictness, supervision, supremacy, sway. **2** button, dial, handle, key, lever, switch. ● *vb* **1** administer, *inf* be at the helm, be in charge, *inf* boss, command, conduct, cope with, deal with, direct, dominate, engineer, govern, guide, handle, have control of, lead, look after, manage, manipulate, order about, oversee, regiment, regulate, rule, run, superintend, supervise. **2** *control animals.* check, confine, contain, curb, hold back, keep in check, master, repress, restrain, subdue, suppress.

controversial *adj* **1** arguable, controvertible, debatable, disputable, doubtful, problematical, questionable. *Opp* ACCEPTED. **2** argumentative, contentious, dialectic, litigious, polemical, provocative.

controversy *n* altercation, argument, confrontation, contention, debate, disagreement, dispute, dissension, issue, polemic, quarrel, war of words, wrangle.

convalesce *vb* get better, improve, make progress, mend, recover, recuperate, regain strength.

convalescent *adj* getting better, healing, improving, making progress, *inf* on the mend, recovering, recuperating.

convene *vb* bring together, call, convoke, summon. ▷ GATHER.

convenient *adj* accessible, appropriate, at hand, available, commodious, expedient, handy, helpful, labour-saving, nearby, neat, opportune, serviceable, suitable, timely, usable, useful. *Opp* INCONVENIENT.

convention *n* **1** custom, etiquette, formality, matter of form, practice, rule, tradition. **2** ▷ ASSEMBLY.

conventional *adj* **1** accepted, accustomed, commonplace, correct, customary, decorous, expected, formal, habitual, mainstream, orthodox, prevalent, received, *inf* run-of-the-mill, standard, straight, traditional, unadventurous, unimaginative, unoriginal, unsurprising. ▷ ORDINARY. **2** [*derog*] bourgeois, conservative, hidebound, pedestrian, reactionary, rigid, stereotyped, *inf* stuffy. *Opp* UNCONVENTIONAL.

converge *vb* coincide, combine, come together, join, link up, meet, merge, unite. *Opp* DIVERGE.

conversation *n inf* chat, *inf* chin-wag, colloquy, communication, conference, dialogue, discourse, discussion, exchange of views, gossip, *inf* heart-to-heart, intercourse, *inf* natter, palaver, phone-call, *inf* pow-wow, tête-à-tête. ▷ TALK.

convert *vb* change someone's mind, convince, persuade, re-educate, reform, regenerate, rehabilitate, save, win over. ▷ CHANGE.

convey *vb* **1** bear, bring, carry, conduct, deliver, export, ferry, fetch, forward, import, move, send, shift, ship, shuttle, take,

taxi, transfer, transport.
2 *convey a message.* communicate, disclose, impart, imply, indicate, mean, relay, reveal, signify, tell, transmit.

convict *n* condemned person, criminal, culprit, felon, malefactor, prisoner, wrongdoer.
● *vb* condemn, declare guilty, prove guilty, sentence.
Opp ACQUIT.

conviction *n* 1 assurance, certainty, confidence, firmness. 2 *religious conviction.* belief, creed, faith, opinion, persuasion, position, principle, tenet, view.

convince *vb* assure, *inf* bring round, convert, persuade, prove to, reassure, satisfy, sway, win over. **convincing** ▷ PERSUASIVE.

convulsion *n* 1 disturbance, eruption, outburst, tremor, turbulence, upheaval.
2 [*medical*] attack, fit, paroxysm, seizure, spasm.

convulsive *adj* jerky, shaking, spasmodic, *inf* twitchy, uncontrolled, uncoordinated, violent, wrenching.

cook *vb* concoct, heat up, make, prepare, warm up. □ *bake, barbecue, boil, braise, brew, broil, casserole, coddle, fry, grill, pickle, poach, roast, sauté, scramble, simmer, steam, stew, toast.* **cook up** ▷ PLOT.

cooking *n* baking, catering, cookery, cuisine.

cool *adj* 1 chilled, chilly, coldish, iced, refreshing, unheated. ▷ COLD. *Opp* HOT. 2 calm, collected, composed, dignified, elegant, *inf* laid-back, level-headed, phlegmatic, quiet, relaxed, self-possessed, sensible,

serene, unexcited, unflustered, unruffled, urbane. ▷ BRAVE. 3 [*derog*] aloof, apathetic, cold-blooded, dispassionate, distant, frigid, half-hearted, indifferent, lukewarm, negative, offhand, reserved, *inf* stand-offish, unconcerned, unemotional, unenthusiastic, unfriendly, uninvolved, unresponsive, unsociable, unwelcoming. *Opp* PASSIONATE. 4 [*inf*] *cool customer.* ▷ INSOLENT.
● *vb* 1 chill, freeze, ice, refrigerate. *Opp* HEAT. 2 *cool your enthusiasm.* abate, allay, assuage, calm, dampen, diminish, lessen, moderate, *inf* pour cold water on, quiet, temper. *Opp* INFLAME.

cooperate *vb* act in concert, collaborate, combine, conspire, help each other, *inf* join forces, *inf* pitch in, *inf* play along, *inf* play ball, *inf* pull together, support each other, unite, work as a team, work together. *Opp* COMPETE.

cooperation *n* assistance, collaboration, cooperative effort, coordination, help, joint action, mutual support, teamwork. *Opp* COMPETITION.

cooperative *adj* 1 accommodating, comradely, constructive, hard-working, helpful to each other, keen, obliging, supportive, united, willing, working as a team. 2 *cooperative effort.* collective, combined, communal, concerted, coordinated, corporate, joint, shared.

cope *vb* get by, make do, manage, survive, win through. **cope with** ▷ ENDURE, MANAGE.

copious *adj* abundant, ample, bountiful, extravagant, generous, great, huge, inexhaustible, large, lavish, liberal, luxuriant, overflowing, plentiful, profuse, unsparing, unstinting. *Opp* SCARCE.

copy *n* 1 carbon copy, clone, counterfeit, double, duplicate, facsimile, fake, forgery, imitation, likeness, model, pattern, photocopy, print, replica, representation, reproduction, tracing, transcript, twin, Xerox. 2 *copy of a book*. edition, volume. ● *vb* 1 borrow, counterfeit, crib, duplicate, emulate, follow, forge, imitate, photocopy, plagiarize, print, repeat, reproduce, simulate, transcribe. 2 ape, imitate, impersonate, mimic, parrot.

cord *n* cable, catgut, lace, line, rope, strand, string, twine, wire.

cordon *n* barrier, chain, fence, line, ring, row. **cordon off** ▷ ISOLATE.

core *n* 1 centre, heart, inside, middle, nucleus. 2 *core of a problem*. central issue, crux, essence, gist, heart, kernel, *sl* nitty-gritty, nub.

cork *n* bung, plug, stopper.

corner *n* 1 angle, crook, joint. 2 bend, crossroads, intersection, junction, turn, turning. 3 *a quiet corner*. hideaway, hiding-place, hole, niche, nook, recess, retreat. ● *vb* capture, catch, trap.

corporation *n* 1 company, concern, enterprise, firm, organization. 2 council, local government.

corpse *n* body, cadaver, carcass, mortal remains, remains, skeleton, *sl* stiff.

correct *adj* 1 accurate, authentic, confirmed, exact, factual, faithful, faultless, flawless, genuine, literal, precise, reliable, right, strict, true, truthful, verified. 2 *correct manners*. acceptable, appropriate, fitting, just, normal, proper, regular, standard, suitable, tactful, unexceptionable, well-mannered. *Opp* WRONG. ● *vb* 1 adjust, alter, cure, *inf* debug, put right, rectify, redress, remedy, repair. 2 *correct pupils' work*. assess, mark. 3 ▷ REPRIMAND.

correspond *vb* accord, agree, be congruous, be consistent, coincide, concur, conform, correlate, fit, harmonize, match, parallel, square, tally. **corresponding** ▷ EQUIVALENT. **correspond with** communicate with, send letters to, write to.

correspondence *n* letters, memoranda, *inf* memos, messages, notes, writings.

correspondent *n* contributor, journalist, reporter. ▷ WRITER.

corridor *n* hall, hallway, passage, passageway.

corrode *vb* 1 consume, eat into, erode, oxidize, rot, rust, tarnish. 2 crumble, deteriorate, disintegrate, tarnish.

corrugated *adj* creased, *inf* crinkly, fluted, furrowed, lined, puckered, ribbed, ridged, wrinkled.

corrupt *adj inf* bent, bribable, criminal, crooked, debauched, decadent, degenerate, depraved, *inf* dishy, dishonest, dishonourable, dissolute, evil, false, fraudulent, illegal, immoral, iniquitous, low, perverted, prof-

ligate, rotten, sinful, unethical, unprincipled, unscrupulous, unsound, untrustworthy, venal, vicious, wicked. *Opp* HONEST.
● *vb* **1** bribe, divert, *inf* fix, influence, pervert, suborn, subvert. **2** *corrupt the innocent.* debauch, deprave, lead astray, make corrupt, tempt, seduce.

cosmetics *n* make-up, toiletries.

cosmic *adj* boundless, endless, infinite, limitless, universal.

cosmopolitan *adj* international, multicultural, sophisticated, urbane. *Opp* PROVINCIAL.

cost *n* amount, charge, expenditure, expense, fare, figure, outlay, payment, price, rate, tariff, value. ● *vb* be valued at, be worth, fetch, go for, realize, sell for, *inf* set you back.

costume *n* apparel, attire, clothing, dress, fancy-dress, garb, garments, *inf* get-up, livery, outfit, period dress, raiment, robes, uniform, vestments. ▷ CLOTHES.

cosy *adj* comfortable, *inf* comfy, easy, homely, intimate, reassuring, relaxing, restful, secure, snug, soft, warm. *Opp* UNCOMFORTABLE.

council *n* committee, conclave, convention, convocation, corporation, gathering, meeting. ▷ ASSEMBLY.

counsel *n* ▷ LAWYER.
● *vb* advise, discuss (with), give help, guide, listen to your views.

count *vb* **1** add up, calculate, check, compute, enumerate, estimate, figure out, keep account of, *inf* notch up, number, reckon, score, take stock of, tell, total, *inf* tot up, work out. **2** be important, have

significance, matter, signify.
count on ▷ EXPECT.

countenance *n* air, appearance, aspect, demeanour, expression, face, features, look, visage.
● *vb* ▷ APPROVE.

counter *n* **1** bar, sales-point, service-point, table. **2** chip, disc, marker, piece, token.
● *vb* answer, *inf* come back at, contradict, defend yourself against, hit back at, parry, react to, rebut, refute, reply to, resist, ward off.

counteract *vb* act against, annul, be an antidote to, cancel out, counterbalance, fight against, foil, invalidate, militate against, negate, neutralize, offset, oppose, resist, thwart, withstand, work against.

counterbalance *vb* balance, compensate for, counteract, counterpoise, counterweight, equalize.

counterfeit *adj* artificial, bogus, copied, ersatz, fake, false, feigned, forged, fraudulent, imitation, make-believe, meretricious, pastiche, *inf* phoney, *inf* pretend, *inf* pseudo, sham, simulated, spurious, synthetic. *Opp* GENUINE. ● *vb* copy, fake, falsify, feign, forge, imitate, pretend, *inf* put on, sham, simulate.

countless *adj* endless, immeasurable, incalculable, infinite, innumerable, limitless, many, measureless, myriad, numberless, numerous, unnumbered, untold. ▷ FINITE.

country *n* **1** canton, commonwealth, domain, empire, kingdom, land, nation, people, power, principality, realm, state, territory. **2** *open country.*

countryside, green belt, landscape, scenery.

couple *n* brace, duo, pair, twosome. ▷ *vb* 1 combine, connect, fasten, hitch, join, link, match, pair, unite, yoke. 2 ▷ MATE.

coupon *n* tear-off slip, ticket, token, voucher.

courage *n* audacity, boldness, *sl* bottle, bravery, daring, dauntlessness, determination, fearlessness, fibre, firmness, fortitude, gallantry, *inf* grit, *inf* guts, heroism, indomitability, intrepidity, mettle, *inf* nerve, patience, *inf* pluck, prowess, resolution, spirit, *sl* spunk, stoicism, tenacity, valour, will-power.
Opp COWARDICE.

courageous *adj* audacious, bold, brave, cool, daring, dauntless, determined, fearless, gallant, game, *sl* gutsy, heroic, indomitable, intrepid, lion-hearted, noble, *inf* plucky, resolute, spirited, stalwart, stoical, stout-hearted, tough, unafraid, uncomplaining, undaunted, unshrinking, valiant, valorous.
Opp COWARDLY.

course *n* 1 bearings, circuit, direction, line, orbit, path, route, track, way. 2 *course of events*. advance, continuation, development, movement, passage, passing, progress, progression, succession. 3 *course of lectures*. curriculum, programme, schedule, sequence, series, syllabus.

court *n* 1 assizes, bench, court martial, high court, lawcourt, magistrates' court. 2 entourage, followers, palace, retinue. 3 ▷ COURTYARD. ● *vb* 1 *inf* ask

for, attract, invite, provoke, seek, solicit. 2 date, *inf* go out with, make advances to, make love to, try to win, woo.

courteous *adj* civil, considerate, gentlemanly, ladylike, urbane, well-bred, well-mannered.
▷ POLITE.

courtier *n* attendant, follower, lady, lord, noble, page, steward.

courtyard *n* court, enclosure, forecourt, patio, *inf* quad, quadrangle, yard.

cover *n* 1 ▷ COVERING. 2 binding, case, dust-jacket, envelope, file, folder, portfolio, wrapper. 3 camouflage, cloak, concealment, cover-up, deception, disguise, façade, front, hiding-place, mask, pretence, refuge, sanctuary, shelter, smoke-screen. 4 *air cover* defence, guard, protection, support.
● *vb* 1 blot out, bury, camouflage, cap, carpet, cloak, clothe, cloud, coat, conceal, curtain, disguise, drape, dress, encase, enclose, enshroud, envelop, face, hide, hood, mantle, mask, obscure, overlay, overspread, plaster, protect, screen, shade, sheathe, shield, shroud, spread over, surface, tile, veil, veneer, wrap up. 2 *cover expenses*. be enough for, match, meet, pay for, suffice for. 3 *talk covered many subjects*. comprise, contain, deal with, embrace, encompass, include, incorporate, involve, treat.

covering *n* blanket, canopy, cap, carpet, casing, cladding, cloak, coat, coating, cocoon, cover, crust, facing, film, incrustation, layer, lid, mantle, outside, pall, rind, roof, screen, sheath, sheet, shell, shield, shroud, skin, surface, tarpaulin, top, veil,

veneer, wrapping. ▷ BED-
CLOTHES.

coward n *inf* chicken, craven,
deserter, runaway, *inf* wimp.

cowardice n cowardliness,
desertion, evasion, faint-heartedness, *inf* funk, shirking,
spinelessness, timidity. ▷ FEAR.
Opp COURAGE.

cowardly adj abject, afraid,
base, chicken-hearted, cower-
ing, craven, dastardly, faint-
hearted, fearful, *inf* gutless,
inf lily-livered, pusillanimous,
spineless, submissive, timid,
timorous, unchivalrous, ungal-
lant, unheroic, *inf* wimpish,
sl yellow. ▷ FRIGHTENED.
Opp COURAGEOUS.

cower vb cringe, crouch, flinch,
grovel, hide, quail, shiver,
shrink, skulk, tremble.

coy adj arch, bashful, coquettish,
demure, diffident, embarrassed,
evasive, hesitant, modest,
reserved, reticent, retiring, self-
conscious, sheepish, shy, timid,
unforthcoming. *Opp* BOLD.

crack n 1 breach, break, chink,
chip, cleavage, cleft, cranny,
craze, crevice, fissure, flaw,
fracture, gap, opening, rift,
rupture, slit, split. 2 ▷ JOKE.
• vb 1 break, chip, fracture,
snap, splinter, split. 2 ▷ HIT,
SOUND. **crack up** ▷ DISINTE-
GRATE.

craft n 1 handicraft, job, skilled
work, technique, trade.
▷ CRAFTSMANSHIP, CUNNING. 2 *a
sea-going craft*. ▷ VESSEL.
• vb ▷ MAKE.

craftsmanship n art, artistry,
cleverness, craft, dexterity,
expertise, handiwork, knack,
inf know-how, workmanship.
▷ SKILL.

crafty adj artful, astute, calculating, canny, cheating, clever,
conniving, cunning, deceitful,
designing, devious, *inf* dodgy,
inf foxy, furtive, guileful, ingenious, knowing, machiavellian,
manipulative, scheming, shifty,
shrewd, sly, *inf* sneaky, tricky,
wily. *Opp* HONEST, NAÏVE.

craggy adj jagged, rocky, rough,
rugged, steep, uneven.

cram vb 1 compress, crowd,
crush, fill, force, jam, overcrowd, overfill, pack, press,
squeeze, stuff. 2 ▷ STUDY.

cramped adj close, crowded,
narrow, restricted, tight,
uncomfortable. *Opp* ROOMY.

crane n davit, derrick, hoist.

crash n 1 bang, boom, clash,
explosion. ▷ SOUND. 2 accident,
bump, collision, derailment,
disaster, impact, knock, pile-up,
smash, wreck. 3 *crash on the
stock market*. collapse, depression, failure, fall. • vb 1 bump,
collide, knock, lurch, pitch,
smash. ▷ HIT. 2 collapse, crash-
dive, dive, fall, plummet,
plunge, topple.

crate n box, carton, case, pack-
ing-case, tea-chest.

crater n abyss, cavity, chasm,
hole, hollow, opening, pit.

crawl vb 1 clamber, creep, edge,
inch, slither, squirm, worm,
wriggle. 2 [*inf*] be obsequious,
cringe, fawn, flatter, grovel,
sl suck up, toady.

craze n diversion, enthusiasm,
fad, fashion, infatuation,
mania, novelty, obsession,
passion, pastime, rage,
inf thing, trend, vogue.

crazy adj berserk, crazed,
delirious, demented, deranged,
frantic, frenzied, hysterical,

insane, lunatic, *inf* potty, *inf* scatty, unbalanced, unhinged, wild. ▷ MAD. **2** *crazy comedy*. daft, eccentric, farcical, idiotic, *inf* knockabout, ludicrous, ridiculous, *sl* wacky, zany. ▷ ABSURD. **3** *crazy ideas*. confused, foolish, ill-considered, illogical, impractical, irrational, senseless, silly, unrealistic, unreasonable, unwise. ▷ STUPID. **4** ▷ ENTHUSIASTIC. *Opp* SENSIBLE.

creamy *adj* milky, oily, rich, smooth, thick, velvety.

crease *n* corrugation, crinkle, fold, furrow, groove, line, pleat, pucker, ridge, ruck, tuck, wrinkle. ● *vb* crimp, crinkle, crumple, crush, fold, furrow, pleat, pucker, ridge, ruck, rumple, wrinkle.

create *vb old use* beget, begin, be the creator of, breed, bring about, bring into existence, build, cause, compose, conceive, concoct, constitute, construct, design, devise, *inf* dream up, engender, engineer, establish, father, forge, form, found, generate, give rise to, hatch, imagine, institute, invent, make up, manufacture, occasion, originate, produce, set up, shape, sire, think up. ▷ MAKE. *Opp* DESTROY.

creation *n* **1** beginning, birth, building, conception, constitution, construction, establishing, formation, foundation, generation, genesis, inception, institution, making, origin, procreation, production, shaping. **2** achievement, brainchild, concept, effort, handiwork, invention, product, work of art. *Opp* DESTRUCTION.

creative *adj* artistic, clever, fecund, fertile, imaginative, ingenious, inspired, inventive, original, positive, productive, resourceful, talented. *Opp* DESTRUCTIVE.

creator *n* architect, artist, author, begetter, builder, composer, craftsman, designer, deviser, discoverer, initiator, inventor, maker, manufacturer, originator, painter, parent, photographer, potter, producer, sculptor, smith, weaver, writer.

creature *n* beast, being, brute, mortal being, organism. ▷ ANIMAL.

credentials *n* authorization, documents, identity card, licence, passport, permit, proof of identity, warrant.

credible *adj* believable, conceivable, convincing, imaginable, likely, persuasive, plausible, possible, reasonable, tenable, thinkable, trustworthy. *Opp* INCREDIBLE.

credit *n* approval, commendation, distinction, esteem, fame, glory, honour, *inf* kudos, merit, praise, prestige, recognition, reputation, status, tribute. ● *vb* **1** accept, believe, *inf* buy, count on, depend on, endorse, have faith in, reckon on, rely on, subscribe to, *inf* swallow, swear by, trust. *Opp* DOUBT. **2** *credit you with sense*. ascribe to, assign to, attach to, attribute to. **3** *credit £10 to my account*. add, enter. *Opp* DEBIT.

creditable *adj* admirable, commendable, estimable, good, honourable, laudable, meritorious, praiseworthy, respectable, well thought of, worthy. *Opp* UNWORTHY.

credulous adj easily taken in, inf green, gullible, inf soft, trusting, unsuspecting. ▷ NAIVE. Opp SCEPTICAL.

creed n belief, conviction, doctrine, dogma, faith, principle, teaching, tenet.

creek n bay, cove, estuary, harbour, inlet.

creep vb crawl, edge, inch, move quietly, move slowly, pussyfoot, slink, slip, slither, sneak, steal, tiptoe, worm, wriggle, writhe.

creepy adj disturbing, eerie, frightening, ghostly, hair-raising, macabre, ominous, scary, sinister, spine-chilling, inf spooky, supernatural, threatening, uncanny, unearthly, weird.

crest n 1 comb, plume, tuft. 2 crest of a hill. apex, brow, crown, head, peak, pinnacle, ridge, summit, top. 3 badge, coat of arms, design, device, emblem, heraldic device, insignia, seal, shield, sign, symbol.

crevice n break, chink, cleft, crack, cranny, fissure, furrow, groove, rift, slit, split.

crew n band, company, gang, party, team. ▷ GROUP.

crime n delinquency, dishonesty, old use felony, illegality, law-breaking, lawlessness, misconduct, misdeed, misdemeanour, offence, inf racket, sin, transgression of the law, violation, wrongdoing. □ abduction, arson, assassination, blackmail, burglary, extortion, hijacking, hooliganism, kidnapping, manslaughter, misappropriation, mugging, murder, pilfering, piracy, poaching, rape, robbery, shop-lifting, smuggling, stealing, terrorism, theft, treason, vandalism.

criminal adj inf bent, corrupt, inf crooked, culpable, dishonest, felonious, illegal, illicit, indictable, lawless, nefarious, inf shady, unlawful. ▷ WICKED, WRONG. Opp LAWFUL.
● n inf baddy, convict, inf crook, culprit, delinquent, desperado, felon, gangster, knave, lawbreaker, malefactor, miscreant, offender, outlaw, recidivist, ruffian, scoundrel, old use transgressor, villain, wrongdoer. □ bandit, brigand, buccaneer, defaulter, gunman, highwayman, sl hoodlum, hooligan, pickpocket, racketeer, receiver, swindler, thug. ▷ CRIME.

cringe vb blench, cower, crouch, dodge, duck, flinch, grovel, quail, quiver, recoil, shrink back, shy away, tremble, wince.

cripple vb 1 disable, dislocate, fracture, hamper, hamstring, incapacitate, lame, maim, mutilate, paralyse, weaken. 2 damage, make useless, put out of action, sabotage, spoil. **crippled** ▷ HANDICAPPED.

crisis n calamity, catastrophe, climax, critical moment, danger, difficulty, disaster, emergency, predicament, problem, turning point.

crisp adj 1 breakable, brittle, crackly, crispy, crunchy, fragile, friable, hard and dry. 2 ▷ BRACING, BRISK.

criterion n measure, principle, standard, touchstone, yardstick.

critic n 1 analyst, authority, commentator, judge, pundit, reviewer. 2 attacker, detractor.

critical adj 1 captious, carping, censorious, criticizing, deprecatory, depreciatory, derogatory, disapproving, disparaging, fault-finding, hypercritical, judgemental, *inf* nit-picking, *derog* Pharisaical, scathing, slighting, uncomplimentary, unfavourable. *Opp* COMPLIMENTARY. **2** analytical, discerning, discriminating, intelligent, judicious, perceptive, probing, sharp. **3** *critical moment*. basic, crucial, dangerous, decisive, important, key, momentous, pivotal, vital. *Opp* UNIMPORTANT.

criticism *n* **1** censure, condemnation, diatribe, disapproval, disparagement, reprimand, reproach, stricture, tirade, verbal attack. **2** *literary criticism*. analysis, appraisal, appreciation, assessment, commentary, critique, elucidation, evaluation, judgement, valuation.

criticize *vb* **1** belittle, berate, blame, carp, *inf* cast aspersions on, castigate, censure, *old use* chide, condemn, complain about, decry, disapprove of, disparage, fault, find fault with, *inf* flay, *inf* get at, impugn, *inf* knock, *inf* lash, *inf* pan, *inf* pick holes in, *inf* pitch into, *inf* rap, rate, rebuke, reprimand, satirize, scold, *inf* slam, *inf* slate, snipe at. *Opp* PRAISE. **2** analyse, appraise, assess, evaluate, discuss, judge, review.

crockery *n* ceramics, china, crocks, dishes, earthenware, porcelain, pottery, tableware. □ *basin, bowl, coffee-cup, coffee-pot, cup, dinner plate, dish, jug, milk-jug, mug, plate,* Amer *platter, pot, sauceboat, saucer, serving dish, side*

plate, soup bowl, sugar-bowl, teacup, teapot, old use *trencher, tureen.*

crook *n* **1** angle, bend, corner, hook. **2** ▷ CRIMINAL.

crooked *adj* **1** angled, askew, awry, bendy, bent, bowed, contorted, curved, curving, deformed, gnarled, lopsided, misshapen, off-centre, tortuous, twisted, twisty, warped, winding, zigzag. ▷ INDIRECT. **2** ▷ CRIMINAL.

crop *n* gathering, harvest, produce, sowing, vintage, yield. ● *vb* bite off, browse, clip, graze, nibble, shear, snip, trim. ▷ CUT. **crop up** ▷ ARISE.

cross *adj* bad-tempered, cantankerous, crotchety, *inf* grumpy, ill-tempered, irascible, irate, irritable, peevish, short-tempered, testy, tetchy, upset, vexed. ▷ ANGRY, ANNOYED. *Opp* GOOD-TEMPERED.
● *n* **1** intersection, X. **2** *a cross to bear*. affliction, burden, difficulty, grief, misfortune, problem, sorrow, trial, tribulation, trouble, worry. **3** *cross of breeds*. amalgam, blend, combination, cross-breed, half-way house, hybrid, mixture, mongrel. ● *vb* **1** criss-cross, intersect, meet, zigzag. **2** *cross a river*. bridge, ford, go across, pass over, span, traverse. **3** *cross someone*. annoy, block, frustrate, hinder, impede, interfere with, oppose, stand in the way of, thwart. **cross out** ▷ CANCEL. **cross swords** ▷ CONFLICT.

crossing *vb* bridge, causeway, flyover, ford, level-crossing, overpass, pedestrian crossing, pelican crossing, subway, step-

ping-stones, underpass, zebra
crossing. 2 *sea crossing*.
▷ JOURNEY.

crossroads *n* interchange, intersection, junction.

crouch *vb* bend, bow, cower,
cringe, duck, kneel, squat,
stoop.

crowd *n* 1 army, assemblage,
assembly, bunch, circle, cluster, collection, company, crush,
flock, gathering, horde, host,
mass, mob, multitude, pack,
press, rabble, swarm, throng.
▷ GROUP. 2 *a football crowd*.
audience, gate, spectators.
● *vb* assemble, bundle, cluster,
collect, compress, congregate,
cram, crush, flock, gather, get
together, herd, huddle, jam,
jostle, mass, muster, overcrowd, pack, *inf* pile, press,
push, squeeze, swarm, throng.

crowded *adj* congested,
cramped, full, jammed, *inf* jam-
packed, jostling, overcrowded,
overflowing, packed, swarming,
teeming, thronging. *Opp* EMPTY.

crown *n* 1 circlet, coronet,
diadem, tiara. 2 *crown of a hill*.
apex, brow, head, peak, ridge,
summit, top. ● *vb* 1 anoint,
appoint, enthrone, install.
2 cap, complete, conclude,
consummate, culminate, finish
off, perfect, round off, top.

crucial *adj* central, critical, decisive, essential, important,
major, momentous, pivotal,
serious. *Opp* UNIMPORTANT.

crude *adj* 1 natural, raw, unprocessed, unrefined. 2 *crude work*.
amateurish, awkward,
bungling, clumsy, inartistic,
incompetent, inelegant, inept,
makeshift, primitive, rough,
rudimentary, unpolished,

unskilful, unworkmanlike.
Opp REFINED. 3 ▷ VULGAR.

cruel *adj* atrocious, barbaric,
barbarous, beastly, bestial,
bloodthirsty, bloody, brutal,
callous, cold-blooded, cold-
hearted, diabolical, ferocious,
fiendish, fierce, flinty, grim,
hard, hard-hearted, harsh,
heartless, hellish, implacable,
inexorable, inhuman, inhumane, malevolent, merciless,
murderous, pitiless, relentless,
remorseless, ruthless, sadistic,
savage, severe, sharp, spiteful,
stern, stony-hearted, tyrannical, unfeeling, unjust,
unkind, unmerciful, unrelenting, vengeful, venomous,
vicious, violent. *Opp* KIND.

cruelty *n* barbarity, bestiality,
bloodthirstiness, brutality,
callousness, cold-bloodedness,
ferocity, hard-heartedness,
heartlessness, inhumanity,
malevolence, ruthlessness,
sadism, savagery, unkindness,
viciousness, violence.

cruise *n* sail, voyage. ▷ TRAVEL.

crumb *n* bit, bite, fragment,
grain, morsel, particle, scrap,
shred, sliver, speck.

crumble *vb* break into pieces,
break up, crush, decay, decompose, deteriorate, disintegrate,
fall apart, fragment, grind,
perish, pound, powder, pulverize.

crumbly *adj* friable, granular,
powdery. *Opp* SOLID.

crumple *vb* crease, crinkle,
crush, dent, fold, mangle,
pucker, rumple, wrinkle.

crunch *vb* break, champ, chew,
crush, grind, masticate, munch,
scrunch, smash, squash.

crusade n campaign, drive, holy war, jehad, movement, struggle, war.

crush n congestion, jam. ▷ CROWD. ● vb 1 break, bruise, compress, crumple, crunch, grind, mangle, mash, pound, press, pulp, pulverize, shiver, smash, splinter, squash, squeeze. 2 *crush opponents.* humiliate, mortify, overwhelm, quash, rout, thrash, vanquish. ▷ CONQUER.

crust n incrustation, outer layer, outside, rind, scab, shell, skin, surface. 1 ▷ COVERING.

crux n centre, core, crucial issue, essence, heart, nub.

cry n battle-cry, bellow, call, caterwaul, ejaculation, exclamation, hoot, howl, outcry, roar, scream, screech, shout, shriek, whoop, yell, yelp, yowl. ● vb bawl, blubber, grizzle, howl, keen, shed tears, snivel, sob, wail, weep, whimper, whinge. **cry off** ▷ WITHDRAW. **cry out** ▷ SHOUT.

crypt n basement, catacomb, cellar, grave, sepulchre, tomb, undercroft, vault.

cryptic adj arcane, cabbalistic, coded, concealed, enigmatic, esoteric, hidden, mysterious, mystical, obscure, occult, perplexing, puzzling, recondite, secret, unclear, unintelligible, veiled. Opp INTELLIGIBLE.

cuddle vb caress, clasp lovingly, dandle, embrace, fondle, hold closely, huddle against, hug, kiss, make love, nestle against, nurse, pet, snuggle up to.

cudgel n baton, bludgeon, cane, club, cosh, stick, truncheon. ● vb batter, beat, bludgeon, cane, inf clobber, cosh, pound,

pummel, thrash, thump, inf thwack. ▷ HIT.

cue n hint, prompt, reminder, sign, signal.

culminate vb build up to, climax, conclude, reach a finale, rise to a peak. ▷ END.

culpable adj blameworthy, criminal, guilty, knowing, liable, punishable, reprehensible, wrong. ▷ DELIBERATE. Opp INNOCENT.

culprit n delinquent, malefactor, miscreant, offender, troublemaker, wrongdoer. ▷ CRIMINAL.

cult n 1 craze, fan-club, fashion, following, devotees, party, school, trend, vogue. 2 *religious cult.* ▷ DENOMINATION.

cultivate vb 1 dig, farm, fertilize, hoe, manure, mulch, plough, prepare, rake, till, turn, work. 2 grow, plant, produce, raise, sow, take cuttings, tend. 3 *cultivate a friendship.* court, develop, encourage, foster, further, improve, promote, pursue, try to achieve.

cultivated adj 1 agricultural, farmed, planted, prepared, tilled. 2 ▷ CULTURED.

cultivation n agriculture, agronomy, breeding, culture, growing, farming, gardening, horticulture, husbandry, nurturing.

cultural adj aesthetic, artistic, civilized, civilizing, educational, elevating, enlightening, highbrow, improving, intellectual.

culture n 1 art, background, civilization, customs, education, learning, mores, traditions, way of life. 2 ▷ CULTIVATION.

cultured adj artistic, civilized, cultivated, discriminating, educated, elegant, erudite, high-brow, knowledgeable, polished, refined, scholarly, sophisticated, well-bred, well-educated, well-read. Opp IGNORANT.

cunning adj 1 artful, devious, dodgy, guileful, insidious, knowing, machiavellian, sly, subtle, tricky, wily. ▷ CRAFTY. 2 adroit, astute, ingenious, skilful. ▷ CLEVER. • n 1 artfulness, chicanery, craft, craftiness, deceit, deception, deviousness, duplicity, guile, slyness, trickery. 2 cleverness, expertise, ingenuity, skill.

cup n 1 beaker, bowl, chalice, glass, goblet, mug, tankard, teacup, tumbler, wine-glass. 2 award, prize, trophy.

cupboard n cabinet, chiffonier, closet, dresser, filing-cabinet, food-cupboard, larder, locker, sideboard, wardrobe.

curable adj operable, remediable, treatable. Opp INCURABLE.

curb vb bridle, check, contain, control, deter, hamper, hinder, hold back, impede, inhibit, limit, moderate, repress, restrain, restrict, subdue, suppress. Opp ENCOURAGE.

curdle vb clot, coagulate, congeal, go lumpy, go sour, thicken.

cure n 1 antidote, corrective, medication, nostrum, palliative, panacea, prescription, remedy, restorative, solution, therapy, treatment. ▷ MEDICINE. 2 deliverance, healing, recovery, recuperation, restoration, revival. • vb alleviate, correct, counteract, ease, inf fix, heal, help, mend, palliate, put right, rectify, relieve, remedy, repair, restore, solve, treat. Opp AGGRAVATE.

curiosity n inquisitiveness, interest, interference, meddling, nosiness, prying, snooping.

curious adj 1 inquiring, inquisitive, interested, probing, puzzled, questioning, searching. 2 interfering, intrusive, meddlesome, inf nosy, prying. 3 ▷ STRANGE. **be curious** ▷ PRY.

curl n bend, coil, curve, kink, loop, ringlet, scroll, spiral, swirl, turn, twist, wave, whorl. • vb 1 bend, coil, corkscrew, curve, entwine, loop, spiral, turn, twine, twist, wind, wreathe, writhe. 2 *curl your hair*. crimp, frizz, perm.

curly adj crimped, curled, curling, frizzy, fuzzy, kinky, permed, wavy. Opp STRAIGHT.

current adj 1 alive, contemporary, continuing, existing, extant, fashionable, living, modern, ongoing, present, present-day, prevailing, prevalent, reigning, remaining, surviving, inf trendy, up-to-date. 2 *current passport*. usable, valid. Opp OLD. • n course, draught, drift, flow, jet, river, stream, tide, trend, undercurrent, undertow.

curriculum n course, programme of study, syllabus.

curse n blasphemy, exclamation, expletive, imprecation, malediction, oath, obscenity, profanity, swearword. ▷ EVIL. Opp BLESSING. • vb blaspheme, damn, fulminate, swear, utter curses. Opp BLESS. **cursed** ▷ HATEFUL.

cursory adj brief, careless, casual, desultory, fleeting, hasty, hurried, perfunctory, quick, slapdash, superficial. Opp THOROUGH.

curt adj abrupt, blunt, brief, brusque, concise, crusty, gruff, laconic, monosyllabic, offhand, rude, sharp, short, snappy, succinct, tart, terse, unceremonious, uncommunicative, ungracious. ▷ RUDE. Opp EXPANSIVE.

curtail vb abbreviate, abridge, break off, contract, cut short, decrease, diminish, inf dock, guillotine, halt, lessen, lop, prune, reduce, restrict, shorten, stop, terminate, trim, truncate. Opp EXTEND.

curtain n blind, drape, drapery, hanging, screen. • vb drape, mask, screen, shroud, veil. ▷ HIDE.

curtsy vb bend the knee, bow, genuflect, salaam.

curve n arc, arch, bend, bow, bulge, camber, circle, convolution, corkscrew, crescent, curl, curvature, cycloid, loop, meander, spiral, swirl, trajectory, turn, twist, undulation, whorl. • vb arc, arch, bend, bow, bulge, camber, coil, corkscrew, curl, loop, meander, snake, spiral, swerve, swirl, turn, twist, wind. ▷ CIRCLE.

curved adj concave, convex, convoluted, crescent, crooked, curvilinear, curving, curvy, rounded, serpentine, shaped, sinuous, sweeping, swelling, tortuous, turned, undulating, whorled.

cushion n bean-bag, bolster, hassock, headrest, pad, pillow. • vb absorb, bolster, deaden,

lessen, mitigate, muffle, protect from, reduce the effect of, soften, support.

custodian n caretaker, curator, guardian, keeper, overseer, superintendent, warden, warder, inf watch-dog, watchman.

custody n 1 care, charge, guardianship, keeping, observation, possession, preservation, protection, safe-keeping. 2 in police custody. captivity, confinement, detention, imprisonment, incarceration, remand.

custom n 1 convention, etiquette, fashion, form, formality, habit, institution, manner, observance, policy, practice, procedure, routine, tradition, usage, way, wont. 2 A shop need: custom. business, buyers, customers, patronage, support, trade.

customary adj accepted, accustomed, common, commonplace, conventional, established, everyday, expected, fashionable, general, habitual, normal, ordinary, popular, prevailing, regular, routine, traditional, typical, usual, wonted. Opp UNUSUAL.

customer n buyer, client, consumer, patron, purchaser, shopper. Opp SELLER.

cut n 1 gash, graze, groove, incision, laceration, nick, notch, opening, rent, rip, slash, slice, slit, snick, snip, split, stab, tear. ▷ INJURY. 2 cut in prices. cutback, decrease, fall, lowering, reduction, saving. • vb 1 amputate, axe, carve, chip, chisel, chop, cleave, clip, crop, dice, dissect, divide, dock, engrave, fell, gash, gouge, grate, graze,

guillotine, hack, halve, hew,
incise, knife, lacerate, lance,
lop, mince, mow, nick, notch,
open, pare, pierce, poll, pollard,
prune, reap, rive, saw, scalp,
score, sever, share, shave,
shear, shred, slash, slice, slit,
snick, snip, split, stab, subdivide, trim, whittle, wound.
2 abbreviate, abridge, bowdlerize, censor, condense, curtail,
digest, edit, précis, shorten,
summarize, truncate. ▷ RE-
DUCE. **cut and dried**
▷ DEFINITE. **cut in** ▷ INTER-
RUPT. **cut off** ▷ REMOVE, STOP.
cut short ▷ CURTAIL.

cutlery *n inf* eating irons.
□ *breadknife, butter-knife, carving knife, cheese knife, dessert-
spoon, fish knife, fish fork, fork,
knife, ladle, salad servers,
spoon, steak knife, tablespoon,
teaspoon.*

cutter *n* □ *axe, billhook, chisel,
chopper, clippers, harvester,
guillotine, lawnmower, mower,
saw, scalpel, scissors, scythe,
secateurs, shears, sickle.*
▷ KNIFE.

cutting *adj* acute, biting, caustic, incisive, keen, mordant,
sarcastic, satirical, sharp, trenchant. ▷ HURTFUL.

cycle *n* **1** circle, repetition, revolution, rotation, round,
sequence, series. **2** bicycle,
inf bike, moped, *inf* motor bike,
motor cycle, penny-farthing,
scooter, tandem, tricycle.
● *vb* ▷ TRAVEL.

cyclic *adj* circular, recurring,
repeating, repetitive, rotating.

cynical *adj* doubting, *inf* hard,
incredulous, misanthropic,
mocking, negative, pessimistic,
questioning, sceptical, sneering.
Opp OPTIMISTIC.

D

dabble *vb* **1** dip, paddle, splash,
wet. **2** *dabble in a hobby.* potter
about, tinker, work casually.

dabbler *n* amateur, dilettante,
potterer.

dagger *n* bayonet, blade, *old
use* dirk, knife, kris, poniard,
stiletto.

daily *adj* diurnal, everyday,
quotidian, regular.

dainty *adj* **1** charming, delicate,
exquisite, fine, graceful, meticu-
ulous, neat, nice, pretty, skilful.
2 choosy, discriminating, fastidious, finicky, fussy, genteel,
mincing, sensitive, squeamish,
well-mannered. **3** *a dainty
morsel.* appealing, appetizing,
choice, delectable, delicious.
Opp CLUMSY, GROSS.

dally *vb* dawdle, delay, *inf* dilly-
dally, hang about, idle, linger,
loaf, loiter, play about, procrastinate, saunter, *old use* tarry,
waste time.

dam *n* bank, barrage, barrier,
dike, embankment, wall, weir.
● *vb* block, check, hold back,
obstruct, restrict, stanch, stem,
stop.

damage *n* destruction, devastation, harm, havoc, hurt, injury,
loss, mutilation, sabotage.
● *vb* **1** blemish, break, buckle,
burst, *inf* bust, chip, crack,
cripple, deface, destroy, disable,
disfigure, *inf* do mischief to,
flaw, fracture, harm, hurt,
immobilize, impair, incapacitate, injure, make inoperative,
make useless, mar, mark, mutilate, *inf* play havoc with, ruin,

rupture, sabotage, scar, scratch, spoil, strain, vandalize, warp, weaken, wound, wreck.
damaged ▷ FAULTY. **damages** ▷ COMPENSATION. **damaging** ▷ HARMFUL.

damn *vb* attack, berate, castigate, censure, condemn, criticize, curse, denounce, doom, execrate, sentence, swear at.

damnation *n* doom, everlasting fire, hell, perdition, ruin. *Opp* SALVATION.

damp *adj* clammy, dank, dewy, dripping, drizzly, foggy, humid, misty, moist, muggy, perspiring, rainy, soggy, steamy, sticky, sweaty, unaired, unventilated, wet, wettish. *Opp* DRY.
● *vb* 1 dampen, humidify, moisten, sprinkle. 2 ▷ DISCOURAGE.

dance *n* choreography, dancing. □ ball, barn-dance, ceilidh, disco, discothèque, inf hop, inf knees-up, party, inf shindy, social, square dance. □ ballet, ballroom dancing, break-dancing, country dancing, disco dancing, flamenco dancing, folk dancing, Latin-American dancing, limbo dancing, morris dancing, old-time dancing, tap-dancing. □ bolero, cancan, conga, fandango, fling, foxtrot, gavotte, hornpipe, jig, mazurka, minuet, polka, polonaise, quadrille, quickstep, reel, rumba, square dance, tango, waltz. ● *vb* caper, cavort, frisk, frolic, gambol, hop about, jig, jive, jump, leap, prance, rock, skip, *joc* trip the light fantastic, whirl.

danger *n* 1 crisis, distress, hazard, insecurity, jeopardy, menace, peril, pitfall, trouble, uncertainty. 2 *danger of frost*. chance, liability, possibility, risk, threat.

dangerous *adj* 1 alarming, breakneck, *inf* chancy, critical, destructive, explosive, grave, *sl* hairy, harmful, hazardous, insecure, menacing, *inf* nasty, noxious, perilous, precarious, reckless, risky, threatening, toxic, uncertain, unsafe.
2 *dangerous men.* desperate, ruthless, treacherous, unmanageable, unpredictable, violent, volatile, wild. *Opp* HARMLESS.

dangle *vb* be suspended, depend, droop, flap, hang, sway, swing, trail, wave about.

dank *adj* chilly, clammy, damp, moist, unaired.

dappled *adj* blotchy, brindled, dotted, flecked, freckled, marbled, motley, mottled, particoloured, patchy, pied, speckled, spotted, stippled, streaked, varicoloured, variegated.

dare *vb* 1 gamble, have the courage, risk, take a chance, venture. 2 challenge, defy, provoke, taunt. **daring** ▷ BOLD.

dark *adj* 1 black, blackish, cheerless, clouded, cloudy, coal-black, dim, dingy, dismal, drab, dreary, dull, dusky, funereal, gloomy, glowering, glum, grim, inky, moonless, murky, overcast, pitch-black, pitch-dark, *poet* sable, shadowy, shady, sombre, starless, stygian, sullen, sunless, tenebrous, unilluminated, unlighted, unlit. 2 *dark colours.* dense, heavy, strong. 3 *dark complexion.* black, brown, dark-skinned, dusky, swarthy, tanned. 4 ▷ HIDDEN, MYSTERIOUS. *Opp* LIGHT, PALE.

darken *vb* 1 become overcast, cloud over. 2 blacken, dim, eclipse, obscure, overshadow, shade. *Opp* LIGHTEN.

darling *n inf* apple of your eye, beloved, *inf* blue-eyed boy, dear, dearest, favourite, honey, love, loved one, pet, sweet, sweetheart, true love.

dart *n* arrow, bolt, missile, shaft. ● *vb* bound, fling, flit, fly, hurtle, leap, move suddenly, shoot, spring, *inf* whiz, *inf* zip. ▷ DASH.

dash *n* 1 chase, race, run, rush, sprint, spurt. ● *vb* 1 bolt, chase, dart, fly, hasten, hurry, move quickly, race, run, rush, speed, sprint, tear, *inf* zoom. 2 ▷ HIT.

dashing *adj* animated, dapper, dynamic, elegant, lively, smart, spirited, stylish, vigorous.

data *plur n* details, evidence, facts, figures, information, statistics.

date *n* 1 day. ▷ TIME. 2 *date with a friend*. appointment, assignation, engagement, fixture, meeting, rendezvous. **out-of-date** ▷ OBSOLETE. **up-to-date** ▷ MODERN.

daunt *vb* alarm, depress, deter, discourage, dishearten, dismay, intimidate, overawe, put off, unnerve. ▷ FRIGHTEN. *Opp* ENCOURAGE.

dawdle *vb* be slow, dally, delay, *inf* dilly-dally, hang about, idle, lag behind, linger, loaf about, loiter, move slowly, straggle, *inf* take it easy, *inf* take your time, trail behind. *inf* HURRY.

dawn *n* day-break, first light, *inf* peep of day, sunrise. ▷ BEGINNING.

day *n* 1 daylight, daytime, light. 2 age, epoch, era, period, time.

day-dream *n* dream, fantasy, hope, illusion, meditation, pipe-

dream, reverie, vision, woolgathering. ● *vb* dream, fantasize, imagine, meditate.

daze *vb* benumb, paralyse, shock, stun, stupefy. ▷ AMAZE.

dazzle *vb* blind, confuse, disorientate. **dazzling** ▷ BRILLIANT.

dead *adj* 1 cold, dead and buried, deceased, departed, *inf* done for, inanimate, inert, killed, late, lifeless, perished, rigid, stiff. *Opp* ALIVE. 2 *dead language*. died out, extinct, obsolete. 3 *dead with cold*. deadened, insensitive, numb, paralysed, without feeling. 4 *dead battery, engine*. burnt out, defunct, flat, inoperative, not going, not working, no use, out of order, unresponsive, used up, useless, worn out. 5 *a dead party*. boring, dull, moribund, slow, uninteresting. *Opp* LIVELY. 6 *dead centre*. ▷ EXACT. **dead person** ▷ CORPSE. **dead to the world** ▷ ASLEEP.

deaden *vb* 1 anaesthetize, desensitize, dull, numb, paralyse. 2 blunt, check, cushion, damp, diminish, hush, lessen, mitigate, muffle, mute, quieten, reduce, smother, soften, stifle, suppress, weaken.

deadlock *n* halt, impasse, stalemate, standstill, stop, stoppage, tie.

deadly *adj* dangerous, destructive, fatal, lethal, mortal, noxious, terminal. ▷ HARMFUL. *Opp* HARMLESS.

deafen *vb* make deaf, overwhelm. **deafening** ▷ LOUD.

deal *n* 1 agreement, arrangement, bargain, contract, pact, settlement, transaction, understanding. 2 amount, quantity, volume. ● *vb* 1 allot, apportion, assign, dispense, distribute, divide, *inf* dole out, give out, share out. **2** *deal someone a blow.* administer, apply, deliver, give, inflict, mete out. **3** *deal in stocks and shares.* buy and sell, do business, trade, traffic. **deal with** ▷ MANAGE, TREAT.

dealer *n* agent, broker, distributor, merchant, retailer, shopkeeper, stockist, supplier, trader, tradesman, vendor, wholesaler.

dear *adj* **1** adored, beloved, close, darling, intimate, loved, precious, treasured, valued, venerated. ▷ LOVABLE. *Opp* HATEFUL. **2** costly, exorbitant, expensive, high-priced, over-priced, *inf* pricey. *Opp* CHEAP. ● *n* ▷ DARLING.

death *n* **1** decease, demise, dying, loss, passing. ▷ END. **2** casualty, fatality. **put to death** ▷ EXECUTE.

debase *vb* belittle, commercialize, degrade, demean, depreciate, devalue, diminish, lower the tone of, pollute, reduce the value of, ruin, soil, spoil, sully, vulgarize.

debatable *adj* arguable, contentious, controversial, controvertible, disputable, doubtful, dubious, moot (*point*), open to doubt, open to question, problematical, questionable, uncertain, unsettled, unsure. *Opp* CERTAIN.

debate *n* argument, conference, consultation, controversy, deliberation, dialectic, discussion, disputation, dispute, polemic. ● *vb* argue, *inf* chew over, consider, deliberate, discuss, dispute, *inf* mull over,

question, reflect on, weigh up, wrangle.

debit *vb* cancel, remove, subtract, take away. *Opp* CREDIT.

debris *n* bits, detritus, flotsam, fragments, litter, pieces, remains, rubbish, rubble, ruins, waste, wreckage.

debt *n* account, arrears, bill, debit, dues, indebtedness, liability, obligation, score, what you owe. **in debt** bankrupt, defaulting, insolvent. ▷ POOR.

decadent *adj* corrupt, debased, debauched, declining, degenerate, dissolute, immoral, self-indulgent. *Opp* MORAL.

decay *vb* atrophy, break down, corrode, crumble, decompose, degenerate, deteriorate, disintegrate, dissolve, fall apart, fester, go bad, go off, mortify, moulder, oxidize, perish, putrefy, rot, shrivel, spoil, waste away, weaken, wither.

deceit *n* artifice, cheating, chicanery, craftiness, cunning, deceitfulness, dishonesty, dissimulation, double-dealing, duplicity, guile, hypocrisy, insincerity, lying, misrepresentation, pretence, sham, slyness, treachery, trickery, underhandedness, untruthfulness. ▷ DECEPTION. *Opp* HONESTY.

deceitful *adj* cheating, crafty, cunning, deceiving, deceptive, designing, dishonest, double-dealing, duplicitous, false, fraudulent, furtive, hypocritical, insincere, lying, secretive, shifty, sneaky, treacherous, *inf* tricky, *inf* two-faced, underhand, unfaithful, untrustworthy, wily. *Opp* HONEST.

deceive vb inf bamboozle, be an impostor, beguile, betray, blind, bluff, cheat, inf con, defraud, delude, inf diddle, double-cross, dupe, fool, inf fox, inf have on, hoax, hoodwink, inf kid, inf lead on, lie, mislead, mystify, inf outsmart, outwit, pretend, swindle, inf take for a ride, inf take in, trick.

decelerate vb brake, decrease speed, go slower, lose speed, slow down. Opp ACCELERATE.

decent adj 1 acceptable, appropriate, becoming, befitting, chaste, courteous, decorous, delicate, fitting, honourable, modest, polite, presentable, proper, pure, respectable, seemly, sensitive, suitable, tasteful. Opp INDECENT. 2 [inf] a decent meal. agreeable, nice, pleasant, satisfactory. ▷ GOOD. Opp BAD.

deception n bluff, cheat, inf con, confidence trick, cover-up, deceit, fake, feint, inf fiddle, fraud, hoax, imposture, lie, pretence, ruse, sham, stratagem, subterfuge, swindle, trick, wile. ▷ DECEIT.

deceptive adj ambiguous, deceiving, delusive, dishonest, distorted, equivocal, evasive, fallacious, false, fraudulent, illusory, insincere, lying, mendacious, misleading, specious, spurious, treacherous, unreliable, wrong. Opp GENUINE.

decide vb adjudicate, arbitrate, choose, conclude, determine, elect, fix on, judge, make up your mind, opt for, pick, reach a decision, resolve, select, settle. **decided** ▷ DEFINITE.

decipher vb disentangle, inf figure out, read, work out. ▷ DECODE.

decision n conclusion, decree, finding, judgement, outcome, result, ruling, verdict.

decisive adj 1 conclusive, convincing, crucial, final, influential, positive, significant. 2 decisive action. certain, confident, decided, definite, determined, firm, forceful, forthright, incisive, resolute, strong-minded, sure, unhesitating. Opp TENTATIVE.

declaration n affirmation, announcement, assertion, avowal, confirmation, deposition, disclosure, edict, manifesto, notice, proclamation, profession, promulgation, pronouncement, protestation, revelation, statement, testimony.

declare vb affirm, announce, assert, attest, avow, broadcast, certify, claim, confirm, contend, disclose, emphasize, insist, maintain, make known, proclaim, profess, pronounce, protest, report, reveal, show, state, swear, testify, inf trumpet forth, witness. ▷ SAY.

decline n decrease, degeneration, deterioration, diminuendo, downturn, drop, fall, falling off, loss, recession, reduction, slump, worsening. ● vb 1 decrease, degenerate, deteriorate, die away, diminish, drop away, dwindle, ebb, fail, fall off, flag, lessen, peter out, reduce, shrink, sink, slacken, subside, tail off, taper off, wane, weaken, wilt, worsen. Opp IMPROVE. 2 decline an invitation. abstain from, forgo, refuse, reject, *inf* turn down, veto. *Opp* ACCEPT.

decode *vb inf* crack, decipher, explain, figure out, interpret, make out, read, solve, understand, unravel, unscramble.

decompose *vb* break down, decay, disintegrate, go off, moulder, putrefy, rot.

decorate *vb* 1 adorn, array, beautify, *old use* bedeck, colour, deck, *inf* do up, embellish, embroider, festoon, garnish, make beautiful, ornament, paint, paper, *derog* prettify, refurbish, renovate, smarten up, spruce up, *derog* tart up, trim, wallpaper. 2 give a medal to, honour, reward.

decoration *n* 1 accessories, adornment, arabesque, elaboration, embellishment, finery, flourishes, ornament, ornamentation, trappings, trimmings. 2 award, badge, colours, medal, order, ribbon, star.

decorative *adj* elaborate, fancy, non-functional, ornamental, ornate. *Opp* FUNCTIONAL.

decorous *adj* appropriate, becoming, befitting, correct, dignified, fitting, genteel, polite, presentable, proper, refined, respectable, sedate, seemly, staid, suitable, well-behaved. ▷ DECENT. *Opp* INDECOROUS.

decorum *n* correctness, decency, dignity, etiquette, good form, good manners, gravity, modesty, politeness, propriety, protocol, respectability, seemliness.

decoy *n* bait, distraction, diversion, enticement, inducement, lure, red herring, stool-pigeon, trap. ● *vb* allure, attract, bait, draw, entice, inveigle, lead, lure, seduce, tempt, trick.

decrease *n* abatement, contraction, curtailment, cut, cut-back, decline, de-escalation, diminuendo, diminution, downturn, drop, dwindling, easing-off, ebb, fall, falling off, lessening, lowering, reduction, shrinkage, wane. *Opp* INCREASE.
● *vb* 1 abate, curtail, cut, ease off, lower, reduce, slim down, turn down. 2 condense, contract, decline, die away, diminish, dwindle, fall off, lessen, peter out, shrink, slacken, subside, *inf* tail off, taper off, wane. *Opp* INCREASE.

decree *n* act, command, declaration, dictate, dictum, directive, edict, enactment, fiat, injunction, judgement, law, mandate, order, ordinance, proclamation, promulgation, regulation, ruling, statute. ● *vb* command, decide, declare, determine, dictate, direct, ordain, order, prescribe, proclaim, promulgate, pronounce, rule.

decrepit *adj* battered, broken down, derelict, dilapidated, feeble, frail, infirm, ramshackle, tumbledown, weak, worn out. ▷ OLD.

dedicate *vb* 1 commit, consecrate, devote, give, hallow, pledge, sanctify, set apart. 2 *dedicate a book.* address, inscribe. **dedicated** ▷ KEEN, LOYAL.

dedication *n* 1 adherence, allegiance, commitment, devotion, enthusiasm, faithfulness, fidelity, loyalty, single-mindedness, zeal. 2 inscription.

deduce *vb* conclude, divine, draw the conclusion, extrapolate, gather, glean, infer, *inf* put two and two together, reason, surmise, *sl* suss out, understand, work out.

deduct *vb inf* knock off, subtract, take away. *Opp* ADD.

deduction *n* 1 allowance, decrease, diminution, discount, reduction, removal, subtraction, withdrawal. 2 conclusion, finding, inference, reasoning, result.

deed *n* 1 accomplishment, achievement, act, action, adventure, effort, endeavour, enterprise, exploit, feat, performance, stunt, undertaking.
2 ▷ DOCUMENT.

deep *adj* 1 abyssal, bottomless, chasmic, fathomless, profound, unfathomable, unplumbed, yawning. 2 *deep feelings.* earnest, extreme, genuine, heartfelt, intense, serious, sincere. 3 *deep in thought.* absorbed, concentrating, engrossed, immersed, lost, preoccupied, rapt, thoughtful. 4 *deep matters.* abstruse, arcane, esoteric, intellectual, learned, obscure, recondite.
▷ DIFFICULT. 5 *deep sleep.* heavy, sound. 6 *deep colour.* dark, rich, strong, vivid. 7 *deep sound.* bass, booming, growling, low, low-pitched, resonant, reverberating, sonorous. *Opp* SHALLOW, SUPERFICIAL, THIN.

deface *vb* blemish, damage, disfigure, harm, impair, injure, mar, mutilate, ruin, spoil, vandalize.

defeat *n* beating, conquest, downfall, *inf* drubbing, failure, humiliation, *inf* licking, overthrow, *inf* put-down, rebuff, repulse, reverse, rout, setback, subjugation, thrashing, trounc-

ing. *Opp* VICTORY. ● *vb* baulk, beat, best, be victorious over, check, checkmate, *inf* clobber, confound, conquer, crush, destroy, *inf* flatten, foil, frustrate, get the better of, *sl* hammer, *inf* lay low, *inf* lick, master, outdo, outvote, outwit, overcome, overpower, overthrow, overwhelm, prevail over, put down, quell, repulse, rout, ruin, *inf* smash, stop, subdue, subjugate, suppress, *inf* thrash, thwart, triumph over, trounce, vanquish, whip, win a victory over. *Opp* LOSE.
be defeated ▷ LOSE. **defeated** ▷ UNSUCCESSFUL.

defect *n* blemish, *computing* bug, deficiency, error, failing, fault, flaw, imperfection, inadequacy, irregularity, lack, mark, mistake, shortcoming, shortfall, spot, stain, want, weakness, weak point. ● *vb* change sides, desert, go over.

defective *adj* broken, deficient, faulty, flawed, *inf* gone wrong, imperfect, incomplete, *inf* on the blink, unsatisfactory, wanting, weak. *Opp* PERFECT.

defence *n* 1 cover, deterrence, guard, protection, safeguard, security, shelter, shield.
▷ BARRIER. 2 alibi, apologia, apology, case, excuse, explanation, justification, plea, testimony, vindication.

defenceless *adj* exposed, helpless, impotent, insecure, powerless, unguarded, unprotected, vulnerable, weak.

defend *vb* 1 cover, fight for, fortify, guard, keep safe, preserve, protect, safeguard, screen, secure, shelter, shield, *inf* stick up for, watch over.
2 argue for, champion, justify,

plead for, speak up for, stand by, stand up for, support, uphold, vindicate. *Opp* ATTACK.

defendant *n* accused, appellant, offender, prisoner.

defensive *adj* 1 cautious, defending, protective, wary, watchful. 2 apologetic, faint-hearted, self-justifying. *Opp* AGGRESSIVE.

defer *vb* 1 adjourn, delay, hold over, lay aside, postpone, prorogue (*parliament*), put off, *inf* shelve, suspend. 2 ▷ YIELD.

deference *n* acquiescence, compliance, obedience, submission. ▷ RESPECT.

defiant *adj* aggressive, antagonistic, belligerent, bold, brazen, challenging, daring, disobedient, headstrong, insolent, insubordinate, mutinous, obstinate, rebellious, recalcitrant, refractory, self-willed, stubborn, truculent, uncooperative, unruly, unyielding. *Opp* CO-OPERATIVE.

deficient *adj* defective, inadequate, insufficient, lacking, meagre, scanty, scarce, short, sketchy, unsatisfactory, wanting, weak. *Opp* ADEQUATE, EXCESSIVE.

defile *vb* contaminate, corrupt, degrade, desecrate, dirty, dishonour, foul, infect, make dirty, poison, pollute, soil, stain, sully, taint, tarnish.

define *vb* 1 be the boundary of, bound, circumscribe, delineate, demarcate, describe, determine, fix, limit, mark off, mark out, outline, specify. 2 *define a word*. clarify, explain, formulate, give the meaning of, interpret, spell out.

definite *adj* apparent, assured, categorical, certain, clear, clear-cut, confident, confirmed, cut-and-dried, decided, determined, discernible, distinct, emphatic, exact, explicit, express, fixed, incisive, marked, noticeable, obvious, particular, perceptible, plain, positive, precise, pronounced, settled, specific, sure, unambiguous, unequivocal, unmistakable, well-defined. *Opp* VAGUE.

definitely *adv* beyond doubt, certainly, doubtless, for certain, indubitably, positively, surely, unquestionably, without doubt, without fail.

definition *n* 1 clarification, elucidation, explanation, interpretation. 2 clarity, clearness, focus, precision, sharpness.

definitive *adj* agreed, authoritative, complete, conclusive, correct, decisive, final, last (*word*), official, permanent, reliable, settled, standard, ultimate, unconditional. *Opp* PROVISIONAL.

deflect *vb* avert, deviate, divert, fend off, head off, intercept, parry, prevent, sidetrack, swerve, switch, turn aside, veer, ward off.

deformed *adj* bent, buckled, contorted, crippled, crooked, defaced, disfigured, distorted, gnarled, grotesque, malformed, mangled, misshapen, mutilated, twisted, ugly, warped.

defraud *vb inf* con, *inf* diddle, embezzle, *inf* fleece, rob, swindle. ▷ CHEAT.

deft *adj* adept, adroit, agile, clever, dextrous, expert, handy, neat, *inf* nifty, nimble, proficient, quick, skilful. *Opp* CLUMSY.

defy *vb* 1 challenge, confront, dare, disobey, face up to, flout, *inf* kick against, rebel against, refuse to obey, resist, stand up to, withstand. 2 baffle, beat, defeat, elude, foil, frustrate, repel, repulse, resist, thwart, withstand.

degenerate *adj* ▷ CORRUPT.
• *vb* become worse, decline, deteriorate, *inf* go to the dogs, regress, retrogress, sink, slip, weaken, worsen. *Opp* IMPROVE.

degrade *vb* 1 cashier, demote, depose, downgrade. 2 abase, brutalize, cheapen, corrupt, debase, dehumanize, deprave, desensitize, dishonour, harden, humiliate, mortify. **degrading** ▷ SHAMEFUL.

degree *n* 1 calibre, class, grade, order, position, rank, standard, standing, station, status. 2 extent, intensity, level, measure.

deify *vb* idolize, treat as a god, venerate, worship.

deign *vb* concede, condescend, demean yourself, lower yourself, stoop, vouchsafe.

deity *n* creator, divinity, god, goddess, godhead, idol, immortal, power, spirit, supreme being.

dejected *adj* depressed, disconsolate, dispirited, down, downcast, downhearted, heavy-hearted, in low spirits. ▷ SAD.

delay *n* check, deferment, deferral, filibuster, hiatus, hitch, hold-up, interruption, moratorium, pause, postponement, setback, stay *(of execution)*, stoppage, wait. • *vb* 1 check, defer, detain, halt, hinder, hold over, hold up, impede, keep back, keep waiting, make late,

obstruct, postpone, put back, put off, retard, set back, slow down, stay, stop, suspend. 2 be late, be slow, *inf* bide your time, dally, dawdle, *inf* dilly-dally, *inf* drag your feet, *inf* get bogged down, hang about, hang back, hang fire, hesitate, lag, linger, loiter, mark time, pause, *inf* play for time, procrastinate, stall, *old use* tarry, temporize, vacillate, wait. *Opp* HURRY.

delegate *n* agent, ambassador, emissary, envoy, go-between, legate, messenger, nuncio, plenipotentiary, representative, spokesperson. • *vb* appoint, assign, authorize, charge, commission, depute, designate, empower, entrust, mandate, nominate.

delegation *n* commission, deputation, mission.

delete *vb* blot out, cancel, cross out, cut out, edit out, efface, eliminate, eradicate, erase, expunge, obliterate, remove, rub out, strike out, wipe out.

deliberate *adj* 1 arranged, calculated, cold-blooded, conscious, contrived, culpable, designed, intended, intentional, knowing, malicious, organized, planned, pre-arranged, preconceived, premeditated, prepared, purposeful, studied, thought out, wilful, worked out. 2 careful, cautious, circumspect, considered, diligent, measured, methodical, orderly, painstaking, regular, slow, thoughtful, unhurried, watchful. *Opp* HASTY, INSTINCTIVE.
• *vb* ▷ THINK.

delicacy *n* 1 accuracy, care, cleverness, daintiness, discrimination, exquisiteness, fineness, finesse, fragility, intricacy, precision, sensitivity, subtlety, tact. **2** *delicacies to eat.* rarity, speciality, treat.

delicate *adj* **1** dainty, diaphanous, easily broken, easily damaged, elegant, exquisite, fine, flimsy, fragile, frail, gauzy, gentle, feathery, intricate, light, sensitive, slender, soft, tender. *Opp* TOUGH. **2** *delicate work.* accurate, careful, clever, deft, precise, skilled. *Opp* CLUMSY. **3** *delicate flavour, colour.* faint, mild, muted, pale, slight, subtle. **4** *delicate health.* feeble, puny, sickly, squeamish, unhealthy, weak. **5** *delicate problem.* awkward, confidential, embarrassing, private, problematical, prudish, *inf* sticky, ticklish, touchy. **6** *delicate handling.* considerate, diplomatic, discreet, judicious, prudent, sensitive, tactful. *Opp* CRUDE.

delicious *adj* appetizing, choice, delectable, enjoyable, luscious, *inf* mouth-watering, *inf* nice, palatable, savoury, *inf* scrumptious, succulent, tasty, tempting, toothsome, *sl* yummy.

delight *n* bliss, delectation, ecstasy, enchantment, enjoyment, felicity, gratification, happiness, joy, paradise, pleasure, rapture, satisfaction.
● *vb* amuse, bewitch, captivate, charm, cheer, divert, enchant, enrapture, entertain, enthral, entrance, fascinate, gladden, gratify, please, ravish, thrill, transport. *Opp* DISMAY.
delighted ▷ HAPPY, PLEASED.

delightful *adj* agreeable, attractive, captivating, charming, congenial, delectable, diverting, enjoyable, *inf* nice, pleasant,

pleasing, pleasurable, rewarding, satisfying, spell-binding. ▷ BEAUTIFUL.

delinquent *n* culprit, defaulter, hooligan, lawbreaker, malefactor, miscreant, offender, roughneck, ruffian, *inf* tear-away, vandal, wrongdoer, young offender. ▷ CRIMINAL.

delirious *adj inf* beside yourself, crazy, demented, deranged, distracted, ecstatic, excited, feverish, frantic, frenzied, hysterical, incoherent, irrational, light-headed, rambling, wild. ▷ DRUNK, MAD. *Opp* SANE, SOBER.

deliver *vb* **1** bear, bring, carry, cart, convey, distribute, give out, hand over, make over, present, purvey, supply, surrender, take round, transfer, transport, turn over. **2** *deliver a lecture.* announce, broadcast, express, give, make, read. ▷ SPEAK. **3** *deliver a blow.* administer, aim, deal, direct, fire, inflict, launch, strike, throw. ▷ HIT. **4** ▷ RESCUE.

delivery *n* **1** conveyance, dispatch, distribution, shipment, transmission, transportation. **2** *a delivery of goods.* batch, consignment. **3** *delivery of a speech.* enunciation, execution, implementation, performance, presentation. **4** childbirth, confinement, parturition.

deluge *n* downpour, flood, inundation, rainfall, rainstorm, rush, spate. ● *vb* drown, engulf, flood, inundate, overwhelm, submerge, swamp.

delusion *n* dream, fantasy, hallucination, illusion, mirage, misconception, mistake, self-deception.

delve *vb* burrow, dig, explore, investigate, probe, research, search.

demand *n* old use behest, claim, command, desire, expectation, importunity, insistence, need, order, request, requirement, requisition, want. • *vb* call for, claim, cry out for, exact, expect, insist on, necessitate, order, request, require, requisition, want. ▷ ASK. **demanding** ▷ DIFFICULT, IMPORTUNATE. **in demand** ▷ POPULAR.

demean *vb* abase, cheapen, debase, degrade, disgrace, humble, humiliate, lower, make (yourself) cheap, *inf* put (yourself) down, sacrifice (your) pride, undervalue. **demeaning** ▷ SHAMEFUL.

democratic *adj* 1 classless, egalitarian. 2 chosen, elected, elective, popular, representative. *Opp* TOTALITARIAN.

demolish *vb* break down, bulldoze, dismantle, flatten, knock down, level, pull down, raze, tear down, topple, undo, wreck. ▷ DESTROY. *Opp* BUILD.

demon *n* devil, evil spirit, fiend, goblin, imp, spirit.

demonstrable *adj* conclusive, confirmable, evident, incontrovertible, indisputable, irrefutable, palpable, positive, provable, undeniable, unquestionable, verifiable.

demonstrate *vb* 1 confirm, describe, display, embody, establish, evince, exemplify, exhibit, explain, expound, express, illustrate, indicate, manifest, prove, represent, show, substantiate, teach, typify, verify. 2 lobby, march, parade, picket, protest, rally.

demonstration *n* 1 confirmation, description, display, evidence, exhibition, experiment, expression, illustration, indication, manifestation, presentation, proof, representation, show, substantiation, test, trial, verification. 2 *inf* demo, march, parade, picket, protest, rally, sit-in, vigil.

demonstrative *adj* affectionate, effusive, emotional, fulsome, loving, open, uninhibited, unreserved, unrestrained. *Opp* RETICENT.

demote *vb* downgrade, put down, reduce, relegate. *Opp* PROMOTE.

demure *adj* bashful, coy, diffident, modest, prim, quiet, reserved, reticent, retiring, sedate, shy, sober, staid. *Opp* CONCEITED.

den *n* hideaway, hide-out, hiding- place, hole, lair, private place, retreat, sanctuary, secret place, shelter.

denial *n* abnegation, contradiction, disavowal, disclaimer, negation, refusal, refutation, rejection, renunciation, repudiation, veto. *Opp* ADMISSION.

denigrate *vb* belittle, blacken the reputation of, criticize, decry, disparage, impugn, malign, *inf* put down, *inf* run down, sneer at, speak slightingly of, traduce, *inf* turn your nose up, vilify. ▷ DESPISE. *Opp* PRAISE.

denomination *n* 1 category, class, classification, designation, kind, size, sort, species, type, value. 2 church, communion, creed, cult, order, persuasion, schism, school, sect.

denote vb be the sign for, designate, express, indicate, mean, represent, signal, signify, stand for, symbolize.

denouement n climax, inf payoff, resolution, solution, inf sorting out, inf tidying up, unravelling. ▷ END.

denounce vb accuse, attack verbally, betray, blame, brand, censure, complain about, condemn, criticize, declaim against, decry, fulminate against, inf hold forth against, impugn, incriminate, inform against, inveigh against, pillory, report, reveal, stigmatize, inf tell off, vilify, vituperate. Opp PRAISE.

dense adj 1 close, compact, concentrated, heavy, impassable, impenetrable, inf jampacked, lush, massed, packed, solid, thick, tight, viscous. Opp THIN. 2 ▷ STUPID.

dent n concavity, depression, dimple, dint, dip, hollow, indentation, pit. ● vb bend, buckle, crumple, knock in.

denude vb bare, defoliate, deforest, expose, remove, strip, unclothe, uncover. Opp CLOTHE.

deny vb 1 contradict, controvert, disagree with, disclaim, disown, dispute, gainsay, negate, oppose, rebuff, refute, reject, repudiate. Opp AGREE. 2 begrudge, deprive of, disallow, refuse, withhold. Opp GRANT. **deny yourself** ▷ ABSTAIN.

depart vb 1 abscond, begin a journey, inf check out, inf clear off, decamp, disappear, embark, emigrate, escape, exit, go away, sl hit the road, leave, make off, inf make tracks, inf make your

self scarce, migrate, move away, move off, inf push off, quit, retire, retreat, run away, run off, sl scarper, sl scram, set forth, set off, set out, start, take your leave, vanish, withdraw. 2 ▷ DEVIATE. **departed** ▷ DEAD.

department n 1 branch, division, office, part, section, sector, subdivision, unit. 2 [inf] not my department. area, concern, domain, field, function, job, line, province, responsibility, specialism, sphere.

departure n disappearance, embarkation, escape, exit, exodus, going, retirement, retreat, withdrawal. Opp ARRIVAL.

depend vb depend on inf bank on, be dependent on, count on, hinge on, need, pivot on, put your faith in, inf reckon on, rely on, rest on, trust.

dependable adj conscientious, consistent, faithful, honest, regular, reliable, safe, sound, steady, true, trustworthy, unfailing. Opp UNRELIABLE.

dependence n 1 confidence, need, reliance, trust. 2 ▷ ADDICTION.

dependent adj **dependent on** 1 conditional on, connected with, controlled by, determined by, liable to, relative to, subject to, vulnerable to. Opp INDEPENDENT. 2 dependent on drugs. addicted to, enslaved by, inf hooked on, reliant on.

depict vb delineate, describe, draw, illustrate, narrate, outline, paint, picture, portray, represent, reproduce, show, sketch.

deplete vb consume, cut, decrease, drain, lessen, reduce, use up. Opp INCREASE.

deplorable *adj* awful, blameworthy, discreditable, disgraceful, disreputable, dreadful, execrable, lamentable, regrettable, reprehensible, scandalous, shameful, shocking, unfortunate, unworthy. ▷ BAD. *Opp* COMMENDABLE.

deplore *vb* 1 grieve for, lament, mourn, regret. 2 ▷ CONDEMN.

deploy *vb* arrange, bring into action, distribute, manage, position, use systematically, utilize.

deport *vb* banish, exile, expatriate, expel, remove, send abroad, transport.

depose *vb* demote, dethrone, dismiss, displace, get rid of, oust, remove, *inf* topple.

deposit *n* 1 advance payment, down-payment, initial payment, part-payment, retainer, security, stake. 2 accumulation, alluvium, dregs, layer, lees, precipitate, sediment, silt, sludge. • *vb* 1 drop, *inf* dump, lay down, leave, *inf* park, place, precipitate, put down, set down. 2 *deposit money.* bank, pay in, save.

depot *n* 1 arsenal, base, cache, depository, dump, hoard, store, storehouse. 2 *bus depot.* garage, headquarters, station, terminus.

deprave *vb* brutalize, corrupt, debase, degrade, influence, pervert. **depraved** ▷ CORRUPT.

depreciate *vb* 1 become less, decrease, deflate, drop, fall, go down, lessen, lower, reduce, slump, weaken. *Opp* APPRECIATE. 2 ▷ DISPARAGE.

depress *vb* 1 burden, cast down, discourage, dishearten, dismay, dispirit, enervate, grieve, lower the spirits of, make sad,

oppress, sadden, tire, upset, weary. *Opp* CHEER. 2 *depress the market.* bring down, deflate, make less active, push down, undermine, weaken. *Opp* BOOST. **depressed, depressing** ▷ SAD.

depression *n* 1 *inf* blues, dejection, desolation, despair, despondency, gloom, glumness, heaviness, hopelessness, low spirits, melancholy, misery, pessimism, sadness, weariness. *Opp* HAPPINESS. 2 cavity, concavity, dent, dimple, dip, excavation, hole, hollow, impression, indentation, pit, recess, rut, sunken area. *Opp* BUMP. 3 *economic depression.* decline, hard times, recession, slump. *Opp* BOOM, HIGH.

deprive *vb* deprive of deny, dispossess of, prevent from using, refuse, rob of, starve of, strip of, take away, withdraw, withhold. **deprived** ▷ POOR.

deputize *vb* deputize for act as deputy, act as stand-in for, cover for, do the job of, replace, represent, stand in for, substitute for, take over from, understudy.

deputy *n* agent, ambassador, assistant, delegate, emissary, *inf* fill-in, locum, proxy, relief, replacement, representative, reserve, second-in-command, spokesperson, *inf* stand-in, substitute, supply, surrogate, understudy, vice-captain, vice-president.

derelict *adj* abandoned, broken down, decrepit, deserted, desolate, dilapidated, forgotten, forlorn, forsaken, neglected, overgrown, ruined, run-down, tumbledown, uncared-for, untended.

derivation *n* ancestry, descent, etymology, extraction, origin, root. ▷ BEGINNING.

derive *vb* acquire, borrow, collect, crib, draw, extract, gain, gather, get, glean, *inf* lift, obtain, pick up, procure, receive, secure, take. **be derived** ▷ ORIGINATE.

descend *vb* 1 climb down, come down, drop, fall, go down, move down, plummet, plunge, sink, swoop down. 2 decline, dip, incline, slant, slope. 3 alight, disembark, dismount, get down, get off. *Opp* ASCEND. **be descended** ▷ ORIGINATE. **descend on** ▷ ATTACK.

descendant *n* child, heir, scion, successor. *Opp* ANCESTOR.

descendants family, issue, line, lineage, offspring, posterity, progeny, *old use* seed.

descent *n* 1 declivity, dip, drop, fall, incline, slant, slope, way down. *Opp* ASCENT. 2 *aristocratic descent.* ancestry, background, blood, derivation, extraction, family, genealogy, heredity, lineage, origin, parentage, pedigree, stock, strain.

describe *vb* 1 characterize, define, delineate, depict, detail, explain, express, give an account of, narrate, outline, portray, present, recount, relate, report, represent, sketch, speak of, tell about. 2 *describe a circle.* draw, mark out, trace.

description *n* account, characterization, commentary, definition, delineation, depiction, explanation, narration, outline, portrait, portrayal, report, representation, sketch, story, word-picture.

descriptive *adj* colourful, detailed, explanatory, expressive, graphic, illustrative, pictorial, vivid.

desecrate *vb* abuse, contaminate, corrupt, debase, defile, degrade, dishonour, pervert, pollute, profane, treat blasphemously, treat disrespectfully, treat irreverently, vandalize, violate, vitiate. *Opp* REVERE.

desert *adj* arid, barren, desolate, dry, infertile, isolated, lonely, sterile, uncultivated, unfrequented, uninhabited, waterless, wild. *Opp* FERTILE. ● *n* dust bowl, wasteland, wilderness.
   ● *vb* 1 abandon, betray, forsake, give up, jilt, leave, *inf* leave in the lurch, maroon, quit, *inf* rat on, renounce, strand, vacate, *inf* walk out on, *inf* wash your hands of. 2 abscond, decamp, defect, go absent, run away. **deserted** ▷ EMPTY, LONELY.

deserter *n* absconder, absentee, apostate, backslider, betrayer, defector, escapee, fugitive, outlaw, renegade, runaway, traitor, truant, turncoat.

deserve *vb* be good enough for, be worthy of, earn, justify, merit, rate, warrant. **deserving** ▷ WORTHY.

design *n* 1 blueprint, conception, draft, drawing, model, pattern, plan, proposal, prototype, sketch. 2 mark, style, type, version. 3 arrangement, composition, configuration, form, pattern, shape. 4 *wander without design.* aim, end, goal, intention, object, objective, purpose, scheme. ● *vb* conceive, construct, contrive, create, delineate, devise, draft, draw, draw up, fashion, form, intend,

invent, lay out, make, map out,
originate, outline, plan, plot,
project, propose, scheme, shape,
sketch, think up. **designing**
▷ CRAFTY. **have designs**
▷ PLOT.

designer *n* architect, artist,
author, contriver, creator,
deviser, inventor, originator.

desire *n* 1 ache, ambition, appetite, craving, fancy, hankering,
hunger, *inf* itch, longing,
requirement, thirst, urge, want,
wish, yearning, *inf* yen.
2 avarice, covetousness, cupidity, greed, miserliness, rapacity. 3 *sexual desire.* ardour,
libido, love, lust, passion.
● *vb* ache for, ask for, aspire
to, covet, crave, dream of,
fancy, hanker after, *inf* have a
yen for, hope for, hunger for,
inf itch for, like, long for, lust
after, need, pine for, prefer,
pursue, *inf* set your heart on,
set your sights on, strive after,
thirst for, want, wish for, yearn
for.

desolate *adj* 1 abandoned, bare,
barren, benighted, bleak, cheerless, depressing, deserted,
dismal, dreary, empty, forsaken, gloomy, *inf* god-forsaken,
inhospitable, isolated, lonely,
remote, unfrequented, uninhabited, wild, windswept. 2 bereft,
companionless, dejected,
depressed, despairing, disconsolate, distressed, forlorn,
forsaken, inconsolable, lonely,
melancholy, miserable, neglected, solitary, suicidal, wretched.
▷ SAD. *Opp* CHEERFUL.

despair *n* anguish, dejection,
depression, desperation,
despondency, hopelessness,
pessimism, resignation, wretchedness. ▷ MISERY. ● *vb* give in,

give up, lose heart, lose hope,
quit, surrender. *Opp* HOPE.

desperate *adj* 1 *inf* at your wits'
end, beyond hope, despairing,
inconsolable, wretched.
2 *desperate situation.* acute,
bad, critical, dangerous, drastic, grave, hopeless, irretrievable, pressing, serious, severe,
urgent. 3 *desperate criminals.*
dangerous, foolhardy, impetuous, rash, reckless, violent,
wild. 4 ▷ ANXIOUS.

despise *vb* be contemptuous of,
condemn, deride, disapprove of,
disdain, feel contempt for, hate,
have a low opinion of, look
down on, *inf* put down, scorn,
sneer at, spurn, undervalue.
▷ DENIGRATE. *Opp* ADMIRE.

despondent *adj* dejected,
depressed, discouraged,
disheartened, down, downcast,
inf down in the mouth, melancholy, morose, pessimistic, sad,
sorrowful. ▷ MISERABLE.

despotic *adj* absolute, arbitrary,
authoritarian, autocratic,
dictatorial, domineering,
oppressive, totalitarian, tyrannical. *Opp* DEMOCRATIC.

destination *n* goal, objective,
purpose, stopping-place, target,
terminus.

destined *adj* 1 foreordained,
ineluctable, inescapable, inevitable, intended, ordained,
predestined, predetermined,
preordained, unavoidable.
2 *destined to fail.* bound,
certain, doomed, fated, meant.

destiny *n* chance, doom, fate,
fortune, karma, kismet, lot,
luck, providence.

destitute *adj* bankrupt,
deprived, down-and-out, homeless, impecunious, impover-

ished, indigent, insolvent, needy, penniless, poverty-stricken, inf skint. ▷ POOR. Opp WEALTHY.

destroy vb abolish, annihilate, blast, break down, burst, inf bust, crush, inf decimate, demolish, devastate, devour, dismantle, dispose of, do away with, eliminate, eradicate, erase, exterminate, extinguish, extirpate, finish off, flatten, fragment, get rid of, knock down, lay waste, level, liquidate, make useless, nullify, pull down, pulverize, put out of existence, raze, root out, ruin, sabotage, sack, scuttle, shatter, smash, stamp out, undo, uproot, vaporize, wipe out, wreck, write off. ▷ DEFEAT, END, KILL. Opp CONSERVE, CREATE.

destruction n annihilation, damage, inf decimation, demolition, depredation, devastation, elimination, end, eradication, erasure, extermination, extinction, extirpation, havoc, holocaust, liquidation, overthrow, pulling down, ruin, ruination, shattering, smashing, undoing, uprooting, wiping out, wrecking. ▷ KILLING. Opp CONSERVATION, CREATION.

destructive adj adverse, antagonistic, baleful, baneful, calamitous, catastrophic, damaging, dangerous, deadly, deleterious, detrimental, devastating, disastrous, fatal, harmful, injurious, internecine, lethal, malignant, negative, pernicious, pestilential, ruinous, violent. Opp CONSTRUCTIVE.

detach vb cut loose, cut off, disconnect, disengage, disentangle, divide, free, isolate, part,

pull off, release, remove, segregate, separate, sever, take off, tear off, uncouple, undo, unfasten, unfix, unhitch. Opp ATTACH. **detached** ▷ ALOOF, IMPARTIAL, SEPARATE.

detail n aspect, circumstance, complexity, complication, component, element, fact, factor, feature, ingredient, intricacy, item, plur minutiae, nicety, particular, point, refinement, respect, specific, technicality.

detailed adj inf blow-by-blow, complete, complex, comprehensive, descriptive, exact, exhaustive, full, derog fussy, giving all details, derog hair-splitting, intricate, itemized, minute, particularized, specific. Opp GENERAL.

detain vb 1 arrest, capture, confine, gaol, hold, imprison, intern. 2 buttonhole, delay, hinder, hold up, impede, keep, keep waiting, restrain, retard, slow, stop, waylay.

detect vb ascertain, become aware of, diagnose, discern, discover, expose, feel, inf ferret out, find, hear, identify, locate, note, notice, observe, perceive, inf put your finger on, recognize, reveal, scent, see, sense, sight, smell, sniff out, spot, spy, taste, track down, uncover, unearth, unmask.

detective n investigator, policeman, policewoman, inf private eye, sleuth, inf snooper.

detention n captivity, confinement, custody, imprisonment, incarceration, internment.

deter vb check, daunt, discourage, dismay, dissuade, frighten off, hinder, impede, intimidate, obstruct, prevent, put off, repel, send away, stop, *inf* turn off, warn off. *Opp* ENCOURAGE.

deteriorate *vb* crumble, decay, decline, degenerate, depreciate, disintegrate, fall off, get worse, *inf* go downhill, lapse, relapse, slip, weaken, worsen. *Opp* IMPROVE.

determination *n inf* backbone, commitment, courage, dedication, doggedness, drive, firmness, fortitude, *inf* grit, *inf* guts, perseverance, persistence, pertinacity, resoluteness, resolution, resolve, single-mindedness, spirit, steadfastness, *derog* stubbornness, tenacity, will-power.

determine *vb* 1 arbitrate, clinch, conclude, decide, establish, find out, identify, judge, settle. 2 choose, decide on, fix on, resolve, select. 3 *What determined your choice?* affect, condition, dictate, govern, influence, regulate.

determined *adj* adamant, assertive, bent (*on success*), certain, convinced, decided, decisive, definite, dogged, firm, insistent, intent, *derog* obstinate, persistent, pertinacious, purposeful, resolute, resolved, single-minded, steadfast, strong-minded, strong-willed, *derog* stubborn, sure, tenacious, tough, unwavering. *Opp* IRRESOLUTE.

deterrent *n* barrier, caution, check, curb, difficulty, discouragement, disincentive, dissuasion, hindrance, impediment, obstacle, restraint, threat, *inf* turn-off, warning. *Opp* ENCOURAGEMENT.

detest *vb* abhor, abominate, despise, execrate, loathe.
▷ HATE.

detour *n* deviation, diversion, indirect route, roundabout route. **make a detour**
▷ DEVIATE.

detract *vb* detract from diminish, lessen, lower, reduce, take away from.

detrimental *adj* damaging, deleterious, disadvantageous, harmful, hurtful, inimical, injurious, prejudicial, unfavourable. *Opp* ADVANTAGEOUS.

devastate *vb* 1 damage severely, demolish, destroy, flatten, lay waste, level, obliterate, overwhelm, ravage, raze, ruin, sack, waste, wreck. 2 ▷ DISMAY.

develop *vb* 1 advance, age, arise, *inf* blow up, come into existence, evolve, get better, grow, flourish, improve, mature, move on, progress, ripen. *Opp* REGRESS. 2 *develop habits*. acquire, contract, cultivate, evolve, foster, get, pick up. 3 *develop ideas*. amplify, augment, elaborate, enlarge on, expatiate on, unfold, work up. 4 *business developed*. branch out, build up, diversify, enlarge, expand, extend, increase, swell.

development *n* 1 advance, betterment, change, enlargement, evolution, expansion, extension, *inf* forward march, furtherance, gain, growth, improvement, increase, progress, promotion, regeneration, reinforcement, spread. 2 happening, incident, occurrence, outcome, result, upshot. 3 *industrial development*. building, conversion, exploitation, use.

deviate vb branch off, depart, digress, diverge, divert, drift, err, go astray, go round, make a detour, stray, swerve, turn aside, turn off, vary, veer, wander.

device n 1 apparatus, appliance, contraption, contrivance, gadget, implement, instrument, invention, machine, tool, utensil. 2 dodge, expedient, gambit, gimmick, manoeuvre, plan, ploy, ruse, scheme, stratagem, stunt, tactic, trick, wile. 3 *heraldic device*. badge, crest, design, figure, logo, motif, shield, sign, symbol, token.

devil n demon, fiend, imp, spirit. **The Devil** the Adversary, Beelzebub, the Evil One, Lucifer, Mephistopheles, *inf* Old Nick, the Prince of Darkness, Satan.

devilish adj demoniac(al), demonic, diabolical(al), fiendish, hellish, impish, infernal, inhuman, Mephistophelian, satanic. ▷ EVIL. *Opp* ANGELIC.

devious adj 1 circuitous, crooked, deviating, indirect, periphrastic, rambling, roundabout, sinuous, tortuous, wandering, winding. 2 [*derog*] calculating, cunning, deceitful, evasive, insincere, misleading, scheming, *inf* slippery, sly, sneaky, treacherous, underhand, wily. ▷ DISHONEST. *Opp* DIRECT.

devise vb arrange, conceive, concoct, contrive, *inf* cook up, create, design, engineer, form, formulate, frame, imagine, invent, make up, plan, plot, prepare, project, scheme, think out, think up, work out.

devoted adj committed, dedicated, enthusiastic, faithful, loving, staunch, true, unswerving, whole-hearted, zealous. ▷ LOYAL. *Opp* DISLOYAL, HALF-HEARTED.

devotee n *inf* addict, aficionado, *inf* buff, enthusiast, fan, follower, sl freak, supporter.

devotion n allegiance, attachment, commitment, dedication, devotedness, enthusiasm, fanaticism, fervour, loyalty, zeal. ▷ LOVE, PIETY.

devour vb consume, demolish, eat up, engulf, swallow up, take in. ▷ DESTROY, EAT.

devout adj God-fearing, godly, holy, religious, sincere, spiritual. ▷ PIOUS. *Opp* IRRELIGIOUS.

dexterous adj adroit, agile, deft, nimble, quick, sharp, skilful. ▷ CLEVER. *Opp* CLUMSY.

diabolical adj evil, fiendish, inhuman, satanic, wicked. ▷ DEVILISH. *Opp* SAINTLY.

diagnose vb detect, determine, distinguish, find, identify, isolate, name, pinpoint, recognize.

diagnosis n analysis, conclusion, explanation, identification, interpretation, opinion, pronouncement, verdict.

diagram n chart, drawing, figure, flow-chart, graph, illustration, outline, picture, plan, representation, sketch, table.

dial n clock, digital display, face, instrument, pointer, speedometer.

dialect n accent, argot, brogue, cant, creole, idiom, jargon, language, patois, phraseology, pronunciation, register, slang, speech, tongue, vernacular.

dialogue n *inf* chat, *inf* chinwag, colloquy, communication, conference, conversation, debate, discourse, discussion, duologue, exchange, interchange, *old use* intercourse, meeting, oral communication, talk, *inf* tête-à-tête.

diary *n* annals, appointment book, calendar, chronicle, engagement book, journal, log, record.

dictate *vb* 1 read aloud, speak slowly. 2 command, decree, direct, enforce, give orders, impose, *inf* lay down the law, make the rules, ordain, order, prescribe, state categorically.

dictator *n* autocrat, *inf* Big Brother, despot, tyrant. ▷ RULER.

dictatorial *adj* absolute, arbitrary, authoritarian, autocratic, *inf* bossy, despotic, dogmatic, dominant, domineering, illiberal, imperious, intolerant, omnipotent, oppressive, overbearing, repressive, totalitarian, tyrannical, undemocratic. *Opp* DEMOCRATIC.

dictionary *n* concordance, glossary, lexicon, thesaurus, vocabulary, wordbook.

didactic *adj* instructive, lecturing, pedagogic, pedantic.

die *vb* 1 *inf* bite the dust, *inf* breathe your last, cease to exist, come to the end, decease, depart, expire, fall, *inf* give up the ghost, *sl* kick the bucket, lay down your life, lose your life, pass away, *sl* peg out, perish, *sl* pop off, *sl* snuff it, starve. 2 decline, decrease, die away, disappear, droop, dwindle, ebb, end, fade, fail, fizzle out, go out, languish, lessen, peter out, stop, subside, vanish, wane, weaken, wilt, wither.

diet *n* fare, food, intake, nourishment, nutriment, nutrition, sustenance. ● *vb* abstain, *inf* cut down, deny yourself, fast, lose weight, ration yourself, reduce, slim.

differ *vb* 1 be different, be distinct, contrast, deviate, diverge, show differences, vary. 2 argue, be at odds, be at variance, clash, conflict, contradict, disagree, dispute, dissent, fall out, *inf* have a difference, oppose each other, quarrel, take issue with each other. *Opp* AGREE.

difference *n* 1 alteration, change, comparison, contrast, development, deviation, differential, differentiation, discrepancy, disparity, dissimilarity, distinction, diversity, incompatibility, incongruity, inconsistency, modification, nuance, unlikeness, variation, variety. *Opp* SIMILARITY. 2 argument, clash, conflict, controversy, debate, disagreement, disharmony, dispute, dissent, quarrel, strife, tiff, wrangle. *Opp* AGREEMENT.

different *adj* 1 assorted, clashing, conflicting, contradictory, contrasting, deviating, discordant, discrepant, disparate, dissimilar, distinguishable, divergent, diverse, heterogeneous, ill-matched, incompatible, inconsistent, miscellaneous, mixed, multifarious, opposed, opposite, *inf* poles apart, several, sundry, unlike, varied, various. *Opp* SIMILAR. 2 abnormal, altered, anomalous, atypical, bizarre, changed, distinct, distinctive, eccentric, extraordinary, fresh, individual, irregular, new, original, particular, peculiar, personal, revolutionary, separate, singular, special, specific, strange, uncommon, unconventional, unique, unorthodox, unusual. *Opp* CONVENTIONAL.

differentiate *vb* contrast, discriminate, distinguish, tell apart.

difficult *adj* 1 abstruse, advanced, baffling, complex, complicated, deep, *inf* dodgy, enigmatic, hard, intractable, intricate, involved, *inf* knotty, *inf* nasty, obscure, perplexing, problematical, *inf* thorny, ticklish, tricky. 2 arduous, awkward, backbreaking, burdensome, challenging, daunting, demanding, exacting, exhausting, formidable, gruelling, heavy, herculean, *inf* killing, laborious, onerous, punishing, rigorous, severe, strenuous, taxing, tough, uphill. 3 *difficult children.* annoying, disruptive, fussy, headstrong, intractable, obstinate, obstreperous, refractory, stubborn, tiresome, troublesome, trying, uncooperative, unfriendly, unhelpful, unresponsive, unruly. *Opp* COOPERATIVE, EASY.

difficulty *n* adversity, challenge, complication, dilemma, embarrassment, enigma, *inf* fix, *inf* hang-up, hardship, *inf* hiccup, hindrance, hurdle, impediment, *inf* jam, *inf* mess, obstacle, perplexity, *inf* pickle, pitfall, plight, predicament, problem, puzzle, quandary, snag, *inf* spot, straits, *inf* stumbling-block, tribulation, trouble, *inf* vexed question.

diffident *adj* backward, bashful, coy, distrustful, doubtful, fear-

ful, hesitant, hesitating, inhibited, insecure, introvert, meek, modest, nervous, private, reluctant, reserved, retiring, self-effacing, sheepish, shrinking, shy, tentative, timid, timorous, unadventurous, unassuming, underconfident, unsure, withdrawn. *Opp* CONFIDENT.

diffuse *adj* digressive, discursive, long-winded, loose, meandering, rambling, spread out, unstructured, vague, *inf* waffly, wandering. ▷ WORDY. *Opp* CONCISE. • *vb* ▷ SPREAD.

dig *vb* 1 burrow, delve, excavate, gouge, hollow, mine, quarry, scoop, tunnel. 2 cultivate, fork over, *inf* grub up, till, trench, turn over. 3 jab, nudge, poke, prod, punch, shove, thrust. **dig out** ▷ FIND. **dig up** disinter, exhume.

digest *n* ▷ SUMMARY. • *vb* 1 absorb, assimilate, dissolve, ingest, process, utilize. ▷ EAT. 2 consider, ponder, study, take in, understand.

digit *n* 1 figure, integer, number, numeral. 2 finger, toe.

dignified *adj* august, becoming, calm, courtly, decorous, distinguished, elegant, exalted, formal, grand, grave, imposing, impressive, lofty, lordly, majestic, noble, proper, refined, regal, sedate, serious, sober, solemn, stately, tasteful, upright. ▷ PROUD. *Opp* UNBECOMING.

dignitary *n inf* high-up, important person, luminary, notable, official, *inf* VIP, worthy.

dignity *n* calmness, courtliness, decorum, elegance, eminence, formality, glory, grandeur, *Lat* gravitas, gravity, greatness, honour, importance, majesty, nobility, propriety, regality, respectability, seriousness, sobriety, solemnity, stateliness. ▷ PRIDE.

digress vb depart, deviate, diverge, drift, get off the subject, *inf* go off at a tangent, *inf* lose the thread, ramble, stray, veer, wander.

dilapidated adj badly maintained, broken down, crumbling, decayed, decrepit, derelict, falling apart, falling down, in disrepair, in ruins, neglected, ramshackle, rickety, ruined, *inf* run-down, shaky, tottering, tumbledown, uncared-for.

dilemma n *inf* catch-22, deadlock, difficulty, doubt, embarrassment, *inf* fix, impasse, *inf* jam, *inf* mess, *inf* pickle, plight, predicament, problem, quandary, *inf* spot, stalemate.

diligent adj assiduous, busy, careful, conscientious, constant, devoted, earnest, energetic, hardworking, indefatigable, industrious, meticulous, painstaking, persevering, persistent, pertinacious, punctilious, scrupulous, sedulous, studious, thorough, tireless. *Opp* LAZY.

dilute vb adulterate, reduce the strength of, thin, water down, weaken. *Opp* CONCENTRATE.

dim adj 1 bleary, blurred, clouded, cloudy, dark, dingy, dull, faint, fogged, foggy, fuzzy, gloomy, grey, hazy, ill-defined, imperceptible, indistinct, indistinguishable, misty, murky, nebulous, obscure, obscured, pale, shadowy, sombre, unclear, vague, weak. 2 ▷ STUPID.

Opp BRIGHT. ● vb 1 blacken, cloud, darken, dull, make dim, mask, obscure, shade, shroud. 2 become dim, fade, go out, lose brightness, lower. *Opp* BRIGHTEN. **take a dim view** ▷ DISAPPROVE.

dimensions plur n capacity, extent, magnitude, measurements, proportions, scale, scope, size. ▷ MEASUREMENT.

diminish vb 1 abate, become less, contract, curtail, decline, decrease, depreciate, die down, dwindle, ease off, ebb, fade, lessen, *inf* let up, lower, peter out, recede, reduce, shorten, shrink, shrivel, slow down, subside, wane, *inf* wind down. ▷ CUT. *Opp* INCREASE. 2 belittle, cheapen, demean, deprecate, devalue, disparage, minimize, undervalue. *Opp* EXAGGERATE.

diminutive adj microscopic, midget, miniature, minuscule, minute, tiny, undersized. ▷ SMALL.

din n blaring, clamour, clangour, clatter, commotion, crash, hubbub, hullabaloo, noise, outcry, pandemonium, racket, roar, row, rumpus, shouting, tumult, uproar. ▷ SOUND.

dingy adj colourless, dark, depressing, dim, dirty, discoloured, dismal, drab, dreary, dull, faded, gloomy, grimy, murky, old, seedy, shabby, smoky, soiled, sooty, worn. *Opp* BRIGHT.

dining-room n cafeteria, carvery, refectory, restaurant.

dinner n banquet, feast. ▷ MEAL.

dip n 1 concavity, declivity, dent, depression, fall, hollow, incline, slope. 2 *dip in the sea.* bathe, dive, immersion, plunge, soaking, swim. ● *vb* 1 decline, descend, dive, fall, go down, sag, sink, slope down, slump, subside. 2 douse, drop, duck, dunk, immerse, lower, plunge, submerge. **take a dip** ▷ BATHE.

diplomacy *n* adroitness, delicacy, discretion, finesse, negotiation, skill, tact, tactfulness.

diplomat *n* ambassador, consul, government representative, negotiator, official, peacemaker, politician, representative, tactician.

diplomatic *adj* careful, considerate, delicate, discreet, judicious, polite, politic, prudent, sensitive, subtle, tactful, thoughtful, understanding. *Opp* TACTLESS.

direct *adj* 1 non-stop, shortest, straight, unbroken, undeviating, uninterrupted, unswerving. 2 blunt, candid, categorical, clear, decided, explicit, express, forthright, frank, honest, open, outspoken, plain, point-blank, sincere, straightforward, *derog* tactless, to the point, unambiguous, uncomplicated, *derog* undiplomatic, unequivocal, uninhibited, unqualified, unreserved. 3 *direct experience*. empirical, firsthand, *inf* from the horse's mouth, personal. 4 *direct opposites*. absolute, complete, diametrical, exact, head-on, *inf* out-and-out, utter. *Opp* INDIRECT. ● *vb* 1 address, escort, guide, indicate the way, point, route, send, show the way, tell the way, usher. 2 aim, focus, level, target, train, turn. 3 administer, be in charge of, command, conduct, control, govern, handle, lead, manage, mastermind, oversee, regulate,

rule, run, stage-manage, superintend, supervise, take charge of. 4 *direct someone to do something*. advise, bid, charge, command, counsel, enjoin, instruct, order, require, tell.

direction *n* aim, approach, (compass) bearing, course, orientation, path, point of the compass, road, route, tack, track, way. **directions** guidance, guidelines, instructions, orders, plans.

director *n* administrator, *inf* boss, executive, governor, manager, managing director, organizer, president, principal. ▷ CHIEF.

directory *n* catalogue, index, list, register.

dirt *n* 1 dust, excrement, filth, garbage, grime, impurity, mess, mire, muck, ooze, ordure, pollution, slime, sludge, smut, soot, stain. ▷ OBSCENITY. RUBBISH. 2 clay, earth, loam, mud, soil.

dirty *adj* 1 befouled, begrimed, besmirched, bespattered, black, dingy, dusty, filthy, foul, grimy, grubby, marked, messy, mucky, muddy, nasty, scruffy, shabby, slatternly, smeary, smudged, soiled, sooty, sordid, spotted, squalid, stained, sullied, tarnished, travel-stained, uncared for, unclean, untidy, unwashed. 2 *dirty water*. cloudy, contaminated, impure, muddy, murky, poisoned, polluted, tainted, untreated. 3 *dirty tactics*. dishonest, dishonourable, illegal, *inf* low-down, mean, rough, treacherous, unfair, ungentlemanly, unscrupulous, unsporting, unsportsmanlike. ▷ CORRUPT. 4 *dirty talk*. coarse, crude, improper, indecent, offensive, rude, smutty, vulgar.

▷ OBSCENE. *Opp* CLEAN.
● *vb* befoul, foul, make dirty,
mark, *inf* mess up, smear,
smudge, soil, spatter, spot,
stain, streak, tarnish. ▷ DEFILE.
Opp CLEAN.

disability *n* affliction,
complaint, defect, disablement,
handicap, impairment, incapacity, infirmity, weakness.

disable *vb* cripple, damage,
debilitate, enfeeble,
inf hamstring, handicap, immobilize, impair, incapacitate,
injure, lame, maim, make
useless, mutilate, paralyse, put
out of action, ruin, weaken.
disabled ▷ HANDICAPPED.

disadvantage *n* drawback,
handicap, hardship, hindrance,
impediment, inconvenience,
liability, *inf* minus, nuisance,
privation, snag, trouble, weakness.

disagree *vb* argue, bicker, clash,
conflict, contend, differ,
dispute, dissent, diverge, fall
out, fight, quarrel, squabble,
wrangle. **disagree with**
▷ OPPOSE.

disagreeable *adj* disgusting,
distasteful, nasty, objectionable,
obnoxious, offensive, *inf* off-
putting, repellent, sickening,
unsavoury. ▷ UNPLEASANT.
Opp PLEASANT.

disagreement *n* altercation,
argument, clash, conflict,
contention, controversy, debate,
difference, discrepancy, disharmony, disparity, dispute,
dissension, dissent, divergence,
incompatibility, inconsistency,
misunderstanding, opposition,
quarrel, squabble, strife, *inf* tiff,
variance, wrangle. *Opp* AGREE-
MENT.

disappear *vb* 1 become invisible,
cease to exist, clear, die out,
disperse, dissolve, dwindle, ebb,
evanesce, evaporate, fade, melt
away, recede, vanish, vaporize,
wane. ▷ DIE. 2 depart, escape,
flee, fly, go, pass out of sight,
run away, walk away, withdraw. *Opp* APPEAR.

disappoint *vb* be worse than
expected, chagrin, *inf* dash your
hopes, disenchant, disillusion,
dismay, displease, dissatisfy,
fail to satisfy, *inf* let down,
upset, vex. ▷ FRUSTRATE.
Opp SATISFY. **disappointed**
disillusioned, frustrated, *inf* let
down, unsatisfied. ▷ SAD.

disapproval *n* anger, censure,
condemnation, criticism, disap-
probation, disfavour, dislike,
displeasure, dissatisfaction,
hostility, reprimand, reproach.
Opp APPROVAL.

disapprove *vb* **disapprove of**
be displeased by, belittle,
blame, censure, condemn, criticize, denounce, deplore, deprecate, dislike, disparage, frown
on, jeer at, look askance at,
make unwelcome, object to,
regret, reject, *inf* take a dim
view of, take exception to.
Opp APPROVE. **disapproving**
▷ CRITICAL.

disarm *vb* 1 demilitarize, demo-
bilize, disband troops, make
powerless, take weapons from.
2 charm, mollify, pacify,
placate.

disaster *n* accident, act of God,
blow, calamity, cataclysm,
catastrophe, crash, débâcle, failure, fiasco, *inf* flop, *inf* mess-up,
misadventure, mischance,
misfortune, mishap, reverse,
tragedy, *inf* wash-out.
Opp SUCCESS.

disastrous *adj* appalling, awful, calamitous, cataclysmic, catastrophic, crippling, destructive, devastating, dire, dreadful, fatal, ruinous, terrible, tragic. *Opp* SUCCESSFUL.

disbelieve *vb* be sceptical of, discount, discredit, doubt, have no faith in, mistrust, reject, suspect. *Opp* BELIEVE. **disbelieving** ▷ INCREDULOUS.

disc *n* 1 circle, counter, plate, token. 2 album, CD, LP, record, single. 3 [*computing*] CD-ROM, disk, diskette, floppy disk, hard disk.

discard *vb* abandon, cast off, *inf* chuck away, dispense with, dispose of, *inf* ditch, dump, eliminate, get rid of, jettison, junk, reject, scrap, shed, throw away, toss out.

discern *vb* be aware of, be sensitive to, detect, discover, discriminate, distinguish, make out, mark, notice, observe, perceive, recognize, spy. ▷ SEE. **discerning** ▷ PERCEPTIVE.

discernible *adj* detectable, distinguishable, measurable, perceptible. ▷ NOTICEABLE.

discharge *n* 1 release, dismissal. 2 emission, excretion, ooze, pus, secretion, suppuration. ● *vb* 1 belch, eject, emit, expel, exude, give off, give out, pour out, produce, release, secrete, send out, spew, spit out. 2 *discharge guns*. detonate, explode, fire, let off, shoot. 3 *discharge employees*. dismiss, fire, make redundant, remove, sack, throw out. 4 *discharge a prisoner*. absolve, acquit, allow to leave, clear, dismiss, excuse, exonerate, free, let off, liberate, pardon, release. 5 *discharge*

duties. accomplish, carry out, execute, fulfil, perform.

disciple *n* acolyte, adherent, admirer, apostle, apprentice, devotee, follower, learner, proselyte, pupil, scholar, student, supporter.

disciplinarian *n* authoritarian, autocrat, despot, dictator, *inf* hard-liner, *inf* hard taskmaster, martinet, *inf* slavedriver, *inf* stickler, tyrant.

discipline *n* 1 control, drilling, indoctrination, instruction, management, strictness, system, training. 2 good behaviour, obedience, order, orderliness, routine, self-control, self-restraint. ● *vb* 1 break in, coach, control, drill, educate, govern, indoctrinate, instruct, keep in check, manage, restrain, school, train. 2 castigate, chasten, chastise, correct, penalize, punish, rebuke, reprimand, reprove, scold. **disciplined** ▷ OBEDIENT.

disclaim *vb* deny, disown, forswear, reject, renounce, repudiate. *Opp* ACKNOWLEDGE.

disclose *vb* divulge, expose, let out, make known. ▷ REVEAL.

discolour *vb* bleach, dirty, fade, mark, spoil the colour of, stain, tarnish, tinge.

discomfort *n* ache, care, difficulty, distress, hardship, inconvenience, irritation, soreness, uncomfortableness, uneasiness. ▷ PAIN. *Opp* COMFORT.

disconcert *vb* agitate, bewilder, confuse, discomfit, distract, disturb, fluster, nonplus, perplex, *inf* put off, puzzle, *inf* rattle, ruffle, throw off balance, trouble, unsettle, upset, worry. *Opp* REASSURE.

disconnect vb break off, cut off, detach, disengage, divide, part, sever, switch off, take away, turn off, uncouple, undo, unhitch, unhook, unplug.
disconnected ▷ INCOHERENT.

discontented adj annoyed, disgruntled, displeased, dissatisfied, inf fed up, restless, sulky, unhappy, unsettled.

discord n 1 argument, conflict, contention, difference of opinion, disagreement, disharmony, dispute, friction, incompatibility, strife. ▷ QUARREL. 2 [music] cacophony, clash, jangle. ▷ NOISE. Opp HARMONY.

discordant adj 1 conflicting, contrary, differing, disagreeing, dissimilar, divergent, incompatible, incongruous, inconsistent, opposed, opposite. ▷ QUARRELSOME. 2 atonal, cacophonous, clashing, dissonant, grating, grinding, harsh, jangling, jarring, shrill, strident, tuneless, unmusical. Opp HARMONIOUS.

discount n abatement, allowance, concession, cut, deduction, inf mark-down, rebate, reduction. ● vb disbelieve, dismiss, disregard, gloss over, ignore, overlook, reject.

discourage vb 1 cow, damp, dampen, daunt, demoralize, depress, disenchant, dishearten, dismay, dispirit, frighten, inhibit, intimidate, overawe, inf put down, inf put off, scare, inf throw cold water on, unman, unnerve. 2 discourage vandalism. check, deflect, deter, dissuade, hinder, prevent, put an end to, repress, restrain, slow down, stop, suppress. Opp ENCOURAGE.

discouragement n constraint, inf damper, deterrent, disincentive, hindrance, impediment, obstacle, restraint, setback. Opp ENCOURAGEMENT.

discourse n 1 ▷ CONVERSATION. 2 dissertation, essay, monograph, paper, speech, thesis, treatise. ▷ WRITING.
● vb ▷ SPEAK.

discover vb ascertain, bring to light, come across, detect, inf dig up, disclose, inf dredge up, explore, expose, inf ferret out, find, hit on, identify, learn, light upon, locate, notice, observe, perceive, recognize, reveal, search out, spot, sl sus out, track down, turn up, uncover, unearth. ▷ INVENT. Opp HIDE.

discoverer n creator, explorer, finder, initiator, inventor, originator, pioneer, traveller.

discovery n breakthrough, conception, detection, disclosure, exploration, inf find, innovation, invention, recognition, revelation.

discredit vb attack, calumniate, challenge, defame, disbelieve, disgrace, dishonour, disprove, inf explode, prove false, raise doubts about, refuse to believe, ruin the reputation of, show up, slander, slur, smear, vilify.

discreet adj careful, cautious, chary, circumspect, considerate, delicate, diplomatic, guarded, judicious, low-key, mild, muted, polite, politic, prudent, restrained, sensitive, soft, subdued, tactful, thoughtful, understated, wary. Opp INDISCREET.

discrepancy n conflict, difference, disparity, dissimilarity, divergence, incompatibility, incongruity, inconsistency, variance. Opp SIMILARITY.

discretion n circumspection, diplomacy, good sense, judgement, maturity, prudence, responsibility, sensitivity, tact, wisdom. Opp TACTLESSNESS.

discriminate vb 1 differentiate, distinguish, draw a distinction, separate, tell apart. 2 be biased, be intolerant, be prejudiced, show discrimination. **discriminating** ▷ PERCEPTIVE.

discrimination n 1 discernment, good taste, insight, judgement, perceptiveness, refinement, selectivity, subtlety, taste. 2 [derog] bias, bigotry, chauvinism, favouritism, intolerance, male chauvinism, prejudice, racialism, racism, sexism, unfairness. Opp IMPARTIALITY.

discuss vb argue about, confer about, consider, consult about, debate, deliberate, examine, inf put heads together about, talk about, inf weigh up the pros and cons of, write about. ▷ TALK.

discussion n argument, colloquy, confabulation, conference, consideration, consultation, conversation, debate, deliberation, dialogue, discourse, examination, exchange of views, inf powwow, symposium. ▷ TALK.

disdainful adj contemptuous, jeering, mocking, scornful, sneering, supercilious, superior. ▷ PROUD.

disease n affliction, ailment, blight, inf bug, complaint, inf condition, contagion, disorder, infection, infirmity, malady, plague, sickness. ▷ ILLNESS.

diseased adj ailing, infirm, sick, unwell. ▷ ILL.

disembark vb alight, debark, detrain, get off, go ashore, land. Opp EMBARK.

disfigure vb blemish, damage, deface, deform, distort, impair, injure, make ugly, mar, mutilate, ruin, scar, spoil. Opp BEAUTIFY.

disgrace n 1 blot, contumely, degradation, discredit, dishonour, disrepute, embarrassment, humiliation, ignominy, obloquy, odium, opprobrium, scandal, shame, slur, stain, stigma. 2 ▷ OUTRAGE.

disgraceful adj contemptible, degrading, dishonourable, embarrassing, humiliating, ignominious, shameful, shaming, wicked. ▷ BAD.

disgruntled adj annoyed, cross, disaffected, disappointed, discontented, dissatisfied, inf fed up, grumpy, moody, sulky, sullen. ▷ BAD-TEMPERED.

disguise n camouflage, cloak, costume, cover, fancy dress, front, inf get-up, impersonation, make-up, mask, pretence, smoke-screen. • vb blend into the background, camouflage, conceal, cover up, dress up, falsify, gloss over, hide, make inconspicuous, mask, misrepresent, screen, shroud, veil. **disguise yourself as** ▷ IMPERSONATE.

disgust n abhorrence, antipathy, aversion, contempt, detestation, dislike, distaste, hatred, loathing, nausea, outrage, repugnance, repulsion, revulsion, sickness. • vb appal, be distasteful to, displease, horrify, nauseate, offend, outrage, put off, repel, revolt, sicken, shock, *inf* turn your stomach. *Opp* PLEASE. **disgusting** ▷ HATEFUL.

dish *n* 1 basin, bowl, casserole, container, plate, *old use* platter, tureen. 2 concoction, food, item on the menu, recipe. **dish out** ▷ DISTRIBUTE. **dish up** ▷ SERVE.

dishearten *vb* depress, deter, discourage, dismay, put off, sadden. *Opp* ENCOURAGE. **disheartened** ▷ SAD.

dishevelled *adj* bedraggled, disarranged, disordered, knotted, matted, messy, ruffled, rumpled, *inf* scruffy, slovenly, tangled, tousled, uncombed, unkempt, untidy. *Opp* NEAT.

dishonest *adj* and *inf* bent, cheating, corrupt, criminal, crooked, deceitful, deceiving, deceptive, devious, dishonourable, disreputable, false, fraudulent, hypocritical, immoral, insincere, lying, mendacious, misleading, perfidious, *inf* shady, *inf* slippery, specious, swindling, thieving, treacherous, *inf* two-faced, *inf* underhand, unethical, unprincipled, unscrupulous, untrustworthy, untruthful. *Opp* HONEST.

dishonour *n inf* black mark, blot, degradation, discredit, disgrace, humiliation, ignominy, indignity, loss of face, obloquy, opprobrium, reproach, scandal, shame, slander, slur, stain, stigma. *Opp* HONOUR.
• *vb* 1 abuse, affront, debase, defile, degrade, disgrace, offend, profane, shame, slight.
2 ▷ RAPE.

dishonourable *adj* base, blameworthy, compromising, despicable, discreditable, disgraceful, disgusting, dishonest, disloyal, disreputable, ignoble, ignominious, improper, infamous, mean, outrageous, perfidious, reprehensible, scandalous, shabby, shameful, shameless, treacherous, unchivalrous, unethical, unprincipled, unscrupulous, untrustworthy, unworthy, wicked. ▷ CORRUPT. *Opp* HONOURABLE.

disillusion *vb* disabuse, disappoint, disenchant, enlighten, reveal the truth to, undeceive.

disinfect *vb* cauterize, chlorinate, clean, cleanse, decontaminate, fumigate, purge, purify, sanitize, sterilize.

disinfectant *n* antiseptic, decontaminant, fumigant, germicide.

disinherit *vb* cut off, cut out of a will, deprive someone of his/her birthright, deprive someone of his/her inheritance.

disintegrate *vb* break into pieces, break up, come apart, crack up, crumble, decay, decompose, degenerate, deteriorate, fall apart, lose coherence, moulder, rot, shatter, smash, splinter.

disinterested *adj* detached, dispassionate, impartial, impersonal, neutral, objective, unbiased, uninvolved, unprejudiced. *Opp* BIASED.

disjointed *adj* aimless, broken up, confused, desultory, disconnected, dislocated, disordered, disunited, divided, incoherent, jumbled, loose, mixed up, muddled, rambling, separate, split up, unconnected, unco-

ordinated, wandering.
Opp COHERENT.

dislike *n* animus, antagonism,
antipathy, aversion, contempt,
detestation, disapproval, disfavour, disgust, distaste, hatred,
hostility, ill will, loathing,
repugnance, revulsion.
● *vb* avoid, despise, detest,
disapprove of, feel dislike for,
scorn, *inf* take against. ▷ HATE.
Opp LOVE.

dislocate *vb* disengage, disjoint,
displace, misplace, *inf* put out,
put out of joint.

disloyal *adj* apostate, faithless,
false, insincere, perfidious,
recreant, renegade, seditious,
subversive, treacherous, treasonable, *inf* two-faced, unfaithful, unreliable, untrue, untrustworthy. *Opp* LOYAL.

disloyalty *n* betrayal, double-
dealing, duplicity, faithlessness,
falseness, inconstancy, infidelity, perfidy, treachery, treason,
unfaithfulness. *Opp* LOYALTY.

dismal *adj* bleak, cheerless,
depressing, dreary, dull, funereal, gloomy, grey, grim, joyless,
miserable, sombre, wretched.
▷ SAD.

dismantle *vb* demolish, knock
down, strike, strip down, take
apart, take down. *Opp* AS-
SEMBLE.

dismay *n* agitation, alarm,
anxiety, apprehension, astonishment, consternation, depression, disappointment, discouragement, distress, dread, gloom,
horror, pessimism, surprise.
▷ FEAR. ● *vb* alarm, appal,
daunt, depress, devastate,
disappoint, discompose,
discourage, disgust, dishearten,
dispirit, distress, horrify, scare,

shock, take aback, unnerve.
▷ FRIGHTEN. *Opp* PLEASE.

dismiss *vb* 1 disband, discard,
free, let go, *inf* pack off, release,
send away, *inf* send packing.
2 belittle, brush aside, discount,
disregard, drop, give up,
inf pooh-pooh, reject, repudiate,
set aside, shelve, shrug off,
wave aside. 3 *dismiss a worker*.
inf axe, *inf* boot, cashier,
disband, discharge, *inf* fire, get
rid of, give notice to, *inf* give
someone his/her cards, give the
push to, lay off, make redundant, sack.

disobedient *adj* anarchic,
contrary, defiant, delinquent,
disorderly, disruptive, fractious, headstrong, insubordinate, intractable, mutinous,
obdurate, obstinate, obstreperous, perverse, rebellious,
recalcitrant, refractory, riotous,
self-willed, stubborn, uncontrollable, undisciplined, ungovernable, unmanageable, unruly,
wayward, wild, wilful.
▷ NAUGHTY. *Opp* OBEDIENT.

disobey *vb* 1 be disobedient,
mutiny, protest, rebel, revolt,
rise up, strike. 2 break, contravene, defy, disregard, flout,
ignore, infringe, oppose, rebel
against, resist, transgress,
violate. *Opp* OBEY.

disorder *n* 1 anarchy, chaos,
clamour, confusion, disarray,
disorderliness, disorganization,
disturbance, fighting, fracas,
fuss, jumble, lawlessness, mess,
muddle, rumpus, *inf* shambles,
tangle, tumult, untidiness,
uproar. ▷ COMMOTION.
Opp ORDER. 2 ▷ ILLNESS.

disorderly *adj* ▷ DISOBEDIENT,
DISORGANIZED.

disorganized adj aimless, careless, chaotic, confused, disorderly, haphazard, illogical, jumbled, messy, muddled, rambling, scatter-brained, inf slapdash, inf slipshod, inf sloppy, slovenly, straggling, unmethodical, unplanned, unstructured, unsystematic, untidy. Opp SYSTEMATIC.

disown vb cast off, disclaim knowledge of, renounce, repudiate.

disparage vb belittle, demean, depreciate, discredit, insult, inf put down, slight, undervalue. ▷ CRITICIZE. **disparaging** ▷ UNCOMPLIMENTARY.

dispassionate adj calm, composed, cool, equable, even-tempered, level-headed, sober. ▷ IMPARTIAL, UNEMOTIONAL. Opp EMOTIONAL.

dispatch n bulletin, communiqué, document, letter, message, report. • vb 1 consign, convey, forward, mail, post, send, ship, transmit. 2 ▷ KILL.

dispense vb 1 allocate, allot, apportion, assign, deal out, disburse, distribute, dole out, give out, issue, measure out, mete out, parcel out, provide, ration out, share. 2 dispense medicine. make up, prepare, supply. **dispense with** ▷ OMIT, REMOVE.

disperse vb 1 break up, decentralize, devolve, disband, dismiss, dispel, dissipate, distribute, divide up, drive away, send away, send in different directions, separate, spread, stray. Opp GATHER. 2 disappear, dissolve, melt away, scatter, spread out, vanish.

displace vb 1 disarrange, dislocate, dislodge, disturb, misplace, move, put out of place, shift. 2 crowd out, depose, dispossess, evict, expel, oust, replace, succeed, supersede, supplant, take the place of, unseat, usurp.

display n 1 array, demonstration, exhibition, manifestation, pageant, parade, presentation, show, spectacle. 2 ceremony, ostentation, pageantry, pomp, showing off. • vb advertise, air, betray, demonstrate, disclose, exhibit, expose, flaunt, flourish, give evidence of, parade, present, produce, put on show, reveal, set out, show, show off, unfold, unfurl, unveil, vaunt. Opp HIDE.

displease vb anger, offend, inf put out, upset. ▷ ANNOY.

disposable adj 1 at your disposal, available, spendable, usable. 2 biodegradable, expendable, non-returnable, replaceable, inf throw-away.

dispose vb adjust, arrange, array, distribute, group, order, organize, place, position, put, set out, situate. **disposed** ▷ LIABLE. **dispose of** ▷ DESTROY, DISCARD.

disproportionate adj excessive, incommensurate, incongruous, inequitable, inordinate, out of proportion, unbalanced, uneven, unreasonable. Opp PROPORTIONAL.

disprove vb confute, contradict, controvert, demolish, discredit, inf explode, invalidate, negate, rebut, refute, show to be wrong. Opp PROVE.

dispute n ▷ QUARREL. • vb argue against, challenge, contest, contradict, controvert, deny, disagree with, doubt, fault, gainsay, impugn, object to, oppose, *inf* pick holes in, quarrel with, query, question, raise doubts about, take exception to. ▷ DEBATE. *Opp* ACCEPT.

disqualify *vb* bar, debar, declare ineligible, exclude, preclude, prohibit, reject, turn down.

disregard *vb* brush aside, despise, discount, dismiss, disobey, exclude, *inf* fly in the face of, forget, ignore, leave out, *inf* make light of, miss out, neglect, omit, overlook, pass over, pay no attention to, *inf* pooh-pooh, reject, shrug off, skip, slight, snub, turn a blind eye to. *Opp* HEED.

disreputable *adj* dishonest, dishonourable, *inf* dodgy, dubious, infamous, questionable, raffish, *inf* shady, suspect, suspicious, unconventional, unreliable, unsound, untrustworthy. *Opp* REPUTABLE.

disrespectful *adj* bad-mannered, blasphemous, derisive, discourteous, disparaging, impolite, impudent, inconsiderate, insolent, insulting, irreverent, mocking, scornful, uncivil, uncomplimentary, unmannerly. ▷ RUDE. *Opp* RESPECTFUL.

disrupt *vb* agitate, break up, confuse, disconcert, dislocate, disorder, disturb, interfere with, interrupt, intrude on, spoil, throw into disorder, unsettle, upset.

dissatisfaction *n* annoyance, chagrin, disappointment, discontentment, dismay, displeasure, disquiet, exasperation, frustration, irritation,

malaise, mortification, regret, unhappiness. *Opp* SATISFACTION.

dissatisfied *adj* disaffected, disappointed, discontented, disgruntled, displeased, fed up, frustrated, unfulfilled, unsatisfied. ▷ UNHAPPY. *Opp* CONTENTED.

dissident *n derog* agitator, apostate, dissenter, independent thinker, nonconformer, protester, rebel, recusant, *inf* refusenik, revolutionary. *Opp* CONFORMIST.

dissimilar *adj* antithetical, clashing, conflicting, contrasting, different, disparate, distinct, distinguishable, divergent, diverse, heterogeneous, incompatible, irreconcilable, opposite, unlike, unrelated, various. *Opp* SIMILAR.

dissipate *vb* 1 break up, diffuse, disappear, disperse, scatter. 2 distribute, fritter away, spread about, squander, throw away, use up, waste. **dissipated** ▷ IMMORAL.

dissociate *vb* back away, cut off, detach, disengage, distance, divorce, isolate, segregate. ▷ SEPARATE. *Opp* ASSOCIATE.

dissolve *vb* 1 become liquid, decompose, deliquesce, dematerialize, diffuse, disappear, disintegrate, disperse, liquefy, melt away, vanish. 2 *dissolve a meeting*. adjourn, break up, cancel, disband, dismiss, divorce, end, sever, split up, suspend, terminate, *inf* wind up.

dissuade *vb* dissuade from advise against, argue out of, deter from, discourage from, persuade not to, put off, remon-

strate against, warn against.
Opp PERSUADE.

distance *n* 1 breadth, extent,
gap, *inf* haul, interval, journey,
length, measurement, mileage,
range, reach, separation, space,
span, stretch, width.
2 aloofness, coolness, haughtiness, isolation, remoteness,
separation, *inf* standoffishness,
unfriendliness. ● *vb* **distance**
yourself be unfriendly, detach
yourself, dissociate yourself,
keep away, keep your distance,
remove yourself, separate yourself, set yourself apart, stay
away. *Opp* INVOLVE.

distant *adj* 1 far, far-away, far-
flung, *inf* god-forsaken, inaccessible, outlying, out-of-the-way,
remote, removed. *Opp* CLOSE.
2 aloof, cool, formal, frigid,
haughty, reserved, reticent,
stiff, unapproachable, unenthusiastic, unfriendly, withdrawn.
Opp FRIENDLY.

distasteful *adj* disgusting,
displeasing, nasty, nauseating,
objectionable, offensive, *inf* off-
putting, repugnant, revolting,
unpalatable. ▷ UNPLEASANT.
Opp PLEASANT.

distinct *adj* 1 apparent, clear,
clear-cut, definite, evident,
noticeable, obvious, palpable,
patent, perceptible, plain,
precise, recognizable, sharp,
unambiguous, unequivocal,
unmistakable, visible, well-
defined. *Opp* INDISTINCT.
2 contrasting, detached, different, discrete, dissimilar, distinguishable, individual, separate,
special, *Lat* sui generis, unconnected, unique.

distinction *n* 1 contrast, difference, differentiation, discrimination, dissimilarity, distinc-

tiveness, dividing line, division,
individuality, particularity,
peculiarity, separation.
Opp SIMILARITY. 2 *distinction of
being first.* celebrity, credit,
eminence, excellence, fame,
glory, greatness, honour, importance, merit, prestige, renown,
reputation, superiority.

distinctive *adj* characteristic,
different, distinguishing, idiosyncratic, individual, inimitable, original, peculiar, personal, singular, special, striking,
typical, uncommon, unique.
Opp COMMON.

distinguish *vb* 1 choose, decide,
differentiate, discriminate,
judge, make a distinction,
separate, tell apart. 2 ascertain,
determine, discern, know, make
out, perceive, pick out, recognize, see, single out, tell.
distinguished ▷ FAMOUS.

distort *vb* 1 bend, buckle,
contort, deform, misshape,
twist, warp, wrench. 2 alter,
exaggerate, falsify, garble,
misrepresent, pervert, slant,
tamper with, twist, violate.
distorted ▷ GNARLED, FALSE.

distract *vb* bewilder, bother,
confound, confuse, deflect,
disconcert, distress, divert,
harass, mystify, perplex, puzzle,
rattle, sidetrack, trouble,
worry. **distracted** ▷ DIS-
TRAUGHT, MAD.

distraction *n* 1 disturbance,
diversion, interference, interruption, temptation, *inf* upset.
2 agitation, befuddlement,
bewilderment, confusion, delirium, frenzy, insanity, madness.
3 ▷ DIVERSION.

distraught *adj* agitated,
inf beside yourself, distracted,

distressed, disturbed, emotional, excited, frantic, hysterical, overcome, overwrought, troubled, upset, worked up.
▷ ANXIOUS. Opp CALM.

distress n adversity, affliction, angst, anguish, anxiety, danger, desolation, difficulty, discomfort, dismay, fright, grief, heartache, misery, pain, poverty, privation, sadness, sorrow, stress, suffering, torment, tribulation, trouble, unhappiness, woe, worry, wretchedness.
▷ PAIN. ● vb afflict, alarm, bother, inf cut up, dismay, disturb, frighten, grieve, harass, harrow, hurt, make miserable, oppress, pain, perplex, plague, sadden, scare, shake, shock, terrify, torment, torture, trouble, upset, vex, worry, wound. Opp COMFORT.

distribute vb allocate, allot, apportion, arrange, assign, circulate, deal out, deliver, inf dish out, dispense, disperse, dispose of, disseminate, divide out, inf dole out, give out, hand round, issue, mete out, partition, pass round, scatter, share out, spread, strew, take round. Opp COLLECT.

district n area, community, department, division, locality, neighbourhood, parish, part, partition, precinct, province, quarter, region, sector, territory, vicinity, ward, zone.

distrust vb be distrustful of, disbelieve, doubt, have misgivings about, have qualms about, mistrust, question, suspect. Opp TRUST.

distrustful adj cautious, chary, cynical, disbelieving, distrust-

ing, doubtful, dubious, sceptical, suspicious, uncertain, uneasy, unsure, wary. Opp TRUSTFUL.

disturb vb 1 agitate, alarm, annoy, bother, discompose, disrupt, distract, distress, excite, fluster, frighten, hassle, interrupt, intrude on, perturb, pester, ruffle, scare, shake, startle, stir up, trouble, unsettle, upset, worry. 2 confuse, disorder, interfere with, jumble up, inf mess about with, move, muddle, rearrange, reorganize.
disturbed ▷ DISTRAUGHT.

disturbance n disruption, interference, upheaval, upset.
▷ COMMOTION.

disunited adj divided, opposed, polarized, split. Opp UNITED.

disunity n difference, disagreement, discord, disharmony, disintegration, division, fragmentation, incoherence, opposition, polarization. Opp UNITY.

disused adj abandoned, archaic, closed, dead, discarded, discontinued, idle, neglected, obsolete, superannuated, unused, withdrawn. ▷ OLD. Opp CURRENT.

ditch n aqueduct, channel, dike, drain, gully, gutter, moat, trench, watercourse.
● vb ▷ ABANDON.

dive vb crash-dive, descend, dip, drop, duck, fall, go snorkelling, go under, jump, leap, nosedive, pitch, plummet, plunge, sink, submerge, subside, swoop.

diverge vb branch, deviate, divide, fork, go off at a tangent, part, radiate, ramify, separate, split, spread, subdivide.
▷ DIFFER. Opp CONVERGE.

diverse adj assorted, different, dissimilar, distinct, divergent,

diversify   do

diversified, heterogeneous, miscellaneous, mixed, multifarious, varied, various.

diversify *vb* branch out, broaden out, develop, divide, enlarge, expand, extend, spread out, vary.

diversion *n* **1** detour, deviation. **2** amusement, distraction, entertainment, fun, game, hobby, interest, pastime, play, recreation, relaxation, sport.

divert *vb* **1** alter, avert, change direction, deflect, deviate, rechannel, redirect, reroute, shunt, sidetrack, switch, turn aside. **2** amuse, beguile, cheer up, delight, distract, engage, entertain, keep happy, occupy, recreate, regale. **diverting** ▷ FUNNY.

divide *vb* **1** branch, detach, diverge, fork, move apart, part, separate, sunder. **2** allocate, allot, apportion, break up, cut up, deal out, dispense, distribute, dole out, give out, halve, measure out, mete out, parcel out, pass round, share out. **3** *divide a party.* cause disagreement in, disunite, polarize, split. **4** *divide into sets.* arrange, categorize, classify, grade, group, sort out, subdivide. *Opp* GATHER, UNITE.

divine *adj* angelic, celestial, godlike, hallowed, heavenly, holy, immortal, mystical, religious, sacred, saintly, seraphic, spiritual, superhuman, supernatural, transcendental. *Opp* MORTAL. ● *n* ▷ CLERGYMAN. ● *vb* ▷ PROPHESY.

divinity *n* **1** ▷ GOD. **2** religion, religious studies, theology.

division *n* **1** allocation, allotment, apportionment, cutting

up, dividing, partition, segmentation, separation, splitting. **2** disagreement, discord, disunity, feud, quarrel, rupture, schism, split. **3** alcove, compartment, part, recess, section, segment. **4** *division between rooms, lands.* border, borderline, boundary line, demarcation, divider, dividing wall, fence, frontier, margin, partition, screen. **5** *division of a business.* branch, department, section, subdivision, unit.

divorce *n* annulment, *inf* breakup, decree nisi, dissolution, separation, *inf* split-up.
● *vb* annul marriage, dissolve marriage, part, separate, *inf* split up.

dizziness *n* faintness, giddiness, light-headedness, vertigo.

dizzy *adj* bewildered, confused, dazed, faint, giddy, lightheaded, muddled, reeling, shaky, swimming, unsteady, *inf* woozy.

do *vb* **1** accomplish, achieve, bring about, carry out, cause, commit, complete, effect, execute, finish, fulfil, implement, initiate, instigate, organize, perform, produce, undertake. **2** *do the garden.* arrange, attend to, cope with, deal with, handle, look after, manage, work at. **3** *do sums.* answer, give your mind to, puzzle out, solve, think out, work out. **4** *Will this do?* be acceptable, be enough, be satisfactory, be sufficient, be suitable, satisfy, serve, suffice. **5** *Do as you like.* act, behave, conduct yourself, perform. **do away with** ▷ ABOLISH. **do up** ▷ DECORATE, FASTEN.

docile *adj* cooperative, domesticated, obedient, submissive, tractable. ▷ TAME.

dock *n* berth, boatyard, dockyard, dry dock, harbour, haven, jetty, landing-stage, marina, pier, port, quay, slipway, wharf. ● *vb* 1 anchor, berth, drop anchor, land, moor, put in, tie up. 2 ▷ CUT.

doctor *n* general practitioner, *inf* GP, *inf* medic, medical officer, medical practitioner, *inf* MO, physician, *derog* quack, surgeon.

doctrine *n* axiom, belief, conviction, *Lat* credo, creed, dogma, maxim, orthodoxy, postulate, precept, principle, teaching, tenet, theory, thesis.

document *n* certificate, charter, chronicle, deed, diploma, form, instrument, legal document, licence, manuscript, *inf* MS, paper, parchment, passport, policy, print-out, record, typescript, visa, warrant, will. ● *vb* ▷ RECORD.

documentary *adj* 1 authenticated, chronicled, recorded, substantiated, written. 2 factual, historical, non-fiction, real life.

dodge *n* contrivance, device, knack, manoeuvre, ploy, *sl* racket, ruse, scheme, stratagem, subterfuge, trick, *inf* wheeze. ● *vb* 1 avoid, duck, elude, escape, evade, fend off, move out of the way, sidestep, swerve, turn away, veer, weave. 2 *dodge work*. shirk, *inf* skive, *inf* wriggle out of. 3 *dodge a question*. equivocate, fudge, hedge, quibble, *inf* waffle.

dog *n* bitch, *inf* bow-wow, *derog* cur, dingo, hound,

mongrel, pedigree, pup, puppy, whelp. ● *vb* ▷ FOLLOW.

dogma *n* article of faith, belief, conviction, creed, doctrine, orthodoxy, precept, principle, teaching, tenet, truth.

dogmatic *adj* assertive, arbitrary, authoritarian, authoritative, categorical, certain, dictatorial, doctrinaire, *inf* hard-line, hidebound, imperious, inflexible, intolerant, legalistic, narrow-minded, obdurate, opinionated, pontifical, positive. ▷ STUBBORN. *Opp* AMENABLE.

dole *n* [*inf*] benefit, income support, social security, unemployment benefit. **dole out** ▷ DISTRIBUTE. **on the dole** ▷ UNEMPLOYED.

doll *n* *inf* dolly, figure, marionette, puppet, rag doll.

domestic *adj* 1 family, household, in the home, private. 2 *domestic air service.* indigenous, inland, internal, national.

domesticated *adj* house-broken, house-trained, tame, tamed, trained. *Opp* WILD.

dominant *adj* 1 biggest, chief, commanding, conspicuous, eye-catching, highest, imposing, largest, main, major, obvious, outstanding, pre-eminent, prevailing, primary, principal, tallest, uppermost, widespread. 2 ascendant, controlling, dominating, domineering, governing, influential, leading, powerful, predominant, presiding, reigning, ruling, supreme.

dominate *vb* 1 be dominant, be in the majority, control, direct, govern, influence, lead, manage, master, monopolize, outnumber, preponderate, prevail, rule, subjugate, take control, tyrannize. **2** dwarf, look down on, overshadow, tower over.

domineering *adj* authoritarian, autocratic, *inf* bossy, despotic, dictatorial, high-handed, oppressive, overbearing, *inf* pushy, strict, tyrannical. *Opp* SUBMISSIVE.

donate *vb* contribute, give, grant, hand over, make a donation, present, subscribe, supply.

donation *n* alms, contribution, freewill offering, gift, offering, present, subscription.

donor *n* backer, benefactor, contributor, giver, philanthropist, provider, sponsor, supplier, supporter.

doom *n* destiny, end, fate, fortune, karma, kismet, lot.

doomed *adj* **1** condemned, destined, fated, intended, ordained, predestined. **2** *a doomed enterprise.* accursed, bedevilled, cursed, damned, hopeless, ill-fated, ill-starred, luckless, star-crossed, unlucky.

door *n* barrier, doorway, entrance, exit, French window, gate, gateway, opening, portal, postern, revolving door, swing door, way out.

dormant *adj* **1** asleep, comatose, hibernating, inactive, inert, passive, quiescent, quiet, resting, sleeping. **2** *dormant talent.* hidden, latent, potential, unrevealed, untapped, unused. *Opp* ACTIVE.

dose *n* amount, dosage, measure, portion, prescribed amount, quantity. • *vb* administer, dispense, prescribe.

dossier *n* file, folder, records, set of documents.

dot *n* decimal point, fleck, full stop, iota, jot, mark, point, speck, spot. • *vb* fleck, mark with dots, punctuate, speckle, spot, stipple.

dote *vb* dote on adore, idolize, worship. ▷ LOVE.

double *adj* coupled, doubled, dual, duple, duplicated, paired, twin, twofold, two-ply. • *n* clone, copy, counterpart, *Ger* doppelgänger, duplicate, *inf* look-alike, opposite, *inf* spitting image, twin. • *vb* duplicate, increase, multiply by two, reduplicate, repeat. **double back** ▷ RETURN. **double up** ▷ COLLAPSE.

double-cross *vb* cheat, deceive, let down, trick. ▷ BETRAY.

doubt *n* **1** agnosticism, anxiety, apprehension, confusion, cynicism, diffidence, disbelief, disquiet, distrust, fear, hesitation, incredulity, indecision, misgiving, mistrust, perplexity, qualm, reservation, scepticism, suspicion, worry. **2** *doubt about meaning.* ambiguity, difficulty, dilemma, problem, query, question, uncertainty. *Opp* CERTAINTY. • *vb* be dubious, be sceptical about, disbelieve, distrust, fear, feel uncertain about, have doubts about, have misgivings about, have reservations about, hesitate, lack confidence, mistrust, query, question, suspect. *Opp* TRUST.

doubtful *adj* **1** agnostic, cynical, diffident, disbelieving, distrustful, dubious, hesitant, incredulous, sceptical, suspicious, tentative, uncertain, unclear, unconvinced, undecided, unsure. **2** *a doubtful decision.* ambiguous, debatable, dubious, equivocal, *inf* iffy, inconclusive, problematical, questionable, suspect, vague, worrying. **3** *a doubtful ally.* irresolute, uncommitted, unreliable, untrustworthy, vacillating, wavering. *Opp* CERTAIN, DEPENDABLE.

dowdy *adj* colourless, dingy, drab, dull, *inf* frumpish, old-fashioned, shabby, *inf* sloppy, slovenly, *inf* tatty, unattractive, unstylish. *Opp* SMART.

downfall *n* collapse, defeat, overthrow, ruin, undoing.

downhearted *adj* dejected, depressed, discouraged, *inf* down, downcast, miserable, unhappy. ▷ SAD.

downward *adj* declining, descending, downhill, easy, falling, going down. *Opp* UPWARD.

downy *adj* feathery, fleecy, fluffy, furry, fuzzy, soft, velvety, woolly.

drab *adj* cheerless, colourless, dingy, dismal, dowdy, dreary, dull, flat, gloomy, grey, grimy, lacklustre, shabby, sombre, unattractive, uninteresting. *Opp* BRIGHT.

draft *n* **1** first version, notes, outline, plan, rough version, sketch. **2** *bank draft.* cheque, order, postal order. ● *vb* block out, compose, delineate, draw up, outline, plan, prepare, put together, sketch out, work out, write a draft of.

drag *vb* **1** draw, haul, lug, pull, tow, trail, tug. **2** *time drags.* be boring, crawl, creep, go slowly, linger, loiter, lose momentum, move slowly, pass slowly.

drain *n* channel, conduit, culvert, dike, ditch, drainage, drainpipe, duct, gutter, outlet, pipe, sewer, trench, water-

course. ● *vb* **1** bleed, clear, draw off, dry out, empty, evacuate, extract, pump out, remove, tap, take off. **2** drip, ebb, leak out, ooze, seep, strain, trickle. **3** *drain resources.* consume, deplete, exhaust, sap, spend, use up.

drama *n* **1** acting, dramatics, dramaturgy, histrionics, improvisation, stagecraft, theatre, theatricals, thespian arts. **2** comedy, dramatization, farce, melodrama, musical, opera, operetta, pantomime, performance, play, production, screenplay, script, show, stage version, TV version, tragedy. **3** *real-life drama.* action, crisis, excitement, suspense, turmoil.

dramatic *adj* **1** histrionic, stage, theatrical, thespian. **2** *dramatic gestures.* exaggerated, flamboyant, large, overdone, showy. **3** ▷ EXCITING.

dramatist *n* dramaturge, playwright, scriptwriter.

dramatize *vb* **1** adapt, make into a play. **2** exaggerate, make too much of, overdo, overplay, overstate.

drape *n* old use arras, curtain, drapery, hanging, screen, tapestry, valance. ● *vb* cover, decorate, festoon, hang, swathe.

drastic *adj* desperate, dire, draconian, extreme, far-reaching, forceful, harsh, radical, rigorous, severe, strong, vigorous.

draught *n* **1** breeze, current, movement, puff, wind. **2** *draught of ale.* dose, drink, gulp, measure, pull, swallow, *inf* swig.

draw *n* **1** attraction, enticement, lure, *inf* pull. **2** dead-heat, dead-

158

lock, stalemate, tie. 3 competition, lottery, raffle. ● vb 1 drag, haul, lug, pull, tow, tug. 2 *draw a crowd.* allure, attract, bring in, coax, entice, invite, lure, persuade, pull in, win over. 3 *draw a sword.* extract, remove, take out, unsheathe, withdraw. 4 *draw lots.* choose, pick, select. 5 *draw a conclusion.* arrive at, come to, deduce, formulate, infer, work out. 6 *draw water.* drain, let (*blood*), pour, pump, syphon, tap. 7 *draw 1-1.* be equal, finish equal, tie. 8 *draw pictures.* depict, map out, mark out, outline, paint, pen, pencil, portray, represent, sketch, trace. **draw out** ▷ EXTEND. **draw up** ▷ DRAFT, HALT.

drawback n defect, difficulty, disadvantage, hindrance, hurdle, impediment, obstacle, obstruction, problem, snag, stumbling block.

drawing n cartoon, design, graphics, illustration, outline, sketch. ▷ PICTURE.

dread n anxiety, apprehension, awe, *inf* cold feet, dismay, fear, *inf* the jitters, nervousness, perturbation, qualm, trepidation, uneasiness, worry. ● vb be afraid of, shrink from, view with horror. ▷ FEAR.

dreadful adj alarming, appalling, awful, dire, distressing, evil, fearful, frightful, ghastly, grisly, gruesome, harrowing, hideous, horrible, horrifying, indescribable, monstrous, shocking, terrible, tragic, unspeakable, upsetting, wicked. ▷ BAD, FRIGHTENING.

dream n 1 daydream, delusion, fantasy, hallucination, illusion, mirage, nightmare, reverie,

trance, vision. 2 ambition, aspiration, idea', pipe-dream, wish. ● vb conjure up, daydream, fancy, fantasize, hallucinate, have a vision, imagine, think. **dream up** ▷ INVENT.

dreary adj bleak, boring, cheerless, depressing, dismal, dull, gloomy, joyless, sombre, uninteresting. ▷ MISERABLE.

dregs n deposit, grounds (*of coffee*), lees, precipitate, remains, residue, sediment.

drench vb douse, drown, flood, inundate, saturate, soak, souse, steep, wet thoroughly.

dress n 1 apparel, attire, clothing, costume, garb, garments, *inf* gear, *inf* get-up, outfit, *old use* raiment. ▷ CLOTHES. 2 frock, gown, robe, shift. ● vb 1 array, attire, clothe, cover, fit out, provide clothes for, put clothes on, robe. 2 *dress a wound.* attend to, bandage, bind up, care for, put a dressing on, tend, treat. *Opp* UNCOVER.

dressing n bandage, compress, plaster, poultice.

dribble vb 1 drool, slaver, slobber. 2 drip, flow, leak, ooze, run, seep, trickle.

drift n 1 accumulation, bank, dune, heap, mound, pile, ridge. 2 *drift of a speech.* ▷ GIST. ● vb 1 be carried, coast, float, meander, move casually, move slowly, ramble, roam, rove, stray, waft, walk aimlessly, wander. 2 *snow drifts.* accumulate, gather, make drifts, pile up.

drill n 1 discipline, exercises, instruction, practice, *sl* square-bashing, training. ● vb 1 coach,

drink

discipline, exercise, indoctrinate, instruct, practise, rehearse, school, teach, train. **2** bore, penetrate, perforate, pierce.

drink *n* **1** beverage, *inf* bevvy, *inf* cuppa, *inf* dram, draught, glass, *inf* gulp, *inf* night-cap, *inf* nip, pint, *joc* potation, sip, swallow, swig, *inf* tipple, tot. **2** alcohol, *inf* booze, *joc* grog, *joc* liquid refreshment, liquor. □ ale, beer, bourbon, brandy, champagne, chartreuse, cider, cocktail, Cognac, crème de menthe, gin, Kirsch, lager, mead, perry, *inf* plonk, port, punch, rum, schnapps, shandy, sherry, vermouth, vodka, whisky, wine. ● *vb* **1** gulp, guzzle, imbibe, *inf* knock back, lap, partake of, *old use* quaff, sip, suck, swallow, swig, *inf* swill. **2** *inf* booze, carouse, get drunk, *inf* indulge, tipple, tope.

drip *n* bead, dribble, drop, leak, splash, spot, tear, trickle. ● *vb* dribble, drizzle, drop, fall in drips, leak, plop, splash, sprinkle, trickle, weep.

drive *n* **1** excursion, jaunt, journey, outing, ride, run, *inf* spin, trip. **2** aggressiveness, ambition, determination, energy, enterprise, enthusiasm, *inf* get-up-and-go, impetus, industry, initiative, keenness, motivation, persistence, *inf* push, vigour, vim, zeal. **3** campaign, crusade, effort. ● *vb* **1** bang, dig, hammer, hit, impel, knock, plunge, prod, push, ram, sink, stab, strike, thrust. **2** coerce, compel, constrain, force, oblige, press, urge. **3** *drive a car.* control, direct, guide, handle, herd, manage, pilot, propel,

drug

send, steer. ▷ TRAVEL. **drive out** ▷ EXPEL.

droop *vb* be limp, bend, dangle, fall, flop, hang, sag, slump, wilt, wither.

drop *n* **1** bead, blob, bubble, dab, drip, droplet, globule, pearl, spot, tear. **2** dash, *inf* nip, small quantity, *inf* tot. **3** *a steep drop.* declivity, descent, dive, escarpment, fall, incline, plunge, precipice, scarp. **4** *a drop in price.* cut, decrease, reduction, slump. *Opp* RISE. ● *vb* **1** collapse, descend, dip, dive, fall, go down, jump down, lower, nose-dive, plummet, *inf* plump, plunge, sink, slump, subside, swoop, tumble. **2** *drop from a team.* eliminate, exclude, leave out, omit. **3** *drop a friend.* abandon, desert, discard, *inf* dump, forsake, give up, jilt, leave, reject, scrap, shed. **drop behind** ▷ LAG. **drop in on** ▷ VISIT. **drop off** ▷ SLEEP.

drown *vb* **1** engulf, flood, immerse, submerge, swamp. ▷ KILL. **2** *noise drowned my voice.* be louder than, overpower, overwhelm, silence.

drowsy *adj* dozing, dozy, heavy-eyed, listless, *inf* nodding off, sleepy, sluggish, somnolent, soporific, tired, weary. *Opp* LIVELY.

drudgery *n* chore, donkey-work, *inf* grind, labour, slavery, *inf* slog, toil, travail. ▷ WORK.

drug *n* **1** cure, medicament, medication, medicine, *old use* physic, remedy, treatment. **2** *inf* dope, narcotic, opiate. □ analgesic, antidepressant, barbiturate, hallucinogen, painkiller, sedative, stimulant, tonic, tranquilliser. □ caffeine, canna-

bis, cocaine, digitalis, hashish, heroin, insulin, laudanum, marijuana, morphia, nicotine, opium, phenobarbitone, quinine. ● *vb* anaesthetize, *inf* dope, dose, give a drug to, *inf* knock out, medicate, poison, sedate, stupefy, tranquillize, treat.

drum *n* 1 ▷ BARREL. 2 □ *bass-drum, bongo-drum, kettledrum, side-drum, snare-drum, tambour, tenor-drum,* plur *timpani, tom-tom.*

drunk *adj* delirious, fuddled, incapable, inebriate, inebriated, intoxicated, maudlin. [*slang*] blotto, bombed, boozed-up, canned, high, legless, merry, paralytic, pickled, pie-eyed, pissed, plastered, sloshed, soused, sozzled, stoned, tanked, tiddly, tight, tipsy. *Opp* SOBER.

drunkard *n* alcoholic, *inf* boozer, *sl* dipso, dipsomaniac, drunk, *inf* sot, tippler, toper, *sl* wino. *Opp* TEETOTALLER.

dry *adj* 1 arid, baked, barren, dead, dehydrated, desiccated, moistureless, parched, scorched, shrivelled, sterile, thirsty, waterless. *Opp* WET. 2 *a dry book.* boring, dreary, dull, flat, prosaic, stale, tedious, tiresome, uninspired, uninteresting. *Opp* LIVELY. 3 *dry humour.* *inf* dead-pan, droll, expressionless, laconic, lugubrious, unsmiling. ● *vb* become dry, dehumidify, dehydrate, desiccate, go hard, make dry, parch, shrivel, wilt, wither.

dual *adj* binary, coupled, double, duplicate, linked, paired, twin.

dubious *adj* 1 ▷ DOUBTFUL. 2 *a dubious character. inf* fishy,

inf shady, suspect, suspicious, unreliable, untrustworthy.

duck *vb* 1 avoid, bend, bob down, crouch, dip down, dodge, evade, sidestep, stoop, swerve, take evasive action. 2 immerse, plunge, push under, submerge.

due *adj* 1 in arrears, outstanding, owed, owing, payable, unpaid. 2 *due consideration.* adequate, appropriate, decent, deserved, expected, fitting, just, mature, merited, proper, requisite, right, rightful, scheduled, sufficient, suitable, well-earned. ● *n* deserts, entitlement, merits, reward, rights. **dues** ▷ DUTY.

dull *adj* 1 dim, dingy, dowdy, drab, dreary, faded, flat, gloomy, lacklustre, lifeless, matt, plain, shabby, sombre, subdued. 2 *a dull sky.* cloudy, dismal, grey, heavy, leaden, murky, overcast, sullen, sunless. 3 *a dull sound.* deadened, indistinct, muffled, muted. 4 *a dull student.* dense, dim, dim-witted, obtuse, slow, *inf* thick, unimaginative, unintelligent, unresponsive. ▷ STUPID. 5 *a dull edge.* blunt, blunted, unsharpened. 6 *dull talk.* boring, commonplace, dry, monotonous, prosaic, stodgy, tame, tedious, unexciting, uninteresting. *Opp* BRIGHT, SHARP.

dumb *adj* inarticulate, *inf* mum, mute, silent, speechless, tongue-tied, unable to speak.

dummy *n* 1 copy, counterfeit, duplicate, imitation, mock-up, model, reproduction, sample, sham, simulation, substitute, toy. 2 doll, figure, manikin, puppet.

dump n 1 junkyard, rubbish-heap, tip. 2 arms dump. arsenal, cache, depot, hoard, store. • vb deposit, discard, dispose of, inf ditch, drop, empty out, get rid of, jettison, offload, inf park, place, put down, reject, scrap, throw away, throw down, tip, unload.

dune n drift, hillock, hummock, mound, sand-dune.

dungeon n old use donjon, gaol, keep, lock-up, oubliette, pit, prison, vault.

duplicate adj alternative, copied, corresponding, identical, matching, second, twin. • n carbon copy, clone, copy, double, facsimile, imitation, likeness, inf look-alike, match, photocopy, photostat, replica, reproduction, twin, Xerox. • vb copy, do again, double up on, photocopy, print, repeat, reproduce, Xerox.

durable adj enduring, hard-wearing, heavy-duty, indes-tructible, long-lasting, perma-nent, resilient, stout, strong, substantial, thick, tough. Opp IMPERMANENT, WEAK.

dusk n evening, gloaming, gloom, sundown, sunset, twilight.

dust n dirt, grime, grit, particles, powder.

dusty adj 1 chalky, crumbly, dry, fine, friable, gritty, powdery, sandy, sooty. 2 a dusty room. dirty, filthy, grimy, grubby, mucky, uncleaned, unswept.

dutiful adj attentive, careful, compliant, conscientious, devo-ted, diligent, faithful, hard-working, loyal, obedient, oblig-ing, punctilious, reliable,

responsible, scrupulous, thor-ough, trustworthy, willing. Opp IRRESPONSIBLE.

duty n 1 allegiance, faithfulness, loyalty, obedience, obligation, onus, responsibility, service. 2 assignment, business, charge, chore, function, job, office, role, stint, task, work. 3 charge, customs, dues, fee, impost, levy, tariff, tax, toll.

dwarf adj ▷ SMALL. • n midget, pigmy. • vb dominate, look bigger than, overshadow, tower over.

dwell vb abide, be accommo-dated, live, lodge, reside, stay. **dwell in** ▷ INHABIT.

dwelling n abode, domicile, habitation, home, lodging, quarters, residence. ▷ HOUSE.

dying adj declining, expiring, fading, failing, moribund, obsol-escent. Opp ALIVE.

dynamic adj active, committed, driving, eager, energetic, enter-prising, enthusiastic, forceful, inf go-ahead, derog go-getting, high-powered, lively, moti-vated, powerful, pushful, derog pushy, spirited, vigorous, zealous. Opp APATHETIC.

E

eager adj agog, animated, anxious (to please), ardent, avid, bursting, committed, crav-ing, desirous, earnest, enthu-siastic, excited, fervent, fervid, hungry, impatient, intent, interested, inf itching, keen, inf keyed up, longing, moti-vated, passionate, inf raring (to *go*), voracious, yearning, zealous. Opp APATHETIC.

eagerness n alacrity, anxiety, appetite, ardour, avidity, commitment, desire, earnestness, enthusiasm, excitement, fervour, hunger, impatience, intentness, interest, keenness, longing, motivation, passion, thirst, zeal. Opp APATHY.

early adj 1 advance, ahead of time, before time, first, forward, premature. Opp LATE. 2 ancient, antiquated, initial, original, primeval, primitive. ▷ OLD. Opp RECENT.

earn vb 1 be paid, inf bring in, inf clear, draw, fetch in, gain, get, inf gross, make, make a profit of, net, realize, receive, inf take home, work for, yield. 2 attain, be worthy of, deserve, merit, qualify for, warrant, win.

earnest adj 1 assiduous, committed, conscientious, dedicated, determined, devoted, diligent, eager, hard-working, industrious, involved, purposeful, resolved, zealous. Opp CASUAL. 2 grave, heartfelt, impassioned, serious, sincere, sober, solemn, thoughtful, well-meant.

earnings n income, salary, stipend, wages. ▷ PAY.

earth n clay, dirt, ground, humus, land, loam, soil, topsoil.

earthenware n ceramics, china, crockery, inf crocks, porcelain, pots, pottery.

earthly adj corporeal, human, material, materialistic, mortal, mundane, physical, secular, temporal, terrestrial, worldly. Opp SPIRITUAL.

earthquake n quake, shock, tremor, upheaval.

earthy adj bawdy, coarse, crude, down to earth, frank, lusty, ribald, uninhibited. ▷ OBSCENE.

ease n 1 aplomb, calmness, comfort, composure, contentment, enjoyment, happiness, leisure, luxury, peace, quiet, relaxation, repose, rest, serenity, tranquillity. 2 dexterity, easiness, effortlessness, facility, nonchalance, simplicity, skill, speed, straightforwardness. Opp DIFFICULTY. ● vb 1 allay, alleviate, assuage, calm, comfort, decrease, lessen, lighten, mitigate, moderate, pacify, quell, quieten, reduce, relax, relieve, slacken, soothe, tranquillize. 2 edge, guide, inch, manoeuvre, move gradually, slide, slip, steer.

easy adj 1 carefree, comfortable, contented, cosy, inf cushy, effortless, leisurely, light, painless, peaceful, pleasant, relaxed, relaxing, restful, serene, soft, tranquil, undemanding, unexacting, unhurried, untroubled. 2 clear, elementary, facile, foolproof, inf idiot-proof, manageable, plain, simple, straightforward, uncomplicated, understandable, user-friendly. 3 ▷ EASYGOING. Opp DIFFICULTY.

easygoing adj accommodating, affable, amenable, calm, carefree, casual, cheerful, docile, even-tempered, flexible, forbearing, inf free and easy, friendly, genial, inf happy-go-lucky, indulgent, informal, inf laid-back, derog lax, lenient, liberal, mellow, natural, nonchalant, open, patient, permissive, placid, relaxed, tolerant, unexcitable, unruffled, derog weak. Opp STRICT.

eat *vb* consume, devour, digest, feed on, ingest, live on, *old use* partake of, swallow. □ *bite, bolt, champ, chew, crunch, gnaw, gobble, gorge, gormandize, graze, grind, gulp, guzzle, inf make a pig of yourself, masticate, munch, nibble, overeat, peck, inf scoff, inf slurp, inf stuff (yourself), taste, inf tuck in, inf wolf.* □ *banquet, breakfast, dine, feast, lunch, snack, old use sup.* **eat away, eat into** ▷ ERODE.

eatable *adj* digestible, edible, fit to eat, good, palatable, safe to eat, wholesome. ▷ TASTY. *Opp* INEDIBLE.

ebb *vb* fall, flow back, go down, recede, retreat, subside. ▷ DECLINE.

eccentric *adj* 1 aberrant, abnormal, anomalous, atypical, bizarre, cranky, curious, freakish, grotesque, idiosyncratic, *sl* kinky, odd, outlandish, out of the ordinary, peculiar, preposterous, quaint, queer, quirky, singular, strange, unconventional, unusual, *sl* wacky, *inf* way-out, *inf* weird, *inf* zany. ▷ ABSURD, MAD. 2 *eccentric circles.* irregular, off-centre.
• *n inf* character, *inf* crackpot, crank, *inf* freak, individualist, nonconformist, *inf* oddball, oddity, *inf* weirdie, *inf* weirdo.

echo *vb* 1 resound, reverberate, ring, sound again. 2 ape, copy, duplicate, emulate, imitate, mimic, mirror, reiterate, repeat, reproduce, say again.

eclipse *vb* 1 block out, blot out, cloud, darken, dim, extinguish, obscure, veil. ▷ COVER. 2 excel, outdo, outshine, overshadow, *inf* put in the shade, surpass, top.

economic *adj* budgetary, business, financial, fiscal, monetary, money-making, trading.

economical *adj* 1 careful, cheese-paring, frugal, parsimonious, prudent, prudent, sparing, thrifty. ▷ MISERLY. *Opp* WASTEFUL. 2 *an economical meal.* cheap, cost-effective, inexpensive, low-priced, moneysaving, reasonable, *inf* value-for-money. *Opp* EXPENSIVE.

economize *vb* be economical, cut back, retrench, save, *inf* scrimp, skimp, spend less, *inf* tighten your belt. *Opp* SQUANDER.

economy *n* 1 frugality, *derog* meanness, *derog* miserliness, parsimony, providence, prudence, saving, thrift. *Opp* WASTE. 2 *the national economy.* budget, economic affairs, wealth. 3 ▷ BREVITY.

ecstasy *n* bliss, delight, delirium, elation, enthusiasm, euphoria, exaltation, fervour, frenzy, gratification, happiness, joy, rapture, thrill, trance, *old use* transport.

ecstatic *adj* blissful, delighted, delirious, elated, enraptured, enthusiastic, euphoric, exhilarated, exultant, fervent, frenzied, gleeful, joyful, orgasmic, overjoyed, *inf* over the moon, rapturous, transported. ▷ HAPPY.

eddy *n* circular movement, maelstrom, swirl, vortex, whirl, whirlpool, whirlwind.
• *n* move in circles, spin, swirl, turn, whirl.

edge *n* 1 border, boundary, brim, brink, circumference, frame, kerb, limit, lip, margin, outline, perimeter, periphery, rim, side, verge. **2** *edge of town.* outlying parts, outskirts, suburbs. **3** *edge on a knife.* acuteness, keenness, sharpness. **4** *edge of a curtain.* edging, fringe, hem, selvage. • *vb* **1** bind, border, fringe, hem, make an edge for, trim. **2** *edge away.* crawl, creep, inch, move stealthily, sidle, slink, steal, work your way, worm.

edible *adj* digestible, eatable, fit to eat, palatable, safe to eat, wholesome. ▷ TASTY. *Opp* INEDIBLE.

edit *vb* adapt, alter, amend, arrange, assemble, compile, get ready, modify, organize, prepare, put together, select, supervise the production of. □ abridge, annotate, bowdlerize, censor, clean up, condense, copy-edit, correct, cut, dub, emend, expurgate, format, polish, proof-read, rearrange, rephrase, revise, rewrite, select, shorten, splice (film).

edition *n* **1** copy, issue, number. **2** impression, printing, print-run, publication, version.

educate *vb* bring up, civilize, coach, counsel, cultivate, discipline, drill, edify, enlighten, guide, improve, inculcate, indoctrinate, inform, instruct, lecture, nurture, rear, school, teach, train, tutor.

educated *adj* cultured, enlightened, erudite, knowledgeable, learned, literate, numerate, sophisticated, trained, well-bred, well-read.

education *n* coaching, curriculum, enlightenment, guidance, indoctrination, instruction, schooling, syllabus, teaching,

training, tuition. □ academy, college, conservatory, polytechnic, sixth-form college, tertiary college, university. ▷ SCHOOL, TEACHING.

eerie *adj inf* creepy, frightening, ghostly, mysterious, *inf* scary, spectral, *inf* spooky, strange, uncanny, unearthly, unnatural, weird.

effect *n* **1** aftermath, conclusion, consequence, impact, influence, issue, outcome, repercussion, result, sequel, upshot. **2** feeling, illusion, impression, sensation, sense. • *vb* accomplish, achieve, bring about, bring in, carry out, cause, create, effectuate, enforce, execute, implement, initiate, make, produce, put into effect, secure.

effective *adj* **1** able, capable, competent, effectual, efficacious, functional, impressive, potent, powerful, productive, proficient, real, serviceable, strong, successful, useful, worthwhile. ▷ EFFICIENT. **2** *an effective argument.* cogent, compelling, convincing, meaningful, persuasive, striking, telling. *Opp* INEFFECTIVE.

effeminate *adj* camp, effete, girlish, *inf* pansy, *inf* sissy, unmanly, weak, womanish. *Opp* MANLY.

effervesce *vb* bubble, ferment, fizz, foam, froth, sparkle.

effervescent *adj* bubbling, bubbly, carbonated, fizzy, foaming, frothy, gassy, sparkling.

efficient *adj* businesslike, cost-effective, economic, productive, streamlined, thrifty. ▷ EFFECTIVE. *Opp* INEFFICIENT.

effort *n* **1** application, diligence, *inf* elbow grease, endeavour, exertion, industry, labour, pains, strain, stress, striving, struggle, toil, *old use* travail, trouble, work. **2** *a brave effort.* attempt, endeavour, go, try, venture. **3** *a successful effort.* accomplishment, achievement, exploit, feat, job, outcome, product, production, result.

effusive *adj* demonstrative, ebullient, enthusiastic, exuberant, fulsome, gushing, lavish, *inf* over the top, profuse, voluble. *Opp* RETICENT.

egoism *n* egocentricity, egotism, narcissism, pride, self-centredness, self-importance, self-interest, selfishness, self-love, self-regard, vanity.

egotistical *adj* egocentric, self-admiring, self-centred, selfish. ▷ CONCEITED.

eject *vb* **1** banish, *inf* boot out, *inf* bundle out, deport, discharge, dismiss, drive out, evict, exile, expel, get rid of, *inf* kick out, oust, push out, put out, remove, sack, send out, shoot out, *inf* shove out, throw out, turn out. **2** ▷ EMIT.

elaborate *adj* **1** complex, complicated, detailed, exhaustive, intricate, involved, meticulous, minute, painstaking, thorough, well worked out. **2** *elaborate décor.* baroque, busy, Byzantine, decorative, fancy, fantastic, fussy, grotesque, intricate, ornamental, ornamented, ornate, rococo, showy. *Opp* SIMPLE. ● *vb* add to, adorn, amplify, complicate, decorate, develop, embellish, enlarge on, enrich, expand, expatiate on, fill out, flesh out, give details of, improve on, ornament. *Opp* SIMPLIFY.

elapse *vb* go by, lapse, pass, slip by.

elastic *adj* bendy, bouncy, ductile, expandable, flexible, plastic, pliable, pliant, resilient, rubbery, *inf* springy, stretchable, *inf* stretchy, yielding. *Opp* RIGID.

elderly *adj* ageing, *inf* getting on, oldish. ▷ OLD.

elect *adj* [*goes after noun*] *president elect.* [*synonyms used after noun*] designate, to be; [*synonyms before noun*] chosen, elected, prospective, selected. ● *vb* adopt, appoint, choose, name, nominate, opt for, pick, select, vote for.

election *n* ballot, choice, plebiscite, poll, referendum, selection, vote, voting.

electioneer *vb* campaign, canvass.

electorate *n* constituents, electors, voters.

electric *adj* **1** battery-operated, electrical, mains-operated. **2** *electric atmosphere.* electrifying. ▷ EXCITING.

electricity *n* current, energy, power, power supply.

elegant *adj* artistic, beautiful, chic, courtly, cultivated, dapper, debonair, dignified, exquisite, fashionable, fine, genteel, graceful, gracious, handsome, luxurious, modish, noble, pleasing, *inf* plush, *inf* posh, refined, smart, soigné(e), sophisticated, splendid, stately, stylish, suave, tasteful, urbane, well-bred. *Opp* INELEGANT.

elegy *n* dirge, lament, requiem.

element *n* **1** component, constituent, detail, essential, factor, feature, fragment, hint, ingredient, part, piece, small amount, trace, unit. **2** *in your element*. domain, environment, habitat, medium, sphere, territory. **elements** ▷ RUDIMENTS, WEATHER.

elementary *adj* basic, early, first, fundamental, initial, introductory, primary, principal, rudimentary, simple, straightforward, uncomplicated, understandable. ▷ EASY. *Opp* ADVANCED.

elevate *vb* exalt, hold up, lift, make higher, promote, rear. ▷ RAISE. **elevated** ▷ HIGH, NOBLE.

elicit *vb* bring out, call forth, derive, draw out, evoke, extort, extract, get, obtain, wrest, wring.

eligible *adj* acceptable, allowed, appropriate, authorized, available, competent, equipped, fit, fitting, proper, qualified, suitable, worthy. *Opp* INELIGIBLE.

eliminate *vb* **1** abolish, annihilate, delete, destroy, dispense with, do away with, eject, end, eradicate, exterminate, extinguish, finish off, get rid of, put an end to, remove, stamp out. ▷ KILL. **2** cut out, drop, exclude, knock out, leave out, omit, reject.

élite *n* aristocracy, best, *inf* cream, first-class people, flower, meritocracy, nobility, top people, *inf* upper crust.

eloquent *adj* articulate, expressive, fluent, forceful, *derog* glib, moving, persuasive, plausible, powerful, unfaltering. *Opp* INARTICULATE.

elude *vb* avoid, circumvent, dodge, *inf* duck, escape, evade,

foil, get away from, *inf* give (someone) the slip, shake off, slip away from.

elusive *adj* **1** *inf* always on the move, evasive, fugitive, hard to find, slippery. **2** *elusive meaning*. ambiguous, baffling, deceptive, hard to pin down, indefinable, intangible, puzzling, shifting.

emaciated *adj* anorectic, atrophied, bony, cadaverous, gaunt, haggard, shrivelled, skeletal, skinny, starved, underfed, undernourished, wasted away, wizened. ▷ THIN.

emancipate *vb* deliver, discharge, enfranchise, free, give rights to, let go, liberate, loose, manumit, release, set free, unchain. *Opp* ENSLAVE.

embankment *n* bank, causeway, dam, earthwork, mound, rampart.

embark *vb* board, depart, go aboard, leave, set out. *Opp* DISEMBARK. **embark on** ▷ BEGIN.

embarrass *vb* abash, chagrin, confuse, discomfit, discompose, disconcert, discountenance, disgrace, distress, fluster, humiliate, *inf* make you blush, mortify, *inf* put you on the spot, shame, *inf* show up, upset. **embarrassed** ▷ ASHAMED. **embarrassing** ▷ AWKWARD, SHAMEFUL.

embellish *vb* adorn, beautify, deck, decorate, embroider, garnish, ornament, *sl* tart up, *inf* titivate. ▷ ELABORATE.

embezzle *vb* appropriate, misapply, misappropriate, peculate, *inf* put your hand in the till, take fraudulently. ▷ STEAL.

embezzlement *n* fraud, misappropriation, misuse of

funds, peculation, stealing, theft.

embittered *adj* acid, bitter, disillusioned, envious, rancorous, resentful, sour. ▷ ANGRY.

emblem *n* badge, crest, device, image, insignia, mark, regalia, seal, sign, symbol, token.

embody *vb* 1 exemplify, express, incarnate, manifest, personify, reify, represent, stand for, symbolize. 2 bring together, combine, comprise, embrace, enclose, gather together, include, incorporate, integrate, involve, take in, unite.

embrace *vb* 1 clasp, cling to, cuddle, enfold, fondle, grasp, hold, hug, kiss, snuggle up to. 2 *embrace new ideas*. accept, espouse, receive, take on, welcome. 3 ▷ EMBODY.

embryonic *adj* early, immature, just beginning, rudimentary, underdeveloped, undeveloped, unformed. *Opp* MATURE.

emerge *vb* appear, arise, be revealed, come out, come to light, come to notice, emanate, *old use* issue forth, leak out, *inf* pop up, proceed, surface, transpire, *inf* turn out.

emergency *n* crisis, danger, difficulty, exigency, predicament, serious situation.

emigrate *vb* depart, go abroad, leave, quit, relocate, resettle, set out.

eminent *adj* august, celebrated, conspicuous, distinguished, elevated, esteemed, exalted, familiar, famous, great, high-ranking, honoured, illustrious, important, notable, noted, noteworthy, outstanding, pre-eminent, prominent, renowned, well-known. *Opp* LOWLY.

emit *vb* belch, discharge, disgorge, ejaculate, eject, exhale, expel, exude, give off, give out, issue, radiate, send out, spew out, spout, transmit, vent, vomit.

emotion *n* agitation, excitement, feeling, fervour, passion, sentiment, warmth. ▷ ANGER, LOVE, etc.

emotional *adj* 1 ardent, demonstrative, enthusiastic, excited, fervent, fiery, heated, hot-headed, impassioned, intense, irrational, moved, passionate, romantic, stirred, touched, warm-hearted, *inf* worked up. ▷ ANGRY, LOVING, etc. 2 *emotional language*. affecting, biased, emotive, heartfelt, heart-rending, inflammatory, loaded, moving, pathetic, poignant, prejudiced, provocative, sentimental, stirring, subjective, tear-jerking, tender, touching. *Opp* UNEMOTIONAL.

emphasis *n* accent, attention, force, gravity, importance, intensity, priority, prominence, strength, stress, urgency, weight.

emphasize *vb* accent, accentuate, bring out, dwell on, focus on, foreground, give emphasis to, highlight, impress, insist on, make obvious, *inf* play up, point up, *inf* press home, *inf* rub it in, show clearly, spotlight, stress, underline, underscore.

emphatic *adj* affirmative, assertive, categorical, confident, dogmatic, definite, firm, forceful, insistent, positive, pronounced, resolute, strong, uncompromising, unequivocal. *Opp* TENTATIVE.

empirical adj experiential, experimental, observed, practical, pragmatic. Opp THEORETICAL.

employ vb 1 commission, engage, enlist, have on the payroll, hire, pay, sign up, take on, use the services of. 2 apply, use, utilize.

employed adj active, busy, earning, engaged, hired, involved, in work, occupied, practising, working. ▷ BUSY. Opp UNEMPLOYED.

employee n old use hand, inf underling, worker. **employees** staff, workforce.

employer n boss, chief, inf gaffer, inf governor, head, manager, owner, proprietor, taskmaster.

employment n business, calling, craft, job, line, livelihood, living, métier, occupation, profession, pursuit, trade, vocation, work.

empty adj 1 bare, blank, clean, clear, deserted, desolate, forsaken, hollow, unfilled, unfurnished, uninhabited, unladen, unoccupied, unused, vacant, void. Opp FULL. 2 empty threats. futile, idle, impotent, ineffective, insincere, meaningless, pointless, purposeless, senseless, silly, unreal, worthless. ● vb clear, discharge, drain, eject, evacuate, exhaust, pour out, remove, take out, unload, vacate, void. Opp FILL.

enable vb aid, allow, approve, assist, authorize, charter, empower, entitle, equip, facilitate, franchise, help, license, make it possible, permit, provide the means, qualify, sanction. Opp PREVENT.

enchant vb allure, beguile, bewitch, captivate, cast a spell on, charm, delight, enrapture, enthral, entrance, fascinate, hypnotize, mesmerize, spellbind. **enchanting** ▷ ATTRACTIVE.

enchantment n charm, conjuration, magic, sorcery, spell, witchcraft, wizardry. ▷ DELIGHT.

enclose vb bound, box, cage, case, cocoon, conceal, confine, contain, cover, encase, encircle, encompass, enfold, envelop, fence in, hedge in, hem in, immure, insert, limit, package, parcel up, pen, restrict, ring, secure, sheathe, shut in, shut up, surround, wall in, wall up, wrap. ▷ IMPRISON.

enclosure n 1 arena, cage, compound, coop, corral, court, courtyard, farmyard, field, fold, paddock, pen, pound, ring, run, sheepfold, stockade, sty, yard. 2 enclosure in an envelope. contents, inclusion, insertion.

encounter n 1 confrontation, meeting. 2 [military] battle, brush, clash, dispute, skirmish, struggle. ▷ FIGHT. ● vb chance upon, clash with, come upon, confront, contend with, inf cross swords with, face, grapple with, happen upon, have an encounter with, meet, inf run into.

encourage vb 1 abet, advocate, animate, applaud, cheer, inf egg on, embolden, give hope to, hearten, incite, inspire, invite, persuade, prompt, rally, reassure, rouse, spur on, support, urge. 2 encourage sales. aid, be an incentive to, be conducive to, boost, engender, foster, further, generate, help, increase, induce, promote, stimulate. *Opp* DISCOURAGE.

encouragement *n* applause, approval, boost, cheer, exhortation, incentive, incitement, inspiration, reassurance, *inf* shot in the arm, stimulation, stimulus, support. *Opp* DISCOURAGEMENT.

encouraging *adj* comforting, heartening, hopeful, inspiring, optimistic, positive, promising, reassuring. ▷ FAVOURABLE.

encroach *vb* enter, impinge, infringe, intrude, invade, make inroads, trespass, violate.

end *n* 1 boundary, edge, extreme, extremity, limit, pole, tip. 2 cessation, close, coda, completion, conclusion, culmination, curtain (*of play*), denouement (*of plot*), ending, expiration, expiry, finale, finish, *inf* pay-off, resolution. 3 *journey's end*. destination, home, termination, terminus. 4 *end of a queue*. back, rear, tail. 5 *end of your life*. destiny, destruction, doom, extinction, fate, passing, ruin. ▷ DEATH. 6 *an end in view*. aim, aspiration, consequence, design, effect, intention, objective, outcome, plan, purpose, result, upshot. *Opp* BEGINNING.
• *vb* 1 abolish, break off, bring to an end, complete, conclude, cut off, destroy, discontinue, *inf* drop, eliminate, exterminate, finalize, *inf* get rid of, halt, phase out, *inf* put an end to, *inf* round off, ruin, scotch, terminate, *inf* wind up. 2 break up, cease, close, come to an end, culminate, die, disappear, expire, fade away, finish, *inf* pack up, reach a climax, stop. *Opp* BEGIN.

endanger *vb* expose to risk, imperil, jeopardize, put at risk, threaten. *Opp* PROTECT.

endearing *adj* appealing, attractive, captivating, charming, disarming, enchanting, engaging, likable, lovable, sweet, winning, winsome. *Opp* REPULSIVE.

endeavour *vb* aim, aspire, attempt, do your best, exert yourself, strive, try.

endless *adj* 1 boundless, immeasurable, inexhaustible, infinite, limitless, measureless, unbounded, unfailing, unlimited. 2 abiding, ceaseless, constant, continual, continuous, enduring, eternal, everlasting, immortal, incessant, interminable, never-ending, nonstop, perpetual, persistent, unbroken, undying, unending, uninterrupted.

endorse *vb* 1 advocate, agree with, approve, authorize, *inf* back, condone, confirm, *inf* sanction, set your seal of approval to, subscribe to, support. 2 *endorse a cheque*. countersign, sign.

endurance *n* determination, fortitude, patience, perseverance, persistence, pertinacity, resolution, stamina, staying-power, strength, tenacity.

endure *vb* 1 carry on, continue, exist, last, live on, persevere, persist, prevail, remain, stay, survive. 2 bear, cope with, experience, go through, *inf* put up with, stand, *inf* stick, *inf* stomach, submit to, suffer, *sl* sweat it out, tolerate, undergo, weather, withstand. **enduring** ▷ ENDLESS.

enemy *n* adversary, antagonist, assailant, attacker, competitor,

foe, opponent, opposition, the
other side, rival, *inf* them.
Opp FRIEND.

energetic *adj* active, animated,
brisk, dynamic, enthusiastic,
fast, forceful, hard-working,
high-powered, indefatigable,
lively, powerful, quick-moving,
spirited, strenuous, tireless,
unflagging, vigorous, zestful.
Opp LETHARGIC.

energy *n* 1 animation, ardour,
inf dash, drive, dynamism,
élan, enthusiasm, exertion, fire,
force, forcefulness, *inf* get-up-
and-go, *inf* go, life, liveliness,
might, *inf* pep, spirit, stamina,
strength, verve, vigour, *inf* vim,
vitality, vivacity, zeal, zest.
Opp LETHARGY. 2 fuel, power.

enforce *vb* administer, apply,
carry out, compel, execute,
implement, impose, inflict,
insist on, prosecute, put into
effect, require, stress.
Opp WAIVE.

engage *vb* 1 contract with,
employ, enlist, hire, recruit,
sign up, take on. 2 *cogs engage.*
bite, fit together, interlock.
3 *engage to do something.*
▷ PROMISE. 4 *engaged me in
gossip.* ▷ OCCUPY. 5 *engage in
sport.* ▷ PARTICIPATE.

engaged *adj* 1 affianced,
betrothed, *old use* plighted, *old
use* promised, *old use* spoken
for. 2 ▷ BUSY.

engagement *n* 1 betrothal,
promise to marry, *old use* troth.
2 *social engagements.* appointment, arrangement, commitment, date, fixture, meeting,
obligation, rendezvous.
3 ▷ BATTLE.

engine *n* 1 machine, motor.
□ diesel, electric, internal-

combustion, jet, outboard,
petrol, steam, turbine, turbo-jet,
turbo-prop. 2 locomotive.

engineer *n* mechanic, technician. ● *vb* ▷ CONSTRUCT, DEVISE.

engrave *vb* carve, chisel, etch,
inscribe. ▷ CUT.

enigma *n* conundrum, mystery,
inf poser, problem, puzzle,
riddle.

enjoy *vb* 1 admire, appreciate,
bask in, be happy in, delight in,
inf go in for, indulge in, *inf* lap
up, luxuriate in, rejoice in,
relish, revel in, savour, take
pleasure from, take pleasure in.
▷ LIKE. 2 benefit from, experience, have, take advantage of,
use. **enjoy yourself** celebrate,
inf gad about, *inf* have a fling,
have a good time, make merry.

enjoyable *adj* agreeable, amusing, delicious, delightful, diverting, entertaining, gratifying,
likeable, *inf* nice, pleasurable,
rewarding, satisfying.
▷ PLEASANT. *Opp* UNPLEASANT.

enlarge *vb* amplify, augment,
blow up, broaden, build up,
develop, dilate, distend, diversify, elongate, expand, extend,
fill out, grow, increase, inflate,
lengthen, magnify, multiply,
spread, stretch, supplement,
swell, wax, widen.
Opp DECREASE. **enlarge on**
▷ ELABORATE.

enlighten *vb* edify, illuminate,
inform, make aware. ▷ TEACH.

enlist *vb* 1 conscript, engage,
enrol, impress, muster, recruit,
sign up. 2 *enlist in the army.*
enrol, enter, join up, register,
sign on, volunteer. 3 *enlist help.*
▷ OBTAIN.

enliven *vb* animate, arouse,
brighten, cheer up, energize,

inspire, *inf* pep up, quicken, rouse, stimulate, vitalize, wake up.

enormous *adj* Brobdingnagian, colossal, elephantine, gargantuan, giant, gigantic, gross, huge, hulking, immense, *inf* jumbo, mammoth, massive, mighty, monstrous, mountainous, prodigious, stupendous, titanic, towering, tremendous, vast. ▷ BIG. *Opp* SMALL.

enough *adj* adequate, ample, as much as necessary, sufficient.

enquire *vb* ask, beg, demand, entreat, implore, inquire, query, question, request.
enquire about ▷ INVESTIGATE.

enrage *vb* incense, inflame, infuriate, madden, provoke. ▷ ANGER.

enslave *vb* disenfranchise, dominate, make slaves of, subject, subjugate, take away the rights of. *Opp* EMANCIPATE.

ensure *vb* confirm, guarantee, make certain, make sure, secure.

entail *vb* call for, demand, give rise to, involve, lead to, necessitate, require.

enter *vb* 1 arrive, come in, get in, go in, infiltrate, invade, move in, step in. *Opp* DEPART. 2 dig into, penetrate, pierce, puncture, push into. 3 *enter a contest.* engage in, enlist in, enrol in, *inf* go in for, join, participate in, sign up for, take part in, take up, volunteer for. 4 *enter names on a list.* add, inscribe, insert, note down, put down, record, register, set down, sign, write. *Opp* REMOVE.
enter into ▷ BEGIN.

enterprise *n* 1 adventure, effort, endeavour, operation,

programme, project, undertaking, venture. 2 adventurousness, ambition, boldness, courage, daring, determination, drive, energy, *inf* get-up-and-go, initiative, *inf* push. 3 business, company, concern, firm, organization.

enterprising *adj* adventurous, ambitious, bold, courageous, daring, determined, eager, energetic, enthusiastic, *inf* goahead, *derog* go-getting, hardworking, imaginative, indefatigable, industrious, intrepid, keen, purposeful, *inf* pushful, *derog* pushy, resourceful, spirited, venturesome, vigorous, zealous. *Opp* UNADVENTUROUS.

entertain *vb* 1 amuse, cheer up, delight, divert, keep amused, make laugh, occupy, please, regale, *inf* tickle. *Opp* BORE. 2 *entertain friends.* accommodate, be host to, be hostess to, cater for, give hospitality to, *inf* put up, receive, treat, welcome. 3 *entertain an idea.* accept, agree to, approve, consent to, consider, contemplate, harbour, support, take seriously. *Opp* IGNORE. **entertaining** ▷ INTERESTING.

entertainer *n* artist, artiste, performer. □ acrobat, actor, actress, ballerina, broadcaster, busker, clown, comedian, comic, compère, conjurer, dancer, disc jockey, DJ, impersonator, jester, juggler, lion-tamer, magician, matador, mime artist, minstrel, singer, stunt man, toreador, trapeze artist, trouper, ventriloquist. ▷ MUSICIAN.

entertainment *n* 1 amusement, distraction, diversion, enjoyment, fun, night-life, pastime, play, pleasure, recreation, sport. **2** divertissement, exhibition, extravaganza, performance, presentation, production, show, spectacle. □ *ballet, bullfight, cabaret, casino, ceilidh, cinema, circus, concert, dance, disco, discothèque, fair, firework display, flower show, gymkhana, motor show, nightclub, pageant, pantomime, play, radio, recital, recitation, revue, rodeo, son et lumière, tattoo, television, variety show, waxworks, zoo.* ▷ DANCE, DRAMA, MUSIC, SPORT.

enthusiasm *n* **1** ambition, ardour, avidity, commitment, drive, eagerness, excitement, exuberance, *derog* fanaticism, fervour, gusto, keenness, panache, passion, relish, spirit, verve, zeal, zest. *Opp* APATHY. **2** craze, diversion, *inf* fad, hobby, interest, passion, pastime.

enthusiast *n* addict, adherent, admirer, aficionado, *inf* buff, champion, devotee, fan, fanatic, *sl* fiend, *sl* freak, lover, supporter, zealot.

enthusiastic *adj* ambitious, ardent, avid, committed, *inf* crazy, delighted, devoted, eager, earnest, ebullient, energetic, excited, exuberant, fervent, fervid, hearty, impassioned, interested, involved, irrepressible, keen, lively, *inf* mad (about), *inf* mad keen, motivated, optimistic, passionate, positive, rapturous, raring (*to go*), spirited, unqualified, unstinting, vigorous, wholehearted, zealous. *Opp* APATHETIC. **be enthusiastic** enthuse, get excited, *inf* go into raptures, *inf* go overboard, rave.

entice *vb* allure, attract, cajole, coax, decoy, inveigle, lead on, lure, persuade, seduce, tempt, trap, wheedle.

entire *adj* complete, full, intact, sound, total, unbroken, undivided, uninterrupted, whole.

entitle *vb* **1** call, christen, designate, dub, name, style, term, title. **2** *A licence entitles you to drive.* allow, authorize, empower, enable, justify, license, permit, qualify, warrant.

entitlement *n* claim, ownership, prerogative, right, title.

entity *n* article, being, object, organism, thing, whole.

entrails *n* bowels, guts, *inf* innards, inner organs, *inf* insides, intestines, viscera.

entrance *n* **1** access, admission, admittance. **2** appearance, arrival, coming, entry. **3** door, doorway, gate, gateway, ingress, opening, portal, turnstile, way in. **4** ante-room, entrance hall, foyer, lobby, passage, passageway, porch, vestibule. *Opp* EXIT.

entrant *n* applicant, candidate, competitor, contender, contestant, entry, participant, player, rival.

entreat *vb* ask, beg, beseech, implore, importune, petition, sue, supplicate. ▷ REQUEST.

entry *n* **1** insertion, item, jotting, listing, note, record. **2** ▷ ENTRANCE. **3** ▷ ENTRANT.

envelop *vb* cloak, cover, enclose, enfold, enshroud, enwrap, shroud, swathe, veil, wrap. ▷ HIDE.

envelope *n* cover, sheath, wrapper, wrapping.

enviable adj attractive, covetable, desirable, favourable, sought-after.

envious adj begrudging, bitter, covetous, dissatisfied, inf green-eyed, inf green with envy, grudging, jaundiced, jealous, resentful.

environment n circumstances, conditions, context, ecosystem, environs, habitat, location, milieu, setting, situation, surroundings, territory.

envisage vb anticipate, contemplate, dream of, envision, fancy, forecast, foresee, imagine, picture, predict, visualize.

envy n bitterness, covetousness, cupidity, desire, discontent, dissatisfaction, ill-will, jealousy, longing, resentment.
• vb begrudge, grudge, resent.

ephemeral adj brief, evanescent, fleeting, fugitive, impermanent, momentary, passing, short-lived, temporary, transient, transitory. Opp PERMANENT.

epidemic adj general, pandemic, prevalent, spreading, universal, widespread. • n outbreak, pestilence, plague, rash, upsurge.

episode n 1 affair, event, happening, incident, matter, occurrence. 2 chapter, instalment, part, passage, scene, section.

epitome n 1 archetype, embodiment, essence, exemplar, incarnation, personification, quintessence, representation, type. 2 ▷ SUMMARY.

equal adj balanced, coextensive, commensurate, congruent, correspondent, egalitarian, even, fair, identical, indistinguishable, interchangeable,

level, like, matched, matching, proportionate, regular, the same, symmetrical, uniform. ▷ EQUIVALENT. Opp UNEQUAL.
• n clone, compeer, counterpart, equivalent, fellow, peer, twin. • vb 1 balance, correspond to, draw with, tie with. 2 No one equals Caruso. be in the same class as, compare with, match, parallel, resemble, rival, vie with.

equality n 1 balance, congruence, correspondence, equivalence, identity, similarity, uniformity. Opp BIAS. 2 social equality. egalitarianism, even-handedness, fairness, justice, parity. Opp INEQUALITY.

equalize vb balance, catch up, compensate, even up, level, make equal, match, regularize, inf square, standardize.

equate vb assume to be equal, compare, juxtapose, liken, match, parallel, set side by side.

equilibrium n balance, equanimity, equipoise, evenness, poise, stability, steadiness, symmetry.

equip vb accoutre, arm, array, attire, caparison, clothe, dress, fit out, fit up, furnish, inf kit out, outfit, provide, stock, supply.

equipment n accoutrements, apparatus, appurtenances, sl clobber, furnishings, inf gear, inf hardware, implements, instruments, kit, machinery, materials, outfit, paraphernalia, plant, inf rig, inf stuff, supplies, tackle, inf things, tools, trappings. ▷ CLOTHES.

equivalent adj alike, analogous, comparable, corresponding, fair, interchangeable, parallel, proportionate, *Lat* pro rata, similar, synonymous. ▷ EQUAL.

equivocal *adj* ambiguous, circumlocutory, equivocating, evasive, noncommittal, oblique, periphrastic, questionable, roundabout, suspect.

equivocate *vb inf* beat about the bush, be equivocal, dodge the issue, fence, *inf* have it both ways, hedge, prevaricate, quibble, waffle.

era *n* age, date, day, epoch, period, time.

eradicate *vb* eliminate, erase, get rid of, root out, uproot. ▷ DESTROY.

erase *vb* cancel, cross out, delete, efface, eradicate, expunge, obliterate, rub out, wipe away, wipe off. ▷ REMOVE.

erect *adj* perpendicular, rigid, standing, straight, upright, vertical. ● *vb* build, construct, elevate, establish, lift up, make upright, pitch (*a tent*), put up, raise, set up.

erode *vb* abrade, corrode, eat away, eat into, gnaw away, grind down, wash away, wear away.

erotic *adj* amatory, amorous, aphrodisiac, arousing, lubricious, lustful, *sl* randy, *sl* raunchy, seductive, sensual, venereal, voluptuous. ▷ SEXY.

err *vb* be mistaken, be naughty, *sl* boob, *inf* get it wrong, go astray, go wrong, misbehave, miscalculate, sin, *inf* slip up, transgress.

errand *n* assignment, commission, duty, job, journey, mission, task, trip.

erratic *adj* 1 aberrant, capricious, changeable, fickle, fitful,

fluctuating, inconsistent, irregular, shifting, spasmodic, sporadic, uneven, unpredictable, unreliable, unstable, unsteady, variable, wayward. *Opp* REGULAR. 2 aimless, directionless, haphazard, meandering, wandering.

error *n inf* bloomer, blunder, *sl* boob, *Lat* corrigendum, *Lat* erratum, fallacy, falsehood, fault, flaw, gaffe, *inf* howler, inaccuracy, inconsistency, inexactitude, lapse, misapprehension, miscalculation, misconception, misprint, mistake, misunderstanding, omission, oversight, sin, *inf* slip-up, solecism, transgression, *old use* trespass, wrongdoing. ▷ WRONG.

erupt *vb* be discharged, be emitted, belch, break out, burst out, explode, gush, issue, pour out, shoot out, spew, spout, spurt, vomit.

eruption *n* burst, discharge, emission, explosion, outbreak, outburst, rash.

escapade *n* adventure, exploit, *inf* lark, mischief, practical joke, *inf* prank, scrape, stunt.

escape *n* 1 bolt, breakout, departure, flight, flit, getaway, jailbreak, retreat, running away. 2 discharge, emission, leak, leakage, seepage. 3 *escape from reality*. avoidance, distraction, diversion, escapism, evasion, relaxation, relief. ● *vb* 1 abscond, *inf* beat it, bolt, break free, break out, *inf* cut and run, decamp, disappear, *sl* do a bunk, elope, flee, fly, get away, *inf* give someone the slip, run away, *sl* scarper, slip away, *inf* slip the net, *inf* take to your heels, *inf* turn tail. 2 discharge, drain, leak, ooze, pour out, run out, seep. **3** *escape the nasty jobs.* avoid, dodge, duck, elude, evade, get away from, shirk, *sl* skive off.

escapism *n* day-dreaming, fantasy, pretence, unreality, wishful thinking.

escort *n* **1** bodyguard, convoy, guard, guide, pilot, protection, protector, safe-conduct. **2** *royal escort.* attendant, entourage, retinue, train. **3** *escort at a dance.* chaperon, companion, *inf* date, partner. • *vb* accompany, attend, chaperon, conduct, guard, *inf* keep an eye on, *inf* keep tabs on, look after, protect, shepherd, stay with, usher, watch.

essence *n* **1** centre, character, core, cornerstone, crux, essential quality, heart, kernel, life, meaning, nature, pith, quiddity, quintessence, soul, spirit, substance. **2** concentrate, decoction, elixir, extract, flavouring, fragrance, perfume, scent, tincture.

essential *adj* basic, characteristic, chief, crucial, elementary, fundamental, important, indispensable, inherent, innate, intrinsic, irreplaceable, key, leading, main, necessary, primary, principal, quintessential, requisite, vital. *Opp* INESSENTIAL.

establish *vb* **1** base, begin, constitute, construct, create, decree, form, found, inaugurate, initiate, institute, introduce, organize, originate, set up, start. **2** *establish yourself in a job.* confirm, ensconce, entrench, install, lodge, secure, settle, station. **3** *establish facts.* accept, agree, authenticate, certify, confirm, corroborate,

decide, demonstrate, fix, prove, ratify, recognize, show to be true, substantiate, verify.

established *adj* deep-rooted, deep-seated, indelible, ineradicable, ingrained, long-lasting, long-standing, permanent, proven, reliable, respected, rooted, secure, traditional, well-known, well-tried. *Opp* NEW.

establishment *n* **1** composition, constitution, creation, formation, foundation, inauguration, inception, institution, introduction, setting up. **2** *a well-run establishment.* business, company, concern, enterprise, factory, household, institution, office, organization, shop.

estate *n* **1** area, development, domain, land. **2** assets, belongings, capital, chattels, effects, fortune, goods, inheritance, lands, possessions, property, wealth.

esteem *n* admiration, credit, estimation, favour, honour, regard, respect, reverence, veneration. • *vb* ▷ RESPECT.

estimate *n* appraisal, approximation, assessment, calculation, conjecture, estimation, evaluation, guess, *inf* guesstimate, judgement, opinion, price, quotation, reckoning, specification, valuation. • *vb* appraise, assess, calculate, compute, conjecture, consider, count up, evaluate, gauge, guess, judge, project, reckon, surmise, think out, weigh up, work out.

estimation *n* appraisal, appreciation, assessment, calculation, computation, consideration, estimate, evaluation, judgement, opinion, rating, view.

estuary n creek, *Scot* firth, fjord, inlet, *Scot* loch, river mouth.

eternal adj ceaseless, deathless, endless, everlasting, heavenly, immeasurable, immortal, infinite, lasting, limitless, measureless, never-ending, permanent, perpetual, timeless, unchanging, undying, unending, unlimited. ▷ CONTINUAL. *Opp* OCCASIONAL, TRANSIENT.

eternity n afterlife, eternal life, immortality, infinity, perpetuity.

ethical adj decent, fair, good, honest, just, moral, noble, principled, righteous, upright, virtuous. *Opp* IMMORAL.

ethnic adj cultural, folk, national, racial, traditional, tribal.

etiquette n ceremony, civility, code of behaviour, conventions, courtesy, decency, decorum, form, formalities, manners, politeness, propriety, protocol, rules of behaviour, standards of behaviour.

evacuate vb 1 clear, deplete, drain, move out, remove, send away, void. 2 abandon, decamp from, desert, empty, forsake, leave, pull out of, quit, relinquish, vacate, withdraw from.

evade vb 1 avoid, *inf* chicken out of, circumvent, dodge, duck, elude, escape from, fend off, flinch from, get away from, shirk, shrink from, shun, sidestep, *inf* skive, steer clear of, turn your back on. 2 *evade a question.* fudge, hedge, parry. ▷ EQUIVOCATE. *Opp* CONFRONT.

evaluate vb appraise, assess, calculate value of, estimate, judge, value, weigh up.

evaporate vb dehydrate, desiccate, disappear, disperse, dissipate, dissolve, dry up, evanesce, melt away, vanish, vaporize.

evasive adj ambiguous, *inf* cagey, circumlocutory, deceptive, devious, disingenuous, equivocal, equivocating, inconclusive, indecisive, indirect, *inf* jesuitical, misleading, noncommittal, oblique, prevaricating, roundabout, *inf* shifty, sophistical, uninformative. *Opp* DIRECT.

even adj 1 flat, flush, horizontal, level, plane, smooth, straight, true. 2 *even pulse.* consistent, constant, equalized, measured, metrical, monotonous, proportional, regular, rhythmical, symmetrical, unbroken, uniform, unvarying. 3 *even scores.* balanced, equal, identical, level, matching, the same. 4 ▷ EVEN-TEMPERED. *Opp* IRREGULAR. **even out** ▷ FLATTEN. **even up** ▷ EQUALIZE. **get even** ▷ RETALIATE.

evening n dusk, *poet* eventide, *poet* gloaming, nightfall, sundown, sunset, twilight.

event n 1 affair, business, chance, circumstance, contingency, episode, eventuality, experience, happening, incident, occurrence. 2 conclusion, consequence, effect, issue, outcome, result, upshot. 3 activity, ceremony, entertainment, function, occasion. 4 *sporting event.* bout, championship, competition, contest, engagement, fixture, game, match, meeting, tournament.

even-tempered adj balanced, calm, composed, cool, equable, even, impassive, imperturbable, pacific, peaceable, peaceful, placid, poised, reliable, self-possessed, serene, stable, steady, tranquil, unemotional, unexcitable, unruffled. Opp EXCITABLE.

eventual *adj* concluding, consequent, destined, due, ensuing, expected, final, last, overall, probable, resultant, resulting, ultimate.

everlasting *adj* ceaseless, deathless, endless, eternal, immortal, incorruptible, infinite, lasting, limitless, measureless, never-ending, permanent, perpetual, persistent, timeless, unchanging, undying, unending. Opp TRANSIENT.

evermore *adv* always, eternally, for ever, unceasingly.

evict *vb* dislodge, dispossess, eject, expel, *sl* give (someone) the boot, *inf* kick out, oust, put out, remove, throw out, *inf* turf out, turn out.

evidence *n* attestation, certification, confirmation, corroboration, data, demonstration, deposition, documentation, facts, grounds, information, proof, sign, statement, statistics, substantiation, testimony. **give evidence** ▷ TESTIFY.

evident *adj* apparent, certain, clear, discernible, manifest, noticeable, obvious, palpable, patent, perceptible, plain, self-explanatory, unambiguous, undeniable, unmistakable, visible. Opp UNCERTAIN.

evil *adj* **1** amoral, atrocious, base, black-hearted, blasphemous, corrupt, criminal, cruel, depraved, devilish, diabolical, dishonest, fiendish, foul, harmful, hateful, heinous, hellish, immoral, impious, infamous, iniquitous, irreligious, machiavellian, malevolent, malicious, malignant, nefarious, pernicious, perverted, reprobate, satanic, sinful, sinister, treacherous, ungodly, unprincipled, unrighteous, vicious, vile, villainous, wicked, wrong. ▷ BAD. Opp GOOD. **2** *evil smell.* foul, nasty, pestilential, poisonous, troublesome, unspeakable, vile. ▷ UNPLEASANT. Opp PLEASANT. ● *n* **1** amorality, blasphemy, corruption, criminality, cruelty, depravity, dishonesty, fiendishness, heinousness, immorality, impiety, iniquity, *old use* knavery, malevolence, malice, mischief, pain, sin, sinfulness, suffering, treachery, turpitude, ungodliness, unrighteousness, vice, viciousness, villainy, wickedness, wrongdoing. ▷ CRIME. **2** *Poverty is an evil.* affliction, bane, calamity, catastrophe, curse, disaster, enormity, hardship, harm, ill, misfortune, wrong.

evocative *adj* atmospheric, convincing, descriptive, emotive, graphic, imaginative, provoking, realistic, stimulating, suggestive, vivid.

evoke *vb* arouse, awaken, call up, conjure up, elicit, excite, inspire, invoke, kindle, produce, provoke, raise, rouse, stimulate, stir up, suggest, summon up.

evolution *n* advance, development, emergence, formation, growth, improvement, maturation, maturing, progress, unfolding.

evolve *vb* derive, descend, develop, emerge, grow,

improve, mature, modify gradually, progress, unfold.

exact adj 1 accurate, correct, dead (centre), detailed, faithful, faultless, flawless, meticulous, painstaking, precise, punctilious, right, rigorous, scrupulous, specific, inf spot-on, strict, true, truthful, veracious. Opp IMPRECISE. 2 exact copy. identical, indistinguishable, literal, perfect. • vb claim, compel, demand, enforce, extort, extract, get, impose, insist on, obtain, require.
exacting ▷ DIFFICULT.

exaggerate vb 1 amplify, embellish, embroider, enlarge, inflate, inf lay it on thick, magnify, make too much of, maximize, overdo, overemphasize, overestimate, overstate, inf pile it on, inf play up. Opp MINIMIZE. 2 ▷ CARICATURE.
exaggerated ▷ EXCESSIVE.

exalt vb boost, elevate, lift, promote, raise, uplift. ▷ PRAISE.
exalted ▷ HIGH.

examination n 1 analysis, appraisal, assessment, audit, catechism, inf exam, inspection, investigation, inf oral, paper, post-mortem, review, scrutiny, study, survey, test, inf viva, Lat viva voce. 2 [medical] inf check-up, scan. 3 police examination. cross-examination, enquiry, inquiry, inquisition, interrogation, probe, questioning, trial.

examine vb 1 analyse, appraise, audit (accounts), check, inf check out, explore, inquire into, inspect, investigate, peruse, probe, research, scan, scrutinize, sift, sort out, study, sl sus out, test, vet, weigh up. 2 examine a witness.

catechize, cross-examine, cross-question, inf grill, interrogate, inf pump, question, sound out, try.

example n 1 case, illustration, instance, occurrence, sample, specimen. 2 example to follow. ideal, lesson, model, paragon, pattern, prototype. **make an example of** ▷ PUNISH.

exasperate vb inf aggravate, drive mad, gall, infuriate, irk, irritate, inf needle, pique, provoke, rile, vex. ▷ ANNOY.

excavate vb burrow, dig, gouge out, hollow out, mine, scoop out, unearth.

exceed vb beat, be more than, do more than, go beyond, go over, outnumber, outshine, outstrip, overstep, overtake, pass, transcend. ▷ EXCEL.

exceedingly adv amazingly, especially, exceptionally, excessively, extraordinarily, extremely, outstandingly, specially, unusually, very.

excel vb beat, be excellent, better, do best, eclipse, outclass, outdo, outshine, shine, stand out, surpass, top. ▷ EXCEED.

excellent adj inf ace, admirable, inf brilliant, old use capital, champion, choice, consummate, sl cracking, distinguished, esteemed, estimable, exceptional, exemplary, extraordinary, inf fabulous, inf fantastic, fine, first-class, first-rate, flawless, gorgeous, great, high-class, ideal, impressive, magnificent, marvellous, model, notable, outstanding, perfect, inf phenomenal, remarkable, inf smashing, splendid, sterling, inf stunning, inf super, superb, superlative, supreme, surpassing, *inf* terrific, *inf* tip-top, *old use* top-hole, *inf* top-notch, top-ranking, *inf* tremendous, unequalled, wonderful. *Opp* BAD.

except *vb* exclude, leave out, omit.

exception *n* 1 exclusion, omission, rejection. 2 abnormality, anomaly, departure, deviation, eccentricity, freak, irregularity, oddity, peculiarity, quirk, rarity. **take exception** ▷ OBJECT.

exceptional *adj* 1 aberrant, abnormal, anomalous, atypical, curious, deviant, eccentric, extraordinary, extreme, isolated, memorable, notable, odd, out-of-the-ordinary, peculiar, phenomenal, quirky, rare, remarkable, singular, solitary, special, strange, surprising, uncommon, unconventional, unexpected, unheard-of, unique, unparalleled, unprecedented, unpredictable, untypical, unusual. 2 ▷ EXCELLENT. *Opp* ORDINARY.

excerpt *n* citation, clip, extract, fragment, highlight, part, passage, quotation, section, selection.

excess *n* 1 abundance, glut, overabundance, overflow, *inf* overkill, profit, redundancy, superabundance, superfluity, surfeit, surplus. *Opp* SCARCITY. 2 debauchery, dissipation, extravagance, intemperance, over-indulgence, profligacy, wastefulness. *Opp* MODERATION.

excessive *adj* 1 disproportionate, exaggerated, extravagant, extreme, fanatical, immoderate, inordinate, intemperate, needless, overdone, prodigal, profligate, profuse, superfluous,

undue, unnecessary, unneeded, wasteful. ▷ HUGE. *Opp* INADEQUATE. 2 *excessive prices.* exorbitant, extortionate, unjustifiable, unrealistic, unreasonable. *Opp* MODERATE.

exchange *n* deal, interchange, reciprocity, replacement, substitution, *inf* swap, switch. ● *vb* bargain, barter, change, convert (*currency*), interchange, reciprocate, replace, substitute, *inf* swap, switch, *inf* swop, trade, trade in, traffic. **exchange words** ▷ TALK.

excitable *adj inf* bubbly, chattery, edgy, emotional, explosive, fidgety, fiery, highly-strung, hot-tempered, irrepressible, jumpy, lively, mercurial, nervous, passionate, quick-tempered, restive, temperamental, unstable, volatile. *Opp* CALM.

excite *vb* 1 agitate, amaze, animate, arouse, awaken, discompose, disturb, elate, electrify, enthral, exhilarate, fluster, *inf* get going, incite, inflame, interest, intoxicate, make excited, move, perturb, provoke, rouse, stimulate, stir up, thrill, titillate, *inf* turn on, upset, urge, *inf* wind up, *inf* work up. 2 *excite interest.* activate, cause, elicit, encourage, engender, evoke, fire, generate, kindle, motivate, produce, set off, whet. *Opp* CALM.

excited *adj* agitated, boisterous, delirious, eager, enthusiastic, excitable, exuberant, feverish, frantic, frenzied, heated, *inf* het up, hysterical, impassioned, intoxicated, lively, moved, nervous, overwrought, restless, spirited, vivacious, wild. *Opp* APATHETIC.

excitement n action, activity, adventure, agitation, animation, commotion, delirium, drama, eagerness, enthusiasm, furore, fuss, heat, intensity, inf kicks, passion, stimulation, suspense, tension, thrill, unrest.

exciting adj cliff-hanging, dramatic, electric, electrifying, eventful, fast-moving, galvanizing, gripping, heady, hair-raising, inspiring, intoxicating, inf nail-biting, provocative, riveting, rousing, sensational, spectacular, spine-tingling, stimulating, stirring, suspenseful, tense, thrilling. ▷ AMAZING. *Opp* BORING.

exclaim vb bawl, bellow, blurt out, call, cry out, old use ejaculate, shout, utter, vociferate, yell. ▷ SAY.

exclamation n bellow, call, cry, old use ejaculation, expletive, interjection, oath, shout, swearword, utterance, vociferation, yell.

exclude vb ban, banish, bar, blacklist, debar, disallow, disown, eject, except, excommunicate, expel, forbid, interdict, keep out, leave out, lock out, omit, ostracize, oust, outlaw, prohibit, proscribe, put an embargo on, refuse, reject, repudiate, rule out, shut out, veto. ▷ REMOVE. *Opp* INCLUDE.

exclusive adj 1 limiting, restricted, sole, unique, unshared. 2 *an exclusive club.* clannish, classy, closed, fashionable, sl posh, private, restrictive, select, selective, snobbish, inf up-market.

excreta plur n droppings, dung, excrement, faeces, manure, sewage, waste matter.

excrete vb defecate, evacuate the bowels, go to the lavatory, relieve yourself.

excursion n cruise, expedition, jaunt, journey, outing, ramble, tour, trip, voyage. ▷ TRAVEL.

excuse n alibi, apology, defence, explanation, extenuation, justification, mitigation, palliation, plea, pretext, rationalization, reason, vindication.
● vb 1 apologize for, condone, disregard, explain away, forgive, ignore, justify, mitigate, overlook, pardon, pass over, sanction, tolerate, vindicate, warrant. 2 absolve, acquit, clear, discharge, exculpate, exempt, exonerate, free, let off, inf let off the hook, liberate, release. *Opp* BLAME.

execute vb 1 accomplish, achieve, bring off, carry out, complete, discharge, do, effect, enact, finish, implement, perform, inf pull off. 2 kill, put to death. □ *behead, burn, crucify, decapitate, electrocute, garrotte, gas, guillotine, hang, lynch, shoot, stone.*

executive n administrator, inf boss, director, manager, officer. ▷ CHIEF.

exemplary adj admirable, commendable, faultless, flawless, ideal, model, perfect, praiseworthy, unexceptionable.

exemplify vb demonstrate, depict, embody, illustrate, personify, represent, show, symbolize, typify.

exempt vb except, exclude, excuse, free, let off, inf let off the hook, liberate, release, spare.

exercise n 1 action, activity, aerobics, callisthenics, effort, exertion, games, gymnastics, PE, sport, *inf* warm-up, *inf* work-out. **2** *military exercises*. discipline, drill, manoeuvres, operation, practice, training. ● *vb* **1** apply, bring to bear, display, effect, employ, execute, exert, expend, implement, put to use, show, use, utilize, wield. **2** *exercise your body*. discipline, drill, exert, jog, keep fit, practise, train, *inf* work out. **3** ▷ WORRY.

exertion *n* action, effort, endeavour, strain, striving, struggle. ▷ WORK.

exhaust *n* discharge, effluent, emission, fumes, gases, smoke. ● *vb* **1** consume, deplete, dissipate, drain, dry up, empty, expend, finish off, *inf* run through, sap, spend, use up, void. **2** debilitate, enervate, *inf* fag, fatigue, prostrate, tax, tire, wear out, weary. **exhausted** ▷ BREATHLESS, WEARY.

exhausting *adj* arduous, back-breaking, crippling, debilitating, demanding, difficult, enervating, fatiguing, gruelling, hard, laborious, punishing, severe, strenuous, taxing, tiring, wearying.

exhaustion *n* debility, fatigue, lassitude, tiredness, weakness, weariness.

exhaustive *adj inf* all-out, careful, comprehensive, full-scale, intensive, meticulous, thorough. *Opp* INCOMPLETE.

exhibit *vb* **1** arrange, display, offer, present, put up, set up, show. **2** *exhibit knowledge*. air, betray, brandish, demonstrate, disclose, evidence, express, *derog* flaunt, indicate, manifest, *derog* parade, reveal, *derog* show off. *Opp* HIDE.

exhibition *n* demonstration, display, *inf* expo, exposition, presentation, show.

exhilarating *adj* bracing, cheering, enlivening, exciting, invigorating, refreshing, rejuvenating, stimulating, tonic, uplifting. ▷ HAPPY.

exhort *vb* advise, encourage, harangue, *inf* give a pep talk to, lecture, sermonize, urge.

exile *n* **1** banishment, deportation, expatriation, expulsion, transportation. **2** deportee, displaced person, émigré, expatriate, outcast, refugee, wanderer. ● *vb* ban, banish, bar, deport, drive out, eject, evict, expatriate, expel, oust, send away, transport.

exist *vb* **1** be, be found, be in existence, be real, happen, occur. **2** abide, continue, endure, hold out, keep going, last, live, remain alive, subsist, survive. **existing** ▷ ACTUAL, CURRENT, LIVING.

existence *n* actuality, being, continuance, life, living, persistence, reality, survival.

exit *n* **1** barrier, door, doorway, egress, gate, gateway, opening, portal, way out. **2** *a hurried exit*. departure, escape, evacuation, exodus, flight, leave-taking, retreat, withdrawal. ● *vb* ▷ DEPART.

exorbitant *adj* disproportionate, excessive, extortionate, extravagant, high, inordinate, outrageous, profiteering, prohibitive, *inf* sky-high, *inf* steep, *inf* stiff, *inf* swingeing, top, unjustifiable, unrealistic, unreasonable, unwarranted. ▷ EXPENSIVE. *Opp* REASONABLE.

exotic adj **1** alien, faraway, foreign, remote, romantic, unfamiliar, wonderful. **2** bizarre, colourful, different, exciting, extraordinary, foreign-looking, novel, odd, outlandish, peculiar, rare, singular, strange, striking, unfamiliar, unusual, weird. Opp ORDINARY.

expand vb **1** amplify, augment, broaden, build up, develop, diversify, elaborate, enlarge, extend, fill out, heighten, increase, make bigger, make longer, prolong. **2** become bigger, dilate, distend, grow, increase, lengthen, open out, stretch, swell, thicken, widen. Opp CONTRACT.

expanse n area, breadth, extent, range, sheet, space, spread, stretch, sweep, surface, tract.

expansive adj affable, amiable, communicative, effusive, extrovert, friendly, genial, open, outgoing, sociable, well-disposed. ▷ TALKATIVE. Opp TACITURN. **2** ▷ BROAD. Opp NARROW.

expect vb **1** anticipate, await, bank on, bargain for, be prepared for, contemplate, count on, envisage, forecast, foresee, have faith in, hope for, imagine, look forward to, plan for, predict, prophesy, reckon on, wait for. **2** expect obedience. consider necessary, demand, insist on, look for, rely on, require, want. **3** I expect he'll come. assume, believe, conjecture, guess, imagine, judge, presume, presuppose, suppose, surmise, think. **expected** ▷ PREDICTABLE.

expectant adj **1** eager, hopeful, inf keyed up, inf on tenter-

hooks, optimistic, ready. **2** inf expecting, pregnant.

expedient adj advantageous, advisable, appropriate, apropos, beneficial, convenient, desirable, helpful, judicious, opportune, politic, practical, pragmatic, profitable, propitious, prudent, right, sensible, suitable, to your advantage, useful, worthwhile. ● n contrivance, device, inf dodge, manoeuvre, means, measure, method, inf ploy, recourse, resort, ruse, scheme, stratagem, tactics.

expedition n crusade, excursion, exploration, journey, mission, pilgrimage, quest, raid, safari, tour, trek, trip, undertaking, voyage.

expel vb **1** ban, banish, cast out, inf chuck out, dismiss, drive out, eject, evict, exile, exorcise, inf fire, inf kick out, oust, remove, inf sack, send away, throw out, turn out, inf turf out. **2** expel fumes. belch, discharge, emit, exhale, give out, push out, send out, spew out.

expend vb consume, disburse, sl dish out, employ, pay out, spend, use.

expendable adj disposable, inessential, insignificant, replaceable, inf throw-away, unimportant.

expense n charge, cost, disbursement, expenditure, fee, outgoings, outlay, overheads, payment, price, rate, spending.

expensive adj costly, dear, generous, high-priced, overpriced, precious, inf pricey, inf steep, inf up-market, valuable. ▷ EXORBITANT. Opp CHEAP.

experience n 1 familiarity, involvement, observation, participation, practice, taking part. 2 background, expertise, *inf* know-how, knowledge, *Fr* savoir faire, skill, understanding, wisdom. 3 *a nasty experience*. adventure, circumstance, episode, event, happening, incident, occurrence, ordeal, trial. ● vb encounter, endure, face, go through, have a taste of, know, meet, practise, sample, suffer, test out, try, undergo. **experienced** ▷ EXPERT.

experiment n demonstration, investigation, *inf* practical, proof, research, test, trial, try-out. ● vb do experiments, examine, investigate, make tests, probe, research, test, try out.

experimental adj 1 exploratory, on trial, pilot, provisional, tentative, trial. 2 *experimental evidence*. empirical, experiential, proved, tested.

expert adj able, *inf* ace, *inf* brilliant, capable, competent, *inf* crack, experienced, knowing, knowledgeable, master, masterly, practised, professional, proficient, qualified, skilful, skilled, sophisticated, specialized, trained, well-versed, worldly-wise. ▷ CLEVER. *Opp* UNSKILFUL. ● n *inf* ace, authority, connoisseur, *inf* dab hand, genius, *derog* know-all, master, *inf* old hand, professional, pundit, specialist, veteran, virtuoso, *derog* wiseacre, *inf* wizard. *Opp* AMATEUR.

expertise n adroitness, dexterity, expertness, judgement, *inf* know-how, knowledge, *Fr* savoir faire, skill.

expire vb become invalid, cease, come to an end, discontinue, finish, *inf* run out, terminate. ▷ DIE.

explain vb 1 clarify, clear up, decipher, decode, define, demonstrate, describe, disentangle, elucidate, expound, *inf* get across, *inf* get over, gloss, illustrate, interpret, make clear, make plain, provide an explanation, resolve, shed light on, simplify, solve, *inf* sort out, spell out, teach, translate, unravel. 2 *explain a mistake*. account for, excuse, give reasons for, justify, legitimatize, legitimize, make excuses for, rationalize, vindicate.

explanation n 1 account, analysis, clarification, definition, demonstration, description, elucidation, exegesis, explication, exposition, gloss, illustration, interpretation, key, meaning, rubric, significance, solution, translation. 2 cause, excuse, justification, motivation, motive, rationalization, reason, vindication.

explanatory adj descriptive, expository, helpful, illuminating, illustrative, interpretive, revelatory.

explicit adj categorical, clear, definite, detailed, direct, exact, express, frank, graphic, manifest, open, outspoken, patent, plain, positive, precise, put into words, said, specific, *inf* spelt out, spoken, stated, straightforward, unambiguous, unconcealed, unequivocal, unhidden, unreserved, well-defined. *Opp* IMPLICIT.

explode vb 1 backfire, blast, blow up, burst, detonate, erupt, go off, make an explosion, set off, shatter. 2 *explode a theory.* debunk, destroy, discredit, disprove, put an end to, rebut, refute, reject.

exploit n achievement, adventure, attainment, deed, enterprise, feat. ● vb 1 build on, capitalize on, *inf* cash in on, develop, make capital out of, make use of, profit by, profit from, trade on, use, utilize, work on. 2 *exploit people.* *inf* bleed, enslave, ill-treat, impose on, keep down, manipulate, *inf* milk, misuse, oppress, *inf* rip off, *inf* squeeze dry, take advantage of, treat unfairly, withhold rights from.

explore vb 1 break new ground, probe, prospect, reconnoitre, scout, search, survey, tour, travel through. 2 *explore a problem.* analyse, examine, inspect, investigate, look into, probe, research, scrutinize, study.

explosion n 1 bang, blast, boom, burst, clap, crack, detonation, discharge, eruption, firing, report. 2 *explosion of anger.* fit, outbreak, outburst, *inf* paddy, paroxysm, spasm.

explosive adj dangerous, highly-charged, liable to explode, sensitive, unstable, volatile. *Opp* STABLE. ● n cordite, dynamite, gelignite, gunpowder, TNT.

exponent n 1 executant, interpreter, performer, player. 2 advocate, champion, defender, expounder, presenter, propagandist, proponent, supporter, upholder.

expose vb bare, betray, dig up, disclose, display, exhibit, lay

bare, reveal, show (up), uncover, unearth, unmask. ▷ REVEAL. *Opp* HIDE.

express vb air, articulate, disclose, give vent to, make known, phrase, put into words, release, vent, ventilate, voice, word. ▷ COMMUNICATE.

expression n 1 cliché, formula, phrase, phraseology, remark, statement, term, turn of phrase, usage, utterance, wording. ▷ SAYING. 2 articulation, confession, declaration, disclosure, revelation, statement. 3 *expression in your voice.* accent, depth, emotion, expressiveness, feeling, intensity, intonation, nuance, pathos, sensibility, sympathy, tone, understanding. 4 *expression on your face.* air, appearance, aspect, countenance, face, look, mien. □ beam, frown, glare, glower, grimace, grin, laugh, leer, long face, lour, lower, poker-face, pout, scowl, smile, smirk, sneer, wince, yawn.

expressionless adj 1 blank, *inf* dead-pan, emotionless, empty, glassy, impassive, inscrutable, poker-faced, straight-faced, uncommunicative, wooden. 2 boring, dull, flat, monotonous, uninspiring, unmodulated, unvarying. *Opp* EXPRESSIVE.

expressive adj 1 indicative, meaningful, mobile, revealing, sensitive, significant, striking, suggestive, telling. 2 articulate, eloquent, lively, modulated, varied. *Opp* EXPRESSIONLESS.

exquisite adj delicate, elegant, fine, intricate, refined, skilful, well-crafted. ▷ BEAUTIFUL. *Opp* CRUDE.

extend vb **1** add to, broaden, build up, develop, draw out, enlarge, expand, increase, keep going, lengthen, make longer, open up, pad out, perpetuate, prolong, protract, inf spin out, spread, stretch, widen. **2** extend a deadline. defer, delay, postpone, put back, put off. **3** extend your hand. give, hold out, offer, outstretch, present, proffer, put out, raise, reach out, stick out, stretch out. **4** The garden extends to the fence. continue, range, reach.

extensive adj broad, comprehensive, expansive, far-ranging, far-reaching, sweeping, vast, wide, widespread. ▷ LARGE.

extent n amount, area, bounds, breadth, compass, degree, dimensions, distance, expanse, length, limit, magnitude, measure, measurement, proportions, quantity, range, reach, scale, scope, size, space, spread, sweep, width.

exterior adj external, outer, outside, outward, superficial. ● n coating, covering, façade, front, outside, shell, skin, surface. Opp INTERIOR.

exterminate vb annihilate, destroy, eliminate, eradicate, extirpate, get rid of, obliterate, put an end to, root out, terminate. ▷ KILL.

external adj exterior, outer, outside, outward, superficial. Opp INTERNAL.

extinct adj burnt out, dead, defunct, died out, exterminated, extinguished, gone, inactive, vanished. ▷ OLD. Opp LIVING.

extinguish vb blow out, damp down, douse, put out, quench, slake, smother, snuff out,

switch off. ▷ DESTROY. Opp KINDLE.

extort vb blackmail, bully, coerce, exact, extract, force, obtain by force.

extra adj accessory, added, additional, ancillary, auxiliary, excess, further, left-over, more, other, reserve, spare, superfluous, supernumerary, supplementary, surplus, temporary, unneeded, unused, unwanted.

extract n **1** concentrate, concentration, decoction, distillation, essence, quintessence. **2** abstract, citation, inf clip, clipping, cutting, excerpt, passage, quotation, selection. ● vb **1** draw out, extricate, pull out, remove, take out, withdraw. **2** extract a confession. extort, force out, inf winkle out, inf worm out, wrench, wrest, wring. **3** extract what you need. choose, cull, derive, distil, gather, glean, quote, select. ▷ OBTAIN.

extraordinary adj abnormal, amazing, astonishing, astounding, awe-inspiring, bizarre, breathtaking, curious, exceptional, extreme, fantastic, inf funny, incredible, marvellous, miraculous, mysterious, mystical, notable, noteworthy, odd, outstanding, peculiar, inf phenomenal, prodigious, queer, rare, remarkable, inf sensational, signal, singular, special, staggering, strange, striking, stunning, stupendous, surprising, inf unbelievable, uncommon, unheard-of, unimaginable, unique, unprecedented, unusual, inf weird, wonderful. Opp ORDINARY.

extravagance n excess, immoderation, improvidence, lavishness, overindulgence, overspending, prodigality, profligacy, self-indulgence, wastefulness. Opp ECONOMY.

extravagant adj exaggerated, excessive, flamboyant, grandiose, immoderate, improvident, lavish, outrageous, overblown, overdone, pretentious, prodigal, profligate, profuse, reckless, self-indulgent, inf showy, spendthrift, uneconomical, unreasonable, unthrifty, wasteful. ▷ EXPENSIVE. Opp ECONOMICAL.

extreme adj 1 acute, drastic, excessive, greatest, intensest, maximum, severest, inf terrific, utmost. ▷ EXTRAORDINARY. 2 distant, endmost, farthest, furthest, furthermost, last, outermost, remotest, ultimate, uttermost. 3 extreme opinions. absolute, avant-garde, exaggerated, extravagant, extremist, fanatical, inf hard-line, immoderate, intemperate, intransigent, left-wing, militant, obsessive, outrageous, radical, right-wing, uncompromising, inf way-out, zealous. • n bottom, bounds, edge, end, extremity, left wing, limit, maximum, minimum, opposite, pole, right wing, top, ultimate.

extroverted adj active, confident, exhibitionist, outgoing, positive. ▷ SOCIABLE. Opp INTROVERTED.

exuberant adj 1 animated, boisterous, inf bubbly, buoyant, eager, ebullient, effervescent, energetic, enthusiastic, excited, exhilarated, exultant, high-spirited, irrepressible, lively, spirited, sprightly, vivacious. ▷ CHEERFUL. 2 exuberant decoration. baroque, exaggerated, highly-decorated, ornate,

overdone, rich, rococo. 3 exuberant growth. abundant, copious, lush, luxuriant, overflowing, profuse, rank, teeming. Opp AUSTERE.

exultant adj delighted, ecstatic, elated, joyful, jubilant, inf on top of the world, overjoyed, rejoicing. ▷ EXUBERANT.

eye n 1 eyeball, inf peeper. 2 discernment, perception, sight, vision. • vb contemplate, examine, inspect, look at, observe, regard, scrutinize, study, watch. ▷ SEE.

eye-witness n bystander, looker-on, observer, onlooker, passer-by, spectator, watcher, witness.

F

fabric n 1 material, stuff, textile. ▷ CLOTH. 2 fabric of a building. constitution, construction, framework, make-up, structure, substance.

fabulous adj 1 fabled, fairy-tale, fanciful, fictitious, imaginary, legendary, mythical, storybook. 2 ▷ EXCELLENT.

face n 1 appearance, countenance, features, lineaments, look, sl mug, old use physiognomy, visage. ▷ EXPRESSION. 2 face of building. aspect, covering, exterior, façade, facet, front, outside, side, surface. • vb 1 be opposite, front, look towards, overlook. 2 face danger. appear before, brave, come to terms with, confront, cope with, defy, encounter, experience, face up to, meet, oppose, square up to, stand up to, tackle. **3** *face a wall with plaster*. clad, coat, cover, dress, finish, overlay, sheathe, veneer.

facetious *adj* cheeky, flippant, impudent, irreverent. ▷ FUNNY.

facile *adj* **1** cheap, easy, effortless, hasty, obvious, quick, simple, superficial, unconsidered. **2** *facile talker*. fluent, glib, insincere, plausible, ready, shallow, slick, *inf* smooth.

facility *n* **1** adroitness, alacrity, ease, expertise, fluency, *derog* glibness, skill, smoothness. **2** *a useful facility*. amenity, convenience, help, provision, resource, service.

fact *n* actuality, certainty, *Fr* fait accompli, reality, truth. *Opp* FICTION. **the facts** circumstances, data, details, evidence, information, *sl* the lowdown, particulars, statistics.

factor *n* aspect, cause, circumstance, component, consideration, constituent, contingency, detail, determinant, element, fact, influence, ingredient, item, parameter, part, particular.

factory *n* assembly line, forge, foundry, manufacturing plant, mill, plant, refinery, shop-floor, works, workshop.

factual *adj* **1** accurate, *Lat* bona fide, circumstantial, correct, demonstrable, empirical, faithful, genuine, matter-of-fact, objective, plain, prosaic, provable, realistic, straightforward, true, unadorned, unbiased, undistorted, unemotional, unimaginative, unvarnished, valid, verifiable, well-documented. *Opp* FALSE. **2** *a factual film*. biographical, documentary, historical, real-life. *Opp* FICTIONAL.

faculty *n* ability, aptitude, capability, capacity, flair, genius, gift, knack, power, talent.

fade *vb* **1** blanch, bleach, darken, dim, discolour, dull, etiolate, grow pale, whiten. *Opp* BRIGHTEN. **2** become less, decline, decrease, diminish, disappear, dwindle, evanesce, fail, melt away, vanish, wane, weaken. **3** *flowers fade*. droop, flag, perish, shrivel, wilt, wither.

fail *vb* **1** abort, be a failure, be unsuccessful, break down, close down, come to an end, *inf* come to grief, come to nothing, *sl* conk out, *inf* crash, cut out, fall through, *inf* fizzle out, *inf* flop, *inf* fold, fold up, founder, give up, go bankrupt, *inf* go bust, go out of business, meet with disaster, miscarry, misfire, *inf* miss out, peter out, stop working. **2** *fail in health.* decay, decline, deteriorate, diminish, disappear, dwindle, ebb, fade, get worse, give out, melt away, vanish, wane, weaken. **3** *fail to do something.* forget, neglect, omit. **4** *fail someone.* abandon, disappoint, *inf* let down. *Opp* IMPROVE, SUCCEED.

failing *n* blemish, defect, fault, flaw, foible, imperfection, shortcoming, weakness, weak spot.

failure *n* **1** abandonment, defeat, disappointment, disaster, downfall, fiasco, *inf* flop, loss, miscarriage, *inf* wash-out, wreck. **2** breakdown, collapse, crash, stoppage. **3** *failure to do your duty.* dereliction, neglect, omission, remissness. *Opp* SUCCESS.

faint *adj* **1** blurred, blurry, dim, faded, feeble, hazy, ill-defined,

indistinct, misty, muzzy, pale, pastel (*colours*), shadowy, unclear, vague. **2** *faint smell.* delicate, slight. **3** *faint sounds.* distant, hushed, low, muffled, muted, soft, stifled, subdued, thin, weak. **4** *faint in the head.* dizzy, exhausted, feeble, giddy, light-headed, unsteady, vertiginous, weak, *inf* woozy. *Opp* CLEAR, STRONG.
● *vb* become unconscious, black out, collapse, *inf* flake out, *inf* keel over, pass out, swoon.

fair *adj* **1** blond, blonde, flaxen, golden, light, yellow. **2** *fair weather.* bright, clear, clement, cloudless, dry, favourable, fine, pleasant, sunny. *Opp* DARK. **3** *a fair decision.* disinterested, even-handed, fair-minded, honest, honourable, impartial, just, lawful, legitimate, nonpartisan, open-minded, proper, right, unbiased, unprejudiced, upright. *Opp* UNJUST. **4** *a fair standard.* acceptable, adequate, average, indifferent, mediocre, middling, moderate, ordinary, passable, reasonable, respectable, satisfactory, *inf* so-so, tolerable. *Opp* UNACCEPTABLE. **5** ▷ BEAUTIFUL. ● *n* **1** amusement-park, fair-ground, funfair. **2** bazaar, carnival, exhibition, festival, fête, gala, market, sale, show.

fairly *adv* moderately, pretty, quite, rather, reasonably, somewhat, tolerably, up to a point.

faith *n* **1** assurance, belief, certitude, confidence, credence, reliance, sureness, trust. *Opp* DOUBT. **2** conviction, creed, devotion, doctrine, dogma, persuasion, religion.

faithful *adj* **1** constant, dependable, devoted, dutiful, honest,

loyal, reliable, staunch, steadfast, trusted, trusty, trustworthy, unswerving. **2** *a faithful account.* accurate, close, consistent, exact, factual, literal, precise. ▷ TRUE. *Opp* FALSE.

fake *adj* artificial, bogus, concocted, counterfeit, ersatz, factitious, false, fictitious, forged, fraudulent, imitation, invented, made-up, mock, *sl* phoney, pretended, sham, simulated, spurious, synthetic, trumped-up, unfounded, unreal. *Opp* GENUINE. ● *n* **1** copy, counterfeit, duplicate, forgery, hoax, imitation, replica, reproduction, sham, simulation. **2** charlatan, cheat, fraud, hoaxer, humbug, impostor, mountebank, *sl* phoney, quack. ● *vb* affect, copy, counterfeit, dissemble, falsify, feign, forge, fudge, imitate, make believe, mock up, pretend, put on, reproduce, sham, simulate.

fall *n* **1** collapse, crash, decline, decrease, depreciation, descent, dip, dive, downswing, downturn, drop, lowering, nosedive, plunge, reduction, slant, slump, tumble. **2** *fall of a fortress.* capitulation, capture, defeat, overthrow, seizure, submission, surrender. ● *vb* **1** collapse, *inf* come a cropper, crash down, dive, drop down, founder, go down, keel over, overbalance, pitch, plummet, plunge, sink, slump, spiral, stumble, topple, trip over, tumble. **2** become less, become lower, decline, decrease, diminish, dwindle, ebb, lessen, subside. **3** descend, drop, fall away, slope down. **4** *curtains fell in folds.* be suspended, cascade, dangle, dip down, hang. **5** *silence fell.* come,

come about, happen, occur, settle. 6 ▷ DIE. 7 ▷ SURRENDER. **fall apart** ▷ DISINTEGRATE. **fall back** ▷ RETREAT. **fall behind** ▷ LAG. **fall down, fall in** ▷ COLLAPSE. **fall off** ▷ DECLINE. **fall out** ▷ QUARREL. **fall through** ▷ FAIL.

fallacy *n* delusion, error, flaw, miscalculation, misconception, mistake, solecism.

fallible *adj* erring, frail, human, imperfect, liable to make mistakes, uncertain, unpredictable, unreliable, weak. *Opp* INFALLIBLE.

fallow *adj* dormant, resting, uncultivated, unplanted, unsown, unused.

false *adj* 1 deceptive, distorted, erroneous, fabricated, fallacious, faulty, fictitious, flawed, imprecise, inaccurate, incorrect, inexact, invalid, misleading, mistaken, spurious, unfactual, unsound, untrue, wrong. ▷ FAKE. 2 *false friends.* deceitful, dishonest, disloyal, double-dealing, double-faced, faithless, lying, treacherous, unfaithful, unreliable, untrustworthy. *Opp* TRUE. **false name** ▷ PSEUDONYM.

falsehood *n* fabrication, *inf* fib, fiction, lie, prevarication, *inf* story, untruth, *sl* whopper.

falsify *vb* alter, *inf* cook (*the books*), counterfeit, distort, exaggerate, fake, forge, *inf* fudge, imitate, misrepresent, mock up, oversimplify, pervert, simulate, slant, tamper with, tell lies about, twist.

falter *vb* 1 become weaker, flag, flinch, hesitate, hold back, lose confidence, pause, quail, stagger, stumble, totter, vacillate, waver. 2 stammer, stutter. **faltering** ▷ HESITANT.

fame *n* acclaim, celebrity, distinction, eminence, glory, honour, illustriousness, importance, *inf* kudos, name, *derog* notoriety, pre-eminence, prestige, prominence, public esteem, renown, reputation, repute, *inf* stardom.

familiar *adj* 1 accustomed, common, conventional, current, customary, everyday, frequent, habitual, mundane, normal, ordinary, predictable, regular, routine, stock, traditional, usual, well-known. *Opp* STRANGE. 2 *familiar language.* *inf* chatty, close, confidential, *derog* forward, *inf* free-and-easy, *derog* impudent, informal, intimate, near, *derog* presumptuous, relaxed, sociable, unceremonious. ▷ FRIENDLY. *Opp* FORMAL. **familiar with** acquainted with, *inf* at home with, aware of, conscious of, expert in, informed about, knowledgeable about, trained in, versed in.

family *n* 1 brood, children, *inf* flesh and blood, generation, issue, kindred, *old use* kith and kin, litter, *inf* nearest and dearest, offspring, progeny, relations, relatives, *inf* tribe. 2 ancestry, blood, clan, dynasty, extraction, forebears, genealogy, house, line, lineage, pedigree, race, stream, tribe. □ *ancestor, descendant.* □ *aunt, brother, child, cousin, daughter, father, fiancé(e), forefather, foster-child, foster-parent, godchild, godparent, grandchild, grandparent, guardian, husband,* Amer junior, kinsman, kinswoman, mother, nephew, next-of-kin, niece, parent, sibling, sister, son, step-child, step-parent, uncle, ward, widow, widower, wife.

famine *n* dearth, hunger, lack, malnutrition, scarcity, shortage, starvation, want. Opp PLENTY.

famished *adj* craving, famishing, hungry, *inf* peckish, ravenous, starved, starving.

famous *adj* acclaimed, big, celebrated, distinguished, eminent, exalted, famed, glorious, great, historic, honoured, illustrious, important, legendary, lionized, notable, noted, *derog* notorious, outstanding, popular, prominent, proverbial, renowned, revered, time-honoured, venerable, well-known, world-famous. Opp UNKNOWN.

fan *n* 1 blower, extractor, propeller, ventilator. 2 *a soccer fan.* addict, admirer, aficionado, *inf* buff, devotee, enthusiast, fanatic, *inf* fiend, follower, *inf* freak, lover, supporter. ▷ FANATIC.

fanatic *n* activist, adherent, bigot, extremist, fiend, freak, maniac, militant, zealot.

fanatical *adj* bigoted, excessive, extreme, fervent, fervid, immoderate, irrational, maniacal, militant, obsessive, over-enthusiastic, passionate, rabid, single-minded, zealous. Opp MODERATE.

fanciful *adj* capricious, chimerical, fancy, fantastic, illusory, imaginary, imagined, make-believe, unrealistic, whimsical.

fancy *adj* decorative, elaborate, embellished, embroidered,

intricate, ornamented, ornate. ▷ FANCIFUL. ● *n* ▷ IMAGINATION, WHIM. ● *vb* 1 conjure up, dream of, envisage, imagine, picture, visualize. ▷ THINK. 2 be attracted to crave, *inf* have a yen for, like, long for, prefer, want, wish for. ▷ DESIRE.

fantastic *adj* 1 absurd, amazing, elaborate, exaggerated, extraordinary, extravagant, fabulous, fanciful, far-fetched, grotesque, imaginative, implausible, incredible, odd, quaint, remarkable, rococo, strange, surreal, unbelievable, unlikely, unrealistic, weird. 2 ▷ EXCELLENT. Opp ORDINARY.

fantasy *n* chimera, day-dream, delusion, dream, fancy, hallucination, illusion, imagination, invention, make-believe, mirage, pipe-dream, reverie, vision. Opp REALITY.

far *adj* distant, far-away, far-off, outlying, remote. Opp NEAR.

farcical *adj* absurd, foolish, ludicrous, preposterous, ridiculous, silly. ▷ FUNNY.

fare *n* 1 charge, cost, fee, payment, price, ticket. 2 *festive fare.* ▷ FOOD.

farewell *adj* goodbye, last, leaving, parting, valedictory. ● *n* departure, leave-taking, *inf* send-off, valediction. ▷ GOODBYE.

farm *n* farmhouse, farmstead, *old use* grange. □ *arable farm, croft, dairy farm, fish farm, fruit farm, livestock farm, organic farm, plantation, poultry farm, ranch, smallholding.*

farming *n* agriculture, agronomy, crofting, cultivation, food-production, husbandry.

fascinate vb allure, attract, beguile, bewitch, captivate, charm, delight, enchant, engross, enthral, entice, entrance, hypnotize, interest, mesmerize, rivet, spellbind.
fascinating ▷ ATTRACTIVE.

fashion n 1 convention, manner, method, mode, way. 2 craze, cut, inf fad, line, look, pattern, rage, style, taste, trend, vogue.

fashionable adj Fr [à] la mode, chic, contemporary, current, elegant, inf in, in vogue, the latest, modern, modish, popular, smart, inf snazzy, sophisticated, stylish, tasteful, inf trendy, up-to-date, inf with it. Opp UNFASHIONABLE.

fast adv at full tilt, briskly, in no time, post-haste, quickly, rapidly, swiftly. ● adj 1 breakneck, brisk, expeditious, express, hasty, headlong, high-speed, hurried, lively, inf nippy, precipitate, quick, rapid, smart, inf spanking, speedy, supersonic, swift, unhesitating. Opp SLOW. 2 fast on the rocks. attached, bound, fastened, firm, fixed, immobile, immovable, secure, tight. 3 fast colours. indelible, lasting, permanent, stable. 4 fast living. ▷ IMMORAL. ● vb abstain, deny yourself, diet, go hungry, go without food, starve. Opp INDULGE.

fasten vb affix, anchor, attach, batten, bind, bolt, button, buckle, button, chain, clamp, clasp, cling, close, connect, couple, do up, fix, grip, hitch, hook, knot, join, lace, lash, latch on, link, lock, make fast, moor, nail, padlock, paste, peg, pin, rivet, rope, screw down, seal, secure, solder, staple, strap, tack, tape,

tether, tie, unite, weld. ▷ STICK. Opp UNDO.

fastener n bond, connection, connector, coupling, fastening, link, linkage. □ anchor, bolt, buckle, button, catch, chain, clamp, clasp, clip, dowel, dowel-pin, drawing-pin, glue, gum, hasp, hook, knot, lace, latch, lock, mooring, nail, padlock, painter, paste, peg, pin, rivet, rope, safety-pin, screw, seal, Sellotape, solder, staple, strap, string, tack, tape, tether, tie, toggle, Velcro, wedge, zip.

fastidious adj choosy, dainty, delicate, discriminating, finical, finicky, fussy, hard to please, nice, particular, inf pernickety, inf picky, selective, squeamish.

fat adj 1 bloated, inf broad in the beam, bulky, chubby, corpulent, dumpy, flabby, fleshy, gross, heavy, massive, obese, overweight, paunchy, plump, podgy, portly, pot-bellied, pudgy, rotund, round, solid, squat, stocky, stout, thick, tubby, weighty, well-fed. ▷ BIG. 2 fat meat. fatty, greasy, oily. Opp LEAN. ● n □ adipose tissue, blubber, butter, dripping, grease, lard, margarine, oil, suet.

fatal adj 1 deadly, final, incurable, lethal, malignant, mortal, terminal. 2 ▷ DISASTROUS.

fatality n casualty, death, loss.

fate n 1 chance, destiny, doom, fortune, karma, kismet, lot, luck, nemesis, inf powers above, predestination, providence, the stars. 2 death, demise, destruction, disaster, downfall, end, ruin.

fated adj certain, cursed, damned, decreed, destined,

doomed, foreordained, inescapable, inevitable, intended, predestined, predetermined, preordained, sure.

father n begetter, *inf* dad, *inf* daddy, *inf* pa, *inf* papa, parent, *old use* pater, *inf* pop, sire.

fatigue n debility, exhaustion, feebleness, languor, lassitude, lethargy, tiredness, weakness, weariness. • *vb* debilitate, drain, enervate, exhaust, tire, weaken, weary. **fatigued** ▷ WEARY.

fault n 1 blemish, defect, deficiency, demerit, failing, failure, fallacy, flaw, foible, frailty, imperfection, inaccuracy, malfunction, snag, weakness. 2 blunder, *inf* boob, error, failing, *Fr* faux pas, gaffe, *inf* howler, indiscretion, lapse, miscalculation, misconduct, misdeed, mistake, negligence, offence, omission, oversight, peccadillo, shortcoming, sin, slip, transgression, *old use* trespass, vice, wrongdoing. 3 *It was my fault.* accountability, blame, culpability, guilt, liability, responsibility. • *vb* ▷ CRITICIZE.

faultless adj accurate, correct, exemplary, flawless, ideal, in mint condition, irreproachable, sinless, unimpeachable. ▷ PERFECT. Opp FAULTY.

faulty adj broken, damaged, defective, deficient, flawed, illogical, imperfect, inaccurate, incomplete, incorrect, inoperative, invalid, not working, out of order, shop-soiled, unusable, useless. Opp FAULTLESS.

favour n 1 acceptance, approbation, approval, bias, favourit-

ism, friendliness, goodwill, grace, liking, partiality, preference, support. 2 *Do me a favour.* benefit, courtesy, gift, good deed, good turn, indulgence, kindness, service. • *vb* 1 approve of, be in sympathy with, champion, choose, commend, esteem, *inf* fancy, *inf* go for, like, opt for, prefer, show favour to, think well of, value. Opp DISLIKE. 2 abet, advance, back, be advantageous to, befriend, forward, promote, support. ▷ HELP. Opp HINDER.

favourable adj 1 advantageous, appropriate, auspicious, beneficial, benign, convenient, following (*wind*), friendly, generous, helpful, kind, opportune, positive, promising, propitious, reassuring, suitable, supportive, sympathetic, understanding, well-disposed. 2 *a favourable review.* approving, commendatory, complimentary, congratulatory, encouraging, enthusiastic, laudatory. 3 *a favourable reputation.* agreeable, desirable, enviable, good, pleasing, satisfactory. Opp UNFAVOURABLE.

favourite adj beloved, best, choice, chosen, dearest, esteemed, ideal, liked, loved, popular, preferred, selected, well-liked. • n 1 choice, pick, preference. 2 *inf* apple of your eye, darling, idol, pet.

fear n alarm, anxiety, apprehension, apprehensiveness, awe, concern, consternation, cowardice, cravenness, diffidence, dismay, doubt, dread, faint-heartedness, foreboding, fright, *inf* funk, horror, misgiving, nervousness, panic, phobia, qualm, suspicion, terror, timid-

ity, trepidation, uneasiness,
worry. ▷ PHOBIA. *Opp* COURAGE.
● *vb* be afraid of, dread, quail
at, shrink from, suspect, tremble at, worry about.

fearful *adj* 1 alarmed, apprehensive, frightened, nervous,
panic-stricken, scared, terrified,
timid. ▷ AFRAID. *Opp* FEARLESS.
2 ▷ FEARSOME.

fearless *adj* bold, brave, dauntless, intrepid, resolute, stoical,
unafraid, unconcerned,
undaunted, valiant, valorous.
▷ COURAGEOUS. *Opp* FEARFUL.

fearsome *adj* appalling, awe-
inspiring, awesome, daunting,
dreadful, fearful, frightful,
intimidating, terrible, terrifying. ▷ FRIGHTENING.

feasible *adj* 1 achievable, attainable, easy, possible, practicable,
practical, realizable, viable,
workable. *Opp* IMPRACTICAL. 2 *a
feasible scenario*. credible,
likely, plausible, reasonable.
Opp IMPLAUSIBLE.

feast *n* banquet, *sl* blow-out,
dinner, *inf* spread. ▷ MEAL.
● *vb* dine, gorge, gormandize,
inf wine and dine. ▷ EAT.

feat *n* accomplishment, achievement, act, action, attainment,
deed, exploit, performance.

feather *n* plume, quill. **feathers**
down, plumage.

feathery *adj* downy, fluffy, light,
wispy.

feature *n* 1 aspect, attribute,
characteristic, circumstance,
detail, facet, hall mark, idiosyncrasy, mark, peculiarity, point,
property, quality, trait.
2 *newspaper feature*. article,
column, item, piece, report,
story. ● *vb* 1 emphasize, focus
on, give prominence to, high-

light, *inf* play up, present,
promote, show up, *inf* spotlight,
inf star, stress. 2 *feature in a
film*. act, appear, figure, participate, perform, play a role, star,
take a part. **features** ▷ FACE.

fee *n* bill, charge, cost, dues,
emolument, fare, payment,
price, remuneration, subscription, sum, tariff, terms, toll,
wage.

feeble *adj* 1 ailing, debilitated,
decrepit, delicate, enfeebled,
exhausted, faint, fragile, frail,
helpless, ill, impotent, inadequate, ineffective, infirm,
languid, listless, poorly, powerless, puny, sickly, slight,
useless, weak. *Opp* STRONG.
2 effete, feckless, hesitant,
incompetent, indecisive, ineffectual, irresolute, *inf* namby-
pamby, spineless, vacillating,
weedy, wimpish, *inf* wishy-
washy. 3 *feeble excuses*. flimsy,
insubstantial, lame, paltry,
poor, tame, thin, unconvincing.

feed *vb* 1 cater for, give food to,
nourish, nurture, provender,
provide for, provision,
strengthen, suckle, support,
sustain, *inf* wine and dine.
2 dine, eat, fare, graze, pasture.
feed on ▷ EAT.

feel *vb* 1 caress, finger, fondle,
handle, hold, manipulate, maul,
inf paw, pet, stroke, touch.
2 *feel your way*. explore,
fumble, grope. 3 *feel the cold*.
be aware of, be conscious of,
detect, discern, experience,
know, notice, perceive, sense,
suffer, undergo. 4 *It feels cold*.
appear, give a feeling of, seem.
5 *feel something's true*. believe,
consider, deem, guess, *inf* have
a feeling, *inf* have a hunch,
intuit, judge, think.

feeling n 1 sensation, sense of touch, sensitivity. 2 ardour, emotion, fervour, passion, sentiment, warmth. 3 *religious feelings.* attitude, belief, consciousness, guess, hunch, idea, impression, instinct, intuition, notion, opinion, perception, thought, view. 4 *a feeling for music.* fondness, responsiveness, sensibility, sympathy, understanding. 5 [*inf*] *a party feeling.* atmosphere, aura, mood, tone, *inf* vibrations.

fell vb bring down, chop down, cut down, flatten, *inf* floor, knock down, mow down, prostrate. ▷ KILL.

female adj ▷ FEMININE. *Opp* MALE. • n □ aunt, *old use* damsel, daughter, *old use* débutante, fiancée, girl, girlfriend, grandmother, lady, *inf* lass, lesbian, *old use* maid, *old use* maiden, *old use* mistress, mother, niece, sister, spinster, *old use or sexist* wench, wife, woman. □ bitch, cow, doe, ewe, hen, lioness, mare, nanny-goat, sow, tigress, vixen.

feminine adj *derog of men* effeminate, female, *derog* girlish, ladylike, womanly. *Opp* MASCULINE.

fen n bog, lowland, marsh, morass, quagmire, slough, swamp.

fence n barricade, barrier, fencing, hedge, hurdle, obstacle, paling, palisade, railing, rampart, stockade, wall, wire. • vb 1 bound, circumscribe, confine, coop up, encircle, enclose, hedge in, immure, pen, restrict, surround, wall in. 2 ▷ FIGHT.

fend vb fend for yourself care for yourself, do for yourself,

inf get along, *inf* get by, look after yourself, *inf* scrape along, support yourself, survive. fend off ▷ REPEL.

ferment n ▷ COMMOTION. • vb 1 boil, bubble, effervesce, *inf* fizz, foam, froth, rise, seethe, work. 2 agitate, excite, foment, incite, instigate, provoke, rouse, stir up.

ferocious adj bestial, bloodthirsty, brutal, cruel, feral, fiendish, fierce, harsh, inhuman, merciless, murderous, pitiless, sadistic, savage, vicious, wild. *Opp* GENTLE.

ferry n ▷ VESSEL. • vb carry, export, fetch, import, shift, ship, shuttle, take across, taxi, transport. ▷ CONVEY.

fertile adj abundant, fecund, fertilized, flourishing, fruitful, lush, luxuriant, productive, prolific, rich, teeming, well-fertilized. *Opp* STERILE.

fertilize vb 1 impregnate, inseminate, pollinate. 2 cultivate, dress, enrich, feed, make fertile, manure, mulch, nourish, top-dress.

fertilizer n compost, dressing, dung, manure, mulch, nutrient.

fervent adj animated, ardent, avid, burning, committed, devout, eager, earnest, emotional, enthusiastic, excited, fanatical, fervid, fiery, frenzied, heated, impassioned, intense, keen, passionate, rapturous, spirited, vehement, vigorous, warm, wholehearted, zealous. *Opp* COOL.

fervour n ardour, eagerness, energy, enthusiasm, excitement, fervency, fire, heat, intensity, keenness, passion, sparkle, spirit, vehemence, vigour, warmth, zeal.

fester vb become infected, become inflamed, become poisoned, decay, discharge, gather, go bad, go septic, mortify, ooze, putrefy, rot, run, suppurate, ulcerate.

festival n anniversary, carnival, celebration, commemoration, fair, feast, fête, fiesta, gala, holiday, jamboree, jubilee. ▷ FESTIVITY.

festive adj celebratory, cheerful, cheery, convivial, gay, gleeful, jolly, jovial, joyful, joyous, light-hearted, merry, uproarious. ▷ HAPPY.

festivity n celebration, conviviality, entertainment, feasting, festive occasion, inf jollification, jollity, jubilation, merry-making, merriment, mirth, rejoicing, revelry, revels. ▷ PARTY.

fetch vb 1 bear, bring, call for, carry, collect, convey, get, import, obtain, pick up, retrieve, transfer, transport. 2 fetch a good price. be bought for, bring in, earn, go for, make, produce, raise, realize, sell for. **fetching** ▷ ATTRACTIVE.

feud n animosity, antagonism, inf bad blood, conflict, dispute, enmity, grudge, hostility, rivalry, strife, vendetta. ▷ QUARREL.

fever n delirium, feverishness, high temperature.

feverish adj 1 burning, febrile, fevered, flushed, hot, inflamed, trembling. Opp COOL. 2 feverish activity. agitated, excited, frantic, frenetic, frenzied, hectic, hurried, impatient, passionate, restless.

few adj inf few and far between, hardly any, inadequate, infrequent, rare, scarce, sparse, sporadic, inf thin on the ground, uncommon. Opp MANY.

fibre n 1 filament, hair, strand, thread. 2 moral fibre. backbone, character, determination, spirit, tenacity, toughness. ▷ COURAGE.

fickle adj capricious, changeable, changing, disloyal, erratic, faithless, flighty, inconsistent, inconstant, mercurial, mutable, treacherous, undependable, unfaithful, unpredictable, unreliable, unstable, unsteady, inf up and down, vacillating, variable, volatile. Opp CONSTANT.

fiction n concoction, deception, fabrication, fantasy, figment of the imagination, flight of fancy, invention, lies, story-telling, inf tall story. ▷ WRITING. Opp FACT.

fictional adj fabulous, fanciful, imaginary, invented, legendary, made-up, make-believe, mythical, story-book. Opp FACTUAL.

fictitious adj apocryphal, assumed, fabricated, deceitful, fraudulent, imagined, invented, made-up, spurious, unreal, untrue. ▷ FALSE. Opp GENUINE.

fiddle vb interfere, meddle, play about, tamper. ▷ FIDGET. **fiddling** ▷ TRIVIAL.

fidget vb be restless, inf fiddle about, fret, frisk about, fuss, jerk about, inf jiggle, inf mess about, move restlessly, inf play about, shuffle, squirm, twitch, worry, wriggle about.

fidgety adj agitated, frisky, impatient, jittery, jumpy, nervous, on edge, restive, rest-

less, *inf* twitchy, uneasy.
Opp CALM.

field *n* 1 arable land, clearing, enclosure, grassland, *poet* glebe, green, *old use* mead, meadow, paddock, pasture. 2 *a games field.* arena, ground, pitch, playing-field, recreation ground, stadium. 3 *field of activity.* area, *inf* department, domain, province, sphere, subject, territory.

fiend *n* 1 demon, devil, evil spirit, goblin, hobgoblin, imp, Satan, spirit. 2 ▷ FANATIC.

fierce *adj* 1 angry, barbaric, barbarous, bloodthirsty, bloody, brutal, cold-blooded, cruel, dangerous, fearsome, ferocious, fiendish, fiery, homicidal, inhuman, merciless, murderous, pitiless, ruthless, sadistic, savage, untamed, vicious, violent, wild. 2 *fierce opposition.* active, aggressive, competitive, eager, furious, heated, intense, keen, passionate, relentless, strong, unrelenting.
Opp GENTLE.

fiery *adj* 1 ablaze, afire, aflame, aglow, blazing, burning, fierce, flaming, glowing, heated, hot, incandescent, raging, red, red-hot. 2 *a fiery temper.* angry, ardent, choleric, excitable, fervent, furious, hot-headed, intense, irascible, irritable, livid, mad, passionate, touchy, violent. *Opp* COOL.

fight *n* action, affray, attack, battle, bout, brawl, *inf* brush, *inf* bust-up, clash, combat, competition, conflict, confrontation, contest, counter-attack, dispute, dogfight, duel, *inf* dust-up, encounter, engagement, feud, *old use* fisticuffs, fracas, fray, *inf* free-for-all, hostilities, joust, match, mêlée, *inf* punch-up, raid, riot, rivalry, row, scramble, scrap, scrimmage, scuffle, *inf* set-to, skirmish, squabble, strife, struggle, tussle, war, wrangle.
▷ QUARREL. ● *vb* 1 attack, battle, box, brawl, *inf* brush, clash, compete, conflict, contend, do battle, duel, engage, exchange blows, fence, feud, grapple, have a fight, joust, quarrel, row, scrap, scuffle, skirmish, spar, squabble, stand up (to), strive, struggle, *old use* tilt, tussle, wage war, wrestle. 2 *fight a decision.* campaign against, contest, defy, oppose, protest against, resist, take a stand against.

fighter *n* aggressor, antagonist, attacker, belligerent, campaigner, combatant, contender, contestant, defender, □ *archer, boxer, inf brawler, champion, duellist, freedom-fighter, gladiator, guerrilla, gunman, knight, marine, marksman, mercenary, partisan, prize-fighter, pugilist, sniper, swordsman, terrorist, warrior, wrestler.* ▷ SOLDIER.

figure *n* 1 amount, cipher, digit, integer, number, numeral, sum, symbol, value. 2 diagram, drawing, graph, illustration, outline, picture, plate, representation. 3 *plump figure.* body, build, form, outline, physique, shape, silhouette. 4 *bronze figure.* ▷ SCULPTURE. 5 *well-known figure.* ▷ PERSON.
● *vb* ▷ FEATURE. **figure out** ▷ CALCULATE, UNDERSTAND.
figures ▷ STATISTICS.

file *n* 1 binder, box-file, case, cover, documentation, document-case, dossier, folder, portfolio, ring-binder. 2 *single file.*

column, line, procession, queue, rank, row, stream, string, train. ● *vb* 1 arrange, categorize, classify, enter, pigeon-hole, organize, put away, record, register, store, systematize. 2 *file through a door*. march, parade, proceed in a line, stream, troop.

fill *vb* 1 be full of, block, *inf* bung up, caulk, clog, close up, cram, crowd, flood, inflate, jam, load, obstruct, pack, plug, refill, replenish, seal, stock up, stop up, *inf* stuff, *inf* top up. *Opp* EMPTY. 2 *fill a need*. answer, fulfil, furnish, meet, provide, satisfy, supply. 3 *fill a post*. execute, hold, occupy, take over, take up. **fill out** ▷ SWELL.

filling *n* contents, *inf* innards, insides, padding, stuffing, wadding.

film *n* 1 coat, coating, cover, covering, haze, layer, membrane, mist, overlay, screen, sheet, skin, slick, tissue, veil. 2 cartoon, *old use* flick, motion picture, movie, picture, video, videotape.

filter *n* colander, gauze, membrane, mesh, riddle, screen, sieve, strainer. ● *vb* clarify, filtrate, percolate, purify, refine, screen, sieve, sift, strain.

filth *n* decay, dirt, effluent, garbage, grime, *inf* gunge, impurity, muck, mud, ordure, pollution, putrescence, refuse, rubbish, scum, sewage, slime, sludge, trash. ▷ EXCRETA.

filthy *adj* 1 begrimed, caked, defiled, dirty, disgusting, dusty, foul, grimy, grubby, impure, messy, mucky, muddy, nasty, polluted, scummy, slimy, smelly, soiled, sooty, sordid,

squalid, stinking, tainted, uncleaned, unkempt, unwashed, vile. 2 ▷ OBSCENE. *Opp* CLEAN.

final *adj* clinching, closing, concluding, conclusive, decisive, dying, end, eventual, finishing, last, settled, terminal, terminating, ultimate. *Opp* INITIAL.

finalize *vb* clinch, complete, conclude, settle, *inf* sew up, *inf* wrap up.

finance *n* accounting, banking, business, commerce, economics, investment, stocks and shares. ● *vb* back, fund, guarantee, invest in, pay for, provide money for, subsidize, support, underwrite. **finances** assets, bank account, budget, capital, cash, funds, holdings, income, money, resources, wealth, *inf* the wherewithal.

financial *adj* economic, fiscal, monetary, pecuniary.

find *vb* 1 acquire, arrive at, become aware of, *inf* bump into, chance upon, come across, come upon, detect, diagnose, dig out, dig up, discover, encounter, espy, expose, *inf* ferret out, happen on, hit on, identify, learn, light on, locate, meet, note, notice, observe, *inf* put your finger on, reach, recognize, reveal, spot, stumble on, uncover, unearth. 2 *find lost property*. get back, recover, rediscover, regain, repossess, retrieve, trace, track down. 3 *found me a job*. give, pass on, procure, provide, supply. *Opp* LOSE.

finding *n* conclusion, decision, decree, judgement, pronouncement, verdict.

fine adj 1 admirable, beautiful, choice, classic, commendable, excellent, first-class, handsome, noble, select, superior, worthy. ▷ GOOD. 2 *fine workmanship.* consummate, craftsmanlike, meticulous, skilful, skilled. 3 *fine sand.* minute, powdery, soft. 4 *fine fabric.* dainty, delicate, exquisite, flimsy, fragile, silky. 5 *a fine point.* acute, keen, narrow, sharp, slender, slim, thin. 6 *a fine distinction.* fine-drawn, discriminating, hair-splitting, nice, precise, subtle. 7 *fine weather.* bright, clear, cloudless, dry, fair, nice, pleasant, sunny. ● n charge, forfeit, penalty.

finish n 1 cessation, close, completion, conclusion, culmination, end, ending, finale, resolution, result, termination. 2 *finish on furniture.* appearance, completeness, gloss, lustre, patina, perfection, polish, shine, smoothness, surface, texture. ● vb 1 accomplish, achieve, break off, bring to an end, cease, clinch, complete, conclude, discontinue, end, finalize, fulfil, halt, pack up, perfect, phase out, reach the end, round off, say goodbye, sign off, stop, take your leave, terminate, *inf* wind up, *inf* wrap up. 2 consume, drink up, eat up, empty, exhaust, expend, get through, *inf* polish off, *inf* say goodbye to, to use up. **finish off** ▷ KILL.

finite adj bounded, calculable, controlled, countable, definable, defined, determinate, fixed, known, limited, measurable, numbered, rationed, restricted. *Opp* INFINITE.

fire n 1 blaze, burning, combustion, conflagration, flames, holocaust, inferno, pyre. 2 fireplace, grate, hearth. □ boiler, bonfire, brazier, convector, electric fire, forge, furnace, gas fire, immersion-heater, incinerator, kiln, oven, radiator, stove. 3 *fire in your veins.* ▷ PASSION. ● vb 1 bake, burn, heat, ignite, kindle, light, put a light to, set alight, set fire to, spark off. 2 animate, awaken, enkindle, enliven, excite, incite, inflame, inspire, motivate, rouse, stimulate, stir. 3 *fire a gun or missile.* catapult, detonate, discharge, explode, launch, let off, propel, set off, shoot, trigger off. 4 *fire a worker.* dismiss, make redundant, sack, throw out. **fire at** ▷ BOMBARD. **hang fire** ▷ DELAY.

fireproof adj flameproof, incombustible, non-flammable. *Opp* INFLAMMABLE.

fire-raiser n arsonist, pyromaniac.

firm adj 1 compact, compressed, congealed, dense, hard, inelastic, inflexible, rigid, set, solid, stable, stiff, unyielding. 2 *firm on the rocks.* anchored, embedded, fast, fastened, fixed, immovable, secure, steady, tight. 3 *firm convictions.* adamant, decided, determined, dogged, obstinate, persistent, resolute, unshakeable, unwavering. 4 *a firm price.* agreed, settled, unchangeable. 5 *firm friends.* constant, dependable, devoted, faithful, loyal, reliable. ● n business, company, concern, corporation, establishment, organization, partnership.

first adj 1 cardinal, chief, dominant, foremost, head, highest, key, leading, main, outstanding, paramount, predominant, primary, prime, principal, top, uppermost. 2 *first steps.* basic, elementary, fundamental, initial, introductory, preliminary, rudimentary. 3 *first inhabitants.* aboriginal, archetypal, earliest, eldest, embryonic, oldest, original, primeval. **first-class, first-rate** ▷ EXCELLENT.

fish n ▷ *brill, brisling, carp, catfish, chub, cod, coelacanth, conger, cuttlefish, dab, dace, eel, flounder, goldfish, grayling, gudgeon, haddock, hake, halibut, herring, jellyfish, lamprey, ling, mackerel, minnow, mullet, perch, pike, pilchard, piranha, plaice, roach, salmon, sardine, sawfish, shark, skate, sole, sprat, squid, starfish, stickleback, sturgeon, swordfish, inf tiddler, trout, tuna, turbot, whitebait, whiting.* ● vb angle, go fishing, trawl.

fisher n angler, fisherman, trawlerman.

fit adj 1 adapted, adequate, applicable, apposite, appropriate, apropos, apt, becoming, befitting, correct, decent, equipped, fitting, good enough, proper, right, satisfactory, seemly, sound, suitable, suited, timely. 2 able, capable, competent, in good form, on form, prepared, ready, strong, well enough. ▷ HEALTHY. Opp UNFIT. ● n attack, bout, convulsion, eruption, explosion, outbreak, outburst, paroxysm, seizure, spasm, spell. ● vb 1 accord with, become, be fitting for, conform with, correspond to, correspond with, go with, harmonize with,

suit. 2 *fit things into place.* arrange, assemble, build, construct, dovetail, install, interlock, join, match, position, put in place, put together. **fit out, fit up** ▷ EQUIP.

fix n inf catch-22, corner, difficulty, dilemma, inf hole, inf jam, mess, inf pickle, plight, predicament, problem, quandary. ● vb 1 attach, bind, connect, embed, implant, install, join, link, make firm, plant, position, secure, stabilize, stick. ▷ FASTEN. 2 *fix a price.* agree, appoint, arrange, arrive at, conclude, confirm, decide, define, establish, finalize, name, ordain, set, settle, sort out, specify. 3 *fix a broken window.* correct, make good, mend, put right, rectify, remedy, repair.

fixture n date, engagement, event, game, match, meeting.

fizz vb bubble, effervesce, fizzle, foam, froth, hiss, sizzle, sparkle, sputter.

fizzy adj bubbly, effervescent, foaming, sparkling.

flag n banner, bunting, colours, ensign, jack, pennant, pennon, standard, streamer.
● vb 1 ▷ SIGNAL. 2 *enthusiasm flagged.* ▷ DECLINE.

flake n bit, chip, leaf, scale, scurf, shaving, slice, sliver, splinter, wafer.

flame n blaze, light, tongue. ▷ FIRE. ● vb ▷ FLARE.

flap vb beat, flutter, oscillate, slap, sway, swing, thrash about, thresh about, wag, waggle, wave about.

flare vb 1 blaze, brighten, burst out, erupt, flame, shine. ▷ BURN. 2 ▷ WIDEN.

flash *vb* coruscate, dazzle, flicker, glare, glint, glitter, light up, reflect, scintillate, shine, spark, sparkle, twinkle.
▷ BURN.

flat *adj* **1** calm, even, horizontal, level, smooth, unbroken, unruffled. **2** outstretched, prone, prostrate, recumbent, spread-eagled, spread out, supine. **3** *a flat voice.* bland, boring, dead, dry, dull, featureless, insipid, lacklustre, lifeless, monotonous, spiritless, stale, tedious, tired, unexciting, uninteresting, unmodulated, unvarying. **4** *a flat tyre.* blown out, burst, deflated, punctured. ● *n* apartment, bedsitter, flatlet, maisonette, penthouse, rooms, suite.

flatten *vb* **1** compress, even out, iron out, level out, press, roll, smooth, straighten. **2** crush, demolish, devastate, level, raze, run over, squash, trample.
▷ DESTROY. **3** *flatten an opponent.* fell, floor, knock down, prostrate. ▷ DEFEAT.

flatter *vb* be flattering to, *inf* butter up, compliment, court, curry favour with, fawn on, humour, *inf* play up to, praise, *sl* suck up to, *inf* toady to. *Opp* INSULT. **flattering**
▷ COMPLIMENTARY, OBSEQUIOUS.

flatterer *n inf* crawler, *inf* creep, groveller, lackey, sycophant, time-server, *inf* toady, *inf* yes-man.

flattery *n* adulation, blandishments, *inf* blarney, *inf* boot-licking, cajolery, fawning, *inf* flannel, insincerity, obsequiousness, servility, *inf* soft soap, sycophancy, unctuousness.

flavour *n* **1** savour, taste.
▷ FLAVOURING. **2** air, ambience,

atmosphere, aura, character, characteristic, feel, feeling, property, quality, spirit, stamp, style. ● *vb* add flavour to, add taste to, season, spice.

flavouring *n* additive, essence, extract, seasoning.

flaw *n* break, defect, error, fallacy, fault, imperfection, inaccuracy, loophole, mistake, shortcoming, slip, split, weakness. ▷ BLEMISH. **flawed**
▷ IMPERFECT.

flawless *adj* accurate, clean, faultless, immaculate, mint, pristine, sound, spotless, undamaged, unmarked.
▷ PERFECT. *Opp* IMPERFECT.

flee *vb* abscond, *inf* beat a retreat, *sl* beat it, bolt, clear off, cut and run, decamp, disappear, escape, fly, get away, hurry off, *inf* make a run for it, make off, retreat, run away, *sl* scarper, take flight, *inf* take to your heels, vanish, withdraw.

fleet *n* armada, convoy, flotilla, navy, squadron, task force.

fleeting *adj* brief, ephemeral, evanescent, fugitive, impermanent, momentary, mutable, passing, short, short-lived, temporary, transient, transitory. *Opp* PERMANENT.

flesh *n* carrion, fat, meat, muscle, tissue.

flex *n* cable, cord, extension, lead, wire. ● *vb* ▷ BEND.

flexible *adj* **1** bendable, *inf* bendy, elastic, flexile, floppy, giving, limp, plastic, pliable, pliant, rubbery, soft, springy, stretchy, supple, whippy, willowy, yielding. **2** adjustable, alterable, fluid, mutable, open, provisional, variable. **3** *a flexible person.* accommodating, adaptable, amenable, compliant, conformable, cooperative, docile, easygoing, malleable, open-minded, responsive, tractable, willing. *Opp* RIGID.

flicker *vb* blink, flap, flutter, glimmer, gutter, quiver, shake, shimmer, sparkle, tremble, twinkle, vibrate, waver.

flight *n* **1** journey, trajectory. **2** ▷ ESCAPE.

flimsy *adj* **1** breakable, brittle, delicate, fine, fragile, frail, insubstantial, light, loose, slight, thin, weak. **2** *a flimsy building.* decrepit, dilapidated, gimcrack, jerry-built, makeshift, rickety, shaky, tottering, wobbly. **3** *a flimsy argument.* feeble, implausible, inadequate, superficial, trivial, unbelievable, unconvincing, unsatisfactory. *Opp* STRONG.

flinch *vb* blench, cower, cringe, dodge, draw back, duck, falter, jerk away, jump, quail, quake, recoil, shrink back, shy away, start, swerve, wince. **flinch from** ▷ EVADE.

fling *vb* bowl, *inf* bung, cast, *inf* chuck, heave, hurl, launch, lob, pelt, pitch, propel, send, *inf* shy, *inf* sling, throw, toss.

flippant *adj* cheeky, facetious, facile, *inf* flip, frivolous, lighthearted, shallow, superficial, thoughtless, unserious. *Opp* SERIOUS.

flirt *n female* coquette, *male* philanderer, *inf* tease. • *vb sl* chat someone up, lead someone on, make love, philander, toy with someone's affections.

flirtatious *adj* amorous, coquettish, flirty, *derog* philandering,

playful, *derog* promiscuous, teasing.

float *vb* **1** be buoyed, be suspended, bob, drift, glide, hang, hover, sail, swim, waft. **2** *float a ship.* launch. *Opp* SINK.

flock *n* assembly, congregation, crowd, drove, gathering, herd, horde, multitude, swarm. ▷ GROUP. • *vb* ▷ GATHER.

flog *vb* beat, birch, cane, chastise, flagellate, flay, lash, scourge, thrash, whip. ▷ HIT.

flood *n* **1** cataract, deluge, downpour, flash-flood, inundation, overflow, rush, spate, stream, tidal wave, tide, torrent. **2** abundance, excess, glut, plethora, quantity, superfluity, surfeit, surge. • *vb* cover, deluge, drown, engulf, fill up, immerse, inundate, overflow, overwhelm, saturate, sink, submerge, swamp.

floor *n* **1** floorboards, flooring. **2** deck, level, storey, tier.

flop *vb* **1** collapse, dangle, droop, drop, fall, flag, flap about, hang down, sag, slump, topple, tumble, wilt. **2** ▷ FAIL.

floppy *adj* dangling, droopy, flabby, hanging, loose, limp, pliable, soft. ▷ FLEXIBLE. *Opp* RIGID.

flounder *vb* **1** blunder, flail, fumble, grope, move clumsily, plunge about, stagger, struggle, stumble, tumble, wallow. **2** falter, get confused, make mistakes, talk aimlessly.

flourish *n* ▷ GESTURE. • *vb* **1** be fruitful, be successful, bloom, blossom, boom, burgeon, develop, do well, flower, grow, increase, *inf* perk up, progress, prosper, strengthen, succeed, thrive. **2** *flourish an umbrella.*

brandish, flaunt, gesture with, shake, swing, twirl, wag, wave, wield.

flow n cascade, course, current, drift, ebb, effusion, flood, gush, outpouring, spate, spurt, stream, tide, trickle. ● vb bleed, cascade, course, dribble, drift, drip, ebb, flood, flush, glide, gush, issue, leak, move in a stream, ooze, overflow, pour, purl, ripple, roll, run, seep, spill, spring, spurt, squirt, stream, swirl, trickle, well, well up.

flower n 1 bloom, blossom, bud, floret, petal. □ begonia, bluebell, buttercup, campanula, campion, candytuft, carnation, catkin, celandine, chrysanthemum, coltsfoot, columbine, cornflower, cowslip, crocus, crowfoot, cyclamen, daffodil, dahlia, daisy, dandelion, forget-me-not, foxglove, freesia, geranium, gladiolus, gypsophila, harebell, hollyhock, hyacinth, iris, jonquil, kingcup, lilac, lily, lupin, marguerite, marigold, montbretia, nasturtium, orchid, pansy, pelargonium, peony, periwinkle, petunia, phlox, pink, polyanthus, poppy, primrose, rhododendron, rose, saxifrage, scabious, scarlet pimpernel, snowdrop, speedwell, sunflower, tulip, violet, wallflower, waterlily. ● vb bloom, blossom, poet blow, bud, burgeon, come out, have flowers, open out, unfold. ▷ FLOURISH. **bunch of flowers** arrangement, bouquet, corsage, garland, posy, spray, wreath.

fluctuate vb alternate, be unsteady, change, go up and down, oscillate, seesaw, shift, swing, vacillate, vary, waver.

fluent adj articulate, effortless, eloquent, expressive, derog facile, felicitous, flowing, derog glib, natural, polished, ready, smooth, voluble, unhesitating. Opp HESITANT.

fluff n down, dust, feathers, floss, fuzz, thistledown.

fluffy adj downy, feathery, fibrous, fleecy, furry, fuzzy, hairy, light, silky, soft, velvety, wispy, woolly.

fluid adj 1 aqueous, flowing, gaseous, liquefied, liquid, melted, molten, running, inf runny, sloppy, watery. Opp SOLID. 2 a fluid situation. adjustable, alterable, changing, flexible, mutable, open, variable, undefined. ● n gas, liquid, liquor, plasma, vapour.

fluke n accident, chance, serendipity, stroke of good luck, twist of fate.

flush vb 1 blush, colour, glow, go red, redden. 2 flush a lavatory. clean out, cleanse, flood, inf pull the plug, rinse out, wash out. 3 flush from a hiding-place. chase out, drive out, expel, send up.

fluster vb agitate, bewilder, bother, distract, flurry, perplex, put off, put out, inf rattle, inf throw, upset. ▷ CONFUSE.

flutter vb bat (eyelid), flap, flicker, flit, fluctuate, move agitatedly, oscillate, palpitate, quiver, shake, tremble, twitch, vacillate, vibrate, wave.

fly vb 1 ascend, flit, glide, hover, rise, sail, soar, swoop, take flight, take wing. 2 fly a plane. aviate, pilot, take off in. 3 fly a flag. display, flap, flutter, hang up, hoist, raise, show, wave. 4 fly from danger. flee, hurry,

move quickly, run. ▷ ESCAPE.
fly at ▷ ATTACK. **fly in the
face of** ▷ DISREGARD.

flying *n* aeronautics, air-travel,
aviation, flight, *inf* jetting.

foam *n* 1 bubbles, effervescence,
froth, head (*on beer*), lather,
scum, spume, suds. 2 sponge.
● *vb* boil, bubble, efferyesce,
fizz, froth, lather, make foam.

focus *n* 1 clarity, correct adjustment, sharpness. 2 centre, core,
focal point, heart, hub, pivot,
target. ● *vb* aim, centre, concentrate, direct attention, fix attention, home in, spotlight.

fog *n* bad visibility, cloud, haze,
miasma, mist, smog, vapour.

foggy *adj* blurred, blurry, clouded, cloudy, dim, hazy, indistinct, misty, murky, obscure.
Opp CLEAR.

foil *vb* baffle, block, check,
circumvent, frustrate, halt,
hamper, hinder, obstruct,
outwit, prevent, stop, thwart.
▷ DEFEAT.

foist *vb* *inf* fob off, get rid of,
impose, offload, palm off.

fold *n* 1 bend, corrugation,
crease, crinkle, furrow, gather,
hollow, knife-edge, line, pleat,
pucker, wrinkle. 2 *fold for
sheep.* ▷ ENCLOSURE.
● *vb* 1 bend, crease, crimp,
crinkle, double over, jack-knife,
overlap, pleat, ply, pucker, tuck
in, turn over. 2 close, collapse,
let down, put down, shut.
3 *fold in your arms.* clasp, clip,
embrace, enclose, enfold,
entwine, envelop, hold, hug,
wrap. 4 *business folded.*
▷ FAIL.

folk *n* clan, nation, people, the
population, the public, race,
society, tribe.

follow *vb* 1 accompany, chase,
come after, dog, escort, go after,
hound, hunt, keep pace with,
pursue, replace, shadow, stalk,
succeed, supersede, supplant,
inf tag along with, tail, take the
place of, track, trail. 2 *follow a
path.* keep to, trace. 3 *follow
rules.* abide by, adhere to,
attend to, comply with, conform
to, heed, honour, obey, observe,
pay attention to, stick to,
submit to, take notice of.
4 *follow my example.* adopt, be
guided by, conform to, copy,
imitate, mimic, mirror. 5 *follow
an argument.* appreciate,
comprehend, grasp, keep up
with, take in, understand.
6 *follow football.* admire, be a
fan of, keep abreast of, know
about, take an interest in,
support. 7 *It doesn't follow.* be
inevitable, be logical, come
about, ensue, happen, have the
consequence, mean, result.
following ▷ SUBSEQUENT.

folly *n* foolishness, insanity,
lunacy, madness. ▷ STUPIDITY.

foment *vb* arouse, incite, instigate, kindle, provoke, rouse,
stir up. ▷ STIMULATE.

fond *adj* 1 adoring, affectionate,
caring, loving, tender, warm.
2 *a fond hope.* ▷ FOOLISH. **be
fond of** ▷ LOVE.

fondle *vb* caress, cuddle, handle,
pat, pet, snuggle, squeeze,
touch.

food *n* aliment, *old use* bread, *old
use* comestibles, cooking,
cuisine, delicacies, diet,
inf eatables, *inf* eats, fare, feed,
fodder, foodstuff, forage,
inf grub, *inf* junk food, *old
use* meat, *sl* nosh, nourishment,
nutriments, provender, provisions, rations, recipe, refresh-

ments, sustenance, swill, *old use* tuck, *old use* viands, *old use* victuals. ▷ MEAL.

fool *n* 1 [*most synonyms inf*] ass, blockhead, booby, buffoon, dimwit, dope, dunce, dunderhead, dupe, fat-head, half-wit, ignoramus, mug, muggins, mutt, ninny, nit, nitwit, simpleton, sucker, twerp, wally. ▷ IDIOT. 2 clown, comedian, comic, coxcomb, entertainer, jester.
● *vb inf* bamboozle, bluff, cheat, *inf* con, cozen, deceive, defraud, delude, dupe, fleece, gull, *inf* have on, hoax, hoodwink, *inf* kid, mislead, *inf* string along, swindle, take in, tease, trick. **fool about** ▷ MISBEHAVE.

foolish *adj* absurd, asinine, brainless, childish, crazy, daft, *inf* dopey, *inf* dotty, fatuous, feather-brained, feeble-minded, *old use* fond, frivolous, *inf* half-baked, hare-brained, idiotic, illogical, immature, inane, infantile, irrational, *inf* jokey, laughable, light-hearted, ludicrous, mad, meaningless, mindless, misguided, naïve, nonsensical, playful, pointless, preposterous, ridiculous, scatter-brained, *inf* scatty, senseless, shallow, silly, simple, simple-minded, simplistic, *inf* soppy, stupid, thoughtless, unintelligent, unreasonable, unsound, unwise, witless. *Opp* WISE.

foot *n* 1 claw, hoof, paw, trotter. 2 ▷ BASE.

footprint *n* footmark, spoor, track.

forbid *vb* ban, bar, debar, deny, deter, disallow, exclude, interdict, make illegal, outlaw, preclude, prevent, prohibit, proscribe, refuse, rule out, say no to, stop, veto. *Opp* ALLOW.

forbidden *adj* 1 against the law, taboo, unlawful, wrong. 2 *a forbidden area.* closed, out of bounds, restricted, secret.

forbidding *adj* gloomy, grim, menacing, ominous, stern, threatening, uninviting, unwelcoming. ▷ UNFRIENDLY. *Opp* FRIENDLY.

force *n* 1 aggression, *inf* arm-twisting, coercion, compulsion, constraint, drive, duress, effort, might, power, pressure, strength, vehemence, vigour, violence. 2 effect, energy, impact, intensity, momentum, shock. 3 *a military force.* army, body, group, troops. 4 *force of an argument.* cogency, effectiveness, persuasiveness, rightness, thrust, validity, weight.
● *vb* 1 bulldoze, coerce, compel, constrain, drive, impel, impose on, make, oblige, order, press-gang, pressurize. 2 *force a door.* break open, burst open, prise open, smash, use force on, wrench. 3 *force something on someone.* impose, inflict.

foreboding *n* anxiety, apprehension, dread, fear, feeling, foreshadowing, forewarning, intimation, intuition, misgiving, omen, portent, premonition, presentiment, suspicion, warning, worry.

forecast *n* augury, expectation, outlook, prediction, prognosis, prognostication, projection, prophecy. ● *vb* ▷ FORESEE.

forefront *n* avant-garde, front, lead, vanguard.

foreign *adj* 1 distant, exotic, faraway, outlandish, remote, strange, unfamiliar, unknown.

2 alien, external, immigrant, imported, incoming, international, outside, overseas, visiting. 3 *foreign ideas*. extraneous, odd, uncharacteristic, unnatural, untypical, unusual, unwanted. *Opp* NATIVE.

foreigner *n* alien, immigrant, newcomer, outsider, overseas visitor, stranger. *Opp* NATIVE.

foremost *adj* first, leading, main, primary, supreme. ▷ CHIEF.

forerunner *n* advance messenger, harbinger, herald, precursor, predecessor. ▷ ANCESTOR.

foresee *vb* anticipate, envisage, expect, forecast, picture. ▷ FORETELL.

foresight *n* anticipation, caution, far-sightedness, forethought, looking ahead, perspicacity, planning, preparation, prudence, readiness, vision.

forest *n* coppice, copse, jungle, plantation, trees, woodland, woods.

foretaste *n* advance warning, augury, example, foreknowledge, forewarning, indication, omen, premonition, preview, sample, specimen, *inf* tip-off, trailer, *inf* try-out.

foretell *vb* augur, *old use* bode, forebode, foreshadow, forewarn, give a foretaste of, herald, portend, predict, presage, prognosticate, prophesy, signify. ▷ FORESEE.

forethought *n* anticipation, caution, far-sightedness, foresight, looking ahead, perspicacity, planning, preparation, prudence, readiness, vision.

forewarning *n* advance warning, augury, omen, premonition, *inf* tip-off. ▷ FORETASTE.

forfeit *n* confiscation, damages, fee, fine, penalty, sequestration. ● *vb* abandon, give up, let go, lose, pay up, relinquish, renounce, surrender.

forge *n* furnace, smithy, workshop. ● *vb* 1 beat into shape, cast, construct, hammer out, manufacture, mould, shape, work. 2 coin, copy, counterfeit, fake, falsify, imitate, make illegally, reproduce. **forge ahead** ▷ ADVANCE.

forgery *n* copy, counterfeit, *inf* dud, fake, fraud, imitation, *inf* phoney, replica, reproduction.

forget *vb* 1 be forgetful, dismiss from your mind, disregard, fail to remember, ignore, leave out, lose track (of), miss out, neglect, omit, overlook, skip, suffer from amnesia, unlearn. 2 be without, leave behind, lose. *Opp* REMEMBER.

forgetful *adj* absent-minded, amnesiac, careless, distracted, inattentive, neglectful, negligent, oblivious, preoccupied, unconscious, unmindful, unreliable, vague, *inf* woolly-minded.

forgivable *adj* allowable, excusable, justifiable, negligible, pardonable, petty, understandable, venial. *Opp* UNFORGIVABLE.

forgive *vb* 1 absolve, acquit, clear, exculpate, excuse, exonerate, indulge, *inf* let off, pardon, spare. 2 *forgive a crime*. condone, ignore, make allowances for, overlook, pass over.

forgiveness *n* absolution, amnesty, clemency, compassion, exculpation, exoneration, grace, indulgence, leniency, mercy, pardon, reprieve, tolerance. *Opp* RETRIBUTION.

forgiving *adj* clement, compassionate, forbearing, generous, magnanimous, merciful, tolerant, understanding. ▷ KIND. *Opp* VENGEFUL.

forgo *vb* abandon, abstain from, do without, forswear, give up, go without, omit, pass up, relinquish, renounce, sacrifice, turn down, waive.

forked *adj* branched, cleft, divergent, divided, fork-like, pronged, split, V-shaped.

forlorn *adj* abandoned, alone, bereft, deserted, forsaken, friendless, lonely, outcast, solitary, unloved. ▷ SAD.

form *n* 1 appearance, arrangement, cast, character, configuration, design, format, framework, genre, guise, kind, manifestation, manner, model, mould, nature, pattern, plan, semblance, sort, species, structure, style, system, type, variety. 2 *human form*. anatomy, body, build, figure, frame, outline, physique, shape, silhouette. 3 *your form in school*. class, grade, group, level, set, stream, tutor-group. 4 *good form*. behaviour, convention, custom, etiquette, fashion, manners, practice. 5 *an application form*. document, paper. 6 *in good form*. condition, *inf* fettle, fitness, health, performance, spirits. 7 ▷ SEAT. ● *vb* 1 bring into existence, cast, constitute, construct, create, design, establish, forge, found, give form to, make, model, mould, organize, produce, shape. 2 appear, arise, come into existence, develop, grow, materialize, take shape.

3 *form a team*. act as, compose, comprise, make up, serve as. 4 *form a habit*. acquire, cultivate, develop, get.

formal *adj* 1 aloof, ceremonial, ceremonious, conventional, cool, correct, customary, dignified, *inf* dressed-up, orthodox, *inf* posh, *derog* pretentious, proper, punctilious, ritualistic, solemn, sophisticated, stately, *inf* starchy, stiff-necked, unbending, unfriendly. 2 *formal language*. academic, impersonal, official, precise, reserved, specialist, stilted, technical, unemotional. 3 *a formal agreement*. binding, contractual, enforceable, legal, *inf* signed and sealed. 4 *a formal design*. calculated, geometrical, orderly, organized, regular, rigid, symmetrical. *Opp* INFORMAL.

format *n* appearance, design, layout, plan, shape, size, style.

former *adj* bygone, departed, ex-, last, late, old, one-time, past, previous, prior, recent. **the former** earlier, first, first-mentioned. *Opp* LATTER.

formidable *adj* awe-inspiring, awesome, challenging, daunting, difficult, dreadful, fearful, frightening, intimidating, large-scale, *inf* mind-boggling, onerous, overwhelming, prodigious, taxing. *Opp* EASY.

formula *n* 1 form of words, ritual, rubric, spell, wording. 2 *formula for success*. blueprint, method, prescription, procedure, recipe, rule, technique, way.

formulate *vb* 1 articulate, codify, define, express clearly, set out in detail, specify, systematize. 2 concoct, create, devise, evolve, form, invent, map out, originate, plan, work out.

forsake *vb* abandon, break off from, desert, forgo, forswear, give up, jettison, jilt, leave, quit, renounce, repudiate, surrender, throw over, *inf* turn your back on, vacate.

fort *n* camp, castle, citadel, fortification, fortress, garrison, stronghold, tower.

forthright *adj* blunt, candid, decisive, direct, outspoken, plain-speaking, straightforward, unequivocal, unhesitating, uninhibited. ▷ FRANK. *Opp* EVASIVE.

fortify *vb* 1 buttress, defend, garrison, protect, reinforce, secure against attack, shore up. 2 bolster, boost, brace, buoy up, cheer, embolden, encourage, hearten, invigorate, lift the morale of, reassure, stiffen the resolve of, strengthen, support, sustain. *Opp* WEAKEN.

fortitude *n* backbone, bravery, courage, determination, endurance, firmness, heroism, patience, resolution, stoicism, tenacity, valour, will-power. ▷ COURAGE. *Opp* COWARDICE.

fortunate *adj* auspicious, blessed, favourable, lucky, opportune, propitious, prosperous, providential, timely. ▷ HAPPY.

fortune *n* 1 accident, chance, destiny, fate, fortuity, karma, kismet, luck, providence. 2 affluence, assets, estate, holdings, inheritance, means, *inf* millions, money, opulence, *inf* pile, possessions, property, prosperity, riches, treasure, wealth.

fortune-teller *n* clairvoyant, crystal-gazer, futurologist, oracle, palmist, prophet, seer, soothsayer, stargazer, sybil.

forward *adj* 1 advancing, front, frontal, head-first, leading, onward, progressive. 2 *forward planning*. advance, early, forward-looking, future, well-advanced. 3 *a forward child*. advanced, assertive, bold, brazen, cheeky, confident, familiar, *inf* fresh, impertinent, impudent, insolent, over-confident, precocious, presumptuous, pushful, *inf* pushy, shameless, uninhibited. *Opp* BACKWARD. ● *vb* 1 dispatch, expedite, freight, post on, re-address, send, send on, ship, transmit, transport. 2 *forward your career*. accelerate, advance, encourage, facilitate, foster, further, hasten, help along, *inf* lend a helping hand to, promote, speed up, support. ▷ HELP. *Opp* HINDER.

foster *vb* 1 advance, cultivate, encourage, further, nurture, promote, stimulate. ▷ HELP. 2 *foster a child*. adopt, bring up, care for, look after, maintain, nourish, nurse, raise, rear, take care of.

foul *adj* 1 bad, contaminated, disagreeable, disgusting, fetid, filthy, hateful, impure, infected, loathsome, nasty, nauseating, nauseous, noisome, obnoxious, offensive, polluted, putrid, repellent, repugnant, repulsive, revolting, rotten, sickening, smelly, squalid, stinking, vile. ▷ DIRTY, SMELLING. 2 *foul crimes*. abhorrent, abominable, atrocious, beastly, cruel, evil, ignominious, monstrous, scandalous, shameful, vicious,

villainous, violent, wicked.
3 *foul language.* abusive,
bawdy, blasphemous, coarse,
common, crude, impolite,
improper, indecent, insulting,
licentious, offensive, rude,
uncouth, vulgar. ▷ OBSCENE.
4 *foul weather.* foggy, rainy,
rough, stormy, violent, windy.
▷ UNPLEASANT. **5** *foul play.*
against the rules, dishonest,
forbidden, illegal, invalid,
prohibited, unfair, unsportsmanlike. *Opp* CLEAN, FAIR.
● *n* infringement, violation.
● *vb* ▷ DIRTY. **foul up**
▷ MUDDLE.

found *vb* **1** begin, bring about,
create, endow, establish, fund,
inf get going, inaugurate, initiate, institute, organize, originate, provide money for, raise,
set up, start. **2** base, build, construct, erect, ground, rest, set.

foundation *n* **1** beginning,
endowment, establishment,
founding, inauguration, initiation, institution, organizing,
setting up, starting. **2** base,
basement, basis, bottom,
cornerstone, foot, footing,
substructure, underpinning.
3 *foundations of science.* basic
principle, element, essential,
fundamental, origin,
plur rudiments.

founder *vb* abort, be wrecked,
inf come to grief, fail, fall
through, go down, miscarry,
sink.

fountain *n* font, fount, fountainhead, jet, source, spout, spray,
spring, well, well-spring.

foyer *n* ante-room, entrance,
entrance hall, hall, lobby,
reception.

fraction *n* division, part,
portion, section, subdivision.

fracture *n* break, breakage, chip,
cleavage, cleft, crack, fissure,
gap, opening, rent, rift, rupture,
split. ● *vb* breach, break, cause
a fracture in, chip, cleave,
crack, rupture, separate, split,
suffer a fracture in.

fragile *adj* ▷ FRAIL.

fragment *n* atom, bit, chip,
crumb, *plur* debris, morsel,
part, particle, piece, portion,
remnant, scrap, shard, shiver,
shred, sliver, *plur* smithereens,
snippet, speck. ● *vb* ▷ BREAK.

fragmentary *adj inf* bitty,
broken, disconnected, disinte-
grated, disjointed, fragmented,
imperfect, in bits, incoherent,
incomplete, in fragments,
partial, scattered, scrappy,
sketchy, uncoordinated.
Opp COMPLETE.

fragrance *n* aroma, bouquet,
nose (*of wine*), odour, perfume,
redolence, scent, smell.

fragrant *adj* aromatic, odorous,
perfumed, redolent, scented,
sweet-smelling.

frail *adj* breakable, brittle,
dainty, delicate, easily damaged, feeble, flimsy, fragile,
insubstantial, light, *derog* puny,
rickety, slight, thin, unsound,
unsteady, vulnerable, weak,
derog weedy. ▷ ILL.
Opp STRONG.

frame *n* **1** bodywork, chassis,
construction, scaffolding, structure. ▷ FRAMEWORK. **2** *photo
frame.* border, case, casing,
edge, edging, mount, mounting.
● *vb* **1** box in, enclose, mount,
set off, surround. **2** ▷ COMPOSE.
frame of mind ▷ ATTITUDE.

framework *n* bare bones,
frame, outline, plan, shell, skeleton, support, trellis.

frank adj blunt, candid, direct, downright, explicit, forthright, genuine, inf heart-to-heart, honest, ingenuous, inf no-nonsense, open, outright, outspoken, plain, plain-spoken, revealing, serious, sincere, straightforward, straight from the heart, to the point, trustworthy, truthful, unconcealed, undisguised, unreserved. Opp INSINCERE.

frantic adj agitated, anxious, berserk, inf beside yourself, crazy, delirious, demented, deranged, desperate, distraught, excitable, feverish, inf fraught, frenetic, frenzied, furious, hectic, hurried, hysterical, mad, overwrought, panicky, rabid, uncontrollable, violent, wild, worked up. Opp CALM.

fraud n 1 cheating, chicanery, inf con-trick, counterfeit, deceit, deception, dishonesty, double-dealing, duplicity, fake, forgery, hoax, imposture, pretence, inf put-up job, ruse, sham, inf sharp practice, swindle, trick, trickery. 2 charlatan, cheat, inf con-man, hoaxer, humbug, impostor, mountebank, sl phoney, inf quack, rogue, scoundrel, swindler.

fraudulent adj inf bent, bogus, cheating, corrupt, counterfeit, criminal, inf crooked, deceitful, devious, inf dirty, dishonest, double-dealing, duplicitous, fake, false, forged, illegal, lying, sl phoney, sham, specious, swindling, underhand, unscrupulous. Opp HONEST.

fray n brawl, commotion, conflict, disturbance, fracas, mêlée, quarrel, rumpus. ▷ FIGHT.

frayed adj chafed, rough-edged, tattered, threadbare, unravelled, worn. ▷ RAGGED.

freak adj aberrant, abnormal, anomalous, atypical, bizarre, exceptional, extraordinary, freakish, odd, peculiar, queer, rare, uncountable, unforeseeable, unpredictable, unusual, weird. Opp NORMAL.
● n 1 aberration, abnormality, abortion, anomaly, curiosity, deformity, irregularity, monster, monstrosity, mutant, oddity, inf one-off, quirk, rarity, sport, variant. 2 ▷ FANATIC.

free adj 1 able, allowed, at leisure, at liberty, idle, independent, loose, not working, uncommitted, unconfined, unconstrained, unencumbered, unfixed, unrestrained, untrammelled. 2 free from slavery. emancipated, freeborn, let go, liberated, released, unchained, unfettered, unshackled. 3 a free country. autonomous, democratic, independent, self-governing, sovereign. 4 free access. accessible, clear, open, permitted, unhindered, unimpeded, unrestricted. 5 free gifts. complimentary, gratis, sl on the house, unasked-for, unsolicited, without charge. 6 free space. available, empty, uninhabited, unoccupied, vacant. 7 free with money. bounteous, casual, charitable, generous, lavish, liberal, munificent, ready, unstinting, willing. ● vb 1 absolve, acquit, clear, deliver, discharge, disenthral, emancipate, enfranchise, exculpate, exonerate, let go, let off, let out, liberate, loose, make free, manumit, pardon, parole, ransom, release, reprieve, rescue, save, set free, spare,

turn loose, unchain, unfetter, unleash, unlock, unloose. *Opp* CONFINE. **2** *free tangled ropes.* clear, disengage, disentangle, extricate, loose, unbind, undo, unknot, untie. *Opp* TANGLE.
free and easy ▷ INFORMAL.

freedom *n* **1** autonomy, independence, liberty, self-determination, self-government, sovereignty. *Opp* CAPTIVITY. **2** deliverance, emancipation, exemption, immunity, liberation, release. **3** *freedom to choose.* ability, *Fr* carte blanche, discretion, free hand, latitude, leeway, leisure, licence, opportunity, permission, power, privilege, right, scope.

freeze *vb* **1** become ice, become solid, congeal, harden, ice over, ice up, solidify, stiffen. **2** chill, cool, make cold, numb. **3** *freeze food.* chill, deep-freeze, dry-freeze, ice, refrigerate. **4** *freeze the frame.* fix, hold, immobilize, keep still, paralyse, peg, petrify, stand still, stick, stop. **freezing** ▷ COLD.

freight *n* cargo, consignment, goods, haul, load, merchandise, payload, shipment.

frenzy *n* agitation, delirium, derangement, excitement, fever, fit, fury, hysteria, insanity, lunacy, madness, mania, outburst, paroxysm, passion, turmoil.

frequent *adj* common, constant, continual, countless, customary, everyday, familiar, habitual, incessant, innumerable, many, normal, numerous, ordinary, persistent, recurrent, recurring, regular, reiterative, repeated, usual. *Opp* INFREQUENT. ● *vb* ▷ HAUNT.

fresh *adj* **1** additional, alternative, different, extra, just arrived, new, recent, supplementary, unfamiliar, up-to-date. **2** alert, energetic, healthy, invigorated, lively, *inf* perky, rested, revived, sprightly, spry, tingling, vigorous, vital. **3** *a fresh recruit.* callow, *inf* green, inexperienced, naive, raw, unsophisticated, untried, *inf* wet behind the ears. **4** *fresh water.* clear, drinkable, potable, pure, refreshing, sweet, uncontaminated. **5** *fresh air.* airy, circulating, cool, unpolluted, ventilated. **6** *a fresh wind.* bracing, breezy, invigorating, moderate, sharp, stiff, strongish. **7** *fresh food.* healthy, natural, newly gathered, unprocessed, untreated, wholesome. **8** *fresh sheets.* clean, crisp, laundered, unironed, unused, washed-and-ironed. **9** *fresh colours.* bright, clean, glowing, just painted, renewed, restored, sparkling, unfaded, vivid. *Opp* OLD, STALE.

fret *vb* **1** agonize, be anxious, brood, lose sleep, worry. **2** ▷ ANNOY.

fretful *adj* anxious, distressed, disturbed, edgy, irritable, irritated, jittery, peevish, petulant, restless, testy, touchy, worried. ▷ BAD-TEMPERED. *Opp* CALM.

friction *n* **1** abrading, abrasion, attrition, chafing, fretting, grating, resistance, rubbing, scraping. **2** ▷ CONFLICT.

friend *n* acquaintance, associate, *inf* buddy, *inf* chum, companion, comrade, confidant(e), *inf* crony, intimate, *inf* mate, *inf* pal, partner, pen-friend, playfellow, playmate, supporter, well-wisher. ▷ ALLY.

LOVER. *Opp* ENEMY. **be friends**
▷ ASSOCIATE. **make friends
with** ▷ BEFRIEND.

friendless *adj* abandoned, alienated, alone, deserted, estranged,
forlorn, forsaken, isolated,
lonely, ostracized, shunned,
shut out, solitary, unattached,
unloved.

friendliness *n* benevolence,
camaraderie, conviviality,
devotion, esteem, familiarity,
goodwill, helpfulness, hospitality, kindness, neighbourliness,
regard, sociability, warmth.
Opp HOSTILITY.

friendly *adj* accessible, affable,
affectionate, agreeable, amiable,
amicable, approachable,
attached, benevolent, benign,
inf chummy, civil, close, clubbable, companionable, compatible, comradely, conciliatory,
congenial, convivial, cordial,
demonstrative, expansive,
favourable, genial, good-
natured, gracious, helpful,
hospitable, intimate, kind,
kind-hearted, kindly, likeable,
inf matey, neighbourly, outgoing, *inf* pally, sympathetic,
tender, *inf* thick, warm,
welcoming, well-disposed.
▷ FAMILIAR, LOVING, SOCIABLE.
Opp UNFRIENDLY.

friendship *n* affection, alliance,
amity, association, attachment,
closeness, comradeship, fellowship, fondness, harmony, intimacy, rapport, relationship.
▷ FRIENDLINESS, LOVE.
Opp HOSTILITY.

fright *n* 1 jolt, scare, shock,
surprise. 2 alarm, apprehension, consternation, dismay,
dread, fear, horror, panic,
terror, trepidation.

frighten *vb* agitate, alarm, appal,
browbeat, bully, cow, *inf* curdle
your blood, daunt, dismay,
distress, harrow, horrify, intimidate, make afraid, *inf* make
your blood run cold, make your
hair stand on end, menace,
panic, persecute, *inf* petrify,
inf put the wind up, scare,
inf scare stiff, shake, shock,
startle, terrify, terrorize,
threaten, traumatize, tyrannize,
unnerve, upset. ▷ DISCOURAGE.
Opp REASSURE.

frightened *adj* afraid, aghast,
alarmed, anxious, appalled,
apprehensive, *inf* chicken,
cowardly, craven, daunted,
fearful, harrowed, horrified,
horror-struck, panicky, panic-
stricken, petrified, scared,
shocked, terrified, terror-
stricken, trembling, unnerved,
upset, *inf* windy.

frightening *adj* alarming,
appalling, blood-curdling,
inf creepy, daunting, dire,
dreadful, eerie, fearful, fearsome, formidable, ghostly,
grim, hair-raising, horrifying,
intimidating, petrifying, scary,
sinister, spine-chilling,
inf spooky, terrifying, traumatic, uncanny, unnerving,
upsetting, weird, worrying.
▷ FRIGHTFUL.

frightful *adj* 1 awful, ghastly,
grisly, gruesome, harrowing,
hideous, horrible, horrid,
horrific, macabre, shocking,
terrible. ▷ FRIGHTENING.
2 ▷ BAD.

fringe *n* 1 borders, boundary,
edge, limits, marches, margin,
outskirts, perimeter, periphery.
2 border, edging, flounce, frill,
gathering, ruffle, trimming,
valance.

frisky *adj* active, animated, coltish, frolicsome, high-spirited, jaunty, lively, perky, playful, skittish, spirited, sprightly.

frivolity *n* childishness, facetiousness, flippancy, levity, light-heartedness, nonsense, playing about, silliness, triviality. ▷ FUN.

frivolous *adj* casual, childish, facetious, flighty, *inf* flip, flippant, foolish, inconsequential, insignificant, irresponsible, jocular, joking, minor, nugatory, paltry, petty, pointless, puerile, ridiculous, shallow, silly, stupid, superficial, trifling, trivial, trumpery, unimportant, unserious, vacuous, worthless. *Opp* SERIOUS.

frock *n* dress, gown, robe.

frolic *vb* caper, cavort, curvet, dance, frisk about, gambol, have fun, hop about, *inf* horse about, jump about, lark around, leap about, *inf* make whoopee, play about, prance, revel, rollick, romp, skip, skylark, sport.

front *adj* facing, first, foremost, leading, most advanced.
● *n* 1 anterior, bow (*of ship*), façade, face, facing, forefront, foreground, frontage, head, nose, obverse, van, vanguard. 2 battle area, danger zone, front line. 3 *a brave front*. appearance, aspect, bearing, blind, *inf* cover-up, demeanour, disguise, expression, look, mask, pretence, show. *Opp* BACK.

frontal *adj* direct, facing, head-on, oncoming, straight.

frontier *n* border, borderline, boundary, bounds, limit, marches, pale.

froth *n* bubbles, effervescence, foam, head (*on beer*), lather, scum, spume, suds.

frown *vb inf* give a dirty look, glare, glower, grimace, knit your brows, look sullen, lour, lower, scowl. **frown on** ▷ DISAPPROVE.

fruit *n* □ apple, apricot, avocado, banana, berry, bilberry, blackberry, cherry, coconut, crabapple, cranberry, currant, damson, date, fig, gooseberry, grape, grapefruit, greengage, guava, hip, kiwi fruit, lemon, lichee, lime, litchi, loganberry, lychee, mango, medlar, melon, mulberry, nectarine, olive, orange, papaw, pawpaw, peach, pear, pineapple, plum, pomegranate, prune, quince, raisin, raspberry, satsuma, sloe, strawberry, sultana, tangerine, tomato, ugli.

fruitful *adj* 1 abundant, bounteous, bountiful, copious, fecund, fertile, flourishing, lush, luxurious, plenteous, productive, profuse, prolific, rich. 2 advantageous, beneficial, effective, gainful, profitable, rewarding, successful, useful, well-spent, worthwhile. *Opp* FRUITLESS.

fruitless *adj* 1 barren, sterile, unfruitful, unproductive. 2 abortive, bootless, disappointing, futile, ineffective, ineffectual, pointless, profitless, unavailing, unprofitable, unrewarding, unsuccessful, useless, vain. *Opp* FRUITFUL.

frustrate *vb* baffle, balk, baulk, block, check, disappoint, discourage, foil, halt, hamstring, hinder, impede, inhibit, nullify, prevent, *inf* scotch, stop, stymie, thwart. ▷ DEFEAT. *Opp* ENCOURAGE.

frustrated adj disappointed, embittered, loveless, lovesick, resentful, thwarted, unfulfilled, unsatisfied.

fuel n □ anthracite, butane, charcoal, coal, coke, derv, diesel, electricity, gas, gasoline, kindling, logs, methylated spirit, nuclear fuel, oil, paraffin, peat, petrol, propane, tinder, wood.
 • vb encourage, feed, inflame, keep going, nourish, put fuel on, stoke up, supply with fuel.

fugitive adj ▷ TRANSIENT.
 • n deserter, escapee, escaper, refugee, renegade, runaway.

fulfil vb 1 accomplish, achieve, bring about, bring off, carry off, carry out, complete, consummate, discharge, do, effect, effectuate, execute, implement, make come true, perform, realize. 2 fulfil a need. answer, comply with, conform to, meet, obey, respond to, satisfy.

full adj 1 brimming, bursting, inf chock-a-block, inf chock-full, congested, crammed, crowded, filled, jammed, inf jam-packed, loaded, overflowing, packed, replete, solid, stuffed, topped-up, well-filled, well-stocked, well-supplied. 2 a full stomach. gorged, sated, satiated, satisfied, well-fed. 3 the full story. complete, comprehensive, detailed, entire, exhaustive, plenary, thorough, total, unabridged, uncensored, uncut, unedited, unexpurgated, whole. 4 full speed. extreme, greatest, highest, maximum, top, utmost. 5 a full figure. ample, broad, buxom, fat, large, plump, rounded, voluptuous, well-built. 6 a full skirt. baggy, generous, voluminous, wide. Opp EMPTY, INCOMPLETE, SMALL.

full-grown adj adult, grown-up, mature, ready, ripe.

fumble vb grope at, feel, handle awkwardly, mishandle, stumble, touch clumsily.

fume vb emit fumes, smoke, smoulder. **fuming** ▷ ANGRY.

fumes plur n exhaust, fog, gases, pollution, smog, smoke, vapour.

fun n amusement, clowning, diversion, enjoyment, entertainment, festivity, inf fooling around, frolic, inf fun-and-games, gaiety, games, inf high jinks, high spirits, horseplay, jocularity, jokes, joking, joc jollification, jollity, laughter, merriment, merrymaking, mirth, pastimes, play, playfulness, pleasure, pranks, recreation, romp, inf skylarking, sport, teasing, tomfoolery. ▷ FRIVOLITY. **make fun of** ▷ MOCK.

function n 1 aim, purpose, Fr raison d'être, use. ▷ JOB. 2 an official function. affair, ceremony, inf do, event, occasion, party, reception. • vb act, behave, go, operate, perform, run, work.

functional adj functioning, practical, serviceable, useful, utilitarian, working. Opp DECORATIVE.

fund n cache, hoard, inf kitty, mine, pool, reserve, reservoir, stock, store, supply, treasurehouse. **funds** capital, endowments, investments, reserves, resources, riches, savings, wealth. ▷ MONEY.

fundamental adj axiomatic, basic, cardinal, central, crucial, elementary, essential, important, key, main, necessary, primary, prime, principal, quintessential, rudimentary, underlying. Opp INESSENTIAL.

funeral n burial, cremation, entombment, exequies, interment, obsequies, Requiem Mass, wake.

funereal adj dark, depressing, dismal, gloomy, grave, mournful, sepulchral, solemn, sombre. ▷ SAD. Opp CHEERFUL.

funnel n chimney, smoke-stack. ● vb channel, direct, filter, pour.

funny adj 1 absurd, amusing, comic, comical, crazy, inf daft, diverting, droll, eccentric, entertaining, facetious, farcical, foolish, grotesque, hilarious, humorous, inf hysterical, ironic, jocose, jocular, inf killing, laughable, ludicrous, mad, merry, nonsensical, preposterous, inf priceless, inf rich, ridiculous, risible, sarcastic, sardonic, satirical, inf side-splitting, silly, slapstick, uproarious, waggish, witty, zany. Opp SERIOUS.
2 ▷ PECULIAR.

fur n bristles, coat, down, fleece, hair, hide, pelt, skin, wool.

furious adj 1 boiling, enraged, fuming, incensed, infuriated, irate, livid, mad, raging, savage, wrathful. ▷ ANGRY.
2 furious activity. agitated, fierce, frantic, frenzied, intense, tempestuous, tumultuous, turbulent, violent, wild. Opp CALM.

furnish vb 1 decorate, equip, fit out, fit up, inf kit out. 2 furnish information. afford, give, grant, provide, supply.

furniture n antiques, chattels, effects, equipment, fitments, fittings, fixtures, furnishings,

household goods, inf movables, possessions. □ armchair, bed, bench, bookcase, bunk, bureau, cabinet, chair, chesterfield, chest of drawers, chiffonier, commode, cot, couch, cradle, cupboard, cushion, desk, divan, drawer, dresser, dressing-table, easel, fender, filing-cabinet, fireplace, mantelpiece, ottoman, overmantel, pelmet, pew, pouffe, rocking-chair, seat, settee, sideboard, sofa, stool, suite, table, trestle-table, wardrobe, workbench.

furrow n channel, corrugation, crease, cut, ditch, drill, fissure, fluting, gash, groove, hollow, line, rut, score, scratch, track, trench, wrinkle.

furrowed adj 1 creased, crinkled, corrugated, fluted, grooved, ploughed, ribbed, ridged, rutted, scored.
2 furrowed brow. frowning, lined, worried, wrinkled. Opp SMOOTH.

furry adj bristly, downy, feathery, fleecy, fuzzy, hairy, woolly.

further adj accessory, additional, another, auxiliary, extra, fresh, more, new, other, spare, supplementary.

furthermore adv additionally, also, besides, moreover, too.

furtive adj clandestine, concealed, conspiratorial, covert, deceitful, disguised, hidden, mysterious, private, secret, secretive, shifty, sly, inf sneaky, stealthy, surreptitious, underhand, untrustworthy. ▷ CRAFTY. Opp BLATANT.

fury n ferocity, fierceness, force, intensity, madness, power, rage, savagery, tempestuousness, turbulence, vehemence, violence, wrath. ▷ ANGER.

fuse *vb* amalgamate, blend, coalesce, combine, commingle, compound, consolidate, join, meld, melt, merge, mix, solder, unite, weld.

fusillade *n* barrage, burst, firing, outburst, salvo, volley.

fuss *n* ▷ COMMOTION.
 ● *vb* agitate, bother, complain, *inf* create, fidget, *inf* flap, *inf* get worked up, grumble, make a commotion, worry.

fussy *adj* **1** carping, choosy, difficult, discriminating, *inf* faddy, fastidious, *inf* finicky, hard to please, niggling, *inf* nit-picking, particular, *inf* pernickety, scrupulous, squeamish. **2** *fussy decorations.* Byzantine, complicated, detailed, elaborate, fancy, ornate, overdone, rococo.

futile *adj* abortive, absurd, barren, bootless, empty, foolish, forlorn, fruitless, hollow, impotent, ineffective, ineffectual, pointless, profitless, silly, sterile, unavailing, unproductive, unprofitable, unsuccessful, useless, vain, wasted, worthless. *Opp* FRUITFUL.

future *adj* approaching, awaited, coming, destined, expected, forthcoming, impending, intended, planned, prospective, subsequent, unborn.
 ● *n* expectations, outlook, prospects, time to come, tomorrow. *Opp* PAST.

fuzz *n* down, floss, fluff, hair.

fuzzy *adj* **1** downy, feathery, fleecy, fluffy, frizzy, furry, linty, woolly. **2** bleary, blurred, cloudy, dim, faint, hazy, illdefined, indistinct, misty, obscure, out of focus, shadowy, unclear, unfocused, vague. *Opp* CLEAR.

G

gadget *n* apparatus, appliance, contraption, contrivance, device, implement, instrument, invention, machine, tool, utensil.

gag *n* ▷ JOKE. ● *vb* check, curb, keep quiet, muffle, muzzle, prevent from speaking, quiet, silence, stifle, still, suppress.

gaiety *n* brightness, cheerfulness, colourfulness, delight, exhilaration, felicity, glee, happiness, high spirits, hilarity, jollity, joyfulness, joyousness, light-heartedness, liveliness, merriment, merrymaking, mirth.

gain *n* achievement, acquisition, advantage, asset, attainment, benefit, dividend, earnings, income, increase, proceeds, profit, return, revenue, winnings, yield. *Opp* LOSS.
 ● *vb* **1** acquire, bring in, capture, collect, earn, garner, gather in, get, harvest, make, net, obtain, pick up, procure, profit, realize, reap, receive, win. *Opp* LOSE. **2** *gain your objective.* achieve, arrive at, attain, get to, reach, secure. *Opp* MISS. **gain on** approach, catch up with, close the gap, close with, go faster than, leave behind, overhaul, overtake.

gainful *adj* advantageous, beneficial, fruitful, lucrative, paid, productive, profitable, remunerative, rewarding, useful, worthwhile.

gala *n* carnival, celebration, fair, festival, festivity, fête, *inf* jamboree, party.

gale n blast, cyclone, hurricane, outburst, storm, tempest, tornado, typhoon, wind.

gallant adj attentive, chivalrous, courageous, courteous, courtly, dashing, fearless, gentlemanly, gracious, heroic, honourable, intrepid, magnanimous, noble, polite, valiant, well-bred. ▷ BRAVE. Opp VILLAINOUS.

gallows n gibbet, scaffold.

gamble vb back, bet, chance, draw lots, game, inf have a flutter, hazard, lay bets, risk money, speculate, stake money, inf take a chance, take risks, inf try your luck, venture, wager.

game adj ▷ BRAVE, WILLING.
• n 1 amusement, diversion, entertainment, frolic, fun, jest, joke, inf lark, inf messing about, pastime, play, playing, recreation, romp, sport. 2 competition, contest, match, round, tournament. ▷ SPORT. 3 animals, game-birds, prey, quarry. **give the game away** ▷ REVEAL.

gang n band, crew, crowd, mob, pack, ring, team. ▷ GROUP. **gang together, gang up** ▷ COMBINE.

gangster n bandit, brigand, criminal, inf crook, desperado, gunman, hoodlum, hooligan, mafioso, mugger, racketeer, robber, ruffian, thug, tough.

gaol n borstal, cell, custody, dungeon, guardhouse, jail, Amer penitentiary, prison.
• vb confine, detain, imprison, incarcerate, intern, inf send down, send to prison, inf shut away, shut up.

gaoler n guard, jailer, prison officer, sl screw, warder.

gap n 1 aperture, breach, break, cavity, chink, cleft, crack, cranny, crevice, gulf, hole, opening, rent, rift, rip, space, void. 2 breathing-space, discontinuity, hiatus, interlude, intermission, interruption, interval, lacuna, lapse, lull, pause, recess, respite, rest, suspension, wait. 3 gap between political parties. difference, disagreement, discrepancy, disparity, distance, divergence, division, incompatibility, inconsistency.

gape vb 1 open, part, split, yawn. 2 inf gawp, gaze, inf goggle, stare.

garbage n debris, detritus, junk, litter, muck, refuse, scrap, trash, waste. ▷ RUBBISH.

garble vb corrupt, distort, falsify, misconstrue, misquote, misrepresent, mutilate, pervert, slant, twist, warp. ▷ CONFUSE.

garden n allotment, patch, plot, yard. □ arbour, bed, border, herbaceous border, lawn, orchard, patio, pergola, rock garden, rose garden, shrubbery, terrace, vegetable garden, walled garden, water garden, windowbox. **gardens** grounds, park.

gardening n cultivation, horticulture.

garish adj bright, Brummagem, cheap, crude, flamboyant, flashy, gaudy, harsh, loud, lurid, meretricious, ostentatious, raffish, showy, startling, tasteless, tawdry, vivid, vulgar. Opp DRAB, TASTEFUL.

garment n apparel, attire, clothing, costume, dress, garb, habit, outfit. ▷ CLOTHES.

garrison n 1 contingent, detachment, force, unit. 2 barracks, camp, citadel, fort, fortification, fortress, station, stronghold.

gas *n* exhalation, exhaust, fumes, miasma, vapour.

gash *vb* chop, cleave, cut, incise, lacerate, score, slash, slit, split, wound.

gasp *vb* blow, breathe with difficulty, choke, fight for breath, gulp, *inf* huff and puff, pant, puff, snort, wheeze. **gasping** ▷ BREATHLESS, THIRSTY.

gate *n* access, barrier, door, entrance, entry, exit, gateway, kissing-gate, opening, passage, *poet* portal, portcullis, turnstile, way in, way out, wicket, wicket-gate.

gather *vb* 1 accumulate, amass, assemble, bring together, build up, cluster, collect, come together, concentrate, congregate, convene, crowd, flock, forgather, get together, group, grow, heap up, herd, hoard, huddle together, marshal, mass, meet, mobilize, muster, pick up, pile up, rally, round up, stockpile, store up, swarm, throng. *Opp* DISPERSE. 2 *gather flowers.* cull, garner, glean, harvest, pick, pluck, reap. 3 *I gather he's ill.* assume, be led to believe, conclude, deduce, guess, infer, learn, surmise, understand.

gathering *n* assembly, conclave, congress, convention, convocation, function, *inf* get-together, meeting, party, rally, social. ▷ GROUP.

gaudy *adj* bright, Brummagem, cheap, crude, flamboyant, flashy, garish, harsh, loud, lurid, meretricious, ostentatious, raffish, showy, startling,

tasteless, tawdry, vivid, vulgar. *Opp* DRAB, TASTEFUL.

gauge *n* 1 bench-mark, criterion, guide-line, measurement, norm, standard, test, yardstick. 2 capacity, dimensions, extent, measure, size, span, thickness, width. ● *vb* ▷ ESTIMATE, MEASURE.

gaunt *adj* 1 bony, cadaverous, emaciated, haggard, hollow-eyed, lanky, lean, pinched, raw-boned, scraggy, scrawny, skeletal, starving, underweight, wasted away. ▷ THIN. *Opp* PLUMP. 2 *a gaunt ruin.* bare, bleak, desolate, dreary, forbidding, grim, stark, stern, unfriendly. *Opp* ATTRACTIVE.

gawky *adj* awkward, blundering, clumsy, gangling, gauche, inept, lumbering, maladroit, uncoordinated, ungainly, ungraceful, unskilful. *Opp* GRACEFUL.

gay *adj* 1 animated, bright, carefree, cheerful, colourful, festive, fun-loving, jolly, jovial, joyful, light-hearted, lively, merry, sparkling, sunny, vivacious. ▷ HAPPY. 2 ▷ HOMOSEXUAL.

gaze *vb* contemplate, gape, look, regard, stare, view, wonder (at).

gear *n* accessories, accoutrements, apparatus, appliances, baggage, belongings, equipment, *inf* get-up, harness, implements, instruments, kit, luggage, materials, paraphernalia, rig, stuff, tackle, things, tools, trappings. ▷ CLOTHES.

gem *n* gemstone, jewel, precious stone, *sl* sparkler.

general *adj* 1 accepted, accustomed, collective, common, communal, conventional, customary, everyday, familiar, habitual, normal, ordinary, popular, prevailing, prevalent, public, regular, *inf* run-of-the-mill, shared, typical, usual. **2** *general discussion.* across-the-board, all-embracing, blanket, broad-based, catholic, comprehensive, diversified, encyclopaedic, extensive, far-ranging, far-reaching, global, heterogeneous, hybrid, inclusive, sweeping, universal, wholesale, wide-ranging, widespread, worldwide. **3** *a general idea.* approximate, broad, ill-defined, imprecise, indefinite, inexact, in outline, loose, simplified, superficial, unclear, undefined, unspecific, vague. Opp SPECIFIC.

generally *adv* as a rule, broadly, chiefly, commonly, in the main, mainly, mostly, normally, on the whole, predominantly, principally, usually.

generate *vb* beget, breed, bring about, cause, create, engender, father, give rise to, make, originate, procreate, produce, propagate, sire, spawn, *inf* whip up.

generosity *n* bounty, largesse, liberality, munificence, philanthropy.

generous *adj* **1** benevolent, big-hearted, bounteous, bountiful, charitable, disinterested, forgiving, *inf* free, impartial, kind, liberal, magnanimous, munificent, noble, open, open-handed, philanthropic, public-spirited, unmercenary, unprejudiced, unselfish, unsparing, unstinting. **2** *generous gifts.* handsome, princely, undeserved, unearned, valuable. ▷ EXPENSIVE. **3** *generous portions.* abundant, ample, copious, lavish,

plentiful, sizeable, substantial. ▷ BIG. Opp MEAN, SELFISH.

genial *adj* affable, agreeable, amiable, cheerful, convivial, cordial, easygoing, good-natured, happy, jolly, jovial, kindly, pleasant, relaxed, sociable, sunny, warm, warm-hearted. ▷ FRIENDLY. Opp UNFRIENDLY.

genitals *n* genitalia, *inf* private parts, pudenda, sex organs.

genius *n* **1** ability, aptitude, bent, brains, brilliance, capability, flair, gift, intellect, intelligence, knack, talent, wit. **2** academic, *inf* egghead, expert, intellectual, *derog* know-all, mastermind, thinker, virtuoso.

genteel *adj derog* affected, chivalrous, courtly, gentlemanly, ladylike, mannered, overpolite, patrician, *inf* posh, refined, stylish, *inf* upper-crust. ▷ POLITE.

gentle *adj* **1** amiable, biddable, compassionate, docile, easygoing, good-tempered, harmless, humane, kind, kindly, lenient, loving, meek, merciful, mild, moderate, obedient, pacific, passive, peace-loving, pleasant, quiet, soft-hearted, sweet-tempered, sympathetic, tame, tender. **2** *gentle music.* low, muted, peaceful, reassuring, relaxing, soft, soothing. **3** *gentle wind.* balmy, delicate, faint, light, soft, warm. **4** *a gentle hint.* indirect, polite, subtle, tactful. **5** *a gentle hill.* easy, gradual, imperceptible, moderate, slight, steady. Opp HARSH, SEVERE.

genuine *adj* **1** actual, authentic, authenticated, *Lat* bona fide, legitimate, original, proper, *sl* pukka, real, sterling, veritable. **2** *genuine feelings*. candid, devout, earnest, frank, heartfelt, honest, sincere, true, unaffected, unfeigned. Opp FALSE.

germ *n* **1** basis, beginning, embryo, genesis, cause, nucleus, origin, root, seed, source, start. **2** bacterium, *inf* bug, microbe, micro-organism, virus.

germinate *vb* begin to grow, bud, develop, grow, root, shoot, spring up, sprout, start growing, take root.

gesture *n* action, flourish, gesticulation, indication, motion, movement, sign, signal. • *vb* gesticulate, indicate, motion, sign, signal. □ *beckon, bow, nod, point, salute, shake your head, shrug, smile, wave, wink.*

get *vb* **1** acquire, be given, bring, buy, come by, come in possession of, earn, fetch, gain, get hold of, inherit, *inf* land, *inf* lay hands on, obtain, pick up, procure, purchase, receive, retrieve, secure, take, win. **2** *get her by phone*. contact, get in touch with, reach, speak to. **3** *get a cold*. catch, come down with, contract, develop, fall ill with, suffer from. **4** *get a criminal*. apprehend, arrest, capture, catch, *inf* collar, *inf* nab, *sl* pinch, seize. **5** *get him to help*. cajole, cause, induce, influence, persuade, prevail on, *inf* twist someone's arm, wheedle. **6** *get tea*. cook, make ready, prepare. **7** *get what he means*. absorb, appreciate, apprehend, comprehend, fathom, follow, glean, grasp, know, take in, understand, work out. **8** *get what he says*. catch, distin-

guish, hear, make out. **9** *get somewhere*. arrive, come, go, journey, reach, travel. **10** *get cold*. become, grow, turn. **get across** ▷ COMMUNICATE. **get ahead** ▷ PROSPER. **get at** ▷ CRITICIZE. **get away** ▷ ESCAPE. **get down** ▷ DESCEND. **get in** ▷ ENTER. **get off** ▷ DESCEND. **get on** ▷ PROSPER. **get out** ▷ LEAVE. **get together** ▷ GATHER.

getaway *n* escape, flight, retreat.

ghastly *adj* appalling, awful, deathlike, dreadful, frightening, frightful, grim, grisly, gruesome, hideous, horrible, macabre, nasty, shocking, terrible, upsetting. ▷ UNPLEASANT.

ghost *n* apparition, banshee, *inf* bogey, *Ger* doppelgänger, ghoul, hallucination, illusion, phantasm, phantom, poltergeist, shade, shadow, spectre, spirit, *inf* spook, vision, visitant, wraith. **give up the ghost** ▷ DIE.

ghostly *adj* creepy, disembodied, eerie, frightening, illusory, phantasmal, scary, sinister, spectral, *inf* spooky, supernatural, uncanny, unearthly, weird, wraith-like.

giant *adj* ▷ GIGANTIC. • *n* colossus, Goliath, leviathan, monster, ogre, superhuman, titan, *inf* whopper.

giddiness *n* dizziness, faintness, unsteadiness, vertigo.

giddy *adj* dizzy, faint, lightheaded, reeling, silly, spinning, unbalanced, unsteady, vertiginous.

gift *n* **1** benefaction, bonus, bounty, charity, contribution, donation, favour, *inf* give-away, grant, gratuity, *inf* hand-out, honorarium, largesse, offering, present, tip. **2** ability, aptitude, bent, capability, capacity, facility, flair, genius, knack, power, strength, talent.

gifted *adj* able, capable, expert, skilful, skilled, talented.
▷ CLEVER.

gigantic *adj* Brobdingnagian, colossal, elephantine, enormous, gargantuan, giant, herculean, huge, immense, *inf* jumbo, king-size, mammoth, massive, mighty, monstrous, prodigious, titanic, towering, vast. ▷ BIG. *Opp* SMALL.

giggle *vb* snicker, snigger, titter. ▷ LAUGH.

gimcrack *adj* cheap, *inf* cheap and nasty, flimsy, rubbishy, shoddy, tawdry, trashy, trumpery, useless, worthless.

gimmick *n* device, ploy, ruse, stratagem, stunt, subterfuge, trick.

girder *n* bar, beam, joist, rafter.

girdle *n* band, belt, corset, waistband. ● *vb* ▷ SURROUND.

girl *n sl* bird, *old use* damsel, daughter, débutante, fiancée, girlfriend, hoyden, lass, *old use* maid, *old use* maiden, *inf* miss, schoolgirl, tomboy, virgin, *old use or sexist* wench. ▷ WOMAN.

girth *n* circumference, measurement round, perimeter.

gist *n* core, direction, drift, essence, general sense, main idea, meaning, nub, pith, point, quintessence, significance.

give *vb* **1** accord, allocate, allot, allow, apportion, assign, award, bestow, confer, contribute, deal out, *inf* dish out, distribute, *inf* dole out, donate, endow, entrust, *inf* fork out, furnish,

give away, give out, grant, hand over, lend, let (someone) have, offer, pass over, pay, present, provide, ration out, render, share out, supply. **2** *give information*. deliver, display, express, impart, issue, notify, publish, put across, put into words, reveal, set out, show, tell, transmit. **3** *give a shout*. emit, let out, utter, voice. **4** *give medicine*. administer, dispense, dose with, impose, inflict, mete out, prescribe. **5** *give a party*. arrange, organize, provide, put on, run, set up. **6** *give trouble*. cause, create, engender, occasion. **7** *give under pressure*. be flexible, bend, buckle, collapse, distort, fail, fall apart, give way, warp, yield. *Opp* RECEIVE, TAKE. **give away** ▷ BETRAY. **give in** ▷ SURRENDER. **give off, give out** ▷ EMIT. **give up** ▷ ABANDON, SURRENDER.

glad *adj* **1** content, delighted, gratified, joyful, overjoyed, pleased. ▷ HAPPY. *Opp* GLOOMY. **2** *glad to help*. disposed, eager, inclined, keen, ready, willing. *Opp* RELUCTANT.

glamorize *vb* idealize, romanticize.

glamorous *adj* alluring, appealing, colourful, dazzling, enviable, exciting, exotic, fascinating, glittering, prestigious, romantic, smart, spectacular, wealthy. ▷ BEAUTIFUL.

glamour *n* allure, appeal, attraction, brilliance, charm, excitement, fascination, glitter, highlife, lustre, magic, romance. ▷ BEAUTY.

glance *vb* glimpse, have a quick look, peek, peep, scan, skim, *sl* take a dekko. ▷ LOOK.

glare vb 1 frown, inf give a nasty look, glower, inf look daggers, lour, lower, scowl, stare angrily. 2 blaze, dazzle, flare, reflect, shine. ▷ LIGHT. **glaring** ▷ BRIGHT.

glass n 1 crystal, glassware. 2 glazing, pane, plate-glass, window. 3 looking-glass, mirror, reflector. 4 beaker, drinking-glass, goblet, tumbler, wine-glass. 5 optical instrument. □ binoculars, field-glasses, goggles, magnifying glass, microscope, opera-glasses, telescope, spyglass. **glasses** inf specs, spectacles. □ bifocals, contact-lenses, eyeglass, lorgnette, monocle, pince-nez, reading glasses, sun-glasses, trifocals.

glasshouse n conservatory, greenhouse, hothouse, orangery, vinery.

glassy adj 1 glazed, gleaming, glossy, icy, polished, shining, shiny, smooth, vitreous. 2 glassy stare. ▷ EXPRESSIONLESS.

glaze vb burnish, enamel, gloss, lacquer, polish, shellac, shine, varnish.

gleam vb flash, glimmer, glint, glisten, glow, reflect, shine. ▷ LIGHT. **gleaming** ▷ BRIGHT.

gleeful adj cheerful, delighted, ecstatic, exuberant, exultant, gay, joyful, joyful, jubilant, overjoyed, pleased, rapturous, triumphant. ▷ HAPPY. Opp SAD.

glib adj articulate, facile, fast-talking, fluent, insincere, plausible, quick, ready, shallow, slick, smooth, smooth-tongued, suave, superficial, unctuous. ▷ TALKATIVE. Opp INARTICULATE, SINCERE.

glide vb coast, drift, float, fly, free-wheel, glissade, hang, hover, move smoothly, sail, skate, ski, skid, skim, slide, slip, soar, stream.

glimpse n glance, look, peep, sight, inf squint, view.
● vb discern, distinguish, espy, get a glimpse of, make out, notice, observe, see briefly, sight, spot, spy.

glisten vb flash, gleam, glimmer, glint, glitter, reflect, shine. ▷ LIGHT.

glitter vb coruscate, flash, scintillate, spark, sparkle, twinkle. ▷ LIGHT. **glittering** ▷ BRIGHT.

gloat vb boast, brag, inf crow, exult, glory, rejoice, inf rub it in, show off, triumph.

global adj broad, far-reaching, international, pandemic, total, universal, wide-ranging, worldwide. Opp LOCAL.

globe n 1 ball, globule, orb, sphere. 2 earth, planet, world.

gloom n blackness, cloudiness, darkness, dimness, dullness, dusk, murk, murkiness, obscurity, semi-darkness, shade, shadow, twilight. ▷ DEPRESSION.

gloomy adj 1 cheerless, cloudy, dark, depressing, dim, dingy, dismal, dreary, dull, glum, grim, heavy, joyless, murky, obscure, overcast, shadowy, shady, sombre. 2 a gloomy mood. depressed, downhearted, lugubrious, mournful, pessimistic, saturnine. ▷ SAD. Opp CHEERFUL.

glorious adj 1 celebrated, distinguished, eminent, famed, famous, heroic, illustrious, noble, noted, renowned, triumphant. 2 glorious weather. beautiful, bright, brilliant, dazzling, delightful, excellent, fine, gorgeous, grand, impressive, lovely, magnificent, majestic, marvellous, outstanding, pleasurable, resplendent, spectacular, splendid, *inf* super, superb, wonderful. *Opp* ORDINARY.

glory *n* 1 credit, distinction, eminence, fame, honour, *inf* kudos, praise, prestige, renown, repute, reputation, success, triumph. 2 *glory to God*. adoration, exaltation, glorification, gratitude, homage, praise, thanksgiving, veneration, worship. 3 *glory of sunrise*. brightness, brilliance, grandeur, magnificence, majesty, radiance, splendour, wonder. ▷ BEAUTY.

gloss *n* 1 brightness, brilliance, burnish, finish, glaze, gleam, lustre, polish, sheen, shine, varnish. 2 annotation, comment, definition, elucidation, exegesis, explanation, footnote, marginal note, note, paraphrase. ● *vb* annotate, comment on, define, elucidate, explain, interpret, paraphrase. **gloss over** ▷ CONCEAL.

glossary *n* dictionary, phrasebook, vocabulary, word-list.

glossy *adj* bright, burnished, glassy, glazed, gleaming, glistening, lustrous, polished, reflective, shiny, silky, sleek, smooth, waxed. *Opp* DULL.

glove *n* gauntlet, mitt, mitten.

glow *n* 1 burning, fieriness, heat, incandescence, luminosity, lustre, phosphorescence, radiation, red-heat, redness. 2 ardour, blush, enthusiasm, fervour, flush, passion, rosiness, warmth. ● *vb* blush, flush,

gleam, incandesce, light up, phosphoresce, radiate heat, redden, smoulder, warm up. ▷ LIGHT.

glower *vb* frown, glare, lour, lower, scowl, stare angrily.

glowing *adj* 1 aglow, bright, hot, incandescent, lambent, luminous, phosphorescent, radiant, red, red-hot, white-hot. 2 *glowing praise*. complimentary, enthusiastic, fervent, passionate, warm.

glue *n* adhesive, cement, fixative, gum, paste, sealant, size, wallpaper-paste. ● *vb* affix, bond, cement, fasten, fix, gum, paste, seal, stick.

glum *adj* cheerless, displeased, gloomy, grim, heavy, joyless, lugubrious, moody, mournful, *inf* out of sorts, saturnine, sullen. ▷ SAD. *Opp* CHEERFUL.

glut *n* abundance, excess, overabundance, overflow, overprovision, plenty, superfluity, surfeit, surplus. *Opp* SCARCITY.

glutton *n joc* good trencherman, gormandizer, gourmand, *inf* greedy-guts, guzzler, *inf* pig.

gluttonous *adj* gormandizing, greedy, *inf* hoggish, *inf* piggish, insatiable, ravenous, voracious.

gnarled *adj* bent, bumpy, contorted, crooked, distorted, knobbly, knotted, knotty, lumpy, rough, rugged, twisted, warped.

gnaw *vb* bite, chew, erode, wear away. ▷ EAT.

go *n* attempt, chance, *inf* crack, opportunity, *inf* shot, *inf* stab, try, turn. ● *vb* 1 advance, begin, be off, commence, decamp, depart, disappear, embark, escape, get away, get going, get moving, get out, get under way, leave, make off, move, *inf* nip along, pass along, pass on, proceed, retire, retreat, run, set off, set out, *inf* shove off, start, take off, take your leave, vanish, *old use* wend your way, withdraw. ▷ RUN, TRAVEL, WALK. **2** die, fade, fail, give way. **3** extend, lead, reach, stretch. **4** *car won't go*. act, function, operate, perform, run, work. **5** *bomb went bang*. give off, make, produce, sound. **6** *Time goes slowly*. elapse, lapse, pass. **7** *go sour*. become, grow, turn. **8** *Milk goes in the fridge*. belong, feel at home, have a proper place, live. **go away** ▷ DEPART. **go down** ▷ DESCEND, SINK. **go in** ▷ LIKE. **go into** ▷ INVESTIGATE. **go off** ▷ EXPLODE. **go on** ▷ CONTINUE. **go through** ▷ SUFFER. **go to** ▷ VISIT. **go together** ▷ MATCH. **go with** ▷ ACCOMPANY. **go without** ▷ ABSTAIN.

goad *vb* badger, *inf* chivvy, egg on, *inf* hassle, needle, prick, prod, prompt, spur, urge. ▷ STIMULATE.

go-ahead *adj* ambitious, enterprising, forward-looking, progressive, resourceful. • *n* approval, *inf* green light, permission, sanction, *inf* sayso, *inf* thumbs-up.

goal *n* aim, ambition, aspiration, design, end, ideal, intention, object, objective, purpose, target.

gobble *vb* bolt, devour, gulp, guzzle. ▷ EAT.

go-between *n* agent, broker, envoy, intermediary, liaison, mediator, messenger, middleman, negotiator. **act as go-between** ▷ MEDIATE.

god, goddess *ns* deity, divinity, godhead, spirit. **God** the Almighty, the Creator, the supreme being. **the gods** the immortals, the pantheon, the powers above.

godsend *n inf* bit of good luck, blessing, boon, gift, miracle, *inf* stroke of good fortune, windfall.

golden *adj* **1** aureate, gilded, gilt. **2** *golden hair*. blond, blonde, flaxen, yellow.

good *adj* **1** acceptable, admirable, agreeable, appropriate, approved of, commendable, delightful, enjoyable, esteemed, *inf* fabulous, fair, *inf* fantastic, fine, gratifying, happy, *inf* incredible, lovely, marvellous, nice, perfect, *inf* phenomenal, pleasant, pleasing, praiseworthy, proper, remarkable, right, satisfactory, *inf* sensational, sound, splendid, suitable, *inf* super, superb, useful, valid, valuable, wonderful, worthy. ▷ EXCELLENT. **2** *a good person*. angelic, benevolent, caring, charitable, chaste, considerate, decent, dependable, dutiful, ethical, friendly, helpful, holy, honest, honourable, humane, incorruptible, innocent, just, law-abiding, loyal, merciful, moral, noble, obedient, personable, pure, reliable, religious, righteous, saintly, sound, *inf* straight, thoughtful, true, trustworthy, upright, virtuous, well-behaved, well-mannered, worthy. ▷ KIND. **3** *a good worker*. able, accomplished, capable, conscientious, efficient, gifted, proficient, skilful, skilled, talented. ▷ CLEVER. **4** *good work*. careful, competent, correct, creditable, efficient, meritorious, neat, orderly, presentable, professional, thorough, well-done. **5** *good food.* beneficial, delicious, eatable, healthy, nourishing, nutritious, tasty, well-cooked, wholesome. **6** *a good book.* classic, exciting, great, interesting, readable, well-written. *Opp* BAD. **good-humoured** ▷ GOOD-TEMPERED. **good-looking** ▷ HANDSOME. **good-natured** ▷ GOOD-TEMPERED. **good person** *inf* angel, *inf* jewel, philanthropist, *inf* saint, Samaritan, worthy. **goods 1** belongings, chattels, effects, possessions, property. **2** commodities, freight, load, merchandise, produce, stock, wares.

goodbye *n* farewell, departure, leave-taking, parting words, send-off, valediction. □ *adieu, adios, arrivederci, auf Wiedersehen, au revoir, bon voyage, cheerio, ciao, so long.*

good-tempered *adj* accommodating, amenable, amiable, benevolent, benign, cheerful, cheery, considerate, cooperative, cordial, friendly, genial, good-humoured, good-natured, helpful, in a good mood, obliging, patient, pleasant, relaxed, smiling, sympathetic, thoughtful, willing. ▷ KIND. *Opp* BAD-TEMPERED.

gorge *vb* be greedy, fill up, gormandize, guzzle, indulge yourself, *inf* make a pig of yourself, overeat, *inf* stuff yourself. ▷ EAT.

gorgeous *adj* colourful, dazzling, glorious, magnificent, resplendent, showy, splendid, sumptuous. ▷ BEAUTIFUL.

gory *adj* blood-stained, bloody, grisly, gruesome, sanguinary, savage.

gospel *n* creed, doctrine, good news, good tidings, message, religion, revelation, teaching, testament.

gossip *n* **1** casual talk, chatter, *inf* the grapevine, hearsay, prattle, rumour, scandal, small talk, *inf* tattle, *inf* tittle-tattle. **2** *inf* blab, busybody, chatterbox, *inf* Nosey Parker, rumour-monger, scandalmonger, telltale. ● *vb inf* blab, chat, chatter, *inf* natter, prattle, spread scandal, *inf* tattle, tell tales, *inf* tittle-tattle. ▷ TALK.

gouge *vb* chisel, dig, gash, hollow, incise, scoop. ▷ CUT.

gourmet *n Fr* bon viveur, connoisseur, epicure, gastronome, *derog* gourmand.

govern *vb* **1** administer, be in charge of, command, conduct affairs, control, direct, guide, head, lead, look after, manage, oversee, preside over, reign, rule, run, steer, superintend, supervise. **2** *govern your anger.* bridle, check, control, curb, discipline, keep in check, keep under control, master, regulate, restrain, tame.

government *n* administration, authority, bureaucracy, conduct of state affairs, constitution, control, direction, domination, management, oversight, regime, regulation, rule, sovereignty, supervision, surveillance, sway. □ *commonwealth, democracy, dictatorship, empire, federation, kingdom, monarchy, oligarchy, republic.*

gown *n* dress, frock. ▷ CLOTHES.

grab vb appropriate, arrogate, inf bag, capture, catch, clutch, inf collar, commandeer, expropriate, get hold of, grasp, hold, inf nab, pluck, seize, snap up, snatch, usurp.

grace n 1 attractiveness, beauty, charm, ease, elegance, fluidity, gracefulness, loveliness, poise, refinement, softness, tastefulness. 2 God's grace. beneficence, benevolence, compassion, favour, forgiveness, goodness, graciousness, kindness, love, mercy. 3 grace before meals. blessing, prayer, thanksgiving.

graceful adj 1 agile, balletic, deft, dignified, easy, elegant, flowing, fluid, natural, nimble, pliant, slender, slim, smooth, supple, willowy. ▷ BEAUTIFUL. 2 graceful compliments. courteous, courtly, delicate, kind, polite, refined, suave, tactful, urbane. Opp GRACELESS.

graceless adj 1 awkward, clumsy, gangling, gawky, inelegant, maladroit, uncoordinated, ungainly. ▷ CLUMSY. Opp GRACEFUL. 2 graceless manners. boorish, gauche, inept, tactless, uncouth. ▷ RUDE.

gracious adj 1 affable, agreeable, civilized, cordial, courteous, dignified, elegant, friendly, good-natured, pleasant, polite, with grace. ▷ KIND. 2 clement, compassionate, forgiving, generous, indulgent, lenient, magnanimous, pitying, sympathetic. ▷ MERCIFUL. 3 gracious living. affluent, expensive, lavish, luxurious, opulent, self-indulgent, sumptuous.

grade n category, class, condition, degree, echelon, estate, level, mark, notch, point, position, quality, rank, rung, situation, standard, standing, status, step. ● vb 1 arrange, categorize, classify, differentiate, group, organize, range, size, sort. 2 grade students' work. assess, evaluate, mark, rank, rate.

gradient n ascent, bank, declivity, hill, incline, rise, slope.

gradual adj continuous, easy, even, gentle, leisurely, moderate, regular, slow, steady, unhurried, unspectacular. Opp SUDDEN.

graduate vb 1 become a graduate, be successful, get a degree, pass, qualify. 2 graduate a measuring-rod. calibrate, divide into graded sections, gradate, mark off, mark with a scale.

graft vb implant, insert, join, splice.

grain n 1 atom, bit, crumb, fleck, fragment, granule, iota, jot, mite, molecule, morsel, mote, particle, scrap, seed, speck, trace. 2 ▷ CEREAL.

grand adj 1 aristocratic, august, dignified, eminent, glorious, great, important, imposing, impressive, lordly, magnificent, majestic, noble, opulent, palatial, regal, royal, splendid, stately, sumptuous, superb. ▷ BIG. 2 [derog] haughty, inf high-and-mighty, lofty, patronizing, pompous, posh, inf upper crust. ▷ GRANDIOSE. Opp MODEST.

grandiloquent adj bombastic, elaborate, florid, flowery, fustian, high-flown, inflated, melodramatic, ornate, poetic, pompous, rhetorical, turgid. ▷ GRANDIOSE. Opp SIMPLE.

grandiose adj affected, ambitious, exaggerated, extravagant, flamboyant, *inf* flashy, grand, highfalutin, ostentatious, overdone, *inf* over the top, pretentious, showy. ▷ GRANDILOQUENT. *Opp* MODEST.

grant *n* allocation, allowance, annuity, award, benefaction, bursary, concession, contribution, donation, endowment, expenses, gift, honorarium, investment, loan, pension, scholarship, sponsorship, subsidy, subvention.
● *vb* 1 allocate, allot, allow, assign, award, bestow, confer, donate, give, pay, provide, supply. 2 *grant that I'm right.* accede, accept, acknowledge, admit, agree, concede, consent, vouchsafe.

graph *n* chart, column-graph, diagram, grid, pie chart, table.

graphic *adj* clear, descriptive, detailed, lifelike, lucid, photographic, plain, realistic, representational, vivid, well-drawn.

grapple *vb* clutch (at), grab, seize, tackle, wrestle. ▷ GRASP, FIGHT. **grapple with** *grapple with a problem.* attend to, come to grips with, contend with, cope with, deal with, engage with, get involved with, handle, *inf* have a go at, manage, try to solve.

grasp *vb* 1 catch, clasp, clutch, get hold of, *inf* get your hands on, grab, grapple with, grip, hang on to, hold, *inf* nab, seize, snatch, take hold of. 2 *grasp an idea.* appreciate, apprehend, comprehend, *inf* cotton on to, follow, *inf* get the drift of, get the hang of, get the point of, learn, master, realize, take in, understand. **grasping** ▷ GREEDY.

grass *n* downland, field, grassland, green, lawn, meadow, pasture, playing-field, prairie, savannah, steppe, *poet* sward, turf, veld. ● *vb* ▷ INFORM.

grate *n* fireplace, hearth.
● *vb* cut, grind, rasp, shred, triturate. **grate on** ▷ ANNOY. **grating** ▷ ANNOYING, HARSH.

grateful *adj* appreciative, beholden, gratified, indebted, obliged, thankful. *Opp* UNGRATEFUL.

gratify *vb* delight, fulfil, indulge, pander to, please, satisfy.

gratis *adj* complimentary, free, free of charge, gratuitous, without charge.

gratitude *n* appreciation, gratefulness, thankfulness, thanks.

gratuitous *adj* 1 ▷ GRATIS. 2 *gratuitous insults.* baseless, groundless, inappropriate, needless, unasked-for, uncalled-for, undeserved, unjustifiable, unmerited, unnecessary, unprovoked, unsolicited, unwarranted. *Opp* JUSTIFIABLE.

gratuity *n* bonus, *inf* perk, *Fr* pourboire, present, recompense, reward, tip.

grave *adj* 1 acute, critical, crucial, dangerous, important, *inf* life and death, major, momentous, perilous, pressing, serious, severe, significant, terminal (*illness*), threatening, urgent, vital, weighty, worrying. 2 *a grave offence.* criminal, indictable, punishable. 3 *a grave look.* dignified, earnest, grim, long-faced, pensive, sedate, serious, severe, sober, solemn, sombre, subdued, thoughtful, unsmiling. ▷ SAD. *Opp* CHEERFUL, TRIVIAL.
● *n* barrow, burial-place, crypt, *inf* last resting-place, mauso-

leum, sepulchre, tomb, tumulus, vault. ▷ GRAVESTONE.

gravel n grit, pebbles, shingle, stones.

gravestone n headstone, memorial, monument, tombstone.

graveyard n burial-ground, cemetery, churchyard, necropolis.

gravity n 1 acuteness, danger, importance, magnitude, momentousness, seriousness, severity, significance, weightiness. 2 *behave with gravity*. ceremony, dignity, earnestness, *Lat* gravitas, pomp, reserve, sedateness, sobriety, solemnity. 3 *force of gravity*. attraction, gravitation, heaviness, ponderousness, pull, weight.

graze n abrasion, laceration, raw spot, scrape, scratch. ▷ WOUND.

grease n fat, lubrication, oil.

greasy adj 1 buttery, fatty, oily, slippery, slithery, smeary, waxy. 2 *greasy manner*. fawning, flattering, fulsome, grovelling, ingratiating, slick, *inf* smarmy, sycophantic, toadying, unctuous.

great adj 1 colossal, enormous, extensive, giant, gigantic, grand, huge, immense, large, massive, prodigious, *inf* tremendous, vast. ▷ BIG. 2 *great pain*. acute, considerable, excessive, extreme, intense, marked, pronounced. ▷ SEVERE. 3 *great events*. grand, imposing, large-scale, momentous, serious, significant, spectacular, weighty. ▷ IMPORTANT. 4 *great music*. brilliant, classic, *inf* fabulous, famous, *inf* fantastic, fine, first-rate, outstanding, wonderful. ▷ EXCELLENT. 5 *a great athlete*. able, cele-

brated, distinguished, eminent, gifted, notable, noted, prominent, renowned, talented, well-known. ▷ FAMOUS. 6 *a great friend*. chief, close, dedicated, devoted, faithful, fast, loyal, main, true, valued. 7 *a great reader*. active, ardent, assiduous, eager, enthusiastic, frequent, habitual, keen, passionate, zealous. 8 ▷ GOOD. *Opp* SMALL, UNIMPORTANT.

greed n 1 appetite, craving, gluttony, gormandizing, hunger, insatiability, intemperance, overeating, ravenousness, self-indulgence, voraciousness, voracity. 2 *greed for wealth*. acquisitiveness, avarice, covetousness, cupidity, desire, rapacity, self-interest. ▷ SELFISHNESS.

greedy adj 1 famished, gluttonous, gormandizing, *inf* hoggish, hungry, insatiable, intemperate, omnivorous, *inf* piggish, ravenous, self-indulgent, starving, voracious. *Opp* ABSTEMIOUS. 2 *greedy for wealth*. acquisitive, avaricious, avid, covetous, desirous, eager, grasping, materialistic, mean, mercenary, miserly, *inf* money-grubbing, rapacious, selfish. *Opp* UNSELFISH. **be greedy** ▷ GORGE. **greedy person** ▷ GLUTTON.

green adj 1 grassy, greenish, leafy, verdant. □ emerald, grass-green, jade, khaki, lime, olive, pea-green, turquoise. 2 ▷ IMMATURE.

greenery n foliage, leaves, plants, vegetation.

greet vb accost, acknowledge, address, give a greeting to, hail, receive, salute, *inf* say hello to, usher in, welcome.

greeting n salutation, reception, welcome. **greetings** compliments, congratulations, felicitations, good wishes, regards.

grey adj ashen, blackish, colourless, greying, grizzled, grizzly, hoary, leaden, livid, pearly, silver, silvery, slate-grey, smoky, sooty, whitish.
▷ GLOOMY.

grid n framework, grating, grille, lattice, network.

grief n affliction, anguish, dejection, depression, desolation, despondency, distress, heartache, heartbreak, melancholy, misery, mourning, pain, regret, remorse, sadness, sorrow, suffering, tragedy, unhappiness, woe, wretchedness.
▷ PAIN. Opp HAPPINESS. **come to grief** ▷ FAIL.

grievance n 1 calamity, damage, hardship, harm, indignity, injury, injustice. 2 allegation, inf bone to pick, charge, complaint, inf gripe, objection.

grieve vb 1 afflict, cause grief, depress, dismay, distress, hurt, pain, sadden, upset, wound. Opp PLEASE. 2 be in mourning, feel grief, inf eat your heart out, fret, lament, mope, mourn, suffer, wail, weep. Opp REJOICE.

grim adj alarming, appalling, awful, cruel, dire, dour, dreadful, fearsome, fierce, forbidding, formidable, frightening, frightful, frowning, ghastly, grisly, gruesome, harsh, hideous, horrible, inf horrid, inexorable, inflexible, joyless, louring, menacing, merciless, ominous, pitiless, relentless, ruthless, savage, severe, sinister, stark, stern, sullen, surly, terrible, threatening, unattractive,

uncompromising, unfriendly, unpleasant, unrelenting, unsmiling, unyielding.
▷ GLOOMY. Opp CHEERFUL.

grime n dirt, dust, filth, grit, muck, scum, soot.

grind vb 1 abrade, comminute, crumble, crush, erode, granulate, grate, mill, pound, powder, pulverize, rasp, triturate. 2 file, polish, sand, sandpaper, scrape, sharpen, smooth, wear away, whet. 3 *grind your teeth.* gnash, grate, grit, rub together. **grind away** ▷ WORK. **grind down** ▷ OPPRESS.

grip n clasp, clutch, grasp, handclasp, hold, purchase, stranglehold. ▷ CONTROL. • vb 1 clasp, clutch, get a grip of, grab, grasp, hold, seize, take hold of. 2 *grip the imagination.* absorb, compel, engage, engross, enthral, entrance, fascinate, hypnotize, mesmerize, rivet, spellbind. **come to grips with** ▷ TACKLE.

grisly adj appalling, awful, bloody, disgusting, dreadful, fearful, frightful, ghastly, ghoulish, gory, grim, gruesome, hair-raising, hideous, horrible, inf horrid, horrifying, macabre, nauseating, repellent, repulsive, revolting, sickening, terrible.

gristly adj leathery, rubbery, tough, uneatable.

gritty adj abrasive, dusty, grainy, granular, gravelly, harsh, rasping, rough, sandy.

groan vb 1 cry out, lament, moan, sigh, wail, whimper, whine. 2 ▷ COMPLAIN.

groom n 1 ostler, stable-lad, stableman. 2 bridegroom, husband. • vb 1 brush, clean,

make neat, neaten, preen,
smarten up, spruce up, tidy,
inf titivate. 2 *groom someone for
a job.* coach, drill, educate, get
ready, prepare, prime, train up,
tutor.

groove n channel, cut, fluting,
furrow, gouge, gutter, hollow,
indentation, rut, score, scratch,
slot, striation, track.

grope *vb* cast about, feel about,
fish, flounder, fumble, search
blindly.

gross *adj* 1 bloated, massive,
obese, overweight, repellent,
repulsive, revolting. ▷ FAT.
2 churlish, coarse, crude, rude,
unrefined, unsophisticated,
vulgar. 3 *gross injustice.*
blatant, flagrant, glaring, manifest, monstrous, obvious, outrageous, shameful. 4 *gross
income.* before tax, inclusive,
overall, total, whole.

grotesque *adj* absurd, bizarre,
curious, deformed, distorted,
fantastic, freakish, gnarled,
incongruous, ludicrous,
macabre, malformed,
misshapen, monstrous, outlandish, preposterous, queer, ridiculous, strange, surreal, twisted,
ugly, unnatural, weird.

ground n 1 clay, dirt, earth,
loam, mud, soil. 2 area, land,
property, surroundings,
terrain. 3 campus, estate,
garden, park. 4 *sports ground.*
arena, court, field, pitch, play-
ground, playing-field, recreation ground, stadium.
5 *grounds for complaint.* argument, base, basis, case, cause,
excuse, evidence, foundation,
justification, motive, proof,
rationale, reason. ● *vb* 1 base,
establish, found, set, settle.
2 coach, educate, instruct,

prepare, teach, train, tutor.
3 beach, run ashore, shipwreck,
strand, wreck.

groundless *adj* baseless,
chimerical, false, gratuitous,
hypothetical, illusory, imaginary, irrational, motiveless,
needless, speculative, suppositional, uncalled-for, unfounded,
unjustifiable, unjustified,
unproven, unreasonable,
unsound, unsubstantiated,
unsupported, unwarranted.

group n 1 [*people*] alliance,
assemblage, assembly, association, band, bevy, body, brotherhood, *inf* bunch, cadre, cartel,
caste, caucus, circle, clan, class,
derog clique, club, cohort,
colony, committee, community,
company, conclave, congregation, consortium, contingent,
corps, coterie, coven, crew,
crowd, delegation, faction,
family, federation, force, fraternity, gang, gathering, guild,
horde, host, knot, league,
meeting, *derog* mob, multitude,
number, organization, party,
phalanx, picket, platoon, posse,
derog rabble, ring, sect,
derog shower, sisterhood, society, squad, squadron, swarm,
team, throng, troop, troupe,
union, unit. 2 [*things, animals*]
accumulation, agglomeration,
assemblage, assortment, batch,
battery (*guns*), brood (*chicks*),
bunch, bundle, category, class,
clump, cluster, clutch (*eggs*),
collection, combination,
conglomeration, constellation,
convoy, covey (*birds*), fleet,
flock, gaggle (*geese*), galaxy,
grouping, heap, herd, hoard,
host, litter, mass, pack, pile,
pride (*lions*), school, set, shoal
(*fish*), species. 3 ▷ MUSICIAN.

● *vb* 1 arrange, assemble, assort, bracket together, bring together, categorize, classify, collect, deploy, gather, herd, marshal, order, organize, put together, set out, sort. 2 associate, band, cluster, come together, congregate, crowd, flock, gather, get together, herd, make groups, swarm, team up, throng.

grovel *vb* abase yourself, be humble, cower, *inf* crawl, *inf* creep, cringe, demean yourself, fawn, flatter, ingratiate yourself, *inf* kowtow, *inf* lick someone's boots, prostrate yourself, snivel, *inf* suck up, *inf* toady. **grovelling** ▷ OBSEQUIOUS.

grow *vb* 1 augment, become bigger, broaden, build up, burgeon, come to life, develop, emerge, enlarge, evolve, expand, extend, fill out, flourish, flower, germinate, improve, increase, lengthen, live, make progress, mature, multiply, mushroom, progress, proliferate, prosper, put on growth, ripen, rise, shoot up, spread, spring up, sprout, survive, swell, thicken, thrive. 2 *grow roses.* cultivate, farm, help along, nurture, produce, propagate, raise. 3 *grow older.* become, get, turn.

grown-up *adj* adult, fully-grown, mature, well-developed.

growth *n* 1 accretion, advance, augmentation, broadening, burgeoning, development, enlargement, evolution, expansion, extension, flowering, getting bigger, growing, improvement, increase, maturation, maturing, progress, proliferation, prosperity, spread,

success. 2 crop, harvest, plants, produce, vegetation, yield. 3 cancer, cyst, excrescence, lump, swelling, tumour.

grub *n* 1 caterpillar, larva, maggot. 2 ▷ FOOD. ● *vb* ▷ DIG.

grudge *n* ▷ RESENTMENT.
● *vb* begrudge, covet, envy, resent.

grudging *adj* cautious, envious, guarded, half-hearted, hesitant, jealous, reluctant, resentful, secret, unenthusiastic, ungracious, unkind, unwilling. *Opp* ENTHUSIASTIC.

gruelling *adj* arduous, backbreaking, crippling, demanding, exhausting, fatiguing, laborious, punishing, severe, stiff, strenuous, taxing, tiring, tough, uphill, wearying. ▷ DIFFICULT. *Opp* EASY.

gruesome *adj* appalling, awful, bloody, disgusting, dreadful, fearful, fearsome, frightful, ghastly, ghoulish, gory, grim, grisly, hair-raising, hideous, horrible, *inf* horrid, horrific, horrifying, macabre, repellent, repugnant, revolting, shocking, sickening, terrible.

gruff *adj* 1 guttural, harsh, hoarse, husky, rasping, rough, throaty. 2 ▷ BAD-TEMPERED.

grumble *vb inf* beef, fuss, *inf* gripe, *inf* grouch, grouse, make a fuss, *inf* moan, object, protest, *inf* whinge. ▷ COMPLAIN.

guarantee *n* assurance, bond, oath, obligation, pledge, promise, surety, undertaking, warranty, word of honour.
● *vb* 1 assure, certify, give a guarantee, pledge, promise, swear, undertake, vouch, vow.

2 ensure, make sure of, reserve, secure, stake a claim to.

guard n bodyguard, *inf* bouncer, custodian, escort, guardian, *sl* heavy, lookout, *sl* minder, patrol, picket, *sl* screw, security-guard, sentinel, sentry, warder, watchman. ● *vb* be on guard over, care for, defend, keep safe, keep watch on, look after, mind, oversee, patrol, police, preserve, prevent from escaping, protect, safeguard, secure, shelter, shield, stand guard over, supervise, tend, watch, watch over. **on your guard** ▷ ALERT.

guardian n 1 adoptive parent, foster-parent. 2 champion, custodian, defender, keeper, preserver, protector, trustee, warden. ▷ GUARD.

guess n assumption, conjecture, estimate, feeling, *sl* guesstimate, guesswork, hunch, hypothesis, intuition, opinion, prediction, *inf* shot in the dark, speculation, supposition, surmise, suspicion, theory. ● *vb* assume, conclude, conjecture, divine, estimate, expect, fancy, feel, have a hunch, have a theory, *inf* hazard a guess, hypothesize, imagine, intuit, judge, make a guess, postulate, predict, *inf* reckon, speculate, suppose, surmise, suspect, think likely, work out.

guest n 1 caller, company, visitor. 2 *hotel guests.* boarder, customer, lodger, patron, resident, tenant.

guidance n advice, briefing, counselling, direction, guidelines, guiding, help, instruction, leadership, management, *inf* spoon-feeding, *inf* taking by the hand, teaching, tips.

guide n 1 courier, escort, leader, navigator, pilot. 2 adviser, counsellor, director, guru, mentor. 3 atlas, directory, gazetteer, guidebook, handbook, *Lat* vade mecum. ● *vb* 1 conduct, direct, escort, lead, manoeuvre, navigate, pilot, shepherd, show the way, steer, supervise, usher. 2 advise, brief, control, counsel, educate, give guidance to, govern, help along, influence, instruct, regulate, *inf* take by the hand, teach, train, tutor. *Opp* MISLEAD.

guilt n 1 blame, blameworthiness, criminality, culpability, fault, guiltiness, liability, responsibility, sinfulness, wickedness, wrongdoing. 2 *a look of guilt.* bad conscience, contriteness, contrition, dishonour, guilty feelings, penitence, regret, remorse, self-accusation, self-reproach, shame, sorrow. *Opp* INNOCENCE.

guiltless adj above suspicion, blameless, clear, faultless, free, honourable, immaculate, innocent, in the right, irreproachable, pure, sinless, untarnished, untroubled, virtuous. *Opp* GUILTY.

guilty adj 1 at fault, blameable, blameworthy, culpable, in the wrong, liable, reprehensible, responsible. 2 *a guilty look.* apologetic, ashamed, conscience-stricken, contrite, penitent, *inf* red-faced, regretful, remorseful, repentant, rueful, shamefaced, sheepish, sorry. *Opp* GUILTLESS, SHAMELESS.

gullible adj credulous, easily taken in, *inf* green, impressionable, inexperienced, innocent, naïve, suggestible, trusting, unsophisticated, unsuspecting, unwary. *Opp* WARY.

gulp *n* mouthful, swallow, *inf* swig. ● *vb* 1 bolt down, gobble, swallow, *inf* wolf. ▷ EAT. 2 *inf* knock back, quaff, *inf* swig. ▷ DRINK. 3 *gulp back tears*. check, choke back, stifle, suppress.

gumption *n* cleverness, *inf* common sense, enterprise, initiative, judgement, *inf* nous, resourcefulness, sense, wisdom.

gun *n plur* artillery, firearm. □ airgun, automatic, blunderbuss, cannon, machine-gun, mortar, musket, pistol, revolver, rifle, shot-gun, plur *small arms*, sub-machine-gun, tommy-gun. **gun down** ▷ SHOOT.

gunfire *n* cannonade, cross-fire, firing, gunshots, salvo.

gunman *n* assassin, bandit, criminal, desperado, fighter, gangster, killer, murderer, sniper, terrorist.

gurgle *vb* babble, bubble, burble, ripple, purl, splash.

gush *n* burst, cascade, eruption, flood, flow, jet, outpouring, overflow, rush, spout, spurt, squirt, stream, tide, torrent. ● *vb* 1 come in a gush, cascade, flood, flow freely, overflow, pour, run, rush, spout, spurt, squirt, stream, well up. 2 be enthusiastic, be sentimental, bubble over, fuss, *inf* go on, prattle on, talk on. **gushing** ▷ EFFUSIVE, SENTIMENTAL.

gusto *n* appetite, delight, enjoyment, enthusiasm, excitement, liveliness, pleasure, relish, satisfaction, spirit, verve, vigour, zest.

gut *vb* 1 clean, disembowel, draw, eviscerate, remove the

guts of. 2 *gut a building*. clear, despoil, empty, loot, pillage, plunder, ransack, ravage, remove the contents of, sack, strip.

guts *plur n* 1 alimentary canal, belly, bowels, entrails, *inf* innards, insides, intestines, stomach, viscera. 2 ▷ COURAGE.

gutter *n* channel, conduit, ditch, drain, duct, guttering, sewer, sluice, trench, trough.

gypsy *n* nomad, Romany, traveller, wanderer.

gyrate *vb* circle, pirouette, revolve, rotate, spin, spiral, swivel, turn, twirl, wheel, whirl.

H

habit *n* 1 convention, custom, pattern, policy, practice, routine, rule, usage, *old use* wont. 2 attitude, bent, disposition, inclination, manner, mannerism, penchant, predisposition, proclivity, propensity, quirk, tendency, way. 3 *bad habit*. addiction, compulsion, craving, dependence, fixation, obsession, vice.

habitable *adj* in good repair, inhabitable, liveable, usable. *Opp* UNINHABITABLE.

habitual *adj* 1 accustomed, common, conventional, customary, established, expected, familiar, fixed, frequent, natural, normal, ordinary, predictable, regular, ritual, routine, set, settled, standard, traditional, typical, usual, *old use* wonted. 2 addictive, beset-

ting, chronic, established, ineradicable, ingrained, obsessive, persistent, recurrent.
3 *habitual smokers.* addicted, conditioned, confirmed, dependent, hardened, *inf* hooked, inveterate, persistent.

hack *vb* carve, chop, gash, hew, mangle, mutilate, slash. ▷ CUT.

hackneyed *adj* banal, clichéd, cliché-ridden, commonplace, conventional, *inf* corny, familiar, feeble, obvious, overused, pedestrian, platitudinous, predictable, stale, stereotyped, stock, threadbare, tired, trite, uninspired, unoriginal. *Opp* NEW.

haggard *adj inf* all skin and bone, careworn, drawn, emaciated, exhausted, gaunt, hollow-cheeked, hollow-eyed, pinched, run-down, scraggy, scrawny, shrunken, thin, tired out, ugly, unhealthy, wasted, weary, withered, worn out, *inf* worried to death. *Opp* HEALTHY.

haggle *vb* argue, bargain, barter, discuss terms, negotiate, quibble, wrangle. ▷ QUARREL.

hail *vb* 1 accost, address, call to, greet, signal to. 2 ▷ ACCLAIM.

hair *n* 1 beard, bristles, curls, fleece, fur, hank, locks, mane, *inf* mop, moustache, shock, tresses, whiskers. 2 coiffure, cut, haircut, *inf* hair-do, hairstyle, style. □ bob, braid, bun, crew-cut, dreadlocks, fringe, Mohican, *inf* perm, permanent wave, pigtail, plait, pony-tail, quiff, ringlets, short back and sides, sideboards, sideburns, tonsure, topknot. 3 *false hair.* hair-piece, toupee, wig.

hairdresser *n* barber, coiffeur, coiffeuse, hair-stylist.

hairless *adj* bald, bare, clean-shaven, naked, shaved, shaven, smooth. *Opp* HAIRY.

hairy *adj* bearded, bristly, downy, feathery, fleecy, furry, fuzzy, hirsute, long-haired, shaggy, stubbly, woolly. *Opp* HAIRLESS.

half-hearted *adj* apathetic, cool, easily distracted, feeble, indifferent, ineffective, lackadaisical, listless, lukewarm, nonchalant, passive, perfunctory, phlegmatic, uncaring, uncommitted, unconcerned, unenthusiastic, unreliable, wavering, weak, *inf* wishy-washy. *Opp* ENTHUSIASTIC.

hall *n* 1 auditorium, concert-hall, lecture room, theatre. 2 corridor, entrance-hall, foyer, hallway, lobby, passage, passageway, vestibule.

hallowed *adj* blessed, consecrated, dedicated, holy, honoured, revered, reverenced, sacred, sacrosanct, worshipped.

hallucinate *vb* day-dream, dream, fantasize, *inf* have a trip, have hallucinations, *inf* see things, see visions.

hallucination *n* apparition, chimera, day-dream, delusion, dream, fantasy, figment of the imagination, illusion, mirage, vision. ▷ GHOST.

halt *n* break, cessation, close, end, interruption, pause, standstill, stop, stoppage, termination. ● *vb* 1 arrest, block, break off, cease, check, curb, end, impede, obstruct, stop, terminate. 2 come to a halt, come to rest, desist, discontinue, draw up, pull up, quit, stop, wait. *Opp* START. **halting**
▷ HESITANT, IRREGULAR.

halve *vb* bisect, cut by half, cut in half, decrease, divide into halves, lessen, reduce by half, share equally, split in two.

hammer *n* mallet, sledge-hammer. • *vb inf* bash, batter, beat, drive, knock, pound, smash, strike. ▷ DEFEAT, HIT.

hamper *vb* baulk, block, curb, curtail, delay, encumber, entangle, fetter, foil, frustrate, handicap, hinder, hold back, hold up, impede, inhibit, interfere with, obstruct, prevent, restrain, restrict, retard, shackle, slow down, thwart, trammel. *Opp* HELP.

hand *n* 1 fist, *sl* mitt, palm, *inf* paw. 2 *hand on a dial*. index, indicator, pointer. 3 [*old use*] *factory hands*. ▷ WORKER. • *vb* convey, deliver, give, offer, pass, present, submit. **at hand** ▷ HANDY. **give a hand** ▷ HELP. **hand down** ▷ BEQUEATH. **hand over** ▷ SURRENDER. **hand round** ▷ DISTRIBUTE. **lend a hand** ▷ HELP. **to hand** ▷ HANDY.

handicap *n* 1 barrier, burden, disadvantage, difficulty, drawback, encumbrance, hindrance, impediment, inconvenience, limitation, *inf* minus, nuisance, obstacle, problem, restraint, restriction, shortcoming, stumbling-block. *Opp* ADVANTAGE. 2 defect, disability, impairment. • *vb* be a handicap to, burden, check, curb, disable, disadvantage, encumber, hamper, hinder, hold back, impede, limit, restrain, restrict, retard, trammel. *Opp* HELP.

handicapped *adj* [*Some synonyms may cause offence*] autistic, bedridden, blind, crippled, deaf, disabled, disadvantaged, dumb, dyslexic, incapacitated, invalid, lame, limbless, maimed, mute, paralysed, paraplegic, retarded, slow, spastic, unsighted. ▷ ILL.

handiwork *n* achievement, creation, doing, invention, production, responsibility, work.

handle *n* grip, haft, handgrip, helve, hilt, knob, stock (*of rifle*). • *vb* 1 caress, feel, finger, fondle, grasp, hold, *inf* maul, pat, *inf* paw, stroke, touch, treat. 2 *handle situations, people*. conduct, contend with, control, cope with, deal with, direct, guide, look after, manage, manipulate, tackle, treat. ▷ ORGANIZE. 3 *car handles well*. manoeuvre, operate, respond, steer, work. 4 *handle goods*. deal in, do trade in, market, sell, stock, touch, traffic in.

handsome *adj* 1 admirable, attractive, beautiful, comely, elegant, fair, fine-looking, good-looking, personable, tasteful. *Opp* UGLY. 2 *handsome gift*. big, bountiful, generous, goodly, gracious, large, liberal, magnanimous, munificent, sizeable, unselfish, valuable. *Opp* MEAN.

handy *adj* 1 convenient, easy to use, helpful, manageable, practical, serviceable, useful, well-designed, worth having. 2 *handy with tools*. adept, capable, clever, competent, practical, proficient, skilful. 3 *keep tools handy*. accessible, at hand, available, close at hand, easy to reach, get-at-able, nearby, reachable, ready, to hand. *Opp* AWKWARD, INACCESSIBLE.

hang vb 1 be suspended, dangle, depend, droop, flap, flop, sway, swing, trail down. 2 *hang washing*. attach, drape, fasten, fix, peg up, pin up, stick up, suspend. 3 *hang in the air*. drift, float, hover. **hang about** ▷ DAWDLE. **hang back** ▷ HESITATE. **hanging** ▷ PENDENT. **hangings** ▷ DRAPE. **hang on** ▷ WAIT. **hang on to** ▷ KEEP.

hank n coil, length, loop, piece, skein.

hanker vb ache, covet, crave, desire, fancy, *inf* have a yen, hunger, itch, long, pine, thirst, want, wish, yearn.

haphazard adj accidental, adventitious, arbitrary, casual, chance, chaotic, confusing, disorderly, disorganized, fortuitous, *inf* higgledy-piggledy, *inf* hit-or-miss, illogical, irrational, random, serendipitous, unforeseen, unplanned, unstructured, unsystematic. *Opp* ORDERLY.

happen vb arise, befall, *old use* betide, chance, come about, crop up, emerge, follow, materialize, occur, result, take place, *inf* transpire, *inf* turn out. **happen on** ▷ FIND.

happening n accident, affair, chance, circumstance, episode, event, incident, occasion, occurrence, phenomenon.

happiness n bliss, cheer, cheerfulness, contentment, delight, ecstasy, elation, enjoyment, euphoria, exhilaration, exuberance, felicity, gaiety, gladness, glee, *inf* heaven, high spirits, joy, joyfulness, joyousness, jubilation, light-heartedness, merriment, pleasure, pride,

rapture, well-being. *Opp* SADNESS.

happy adj 1 beatific, blessed, blissful, *poet* blithe, buoyant, cheerful, cheery, contented, delighted, ecstatic, elated, enraptured, euphoric, exhilarated, exuberant, exultant, felicitous, festive, gay, glad, gleeful, good-humoured, gratified, grinning, halcyon (*days*), *inf* heavenly, high-spirited, idyllic, jocose, jocular, jocund, joking, jolly, jovial, joyful, joyous, jubilant, laughing, light-hearted, lively, merry, *inf* on top of the world, overjoyed, *inf* over the moon, pleased, proud, radiant, rapturous, rejoicing, relaxed, satisfied, smiling, *inf* starry-eyed, sunny, thrilled, triumphant. *Opp* SAD. 2 *a happy accident*. advantageous, appropriate, apt, auspicious, beneficial, convenient, favourable, felicitous, fortuitous, fortunate, lucky, opportune, propitious, timely, welcome, well-timed.

harangue n diatribe, exhortation, lecture, *inf* pep talk, tirade. ▷ SPEECH. ● vb chivvy, encourage, exhort, lecture, pontificate, preach, sermonize. ▷ SPEAK, TALK.

harass vb annoy, attack, badger, bait, bother, chivvy, disturb, harry, *inf* hassle, hound, irritate, molest, nag, persecute, pester, *inf* pick on, *inf* plague, torment, trouble, vex, worry.

harassed adj *inf* at the end of your tether, careworn, distraught, distressed, exhausted, frayed, pressured, strained, stressed, tired, weary, worn out.

harbour n anchorage, dock, haven, jetty, landing-stage,

marina, mooring, pier, port, quay, safe haven, shelter, wharf. • vb 1 conceal, give asylum to, give refuge to, give sanctuary to, hide, protect, shelter, shield. 2 *harbour a grudge*. cherish, cling on to, hold on to, keep in mind, maintain, nurse, nurture, retain.

hard adj 1 adamantine, compact, compressed, dense, firm, flinty, frozen, hardened, impenetrable, impervious, inflexible, rigid, rocky, solid, solidified, steely, stiff, stony, unbreakable, unyielding. 2 *hard labour*. arduous, back-breaking, exhausting, fatiguing, formidable, gruelling, harsh, heavy, laborious, onerous, rigorous, severe, stiff, strenuous, taxing, tiring, tough, uphill, wearying. 3 *a hard problem*. baffling, complex, complicated, confusing, difficult, enigmatic, insoluble, intricate, involved, knotty, perplexing, puzzling, tangled, *inf* thorny. 4 *a hard heart*. callous, cold, cruel, *inf* hard-boiled, hard-hearted, harsh, heartless, hostile, inflexible, intolerant, merciless, obdurate, pitiless, ruthless, severe, stern, strict, unbending, unfeeling, unfriendly, unkind. 5 *a hard blow*. forceful, heavy, powerful, strong, violent. 6 *hard times*. austere, bad, calamitous, disagreeable, distressing, grim, intolerable, painful, unhappy, unpleasant. 7 *a hard worker*. assiduous, conscientious, devoted, indefatigable, industrious, keen, persistent, unflagging, untiring, zealous. Opp EASY, SOFT. **hard-headed** ▷ BUSINESSLIKE. **hard-hearted**

▷ CRUEL. **hard up** ▷ POOR. **hard-wearing** ▷ DURABLE.

harden vb bake, cake, clot, coagulate, congeal, freeze, gel, jell, ossify, petrify, reinforce, set, solidify, stiffen, strengthen, toughen. Opp SOFTEN.

hardly adv barely, faintly, only just, rarely, scarcely, seldom, with difficulty.

hardship n adversity, affliction, austerity, bad luck, deprivation, destitution, difficulty, distress, misery, misfortune, need, privation, suffering, *inf* trials and tribulations, trouble, unhappiness, want.

hardware n equipment, implements, instruments, ironmongery, machinery, tools.

hardy adj 1 durable, fit, healthy, hearty, resilient, robust, rugged, strong, sturdy, tough, vigorous. Opp TENDER. 2 ▷ BOLD.

harm n abuse, damage, detriment, disadvantage, disservice, havoc, hurt, inconvenience, injury, loss, mischief, misfortune, pain, unhappiness, *inf* upset, wrong. ▷ EVIL. • vb abuse, be harmful to, damage, hurt, ill-treat, impair, injure, maltreat, misuse, ruin, spoil, wound. Opp BENEFIT.

harmful adj addictive, bad, baleful, damaging, dangerous, deadly, deleterious, destructive, detrimental, disadvantageous, evil, fatal, hurtful, injurious, lethal, malign, negative, noxious, pernicious, poisonous, prejudicial, ruinous, unfavourable, unhealthy, unpleasant, unwholesome. Opp BENEFICIAL, HARMLESS.

harmless *adj* acceptable, benign, gentle, innocent, innocuous, inoffensive, mild, non-addictive, non-toxic, safe, tame, unobjectionable. *Opp* HARMFUL.

harmonious *adj* 1 concordant, consonant, *inf* easy on the ear, euphonious, harmonizing, melodious, musical, sweet-sounding, tonal, tuneful. *Opp* DISCORDANT. 2 a *harmonious meeting*. agreeable, amicable, compatible, congenial, congruous, cooperative, friendly, integrated, like-minded, sympathetic.

harmonize *vb* agree, balance, be in harmony, blend, cooperate, coordinate, correspond, go together, match, suit each other, tally, tone in.

harmony *n* 1 assonance, concord, consonance, euphony, tunefulness. 2 accord, agreement, amity, balance, compatibility, conformity, congruence, cooperation, friendliness, goodwill, like-mindedness, peace, rapport, sympathy, togetherness, understanding. *Opp* DISCORD.

harness *n* equipment, *inf* gear, straps, tackle. ● *vb* control, domesticate, exploit, keep under control, make use of, mobilize, tame, use, utilize.

harsh *adj* 1 abrasive, bristly, coarse, hairy, rough, scratchy. 2 *harsh sounds*. cacophonous, croaking, croaky, disagreeable, discordant, dissonant, grating, gravelly, grinding, gruff, guttural, hoarse, husky, irritating, jarring, rasping, raucous, rough, screeching, shrill, squawking, stertorous, strident, unpleasant. 3 *harsh colours*,

light. bright, brilliant, dazzling, gaudy, glaring, lurid. 4 *harsh smell*. acrid, bitter, sour, unpleasant. 5 *harsh conditions*. arduous, austere, comfortless, difficult, hard, severe, stressful, tough. 6 *harsh criticism, treatment*. abusive, acerbic, bitter, blunt, brutal, cruel, Draconian, frank, hard-hearted, hurtful, impolite, merciless, outspoken, pitiless, severe, sharp, stern, strict, uncivil, unforgiving, unkind, unrelenting, unsympathetic, untempered. *Opp* GENTLE.

harvest *n* crop, gathering-in, produce, reaping, return, yield. ● *vb* bring in, collect, garner, gather, glean, mow, pick, reap, take in.

hash *n* 1 goulash, stew. 2 *inf* botch, confusion, farrago, *inf* hotchpotch, jumble, mess, *inf* mishmash, mixture. **make a hash of** ▷ BUNGLE.

hassle *n* altercation, argument, bother, confusion, difficulty, disagreement, disturbance, fighting, fuss, harassment, inconvenience, making difficulties, nuisance, persecution, problem, struggle, trouble, upset. ● *vb* ▷ HARASS, QUARREL.

haste *n* dispatch, hurry, impetuosity, precipitateness, quickness, rashness, recklessness, rush, urgency. ▷ SPEED.

hasty *adj* 1 abrupt, fast, foolhardy, headlong, hot-headed, hurried, ill-considered, immediate, impetuous, impulsive, incautious, instantaneous, *inf* pell-mell, precipitate, quick, rapid, rash, reckless, speedy, sudden, summary (*justice*), swift. 2 *hasty work*. brief, careless, cursory, hurried, ill-considered, perfunctory, rushed, short, slapdash, superficial, thoughtless, unthinking. *Opp* CAREFUL, SLOW.

hat *n* head-dress. □ *Balaclava, bearskin, beret, biretta, boater, bonnet, bowler, busby, cap, coronet, crash-helmet, crown, deerstalker, diadem, fez, fillet, headband, helmet, hood, mitre, skullcap, sombrero, sou'wester, stetson, sun-hat, tiara, top hat, toque, trilby, turban, wig, wimple, yarmulke.*

hatch *vb* 1 brood, incubate. 2 conceive, concoct, contrive, *inf* cook up, design, devise, *inf* dream up, formulate, invent, plan, plot, scheme, think up.

hate *n* 1 ▷ HATRED. 2 *a pet hate.* abomination, aversion, *Fr* bête noire, dislike, loathing. ● *vb* abhor, abominate, be averse to, be hostile to, be revolted by, *inf* can't bear, *inf* can't stand, deplore, despise, detest, dislike, execrate, fear, find intolerable, loathe, object to, recoil from, resent, scorn, shudder at. *Opp* LIKE, LOVE.

hateful *adj* abhorred, abhorrent, abominable, accursed, awful, contemptible, cursed, *inf* damnable, despicable, detestable, disgusting, distasteful, execrable, foul, hated, heinous, horrible, *inf* horrid, loathsome, nasty, nauseating, obnoxious, odious, offensive, repellent, repugnant, repulsive, revolting, vile. ▷ EVIL. *Opp* LOVABLE.

hatred *n* abhorrence, animosity, antagonism, antipathy, aversion, contempt, detestation, dislike, enmity, execration, hate, hostility, ill-will, intolerance, loathing, misanthropy,

odium, repugnance, revulsion. *Opp* LOVE.

haughty *adj* arrogant, boastful, bumptious, cavalier, *inf* cocky, conceited, condescending, disdainful, egotistical, *inf* high-and-mighty, *inf* hoity-toity, imperious, lofty, lordly, offhand, patronizing, pompous, presumptuous, pretentious, proud, self-admiring, self-important, smug, snobbish, *inf* snooty, *inf* stuck-up, supercilious, superior, *inf* uppish, vain. *Opp* MODEST.

haul *vb* carry, cart, convey, drag, draw, heave, *inf* lug, move, pull, tow, trail, transport, tug.

haunt *vb* 1 frequent, *inf* hang around, keep returning to, loiter about, patronize, spend time at, visit regularly. 2 *haunt the mind.* beset, linger in, obsess, plague, prey on, torment.

have *vb* 1 be in possession of, keep, maintain, own, possess, use, utilize. 2 *house has six rooms.* comprise, consist of, contain, embody, hold, include, incorporate, involve. 3 *have fun, illness.* be subject to, endure, enjoy, experience, feel, go through, know, live through, put up with, suffer, tolerate, undergo. 4 *have presents.* accept, acquire, be given, gain, get, obtain, procure, receive. 5 *thieves had the lot. inf* get away with, remove, retain, secure, steal, take. 6 *have a snack.* consume, eat, drink, partake of, swallow. 7 *have a party.* arrange, hold, organize, prepare, set up. 8 *have guests.* be host to, cater for, entertain, put up. **have on** ▷ HOAX.

have to be compelled to, be forced to, have an obligation to, must, need to, ought to, should. **have up** ▷ ARREST.

haven *n* asylum, refuge, retreat, safety, sanctuary, shelter. ▷ HARBOUR.

havoc *n* carnage, chaos, confusion, damage, desolation, destruction, devastation, disorder, disruption, *inf* mayhem, *inf* rack and ruin, ruin, *inf* shambles, upset, waste, wreckage.

hazard *n* chance, danger, jeopardy, peril, risk, threat. ● *vb* dare, gamble, jeopardize, risk, stake, take a chance with, venture.

hazardous *adj* chancy, dangerous, *inf* dicey, fraught with danger, parlous, perilous, precarious, risky, *inf* ticklish, *inf* tricky, uncertain, unpredictable, unsafe. *Opp* SAFE.

haze *n* cloud, film, fog, mist, steam, vapour.

hazy *adj* 1 blurred, blurry, clouded, cloudy, dim, faint, foggy, fuzzy, indefinite, milky, misty, obscure, unclear. 2 ▷ VAGUE. *Opp* CLEAR.

head *adj* ▷ CHIEF. ● *n* 1 brain, cranium, skull. 2 *head for figures*. ability, brains, capacity, imagination, intelligence, intellect, mind, understanding. 3 *head of a mountain*. apex, crown, highest point, peak, summit, top, vertex. 4 boss, director, employer, leader, manager, ruler. ▷ CHIEF. 5 *head of a school*. headmaster, headmistress, headteacher, principal. 6 *head of a river*. ▷ SOURCE. ● *vb* 1 be in charge of, command, control, direct,

govern, guide, lead, manage, rule, run, superintend, supervise. 2 *head for home*. aim, go, make, *inf* make a beeline, point, set out, start, steer, turn. **head off** ▷ DEFLECT. **lose your head** ▷ PANIC. **off your head** ▷ MAD.

heading *n* caption, headline, rubric, title.

headquarters *n* administration, base, depot, head office, *inf* HQ, main office, *inf* nerve-centre.

heal *vb* 1 become healthy, get better, improve, knit, mend, recover, recuperate, unite. 2 cure, make better, minister to, nurse, rejuvenate, remedy, renew, restore, revitalize, tend, treat. 3 *heal differences*. patch up, put right, reconcile, repair, settle.

health *n* 1 condition, constitution, fettle, form, shape, trim. 2 *the picture of health*. fitness, robustness, soundness, strength, vigour, well-being.

healthy *adj* 1 active, blooming, fine, fit, flourishing, good, *inf* hale-and-hearty, hearty, *inf* in fine fettle, in good shape, lively, perky, robust, sound, strong, sturdy, vigorous, well. 2 bracing, health-giving, hygienic, invigorating, salubrious, sanitary, wholesome. *Opp* ILL, UNHEALTHY.

heap *n* accumulation, assemblage, bank, collection, hill, hoard, mass, mound, mountain, pile, stack. ● *vb* accumulate, amass, bank up, collect, gather, hoard, mass, pile, stack, stockpile, store. **heaps** ▷ PLENTY.

hear *vb* 1 attend to, catch, *old use* hearken to, heed, listen to, overhear, pay attention to, pick up. 2 *hear evidence*. examine, investigate, judge, try. 3 *hear news*. be told, discover, find out, gather, get, *inf* get wind of, learn, receive.

hearing *n* case, inquest, inquiry, trial.

heart *n* 1 *sl* ticker. 2 centre, core, crux, essence, focus, hub, inside, kernel, marrow, middle, *sl* nitty-gritty, nub, nucleus, pith. 3 affection, compassion, concern, courage, feeling, goodness, humanity, kindness, love, pity, sensitivity, sympathy, tenderness, understanding, warmth.

heartbreaking *adj* bitter, distressing, grievous, heart-rending, pitiful, tragic.

heartbroken *adj* broken-hearted, dejected, desolate, despairing, dispirited, grieved, inconsolable, miserable, *inf* shattered. ▷ SAD.

hearten *vb* boost, cheer up, encourage, strengthen, uplift.

heartless *adj* callous, cold, icy, inhuman, pitiless, ruthless, steely, stony, unconcerned, unemotional, unkind, unsympathetic. ▷ CRUEL.

hearty *adj* 1 enthusiastic, exuberant, friendly, genuine, healthy, heartfelt, lively, positive, robust, sincere, spirited, strong, vigorous, warm. *Opp* HALF-HEARTED. 2 *a hearty dinner*. ▷ BIG.

heat *n* 1 calorific value, fever, fieriness, glow, hotness, incandescence, warmth. 2 closeness, heat-wave, high temperature, hot weather, humidity, sultriness, torridity, warmth. 3 *heat of the moment*. anger, ardour, eagerness, enthusiasm, excite-ment, fervour, feverishness, fury, impetuosity, violence. ▷ PASSION. *Opp* COLD. ● *vb* bake, blister, boil, burn, cook, *inf* frizzle, fry, grill, inflame, make hot, melt, reheat, roast, scald, scorch, simmer, sizzle, smoulder, steam, stew, swelter, toast, warm. *Opp* COOL. **heated** ▷ FERVENT, HOT.

heath *n* common land, moor, moorland, open country, waste land, wilderness.

heathen *adj* atheistic, barbaric, godless, idolatrous, infidel, irreligious, pagan, philistine, savage, unenlightened. ● *n* atheist, barbarian, heretic, idolater, infidel, pagan, philistine, savage, sceptic, unbeliever.

heave *vb* 1 drag, draw, haul, hoist, lift, lug, move, pull, raise, tow, tug. 2 ▷ THROW. **heave into sight** ▷ APPEAR. **heave up** ▷ VOMIT.

heaven *n* 1 after-life, Elysium, eternal rest, the hereafter, the next world, nirvana, paradise. 2 bliss, contentment, delight, ecstasy, felicity, happiness, joy, perfection, pleasure, rapture, Utopia. *Opp* HELL.

heavenly *adj* angelic, beatific, beautiful, blissful, celestial, delightful, divine, exquisite, glorious, lovely, other-worldly, *inf* out of this world, saintly, spiritual, sublime, unearthly, wonderful.

heavy *adj* 1 bulky, burdensome, compact, concentrated, dense, hefty, immovable, large, leaden, massive, ponderous, unwieldy, weighty. ▷ BIG, FAT. 2 *heavy work*. arduous, demanding, difficult, hard, exhausting, laborious, onerous, strenuous, tough. **3** *heavy rain*. penetrating, pervasive, severe, torrential. **4** *a heavy crop*. abundant, copious, laden, loaded, profuse, thick. **5** *a heavy heart*. burdened, depressed, gloomy, miserable, sorrowful. ▷ SAD. **6** [*inf*] *a heavy lecture*. deep, dull, intellectual, intense, serious, tedious, wearisome. *Opp* LIGHT. **heavy-handed** ▷ CLUMSY. **heavy-hearted** ▷ SAD.

hectic *adj* animated, boisterous, brisk, bustling, busy, chaotic, excited, feverish, frantic, frenetic, frenzied, hurried, hyperactive, lively, mad, overactive, restless, riotous, rumbustious, *inf* rushed off your feet, turbulent, wild. *Opp* LEISURELY.

hedge *n* barrier, fence, hedgerow, screen. ● *vb inf* beat about the bush, be evasive, equivocate, *inf* hum and haw, quibble, stall, temporize, waffle. **hedge in** ▷ ENCLOSE.

hedonistic *adj* epicurean, extravagant, intemperate, luxurious, pleasure-loving, self-indulgent, sensual, sybaritic, voluptuous. *Opp* PURITANICAL.

heed *vb* attend to, bear in mind, concern yourself about, consider, follow, keep to, listen to, mark, mind, note, notice, obey, observe, pay attention to, regard, take notice of. *Opp* DISREGARD.

heedful *adj* attentive, careful, concerned, considerate, mindful, observant, sympathetic, taking notice, vigilant, watchful. *Opp* HEEDLESS.

heedless *adj* blind, careless, deaf, inattentive, inconsiderate, neglectful, oblivious, reckless, regardless, thoughtless, uncaring, unconcerned, unmindful, unobservant, unsympathetic. *Opp* HEEDFUL.

heel *vb* careen, incline, lean, list, tilt, tip.

hefty *adj* beefy, brawny, bulky, burly, heavy, heavyweight, hulking, husky, large, massive, mighty, muscular, powerful, robust, rugged, solid, substantial, *inf* strapping, strong, tough. ▷ BIG. *Opp* SLIGHT.

height *n* **1** altitude, elevation, level, tallness, vertical measurement. **2** crag, fell, hill, mound, mountain, peak, prominence, ridge, summit, top. **3** *height of your career*. acme, apogee, climax, crest, culmination, extreme, high point, maximum, peak, pinnacle, zenith.

heighten *vb* add to, amplify, augment, boost, build up, elevate, enhance, improve, increase, intensify, lift up, magnify, make higher, maximize, raise, reinforce, sharpen, strengthen, supplement. *Opp* LOWER, REDUCE.

hell *n* **1** eternal punishment, Hades, infernal regions, lower regions, nether world, *sl* the other place, underworld. **2** ▷ MISERY. *Opp* HEAVEN.

help *n* advice, aid, assistance, avail, backing, benefit, boost, collaboration, contribution, co-operation, encouragement, friendship, guidance, moral support, patronage, relief, remedy, succour, support. *Opp* HINDRANCE. ● *vb* **1** abet, advise, aid, aid and abet, assist, back, befriend, be helpful, boost, collaborate, contribute, cooperate, encourage, facilitate, forward, further the interests of, *inf* give a hand, *inf* lend a hand, profit, promote, prop up, *inf* rally round, serve, side with, *derog* spoonfeed, stand by, subsidize, succour, support, take pity on. Opp HINDER. **2** *linctus helps a cough.* alleviate, benefit, cure, ease, improve, lessen, make easier, relieve, remedy. **3** *can't help it.* ▷ AVOID, PREVENT.

helper *n* abettor, accessory, accomplice, ally, assistant, associate, collaborator, colleague, confederate, deputy, helpmate, *inf* henchman, partner, *inf* right-hand man, second, supporter, *inf* willing hands.

helpful *adj* **1** accommodating, benevolent, caring, considerate, constructive, cooperative, favourable, friendly, helping, kind, neighbourly, obliging, practical, supportive, sympathetic, thoughtful, willing. **2** *a helpful comment.* advantageous, beneficial, informative, instructive, profitable, useful, valuable, worthwhile. **3** *a helpful tool.* convenient, easy to use, handy, manageable, practical, serviceable, useful, well-designed, worth having. Opp UNHELPFUL, USELESS.

helping *adj* ▷ HELPFUL.
● *n* amount, *inf* dollop, plateful, portion, ration, serving, share.

helpless *adj* abandoned, crippled, defenceless, dependent, deserted, destitute, disabled, exposed, feeble, handicapped, impotent, incapable, in difficulties, infirm, lame, marooned, powerless, stranded, unprotected, vulnerable. Opp INDEPENDENT.

herald *n* **1** announcer, courier, messenger, town crier. **2** *herald of spring.* forerunner, harbinger, omen, precursor, sign.
● *vb* advertise, announce, indicate, make known, proclaim, promise, publicize. ▷ FORETELL.

herd *n* bunch, flock, mob, pack, swarm, throng. ▷ GROUP.
● *vb* assemble, collect, congregate, drive, gather, group together, round up, shepherd.

hereditary *adj* **1** ancestral, bequeathed, family, handed down, inherited, passed down, passed on, willed. **2** congenital, constitutional, genetic, inborn, inbred, inherent, inheritable, innate, native, natural, transmissible, transmittable.

heresy *n* blasphemy, dissent, idolatry, nonconformity, rebellion, *inf* stepping out of line, unorthodox ideas.

heretic *n* apostate, blasphemer, dissenter, free-thinker, iconoclast, nonconformist, rebel, renegade, unorthodox thinker. Opp BELIEVER.

heretical *adj* apostate, atheistic, blasphemous, dissenting, free-thinking, heathen, iconoclastic, idolatrous, impious, irreligious, nonconformist, pagan, rebellious, unorthodox. Opp ORTHODOX.

heritage *n* birthright, culture, history, inheritance, legacy, past, tradition.

hermit *n* anchoress, anchorite, eremite, monk, recluse, solitary.

hero, heroine *ns* champion, conqueror, daredevil, exemplar, ideal, idol, luminary, protagonist, star, superman, *inf* superstar, superwoman, victor, winner.

heroic adj adventurous, audacious, bold, brave, chivalrous, courageous, daring, dauntless, doughty, epic, fearless, gallant, herculean, intrepid, lion-hearted, noble, selfless, staunch, steadfast, stout-hearted, superhuman, unafraid, valiant, valorous. Opp COWARDLY.

hesitant adj cautious, diffident, dithering, faltering, half-hearted, halting, hesitating, indecisive, irresolute, nervous, inf shilly-shallying, shy, stammering, stumbling, stuttering, tentative, timid, uncertain, uncommitted, undecided, underconfident, unsure, vacillating, wary, wavering. Opp DECISIVE, FLUENT.

hesitate vb 1 be hesitant, be indecisive, inf be in two minds, delay, demur, inf dilly-dally, dither, equivocate, falter, halt, hang back, haver, inf hum and haw, pause, put it off, inf shilly-shally, shrink back, teeter, temporize, think twice, vacillate, wait, waver. 2 stammer, stumble, stutter.

hesitation n caution, delay, diffidence, dithering, doubt, indecision, irresolution, nervousness, reluctance, inf shilly-shallying, uncertainty, vacillation, wavering.

hidden adj 1 camouflaged, concealed, covered, disguised, enclosed, invisible, obscured, out of sight, private, shrouded, inf under wraps, undetectable, unnoticeable, unseen, veiled. Opp VISIBLE. 2 hidden meaning. abstruse, arcane, coded, covert, cryptic, dark, esoteric, implicit, mysterious, mystical, obscure, occult, recondite, secret, unclear. Opp OBVIOUS.

hide n fur, leather, pelt, skin.
● vb 1 blot out, bury, camouflage, cloak, conceal, cover, curtain, disguise, eclipse, enclose, mantle, mask, obscure, put away, put out of sight, screen, secrete, shelter, shroud, veil, wrap up. 2 go into hiding. inf go to ground, inf hole up, keep hidden, inf lie low, lurk, shut yourself away, take cover. 3 hide facts. censor, inf hush up, repress, silence, suppress, withhold.

hideous adj appalling, beastly, disgusting, dreadful, frightful, ghastly, grim, grisly, grotesque, gruesome, macabre, nauseous, odious, repellent, repulsive, revolting, shocking, sickening, terrible. ▷ UGLY. Opp BEAUTIFUL.

hiding-place n den, haven, hide, hideaway, inf hide-out, inf hidey-hole, lair, refuge, retreat, sanctuary.

hierarchy n grading, ladder, inf pecking-order, ranking, scale, sequence, series, social order, system.

high adj 1 elevated, extending upwards, high-rise, lofty, raised, soaring, tall, towering. 2 aristocratic, chief, distinguished, eminent, exalted, important, leading, powerful, prominent, royal, top, upper. 3 high prices. dear, excessive, exorbitant, expensive, extravagant, outrageous, inf steep, unreasonable. 4 high winds. exceptional, extreme, great, intense, inf stiff, stormy, strong. 5 a high reputation. favourable, good, noble, respected, virtuous. 6 high sounds. acute, high-pitched, penetrating, piercing, sharp, shrill, soprano, squeaky, treble.

Opp LOW. **high-and-mighty**
▷ ARROGANT. **high-class**
▷ EXCELLENT. **high-handed**
▷ ARROGANT. **high-minded**
▷ MORAL. **high-powered**
▷ POWERFUL. **high-speed**
▷ FAST. **high-spirited**
▷ LIVELY.

highbrow *adj* **1** academic, bookish, brainy, cultured, intellectual, *derog* pretentious, sophisticated. **2** *highbrow books*. classical, cultural, deep, difficult, educational, improving, serious. *Opp* LOWBROW.

highlight *n* best moment, climax, high spot, peak, top point.

hilarious *adj* boisterous, cheerful, cheering, entertaining, jolly, jovial, lively, merry, mirthful, rollicking, side-splitting, uproarious. ▷ FUNNY.

hill *n* **1** elevation, eminence, foothill, height, hillock, hillside, hummock, knoll, mound, mount, mountain, peak, prominence, ridge, summit. □ brae, down, fell, pike, stack, tor, wold. **2** acclivity, ascent, declivity, drop, gradient, incline, ramp, rise, slope.

hinder *vb* arrest, bar, be a hindrance to, check, curb, delay, deter, endanger, frustrate, get in the way of, hamper, handicap, hit, hold back, hold up, impede, keep back, limit, obstruct, oppose, prevent, restrain, restrict, retard, sabotage, slow down, slow up, stand in the way of, stop, thwart. *Opp* HELP.

hindrance *n* bar, barrier, burden, check, curb, deterrent, difficulty, disadvantage, *inf* drag, drawback, encumbrance, handicap, hitch, impediment, inconvenience, limitation, obstacle, obstruction, restraint, restriction, snag, stumbling-block. *Opp* HELP.

hinge *n* articulation, joint, pivot.
• *vb* depend, hang, rest, revolve, turn.

hint *n* **1** allusion, clue, idea, implication, inkling, innuendo, insinuation, pointer, shadow, sign, suggestion, tip, *inf* tip-off. **2** *a hint of herbs*. dash, taste, tinge, touch, trace, undertone, whiff. • *vb* allude, give a hint, imply, indicate, insinuate, intimate, mention, suggest, tip off.

hire *vb* book, charter, employ, engage, lease, pay for the use of, rent, sign on, take on. **hire out** lease out, let, rent out, take payment for.

hiss *vb* buzz, fizz, purr, rustle, sizzle, whir, whizz.

historic *adj* celebrated, eminent, epoch-making, famed, famous, important, momentous, notable, outstanding, remarkable, renowned, significant, well-known. *Opp* INSIGNIFICANT.

historical *adj* actual, authentic, documented, factual, real, real-life, recorded, true, verifiable. *Opp* FICTITIOUS.

history *n* **1** antiquity, bygone days, heritage, historical events, the old days, the past. **2** annals, biography, chronicles, diaries, narratives, records.

histrionic *adj* actorish, dramatic, theatrical.

hit *n* **1** blow, bull's eye, collision, impact, shot, stroke. **2** success, triumph, *inf* winner.
• *vb* **1** bang, bash, baste, batter, beat, belt, biff, birch, box,

bludgeon, buffet, bump, butt, cane, cannon into, clap, clip, clobber, clock, clonk, clout, club, collide with, cosh, crack, crash into, cudgel, cuff, dash, deliver a blow, drive, elbow, flagellate, flail, flick, flip, flog, hammer, head, head-butt, impact, jab, jar, jog, kick, knee, knock, lam, lambaste, lash, nudge, pat, poke, pound, prod, pummel, punch, punt, putt, ram, rap, run into, scourge, slam, slap, slog, slosh, slug, smack, smash, smite, sock, spank, stab, strike, stub, swat, swipe, tan, tap, thrash, thump, thwack, wallop, whack, wham, whip. **2** *The slump hit sales.* affect, attack, bring disaster to, check, damage, do harm to, harm, have an effect on, hinder, hurt, make suffer, ruin. **hit back** ▷ RETALIATE. **hit on** ▷ DISCOVER.

hoard *n* accumulation, cache, collection, fund, heap, pile, reserve, stockpile, store, supply, treasure-trove. ● *vb* accumulate, amass, assemble, collect, gather, keep, lay in, lay up, mass, pile up, put away, put by, save, stockpile, store, treasure. *Opp* SQUANDER, USE.

hoarse *adj* croaking, grating, gravelly, growling, gruff, harsh, husky, rasping, raucous, rough, throaty.

hoax *n* cheat, *inf* con, confidence trick, deception, fake, fraud, humbug, imposture, joke, *inf* leg-pull, practical joke, spoof, swindle, trick. ● *vb* bluff, cheat, *inf* con, cozen, deceive, defraud, delude, dupe, fool, gull, *inf* have on, hoodwink, lead on, mislead, *inf* pull someone's leg,

swindle, *inf* take for a ride, take in, trick. ▷ TEASE.

hoaxer *n inf* con-man, impostor, joker, practical joker, trickster. ▷ CHEAT.

hobble *vb* dodder, falter, limp, shuffle, stagger, stumble, totter. ▷ WALK.

hobby *n* amateur interest, avocation, diversion, interest, pastime, pursuit, recreation, relaxation, sideline.

hoist *n* block-and-tackle, crane, davit, jack, lift, pulley, tackle, winch, windlass. ● *vb* elevate, heave, lift, pull up, raise, winch up.

hold *n* **1** clasp, clutch, foothold, grasp, grip, purchase, toehold. **2** *a hold over someone.* ascendancy, authority, control, dominance, influence, leverage, mastery, power, sway.

● *vb* **1** bear, carry, catch, clasp, clench, cling to, clutch, cradle, embrace, enfold, grasp, grip, hang on to, have, hug, keep, possess, retain, seize, support, take. **2** *hold a suspect.* arrest, confine, coop up, detain, imprison, keep in custody, restrain. **3** *hold an opinion.* believe in, stick to, subscribe to, swear to. **4** *hold a pose.* continue, keep up, maintain, occupy, preserve, retain, sustain. **5** *hold a party.* celebrate, conduct, convene, have, organize. **6** *jug holds a litre.* contain, enclose, have a capacity of, include. **7** *My offer holds.* be unaltered, carry on, continue, endure, hold out, keep on, last, persist, remain unchanged, stay. **hold back** ▷ RESTRAIN. **hold forth** ▷ SPEAK, TALK. **hold out** ▷ OFFER, PERSIST. **hold over,**

hold up ▷ DELAY. **hold-up** ▷ ROBBERY.

hole n 1 abyss, burrow, cave, cavern, cavity, chamber, chasm, crater, dent, depression, excavation, fault, fissure, hollow, indentation, niche, pit, pocket, pot-hole, recess, shaft, tunnel. 2 aperture, breach, break, chink, crack, cut, eyelet, fissure, gap, gash, leak, opening, orifice, perforation, puncture, rip, slit, slot, split, tear, vent.

holiday n bank holiday, break, day off, furlough, half-term, leave, recess, respite, rest, sabbatical, time off, vacation.

holiness n devotion, divinity, faith, godliness, piety, derog religiosity, sacredness, saintliness, derog sanctimoniousness, sanctity, venerability.

hollow adj 1 empty, unfilled, vacant, void. 2 cavernous, concave, deep, depressed, dimpled, indented, recessed, sunken. 3 *a hollow laugh, victory*. cynical, false, futile, insincere, insubstantial, meaningless, pointless, valueless, worthless. ● n bowl, cave, cavern, cavity, concavity, crater, dent, depression, dimple, dint, dip, dish, excavation, furrow, hole, indentation, pit, trough. ▷ VALLEY. **hollow out** ▷ EXCAVATE.

holocaust n 1 conflagration, firestorm, inferno. 2 annihilation, bloodbath, destruction, devastation, extermination, genocide, massacre, pogrom.

holy adj 1 blessed, consecrated, dedicated, devoted, divine, hallowed, heavenly, revered, sacred, sacrosanct, venerable. 2 *holy pilgrims*. devout, faithful, God-fearing, godly, immaculate, derog pietistic, pious, prayerful, pure, religious, reverent, reverential, righteous, saintly, derog sanctimonious, sinless, unsullied. Opp IRRELIGIOUS.

home n 1 abode, accommodation, base, domicile, dwelling, dwelling-place, habitation, household, lodging, quarters, residence. ▷ HOUSE. 2 birthplace, native land. 3 derog institution. □ old use *almshouse, convalescent home, hospice, nursing-home, old use poorhouse, rest home, retirement home, retreat, shelter*.

homeless adj abandoned, destitute, dispossessed, down-and-out, evicted, exiled, forsaken, itinerant, nomadic, outcast, rootless, unhoused, vagrant, wandering. ● plur n beggars, refugees, tramps, vagabonds, vagrants.

homely adj comfortable, congenial, cosy, easygoing, friendly, informal, intimate, modest, natural, relaxed, simple, unaffected, unassuming, unpretentious, unsophisticated. ▷ FAMILIAR. Opp FORMAL, SOPHISTICATED.

homogeneous adj akin, alike, comparable, compatible, consistent, identical, indistinguishable, matching, similar, uniform, unvarying. Opp DIFFERENT.

homosexual adj inf camp, gay, lesbian, derog queer.

honest adj above-board, blunt, candid, conscientious, direct, equitable, fair, forthright,

frank, genuine, good, honourable, impartial, incorrupt-
ible, just, law-abiding, legal, legitimate, moral, *inf* on the level,
open, outspoken, plain, principled, pure, reliable, respectable, scrupulous, sincere,
square (*deal*), straight, straightforward, trustworthy, trusty,
truthful, unbiased, unequivocal, unprejudiced, upright,
veracious, virtuous.
Opp DISHONEST.

honesty *n* 1 fairness, goodness,
honour, integrity, morality,
probity, rectitude, reliability,
scrupulousness, sense of
justice, trustworthiness, truthfulness, uprightness, veracity,
virtue. *Opp* DECEIT. 2 bluntness,
candour, directness, frankness,
outspokenness, plainness,
sincerity, straightforwardness.

honorary *adj* nominal, titular,
unofficial, unpaid.

honour *n* 1 acclaim, accolade,
compliment, credit, esteem,
fame, good name, *inf* kudos,
regard, renown, reputation,
repute, respect, reverence,
veneration. 2 distinction, duty,
importance, pleasure, privilege.
3 *a sense of honour*. decency,
dignity, honesty, integrity,
loyalty, morality, nobility, principle, rectitude, righteousness,
sincerity, uprightness, virtue.
● *vb* acclaim, admire, applaud,
celebrate, commemorate,
commend, dignify, esteem, give
credit to, glorify, pay homage
to, pay respects to, pay tribute
to, praise, remember, respect,
revere, reverence, show respect
to, sing the praises of, value,
venerate, worship.

honourable *adj* admirable,
chivalrous, creditable, decent,

estimable, ethical, fair, good,
high-minded, irreproachable,
just, law-abiding, loyal, moral,
noble, principled, proper, reputable, respectable, respected,
righteous, sincere, *inf* straight,
trustworthy, trusty, upright,
venerable, virtuous, worthy.
▷ HONEST. *Opp* DISHONOURABLE.

hoodwink *vb* bluff, cheat,
inf con, cozen, deceive, defraud,
delude, dupe, fool, gull, *inf* have
on, hoax, lead on, mislead,
inf pull the wool over someone's eyes, swindle, *inf* take for
a ride, take in, trick.

hook *n* barb, crook, peg.
▷ FASTENER. ● *vb* 1 ▷ FASTEN.
2 *hook a fish*. capture, catch,
take.

hooligan *n* bully, delinquent,
hoodlum, lout, mugger, rough,
ruffian, *inf* tearaway, thug,
tough, trouble-maker, vandal,
inf yob. ▷ CRIMINAL.

hoop *n* band, circle, girdle, loop,
ring.

hop *vb* bound, caper, dance,
jump, leap, limp, prance, skip,
spring, vault.

hope *n* 1 ambition, aspiration,
craving, day-dream, desire,
dream, longing, wish, yearning.
2 *hope of better weather*.
assumption, conviction, expectation, faith, likelihood, optimism, promise, prospect.
● *vb inf* anticipate, aspire, be
hopeful, believe, contemplate,
count on, desire, expect, foresee, have faith, have hope, look
forward (to), trust, wish.
Opp DESPAIR.

hopeful *adj* 1 assured, confident,
expectant, optimistic, positive,
sanguine. 2 *hopeful signs*.
auspicious, cheering, encourag-

ing, favourable, heartening, promising, propitious, reassuring. Opp HOPELESS.

hopefully adv 1 confidently, expectantly, optimistically, with hope. 2 [inf] *Hopefully I'll be better tomorrow.* all being well, most likely, probably. [Many think this use of *hopefully* is wrong]

hopeless adj 1 defeatist, demoralized, despairing, desperate, disconsolate, fatalist, negative, pessimistic, resigned, wretched. 2 *a hopeless situation.* daunting, depressing, impossible, incurable, irremediable, irreparable, irreversible. 3 [inf] *He's hopeless!* feeble, inadequate, incompetent, inefficient, poor, useless, weak, worthless. Opp HOPEFUL.

horde n band, crowd, gang, mob, swarm, throng, tribe. ▷ GROUP.

horizontal adj even, flat, level, lying down, prone, prostrate, supine. Opp VERTICAL.

horrible adj awful, beastly, disagreeable, dreadful, ghastly, hateful, horrid, loathsome, macabre, nasty, objectionable, odious, offensive, revolting, terrible, unkind. ▷ HORRIFIC, UNPLEASANT. Opp PLEASANT.

horrific adj appalling, atrocious, blood-curdling, disgusting, dreadful, frightening, frightful, grisly, gruesome, hair-raising, harrowing, horrendous, horrifying, nauseating, shocking, sickening, spine-chilling, unacceptable, unnerving, unthinkable.

horrify vb alarm, appal, disgust, frighten, harrow, nauseate, outrage, scare, shock, sicken,

stun, terrify, unnerve. **horrifying** ▷ HORRIFIC.

horror n 1 abhorrence, antipathy, aversion, detestation, disgust, dislike, dismay, distaste, dread, fear, hatred, loathing, panic, repugnance, revulsion, terror. 2 awfulness, frightfulness, ghastliness, gruesomeness, hideousness.

horse n bronco, carthorse, *old use* charger, cob, colt, filly, foal, *childish* gee-gee, gelding, hack, hunter, *old use* jade, mare, mount, mule, mustang, *inf* nag, *old use* palfrey, piebald, pony, race-horse, roan, skewbald, stallion, steed, warhorse.

horseman, horsewoman ns cavalryman, equestrian, jockey, rider.

hospitable adj cordial, courteous, generous, gracious, receptive, sociable, welcoming. ▷ FRIENDLY. Opp INHOSPITABLE.

hospital n clinic, convalescent home, dispensary, health centre, hospice, infirmary, medical centre, nursing home, sanatorium, sick bay.

hospitality n 1 accommodation, catering, entertainment. 2 cordiality, courtesy, friendliness, generosity, sociability, warmth, welcome.

host n 1 army, crowd, mob, multitude, swarm, throng, troop. ▷ GROUP. 2 ▷ COMPÈRE.

hostage n captive, pawn, prisoner, surety.

hostile adj 1 aggressive, antagonistic, antipathetic, attacking, averse, bellicose, belligerent, combative, confrontational, ill-disposed, inhospitable, inimical, malevolent, militant, opposed, oppressive, pugna-

cious, resentful, rival, unfriendly, unsympathetic, unwelcoming, warlike, warring. ▷ ANGRY. Opp FRIENDLY.
2 *hostile conditions.* adverse, contrary, opposing, unfavourable, unhelpful, unpropitious. ▷ BAD. Opp FAVOURABLE.

hostility *n* aggression, animosity, animus, antagonism, bad feeling, belligerence, confrontation, dissension, enmity, estrangement, friction, incompatibility, malevolence, malice, opposition, pugnacity, rancour, resentment, strife, unfriendliness. ▷ HATRED. Opp FRIENDSHIP. **hostilities** ▷ WAR.

hot *adj* **1** baking, blistering, boiling, burning, close, fiery, flaming, humid, oppressive, *inf* piping, red-hot, roasting, scalding, scorching, searing, sizzling, steamy, stifling, sultry, summery, sweltering, thermal, torrid, tropical, warm, whitehot. **2** *hot temper.* ardent, eager, emotional, excited, fervent, fervid, feverish, fierce, heated, hotheaded, impatient, impetuous, inflamed, intense, passionate, violent. **3** *hot taste.* acrid, biting, gingery, peppery, piquant, pungent, spicy, strong. Opp COLD, COOL. **hot-tempered** ▷ BAD-TEMPERED. **hot under the collar** ▷ ANGRY.

hotel *n* guest house, hostel, *joc* hostelry, inn, lodge, motel, pension. ▷ ACCOMMODATION.

hound *n* ▷ DOG. ● *vb* annoy, badger, chase, harass, harry, hunt, nag, persecute, pester, pursue.

house *n old use* abode, domicile, dwelling, dwelling-place, habitation, home, homestead, household, place, residence. □ *apartment,* *inf* back-to-back, bungalow, chalet, cottage, council house, croft, detached house, farmhouse, flat, grange, hovel, homestead, hut, igloo, lodge, maisonette, manor, manse, mansion, penthouse, *inf* prefab, public house, rectory, *inf* semi, semi-detached house, shack, shanty, terraced house, thatched house, *inf* two-up two-down, vicarage, villa. ● *vb* accommodate, billet, board, domicile, harbour, keep, lodge, place, *inf* put up, quarter, shelter, take in.

household *n* establishment, family, home, ménage, *inf* set-up.

hovel *n* cottage, *inf* dump, hole, hut, shack, shanty, shed.

hover *vb* **1** be suspended, drift, float, flutter, fly, hang, poise. **2** be indecisive, dally, dither, *inf* hang about, hang around, hesitate, linger, loiter, pause, vacillate, wait about, waver.

howl *vb* bay, bellow, cry, roar, shout, ululate, wail, yowl.

hub *n* axis, centre, core, focal point, focus, heart, middle, nucleus, pivot.

huddle *n* ▷ GROUP. ● *vb* **1** cluster, converge, crowd, flock, gather, group, heap, herd, jam, jumble, pile, press, squeeze, swarm, throng. **2** cuddle, curl up, hug, nestle, snuggle.

hue *n* cast, complexion, dye, nuance, shade, tincture, tinge, tint, tone. ▷ COLOUR. **hue and cry** ▷ OUTCRY.

hug *vb* clasp, cling to, crush, cuddle, embrace, enfold, fold in your arms, hold close, huddle together, nestle together, nurse, snuggle against, squeeze.

huge *adj* 1 Brobdingnagian, colossal, elephantine, enormous, gargantuan, giant, gigantic, *inf* hulking, immense, imposing, impressive, *inf* jumbo, majestic, mammoth, massive, mighty, *inf* monster, monstrous, monumental, mountainous, prodigious, stupendous, titanic, towering, *inf* tremendous, vast, weighty, *inf* whopping. ▷ BIG. 2 *huge number*. ▷ INFINITE. *Opp* SMALL.

hulk *n* 1 body, carcass, frame, hull, shell, wreck. 2 *a clumsy hulk*. lout, lump, oaf.

hulking *adj* awkward, bulky, cumbersome, heavy, ungainly, unwieldy. ▷ BIG, CLUMSY.

hull *n* body, framework, structure.

hum *vb* buzz, drone, murmur, purr, sing, thrum, vibrate, whirr. **hum and haw** ▷ HESITATE.

human *adj* 1 anthropoid, hominid, hominoid, mortal. 2 *human feeling*. kind, rational, reasonable, sensible, sensitive, sympathetic, thoughtful. ▷ HUMANE. *Opp* INHUMAN. **human beings** folk, humanity, mankind, men and women, mortals, people.

humane *adj* altruistic, benevolent, charitable, civilized, compassionate, feeling, forgiving, good, human, humanitarian, kind-hearted, loving, magnanimous, merciful, philanthropic, pitying, refined, sympathetic, tender, understanding, unselfish, warm-hearted. ▷ KIND. *Opp* INHUMANE.

humble *adj* 1 deferential, docile, meek, modest, *derog* obsequi-

ous, polite, reserved, respectful, self-effacing, *derog* servile, submissive, subservient, *derog* sycophantic, unassertive, unassuming, unostentatious, unpresuming, unpretentious. *Opp* PROUD. 2 *humble birth*. base, commonplace, ignoble, inferior, insignificant, low, lowly, mean, obscure, ordinary, plebeian, poor, simple, undistinguished, unimportant, unprepossessing, unremarkable. • *vb* ▷ HUMILIATE.

humid *adj* clammy, damp, dank, moist, muggy, steamy, sticky, sultry, sweaty.

humiliate *vb* abase, abash, break, break someone's spirit, bring someone down, chagrin, chasten, crush, deflate, degrade, demean, discredit, disgrace, embarrass, humble, make someone ashamed, *inf* make someone eat humble pie, *inf* make someone feel small, mortify, *inf* put someone down, *inf* put someone in his/her place, shame, *inf* show someone up, *inf* take someone down a peg. **humiliating** ▷ SHAMEFUL.

humiliation *n* abasement, chagrin, degradation, discredit, disgrace, dishonour, embarrassment, ignominy, indignity, loss of face, mortification, obloquy, shame.

humility *n* deference, humbleness, lowliness, meekness, modesty, self-abasement, self-effacement, *derog* servility, shyness, unpretentiousness. *Opp* PRIDE.

humorous *adj* absurd, amusing, comic, comical, diverting, droll, entertaining, facetious, farcical, funny, hilarious, *inf* hysterical, ironic, jocose, jocular, *inf* killing, laughable, merry, *inf* priceless, risible, sarcastic, sardonic, satirical, *inf* side-splitting, slapstick, uproarious, waggish, whimsical, witty, zany. *Opp* SERIOUS.

humour *n* 1 absurdity, badinage, banter, comedy, drollness, facetiousness, fun, incongruity, irony, jesting, jocularity, jokes, joking, merriment, quips, raillery, repartee, satire, *inf* sense of fun, waggishness, wit, witticism, wittiness. 2 *in a good humour*. disposition, frame of mind, mood, spirits, state of mind, temper.

hump *n* 1 bulge, bump, curve, growth, hunch, knob, lump, node, projection, protrusion, protuberance, swelling, tumescence. 2 *hump in the ground*. barrow, hillock, hummock, mound, rise, tumulus.
• *vb* 1 arch, bend, crook, curl, curve, hunch, raise. 2 *hump a load*. drag, heave, hoist, lift, lug, raise, shoulder.

hunch *n* 1 ▷ HUMP. 2 feeling, guess, idea, impression, inkling, intuition, premonition, presentiment, suspicion.
• *vb* arch, bend, crook, curl, curve, huddle, hump, raise, shrug.

hunger *n* 1 appetite, craving, greed, ravenousness, voracity. 2 deprivation, famine, lack of food, malnutrition, starvation, want. • *vb* ▷ DESIRE.

hungry *adj* aching, avid, covetous, craving, eager, emaciated, famished, famishing, greedy, longing, *inf* peckish, ravenous, starved, starving, underfed, undernourished, voracious.

hunt *n* chase, pursuit, quest, search. ▷ HUNTING.

• *vb* 1 chase, course, dog, ferret, hound, poach, pursue, stalk, track, trail. 2 *hunt for lost property*. *inf* check out, enquire after, ferret out, look for, rummage, search for, seek, trace, track down.

hunter *n* huntsman, huntswoman, predator, stalker, trapper.

hunting *n* blood-sports, coursing, poaching, stalking, trapping.

hurdle *n* 1 barricade, barrier, fence, hedge, jump, obstacle, wall. 2 bar, check, complication, difficulty, handicap, hindrance, impediment, obstruction, problem, restraint, snag, stumbling block.

hurl *vb* cast, catapult, chuck, dash, fire, fling, heave, launch, *inf* let fly, pelt, pitch, project, propel, send, shy, sling, throw, toss.

hurricane *n* cyclone, storm, tempest, tornado, typhoon, whirlwind.

hurry *n* ▷ HASTE. • *vb* 1 *inf* belt, *inf* buck up, chase, dash, dispatch, *inf* fly, *inf* get a move on, hasten, hurtle, hustle, make haste, move quickly, rush, *inf* shift, speed, *inf* step on it, work faster. 2 *hurry a process*. accelerate, expedite, press on with, quicken, speed up. *Opp* DELAY. **hurried** ▷ HASTY.

hurt *vb* 1 ache, be painful, burn, pinch, smart, sting, suffer pain, throb, tingle. 2 *hurt physically*. abuse, afflict, agonize, bruise, cause pain to, cripple, cut, disable, injure, maim, misuse, mutilate, torture, wound. 3 *hurt mentally*. affect, aggrieve, be hurtful to, *inf* cut to the quick, depress, distress, grieve, humiliate, insult, offend, pain, sadden, torment, upset. **4** *hurt things.* damage, harm, impair, mar, ruin, sabotage, spoil.

hurtful *adj* biting, cruel, cutting, damaging, derogatory, detrimental, distressing, hard to bear, harmful, injurious, malicious, nasty, painful, sarcastic, scathing, spiteful, uncharitable, unkind, upsetting, vicious, wounding. *Opp* KIND.

hurtle *vb* charge, chase, dash, fly, plunge, race, rush, shoot, speed, tear.

hush *int* be quiet! be silent! *inf* hold your tongue! *sl* pipe down! *inf* shut up! • *vb* ▷ SILENCE. **hush up** ▷ SUPPRESS.

hustle *vb* **1** bustle, hasten, hurry, jostle, rush, scamper, scurry. **2** *hustled me away.* coerce, compel, force, push, shove, thrust.

hut *n* cabin, den, hovel, lean-to, shack, shanty, shed, shelter.

hybrid *n* amalgam, combination, composite, compound, cross, cross-breed, half-breed, mixture, mongrel.

hygiene *n* cleanliness, health, sanitariness, sanitation, wholesomeness.

hygienic *adj* aseptic, clean, disinfected, germ-free, healthy, pure, salubrious, sanitary, sterile, sterilized, unpolluted, wholesome. *Opp* UNHEALTHY.

hypnotic *adj* fascinating, irresistible, magnetic, mesmeric, mesmerizing, sleep-inducing, soothing, soporific, spellbinding.

hypnotize *vb* bewitch, captivate, cast a spell over, dominate, enchant, entrance, fascinate, gain power over, magnetize, mesmerize, *inf* put to sleep, spellbind, *inf* stupefy.

hypocrisy *n* cant, deceit, deception, double-dealing, double standards, double-talk, doublethink, duplicity, falsity, *inf* humbug, inconsistency, insincerity.

hypocritical *adj* deceptive, double-dealing, double-faced, duplicitous, false, inconsistent, insincere, Pharisaical, *inf* phoney, self-deceiving, self-righteous, *inf* two-faced.

hypothesis *n* conjecture, guess, postulate, premise, proposition, speculation, supposition, theory, thesis.

hypothetical *adj* academic, alleged, assumed, conjectural, groundless, imaginary, presumed, putative, speculative, supposed, suppositional, theoretical, unreal.

hysteria *n* frenzy, hysterics, madness, mania, panic.

hysterical *adj* berserk, beside yourself, crazed, delirious, demented, distraught, frantic, frenzied, irrational, mad, overemotional, rabid, raving, uncontrollable, wild.

I

ice *n* black ice, floe, frost, glacier, iceberg, icicle, rime.

icy *adj* **1** arctic, chilling, freezing, frosty, frozen, glacial, polar, Siberian. ▷ COLD. **2** *icy roads.* glassy, slippery, *inf* slippy, slithery.

idea n 1 abstraction, attitude, belief, concept, conception, conjecture, construct, conviction, doctrine, hypothesis, notion, opinion, philosophy, principle, sentiment, teaching, tenet, theory, thought, view. 2 *a bright idea.* brainwave, design, fancy, guess, inspiration, plan, proposal, scheme, suggestion. 3 *idea of a poem.* intention, meaning, point. 4 *idea of what to expect.* clue, guidelines, impression, inkling, intimation, model, pattern, perception, suspicion, vision.

ideal adj 1 best, classic, complete, excellent, faultless, model, optimum, perfect, supreme, unsurpassable. 2 *an ideal world.* chimerical, dream, hypothetical, illusory, imaginary, unattainable, unreal, Utopian, visionary. • n 1 acme, criterion, epitome, exemplar, model, paragon, pattern, standard. 2 ▷ PRINCIPLE.

idealistic adj high-minded, impractical, over-optimistic, quixotic, romantic, starry-eyed, unrealistic. *Opp* REALISTIC.

idealize vb apotheosize, deify, exalt, glamorize, glorify, *inf* put on a pedestal, romanticize. ▷ IDOLIZE.

identical adj alike, comparable, congruent, corresponding, duplicate, equal, equivalent, indistinguishable, interchangeable, like, matching, the same, similar, twin. *Opp* DIFFERENT.

identifiable adj detectable, discernible, distinctive, distinguishable, familiar, known, named, noticeable, perceptible, recognizable, unmistakable. *Opp* UNIDENTIFIABLE.

identify vb 1 distinguish, label, mark, name, pick out, pinpoint, *inf* put a name to, recognize, single out, specify, spot. 2 *identify an illness.* detect, diagnose, discover. **identify with** empathize with, feel for, *inf* put yourself in the shoes of, relate to, sympathize with.

identity n 1 *inf* ID, name. 2 character, distinctiveness, individuality, nature, particularity, personality, selfhood, singularity, uniqueness.

ideology n assumptions, beliefs, creed, convictions, ideas, philosophy, principles, tenets, theories, underlying attitudes.

idiom n argot, cant, choice of words, dialect, expression, jargon, language, manner of speaking, parlance, phrase, phraseology, phrasing, turn of phrase, usage.

idiomatic adj colloquial, natural, vernacular, well-phrased.

idiosyncrasy n characteristic, eccentricity, feature, habit, individuality, mannerism, oddity, peculiarity, quirk, trait.

idiosyncratic adj characteristic, distinctive, eccentric, individual, odd, peculiar, personal, quirky, singular, unique. *Opp* COMMON.

idiot n [*most synonyms inf*] ass, blockhead, bonehead, booby, chump, clot, cretin, dim-wit, dolt, dope, duffer, dumb-bell, dummy, dunce, dunderhead, fat-head, fool, half-wit, ignoramus, imbecile, moron, nincompoop, ninny, nitwit, simpleton, twerp, twit.

idiotic adj absurd, asinine, crazy, foolish, half-witted, imbecile, insane, irrational, mad, moronic, nonsensical, ridiculous, senseless. ▷ STUPID. *Opp* SENSIBLE.

idle *adj* 1 dormant, inactive, inoperative, in retirement, not working, redundant, retired, unemployed, unoccupied, unproductive, unused. 2 apathetic, good-for-nothing, indolent, lackadaisical, lazy, shiftless, slothful, slow, sluggish, torpid, uncommitted, work-shy. 3 *idle speculation.* casual, frivolous, futile, pointless, worthless. *Opp* BUSY.
• *vb* be lazy, dawdle, do nothing, *inf* hang about, *inf* kill time, laze, loaf, loll, lounge about, *inf* mess about, potter, slack, stagnate, take it easy, vegetate. *Opp* WORK.

idler *n* good-for-nothing, *inf* layabout, *inf* lazybones, loafer, malingerer, shirker, *inf* skiver, slacker, sluggard, wastrel.

idol *n* 1 deity, effigy, fetish, god, graven image, icon, statue. 2 *pop idol.* celebrity, *inf* darling, favourite, hero, *inf* pin-up, star, *inf* superstar.

idolize *vb* adore, adulate, hero-worship, lionize, look up to, revere, reverence, venerate, worship. ▷ IDEALIZE.

idyllic *adj* Arcadian, bucolic, charming, delightful, happy, idealized, lovely, pastoral, peaceful, perfect, picturesque, rustic, unspoiled.

ignite *vb* burn, catch fire, fire, kindle, light, set alight, set on fire, spark off, touch off.

ignoble *adj* base, churlish, cowardly, despicable, disgraceful, dishonourable, infamous, low, mean, selfish, shabby,

uncharitable, unchivalrous, unworthy. *Opp* NOBLE.

ignorance *n* inexperience, innocence, unawareness, unconsciousness, unfamiliarity. ▷ STUPIDITY. *Opp* KNOWLEDGE.

ignorant *adj* 1 ill-informed, innocent, lacking knowledge, oblivious, unacquainted, unaware, unconscious, unfamiliar (with), uninformed, unwitting. 2 benighted, *inf* clueless, illiterate, uncouth, uncultivated, uneducated, unenlightened, unlettered, unscholarly, unsophisticated. ▷ IMPOLITE, STUPID. *Opp* CLEVER, KNOWLEDGEABLE.

ignore *vb* disobey, disregard, leave out, miss out, neglect, omit, overlook, pass over, reject, *inf* shut your eyes to, skip, slight, snub, take no notice of, *inf* turn a blind eye to.

ill *adj* 1 ailing, bad, bedridden, bilious, *inf* dicky, diseased, feeble, frail, *inf* funny, *inf* groggy, indisposed, infected, infirm, invalid, nauseated, nauseous, *inf* off-colour, *inf* out of sorts, pasty, poorly, queasy, queer, *inf* seedy, sick, sickly, suffering, *inf* under the weather, unhealthy, unwell, valetudinarian, weak. *Opp* HEALTHY. 2 *ill effects.* bad, damaging, detrimental, evil, harmful, injurious, unfavourable, unfortunate, unlucky. *Opp* GOOD. • *plur n* the infirm, invalids, patients, the sick, sufferers, victims. **be ill** ail, languish, sicken. **ill-advised** ▷ MISGUIDED. **ill-bred** ▷ RUDE. **ill-fated** ▷ UNLUCKY. **ill-humoured** ▷ BAD-TEMPERED. **ill-mannered** ▷ RUDE. **ill-natured** ▷ UNKIND. **ill-omened** ▷ UNLUCKY. **ill-**

tempered ▷ BAD-TEMPERED.
ill-treat ▷ MISTREAT.

illegal *adj* actionable, against the law, banned, black-market, criminal, felonious, forbidden, illicit, invalid, irregular, outlawed, prohibited, proscribed, unauthorized, unconstitutional, unlawful, unlicensed, wrong, wrongful. ▷ ILLEGITIMATE. *Opp* LEGAL.

illegible *adj* indecipherable, indistinct, obscure, unclear, unreadable. *Opp* LEGIBLE.

illegitimate *adj* 1 against the rules, improper, inadmissible, incorrect, invalid, irregular, spurious, unauthorized, unjustifiable, unreasonable, unwarranted. ▷ ILLEGAL. 2 bastard, born out of wedlock, natural. *Opp* LEGITIMATE.

illiterate *adj* unable to read, uneducated, unlettered. ▷ IGNORANT. *Opp* LITERATE.

illness *n* abnormality, affliction, ailment, allergy, attack, blight, *inf* bug, complaint, condition, contagion, disability, disease, disorder, epidemic, fever, fit, health problem, indisposition, infection, infirmity, malady, malaise, pestilence, plague, sickness, *inf* trouble, *inf* turn, *inf* upset, weakness. ▷ WOUND.

illogical *adj* absurd, fallacious, inconsequential, inconsistent, invalid, irrational, senseless, unreasonable, unsound. ▷ SILLY. *Opp* LOGICAL.

illuminate *vb* 1 brighten, decorate with lights, light up, make brighter, reveal. 2 clarify, clear up, elucidate, enlighten, explain, explicate, throw light on.

illusion *n* 1 apparition, conjuring trick, day-dream, deception, delusion, dream, fancy, fantasy, figment of the imagination, hallucination, mirage. 2 *under an illusion.* error, false impression, misapprehension, misconception, mistake.

illusory *adj* chimerical, deceptive, deluding, delusive, fallacious, false, illusive, imagined, misleading, mistaken, sham, unreal, untrue. ▷ IMAGINARY. *Opp* REAL.

illustrate *vb* 1 demonstrate, elucidate, exemplify, explain, instance, show. 2 adorn, decorate, embellish, illuminate, ornament. 3 depict, draw pictures of, picture, portray.

illustration *n* 1 case in point, demonstration, example, exemplar, instance, sample, specimen. 2 decoration, depiction, diagram, drawing, figure, photograph, picture, sketch. ▷ IMAGE.

image *n* 1 imitation, likeness, projection, reflection, representation. ▷ PICTURE. 2 carving, effigy, figure, icon, idol, statue. 3 *the image of her mother.* counterpart, double, likeness, spitting-image, twin.

imaginary *adj* fabulous, fanciful, fictional, fictitious, hypothetical, imagined, insubstantial, invented, legendary, made-up, mythical, mythological, non-existent, supposed, unreal, visionary. ▷ ILLUSORY. *Opp* REAL.

imagination *n* artistry, creativity, fancy, ingenuity, insight, inspiration, inventiveness, *inf* mind's eye, originality, resourcefulness, sensitivity, thought, vision.

imaginative adj artistic, attractive, beautiful, clever, creative, fanciful, ingenious, innovative, inspired, inspiring, inventive, original, poetic, resourceful, sensitive, thoughtful, unusual, visionary, vivid. Opp UNIMAGINATIVE.

imagine vb 1 conceive, conjure up, inf cook up, create, dream up, envisage, fancy, fantasize, invent, make believe, make up, picture, pretend, see, think of, think up, visualize. 2 assume, believe, conjecture, guess, infer, judge, presume, suppose, surmise, suspect, think.

imitate vb 1 ape, burlesque, caricature, counterfeit, duplicate, echo, guy, mimic, parody, parrot, portray, reproduce, satirize, send up, simulate, inf take off, travesty. ▷ IMPERSONATE. 2 copy, emulate, follow, match, model yourself on.

imitation adj artificial, copied, counterfeit, dummy, ersatz, man-made, mock, model, inf phoney, reproduction, sham, simulated, synthetic. Opp REAL. • n 1 copying, duplication, emulation, mimicry, repetition. 2 inf clone, copy, counterfeit, dummy, duplicate, fake, forgery, impersonation, impression, likeness, inf mock-up, model, parody, reflection, replica, reproduction, sham, simulation, inf take-off, toy, travesty.

immature adj adolescent, babyish, backward, callow, childish, inf green, inexperienced, infantile, juvenile, new, puerile, undeveloped, unripe, young, youthful. Opp MATURE.

immediate adj 1 instant, instantaneous, prompt, quick, speedy, sudden, swift, unhesitating, unthinking. 2 immediate need. current, present, pressing, top-priority, urgent. 3 immediate neighbours. adjacent, close, closest, direct, near, nearest, neighbouring, next.

immediately adv at once, directly, forthwith, instantly, now, promptly, inf right away, straight away, unhesitatingly.

immense adj Brobdingnagian, colossal, elephantine, enormous, gargantuan, giant, gigantic, great, huge, inf hulking, immeasurable, imposing, impressive, incalculable, inf jumbo, large, mammoth, massive, mighty, inf monster, monstrous, monumental, mountainous, prodigious, stupendous, titanic, towering, inf tremendous, vast, inf whopping. ▷ BIG. Opp SMALL.

immerse vb bathe, dip, drench, drown, duck, dunk, inundate, lower, plunge, sink, submerge. **immersed** ▷ BUSY, INTERESTED.

immersion n baptism, dipping, ducking, plunge, submersion.

immigrant n alien, arrival, incomer, newcomer, outsider, settler.

imminent adj about to happen, approaching, close, coming, foreseeable, forthcoming, impending, looming, menacing, near, threatening.

immobile adj 1 ▷ IMMOVABLE. 2 frozen, inexpressive, inflexible, rigid. Opp MOBILE.

immobilize vb cripple, damage, disable, make immobile, paralyse, put out of action, sabotage, stop.

immoral adj abandoned, base, conscienceless, corrupt,

debauched, degenerate, depraved, dishonest, dissipated, dissolute, evil, *inf* fast, impure, indecent, irresponsible, licentious, loose, low, profligate, promiscuous, *inf* rotten, sinful, unchaste, unethical, unprincipled, unscrupulous, vicious, villainous, wanton, wrong.
▷ WICKED. Opp MORAL.

immoral person blackguard, cheat, degenerate, liar, libertine, profligate, rake, reprobate, scoundrel, sinner, villain, wrongdoer.

immortal *adj* 1 ageless, ceaseless, deathless, endless, eternal, everlasting, incorruptible, indestructible, never-ending, perpetual, sempiternal, timeless, unchanging, undying, unending, unfading. 2 *immortal beings.* divine, godlike, legendary, mythical. Opp MORTAL.

immortalize *vb* apotheosize, beatify, canonize, commemorate, deify, enshrine, keep alive, make immortal, make permanent, memorialize, perpetuate.

immovable *adj* 1 anchored, fast, firm, fixed, immobile, immobilized, motionless, paralysed, riveted, rooted, secure, set, settled, solid, static, stationary, still, stuck, unmoving.
2 ▷ IMMUTABLE.

immune *adj* exempt, free, immunized, inoculated, invulnerable, protected, resistant, safe, unaffected, vaccinated.
Opp VULNERABLE.

immunize *vb* inoculate, vaccinate.

immutable *adj* constant, dependable, enduring, eternal, fixed, invariable, lasting, obdurate, permanent, perpetual, reli-

able, settled, stable, steadfast, unalterable, unchangeable, unswerving, unvarying.
▷ RESOLUTE. Opp CHANGEABLE.

impact *n* 1 bang, blow, bump, collision, concussion, contact, crash, knock, smash. 2 bearing, consequence, effect, force, impression, influence, repercussions, reverberations, shock, thrust. ● *vb* ▷ HIT.

impair *vb* cripple, damage, harm, injure, mar, ruin, spoil, weaken.

impale *vb* pierce, run through, skewer, spear, spike, spit, stab, stick, transfix.

impartial *adj* balanced, detached, disinterested, dispassionate, equitable, even-handed, fair, fair-minded, just, neutral, non-partisan, objective, openminded, unbiased, uninvolved, unprejudiced. Opp BIASED.

impartiality *n* balance, detachment, disinterest, fairness, justice, neutrality, objectivity, open-mindedness. Opp BIAS.

impassable *adj* blocked, closed, obstructed, unusable.

impatient *adj* 1 anxious, eager, keen, impetuous, precipitate, *inf* raring. 2 agitated, chafing, edgy, fidgety, fretful, irritable, nervous, restive, restless, uneasy. 3 *an impatient manner.* abrupt, brusque, curt, hasty, intolerant, irascible, irritable, quick-tempered, short-tempered, snappish, snappy, testy.
Opp APATHETIC, PATIENT.

impede *vb* arrest, bar, be an impediment to, check, curb, delay, deter, frustrate, get in the way of, hamper, handicap, hinder, *inf* hit, hold back, hold up, keep back, limit, obstruct, oppose, prevent, restrain, restrict, retard, sabotage, slow down, slow up, stand in the way of, stop, thwart. Opp HELP.

impediment n 1 bar, barrier, burden, check, curb, deterrent, difficulty, disadvantage, inf drag, drawback, encumbrance, hindrance, inconvenience, limitation, obstacle, obstruction, restraint, restriction, snag, stumbling-block. 2 ▷ HANDICAP.

impending adj about to happen, approaching, close, coming, foreseeable, forthcoming, imminent, looming, menacing, near, inf on the horizon, threatening.

impenetrable adj 1 dense, hard, resilient, solid, strong. ▷ IMPERVIOUS. 2 impregnable, invincible, inviolable, invulnerable, safe, secure, unassailable, unconquerable. Opp VULNERABLE. 3 impenetrable language. inaccessible, incomprehensible, inscrutable, unfathomable, inf unget-at-able. Opp ACCESSIBLE.

imperceptible adj faint, gradual, inappreciable, inaudible, indistinguishable, infinitesimal, insignificant, invisible, microscopic, minute, negligible, slight, small, subtle, tiny, unclear, undetectable, unnoticeable, vague. ▷ SMALL. Opp PERCEPTIBLE.

imperceptive adj impercipient, inattentive, slow, uncritical, undiscriminating, unobservant, unresponsive ▷ STUPID. Opp PERCEPTIVE.

imperfect adj blemished, broken, chipped, cracked,

damaged, defective, deficient, faulty, flawed, incomplete, incorrect, marred, partial, patchy, shop-soiled, spoilt, unfinished, wanting. Opp PERFECT.

imperfection n blemish, damage, defect, deficiency, error, failing, fault, flaw, foible, frailty, inadequacy, infirmity, peccadillo, shortcoming, weakness. Opp PERFECTION.

impermanent adj changing, destructible, ephemeral, evanescent, fleeting, momentary, passing, shifting, short-lived, temporary, transient, transitory, unstable. ▷ CHANGEABLE. Opp PERMANENT.

impersonal adj aloof, businesslike, cold, cool, correct, detached, disinterested, dispassionate, distant, formal, hard, inhuman, mechanical, objective, official, remote, stiff, unapproachable, unemotional, unfriendly, unprejudiced, unsympathetic, without emotion, wooden. Opp FRIENDLY.

impersonate vb disguise yourself as, do impressions of, dress up as, masquerade as, mimic, pass yourself off as, portray, pose as, pretend to be, inf take off. ▷ IMITATE.

impertinent adj bold, brazen, cheeky, inf cocky, inf cool, discourteous, disrespectful, forward, fresh, impolite, impudent, insolent, insubordinate, insulting, irreverent, pert, saucy. ▷ RUDE. Opp RESPECTFUL.

impervious adj 1 hermetic, impenetrable, impermeable, non-porous, solid, waterproof,

water-repellent, watertight.
Opp POROUS. 2 ▷ RESISTANT.

impetuous *adj* abrupt, careless,
eager, hasty, headlong, hot-
headed, impulsive, incautious,
offhand, precipitate, quick,
rash, reckless, speedy, spontaneous, *inf* spur-of-the-moment,
inf tearing, thoughtless, unplanned, unpremeditated, unthinking, violent. Opp CAUTIOUS.

impetus *n* boost, drive, encouragement, energy, fillip, force,
impulse, incentive, inspiration,
momentum, motivation, power,
push, spur, stimulation, stimulus, thrust.

impiety *n* blasphemy, godless-
ness, irreverence, profanity,
sacrilege, sinfulness, ungodliness, unrighteousness, wickedness. Opp PIETY.

impious *adj* blasphemous,
godless, irreligious, irreverent,
profane, sacrilegious, sinful,
unholy. ▷ WICKED. Opp PIOUS.

implausible *adj* doubtful, dubious, far-fetched, feeble, improbable, questionable, suspect,
unconvincing, unlikely, unreasonable, weak. Opp PLAUSIBLE.

implement *n* apparatus, appliance, contrivance, device,
gadget, instrument, mechanism,
tool, utensil. ● *vb* accomplish, achieve, bring about, carry out,
effect, enforce, execute, fulfil,
perform, put into effect, put into
practice, realize, try out.

implicate *vb* associate, concern,
connect, embroil, enmesh,
ensnare, entangle, entrap,
include, incriminate, inculpate,
involve, show involvement in.

implication *n* 1 hidden meaning, hint, innuendo, insinua-

tion, overtone, purport, significance. 2 *implication in crime*.
association, connection,
embroilment, entanglement,
inclusion, involvement.

implicit *adj* 1 hinted at, implied,
indirect, inherent, insinuated,
tacit, understood, undeclared,
unexpressed, unsaid, unspoken,
unstated, unvoiced. Opp EXPLI-
CIT. 2 *implicit faith*. ▷ ABSO-
LUTE.

imply *vb* 1 hint, indicate, insinuate, intimate, mean, point to,
suggest. 2 ▷ SIGNIFY.

impolite *adj* discourteous, disrespectful, ill-bred, ill-mannered,
uncivil, vulgar. ▷ RUDE.
Opp POLITE.

import *vb* bring in, buy in, introduce, ship in. ▷ CONVEY.

important *adj* 1 basic, big,
cardinal, central, chief, consequential, critical, epoch-
making, essential, foremost,
fundamental, grave, historic,
key, main, major, momentous,
newsworthy, noteworthy, once
in a lifetime, outstanding, pressing, primary, principal, rare,
salient, serious, signal, significant, strategic, substantial,
urgent, valuable, vital, weighty.
2 celebrated, distinguished,
eminent, famous, great, high-
ranking, influential, known,
leading, notable, noted, powerful, pre-eminent, prominent,
renowned, top-level, well-
known. Opp UNIMPORTANT. **be
important** ▷ MATTER.

importunate *adj* demanding,
impatient, insistent, persistent,
pressing, relentless, urgent,
unremitting.

importune *vb* badger, harass,
hound, pester, plague, plead

with, press, solicit, urge.
▷ ASK.

impose vb charge with, decree,
dictate, enforce, exact, fix, foist,
force, inflict, insist on, introduce, lay, levy, prescribe, set.
impose on ▷ BURDEN, EXPLOIT.
imposing ▷ IMPRESSIVE.

impossible adj hopeless, impracticable, impractical, inconceivable, insoluble, insuperable,
insurmountable, inf not on, out
of the question, unachievable,
unattainable, unimaginable,
unobtainable, unthinkable,
unviable, unworkable.
Opp POSSIBLE.

impotent adj debilitated,
decrepit, emasculated, enervated, helpless, inadequate, incapable, incompetent, ineffective,
ineffectual, inept, infirm, powerless, unable. ▷ WEAK.
Opp POTENT.

impracticable adj not feasible,
unachievable, unworkable,
useless. ▷ IMPOSSIBLE.
Opp PRACTICABLE.

impractical adj academic, idealistic, quixotic, romantic, theoretical, unrealistic, visionary.
Opp PRACTICAL.

imprecise adj ambiguous,
approximate, careless, estimated, fuzzy, guessed, hazy, ill-
defined, inaccurate, inexact,
inexplicit, loose, inf sloppy,
undefined, unscientific, vague,
inf waffly, inf woolly.
Opp PRECISE.

impregnable adj impenetrable,
invincible, inviolable, invulnerable, safe, secure, strong, unassailable, unconquerable.
Opp VULNERABLE.

impress vb 1 affect, be memorable to, excite, influence,

inspire, leave its mark on,
move, persuade, inf stick in the
mind of, stir, touch. 2 impress a
mark. emboss, engrave,
imprint, mark, print, stamp.

impression n 1 effect, impact,
influence, mark. 2 belief,
consciousness, fancy, feeling,
hunch, idea, memory, notion,
opinion, recollection, sense,
suspicion, view. 3 dent, hollow,
imprint, indentation, mark,
print, stamp. 4 imitation,
impersonation, mimicry,
parody, inf take-off. 5 impression of a book. edition, printing,
reprint.

impressionable adj easily
influenced, gullible, inexperienced, naïve, persuadable,
receptive, responsive, suggestible, susceptible.

impressive adj affecting,
august, awe-inspiring,
awesome, commanding, distinguished, evocative, exciting,
formidable, grand, derog grandiose, great, imposing, magnificent, majestic, memorable,
moving, powerful, redoubtable,
remarkable, splendid, stately,
stirring, striking, touching.
▷ BIG. Opp INSIGNIFICANT.

imprison vb cage, commit to
prison, confine, detain, gaol,
immure, incarcerate, intern,
jail, keep in custody, keep
under house arrest, inf keep
under lock and key, lock away,
lock up, inf put away, remand,
inf send down, shut in, shut up.
Opp FREE.

imprisonment n confinement,
custody, detention, duress, gaol,
house arrest, incarceration,
internment, jail, remand,
restraint.

improbable *adj* absurd, doubtful, dubious, far-fetched, *inf* hard to believe, implausible, incredible, preposterous, questionable, unbelievable, unconvincing, unexpected, unlikely. *Opp* PROBABLE.

impromptu *adj inf* ad-lib, extempore, extemporized, improvised, impulsive, made-up, offhand, *inf* off the cuff, *inf* off the top of your head, *inf* on the spur of the moment, spontaneous, unplanned, unpremeditated, unprepared, unrehearsed, unscripted. ▷ IMPULSIVE. *Opp* REHEARSED.

improper *adj* 1 ill-judged, ill-timed, inappropriate, incorrect, infelicitous, inopportune, irregular, mistaken, out of place, uncalled-for, unfit, unseemly, unsuitable, unwarranted. ▷ WRONG. 2 ▷ INDECENT. *Opp* PROPER.

impropriety *n* inappropriateness, incorrectness, indecency, indelicacy, infelicity, insensitivity, irregularity, rudeness, unseemliness. ▷ OBSCENITY. *Opp* PROPRIETY.

improve *vb* 1 advance, develop, get better, grow, increase, *inf* look up, move on, progress, *inf* take a turn for the better. 2 *improve after illness.* convalesce, *inf* pick up, rally, recover, recuperate, revive, strengthen, *inf* turn the corner. 3 *improve your ways.* ameliorate, amend, better, correct, enhance, enrich, make better, mend, polish (up), purify, refine, reform, revise. 4 *improve a home.* decorate, extend, modernize, rebuild, recondition, refurbish, reno-

vate, repair, touch up, update, upgrade. *Opp* WORSEN.

improvement *n* 1 advance, amelioration, betterment, correction, development, enhancement, gain, increase, progress, rally, recovery, reformation, upswing, upturn. 2 *home improvements.* alteration, extension, *inf* face-lift, modernization, modification, renovation.

improvise *vb* 1 *inf* ad-lib, concoct, contrive, devise, invent, make do, make up, *inf* throw together. 2 extemporize, perform impromptu, play by ear, vamp.

impudent *adj* audacious, bold, *inf* cheeky, disrespectful, forward, *inf* fresh, impertinent, insolent, pert, presumptuous, saucy. ▷ RUDE. *Opp* RESPECTFUL.

impulse *n* 1 drive, force, impetus, motive, pressure, push, stimulus, thrust. 2 caprice, desire, instinct, urge, whim.

impulsive *adj* automatic, emotional, hare-brained, hasty, headlong, hot-headed, impetuous, instinctive, intuitive, involuntary, madcap, precipitate, rash, reckless, *inf* snap, spontaneous, *inf* spur-of-the-moment, sudden, thoughtless, unconscious, unplanned, unpremeditated, unthinking, wild. ▷ IMPROMPTU. *Opp* DELIBERATE.

impure *adj* 1 adulterated, contaminated, defiled, foul, infected, polluted, tainted, unclean, unwholesome. ▷ DIRTY. 2 ▷ INDECENT.

impurity *n* contamination, defilement, infection, pollution, taint. ▷ DIRT.

inaccessible adj cut off, deserted, desolate, god-forsaken, impassable, impenetrable, inconvenient, isolated, lonely, inf off the beaten track, outlying, out of reach, out-of-the-way, private, remote, solitary, unavailable, unfrequented, inf unget-at-able, unobtainable, unreachable, unusable. Opp ACCESSIBLE.

inaccurate adj erroneous, fallacious, false, faulty, flawed, imperfect, imprecise, incorrect, inexact, misleading, mistaken, unfaithful, unreliable, unsound, untrue, vague, wrong. Opp ACCURATE.

inactive adj asleep, dormant, hibernating, idle, immobile, inanimate, indolent, inert, languid, lazy, lethargic, out of action, passive, quiescent, quiet, sedentary, sleepy, slothful, slow, sluggish, somnolent, torpid, unemployed, unoccupied, vegetating. Opp ACTIVE.

inadequate adj deficient, disappointing, faulty, imperfect, incompetent, incomplete, ineffective, insufficient, limited, meagre, mean, niggardly, inf pathetic, scanty, scarce, inf skimpy, sparse, unacceptable, unsatisfactory, unsuitable. Opp ADEQUATE.

inadvisable adj foolish, ill-advised, imprudent, misguided, unwise. ▷ SILLY. Opp WISE.

inanimate adj cold, dead, dormant, immobile, inactive, insentient, lifeless, motionless, spiritless, unconscious. Opp ANIMATE.

inappropriate adj ill-judged, ill-suited, ill-timed, improper, inapplicable, inapposite, incom-patible, incongruous, incorrect, inept, inopportune, irrelevant, out of place, tactless, tasteless, unbecoming, unbefitting, unfit, unseasonable, unseemly, unsuitable, unsuited, untimely, wrong. Opp APPROPRIATE.

inarticulate adj dumb, faltering, halting, hesitant, mumbling, mute, shy, silent, speechless, stammering, stuttering, tongue-tied, voiceless. ▷ INCOHERENT. Opp ARTICULATE.

inattentive adj absent-minded, abstracted, careless, day-dreaming, distracted, dreaming, drifting, heedless, inf in a world of your own, lacking concentration, negligent, preoccupied, rambling, remiss, slack, unobservant, vague, wandering, wool-gathering. Opp ATTENTIVE.

inaudible adj imperceptible, mumbled, quiet, silenced, silent, stifled, undetectable, undistinguishable, unheard. ▷ FAINT. Opp AUDIBLE.

incapable adj 1 clumsy, helpless, impotent, inadequate, incompetent, ineffective, ineffectual, inept, powerless, stupid, unable, unfit, unqualified, useless, weak. Opp CAPABLE. 2 ▷ DRUNK.

incentive n bait, inf carrot, encouragement, enticement, impetus, incitement, inducement, lure, motivation, reward, stimulus, inf sweetener.

incessant adj ceaseless, chronic, constant, continual, continuous, endless, eternal, everlasting, interminable, never-ending, non-stop, perennial, permanent, perpetual, persistent, relentless, unbroken, unceasing, unending, unremitting. Opp INTERMITTENT, TEMPORARY.

incident n 1 affair, circumstance, episode, event, fact, happening, occasion, occurrence, proceeding. 2 *a nasty incident.* accident, confrontation, disturbance, fight, scene, upset. ▷ COMMOTION.

incidental adj accidental, adventitious, attendant, casual, chance, fortuitous, inessential, minor, odd, random, secondary, serendipitous, subordinate, subsidiary, unplanned. Opp ESSENTIAL.

incipient adj beginning, developing, early, embryonic, growing, new, rudimentary, starting.

incisive adj acute, clear, concise, cutting, decisive, direct, penetrating, percipient, precise, sharp, telling, trenchant. Opp VAGUE.

incite vb awaken, encourage, excite, fire, foment, inflame, inspire, prompt, provoke, rouse, spur on, stimulate, stir, urge, whip up, work up.

inclination n affection, bent, bias, disposition, fondness, habit, instinct, leaning, liking, partiality, penchant, predilection, predisposition, preference, proclivity, propensity, readiness, tendency, trend, willingness. ▷ DESIRE.

incline n acclivity, ascent, declivity, descent, drop, grade, gradient, hill, pitch, ramp, rise, slope. • vb angle, ascend, bank, bend, bow, descend, drop, gravitate, lean, rise, slant, slope, tend, tilt, tip, veer. **inclined (to)** ▷ LIABLE.

include vb 1 add in, blend in, combine, comprehend, comprise, consist of, contain, embody, embrace, encompass, incorporate, involve, make room for, mix, subsume, take in. 2 *The price includes tea.* allow for, cover, take into account. Opp EXCLUDE.

incoherent adj confused, disconnected, disjointed, disordered, disorganized, garbled, illogical, incomprehensible, inconsistent, irrational, jumbled, mixed up, muddled, rambling, scrambled, unclear, unconnected, unstructured, unsystematic. ▷ INARTICULATE. Opp COHERENT.

incombustible adj fireproof, fire-resistant, flameproof, nonflammable. Opp COMBUSTIBLE.

income n earnings, gain, interest, pay, pension, proceeds, profits, receipts, return, revenue, salary, takings, wages. Opp EXPENSE.

incoming adj 1 approaching, arriving, entering, coming, landing, new, next, returning. 2 *incoming tide.* flowing, rising. Opp OUTGOING.

incompatible adj antipathetic, at variance, clashing, conflicting, contradictory, contrasting, different, discordant, discrepant, incongruous, inconsistent, irreconcilable, mismatched, opposed, unsuited. Opp COMPATIBLE.

incompetent adj 1 bungling, clumsy, feckless, gauche, helpless, *inf* hopeless, incapable, ineffective, ineffectual, inefficient, inexperienced, maladroit, unfit, unqualified, unskilled, untrained. 2 bungled, inade-

quate, inexpert, unacceptable,
unsatisfactory, unskilful,
useless. *Opp* COMPETENT.

incomplete *adj* abbreviated,
abridged, *inf* bitty, deficient,
edited, expurgated, faulty, fragmentary, imperfect, insufficient, partial, selective, shortened, sketchy, unfinished,
unpolished, wanting.
Opp COMPLETE.

incomprehensible
adj abstruse, arcane, baffling,
beyond comprehension, cryptic,
deep, enigmatic, esoteric, illegible, impenetrable, indecipherable, meaningless, mysterious,
mystifying, obscure, opaque,
inf over my head, perplexing,
puzzling, recondite, strange, too
difficult, unclear, unfathomable, unintelligible.
Opp COMPREHENSIBLE.

inconceivable *adj* implausible,
impossible to understand,
incredible, *inf* mind-boggling,
staggering, unbelievable,
undreamed-of, unimaginable,
unthinkable. *Opp* CREDIBLE.

inconclusive *adj* ambiguous,
equivocal, indecisive, indefinite, interrogative, open, open-
ended, questionable, uncertain,
unconvincing, unresolved,
inf up in the air.
Opp CONCLUSIVE.

incongruous *adj* clashing,
conflicting, contrasting,
discordant, ill-matched, ill-
suited, inappropriate, incompatible, inconsistent, irreconcilable, odd, out of keeping, out of
place, surprising, uncoordinated, unsuited. ▷ ABSURD.
Opp COMPATIBLE.

inconsiderate *adj* careless,
cruel, heedless, insensitive,
intolerant, negligent, rude,

self-centred, selfish, tactless,
thoughtless, uncaring, unconcerned, unfriendly, ungracious,
unhelpful, unkind, unsympathetic, unthinking. *Opp* CON-
SIDERATE.

inconsistent *adj* capricious,
changeable, erratic, fickle,
inconstant, patchy, unpredictable, unreliable, unstable,
inf up-and-down, variable.
▷ INCOMPATIBLE. *Opp* CON-
SISTENT.

inconspicuous *adj* camouflaged, concealed, discreet,
hidden, insignificant, in the
background, invisible, modest,
ordinary, out of sight, plain,
restrained, retiring, self-effacing, small, unassuming, unobtrusive, unostentatious.
Opp CONSPICUOUS.

inconvenience *n* annoyance,
bother, discomfort, disruption,
drawback, encumbrance,
hindrance, impediment, irritation, nuisance, trouble.
● *vb* annoy, bother, discommode, disturb, incommode, irk,
irritate, *inf* put out, trouble.

inconvenient *adj* annoying,
awkward, bothersome, cumbersome, difficult, embarrassing,
ill-timed, inopportune, irksome,
irritating, tiresome, troublesome, unsuitable, untimely,
untoward, unwieldy.
Opp CONVENIENT.

incorporate *vb* admit, combine,
comprehend, comprise, consist
of, contain, embody, embrace,
encompass, include, involve,
mix in, subsume, take in, take
into account, unite.
Opp EXCLUDE.

incorrect *adj* erroneous, fallacious, false, faulty, imprecise,

improper, inaccurate, inexact,
mendacious, misinformed,
misleading, mistaken, specious,
untrue. Opp CORRECT.

incorrigible adj confirmed,
inf dyed-in-the-wool, habitual,
hardened, inf hopeless, impenitent, incurable, inveterate, irredeemable, obdurate, shameless,
unalterable, unreformable,
unrepentant. ▷ WICKED.

incorruptible adj 1 honest,
honourable, just, moral, sound,
inf straight, true, trustworthy,
unbribable, upright.
Opp CORRUPT. 2 ▷ EVERLASTING.

increase n addition, amplification, augmentation, boost,
build-up, crescendo, development, enlargement, escalation,
expansion, extension, gain,
growth, increment, inflation,
intensification, proliferation,
rise, spread, upsurge, upturn.
• vb 1 add to, advance, amplify,
augment, boost, broaden, build
up, develop, enlarge, expand,
extend, improve, lengthen,
magnify, make bigger, maximize, multiply, prolong, put up,
raise, inf step up, strengthen,
stretch, swell, widen, 2 escalate,
gain, get bigger, grow, intensify, proliferate, inf snowball,
spread, wax. Opp DECREASE.

incredible adj beyond belief,
far-fetched, implausible,
impossible, improbable, inconceivable, miraculous, surprising, unbelievable, unconvincing, unimaginable, unlikely,
untenable, unthinkable.
▷ EXTRAORDINARY. Opp CRED-
IBLE.

incredulous adj disbelieving,
distrustful, doubtful, dubious,
mistrustful, questioning, sceptical, suspicious, unbelieving,

uncertain, unconvinced.
Opp CREDULOUS.

incriminate vb accuse, blame,
charge, embroil, implicate,
inculpate, indict, involve,
inf point the finger at.
Opp EXCUSE.

incur vb earn, expose yourself
to, get, lay yourself open to,
provoke, run up, suffer.

incurable adj 1 fatal, hopeless,
inoperable, irremediable, irreparable, terminal, untreatable.
Opp CURABLE. 2 ▷ INCORRIGIBLE.

indebted adj old use beholden,
bound, grateful, obliged, thankful, under an obligation.

indecent adj inf blue, coarse,
crude, dirty, immodest, impolite, improper, impure, indelicate, insensitive, naughty,
obscene, offensive, risqué, rude,
inf sexy, inf smutty, suggestive,
titillating, unprintable, unrepeatable, unsuitable, vulgar.
▷ INDECOROUS. Opp DECENT.

indecisive adj doubtful, equivo-
cal, evasive, inf in two minds,
irresolute, undecided.
▷ HESITANT, INDEFINITE.
Opp DECISIVE. **be indecisive**
▷ HESITATE.

indecorous adj churlish, ill-
bred, inappropriate, inf in bad
taste, tasteless, unbecoming,
uncouth, undignified,
unseemly, vulgar. ▷ INDECENT.
Opp DECOROUS.

indefensible adj incredible,
insupportable, unjustifiable,
unpardonable, unreasonable,
unsound, untenable, vulnerable, weak. ▷ WRONG.

indefinite adj ambiguous, blurred, confused, dim, general, ill-
defined, imprecise, indeterminate, inexact, inexplicit,

inf leaving it open, neutral, obscure, uncertain, unclear, unsettled, unspecific, unspecified, unsure, vague.
▷ INDECISIVE. *Opp* DEFINITE.

indelible *adj* fast, fixed, indestructible, ineffaceable, ineradicable, ingrained, lasting, unfading, unforgettable.
▷ PERMANENT.

indentation *n* cut, dent, depression, dimple, dip, furrow, groove, hollow, indent, mark, nick, notch, pit, recess, score, serration, toothmark, zigzag.

independence *n* 1 autonomy, freedom, individualism, liberty, nonconformity, self-confidence, self-reliance, self-sufficiency. 2 autarchy, home rule, self-determination, self-government, self-rule, sovereignty.

independent *adj* 1 carefree, *inf* footloose, free, freethinking, individualistic, nonconformist, non-partisan, open-minded, private, self-confident, self-reliant, separate, spontaneous, unbeholden, unbiased, uncommitted, unconventional, unprejudiced, untrammelled, without ties. 2 autonomous, liberated, neutral, non-aligned, self-determining, self-governing, sovereign.

indescribable *adj* beyond words, indefinable, inexpressible, stunning, unspeakable, unutterable.

indestructible *adj* durable, enduring, eternal, everlasting, immortal, imperishable, ineradicable, lasting, permanent, shatter-proof, solid, strong, tough, toughened, unbreakable.

index *n* 1 catalogue, directory, guide, key, register, table (*of contents*). 2 ▷ INDICATOR.

indicate *vb* announce, betoken, communicate, convey, denote, describe, designate, display, evidence, express, give an indication (*of*), give notice of, imply, intimate, make known, manifest, mean, notify, point out, register, reveal, say, show, signal, signify, specify, spell, stand for, suggest, symbolize, warn.

indication *n* augury, clue, evidence, forewarning, hint, inkling, intimation, omen, portent, sign, signal, suggestion, symptom, token, warning.

indicator *n* clock, dial, display, gauge, index, instrument, marker, meter, needle, pointer, screen, sign, signal.

indifferent *adj* 1 aloof, apathetic, blasé, bored, casual, cold, cool, detached, disinterested, dispassionate, distant, half-hearted, impassive, incurious, insouciant, neutral, nonchalant, not bothered, uncaring, unconcerned, unemotional, unenthusiastic, unexcited, unimpressed, uninterested, uninvolved, unmoved.
▷ IMPARTIAL. *Opp* ENTHUSIASTIC. 2 commonplace, fair, mediocre, middling, moderate, *inf* nothing to write home about, *inf* poorish, undistinguished, unexciting.
▷ ORDINARY. *Opp* EXCELLENT.

indigestion *n* dyspepsia, flatulence, heartburn.

indignant *adj inf* aerated, annoyed, cross, disgruntled, exasperated, furious, heated, infuriated, *inf* in high dudgeon, irate, irked, irritated, livid, mad, *inf* miffed, *inf* peeved,

piqued, provoked, *inf* put out, riled, sore, upset, vexed.
▷ ANGRY.

indirect *adj* **1** *inf* all round the houses, ambagious, bendy, circuitous, devious, erratic, long, meandering, oblique, rambling, roundabout, roving, tortuous, twisting, winding, zigzag. **2** *an indirect insult*. ambiguous, backhanded, circumlocutory, disguised, equivocal, euphemistic, evasive, implicit, implied, oblique. *Opp* DIRECT.

indiscreet *adj* careless, foolish, ill-advised, ill-considered, ill-judged, impolite, impolitic, incautious, injudicious, insensitive, tactless, undiplomatic, unguarded, unthinking, unwise. *Opp* DISCREET.

indiscriminate *adj* aimless, careless, casual, confused, desultory, general, haphazard, *inf* hit or miss, imperceptive, miscellaneous, mixed, promiscuous, random, uncritical, undifferentiated, undiscerning, undiscriminating, uninformed, unplanned, unselective, unsystematic, wholesale. *Opp* SELECTIVE.

indispensable *adj* basic, central, compulsory, crucial, essential, imperative, important, key, mandatory, necessary, needed, obligatory, required, requisite, vital. *Opp* UNNECESSARY.

indisputable *adj* absolute, accepted, acknowledged, axiomatic, beyond doubt, certain, clear, definite, evident, incontestable, incontrovertible, indubitable, irrefutable, positive, proved, proven, self-evident, sure, unanswerable, unargu-

able, undeniable, undisputed, undoubted, unimpeachable, unquestionable. *Opp* DEBATABLE.

indistinct *adj* **1** bleary, blurred, confused, dim, dull, faint, fuzzy, hazy, ill-defined, indefinite, misty, obscure, shadowy, unclear, vague. **2** deadened, muffled, mumbled, muted, slurred, unintelligible, woolly. *Opp* DISTINCT.

indistinguishable *adj* alike, identical, interchangeable, the same, twin, undifferentiated. *Opp* DIFFERENT.

individual *adj* characteristic, different, distinct, distinctive, exclusive, idiosyncratic, individualistic, particular, peculiar, personal, private, separate, singular, special, specific, unique. *Opp* COLLECTIVE, GENERAL. ● *n* ▷ PERSON.

indoctrinate *vb* brainwash, implant, instruct, re-educate, train. ▷ TEACH.

induce *vb* **1** coax, encourage, incite, influence, inspire, motivate, persuade, press, prevail on, stimulate, sway, *inf* talk into, tempt, urge. *Opp* DISCOURAGE. **2** *induce a fever*. bring on, cause, effect, engender, generate, give rise to, lead to, occasion, produce, provoke.

inducement *n* attraction, bait, bribe, encouragement, enticement, incentive, spur, stimulus, *inf* sweetener.

indulge *vb* be indulgent to, cosset, favour, give in to, gratify, humour, mollycoddle, pamper, pander to, spoil, *inf* spoonfeed, treat. *Opp* DEPRIVE. **indulge in**

▷ ENJOY. **indulge yourself** be self-indulgent, drink too much, eat too much, give in to temptation, overdo it, overeat, spoil yourself, succumb, yield.

indulgent adj compliant, easy-going, fond, forbearing, forgiving, genial, kind, lenient, liberal, overgenerous, patient, permissive, tolerant. Opp STRICT.

industrious adj assiduous, busy, conscientious, diligent, dynamic, earnest, energetic, enterprising, hard-working, involved, keen, laborious, persistent, pertinacious, productive, sedulous, tireless, unflagging, untiring, zealous. Opp LAZY.

industry n 1 business, commerce, manufacturing, production, trade. 2 activity, application, commitment, determination, diligence, dynamism, effort, energy, enterprise, industriousness, keenness, labour, perseverance, persistence, sedulousness, tirelessness, toil, zeal. ▷ WORK. Opp LAZINESS.

inedible adj bad for you, harmful, indigestible, nauseating, inf off, poisonous, rotten, tough, uneatable, unpalatable, unwholesome. Opp EDIBLE.

ineffective adj 1 fruitless, futile, inf hopeless, inept, unconvincing, unproductive, unsuccessful, useless, vain, worthless. 2 disorganized, feckless, feeble, idle, impotent, inadequate, incapable, incompetent, ineffectual, inefficient, powerless, shiftless, unenterprising, weak. Opp EFFECTIVE.

inefficient adj 1 extravagant, prodigal, uneconomic, wasteful.

2 ▷ INEFFECTIVE. Opp EFFICIENT.

inelegant adj awkward, clumsy, crude, gauche, graceless, inartistic, rough, uncouth, ungainly, unpolished, unskilful, unsophisticated, unstylish. ▷ UGLY. Opp ELEGANT.

ineligible adj disqualified, inappropriate, inf out of the running, inf ruled out, unacceptable, unauthorized, unfit, unqualified, unsuitable, unworthy. Opp ELIGIBLE.

inept adj 1 awkward, bumbling, bungling, clumsy, gauche, incompetent, inexpert, maladroit, unskilful, unskilled. 2 ▷ INAPPROPRIATE.

inequality n contrast, difference, discrepancy, disparity, dissimilarity, imbalance, incongruity, prejudice. Opp EQUALITY.

inert adj apathetic, dormant, idle, immobile, inactive, inanimate, lifeless, passive, quiescent, quiet, slow, sluggish, static, stationary, still, supine, torpid. Opp LIVELY.

inertia n apathy, deadness, idleness, immobility, inactivity, indolence, lassitude, laziness, lethargy, listlessness, numbness, passivity, sluggishness, torpor. Opp LIVELINESS.

inessential adj dispensable, expendable, minor, needless, non-essential, optional, ornamental, secondary, spare, superfluous, unimportant, unnecessary. Opp ESSENTIAL.

inevitable adj assured, inf bound to happen, certain, destined, fated, ineluctable, inescapable, inexorable, ordained, predictable, sure, unavoidable. ▷ RELENTLESS.

inexcusable adj ▷ UNFORGIVABLE.

inexpensive adj ▷ CHEAP.

inexperienced adj inf born yesterday, callow, inf green, immature, inexpert, innocent, naïve, new, probationary, raw, unaccustomed, unfledged, uninitiated, unskilled, unsophisticated, untried, inf wet behind the ears, young. Opp EXPERT.

inexplicable adj baffling, bewildering, confusing, enigmatic, incomprehensible, inscrutable, insoluble, mysterious, mystifying, perplexing, puzzling, strange, unaccountable, unexplainable, unfathomable, unsolvable. Opp STRAIGHTFORWARD.

infallible adj certain, dependable, faultless, foolproof, impeccable, perfect, reliable, sound, sure, trustworthy, unbeatable, unerring, unfailing. Opp FALLIBLE.

infamous adj disgraceful, disreputable, ill-famed, notorious, outrageous, well-known. ▷ WICKED.

infant n baby, inf toddler, inf tot. ▷ CHILD.

infantile adj [derog] adolescent, babyish, childish, immature, juvenile, puerile. ▷ SILLY. Opp MATURE.

infatuated adj besotted, charmed, enchanted, inf head over heels, in love, obsessed, inf smitten.

infatuation n inf crush, obsession, passion. ▷ LOVE.

infect vb 1 blight, contaminate, defile, poison, pollute, spoil, taint. 2 affect, influence, inspire, touch. **infected** ▷ SEPTIC.

infection n blight, contagion, contamination, epidemic, pestilence, pollution, virus. ▷ ILLNESS.

infectious adj catching, communicable, contagious, spreading, transmissible, transmittable.

infer vb assume, conclude, deduce, derive, draw a conclusion, extrapolate, gather, guess, reach the conclusion, surmise, understand, work out.

inferior adj 1 humble, junior, lesser, lower, lowly, mean, menial, secondary, second-class, servile, subordinate, subsidiary, unimportant. 2 cheap, indifferent, mediocre, poor, shoddy, tawdry, inf tinny. Opp SUPERIOR.
• n ▷ SUBORDINATE.

infertile adj barren, sterile, unfruitful, unproductive.

infest vb infiltrate, overrun, pervade, plague. **infested** alive, crawling, swarming, teeming, verminous.

infidelity n 1 adultery, unfaithfulness. 2 ▷ DISLOYALTY.

infiltrate vb enter secretly, insinuate, intrude, penetrate, spy on.

infinite adj astronomical, big, boundless, countless, endless, eternal, everlasting, immeasurable, immense, incalculable, indeterminate, inestimable, inexhaustible, innumerable, interminable, limitless, multitudinous, never-ending, numberless, perpetual, uncountable, undefined, unending, unfathomable, unlimited, unnumbered, untold. ▷ HUGE. Opp FINITE.

infinity n endlessness, eternity, infinite distance, infinite quantity, infinitude, perpetuity, space.

infirm adj bedridden, crippled, elderly, feeble, frail, lame, old, poorly, senile, sickly, unwell. ▷ ILL, WEAK. Opp HEALTHY.

inflame vb arouse, encourage, excite, fire, foment, goad, ignite, incense, incite, kindle, madden, provoke, rouse, stimulate, stir up, work up. ▷ ANGER. Opp COOL. **inflamed** ▷ PASSIONATE, SEPTIC.

inflammable adj burnable, combustible, flammable, volatile. Opp INCOMBUSTIBLE.

inflammation n abscess, boil, infection, irritation, redness, sore, soreness, swelling.

inflate vb 1 blow up, dilate, distend, enlarge, puff up, pump up, swell. 2 ▷ EXAGGERATE.

inflexible adj 1 adamantine, firm, hard, hardened, immovable, rigid, solid, stiff, unbending, unyielding. 2 adamant, entrenched, fixed, immutable, inexorable, intractable, intransigent, obdurate, obstinate, inf pig-headed, refractory, resolute, rigorous, strict, stubborn, unalterable, unchangeable, uncompromising, unhelpful. Opp FLEXIBLE.

inflict vb administer, apply, deal out, enforce, force, impose, mete out, perpetrate, wreak.

influence n ascendancy, authority, control, direction, dominance, effect, guidance, hold, impact, leverage, power, pressure, pull, sway, weight.
● vb 1 affect, bias, change, control, direct, dominate, exert influence on, guide, impinge on, impress, manipulate, modify, motivate, move, persuade, prejudice, prompt, put pressure on, stir, sway.

2 influence a judge. bribe, corrupt, lead astray, suborn, tempt.

influential adj authoritative, compelling, controlling, convincing, dominant, effective, far-reaching, forceful, guiding, important, inspiring, leading, moving, persuasive, potent, powerful, prestigious, significant, strong, telling, weighty. Opp UNIMPORTANT.

influx n flood, flow, inflow, inundation, invasion, rush, stream.

inform vb 1 advise, apprise, brief, communicate to, enlighten, inf fill in, give information to, instruct, leak, notify, inf put in the picture, teach, tell, inf tip off. 2 inf blab, give information, sl grass, sl peach, sl rat, inf sneak, inf split on, inf tell, inf tell tales. **inform against** ▷ BETRAY. **informed** ▷ KNOWLEDGEABLE.

informal adj 1 approachable, casual, comfortable, cosy, easy, easygoing, everyday, familiar, free and easy, friendly, homely, natural, ordinary, relaxed, simple, unceremonious, unofficial, unpretentious, unsophisticated. 2 informal language. chatty, colloquial, personal, slangy, vernacular. 3 an informal design. asymmetrical, flexible, fluid, intuitive, irregular, spontaneous. Opp FORMAL.

information n 1 announcement, briefing, bulletin, communication, enlightenment, instruction, message, news, report, statement, old use tidings, inf tip-off, word. 2 data, database, dossier, evidence, facts, intelligence, knowledge, statistics.

informative adj communicative, edifying, educational, enlightening, factual, giving information, helpful, illuminating, instructive, meaningful, revealing, useful. Opp MEANINGLESS.

informer n sl grass, informant, spy, sl stool-pigeon, inf tell-tale, traitor.

infrequent adj exceptional, intermittent, irregular, occasional, inf once in a blue moon, rare, spasmodic, uncommon, unusual. Opp FREQUENT.

infringe vb breach, break, contravene, defy, disobey, disregard, flout, ignore, overstep, sin against, transgress, violate.

ingenious adj adroit, artful, astute, brilliant, clever, complex, crafty, creative, cunning, deft, imaginative, inspired, intelligent, intricate, inventive, neat, original, resourceful, shrewd, skilful, inf smart, subtle, talented. Opp UNIMAGINATIVE.

ingenuous adj artless, childlike, frank, guileless, honest, innocent, naïve, open, plain, simple, sincere, trusting, unaffected, uncomplicated, unsophisticated. Opp SOPHISTICATED.

ingredient n component, constituent, element, factor, plur makings, part.

inhabit vb old use abide in, colonize, dwell in, live in, make your home in, occupy, people, populate, possess, reside in, settle in, set up home in.

inhabitable adj habitable, in good repair, liveable, usable. Opp UNINHABITABLE.

inhabitant n citizen, old use denizen, dweller, inmate, native, occupant, occupier, plur population, resident, settler, tenant, plur townsfolk, plur townspeople.

inherent adj built-in, congenital, essential, fundamental, hereditary, immanent, inborn, inbred, indwelling, ingrained, intrinsic, native, natural.

inherit vb be the inheritor of, be left, inf come into, receive as an inheritance, succeed to. **inherited** ▷ HEREDITARY.

inheritance n bequest, birthright, estate, fortune, heritage, legacy, patrimony.

inhibit vb bridle, check, control, curb, discourage, frustrate, hinder, hold back, prevent, quell, repress, restrain. **inhibited** ▷ REPRESSED, SHY.

inhibition n 1 bar, barrier, check, constraint, curb, impediment, interference, restraint, stricture. 2 blockage, diffidence, inf hang-up, repression, reserve, self-consciousness, shyness.

inhospitable adj antisocial, reclusive, reserved, solitary, standoffish, unkind, unsociable, unwelcoming. ▷ UNFRIENDLY. 2 bleak, cold, comfortless, desolate, grim, hostile, lonely. Opp HOSPITABLE.

inhuman adj animal, barbaric, barbarous, bestial, bloodthirsty, brutish, diabolical, fiendish, merciless, pitiless, ruthless, savage, unnatural, vicious. ▷ INHUMANE. Opp HUMAN.

inhumane adj cold-hearted, cruel, hard, hard-hearted, heartless, inconsiderate, insensitive, uncaring, uncharitable, uncivilized, unfeeling, unkind, unsympathetic. ▷ INHUMAN. *Opp* HUMANE.

initial *adj* beginning, commencing, earliest, first, inaugural, incipient, introductory, opening, original, primary, starting. *Opp* FINAL.

initiate *vb* activate, actuate, begin, commence, enter upon, get going, get under way, inaugurate, instigate, institute, introduce, launch, originate, set going, set in motion, set up, start, take the initiative, trigger.

initiative *n* ambition, drive, dynamism, enterprise, *inf* get-up-and-go, inventiveness, lead, leadership, originality, resourcefulness. **take the initiative** ▷ INITIATE.

injection *n inf* fix, inoculation, *inf* jab, vaccination.

injure *vb* break, crush, cut, damage, deface, disfigure, harm, hurt, ill-treat, impair, mar, ruin, spoil, vandalize. ▷ WOUND.

injurious *adj* 1 damaging, deleterious, destructive, detrimental, harmful, insalubrious, painful, ruinous. 2 ▷ ABUSIVE.

injury *n* damage, harm, hurt, mischief. ▷ WOUND.

injustice *n* bias, bigotry, discrimination, dishonesty, favouritism, illegality, inequality, inequity, one-sidedness, oppression, partiality, partisanship, prejudice, unfairness, unlawfulness, wrong, wrongness. *Opp* JUSTICE.

inn *n old use* hostelry, hotel, *inf* local, pub, tavern.

inner *adj* central, concealed, hidden, innermost, inside, interior, internal, intimate,

inward, mental, middle, private, secret. *Opp* OUTER.

innocence *n* 1 goodness, honesty, incorruptibility, purity, righteousness, sinlessness, virtue. 2 [*derog*] gullibility, inexperience, naïvety, simple-mindedness.

innocent *adj* 1 above suspicion, angelic, blameless, chaste, childlike, faultless, free from blame, guiltless, harmless, honest, immaculate, incorrupt, inoffensive, pure, righteous, sinless, spotless, untainted, virginal, virtuous. *Opp* CORRUPT, GUILTY. 2 artless, childlike, credulous, *inf* green, guileless, gullible, inexperienced, ingenuous, naïve, simple, simple-minded, trusting, unsophisticated.

innovation *n* change, departure, invention, new feature, novelty, reform, revolution.

innovator *n* discoverer, experimenter, inventor, pioneer, reformer, revolutionary.

innumerable *adj* countless, many, numberless, uncountable, untold. ▷ INFINITE.

inquest *n* hearing. ▷ INQUIRY.

inquire *vb* ask, explore, investigate, seek information, *inf* probe, search, survey. ▷ ENQUIRE.

inquiry *n* cross-examination, examination, inquest, inquisition, interrogation, investigation, poll, *inf* post-mortem, *inf* probe, referendum, review, study, survey.

inquisitive *adj* curious, impertinent, indiscreet, inquiring, interfering, intrusive, investigative, meddlesome, meddling, *inf* nosy, probing, prying, ques-

tioning, sceptical, searching,
inf snooping, spying. **be
inquisitive** ▷ PRY.

insane *adj inf* crazy, deranged,
lunatic, *inf* mental, psychotic,
unbalanced, unhinged. ▷ MAD.
Opp SANE.

inscription *n* dedication,
engraving, epigraph, superscription, writing.

insect *n inf* bug, *inf* creepy-
crawly. □ ant, aphid, bee, beetle,
blackfly, butterfly, cicada, cock-
chafer, cockroach, crane-fly,
cricket, daddy-long-legs, damsel-
fly, dragonfly, earwig, firefly,
fly, glow-worm, gnat, grasshop-
per, hornet, ladybird, locust,
mantis, mayfly, midge,
mosquito, moth, sawfly, termite,
tsetse (fly), wasp, weevil.

insecure *adj* 1 dangerous,
flimsy, loose, precarious, rickety, rocky, shaky, unsafe,
unsound, unstable, unsteady,
unsupported, weak, wobbly.
2 *an insecure feeling.* anxious,
apprehensive, defenceless,
exposed, open, uncertain,
underconfident, unprotected,
vulnerable, worried.
Opp SECURE.

insensible *adj* anaesthetized,
benumbed, *inf* dead to the
world, inert, insensate, insentient, knocked out, numb, *inf* out,
senseless, unaware, unconscious. *Opp* CONSCIOUS.

insensitive *adj* 1 anaesthetized,
dead, numb, unresponsive.
2 boorish, callous, crass, cruel,
imperceptive, obtuse, tactless,
inf thick-skinned, thoughtless,
uncaring, unfeeling, unsympathetic. *Opp* SENSITIVE.

inseparable *adj* always
together, attached, indissoluble,
indivisible, integral.

insert *vb* drive in, embed,
implant, intercalate, interject,
interleave, interpolate, interpose, introduce, place in,
inf pop in, push in, put in, stick
in, tuck in.

inside *adj* central, indoor, inner,
innermost, interior, internal.
● *n* bowels, centre, contents,
core, heart, indoors, interior,
lining, middle. *Opp* OUTSIDE.
insides ▷ ENTRAILS.

insidious *adj* creeping, deceptive, furtive, pervasive, secretive, stealthy, subtle, surreptitious, treacherous, underhand.
▷ CRAFTY.

insignificant *adj* forgettable,
inconsiderable, irrelevant,
insubstantial, lightweight,
meaningless, minor, negligible,
paltry, small, trifling, trivial,
undistinguished, unimportant,
unimpressive, valueless, worthless. *Opp* SIGNIFICANT.

insincere *adj* artful, crafty,
deceitful, deceptive, devious,
dishonest, disingenuous,
dissembling, false, feigned, flattering, *inf* foxy, hollow, hypocritical, lying, *inf* mealy-
mouthed, mendacious, perfidious, *inf* phoney, pretended,
inf put on, *inf* smarmy, sycophantic, treacherous, *inf* two-
faced, untrue, untruthful, wily.
Opp SINCERE.

insist *vb* 1 assert, asseverate,
aver, avow, declare, emphasize,
hold, maintain, state, stress,
swear, take an oath, vow.
2 assert yourself, be assertive,
command, persist, *inf* put your
foot down, stand firm, *inf* stick
to your guns. **insist on**
▷ DEMAND.

insistent *adj* assertive, demanding, dogged, emphatic, firm,

forceful, importunate, inexorable, obstinate, peremptory, persistent, relentless, repeated, resolute, stubborn, unrelenting, unremitting, urgent.

insolence n arrogance, boldness, inf cheek, defiance, disrespect, effrontery, impertinence, impudence, incivility, insubordination, inf lip, presumptuousness, rudeness, inf sauce.

insolent adj arrogant, audacious, bold, brazen, inf cheeky, contemptuous, defiant, disdainful, disrespectful, forward, inf fresh, impertinent, impolite, impudent, insubordinate, insulting, offensive, pert, presumptuous, saucy, shameless, sneering, uncivil. ▷ RUDE. Opp POLITE.

insoluble adj baffling, enigmatic, incomprehensible, inexplicable, mystifying, puzzling, strange, unaccountable, unanswerable, unfathomable, unsolvable. Opp SOLUBLE.

insolvent adj bankrupt, inf bust, failed, ruined. ▷ POOR.

inspect vb check, examine, sl give it the once over, investigate, peruse, pore over, scan, scrutinize, study, survey, vet.

inspection n check, check-up, examination, inf going-over, investigation, review, scrutiny, survey.

inspector n controller, examiner, investigator, official, scrutineer, superintendent, supervisor, tester.

inspiration n 1 creativity, genius, imagination, muse. 2 enthusiasm, impulse, incitement, influence, motivation, prompting, spur, stimulation,

stimulus. 3 a sudden inspiration. brainwave, idea, insight, revelation, thought.

inspire vb activate, animate, arouse, awaken, inf egg on, encourage, energize, enthuse, fire, galvanize, influence, inspirit, instigate, kindle, motivate, prompt, provoke, quicken, reassure, set off, spark off, spur, stimulate, stir, support.

instability n capriciousness, change, changeableness, fickleness, fluctuation, flux, impermanence, inconstancy, insecurity, mutability, precariousness, shakiness, transience, uncertainty, unpredictability, unreliability, unsteadiness, inf ups-and-downs, vacillation, variability, variations, weakness. Opp STABILITY.

install vb ensconce, establish, fit, fix, instate, introduce, place, plant, position, put in, settle, set up, situate, station. Opp REMOVE.

instalment n 1 payment, rent, rental. 2 chapter, episode, part.

instance n case, example, exemplar, illustration, occurrence, precedent, sample.

instant adj direct, fast, immediate, instantaneous, on-the-spot, prompt, quick, rapid, speedy, split-second, swift, unhesitating, urgent. • n flash, inf jiffy, moment, point of time, second, split second, inf tick, inf trice, inf twinkling.

instigate vb activate, begin, be the instigator of, bring about, cause, encourage, foment, generate, incite, initiate, inspire, kindle, prompt, provoke, set up, start, stimulate, stir up, urge, inf whip up.

instigator n agitator, fomenter, inciter, initiator, inspirer, leader, mischief-maker, provoker, ringleader, trouble-maker.

instil vb inf din into, imbue, implant, inculcate, indoctrinate, infuse, ingrain, inject, insinuate, introduce.

instinct n bent, faculty, feel, feeling, guesswork, hunch, impulse, inclination, instinctive urge, intuition, presentiment, propensity, sixth-sense, the subconscious, tendency, urge.

instinctive adj automatic, congenital, constitutional, inf gut, impulsive, inborn, inbred, inherent, innate, instinctual, intuitive, involuntary, irrational, mechanical, native, natural, reflex, spontaneous, subconscious, unconscious, unreasoning, unthinking, visceral. Opp DELIBERATE.

institute n ▷ INSTITUTION.
● vb begin, create, establish, fix up, found, inaugurate, initiate, introduce, launch, open, organize, originate, pioneer, set up, start.

institution n 1 creation, establishing, formation, founding, inauguration, inception, initiation, introduction, launching, opening, setting-up. 2 academy, asylum, establishment, foundation, home, hospital, institute, organization, school, inf set-up. 3 convention, custom, habit, practice, ritual, routine, rule, tradition.

instruct vb 1 coach, drill, educate, indoctrinate, inform, lecture, prepare, school, teach, train, tutor. 2 authorize, brief, charge, command, direct,

enjoin, give the order, order, require, tell.

instruction n 1 briefing, coaching, demonstration, drill, education, guidance, indoctrination, lecture, lesson, schooling, teaching, training, tuition, tutorial, tutoring. 2 authorization, brief, charge, command, direction, directive, order, requisition.

instructive adj didactic, edifying, educational, enlightening, helpful, illuminating, improving, informational, informative, instructional, revealing.

instructor n adviser, coach, trainer, tutor. ▷ TEACHER.

instrument n apparatus, appliance, contraption, device, equipment, gadget, implement, machine, mechanism, tool, utensil. **musical instrument** □ accordion, bagpipes, banjo, bassoon, bugle, castanets, celesta, cello, clarinet, clavichord, clavier, concertina, cor anglais, cornet, cymbals, double-bass, drum, dulcimer, euphonium, fiddle, fife, flugelhorn, flute, fortepiano, French horn, glockenspiel, gong, guitar, harmonica, harmonium, harp, harpsichord, horn, hurdy-gurdy, kettledrum, keyboard, lute, lyre, mouth-organ, oboe, organ, piano, piccolo, pipes, recorder, saxophone, sitar, spinet, synthesizer, tambourine, timpani, triangle, trombone, trumpet, tuba, tubular bells, ukulele, viol, viola, violin, virginals, xylophone, zither.

instrumental adj active, advantageous, beneficial, contributory, helpful, influential, supportive, useful, valuable.

insubordinate *adj* defiant, disobedient, insurgent, mutinous, rebellious, riotous, seditious, undisciplined, unruly. ▷ IMPERTINENT. *Opp* OBEDIENT.

insufficient *adj* deficient, disappointing, inadequate, incomplete, little, meagre, mean, niggardly, *inf* pathetic, poor, scanty, scarce, short, skimpy, sparse, unsatisfactory. *Opp* EXCESSIVE, SUFFICIENT.

insular *adj* closed, cut-off, isolated, limited, narrow, narrow-minded, parochial, provincial, remote, separated. *Opp* BROAD-MINDED, COSMOPOLITAN.

insulate *vb* 1 cocoon, cover, cushion, enclose, isolate, lag, protect, shield, surround, wrap up. 2 cut off, detach, isolate, keep apart, quarantine, segregate, separate.

insult *n* abuse, affront, aspersion, *inf* cheek, contumely, defamation, impudence, indignity, insulting behaviour, libel, *inf* put-down, rudeness, slander, slight, slur, snub. ● *vb* abuse, affront, be rude to, *inf* call names, *inf* cock a snook at, defame, dishonour, disparage, libel, mock, offend, outrage, patronize, revile, slander, slang, slight, sneer at, snub, *inf* thumb your nose at, vilify. *Opp* COMPLIMENT. **insulting** ▷ RUDE.

insuperable *adj* insurmountable, overwhelming, unconquerable. ▷ IMPOSSIBLE.

insurance *n* assurance, cover, indemnification, indemnity, policy, protection, security.

insure *vb* cover yourself, indemnify, protect, take out insurance.

intact *adj* complete, entire, integral, solid, sound, unbroken, undamaged, whole. ▷ PERFECT.

intangible *adj* abstract, airy, disembodied, elusive, ethereal, evanescent, fleeting, impalpable, imperceptible, imponderable, incorporeal, indefinite, insubstantial, invisible, shadowy, unreal, vague. *Opp* TANGIBLE.

integral *adj* 1 basic, constituent, essential, fundamental, indispensable, intrinsic, irreplaceable, necessary, requisite. *Opp* INESSENTIAL. 2 *an integral unit.* attached, complete, full, indivisible, whole. *Opp* SEPARATE.

integrate *vb* amalgamate, assemble, blend, bring together, coalesce, combine, consolidate, desegregate, fuse, harmonize, join, knit, merge, mix, put together, unify, unite, weld. *Opp* SEPARATE.

integrity *n* 1 decency, fidelity, goodness, honesty, honour, incorruptibility, loyalty, morality, principle, probity, rectitude, reliability, righteousness, sincerity, trustworthiness, uprightness, veracity, virtue. 2 ▷ UNITY.

intellect *n inf* brains, cleverness, genius, mind, rationality, reason, sense, understanding, wisdom, *old use* wit. ▷ INTELLIGENCE.

intellectual *adj* 1 academic, *inf* bookish, cerebral, cultured, educated, scholarly, studious, thinking, thoughtful. ▷ INTELLIGENT. 2 cultural, deep, difficult, educational, highbrow, improving, thought-provoking. ● *n* academic, *inf* egghead, genius, highbrow, intellectual person, *inf* mastermind, *inf* one of the intelligentsia, savant, thinker.

intelligence *n* **1** ability, acumen, alertness, astuteness, brainpower, *inf* brains, brightness, brilliance, capacity, cleverness, discernment, genius, *inf* grey matter, insight, intellect, judgement, keenness, mind, *inf* nous, perceptiveness, perspicaciousness, perspicacity, quickness, reason, sagacity, sense, sharpness, shrewdness, understanding, wisdom, wit, wits. **2** data, facts, information, knowledge, *inf* low-down, news, notification, report, *inf* tip-off, warning. **3** espionage, secret service, spying.

intelligent *adj* able, acute, alert, astute, brainy, bright, brilliant, *inf* canny, clever, discerning, educated, intellectual, knowing, penetrating, perceptive, percipient, perspicacious, profound, quick, ratiocinative, rational, reasonable, sagacious, sensible, sharp, shrewd, *inf* smart, thinking, thoughtful, trenchant, wise, *inf* with it, witty. *Opp* STUPID.

intelligible *adj* clear, comprehensible, decipherable, fathomable, legible, logical, lucid, meaningful, plain, straightforward, unambiguous, understandable. *Opp* INCOMPREHENSIBLE.

intend *vb* aim, aspire, contemplate, design, determine, have in mind, mean, plan, plot, propose, purpose, resolve, scheme.

intense *adj* **1** ardent, burning, consuming, deep, eager, earnest, emotional, fanatical,

fervent, fervid, impassioned, passionate, powerful, profound, serious, strong, towering, vehement, violent, zealous. *Opp* COOL, HALF-HEARTED. **2** *intense pain.* acute, agonizing, excruciating, extreme, fierce, great, harsh, keen, severe, sharp. *Opp* SLIGHT.

intensify *vb* add to, aggravate, augment, become greater, boost, build up, deepen, emphasize, escalate, fire, focus, fuel, heighten, *inf* hot up, increase, magnify, make greater, quicken, raise, redouble, reinforce, sharpen, *inf* step up, strengthen, whet. *Opp* REDUCE.

intensive *adj inf* all-out, comprehensive, concentrated, detailed, exhaustive, high-powered, thorough, unremitting.

intent *adj* absorbed, attentive, bent, committed, concentrated, concentrating, determined, eager, engrossed, enthusiastic, firm, focused, keen, occupied, preoccupied, resolute, set, steadfast, watchful, zealous. *Opp* CASUAL. ● *n* ▷ INTENTION.

intention *n* aim, ambition, design, end, goal, intent, object, objective, plan, point, purpose, target.

intentional *adj* calculated, conscious, contrived, deliberate, designed, intended, knowing, planned, pre-arranged, preconceived, premeditated, prepared, studied, wilful. *Opp* ACCIDENTAL.

intercept *vb* ambush, arrest, block, catch, check, cut off, deflect, head off, impede, interrupt, obstruct, stop, thwart, trap.

intercourse n 1 communication, conversation, dealings, interaction, traffic. 2 *sexual intercourse.* carnal knowledge, coition, coitus, congress, copulation, intimacy, love-making, mating, rape, sex, union.

interest n 1 attention, attentiveness, care, commitment, concern, curiosity, involvement, notice, regard, scrutiny. 2 *of no interest.* consequence, importance, moment, note, significance, value. 3 *leisure interests.* activity, diversion, hobby, pastime, preoccupation, pursuit, relaxation. ● vb absorb, appeal to, arouse the curiosity of, attract, capture the imagination of, captivate, concern, divert, enchant, engage, engross, entertain, enthral, fascinate, intrigue, involve, occupy, preoccupy, stimulate, *inf* turn on. ▷ EXCITE. *Opp* BORE.

interested adj 1 absorbed, attentive, curious, engrossed, enthusiastic, immersed, intent, involved, keen, occupied, preoccupied, rapt, responsive, riveted. *Opp* UNINTERESTED. 2 concerned, involved, partial. ▷ BIASED.

interesting adj absorbing, appealing, attractive, challenging, compelling, curious, engaging, engrossing, entertaining, enthralling, fascinating, gripping, imaginative, important, intriguing, inviting, original, piquant, *often ironic* riveting, spellbinding, unpredictable, unusual, varied. *Opp* BORING.

interfere vb be a busybody, butt in, interrupt, intervene, intrude, meddle, obtrude, *inf* poke your nose in, pry,

snoop, *inf* stick your oar in, tamper. **interfere with** ▷ OBSTRUCT. **interfering** ▷ NOSY.

interim adj half-time, halfway, provisional, stopgap, temporary.

interior adj ▷ INTERNAL. ● n centre, core, depths, heart, inside, middle, nucleus.

interlude n entr'acte, intermezzo, intermission. ▷ INTERVAL.

intermediary n agent, ambassador, arbiter, arbitrator, broker, go-between, mediator, middleman, negotiator, referee, spokesperson, umpire.

intermediate adj average, *inf* betwixt and between, halfway, intermediary, intervening, mean, medial, median, middle, midway, *inf* neither one thing nor the other, neutral, *inf* sitting on the fence, transitional.

intermittent adj broken, discontinuous, erratic, fitful, irregular, occasional, *inf* on and off, periodic, random, recurrent, spasmodic, sporadic. *Opp* CONTINUOUS.

internal adj 1 inner, inside, interior. *Opp* EXTERNAL. 2 confidential, hidden, intimate, inward, personal, private, secret, undisclosed.

international adj cosmopolitan, global, intercontinental, universal, worldwide.

interpret vb clarify, clear up, construe, decipher, decode, define, elucidate, explain, explicate, expound, gloss, make clear, make sense of, paraphrase, render, rephrase, reword, simplify, sort out, translate, understand, unravel, work out.

interpretation n clarification, definition, elucidation, explanation, gloss, paraphrase, reading, rendering, translation, understanding, version.

interrogation n cross-examination, debriefing, examination, grilling, inquisition, questioning, *inf* third degree.

interrogative adj asking, inquiring, inquisitive, interrogatory, investigatory, questioning.

interrupt vb 1 *inf* barge in, break in, butt in, *inf* chime in, *inf* chip in, cut in, disrupt, disturb, heckle, hold up, interfere, intervene, intrude, punctuate, obstruct, spoil. 2 break off, call a halt to, cut off, cut short, discontinue, halt, stop, suspend, terminate.

interruption n break, check, disruption, division, gap, halt, hiatus, interference, intrusion, stop, suspension. ▷ INTERVAL.

intersect vb bisect each other, converge, criss-cross, cross, divide, meet, pass across each other.

interval n 1 adjournment, break, *inf* breather, breathing-space, delay, distance, gap, hiatus, interruption, lapse, lull, opening, pause, recess, respite, rest, space, void, wait. 2 entr'acte, interlude, intermezzo, intermission.

intervene vb 1 come between, elapse, happen, occur, pass. 2 arbitrate, butt in, intercede, interfere, interpose, interrupt, intrude, mediate, *inf* step in.

interview n appraisal, audience, duologue, formal discussion,

meeting, questioning, selection procedure, vetting.
● vb appraise, ask questions, evaluate, examine, interrogate, question, sound out, vet.

interweave vb criss-cross, entwine, interlace, intertwine, knit, tangle, weave together.

intestines *plur* n bowels, entrails, innards, insides, offal.

intimate adj 1 affectionate, close, familiar, informal, loving, sexual. ▷ FRIENDLY. 2 *intimate details.* confidential, detailed, exhaustive, personal, private, secret. ● n ▷ FRIEND. ● vb ▷ INDICATE.

intimidate vb alarm, browbeat, bully, coerce, cow, daunt, dismay, frighten, hector, make afraid, menace, overawe, persecute, petrify, scare, terrify, terrorize, threaten, tyrannize.

intolerable adj excruciating, impossible, insufferable, insupportable, unacceptable, unbearable, unendurable.
Opp TOLERABLE.

intolerant adj biased, bigoted, chauvinistic, classist, discriminatory, dogmatic, illiberal, narrow-minded, one-sided, opinionated, prejudiced, racist, sexist, uncharitable, unsympathetic, xenophobic.
Opp TOLERANT.

intonation n accent, delivery, inflection, modulation, pronunciation, sound, speech pattern, tone.

intoxicate vb addle, inebriate, make drunk, stupefy. **intoxicated** ▷ DRUNK, EXCITED. **intoxicating** ▷ ALCOHOLIC, EXCITING.

intricate adj complex, complicated, convoluted, delicate, detailed, elaborate, entangled,

fancy, *inf* fiddly, involved,
inf knotty, labyrinthine, ornate,
sophisticated, tangled, tortuous.
Opp SIMPLE.

intrigue *n* ▷ PLOT. • *vb* 1 appeal
to, arouse the curiosity of,
attract, beguile, captivate,
capture the interest of, engage,
engross, excite the curiosity of,
fascinate, interest, stimulate,
inf turn on. Opp BORE.

intrinsic *adj* basic, essential,
fundamental, immanent,
inborn, inbred, in-built, inherent, native, natural, proper,
real.

introduce *vb* 1 acquaint, make
known, present. 2 announce,
give an introduction to, lead
into, preface. 3 add, advance,
bring in, bring out, broach,
create, establish, inaugurate,
initiate, inject, insert, interpose, launch, make available,
offer, phase in, pioneer, put
forward, set up, start, suggest,
usher in. ▷ BEGIN.

introduction *n* foreword,
inf intro, *inf* lead-in, opening,
overture, preamble, preface,
prelude, prologue.
▷ BEGINNING.

introductory *adj* basic, early,
first, fundamental, inaugural,
initial, opening, prefatory,
preliminary, preparatory, starting. Opp FINAL.

introverted *adj* contemplative,
introspective, inward-looking,
meditative, pensive, quiet,
reserved, retiring, self-
contained, shy, thoughtful,
unsociable, withdrawn.
Opp EXTROVERTED.

intrude *vb* break in, butt in,
eavesdrop, encroach, gatecrash,
interfere, interpose, interrupt,

intervene, join uninvited,
obtrude, *inf* snoop.

intruder *n* 1 eavesdropper, gatecrasher, infiltrator, interloper,
inf uninvited guest. 2 burglar,
housebreaker, invader,
prowler, raider, robber,
inf snooper, thief, trespasser.

intuition *n* insight, perceptiveness, percipience. ▷ INSTINCT.

invade *vb* descend on, encroach
on, enter, impinge on, infest,
infringe, march into, occupy,
overrun, penetrate, raid,
subdue, violate. ▷ ATTACK.

invalid *adj* 1 null and void, out-
of-date, unacceptable, unusable,
void, worthless. 2 fallacious,
false, illogical, incorrect, irrational, spurious, unconvincing,
unfounded, unreasonable,
unscientific, unsound, untenable, untrue, wrong. Opp VALID.
3 ▷ ILL. • *n* cripple, incurable,
patient, sufferer, valetudinarian.

invaluable *adj* incalculable,
inestimable, irreplaceable,
precious, priceless, useful.
▷ VALUABLE. Opp WORTHLESS.

invariable *adj* certain, changeless, constant, eternal, even,
immutable, inflexible, permanent, predictable, regular, reliable, rigid, solid, stable, steady,
unalterable, unchangeable,
unchanging, unfailing, uniform,
unvarying, unwavering.
Opp VARIABLE.

invasion *n* 1 encroachment,
incursion, infiltration, inroad,
intrusion, onslaught, raid,
violation. ▷ ATTACK. 2 colony,
flood, horde, infestation, spate,
stream, swarm, throng.

invasive *adj* burgeoning,
increasing, mushrooming,

profuse, proliferating, relentless, unstoppable.

invent *vb* coin, conceive, concoct, construct, contrive, *inf* cook up, create, design, devise, discover, *inf* dream up, fabricate, formulate, *inf* hit upon, imagine, improvise, make up, originate, plan, put together, think up, trump up.

invention *n* 1 brainchild, coinage, contrivance, creation, design, discovery. 2 contraption, device, gadget. 3 deceit, fabrication, falsehood, fantasy, fiction, figment, lie. 4 ▷ INVENTIVENESS.

inventive *adj* clever, creative, enterprising, fertile, imaginative, ingenious, innovative, inspired, original, resourceful. *Opp* BANAL.

inventiveness *n* creativity, genius, imagination, ingenuity, inspiration, invention, originality, resourcefulness.

inventor *n* architect, author, *inf* boffin, creator, designer, discoverer, maker, originator.

inverse *adj* opposite, reversed, transposed.

invert *vb* capsize, overturn, reverse, transpose, turn upside down, upset.

invest *vb* 1 buy stocks and shares, play the market, speculate. 2 lay out, put to work, *inf* sink, use profitably, venture. **invest in** ▷ BUY.

investigate *vb* analyse, consider, enquire about, examine, explore, follow up, gather evidence about, *inf* go into, inquire into, look into, probe, research, scrutinize, sift (*evidence*), study, *inf* suss out, weigh up.

investigation *n* enquiry, examination, inquiry, inquisition, inspection, *inf* post-mortem, *inf* probe, quest, research, review, scrutiny, search, study, survey.

invidious *adj* discriminatory, objectionable, offensive, undesirable, unfair, unjust, unwarranted.

invigorating *adj* bracing, enlivening, exhilarating, fresh, healthful, health-giving, healthy, refreshing, rejuvenating, revitalizing, salubrious, stimulating, tonic, vitalizing. *Opp* EXHAUSTING.

invincible *adj* impregnable, indestructible, indomitable, insuperable, invulnerable, strong, unassailable, unbeatable, unconquerable, unstoppable.

invisible *adj* camouflaged, concealed, covered, disguised, hidden, imperceptible, inconspicuous, obscured, out of sight, secret, undetectable, unnoticeable, unnoticed, unseen. *Opp* VISIBLE.

invite *vb* 1 ask, encourage, request, summon, urge. 2 attract, entice, solicit, tempt. **inviting** ▷ ATTRACTIVE.

invoice *n* account, bill, list, statement.

invoke *vb* appeal to, call for, cry out for, entreat, implore, pray for, solicit, supplicate.

involuntary *adj* automatic, conditioned, impulsive, instinctive, mechanical, reflex, spontaneous, unconscious, uncontrollable, unintentional, unthinking, unwitting. *Opp* DELIBERATE.

involve *vb* 1 comprise, contain, embrace, entail, hold, include, incorporate, take in. 2 affect, concern, interest, touch. 3 *involve in crime.* embroil, implicate, include, incriminate, inculpate, *inf* mix up. **involved** ▷ BUSY, COMPLEX.

involvement *n* 1 activity, interest, participation. 2 association, complicity, entanglement, partnership.

ironic *adj* derisive, double-edged, ironical, mocking, sarcastic, satirical, wry.

irony *n* double meaning, mockery, paradox, sarcasm, satire.

irrational *adj* absurd, arbitrary, biased, crazy, emotional, emotive, illogical, insane, mad, nonsensical, prejudiced, senseless, subjective, surreal, unconvincing, unintelligent, unreasonable, unreasoning, unsound, unthinking, wild. ▷ SILLY. *Opp* RATIONAL.

irregular *adj* 1 erratic, fitful, fluctuating, halting, haphazard, intermittent, occasional, random, spasmodic, sporadic, unequal, unpredictable, unpunctual, variable, varying, wavering. 2 abnormal, anomalous, eccentric, exceptional, extraordinary, illegal, improper, odd, peculiar, quirky, unconventional, unofficial, unplanned, unscheduled, unusual. 3 *irregular surface.* broken, bumpy, jagged, lumpy, patchy, pitted, ragged, rough, uneven, up and down. *Opp* REGULAR.

irrelevant *adj inf* beside the point, extraneous, immaterial, impertinent, inapplicable, inapposite, inappropriate, inessen-

tial, malapropos, *inf* neither here nor there, pointless, unconnected, unnecessary, unrelated. *Opp* RELEVANT.

irreligious *adj* agnostic, atheistic, godless, heathen, humanist, impious, irreverent, pagan, sinful, uncommitted, unconverted, ungodly, unrighteous, wicked. *Opp* RELIGIOUS.

irreparable *adj* hopeless, incurable, irrecoverable, irremediable, irretrievable, irreversible, lasting, permanent, unalterable.

irreplaceable *adj* inimitable, priceless, unique. ▷ RARE.

irrepressible *adj* boisterous, bouncy, *inf* bubbling, buoyant, ebullient, resilient, uncontrollable, ungovernable, uninhibited, unmanageable, unrestrainable, unstoppable, vigorous. ▷ LIVELY. *Opp* LETHARGIC.

irresistible *adj* compelling, inescapable, inexorable, irrepressible, not to be denied, overpowering, overriding, overwhelming, persuasive, powerful, relentless, seductive, strong, unavoidable, uncontrollable. *Opp* WEAK.

irresolute *adj* doubtful, fickle, flexible, *inf* hedging your bets, indecisive, open to compromise, tentative, uncertain, undecided, vacillating, wavering, weak, weak-willed. ▷ HESITANT. *Opp* RESOLUTE.

irresponsible *adj* antisocial, careless, conscienceless, devil-may-care, feckless, immature, immoral, inconsiderate, negligent, rash, reckless, selfish, shiftless, thoughtless, unethical, unreliable, unthinking, untrustworthy, wild. *Opp* RESPONSIBLE.

irreverent *adj* blasphemous, disrespectful, impious, irreligious, profane, sacrilegious, ungodly, unholy. ▷ RUDE. *Opp* REVERENT.

irrevocable *adj* binding, final, fixed, hard and fast, immutable, irreparable, irretrievable, irreversible, permanent, settled, unalterable, unchangeable.

irrigate *vb* flood, inundate, supply water to, water.

irritable *adj* bad-tempered, cantankerous, choleric, crabby, cross, crotchety, crusty, curmudgeonly, dyspeptic, easily annoyed, edgy, fractious, grumpy, ill-humoured, ill-tempered, impatient, irascible, oversensitive, peevish, pettish, petulant, *inf* prickly, querulous, *inf* ratty, short-tempered, snappy, testy, tetchy, touchy, waspish. ▷ ANGRY. *Opp* EVEN-TEMPERED.

irritate *vb* 1 cause irritation, itch, rub, tickle, tingle. 2 ▷ ANNOY.

island *n plur* archipelago, atoll, coral reef, isle, islet.

isolate *vb* cloister, cordon off, cut off, detach, exclude, insulate, keep apart, place apart, quarantine, seclude, segregate, separate, sequester, set apart, shut off, shut out, single out. **isolated** ▷ SOLITARY.

issue *n* 1 affair, argument, controversy, dispute, matter, point, problem, question, subject, topic. 2 conclusion, consequence, effect, end, impact, outcome, *inf* payoff, repercussions, result, upshot. 3 *issue of a magazine.* copy, edition, instalment, number, printing, publication, version.

● *vb* 1 appear, come out, emerge, erupt, flow out, gush, leak, rise, spring. 2 announce, bring out, broadcast, circulate, declare, disseminate, distribute, give out, make public, print, produce, promulgate, publicize, publish, put out, release, send out, supply.

itch *n* 1 irritation, prickling, tickle, tingling. 2 ache, craving, desire, hankering, hunger, impatience, impulse, longing, need, restlessness, thirst, urge, wish, yearning, *inf* yen.

● *vb* 1 be irritated, prickle, tickle, tingle. 2 ▷ DESIRE.

item *n* 1 article, bit, component, contribution, entry, ingredient, lot, matter, object, particular, thing. 2 *item in a newspaper.* account, article, feature, notice, piece, report.

J

jab *vb* dig, elbow, nudge, poke, prod, stab, thrust. ▷ HIT.

jacket *n* casing, cover, covering, envelope, folder, sheath, skin, wrapper, wrapping. ▷ COAT.

jaded *adj* 1 ▷ WEARY. 2 bored, *inf* fed up, gorged, listless, sated, satiated, *inf* sick and tired, surfeited. *Opp* LIVELY.

jagged *adj* angular, barbed, broken, chipped, denticulate, indented, irregular, notched, ragged, rough, serrated, sharp, snagged, spiky, toothed, uneven, zigzag. *Opp* SMOOTH.

jail, jailer *ns* ▷ GAOL, GAOLER.

jam *n* 1 blockage, bottleneck, congestion, crush, obstruction, press, squeeze, stoppage, throng. ▷ CROWD. **2** difficulty, dilemma, embarrassment, *inf* fix, *inf* hole, *inf* hot water, *inf* pickle, plight, predicament, quandary, tight corner, trouble. **3** conserve, jelly, marmalade, preserve. ● *vb* **1** block, *inf* bung up, clog, congest, cram, crowd, crush, fill, force, pack, obstruct, overcrowd, ram, squash, squeeze, stop up, stuff. **2** prop, stick, wedge.

jar *n* amphora, carafe, container, crock, ewer, glass, jug, mug, pitcher, pot, receptacle, urn, vessel. ▷ BOTTLE. *vb* **1** jerk, jog, jolt, *inf* rattle, shake, shock, upset. **2** *That noise jars on me.* grate, grind, *inf* jangle. ▷ ANNOY. **jarring** ▷ HARSH.

jargon *n* argot, cant, creole, dialect, idiom, language, patois, slang, vernacular.

jaunt *n* excursion, expedition, outing, tour, trip. ▷ JOURNEY.

jaunty *adj* alert, breezy, bright, brisk, buoyant, carefree, *inf* cheeky, debonair, frisky, lively, perky, spirited, sprightly. ▷ HAPPY.

jazzy *adj* **1** animated, rhythmic, spirited, swinging, syncopated, vivacious. ▷ LIVELY. *Opp* SEDATE. **2** *jazzy colours.* bold, clashing, contrasting, flashy, gaudy, loud.

jealous *adj* **1** bitter, covetous, envious, *inf* green-eyed, *inf* green with envy, grudging, jaundiced, resentful. **2** *jealous of your reputation.* careful, possessive, protective, vigilant, watchful.

jeer *vb* barrack, boo, chaff, deride, disapprove, gibe, heckle, hiss, *inf* knock, laugh,

make fun (of), mock, scoff, sneer, taunt, *inf* twit. ▷ RIDICULE. *Opp* CHEER.

jeopardize *vb* endanger, gamble, imperil, menace, put at risk, risk, threaten, venture.

jerk *vb* jar, jiggle, jog, jolt, lurch, move jerkily, move suddenly, pluck, pull, *inf* rattle, shake, tug, tweak, twist, twitch, wrench, *inf* yank.

jerky *adj* bouncy, bumpy, convulsive, erratic, fitful, jolting, jumpy, rough, shaky, spasmodic, *inf* stopping and starting, twitchy, uncontrolled, uneven. *Opp* STEADY.

jest *n*, *vb* ▷ JOKE.

jester *n* buffoon, clown, comedian, comic, fool, joker.

jet *adj* ▷ BLACK. ● *n* **1** flow, fountain, gush, rush, spout, spray, spurt, squirt, stream. **2** nozzle, sprinkler.

jetty *n* breakwater, groyne, landing-stage, mole, pier, quay, wharf.

jewel *n* brilliant, gem, gemstone, ornament, precious stone, *inf* rock, *inf* sparkler. ▷ JEWELLERY. □ amber, cairngorm, carnelian, coral, diamond, emerald, garnet, ivory, jade, jasper, jet, lapis lazuli, moonstone, onyx, opal, pearl, rhinestone, ruby, sapphire, topaz, turquoise.

jeweller *n* goldsmith, silversmith.

jewellery *n* gems, jewels, ornaments, treasure, *inf* sparklers. □ bangle, beads, bracelet, brooch, chain, charm, clasp, cuff-links, earring, locket, necklace, pendant, pin, ring, signet ring, tie-pin, watch, watch-chain.

jilt *vb* abandon, break with, desert, *inf* ditch, drop, *inf* dump, forsake, *inf* give someone the brush-off, leave behind, *inf* leave in the lurch, renounce, repudiate, *inf* throw over, *inf* wash your hands of.

jingle *n* 1 doggerel, rhyme, song, tune, verse. 2 chinking, clinking, jangling, ringing, tinkling, tintinnabulation. ● *vb* chime, chink, clink, jangle, ring, tinkle. ▷ SOUND.

job *n* 1 activity, assignment, charge, chore, duty, errand, function, housework, mission, operation, project, pursuit, responsibility, role, stint, task, undertaking, work.
2 appointment, business, calling, career, craft, employment, livelihood, living, métier, occupation, position, post, profession, sinecure, trade, vocation.

jobless *adj* out of work, redundant, unemployed, unwaged.

jocular *adj* cheerful, gay, glad, gleeful, happy, jocund, jokey, joking, jolly, jovial, joyous, jubilant, merry, overjoyed, rejoicing. *Opp* SAD, SERIOUS.

jog *vb* 1 bounce, jar, jerk, joggle, jolt, knock, nudge, shake.
▷ HIT. 2 *jog the memory*. activate, arouse, prompt, refresh, remind, set off, stimulate, stir. 3 *jog round the park*. exercise, lope, run, trot.

join *n* connection, joint, knot, link, mend, seam. ● *vb* 1 add, amalgamate, attach, combine, connect, couple, dock, dovetail, fit, fix, juxtapose, knit, link, marry, merge, put together, splice, tack on, unite, yoke.
▷ FASTEN. *Opp* SEPARATE.
2 abut, adjoin, border on, come

together, converge, meet, touch, verge on. 3 *join a crowd*. accompany, associate with, follow, go with, *inf* latch on to, tag along with, team up with. 4 *join a club*. affiliate with, become a member of, enlist in, enrol in, participate in, register for, sign up for, subscribe to, volunteer for. *Opp* LEAVE.

joint *adj* collaborative, collective, combined, common, communal, concerted, cooperative, corporate, general, mutual, shared, united. *Opp* SEPARATE. ● *n* articulation, connection, hinge, junction, union.

joist *n* beam, girder, rafter.

joke *n* *inf* crack, funny story, *inf* gag, *old use* jape, jest, laugh, *inf* one-liner, pleasantry, pun, quip, wisecrack, witticism.
● *vb* banter, be facetious, clown, fool about, have a laugh, jest, make jokes, quip, tease.

jolly *adj* cheerful, delighted, gay, glad, gleeful, grinning, high-spirited, jocose, jocular, jocund, joking, jovial, joyful, joyous, jubilant, laughing, merry, playful, rejoicing, rosy-faced, smiling, sportive. ▷ HAPPY. *Opp* SAD.

jolt *vb* 1 bounce, bump, jar, jerk, jog, shake, twitch. ▷ HIT. 2 *jolted me into action*. astonish, disturb, nonplus, shake up, shock, startle, stun, surprise.

jostle *vb* crowd in on, hustle, press, push, shove.

jot *vb* **jot down** note, scribble, take down. ▷ WRITE.

journal *n* 1 gazette, magazine, monthly, newsletter, newspaper, paper, periodical, publication, review, weekly. 2 account, annals, chronicle, diary, dossier, history, log, memoir, record, scrapbook.

journalist *n* broadcaster, columnist, contributor, correspondent, *derog* hack, *inf* newshound, newspaperman, newspaperwoman, pressman, reporter, writer.

journey *n* excursion, expedition, itinerary, jaunt, mission, odyssey, outing, peregrination, progress, route, tour, transition, travelling, trip, wandering. □ cruise, drive, flight, hike, joy-ride, pilgrimage, ramble, ride, run, safari, sail, sea crossing, sea passage, trek, voyage, walk. ● *vb* ▷ TRAVEL.

joy *n* bliss, cheer, cheerfulness, delight, ecstasy, elation, euphoria, exaltation, exhilaration, exultation, felicity, gaiety, gladness, glee, gratification, happiness, high spirits, hilarity, jocularity, joviality, joyfulness, joyousness, jubilation, light-heartedness, merriment, mirth, pleasure, rapture, rejoicing, triumph. *Opp* SORROW.

joyful *adj* buoyant, cheerful, delighted, ecstatic, elated, euphoric, exhilarated, exultant, gay, glad, gleeful, jocund, jolly, jovial, joyous, jubilant, light-hearted, merry, overjoyed, pleased, rapturous, rejoicing, triumphant. ▷ HAPPY. *Opp* SAD.

jubilee *n* anniversary, celebration, commemoration, festival.

judge *n* 1 *sl* beak, justice, magistrate. 2 adjudicator, arbiter, arbitrator, moderator, referee, umpire. 3 *judge of wine.* authority, connoisseur, critic, expert, reviewer. ● *vb* 1 condemn,

convict, examine, pass judgement on, pronounce judgement on, punish, sentence, try. 2 adjudicate, mediate, moderate, referee, umpire. 3 believe, conclude, consider, decide, decree, deem, determine, estimate, gauge, guess, reckon, rule, suppose. 4 *judge others.* appraise, assess, criticize, evaluate, give your opinion of, rate, rebuke, scold, sit in judgement on, size up, weigh.

judgement *n* 1 arbitration, award, conclusion, conviction, decision, decree, *old use* doom, finding, outcome, penalty, punishment, result, ruling, verdict. 2 *use your judgement.* acumen, common sense, discernment, discretion, discrimination, expertise, good sense, reason, wisdom. ▷ INTELLIGENCE. 3 *in my judgement.* assessment, belief, estimation, evaluation, idea, impression, mind, notion, opinion, point of view, valuation.

judicial *adj* 1 forensic, legal, official. 2 ▷ JUDICIOUS.

judicious *adj* appropriate, astute, careful, circumspect, considered, diplomatic, discerning, discreet, discriminating, enlightened, expedient, judicial, politic, prudent, sage, sensible, shrewd, sober, thoughtful, well-advised, well-judged. ▷ WISE.

jug *n* bottle, carafe, container, decanter, ewer, flagon, flask, jar, pitcher, vessel.

juggle *vb* alter, *inf* cook, *inf* doctor, falsify, *inf* fix, manipulate, misrepresent, move about, rearrange, rig, tamper.

juice n drink, extract, fluid, liquid, sap.

juicy adj lush, moist, soft, inf squelchy, succulent, wet. Opp DRY.

jumble n chaos, clutter, confusion, disarray, disorder, farrago, hotchpotch, mess, muddle, tangle. ● vb confuse, disarrange, disorganize, inf mess up, mingle, mix up, muddle, shuffle, tangle. Opp ARRANGE.

jump n 1 bounce, bound, hop, leap, pounce, skip, spring, vault. 2 ditch, fence, gap, gate, hurdle, obstacle. 3 a jump in prices. ▷ RISE. ● vb 1 bounce, bound, caper, dance, frisk, frolic, gambol, hop, leap, pounce, prance, skip, spring. 2 jump a fence. clear, hurdle, vault. 3 jump in surprise. flinch, recoil, start, wince. **jump on** ▷ ATTACK. **make someone jump** ▷ STARTLE.

junction n confluence, connection, corner, crossroads, interchange, intersection, joining, juncture, inf link-up, meeting, points, T-junction, union.

jungle n forest, rain-forest, tangle, undergrowth, woods.

junior adj inferior, lesser, lower, minor, secondary, subordinate, subsidiary, younger. Opp SENIOR.

junk n clutter, debris, flotsam-and-jetsam, garbage, litter, lumber, oddments, odds and ends, refuse, rubbish, rummage, scrap, trash, waste. ● vb ▷ DISCARD.

just adj apt, deserved, equitable, ethical, even-handed, fair, fair-minded, honest, impartial, justified, lawful, legal, legitim-

ate, merited, neutral, proper, reasonable, rightful, right-minded, unbiased, unprejudiced, upright. ▷ MORAL. Opp UNJUST.

justice n 1 equity, even-handedness, fair-mindedness, fair play, impartiality, integrity, legality, neutrality, objectivity, right. ▷ MORALITY. 2 the law, legal proceedings, the police, punishment, retribution, vengeance.

justifiable adj acceptable, allowable, defensible, excusable, forgivable, justified, lawful, legitimate, pardonable, permissible, reasonable, understandable, warranted. Opp UNJUSTIFIABLE.

justify vb condone, defend, exculpate, excuse, exonerate, explain, explain away, forgive, legitimate, legitimize, pardon, rationalize, substantiate, support, sustain, uphold, validate, vindicate, warrant.

jut vb beetle, extend, overhang, poke out, project, protrude, stick out. Opp RECEDE.

juvenile adj 1 babyish, childish, immature, infantile, puerile, unsophisticated. 2 adolescent, inf teenage, underage, young, youthful. Opp MATURE.

K

keen adj 1 active, ambitious, anxious, ardent, assiduous, avid, bright, clever, committed, dedicated, devoted, diligent, eager, enthusiastic, fervent, fervid, industrious, intelligent, intense, intent, interested, motivated, passionate, quick, zealous. **2** *a keen knife.* knife-edged, piercing, razor-sharp, sharp, sharpened. **3** *a keen wit.* acerbic, acid, acute, biting, clever, cutting, discerning, incisive, lively, mordant, observant, pungent, rapier-like, sarcastic, satirical, scathing, shrewd, sophisticated, stinging. **4** *keen eyesight.* acute, clear, fine, perceptive, sensitive. **5** *a keen wind.* bitter, cold, extreme, icy, intense, penetrating, severe. **6** *keen prices.* competitive, low, rock-bottom. *Opp* APATHETIC, DULL.

keep *vb* **1** accumulate, amass, conserve, guard, hang on to, hoard, hold, maintain, preserve, protect, put aside, put away, retain, safeguard, save, store, stow away, withhold. **2** *keep going.* carry on, continue, do again and again, do for a long time, keep on, persevere in, persist in. **3** *keep left.* remain, stay. **4** *keep a family.* be responsible for, care for, cherish, feed, finance, foster, guard, have charge of, look after, maintain, manage, mind, own, pay for, protect, provide for, subsidize, support, take charge of, tend, watch over. **5** *keep a birthday.* celebrate, commemorate, mark, observe, solemnize. **6** *food keeps in the fridge.* be preserved, be usable, last, survive, stay fresh, stay good. **7** *won't keep you.* block, check, confine, curb, delay, detain, deter, get in the way of, hamper, hinder, hold up, impede, imprison, obstruct, prevent, restrain, retard. **keep still** ▷ STAY. **keep to**

▷ FOLLOW, OBEY. **keep up**
▷ PROLONG, SUSTAIN.

keeper *n* caretaker, curator, custodian, gaoler, guard, guardian, *inf* minder, warden, warder.

kernel *n* centre, core, essence, heart, middle, nub, pith.

key *n* **1** answer, clarification, clue, explanation, indicator, pointer, secret, solution. **2** *key to a map.* glossary, guide, index, legend.

keyboard *n* □ accordion, celesta, clavichord, clavier, fortepiano, harmonium, harpsichord, organ, piano, old use *pianoforte*, spinet, synthesizer, virginals.

kick *vb* boot, heel, punt. ▷ HIT.

kidnap *vb* abduct, capture, carry off, run away with, seize, snatch.

kill *vb* annihilate, assassinate, be the killer of, *sl* bump off, butcher, cull, decimate, destroy, *inf* dispatch, *inf* do away with, *sl* do in, execute, exterminate, *inf* finish off, *inf* knock off, liquidate, martyr, massacre, murder, put down, put to death, put to sleep, slaughter, slay, *inf* snuff out, take life, *Amer sl* waste. □ *behead, brain, choke, crucify, decapitate, disembowel, drown, electrocute, eviscerate, garrotte, gas, guillotine, hang, knife, lynch, poison, pole-axe, shoot, smother, stab, starve, stifle, stone, strangle, suffocate, throttle.*

killer *n* assassin, butcher, cutthroat, destroyer, executioner, exterminator, gunman, *sl* hit man, murderer, slayer.

killing *n* annihilation, assassination, bloodbath, bloodshed, butchery, carnage, decimation,

destruction, elimination, eradication, euthanasia, execution,
extermination, extinction, fratricide, genocide, homicide,
infanticide, liquidation,
manslaughter, martyrdom,
massacre, matricide, murder,
parricide, patricide, pogrom,
regicide, slaughter, sororicide,
suicide, unlawful killing, uxoricide.

kin *n* clan, family, *inf* folks,
kindred, kith and kin, relations, relatives.

kind *adj* accommodating, affable,
affectionate, agreeable, altruistic, amenable, amiable,
amicable, approachable, attentive, avuncular, beneficent,
benevolent, benign, bountiful,
brotherly, caring, charitable,
comforting, compassionate,
congenial, considerate, cordial,
courteous, encouraging,
fatherly, favourable, friendly,
generous, genial, gentle, good-
natured, good-tempered,
gracious, helpful, hospitable,
humane, humanitarian, indulgent, kind-hearted, kindly, lenient, loving, merciful, mild,
motherly, neighbourly, nice,
obliging, patient, philanthropic,
pleasant, polite, public-spirited,
sensitive, sisterly, soft-hearted,
sweet, sympathetic, tactful,
tender, tender-hearted, thoughtful, tolerant, understanding,
unselfish, warm, warm-hearted,
well-intentioned, well-meaning,
well-meant. *Opp* UNKIND.
● *n* brand, breed, category,
class, description, family, form,
genre, genus, make, manner,
nature, persuasion, race, set,
sort, species, style, type,
variety.

kindle *vb* 1 burn, fire, ignite,
light, set alight, set fire to,
spark off. 2 ▷ AROUSE.

king *n* 1 crowned head, His
Majesty, monarch, ruler, sovereign. 2 ▷ CHIEF.

kingdom *n* country, empire,
land, monarchy, realm.

kink *n* 1 bend, coil, crimp,
crinkle, curl, knot, loop, tangle,
twist, wave. 2 ▷ QUIRK.

kiosk *n* booth, stall. □ *bookstall,
news-stand, telephone-box.*

kiss *vb* caress, embrace, *sl* neck,
osculate, *old use* spoon.
▷ TOUCH.

kit *n* accoutrements, apparatus,
appurtenances, baggage, effects,
equipment, gear, *joc* impedimenta, implements, luggage,
outfit, paraphernalia, rig,
supplies, tackle, tools, tools of
the trade, utensils.

kitchen *n* cookhouse, galley,
kitchenette, scullery.

knack *n* ability, adroitness, aptitude, art, bent, dexterity,
expertise, facility, flair, genius,
gift, habit, intuition, *inf* know-
how, skill, talent, trick, *inf* way.

knapsack *n* backpack, haversack, rucksack.

knead *vb* manipulate, massage,
pound, press, pummel, squeeze,
work.

kneel *vb* bend, bow, crouch, fall
to your knees, genuflect, stoop.

knickers *n old use* bloomers,
boxer-shorts, briefs, drawers,
panties, pants, shorts, trunks,
underpants.

knife *n* blade. □ *butter-knife,
carving-knife, clasp-knife,
cleaver, dagger, flick-knife,
machete, penknife, pocket-knife,
scalpel, sheath knife.* ● *vb* cut,

pierce, slash, stab.
▷ KILL, WOUND.

knit *vb* 1 crochet, weave. 2 bind,
combine, connect, fasten, heal,
interlace, interweave, join,
knot, link, marry, mend, tie,
unite. **knit your brow**
▷ FROWN.

knob *n* boss, bulge, bump,
handle, lump, projection, protrusion, protuberance, stud,
swelling.

knock *vb* 1 bang, *inf* bash, buffet,
bump, pound, rap, smack, *old
use* smite, strike, tap, thump.
▷ HIT. 2 ▷ CRITICIZE. **knock
down** ▷ DEMOLISH. **knock off**
▷ CEASE. **knock out** ▷ STUN.

knot *n* 1 bond, bow, ligature,
tangle, tie. 2 ▷ GROUP.
● *vb* bind, do up, entangle,
entwine, join, knit, lash, link,
tether, tie, unite. ▷ FASTEN.
Opp UNTIE.

know *vb* 1 be certain, have
confidence, have no doubt.
2 *know facts.* be cognizant of, be
familiar with, be knowledgeable about, comprehend,
discern, have experience of,
have in mind, realize, remember, understand. 3 *know a
person.* be acquainted with, be
a friend of, be friends with.
4 differentiate, distinguish,
identify, make out, perceive,
recognize, see.

know-all *n* expert, pundit,
inf show-off, wiseacre.

knowing *adj* astute, clever,
conspiratorial, cunning,
discerning, experienced, expressive, meaningful, perceptive,
shrewd. ▷ CUNNING, KNOWL-
EDGEABLE. *Opp* INNOCENT.

knowledge *n* 1 data, facts, information, intelligence, *sl* low-

down. 2 acquaintance, awareness, background, cognition,
competence, consciousness,
education, erudition, experience, expertise, familiarity,
grasp, insight, *inf* know-how,
learning, lore, memory,
science, scholarship, skill,
sophistication, technique, training. *Opp* IGNORANCE.

knowledgeable *adj Fr* au fait,
aware, cognizant, conversant,
educated, enlightened, erudite,
experienced, expert, familiar
(with), *sl* genned up, informed,
inf in the know, learned, scholarly, versed (in), well-
informed. *Opp* IGNORANT.

L

label *n* brand, docket, hallmark,
identification, imprint, logo,
marker, sticker, tag, ticket,
trademark. ● *vb* brand, call,
categorize, class, classify,
define, describe, docket,
identify, mark, name, pigeon-
hole, stamp, tag.

laborious *adj* 1 arduous, back-
breaking, difficult, exhausting,
fatiguing, gruelling, hard,
heavy, herculean, onerous, stiff,
strenuous, taxing, tiresome,
tough, uphill, wearisome,
wearying. *Opp* EASY. 2 *a laborious style.* artificial, contrived,
forced, heavy, laboured, overdone, overworked, pedestrian,
ponderous, strained, unnatural.
Opp FLUENT.

labour *n* 1 *inf* donkey-work,
drudgery, effort, exertion,
industry, navvying, *inf* pains,

slavery, strain, *inf* sweat, toil, work. **2** employees, *old use* hands, wage-earners, workers, workforce. **3** childbirth, contractions, delivery, labour pains, parturition, *old use* travail. ● *vb* drudge, exert yourself, navvy, *inf* slave, strain, strive, struggle, *inf* sweat, toil, travail. ▷ WORK. **laboured** ▷ LABORIOUS.

labourer *n* blue-collar worker, employee, *old use* hand, manual worker, *inf* navvy, wage-earner, worker.

labour-saving *adj* convenient, handy, helpful, time-saving.

labyrinth *n* complex, jungle, maze, network, tangle.

lace *n* **1** filigree, mesh, net, netting, openwork, tatting, web. **2** bootlace, cord, shoelace, string, thong. ● *vb* ▷ FASTEN.

lacerate *vb* claw, cut, gash, graze, mangle, rip, scrape, scratch, slash, tear. ▷ WOUND.

lack *n* absence, dearth, deficiency, deprivation, famine, insufficiency, need, paucity, privation, scarcity, shortage, want. *Opp* PLENTY. ● *vb* be lacking in, be short of, be without, miss, need, require, want.

lacking *adj* defective, deficient, inadequate, insufficient, short, unsatisfactory, weak. ▷ STUPID.

laden *adj* burdened, *inf* chock-full, fraught, full, hampered, loaded, oppressed, piled high, weighed down.

lady *n* **1** wife, woman. ▷ FEMALE. **2** aristocrat, peeress. ▷ TITLE.

ladylike *adj* aristocratic, courtly, cultured, dainty, decorous, elegant, genteel, modest, noble, polished, posh, prim and proper, *derog* prissy, refined, respectable, well-born, well-bred. ▷ POLITE.

lag *vb* **1** be slow, *inf* bring up the rear, come last, dally, dawdle, delay, drop behind, fall behind, go too slow, hang about, hang back, idle, linger, loiter, saunter, straggle, trail. **2** *lag pipes*. insulate, wrap up.

lair *n* den, hide-out, hiding-place, refuge, resting-place, retreat, shelter.

lake *n* boating-lake, lagoon, lido, *Scot* loch, mere, pool, pond, reservoir, sea, tarn, water.

lame *adj* **1** crippled, disabled, halting, handicapped, hobbled, hobbling, incapacitated, limping, maimed, spavined. **2** *a lame leg*. dragging, game, *inf* gammy, injured, stiff. **3** *a lame excuse*. feeble, flimsy, inadequate, poor, tame, thin, unconvincing, weak. ● *vb* cripple, disable, hobble, incapacitate, maim. **be lame** ▷ LIMP.

lament *n* dirge, elegy, lamentation, moaning, monody, mourning, requiem, threnody. ● *vb* bemoan, bewail, complain, cry, deplore, express your sorrow, grieve, keen, mourn, regret, shed tears, sorrow, wail, weep.

lamentable *adj* deplorable, regrettable, unfortunate, unhappy. ▷ SAD.

lamentation *n* complaints, crying, grief, grieving, lamenting, moaning, mourning, regrets, sobbing, tears, wailing, weeping.

lamp *n* bulb, fluorescent lamp, headlamp, lantern, standard lamp, street light, torch. ▷ LIGHT.

land n 1 coast, ground, landfall, shore, *joc* terra firma. 2 *lie of the land*. geography, landscape, terrain, topography. 3 country, fatherland, homeland, motherland, nation, region, state, territory. 4 earth, farmland, soil. 5 *land you own*. estate, grounds, property. ● *vb* 1 alight, arrive, berth, come ashore, come to rest, disembark, dismount, dock, end a journey, get down, go ashore, light, reach landfall, settle, touch down. 2 *land yourself a job*. ▷ GET.

landing n 1 docking, re-entry, return, splashdown, touchdown. 2 alighting, arrival, deplaning, disembarkation. 3 ▷ LANDING-STAGE.

landing-stage n berth, dock, harbour, jetty, landing, pier, quay, wharf.

landlady, landlord ns 1 host, hostess, hotelier, *old use* innkeeper, licensee, publican, restaurateur. 2 landowner, lessor, letter, manager, manageress, owner, proprietor.

landmark n 1 feature, guidepost, high point, identification, visible feature. 2 milestone, new era, turning-point, watershed.

landscape n aspect, countryside, outlook, panorama, prospect, rural scene, scene, scenery, view, vista.

language n 1 parlance, speech, tongue. □ *argot, cant, colloquialism, dialect, formal language, idiolect, idiom, informal language, jargon, journalese, lingua franca, inf lingo, patois, register, slang, vernacular*. 2 linguistics. □ *etymology, lexicography, orthography, philo-*

logy, phonetics, psycholinguistics, semantics, semiotics, sociolinguistics. 3 *computer language*. code, system of signs.

languid adj apathetic, *inf* droopy, feeble, inactive, inert, lackadaisical, lazy, lethargic, slow, sluggish, torpid, unenthusiastic, weak. *Opp* ENERGETIC.

languish vb decline, flag, lose momentum, mope, pine, slow down, stagnate, suffer, sulk, waste away, weaken, wither. *Opp* FLOURISH.

lank adj 1 drooping, lifeless, limp, long, straight, thin. 2 ▷ LANKY.

lanky adj angular, awkward, bony, gangling, gaunt, lank, lean, long, scraggy, scrawny, skinny, tall, thin, ungraceful, weedy. *Opp* GRACEFUL, STURDY.

lap n 1 knees, thighs. 2 circle, circuit, course, orbit, revolution. ● *vb* ▷ DRINK.

lapse n 1 backsliding, blunder, decline, error, failing, fault, flaw, mistake, omission, relapse, shortcoming, slip, *inf* slip-up, temporary failure, weakness. 2 *lapse of time*. break, gap, hiatus, *inf* hold-up, intermission, interruption, interval, lacuna, lull, pause. ● *vb* 1 decline, deteriorate, diminish, drop, fall, sink, slide, slip, slump, subside. 2 *My membership lapsed*. become invalid, expire, finish, run out, stop, terminate.

large adj above average, abundant, ample, big, bold, broad, bulky, burly, capacious, colossal, commodious, considerable, copious, elephantine, enormous, extensive, fat, formidable, gargantuan, generous, giant, gigantic, grand, great, heavy, hefty, high, huge, *inf* hulking, immense, immeasurable, impressive, incalculable, infinite, *inf* jumbo, *inf* king-sized, largish, lofty, long, mammoth, massive, mighty, monstrous, monumental, mountainous, outsize, overgrown, oversized, prodigious, *inf* roomy, sizeable, spacious, substantial, swingeing (*increase*), tall, thick, *inf* thumping, *inf* tidy (*sum*), titanic, towering, *inf* tremendous, vast, voluminous, weighty, *inf* whacking, *inf* whopping, wide. *Opp* SMALL.

larva n caterpillar, grub, maggot.

lash n ▷ WHIP. ● vb 1 beat, birch, cane, flail, flog, scourge, strike, thrash, whip. ▷ HIT.
2 ▷ CRITICIZE.

last adj closing, concluding, final, furthest, hindmost, latest, most recent, rearmost, terminal, terminating, ultimate. *Opp* FIRST. ● vb carry on, continue, endure, hold, hold out, keep on, linger, live, persist, remain, stay, survive, *inf* wear well. *Opp* DIE, FINISH.

lasting ▷ PERMANENT.

late adj 1 behindhand, belated, delayed, dilatory, overdue, slow, tardy, unpunctual. 2 *a late edition.* current, last, new, recent, up-to-date. 3 *the late king.* dead, deceased, departed, ex-, former, past, previous.

latent adj dormant, hidden, invisible, potential, undeveloped, undiscovered.

latitude n *inf* elbow-room, freedom, leeway, liberty, room, scope, space.

latter adj closing, concluding, last, last-mentioned, later, recent, second. *Opp* FORMER.

lattice n criss-cross, framework, grid, mesh, trellis.

laugh vb beam, be amused, burst into laughter, chortle, chuckle, *sl* fall about, giggle, grin, guffaw, roar with laughter, simper, smile, smirk, sneer, snicker, snigger, *inf* split your sides, titter. **laugh at** ▷ RIDICULE.

laughable adj absurd, derisory, ludicrous, preposterous, ridiculous. ▷ FUNNY.

laughing-stock n butt, figure of fun, victim.

laughter n chuckling, giggling, guffawing, hilarity, *inf* hysterics, laughing, laughs, merriment, mirth, snickering, sniggering, tittering. ▷ RIDICULE.

launch vb 1 begin, embark on, establish, float, found, inaugurate, initiate, open, organize, set in motion, set off, set up, start. 2 blast off, catapult, dispatch, fire, propel, send off, set off, shoot.

lavatory n bathroom, cloakroom, convenience, *inf* Gents, *inf* Ladies, latrine, *inf* loo, *inf* men's room, *childish* potty, *old use* privy, public convenience, toilet, urinal, water-closet, WC, *inf* women's room.

lavish adj 1 abundant, bountiful, copious, exuberant, free, generous, liberal, luxuriant, luxurious, munificent, opulent, plentiful, profuse, sumptuous, unselfish, unsparing, unstinting. 2 excessive, extravagant, improvident, prodigal, self-indulgent, wasteful. *Opp* ECONOMICAL.

law n 1 act, bill [= *draft law*], bylaw, commandment, decree, directive, edict, injunction, mandate, measure, order, ordinance, pronouncement, regulation, rule, statute. 2 *laws of science*. axiom, formula, postulate, principle, proposition, theory. 3 *laws of decency*. code, convention, practice. 4 *court of law*. justice, litigation.

law-abiding adj compliant, decent, disciplined, good, honest, obedient, orderly, peaceable, peaceful, respectable, well-behaved. Opp LAWLESS.

lawful adj allowable, allowed, authorized, constitutional, documented, just, justifiable, legal, legitimate, permissible, permitted, prescribed, proper, recognized, regular, right, rightful, valid. Opp ILLEGAL.

lawless adj anarchic, anarchical, badly-behaved, chaotic, disobedient, disorderly, ill-disciplined, insubordinate, mutinous, rebellious, riotous, rowdy, seditious, turbulent, uncontrolled, undisciplined, ungoverned, unregulated, unrestrained, unruly, wild. ▷ WICKED. Opp LAW-ABIDING.

lawlessness n anarchy, chaos, disobedience, disorder, mob-rule, rebellion, rioting. Opp ORDER.

lawyer n advocate, barrister, counsel, legal representative, member of the bar, solicitor.

lax adj careless, casual, easygoing, flexible, indulgent, lenient, loose, neglectful, negligent, permissive, relaxed, remiss, slack, slipshod, unreliable, vague. Opp STRICT.

laxative n aperient, enema, purgative.

lay vb 1 apply, arrange, deposit, leave, place, position, put down, rest, set down, set out, spread. 2 *lay foundations*. build, construct, establish. 3 *lay the blame on someone*. ascribe, assign, attribute, burden, charge, impose, plant, *inf* saddle. 4 *lay plans*. concoct, create, design, organize, plan, set up. **lay bare** ▷ REVEAL. **lay bets** ▷ GAMBLE. **lay by** ▷ STORE. **lay down the law** ▷ DICTATE. **lay in** ▷ STORE. **lay into** ▷ ATTACK. **lay low** ▷ DEFEAT. **lay off something** ▷ CEASE. **lay someone off** ▷ DISMISS. **lay to rest** ▷ BURY. **lay up** ▷ STORE. **lay waste** ▷ DESTROY.

layer n 1 coat, coating, covering, film, sheet, skin, surface, thickness. 2 *layer of rock*. seam, stratum, substratum. **in layers** laminated, layered, sandwiched, stratified.

layman n 1 amateur, non-specialist, untrained person. Opp PROFESSIONAL. 2 [*church*] layperson, member of the congregation, parishioner, unordained person. Opp CLERGYMAN.

laze vb be lazy, do nothing, idle, lie about, loaf, lounge, relax, sit about, unwind.

laziness n dilatoriness, idleness, inactivity, indolence, lethargy, loafing, lounging about, shiftlessness, slackness, sloth, slowness, sluggishness, torpor. Opp INDUSTRY.

lazy adj 1 dilatory, easily pleased, easygoing, idle, inactive, indolent, languid, lethargic, listless, shiftless,

inf skiving, slack, slothful, slow, sluggish, torpid, unenterprising, work-shy. **2** peaceful, quiet, relaxing. *Opp* ENERGETIC, INDUSTRIOUS. **be lazy** ▷ LAZE.
lazy person ▷ SLACKER.

lead *n* **1** direction, example, guidance, leadership, model, pattern, precedent. **2** clue, hint, line, tip, tip-off. **3** *lead in a race.* first place, front, spearhead, van, vanguard. **4** *lead in a play.* chief part, hero, heroine, principal, protagonist, starring role, title role. **5** cable, flex, wire. **6** *dog's lead.* chain, leash, strap. ● *vb* **1** conduct, draw, escort, guide, influence, pilot, prompt, show the way, steer, usher. **2** be in charge of, captain, command, direct, govern, head, manage, preside over, rule, *inf* skipper, superintend, supervise. **3** be first, be in front, be in the lead, go first, head the field. **4** *lead the field.* beat, defeat, excel, outdo, outstrip, precede, surpass, vanquish. *Opp* FOLLOW. **lead astray** ▷ MISLEAD. **leading** ▷ CHIEF, INFLUENTIAL. **lead off** ▷ BEGIN.

leader *n* **1** ayatollah, boss, captain, chieftain, commander, conductor, courier, demagogue, director, figure-head, godfather, guide, head, patriarch, premier, prime minister, principal, ringleader, superior, *inf* supremo. ▷ CHIEF, RULER. **2** *leader in a newspaper.* editorial, leading article.

leaf *n* **1** blade, foliage, frond, greenery. **2** folio, page, sheet.

leaflet *n* advertisement, bill, booklet, brochure, circular, flyer, folder, handbill, handout, notice, pamphlet.

league *n* alliance, association, coalition, confederation, *derog* conspiracy, federation, fraternity, guild, society, union. ▷ GROUP. **be in league with** ▷ CONSPIRE.

leak *n* **1** discharge, drip, emission, escape, exudation, leakage, oozing, seepage, trickle. **2** aperture, break, chink, crack, crevice, cut, fissure, flaw, hole, opening, perforation, puncture, rent, split, tear. **3** *security leak.* disclosure, revelation. ● *vb* **1** discharge, drip, escape, exude, ooze, percolate, seep, spill, trickle. **2** *leak secrets.* disclose, divulge, give away, let out, let slip, *inf* let the cat out of the bag about, make known, pass on, reveal, *inf* spill the beans about.

leaky *adj* cracked, dripping, holed, perforated, punctured.

lean *adj* angular, bony, emaciated, gangling, gaunt, hungry-looking, lanky, long, rangy, scraggy, scrawny, skinny, slender, slim, spare, thin, weedy, wiry. *Opp* FAT. ● *vb* **1** careen, heel over, incline, keel over, list, slant, slope, tilt, tip. **2** loll, prop yourself up, recline, rest, support yourself.

leaning *n* bent, bias, favouritism, inclination, instinct, liking, partiality, penchant, predilection, preference, propensity, readiness, taste, tendency, trend.

leap *vb* **1** bound, clear (*a fence*), hop over, hurdle, jump, leap-frog, skip over, spring, vault. **2** caper, cavort, dance, frisk, frolic, gambol, hop, prance, romp. **3** *leap on someone.* ambush, attack, pounce.

learn *vb* acquire, ascertain, assimilate, become aware of, become proficient in, be taught, *inf* catch on, commit to memory, discover, find out, gain, gain understanding of, gather, grasp, master, memorize, *inf* mug up, pick up, remember, study, *inf* swot up. **learned** ▷ ACADEMIC, EDUCATED.

learner *n* apprentice, beginner, cadet, initiate, L-driver, novice, pupil, scholar, starter, student, trainee, tiro.

learning *n* culture, education, erudition, information, knowledge, lore, scholarship, wisdom.

lease *n* agreement, contract.
● *vb* charter, hire out, let, rent out, sublet.

least *adj* fewest, lowest, minimum, negligible, poorest, slightest, smallest, tiniest.

leather *n* chamois, hide, skin, suede.

leave *n* **1** authorization, consent, dispensation, liberty, licence, permission, sanction. **2** *leave from work.* absence, free time, furlough, holiday, recess, sabbatical, time off, vacation.
● *vb* **1** *inf* be off, *inf* check out, decamp, depart, disappear, *sl* do a bunk, escape, exeunt [*they go out*], exit [*he/she goes out*], get away, get out, go away, go out, *sl* hop it, *inf* pull out, *si* push off, retire, retreat, run away, say goodbye, set off, *inf* take off, take your leave, withdraw. **2** abandon, desert, evacuate, forsake, vacate. **3** *leave your job. inf* chuck in, *inf* drop out of, give up, quit, relinquish, renounce, resign from, retire from, *inf* walk out of, *inf* wash

your hands of. **4** *leave it there.* allow to stay, *inf* let alone, let be. **5** *left it here.* deposit, place, position, put down, set down. **6** *left it somewhere.* forget, lose, mislay. **7** *leave it to you.* assign, cede, consign, entrust, refer, relinquish. **8** *leave in a will.* bequeath, hand down, will. **leave off** ▷ STOP. **leave out** ▷ OMIT.

lecture *n* **1** address, discourse, disquisition, instruction, lesson, paper, speech, talk, treatise. **2** *lecture on bad manners.* diatribe, harangue, sermon. ▷ REPRIMAND.
● *vb* **1** be a lecturer, teach. **2** discourse, give a lecture, harangue, *inf* hold forth, pontificate, preach, sermonize, speak, talk formally. **3** ▷ REPRIMAND.

lecturer *n* don, fellow, instructor, professor, speaker, teacher, tutor.

ledge *n* mantel, overhang, projection, ridge, shelf, sill, step, window-sill.

left *adj, n* **1** left-hand, port [= *left facing bow of ship*], sinistral. **2** *left wing in politics.* communist, Labour, leftist, liberal, Marxist, progressive, radical, *derog* red, revolutionary, socialist. *Opp* RIGHT.

leg *n* **1** limb, member, *inf* peg, *inf* pin, shank. □ ankle, calf, foot, hock, knee, shin, thigh. **2** brace, column, pillar, prop, support, upright. **3** *leg of a journey.* lap, length, part, section, stage, stretch. **pull someone's leg** ▷ HOAX.

legacy *n* bequest, endowment, estate, inheritance.

legal *adj* **1** above-board, acceptable, admissible, allowable, allowed, authorized, constitutional, just, lawful, legalized, legitimate, licensed, licit, permitted, permissible, proper, regular, right, rightful, valid. *Opp* ILLEGAL. **2** *legal proceedings*. forensic, judicial, judiciary.

legalize *vb* allow, authorize, legitimate, legitimize, license, make legal, normalize, permit, regularize, validate. *Opp* BAN.

legend *n* epic, folk-tale, myth, saga, tradition. ▷ STORY.

legendary *adj* **1** apocryphal, epic, fabled, fabulous, fictional, fictitious, imaginary, invented, made-up, mythical, non-existent, story-book, traditional. **2** *a legendary name*. ▷ FAMOUS.

legible *adj* clear, decipherable, distinct, intelligible, neat, plain, readable, understandable. *Opp* ILLEGIBLE.

legitimate *adj* **1** authentic, genuine, proper, real, regular, true. ▷ LEGAL. **2** *a legitimate deception*. ethical, just, justifiable, moral, proper, reasonable, right. *Opp* ILLEGITIMATE.
● *vb* ▷ LEGALIZE.

leisure *n* breathing-space, ease, holiday, liberty, opportunity, quiet, recreation, relaxation, relief, repose, respite, rest, spare time, time off.

leisurely *adj* easy, gentle, lingering, peaceful, relaxed, relaxing, restful, unhurried. ▷ SLOW. *Opp* BRISK.

lend *vb* advance, loan. *Opp* BORROW.

length *n* **1** distance, extent, footage, measure, measurement, mileage, reach, size, span, stretch. **2** duration, period, stretch, term.

lengthen *vb* continue, drag out, draw out, elongate, enlarge, expand, extend, get longer, increase, make longer, *inf* pad out, prolong, protract, pull out, stretch. *Opp* SHORTEN.

lenient *adj* charitable, easygoing, forbearing, forgiving, gentle, humane, indulgent, merciful, mild, permissive, soft, soft-hearted, sparing, tolerant. ▷ KIND. *Opp* STRICT.

less *adj* fewer, reduced, shorter, smaller. *Opp* MORE.

lessen *vb* **1** assuage, cut, deaden, decrease, ease, lighten, lower, make less, minimize, mitigate, reduce, relieve, tone down. **2** abate, become less, decline, decrease, die away, diminish, dwindle, ease off, let up, moderate, slacken, subside, tail off, weaken. *Opp* INCREASE.

lesson *n* **1** class, drill, instruction, laboratory, lecture, practical, seminar, session, task, teaching, tutorial, workshop. **2** *a moral lesson*. admonition, example, moral, warning.

let *vb* **1** agree to, allow to, authorize, consent to, enable to, give permission to, license to, permit to, sanction to. **2** *let a house*. charter, contract out, hire, lease, rent. **let alone, let be** ▷ LEAVE. **let go, let loose** ▷ LIBERATE. **let off** ▷ FIRE. **let out** ▷ LIBERATE. **let someone off** ▷ ACQUIT. **let up** ▷ LESSEN.

letdown *n* anti-climax, disappointment, disillusionment, *inf* wash-out.

lethal *adj* deadly, fatal, mortal, poisonous.

lethargic *adj* apathetic, comatose, dull, heavy, inactive, indifferent, indolent, languid, lazy, listless, phlegmatic, sleepy, slow, slothful, sluggish, torpid. ▷ WEARY. *Opp* ENERGETIC.

lethargy *n* apathy, idleness, inactivity, indolence, inertia, laziness, listlessness, slothfulness, slowness, sluggishness, torpor, weariness. *Opp* ENERGY.

letter *n* **1** character, consonant, sign, symbol, vowel. **2** *old use* billet-doux, card, communication, dispatch, epistle, message, missive, note, postcard. **letters** correspondence, junk mail, mail, post.

level *adj* **1** even, flat, flush, horizontal, plane, regular, smooth, straight, true, uniform. **2** horizontal. **3** *level scores.* balanced, even, equal, matching, *inf* neck-and-neck, the same. *Opp* UNEVEN.
● *n* **1** altitude, depth, elevation, height, value. **2** degree, echelon, grade, plane, position, rank, *inf* rung on the ladder, stage, standard, standing, status. **3** *level in a building.* floor, storey. ● *vb* **1** even out, flatten, rake, smooth. **2** bulldoze, demolish, destroy, devastate, knock down, lay low, raze, tear down, wreck. **level-headed** ▷ SENSIBLE.

lever *vb* force, prise, wrench.

liable *adj* **1** accountable, answerable, blameworthy, responsible. **2** *liable to fall over.* apt, disposed, inclined, in the habit of, likely, minded, predisposed, prone, ready, susceptible, tempted, vulnerable, willing.

liaison *n* **1** communication, contact, cooperation, liaising, linkage, links, mediation, relationship, tie. **2** ▷ AFFAIR.

liar *n* deceiver, false witness, *inf* fibber, perjurer, *inf* storyteller.

libel *n* calumny, defamation, denigration, insult, lie, misrepresentation, obloquy, scandal, slander, slur, smear, vilification. ● *vb* blacken the name of, calumniate, defame, denigrate, disparage, malign, misrepresent, slander, slur, smear, write lies about, traduce, vilify.

libellous *adj* calumnious, cruel, damaging, defamatory, disparaging, false, hurtful, insulting, lying, malicious, mendacious, scurrilous, slanderous, untrue, vicious.

liberal *adj* **1** abundant, ample, bounteous, bountiful, copious, free, generous, lavish, munificent, open-handed, plentiful, unstinting. **2** *liberal attitudes.* big-hearted, broad-minded, charitable, easygoing, enlightened, fair-minded, humanitarian, indulgent, impartial, latitudinarian, lenient, magnanimous, open-minded, permissive, philanthropic, tolerant, unbiased, unbigoted, unopinionated, unprejudiced, unselfish. *Opp* NARROW-MINDED. **3** *liberal politics.* progressive, radical, reformist. *Opp* CONSERVATIVE.

liberalize *vb* broaden, ease, enlarge, make more liberal, moderate, open up, relax, soften, widen.

liberate *vb* deliver, discharge, disenthral, emancipate, enfranchise, free, let go, let loose, let out, loose, manumit, ransom, release, rescue, save, set free, untie. *Opp* CAPTURE, SUBJUGATE.

liberty n autonomy, emancipation, independence, liberation, release, self-determination, self-rule. ▷ FREEDOM. **at liberty** ▷ FREE.

licence n 1 certificate, credentials, document, papers, permit, warrant. 2 ▷ FREEDOM.

license vb 1 allow, approve, authorize, certify, commission, empower, entitle, give a licence to, permit, sanction, validate. 2 buy a licence for, make legal.

lid n cap, cover, covering, top.

lie n deceit, dishonesty, disinformation, fabrication, falsehood, falsification, inf fib, fiction, invention, misrepresentation, prevarication, untruth, inf whopper. Opp TRUTH.
 • vb 1 inf be economical with the truth, bluff, commit perjury, deceive, falsify the facts, inf fib, perjure yourself, prevaricate, tell lies. 2 be horizontal, be prone, be prostrate, be recumbent, be supine, lean back, lounge, recline, repose, rest, sprawl, stretch out. 3 *The house lies in a valley.* be, be found, be located, be situated, exist. **lie low** ▷ HIDE.

life n 1 being, existence, living. 2 activity, animation, dash, élan, energy, enthusiasm, exuberance, inf go, liveliness, soul, sparkle, spirit, sprightliness, verve, vigour, vitality, vivacity, zest. 3 autobiography, biography, memoir, story.

lifeless adj 1 comatose, dead, deceased, inanimate, inert, insensate, insensible, killed, motionless, unconscious. 2 *lifeless desert.* arid, bare, barren, desolate, empty, sterile, uninhabited, waste. 3 *a lifeless*

performance. apathetic, boring, dull, flat, heavy, lacklustre, lethargic, slow, torpid, unexciting, wooden. Opp LIVELY, LIVING.

lifelike adj authentic, convincing, faithful, graphic, natural, photographic, realistic, true-to-life, vivid. Opp UNREALISTIC.

lift n elevator, hoist. • vb 1 buoy up, carry, elevate, heave up, hoist, jack up, pick up, pull up, raise, rear. 2 ascend, fly, lift off, rise, soar. 3 boost, cheer, enhance, improve, promote. 4 ▷ STEAL.

light adj 1 lightweight, portable, underweight, weightless. Opp HEAVY. 2 bright, illuminated, lit-up, well-lit. Opp DARK. 3 *light work.* ▷ EASY. 4 *a light wind.* ▷ GENTLE. 5 *a light touch.* ▷ DELICATE. 6 *light colours.* ▷ PALE. 7 *a light heart.* ▷ CHEERFUL. 8 *light traffic.* ▷ SPARSE. • n 1 beam, blaze, brightness, brilliance, effulgence, flare, flash, fluorescence, glare, gleam, glint, glitter, glow, halo, illumination, incandescence, luminosity, lustre, phosphorescence, radiance, ray, reflection, scintillation, shine, sparkle, twinkle. □ candlelight, daylight, firelight, gaslight, moonlight, starlight, sunlight, torchlight, twilight. □ arc light, beacon, bulb, candelabra, candle, chandelier, electric light, flare, floodlight, fluorescent lamp, headlamp, headlight, lamp, lantern, laser, lighthouse, lightship, neon light, pilot light, searchlight, spotlight, standard lamp, street light, strobe, stroboscope, taper, torch, traffic lights.
 • vb 1 fire, ignite, kindle, put a match to, set alight, set fire to,

switch on. *Opp* EXTINGUISH.
2 ▷ LIGHTEN. **bring to light**
▷ DISCOVER. **give light, reflect
light** be bright, be luminous,
be phosphorescent, blaze, blink,
burn, coruscate, dazzle, flash,
flicker, glare, gleam, glimmer,
glint, glisten, glitter, glow, radiate, reflect, scintillate, shimmer, shine, spark, sparkle,
twinkle. **light-headed** ▷ DIZZY.
light-hearted ▷ CHEERFUL.
light up ▷ LIGHTEN. **shed
light on** ▷ EXPLAIN.

lighten *vb* 1 cast light on, floodlight, illuminate, irradiate,
light up, shed light on, shine
on. 2 *The sky lightened.* become
lighter, brighten, cheer up,
clear. 3 ▷ LESSEN.

lighthouse *n* beacon, light,
lightship, warning-light.

like *adj* akin to, analogous to,
close to, cognate with, comparable to, congruent with, corresponding to, equal to, equivalent to, identical to, parallel to,
similar to. • *n* liking, partiality,
predilection, preference.
• *vb* admire, approve of, appreciate, be attracted to, be fond
of, be interested in, be keen on,
be partial to, be pleased by,
delight in, enjoy, find pleasant,
sl go for, *inf* go in for, have a
high regard for, prefer, relish,
revel in, take pleasure in,
inf take to, welcome. ▷ LOVE.
Opp HATE.

likeable *adj* admirable, attractive, charming, congenial,
endearing, interesting, lovable,
nice, personable, pleasant,
pleasing. ▷ FRIENDLY.
Opp HATEFUL.

likelihood *n* chance, hope, possibility, probability, prospect.

likely *adj* 1 anticipated, expected, feasible, foreseeable, plausible, possible, predictable,
probable, reasonable, unsurprising. 2 *a likely candidate.*
able, acceptable, appropriate,
convincing, credible, favourite,
fitting, hopeful, promising,
qualified, suitable, *inf* tipped to
win. 3 *likely to come.* apt,
disposed, inclined, liable,
prone, ready, tempted, willing.
Opp UNLIKELY.

liken *vb* compare, equate, juxtapose, match.

likeness *n* 1 affinity, analogy,
compatibility, congruity, correspondence, resemblance, similarity. *Opp* DIFFERENCE. 2 copy,
depiction, drawing, duplicate,
facsimile, image, model,
picture, portrait, replica, representation, reproduction, study.

liking *n* affection, affinity, appetite, eye, fondness, inclination,
partiality, penchant, predilection, predisposition, preference,
propensity, *inf* soft spot, taste,
weakness. ▷ LOVE. *Opp* HATRED.

limb *n* appendage, member,
offshoot, projection. □ *arm,
bough, branch, flipper, foreleg,
forelimb, leg, wing.*

limber *vb* **limber up** exercise,
get ready, loosen up, prepare,
warm up.

limbo *n* **in limbo** abandoned,
forgotten, in abeyance, left out,
neglected, neither one thing
nor the other, *inf* on hold,
inf on the back burner, unattached.

limit *n* 1 barrier, boundary,
bounds, brink, confines, demarcation line, edge, end, extent,
extreme point, frontier, perimeter. 2 ceiling, check, curb,

cut-off point, deadline, inhibition, limitation, maximum, restraint, restriction, stop, threshold. • vb bridle, check, circumscribe, confine, control, curb, define, fix, hold in check, put a limit on, ration, restrain, restrict. **limited** ▷ FINITE, INADEQUATE.

limitation n 1 ▷ LIMIT. 2 defect, deficiency, fault, inadequacy, shortcoming, weakness.

limitless adj boundless, countless, endless, everlasting, immeasurable, incalculable, inexhaustible, infinite, innumerable, never-ending, numberless, perpetual, renewable, unbounded, unconfined, unending, unimaginable, unlimited, unrestricted. ▷ VAST. Opp FINITE.

limp adj inf bendy, drooping, flabby, flaccid, flexible, inf floppy, lax, loose, pliable, sagging, slack, soft, weak, wilting, yielding. ▷ WEARY. Opp RIGID. • vb be lame, falter, hobble, hop, stagger, totter.

line n 1 band, borderline, boundary, contour, contour line, dash, mark, streak, striation, strip, stripe, stroke, trail. 2 corrugation, crease, inf crow's feet, fold, furrow, groove, score, wrinkle. 3 cable, cord, flex, hawser, lead, rope, string, thread, wire. 4 chain, column, cordon, crocodile, file, procession, queue, rank, row, series. 5 railway line. branch, main line, route, service, track. • vb 1 mark with lines, rule, score, streak, striate, underline. 2 line the street. border, edge, fringe. 3 line a garment. cover the inside, insert a lining, pad, reinforce. **line up** ▷ ALIGN, QUEUE.

linger vb continue, dally, dawdle, delay, dither, endure, hang about, hover, idle, lag, last, loiter, pause, persist, procrastinate, remain, inf shilly-shally, stay, stay behind, inf stick around, survive, temporize, wait about. Opp HURRY.

lining n inner coat, inner layer, interfacing, liner, padding.

link n 1 bond, connection, connector, coupling, join, joint, linkage, tie, yoke. ▷ FASTENER. 2 affiliation, alliance, association, communication, interdependence, liaison, partnership, relationship, inf tie-up, twinning, union. • vb 1 amalgamate, associate, attach, compare, concatenate, connect, couple, interlink, join, juxtapose, make a link, merge, network, relate, see a link, twin, unite, yoke. ▷ FASTEN.

lip n brim, brink, edge, rim.

liquefy vb become liquid, dissolve, liquidize, melt, run, thaw. Opp SOLIDIFY.

liquid adj aqueous, flowing, fluid, liquefied, melted, molten, running, inf runny, sloppy, inf sloshy, thin, watery, wet. Opp SOLID. • n fluid, juice, liquor, solution, stock.

liquidate vb annihilate, destroy, inf do away with, inf get rid of, remove, silence, wipe out. ▷ KILL.

liquor n 1 alcohol, sl booze, sl hard stuff, intoxicants, sl shorts, spirits, strong drink. 2 ▷ LIQUID.

list n catalogue, column, directory, file, index, inventory, listing, register, roll, roster, rota, schedule, shopping-list, table.

• *vb* 1 catalogue, enumerate, file, index, itemize, make a list of, note, record, register, tabulate, write down. 2 bank, careen, heel, incline, keel over, lean, slant, slope, tilt, tip.

listen *vb* attend, concentrate, eavesdrop, *old use* hark, hear, heed, *inf* keep your ears open, lend an ear, overhear, pay attention, take notice.

listless *adj* apathetic, enervated, feeble, heavy, languid, lazy, lethargic, lifeless, phlegmatic, sluggish, tired, torpid, unenthusiastic, uninterested, weak. ▷ WEARY. *Opp* LIVELY.

literal *adj* close, exact, faithful, matter of fact, plain, prosaic, strict, unimaginative, verbatim, word for word.

literary *adj* 1 cultured, educated, erudite, imaginative, learned, refined, scholarly, well-read, widely-read. 2 *literary style*. ornate, *derog* pedantic, poetic, polished, rhetorical, *derog* self-conscious, sophisticated, stylish.

literate *adj* 1 educated, well-read. 2 accurate, correct, readable, well-written.

literature *n* books, brochures, circulars, creative writing, handbills, handouts, leaflets, pamphlets, papers, writings. □ *autobiography, biography, comedy, crime fiction, criticism, drama, epic, essay, fantasy, fiction, folk-tale, journalism, myth and legend, novels, parody, poetry, propaganda, prose, romance, satire, science fiction, tragedy.* ▷ WRITING.

lithe *adj* agile, flexible, limber, lissom, loose-jointed, pliable, pliant, supple. *Opp* STIFF.

litter *n* bits and pieces, clutter, debris, fragments, garbage, jumble, junk, mess, odds and ends, refuse, rubbish, trash, waste. • *vb* clutter, fill with litter, make untidy, *inf* mess up, scatter, strew.

little *adj* 1 *inf* baby, bantam, compact, concise, diminutive, *inf* dinky, dwarf, exiguous, fine, fractional, infinitesimal, lean, lilliputian, microscopic, midget, *inf* mini, miniature, minuscule, minute, narrow, petite (*woman*), *inf* pint-sized, *inf* pocket-sized, *inf* poky, portable, pygmy, short, slender, slight, small, *inf* teeny, thin, tiny, toy, undergrown, undersized, *inf* wee, *inf* weeny. *Opp* BIG. 2 *little food*. inadequate, insufficient, meagre, mean, *inf* measly, miserly, modest, niggardly, parsimonious, *inf* piddling, scanty, skimpy, stingy, ungenerous, unsatisfactory. 3 *of little importance*. inconsequential, insignificant, minor, negligible, nugatory, slim (*chance*), slight, trifling, trivial, unimportant.

live *adj* 1 ▷ LIVING. 2 *a live fire*. ▷ ALIGHT. 3 *a live issue*. contemporary, current, important, pressing, relevant, topical, vital. *Opp* DEAD. • *vb* 1 breathe, continue, endure, exist, flourish, function, last, persist, remain, stay alive, survive. *Opp* DIE. 2 be accommodated, dwell, lodge, reside, room, stay. 3 *live on £20 a week*. fare, *inf* get along, keep going, make a living, pay the bills, subsist. **live in** ▷ INHABIT. **live on** ▷ EAT.

liveliness *n* activity, animation, boisterousness, bustle, dynamism, energy, enthusiasm, exuberance, *inf* go, gusto, high spirits, spirit, sprightliness, verve, vigour, vitality, vivacity, zeal. *Opp* APATHY.

lively *adj* active, agile, alert, animated, boisterous, bubbly, bustling, busy, cheerful, colourful, dashing, eager, energetic, enthusiastic, exciting, expressive, exuberant, frisky, gay, high-spirited, irrepressible, jaunty, jazzy, jolly, merry, nimble, *inf* perky, playful, quick, spirited, sprightly, stimulating, strong, vigorous, vital, vivacious, vivid, *inf* zippy. ▷ HAPPY. *Opp* APATHETIC.

livestock *n* cattle, farm animals.

living *adj* active, actual, alive, animate, breathing, existing, extant, flourishing, functioning, live, living, *old use* quick, sentient, surviving, vigorous, vital. ▷ LIVELY. *Opp* DEAD, EXTINCT. • *n* income, livelihood, occupation, subsistence, way of life.

load *n* burden, cargo, consignment, freight, lading, lorry-load, shipment, van-load. **2** *load of responsibility*. *inf* albatross, anxiety, care, *inf* cross, encumbrance, *inf* millstone, onus, trouble, weight, worry. • *vb* **1** burden, encumber, fill, heap, overwhelm, pack, pile, ply, saddle, stack, stow, weigh down. **2** *load a gun*. charge, prime. **loaded** ▷ BIASED, LADEN, WEALTHY.

loafer *n* idler, *inf* good-for-nothing, layabout, *inf* lazybones, lounger, shirker, *sl* skiver, vagrant, wastrel.

loan *n* advance, credit, mortgage. • *vb* advance, allow, credit, lend.

loathe *vb* abhor, abominate, be averse to, be revolted by, despise, detest, dislike, execrate, find intolerable, hate, object to, recoil from, resent, scorn, shudder at. *Opp* LOVE.

lobby *n* **1** ante-room, corridor, entrance hall, entry, foyer, hall, hallway, porch, reception, vestibule. **2** *environmental lobby*. campaign, campaigners, pressure-group, supporters. • *vb* persuade, petition, pressurize, try to influence, urge.

local *adj* **1** adjacent, adjoining, nearby, neighbouring, serving the locality. **2** *local politics*. community, limited, narrow, neighbourhood, parochial, particular, provincial, regional. *Opp* GENERAL, NATIONAL. • *n* **1** inhabitant, resident, townsman, townswoman. **2** ▷ PUB.

locality *n* area, catchment area, community, district, location, neighbourhood, parish, region, residential area, town, vicinity, zone.

localize *vb* concentrate, confine, contain, enclose, keep within bounds, limit, narrow down, pin down, restrict. *Opp* SPREAD.

locate *vb* **1** come across, detect, discover, find, identify, *inf* lay your hands on, *inf* run to earth, search out, track down, unearth. **2** build, establish, find a place for, found, place, position, put, set up, site, situate, station.

location *n* **1** locale, locality, place, point, position, setting, site, situation, spot, venue, whereabouts. **2** *film locations*. background, scene, setting.

lock *n* bar, bolt, catch, clasp, fastening, hasp, latch, padlock.

• *vb* bolt, close, fasten, padlock, seal, secure, shut. **lock away** ▷ IMPRISON. **lock out** ▷ EXCLUDE. **lock up** ▷ IMPRISON.

lodge *n* ▷ HOUSE.
• *vb* 1 accommodate, billet, board, house, *inf* put up. 2 abide, dwell, live, *inf* put up, reside, stay, stop. 3 *lodge a complaint.* enter, file, make formally, put on record, record, register, submit.

lodger *n* boarder, guest, inmate, paying guest, resident, tenant.

lodgings *n* accommodation, apartment, billet, boarding-house, *inf* digs, lodging-house, *sl* pad, quarters, rooms, shelter, *sl* squat, temporary home.

lofty *adj* 1 elevated, high, imposing, majestic, noble, soaring, tall, towering. 2 ▷ ARROGANT.

log *n* 1 timber, wood. 2 account, diary, journal, record.

logic *n* clarity, deduction, intelligence, logical thinking, ratiocination, rationality, reasonableness, reasoning, sense, validity.

logical *adj* clear, cogent, coherent, consistent, deductive, intelligent, methodical, rational, reasonable, sensible, sound, *inf* step-by-step, structured, systematic, valid, well-reasoned, well-thought-out, wise. *Opp* ILLOGICAL.

loiter *vb* be slow, dally, dawdle, hang back, linger, *inf* loaf about, *inf* mess about, skulk, *inf* stand about, straggle.

lone *adj* isolated, separate, single, solitary, solo, unaccompanied. ▷ LONELY.

lonely *adj* 1 abandoned, alone, forlorn, forsaken, friendless, lonesome, loveless, neglected, outcast, reclusive, retiring, solitary, unsociable, withdrawn. 2 SAD. 2 *inf* cut off, deserted, desolate, distant, far-away, isolated, *inf* off the beaten track, out of the way, remote, secluded, unfrequented, uninhabited.

long *adj* big, drawn out, elongated, endless, extended, extensive, great, interminable, large, lasting, lengthy, longish, prolonged, protracted, slow, stretched, sustained, time-consuming, unending.
• *vb* crave, hanker, have a longing (for), hunger, *inf* itch, pine, thirst, wish, yearn. **long for** ▷ DESIRE. **long-lasting, long-lived** ▷ PERMANENT. **long-standing** ▷ OLD. **long-suffering** ▷ PATIENT. **long-winded** ▷ TEDIOUS.

longing *n* appetite, craving, desire, hankering, hunger, *inf* itch, need, thirst, urge, wish, yearning, *inf* yen.

look *n* 1 glance, glimpse, observation, peek, peep, sight, *inf* squint, view. 2 air, appearance, aspect, attractiveness, bearing, beauty, complexion, countenance, demeanour, expression, face, looks, manner, mien. • *vb* 1 behold, *inf* cast your eye, consider, contemplate, examine, eye, gape, *inf* gawp, gaze, glance, glimpse, goggle, have a look, inspect, observe, ogle, pay attention (to), peek, peep, peer, read, regard, scan, scrutinize, see, skim through, squint, stare, study, survey, *sl* take a dekko, take note (of), view, watch. 2 *The house looks south.* face, overlook. 3 *look pleased.* appear,

seem. **look after** ▷ TEND. **look
down on** ▷ DESPISE. **look for**
▷ SEEK. **look into** ▷ INVEST-
IGATE. **look out** ▷ BEWARE.
look up to ▷ ADMIRE.

look-out *n* guard, sentinel,
sentry, watchman.

loom *vb* appear, arise, dominate,
emerge, hover, impend, materialize, menace, rise, stand out,
stick up, take shape, threaten,
tower.

loop *n* bend, bow, circle, coil,
curl, eye, hoop, kink, noose,
ring, turn, twist, whorl.
● *vb* bend, coil, curl, entwine,
make a loop, turn, twist, wind.

loophole *n* escape, *inf* get-out,
inf let-out, outlet, way out.

loose *adj* 1 detachable, detached,
disconnected, independent,
insecure, loosened, movable,
moving, scattered, shaky, unattached, unconnected,
unfastened, unsteady, wobbly.
2 *loose animals*. at large, at
liberty, escaped, free, free-
range, released, roaming,
uncaged, unconfined, unfettered, unrestricted, untied.
3 *loose hair*. dangling, hanging,
spread out, straggling, trailing.
4 *loose clothing*. baggy,
inf floppy, loose-fitting, slack,
unbuttoned. 5 *loose thinking*.
broad, careless, casual, diffuse,
general, ill-defined, illogical,
imprecise, inexact, informal,
lax, rambling, rough, *inf*
sloppy, unscientific, unstructured, vague. *Opp* PRECISE,
SECURE, TIGHT. 6 ▷ IMMORAL.
● *vb* ▷ FREE, LOOSEN.

loosen *vb* 1 ease off, free, let go,
loose, make loose, relax,
release, separate, slacken,

unfasten, unloose, untie.
▷ UNDO. 2 become loose, come
adrift, open up. *Opp* TIGHTEN.

loot *n* booty, contraband, haul,
inf ill-gotten gains, plunder,
prize, spoils, *inf* swag, takings.
● *vb* despoil, pillage, plunder,
raid, ransack, ravage, rifle, rob,
sack, steal from.

lopsided *adj* askew, asymmetrical, awry, *inf* cockeyed,
crooked, one-sided, tilting,
unbalanced, unequal, uneven.

lord *n* aristocrat, noble, peer.
□ baron, count, duke, earl, old
use thane, viscount. ▷ RULER.

lose *vb* 1 be deprived of, cease to
have, drop, find yourself without, forfeit, forgo, leave (somewhere), mislay, misplace, miss,
part with, stray from. *Opp* FIND.
2 admit defeat, be defeated,
capitulate, *inf* come to grief,
fail, get beaten, get thrashed,
succumb, suffer defeat.
Opp WIN. 3 *lose your chance*.
fritter, let slip, squander, waste.
4 *lose pursuers*. escape from,
evade, get rid of, give the slip,
leave behind, outrun, shake off,
throw off. **losing** ▷ UNSUC-
CESSFUL.

loser *n* the defeated, runner-up,
the vanquished. *Opp* WINNER.

loss *n* bereavement, damage,
defeat, deficit, depletion,
deprivation, destruction,
diminution, disappearance,
erosion, failure, forfeiture,
impairment, privation, reduction, sacrifice. *Opp* GAIN.

losses casualties, deaths, death
toll, fatalities.

lost *adj* 1 abandoned, departed,
destroyed, disappeared, extinct,
forgotten, gone, irrecoverable,
irretrievable, left behind,

mislaid, misplaced, missing, strayed, untraceable, vanished. **2** absorbed, day-dreaming, dreamy, distracted, engrossed, preoccupied, rapt. **3** corrupt, damned, fallen. ▷ WICKED.

lot n *a lot in a sale.* ▷ ITEM. **a lot of, lots of** ▷ PLENTY. **draw lots** ▷ GAMBLE. **the lot** all (of), everything, the whole thing, *inf* the works.

lotion n balm, cream, embrocation, liniment, ointment, pomade, salve, unguent.

lottery n **1** raffle, sweepstake. **2** gamble, speculation, venture.

loud adj **1** audible, blaring, booming, clamorous, clarion (*call*), deafening, ear-splitting, echoing, fortissimo, high, noisy, penetrating, piercing, raucous, resounding, reverberant, reverberating, roaring, rowdy, shrieking, shrill, sonorous, stentorian, strident, thundering, thunderous, vociferous. **2** *loud colours.* ▷ GAUDY. *Opp* QUIET.

lounge n drawing-room, front room, living-room, parlour, salon, sitting-room. ● vb be idle, be lazy, dawdle, hang about, idle, *inf* kill time, laze, loaf, lie around, loiter, *inf* loll about, *inf* mess about, *inf* mooch about, relax, *inf* skive, slouch, slump, sprawl, stand about, take it easy, vegetate, waste time.

lout n boor, churl, rude person, oaf, *inf* yob.

lovable adj adorable, appealing, attractive, charming, cuddly, *inf* cute, *inf* darling, dear, enchanting, endearing, engaging, fetching, likeable, lovely,

pleasing, taking, winning, winsome. *Opp* HATEFUL.

love n **1** admiration, adoration, adulation, affection, ardour, attachment, attraction, desire, devotion, fancy, fervour, fondness, infatuation, liking, passion, regard, tenderness, warmth. ▷ FRIENDSHIP. **2** beloved, darling, dear, dearest, loved one. ▷ LOVER. ● vb **1** admire, adore, be charmed by, be fond of, be infatuated by, be in love with, care for, cherish, desire, dote on, fancy, *inf* have a crush on, have a passion for, idolize, lose your heart to, lust after, treasure, value, want, worship. ▷ LIKE. *Opp* HATE. **in love** besotted, devoted, enamoured, fond, *inf* head over heels, infatuated. **love affair** affair, amour, courtship, intrigue, liaison, relationship, romance. **make love** be intimate, *inf* canoodle, caress, copulate, court, cuddle, embrace, flirt, fornicate, have intercourse, have sex, kiss, mate, *sl* neck, *inf* pet, philander, *old use* spoon, woo. ▷ SEX.

loved adj beloved, cherished, darling, dear, dearest, esteemed, favourite, precious, treasured, valued, wanted.

loveless adj cold, frigid, heartless, passionless, undemonstrative, unfeeling, unloving, unresponsive. *Opp* LOVING. ▷ UNLOVED.

lovely adj appealing, attractive, charming, delightful, enjoyable, fine, good, nice, pleasant, pretty, sweet. ▷ BEAUTIFUL. *Opp* NASTY.

lover n admirer, boyfriend, companion, concubine,

fiancé(e), *old use* follower, friend, gigolo, girlfriend, *inf* intended, mate, mistress, *old use* paramour, suitor, sweetheart, *sl* toy boy, valentine.

lovesick *adj* frustrated, languishing, lovelorn, pining.

loving *adj* admiring, adoring, affectionate, amorous, ardent, attached, brotherly, caring, close, concerned, dear, demonstrative, devoted, doting, fatherly, fond, friendly, inseparable, kind, maternal, motherly, passionate, paternal, protective, sisterly, tender, warm.
▷ FRIENDLY, SEXY.
Opp LOVELESS.

low *adj* 1 flat, low-lying, sunken. 2 *low trees.* little, short, squat, stumpy, stunted. 3 *low status.* abject, base, degraded, humble, inferior, junior, lesser, lower, lowly, menial, miserable, modest, servile. 4 *low behaviour.* churlish, coarse, common, cowardly, crude, *old use* dastardly, disreputable, ignoble, mean, nasty, vulgar, wicked.
▷ IMMORAL. 5 *low sounds.* gentle, indistinct, muffled, murmurous, muted, pianissimo, quiet, soft, subdued, whispered. 6 *low notes.* bass, deep, reverberant. *Opp* HIGH. **in low spirits** ▷ SAD. **low point** ▷ NADIR.

lowbrow *adj* accessible, easy, ordinary, pop, popular, *derog* rubbishy, simple, straightforward, *derog* trashy, *derog* uncultured, undemanding, unpretentious, unsophisticated. *Opp* HIGHBROW.

lower *vb* 1 dip, drop, haul down, let down, take down. 2 *lower prices.* bring down, cut, decrease, discount, lessen,

mark down, reduce, *inf* slash. 3 *lower the volume.* abate, diminish, quieten, tone down, turn down. 4 *lower yourself.* abase, belittle, debase, degrade, demean, discredit, disgrace, humble, humiliate, stoop. *Opp* RAISE.

lowly *adj* base, humble, insignificant, little-known, low, low-born, meek, modest, obscure, unimportant.
▷ ORDINARY. *Opp* EMINENT.

loyal *adj* committed, constant, dedicated, dependable, devoted, dutiful, faithful, honest, patriotic, reliable, sincere, stable, staunch, steadfast, steady, true, trustworthy, trusty, unswerving, unwavering. *Opp* DISLOYAL.

loyalty *n* allegiance, constancy, dedication, dependability, devotion, duty, faithfulness, fealty, fidelity, honesty, patriotism, reliability, staunchness, steadfastness, trustworthiness. *Opp* DISLOYALTY.

lubricate *vb* grease, oil.

luck *n* 1 accident, chance, coincidence, destiny, fate, *inf* fluke, fortune, serendipity. 2 *wished her luck.* inf break, good fortune, happiness, prosperity, success.

lucky *adj* 1 accidental, appropriate, chance, *inf* fluky, fortuitous, opportune, providential, timely, unintentional, unplanned, welcome. 2 blessed, favoured, fortunate, successful.
▷ HAPPY. 3 *lucky number.* advantageous, auspicious. *Opp* UNLUCKY.

luggage *n* baggage, belongings, *inf* gear, impedimenta, paraphernalia, *inf* things. □ bag, *basket, box, brief-case, case, chest, hamper, handbag, hand luggage, haversack, holdall, knapsack, pannier,* old use *portmanteau, purse, rucksack, satchel, suitcase, trunk, wallet.*

lukewarm *adj* 1 room temperature, tepid, warm. 2 apathetic, cool, half-hearted, indifferent, unenthusiastic.

lull *n* break, calm, delay, gap, halt, hiatus, interlude, interruption, interval, lapse, *inf* let-up, pause, respite, rest, silence.
• *vb* calm, hush, pacify, quell, quieten, soothe, subdue, tranquillize.

lumber *n* 1 beams, boards, planks, timber, wood. 2 bits and pieces, clutter, jumble, junk, litter, odds and ends, rubbish, trash, *inf* white elephants. • *vb* 1 blunder, move clumsily, shamble, trudge. 2 ▷ BURDEN.

luminous *adj* bright, glowing, luminescent, lustrous, phosphorescent, radiant, refulgent, shining. ▷ LIGHT.

lump *n* 1 ball, bar, bit, block, cake, chunk, clod, clot, cube, *inf* dollop, gob, gobbet, hunk, ingot, mass, nugget, piece, slab, wad, wedge, *inf* wodge. 2 boil, bulge, bump, carbuncle, cyst, excrescence, growth, hump, knob, node, nodule, protrusion, protuberance, spot, swelling, tumescence, tumour. • *vb* **lump together** ▷ COMBINE.

lunacy *n* delirium, dementia, derangement, frenzy, hysteria, illogicality, insanity, madness, mania, psychosis, unreason. ▷ STUPIDITY.

lunatic *adj* ▷ MAD. • *n inf* crackpot, *inf* crank, *inf* loony,

madman, madwoman, maniac, *inf* mental case, *inf* nutcase, *inf* nutter, psychopath, psychotic.

lunge *vb* 1 jab, stab, strike, thrust. 2 charge, dash, dive, lurch, plunge, pounce, rush, spring, throw yourself.

lurch *vb* heave, lean, list, lunge, pitch, plunge, reel, roll, stagger, stumble, sway, totter, wallow. **leave in the lurch** ▷ ABANDON.

lure *vb* allure, attract, bait, charm, coax, decoy, draw, entice, induce, inveigle, invite, lead on, persuade, seduce, tempt.

lurid *adj* 1 bright, gaudy, glaring, glowing, striking, vivid. 2 ▷ SENSATIONAL.

lurk *vb* crouch, hide, lie in wait, lie low, prowl, skulk, steal.

luscious *adj* appetizing, delectable, delicious, juicy, mouthwatering, rich, succulent, sweet, tasty.

lust *n* 1 carnality, concupiscence, desire, lasciviousness, lechery, libido, licentiousness, passion, sensuality, sexuality. 2 appetite, craving, greed, hunger, itch, longing.

lustful *adj* carnal, concupiscent, erotic, lascivious, lecherous, lewd, libidinous, licentious, on heat, passionate, *sl* randy, salacious, sensual, *sl* turned on. ▷ SEXY.

lustrous *adj* burnished, glazed, gleaming, glossy, metallic, polished, reflective, sheeny, shiny.

luxuriant *adj* 1 abundant, ample, copious, dense, exuberant, fertile, flourishing, green, lush, opulent, plenteous, plentiful, profuse, prolific, rank, rich, teeming, thick, thriving, verdant. 2 ▷ ORNATE. *Opp* SPARSE.

luxurious *adj* comfortable, costly, expensive, extravagant, grand, hedonistic, lavish, lush, magnificent, opulent, pampered, *inf* plush, *inf* posh, rich, *inf* ritzy, self-indulgent, splendid, sumptuous, sybaritic, voluptuous. *Opp* SPARTAN.

luxury *n* affluence, comfort, ease, enjoyment, extravagance, grandeur, hedonism, high living, indulgence, magnificence, opulence, pleasure, relaxation, self-indulgence, splendour, sumptuousness, voluptuousness.

lying *adj* crooked, deceitful, deceptive, dishonest, double-dealing, duplicitous, false, hypocritical, inaccurate, insincere, mendacious, misleading, perfidious, unreliable, untrustworthy, untruthful. *Opp* TRUTHFUL. ● *n* deceit, deception, dishonesty, duplicity, falsehood, *inf* fibbing, hypocrisy, mendacity, perfidy, perjury, prevarication.

lyrical *adj* emotional, expressive, impassioned, inspired, melodious, musical, poetic, rapturous, rhapsodic, song-like, sweet, tuneful. *Opp* PROSAIC.

M

macabre *adj* eerie, fearsome, frightful, ghoulish, grim, grisly, grotesque, gruesome, morbid, *inf* sick, unhealthy, weird.

machine *n* appliance, contraption, contrivance, device, engine, gadget, implement, instrument, mechanism, motor, robot, tool. ▷ MACHINERY.

machinery *n* 1 apparatus, equipment, gear, machines, plant. 2 constitution, method, organization, procedure, structure, system.

mackintosh *n* anorak, cape, mac, sou'wester, waterproof. ▷ COAT.

mad *adj* 1 *inf* batty, berserk, *inf* bonkers, *inf* certified, *inf* crackers, crazed, crazy, *inf* daft, delirious, demented, deranged, disordered, distracted, *inf* dotty, eccentric, fanatical, frantic, frenzied, hysterical, insane, irrational, *inf* loony, lunatic, maniacal, manic, *inf* mental, moonstruck, *Lat* non compos mentis, *inf* nutty, *inf* off your head, *inf* off your rocker, *inf* out of your mind, possessed, *inf* potty, psychotic, *inf* queer in the head, *inf* round the bend, *inf* round the twist, *inf* screwy, *inf* touched, unbalanced, unhinged, unstable, *inf* up the pole, wild. *Opp* SANE. 2 *a mad comedy*. ▷ ABSURD. 3 ▷ ANGRY. 4 ▷ ENTHUSIASTIC.

madden *vb* anger, craze, derange, *inf* drive crazy, enrage, exasperate, excite, incense, inflame, infuriate, irritate, make you mad, *inf* make your blood boil, *inf* make you see red, provoke, *inf* send you round the bend, unhinge, vex.

madman, madwoman *ns* *inf* crackpot, *inf* crank, eccentric, *inf* loony, lunatic, maniac, *inf* mental case, *inf* nutcase, *inf* nutter, psychopath, psychotic.

madness *n* delirium, dementia, derangement, eccentricity, folly, frenzy, hysteria, illogicality, insanity, lunacy, mania, mental illness, psychosis, unreason. ▷ STUPIDITY.

magazine *n* **1** comic, journal, monthly, newspaper, pamphlet, paper, periodical, publication, quarterly, weekly. **2** *magazine of weapons*. ammunition dump, armoury, arsenal, storehouse.

magic *adj* **1** conjuring, miraculous, mystic, necromantic, supernatural. **2** bewitching, charming, enchanting, entrancing, magical, spellbinding. ● *n* **1** black magic, charm, enchantment, hocus-pocus, incantation, *inf* mumbo-jumbo, necromancy, occultism, sorcery, spell, voodoo, witchcraft, witchery, wizardry. **2** conjuring, illusion, legerdemain, sleight of hand, trickery, tricks.

magician *n* conjuror, enchanter, enchantress, illusionist, magus, necromancer, sorcerer, *old use* warlock, witch, witchdoctor, wizard.

magnetic *adj* alluring, attractive, bewitching, captivating, charismatic, charming, compelling, engaging, enthralling, entrancing, fascinating, hypnotic, inviting, irresistible,

seductive, spellbinding. *Opp* REPULSIVE.

magnetism *n* allure, appeal, attractiveness, charisma, charm, drawing power, fascination, irresistibility, lure, power, pull, seductiveness.

magnificent *adj* awe-inspiring, beautiful, distinguished, excellent, fine, glorious, gorgeous, grand, grandiose, great, imposing, impressive, majestic, marvellous, noble, opulent, *inf* posh, regal, resplendent, rich, spectacular, splendid, stately, sumptuous, superb, wonderful. *Opp* ORDINARY.

magnify *vb* **1** amplify, augment, *inf* blow up, enlarge, expand, increase, intensify, make larger. *Opp* SHRINK. **2** *magnify difficulties*. *inf* blow up out of proportion, dramatize, exaggerate, heighten, inflate, make too much of, maximize, overdo, overestimate, overstate. *Opp* MINIMIZE.

magnitude *n* bigness, enormousness, extent, greatness, immensity, importance, size.

mail *n* correspondence, letters, parcels, post. ● *vb* dispatch, forward, post, send.

maim *vb* cripple, disable, hamstring, handicap, incapacitate, lame, mutilate. ▷ WOUND.

main *adj* basic, biggest, cardinal, central, chief, critical, crucial, dominant, dominating, essential, first, foremost, fundamental, greatest, largest, leading, major, most important, outstanding, paramount, predominant, pre-eminent, prevailing, primary, prime, principal, special, strongest, supreme, top, vital. *Opp* MINOR.

mainly *adv* above all, as a rule, chiefly, especially, essentially, first and foremost, generally, in the main, largely, mostly, normally, on the whole, predominantly, primarily, principally, usually.

maintain *vb* 1 carry on, continue, hold to, keep going, keep up, perpetuate, persevere in, persist in, preserve, retain, stick to, sustain. 2 *maintain a car.* care for, keep in good condition, look after, service, take care of. 3 *maintain a family.* feed, keep, pay for, provide for, stand by, support. 4 *maintain your innocence.* affirm, allege, argue, assert, aver, claim, contend, declare, defend, insist, proclaim, profess, state, uphold.

maintenance *n* 1 care, conservation, looking after, preservation, repairs, servicing, upkeep. 2 alimony, allowance, contribution, subsistence, support.

majestic *adj* august, awe-inspiring, awesome, dignified, distinguished, elevated, exalted, glorious, grand, grandiose, imperial, imposing, impressive, kingly, lofty, lordly, magisterial, magnificent, monumental, noble, pompous, princely, queenly, regal, royal, splendid, stately, striking, sublime.

majesty *n* awesomeness, dignity, glory, grandeur, kingliness, loftiness, magnificence, nobility, pomp, royalty, splendour, stateliness, sublimity.

major *adj* bigger, chief, considerable, extensive, greater, important, key, larger, leading, outstanding, principal, serious, significant. ▷ MAIN. *Opp* MINOR.

majority *n* 1 *inf* best part, *inf* better part, bulk, greater number, mass, preponderance. 2 adulthood, coming of age, manhood, maturity, womanhood. **be in the majority** ▷ DOMINATE.

make *n* brand, kind, model, sort, type, variety. ● *vb* 1 assemble, beget, bring about, build, compose, constitute, construct, contrive, craft, create, devise, do, engender, erect, execute, fabricate, fashion, forge, form, frame, generate, invent, make up, manufacture, mass-produce, originate, produce, put together, think up. 2 *make dinner.* concoct, cook, *inf* fix, prepare. 3 *make clothes.* knit, *inf* run up, sew, weave. 4 *make an effigy.* carve, cast, model, mould, sculpt, shape. 5 *make a speech.* deliver, pronounce, utter. ▷ SPEAK. 6 *made her chairperson.* appoint, elect, nominate, ordain. 7 *make P into B.* alter, change, convert, modify, transform, turn. 8 *make a fortune.* earn, gain, get, obtain, receive. 9 *make a good employee.* become, change into, grow into, turn into. 10 *make your objective.* accomplish, achieve, arrive at, attain, catch, get to, reach, win. 11 *2 + 2 makes 4.* add up to, amount to, come to, total. 12 *make rules.* agree, arrange, codify, establish, decide on, draw up, fix, write. 13 *make her happy.* cause to become, render. 14 *make trouble.* bring about, carry out, cause, give rise to, provoke, result in. 15 *make them obey.* coerce, compel, constrain, force, induce, oblige, order, pressurize, prevail on,

require. **make amends**
▷ COMPENSATE. **make believe**
▷ IMAGINE. **make fun of**
▷ RIDICULE. **make good**
▷ PROSPER. **make love** ▷ LOVE.
make off ▷ DEPART. **make off
with** ▷ STEAL. **make out**
▷ UNDERSTAND. **make up**
▷ INVENT. **make up for**
▷ COMPENSATE. **make up your
mind** ▷ DECIDE.

make-believe *adj* fanciful,
feigned, imaginary, made-up,
mock, *inf* pretend, pretended,
sham, simulated, unreal.
● *n* dream, fantasy, play-acting,
pretence, self-deception,
unreality.

maker *n* architect, author,
builder, creator, director, manufacturer, originator, producer.

makeshift *adj* emergency,
improvised, provisional, stopgap, temporary.

maladjusted *adj* disturbed,
muddled, neurotic, unbalanced.

male *adj* manly, masculine,
virile. ● *n* □ bachelor, *inf* bloke,
boy, boyfriend, *inf* bridegroom,
brother, chap, *inf* codger, father,
fellow, gentleman, groom,
inf guy, husband, lad, lover,
man, son, *inf* squire, uncle,
widower. □ buck, bull, cock, dog,
ram, stallion, tom(cat).
Opp FEMALE.

malefactor *n* delinquent, lawbreaker, offender, villain,
wrongdoer. ▷ CRIMINAL.

malice *n* animosity,
inf bitchiness, bitterness,
inf cattiness, enmity, hatred,
hostility, ill-will, malevolence,
maliciousness, malignity, nasti-
ness, rancour, spite, spitefulness, vengefulness, venom,
viciousness, vindictiveness.

malicious *adj inf* bitchy, bitter,
inf catty, evil, evil-minded,
hateful, ill-natured, malevolent,
malignant, mischievous, nasty,
rancorous, revengeful, sly,
spiteful, vengeful, venomous,
vicious, villainous, vindictive,
wicked. *Opp* KIND.

malignant *adj* dangerous,
deadly, destructive, fatal, harmful, injurious, life-threatening,
poisonous, *inf* terminal, uncontrollable, virulent.
▷ MALICIOUS.

malleable *adj* ductile, plastic,
pliable, soft, tractable, workable. *Opp* BRITTLE.

malnutrition *n* famine, hunger,
starvation, undernourishment.

man *n* 1 [*either sex*] ▷ MANKIND.
2 ▷ MALE. ● *vb* cover, crew,
provide staff for, staff.

manage *vb* 1 administer, be in
charge of, be manager of,
command, conduct, control,
direct, dominate, govern, head,
lead, look after, mastermind,
operate, organize, oversee,
preside over, regulate, rule,
run, superintend, supervise,
take care of, take control of,
take over. 2 *manage your jobs.*
accomplish, achieve, bring
about, carry out, contend with,
cope with, deal with, do, finish,
get through, handle, manipulate, muddle through,
perform, sort out, succeed in,
undertake. 3 *Can you manage?*
cope, fend for yourself,
inf make it, scrape by, shift for
yourself, succeed, survive.
4 *can manage £10.* afford, spare.

manageable *adj* 1 acceptable,
convenient, easy to manage,
handy, neat, reasonable.
Opp AWKWARD. 2 amenable,

compliant, controllable, disciplined, docile, governable, submissive, tame, tractable. ▷ OBEDIENT. *Opp* DISOBEDIENT.

manager, manageress *ns* administrator, *inf* boss, chief, controller, director, executive, foreman, forewoman, governor, head, organizer, overseer, proprietor, ruler, superintendent, supervisor. ▷ CHIEF.

mandatory *adj* compulsory, essential, necessary, needed, obligatory, required, requisite.

mangle *vb* butcher, cripple, crush, cut, damage, deform, disfigure, hack, injure, lacerate, maim, maul, mutilate, ruin, spoil, squash, tear, wound.

mangy *adj* dirty, filthy, motheaten, nasty, scabby, scruffy, shabby, slovenly, squalid, *inf* tatty, unkempt, wretched.

manhandle *vb* 1 carry, haul, heave, hump, lift, manoeuvre, move, pull, push. 2 abuse, batter, *inf* beat up, ill-treat, knock about, maltreat, mistreat, misuse, *inf* rough up, treat roughly.

mania *n* craving, craze, enthusiasm, fad, fetish, frenzy, infatuation, obsession, passion, preoccupation, rage. ▷ MADNESS.

maniac *n* lunatic, psychopath, psychotic. ▷ MADMAN.

manifest *adj* apparent, blatant, clear, conspicuous, discernible, evident, explicit, glaring, noticeable, obvious, patent, plain, recognizable, undisguised, visible. ● *vb* ▷ SHOW.

manifesto *n* declaration, policy statement.

manipulate *vb* 1 feel, massage, rub, stimulate. 2 *manipulate*

people. control, direct, engineer, exploit, guide, handle, influence, manage, manoeuvre, orchestrate, steer.

mankind *n Lat* homo sapiens, human beings, humanity, humankind, the human race, man, men and women, mortals, people.

manly *adj* chivalrous, gallant, heroic, *inf* macho, male, mannish, masculine, strong, swashbuckling, vigorous, virile. ▷ BRAVE. *Opp* EFFEMINATE.

man-made *adj* artificial, imitation, manufactured, mass-produced, processed, simulated, synthetic, unnatural. *Opp* NATURAL.

manner *n* 1 approach, fashion, means, method, mode, procedure, process, style, technique, way. 2 air, aspect, attitude, bearing, behaviour, character, conduct, demeanour, deportment, disposition, look, mien. 3 *all manner of things*. genre, kind, sort, type, variety.

manners *plur n* behaviour, breeding, civility, conduct, courtesy, decorum, etiquette, gentility, politeness, protocol, refinement, social graces.

mannerism *n* characteristic, habit, idiosyncrasy, peculiarity, quirk, trait.

manoeuvre *n* device, dodge, gambit, intrigue, move, operation, plan, plot, ploy, ruse, scheme, stratagem, strategy, tactics, trick. ● *vb* contrive, engineer, guide, jockey, manipulate, move, navigate, negotiate, pilot, steer.

manoeuvres army exercise, operation, training.

mansion n castle, château, manor, manor-house, palace, stately home, villa. ▷ HOUSE.

mantle n cape, cloak, covering, hood, shawl, shroud, wrap. • vb ▷ COVER.

manufacture vb assemble, build, construct, create, fabricate, make, mass-produce, prefabricate, process, put together, inf turn out. **manufactured** ▷ MAN-MADE.

manufacturer n factory-owner, industrialist, maker, producer.

manure n compost, dung, fertilizer, inf muck.

manuscript n document, papers, script. ▷ BOOK.

many adj abundant, assorted, copious, countless, diverse, frequent, innumerable, multifarious, myriad, numberless, numerous, profuse, inf umpteen, uncountable, untold, varied, various. Opp FEW.

map n chart, diagram, plan.

mar vb blight, blot, damage, deface, disfigure, harm, hurt, impair, ruin, spoil, stain, taint, tarnish, wreck.

marauder n bandit, buccaneer, invader, pirate, plunderer, raider.

march n cortège, demonstration, march-past, parade, procession, progress. • vb file, pace, parade, step, stride, troop. ▷ WALK.

margin n 1 border, boundary, brink, edge, frieze, perimeter, periphery, rim, side, verge. 2 allowance, latitude, leeway, room, scope, space.

marginal adj borderline, doubtful, insignificant, minimal, negligible, peripheral, slight, small, unimportant.

marital adj conjugal, matrimonial, nuptial.

mark n 1 blemish, blot, blotch, dent, dot, fingermark, plur graffiti, impression, line, marking, pockmark, print, scar, scratch, scribble, smear, smudge, smut, inf splotch, spot, stain, plur stigmata, streak, trace, vestige. 2 mark of breeding. characteristic, feature, indication, indicator, marker, token. 3 identifying mark. badge, brand, device, emblem, fingerprint, hallmark, label, seal, sign, stamp, standard, symbol, trademark.
• vb 1 blemish, blot, brand, bruise, cut, damage, deface, dent, dirty, disfigure, draw on, make a mark on, mar, scar, scratch, scrawl over, scribble on, smudge, spot, stain, stamp, streak, tattoo, write on. 2 mark pupils' work. appraise, assess, correct, evaluate, grade, tick. 3 mark my words. attend to, heed, listen to, mind, note, notice, observe, pay attention to, take note of, take seriously, inf take to heart, watch.

market n auction, bazaar, exchange, fair, marketplace, sale. ▷ SHOP. • vb advertise, deal in, make available, merchandise, peddle, promote, put on the market, retail, sell, inf tout, trade, trade in, try to sell, vend.

marksman n crack shot, gunman, sharpshooter, sniper.

maroon vb abandon, cast away, desert, forsake, isolate, leave, put ashore, strand.

marriage n 1 matrimony, partnership, union, wedlock. 2 nuptials, union, wedding.

□ bigamy, monogamy, poly-
gamy.

marriageable adj adult,
mature, nubile.

marry vb espouse, inf get
hitched, inf get spliced, join in
matrimony, inf tie the knot,
unite, wed.

marsh n bog, fen, marshland,
morass, mud, mudflats, quagmire, quicksands, saltings, salt-
marsh, old use slough, swamp,
wetland.

marshal vb arrange, assemble,
collect, deploy, draw up, gather,
group, line up, muster, organize, set out.

martial adj aggressive, bellicose, belligerent, militant, military, pugnacious, soldierly,
warlike. Opp PEACEABLE.

marvel n miracle, phenomenon,
wonder. ● vb marvel at
admire, applaud, be amazed by,
be astonished by, be surprised
by, gape at, praise, wonder at.

marvellous adj admirable,
amazing, astonishing, astounding, breathtaking, excellent,
exceptional, extraordinary,
inf fabulous, inf fantastic, glorious, impressive, incredible,
magnificent, miraculous, out of
the ordinary, inf out of this
world, phenomenal, praiseworthy, prodigious, remarkable,
inf sensational, spectacular,
splendid, staggering, stunning,
stupendous, inf super, superb,
surprising, inf terrific, unbelievable, wonderful, wondrous.
Opp ORDINARY.

masculine adj boyish, inf butch,
gentlemanly, heroic, inf macho,
male, manly, mannish, muscular, powerful, strong, vigorous,
virile. Opp FEMININE.

mash vb beat, crush, grind,
mangle, pound, pulp, pulverize,
smash, squash.

mask n camouflage, cloak, cover,
cover-up, disguise, façade,
front, guise, screen, shield, veil,
visor. ● vb blot out, camouflage,
cloak, conceal, cover, disguise,
hide, obscure, screen, shield,
shroud, veil.

masonry n bricks, brickwork,
stone, stonework.

mass adj comprehensive,
general, large-scale, popular,
universal, wholesale, widespread. ● n 1 accumulation,
agglomeration, aggregation,
body, bulk, inf chunk, collection, concretion, conglomeration, inf dollop, heap, hoard,
inf hunk, inf load, lot, lump,
mound, mountain, pile, profusion, quantity, stack, volume.
2 ▷ GROUP. ● vb accumulate,
aggregate, amass, assemble,
collect, congregate, convene,
flock together, gather, marshal,
meet, mobilize, muster, pile up,
rally.

massacre vb annihilate, slaughter. ▷ KILL.

massage vb knead, manipulate,
rub.

mast n aerial, flagpole, maypole,
pylon, transmitter.

master n 1 inf boss, employer,
governor, keeper, lord, overseer, owner, person in charge,
proprietor, ruler, taskmaster.
▷ CHIEF. 2 captain, skipper.
3 master of an art. inf ace,
authority, expert, genius,
mastermind, maestro, virtuoso.
4 ▷ TEACHER. ● vb 1 become
expert in, inf get off by heart,
inf get the hang of, grasp,
know, learn, understand.
2 break in, bridle, check,

conquer, control, curb, defeat, dominate, *inf* get the better of, govern, manage, overcome, overpower, quell, regulate, repress, rule, subdue, subjugate, suppress, tame, triumph over, vanquish.

masterly *adj* accomplished, adroit, consummate, dexterous, excellent, expert, masterful, matchless, practised, proficient, skilful, skilled, unsurpassable.

mastermind *n* architect, brains, conceiver, contriver, creator, engineer, expert, genius, intellectual, inventor, manager, originator, planner, prime mover. ● *vb* carry through, conceive, contrive, devise, direct, engineer, execute, manage, organize, originate, plan, plot. ▷ MANAGE.

masterpiece *n* best work, *Fr* chef-d'oeuvre, classic, *inf* hit, *Lat* magnum opus, masterwork, *Fr* pièce de résistance.

match *n* 1 bout, competition, contest, duel, game, test match, tie, tournament, tourney. 2 *met my match.* complement, counterpart, double, equal, equivalent, twin. 3 *a good match.* combination, fit, pair, similarity. 4 *a love match.* alliance, friendship, marriage, partnership, relationship, union. ● *vb* 1 agree, accord, be compatible, be equivalent, be the same, be similar, blend, coincide, combine, compare, coordinate, correspond, fit, *inf* go together, harmonize, suit, tally, tie in, tone in. *Opp* CONTRAST. 2 ally, combine, fit, join, link up, marry, mate, pair off, pair up, put together, team up. *Opp* SPLIT. **matching** ▷ SIMILAR.

mate *n* 1 *inf* better half, companion, consort, helpmeet, husband, partner, spouse, wife. ▷ FRIEND. 2 assistant, associate, collaborator, colleague, helper. ● *vb* become partners, copulate, couple, have intercourse, *inf* have sex, join, marry, *inf* pair up, unite, wed.

material *adj* concrete, corporeal, palpable, physical, solid, substantial, tangible. ● *n* 1 fabric, stuff, textile. ▷ CLOTH. 2 components, constituents, content, data, facts, ideas, information, matter, notes, resources, statistics, stuff, subject matter, substance, supplies, things.

materialize *vb* appear, become visible, emerge, occur, take shape, *inf* turn up.

mathematics *n* mathematical science, *inf* maths, number work. □ addition, algebra, arithmetic, calculus, division, geometry, multiplication, operational research, statistics, subtraction, trigonometry.

matted *adj* knotted, tangled, uncombed, unkempt. ▷ DISHEVELLED.

matter *n* 1 body, material, stuff, substance. 2 discharge, pus, suppuration. 3 *a matter of life and death.* affair, business, concern, episode, event, fact, incident, issue, occurrence, question, situation, subject, thing, topic. 4 *What's the matter?* difficulty, problem, trouble, upset, worry. ● *vb* be important, be of consequence, be significant, count, make a difference, mean something, signify. **matter-of-fact** ▷ PROSAIC.

mature adj 1 adult, advanced, experienced, full-grown, grown-up, nubile, of age, perfect, sophisticated, well-developed. 2 mellow, ready, ripe, seasoned. *Opp* IMMATURE. • *vb* age, come to fruition, develop, grow up, mellow, reach maturity, ripen.

maturity n adulthood, completion, majority, mellowness, perfection, readiness, ripeness.

maul vb claw, injure, *inf* knock about, lacerate, mangle, manhandle, mutilate, paw, savage, treat roughly, wound.

maximize vb 1 add to, augment, build up, increase, make the most of. 2 inflate, magnify, overdo, overstate.
▷ EXAGGERATE. *Opp* MINIMIZE.

maximum adj biggest, extreme, full, fullest, greatest, highest, largest, maximal, most, peak, supreme, top, topmost, utmost, uttermost. • n apex, ceiling, climax, extreme, highest point, peak, pinnacle, top, upper limit, zenith. *Opp* MINIMUM.

maybe adv conceivably, perhaps, possibly.

maze n complex, confusion, convolution, labyrinth, network, tangle, web.

meadow n field, *old use* mead, paddock, pasture.

meagre adj deficient, inadequate, insufficient, lean, mean, paltry, poor, puny, scanty, skimpy, slight, sparse, thin, unsatisfying. ▷ SMALL. *Opp* GENEROUS.

meal n *inf* blow-out, *old use* collation, repast, *inf* spread. □ *banquet, barbecue, breakfast, buffet, dinner, inf elevenses, feast, high tea, lunch, luncheon, picnic, snack, supper, take-away, tea, tea-break, old use tiffin.*

mean adj 1 beggarly, *inf* cheeseparing, close, close-fisted, illiberal, *inf* mingy, miserly, niggardly, parsimonious, *inf* penny-pinching, selfish, sparing, stingy, *inf* tight, tight-fisted, ungenerous. 2 *a mean disposition*. callous, churlish, contemptible, cruel, despicable, hard-hearted, ignoble, ill-tempered, malicious, nasty, shabby, shameful, small-minded, *inf* sneaky, spiteful, uncharitable, unkind, vicious. 3 *a mean dwelling*. base, common, humble, inferior, insignificant, low, lowly, miserable, poor, shabby, squalid, wretched. *Opp* GENEROUS, VALUABLE. • *vb* 1 augur, betoken, communicate, connote, convey, denote, *inf* drive at, express, foretell, *inf* get over, herald, hint at, imply, indicate, intimate, portend, presage, refer to, represent, say, show, signal, signify, specify, spell out, stand for, suggest, symbolize. 2 *I mean to succeed*. aim, desire, have in mind, hope, intend, plan, propose, purpose, want, wish. 3 *The job means long hours*. entail, involve, necessitate.

meander vb ramble, rove, snake, twist and turn, wander, wind, zigzag. **meandering** ▷ TWISTY.

meaning n connotation, content, definition, denotation, drift, explanation, force, gist, idea, implication, import, importance, interpretation, message, point, purport, purpose, relevance, sense, significance, signification, substance, thrust, value.

meaningful adj deep, eloquent, expressive, meaning, pointed, positive, pregnant, relevant, serious, significant, suggestive, telling, tell-tale, weighty, worth-while. Opp MEANINGLESS.

meaningless adj 1 absurd, coded, incomprehensible, incoherent, inconsequential, irrelevant, nonsensical, pointless, senseless. 2 *meaningless compliments*. empty, flattering, hollow, insincere, shallow, silly, sycophantic, vacuous, worthless. Opp MEANINGFUL.

means n 1 ability, capacity, channel, course, fashion, machinery, manner, medium, method, mode, process, way. 2 *private means*. ▷ WEALTH.

measurable adj appreciable, considerable, perceptible, quantifiable, reasonable, significant. Opp NEGLIGIBLE.

measure n 1 allocation, allowance, amount, amplitude, extent, magnitude, portion, quantity, quota, range, ration, scope, size, unit. ▷ MEASUREMENT. 2 criterion, inf litmus test, standard, test, touchstone, yardstick. 3 *measures to curb crime*. act, action, bill, control, course of action, expedient, law, means, procedure, step.
• vb assess, calculate, calibrate, compute, count, determine, estimate, gauge, judge, mark out, meter, plumb (depth), quantify, rank, rate, reckon, survey, take measurements of, weigh. **measure out** ▷ DISPENSE.

measurement n amount, calculation, dimensions, extent, figure, mensuration, size. ▷ MEASURE. □ area, breadth, bulk, capacity, depth, distance, height, length, mass, speed, time, volume, weight, width. □ acreage, footage, mileage, tonnage.

meat n flesh. ▷ FOOD. □ bacon, beef, chicken, game, gammon, ham, lamb, mutton, pork, poultry, turkey, veal, venison. □ brawn, breast, burger, brisket, chine, chops, chuck, cutlet, fillet, flank, hamburger, leg, loin, mince, offal, pâté, potted meat, rib, rissole, rump, sausage, scrag, shoulder, silverside, sirloin, spare-rib, steak, topside, tripe.

mechanic n engineer, technician.

mechanical adj 1 automated, automatic, machine-driven, technological. 2 cold, habitual, impersonal, inhuman, instinctive, lifeless, matter-of-fact, perfunctory, reflex, routine, soulless, unconscious, unemotional, unfeeling, unimaginative, uninspired, unthinking. Opp HUMAN.

mechanize vb automate, bring up to date, computerize, equip with machines, modernize.

medal n award, decoration, honour, medallion, prize, reward, trophy.

medallist n champion, victor, winner.

meddle vb inf be a busybody, butt in, interfere, inf poke your nose in, pry, snoop, tamper.

mediate vb act as go-between, act as mediator, arbitrate, intercede, liaise, negotiate.

mediator n arbiter, arbitrator, broker, conciliator, go-between, intercessor, intermediary, judge, liaison officer, middleman, moderator, negotiator, peacemaker, referee, umpire.

medicinal *adj* curative, healing, medical, remedial, restorative, therapeutic.

medicine *n* **1** healing, surgery, therapeutics, therapy, treatment. **2** cure, dose, drug, medicament, medication, nostrum, panacea, *old use* physic, prescription, remedy, treatment. □ anaesthetic, antibiotic, antidote, antiseptic, aspirin, capsule, gargle, herbal remedy, iodine, inhaler, linctus, lotion, lozenge, narcotic, ointment, painkiller, pastille, penicillin, pill, sedative, suppository, tablet, tonic, tranquillizer.

mediocre *adj* amateurish, average, *inf* common-or-garden, commonplace, everyday, fair, indifferent, inferior, medium, middling, moderate, ordinary, passable, pedestrian, poorish, *inf* run-of-the-mill, second-rate, *inf* so-so, undistinguished, unexceptional, unexciting, uninspired, unremarkable, weakish. *Opp* OUTSTANDING.

meditate *vb* be lost in thought, brood, celebrate, chew over, cogitate, consider, contemplate, deliberate, mull things over, muse, ponder, pray, reflect, ruminate, think, turn over.

meditation *n* cerebration, contemplation, deliberation, musing, prayer, reflection, rumination, thought, yoga.

meditative *adj* brooding, contemplative, pensive, prayerful, rapt, reflective, ruminative, thoughtful.

medium *adj* average, intermediate, mean, medial, median, mid, middle, middling, mid-sized, midway, moderate, normal, ordinary, standard, usual.

● *n* **1** average, centre, compromise, mean, middle, midpoint, norm. **2** approach, channel, form, means, method, mode, vehicle, way. **3** clairvoyant, seer, spiritualist. **the media**, **mass media** ▷ COMMUNICATION.

meek *adj* acquiescent, compliant, deferential, docile, forbearing, gentle, humble, long-suffering, lowly, mild, modest, non-militant, obedient, patient, peaceable, quiet, resigned, retiring, self-effacing, shy, soft, spineless, submissive, tame, timid, tractable, unambitious, unassuming, unprotesting, weak, *inf* wimpish. *Opp* AGGRESSIVE.

meet *vb* **1** *inf* bump into, chance upon, collide with, come across, confront, contact, encounter, face, happen on, have a meeting with, run across, run into, see. **2** be introduced to, make the acquaintance of. **3** come and fetch, greet, *inf* pick up, rendezvous with, welcome. **4** assemble, collect, come together, congregate, convene, forgather, gather, have a meeting, muster, rally, rendezvous. **5** *The ends don't meet.* abut, adjoin, come together, connect, converge, cross, intersect, join, link up, merge, touch, unite. **6** *meet a request.* acquiesce in, agree to, answer, comply with, deal with, fulfil, *inf* measure up to, observe, pay, satisfy, settle, take care of. **7** *meet difficulties.* encounter, endure, experience, go through, suffer, undergo.

meeting *n* **1** assembly, gathering, *inf* get-together, *inf* powwow. □ audience, board, briefing, cabinet, caucus, *committee, conclave, conference, congregation, congress, convention, council, discussion group, forum, prayer meeting, rally, seminar, service, synod.* **2** *appointment, assignation, date, engagement, inf* get-together, rendezvous, *old use* tryst. **3** *chance meeting.* confrontation, contact, encounter. **4** *meeting of lines, roads.* confluence (*of rivers*), convergence, crossing, crossroads, intersection, joining, junction, T-junction, union.

melancholy *adj* cheerless, dejected, depressed, depressing, despondent, disconsolate, dismal, dispirited, dispiriting, *inf* down, down-hearted, forlorn, gloomy, glum, joyless, lifeless, low, lugubrious, melancholic, miserable, moody, morose, mournful, sombre, sorrowful, unhappy, woebegone, woeful. ▷ SAD.
Opp CHEERFUL. ● *n* ▷ SADNESS.

mellow *adj* **1** mature, rich, ripe, smooth, sweet. **2** *mellow mood.* agreeable, genial, amiable, comforting, cordial, genial, gentle, happy, kindly, peaceful, pleasant, reassuring, soft, subdued, warm.
Opp HARSH. ● *vb* age, develop, improve with age, mature, ripen, soften, sweeten.

melodious *adj* dulcet, *inf* easy on the ear, euphonious, harmonious, lyrical, mellifluous, melodic, sweet, tuneful.

melodramatic *adj* emotional, exaggerated, *inf* hammy, histrionic, overdone, overdrawn, *inf* over the top, sensationalized, sentimental, theatrical.

melody *n* air, song, strain, subject, theme, tune.

melt *vb* deliquesce, dissolve, liquefy, soften, thaw, unfreeze.
melt away ▷ DISAPPEAR.

member *n* associate, colleague, fellow, life-member, paid-up member.

memorable *adj* catchy (*tune*), distinguished, extraordinary, haunting, historic, impressive, indelible, ineradicable, never-to-be-forgotten, notable, outstanding, remarkable, striking, unforgettable.

memorial *n* cairn, cenotaph, gravestone, headstone, monument, plaque, reminder, statue, tablet, tomb.

memorize *vb* commit to memory, *inf* get off by heart, learn, learn by rote, learn parrot-fashion, remember, retain.

memory *n* **1** ability to remember, recall, retention. **2** impression, recollection, reminder, reminiscence, souvenir. **3** *memory of the dead.* fame, honour, name, remembrance, reputation, respect.

menace *n* danger, peril, threat, warning. ● *vb* alarm, bully, cow, intimidate, terrify, terrorize, threaten. ▷ FRIGHTEN.

mend *vb* **1** fix, patch up, put right, rectify, remedy, renew, renovate, repair, restore. □ *beat out, darn, patch, replace parts, sew up, solder, stitch up, touch up, weld.* **2** *mend your ways.* ameliorate, amend, correct, cure, improve, make better, reform, revise. **3** *mend after illness.* convalesce, get better, heal, improve, recover, recuperate.

menial *adj* base, boring, common, degrading, demeaning, humble, inferior, insignifi-

cant, low, lowly, servile, slavish, subservient, unskilled,
unworthy. ● *n inf* dogsbody,
lackey, minion, slave, underling. ▷ SERVANT.

mental *adj* 1 abstract, cerebral,
cognitive, conceptual, intellectual, rational, theoretical.
2 *mental illness.* emotional,
psychological, subjective,
temperamental. ▷ MAD.

mentality *n* attitude, bent, character, disposition, frame of
mind, inclination, *inf* make-up,
outlook, personality, predisposition, propensity, psychology,
set, temperament, way of thinking.

mention *vb* acknowledge, allude
to, animadvert on, bring up,
broach, cite, comment on,
disclose, draw attention to,
enumerate, hint at, *inf* let drop,
let out, make known, make
mention, name, note, observe,
pay tribute to, point out, quote,
recognize, refer to, remark,
report, reveal, say, speak about,
touch on, write about.

mercenary *adj* acquisitive,
avaricious, covetous, grasping,
greedy, *inf* money-mad, venal.
● *n* ▷ FIGHTER.

merchandise *n* commodities,
goods, items for sale, produce,
products, stock.
● *vb* ▷ ADVERTISE.

merchant *n* broker, dealer,
distributor, retailer, salesman,
seller, shopkeeper, stockist,
supplier, trader, tradesman,
tradeswoman, vendor, wholesaler.

merciful *adj* beneficent, benevolent, charitable, clement,
compassionate, forbearing,
forgiving, generous, gracious,

humane, humanitarian, indulgent, kind, kind-hearted,
kindly, lenient, liberal,
magnanimous, mild, pitying,
inf soft, soft-hearted, sympathetic, tender-hearted, tolerant.
Opp MERCILESS.

merciless *adj* barbaric, barbarous, brutal, callous, cold, cruel,
cut-throat, hard, hard-hearted,
harsh, heartless, indifferent,
inexorable, inflexible, inhuman,
inhumane, intolerant, malevolent, pitiless, relentless,
remorseless, rigorous, ruthless,
savage, severe, stern, stony-
hearted, strict, tyrannical,
unbending, unfeeling, unforgiving, unkind, unmerciful, unrelenting, unremitting, vicious.
Opp MERCIFUL.

mercy *n* beneficence, benignity,
charity, clemency, compassion,
feeling, forbearance, forgiveness, generosity, grace,
humaneness, humanity, indulgence, kind-heartedness, kindness, leniency, love, pity,
quarter, sympathy, understanding.

merge *vb* 1 amalgamate, blend,
coalesce, combine, come
together, confederate, consoli-
ate, fuse, integrate, join
together, link up, mingle, mix,
pool, put together, unite.
2 *motorways merge.* converge,
join, meet. *Opp* SEPARATE.

merit *n* credit, distinction, excellence, good, goodness, importance, quality, strength, talent,
value, virtue, worth, worthiness. ● *vb* be entitled to, be
worthy of, deserve, earn, have
a right to, incur, justify, rate,
warrant.

meritorious *adj* admirable,
commendable, estimable, exem-

plary, honourable, laudable, praiseworthy, worthy.

merriment *n* amusement, cheerfulness, conviviality, exuberance, gaiety, glee, good cheer, high spirits, hilarity, jocularity, joking, jollity, joviality, *inf* larking about, laughter, levity, light-heartedness, liveliness, mirth, vivacity. ▷ MERRYMAKING.

merry *adj* bright, *inf* bubbly, carefree, cheerful, cheery, *inf* chirpy, convivial, festive, fun-loving, gay, glad, hilarious, jocular, jolly, jovial, joyful, joyous, light-hearted, lively, mirthful, rollicking, spirited, vivacious. ▷ HAPPY. *Opp* SERIOUS.

merrymaking *n* carousing, celebration, conviviality, festivity, frolic, fun, *inf* fun and games, *inf* jollification, *inf* junketing, merriment, revelry, roistering, sociability, *old use* wassailing. ▷ PARTY.

mesh *n* grid, lace, lacework, lattice, lattice-work, net, netting, network, reticulation, screen, sieve, tangle, tracery, trellis, web, webbing.

mess *n* 1 chaos, clutter, confusion, dirt, disarray, disorder, hotchpotch, jumble, litter, *inf* mishmash, muddle, *inf* shambles, tangle, untidiness. ▷ CONFUSION, DIRT. 2 *made a mess of it. inf* botch, failure, *inf* hash, *inf* mix-up. 3 *got into a mess.* difficulty, dilemma, *inf* fix, *inf* jam, *inf* pickle, plight, predicament, problem, trouble. ● *vb* **mess about** amuse yourself, loaf, loiter, lounge about, *inf* monkey about, *inf* muck about, *inf* play about. **make a mess of**

▷ BUNGLE, MUDDLE. **mess up** ▷ MUDDLE. **mess up a job** ▷ BUNGLE.

message *n* announcement, bulletin, cable, communication, communiqué, dispatch, information, intelligence, letter, memo, memorandum, missive, news, note, notice, report, statement, *old use* tidings.

messenger *n* bearer, carrier, courier, dispatch-rider, emissary, envoy, errand-boy, errand-girl, go-between, harbinger, herald, intermediary, legate, Mercury, messengerboy, messenger-girl, nuncio, postman, runner.

messy *adj* blowzy, careless, chaotic, cluttered, dirty, dishevelled, disorderly, filthy, grubby, mucky, muddled, *inf* shambolic, slapdash, sloppy, slovenly, unkempt, untidy. *Opp* NEAT.

metallic *adj* 1 gleaming, lustrous, shiny. 2 clanking, clinking, ringing.

metaphorical *adj* allegorical, figurative, non-literal, symbolic. *Opp* LITERAL.

method *n* 1 approach, fashion, *inf* knack, manner, means, methodology, mode, *Lat* modus operandi, plan, procedure, process, programme, recipe, scheme, style, technique, trick, way. 2 arrangement, design, discipline, neatness, order, orderliness, organization, pattern, routine, structure, system.

methodical *adj* businesslike, careful, deliberate, disciplined, logical, meticulous, neat, ordered, orderly, organized, painstaking, precise, rational, regular, routine, structured, systematic, tidy. *Opp* DISORGANIZED.

meticulous *adj* accurate, exact, exacting, fastidious, *inf* finicky, painstaking, particular, perfectionist, precise, punctilious, scrupulous, thorough. *Opp* CARELESS.

microbe *n* bacillus, bacterium, *inf* bug, germ, micro-organism, virus.

middle *adj* central, centre, halfway, inner, inside, intermediate, intervening, mean, medial, median, mid, middle-of-the-road, midway, neutral.
● *n* bull's eye, centre, core, crown (*of road*), focus, half-way point, heart, hub, inside, middle position, midpoint, midst, nucleus.

middling *adj* average, fair, *inf* fair to middling, indifferent, mediocre, moderate, modest, *inf* nothing to write home about, ordinary, passable, run-of-the-mill, *inf* so-so, unremarkable. *Opp* OUTSTANDING.

might *n* capability, capacity, energy, force, muscle, potency, power, strength, superiority, vigour.

mighty *adj* brawny, dominant, doughty, energetic, enormous, forceful, great, hefty, muscular, potent, powerful, robust, *inf* strapping, strong, sturdy, vigorous, weighty. ▷ BIG. *Opp* WEAK.

migrate *vb* emigrate, go, immigrate, move, relocate, resettle, settle, travel.

mild *adj* 1 affable, amiable, conciliatory, docile, easygoing, equable, forbearing, forgiving, gentle, good-tempered, harmless, indulgent, inoffensive,

kind, kindly, lenient, meek, merciful, modest, non-violent, pacific, peaceable, placid, quiet, *inf* soft, soft-hearted, submissive, sympathetic, tractable, unassuming, understanding, yielding. 2 *mild weather.* balmy, calm, clement, fair, peaceful, pleasant, serene, temperate, warm. 3 *a mild illness.* insignificant, minor, modest, slight, trivial, unimportant. 4 *mild flavour.* bland, delicate, faint, mellow, soothing, subtle. *Opp* SEVERE, STRONG.

mildness *n* affability, amiability, clemency, docility, forbearance, gentleness, kindness, leniency, moderation, placidity, softness, sympathy, tenderness. *Opp* ASPERITY.

militant *adj* active, aggressive, assertive, attacking, combative, fierce, hostile, positive, pugnacious. *Opp* PASSIVE. ● *n* activist, extremist, *inf* hawk, partisan.

militaristic *adj* bellicose, belligerent, combative, fond of fighting, hawkish, hostile, pugnacious, warlike. *Opp* PEACEABLE.

military *adj* armed, belligerent, combatant, enlisted, fighting, martial, uniformed, warlike. *Opp* CIVIL.

militate *vb* **militate against** cancel out, counter, counteract, countervail, discourage, hinder, oppose, prevent, resist.

milk *vb* bleed, drain, exploit, extract, tap, wring.

milky *adj* chalky, cloudy, misty, opaque, whitish. *Opp* CLEAR.

mill *n* 1 factory, foundry, plant, shop, works, workshop. 2 crusher, grinder, quern, water- mill, windmill.
● *vb* crush, granulate, grate,

grind, pound, powder, pulverize. **mill about** move aimlessly, seethe, swarm, throng, wander.

mimic n caricaturist, imitator, impersonator, impressionist.
● vb ape, caricature, copy, do impressions of, echo, imitate, impersonate, lampoon, look like, inf make fun of, mirror, mock, parody, parrot, pretend to be, reproduce, ridicule, satirize, simulate, sound like, inf take off.

mind n 1 astuteness, brain, brainpower, brains, cleverness, inf grey matter, head, insight, intellect, intelligence, judgement, memory, mental power, perception, psyche, rationality, reason, reasoning, remembrance, sagacity, sapience, sense, shrewdness, thinking, understanding, wisdom, wit, wits. 2 attitude, belief, bias, disposition, humour, inclination, intention, opinion, outlook, persuasion, plan, point of view, position, view, viewpoint, way of thinking, wishes.
● vb 1 attend to, care for, guard, keep an eye on, look after, take care of, take charge of, watch. 2 mind the warning. be careful about, beware of, heed, listen to, look out for, mark, note, obey, pay attention to, remember, take notice of, watch out for. 3 won't mind if he's late. be annoyed, be bothered, be offended, be resentful, bother, care, complain, disapprove, grumble, object, take offence, worry. **be in two minds** ▷ HESITATE.
make up your mind
▷ DECIDE. **out of your mind**
▷ MAD.

mindful adj alert, attentive, aware, conscious, heedful,

inf on the lookout, vigilant, watchful. ▷ CAREFUL. Opp CARELESS.

mindless adj brainless, fatuous, idiotic, obtuse, senseless, thick, thoughtless, unintelligent, unthinking, witless. ▷ STUPID. Opp INTELLIGENT.

mine n 1 coalfield, colliery, excavation, opencast mine, pit, quarry, shaft, tunnel, working. 2 mine of information. fund, repository, source, store, storehouse, supply, treasury, vein, wealth. ● vb dig, excavate, extract, quarry, remove, scoop out, unearth.

mineral n metal, ore, rock.

mingle vb amalgamate, associate, blend, circulate, combine, commingle, get together, fraternize, inf hobnob, intermingle, intermix, join, merge, mix, move about, inf rub shoulders, socialize, unite.

miniature adj baby, diminutive, dwarf, pygmy, reduced, scaled-down, small-scale, tiny, toy. ▷ SMALL.

minimal adj least, minimum, negligible, nominal, slightest, smallest, token.

minimize vb 1 cut down, decrease, diminish, lessen, pare, prune, reduce. 2 minimize problems. belittle, decry, devalue, depreciate, gloss over, make light of, play down, underestimate, undervalue. Opp MAXIMIZE.

minimum adj bottom, least, littlest, lowest, minimal, minutest, nominal, inf rock bottom, slightest, smallest.
● n least, lowest, minimum amount, minimum quantity, nadir. Opp MAXIMUM.

minister n ▷ CLERGYMAN, OFFI-
CIAL. ● vb **minister to** aid,
assist, attend to, care for, help,
look after, nurse, see to,
support, wait on.

minor adj inconsequential, inferior, insignificant, lesser, little,
negligible, petty, secondary,
smaller, subordinate, subsidiary, trivial, unimportant.
▷ SMALL. Opp MAJOR.
● n ▷ ADOLESCENT, CHILD.

minstrel n balladeer, bard,
entertainer, jongleur, musician,
singer, troubadour.

mint adj brand-new, first-class,
fresh, immaculate, new, perfect,
unblemished, unmarked,
unused. ● n fortune, heap,
inf packet, pile, stack, unlimited supply, vast amount.
● vb cast, coin, forge, make,
manufacture, produce, stamp
out, strike.

minute adj diminutive, dwarf,
infinitesimal, insignificant, lilliputian, microscopic, inf mini,
miniature, minuscule, inf pint-
sized, pocket, pygmy, tiny.
▷ SMALL.

minutes plur n log, notes,
proceedings, record, résumé,
summary, transactions.

miracle n marvel, miraculous
event, mystery, wonder.

miraculous adj abnormal,
extraordinary, incredible, inexplicable, magic, magical,
mysterious, paranormal,
phenomenal, preternatural,
remarkable, supernatural,
unaccountable, unbelievable,
unexplainable. ▷ MARVELLOUS.

mirage n delusion, hallucination, illusion, vision.

mire n bog, fen, marsh, morass,
mud, ooze, quagmire, quick-

sand, slime, old use slough,
swamp. ▷ DIRT.

mirror n glass, looking-glass,
reflector, speculum. ● vb echo,
reflect, repeat, send back.

misadventure n accident,
calamity, catastrophe, disaster,
ill fortune, mischance, misfortune, mishap.

misanthropic adj anti-social,
cynical, mean, nasty, surly,
unfriendly, unpleasant, unsociable. Opp PHILANTHROPIC.

misappropriate vb defalcate,
embezzle, expropriate, peculate.
▷ STEAL.

misbehave vb be a nuisance, be
bad, behave badly, be mischievous, inf blot your copybook,
inf carry on, commit an offence,
default, disobey, do wrong, err,
fool about, make mischief,
inf mess about, inf muck
about, offend, inf play about,
play up, inf raise Cain, sin,
transgress.

misbehaviour n badness, delinquency, disobedience, disorderliness, horseplay, indiscipline,
insubordination, mischief,
mischief-making, misconduct,
misdemeanour, naughtiness,
rowdyism, rudeness, sin,
vandalism, wrongdoing.

miscalculate vb inf boob, err,
inf get it wrong, go wrong,
make a mistake, miscount,
misjudge, misread, overestimate, overrate, overvalue,
inf slip up, underestimate,
underrate.

miscarriage n 1 abortion,
premature birth, termination of
pregnancy. 2 miscarriage of
justice. breakdown, collapse,
defeat, error, failure, perversion.

miscarry vb 1 abort, inf lose a baby, suffer a miscarriage. 2 break down, inf come to grief, come to nothing, fail, fall through, founder, go wrong, misfire. Opp SUCCEED.

miscellaneous adj assorted, different, old use divers, diverse, heterogeneous, manifold, mixed, motley, multifarious, sundry, varied, various.

miscellany n assortment, diversity, gallimaufry, hotchpotch, jumble, medley, mélange, inf mixed bag, mixture, pot-pourri, inf ragbag, variety.

mischief n 1 devilment, devilry, escapade, impishness, misbehaviour, misconduct, inf monkey business, naughtiness, playfulness, prank, rascality, roguishness, scrape, inf shenanigans, trouble. 2 damage, difficulty, evil, harm, hurt, injury, misfortune, trouble.

mischievous adj annoying, badly behaved, boisterous, disobedient, elvish, fractious, frolicsome, full of mischief, impish, lively, naughty, playful, inf puckish, rascally, roguish, sportive, uncontrollable, inf up to no good. ▷ WICKED. Opp WELL-BEHAVED.

miser n hoarder, miserly person, niggard, inf Scrooge, inf skinflint. Opp SPENDTHRIFT.

miserable adj 1 broken-hearted, crestfallen, inf cut up, dejected, depressed, desolate, despairing, despondent, disappointed, disconsolate, dismayed, dispirited, distressed, doleful, inf down, downcast, downhearted, forlorn, friendless, gloomy, glum, grief-stricken, heartbroken, hopeless, in low spirits, inf in the doldrums, inf in the dumps, joyless, lachrymose, languishing, lonely, low, melancholy, mournful, moping, sad, sorrowful, suicidal, tearful, uneasy, unfortunate, unhappy, unlucky, woebegone, woeful, wretched. 2 churlish, cross, disagreeable, discontented, inf grumpy, ill-natured, mean, miserly, morose, pessimistic, sour, sulky, sullen, surly, taciturn, unfriendly, unhelpful, unsociable. 3 miserable living conditions. abject, awful, bad, deplorable, destitute, disgraceful, distressing, heart-breaking, hopeless, impoverished, inadequate, inhuman, lamentable, pathetic, pitiable, pitiful, poor, shameful, sordid, soul-destroying, squalid, vile, uncivilized, uncomfortable, vile, worthless, wretched. 4 miserable weather. cheerless, damp, depressing, dismal, dreary, grey, inclement, sunless, unpleasant, wet. Opp HAPPY, PLEASANT.

miserly adj avaricious, inf cheese-paring, inf close, inf close-fisted, covetous, economical, grasping, greedy, mean, mercenary, mingy, niggardly, parsimonious, penny-pinching, penurious, sparing, stingy, inf tight, inf tight-fisted. Opp GENEROUS.

misery n 1 angst, anguish, anxiety, bitterness, dejection, depression, despair, desperation, despondency, discomfort, distress, dolour, gloom, grief, heartache, heartbreak, inf hell, hopelessness, melancholy, sadness, sorrow, suffering,

unhappiness, woe, wretchedness. *Opp* HAPPINESS.
2 adversity, affliction, deprivation, destitution, indigence, misfortune, need, oppression, penury, poverty, privation, squalor, suffering, *inf* trials and tribulations, tribulation, trouble, want, wretchedness.

misfire *vb* abort, fail, fall through, *inf* flop, founder, go wrong, miscarry. *Opp* SUCCEED.

misfortune *n* accident, adversity, affliction, bad luck, blow, calamity, catastrophe, contretemps, curse, disappointment, disaster, evil, hard luck, hardship, ill-luck, misadventure, mischance, mishap, reverse, setback, tragedy, trouble, vicissitude.

misguided *adj* erroneous, foolish, ill-advised, ill-judged, inappropriate, incorrect, inexact, misinformed, misjudged, misled, mistaken, unfounded, unjust, unsound, unwise.
▷ WRONG.

misjudge *vb* get wrong, guess wrongly, *inf* jump to the wrong conclusion, make a mistake, misinterpret, overestimate, overvalue, underestimate, undervalue. ▷ MISCALCULATE.

mislay *vb* lose, mislocate, misplace, put in the wrong place.

mislead *vb* bluff, confuse, delude, fool, give misleading information to, give a wrong impression to, lead astray, *inf* lead up the garden path, lie to, misdirect, misguide, misinform, outwit, *inf* take for a ride, take in, *inf* throw off the scent, trick. ▷ DECEIVE. **misleading**
▷ DECEPTIVE, PUZZLING.

miss *vb* 1 absent yourself from, avoid, be absent from, be too late for, dodge, escape, evade, fail to keep, forget, forgo, let go, lose, play truant from, *inf* skive off. 2 *miss a target.* be wide of, fail to hit, fall short of. 3 *miss absent friends.* feel nostalgia for, grieve for, lament, long for, need, pine for, want, yearn for. **miss out**
▷ OMIT.

misshapen *adj* awry, bent, contorted, corkscrew, crippled, crooked, crumpled, deformed, disfigured, distorted, gnarled, grotesque, knotted, malformed, monstrous, screwed up, tangled, twisted, twisty, ugly, warped. *Opp* PERFECT.

missile *n* projectile. □ *arrow, ballistic missile, bomb, boomerang, brickbat, bullet, dart, grenade, guided missile, rocket, shell, shot, torpedo.* ▷ WEAPON.

missing *adj* absent, disappeared, lost, mislaid, *inf* skiving, straying, truant, unaccounted-for. *Opp* PRESENT.

mission *n* 1 delegation, deputation, expedition, exploration, journey, sortie, task-force, voyage. 2 *mission in life.* aim, assignment, calling, commitment, duty, function, goal, job, life's work, métier, objective, occupation, profession, purpose, quest, undertaking, vocation. 3 *evangelical mission.* campaign, crusade, holy war.

missionary *n* campaigner, crusader, evangelist, minister, preacher, proselytizer.

mist *n* 1 cloud, drizzle, fog, haze, smog, vapour. 2 condensation, film, steam.

mistake n inf bloomer, blunder, inf boob, inf botch, inf clanger, erratum, error, false step, fault, Fr faux pas, gaffe, inf howler, inaccuracy, indiscretion, lapse, misapprehension, miscalculation, misconception, misjudgement, misprint, misspelling, misunderstanding, omission, oversight, slip, slip-up, solecism, wrong move. ● vb confuse, inf get the wrong end of the stick, get wrong, misconstrue, misinterpret, misjudge, misread, misunderstand, mix up, inf take the wrong way.

mistaken adj erroneous, distorted, false, faulty, ill-judged, inaccurate, inappropriate, incorrect, inexact, misguided, misinformed, unfounded, unjust, unsound. ▷ WRONG. Opp CORRECT.

mistimed adj badly timed, early, inconvenient, inopportune, late, unseasonable, untimely. Opp OPPORTUNE.

mistreat vb abuse, batter, damage, harm, hurt, ill-treat, ill-use, injure, inf knock about, maltreat, manhandle, misuse, molest, treat roughly.

mistress n [mostly old use] 1 chief, head, keeper, owner, person in charge, proprietor. 2 ▷ TEACHER. 3 ▷ LOVER.

mistrust n apprehension, inf chariness, distrust, doubt, misgiving, reservation, scepticism, suspicion, uncertainty, unsureness, wariness. ● vb be sceptical about, be suspicious of, be wary of, disbelieve, distrust, doubt, fear, have doubts about, have misgivings about, have reservations about, question, suspect. Opp TRUST.

misty adj bleary, blurred, blurry, clouded, cloudy, dim, faint, foggy, fuzzy, hazy, indistinct, murky, obscure, opaque, shadowy, smoky, steamy, unclear, vague. Opp CLEAR.

misunderstand vb inf get the wrong end of the stick, get wrong, misapprehend, miscalculate, misconceive, misconstrue, mishear, misinterpret, misjudge, misread, miss the point of, mistake, mistranslate. Opp UNDERSTAND.

misunderstanding n 1 error, failure of understanding, false impression, misapprehension, miscalculation, misconception, misconstruction, misinterpretation, misjudgement, misreading, mistake, inf mix up, wrong idea. 2 argument, inf contretemps, controversy, difference of opinion, disagreement, discord, dispute. ▷ QUARREL.

misuse n abuse, careless use, corruption, ill-treatment, illuse, maltreatment, misapplication, misappropriation, mishandling, mistreatment, perversion. ● vb 1 damage, harm, mishandle, treat carelessly. 2 misuse an animal. abuse, batter, damage, harm, hurt, ill-treat, ill-use, injure, inf knock about, maltreat, manhandle, mistreat, molest, treat roughly. 3 misuse funds. fritter away, misappropriate, squander, use wrongly, waste.

mitigate vb abate, allay, alleviate, decrease, ease, extenuate, lessen, lighten, make milder, moderate, palliate, qualify, reduce, relieve, soften, inf take the edge off, temper, tone down. Opp AGGRAVATE.

mix n amalgam, assortment, blend, combination, compound, range, variety. • vb 1 alloy, amalgamate, blend, coalesce, combine, commingle, compound, confuse, diffuse, emulsify, fuse, homogenize, integrate, intermingle, join, jumble up, make a mixture, meld, merge, mingle, mix up, muddle, put together, shuffle, stir together, unite. *Opp* SEPARATE. 2 *mix with people*. ▷ SOCIALIZE.

mixed adj 1 assorted, different, diverse, heterogeneous, miscellaneous, varied, various. 2 *mixed with other things*. adulterated, alloyed, diluted, impure. 3 *mixed ingredients*. amalgamated, combined, composite, hybrid, integrated, joint, mongrel, united. 4 *mixed feelings*. ambiguous, ambivalent, confused, equivocal, muddled, uncertain.

mixture n 1 alloy, amalgam, amalgamation, association, assortment, blend, collection, combination, composite, compound, concoction, conglomeration, emulsion, farrago, fusion, gallimaufry, *inf* hotchpotch, intermingling, jumble, medley, mélange, merger, mess, mingling, miscellany, *inf* mishmash, mix, *inf* motley collection, pastiche, pot-pourri, selection, suspension, synthesis, variety. 2 cross-breed, half-caste, hybrid, mongrel.

moan n complaint, grievance, lament, lamentation. • vb 1 complain, grieve, *inf* grouse, grumble, lament. 2 cry, groan, keen, sigh, ululate, wail, weep, whimper, whine. ▷ SOUND.

mob n *inf* bunch, crowd, gang, herd, horde, host, multitude, pack, press, rabble, riot, *inf* shower, swarm, throng. ▷ GROUP. • vb besiege, crowd round, hem in, jostle, surround, swarm round, throng round.

mobile adj 1 itinerant, motorized, movable, portable, transportable, travelling, unfixed. 2 able to move, active, agile, independent, moving, nimble, *inf* on the go, *inf* up and about. 3 *mobile features*. animated, changeable, changing, expressive, flexible, fluid, plastic, shifting. *Opp* IMMOVABLE.

mobilize vb activate, assemble, call up, conscript, enlist, enrol, gather, get together, levy, marshal, muster, organize, rally, stir up, summon.

mock adj artificial, counterfeit, ersatz, fake, false, imitation, make-believe, man-made, *inf* pretend, simulated, sham, substitute. • vb decry, deride, disparage, flout, gibe at, insult, jeer at, lampoon, laugh at, make fun of, make sport of, parody, poke fun at, ridicule, satirize, scoff at, scorn, *inf* send up, sneer at, tantalize, taunt, tease, travesty. ▷ MIMIC.

mockery n derision, insults, jeering, laughter, ridicule, scorn. □ burlesque, caricature, lampoon, parody, sarcasm, satire, inf send-up, inf spoof, inf take-off, travesty.

mocking adj contemptuous, derisive, disparaging, disrespectful, insulting, irreverent, jeering, rude, sarcastic, satirical, scornful, taunting, teasing, uncomplimentary, unkind. *Opp* RESPECTFUL.

mode *n* **1** approach, configuration, manner, medium, method, *Lat* modus operandi, procedure, set-up, system, technique, way. **2** ▷ FASHION.

model *adj* **1** imitation, miniature, scaled-down, toy. **2** *model pupil.* exemplary, ideal, perfect, unequalled. ● *n* **1** archetype, copy, dummy, effigy, facsimile, image, imitation, likeness, miniature, *inf* mock-up, paradigm, prototype, replica, representation, scale model, toy. **2** *model of excellence.* byword, epitome, example, exemplar, ideal, nonpareil, paragon, pattern, standard, yardstick. **3** *artist's model.* poser, sitter, subject. **4** *latest model.* brand, design, kind, mark, type, version. **5** *fashion model.* mannequin. ● *vb* carve, fashion, form, make, mould, sculpt, shape. **model yourself on** ▷ IMITATE.

moderate *adj* **1** average, balanced, calm, cautious, commonsensical, cool, deliberate, fair, judicious, medium, middle, *inf* middle-of-the-road, middling, modest, normal, ordinary, rational, reasonable, respectable, sensible, sober, steady, temperate, unexceptional, usual. *Opp* EXTREME. **2** *moderate winds.* gentle, light, mild. ● *vb* **1** abate, become less extreme, decline, decrease, die down, ease off, subside. **2** blunt, calm, check, curb, dull, ease, keep down, lessen, make less extreme, mitigate, modify, modulate, mollify, reduce, regulate, restrain, slacken, subdue, temper, tone down.

moderately *adv* comparatively, fairly, passably, *inf* pretty, quite, rather, reasonably, somewhat, to some extent.

moderation *n* balance, caution, common sense, fairness, reasonableness, restraint, reticence, sobriety, temperance.

modern *adj* advanced, avant-garde, contemporary, current, fashionable, forward-looking, fresh, futuristic, in vogue, latest, modish, new, newfangled, novel, present, present-day, progressive, recent, stylish, *inf* trendy, up-to-date, up-to-the-minute, *inf* with it. *Opp* OLD.

modernize *vb* bring up-to-date, *inf* do up, improve, make modern, rebuild, redesign, redo, refurbish, regenerate, rejuvenate, renovate, revamp, update.

modest *adj* **1** diffident, humble, inconspicuous, lowly, meek, plain, quiet, reserved, restrained, reticent, retiring, self-effacing, simple, unassuming, unobtrusive, unostentatious, unpretentious. *Opp* CONCEITED. **2** bashful, chaste, coy, decent, demure, discreet, proper, seemly, self-conscious, shamefaced, shy, simple. **3** *a modest income.* limited, medium, middling, moderate, normal, ordinary, reasonable, unexceptional. *Opp* EXCESSIVE.

modesty *n* **1** humbleness, humility, lowliness, meekness, reserve, restraint, reticence, self-effacement, simplicity. *Opp* OSTENTATION. **2** *modesty about undressing.* bashfulness, coyness, decency, demureness, discretion, propriety, seemliness, self-consciousness, shame, shyness.

modify vb adapt, adjust, alter, amend, change, convert, improve, reconstruct, redesign, remake, remodel, reorganize, revise, reword, rework, transform, vary. ▷ MODERATE.

modulate vb adjust, balance, change key, change the tone, lower the tone, moderate, regulate, soften, tone down.

moist adj affected by moisture, clammy, damp, dank, dewy, humid, misty, inf muggy, rainy, inf runny, steamy, watery, wettish. ▷ WET. Opp DRY.

moisten vb damp, dampen, humidify, make moist, moisturize, soak, spray, wet. Opp DRY.

moisture n condensation, damp, dampness, dankness, dew, humidity, liquid, precipitation, spray, steam, vapour, water, wet, wetness.

molest vb abuse, accost, annoy, assault, attack, badger, bother, disturb, harass, harry, hassle, hector, ill-treat, interfere with, irk, irritate, manhandle, mistreat, inf needle, persecute, pester, plague, set on, tease, torment, vex, worry.

molten adj fluid, liquid, liquefied, melted, soft.

moment n 1 flash, instant, inf jiffy, minute, second, split second, inf tick, inf trice, inf twinkling of an eye, inf two shakes. 2 a historic moment. hour, juncture, occasion, opportunity, point in time, stage, time.

momentary adj brief, ephemeral, evanescent, fleeting, fugitive, hasty, passing, quick, short, short-lived, temporary, transient, transitory. Opp PERMANENT.

momentous adj consequential, critical, crucial, decisive, epoch-making, fateful, grave, historic, important, portentous, serious, significant, weighty. Opp UNIMPORTANT.

monarch n crowned head, emperor, empress, king, potentate, queen, ruler, tsar.

monarchy n empire, domain, kingdom, realm.

money n affluence, arrears, assets, bank-notes, inf bread, capital, cash, change, cheque, coin, copper, credit card, credit transfer, currency, damages, debt, dividend, inf dough, dowry, earnings, endowment, estate, expenditure, finance, fortune, fund, grant, income, interest, investment, legal tender, loan, inf lolly, old use lucre, mortgage, inf nest-egg, notes, outgoings, patrimony, pay, penny, pension, pocket-money, proceeds, profit, inf the ready, remittance, resources, revenue, riches, salary, savings, silver, sterling, takings, tax, traveller's cheque, wage, wealth, inf the wherewithal, winnings.

mongrel n cross-breed, cur, half-breed, hybrid, mixed breed.

monitor n 1 detector, guardian, prefect, supervisor, watchdog. 2 TV monitor. screen, set, television, TV, VDU, visual display unit. ● vb audit, check, examine, inf keep an eye on, oversee, record, supervise, trace, track, watch.

monk n brother, friar, hermit.

monkey n ape, primate, simian. □ baboon, chimpanzee, gibbon, gorilla, marmoset, orang-utan.

monopolize vb control, inf corner the market in, dominate, have a monopoly of, inf hog, keep for yourself, own, shut others out of, take over. Opp SHARE.

monotonous adj boring, colourless, dreary, dull, featureless, flat, level, repetitious, repetitive, soporific, tedious, tiresome, tiring, toneless, unchanging, uneventful, unexciting, uniform, uninteresting, unvarying, wearisome. Opp INTERESTING.

monster n abortion, beast, bogey-man, brute, demon, devil, fiend, freak, giant, horror, monstrosity, monstrous creature, mutant, ogre, troll.

monstrous adj 1 colossal, elephantine, enormous, gargantuan, giant, gigantic, great, huge, hulking, immense, inf jumbo, mammoth, mighty, prodigious, titanic, towering, tremendous, vast. ▷ BIG. 2 a monstrous crime. abhorrent, atrocious, awful, beastly, brutal, cruel, devilish, dreadful, disgusting, evil, ghoulish, grisly, gross, gruesome, heinous, hideous, inf horrendous, horrible, horrific, horrifying, inhuman, nightmarish, obscene, outrageous, repulsive, shocking, terrible, ugly, villainous, wicked. ▷ EVIL.

monument n cairn, cenotaph, cross, gravestone, headstone, mausoleum, memorial, obelisk, pillar, prehistoric remains, relic, reminder, shrine, tomb, tombstone.

monumental adj 1 awe-inspiring, awesome, classic, enduring, epoch-making, grand, historic, impressive, lasting, large-scale, major, memorable, unforgettable. ▷ BIG. 2 a monumental plaque. commemorative, memorial.

mood n 1 attitude, disposition, frame of mind, humour, inclination, nature, spirit, state of mind, temper, vein. 2 atmosphere, feeling, tone. ▷ ANGRY, HAPPY, SAD, etc. **in the mood** ▷ READY.

moody adj abrupt, bad-tempered, cantankerous, capricious, changeable, crabby, cross, crotchety, depressed, depressive, disgruntled, erratic, fickle, gloomy, grumpy, inf huffy, ill-humoured, inconstant, irritable, melancholy, mercurial, miserable, morose, peevish, petulant, inf short, short-tempered, snappy, sulky, sullen, temperamental, testy, inf touchy, unpredictable, unreliable, unstable, volatile. ▷ SAD.

moor n fell, heath, moorland, wasteland. ● vb anchor, berth, dock, make fast, secure, tie up. ▷ FASTEN.

mope vb be sad, brood, despair, grieve, languish, inf moon, pine, sulk.

moral adj 1 blameless, chaste, decent, ethical, good, high-minded, honest, honourable, incorruptible, innocent, irreproachable, just, law-abiding, noble, principled, proper, pure, respectable, responsible, right, righteous, sinless, trustworthy, truthful, upright, upstanding, virtuous. 2 a moral tale. allegorical, cautionary, didactic, moralistic, moralizing. Opp IMMORAL. ● n lesson, maxim, meaning, message, point, precept, principle, teaching. **morals** ▷ MORALITY.

moral tale allegory, cautionary tale, fable, parable.

morale n attitude, cheerfulness, confidence, Fr esprit de corps, inf heart, mood, self-confidence, self-esteem, spirit, state of mind.

morality n behaviour, conduct, decency, ethics, ethos, fairness, goodness, honesty, ideals, integrity, justice, morals, principles, propriety, rectitude, righteousness, rightness, scruples, standards, uprightness, virtue.

moralize vb lecture, philosophize, pontificate, preach, sermonize.

morbid adj black (humour), brooding, dejected, depressed, ghoulish, gloomy, grim, grotesque, gruesome, lugubrious, macabre, melancholy, monstrous, morose, pathological, pessimistic, inf sick, sombre, unhappy, unhealthy, unpleasant, unwholesome. Opp CHEERFUL.

more adj added, additional, extra, further, increased, longer, new, other, renewed, supplementary. Opp LESS.

moreover adv also, as well, besides, further, furthermore, in addition, old use to boot, too.

morose adj bad-tempered, churlish, depressed, gloomy, glum, grim, humourless, ill-natured, melancholy, moody, mournful, pessimistic, saturnine, sour, sulky, sullen, surly, taciturn, unhappy, unsociable. ▷ SAD. Opp CHEERFUL.

morsel n bite, crumb, fragment, gobbet, mouthful, nibble, piece, sample, scrap, small amount,

soupçon, spoonful, taste, titbit. ▷ BIT.

mortal adj 1 ephemeral, human, passing, temporal, transient. Opp IMMORTAL. 2 mortal sickness. deadly, fatal, lethal, terminal. 3 mortal enemies. deadly, implacable, irreconcilable, remorseless, sworn, unrelenting. ● n creature, human being, man, person, soul, woman.

mortality n 1 corruptibility, humanity, impermanence, transience. 2 infant mortality. death-rate, dying, fatalities, loss of life.

mortify vb abash, chagrin, chasten, inf crush, deflate, embarrass, humble, humiliate, inf put down, shame.

mostly adv chiefly, commonly, generally, largely, mainly, normally, predominantly, primarily, principally, typically, usually.

moth-eaten adj antiquated, decrepit, holey, mangy, ragged, shabby, inf tatty. ▷ OLD.

mother n old use dam, inf ma, inf mamma, old use mater, inf mum, inf mummy, parent. ● vb care for, cherish, coddle, comfort, cuddle, fuss over, indulge, look after, love, nourish, nurse, nurture, pamper, protect, spoil, take care of.

motherly adj caring, kind, maternal, protective. ▷ LOVING.

motif n decoration, design, device, figure, idea, leitmotif, ornament, pattern, symbol, theme.

motion n action, activity, agitation, change, commotion, development, evolution, move, movement, progress, rise and fall, stir, stirring, to and

fro, travel, travelling, trend.
● *vb* ▷ GESTURE.

motionless *adj* at rest, calm,
frozen, immobile, inanimate,
inert, lifeless, paralysed, peaceful, resting, stagnant, static,
stationary, still, stock-still,
unmoving. *Opp* MOVING.

motivate *vb* activate, actuate,
arouse, cause, drive, egg on,
encourage, excite, galvanize,
goad, incite, induce, influence,
inspire, instigate, move, occasion, persuade, prompt,
provoke, push, rouse, spur,
stimulate, stir, urge.

motive *n* aim, ambition, cause,
drive, encouragement, end,
enticement, grounds, impulse,
incentive, incitement, inducement, inspiration, instigation,
intention, lure, motivation,
object, provocation, purpose,
push, rationale, reason, spur,
stimulation, stimulus, thinking.

motor *n* ▷ ENGINE, VEHICLE.
● *vb* drive, go by car. ▷ TRAVEL.

mottled *adj* blotchy, brindled,
dappled, flecked, freckled,
marbled, patchy, spattered,
speckled, spotted, spotty,
streaked, streaky, variegated.

motto *n* adage, aphorism, catch-
phrase, maxim, precept, proverb, rule, saw, saying, slogan.

mould *n* blight, fungus, growth,
mildew. ● *vb* cast, fashion,
forge, form, model, *inf* sculpt,
shape, stamp, work.

mouldy *adj* carious, damp,
decaying, decomposing, fusty,
mildewed, mouldering, musty,
putrefying, rotten, stale.

mound *n* bank, dune, elevation,
heap, hill, hillock, hummock,
hump, knoll, pile, stack, tumulus.

mount *n* ▷ MOUNTAIN.
● *vb* 1 ascend, clamber up,
climb, fly up, go up, rise, rocket
upwards, scale, shoot up, soar.
Opp DESCEND. 2 *mount a horse.*
get astride, get on, jump onto.
3 *savings mount.* accumulate,
build up, escalate, expand, get
bigger, grow, increase, intensify, multiply, pile up, swell.
Opp DECREASE. 4 *mount a
picture.* display, exhibit, frame,
install, prepare, put in place,
put on, set up.

mountain *n* alp, arête, *Scot* ben,
elevation, eminence, height,
hill, mound, mount, peak,
prominence, range, ridge,
sierra, summit, tor, volcano.

mountainous *adj* alpine,
craggy, daunting, formidable,
high, hilly, precipitous, rocky,
rugged, steep, towering.
▷ BIG.

mourn *vb* bemoan, bewail, fret,
go into mourning, grieve, keen,
lament, mope, pine, regret,
wail, weep. *Opp* REJOICE.

mournful *adj* dismal,
distressed, distressing, doleful,
funereal, gloomy, grief-stricken,
grieving, heartbreaking, heartbroken, lamenting, lugubrious,
melancholy, plaintive, plangent, sad, sorrowful, tearful,
tragic, unhappy, woeful.
Opp CHEERFUL.

mouth *n* 1 *inf* chops, *sl* gob,
jaws, *sl* kisser, lips, maw,
muzzle, palate. 2 *mouth of cave.*
aperture, door, doorway,
entrance, exit, gate, gateway,
inlet, opening, orifice, outlet,
vent, way in. 3 *mouth of a river.*
delta, estuary, outflow.
● *vb* articulate, enunciate, form,
pronounce. ▷ SAY.

mouthful *n* bite, gobbet, gulp, morsel, sip, spoonful, swallow, taste.

movable *adj* adjustable, changeable, detachable, floating, mobile, portable, transferable, transportable, unfixed, variable. *Opp* IMMOVABLE.

move *n* 1 act, action, deed, device, dodge, gambit, manoeuvre, measure, movement, ploy, ruse, step, stratagem, *inf* tack, tactic. 2 *a career move.* change, changeover, relocation, shift, transfer. 3 *your move.* chance, go, opportunity, turn. ● *vb* 1 move about. be agitated, be astir, budge, change places, change position, fidget, flap, roll, shake, shift, stir, swing, toss, tremble, turn, twist, twitch, wag, *inf* waggle, wave, *inf* wiggle. 2 move along. cruise, fly, jog, journey, make headway, make progress, march, pass, proceed, travel, walk. 3 move quickly. bolt, *inf* bowl along, canter, career, dash, dart, flit, flounce, fly, gallop, hasten, hurry, hurtle, hustle, *inf* nip, race, run, rush, shoot, speed, stampede, streak, sweep along, sweep past, *inf* tear, *inf* zip, *inf* zoom. 4 move slowly. amble, crawl, dawdle, drift, stroll. 5 move gracefully. dance, flow, glide, skate, skim, slide, slip, sweep. 6 move awkwardly. dodder, falter, flounder, lumber, lurch, pitch, shuffle, stagger, stumble, sway, totter, trip, trundle. 7 move stealthily. crawl, creep, edge, slink, slither. 8 move things. carry, export, import, shift, ship, relocate, transfer, transplant, transport, transpose. 9 moved him to act.

encourage, impel, influence, inspire, persuade, prompt, stimulate, urge. 10 *move the crowd's feelings.* affect, arouse, enrage, fire, impassion, rouse, stir, touch. 11 *moved to improve the situation.* act, do something, make a move, take action.
move away ▷ DEPART. **move back** ▷ RETREAT. **move down** ▷ DESCEND. **move in** ▷ ENTER. **move round** ▷ CIRCULATE, ROTATE. **move towards** ▷ APPROACH. **move up** ▷ ASCEND.

movement *n* 1 action, activity, migration, motion, shifting, stirring. ▷ GESTURE, MOVE. 2 *movement towards green issues.* change, development, drift, evolution, progress, shift, swing, tendency, trend. 3 *a political movement.* campaign, crusade, drive, faction, group, organization, party. 4 *military movements.* exercise, operation.

movie *n* film, *inf* flick, motion picture.

moving *adj* 1 active, alive, astir, dynamic, flowing, going, in motion, mobile, movable, on the move, travelling, under way. *Opp* MOTIONLESS. 2 *a moving tale.* affecting, emotional, emotive, exciting, heart-rending, heart-warming, inspirational, inspiring, pathetic, poignant, spine-tingling, stirring, *inf* tear-jerking, thrilling, touching.

mow *vb* clip, cut, scythe, shear, trim.

muck *n* dirt, droppings, dung, excrement, faeces, filth, grime, *inf* gunge, manure, mess, mire, mud, ooze, ordure, rubbish, scum, sewage, slime, sludge.

mucky adj dirty, filthy, foul, grimy, grubby, messy, muddy, scummy, slimy, soiled, sordid, squalid. Opp CLEAN.

mud n clay, dirt, mire, muck, ooze, silt, slime, sludge, slurry, soil.

muddle n chaos, clutter, confusion, disorder, inf hotchpotch, jumble, mess, inf mishmash, inf mix up, inf shambles, tangle, untidiness. ● vb 1 bemuse, bewilder, confound, confuse, disorient, disorientate, mislead, perplex, puzzle. Opp CLARIFY. 2 disarrange, disorder, disorganize, entangle, inf foul up, jumble, make a mess of, inf mess up, mix up, scramble, shuffle, tangle. Opp TIDY.

muddy adj 1 caked, dirty, filthy, messy, mucky, soiled. 2 muddy water. cloudy, impure, misty, opaque. 3 muddy ground. boggy, marshy, sloppy, sodden, soft, spongy, waterlogged, wet. Opp CLEAN, FIRM.

muffle vb 1 cloak, conceal, cover, enclose, enfold, envelop, shroud, swathe, wrap up. 2 muffle noise. damp, dampen, deaden, disguise, dull, hush, mask, mute, quieten, silence, soften, stifle, still, suppress, tone down.

muffled adj damped, deadened, dull, fuzzy, indistinct, muted, silenced, stifled, suppressed, unclear, woolly. Opp CLEAR.

mug n beaker, cup, old use flagon, pot, tankard. ● vb assault, beat up, jump on, molest, set on, steal from. ▷ ATTACK.
mug up ▷ LEARN.

mugger n attacker, hooligan, robber, ruffian, thief, thug. ▷ CRIMINAL.

mugging n attack, robbery, street crime. ▷ CRIME.

muggy adj clammy, close, damp, humid, moist, oppressive, steamy, sticky, stuffy, sultry, warm.

multiple adj complex, compound, double, many, numerous, plural, quadruple, quintuple, triple.

multiplicity n abundance, array, complex, diversity, number, plurality, profusion, variety.

multiply vb 1 double, quadruple, quintuple, inf times, triple. 2 become numerous, breed, increase, proliferate, propagate, reproduce, spread.

multitude n crowd, host, large number, legion, lots, mass, myriad, swarm, throng. ▷ GROUP.

mumble vb be inarticulate, murmur, mutter, speak indistinctly, swallow your words.

munch vb bite, chew, champ, chomp, crunch, eat, gnaw, masticate.

mundane adj banal, common, commonplace, down-to-earth, dull, everyday, familiar, human, material, physical, practical, quotidian, routine, temporal, worldly. ▷ ORDINARY. Opp EXTRAORDINARY, SPIRITUAL.

municipal adj borough, city, civic, community, district, local, public, town, urban.

murder n assassination, fratricide, genocide, homicide, infanticide, killing, manslaughter, matricide, parricide, patricide, regicide, sororicide, unlawful killing, uxoricide. ● vb ▷ KILL.

murderer n assassin, inf butcher, cutthroat, gunman, homicide, killer, slayer.

murderous adj barbarous, bloodthirsty, bloody, brutal, cruel, dangerous, deadly, fell, ferocious, fierce, homicidal, inhuman, pitiless, ruthless, savage, vicious, violent.

murky adj clouded, cloudy, dark, dim, dismal, dreary, dull, foggy, funereal, gloomy, grey, misty, muddy, obscure, overcast, shadowy, sombre. Opp CLEAR.

murmur n background noise, buzz, drone, grumble, hum, mutter, rumble, susurration, undertone, whisper. ● vb drone, hum, moan, mumble, mutter, rumble, speak in an undertone, whisper. ▷ GRUMBLE, TALK.

muscular adj athletic, inf beefy, brawny, broad-shouldered, burly, hefty, inf hulking, husky, powerful, powerfully built, robust, sinewy, inf strapping, strong, sturdy, tough, well-built, well-developed, wiry. Opp WEAK.

muse vb cogitate, consider, contemplate, deliberate, meditate, mull over, ponder, reflect, ruminate, study, think.

mushy adj pulpy, spongy, squashy. ▷ SOFT.

music n harmony. □ blues, chamber music, choral music, classical music, dance music, disco music, folk, instrumental music, jazz, orchestral music, plainsong, pop, ragtime, reggae, rock, soul, swing. □ anthem, ballad, cadenza, calypso, canon, cantata, canticle, carol, chant, concerto, dance, dirge, duet, étude, fanfare, fugue, hymn, improvisation, intermezzo, lullaby, march, musical, nocturne, nonet, octet, opera, operetta, oratorio, overture, prelude, quartet, quintet, rhapsody, rondo, scherzo, sea shanty, septet, sextet, sonata, song, spiritual, symphony, toccata, trio.

musical adj euphonious, harmonious, lyrical, melodious, pleasant, sweet-sounding, tuneful.
musical instrument
▷ INSTRUMENT.

musician n composer, musicmaker, performer, player, singer. □ accompanist, bass, bugler, cellist, clarinettist, conductor, contralto, drummer, fiddler, flautist, guitarist, harpist, instrumentalist, maestro, minstrel, oboist, organist, percussionist, pianist, piper, soloist, soprano, tenor, timpanist, treble, trombonist, trumpeter, violinist, virtuoso, vocalist. **musicians** □ band, choir, chorus, consort, duet, duo, ensemble, group, nonet, octet, orchestra, quartet, quintet, septet, sextet, trio.

muster vb assemble, call together, collect, come together, convene, convoke, gather, get together, group, marshal, mobilize, rally, round up, summon.

musty adj airless, damp, dank, fusty, mildewed, mildewy, mouldy, smelly, stale, stuffy, unventilated.

mutant n abortion, anomaly, deviant, freak, monster, monstrosity, sport, variant.

mutation n alteration, deviance, evolution, metamorphosis, modification, transfiguration, transformation, transmutation, variation. ▷ CHANGE.

mute *adj* dumb, quiet, silent, speechless, tacit, taciturn, tight-lipped, tongue-tied, voiceless. ● *vb* damp, dampen, deaden, dull, hush, make quieter, mask, muffle, quieten, silence, soften, stifle, still, suppress, tone down.

mutilate *vb* cripple, damage, deface, disable, disfigure, dismember, injure, lame, maim, mangle, mar, spoil, vandalize, wound.

mutinous *adj* contumacious, defiant, disobedient, insubordinate, insurgent, insurrectionary, rebellious, refractory, revolutionary, seditious, subversive, ungovernable, unmanageable, unruly. *Opp* OBEDIENT.

mutiny *n* defiance, disobedience, insubordination, insurgency, insurrection, rebellion, revolt, revolution, sedition, subversion, unruliness, uprising. ● *vb* agitate, be mutinous, disobey, rebel, revolt, rise up, strike.

mutter *vb* drone, grumble, mumble, murmur, speak in an undertone, whisper. ▷ GRUMBLE, TALK.

mutual *adj* common, interactive, joint, reciprocal, reciprocated, requited, shared.

muzzle *n* jaws, mouth, nose, snout. ● *vb* censor, gag, restrain, silence, stifle, suppress.

mysterious *adj* arcane, baffling, bewildering, bizarre, confusing, cryptic, curious, dark, enigmatic, incomprehensible, inexplicable, inscrutable, insoluble, magical, miraculous, mystical, mystifying, obscure, perplexing, puzzling, recondite, secret, strange, uncanny, unexplained, unfathomable, unknown, weird. *Opp* STRAIGHTFORWARD.

mystery *n* conundrum, enigma, miracle, problem, puzzle, question, riddle, secret.

mystical *adj* abnormal, arcane, cabalistic, ineffable, metaphysical, mysterious, occult, other-worldly, preternatural, religious, spiritual, supernatural. *Opp* MUNDANE.

mystify *vb* baffle, *inf* bamboozle, *inf* beat, bewilder, confound, confuse, *inf* flummox, fool, hoax, perplex, puzzle, *inf* stump.

myth *n* **1** allegory, fable, legend, mythology, symbolism. **2** fabrication, falsehood, fiction, invention, make-believe, pretence, untruth.

mythical *adj* **1** allegorical, fabled, fabulous, legendary, mythic, mythological, poetic, symbolic. **2** false, fanciful, fictional, imaginary, invented, make-believe, non-existent, pretended, unreal. *Opp* REAL.

N

nadir *n* bottom, depths, low point, zero. *Opp* ZENITH.

nag *n* ▷ HORSE. ● *vb* annoy, badger, chivvy, find fault with, goad, *inf* go on at, harass, hector, *inf* henpeck, keep complaining, pester, *inf* plague, scold, worry.

nail *n* pin, spike, stud, tack.
- *vb* ▷ FASTEN.

naïve *adj* artless, *inf* born yesterday, candid, childlike, credulous, *inf* green, guileless, gullible, inexperienced, ingenuous, innocent, open, simple, simpleminded, stupid, trustful, trusting, unsophisticated, unsuspecting, unwary. *Opp* ARTFUL.

naked *adj* bare, denuded, disrobed, exposed, in the nude, nude, stark-naked, stripped, unclothed, unconcealed, uncovered, undraped, undressed.

name *n* **1** alias, appellation, Christian name, first name, forename, given name, *inf* handle, identity, nickname, nom de plume, pen name, personal name, pseudonym, sobriquet, surname, title. **2** denomination, designation, epithet, term. ● *vb* **1** baptize, call, christen, dub, style. **2** *name a book.* entitle, label. **3** *named him man of the match.* appoint, choose, commission, delegate, designate, elect, nominate, select, single out, specify. **named** ▷ SPECIFIC.

nameless *adj* **1** anonymous, incognito, unheard-of, unidentified, unnamed, unsung. **2** *nameless horrors.* dreadful, horrible, indescribable, inexpressible, shocking, unmentionable, unspeakable, unutterable.

nap *n* catnap, doze, *inf* forty winks, rest, *inf* shut-eye, siesta, sleep, snooze.

narrate *vb* chronicle, describe, detail, recount, rehearse, relate, repeat, report, retail, tell, unfold.

narration *n* commentary, reading, recital, recitation, relation,

storytelling, telling, voiceover.

narrative *n* account, chronicle, description, history, report, story, tale, *inf* yarn.

narrator *n* author, chronicler, raconteur, reporter, storyteller.

narrow *adj* attenuated, close, confined, constricted, constricting, cramped, enclosed, fine, limited, restricted, slender, slim, thin, tight. *Opp* WIDE.

narrow-minded *adj* biased, bigoted, conservative, conventional, hidebound, illiberal, inflexible, insular, intolerant, narrow, old-fashioned, parochial, petty, prejudiced, prim, prudish, puritanical, reactionary, rigid, small-minded, straitlaced, *inf* stuffy. *Opp* BROADMINDED.

nasty *adj* [*Nasty* refers to anything you do not like. The range of synonyms is almost limitless: we give only a selection here.] bad, beastly, dangerous, difficult, dirty, disagreeable, disgusting, distasteful, foul, hateful, horrible, loathsome, *sl* lousy, objectionable, obnoxious, obscene, *inf* offputting, repulsive, revolting, severe, sickening, unkind, unpleasant. *Opp* NICE.

nation *n* civilization, community, country, domain, land, people, population, power, race, realm, society, state, superpower.

national *adj* **1** ethnic, popular, racial. **2** *a national emergency.* countrywide, general, nationwide, state, widespread.
- *n* citizen, inhabitant, native, resident, subject.

nationalism n chauvinism, jingoism, loyalty, patriotism, xenophobia.

native adj 1 aboriginal, indigenous, local, original. 2 *native wit*. congenital, hereditary, inborn, inbred, inherent, inherited, innate, mother (*wit*), natural. • n aborigine, life-long resident.

natural adj 1 common, everyday, habitual, normal, ordinary, predictable, regular, routine, standard, typical, usual. 2 *natural feelings*. healthy, hereditary, human, inborn, inherited, innate, instinctive, intuitive, kind, maternal, native, paternal, proper, right. 3 *a natural smile*. artless, authentic, candid, genuine, guileless, sincere, spontaneous, unaffected, unpretentious, unselfconscious, unstudied. 4 *natural resources*. crude (*oil*), raw, unadulterated, unprocessed, unrefined. 5 *a natural leader*. born, congenital, untaught. Opp UNNATURAL.

nature n 1 countryside, creation, ecology, environment, natural history, scenery, wildlife. 2 attributes, character, complexion, constitution, disposition, essence, humour, make-up, manner, personality, properties, quality, temperament, traits. 3 category, description, kind, sort, species, type, variety.

naughty adj 1 bad, badly-behaved, bad-mannered, boisterous, contrary, defiant, delinquent, disobedient, disorderly, disruptive, fractious, headstrong, impish, impolite, incorrigible, insubordinate, intractable, misbehaved, mischievous, obstinate, obstreperous, perverse, playful, puckish, rascally, rebellious, refractory, roguish, rude, self-willed, stubborn, troublesome, uncontrollable, undisciplined, ungovernable, unmanageable, unruly, wayward, wicked, wild, wilful. 2 [inf] cheeky, improper, ribald, risqué, shocking, inf smutty, vulgar. ▷ OBSCENE. Opp POLITE, WELL BEHAVED.

nauseate vb disgust, offend, repel, revolt, sicken.

nauseous adj disgusting, foul, loathsome, nauseating, offensive, repulsive, revolting, sickening, stomach-turning.

nautical adj marine, maritime, naval, seafaring, seagoing, yachting.

navigate vb captain, direct, drive, guide, handle, manoeuvre, map-read, pilot, sail, skipper, steer.

navy n armada, convoy, fleet, flotilla.

near adj 1 abutting, adjacent, adjoining, bordering, close, connected, contiguous, immediate, nearby, neighbouring, next-door. 2 *Christmas is near*. approaching, coming, forthcoming, imminent, impending, looming, inf round the corner. 3 *near friends*. close, dear, familiar, intimate, related. Opp DISTANT.

nearly adv about, all but, almost, approaching, approximately, around, as good as, close to, just about, not quite, practically, roughly, virtually.

neat adj 1 adroit, clean, dainty, deft, dexterous, elegant, inf natty, orderly, organized, pretty, inf shipshape, smart, inf spick and span, spruce,

straight, systematic, tidy, trim, uncluttered, well-kept.
2 accurate, expert, methodical, meticulous, precise, skilful.
3 *neat alcohol.* pure, *inf* straight, unadulterated, undiluted. *Opp* CLUMSY, UNTIDY.

necessary *adj* compulsory, destined, essential, fated, imperative, important, indispensable, ineluctable, inescapable, inevitable, inexorable, mandatory, needed, needful, obligatory, predestined, required, requisite, unavoidable, vital. *Opp* UNNECESSARY.

necessity *n* **1** compulsion, essential, inevitability, *inf* must, need, obligation, prerequisite, requirement, requisite, *Lat* sine qua non. **2** beggary, destitution, hardship, indigence, need, penury, poverty, privation, shortage, suffering, want.

need *n* call, demand, lack, requirement, want.
▷ NECESSITY. ● *vb* be short of, call for, crave, demand, depend on, lack, miss, rely on, require, want.

needless *adj* excessive, gratuitous, pointless, redundant, superfluous, unnecessary.

needy *adj* badly off, destitute, *inf* hard up, impecunious, impoverished, indigent, necessitous, penurious, poverty-stricken, underpaid. ▷ POOR.

negate *vb* annul, cancel out, deny, gainsay, invalidate, nullify, oppose.

negative *adj* adversarial, antagonistic, *inf* anti, contradictory, destructive, disagreeing, dissenting, grudging, nullifying, obstructive, opposing, pessimistic, uncooperative,

unenthusiastic, unresponsive, unwilling. ● *n* denial, no, refusal, rejection, veto. *Opp* POSITIVE.

neglect *n* carelessness, dereliction of duty, disregard, inadvertence, inattention, indifference, negligence, oversight, slackness. ● *vb* abandon, be remiss about, disregard, forget, ignore, leave alone, let slide, lose sight of, miss, omit, overlook, pay no attention to, shirk, skip. **neglected** ▷ DERELICT.

negligent *adj* careless, forgetful, heedless, inattentive, inconsiderate, indifferent, irresponsible, lax, offhand, reckless, remiss, slack, sloppy, slovenly, thoughtless, uncaring, unthinking. *Opp* CAREFUL.

negligible *adj* imperceptible, inconsequential, inconsiderable, insignificant, minor, nugatory, paltry, petty, slight, small, tiny, trifling, trivial, unimportant. *Opp* CONSIDERABLE.

negotiate *vb* arbitrate, bargain, come to terms, confer, deal, discuss terms, haggle, intercede, make arrangements, mediate, parley, transact.

negotiation *n* arbitration, bargaining, conciliation, debate, diplomacy, discussion, mediation, parleying, transaction.

negotiator *n* agent, ambassador, arbitrator, broker, conciliator, diplomat, go-between, intercessor, intermediary, mediator, middleman.

neighbourhood *n* area, community, district, environs, locality, place, purlieus, quarter, region, surroundings, vicinity, zone.

neighbouring *adj* adjacent, adjoining, attached, bordering, close, closest, connecting, contiguous, near, nearby, nearest, next-door, surrounding.

neighbourly *adj* civil, considerate, friendly, helpful, kind, sociable, thoughtful, well-disposed.

nerve *n* coolness, determination, firmness, fortitude, resolution, resolve, will-power. ▷ COURAGE.

nervous *adj* afraid, agitated, anxious, apprehensive, disturbed, edgy, excitable, fearful, fidgety, flustered, fretful, highly-strung, ill-at-ease, *inf* in a tizzy, insecure, *inf* jittery, *inf* jumpy, *inf* nervy, neurotic, on edge, *inf* on tenterhooks, *inf* rattled, restive, restless, ruffled, shaky, shy, strained, tense, timid, *inf* touchy, *inf* twitchy, uneasy, unnerved, unsettled, *inf* uptight, worried. ▷ FRIGHTENED. *Opp* CALM.

nestle *vb* cuddle, curl up, huddle, nuzzle, snuggle.

net *n* lace, lattice-work, mesh, netting, network, web.
● *vb* 1 catch, capture, enmesh, ensnare, trammel, trap. 2 *net £200 a week.* accumulate, bring in, clear, earn, get, make, realize, receive, *inf* take home.

network *n* 1 *inf* criss-cross, grid, labyrinth, lattice, maze, mesh, net, netting, tangle, tracery, web. 2 complex, organization, system.

neurosis *n* abnormality, anxiety, depression, mental condition, obsession, phobia.

neurotic *adj* anxious, distraught, disturbed, irrational, maladjusted, nervous,

obsessive, overwrought, unbalanced, unstable.

neuter *adj* ambiguous, ambivalent, asexual, indeterminate, uncertain. ● *vb* castrate, *inf* doctor, emasculate, geld, spay, sterilize.

neutral *adj* 1 detached, disinterested, dispassionate, fair, impartial, indifferent, non-aligned, non-belligerent, non-partisan, objective, unaffiliated, unaligned, unbiased, uncommitted, uninvolved, unprejudiced. *Opp* BIASED. 2 *neutral colours.* characterless, colourless, dull, drab, indefinite, indeterminate, intermediate, neither one thing nor the other, pale, vague. *Opp* DISTINCTIVE.

neutralize *vb* annul, cancel out, compensate for, counteract, counterbalance, invalidate, make ineffective, make up for, negate, nullify, offset, wipe out.

new *adj* 1 brand-new, clean, different, fresh, mint, strange, unfamiliar, unheard of, untried, unused. 2 *new ideas.* advanced, contemporary, current, different, fashionable, latest, modern, modernistic, newfangled, novel, original, recent, revolutionary, *inf* trendy, up-to-date. 3 *new data.* added, additional, changed, extra, further, just arrived, supplementary, unexpected, unknown. *Opp* OLD.

newcomer *n* alien, arrival, immigrant, new boy, new girl, outsider, settler, stranger.

news *n* account, advice, announcement, bulletin, communication, communiqué, dispatch, headlines, information, intelligence, *inf* the latest, message, newscast, newsflash, newsletter, notice, press-release, proclamation, report, rumour, statement, *old use* tidings, word.

newspaper *n inf* daily, gazette, journal, paper, periodical, *inf* rag, tabloid.

next *adj* 1 adjacent, adjoining, closest, nearest, neighbouring, next-door. 2 *the next moment*. following, soonest, subsequent, succeeding.

nice *adj* 1 accurate, careful, delicate, discriminating, exact, fine, hair-splitting, meticulous, precise, punctilious, scrupulous, subtle. 2 *nice manners*. dainty, elegant, fastidious, fussy, particular, *inf* pernickety, polished, refined, well-mannered. 3 [*inf*: In this sense, nice refers to anything which you like. The range of synonyms is almost limitless: we give only a selection here.] acceptable, agreeable, amiable, attractive, beautiful, delicious, delightful, friendly, good, gratifying, kind, likeable, pleasant, satisfactory, welcome. *Opp* NASTY.

niche *n* alcove, corner, hollow, nook, recess.

nickname *n* alias, sobriquet.

niggardly *adj* mean, miserly, parsimonious, stingy.

nimble *adj* acrobatic, active, adroit, agile, brisk, deft, dextrous, limber, lithe, lively, *inf* nippy, quick-moving, sprightly, spry, swift. *Opp* CLUMSY.

nip *vb* bite, clip, pinch, snag, snap at, squeeze.

nobility *n* 1 dignity, glory, grandeur, greatness, high-

mindedness, integrity, magnanimity, morality, nobleness, uprightness, virtue, worthiness. 2 *the nobility*. aristocracy, élite, gentry, nobles, peerage, the ruling classes, *inf* the upper crust.

noble *adj* 1 aristocratic, *inf* blue-blooded, courtly, distinguished, élite, gentle, high-born, high-ranking, patrician, princely, royal, thoroughbred, titled, upper-class. 2 *noble deeds*. brave, chivalrous, courageous, gallant, glorious, heroic. 3 *noble thoughts*. elevated, high-flown, honourable, lofty, magnanimous, moral, upright, virtuous, worthy. 4 *noble music*. dignified, elegant, grand, great, imposing, impressive, magnificent, majestic, splendid, stately. *Opp* BASE, COMMON.
● *n* aristocrat, gentleman, gentlewoman, grandee, lady, lord, nobleman, noblewoman, patrician, peer, peeress.

nod *vb* bend, bob, bow. **nod off** ▷ SLEEP.

noise *n inf* babel, bawling, bedlam, blare, cacophony, *inf* caterwauling, clamour, clangour, clatter, commotion, din, discord, *inf* fracas, hubbub, *inf* hullabaloo, outcry, pandemonium, *inf* racket, row, *inf* rumpus, screaming, screeching, shouting, shrieking, tumult, uproar, yelling. ▷ SOUND. *Opp* SILENCE.

noiseless *adj* inaudible, mute, muted, quiet, silent, soft, soundless, still. *Opp* NOISY.

noisy *adj* blaring, boisterous, booming, cacophonous, chattering, clamorous, deafening, discordant, dissonant, ear-splitting, fortissimo, harsh, loud, raucous, resounding, reverberating, rowdy, screaming, screeching, shrieking, shrill, strident, talkative, thunderous, tumultuous, unmusical, uproarious, vociferous. *Opp* NOISELESS.

nomadic *adj* itinerant, peripatetic, roving, travelling, vagrant, wandering, wayfaring.

nominal *adj* **1** formal, in name only, ostensible, self-styled, *inf* so-called, supposed, theoretical, titular. **2** *a nominal sum.* insignificant, minimal, minor, small, token.

nominate *vb* appoint, choose, designate, elect, name, propose, put forward, *inf* put up, recommend, select, specify.

non-existent *adj* chimerical, fictional, fictitious, hypothetical, imaginary, imagined, legendary, made-up, mythical, unreal. *Opp* REAL.

nonplus *vb* amaze, baffle, confound, disconcert, dumbfound, flummox, perplex, puzzle, render speechless.

nonsense *n* **1** [Most synonyms *inf*] balderdash, bilge, boloney, bosh, bunk, bunkum, claptrap, codswallop, double-Dutch, drivel, eyewash, fiddlesticks, foolishness, gibberish, gobbledegook, mumbo jumbo, piffle, poppycock, rot, rubbish, silliness, stuff and nonsense, stupidity, tommy-rot, trash, tripe, twaddle. **2** *The plan was a nonsense.* absurdity, inanity, mistake, nonsensical idea.

nonsensical *adj* absurd, asinine, crazy, *inf* daft, fatuous, foolish, idiotic, illogical, impractical, inane, incomprehensible, irrational, insane,

ludicrous, mad, meaningless, preposterous, ridiculous, senseless, stupid, unreasonable. ▷ SILLY. *Opp* SENSIBLE.

non-stop *adj* ceaseless, constant, continual, continuous, endless, eternal, incessant, interminable, perpetual, persistent, *inf* round-the-clock, steady, unbroken, unending, uninterrupted, unremitting.

norm *n* criterion, measure, model, pattern, rule, standard, type, yardstick.

normal *adj* **1** accepted, accustomed, average, common, commonplace, conventional, customary, established, everyday, familiar, general, habitual, natural, ordinary, orthodox, predictable, prosaic, quotidian, regular, routine, *inf* run-of-the-mill, standard, typical, universal, unsurprising, usual. **2** *a normal person.* balanced, healthy, rational, reasonable, sane, stable, *inf* straight, well-adjusted. *Opp* ABNORMAL.

normalize *vb* legalize, regularize, regulate, return to normal.

nose *n* **1** nostrils, proboscis, snout. **2** *nose of a boat.* bow, front, prow. ● *vb* enter cautiously, insinuate yourself, intrude, nudge your way, penetrate, probe, push, shove. **nose about** ▷ PRY.

nostalgia *n* longing, memory, pining, regret, reminiscence, sentiment, sentimentality, yearning.

nostalgic *adj* emotional, maudlin, regretful, romantic, sentimental, wistful, yearning.

nosy *adj* curious, eavesdropping, inquisitive, interfering, meddlesome, prying.

notable *adj* celebrated, conspicuous, distinctive, distinguished, eminent, evident, extraordinary, famous, illustrious, important, impressive, memorable, noted, noteworthy, noticeable, obvious, outstanding, preeminent, prominent, rare, remarkable, renowned, singular, striking, uncommon, unforgettable, unusual, well-known. *Opp* ORDINARY.

note *n* 1 billet-doux, chit, communication, correspondence, epistle, jotting, letter, *inf* memo, memorandum, message, postcard. 2 annotation, comment, cross-reference, explanation, footnote, gloss, jotting, marginal note. 3 *a note in your voice.* feeling, quality, sound, tone. 4 *a £5 note.* banknote, bill, currency, draft. • *vb* 1 enter, jot down, record, scribble, write down. 2 *note mentally.* detect, discern, discover, feel, find, heed, mark, mind, notice, observe, pay attention to, remark, register, see, spy, take note of. **noted** ▷ FAMOUS.

noteworthy *adj* exceptional, extraordinary, rare, remarkable, uncommon, unique, unusual. *Opp* ORDINARY.

nothing *n cricket* duck, *tennis* love, *old use* naught, *football* nil, nought, zero, *sl* zilch.

notice *n* 1 advertisement, announcement, handbill, handout, intimation, leaflet, message, note, notification, placard, poster, sign, warning. 2 attention, awareness, cognizance, consciousness, heed, note, regard. • *vb* be aware, detect, discern, discover, feel, find, heed, make out, mark, mind,

note, observe, pay attention to, perceive, register, remark, see, spy, take note. **give notice** ▷ NOTIFY, WARN.

noticeable *adj* appreciable, audible, clear, clear-cut, considerable, conspicuous, detectable, discernible, distinct, distinguishable, manifest, marked, measurable, notable, observable, obtrusive, obvious, overt, palpable, perceivable, perceptible, plain, prominent, pronounced, salient, significant, striking, unconcealed, unmistakable, visible. *Opp* IMPERCEPTIBLE.

notify *vb* acquaint, advise, alert, announce, apprise, give notice, inform, make known, proclaim, publish, report, tell, warn.

notion *n* apprehension, belief, concept, conception, fancy, hypothesis, idea, impression, *inf* inkling, opinion, sentiment, theory, thought, understanding, view.

notorious *adj* disgraceful, disreputable, flagrant, ill-famed, infamous, outrageous, overt, patent, scandalous, shocking, talked about, undisguised, undisputed, well-known. ▷ FAMOUS, WICKED.

nourish *vb* feed, maintain, nurse, nurture, provide for, strengthen, support, sustain. **nourishing** ▷ NUTRITIOUS.

nourishment *n* diet, food, goodness, nutrient, nutriment, nutrition, sustenance, *old use* victuals.

novel *adj* different, fresh, imaginative, innovative, new, odd, original, rare, singular, startling, strange, surprising, uncommon, unconventional,

unfamiliar, untested, unusual.
Opp FAMILIAR. ● *n* best-seller,
inf blockbuster, fiction, novel-
ette, novella, romance, story.
▷ WRITING.

novelty *n* 1 freshness, newness,
oddity, originality, strangeness,
surprise, unfamiliarity, uniqueness. 2 bauble, curiosity,
gimmick, knick-knack, ornament, souvenir, trifle, trinket.

novice *n* amateur, apprentice,
beginner, *inf* greenhorn, inexperienced person, initiate, learner, probationer, tiro, trainee.

now *adv* at once, at present,
here and now, immediately,
instantly, just now, nowadays,
promptly, *inf* right now,
straight away, today.

noxious *adj* corrosive, foul,
harmful, nasty, noisome, objectionable, poisonous, polluting,
sulphureous, sulphurous,
unwholesome.

nub *n* centre, core, crux, essence,
gist, heart, kernel, nucleus,
pith, point.

nucleus *n* centre, core, heart,
kernel, middle.

nude *adj* bare, disrobed,
exposed, in the nude, naked,
stark-naked, stripped, unclothed, uncovered, undressed.

nudge *vb* bump, dig, elbow, hit,
jab, jog, jolt, poke, prod, push,
shove, touch.

nuisance *n* annoyance, bother,
burden, inconvenience, irritant,
irritation, *inf* pain, pest, plague,
trouble, vexation, worry.

nullify *vb* abolish, annul, cancel,
do away with, invalidate,
negate, neutralize, quash,
repeal, rescind, revoke, stultify.

numb *adj* anaesthetized,
inf asleep, benumbed, cold,

dead, deadened, frozen, immobile, insensible, insensitive,
paralysed, senseless, suffering
from pins and needles.
Opp SENSITIVE. ● *vb* anaesthetize, benumb, deaden, desensitize, drug, dull, freeze, immobilize, make numb, paralyse,
stun, stupefy.

number *n* 1 digit, figure, integer, numeral, unit. 2 aggregate,
amount, *inf* bunch, collection,
crowd, multitude, quantity,
sum, total. ▷ GROUP. 3 *musical
number.* item, piece, song. 4 *a
number of a magazine.* copy,
edition, impression, issue,
printing, publication. ● *vb* add
up to, total, work out at.
▷ COUNT.

numerous *adj* abundant, copious, countless, endless,
incalculable, infinite, innumerable, many, multitudinous,
myriad, numberless, plentiful,
several, uncountable, untold.
Opp FEW.

nun *n* abbess, mother-superior,
novice, prioress, sister.

nurse *n* 1 district-nurse, *old
use* matron, sister. 2 nanny,
nursemaid. ● *vb* 1 care for, look
after, minister to, nurture,
tend, treat. 2 breast-feed, feed,
suckle, wet-nurse. 3 cherish,
coddle, cradle, cuddle, dandle,
hold, hug, mother, pamper.

nursery *n* 1 crèche, kindergarten, nursery school. 2 garden
centre, market garden.

nurture *vb* bring up, cultivate,
educate, feed, look after, nourish, nurse, rear, tend, train.

nut *n* kernel. □ *almond, brazil,
cashew, chestnut, cob-nut, coconut, filbert, hazel, peanut,
pecan, pistachio, walnut.*

nutrient n fertilizer, goodness, nourishment.

nutriment n food, goodness, nourishment, nutrition, sustenance.

nutritious adj alimentary, beneficial, good for you, health-giving, healthy, nourishing, sustaining, wholesome.

O

oasis n 1 spring, watering-hole, well. 2 asylum, haven, refuge, resort, retreat, safe harbour, sanctuary.

oath n 1 assurance, avowal, guarantee, pledge, promise, undertaking, vow, word of honour. 2 blasphemy, curse, exclamation, expletive, inf four-letter word, imprecation, malediction, obscenity, profanity, swearword.

obedient adj acquiescent, amenable, biddable, compliant, conformable, deferential, disciplined, docile, duteous, dutiful, law-abiding, manageable, submissive, subservient, tamed, tractable, well-behaved, well-trained. Opp DISOBEDIENT.

obese adj corpulent, gross, overweight. ▷ FAT.

obey vb abide by, accept, acquiesce in, act in accordance with, adhere to, agree to, be obedient to, be ruled by, bow to, carry out, comply with, conform to, defer to, do what you are told, execute, follow, fulfil, give in to, heed, honour, implement, keep to, mind, observe, perform,

inf stick to, submit to, take orders from. Opp DISOBEY.

object n 1 article, body, entity, item, thing. 2 aim, end, goal, intent, intention, objective, point, purpose, reason. 3 object of ridicule. butt, destination, target. ● vb argue, be opposed, carp, cavil, complain, demur, disapprove, dispute, dissent, expostulate, sl grouse, grumble, make an objection, inf mind, inf moan, oppose, protest, quibble, raise objections, raise questions, remonstrate, take a stand, take exception. Opp ACCEPT, AGREE.

objection n argument, cavil, challenge, complaint, demur, demurral, disapproval, exception, opposition, outcry, protest, query, question, quibble, refusal, remonstration.

objectionable adj abhorrent, detestable, disagreeable, disgusting, dislikeable, displeasing, distasteful, foul, hateful, insufferable, intolerable, loathsome, nasty, nauseating, noisome, obnoxious, odious, offensive, inf off-putting, repellent, repugnant, repulsive, revolting, sickening, unacceptable, undesirable, unwanted. Opp ACCEPTABLE.

objective adj detached, disinterested, dispassionate, factual, impartial, impersonal, neutral, open-minded, outward-looking, rational, scientific, unbiased, uncoloured, unemotional, unprejudiced. 2 objective evidence. empirical, existing, observable, real. Opp SUBJECTIVE. ● n aim, ambition, aspiration, design, destination, end, goal, hope, intent,

348

intention, object, point, purpose, target.

obligation *n* commitment, compulsion, constraint, contract, duty, liability, need, requirement, responsibility. ▷ PROMISE. *Opp* OPTION.

obligatory *adj* binding, compulsory, essential, mandatory, necessary, required, requisite, unavoidable. *Opp* OPTIONAL.

oblige *vb* 1 coerce, compel, constrain, force, make, require. 2 *Please oblige me.* accommodate, gratify, indulge, please. **obliged** ▷ BOUND, GRATEFUL. **obliging** ▷ HELPFUL, POLITE.

oblique *adj* 1 angled, askew, aslant, canted, declining, diagonal, inclined, leaning, listing, raked, rising, skewed, slanted, slanting, slantwise, sloping, tilted. 2 *an oblique insult.* backhanded, circuitous, circumlocutory, devious, implicit, implied, indirect, roundabout. ▷ EVASIVE. *Opp* DIRECT.

obliterate *vb* blot out, cancel, cover over, delete, destroy, efface, eliminate, eradicate, erase, expunge, extirpate, leave no trace of, rub out, wipe out.

oblivion *n* 1 anonymity, darkness, disregard, extinction, limbo, neglect, obscurity. 2 amnesia, coma, forgetfulness, ignorance, insensibility, obliviousness, unawareness, unconsciousness.

oblivious *adj* forgetful, heedless, ignorant, insensible, insensitive, unacquainted, unaware, unconscious, unfeeling, uninformed, unmindful, unresponsive. *Opp* AWARE.

obscene *adj* abominable, bawdy, *inf* blue, coarse, corrupting, crude, debauched, degenerate, depraved, dirty, disgusting, distasteful, filthy, foul, foulmouthed, gross, immodest, immoral, improper, impure, indecent, indecorous, indelicate, *inf* kinky, lecherous, lewd, loathsome, nasty, *inf* off-colour, offensive, outrageous, perverted, pornographic, prurient, repulsive, ribald, risqué, rude, salacious, scatological, scurrilous, shameful, shameless, shocking, *inf* sick, smutty, suggestive, unchaste, vile, vulgar. ▷ OBJECTIONABLE, SEXY. *Opp* DECENT.

obscenity *n* abomination, blasphemy, coarseness, dirtiness, evil, filth, foulness, grossness, immorality, impropriety, indecency, lewdness, licentiousness, offensiveness, outrage, perversion, pornography, profanity, scurrility, vileness. ▷ SWEARWORD.

obscure *adj* 1 blurred, clouded, concealed, covered, dark, dim, faint, foggy, hazy, hidden, inconspicuous, indefinite, indistinct, masked, misty, murky, nebulous, secret, shadowy, shady, shrouded, unclear, unlit, unrecognizable, vague, veiled. *Opp* CLEAR. 2 *an obscure joke.* arcane, baffling, complex, cryptic, delphic, enigmatic, esoteric, incomprehensible, mystifying, perplexing, puzzling, recherché, recondite, strange. *Opp* OBVIOUS. 3 *an obscure poet.* forgotten, minor, undistinguished, unfamiliar, unheard of, unimportant, unknown, unnoticed. *Opp* FAMOUS. ● *vb* block out, blur, cloak, cloud, conceal, cover, darken, disguise, eclipse, envelop, hide, make obscure, mask, obfuscate, overshadow, screen, shade, shroud, veil. *Opp* CLARIFY.

obsequious *adj* abject, *inf* bootlicking, crawling, cringing, deferential, effusive, fawning, flattering, fulsome, *inf* greasy, grovelling, ingratiating, insincere, mealy-mouthed, menial, *inf* oily, servile, *inf* smarmy, submissive, subservient, sycophantic, unctuous. **be obsequious** ▷ GROVEL.

observant *adj* alert, astute, attentive, aware, careful, eagle-eyed, heedful, mindful, on the lookout, *inf* on the qui vive, perceptive, percipient, quick, sharp-eyed, shrewd, vigilant, watchful, with eyes peeled. *Opp* INATTENTIVE.

observation *n* **1** attention (to), examination, inspection, monitoring, scrutiny, study, surveillance, viewing, watching. **2** comment, note, opinion, reaction, reflection, remark, response, sentiment, statement, thought, utterance.

observe *vb* **1** consider, contemplate, detect, discern, examine, *inf* keep an eye on, look at, monitor, note, notice, perceive, regard, scrutinize, see, spot, spy, stare at, study, view, watch, witness. **2** *observe rules.* abide by, adhere to, comply with, conform to, follow, heed, honour, keep, obey, pay attention to, respect. **3** *observe Easter.* celebrate, commemorate, keep, mark, recognize, remember, solemnize. **4** *observed that it was badly acted.* animadvert (on), comment, declare, explain,

make an observation, mention, reflect, remark, say, state.

observer *n* beholder, bystander, commentator, eyewitness, looker-on, onlooker, spectator, viewer, watcher, witness.

obsess *vb* become an obsession with, bedevil, consume, control, dominate, grip, haunt, monopolize, plague, possess, preoccupy, rule, take hold of.

obsession *n* addiction, *inf* bee in your bonnet, conviction, fetish, fixation, *inf* hang-up, *inf* hobby-horse, *Fr* idée fixe, infatuation, mania, passion, phobia, preoccupation, *sl* thing.

obsessive *adj* addictive, compulsive, consuming, controlling, dominating, haunting, passionate.

obsolescent *adj* ageing, aging, declining, dying out, fading, going out of use, losing popularity, moribund, *inf* on the way out, waning.

obsolete *adj* anachronistic, antiquated, antique, archaic, dated, dead, discarded, disused, extinct, old-fashioned, *inf* old hat, out-dated, out-of-date, outmoded, passé, primitive, superannuated, superseded, unfashionable. ▷ OLD. *Opp* CURRENT.

obstacle *n* bar, barricade, barrier, block, blockage, catch, check, difficulty, hindrance, hurdle, impediment, obstruction, problem, restriction, snag, *inf* stumbling block.

obstinate *adj* adamant, *sl* bloody-minded, defiant, determined, dogged, firm, headstrong, immovable, inflexible, intractable, intransigent, *inf* mulish, obdurate, persistent, pertinacious, perverse, *inf* pig-headed, refractory, resolute, rigid, self-willed, single-minded, *inf* stiff-necked, stubborn, tenacious, uncooperative, unreasonable, unyielding, wilful, wrong-headed. *Opp* AMENABLE.

obstreperous *adj* awkward, boisterous, disorderly, irrepressible, naughty, rough, rowdy, *inf* stroppy, turbulent, uncontrollable, undisciplined, unmanageable, unruly, vociferous, wild. ▷ NOISY. *Opp* WELL-BEHAVED.

obstruct *vb* arrest, bar, block, bring to a standstill, check, curb, delay, deter, frustrate, halt, hamper, hinder, hold up, impede, inhibit, interfere with, interrupt, occlude, prevent, restrict, retard, slow down, stand in the way of, *inf* stonewall, stop, *inf* stymie, thwart. *Opp* HELP.

obtain *vb* 1 acquire, attain, be given, bring, buy, capture, come by, come into possession of, earn, elicit, enlist ⟨help⟩, extort, extract, find, gain, get, get hold of, *inf* lay your hands on, *inf* pick up, procure, purchase, receive, secure, seize, take possession of, win. 2 *rules still obtain*. apply, be in force, be in use, be relevant, be valid, exist, prevail, stand.

obtrusive *adj* blatant, conspicuous, forward, importunate, inescapable, interfering, intrusive, meddling, meddlesome, noticeable, out of place, prominent, unwanted, unwelcome. ▷ OBVIOUS. *Opp* INCONSPICUOUS.

obtuse *adj* dense, dull, imperceptive, slow, slow-witted. ▷ STUPID. *Opp* CLEVER.

obviate *vb* avert, forestall, make unnecessary, preclude, prevent, remove, take away.

obvious *adj* apparent, bald, blatant, clear, clear-cut, conspicuous, distinct, evident, eye-catching, flagrant, glaring, gross, inescapable, intrusive, manifest, notable, noticeable, obtrusive, open, overt, palpable, patent, perceptible, plain, prominent, pronounced, recognizable, self-evident, self-explanatory, straightforward, unconcealed, undisguised, undisputed, unmistakable, visible. *Opp* HIDDEN, OBSCURE.

occasion *n* 1 chance, circumstance, moment, occurrence, opportunity, time. 2 *no occasion for rudeness*. call, cause, excuse, grounds, justification, need, reason. 3 *a happy occasion*. affair, celebration, ceremony, event, function, *inf* get-together, happening, incident, occurrence, party.

occasional *adj* casual, desultory, fitful, infrequent, intermittent, irregular, odd, *inf* once in a while, periodic, random, rare, scattered, spasmodic, sporadic, uncommon, unpredictable. *Opp* FREQUENT, REGULAR.

occult *adj* ▷ SUPERNATURAL.
  ● *n* black arts, black magic, cabbalism, diabolism, occultism, sorcery, the supernatural, witchcraft.

occupant *n* denizen, householder, incumbent, inhabitant, lessee, lodger, occupier, owner, resident, tenant.

occupation *n* 1 incumbency, lease, occupancy, possession, residency, tenancy, tenure, use. 2 appropriation, colonization, conquest, invasion, oppression, seizure, subjection, subjugation, suzerainty, *inf* takeover, usurpation. **3** appointment, business, calling, career, employment, job, *inf* line, métier, position, post, profession, situation, trade, vocation, work. **4** *leisure occupation*. activity, diversion, entertainment, hobby, interest, pastime, pursuit, recreation.

occupy *vb* **1** dwell in, inhabit, live in, move into, reside in, take up residence in, tenant. **2** *occupy space*. fill, take up, use, utilize. **3** capture, colonize, conquer, garrison, invade, overrun, possess, subjugate, take over, take possession of. **4** *occupy your time*. absorb, busy, divert, engage, engross, involve, preoccupy. **occupied** ▷ BUSY.

occur *vb* appear, arise, befall, be found, chance, come about, come into being, *old use* come to pass, *inf* crop up, develop, exist, happen, manifest itself, materialize, *inf* show up, take place, *inf* transpire, *inf* turn out, *inf* turn up.

occurrence *n* affair, case, circumstance, development, event, happening, incident, manifestation, matter, occasion, phenomenon, proceeding.

odd *adj* **1** *odd numbers*. uneven. *Opp* EVEN. **2** *an odd sock*. extra, left over, *inf* one-off, remaining, single, spare, superfluous, surplus, unmatched, unused. **3** *odd jobs*. casual, irregular, miscellaneous, occasional, part-time, random, sundry, varied, various. **4** *odd behaviour*. abnormal, anomalous, atypical, bizarre, *inf* cranky, curious,

deviant, different, eccentric, exceptional, extraordinary, freak, funny, idiosyncratic, incongruous, inexplicable, *inf* kinky, outlandish, out of the ordinary, peculiar, puzzling, queer, rare, singular, strange, uncharacteristic, uncommon, unconventional, unexpected, unusual, weird. *Opp* NORMAL.

oddments *plur n* bits, bits and pieces, fragments, *inf* junk, leftovers, litter, odds and ends, offcuts, remnants, scraps, shreds, unwanted pieces.

odious *adj* detestable, execrable, loathsome, offensive, repugnant, repulsive. ▷ HATEFUL.

odorous *adj* fragrant, odoriferous, perfumed, scented. ▷ SMELLING.

odour *n* aroma, bouquet, fragrance, nose, redolence, scent, smell, stench, *inf* stink.

odourless *adj* deodorized, unscented. *Opp* ODOROUS.

offence *n* **1** breach, crime, fault, felony, infringement, lapse, malefaction, misdeed, misdemeanour, outrage, peccadillo, sin, transgression, trespass, violation, wrong, wrongdoing. **2** anger, annoyance, disgust, displeasure, hard feelings, indignation, irritation, pique, resentment, *inf* upset. **give offence** ▷ OFFEND.

offend *vb* **1** affront, anger, annoy, cause offence, chagrin, disgust, displease, embarrass, give offence, hurt your feelings, insult, irritate, make angry, *inf* miff, outrage, pain, provoke, *inf* put your back up, revolt, rile, sicken, slight, snub, upset, vex. **2** *offend against the law*. do wrong, transgress, violate. **be**

offended be annoyed, *inf* take umbrage.

offender *n* criminal, culprit, delinquent, evil-doer, guilty party, lawbreaker, malefactor, miscreant, outlaw, sinner, transgressor, wrongdoer.

offensive *adj* 1 abusive, annoying, antisocial, coarse, detestable, disagreeable, disgusting, displeasing, disrespectful, embarrassing, foul, impolite, improper, indecent, insulting, loathsome, nasty, nauseating, nauseous, noxious, objectionable, obnoxious, *inf* off-putting, repugnant, revolting, rude, sickening, unpleasant, unsavoury, vile, vulgar. ▷ OBSCENE. *Opp* PLEASANT. 2 *offensive action.* aggressive, antagonistic, attacking, belligerent, hostile, threatening, warlike. *Opp* PEACEABLE. ● *n* ▷ ATTACK.

offer *n* bid, proposal, proposition, suggestion, tender.
● *vb* 1 bid, extend, give the opportunity of, hold out, make an offer of, make available, proffer, put forward, put up, suggest. 2 *offer to help.* come forward, propose, *inf* show willing, volunteer.

offering *n* contribution, donation, gift, oblation, offertory, present, sacrifice.

offhand *adj* 1 abrupt, aloof, careless, cavalier, cool, curt, off-handed, perfunctory, unceremonious, uncooperative, uninterested. ▷ CASUAL.
2 ▷ IMPROMPTU.

office *n* 1 bureau, room, workplace, workroom.
2 appointment, assignment, commission, duty, function, job, occupation, place, position,

post, responsibility, role, situation, work.

officer *n* 1 adjutant, aide-decamp, CO, commandant, commanding officer. 2 *police officer.* constable, PC, policeman, policewoman, WPC.
3 ▷ OFFICIAL.

official *adj* accredited, approved, authentic, authoritative, authorized, bona fide, certified, formal, lawful, legal, legitimate, licensed, organized, proper, recognized, true, trustworthy, valid. ▷ FORMAL. ● *n* administrator, agent, appointee, authorized person, bureaucrat, dignitary, executive, functionary, mandarin, officer, organizer, representative, responsible person. □ *bailiff, captain, chief, clerk of court, commander, commissioner, consul, customs officer, director, elder (of church), equerry, governor, manager, marshal, mayor, mayoress, minister, monitor, ombudsman, overseer, prefect, president, principal, proctor, proprietor, registrar, sheriff, steward, superintendent, supervisor, usher.*

officiate *vb* adjudicate, be in charge, be responsible, chair (*a meeting*), conduct, have authority, manage, preside, referee, *inf* run (*a meeting*), umpire.

officious *adj inf* bossy, bumptious, *inf* cocky, dictatorial, forward, impertinent, interfering, meddlesome, meddling, overzealous, *inf* pushy, self-appointed, self-important.

offset *vb* cancel out, compensate for, counteract, counterbalance, make amends for, make good, make up for, redress.
▷ BALANCE.

offshoot n branch, by-product, derivative, development, *inf* spin-off, subsidiary product.

offspring n [*sing*] baby, child, descendant, heir, successor. [*plur*] brood, family, fry, issue, litter, progeny, *old use* seed, spawn, young.

often adv again and again, *inf* all the time, commonly, constantly, continually, frequently, generally, habitually, many times, regularly, repeatedly, time after time, time and again, usually.

oil vb grease, lubricate.

oily adj 1 buttery, fat, fatty, greasy, oleaginous. 2 *an oily manner*. ▷ OBSEQUIOUS.

ointment n balm, cream, embrocation, emollient, liniment, lotion, paste, salve, unguent.

old adj 1 ancient, antediluvian, antiquated, antique, crumbling, decayed, decaying, decrepit, dilapidated, early, historic, medieval, obsolete, primitive, quaint, ruined, superannuated, time-worn, venerable, veteran, vintage. ▷ OLD-FASHIONED. 2 *old times*. bygone, classical, forgotten, former, (*time*) immemorial, *old use* olden, past, prehistoric, previous, primeval, primitive, primordial, remote. 3 *old people*. advanced in years, aged, *inf* doddery, elderly, geriatric, *inf* getting on, grey-haired, hoary, *inf* in your dotage, long-lived, oldish, *inf* past it, senile. 4 *old customs*. age-old, enduring, established, lasting, long-standing, time-honoured, traditional, well-established. 5 *old clothes*. moth-eaten, ragged, scruffy, shabby, threadbare,

worn, worn-out. 6 *old bread*. dry, stale. 7 *old tickets*. cancelled, expired, invalid, used. 8 *an old hand*. experienced, expert, familiar, mature, practised, skilled, veteran. Opp NEW, YOUNG. **old age** *inf* declining years, decrepitude, *inf* dotage, senility. **old person** centenarian, *inf* fogey, *inf* fogy, nonagenarian, octogenarian, pensioner, septuagenarian.

old-fashioned adj anachronistic, antiquated, archaic, backward-looking, conventional, dated, fusty, hackneyed, narrow-minded, obsolete, old, *inf* old hat, outdated, out-of-date, out-of-touch, outmoded, passé, pedantic, prim, proper, prudish, reactionary, time-honoured, traditional, unfashionable. Opp MODERN. **old-fashioned person** *inf* fogey, *inf* fogy, *inf* fuddy-duddy, pedant, reactionary, *inf* square.

omen n augury, auspice, foreboding, forewarning, harbinger, indication, portent, premonition, presage, prognostication, sign, token, warning, *inf* writing on the wall.

ominous adj baleful, dire, fateful, forbidding, foreboding, grim, ill-omened, ill-starred, inauspicious, lowering, menacing, portentous, prophetic, sinister, threatening, unfavourable, unlucky, unpromising, unpropitious, warning. Opp AUSPICIOUS.

omission n 1 deletion, elimination, exception, excision, exclusion. 2 failure, gap, neglect, negligence, oversight, shortcoming.

omit *vb* 1 cross out, cut, dispense with, drop, edit out, eliminate, erase, except, exclude, ignore, jump, leave out, miss out, overlook, pass over, reject, skip, strike out. 2 fail, forget, neglect.

omnipotent *adj* all-powerful, almighty, invincible, supreme, unconquerable.

oncoming *adj* advancing, approaching, facing, looming, nearing.

onerous *adj* burdensome, demanding, heavy, laborious, taxing. ▷ DIFFICULT.

one-sided *adj* 1 biased, bigoted, partial, partisan, prejudiced. 2 *one-sided game*. ill-matched, unbalanced, unequal, uneven.

onlooker *n* bystander, eyewitness, looker-on, observer, spectator, watcher, witness.

only *adj* lone, one, single, sole, solitary, unique. ● *adv* barely, exclusively, just, merely, simply, solely.

ooze *vb* bleed, discharge, emit, exude, leak, secrete, seep, weep.

opaque *adj* cloudy, dark, dim, dull, filmy, hazy, impenetrable, muddy, murky, obscure, turbid, unclear. *Opp* CLEAR.

open *adj* 1 agape, ajar, gaping, unbolted, unfastened, unlocked, unsealed, unwrapped, wide, wide-open, yawning. 2 accessible, available, exposed, free, public, revealed, unenclosed, unprotected, unrestricted. 3 *open space*. bare, broad, clear, empty, extensive, spacious, treeless, uncrowded, undefended, unfenced, unobstructed, vacant. 4 *open arms*. extended, outstretched, spread out, unfolded. 5 *open nature*. artless,

candid, communicative, flexible, frank, generous, guileless, honest, innocent, magnanimous, open-minded, responsive, sincere, straightforward, transparent, uninhibited. 6 *open defiance*. apparent, barefaced, blatant, conspicuous, downright, evident, flagrant, obvious, outspoken, overt, plain, unconcealed, undisguised, visible. 7 *an open question*. arguable, debatable, moot, problematical, unanswered, undecided, unresolved, unsettled. *Opp* CLOSED, HIDDEN.

● *vb* 1 unbar, unblock, unbolt, unclose, uncork, undo, unfasten, unfold, unfurl, unlatch, unlock, unroll, unseal, untie, unwrap. 2 become open, gape, yawn. 3 *open proceedings*. activate, begin, commence, establish, *inf* get going, inaugurate, initiate, *inf* kick off, launch, set in motion, set up, start. *Opp* CLOSE.

opening *adj* first, inaugural, initial, introductory. *Opp* FINAL. ● *n* 1 aperture, breach, break, chink, cleft, crack, crevice, cut, door, doorway, fissure, gap, gash, gate, gateway, hatch, hole, leak, mouth, orifice, outlet, rent, rift, slit, slot, space, split, tear, vent. 2 beginning, birth, commencement, dawn, inauguration, inception, initiation, launch, outset, start. 3 *a business opening*. *inf* break, chance, opportunity, way in.

operate *vb* 1 act, function, go, perform, run, work. 2 *operate a machine*. control, deal with, drive, handle, manage, use, work. 3 *operate on a patient*. do an operation, perform surgery.

operation *n* 1 control, direction, function, functioning, management, operating, performance, running, working. 2 action, activity, business, campaign, effort, enterprise, exercise, manoeuvre, movement, procedure, proceeding, process, project, transaction, undertaking, venture. 3 [*medical*] biopsy, surgery, transplant.

operational *adj* functioning, going, in operation, in use, in working order, operating, operative, running, *inf* up and running, usable, working.

operative *adj* 1 ▷ OPERATIONAL. 2 *the operative word.* crucial, important, key, principal, relevant, significant. ● *n* ▷ WORKER.

opinion *n* assessment, attitude, belief, comment, conclusion, conjecture, conviction, estimate, feeling, guess, idea, impression, judgement, notion, perception, point of view, sentiment, theory, thought, view, viewpoint, way of thinking.

opponent *n* adversary, antagonist, challenger, competitor, contender, contestant, enemy, foe, opposer, opposition, rival. *Opp* ALLY.

opportune *adj* advantageous, appropriate, auspicious, beneficial, convenient, favourable, felicitous, fortunate, good, happy, lucky, propitious, right, suitable, timely, well-timed. *Opp* INCONVENIENT.

opportunity *n inf* break, chance, moment, occasion, opening, possibility, time.

oppose *vb* argue with, attack, be at variance with, be opposed to, challenge, combat, compete against, confront, contend with,

contest, contradict, controvert, counter, counterattack, defy, disagree with, disapprove of, dissent from, face, fight, object to, obstruct, *inf* pit your wits against, quarrel with, resist, rival, stand up to, *inf* take a stand against, take issue with, withstand. *Opp* SUPPORT.

opposed ▷ HOSTILE, OPPOSITE.

opposite *adj* 1 antithetical, conflicting, contradictory, contrasting, converse, different, hostile, incompatible, inconsistent, opposed, opposing, rival. 2 contrary, reverse. 3 *your opposite number.* corresponding, equivalent, facing, matching, similar. ● *n* antithesis, contrary, converse, reverse.

opposition *n* antagonism, antipathy, competition, defiance, disapproval, enmity, hostility, objection, resistance, scepticism, unfriendliness. ▷ OPPONENT. *Opp* SUPPORT.

oppress *vb* abuse, afflict, burden, crush, depress, encumber, enslave, exploit, grind down, harass, intimidate, keep under, maltreat, overburden, persecute, pressurize, *inf* ride roughshod over, subdue, subjugate, terrorize, *inf* trample on, tyrannize, weigh down.

oppressed *adj* browbeaten, downtrodden, enslaved, exploited, misused, persecuted, subjugated, tyrannized.

oppression *n* abuse, despotism, enslavement, exploitation, harassment, injustice, maltreatment, persecution, pressure, subjection, subjugation, suppression, tyranny.

oppressive *adj* 1 brutal, cruel, despotic, harsh, repressive, tyrannical, undemocratic, unjust. **2** airless, close, heavy, hot, humid, muggy, stifling, stuffy, suffocating, sultry.

optimism *n* buoyancy, cheerfulness, confidence, hope, idealism, positiveness. *Opp* PESSIMISM.

optimistic *adj* buoyant, cheerful, confident, expectant, hopeful, idealistic, *inf* looking on the bright side, positive, sanguine. *Opp* PESSIMISTIC.

optimum *adj* best, finest, first-class, first-rate, highest, ideal, maximum, most favourable, perfect, prime, superlative, top.

option *n* alternative, chance, choice, election, possibility, selection.

optional *adj* avoidable, discretionary, dispensable, elective, inessential, possible, unnecessary, unforced, voluntary. *Opp* COMPULSORY.

oral *adj* by mouth, said, spoken, unwritten, uttered, verbal, vocal, voiced.

oratory *n* declamation, eloquence, enunciation, fluency, *inf* gift of the gab, grandiloquence, magniloquence, rhetoric, speaking, speech making.

orbit *n* circuit, course, path, revolution, trajectory.
• *vb* circle, encircle, go round, travel round.

orbital *adj* circular, encircling.

orchestrate *vb* **1** arrange, compose. **2** ▷ ORGANIZE.

ordeal *n* affliction, anguish, difficulty, distress, hardship, misery, *inf* nightmare, pain, suffering, test, torture, trial, tribulation, trouble.

order *n* **1** arrangement, array, classification, codification, disposition, lay-out, *inf* line-up, neatness, organization, pattern, progression, sequence, series, succession, system, tidiness. **2** calm, control, discipline, good behaviour, government, harmony, law and order, obedience, orderliness, peace, peacefulness, quiet, rule. **3** *social orders.* caste, category, class, degree, group, hierarchy, kind, level, rank, sort, status. **4** *in good order.* condition, repair, state. **5** *orders to be obeyed.* command, decree, direction, directive, edict, fiat, injunction, instruction, law, mandate, ordinance, regulation, requirement, rule. **6** *an order for goods.* application, booking, commission, demand, mandate, request, requisition, reservation. **7** *religious orders.* association, brotherhood, community, fraternity, group, guild, lodge, sect, sisterhood, society, sodality, sorority. *Opp* DISORDER.
• *vb* **1** arrange, categorize, classify, codify, lay out, organize, put in order, sort out, tidy up. **2** *old use* bid, charge, command, compel, decree, demand, direct, enjoin, instruct, ordain, require, tell. **3** apply for, ask for, book, reserve, requisition, send away for.

orderly *adj* **1** careful, methodical, neat, organized, regular, symmetrical, systematic, tidy, well-arranged, well-organized, well-prepared. *Opp* CONFUSED, DISORGANIZED. **2** civilized, controlled, decorous, disciplined, law-abiding, peaceable, polite, restrained, well-behaved, well-mannered. *Opp* UNDISCIPLINED.

ordinary *adj* accustomed, average, common, *inf* common or garden, commonplace, conventional, customary, established, everyday, fair, familiar, habitual, humble, *inf* humdrum, indifferent, mediocre, medium, middling, moderate, modest, mundane, nondescript, normal, orthodox, passable, pedestrian, plain, prosaic, quotidian, reasonable, regular, routine, *inf* run-of-the-mill, satisfactory, simple, *inf* so-so, standard, stock, traditional, typical, undistinguished, unexceptional, unexciting, unimpressive, uninspired, uninteresting, unpretentious, unremarkable, unsurprising, usual, well-known, workaday. *Opp* EXTRAORDINARY.

organic *adj* 1 animate, biological, growing, live, living, natural. 2 *an organic whole.* coherent, coordinated, evolving, integral, integrated, methodical, organized, structured, systematic.

organism *n* animal, being, cell, creature, living thing, plant.

organization *n* 1 arrangement, categorization, classification, codification, composition, coordination, logistics, organizing, planning, regimentation, *inf* running, structuring. 2 *a business organization.* alliance, association, body, business, club, combine, company, concern, confederation, conglomerate, consortium, corporation, federation, firm, group, institute, institution, league, network, *inf* outfit, party, society, syndicate, union.

organize *vb* 1 arrange, catalogue, categorize, classify, codify, compose, coordinate, group, order, *inf* pigeon-hole, put in order, rearrange, regiment, *inf* run, sort, sort out, structure, systematize, tabulate, tidy up. *Opp* JUMBLE. 2 build, coordinate, create, deal with, establish, make arrangements for, manage, mobilize, orchestrate, plan, put together, run, *inf* see to, set up, take care of.
organized ▷ OFFICIAL, SYSTEMATIC.

orgy *n* Bacchanalia, *inf* binge, debauch, *inf* fling, party, *inf* rave-up, revel, revelry, Saturnalia, *inf* spree.

orient *vb* acclimatize, accommodate, accustom, adapt, adjust, condition, familiarize, orientate, position.

oriental *adj* Asiatic, eastern, far-eastern.

origin *n* 1 base, basis, beginning, birth, cause, commencement, cradle, creation, dawn, derivation, foundation, fount, fountainhead, genesis, inauguration, inception, launch, outset, provenance, root, source, start, well-spring. *Opp* END. 2 *humble origins.* ancestry, background, descent, extraction, family, genealogy, heritage, lineage, parentage, pedigree, start in life, stock.

original *adj* 1 aboriginal, archetypal, earliest, first, initial, native, primal, primitive, primordial. 2 *original antiques.* actual, authentic, genuine, real, true, unique. 3 *original ideas.* creative, first-hand, fresh, imaginative, ingenious, innovative, inspired, inventive, new, novel, resourceful, thoughtful, unconventional, unfamiliar, unique, unusual. *Opp* HACKNEYED.

originate vb 1 arise, be born, be derived, be descended, begin, come, commence, crop up, derive, emanate, emerge, issue, proceed, spring up, start, stem. 2 beget, be the inventor of, bring about, coin, conceive, create, design, discover, engender, found, give birth to, inaugurate, initiate, inspire, institute, introduce, invent, launch, mastermind, pioneer, produce, think up.

ornament n accessory, adornment, bauble, beautification, decoration, embellishment, embroidery, enhancement, filigree, frill, frippery, garnish, gewgaw, ornamentation, tracery, trimming, trinket.
▷ JEWELLERY. • vb adorn, beautify, deck, decorate, dress up, elaborate, embellish, emblazon, emboss, embroider, enhance, festoon, garnish, prettify, trim.

ornamental adj attractive, decorative, fancy, flashy, pretty, showy.

ornate adj arabesque, baroque, inf busy, decorated, elaborate, fancy, florid, flamboyant, flowery, fussy, luxuriant, ornamented, overdone, pretentious, rococo. Opp PLAIN.

orphan n foundling, stray, waif.

orthodox adj accepted, accustomed, approved, authorized, common, conformist, conservative, conventional, customary, established, mainstream, normal, official, ordinary, prevailing, recognized, regular, standard, traditional, usual, well-established. Opp UNCONVENTIONAL.

ostensible adj alleged, apparent, outward, pretended, professed,

inf put-on, reputed, specious, supposed, visible. Opp REAL.

ostentation n affectation, display, exhibitionism, flamboyance, inf flashiness, flaunting, parade, pretention, pretentiousness, self-advertisement, show, showing-off, inf swank. Opp MODESTY.

ostentatious adj flamboyant, inf flashy, pretentious, showy, inf swanky, vainglorious.
▷ BOASTFUL. Opp MODEST.

ostracize vb avoid, banish, inf black, blackball, blacklist, boycott, cast out, cold-shoulder, inf cut, inf cut dead, exclude, excommunicate, expel, isolate, reject, inf send to Coventry, shun, shut out, snub. Opp BEFRIEND.

oust vb banish, drive out, eject, expel, inf kick out, remove, replace, inf sack, supplant, take over from, unseat.

outbreak n epidemic, inf flareup, plague, rash, upsurge.

outburst n attack, effusion, eruption, explosion, fit, flood, outbreak, outpouring, paroxysm, rush, spasm, surge, upsurge.

outcast n castaway, displaced person, exile, leper, outlaw, outsider, pariah, refugee, reject, untouchable.

outcome n conclusion, consequence, effect, end-product, result, sequel, upshot.

outcry n cry of disapproval, dissent, hue and cry, objection, opposition, protest, protestation, remonstrance.

outdo vb beat, defeat, exceed, excel, inf get the better of, outbid, outdistance, outrun, outshine, outstrip, outweigh, overcome, surpass, top, trump.

outdoor *adj* alfresco, open-air, out of doors, outside.

outer *adj* 1 exterior, external, outside, outward, superficial, surface. 2 distant, further, outlying, peripheral, remote. *Opp* INNER.

outfit *n* 1 accoutrements, attire, costume, ensemble, equipment, garb, *inf* gear, *inf* get-up, *inf* rig, suit, trappings, *inf* turn-out. 2 ▷ ORGANIZATION.

outgoing *adj* 1 *outgoing president*. departing, emeritus, ex-, former, last, leaving, past, retiring. 2 *outgoing tide*. ebbing, falling, retreating. 3 ▷ SOCIABLE. *Opp* INCOMING. **outgoings** ▷ EXPENSE.

outing *n* excursion, expedition, jaunt, picnic, ride, tour, trip.

outlast *vb* outlive, survive.

outlaw *n* bandit, brigand, criminal, deserter, desperado, fugitive, highwayman, marauder, outcast, renegade, robber. ● *vb* ban, exclude, forbid, prohibit, proscribe. ▷ BANISH.

outlet *n* 1 channel, discharge, duct, egress, escape route, exit, mouth, opening, orifice, safety valve, vent, way out. 2 ▷ SHOP.

outline *n* 1 abstract, *inf* bare bones, diagram, digest, draft, framework, plan, précis, résumé, *inf* rough idea, *inf* rundown, scenario, skeleton, sketch, summary, synopsis, thumbnail sketch. 2 contour, figure, form, profile, shadow, shape, silhouette. ● *vb* delineate, draft, give the outline, give the gist of, plan out, précis, rough out, sketch out, summarize.

outlook *n* 1 aspect, panorama, scene, sight, vantage point, view, vista. 2 *your mental outlook*. angle, attitude, frame of mind, opinion, perspective, point of view, position, slant, standpoint, viewpoint. 3 *the weather outlook*. expectations, forecast, *inf* look-out, prediction, prognosis, prospect.

outlying *adj* distant, far-away, far-flung, far-off, outer, outermost, remote. *Opp* CENTRAL.

output *n* achievement, crop, harvest, production, productivity, result, yield.

outrage *n* 1 atrocity, crime, *inf* disgrace, enormity, indignity, outrageous act, scandal, *inf* sensation, violation. 2 anger, bitterness, disgust, fury, horror, indignation, resentment, revulsion, shock, wrath. ● *vb* ▷ ANGER.

outrageous *adj* 1 abominable, atrocious, barbaric, beastly, bestial, criminal, cruel, disgraceful, disgusting, execrable, infamous, iniquitous, monstrous, nefarious, notorious, offensive, preposterous, revolting, scandalous, shocking, unspeakable, unthinkable, vile, villainous, wicked. 2 *outrageous prices*. excessive, extortionate, extravagant, immoderate, unreasonable. *Opp* REASONABLE.

outside *adj* 1 exterior, external, facing, outer, outward, superficial, surface, visible. 2 *outside interference*. alien, extraneous, foreign. 3 *outside chance*. ▷ REMOTE. ● *n* appearance, case, casing, exterior, façade, face, front, look, shell, skin, surface.

outsider *n* alien, foreigner, *inf* gatecrasher, guest, immigrant, interloper, intruder, invader, newcomer, non-member, non-resident, outcast, stranger, trespasser, visitor.

outskirts *plur n* borders, edge, environs, fringe, margin, outer areas, periphery, purlieus, suburbs. *Opp* CENTRE.

outspoken *adj* blunt, candid, direct, explicit, forthright, frank, plain-spoken, tactless, unambiguous, undiplomatic, unequivocal, unreserved. ▷ HONEST. *Opp* EVASIVE.

outstanding *adj* **1** above the rest, celebrated, conspicuous, distinguished, dominant, eminent, excellent, exceptional, extraordinary, first-class, first-rate, great, important, impressive, memorable, notable, noteworthy, noticeable, predominant, pre-eminent, prominent, remarkable, singular, special, striking, superior, top rank, unrivalled. ▷ FAMOUS. *Opp* ORDINARY. **2** ▷ OVERDUE.

outward *adj* apparent, evident, exterior, external, manifest, noticeable, observable, obvious, ostensible, outer, outside, superficial, surface, visible.

outwit *vb* deceive, dupe, fool, *inf* get the better of, gull, hoax, hoodwink, make a fool of, outfox, outmanoeuvre, *inf* outsmart, *inf* put one over on, *inf* take in, trick. ▷ CHEAT.

oval *adj* egg-shaped, ellipsoidal, elliptical, oviform, ovoid.

ovation *n* acclaim, acclamation, applause, cheering, plaudits, praise.

overcast *adj* black, clouded, cloudy, dark, dismal, dull, gloomy, grey, leaden, lowering, murky, sombre, starless, stormy, sunless, threatening. *Opp* CLOUDLESS.

overcoat *n* greatcoat, mackintosh, top-coat, trench-coat.

overcome *vb* at a loss, beaten, *inf* bowled over, *inf* done in, exhausted, overwhelmed, prostrate, speechless. ● *vb* ▷ OVERTHROW.

overcrowded *adj* congested, crammed, crawling, filled to capacity, full, jammed, *inf* jampacked, overloaded, packed.

overdue *adj* **1** belated, delayed, late, slow, tardy, unpunctual. *Opp* EARLY. **2** *overdue bills*. due, outstanding, owing, unpaid, unresolved, unsettled.

overeat *vb* be greedy, eat too much, feast, gorge, gormandize, *inf* guzzle, indulge yourself, *inf* make a pig of yourself, over-indulge, *inf* stuff yourself.

overflow *vb* brim over, flood, pour over, run over, spill, well up.

overgrown *adj* **1** outsize, over-sized. ▷ BIG. **2** *overgrown garden*. overrun, rank, tangled, uncut, unkempt, untidy, untrimmed, unweeded, weedy, wild.

overhang *vb* beetle, bulge, jut, project, protrude, stick out.

overhaul *vb* **1** check over, examine, *inf* fix, inspect, mend, rebuild, recondition, refurbish, renovate, repair, restore, service. **2** ▷ OVERTAKE.

overhead *adj* aerial, elevated, high, overhanging, raised, upper.

overlook *vb* **1** fail to notice, forget, leave out, miss, neglect, omit. **2** condone, disregard, excuse, gloss over, ignore, let pass, make allowances for, pardon, pass over, pay no attention to, *inf* shut your eyes to, *inf* turn a blind eye to, *inf* write off. 3 *overlook a lake.* face, front, have a view of, look at, look down on, look on to.

overpower *vb* ▷ OVERTHROW.

overpowering *adj* compelling, consuming, inescapable, insupportable, irrepressible, irresistible, overriding, overwhelming, powerful, strong, unbearable, uncontrollable, unendurable.

oversee *vb* administer, be in charge of, control, direct, invigilate, *inf* keep an eye on, preside over, superintend, supervise, watch over.

oversight *n* 1 carelessness, dereliction of duty, error, failure, fault, mistake, omission. 2 *oversight of a job.* administration, control, direction, management, supervision, surveillance.

overstate *vb inf* blow up out of proportion, embroider, exaggerate, magnify, make too much of, maximize, overemphasize, overstress.

overt *adj* apparent, blatant, clear, evident, manifest, obvious, open, patent, plain, unconcealed, undisguised, visible. *Opp* SECRET.

overtake *vb* catch up with, gain on, leave behind, outdistance, outpace, outstrip, overhaul, pass.

overthrow *n* conquest, defeat, destruction, mastery, rout, subjugation, suppression, unseating. ● *vb* beat, bring down, conquer, crush, deal with, defeat, depose, dethrone, get the better of, *inf* lick,

master, oust, overcome, overpower, overturn, overwhelm, rout, *inf* send packing, subdue, *inf* topple, triumph over, unseat, vanquish, win against.

overtone *n* association, connotation, hint, implication, innuendo, reverberation, suggestion, undertone.

overturn *vb* 1 capsize, flip, invert, keel over, knock over, spill, tip over, topple, turn over, *inf* turn turtle, turn upside down, up-end, upset. 2 ▷ OVERTHROW.

overwhelm *vb* 1 engulf, flood, immerse, inundate, submerge, swamp. 2 ▷ OVERTHROW. **overwhelming** ▷ OVERPOWERING.

owe *vb* be in debt, have debts.

owing *adj* due, outstanding, overdue, owed, payable, unpaid, unsettled. **owing to** because of, caused by, on account of, resulting from, thanks to, through.

own *vb* be the owner of, have, hold, possess. **own up** ▷ CONFESS.

owner *n* freeholder, holder, landlady, landlord, possessor, proprietor.

P

pace *n* 1 step, stride. 2 *a fast pace.* gait, *inf* lick, movement, quickness, rate, speed, tempo, velocity. ● *vb* ▷ WALK.

pacify *vb* appease, assuage, calm, conciliate, humour, mollify, placate, quell, quieten, soothe, subdue, tame, tranquillize. *Opp* ANGER.

pack *n* 1 bale, box, bundle, package, packet, parcel. 2 backpack, duffel bag, haversack, kitbag, knapsack, rucksack. 3 ▷ GROUP.
● *vb* 1 bundle (up), fill, load, package, parcel up, put, put together, store, stow, wrap up. 2 compress, cram, crowd, jam, overcrowd, press, ram, squeeze, stuff, tamp down, wedge. **pack off** ▷ DISMISS. **pack up** ▷ FINISH.

pact *n* agreement, alliance, armistice, arrangement, bargain, compact, concord, concordat, contract, covenant, deal, *Fr* entente, league, peace, settlement, treaty, truce, understanding.

pad *n* 1 cushion, filler, hassock, kneeler, padding, pillow, stuffing, wad. 2 jotter, memo pad, notebook, stationery, writing pad. ● *vb* cushion, fill, line, pack, protect, stuff, upholster, wad. **pad out** ▷ EXTEND.

padding *n* 1 filling, protection, upholstery, stuffing, wadding. 2 prolixity, verbiage, verbosity, *inf* waffle, wordiness.

paddle *n* oar, scull.
● *vb* 1 propel, row, scull. 2 dabble, splash about, wade.

paddock *n* enclosure, field, meadow, pasture.

pagan *adj* atheistic, godless, heathen, idolatrous, infidel, irreligious, polytheistic, unchristian. ● *n* atheist, heathen, infidel, savage, unbeliever.

page *n* 1 folio, leaf, recto, sheet, side, verso. 2 errand-boy, messenger, page-boy.

pageant *n* ceremony, display, extravaganza, parade, procession, show, spectacle, tableau.

pageantry *n* ceremony, display, formality, grandeur, magnificence, pomp, ritual, show, spectacle, splendour.

pain *n* ache, aching, affliction, agony, anguish, cramp, crick, discomfort, distress, headache, hurt, irritation, ordeal, pang, smart, smarting, soreness, spasm, stab, sting, suffering, tenderness, throb, throes, toothache, torment, torture, twinge.
● *vb* ▷ HURT.

painful *adj* 1 aching, *inf* achy, agonizing, burning, cruel, excruciating, *old use* grievous, hard to bear, hurting, inflamed, piercing, raw, severe, sharp, smarting, sore, *inf* splitting (*head*), stabbing, stinging, tender, throbbing. 2 distressing, harrowing, hurtful, laborious, *inf* traumatic, trying, unpleasant, upsetting, vexing. 3 *a painful decision.* difficult, hard, troublesome, uncongenial. *Opp* PAINLESS. **be painful** ▷ HURT.

painkiller *n* anaesthetic, analgesic, anodyne, palliative, sedative.

painless *adj* comfortable, easy, effortless, pain-free, simple, trouble-free, undemanding. *Opp* PAINFUL.

paint *n* colour, colouring, dye, pigment, stain, tint. □ *distemper, emulsion, enamel, gloss paint, lacquer, matt paint, oil-colour, oil-paint, oils, pastel, primer, tempera, undercoat, varnish, water-colour, white-wash.* ● *vb* 1 apply paint to, coat, colour, cover, daub, decorate, dye, enamel, gild, lacquer, redecorate, stain, tint, touch up, varnish, whitewash.

2 delineate, depict, describe, picture, portray, represent.

painter *n* artist, decorator, illustrator, miniaturist.

painting *n* fresco, landscape, miniature, mural, oil-painting, portrait, still-life, water-colour.

pair *n* brace, couple, duet, duo, mates, partners, partnership, set of two, twins, twosome. ● *vb* **pair off**, **pair up** couple, double up, find a partner, get together, join up, *inf* make a twosome, match up, *inf* pal up, team up.

palace *n* castle, château, mansion, official residence, stately home. ▷ HOUSE.

palatable *adj* acceptable, agreeable, appetizing, easy to take, eatable, edible, nice to eat, pleasant, tasty. *Opp* UNPALATABLE.

palatial *adj* aristocratic, grand, large-scale, luxurious, majestic, opulent, *inf* posh, splendid, stately, up-market.

pale *adj* **1** anaemic, ashen, blanched, bloodless, cadaverous, colourless, corpse-like, *inf* deathly, drained, etiolated, ghastly, ghostly, ill-looking, pallid, pasty, *inf* peaky, sallow, sickly, unhealthy, wan, *inf* washed-out, *inf* whey-faced, white, whitish. **2** *pale colours*. bleached, dim, faded, faint, light, pastel, subtle, weak. *Opp* BRIGHT. ● *vb* become pale, blanch, blench, dim, etiolate, fade, lighten, lose colour, whiten.

pall *n* cloth, mantle, shroud, veil. ▷ COVERING. ● *vb* become boring, become uninteresting, cloy, irritate, jade, sate, satiate, weary.

palliative *adj* alleviating, calming, reassuring, sedative, soothing. ● *n* painkiller, sedative, tranquillizer.

palpable *adj* apparent, corporeal, evident, manifest, obvious, patent, physical, real, solid, substantial, tangible, touchable, visible. *Opp* INTANGIBLE.

palpitate *vb* beat, flutter, pound, pulsate, quiver, shiver, throb, tremble, vibrate.

paltry *adj* contemptible, inconsequential, insignificant, petty, *inf* piddling, pitiable, puny, trifling, unimportant, worthless. ▷ SMALL. *Opp* IMPORTANT.

pamper *vb* coddle, cosset, humour, indulge, mollycoddle, overindulge, pet, spoil, spoonfeed.

pamphlet *n* booklet, brochure, bulletin, catalogue, circular, flyer, folder, handbill, handout, leaflet, notice, tract.

pan *n* container, utensil. □ *billy-can, casserole, frying-pan, pot, saucepan, skillet.* ● *vb* ▷ CRITICIZE.

panache *n* animation, brio, confidence, dash, élan, energy, enthusiasm, flair, flamboyance, flourish, savoir-faire, self-assurance, spirit, style, swagger, verve, zest.

pandemonium *n* babel, bedlam, chaos, confusion, hubbub, noise, rumpus, turmoil, uproar. ▷ COMMOTION.

pander *n* go-between, *inf* pimp, procurer. ● *vb* **pander to** bow to, cater for, fulfil, gratify, humour, indulge, please, provide, satisfy.

pane *n* glass, light, panel, sheet of glass, window.

panel n 1 insert, pane, panelling, rectangle, *plur* wainscot. 2 committee, group, jury, team.

panic n alarm, consternation, *inf* flap, horror, hysteria, stampede, terror. ● vb become panic-stricken, *inf* fall apart, *inf* flap, *inf* go to pieces, *inf* lose your head, *inf* lose your nerve, over-react, stampede. ▷ FEAR.

panic-stricken adj alarmed, *inf* beside yourself, disorientated, frantic, frenzied, horrified, hysterical, *inf* in a cold sweat, *inf* in a tizzy, jumpy, overexcited, panicky, panicstruck, terror-stricken, undisciplined, unnerved, worked-up. ▷ FRIGHTENED. *Opp* CALM.

panorama n landscape, perspective, prospect, scene, view, vista.

panoramic adj commanding, extensive, scenic, sweeping, wide.

pant vb blow, breathe quickly, gasp, *inf* huff and puff, puff, wheeze. **panting** ▷ BREATHLESS.

pants n 1 *old use* bloomers, boxer shorts, briefs, camiknickers, drawers, knickers, panties, pantihose, shorts, *inf* smalls, trunks, underpants, *inf* undies, Y-fronts. 2 ▷ TROUSERS.

paper n 1 folio, leaf, sheet. □ A4 (A1, A2, etc), card, cardboard, cartridge paper, foolscap, manila, notepaper, papyrus, parchment, postcard, quarto, stationery, tissue-paper, toilet-paper, tracing-paper, vellum, wallpaper, wrapping-paper, writing-paper. 2 certificate, credentials, deed, document, form, *inf* ID, identification, licence, record. 3 *the daily*

paper. *inf* daily, journal, newspaper, *inf* rag, tabloid. 4 *an academic paper.* article, discourse, dissertation, essay, monograph, thesis, treatise.

parable n allegory, exemplum, fable, moral tale. ▷ WRITING.

parade n cavalcade, ceremony, column, cortège, display, file, march-past, motorcade, pageant, procession, review, show, spectacle. ● vb 1 assemble, file past, form up, line up, make a procession, march past, present yourself, process. ▷ DISPLAY.

paradise n Eden, Elysium, heaven, Shangri-La, Utopia.

paradox n absurdity, anomaly, contradiction, incongruity, inconsistency, self-contradiction.

paradoxical adj absurd, anomalous, conflicting, contradictory, illogical, improbable, incongruous, self-contradictory.

parallel adj 1 equidistant. 2 *parallel events.* analogous, cognate, contemporary, corresponding, equivalent, like, matching, similar. ● n 1 analogue, counterpart, equal, likeness, match. 2 analogy, comparison, correspondence, equivalence, kinship, resemblance, similarity. ● vb be parallel to, be parallel with, compare with, correspond to, duplicate, echo, equate with, keep pace with, match, remind you of, run alongside.

paralyse vb anaesthetize, cripple, deactivate, deaden, desensitize, disable, freeze, halt, immobilize, incapacitate, lame, numb, petrify, stop, stun.

paralysed adj crippled, dead, desensitized, disabled, handicapped, immobile, immovable, incapacitated, lame, numb, palsied, paralytic, paraplegic, rigid, unusable, useless.

paralysis n deadness, immobility, numbness, palsy, paraplegia.

paraphernalia plur n accessories, apparatus, baggage, belongings, chattels, inf clobber, effects, equipment, gear, impedimenta, materials, inf odds and ends, possessions, property, inf rig, stuff, tackle, things, trappings.

paraphrase vb explain, interpret, put into other words, rephrase, restate, reword, rewrite, translate.

parcel n bale, box, bundle, carton, case, pack, package, packet. **parcel out** ▷ DIVIDE. **parcel up** ▷ PACK.

parch vb bake, burn, dehydrate, desiccate, dry, scorch, shrivel, wither. **parched** ▷ DRY, THIRSTY.

pardon n absolution, amnesty, condonation, discharge, exculpation, exoneration, forgiveness, indulgence, mercy, release, reprieve. ● vb absolve, condone, exculpate, excuse, exonerate, forgive, free, grant pardon, let off, overlook, release, remit, reprieve, set free, spare.

pardonable adj allowable, condonable, excusable, forgivable, justifiable, minor, negligible, petty, understandable, venial (sin). Opp UNFORGIVABLE.

parent n begetter, father, guardian, mother, procreator, progenitor.

parentage n ancestry, birth, descent, extraction, family, line, lineage, pedigree, stock.

park n common, gardens, green, recreation ground. □ amusement park, arboretum, botanical gardens, car-park, estate, national park, nature reserve, parkland, reserve, theme park. ● vb deposit, leave, place, position, put, station, store. **park yourself** ▷ SETTLE.

parliament n assembly, conclave, congress, convocation, council, diet, government, legislature, lower house, senate, upper house.

parody n burlesque, caricature, distortion, imitation, lampoon, mimicry, satire, inf send-up, inf spoof, inf take-off, travesty. ● vb ape, burlesque, caricature, guy, imitate, lampoon, mimic, satirize, inf send up, inf take off, travesty. ▷ RIDICULE.

parry vb avert, block, deflect, evade, fend off, push away, repel, repulse, stave off, ward off.

part n 1 bit, branch, component, constituent, department, division, element, fraction, fragment, ingredient, parcel, particle, percentage, piece, portion, ramification, scrap, section, sector, segment, shard, share, single item, subdivision, unit. 2 department, faction, party, section, subdivision, unit. 3 part of a book. chapter, episode. 4 part of a town. area, district, neighbourhood, quarter, region, sector, vicinity. 5 part of the body. limb, member, organ. 6 part in a play. cameo, character, role. ● vb 1 cut off, detach, disconnect, divide, pull apart, sepa-

rate, sever, split, sunder.
Opp JOIN. **2** break away, depart,
go away, leave, part company,
quit, say goodbye, separate,
split up, take leave, withdraw.
Opp MEET. **part with**
▷ RELINQUISH. **take part**
▷ PARTICIPATE.

partial *adj* **1** imperfect, incomplete, limited, qualified, unfinished. *Opp* COMPLETE. **2** *partial
judge*. biased, one-sided,
partisan, prejudiced, unfair.
Opp IMPARTIAL. **be partial to**
▷ LIKE.

participate *vb* assist, be active,
be involved, contribute, cooperate, engage, enter, help, join in,
partake, share, take part.

participation *n* activity, assistance, complicity, contribution,
cooperation, engagement,
involvement, partnership, sharing.

particle *n* **1** bit, crumb, dot,
drop, fragment, grain, hint,
iota, jot, mite, morsel, *old
use* mote, piece, scintilla, scrap,
shred, sliver, *inf* smidgen,
speck, trace. **2** atom, electron,
molecule, neutron.

particular *adj* **1** distinct, idiosyncratic, individual, peculiar,
personal, singular, specific,
uncommon, unique, unmistakable. **2** *particular with detail*.
exact, nice, painstaking,
precise, rigorous, scrupulous,
thorough. **3** *gave particular
pleasure*. especial, exceptional,
important, marked, notable,
noteworthy, outstanding, significant, special, unusual.
4 *particular about food*. choosy,
critical, discriminating, fastidious, finical, finicky, fussy,
meticulous, nice, *inf* pernick-

ety, selective. *Opp* GENERAL,
EASYGOING. **particulars**
circumstances, details, facts,
information, *sl* low-down.

parting *n* departure, farewell,
going away, leave-taking, leaving, saying goodbye, separation, splitting up, valediction.

partisan *adj* biased, bigoted,
blinkered, devoted, factional,
fanatical, narrow-minded, one-
sided, partial, prejudiced,
sectarian, unfair. *Opp* IMPARTIAL. ● *n* adherent, devotee,
fanatic, follower, freedom
fighter, guerrilla, resistance
fighter, supporter, underground
fighter, zealot.

partition *n* **1** break-up, division,
separation, splitting up.
2 barrier, panel, room-divider,
screen, wall. ● *vb* cut up,
divide, parcel out, separate off,
share out, split up, subdivide.

partner *n* **1** accessory, accomplice, ally, assistant, associate,
inf bedfellow, collaborator,
colleague, companion, comrade,
confederate, helper, *inf* mate,
sl sidekick. **2** consort, husband,
mate, spouse, wife.

partnership *n* **1** affiliation, alliance, association, combination,
company, confederation, cooperative, syndicate. **2** collaboration, complicity, cooperation. **3** marriage, relationship,
union.

party *n* **1** celebration, *inf* do,
festivity, function, gathering,
inf get-together, *inf* jollification,
inf knees-up, merrymaking,
inf rave-up, *inf* shindig, social
gathering. □ ball, banquet,
barbecue, ceilidh, dance,
inf disco, discothèque, feast,
inf hen-party, house-warming,

orgy, picnic, reception, reunion, inf *stag-party, tea-party, wedding.* **2** *a political party.* alliance, association, bloc, cabal, inf *camp, caucus, clique,* coalition, faction, junta, league, sect, side. ▷ GROUP.

pass *n* **1** canyon, col, cut, defile, gap, gorge, gully, opening, passage, ravine, valley, way through. **2** *identity pass.* authority, authorization, clearance, inf ID, licence, passport, permission, permit, safe-conduct, ticket, warrant.
● *vb* **1** go beyond, go by, move on, move past, outstrip, overhaul, overtake, proceed, progress, inf *thread your way.* **2** *time passes.* disappear, elapse, fade, go away, lapse, tick by, vanish. **3** *pass drinks.* circulate, deal out, deliver, give, hand over, offer, present, share, submit, supply, transfer. **4** *pass a resolution.* agree, approve, authorize, confirm, decree, enact, establish, ordain, pronounce, ratify, validate. **5** *I pass!* inf give in, opt out, say nothing, waive your rights.
pass away ▷ DIE. **pass on** ▷ TRANSFER. **pass out** ▷ FAINT. **pass over** ▷ IGNORE.

passable *adj* **1** acceptable, adequate, admissible, allowable, all right, fair, indifferent, mediocre, middling, moderate, not bad, ordinary, satisfactory, inf so-so, tolerable. Opp UNACCEPTABLE. **2** clear, navigable, open, traversable, unblocked, unobstructed, usable. Opp IMPASSABLE.

passage *n* **1** corridor, entrance, hall, hallway, lobby, passageway, vestibule. **2** *passage of time.* advance, flow, lapse,

march, movement, moving on, passing, progress, progression, transition. **3** *sea passage.* crossing, cruise, voyage. ▷ JOURNEY. **4** *through passage.* pass, route, thoroughfare, tunnel, way through. ▷ OPENING. **5** *passage from a book.* citation, episode, excerpt, extract, paragraph, part, piece, portion, quotation, scene, section, selection.

passenger *n* commuter, rider, traveller, voyager.

passer-by *n* bystander, onlooker, witness.

passion *n* appetite, ardour, avidity, avidness, commitment, craving, craze, desire, drive, eagerness, emotion, enthusiasm, fanaticism, fervency, fervour, fire, flame, frenzy, greed, heat, hunger, infatuation, intensity, keenness, love, lust, mania, obsession, strong feeling, suffering, thirst, urge, urgency, vehemence, zeal, zest.

passionate *adj* ardent, aroused, avid, burning, committed, eager, emotional, enthusiastic, excited, fanatical, fervent, fiery, frenzied, greedy, heated, hot, hungry, impassioned, infatuated, inflamed, intense, lustful, manic, obsessive, roused, sexy, strong, urgent, vehement, violent, worked up, zealous. Opp APATHETIC.

passive *adj* apathetic, complaisant, compliant, deferential, docile, impassive, inert, inactive, long-suffering, malleable, non-violent, patient, phlegmatic, pliable, quiescent, receptive, resigned, sheepish, submissive, supine, tame, tractable, unassertive, unmoved, unresisting, yielding. ▷ CALM. Opp ACTIVE.

past *adj* bygone, dead, *inf* dead and buried, earlier, ended, finished, forgotten, former, gone, historical, late, olden (*days*), *inf* over and done with, previous, recent, sometime. ● *n* antiquity, days gone by, former times, history, old days, olden days, past times. *Opp* FUTURE.

paste *n* 1 adhesive, fixative, glue, gum. 2 pâté, spread. ● *vb* fix, glue, stick. ▷ FASTEN.

pastiche *n* blend, composite, compound, *inf* hotchpotch, mess, miscellany, mixture, *inf* motley collection, patchwork, selection.

pastime *n* activity, amusement, avocation, distraction, diversion, entertainment, fun, game, hobby, leisure activity, occupation, play, recreation, relaxation, sport.

pastoral *adj* 1 agrarian, agricultural, Arcadian, bucolic, country, farming, idyllic, outdoor, provincial, rural, rustic. ▷ PEACEFUL. *Opp* URBAN. 2 *pastoral duties*. clerical, ecclesiastical, parochial, ministerial, priestly.

pasture *n* field, grassland, grazing, mead, meadow, paddock, pasturage.

pat *vb* caress, dab, slap, stroke, tap. ▷ TOUCH.

patch *n* darn, mend, piece, reinforcement, repair. ● *vb* cover, darn, fix, mend, reinforce, repair, sew up, stitch up.

patchy *adj inf* bitty, blotchy, changing, dappled, erratic, inconsistent, irregular, speckled, spotty, uneven, unpredictable, variable, varied, varying. *Opp* UNIFORM.

patent *adj* apparent, blatant, clear, conspicuous, evident, flagrant, manifest, obvious, open, plain, self-evident, transparent, undisguised, visible.

path *n* 1 alley, bridle-path, bridle-way, esplanade, footpath, footway, pathway, pavement, *Amer* sidewalk, towpath, track, trail, walk, walkway, way. ▷ ROAD. 2 approach, course, direction, flight path, orbit, route, trajectory, way.

pathetic *adj* 1 affecting, distressing, emotional, emotive, heart-breaking, heart-rending, lamentable, moving, piteous, pitiable, pitiful, plaintive, poignant, stirring, touching, tragic. ▷ SAD. 2 ▷ INADEQUATE.

pathos *n* emotion, feeling, pity, poignancy, sadness, tragedy.

patience *n* 1 calmness, composure, endurance, equanimity, forbearance, fortitude, leniency, long-suffering, resignation, restraint, self-control, serenity, stoicism, toleration, *inf* unflappability. 2 *work with patience*. assiduity, determination, diligence, doggedness, endurance, firmness, perseverance, persistence, pertinacity, *inf* stickability, tenacity.

patient *adj* 1 accommodating, acquiescent, calm, compliant, composed, docile, easygoing, even-tempered, forbearing, forgiving, lenient, long-suffering, mild, philosophical, quiet, resigned, self-possessed, serene, stoical, submissive, tolerant, uncomplaining. 2 *a patient worker*. assiduous, determined, diligent, dogged, persevering, persistent, steady, tenacious, unhurried, untiring. *Opp* IMPA-

TIENT. ● *n* case, invalid, out-
patient, sufferer.

patriot *n derog* chauvinist, loyal-
ist, nationalist, *derog* xenophobe.

patriotic *adj derog* chauvinistic,
derog jingoistic, loyal, national-
istic, *derog* xenophobic.

patriotism *n derog* chauvinism,
derog jingoism, loyalty, nationalism, *derog* xenophobia.

patrol *n* 1 beat, guard, policing,
sentry-duty, surveillance, vigilance, watch. 2 guard, lookout,
patrolman, sentinel, sentry,
watchman. ● *vb* be on patrol,
defend, guard, inspect, keep a
lookout, make the rounds,
police, protect, stand guard,
tour, walk the beat, watch over.

patron *n* 1 advocate, *inf* angel,
backer, benefactor, champion,
defender, helper, philanthropist, promoter, sponsor,
subscriber, supporter. 2 *patron
of a shop*. client, customer,
frequenter, *inf* regular, shopper.

patronage *n* backing, business,
custom, help, sponsorship,
support, trade.

patronize *vb* 1 back, be a patron
of, bring trade to, buy from,
deal with, encourage, frequent,
give patronage to, shop at,
support. 2 *be patronizing
towards*. humiliate, *inf* look
down on, *inf* look down your
nose at, *inf* put down, talk
down to. **patronizing**
▷ SUPERIOR.

pattern *n* 1 arrangement,
decoration, design, device,
figuration, figure, motif, ornamentation, sequence, shape,
system, tessellation. 2 archetype, criterion, example,

exemplar, guide, ideal, model,
norm, original, paragon,
precedent, prototype, sample,
specimen, standard, yardstick.

pause *n* break, *inf* breather,
breathing space, caesura,
check, delay, gap, halt, hesitation, hiatus, hold-up, interlude,
intermission, interruption,
interval, lacuna, lapse, *inf* let-
up, lull, moratorium, respite,
rest, standstill, stop, stoppage,
suspension, wait. ● *vb* break off,
delay, falter, halt, hang back,
have a pause, hesitate, hold,
mark time, rest, stop, *inf* take a
break, *inf* take a breather, wait.

pave *vb* asphalt, concrete, cover
with paving, flag, *old use* maca-
damize, *inf* make up, surface,
tarmac, tile. **pave the way**
▷ PREPARE.

pavement *n* footpath,
Amer sidewalk. ▷ PATH.

pay *n* cash in hand, compensation, dividend, earnings, emolu-
ments, fee, gain, honorarium,
income, money, payment,
profit, recompense, reimbursement, remittance, return,
salary, settlement, stipend,
take-home pay, wages.

● *vb* 1 *inf* cough up, *inf* fork out,
give, grant, hand over, proffer,
recompense, remunerate,
requite, spend, *inf* stump up.
2 *pay debts*. bear the cost of,
clear, compensate, *inf* foot,
honour, indemnify, meet, pay
back, pay off, pay up, refund,
reimburse, repay, settle.
3 *crime doesn't pay*. avail, benefit, be profitable, pay off,
produce results, prove worthwhile, yield a return. 4 *pay for
mistakes*. be punished, suffer.
▷ ATONE. **pay back** ▷ RETALI-
ATE.

payment n advance, alimony, allowance, charge, commission, compensation, contribution, cost, deposit, disbursement, donation, expenditure, fare, fee, figure, fine, instalment, loan, outgoings, outlay, pocket-money, premium, price, ransom, rate, remittance, reward, royalty, *inf* sub, subscription, subsistence, supplement, surcharge, tip, toll, wage. *Opp* INCOME.

peace n 1 accord, agreement, amity, conciliation, concord, friendliness, harmony, order. *Opp* CONFLICT. 2 alliance, armistice, cease-fire, pact, treaty, truce. *Opp* WAR. 3 *peace of mind.* calm, calmness, peace and quiet, peacefulness, placidity, quiet, repose, serenity, silence, stillness, tranquillity. *Opp* ANXIETY.

peaceable adj amicable, civil, conciliatory, cooperative, friendly, gentle, harmonious, inoffensive, mild, non-violent, pacific, peace-loving, placid, temperate, understanding. *Opp* QUARRELSOME.

peaceful adj balmy, calm, easy, gentle, pacific, placid, pleasant, quiet, relaxing, restful, serene, slow-moving, soothing, still, tranquil, undisturbed, unruffled, untroubled. *Opp* NOISY, STORMY.

peacemaker n adjudicator, appeaser, arbitrator, conciliator, diplomat, intercessor, intermediary, mediator, reconciler, referee, umpire.

peak n 1 apex, brow, cap, crest, crown, eminence, hill, mountain, pinnacle, point, ridge, summit, tip, top. 2 *peak of your career.* acme, apogee, climax, consummation, crisis, crown, culmination, height, highest point, zenith.

peal n carillon, chime, chiming, clangour, knell, reverberation, ringing, tintinnabulation, toll. • *vb* chime, clang, resonate, ring, ring the changes, sound, toll.

peasant n [*derog*] boor, bumpkin, churl, oaf, rustic, serf, swain, village idiot, yokel.

pebbles *plur* n cobbles, gravel, stones.

peculiar adj 1 aberrant, abnormal, anomalous, atypical, bizarre, curious, deviant, eccentric, exceptional, freakish, funny, odd, offbeat, outlandish, out of the ordinary, quaint, queer, quirky, surprising, strange, uncommon, unconventional, unusual, weird. 2 *your peculiar style.* characteristic, different, distinctive, identifiable, idiosyncratic, individual, natural, particular, personal, private, singular, special, unique, unmistakable. *Opp* COMMON, ORDINARY.

peculiarity n abnormality, characteristic, difference, distinctiveness, eccentricity, foible, idiosyncrasy, individuality, mannerism, oddity, outlandishness, quirk, singularity, speciality, trait, uniqueness.

pedantic adj 1 academic, bookish, donnish, dry, formal, humourless, learned, old-fashioned, pompous, scholarly, schoolmasterly, stiff, stilted, *inf* stuffy. 2 *inf* by the book, doctrinaire, exact, fastidious, fussy, inflexible, *inf* nit-picking, precise, punctilious, strict, unimaginative. Opp INFORMAL, LAX.

peddle vb inf flog, hawk, market, inf push, sell, traffic in, vend.

pedestrian adj 1 pedestrianized, traffic-free. 2 banal, boring, dreary, dull, commonplace, flat-footed, lifeless, mundane, prosaic, run-of-the-mill, tedious, unimaginative, uninteresting. ▷ ORDINARY. ● n inf foot-slogger, foot-traveller, stroller, walker.

pedigree adj pure-bred, thoroughbred. ● n ancestry, blood, descent, extraction, family, family history, genealogy, line, lineage, parentage, roots, stock, strain.

pedlar n old use chapman, inf cheapjack, old use colporteur, door-to-door salesman, hawker, inf pusher, seller, street-trader, trafficker, vendor.

peel n coating, rind, skin. ● vb denude, flay, hull, pare, skin, strip. ▷ UNDRESS.

peep vb 1 glance, have a look, peek, squint. ▷ LOOK. 2 ▷ SHOW.

peer n aristocrat, grandee, noble, nobleman, noblewoman, patrician, titled person. □ baron, baroness, countess, duchess, duke, earl, lady, lord, marchioness, marquis, viscount, viscountess. ● vb have a look, look earnestly, spy, squint. ▷ LOOK. **peers** 1 aristocracy, nobility, peerage. 2 colleagues, compeers, confrères, equals, fellows, peer-group.

peevish adj cantankerous, churlish, crabby, crusty, curmudgeonly, grumpy, ill-humoured, irritable, petulant, querulous, testy, touchy, waspish. ▷ BAD-TEMPERED.

peg n bolt, dowel, pin, rod, stick, thole-pin. ● vb ▷ FASTEN.

pelt n coat, fur, hide, skin. ● vb assail, bombard, shower, strafe. ▷ THROW.

pen n 1 coop, Amer corral, enclosure, fold, hutch, pound. 2 ball-point, biro, felt-tip, fountain pen, old use quill.

penalize vb discipline, fine, impose a penalty on, punish.

penalty n fine, forfeit, price. ▷ PUNISHMENT. **pay the penalty** ▷ ATONE.

penance n amends, atonement, contrition, penitence, punishment, reparation. **do penance** ▷ ATONE.

pendent adj dangling, hanging, loose, pendulous, suspended, swaying, swinging, trailing.

pending adj about to happen, forthcoming, inf hanging fire, imminent, impending, inf in the offing, undecided, waiting.

penetrate vb 1 bore through, break through, drill into, enter, get into, get through, infiltrate, lance, make a hole, perforate, pierce, probe, puncture, stab, stick in. 2 damp penetrates, filter through, impregnate, percolate through, permeate, pervade, seep into, suffuse.

penitent adj apologetic, conscience-stricken, contrite, regretful, remorseful, repentant, rueful, shamefaced, sorry. Opp UNREPENTANT.

pennon n banner, flag, pennant, standard, streamer.

pension n annuity, benefit, old age pension, superannuation.

pensive adj brooding, cogitating, contemplative, day-dreaming, inf far-away, inf in a brown study, lost in thought, meditative, reflective, ruminative, thoughtful.

penury *n* beggary, destitution, impoverishment, indigence, lack, need, poverty, scarcity, want.

people *n* **1** folk, human beings, humanity, humans, individuals, ladies and gentlemen, mankind, men and women, mortals, persons. **2** citizenry, citizens, community, electorate, *inf* grass roots, *Gr* hoi polloi, nation, *inf* the plebs, populace, population, the public, society, subjects. **3** *your own people.* clan, family, kinsmen, kith and kin, nation, race, relations, relatives, tribe. • *vb* colonize, fill, inhabit, occupy, overrun, populate, settle.

perceive *vb* **1** become aware of, catch sight of, descry, detect, discern, discover, distinguish, espy, glimpse, hear, identify, make out, notice, note, observe, recognize, see, spot. **2** appreciate, apprehend, comprehend, deduce, feel, *inf* figure out, gather, grasp, infer, know, realize, sense, understand.

perceptible *adj* appreciable, audible, detectable, discernible, distinct, distinguishable, evident, identifiable, manifest, marked, notable, noticeable, observable, obvious, palpable, perceivable, plain, recognizable, unmistakable, visible. *Opp* IMPERCEPTIBLE.

perception *n* appreciation, apprehension, awareness, cognition, comprehension, consciousness, discernment, insight, instinct, intuition, knowledge, observation,

perspective, realization, recognition, sensation, sense, understanding, view.

perceptive *adj* acute, alert, astute, attentive, aware, clever, discerning, discriminating, observant, penetrating, percipient, perspicacious, quick, responsive, sensitive, sharp, sharp-eyed, shrewd, sympathetic, understanding. ▷ INTELLIGENT.

perch *n* rest, resting-place, roost. • *vb* balance, rest, roost, settle, sit.

percussion *n* □ bell, *castanets, celesta, chime bar, cymbal, glockenspiel, gong, kettledrum, maracas, rattle, tambourine, timpani, triangle, tubular bells, vibraphone, whip, wood block, xylophone.* ▷ DRUM.

perdition *n* damnation, doom, downfall, hell, hellfire, ruin, ruination.

perfect *adj* **1** absolute, complete, completed, consummate, excellent, exemplary, faultless, finished, flawless, ideal, immaculate, incomparable, matchless, mint, superlative, unbeatable, undamaged, unexceptionable, unqualified, whole. **2** blameless, irreproachable, pure, sinless, spotless, unimpeachable. **3** accurate, authentic, correct, exact, faithful, immaculate, impeccable, precise, tailor-made, true. *Opp* IMPERFECT. • *vb* bring to fruition, bring to perfection, carry through, complete, consummate, effect, execute, finish, fulfil, make perfect, realize, *inf* see through.

perfection *n* **1** beauty, completeness, excellence, faultlessness, flawlessness, ideal, precision, purity, wholeness. Opp IMPERFECTION. 2 *the perfection of a plan.* accomplishment, achievement, completion, consummation, end, fruition, fulfilment, realization.

perforate vb bore through, drill, penetrate, pierce, prick, punch, puncture, riddle.

perform vb 1 accomplish, achieve, bring about, carry on, carry out, commit, complete, discharge, dispatch, do, effect, execute, finish, fulfil, inf pull off. 2 behave, function, go, operate, run, work. 3 *perform on stage.* act, appear, dance, feature, figure, take part. 4 *perform a play, song.* enact, mount, present, play, produce, put on, render, represent, serenade, sing, stage.

performance n 1 accomplishment, achievement, carrying out, completion, doing, execution, fulfilment. 2 act, behaviour, conduct, deception, exhibition, exploit, feat, play-acting, pretence. 3 *stage performance.* acting, début, impersonation, interpretation, play, playing, portrayal, presentation, production, rendition, representation. □ *concert, dress rehearsal, first night, last night, matinée, première, preview, rehearsal, show, sketch, turn.*

performer n actor, actress, artist, artiste, player, singer, star, inf superstar, thespian, trouper. ▷ ENTERTAINER.

perfume n 1 aroma, bouquet, fragrance, odour, scent. ▷ SMELL. 2 after-shave, eau de Cologne, scent, toilet water.

perfunctory adj apathetic, automatic, brief, cursory, dutiful, fleeting, half-hearted, hurried, inattentive, indifferent, mechanical, offhand, routine, superficial, uncaring, unenthusiastic, uninterested, uninvolved, unthinking. Opp ENTHUSIASTIC.

perhaps adv conceivably, maybe, old use peradventure, old use perchance, possibly.

peril n danger, hazard, insecurity, jeopardy, risk, susceptibility, threat, vulnerability.

perilous adj dangerous, hazardous, insecure, risky, uncertain, unsafe, vulnerable. Opp SAFE.

perimeter n border, borderline, boundary, bounds, circumference, confines, edge, fringe, frontier, limit, margin, periphery, verge.

period n 1 duration, interval, phase, season, session, span, spell, stage, stint, stretch, time, while. 2 aeon, age, epoch, era. ▷ TIME.

periodic adj cyclical, intermittent, occasional, recurrent, repeated, spasmodic, sporadic.

peripheral adj 1 distant, on the perimeter, outer, outermost, outlying. 2 borderline, incidental, inessential, irrelevant, marginal, minor, nonessential, secondary, tangential, unimportant, unnecessary. Opp CENTRAL.

perish vb 1 be destroyed, be killed, die, expire, fall, lose your life, meet your death, pass away. 2 crumble away, decay, decompose, disintegrate, go bad, rot.

perishable adj biodegradable, destructible, liable to perish, unstable. Opp PERMANENT.

perjury n bearing false witness, lying, mendacity.

permanent adj abiding, ceaseless, changeless, chronic, constant, continual, continuous, durable, endless, enduring, eternal, everlasting, fixed, immutable, incessant, incurable, indestructible, indissoluble, ineradicable, interminable, invariable, irreparable, irreversible, lasting, lifelong, long-lasting, never-ending, nonstop, ongoing, perennial, perpetual, persistent, stable, steady, unalterable, unceasing, unchanging, undying, unending. *Opp* TEMPORARY.

permeate vb diffuse, filter through, flow through, impregnate, infiltrate, penetrate, percolate, pervade, saturate, soak through, spread through.

permissible adj acceptable, admissible, allowable, allowed, excusable, lawful, legal, legitimate, licit, permitted, proper, right, sanctioned, tolerable, valid, venial (*sin*). *Opp* UNACCEPTABLE.

permission n acquiescence, agreement, approbation, approval, assent, authority, authorization, consent, dispensation, franchise, *inf* go-ahead, *inf* green light, leave, licence, *inf* rubber stamp, sanction, seal of approval, stamp of approval, support. ▷ PERMIT.

permissive adj acquiescent, consenting, easygoing, indulgent, latitudinarian, lenient, liberal, libertarian, tolerant.

permit n authority, authorization, certification, charter, licence, order, pass, passport, ticket, visa, warrant.

● vb admit, agree to, allow, approve of, authorize, consent to, endorse, enfranchise, give an opportunity for, give permission for, give your blessing to, legalize, license, make possible, sanction, *old use* suffer, support, tolerate.

perpendicular adj at right angles, erect, plumb, straight up and down, upright, vertical.

perpetual adj abiding, ageless, ceaseless, chronic, constant, continual, continuous, endless, enduring, eternal, everlasting, frequent, immortal, immutable, incessant, incurable, indestructible, ineradicable, interminable, invariable, lasting, long-lasting, never-ending, nonstop, ongoing, perennial, permanent, persistent, protracted, recurrent, recurring, repeated, *old use* sempiternal, timeless, unceasing, unchanging, undying, unending, unfailing, unremitting. *Opp* TEMPORARY.

perpetuate vb continue, eternalize, eternize, extend, immortalize, keep going, maintain, make permanent, preserve.

perplex vb baffle, *inf* bamboozle, befuddle, bewilder, confound, confuse, disconcert, distract, dumbfound, muddle, mystify, nonplus, puzzle, *inf* stump, *inf* throw, worry.

perquisite n benefit, bonus, *inf* consideration, emolument, extra, fringe benefit, gratuity, *inf* perk, tip.

persecute vb abuse, afflict, annoy, badger, bother, bully, discriminate against, harass, hector, hound, ill-treat, intimidate, maltreat, martyr, molest, oppress, pester, *inf* put the screws on, suppress, terrorize, torment, torture, trouble, tyrannize, victimize, worry.

persist *vb* be diligent, be steadfast, carry on, continue, endure, go on, *inf* hang on, hold out, *inf* keep at it, keep going, *inf* keep it up, keep on, last, linger, persevere, *inf* plug away, remain, *inf* soldier on, stand firm, stay, *inf* stick at it. *Opp* CEASE.

persistent *adj* 1 ceaseless, chronic, constant, continual, continuous, endless, eternal, everlasting, incessant, interminable, lasting, long-lasting, never-ending, obstinate, permanent, perpetual, persisting, recurrent, recurring, remaining, repeated, unending, unrelenting, unrelieved, unremitting. *Opp* BRIEF, INTERMITTENT. 2 assiduous, determined, dogged, hard-working, indefatigable, patient, persevering, pertinacious, relentless, resolute, steadfast, steady, stubborn, tenacious, tireless, unflagging, untiring, unwavering, zealous. *Opp* LAZY.

person *n* adolescent, adult, baby, being, *inf* body, character, child, *inf* customer, figure, human, human being, individual, infant, mortal, personage, soul, *inf* type, woman. ▷ MAN, PEOPLE, WOMAN.

persona *n* character, exterior, façade, guise, identity, image, part, personality, role, self-image.

personal *adj* 1 distinct, distinctive, exclusive, idiosyncratic, individual, inimitable, particular, peculiar, private, special, unique, your own. *Opp* GEN-

ERAL. 2 *a personal appearance.* actual, in person, in the flesh, live, physical. 3 *personal letters.* confidential, friendly, individual, informal, intimate, private, secret. *Opp* PUBLIC. 4 *personal friends.* bosom, close, dear, familiar, intimate, known. 5 *personal remarks.* belittling, critical, derogatory, disparaging, insulting, offensive, pejorative, rude, slighting, unfriendly. 6 *personal knowledge.* direct, empirical, experiential, first-hand.

personality *n* 1 attractiveness, character, charisma, charm, disposition, identity, individuality, magnetism, *inf* make-up, nature, persona, psyche, temperament. 2 *inf* big name, celebrity, idol, luminary, name, public figure, star, superstar.

personification *n* allegorical representation, embodiment, epitome, human likeness, incarnation, living image, manifestation.

personify *vb* allegorize, embody, epitomize, exemplify, give human shape to, incarnate, manifest, personalize, represent, stand for, symbolize, typify.

personnel *n* employees, manpower, people, staff, workforce, workers.

perspective *n* angle, approach, attitude, outlook, point of view, position, prospect, slant, standpoint, view, viewpoint.

persuade *vb* bring round, cajole, coax, convert, convince, entice, exhort, importune, induce, influence, inveigle, press, prevail upon, prompt, talk into, tempt, urge, use persuasion,

wheedle (into), win over.
Opp DISSUADE.

persuasion *n* 1 argument, blandishment, brainwashing, cajolery, coaxing, conditioning, enticement, exhortation, inducement, persuading, propaganda, reasoning. 2 affiliation, belief, conviction, creed, denomination, faith, religion, sect.

persuasive *adj* cogent, compelling, conclusive, convincing, credible, effective, efficacious, eloquent, forceful, influential, logical, plausible, potent, reasonable, sound, strong, telling, unarguable, valid, watertight. *Opp* UNCONVINCING.

pertain *vb* appertain, apply, be relevant, have bearing, have reference, have relevance, refer. **pertain to** affect, concern.

pertinent *adj* apposite, appropriate, apropos, apt, fitting, germane, relevant, suitable. *Opp* IRRELEVANT.

perturb *vb* agitate, alarm, bother, confuse, discompose, discomfit, disconcert, disquiet, distress, disturb, fluster, frighten, make anxious, ruffle, scare, shake, trouble, unnerve, unsettle, upset, vex, worry. *Opp* REASSURE.

peruse *vb* examine, inspect, look over, read, run your eye over, scan, scrutinize, study.

pervade *vb* affect, diffuse, fill, filter through, flow through, impregnate, penetrate, percolate, permeate, saturate, spread through, suffuse.

pervasive *adj* general, inescapable, insidious, omnipresent, penetrating, permeating,

pervading, prevalent, rife, ubiquitous, universal, widespread.

perverse *adj* adamant, contradictory, contrary, disobedient, fractious, headstrong, illogical, inappropriate, inflexible, intractable, intransigent, obdurate, obstinate, peevish, *inf* pig-headed, rebellious, refractory, self-willed, stubborn, tiresome, uncooperative, unhelpful, unreasonable, wayward, wilful, wrong-headed. *Opp* REASONABLE.

perversion *n* 1 corruption, distortion, falsification, misrepresentation, misuse, twisting. 2 aberration, abnormality, depravity, deviance, deviation, immorality, impropriety, *inf* kinkiness, perversity, unnaturalness, vice, wickedness.

pervert *n* debauchee, degenerate, deviant, perverted person, profligate. • *vb* 1 bend, deflect, distort, divert, falsify, misrepresent, perjure, subvert, twist, undermine. 2 *pervert a witness.* bribe, corrupt, lead astray.

perverted *adj* abnormal, amoral, bad, corrupt, debauched, degenerate, depraved, deviant, dissolute, eccentric, evil, immoral, improper, *inf* kinky, profligate, sick, twisted, unnatural, unprincipled, warped, wicked, wrong. ▷ OBSCENE. *Opp* NATURAL.

pessimism *n* cynicism, despair, despondency, fatalism, gloom, hopelessness, negativeness, resignation, unhappiness. *Opp* OPTIMISM.

pessimistic *adj* bleak, cynical, defeatist, despairing, despondent, fatalistic, gloomy, hopeless, melancholy, morbid, negative, resigned, unhappy. ▷ SAD. *Opp* OPTIMISTIC.

pest n 1 annoyance, bane, bother, curse, irritation, nuisance, *inf* pain in the neck, *inf* thorn in your flesh, trial, vexation. 2 *inf* bug, *inf* creepy-crawly, insect, parasite, *plur* vermin.

pester vb annoy, badger, bait, beseige, bother, *inf* get under someone's skin, harass, harry, *inf* hassle, irritate, molest, nag, nettle, plague, provoke, torment, trouble, worry.

pestilence n blight, curse, epidemic, pandemic, plague, scourge. ▷ ILLNESS.

pet n *inf* apple of your eye, darling, favourite, idol.
• vb caress, cuddle, fondle, kiss, nuzzle, pat, stroke. ▷ TOUCH.

petition n appeal, application, entreaty, list of signatures, plea, request, solicitation, suit, supplication. • vb appeal to, call upon, deliver a petition to, entreat, importune, solicit, sue, supplicate to. ▷ ASK.

petty adj 1 inconsequential, insignificant, minor, niggling, small, trivial, trifling. ▷ UNIMPORTANT. *Opp* IMPORTANT. 2 *petty complaints.* grudging, mean, nit-picking, small-minded, ungenerous. *Opp* GENEROUS.

phase n development, period, season, spell, stage, state, step. ▷ TIME. **phase in** ▷ INTRODUCE. **phase out** ▷ FINISH.

phenomenal adj amazing, astonishing, astounding, exceptional, extraordinary, *inf* fantastic, incredible, marvellous,

inf mind-boggling, miraculous, notable, outstanding, prodigious, rare, remarkable, *inf* sensational, singular, staggering, stunning, unbelievable, unorthodox, unusual, *inf* wonderful. *Opp* ORDINARY.

phenomenon n 1 circumstance, event, experience, fact, happening, incident, occasion, occurrence, sight. 2 *an unusual phenomenon.* curiosity, marvel, miracle, phenomenal person, phenomenal thing, prodigy, rarity, sensation, spectacle, wonder.

philanthropic adj altruistic, beneficent, benevolent, bountiful, caring, charitable, generous, humane, humanitarian, magnanimous, munificent, public-spirited, ungrudging. ▷ KIND. *Opp* MISANTHROPIC.

philanthropist n altruist, benefactor, donor, giver, *inf* Good Samaritan, humanitarian, patron, provider, sponsor.

philistine adj boorish, ignorant, lowbrow, materialistic, uncivilized, uncultivated, uncultured, unenlightened, unlettered, vulgar.

philosopher n sage, student of philosophy, thinker.

philosophical adj 1 abstract, academic, analytical, erudite, esoteric, ideological, impractical, intellectual, learned, logical, metaphysical, rational, reasoned, scholarly, theoretical, thoughtful, wise. 2 calm, collected, composed, detached, equable, imperturbable, judicious, patient, reasonable, resigned, serene, sober, stoical, unemotional, unruffled. *Opp* EMOTIONAL.

philosophize vb analyse, moralize, pontificate, preach, rationalize, reason, sermonize, theorize, think things out.

philosophy n 1 epistemology, ideology, logic, metaphysics, rationalism, thinking. 2 *philosophy of life.* attitude, convictions, outlook, set of beliefs, tenets, values, viewpoint, wisdom.

phlegmatic adj apathetic, cold, cool, frigid, impassive, imperturbable, indifferent, lethargic, passive, placid, slow, sluggish, stoical, stolid, torpid, undemonstrative, unemotional, unenthusiastic, unfeeling, uninvolved, unresponsive. Opp EXCITABLE.

phobia n anxiety, aversion, dislike, dread, inf hang-up, hatred, horror, loathing, neurosis, obsession, repugnance, revulsion. ▷ FEAR. ● *agoraphobia* (open space), *arachnophobia* (spiders), *claustrophobia* (enclosed space), *xenophobia* (foreigners).

phone vb call, dial, inf give a buzz, ring, telephone.

phoney adj affected, artificial, assumed, bogus, cheating, contrived, counterfeit, deceitful, ersatz, factitious, fake, faked, false, fictitious, fraudulent, hypocritical, imitation, insincere, mock, pretended, inf pseudo, inf put-on, inf put-up, sham, spurious, synthetic, trick, unreal. Opp REAL.

photocopy vb copy, duplicate, photostat, print off, reproduce, inf run off.

photograph n enlargement, exposure, negative, inf photo, picture, plate, positive, print, shot, slide, inf snap, snapshot,

transparency. ● vb film, shoot, snap, take a photograph of.

photographic adj 1 accurate, exact, faithful, graphic, lifelike, naturalistic, realistic, representational, true to life. 2 *photographic memory.* pictorial, retentive, visual.

phrase n clause, expression. ▷ SAYING. ● vb ▷ SAY.

phraseology n diction, expression, idiom, language, parlance, phrasing, style, turn of phrase, wording.

physical adj actual, bodily, carnal, concrete, corporal, corporeal, earthly, fleshly, incarnate, material, mortal, palpable, physiological, real, solid, substantial, tangible. Opp INTANGIBLE, SPIRITUAL.

physician n consultant, doctor, general practitioner, inf GP, inf medic, medical practitioner, specialist.

physiological adj anatomical, bodily, physical. Opp PSYCHOLOGICAL.

physique n body, build, figure, form, frame, muscles, physical condition, shape.

pick n 1 choice, election, option, preference, selection. 2 best, cream, élite, favourite, flower, pride. ● vb 1 cast (*actor*), choose, decide on, elect, fix on, make a choice of, name, nominate, opt for, prefer, select, settle on, single out, vote for. 2 *pick flowers.* collect, cull, cut, gather, harvest, pluck, pull off, take. **pick on** ▷ BULLY. **pick up** ▷ GET, IMPROVE.

pictorial adj diagrammatic, graphic, illustrated, realistic, representational, vivid.

picture n 1 delineation, depiction, image, likeness, outline, portrayal, profile, representation. □ abstract, cameo, caricature, cartoon, collage, design, doodle, drawing, engraving, etching, fresco, plur graffiti, plur graphics, icon, identikit, illustration, landscape, montage, mosaic, mural, oil-painting, old master, painting, photofit, photograph, pin-up, plate, portrait, print, reproduction, self-portrait, silhouette, sketch, slide, inf snap, snapshot, still life, transfer, transparency, triptych, Fr trompe l'oeil, video, vignette. 2 film, movie, moving picture, video. ▷ FILM.
● vb 1 caricature, delineate, depict, display, doodle, draw, engrave, etch, evoke, film, illustrate, outline, paint, photograph, portray, print, represent, show, sketch, video. 2 picture the future. conceive, describe, dream up, envisage, envision, fancy, imagine, see in your mind's eye, think up, visualize.

picturesque adj 1 attractive, charming, colourful, idyllic, lovely, pleasant, pretty, quaint, scenic, inf story-book. ▷ BEAUTIFUL. Opp UNATTRACTIVE. 2 picturesque language. colourful, descriptive, expressive, graphic, imaginative, poetic, vivid. Opp PROSAIC.

pie n flan, pasty, patty, quiche, tart, tartlet, turnover, vol-au-vent.

piece n 1 bar, bit, bite, block, chip, chunk, crumb, division, inf dollop, fraction, fragment, grain, helping, hunk, length, lump, morsel, part, particle, portion, quantity, remnant, sample, scrap, section, segment, shard, share, shred, slab, slice, sliver, snippet, speck, stick, tablet, inf titbit, wedge. 2 component, constituent, element, spare part, unit. 3 piece of music. work. article, composition, example, instance, item, number, passage, specimen, work. ▷ MUSIC, WRITING.
piece together ▷ ASSEMBLE.

pied adj dappled, flecked, mottled, particoloured, patchy, piebald, spotted, variegated.

pier n 1 breakwater, jetty, landing-stage, quay, wharf. ▷ DOCK. 2 buttress, column, pile, pillar, post, support, upright.

pierce vb bayonet, bore through, cut, drill, enter, go through, impale, jab, lance, make a hole in, penetrate, perforate, poke through, prick, punch, puncture, riddle, skewer, spear, spike, spit, stab, stick into, thrust into, transfix, tunnel through, wound. **piercing** ▷ SHARP.

piety n dedication, devotion, devotedness, devoutness, faith, godliness, holiness, piousness, religion, derog religiosity, saintliness, sanctity. Opp IMPIETY.

pig n boar, hog, inf piggy, piglet, runt, sow, swine.

pile n 1 abundance, accumulation, agglomeration, collection, concentration, conglomeration, deposit, heap, hoard, inf load, mass, mound, inf mountain, plethora, quantity, stack, stockpile, supply, inf tons. 2 column, pier, post, support, upright.
● vb accumulate, amass, assemble, bring together, build up, collect, concentrate, deposit,

gather, heap, hoard, load, mass, stack up, stockpile, store.

pilfer *vb inf* filch, *inf* pinch, rob, shoplift. ▷ STEAL.

pilgrim *n* crusader, *old use* palmer. ▷ TRAVELLER.

pill *n* bolus, capsule, lozenge, pastille, pellet, pilule, tablet. ▷ MEDICINE.

pillage *n* buccaneering, depredation, despoliation, devastation, looting, marauding, piracy, plunder, plundering, ransacking, rape, rapine, robbery, robbing, sacking, stealing, stripping. ● *vb* despoil, devastate, loot, maraud, plunder, raid, ransack, ravage, raze, rob, sack, steal, strip, vandalize.

pillar *n* baluster, caryatid, column, pier, pilaster, pile, post, prop, shaft, stanchion, support, upright.

pilot *n* 1 airman, *old use* aviator, captain, flier. 2 coxswain, helmsman, navigator, steersman. ● *vb* conduct, convey, direct, drive, fly, guide, lead, navigate, shepherd, steer.

pimple *n* blackhead, boil, eruption, pustule, spot, swelling, *sl* zit. **pimples** acne, rash.

pin *n old use* bodkin, bolt, brooch, clip, dowel, drawing-pin, hatpin, nail, peg, rivet, safety-pin, spike, staple, thole, tiepin. ● *vb* clip, nail, pierce, staple, tack, transfix. ▷ FASTEN.

pinch *vb* 1 crush, grip, hurt, nip, press, squeeze, tweak. 2 ▷ STEAL.

pine *vb* mope, mourn, sicken, waste away. **pine for** ▷ WANT.

pinnacle *n* 1 acme, apex, cap, climax, consummation, crest, crown, crowning point, height, highest point, peak, summit,

top, zenith. 2 *pinnacle on a roof.* spire, steeple, turret.

pioneer *n* 1 colonist, discoverer, explorer, frontiersman, frontierswoman, pathfinder, settler, trail-blazer. 2 innovator, inventor, originator, pace-maker, trend-setter. ● *vb* begin, *inf* bring out, create, develop, discover, establish, experiment with, found, inaugurate, initiate, institute, introduce, invent, launch, open up, originate, set up, start.

pious *adj* 1 dedicated, devoted, devout, faithful, god-fearing, godly, good, holy, moral, religious, reverent, reverential, saintly, sincere, spiritual, virtuous. *Opp* IMPIOUS. 2 *[derog]* *inf* goody-goody, *inf* holier-than-thou, hypocritical, insincere, mealy-mouthed, pietistic, Pharisaical, sanctimonious, self-righteous, self-satisfied, *inf* smarmy, unctuous. *Opp* SINCERE.

pip *n* 1 pit, seed, stone. 2 mark, spot, star. 3 bleep, blip, sound, stroke.

pipe *n* conduit, channel, duct, hose, hydrant, line, main, pipeline, piping, tube. ● *vb* 1 carry along a pipe, carry along a wire, channel, convey, deliver, supply, transmit. 2 *pipe a tune.* blow, play, sound, *inf* tootle, whistle. **pipe up** ▷ SPEAK.

piping ▷ HOT, SHRILL.

piquant *adj* 1 appetizing, pungent, salty, sharp, spicy, tangy, tart, tasty. *Opp* BLAND. 2 *a piquant notion.* arresting, exciting, interesting, provocative, stimulating. *Opp* BANAL.

pirate *n* buccaneer, *old use* corsair, marauder, privateer,

sea rover. ▷ THIEF. ● *vb* ▷ PLA-
GIARIZE.

pit *n* 1 abyss, chasm, crater,
depression, ditch, excavation,
hole, hollow, pothole, rut,
trench, well. 2 coal-mine,
colliery, mine, mineshaft,
quarry, shaft, working.

pitch *n* 1 bitumen, tar. 2 *pitch of
a roof*. angle, gradient, incline,
slope, steepness, tilt. 3 *musical
pitch*. frequency, tuning.
4 *soccer pitch*. arena, ground,
playing-field, stadium.
● *vb* 1 erect, put up, raise, set
up. 2 *pitch stones*. bowl,
inf bung, cast, *inf* chuck, fire,
fling, heave, hurl, launch, lob,
sling, throw, toss. 3 *pitch into
the water*. dive, drop, fall headlong, plunge, plummet, *inf* take
a nosedive, topple. **pitch about**
▷ TOSS. **pitch in** ▷ COOPERATE.
pitch into ▷ ATTACK.

piteous *adj* affecting, distressing, heartbreaking, heart-rending, lamentable, miserable,
moving, pathetic, pitiable, pitiful, plaintive, poignant, touching, woeful, wretched. ▷ SAD.

pitfall *n* catch, danger, difficulty, hazard, peril, snag, trap.

pitiful *adj* 1 abject, contemptible, deplorable, hopeless,
inadequate, incompetent, insignificant, laughable, mean,
inf miserable, *inf* pathetic, pitiable, ridiculous, sorry, trifling,
unimportant, useless, worthless.
Opp ADMIRABLE. 2 ▷ PITIFUL.

pitiless *adj* bloodthirsty, brutal,
callous, cruel, ferocious, hard,
heartless, inexorable, inhuman,
merciless, relentless, ruthless,
sadistic, unfeeling, unrelenting,
unrelieved, unremitting,
unsympathetic. *Opp* MERCIFUL.

pitted *adj* dented, eaten away,
eroded, *inf* holey, marked, pock-
marked, rough, scarred,
uneven. *Opp* SMOOTH.

pity *n* charity, clemency,
commiseration, compassion,
condolence, feeling, forbearance, forgiveness, grace,
humanity, kindness, leniency,
love, mercy, regret, *old use*
ruth, softness, sympathy,
tenderness, understanding,
warmth. *Opp* CRUELTY.
● *vb inf* bleed for, commiserate
with, *inf* feel for, feel sorry for,
show pity for, sympathize with,
weep for.

pivot *n* axis, axle, centre,
fulcrum, gudgeon, hinge, hub,
pin, point of balance, spindle,
swivel. ● *vb* hinge, revolve,
rotate, spin, swivel, turn, twirl,
whirl.

placard *n* advert, advertisement,
bill, notice, poster, sign.

placate *vb* appease, calm,
conciliate, humour, mollify,
pacify, soothe.

place *n* 1 area, country, district,
locale, location, locality, locus,
neighbourhood, part, point,
position, quarter, region, scene,
setting, site, situation, *inf* spot,
town, venue, vicinity,
inf whereabouts. 2 *a place in
society*. condition, degree,
estate, function, grade, job,
mission, niche, office, position,
rank, role, standing, station,
status. 3 *a place to live*.
▷ HOUSE. 4 *a place to sit*.
▷ SEAT. ● *vb* 1 deposit, dispose,
inf dump, lay, leave, locate,
pinpoint, plant, position, put
down, rest, set down, set out,
settle, situate, stand, station,
inf stick. 2 arrange, categorize,

class, classify, grade, order, position, put in order, rank, sort. **3** *can't place it.* identify, put a name to, put into context, recognize, remember.

placid *adj* **1** collected, composed, cool, equable, even-tempered, imperturbable, level-headed, mild, phlegmatic, restful, sensible, stable, steady, unexcitable, untroubled. *Opp* EXCITABLE, STORMY. **2** calm, motionless, peaceful, quiet, tranquil, unruffled, untroubled. *Opp* EXCITABLE, STORMY.

plagiarize *vb* appropriate, borrow, copy, *inf* crib, imitate, infringe copyright, *inf* lift, pirate, purloin, reproduce. ▷ STEAL.

plague *n* **1** affliction, bane, blight, calamity, contagion, epidemic, infection, outbreak, pandemic, pestilence. ▷ ILLNESS. **2** infestation, invasion, nuisance, scourge, swarm, visitation. ● *vb* afflict, annoy, be a nuisance to, bother, distress, disturb, harass, harry, hound, irritate, molest, *inf* nag, persecute, pester, torment, torture, trouble, vex, worry.

plain *adj* **1** apparent, audible, certain, clear, comprehensible, definite, distinct, evident, intelligible, legible, lucid, manifest, obvious, patent, simple, transparent, unambiguous, understandable, unmistakable, visible, well-defined. *Opp* OBSCURE. **2** *plain speech.* basic, blunt, candid, direct, downright, explicit, forthright, frank, honest, informative, outspoken, plain-spoken, prosaic, sincere, straightforward, unequivocal, unvarnished. **3** *plain living.* austere, drab, everyday, frugal, homely, modest, ordinary, simple, Spartan, stark, unadorned, unattractive, undecorated, unexciting, unprepossessing, unpretentious, unremarkable, workaday. *Opp* SOPHISTICATED. ● *n* grassland, pasture, pampas, prairie, savannah, steppe, tundra, veld.

plaintive *adj* doleful, melancholy, mournful, plangent, sorrowful, wistful. ▷ SAD.

plan *n* **1** *inf* bird's-eye view, blueprint, chart, design, diagram, drawing, layout, map, representation, sketch-map. **2** *a plan of action.* aim, course of action, design, formula, idea, intention, method, plot, policy, procedure, programme, project, proposal, proposition, *inf* scenario, scheme, strategy, system. ● *vb* **1** arrange, concoct, contrive, design, devise, draw up a plan, formulate, invent, map out, *inf* mastermind, organize, outline, plot, prepare, scheme, think out, work out. **2** *I plan to go away.* aim, conspire, contemplate, envisage, expect, intend, mean, propose, think of. **planned** ▷ DELIBERATE.

plane *adj* even, flat, flush, level, smooth, uniform. ● *n* **1** flat surface, level, surface. **2** ▷ AIRCRAFT.

planet *n* globe, orb, satellite, sphere, world. □ *Earth, Jupiter, Mars, Mercury, Neptune, Pluto, Saturn, Uranus, Venus.*

plank *n* beam, board, planking, timber.

planning *n* arrangement, design, drafting, forethought, organization, preparation, setting up, thinking out.

plant *n* greenery, growth, undergrowth, vegetation. □ *annual, bulb, cactus, cereal, climber, fern, flower, fungus, grass, herb, lichen, moss, perennial, shrub, tree, vegetable, vine, water-plant, weed.* ▷ FLOWER, TREE, VEGETABLE. **2** *a manufacturing plant.* factory, foundry, mill, shop, works, workshop. **3** *industrial plant.* apparatus, equipment, machinery, machines.
● *vb* **1** bed out, set out, sow, transplant. **2** locate, place, position, put, situate, station.

plaster *n* **1** mortar, stucco. **2** dressing, sticking-plaster.
● *vb* apply, bedaub, coat, cover, daub, smear, spread.

plastic *adj* ductile, flexible, malleable, pliable, shapable, soft, supple, workable. □ *bakelite, celluloid, polystyrene, polythene, polyurethane, polyvinyl, PVC, vinyl.*

plate *n* **1** *old use* charger, dinner-plate, dish, platter, salver, side-plate, soup-plate, *old use* trencher. **2** lamina, lamination, layer, leaf, pane, panel, sheet, slab, stratum. **3** *plates in a book.* illustration, *inf* photo, photograph, picture, print. **4** *a dental plate.* dentures, false teeth. ● *vb* anodize, coat, cover, electroplate, galvanize (*with zinc*), gild (*with gold*).

platform *n* **1** dais, podium, rostrum, stage, stand. **2** *political platform.* ▷ POLICY.

platitude *n* banality, cliché, commonplace, truism.

plausible *adj* **1** acceptable, believable, conceivable, credible, imaginable, likely, logical, persuasive, possible, probable, rational, reasonable, sensible, tenable, thinkable. *Opp* IM-

PLAUSIBLE. **2** deceptive, glib, meretricious, misleading, specious, smooth, sophistical.

play *n* **1** amusement, diversion, entertainment, frivolity, fun, *inf* fun and games, *inf* horse-play, joking, make-believe, merrymaking, playing, pretending, recreation, revelry, *inf* skylarking, sport. **2** *play in moving parts.* flexibility, freedom, freedom of movement, *inf* give, latitude, leeway, looseness, movement, tolerance. **3** ▷ DRAMA. ● *vb* **1** amuse yourself, caper, cavort, disport yourself, enjoy yourself, fool about, frisk, frolic, gambol, *inf* have a good time, have fun, *inf* mess about, romp, sport. **2** *play a game.* join in, participate, take part. **3** *play an opponent.* challenge, compete against, oppose, rival, take on, vie with. **4** *play a role.* act, depict, impersonate, perform, portray, pretend to be, represent, take the part of. **5** *play an instrument.* make music on, perform on, strum. **6** *play the radio.* have on, listen to, operate, put on, switch on. **play about** ▷ MISBEHAVE. **play along, play ball** ▷ COOPERATE. **play down** ▷ MINIMIZE. **play for time** ▷ DELAY. **play it by ear** ▷ IMPROVISE. **play up** ▷ MISBEHAVE. **play up to** ▷ FLATTER.

player *n* **1** athlete, competitor, contestant, participant, sportsman, sportswoman. **2** actor, actress, artiste, entertainer, instrumentalist, musician, performer, soloist, Thespian, trouper. ▷ ENTERTAINER, MUSICIAN.

playful *adj* active, cheerful, coltish, facetious, flirtatious, frisky, frolicsome, fun-loving, good-natured, high-spirited, humorous, impish, jesting, *inf* jokey, joking, kittenish, light-hearted, lively, mischievous, puckish, roguish, skittish, spirited, sportive, sprightly, teasing, *inf* tongue-in-cheek, vivacious, waggish. *Opp* SERIOUS.

plea *n* 1 appeal, entreaty, invocation, petition, prayer, request, solicitation, suit, supplication. 2 argument, excuse, explanation, justification, pretext, reason.

plead *vb* 1 appeal, ask, beg, beseech, cry out, demand, entreat, implore, importune, petition, request, seek, solicit, supplicate. 2 allege, argue, assert, aver, declare, maintain, reason, swear.

pleasant *adj* acceptable, affable, agreeable, amiable, approachable, attractive, balmy, beautiful, charming, cheerful, congenial, decent, delicious, delightful, enjoyable, entertaining, excellent, fine, friendly, genial, gentle, good, gratifying, *inf* heavenly, hospitable, kind, likeable, lovely, mellow, mild, nice, palatable, peaceful, pleasing, pleasurable, pretty, reassuring, relaxed, satisfying, soothing, sympathetic, warm, welcome, welcoming. *Opp* ANNOYING, UNPLEASANT.

please *vb* 1 amuse, cheer up, content, delight, divert, entertain, give pleasure to, gladden, gratify, humour, make happy, satisfy, suit. 2 *Do what you please.* ▷ WANT. **pleasing** ▷ PLEASANT.

pleased *adj inf* chuffed, *derog* complacent, contented, delighted, elated, euphoric, glad, grateful, gratified, *sl* over the moon, satisfied, thankful, thrilled. ▷ HAPPY. *Opp* ANNOYED.

pleasure *n* 1 bliss, comfort, contentment, delight, ecstasy, enjoyment, euphoria, fulfilment, gladness, gratification, happiness, joy, rapture, satisfaction, solace. 2 amusement, diversion, entertainment, fun, luxury, recreation, self-indulgence.

pleat *n* crease, flute, fold, gather, tuck.

plebiscite *n* ballot, poll, referendum, vote.

pledge *n* 1 assurance, covenant, guarantee, oath, pact, promise, undertaking, vow, warranty, word. 2 *a pledge left at a pawnbroker's.* bail, bond, collateral, deposit, pawn, security, surety. ● *vb* agree, commit yourself, contract, give your word, guarantee, promise, swear, undertake, vouch, vouchsafe, vow.

plenary *adj* full, general, open.

plentiful *adj* abounding, abundant, ample, bounteous, bountiful, bristling, bumper (*crop*), copious, generous, inexhaustible, lavish, liberal, overflowing, plenteous, profuse, prolific. *Opp* SCARCE. **be plentiful** ▷ ABOUND.

plenty *n* abundance, adequacy, affluence, cornucopia, excess, fertility, flood, fruitfulness, glut, *inf* heaps, *inf* lashings, *inf* loads, a lot, *inf* lots, *inf* masses, much, more than enough, *inf* oceans, *inf* oodles, *inf* piles, plenitude, plentifulness, plethora, prodigality, profusion, prosperity, quantities, *inf* stacks, sufficiency, superabundance, surfeit, surplus, *inf* tons, wealth. *Opp* SCARCITY.

pliable *adj* 1 bendable, *inf* bendy, ductile, flexible, plastic, pliant, springy, supple. 2 *a pliable character*. adaptable, compliant, docile, easily influenced, easily led, easily persuaded, impressionable, manageable, persuadable, receptive, responsive, susceptible, suggestible, tractable, yielding.

plod *vb* 1 slog, tramp, trudge. ▷ WALK. 2 drudge, grind on, labour, persevere, *inf* peg away, *inf* plug away, toil. ▷ WORK.

plot *n* 1 acreage, allotment, area, estate, garden, lot, parcel, patch, smallholding, tract. 2 *a plot of a novel*. chain of events, narrative, organization, outline, scenario, story, story-line, thread. 3 *a subversive plot*. cabal, conspiracy, intrigue, machination, plan, scheme.
● *vb* 1 chart, compute, draw, map out, mark, outline, plan, project. 2 *plot to rob a bank*. collude, conspire, have designs, intrigue, machinate, scheme. 3 *plot a crime*. arrange, *inf* brew, conceive, concoct, *inf* cook up, design, devise, dream up, hatch.

pluck *n* ▷ COURAGE. *vb* 1 collect, gather, harvest, pick, pull off, remove. 2 grab, jerk, pull, seize, snatch, tear away, tweak, yank. 3 *pluck a chicken*. denude, remove feathers from, strip. 4 *pluck a violin*. play pizzicato, strum, twang.

plug *n* 1 bung, cork, stopper. 2 ▷ ADVERTISEMENT.
● *vb* 1 block up, *inf* bung up, close, cork, fill, jam, seal, stop

up, stuff up. 2 advertise, commend, mention frequently, promote, publicize, puff, recommend. **plug away** ▷ WORK.

plumb *adv* 1 accurately, *inf* dead, exactly, precisely, *inf* slap. 2 perpendicularly, vertically. ● *vb* fathom, measure, penetrate, probe, sound.

plumbing *n* heating system, pipes, water-supply.

plume *n* feather, *plur* plumage, quill.

plump *adj* ample, buxom, chubby, dumpy, overweight, podgy, portly, pudgy, *inf* roly-poly, rotund, round, squat, stout, tubby, *inf* well-upholstered. ▷ FAT. *Opp* THIN. **plump for** ▷ CHOOSE.

plunder *n* booty, contraband, loot, pickings, pillage, prize, spoils, swag, takings.
● *vb* capture, despoil, devastate, lay waste, loot, maraud, pillage, raid, ransack, ravage, rifle, rob, sack, seize, spoil, steal from, strip, vandalize.

plunge *vb* 1 descend, dip, dive, drop, engulf, fall, fall headlong, hurtle, immerse, jump, leap, lower, nosedive, pitch, plummet, sink, submerge, swoop, tumble. 2 force, push, stick, thrust.

poach *vb* 1 hunt, steal. 2 ▷ COOK.

pocket *n* bag, container, pouch, receptacle. ● *vb* ▷ TAKE.

pod *n* case, hull, shell.

poem *n* *inf* ditty, *inf* jingle, piece of poetry, rhyme, verse. □ *ballad, ballade, doggerel, eclogue, elegy, epic, epithalamium, haiku, idyll, lay, limerick, lyric, nursery-rhyme, pastoral, ode, sonnet, vers libre.* ▷ VERSE.

poet n bard, lyricist, minstrel, poetaster, rhymer, rhymester, sonneteer, versifier. ▷ WRITER.

poetic adj emotive, *derog* flowery, imaginative, lyrical, metrical, musical, poetical. *Opp* PROSAIC.

poignant adj affecting, distressing, heartbreaking, heartfelt, heart-rending, moving, painful, pathetic, piquant, piteous, pitiful, stirring, tender, touching, upsetting. ▷ SAD.

point n 1 apex, peak, prong, sharp end, spike, spur, tine, tip. 2 *a point in space*. location, place, position, site, situation, spot. 3 *a point in time*. instant, juncture, moment, second, stage, time. 4 *decimal point*. dot, full stop, mark, speck, spot. 5 *the point of an argument*. aim, burden, crux, drift, end, essence, gist, goal, heart, import, intention, meaning, motive, nub, object, objective, pith, purpose, quiddity, relevance, significance, subject, substance, theme, thrust, use, usefulness. 6 *points to raise*. aspect, detail, idea, item, matter, particular, question, thought, topic. 7 *good points in her character*. attribute, characteristic, facet, feature, peculiarity, property, quality, trait.
• vb 1 call attention to, direct attention to, draw attention to, indicate, point out, show, signal. 2 aim, direct, guide, lead, steer. **pointed** ▷ SHARP. **to the point** ▷ RELEVANT.

pointer n arrow, hand (*of clock*), indicator.

pointless adj aimless, fatuous, fruitless, futile, inane, ineffective, senseless, silly, unproductive, useless, vain, worthless. ▷ STUPID.

poise n aplomb, assurance, balance, calmness, composure, coolness, dignity, equanimity, equilibrium, equipoise, imperturbability, presence, sang-froid, self-confidence, self-control, self-possession, serenity, steadiness.
• vb balance, be poised, hover, keep in balance, support, suspend.

poised adj 1 balanced, hovering, in equilibrium, standing, steady, teetering, wavering. 2 *poised to begin*. keyed up, prepared, ready, set, standing by, waiting. 3 *a poised performer*. assured, calm, composed, cool, cool-headed, dignified, self-confident, self-possessed, serene, suave, *inf* unflappable, unruffled, urbane.

poison n bane, toxin, venom.
• vb 1 adulterate, contaminate, infect, pollute, taint. ▷ KILL. 2 *poison the mind*. corrupt, defile, deprave, envenom, pervert, prejudice, subvert, warp. **poisoned** ▷ DIRTY, POISONOUS.

poisonous adj deadly, fatal, infectious, lethal, mephitic, miasmic, mortal, noxious, poisoned, septic, toxic, venomous, virulent.

poke vb butt, dig, elbow, goad, jab, jog, nudge, prod, stab, stick, thrust. ▷ HIT. **poke about** ▷ SEARCH. **poke fun at** ▷ RIDICULE. **poke out** ▷ PROTRUDE.

poky adj confined, cramped, inconvenient, restrictive, uncomfortable. ▷ SMALL. *Opp* SPACIOUS.

polar adj antarctic, arctic, freezing, glacial, icy, Siberian. ▷ COLD.

polarize vb diverge, divide, move to opposite positions, separate, split.

pole n 1 bar, beanpole, column, flag-pole, mast, post, rod, shaft, spar, staff, stake, standard, stick, stilt, upright. 2 opposite poles. end, extreme, limit. **poles apart** ▷ DIFFERENT.

police n sl the Bill, constabulary, sl the fuzz, inf the law, police force, policemen.
• vb control, guard, keep in order, keep the peace, monitor, oversee, patrol, protect, provide a police presence, supervise, watch over.

policeman, policewoman inf bobby, constable, sl cop, sl copper, detective, Fr gendarme, inspector, officer, PC, police constable, sl rozzer, woman police constable, WPC.

policy n 1 approach, code of conduct, custom, guidelines, inf line, method, practice, principles, procedure, protocol, regulations, rules, stance, strategy, tactics. 2 intentions, manifesto, plan of action, platform, programme, proposals.

polish n 1 brightness, brilliance, finish, glaze, gleam, gloss, lustre, sheen, shine, smoothness, sparkle. 2 beeswax, French polish, oil, shellac, varnish, wax. 3 His manners show polish. inf class, elegance, finesse, grace, refinement, sophistication, style, suavity, urbanity. • vb brighten, brush up, buff up, burnish, French-polish, gloss, rub down, rub up, shine, smooth, wax. **polish off**

▷ FINISH. **polish up** ▷ IMPROVE.

polished adj 1 bright, burnished, glassy, gleaming, glossy, lustrous, shining, shiny. 2 polished manners. civilized, inf classy, cultivated, cultured, debonair, elegant, expert, faultless, fine, finished, flawless, genteel, gracious, impeccable, perfect, perfected, polite, inf posh, refined, soigné(e), sophisticated, suave, urbane. Opp ROUGH.

polite adj agreeable, attentive, chivalrous, civil, considerate, correct, courteous, courtly, cultivated, deferential, diplomatic, discreet, euphemistic, formal, gallant, genteel, gentlemanly, gracious, ladylike, obliging, polished, proper, respectful, tactful, thoughtful, well-bred, well-mannered, well-spoken. Opp RUDE.

political adj 1 administrative, civil, diplomatic, governmental, legislative, parliamentary, state. 2 activist, factional, militant, partisan, party-political. □ anarchist, capitalist, communist, conservative, democrat, fascist, Labour, leftist, left-wing, liberal, Marxist, moderate, monarchist, nationalist, Nazi, parliamentarian, radical, republican, revolutionary, rightist, right-wing, socialist, Tory, old use Whig.

politics n diplomacy, government, political affairs, political science, public affairs, statecraft, statesmanship. □ anarchy, capitalism, communism, democracy, dictatorship, martial law, monarchy, oligarchy, republic.

poll n 1 ballot, election, vote. 2 canvass, census, plebiscite, referandum, survey. • vb ballot, canvass, question, sample, survey.

pollute vb adulterate, befoul, blight, contaminate, corrupt, defile, dirty, foul, infect, poison, soil, taint.

pomp n brilliance, ceremonial, ceremony, display, formality, glory, grandeur, magnificence, ostentation, pageantry, ritual, show, solemnity, spectacle, splendour.

pompous adj affected, arrogant, bombastic, conceited, grandiloquent, grandiose, haughty, inf high-falutin, imperious, long-winded, magisterial, ornate, ostentatious, overbearing, pedantic, pontifical, posh, pretentious, self-important, sententious, showy, smug, snobbish, inf snooty, inf stuck-up, inf stuffy, supercilious, turgid, vain, vainglorious.
▷ PROUD. Opp MODEST.

ponderous adj 1 awkward, bulky, burdensome, cumbersome, heavy, hefty, huge, massive, unwieldy, weighty.
Opp LIGHT. 2 a ponderous style. dreary, dull, elephantine, heavy-handed, humourless, inflated, laboured, lifeless, long-winded, overdone, pedestrian, plodding, prolix, slow, stilted, stodgy, tedious, tiresome, verbose, inf windy.
Opp LIVELY.

pool n lagoon, lake, mere, oasis, paddling-pool, pond, puddle, swimming-pool, tarn.
• vb ▷ COMBINE.

poor adj 1 badly off, bankrupt, beggarly, inf broke, deprived, destitute, disadvantaged, inf down-and-out, inf hard up,

homeless, impecunious, impoverished, in debt, indigent, insolvent, necessitous, needy, inf on your uppers, penniless, penurious, poverty-stricken, sl skint, straitened, underpaid, underprivileged. 2 poor soil. barren, exhausted, infertile, sterile, unfruitful, unproductive. 3 a poor salary. inadequate, insufficient, low, meagre, mean, scanty, small, sparse, unprofitable, unrewarding. 4 poor in health. inf below par, poorly.
▷ ILL. 5 poor quality. amateurish, bad, cheap, defective, deficient, disappointing, faulty, imperfect, inferior, low-grade, mediocre, paltry, second-rate, shoddy, substandard, unacceptable, unsatisfactory, useless, worthless. 6 poor child! forlorn, hapless, ill-fated, luckless, miserable, pathetic, pitiable, sad, unfortunate, unhappy, unlucky, wretched. Opp GOOD, LARGE, LUCKY, RICH. • plur n beggars, the destitute, down-and-outs, the homeless, paupers, tramps, the underprivileged, vagrants, wretches.

populace n commonalty, derog Gk hoi polloi, masses, people, public, derog rabble, derog riff-raff.

popular adj 1 accepted, acclaimed, inf all the rage, approved, celebrated, famous, fashionable, favoured, favourite, inf in, in demand, liked, lionized, loved, renowned, sought-after, inf trendy, well-known, well-liked, well-received. Opp UNPOPULAR. 2 popular opinion. average, common, conventional, current, democratic, general, of the people, ordinary, predominant, prevailing, representative, standard, universal.

popularize vb **1** make popular, promote, spread. **2** *popularize classics*. make easy, simplify, *derog* tart up.

populate vb colonize, dwell in, fill, inhabit, live in, occupy, overrun, people, reside in, settle.

population n citizenry, citizens, community, denizens, folk, inhabitants, natives, occupants, people, populace, public, residents.

populous adj crowded, full, heavily populated, jammed, overcrowded, overpopulated, packed, swarming, teeming.

porch n doorway, entrance, lobby, portico.

pore vb **pore over** examine, go over, peruse, read, scrutinize, study.

pornographic adj arousing, *inf* blue, erotic, explicit, exploitative, sexual, sexy, titillating. ▷ OBSCENE.

porous adj absorbent, cellular, holey, penetrable, permeable, pervious, spongy. *Opp* IMPERVIOUS.

port n anchorage, dock, dockyard, harbour, haven, marina, mooring, sea-port.

portable adj compact, convenient, easy to carry, handy, light, lightweight, manageable, mobile, movable, pocket, pocket-sized, small, transportable. *Opp* UNWIELDY.

porter n **1** caretaker, concierge, door-keeper, doorman, gatekeeper, janitor, security-guard, watchman. **2** baggage-handler, bearer, carrier.

portion n allocation, allowance, bit, chunk, division, fraction, fragment, helping, hunk, measure, part, percentage, piece, quantity, quota, ration, scrap, section, segment, serving, share, slice, sliver, subdivision, wedge. **portion out** ▷ SHARE.

portrait n depiction, image, likeness, picture, portrayal, profile, representation, self-portrait. ▷ PICTURE.

portray vb **1** delineate, depict, describe, evoke, illustrate, paint, picture, represent, show. **2** ▷ IMPERSONATE.

pose n **1** attitude, position, posture, stance. **2** act, affectation, attitudinizing, façade, masquerade, pretence.
● vb **1** keep still, model, sit, strike a pose. **2** attitudinize, *inf* be a poser, be a poseur, posture, *inf* put on airs, show off. **3** *pose a question*. advance, ask, broach, posit, postulate, present, put forward, submit, suggest. **pose as** ▷ IMPERSONATE.

poser n **1** dilemma, enigma, problem, puzzle, question, riddle. **2** ▷ POSEUR.

poseur n attitudinizer, exhibitionist, fraud, impostor, masquerader, *inf* phoney, *inf* poser, pretender, *inf* show-off.

posh adj *inf* classy, elegant, fashionable, formal, grand, lavish, luxurious, ostentatious, rich, showy, smart, snobbish, stylish, sumptuous, *inf* swanky, *inf* swish.

position n **1** locality, location, locus, place, placement, point, reference, site, situation, spot, whereabouts. **2** *an awkward*

position. circumstances, condition, predicament, situation, state. **3** *position of the body.* angle, pose, posture, stance. **4** *intellectual position.* assertion, attitude, contention, hypothesis, opinion, outlook, perspective, principle, proposition, standpoint, thesis, view, viewpoint. **5** *position in a firm.* appointment, degree, employment, function, grade, job, level, niche, occupation, place, post, rank, role, standing, station, status, title.
● *vb* arrange, deploy, dispose, fix, locate, place, put, settle, site, situate, stand, station.

positive *adj* **1** affirmative, assured, categorical, certain, clear, conclusive, confident, convinced, decided, definite, emphatic, explicit, firm, incontestable, incontrovertible, irrefutable, real, sure, undeniable, unequivocal. **2** *positive advice.* beneficial, constructive, helpful, optimistic, practical, useful, worthwhile. *Opp* NEGATIVE.

possess *vb* **1** be in possession of, enjoy, have, hold, own. **2** be gifted with, embody, embrace, include. **3** *possess territory.* acquire, control, dominate, govern, invade, occupy, rule, seize, take over. **4** *possess a person.* bewitch, captivate, cast a spell over, charm, enthral, haunt, hypnotize, obsess.

possessions *plur n* assets, belongings, chattels, effects, estate, fortune, goods, property, riches, things, wealth, worldly goods.

possessive *adj* clinging, dominating, domineering, jealous, overbearing, proprietorial, protective, selfish. ▷ GREEDY.

possibility *n* capability, chance, danger, feasibility, likelihood, odds, opportunity, plausibility, potential, potentiality, practicality, probability, risk.

possible *adj* achievable, admissible, attainable, conceivable, credible, *inf* doable, feasible, imaginable, likely, obtainable, *inf* on, plausible, potential, practicable, practical, probable, prospective, realizable, reasonable, tenable, thinkable, viable, workable. *Opp* IMPOSSIBLE.

possibly *adv* God willing, *inf* hopefully, if possible, maybe, *old use* peradventure, *old use* perchance, perhaps.

post *n* **1** baluster, bollard, brace, capstan, column, gate-post, leg, newel, pale, paling, picket, pier, pile, pillar, pole, prop, pylon, shaft, stake, stanchion, standard, starting-post, strut, support, upright, winning-post. **2** *a sentry's post.* location, place, point, position, station. **3** *post in a firm.* appointment, assignment, employment, function, job, occupation, office, place, position, situation, task, work. **4** airmail, cards, delivery, junk mail, letters, mail, packets, parcels, postcards.
● *vb* **1** advertise, announce, display, pin up, proclaim, promulgate, publicize, publish, put up, stick up. **2** *post a letter.* dispatch, mail, send, transmit. **3** *post a sentry.* appoint, assign, locate, place, position, set, situate, station.

poster *n* advertisement, announcement, bill, broadsheet, circular, display, flyer, notice, placard, sign.

posterity n descendants, future generations, heirs, issue, offspring, progeny, successors.

postpone vb adjourn, defer, delay, extend, hold over, keep in abeyance, lay aside, put back, put off, *inf* put on ice, *inf* put on the back burner, *inf* shelve, stay, suspend, temporize.

postscript n addendum, addition, afterthought, codicil (*to will*), epilogue, *inf* PS.

postulate vb assume, hypothesize, posit, propose, suppose, theorize.

posture n 1 appearance, bearing, carriage, deportment, pose, position, stance. 2 ▷ ATTITUDE.

posy n bouquet, bunch of flowers, buttonhole, corsage, nosegay, spray.

pot n basin, bowl, casserole, cauldron, container, crock, crucible, dish, jar, pan, saucepan, stewpot, teapot, urn, vessel.

potent adj 1 effective, forceful, formidable, influential, intoxicating (*drink*), mighty, overpowering, overwhelming, powerful, puissant, strong, vigorous. ▷ STRONG. 2 *a potent argument*. ▷ PERSUASIVE. *Opp* WEAK.

potential adj 1 aspiring, budding, embryonic, future, *inf* hopeful, intending, latent, likely, possible, probable, promising, prospective, *inf* would-be. 2 *potential disaster*. imminent, impending, looming, threatening. • n aptitude, capability, capacity, possibility, resources.

potion n brew, concoction, decoction, dose, draught, drink, drug, elixir, liquid, medicine, mixture, philtre, potation, tonic.

potter vb dabble, do odd jobs, fiddle about, loiter, mess about, tinker, work.

pottery n ceramics, china, crockery, crocks, earthenware, porcelain, stoneware, terracotta.

pouch n bag, pocket, purse, reticule, sack, wallet.

poultry n □ bantam, chicken, duck, fowl, goose, guinea-fowl, hen, pullet, turkey.

pounce vb ambush, attack, drop on, jump on, leap on, seize, snatch, spring at, strike, swoop down on, take by surprise.

pound n compound, corral, enclosure, pen. • vb batter, beat, crush, grind, hammer, knead, mash, powder, pulp, pulverize, smash. ▷ HIT.

pour vb 1 cascade, course, discharge, disgorge, flood, flow, gush, run, spew, spill, spout, spurt, stream. 2 *pour wine*. decant, empty, serve, tip.

poverty n 1 beggary, bankruptcy, debt, destitution, hardship, impecuniousness, indigence, insolvency, necessity, need, penury, privation, want. 2 *a poverty of talent*. absence, dearth, insufficiency, lack, paucity, scarcity, shortage. *Opp* WEALTH.

powder n dust, particles, talc. • vb 1 atomize, comminute, crush, granulate, grind, pound, pulverize, reduce to powder. 2 besprinkle, coat, cover with powder, dredge, dust, sprinkle.

powdered adj 1 ▷ POWDERY. 2 dehydrated, dried, freeze-dried.

powdery *adj* chalky, crumbly,
crushed, disintegrating, dry,
dusty, fine, friable, granular,
granulated, ground, loose,
powdered, pulverized, sandy.
Opp SOLID. WET.

power *n* **1** ability, capability,
capacity, competence, drive,
energy, faculty, force, might,
muscle, potential, skill, talent,
vigour. **2** *power to arrest.*
authority, privilege, right.
3 *power of a tyrant.* ascendancy,
inf clout, command, control,
dominance, domination, dominion, influence, mastery,
omnipotence, oppression,
potency, rule, sovereignty,
supremacy, sway. ▷ STRENGTH.
Opp WEAKNESS.

powerful *adj* authoritative,
cogent, commanding, compelling, consuming, convincing,
dominant, dynamic, effective,
effectual, energetic, forceful,
high-powered, influential,
invincible, irresistible, mighty,
muscular, omnipotent, overpowering, overwhelming,
persuasive, potent, sovereign,
vigorous, weighty. ▷ STRONG.
Opp POWERLESS.

powerless *adj* defenceless,
disabled, feeble, helpless, impotent, incapable, incapacitated,
ineffective, ineffectual, paralysed, unable, unfit. ▷ WEAK.
Opp POWERFUL.

practicable *adj* achievable,
attainable, *inf* doable, feasible,
performable, possible, practical,
realistic, sensible, viable, workable. *Opp* IMPRACTICABLE.

practical *adj* **1** applied, empirical, experimental. **2** businesslike, capable, competent,
down-to-earth, efficient, expert,
hard-headed, matter-of-fact,

inf no-nonsense, pragmatic,
proficient, realistic, sensible,
skilled. **3** *a practical tool.*
convenient, functional, handy,
usable, useful, utilitarian.
4 ▷ PRACTICABLE. *Opp* IMPRAC-
TICAL, THEORETICAL. **practical
joke** ▷ TRICK.

practically *adv* almost, close to,
just about, nearly, to all intents
and purposes, virtually.

practice *n* **1** action, actuality,
application, doing, effect, operation, reality, use. **2** *inf* dummy-
run, exercise, practising, preparation, rehearsal, *inf* run-
through, training, *inf* try-out,
inf work-out. **3** *common practice.* convention, custom, habit,
modus operandi, routine, tradition, way, wont. **4** *a doctor's
practice.* business, office, work.

practise *vb* **1** do exercises, drill,
exercise, prepare, rehearse,
train, warm up, *inf* work out.
2 *practise what you preach.*
apply, carry out, do, engage in,
follow, make a practice of,
perform, put into practice.

praise *n* **1** acclaim, acclamation,
accolade, admiration, adula-
tion, applause, approbation,
approval, commendation,
compliment, congratulation,
encomium, eulogy, homage,
honour, ovation, panegyric,
plaudits, testimonial, thanks,
tribute. **2** *praise to God.* adoration, devotion, glorification,
worship. ● *vb* **1** acclaim,
admire, applaud, cheer, clap,
commend, compliment, congratulate, *inf* crack up, eulogize,
extol, give a good review of,
marvel at, offer praise to, pay
tribute to, *inf* rave about,
recommend, *inf* say nice things
about, show approval of.

Opp CRITICIZE. 2 *praise God.*
adore, exalt, glorify, honour,
laud, magnify, worship.
Opp CURSE.

praiseworthy *adj* admirable,
commendable, creditable,
deserving, laudable, meritorious, worthy. ▷ GOOD. Opp BAD.

pram *n* baby-carriage, *old
use* perambulator, push-chair.

prance *vb* bound, caper, cavort,
dance, frisk, frolic, gambol,
hop, jig about, jump, leap, play,
romp, skip, spring.

prattle *vb* babble, blather, chatter, gabble, maunder, *inf* rattle
on, *inf* witter on.

pray *vb* beseech, call upon,
invoke, say prayers, supplicate.
▷ ASK.

prayer *n* collect, devotion,
entreaty, invocation, litany,
meditation, petition, praise,
supplication.

prayer-book *n* breviary, missal.

preach *vb* 1 deliver a sermon,
evangelize, expound, proalsey-
tize, spread the Gospel.
2 expatiate, give moral advice,
harangue, *inf* lay down the law,
lecture, moralize, pontificate,
sermonize.

preacher *n* cleric, crusader,
divine, ecclesiastic, evangelist,
minister, missionary, moralist,
pastor, revivalist. ▷ CLERGY-
MAN.

prearranged *adj* arranged
beforehand, fixed, planned,
predetermined, prepared,
rehearsed, thought out.
Opp SPONTANEOUS.

precarious *adj* dangerous,
inf dicey, *inf* dodgy, dubious,
hazardous, insecure, perilous,
risky, rocky, shaky, slippery,
treacherous, uncertain, unreli-

able, unsafe, unstable, unsteady,
vulnerable, wobbly. Opp SAFE.

precaution *n* anticipation,
defence, insurance, preventive
measure, protection, provision,
safeguard, safety measure.

precede *vb* be in front of, come
before, go ahead, go before, go
in front, herald, introduce,
lead, lead into, pave the way
for, preface, prefix, start, usher
in. Opp FOLLOW.

precious *adj* 1 costly, expensive,
invaluable, irreplaceable, priceless, valuable. Opp WORTHLESS.
2 adored, beloved, darling,
dear, loved, prized, treasured,
valued, venerated.

precipice *n* bluff, cliff, crag,
drop, escarpment, precipitous
face, rock.

precipitate *adj* breakneck,
hasty, headlong, meteoric,
premature. ▷ QUICK.
● *vb* accelerate, advance, bring
on, cause, encourage, expedite,
further, hasten, hurry, incite,
induce, instigate, occasion,
provoke, spark off, trigger off.

precipitation *n* ▷ dew, downpour, drizzle, hail, rain, rainfall, shower, sleet, snow, snow-
fall.

precipitous *adj* abrupt, perpendicular, sharp, sheer, steep,
vertical.

precise *adj* 1 accurate, clear-cut,
correct, defined, definite,
distinct, exact, explicit, fixed,
measured, right, specific, unambiguous, unequivocal, well-
defined. Opp IMPRECISE.
2 *precise work.* careful, critical,
exacting, fastidious, faultless,
finicky, flawless, meticulous,
nice, perfect, punctilious, rigorous, scrupulous. Opp CARELESS.

preclude vb avert, avoid, bar, debar, exclude, forestall, frustrate, impede, make impossible, obviate, pre-empt, prevent, prohibit, rule out, thwart.

precocious adj advanced, forward, gifted, mature, quick. ▷ CLEVER. *Opp* BACKWARD.

preconception n assumption, bias, expectation, preconceived idea, predisposition, prejudgement, prejudice, presupposition.

predatory adj acquisitive, avaricious, covetous, extortionate, greedy, hunting, marauding, pillaging, plundering, preying, rapacious, ravenous, voracious.

predecessor n ancestor, antecedent, forebear, forefather, forerunner, precursor.

predetermined adj 1 fated, destined, doomed, ordained, predestined. 2 agreed, prearranged, preplanned, recognized, *inf* set up.

predicament n crisis, difficulty, dilemma, embarrassment, emergency, *inf* fix, impasse, *inf* jam, *inf* mess, *inf* pickle, plight, problem, quandary, situation, state.

predict vb augur, forebode, forecast, foresee, foreshadow, foretell, foretoken, forewarn, hint, intimate, presage, prognosticate, prophesy, tell fortunes.

predictable adj anticipated, certain, expected, foreseeable, foreseen, likely, *inf* on the cards, probable, sure, unsurprising. *Opp* UNPREDICTABLE.

predominant adj ascendant, chief, dominating, leading, main, preponderant, prevailing, prevalent, primary, ruling, sovereign.

predominate vb be in the majority, control, dominate, *inf* have the upper hand, hold sway, lead, outnumber, outweigh, preponderate, prevail, reign, rule.

pre-eminent adj distinguished, eminent, excellent, incomparable, matchless, outstanding, peerless, supreme, unrivalled, unsurpassed.

pre-empt vb anticipate, appropriate, arrogate, expropriate, forestall, seize, take over.

preface n exordium, foreword, introduction, *inf* lead-in, overture, preamble, prelude, proem, prolegomenon, prologue.
 ● vb begin, introduce, lead into, open, precede, prefix, start.

prefer vb advocate, *inf* back, be partial to, choose, fancy, favour, *inf* go for, incline towards, like, like better, opt for, pick out, *inf* plump for, *inf* put your money on, recommend, select, single out, think preferable, vote for, want.

preferable adj advantageous, better, better-liked, chosen, desirable, favoured, likely, nicer, preferred, recommended, wanted. *Opp* OBJECTIONABLE.

preference n 1 choice, fancy, favourite, liking, option, pick, selection, wish. 2 favouritism, inclination, partiality, predilection, prejudice, proclivity.

preferential adj advantageous, better, biased, favourable, favoured, privileged, showing favouritism, special, superior.

pregnant adj 1 carrying a child, expectant, *inf* expecting, gestating, gravid, parturient, *old use* with child. 2 *pregnant remark.* ▷ MEANINGFUL.

prejudice n bias, bigotry, chauvinism, discrimination, dogmatism, fanaticism, favouritism, intolerance, jingoism, leaning, narrow-mindedness, partiality, partisanship, predilection, predisposition, prejudgement, racialism, racism, sexism, unfairness, xenophobia. Opp TOLERANCE.
• vb 1 bias, colour, incline, influence, interfere with, make prejudiced, predispose, sway. 2 *prejudice your chances.* damage, harm, injure, ruin, spoil, undermine.

prejudiced adj biased, bigoted, chauvinist, discriminatory, illiberal, intolerant, jaundiced, jingoistic, leading (*question*), loaded, narrow-minded, one-sided, parochial, partial, partisan, racist, sexist, tendentious, unfair, xenophobic. Opp IMPARTIAL. **prejudiced person** bigot, chauvinist, fanatic, racist, sexist, zealot.

prejudicial adj damaging, deleterious, detrimental, disadvantageous, harmful, inimical, injurious, unfavourable.

preliminary adj advance, earliest, early, experimental, exploratory, first, inaugural, initial, introductory, opening, prefatory, preparatory, qualifying, tentative, trial.
• n ▷ PRELUDE.

prelude n beginning, inf curtain-raiser, exordium, introduction, opener, opening, overture, preamble, precursor, preface, preliminary, preparation, proem, prolegomenon, prologue, start, starter, inf warm-up. Opp CONCLUSION, POSTSCRIPT.

premature adj abortive, before time, early, hasty, ill-timed, precipitate, inf previous, too early, too soon, undeveloped, untimely. Opp LATE.

premeditated adj calculated, conscious, considered, contrived, deliberate, intended, intentional, planned, pre-arranged, preconceived, predetermined, preplanned, studied, wilful. Opp SPONTANEOUS.

premiss n assertion, assumption, basis, grounds, hypothesis, proposition, supposition, thesis.

premonition n anxiety, fear, foreboding, forewarning, inf funny feeling, inf hunch, indication, intuition, misgiving, omen, portent, presentiment, suspicion, warning, worry.

preoccupied adj 1 absorbed, engaged, engrossed, immersed, interested, involved, obsessed, sunk, taken up, wrapped up. 2 absent-minded, abstracted, day-dreaming, distracted, far-away, inattentive, lost in thought, musing, pensive, pondering, rapt, reflecting, thoughtful.

preparation n arrangements, briefing, inf gearing up, getting ready, groundwork, making provision, measures, organization, plans, practice, preparing, setting up, spadework, training.

prepare vb 1 arrange, cook, devise, inf do what's necessary, inf fix up, get ready, make arrangements, make ready, organize, pave the way, plan, process, set up. ▷ MAKE. 2 *prepare for exams.* inf cram, practise, revise, study, inf swot. 3 *prepare pupils for exams.*

brief, coach, educate, equip, instruct, rehearse, teach, train, tutor. **prepared** ▷ PRE-ARRANGED, READY. **prepare yourself** be prepared, be ready, brace yourself, discipline yourself, fortify yourself, steel yourself.

preposterous *adj* bizarre, excessive, extreme, grotesque, monstrous, outrageous, surreal, unreasonable, unthinkable. ▷ ABSURD.

prerequisite *adj* compulsory, essential, indispensable, mandatory, necessary, obligatory, prescribed, required, requisite, specified, stipulated. *Opp* OPTIONAL. • *n* condition, essential, necessity, precondition, proviso, qualification, requirement, requisite, *Lat* sine qua non, stipulation.

prescribe *vb* advise, assign, command, demand, dictate, direct, fix, impose, instruct, lay down, ordain, order, recommend, require, specify stipulate, suggest.

presence *n* 1 attendance, closeness, companionship, company, nearness, propinquity, proximity, society. 2 air, appearance, aura, bearing, comportment, demeanour, impressiveness, mien, personality, poise, self-assurance, self-possession.

present *adj* 1 adjacent, at hand, close, here, in attendance, nearby. 2 contemporary, current, existing, extant, present-day, up-to-date.
• *n* 1 *inf* here and now, today. 2 alms, bonus, bounty, charity, contribution, donation, endowment, gift, grant, gratuity, handout, offering, tip.
• *vb* 1 award, bestow, confer,

dispense, distribute, donate, give, hand over, offer. 2 *present evidence*. adduce, bring forward, demonstrate, display, exhibit, furnish, proffer, put forward, reveal, set out, show, submit. 3 *present a guest*. announce, introduce, make known. 4 *present a play*. act, bring out, perform, put on, stage. **present yourself** ▷ ATTEND, REPORT.

presentable *adj* acceptable, adequate, all right, clean, decent, decorous, fit to be seen, good enough, neat, passable, proper, respectable, satisfactory, suitable, tidy, tolerable, *inf* up to scratch, worthy.

presently *adv* old use anon, before long, by and by, *inf* in a jiffy, shortly, soon.

preserve *n* 1 conserve, jam, jelly, marmalade, 2 *wildlife preserve*. reserve, sanctuary. • *vb* 1 care for, conserve, defend, guard, keep, lay up, look after, maintain, perpetuate, protect, retain, safeguard, save, secure, stockpile, store, support, sustain, uphold, watch over. *Opp* DESTROY. 2 *preserve food*. bottle, can, chill, cure, dehydrate, dry, freeze, freeze-dry, irradiate, jam, pickle, refrigerate, salt, tin. 3 *preserve a corpse*. embalm, mummify.

preside *vb* be in charge, chair, officiate, take charge, take the chair. **preside over** ▷ GOVERN.

press *n* newspapers, magazines, the media. • *vb* 1 apply pressure to, compress, condense, cram, crowd, crush, depress, force, gather, *inf* jam, push, shove, squash, squeeze, subject to pressure. 2 *press laundry*. flatten, iron, smooth. 3 *press* *someone to stay.* ask, beg, bully, coerce, constrain, dragoon, entreat, exhort, implore, importune, induce, *inf* lean on, persuade, pressure, pressurize, put pressure on, request, require, urge. **pressing** ▷ URGENT.

pressure n 1 burden, compression, force, heaviness, load, might, power, stress, weight. 2 *pressure of modern life.* adversity, affliction, constraints, demands, difficulties, exigencies, *inf* hassle, hurry, oppression, problems, strain, stress, urgency. ● vb ask, beg, bully, coerce, constrain, dragoon, entreat, exhort, implore, importune, induce, *inf* lean on, persuade, press, pressurize, put pressure on, request, require, urge.

prestige n cachet, celebrity, credit, distinction, eminence, esteem, fame, glory, good name, honour, importance, influence, *inf* kudos, regard, renown, reputation, respect, standing, stature, status.

prestigious adj acclaimed, august, celebrated, creditable, distinguished, eminent, esteemed, estimable, famed, famous, highly-regarded, high-ranking, honourable, honoured, important, influential, pre-eminent, renowned, reputable, respected, significant, well-known. *Opp* INSIGNIFICANT.

presume vb 1 assume, believe, conjecture, gather, guess, hypothesize, imagine, infer, postulate, suppose, surmise, suspect, *inf* take for granted, *inf* take it, think. 2 *He presumed to correct me.* be presumptuous enough, dare, have the effront-

ery, make bold, take the liberty, venture.

presumptuous adj arrogant, bold, brazen, *inf* cheeky, conceited, forward, impertinent, impudent, insolent, overconfident, *inf* pushy, shameless, unauthorized, unwarranted. ▷ PROUD.

pretence n act, acting, affectation, appearance, artifice, camouflage, charade, counterfeiting, deception, disguise, display, dissembling, dissimulation, excuse, façade, falsification, feigning, feint, fiction, front, guise, hoax, *inf* humbug, hypocrisy, insincerity, invention, lying, make-believe, masquerade, pose, posing, posturing, pretext, ruse, sham, show, simulation, subterfuge, trickery, wile. ▷ DECEIT.

pretend vb 1 act, affect, allege, behave insincerely, bluff, counterfeit, deceive, disguise, dissemble, dissimulate, fake, feign, fool, hoax, hoodwink, imitate, impersonate, *inf* kid, lie, *inf* make out, mislead, playact, play a part, perform, pose, posture, profess, purport, put on an act, sham, simulate, take someone in, trick. 2 ▷ IMAGINE. 3 ▷ CLAIM.

pretender n aspirant, claimant, rival, suitor.

pretentious adj affected, *inf* arty, conceited, exaggerated, extravagant, grandiose, *inf* highfalutin, immodest, inflated, ostentatious, overblown, *inf* over the top, pompous, showy, *inf* snobbish, superficial. *Opp* UNPRETENTIOUS.

pretext n cloak, cover, disguise, excuse, pretence.

pretty adj appealing, attractive, inf bonny, charming, inf cute, dainty, delicate, inf easy on the eye, fetching, good-looking, lovely, nice, pleasing, derog pretty-pretty, winsome. ▷ BEAUTIFUL. Opp UGLY. ● adv fairly, moderately, quite, rather, reasonably, somewhat, tolerably. Opp VERY.

prevail vb be prevalent, hold sway, predominate, preponderate, succeed, triumph, inf win the day. ▷ WIN. **prevailing** ▷ PREVALENT.

prevalent adj accepted, ascendant, chief, common, commonest, current, customary, dominant, dominating, effectual, established, extensive, familiar, fashionable, general, governing, influential, main, mainstream, normal, ordinary, orthodox, pervasive, popular, powerful, predominant, prevailing, principal, ruling, ubiquitous, universal, usual, widespread. Opp UNUSUAL.

prevaricate vb inf beat about the bush, be evasive, cavil, deceive, equivocate, inf fib, hedge, lie, mislead, quibble, temporize.

prevent vb anticipate, avert, avoid, baffle, bar, block, check, control, curb, deter, fend off, foil, forestall, frustrate, hamper, inf head off, inf help (can't help it), hinder, impede, inhibit, inoculate against, intercept, inf nip in the bud, obstruct, obviate, preclude, pre-empt, prohibit, inf put a stop to, restrain, save, stave off, stop, take precautions against, thwart, ward off. ▷ FORBID. Opp ENCOURAGE.

preventive adj anticipatory, counteractive, deterrent, obstructive, precautionary, pre-emptive, preventative.

previous adj 1 above-mentioned, aforementioned, aforesaid, antecedent, earlier, erstwhile, foregoing, former, past, preceding, prior. Opp SUBSEQUENT. 2 ▷ PREMATURE.

prey n kill, quarry, victim. ● vb **prey on** eat, feed on, hunt, kill, live off. ▷ EXPLOIT.

price n 1 amount, charge, cost, inf damage, expenditure, expense, fare, fee, figure, outlay, payment, rate, sum, terms, toll, value, worth. 2 Give me a price. estimate, offer, quotation, valuation. ▷ PAYMENT. **pay the price for** ▷ ATONE.

priceless adj 1 costly, dear, expensive, incalculable, inestimable, invaluable, irreplaceable, precious, inf pricey, rare, valuable. Opp WORTHLESS. 2 ▷ FUNNY.

prick vb 1 bore into, jab, lance, perforate, pierce, punch, puncture, riddle, stab, sting. 2 ▷ STIMULATE.

prickle n 1 barb, bristle, bur, needle, spike, spine, thorn. 2 irritation, itch, pricking, prickling, tingle, tingling. ● vb irritate, itch, make your skin crawl, scratch, sting, tingle.

prickly adj 1 barbed, bristly, rough, scratchy, sharp, spiky, spiny, stubbly, thorny, unshaven. Opp SMOOTH. 2 ▷ IRRITABLE.

pride n 1 Fr amour propre, gratification, happiness, honour, pleasure, satisfaction, self-

respect, self-satisfaction.
▷ DIGNITY. **2** *her pride and joy.*
jewel, treasure, treasured
possession. **3** *pride before a fall.*
arrogance, being proud, *inf* big-
headedness, boastfulness,
conceit, egotism, haughtiness,
hubris, megalomania, narcissism, overconfidence, presumption, self-admiration, self-
esteem, self-importance,
self-love, smugness, snobbery,
snobbishness, vainglory,
vanity. *Opp* HUMILITY.

priest *n* confessor, Druid, lama,
minister, preacher.
▷ CLERGYMAN.

priggish *adj* conservative, fussy,
inf goody-goody, haughty,
moralistic, prudish, self-righteous, sententious, stiff-necked,
inf stuffy. ▷ PRIM.

prim *adj* demure, fastidious,
formal, inhibited, narrow-
minded, precise, *inf* prissy,
proper, prudish, *inf* starchy,
strait-laced. *Opp* BROAD-
MINDED.

primal *adj* **1** early, earliest, first,
original, primeval, primitive,
primordial. **2** ▷ PRIMARY.

primarily *adv* basically, chiefly,
especially, firstly,
fundamentally, generally,
mainly, mostly, particularly,
predominantly, pre-eminently,
principally.

primary *adj* basic, cardinal,
chief, dominant, first, foremost,
fundamental, greatest, important, initial, leading, main,
major, outstanding, paramount,
predominant, pre-eminent,
primal, prime, principal,
supreme, top.

prime *adj* **1** best, first-class, first-
rate, foremost, select, superior,

top, top-quality. ▷ EXCELLENT.
2 ▷ PRIMARY. ● *vb* get ready,
prepare.

primitive *adj* **1** aboriginal,
ancient, barbarian, early, first,
prehistoric, primeval, savage,
uncivilized. **2** *primitive technology.* antediluvian, backward, basic,
inf behind the times, crude,
elementary, obsolete, rough,
rudimentary, simple, simplistic, undeveloped. ▷ OLD.
3 *primitive art.* childlike, crude,
naïve, unpolished, unrefined,
unsophisticated. *Opp* AD-
VANCED, SOPHISTICATED.

principal *adj* basic, cardinal,
chief, dominant, dominating,
first, foremost, fundamental,
greatest, highest, important,
key, leading, main, major,
outstanding, paramount, pre-
eminent, predominant, prevailing, primary, prime, starring,
supreme, top. ● *n* **1** ▷ CHIEF.
2 *the principal in a play.* diva,
hero, heroine, lead, leading
role, prima ballerina, protagonist, star.

principle *n* **1** assumption,
axiom, belief, creed, criterion,
doctrine, dogma, ethic, idea,
ideal, maxim, notion, precept,
proposition, rule, standard,
teaching, tenet, truism, truth,
values. **2** *a person of principle.*
conscience, high-mindedness,
honesty, honour, ideals, integrity, morality, probity, scruples, standards, uprightness,
virtue. **principles** basics,
elements, essentials, fundamentals, laws, philosophy, theory.

print *n* **1** impression, imprint,
indentation, mark, stamp.
2 characters, fount, lettering,
letters, printing, text, type,

typeface. **3** copy, duplicate, engraving, etching, facsimile, linocut, lithograph, monoprint, photograph, reproduction, silk screen, woodcut. ▷ PICTURE.
● *vb* **1** copy, impress, imprint, issue, publish, run off, stamp. **2** ▷ WRITE.

prior *adj* earlier, erstwhile, former, late, old, onetime, previous.

priority *n* first place, greater importance, precedence, preference, prerogative, right-of-way, seniority, superiority, urgency.

prise *vb* force, lever, prize, wrench.

prison *n old use* approved school, *old use* Borstal, cell, *sl* clink, custody, detention centre, dungeon, gaol, guardhouse, house of correction, jail, *inf* lock-up, *Amer* penitentiary, oubliette, reformatory, *sl* stir, youth custody centre.
▷ CAPTIVITY.

prisoner *n* captive, convict, detainee, *inf* gaolbird, hostage, inmate, internee, lifer, *inf* old lag, *inf* trusty.

privacy *n* concealment, isolation, monasticism, quietness, retirement, retreat, seclusion, secrecy, solitude.

private *adj* **1** exclusive, individual, particular, personal, privately owned, reserved. **2** classified, confidential, *inf* hush-hush, *inf* off the record, restricted, secret, top secret, undisclosed. **3** *a private meeting*. clandestine, closed, covert, intimate, surreptitious. **4** *a private hideaway*. concealed, hidden, inaccessible, isolated, little-known, quiet, secluded, sequestered, solitary,

unknown, withdrawn.
Opp PUBLIC.

privilege *n* advantage, benefit, concession, entitlement, exemption, freedom, immunity, licence, prerogative, right.

privileged *adj* **1** advantaged, authorized, élite, entitled, favoured, honoured, immune, licensed, powerful, protected, sanctioned, special, superior. **2** ▷ WEALTHY.

prize *n* accolade, award, jackpot, *inf* purse, reward, trophy, winnings. ● *vb* **1** appreciate, approve of, cherish, esteem, hold dear, like, rate highly, regard, revere, treasure, value. **2** ▷ PRISE.

probable *adj* believable, convincing, credible, expected, feasible, likely, *inf* odds-on, plausible, possible, predictable, presumed, undoubted, unquestioned. *Opp* IMPROBABLE.

probationer *n* apprentice, beginner, inexperienced worker, learner, novice, tiro.

probe *n* enquiry, examination, exploration, inquiry, investigation, research, scrutiny, study.
● *vb* **1** delve, dig, penetrate, plumb, poke, prod. **2** *probe a problem*. examine, explore, go into, inquire into, investigate, look into, research into, scrutinize, study.

problem *n* **1** brain-teaser, conundrum, enigma, mystery, *inf* poser, puzzle, question, riddle. **2** *a worrying problem*. burden, *inf* can of worms, complication, difficulty, dilemma, dispute, *inf* facer, *inf* headache, *inf* hornet's nest, predicament, quandary, setback, snag, trouble, worry.

problematic adj complicated, controversial, debatable, difficult, disputed, doubtful, enigmatic, hard to deal with, inf iffy, intractable, moot (point), problematical, puzzling, questionable, sensitive, taxing, inf tricky, uncertain, unsettling, worrying.
Opp STRAIGHTFORWARD.

procedure n approach, conduct, course of action, inf drill, formula, method, methodology, Lat modus operandi, plan of action, policy, practice, process, routine, scheme, strategy, system, technique, way.

proceed vb 1 advance, carry on, continue, follow, forge ahead, inf get going, go ahead, go on, make headway, make progress, move along, move forward, inf press on, progress. 2 arise, be derived, begin, develop, emerge, grow, originate, spring up, start. ▷ RESULT.

proceedings plur n 1 events, inf goings-on, happenings, things. 2 legal proceedings. action, lawsuit, procedure, process. 3 proceedings of a meeting. annals, business, dealings, inf doings, matters, minutes, records, report, transactions.

proceeds plur n earnings, gain, gate, income, profit, receipts, returns, revenue, takings.
▷ MONEY.

process n 1 function, method, operation, procedure, proceeding, system, technique. 2 process of ageing. course, development, evolution, experience, progression. ● vb 1 alter, change, convert, deal with, make usable, manage, modify, organize, prepare, refine, transform, treat. 2 ▷ PARADE.

procession n cavalcade, chain, column, cortège, file, line, march, march-past, motorcade, pageant, parade, sequence, string, succession, train.

proclaim vb 1 announce, advertise, assert, declare, give out, make known, profess, promulgate, pronounce, publish. 2 ▷ DECREE.

procrastinate vb be dilatory, be indecisive, dally, defer a decision, delay, inf dilly-dally, dither, inf drag your feet, equivocate, evade the issue, hesitate, inf hum and haw, pause, inf play for time, postpone, put things off, inf shilly-shally, stall, temporize, vacillate, waver.

procure vb acquire, buy, come by, find, get, inf get hold of, inf lay your hands on, obtain, inf pick up, purchase, requisition.

prod vb dig, elbow, goad, jab, nudge, poke, push, urge on.
▷ HIT, URGE.

prodigal adj excessive, extravagant, immoderate, improvident, irresponsible, lavish, profligate, reckless, self-indulgent, wasteful.
Opp THRIFTY.

prodigy n curiosity, freak, genius, marvel, miracle, phenomenon, rarity, sensation, talent, virtuoso, inf whizz kid, wonder, Ger Wunderkind.

produce n crop, harvest, output, yield. ▷ PRODUCT. ● vb 1 assemble, bring out, cause, compose, conjure up, construct, create, cultivate, develop, fabricate, form, generate, give rise to, grow, initiate, invent, make, manufacture, originate, provoke, result in, supply, think up, turn out, yield. **2** *produce evidence.* advance, bring out, disclose, display, exhibit, furnish, introduce, offer, present, provide, put forward, reveal, show, supply, throw up. **3** *produce children.* bear, beget, breed, give birth to, raise, rear. **4** *produce a play.* direct, mount, present, put on, stage.

product *n* **1** artefact, by-product, commodity, end-product, goods, merchandise, output, produce, production. **2** consequence, effect, fruit, issue, outcome, result, upshot, yield.

productive *adj* **1** beneficial, busy, constructive, creative, effective, efficient, gainful (*employment*), inventive, profitable, profitmaking, remunerative, rewarding, useful, valuable, worthwhile. **2** *a productive garden.* abundant, bounteous, bountiful, fecund, fertile, fruitful, lush, prolific, vigorous. *Opp* UNPRODUCTIVE.

profess *vb* **1** affirm, announce, assert, asseverate, aver, confess, confirm, declare, maintain, state, vow. **2** *profess to be an expert.* allege, claim, make out, pretend, purport.

profession *n* **1** business, calling, career, craft, employment, job, line of work, métier, occupation, trade, vocation, work. **2** *profession of love.* acknowledgement, affirmation, announcement, assertion, avowal, confession, declaration, statement, testimony.

professional *adj* **1** able, authorized, educated, experienced, expert, knowledgeable, licensed, official, proficient,

qualified, skilled, trained. *Opp* AMATEUR. **2** full-time, paid. **3** *professional work.* businesslike, competent, conscientious, efficient, masterly, proper, skilful, thorough, well-done. *Opp* UNPROFESSIONAL.

● *n* expert, professional player, professional worker.

proficient *adj* able, accomplished, adept, capable, competent, efficient, expert, gifted, professional, skilled, talented. *Opp* INCOMPETENT.

profile *n* **1** contour, outline, shape, side view, silhouette. **2** *personal profile.* account, biography, *Lat* curriculum vitae, sketch, study.

profit *n* advantage, benefit, excess, gain, interest, proceeds, return, revenue, surplus, yield. ● *vb* **1** advance, avail, benefit, further the interests of, pay, serve. ▷ HELP. **2** *profit from a sale.* capitalize (on), *inf* cash in, earn money, gain, *inf* make a killing, make a profit, make money. **profit by, profit from** ▷ EXPLOIT.

profitable *adj* advantageous, beneficial, commercial, enriching, fruitful, gainful, lucrative, money-making, paying, productive, profit-making, remunerative, rewarding, useful, valuable, well-paid, worthwhile. *Opp* UNPROFITABLE.

profiteer *n* black-marketeer, exploiter, extortionist, racketeer. ● *vb* exploit, extort, fleece, overcharge.

profligate *adj* **1** abandoned, debauched, degenerate, depraved, dissolute, immoral, libertine, licentious, loose, perverted, promiscuous, sinful,

sybaritic, unprincipled, wanton. ▷ WICKED.
2 extravagant, prodigal, reckless, spendthrift, wasteful.

profound adj 1 deep, heartfelt, intense, sincere. 2 a profound discussion. abstruse, arcane, erudite, esoteric, imponderable, informed, intellectual, knowledgeable, learned, penetrating, philosophical, recondite, sagacious, scholarly, serious, thoughtful, wise. 3 profound silence. absolute, complete, extreme, fundamental, perfect, thorough, total, unqualified. Opp SUPERFICIAL.

profuse adj abundant, ample, bountiful, copious, extravagant, exuberant, generous, lavish, luxuriant, plentiful, productive, prolific, superabundant, thriving, unsparing, unstinting. Opp MEAN, SPARSE.

programme n 1 agenda, bill of fare, calendar, curriculum, inf line-up, listing, menu, plan, routine, prospectus, schedule, scheme, syllabus, timetable. 2 a TV programme. broadcast, performance, presentation, production, show, transmission.

progress n 1 advance, breakthrough, development, evolution, forward movement, furtherance, gain, growth, headway, improvement, march (of time), maturation, progression, inf step forward.
2 journey, route, travels, way. 3 progress in a career. advancement, betterment, elevation, promotion, rise, inf step up.
● vb advance, inf come on, develop, inf forge ahead, go forward, go on, make headway, make progress, move forward,

press forward, press on, proceed, prosper. ▷ IMPROVE. Opp REGRESS, STAGNATE.

progression n 1 ▷ PROGRESS. 2 chain, concatenation, course, flow, order, row, sequence, series, string, succession.

progressive adj 1 accelerating, advancing, continuing, continuous, developing, escalating, gradual, growing, increasing, ongoing, steady. 2 progressive ideas. advanced, avant-garde, contemporary, dynamic, enterprising, forward-looking, inf go-ahead, modernistic, radical, reformist, revisionist, revolutionary, up-to-date. Opp CONSERVATIVE.

prohibit vb ban, bar, block, censor, check, inf cut out, debar, disallow, exclude, foil, forbid, hinder, impede, inhibit, interdict, make illegal, outlaw, place an embargo on, preclude, prevent, proscribe, restrict, rule out, shut out, stop, taboo, veto. Opp ALLOW.

prohibitive adj discouraging, excessive, exorbitant, impossible, inf out of reach, out of the question, unreasonable, unthinkable.

project n activity, assignment, contract, design, enterprise, idea, job, piece of research, plan, programme, proposal, scheme, task, undertaking, venture. ● vb 1 concoct, contrive, design, devise, invent, plan, propose, scheme, think up. 2 beetle, bulge, extend, jut out, overhang, protrude, stand out, stick out. 3 project into space. cast, inf chuck, fling, hurl, launch, lob, propel, shoot, throw. 4 project light. cast, flash, shine, throw out.

5 *project future profits.* estimate, forecast, predict.

proliferate *vb* burgeon, flourish, grow, increase, multiply, mushroom, reproduce, thrive.

prolific *adj* **1** abundant, bounteous, bountiful, copious, fruitful, numerous, plenteous, profuse, rich. **2** *a prolific writer.* creative, fertile, productive. *Opp* UNPRODUCTIVE.

prolong *vb* delay, *inf* drag out, draw out, elongate, extend, increase, keep up, lengthen, make longer, *inf* pad out, protract, *inf* spin out, stretch out. *Opp* SHORTEN.

prominent *adj* **1** conspicuous, discernible, distinguishable, evident, eye-catching, large, notable, noticeable, obtrusive, obvious, pronounced, recognizable, salient, significant, striking. *Opp* INCONSPICUOUS. **2** bulging, jutting out, projecting, protruding, protuberant, sticking out. **3** celebrated, distinguished, eminent, familiar, foremost, illustrious, important, leading, major, much-publicized, noted, outstanding, public, renowned. ▷ FAMOUS. *Opp* UNKNOWN.

promiscuous *adj* casual, haphazard, indiscriminate, irresponsible, non-selective, random, undiscriminating. ▷ IMMORAL. *Opp* MORAL.

promise *n* **1** assurance, commitment, compact, contract, covenant, guarantee, oath, pledge, undertaking, vow, word, word of honour. **2** *actor with promise.* capability, expectation(s), latent ability, potential, promising qualities, talent. • *vb* **1** agree, assure, commit yourself,

consent, contract, engage, give a promise, give your word, guarantee, pledge, swear, take an oath, undertake, vow. **2** *The clouds promise rain.* augur, *old use* betoken, forebode, foretell, hint at, indicate, presage, prophesy, show signs of, suggest.

promising *adj* auspicious, budding, encouraging, favourable, hopeful, likely, optimistic, propitious, talented, *inf* up-and-coming.

promontory *n* cape, foreland, headland, peninsula, point, projection, ridge, spit, spur.

promote *vb* **1** advance, elevate, exalt, give promotion, move up, prefer, raise, upgrade. **2** *promote a product.* advertise, back, boost, champion, encourage, endorse, further, help, make known, market, patronize, *inf* plug, popularize, publicize, *inf* push, recommend, sell, speak for, sponsor, support. ▷ HELP.

promoter *n* backer, champion, patron, sponsor, supporter.

promotion *n* **1** advancement, elevation, preferment, rise, upgrading. **2** *promotion of a product.* advertising, backing, encouragement, furtherance, marketing, publicity, recommendation, selling, sponsorship.

prompt *adj* eager, efficient, expeditious, immediate, instantaneous, on time, punctual, timely, unhesitating, willing. ▷ QUICK. *Opp* UNPUNCTUAL. • *n* cue, line, reminder. • *vb* advise, coax, egg on, encourage, exhort, help, incite, influence, inspire, jog the memory, motivate, nudge, persuade, prod, provoke, remind, rouse, spur, stimulate, urge.

prone *adj* **1** face down, flat, horizontal, lying, on your front, prostrate, stretched out. *Opp* SUPINE. **2** *prone to colds*. apt, disposed, given, inclined, liable, likely, predisposed, subject, susceptible, tending, vulnerable. *Opp* IMMUNE.

prong *n* point, spike, spur, tine.

pronounce *vb* **1** articulate, aspirate, enunciate, express, put into words, say, sound, speak, utter, vocalize, voice. **2** *pronounce judgement*. announce, assert, asseverate, declare, decree, judge, make known, proclaim, state.
▷ SPEAK.

pronounced *adj* clear, conspicuous, decided, definite, distinct, evident, inescapable, marked, noticeable, obvious, prominent, recognizable, striking, unambiguous, undisguised, unmistakable, well-defined.

pronunciation *n* accent, articulation, delivery, diction, elocution, enunciation, inflection, intonation, modulation, speech.

proof *n* **1** authentication, certification, confirmation, corroboration, demonstration, evidence, facts, grounds, substantiation, testimony, validation, verification. **2** *the proof of the pudding*. criterion, judgement, measure, test, trial.

prop *n* brace, buttress, crutch, post, stay, strut, support, truss, upright. ● *vb* **1** bolster, brace, buttress, hold up, reinforce, shore up, support, sustain. **2** lean, rest, stand.

propaganda *n* advertising, brain-washing, disinformation, indoctrination, persuasion, publicity.

propagate *vb* **1** breed, generate, increase, multiply, produce, proliferate, reproduce. **2** *propagate ideas*. circulate, disseminate, pass on, promote, promulgate, publish, spread, transmit. **3** *propagate plants*. grow from seed, layer, sow, take cuttings.

propel *vb* drive, force, impel, launch, move, *inf* pitchfork, push, send, set in motion, shoot, spur, thrust, urge.

propeller *n* rotor, screw, vane.

proper *adj* **1** becoming, conventional, decent, decorous, delicate, dignified, formal, genteel, gentlemanly, grave, in good taste, ladylike, modest, polite, *derog* prim, *derog* prudish, respectable, sedate, seemly, serious, solemn, tactful, tasteful. **2** acceptable, accepted, advisable, apposite, appropriate, apropos, apt, deserved, fair, fitting, just, lawful, legal, normal, orthodox, rational, sensible, suitable, unexceptionable, usual, valid. **3** *the proper time*. accurate, correct, exact, precise, right. **4** *the proper place*. allocated, distinctive, individual, own, particular, reserved, separate, special, unique. *Opp* IMPROPER.

property *n* **1** assets, belongings, capital, chattels, effects, fortune, *inf* gear, goods, holdings, patrimony, possessions, resources, riches, wealth. **2** acreage, buildings, estate, land, premises. **3** attribute, characteristic, feature, hallmark, idiosyncrasy, oddity, peculiarity, quality, quirk, trait.

prophecy n augury, crystal-gazing, divination, forecast, foretelling, fortune-telling, oracle, prediction, prognosis, prognostication, vaticination.

prophesy vb augur, bode, divine, forecast, foresee, foreshadow, foretell, portend, predict, presage, prognosticate, promise, vaticinate.

prophet n clairvoyant, forecaster, fortune-teller, oracle, seer, sibyl, soothsayer.

prophetic adj apocalyptic, far-seeing, oracular, predictive, prescient, prognostic, prophesying, sibylline.

propitious adj advantageous, auspicious, favourable, fortunate, happy, lucky, opportune, promising, providential, rosy, timely, well-timed.

proportion n 1 balance, comparison, correlation, correspondence, distribution, equivalence, ratio, statistical relationship. 2 allocation, fraction, part, percentage, piece, quota, ration, section, share. ▷ NUMBER, QUANTITY. **proportions** dimensions, extent, magnitude, measurements, size, volume.

proportional adj analogous, balanced, commensurate, comparable, corresponding, equitable, in proportion, just, proportionate, relative, symmetrical. Opp DISPROPORTIONATE.

proposal n bid, declaration, draft, motion, offer, plan, project, proposition, recommendation, scheme, statement, suggestion, tender.

propose vb 1 advance, ask for, inf come up with, present, propound, put forward, recommend, submit, suggest. 2 aim, have in mind, intend, mean, offer, plan, purpose. 3 propose a candidate. nominate, put forward, put up, sponsor.

propriety n appropriateness, aptness, correctness, courtesy, decency, decorum, delicacy, dignity, etiquette, fairness, fitness, formality, gentility, good form, good manners, gravity, justice, modesty, politeness, derog prudishness, refinement, respectability, sedateness, seemliness, sensitivity, suitability, tact, tastefulness. Opp IMPROPRIETY.

prosaic adj 1 clear, direct, down to earth, factual, matter-of-fact, plain, simple, straightforward, to the point, unadorned, understandable, unemotional, unsentimental, unvarnished. 2 [derog] characterless, clichéd, commonplace, dry, dull, flat, hackneyed, lifeless, monotonous, mundane, pedestrian, prosy, routine, stereotyped, trite, unfeeling, unimaginative, uninspired, uninspiring, unpoetic, unromantic. ▷ ORDINARY. Opp POETIC.

prosecute vb 1 accuse, arraign, bring an action against, bring to trial, charge, indict, institute legal proceedings against, prefer charges against, put on trial, sue, take legal proceedings against, take to court. 2 ▷ PURSUE.

prospect n 1 aspect, landscape, outlook, panorama, perspective, scene, seascape, sight, spectacle, view, vista. 2 prospect of fine weather. anticipation,

chance, expectation, hope, like-lihood, opportunity, possibility, probability, promise.
• vb explore, quest, search, survey.

prospective adj anticipated, approaching, awaited, coming, expected, forthcoming, future, imminent, impending, intended, likely, looked-for, negotiable, pending, possible, potential, probable.

prospectus n announcement, brochure, catalogue, leaflet, manifesto, pamphlet, programme, scheme, syllabus.

prosper vb become prosperous, be successful, inf boom, burgeon, develop, do well, fare well, flourish, inf get ahead, inf get on, inf go from strength to strength, grow, inf make good, inf make your fortune, profit, progress, strengthen, succeed, thrive. Opp FAIL.

prosperity n affluence, inf bonanza, inf boom, good fortune, growth, opulence, plenty, profitability, riches, success, wealth.

prosperous adj affluent, inf blooming, inf booming, buoyant, expanding, flourishing, fruitful, healthy, moneyed, money-making, productive, profitable, prospering, rich, successful, thriving, vigorous, wealthy, inf well-heeled, well-off, well-to-do. Opp UNSUCCESSFUL.

prostitute n old use bawd, call girl, old use camp follower, old use courtesan, old use harlot, inf hooker, streetwalker, old use strumpet, inf tart, toy boy, trollop, whore. • vb cheapen, debase, degrade, demean, devalue, lower, misuse.

prostrate adj ▷ OVERCOME, PRONE. • be prostrate yourself abase yourself, bow, kneel, kowtow, lie flat, submit. ▷ GROVEL.

protagonist n chief actor, contender, contestant, hero, heroine, lead, leading figure, principal, title role.

protect vb care for, cherish, conserve, defend, escort, guard, harbour, insulate, keep, keep safe, look after, mind, preserve, provide cover for, safeguard, screen, secure, shield, stand up for, support, take care of, tend, watch over. Opp ENDANGER, NEGLECT.

protection n 1 care, conservation, custody, defence, guardianship, patronage, preservation, safe-keeping, safety, security, tutelage. 2 barrier, buffer, bulwark, cloak, cover, guard, insulation, screen, shelter, shield.

protective adj 1 fireproof, insulating, preservative, protecting, sheltering, shielding, waterproof. 2 protective parents. careful, defensive, heedful, jealous, paternalistic, possessive, solicitous, vigilant, watchful.

protector n benefactor, bodyguard, champion, defender, guard, guardian, sl minder, patron.

protest n 1 complaint, cry of disapproval, demur, demurral, dissent, exception, grievance, inf gripe, inf grouse, grumble, objection, opposition, outcry, protestation, remonstrance. 2 inf demo, demonstration, march, rally. • vb 1 appeal, argue, challenge a decision, complain, cry out, expostulate, express disapproval, fulminate, inf gripe, inf grouse, grumble, make a protest, inf moan, object, remonstrate, take exception. 2 demonstrate, inf hold a demo, march. 3 protest your innocence. affirm, assert, asseverate, aver, declare, insist on, profess, swear.

protracted adj endless, extended, interminable, long-drawn-out, long-winded, never-ending, prolonged, spun-out. ▷ LONG. Opp SHORT.

protrude vb balloon, bulge, extend, jut out, overhang, poke out, project, stand out, stick out, stick up, swell.

protruding adj bulbous, bulging, distended, gibbous, humped, jutting, overhanging, projecting, prominent, protuberant, swollen, tumescent.

proud adj 1 appreciative, delighted, glad, gratified, happy, honoured, pleased, satisfied. 2 a proud bearing. brave, dignified, independent, self-respecting. 3 a proud history. august, distinguished, glorious, great, honourable, illustrious, noble, reputable, respected, splendid, worthy. 4 [derog] arrogant, inf big-headed, boastful, bumptious, inf cocky, inf cocksure, conceited, disdainful, egocentric, egotistical, grand, haughty, inf high and mighty, immodest, lordly, narcissistic, self-centred, self-important, self-satisfied, smug, snobbish, inf snooty, inf stuck-up, supercilious, inf swollen-headed, inf toffee-nosed, vain, vainglorious. Opp MODEST.

provable adj demonstrable, verifiable. Opp UNPROVABLE.

prove vb ascertain, assay, attest, authenticate, inf bear out, certify, check, confirm, corroborate, demonstrate, establish, explain, justify, show to be true, substantiate, test, verify. Opp DISPROVE.

proven adj accepted, proved, reliable, tried and tested, trustworthy, undoubted, unquestionable, valid, verified. Opp DOUBTFUL, THEORETICAL.

proverb n adage, maxim, old use saw. ▷ SAYING.

proverbial adj aphoristic, axiomatic, clichéd, conventional, customary, famous, legendary, time-honoured, traditional, well-known.

provide vb afford, allot, allow, arrange for, cater, contribute, donate, endow, equip, inf fix up with, inf fork out, furnish, give, grant, lay on, lend, make provision, offer, present, produce, purvey, spare, stock, supply, yield.

providence n destiny, divine intervention, fate, fortune, karma, kismet.

provident adj careful, economical, far-sighted, forward-looking, frugal, judicious, prudent, thrifty.

providential adj felicitous, fortunate, happy, lucky, opportune, timely.

provincial adj 1 local, regional. Opp NATIONAL. 2 [derog] backward, boorish, bucolic, insular, narrow-minded, parochial, rural, rustic, small-minded, uncultivated, uncultured, unsophisticated. Opp COSMOPOLITAN.

provisional adj conditional, interim, stopgap, temporary,

tentative, transitional.
Opp DEFINITIVE, PERMANENT.

provisions *plur n* food, foodstuff, groceries, provender,
rations, requirements, stocks,
stores, subsistence, supplies,
old use victuals.

proviso *n* condition, exception,
limitation, provision, qualification, requirement, restriction,
rider, stipulation.

provocation *n inf* aggravation,
cause, challenge, grievance,
grounds, incentive, incitement,
inducement, justification,
motivation, motive, reason,
stimulus, taunts, teasing.

provocative *adj* 1 alluring,
arousing, erotic, pornographic,
inf raunchy, seductive, sensual,
sensuous, *inf* sexy, tantalizing,
tempting. 2 *inf* aggravating,
annoying, infuriating, irksome,
irritating, maddening, provoking, teasing, vexing.

provoke *vb* 1 activate, arouse,
awaken, bring about, call forth,
cause, elicit, encourage, excite,
foment, generate, give rise to,
induce, initiate, inspire, instigate, kindle, motivate, promote,
prompt, spark off, start, stimulate, stir up, urge on, work up.
2 *inf* aggravate, anger, annoy,
enrage, exasperate, gall, *inf* get
on your nerves, goad, incense,
incite, inflame, infuriate,
insult, irk, irritate, madden,
offend, outrage, pique, rile,
rouse, tease, torment, upset,
vex, *inf* wind up, worry.
Opp PACIFY.

prowess *n* 1 ability, adeptness,
adroitness, aptitude, cleverness,
competence, dexterity, excellence, expertise, genius,
mastery, proficiency, skill,

talent. 2 *prowess in battle*. boldness, bravery, courage, daring,
doughtiness, gallantry, heroism, mettle, spirit, valour.

prowl *vb* creep, lurk, roam,
rove, skulk, slink, sneak, steal.
▷ WALK.

proximity *n* 1 closeness, nearness, propinquity. 2 locality,
neighbourhood, vicinity.

prudent *adj* advisable, careful,
cautious, circumspect, discreet,
economical, far-sighted, frugal,
judicious, politic, proper,
provident, reasonable, sagacious, sage, sensible, shrewd,
thoughtful, thrifty, vigilant,
watchful, wise. *Opp* UNWISE.

prudish *adj* decorous, easily
shocked, illiberal, intolerant,
narrow-minded, old-fashioned,
inf old-maidish, priggish, prim,
inf prissy, proper, puritanical,
rigid, shockable, strait-laced,
strict. *Opp* BROAD-MINDED.

prune *vb* clip, cut back, lop, pare
down, trim. ▷ CUT.

pry *vb* be curious, be inquisitive,
be nosy, delve, *inf* ferret,
inquire, interfere, intrude,
investigate, meddle, *inf* nose
about, peer, poke about,
inf poke your nose in, search,
inf snoop, *inf* stick your nose
in. **prying** ▷ INQUISITIVE.

pseudonym *n* alias, assumed
name, false name, incognito,
nickname, *Fr* nom de plume,
pen-name, sobriquet, stage
name.

psychic *adj* clairvoyant, extra-
sensory, magical, mental, metaphysical, mystic, occult, preternatural, psychical, spiritual,
supernatural, telepathic.
● *n* astrologer, clairvoyant,
crystal-gazer, fortune-teller,

medium, mind-reader, spiritualist, telepathist.

psychological *adj* cerebral, emotional, mental, subconscious, subjective, subliminal, unconscious. *Opp* PHYSIOLOGICAL.

pub *n old use* alehouse, bar, *sl* boozer, cocktail lounge, *old use* hostelry, inn, *inf* local, public house, saloon, tavern, wine bar.

puberty *n* adolescence, growing-up, juvenescence, pubescence, sexual maturity, *inf* teens.

public *adj* **1** accessible, available, common, familiar, free, known, open, shared, unconcealed, unrestricted, visible, well-known. **2** *public support*. civic, civil, collective, communal, community, democratic, general, majority, national, popular, social, universal. **3** *a public figure*. ▷ PROMINENT. *Opp* PRIVATE. ● *n* the public. citizens, the community, the country, the nation, people, the populace, society, voters.

publication *n* **1** appearance, issuing, printing, production. ▷ BOOK, MAGAZINE. **2** advertising, announcement, broadcasting, declaration, disclosure, dissemination, proclamation, promulgation, publicizing, reporting.

publicity *n* **1** attention, *inf* ballyhoo, fame, *inf* hype, limelight, notoriety. **2** advertising, marketing, promotion. ▷ ADVERTISEMENT.

publicize *vb* advertise, *sl* hype, *inf* plug, promote, *old use* puff. ▷ PUBLISH.

publish *vb* **1** bring out, circulate, issue, make available,

print, produce, put on sale, release. **2** *publish secrets*. advertise, announce, break the news about, broadcast, communicate, declare, disclose, disseminate, divulge, issue a statement about, *inf* leak, make known, make public, proclaim, promulgate, publicize, *inf* put about, report, reveal, spread.

pucker *vb* compress, contract, crease, crinkle, draw together, purse, screw up, squeeze, tighten, wrinkle.

puerile *adj* babyish, boyish, childish, immature, infantile, juvenile. ▷ SILLY.

puff *n* **1** blast, blow, breath, draught, flurry, gust, whiff, wind. **2** *a puff of smoke*. cloud, wisp. ● *vb* **1** blow, breathe heavily, gasp, huff, pant, wheeze. **2** *puff at a cigar*. *inf* drag, draw, inhale, pull, smoke, suck. **3** *sails puffed by the wind*. balloon, billow, distend, enlarge, inflate, rise, swell.

pugnacious *adj* aggressive, antagonistic, argumentative, bellicose, belligerent, combative, contentious, disputatious, excitable, fractious, hostile, hot-tempered, litigious, militant, unfriendly, warlike. ▷ QUARRELSOME. *Opp* PEACEABLE.

pull *vb* **1** drag, draw, haul, lug, tow, trail. *Opp* PUSH. **2** jerk, tug, pluck, rip, wrench, *inf* yank. **3** *pull a tooth*. extract, pull out, remove, take out. **pull off** ▷ DETACH. **pull out** ▷ WITHDRAW. **pull round** ▷ RECOVER. **pull someone's leg** ▷ TEASE. **pull through** ▷ RECOVER. **pull together** ▷ COOPERATE. **pull up** ▷ HALT.

pulp n mash, mush, paste, pap, purée. ● vb crush, liquidize, mash, pound, pulverize, purée, smash, squash.

pulsate vb beat, drum, oscillate, palpitate, pound, pulse, quiver, reverberate, throb, tick, vibrate.

pulse n beat, drumming, oscillation, pounding, pulsation, rhythm, throb, ticking, vibration.

pump vb drain, draw off, empty, force, raise, siphon. **pump up** blow up, fill, inflate.

punch vb 1 beat, sl biff, box, inf clout, cuff, jab, poke, prod, pummel, slog, sl slug, sl sock, strike, thump. ▷ HIT. 2 ▷ PIERCE.

punctual adj in good time, inf on the dot, on time, prompt. Opp UNPUNCTUAL.

punctuate vb 1 insert punctuation, point. 2 punctuated by applause. break, interrupt, intersperse, inf pepper.

punctuation n marks, points, stops. □ accent, apostrophe, asterisk, bracket, caret, cedilla, colon, comma, dash, exclamation mark, full stop, hyphen, question mark, quotation marks, speech marks, semicolon.

puncture n blow-out, burst, burst tyre, inf flat, flat tyre, hole, leak, opening, perforation, pin-prick, rupture. ● vb deflate, go through, let down, penetrate, perforate, pierce, prick, rupture.

pungent adj 1 aromatic, hot, peppery, piquant, seasoned, sharp, spicy, strong, tangy. 2 acid, acrid, astringent, caustic, inf chemically, harsh, sour, stinging. 3 pungent criticism.

biting, bitter, incisive, mordant, sarcastic, scathing, trenchant.

punish vb castigate, chasten, chastise, correct, discipline, exact retribution from, impose punishment on, inflict punishment on, inf make an example of, pay back, penalize, inf rap over the knuckles, scold, inf teach someone a lesson.

punishment n chastisement, correction, discipline, forfeit, imposition, inf just deserts, penalty, punitive measure, retribution, revenge, sentence. □ banishment, beating, the birch, old use Borstal, the cane, capital punishment, cashiering, confiscation of property, corporal punishment, detention, excommunication, execution, exile, fine, flogging, gaol, inf hiding, imprisonment, jail, keelhauling, lashing, pillory, prison, probation, scourging, spanking, the stocks, torture, whipping.

punitive adj disciplinary, penal, retaliatory, retributive, revengeful, vindictive.

puny adj diminutive, dwarf, feeble, frail, sickly, stunted, underdeveloped, undernourished, undersized. ▷ SMALL. Opp LARGE, STRONG.

pupil n apprentice, beginner, disciple, follower, learner, novice, protégé(e), scholar, schoolboy, schoolchild, schoolgirl, student, tiro.

puppet n doll, dummy, finger-puppet, glove-puppet, hand-puppet, marionette, string-puppet.

purchase n 1 acquisition, inf buy (a good buy), invest-

ment. 2 grasp, grip, hold, leverage, support. • vb acquire, buy,
get, invest in, obtain, pay for,
procure, secure.

pure adj 1 authentic, genuine,
neat, real, solid, sterling,
straight, unadulterated, unalloyed, undiluted. 2 *pure food.*
eatable, germ-free, hygienic,
natural, pasteurized, uncontaminated, untainted, wholesome.
3 *pure water.* clean, clear, distilled, drinkable, fresh, potable,
sterile, unpolluted. 4 *pure in
morals.* blameless, chaste,
decent, good, impeccable, innocent, irreproachable, maidenly,
modest, moral, proper, sinless,
stainless, virginal, virtuous.
5 *pure genius.* absolute,
complete, downright, *inf* out-
and-out, perfect, sheer, thorough, total, true, unmitigated,
unqualified, utter. 6 *pure
science.* abstract, academic,
conjectural, conceptual, hypothetical, speculative, theoretical. Opp IMPURE, PRACTICAL.

purgative n aperient, cathartic,
enema, laxative, purge.

purge vb 1 clean out, cleanse,
clear, depurate, empty, purify,
wash out. 2 *purge your opponents.* eject, eliminate, eradicate, expel, get rid of, liquidate,
oust, remove, root out.

purify vb clarify, clean, cleanse,
decontaminate, depurate, disinfect, distil, filter, fumigate,
make pure, purge, refine, sanitize, sterilize.

puritan n fanatic, *derog* killjoy,
moralist, *derog* prude, zealot.

puritanical adj ascetic, austere,
moralistic, narrow-minded,
pietistic, prim, proper, prudish,
rigid, self-denying, self-discip-

lined, severe, stern, stiff-
necked, strait-laced, strict,
temperate, unbending, uncompromising. Opp HEDONISTIC.

purpose n 1 aim, ambition,
aspiration, design, end, goal,
hope, intent, intention, motivation, motive, object, objective,
outcome, plan, point, rationale,
result, target, wish.
2 determination, devotion,
drive, firmness, persistence,
resolution, resolve, steadfastness, tenacity, will, zeal.
3 *purpose of a tool.* advantage,
application, benefit, good
(*what's the good of it?*), point,
practicality, use, usefulness,
utility, value. • vb ▷ INTEND.

purposeful adj calculated,
decided, decisive, deliberate,
determined, devoted, firm,
persistent, positive, resolute,
steadfast, *derog* stubborn, tenacious, unwavering, wilful,
zealous. ▷ INTENTIONAL.
Opp HESITANT.

purposeless adj aimless, bootless, empty, gratuitous, meaningless, pointless, senseless,
unnecessary, useless, vacuous,
wanton. Opp MEANINGFUL,
USEFUL.

purposely adv consciously,
deliberately, intentionally,
knowingly, on purpose,
wilfully.

purse n bag, handbag, money-
bag, pocketbook, pouch, wallet.

pursue vb 1 chase, follow, go
after, go in pursuit of, harry,
hound, hunt, keep up with, run
after, shadow, stalk, *inf* tail,
trace, track down, trail. 2 aim
for, aspire to, be committed to,
carry on, conduct, continue,
dedicate yourself to, engage in,

follow up, *inf* go for, persevere in, persist in, proceed with, prosecute, *inf* stick with, strive for, try for. 3 *pursue truth*. inquire into, investigate, quest after, search for, seek.

pursuit *n* 1 chase, chasing, following, harrying, *inf* hue and cry, hunt, hunting, pursuing, shadowing, stalking, tracking down, trail. 2 *leisure pursuits*. activity, employment, enthusiasm, hobby, interest, obsession, occupation, pastime, pleasure, speciality, specialization.

push *vb* 1 advance, drive, force, hustle, impel, jostle, move, nudge, poke, press, prod, propel, set in motion, shove, thrust. 2 *push a button*. depress, press. 3 *push into a space*. compress, cram, crowd, crush, insert, jam, pack, put, ram, squash, squeeze. 4 *push someone to act*. browbeat, bully, coerce, compel, constrain, dragoon, encourage, force, hurry, importune, incite, induce, influence, *inf* lean on, motivate, nag, persuade, pressurize, prompt, put pressure on, spur, stimulate, urge. 5 *push a new product*. advertise, boost, make known, market, *inf* plug, promote, publicize. *Opp* PULL. **push around** ▷ BULLY. **push off** ▷ DEPART. **push on** ▷ ADVANCE.

put *vb* 1 arrange, assign, commit, consign, deploy, deposit, dispose, fix, hang, lay, leave, locate, park, place, *inf* plonk, position, rest, set down, settle, situate, stand, station. 2 *put a question*.

express, formulate, frame, phrase, say, state, utter, voice, word, write. 3 *put a proposal*. advance, bring forward, offer, outline, present, propose, submit, suggest, tender. 4 *put blame on someone*. attach, attribute, cast, fix, impose, inflict, lay, *inf* pin. **put across** ▷ COMMUNICATE. **put back** ▷ RETURN. **put by** ▷ SAVE. **put down** ▷ KILL, SUPPRESS. **put in** ▷ INSERT, INSTALL. **put off** ▷ POSTPONE. **put out** ▷ EJECT, EXTINGUISH. **put over** ▷ COMMUNICATE. **put right** ▷ REPAIR. **put someone up** ▷ ACCOMMODATE. **put up** ▷ RAISE. **put your foot down** ▷ INSIST. **put your foot in it** ▷ BLUNDER.

putative *adj* alleged, assumed, conjectural, presumed, reputed, rumoured, supposed, supposititious.

putrefy *vb* decay, decompose, go bad, go off, moulder, rot, spoil.

putrid *adj* bad, corrupt, decaying, decomposing, fetid, foul, mouldy, putrefying, rotten, rotting, spoilt.

puzzle *n inf* brain-teaser, conundrum, difficulty, dilemma, enigma, mystery, paradox, *inf* poser, problem, quandary, question, riddle. ● *vb* baffle, bewilder, confuse, confound, *inf* floor, *inf* flummox, mystify, nonplus, perplex, set thinking, *inf* stump, *inf* stymie, worry. **puzzle out** ▷ SOLVE. **puzzle over** ▷ CONSIDER.

puzzling *adj* ambiguous, baffling, bewildering, confusing, cryptic, enigmatic, impenetrable, inexplicable, insoluble, *inf* mind-boggling, mysterious, mystifying, perplexing, strange, unaccountable, unanswerable, unfathomable, worrying. *Opp* STRAIGHTFORWARD.

pygmy *adj* dwarf, lilliputian, midget, tiny. ▷ SMALL.

Q

quadrangle *n* cloisters, courtyard, enclosure, *inf* quad, yard.

quagmire *n* bog, fen, marsh, mire, morass, mud, quicksand, *old use* slough, swamp.

quail *vb* back away, be apprehensive, blench, cower, cringe, falter, flinch, quake, recoil, show fear, shrink, tremble, wince.

quaint *adj* antiquated, antique, charming, curious, eccentric, fanciful, fantastic, odd, offbeat, old-fashioned, old-world, outlandish, peculiar, picturesque, strange, *inf* twee, unconventional, unexpected, unfamiliar, unusual, whimsical.

quake *vb* convulse, heave, move, quaver, quiver, rock, shake, shiver, shudder, stagger, sway, tremble, vibrate, wobble.

qualification *n* 1 ability, aptitude, capability, capacity, certification, competence, eligibility, experience, fitness, *inf* knowhow, knowledge, proficiency, quality, skill, suitability, training. 2 certificate, degree, diploma, doctorate, first degree, Master's degree, matriculation. 3 *agree without qualification.* caveat, condition, exception, limitation, modification,

proviso, reservation, restriction.

qualified *adj* 1 able, capable, certificated, competent, equipped, experienced, expert, fit, practised, professional, proficient, skilled, trained, well-informed. *Opp* UNSKILLED. 2 *qualified applicants.* appropriate, eligible, suitable. 3 *qualified praise.* cautious, conditional, equivocal, guarded, half-hearted, limited, modified, provisional, reserved, restricted. *Opp* UNCONDITIONAL.

qualify *vb* 1 authorize, empower, entitle, equip, fit, make eligible, permit, sanction. 2 become eligible, get through, *inf* make the grade, meet requirements, pass. 3 *qualify your praise.* abate, lessen, limit, mitigate, moderate, modulate, restrain, restrict, soften, temper, weaken.

quality *n* 1 calibre, class, condition, excellence, grade, rank, sort, standard, status, value, worth. 2 *personal qualities.* attribute, characteristic, distinction, feature, mark, peculiarity, property, trait.

quandary *n inf* catch-22, *inf* cleft stick, confusion, difficulty, dilemma, perplexity, plight, predicament, uncertainty.

quantity *n* aggregate, amount, bulk, consignment, dosage, dose, expanse, extent, length, load, lot, magnitude, mass, measurement, number, part, portion, proportion, quantum, sum, total, volume, weight. ▷ MEASURE.

quarrel *n* altercation, argument, bickering, clash, conflict, confrontation, contention, controversy, debate, difference, disagreement, discord, disharmony, dispute, dissension, division, feud, *inf* hassle, misunderstanding, row, *inf* ructions, rupture, *inf* scene, schism, *inf* slanging match, split, squabble, strife, *inf* tiff, vendetta, wrangle. • *vb* argue, *inf* be at loggerheads, *inf* be at odds, bicker, clash, conflict, contend, *inf* cross swords, differ, disagree, dispute, dissent, *inf* fall out, feud, haggle, misunderstand one another, *inf* row, squabble, wrangle. ▷ FIGHT. **quarrel with** ▷ DISPUTE.

quarrelsome *adj* aggressive, angry, argumentative, bad-tempered, cantankerous, choleric, contentious, contrary, cross, defiant, disagreeable, dyspeptic, explosive, fractious, impatient, irascible, irritable, petulant, peevish, querulous, quick-tempered, *inf* stroppy, testy, truculent, volatile, unfriendly. ▷ PUGNACIOUS. *Opp* PEACEABLE.

quarry *n* 1 game, kill, object, prey, victim. 2 excavation, mine, pit, working. • *vb* dig out, excavate, extract, mine.

quarter *n* area, district, division, locality, neighbourhood, part, region, section, sector, territory, vicinity, zone. • *vb* accommodate, billet, board, house, lodge, *inf* put up, shelter, station. **quarters** abode, accommodation, barracks, billet, domicile, dwelling-place, home, housing, living quarters, lodgings, residence, rooms, shelter.

quash *vb* 1 abolish, annul, cancel, invalidate, overrule,

overthrow, reject, rescind, reverse, revoke. 2 ▷ QUELL.

quaver *vb* falter, fluctuate, oscillate, pulsate, quake, quiver, shake, shiver, shudder, tremble, vibrate, waver.

quay *n* berth, dock, harbour, jetty, landing-stage, pier, wharf.

queasy *adj* bilious, *inf* green, *inf* groggy, nauseated, nauseous, *inf* poorly, *inf* queer, sick, unwell. ▷ ILL.

queer *adj* 1 aberrant, abnormal, anomalous, atypical, bizarre, curious, different, eerie, exceptional, extraordinary, *inf* fishy, freakish, *inf* funny, incongruous, inexplicable, irrational, mysterious, odd, offbeat, outlandish, peculiar, puzzling, quaint, remarkable, *inf* rum, singular, strange, unaccountable, uncanny, uncommon, unconventional, unexpected, unnatural, unorthodox, unusual, weird. 2 *inf* cranky, deviant, eccentric, questionable, *inf* shady (*customer*), *inf* shifty, suspect, suspicious. ▷ MAD. *Opp* NORMAL. 3 ▷ ILL. 4 ▷ HOMOSEXUAL.

quell *vb* 1 crush, overcome, put down, quash, repress, subdue, suppress. 2 *quell fears.* allay, alleviate, calm, mitigate, moderate, mollify, pacify, soothe, tranquillize.

quench *vb* 1 allay, appease, cool, sate, satisfy, slake. 2 *quench a fire.* damp down, douse, extinguish, put out, smother, snuff out, stifle, suppress.

quest *n* crusade, expedition, exploration, hunt, mission, pilgrimage, pursuit, search, voyage of discovery. • *vb* **quest after** ▷ SEEK.

question n 1 inf brain-teaser, conundrum, demand, enquiry, inquiry, inf poser, query, request, riddle. 2 an unresolved question. argument, controversy, debate, difficulty, dispute, doubt, misgiving, mystery, objection, problem, puzzle, uncertainty. • vb 1 ask, catechize, cross-examine, cross-question, debrief, enquire of, examine, inf grill, inquire of, interrogate, interview, probe, inf pump, quiz. 2 question a decision. argue over, be sceptical about, call into question, cast doubt upon, challenge, dispute, doubt, enquire about, impugn, inquire about, object to, oppose, quarrel with, query.

questionable adj arguable, borderline, debatable, disputable, doubtful, dubious, inf iffy, moot, problematical, inf shady (customer), suspect, suspicious, uncertain, unclear, unprovable, unreliable.

questionnaire n catechism, opinion poll, question sheet, quiz, survey, test.

queue n chain, concatenation, column, inf crocodile, file, line, line-up, procession, row, string, succession, tail-back, train. • vb fall in, form a queue, line up, wait in a queue.

quibble n ▷ OBJECTION. • vb inf bandy words, be evasive, carp, cavil, equivocate, inf nit-pick, object, pettifog, inf split hairs, wrangle.

quick adj 1 breakneck, brisk, expeditious, express, fast, old use fleet, headlong, high-speed, inf nippy, precipitate, rapid, inf smart (pace), inf spanking, speedy, swift. 2 a quick reaction. adroit, agile, animated,

brisk, deft, dexterous, energetic, lively, nimble, spirited, spry, vigorous. 3 a quick response. abrupt, early, hasty, hurried, immediate, instant, instantaneous, perfunctory, precipitate, prompt, punctual, ready, sudden, summary, unhesitating. 4 a quick mind. acute, alert, apt, astute, bright, clever, intelligent, perceptive, quick-witted, sharp, shrewd, smart. Opp SLOW. 5 a quick rest. brief, fleeting, momentary, passing, perfunctory, short, short-lived, temporary, transitory. 6 [old use] the quick and the dead. ▷ ALIVE. Opp SLOW.

quicken vb 1 accelerate, expedite, hasten, hurry, go faster, speed up. 2 ▷ AROUSE.

quiet adj 1 inaudible, noiseless, silent, soundless. 2 quiet music. hushed, low, pianissimo, soft, It sotto voce. 3 a quiet person. composed, contemplative, contented, gentle, introverted, meditative, meek, mild, modest, peaceable, reserved, retiring, shy, taciturn, thoughtful, uncommunicative, unforthcoming, unsociable, withdrawn. 4 a quiet life. cloistered, sheltered, tranquil, unadventurous, unexciting, untroubled. 5 a quiet place. isolated, lonely, peaceful, private, secluded, sequestered, undisturbed, unfrequented. 6 quiet weather. calm, motionless, placid, restful, serene, still. Opp BUSY, NOISY, RESTLESS.

quieten vb 1 calm, compose, hush, lull, pacify, sedate, soothe, subdue, tranquillize. 2 deaden, dull, muffle, mute, reduce the volume of, silence, soften, stifle, suppress, tone down.

quirk *n* aberration, caprice, crotchet, eccentricity, idiosyncrasy, kink, oddity, peculiarity, trick, whim.

quit *vb* **1** abandon, decamp from, depart from, desert, exit from, forsake, go away from, leave, walk out (on), withdraw. **2** abdicate, discontinue, drop, give up, leave, *inf* pack it in, relinquish, renounce, repudiate, resign from, retire from, withdraw from. **3** [*inf*] *Quit pushing!* cease, desist from, discontinue, leave off, stop.

quite *adv* [NB: the two senses are almost opposite.] **1** *Yes, I've quite finished.* absolutely, altogether, completely, entirely, perfectly, thoroughly, totally, unreservedly, utterly, wholly. **2** *quite good, but not perfect.* comparatively, fairly, moderately, *inf* pretty, rather, relatively, somewhat, to some extent.

quits *adj* equal, even, level, repaid, revenged, square.

quiver *vb* flicker, fluctuate, flutter, oscillate, palpitate, pulsate, quake, quaver, shake, shiver, shudder, tremble, vibrate, wobble.

quixotic *adj* fanciful, foolhardy, idealistic, impracticable, impractical, romantic, *inf* starry-eyed, unrealistic, unrealizable, unselfish, Utopian, visionary. *Opp* REALISTIC.

quiz *n* competition, exam, examination, questioning, questionnaire, quiz-game, test.
● *vb* ▷ QUESTION.

quizzical *adj* amused, comical, curious, intrigued, perplexed, puzzled, queer, questioning.

quota *n* allocation, allowance, apportionment, assignment, *inf* cut, part, portion, proportion, ration, share.

quotation *n* **1** allusion, citation, *inf* clip, cutting, excerpt, extract, passage, piece, reference, selection. **2** estimate, price, tender, valuation.

quote *vb* **1** cite, instance, mention, produce a quotation from, refer to, repeat, reproduce. **2** *quote a price.* estimate, tender.

R

rabble *n* crowd, gang, herd, *Gk* hoi polloi, horde, mob, *inf* riffraff, swarm, throng. ▷ GROUP.

race *n* **1** breed, clan, ethnic group, family, folk, genus, kind, lineage, nation, people, species, stock, tribe, variety. **2** chase, competition, contention, contest, heat, rivalry. □ cross-country, greyhound race, horse-race, hurdles, marathon, motor-race, regatta, relay, road-race, rowing, scramble, speedway, sprint, steeple-chase, stock-car race, swimming, track event.
● *vb* **1** *I'll race you!* compete with, contest with, have a race with, try to beat. **2** race along. career, dash, *inf* fly, gallop, hasten, hurry, move fast, run, rush, speed, sprint, *inf* tear, *inf* zip, *inf* zoom.

racetrack *n* cinder-track, circuit, dog-track, lap, race-course.

racial *adj* ethnic, folk, genetic, national, tribal.

racism *n* bias, bigotry, chauvinism, discrimination, intolerance, prejudice, racialism, xenophobia. □ *anti-Semitism, apartheid.*

racist *adj* biased, bigoted, chauvinist, discriminatory, intolerant, prejudiced, racialist, xenophobic. □ *anti-Semitic.*

rack *n* frame, framework, holder, scaffold, scaffolding, shelf, stand, support.
● *vb* ▷ TORTURE.

radiant *adj* 1 beaming, bright, brilliant, effulgent, gleaming, glorious, glowing, incandescent, luminous, phosphorescent, refulgent, shining. 2 *The bride was radiant.* ▷ HAPPY.

radiate *vb* beam, diffuse, emanate, emit, give off, gleam, glow, send out, shed, shine, spread, transmit.

radical *adj* 1 basic, cardinal, deep-seated, elementary, essential, fundamental, primary, principal, profound. 2 complete, comprehensive, drastic, entire, exhaustive, thorough, thoroughgoing. 3 *radical politics.* extreme, extremist, fanatical, far-reaching, revolutionary, *derog* subversive.
Opp MODERATE, SUPERFICIAL.

radio *n* CB, *sl* ghettoblaster, portable, receiver, set, *inf* transistor, transmitter, walkie-talkie, *old use* wireless.
● *vb* broadcast, send out, transmit.

rafter *n* beam, girder, joist.

rage *n* ▷ ANGER. ● *vb* be angry, boil, fume, go berserk, lose control, rave, *inf* see red, seethe, storm.

ragged *adj* 1 chafed, frayed, in ribbons, old, patched, patchy, ravelled, rent, ripped, rough, rough-edged, shabby, shaggy, tattered, tatty, threadbare, torn, unkempt, unravelled, untidy, worn out. 2 *ragged line.* denticulated, disorganized, erratic, irregular, jagged, serrated, uneven, zigzag.

rags *plur n* bits and pieces, cloths, fragments, old clothes, remnants, ribbons, scraps, shreds, tatters.

raid *n* assault, attack, blitz, foray, incursion, inroad, invasion, onslaught, sally, sortie, strike, surprise attack, swoop.
● *vb* 1 assault, attack, descend on, invade, pounce on, rush, storm, swoop down on. 2 loot, maraud, pillage, plunder, ransack, rifle, rob, sack, steal from, strip.

raider *n* attacker, brigand, invader, looter, marauder, outlaw, pillager, pirate, plunderer, ransacker, robber, rustler, thief.

railway *n* line, permanent way, *Amer* railroad, rails, track.
□ *branch line, cable railway, funicular, light railway, main line, metro, mineral line, monorail, mountain railway, narrow gauge, rack-and-pinion, rapid transit system, siding, standard gauge, tramway, tube, underground.* ▷ TRAIN.

rain *n* cloudburst, deluge, downpour, drizzle, precipitation, raindrops, rainfall, rainstorm, shower, squall. ● *vb inf* bucket down, drizzle, pelt, pour, *inf* rain cats and dogs, spit, teem.

rainy *adj* damp, drizzly, showery, wet.

raise *vb* **1** elevate, heave up, hoist, hold up, jack up, lift, loft, pick up, put up, rear. **2** *raise prices.* augment, boost, increase, inflate, put up, *inf* up. **3** *raise to a higher rank.* exalt, prefer, promote, upgrade. **4** *raise a monument.* build, construct, create, erect, set up. **5** *raise hopes.* activate, arouse, awaken, build up, buoy up, encourage, engender, enlarge, excite, foment, foster, heighten, incite, kindle, motivate, provoke, rouse, stimulate, uplift. **6** *raise animals, children, crops.* breed, bring up, care for, cultivate, educate, farm, grow, look after, nurture, produce, propagate, rear. **7** *raise money.* amass, collect, get, make, receive, solicit. **8** *raise questions.* advance, bring up, broach, express, instigate, introduce, mention, moot, originate, pose, present, put forward, suggest. *Opp* LOWER, REDUCE. **raise from the dead** ▷ RESURRECT. **raise the alarm** ▷ WARN.

rally *n* **1** assembly, *inf* demo, demonstration, gathering, march, mass meeting, protest. **2** ▷ COMPETITION.
  ● *vb* **1** assemble, convene, get together, marshal, muster, organize, round up, summon. **2** come together, reassemble, reform, regroup. **3** *rally after illness.* ▷ RECOVER.

ram *vb* **1** bump, butt, collide with, crash into, slam into, smash into, strike. ▷ HIT. **2** compress, cram, crowd, crush, drive, force, jam, pack, press, push, squash, squeeze, tamp down, wedge.

ramble *n* hike, tramp, trek, walk. ● *vb* **1** hike, range, roam,

rove, tramp, trek, stroll, wander. ▷ WALK. **2** digress, drift, *inf* lose the thread, maunder, *inf* rabbit on, *inf* rattle on, talk aimlessly, wander, *inf* witter on.

rambling *adj* **1** circuitous, indirect, labyrinthine, meandering, roundabout, tortuous, twisting, wandering, winding, zigzag. *Opp* DIRECT. **2** aimless, circumlocutory, confused, diffuse, digressive, disconnected, discursive, disjointed, illogical, incoherent, jumbled, muddled, periphrastic, unstructured, verbose, wordy. *Opp* COHERENT. **3** *a rambling house.* asymmetrical, extensive, irregular, large, sprawling, straggling, straggly. *Opp* COMPACT.

ramification *n* branch, byproduct, complication, consequence, division, effect, extension, implication, offshoot, result, subdivision, upshot.

ramp *n* acclivity, gradient, incline, rise, slope.

rampage *n* frenzy, riot, tumult, uproar, vandalism, violence.
  ● *vb* behave violently, go berserk, go wild, lose control, race about, run amok, run riot, rush about, storm about. **on the rampage** ▷ WILD.

ramshackle *adj* broken-down, crumbling, decrepit, derelict, dilapidated, flimsy, jerry-built, rickety, ruined, run-down, shaky, tottering, tumbledown, unsafe, unstable, unsteady. *Opp* SOLID.

random *adj* accidental, adventitious, aimless, arbitrary, casual, chance, fortuitous, haphazard, *inf* hit-or-miss, indiscriminate, irregular, serendipitous, stray, unconsidered, unplanned, unpremeditated, unspecific, unsystematic. *Opp* DELIBERATE, SYSTEMATIC.

range *n* 1 area, compass, distance, extent, field, gamut, limit, orbit, radius, reach, scope, span, spectrum, sphere, spread, sweep. 2 *a wide range of goods.* diversity, selection, variety. 3 *range of mountains.* chain, file, line, rank, row, series, string, tier. ● *vb* 1 differ, extend, fluctuate, go, reach, run the gamut, spread, stretch, vary. 2 ▷ RANK. 3 ▷ ROAM.

rank *n* 1 *rank growth.* ▷ ABUNDANT. 2 *rank smell.* ▷ SMELLING. ● *n* 1 column, file, formation, line, order, queue, row, series, tier. 2 birth, blood, caste, class, condition, degree, echelon, estate, grade, level, position, standing, station, status, stratum, title. ● *vb* arrange, array, assort, categorize, class, classify, grade, graduate, line up, order, organize, range, rate, set out in order, sort.

ransack *vb* 1 comb, explore, go through, rake through, rummage through, scour, search, *inf* turn upside down. 2 *ransack a shop.* despoil, loot, pillage, plunder, raid, ravage, rob, sack, strip, wreck.

ransom *n* payment, *inf* payoff, price, redemption. ● *vb* buy the release of, deliver, redeem.

rap *vb* 1 knock, strike, tap. ▷ HIT. 2 ▷ CRITICIZE.

rape *n* 1 assault, sexual attack. 2 ▷ PILLAGE. ● *vb* assault, defile, deflower, dishonour, force yourself on, *inf* have your way with, *old use* ravish, violate.

rapid *adj* alacritous, breakneck, brisk, expeditious, express, fast, *old use* fleet, hasty, headlong, high-speed, hurried, immediate, impetuous, instant, instantaneous, *inf* lightning, *inf* nippy, precipitate, prompt, quick, smooth, speedy, swift, unchecked, uninterrupted. *Opp* SLOW.

rapids *plur n* cataract, current, waterfall, white water.

rapture *n* bliss, delight, ecstasy, elation, euphoria, exaltation, happiness, joy, pleasure, thrill, transport.

rare *adj* abnormal, atypical, curious, exceptional, extraordinary, *inf* few and far between, infrequent, irreplaceable, limited, occasional, odd, out of the ordinary, peculiar, scarce, singular, special, strange, surprising, uncommon, unfamiliar, unusual. *Opp* COMMON.

rascal *n* blackguard, *old use* bounder, devil, good-for-nothing, imp, knave, mischief-maker, miscreant, ne'er-do-well, rapscallion, rogue, *inf* scally-wag, scamp, scoundrel, trouble-maker, villain, wastrel. ▷ CRIMINAL.

rash *adj* careless, foolhardy, hare-brained, hasty, headlong, headstrong, heedless, hot-headed, hurried, ill-advised, ill-considered, impetuous, imprudent, impulsive, incautious, indiscreet, injudicious, madcap, precipitate, reckless, risky, thoughtless, unthinking, wild. *Opp* CAREFUL. ● *n* 1 efflorescence, eruption, spots. 2 *a rash of thefts.* ▷ OUTBREAK.

rasp *vb* 1 abrade, file, grate, rub, scrape. 2 *rasp orders.* croak,

screech, speak hoarsely.
▷ SPEAK. **rasping** ▷ HARSH.

rate n 1 gait, pace, speed, tempo, velocity. 2 amount, charge, cost, fare, fee, figure, payment, price, scale, tariff, wage. ● vb 1 appraise, assess, class, classify, compute, consider, estimate, evaluate, gauge, grade, judge, measure, prize, put a price on, rank, reckon, regard, value, weigh. 2 *rate a prize*. be worthy of, deserve, merit. 3 ▷ REPRIMAND.

rather adv 1 fairly, moderately, *inf* pretty, quite, relatively, slightly, somewhat. 2 *would rather have tea than coffee*. more willingly, preferably, sooner.

ratify vb approve, authorize, confirm, endorse, sanction, sign, validate, verify.

rating n classification, evaluation, grade, grading, mark, order, placing, ranking.

ratio n balance, correlation, correspondence, fraction, percentage, proportion, relationship.

ration n allocation, allotment, allowance, amount, helping, measure, percentage, portion, quota, share. ● vb allocate, allot, apportion, conserve, control, distribute fairly, dole out, give out, limit, parcel out, restrict, share equally. **rations** food, necessaries, necessities, provisions, stores, supplies.

rational adj balanced, clear-headed, commonsense, enlightened, intelligent, judicious, logical, lucid, normal, ratiocinative, reasonable, reasoned, reasoning, sane, sensible,

sound, thoughtful, wise.
Opp IRRATIONAL.

rationale n argument, case, cause, excuse, explanation, grounds, justification, logical basis, principle, reason, reasoning, theory, vindication.

rationalize vb 1 account for, be rational about, elucidate, excuse, explain, justify, make rational, provide a rationale for, ratiocinate, think through, vindicate. 2 ▷ REORGANIZE.

rattle vb 1 clatter, vibrate. 2 agitate, jar, joggle, *inf* jiggle about, jolt, shake about. 3 [*inf*] *rattled him by booing*. alarm, discomfit, discompose, disconcert, disturb, fluster, frighten, make nervous, put off, unnerve, upset, worry. **rattle off** ▷ RECITE. **rattle on** ▷ RAMBLE, TALK.

raucous adj ear-splitting, harsh, husky, grating, jarring, noisy, rasping, rough, screeching, shrill, squawking, strident.

ravage vb damage, despoil, destroy, devastate, lay waste, loot, pillage, plunder, raid, ransack, ruin, sack, spoil, wreak havoc on, wreck.

rave vb 1 be angry, fulminate, fume, rage, rant, roar, storm, thunder. 2 be enthusiastic, enthuse, *inf* go into raptures, *inf* gush, rhapsodize.

ravenous adj famished, hungry, insatiable, ravening, starved, starving, voracious. ▷ GREEDY.

ravish vb 1 bewitch, captivate, capture, charm, delight, enchant, entrance, spellbind, transport. 2 ▷ RAPE. **ravishing** ▷ BEAUTIFUL.

raw adj 1 fresh, rare (*steak*), uncooked, underdone, unprepared, wet (*fish*). **2** *raw materials*. crude, natural, unprocessed, unrefined, untreated. **3** *raw recruits*. inf green, ignorant, immature, inexperienced, innocent, new, unseasoned, untrained, untried. **4** *raw skin*. bloody, chafed, grazed, inflamed, painful, red, rough, scraped, scratched, sensitive, sore, tender, vulnerable. **5** *raw wind*. ▷ COLD.

ray *n* **1** bar, beam, laser, pencil, shaft, streak, stream. **2** *a ray of hope*. flicker, gleam, glimmer, hint, indication, scintilla, sign, trace.

raze *vb* bulldoze, demolish, destroy, flatten, level, tear down.

razor *n* □ cut-throat razor, disposable razor, electric razor, safety razor.

reach *n* compass, distance, orbit, range, scope, sphere.
● *vb* **1** achieve, arrive at, attain, come to, get hold of, get to, go as far as, grasp, inf make, take, touch. **2** *reach for the salt*. put out your hand, stretch, try to get. **3** *reach me by phone*. communicate with, contact, get in touch with. **reach out** ▷ EXTEND.

react *vb* act, answer, behave, conduct yourself, reciprocate, reply, respond, retaliate, retort, take revenge. **react to** ▷ COUNTER.

reaction *n* answer, backlash, inf come-back, counter, countermove, effect, feedback, parry, reciprocation, reflex, rejoinder, reply, reprisal, response, retaliation, retort, revenge, riposte.

reactionary *adj* conservative, die-hard, old-fashioned, rightist,

right-wing, inf stick-in-the-mud, traditionalist, unprogressive. *Opp* PROGRESSIVE.

read *vb* **1** devour, inf dip into, glance at, interpret, look over, peruse, pore over, review, scan, skim, study. **2** *can't read the handwriting*. decipher, decode, interpret, make out, understand.

readable *adj* **1** absorbing, compulsive, easy, engaging, enjoyable, entertaining, gripping, interesting, stimulating, well-written. *Opp* BORING. **2** clear, comprehensible, decipherable, distinct, intelligible, legible, neat, plain, understandable. *Opp* ILLEGIBLE.

readily *adv* cheerfully, eagerly, easily, effortlessly, freely, gladly, happily, promptly, quickly, ungrudgingly, unhesitatingly, voluntarily, willingly.

ready *adj* **1** accessible, inf all set, arranged, at hand, available, complete, convenient, done, finalized, finished, fit, obtainable, prepared, primed, ripe, set, set up, waiting. **2** *ready to help*. agreeable, consenting, content, disposed, eager, equipped, inf game, glad, inclined, in the mood, keen, inf keyed up, liable, likely, minded, of a mind, open, organized, pleased, poised, predisposed, primed, inf psyched up, raring (*to go*), trained, willing. **3** *ready wit*. acute, adroit, alert, apt, facile, immediate, prompt, quick, quick-witted, rapid, sharp, smart, speedy. *Opp* SLOW, UNPREPARED.

real *adj* **1** actual, authentic, certain, corporeal, everyday, existing, factual, genuine, material, natural, ordinary,

palpable, physical, pure, realistic, tangible, visible.
2 authenticated, *Lat* bona fide, legal, legitimate, official, valid, verifiable. 3 *real friends.* dependable, positive, reliable, sound, true, trustworthy, worthy. 4 *real grief.* earnest, heartfelt, honest, sincere, truthful, unaffected, undoubted, unfeigned, unquestionable. *Opp* FALSE.

realism *n* 1 authenticity, fidelity, naturalism, verisimilitude. 2 *realism in business.* clear-sightedness, common sense, objectivity, practicality, pragmatism.

realistic *adj* 1 businesslike, clear-sighted, commonsense, down-to-earth, feasible, hardheaded, *inf* hard-nosed, levelheaded, logical, matter-of-fact, *inf* no-nonsense, objective, possible, practicable, practical, pragmatic, rational, sensible, tough, unemotional, unsentimental, viable, workable. 2 *realistic pictures.* authentic, convincing, faithful, graphic, lifelike, natural, recognizable, representational, true-to-life, truthful, vivid. 3 *realistic prices.* acceptable, adequate, fair, genuine, justifiable, moderate, reasonable. *Opp* UNREALISTIC.

reality *n* actuality, authenticity, certainty, empirical knowledge, experience, fact, life, *inf* nitty-gritty, real life, the real world, truth, verity. *Opp* FANTASY.

realize *vb* 1 accept, appreciate, apprehend, be aware of, become conscious of, *inf* catch on to, comprehend, conceive of, *inf* cotton on to, grasp, know, perceive, recognize, see, sense, *inf* twig, understand, *inf* wake

up to. 2 *realize an ambition.* accomplish, achieve, bring about, complete, effect, effectuate, fulfil, implement, make a reality of, obtain, perform, put into effect. 3 *realize a price.* *inf* bring in, *inf* clear, earn, fetch, make, net, obtain, produce.

realm *n* country, domain, empire, kingdom, monarchy, principality.

reap *vb* 1 cut, garner, gather in, glean, harvest, mow. 2 *reap a reward.* acquire, bring in, collect, get, obtain, receive, win.

rear *adj* back, end, hind, hinder, hindmost, last, rearmost. *Opp* FRONT. ● *n* 1 back, end, stern (*of ship*), tail-end. 2 ▷ BUTTOCKS. ● *vb* 1 breed, bring up, care for, cultivate, educate, feed, look after, nurse, nurture, produce, raise, train. 2 *rear your head.* elevate, hold up, lift, raise, uplift. 3 ▷ BUILD.

rearrange *vb* change round, regroup, reorganize, switch round, swop round, transpose. ▷ CHANGE.

rearrangement *n* anagram, reorganization, transposition. ▷ CHANGE.

reason *n* 1 apology, argument, case, cause, defence, excuse, explanation, grounds, incentive, justification, motive, occasion, pretext, rationale, vindication. 2 brains, common sense, *inf* gumption, intelligence, judgement, logic, mind, *inf* nous, perspicacity, rationality, reasonableness, sanity, sense, understanding, wisdom, wit. ▷ REASONING. 3 *reason for living.* aim, goal, intention, motivation, motive, object, objective, point, purpose, spur, stimulus. ● vb 1 act rationally, calculate, cerebrate, conclude, consider, deduce, estimate, figure out, hypothesize, infer, intellectualize, judge, inf put two and two together, ratiocinate, resolve, theorize, think, use your head, work out. 2 I reasoned with her. argue, debate, discuss, expostulate, remonstrate.

reasonable adj 1 calm, helpful, honest, intelligent, rational, realistic, sane, sensible, sincere, sober, thinking, thoughtful, unemotional, wise. 2 reasonable argument. arguable, believable, credible, defensible, justifiable, logical, plausible, practical, reasoned, sound, tenable, viable, well-thought-out. 3 reasonable prices. acceptable, appropriate, average, cheap, competitive, conservative, fair, inexpensive, moderate, ordinary, proper, right, suitable, tolerable, unexceptionable. Opp IRRATIONAL.

reasoning n analysis, argument, case, derog casuistry, cerebration, deduction, dialectic, hypothesis, line of thought, logic, proof, rationalization, derog sophistry, theorizing, thinking.

reassure vb assure, bolster, buoy up, calm, cheer, comfort, encourage, give confidence to, hearten, inf set someone's mind at rest, support, uplift. Opp ALARM, THREATEN. **reassuring** ▷ SOOTHING, SUPPORTIVE.

rebel adj ▷ REBELLIOUS.
● n anarchist, apostate, dissenter, freedom fighter, heretic,

iconoclast, insurgent, malcontent, maverick, mutineer, nonconformist, recusant, resistance fighter, revolutionary, schismatic. ● vb be a rebel, disobey, dissent, fight, inf kick over the traces, mutiny, refuse to obey, revolt, rise up, inf run riot, inf take a stand. Opp CONFORM. **rebel against** ▷ DEFY.

rebellion n contumacy, defiance, disobedience, insubordination, insurgency, insurrection, mutiny, rebelliousness, resistance, revolt, revolution, rising, schism, sedition, uprising.

rebellious adj inf bolshie, breakaway, contumacious, defiant, difficult, disaffected, disloyal, disobedient, incorrigible, insubordinate, insurgent, intractable, malcontent, mutinous, obstinate, quarrelsome, rebel, recalcitrant, refractory, resistant, revolting, revolutionary, seditious, uncontrollable, ungovernable, unmanageable, unruly, wild. Opp OBEDIENT.

rebirth n reawakening, regeneration, renaissance, renewal, resurgence, resurrection, return, revival.

rebound vb inf backfire, inf boomerang, bounce, misfire, recoil, ricochet, spring back.

rebuff n inf brush-off, check, discouragement, refusal, rejection, slight, snub. ● vb cold-shoulder, decline, discourage, refuse, reject, repulse, slight, snub, spurn, turn down.

rebuild n reassemble, reconstruct, recreate, redevelop, refashion, regenerate, remake. ▷ RECONDITION.

rebuke vb admonish, castigate, censure, chide, reprehend, reproach, reprove, scold, upbraid. ▷ REPRIMAND.

recall vb 1 bring back, call in, summon, withdraw. 2 ▷ REMEMBER.

recede vb abate, decline, dwindle, ebb, fall back, go back, lessen, regress, retire, retreat, return, shrink back, sink, slacken, subside, wane, withdraw.

receipt n 1 account, acknowledgement, bill, proof of purchase, sales slip, ticket. 2 *receipt of goods*. acceptance, delivery, reception. **receipts** gains, gate, income, proceeds, profits, return, takings.

receive vb 1 accept, acquire, be given, be paid, be sent, collect, come by, come into, derive, earn, gain, get, gross, inherit, make, net, obtain, take. 2 *receive an injury*. bear, be subjected to, endure, experience, meet with, suffer, sustain, undergo. 3 *receive visitors*. accommodate, admit, entertain, greet, let in, meet, show in, welcome. *Opp* GIVE.

recent adj brand-new, contemporary, current, fresh, just out, latest, modern, new, novel, present-day, up-to-date, young. *Opp* OLD.

reception n 1 greeting, response, welcome. 2 ▷ PARTY.

receptive adj amenable, favourable, flexible, interested, open, open-minded, responsive, susceptible, sympathetic, tractable, welcoming, well-disposed. *Opp* RESISTANT.

recess n 1 alcove, apse, bay, cavity, corner, cranny, hollow, indentation, niche, nook. 2 adjournment, break, *inf* breather, breathing-space, interlude, intermission, interval, respite, rest, time off.

recession n decline, depression, downturn, slump.

recipe n directions, formula, instructions, method, plan, prescription, procedure, technique.

reciprocal adj corresponding, exchanged, joint, mutual, requited, returned, shared.

reciprocate vb exchange, give the same in return, match, repay, requite, return.

recital n 1 concert, performance, programme. 2 *recital of events*. account, description, narration, narrative, recounting, rehearsal, relation, repetition, story, telling. ▷ RECITATION.

recitation n declaiming, declamation, delivery, monologue, narration, performance, presentation, reading, *old use* rendition, speaking, telling.

recite vb articulate, declaim, deliver, narrate, perform, present, quote, *inf* rattle off, recount, reel off, rehearse, relate, repeat, speak, tell.

reckless adj 1 brash, careless, *inf* crazy, daredevil, *inf* devil-may-care, foolhardy, harebrained, *inf* harum-scarum, hasty, heedless, impetuous, imprudent, impulsive, inattentive, incautious, indiscreet, injudicious, irresponsible, *inf* mad, madcap, negligent, rash, thoughtless, unconsidered, unwise, wild. *Opp* CAREFUL. 2 *reckless criminals*. dangerous, desperate, hardened, violent.

reckon vb 1 add up, appraise, assess, calculate, compute, count, enumerate, estimate, evaluate, figure out, gauge, number, tally, total, value, work out. 2 ▷ THINK.

reclaim vb 1 get back, inf put in for, recapture, recover, regain. 2 *reclaim derelict land.* make usable, regenerate, reinstate, rescue, restore, salvage, save.

recline vb lean back, lie, loll, lounge, repose, rest, sprawl, stretch out.

recluse n anchoress, anchorite, hermit, loner, monk, nun, solitary.

recognizable adj detectable, distinctive, distinguishable, identifiable, known, noticeable, perceptible, undisguised, unmistakable, visible.

recognize vb 1 detect, diagnose, discern, distinguish, identify, know, name, notice, perceive, pick out, place (*can't place him*), inf put a name to, recall, recollect, remember, see, spot. 2 *recognize your faults.* accept, acknowledge, admit to, appreciate, be aware of, concede, confess, grant, realize, understand. 3 *recognize someone's rights.* approve of, inf back, endorse, legitimize, ratify, sanction, support, validate.

recoil vb blench, draw back, falter, flinch, jerk back, jump, quail, shrink, shy away, start, wince. ▷ REBOUND.

recollect vb hark back to, recall, reminisce about, summon up, think back to. ▷ REMEMBER.

recommend vb 1 advise, advocate, counsel, exhort, prescribe, propose, put forward, suggest, urge. 2 applaud, approve of, inf back, commend, favour, inf plug, praise, inf push, inf put in a good word for, speak well of, support, vouch for. ▷ ADVERTISE.

recommendation n advice, advocacy, approbation, approval, inf backing, commendation, counsel, favourable mention, reference, seal of approval, support, testimonial.

reconcile vb bring together, *old use* conciliate, harmonize, make friendly again, placate, reunite, settle differences between. **be reconciled to** accept, adjust to, resign yourself to, submit to.

recondition vb make good, overhaul, rebuild, renew, renovate, repair, restore.

reconnaissance n examination, exploration, inspection, investigation, observation, inf recce, reconnoitring, scouting, spying, survey.

reconnoitre vb inf case, inf check out, examine, explore, gather intelligence (about), inspect, investigate, patrol, scout, scrutinize, spy, survey, sl suss out.

reconsider vb be converted, change your mind, come round, reappraise, reassess, re-examine, rethink, review your position, think better of.

reconstruct vb act out, mock up, recreate, rerun. ▷ REBUILD.

record n 1 account, annals, archives, catalogue, chronicle, diary, documentation, dossier, file, journal, log, memorandum, minutes, narrative, note, register, report, transactions. 2 best performance, best time.

3 ▷ RECORDING. ● *vb* 1 chronicle, document, enter, inscribe, list, log, minute, note, put down, register, set down, take down, transcribe, write down. 2 *record on tape*. keep, preserve, tape, tape-record, video.

recording *n* performance, release. □ *album, audio-tape, cassette, CD, compact disc, digital recording, disc, long-playing record, LP, mono recording, record, single, stereo recording, tape, tape-recording, tele-recording, video, video-cassette, video disc, videotape.*

record-player *n* CD player, gramophone, midi system, *old use* phonograph, record deck, turntable.

recount *vb* communicate, describe, detail, impart, narrate, recite, relate, report, tell, unfold.

recover *vb* 1 find, get back, get compensation for, make good, make up for, recapture, reclaim, recoup, regain, repossess, restore, retrieve, salvage, trace, track down, win back. 2 *inf* be on the mend, come round, convalesce, *inf* get back on your feet, get better, heal, improve, mend, *inf* pull round, *inf* pull through, rally, recuperate, regain your strength, revive, survive, *inf* take a turn for the better.

recovery *n* 1 recapture, reclamation, repossession, restoration, retrieval, salvage, salvaging. 2 *recovery from illness*. advance, convalescence, cure, deliverance, healing, improvement, progress, rally, recuperation, revival, upturn.

recreation *n* amusement, distraction, diversion, enjoyment, entertainment, fun, games, hobby, leisure, pastime, play, pleasure, refreshment, relaxation, sport.

recrimination *n* accusation, *inf* come-back, counter-attack, counter-charge, reprisal, retaliation, retort.

recruit *n* apprentice, beginner, conscript, *inf* greenhorn, initiate, learner, neophyte, *inf* new boy, new girl, novice, tiro, trainee. *Opp* VETERAN.
● *vb* advertise for, conscript, draft in, engage, enlist, enrol, *old use* impress, mobilize, muster, register, sign on, sign up, take on.

rectify *vb* amend, correct, cure, *inf* fix, make good, put right, repair, revise.

recumbent *adj* flat, flat on your back, horizontal, lying down, prone, reclining, stretched out, supine. *Opp* UPRIGHT.

recuperate *vb* convalesce, get better, heal, improve, mend, rally, regain strength, revive. ▷ RECOVER.

recur *vb* be repeated, come back again, happen again, persist, reappear, repeat, return.

recurrent *adj* chronic, cyclical, frequent, intermittent, iterative, periodic, persistent, recurring, regular, repeated, repetitive, returning. ▷ CONTINUAL.

recycle *vb* reclaim, recover, retrieve, reuse, salvage, use again.

red *adj* bloodshot, blushing, embarrassed, fiery, flaming, florid, flushed, glowing, inflamed, rosy, rubicund, ruddy. □ *auburn, blood-red,*

brick-red, cardinal, carmine,
carroty, cerise, cherry, chestnut,
crimson, damask, flame-
coloured, foxy, magenta, maroon,
orange, pink, rose, roseate, ruby,
scarlet, titian, vermilion, wine-
coloured. **red herring** ▷ DECOY.

redden vb blush, colour, flush,
glow.

redeem vb buy back, cash in,
exchange for cash, reclaim,
recover, re-purchase, trade in,
win back. ▷ LIBERATE. **redeem
yourself** ▷ ATONE.

redolent adj 1 aromatic,
fragrant, perfumed, scented,
smelling. 2 redolent of the past.
reminiscent, suggestive.

reduce vb 1 abate, abbreviate,
abridge, clip, compress, curtail,
cut, cut back, cut down, decimate, decrease, detract from,
devalue, dilute, diminish,
inf dock (wages), inf ease up on,
halve, impair, lessen, limit,
lower, make less, minimize,
moderate, narrow, prune,
shorten, shrink, simplify,
inf slash, slim down, tone
down, trim, truncate, weaken,
whittle. 2 become less, contract,
dwindle, shrink. 3 reduce a
liquid. concentrate, condense,
thicken. 4 reduce to rubble.
break up, destroy, grind, pulp,
pulverize, triturate. 5 reduce to
poverty. degrade, demote, downgrade, humble, impoverish,
move down, put down, ruin.
Opp INCREASE, RAISE.

reduction n 1 contraction,
curtailment, inf cutback, decel-
eration (of speed), decimation,
decline, decrease, diminution,
drop, impairment, lessening,
limitation, loss, moderation,
narrowing, remission, shortening, shrinkage, weakening.

2 reduction in price. concession,
cut, depreciation, devaluation,
discount, rebate, refund.
Opp INCREASE.

redundant adj excessive, inessential, non-essential, superfluous, supernumerary, surplus,
too many, unnecessary,
unneeded, unwanted.
Opp NECESSARY.

reek n stench, stink. ▷ SMELL.

reel n bobbin, spool. ● vb falter,
lurch, pitch, rock, roll, spin,
stagger, stumble, sway, totter,
waver, whirl, wobble. **reel off**
▷ RECITE.

refer vb refer to 1 allude to,
bring up, cite, comment on,
draw attention to, make reference to, mention, name, point
to, quote, speak of, specify,
touch on. 2 refer one person to
another. direct to, guide to,
hand over to, pass on to, recommend to, send to. 3 refer to the
dictionary. consult, go to, look
up, resort to, study, turn to.

referee n adjudicator, arbiter,
arbitrator, judge, mediator,
umpire.

reference n 1 allusion, citation,
example, illustration, instance,
intimation, mention, note,
quotation, referral, remark.
2 endorsement, recommendation, testimonial.

refill vb fill up, refuel, renew,
replenish, top up.

refine vb 1 clarify, cleanse,
clear, decontaminate, distil,
process, purify, treat. 2 refine
manners. civilize, cultivate,
improve, perfect, polish.

refined adj 1 aristocratic, civilized, courteous, courtly, cultivated, cultured, delicate, dignified, discerning, discriminating,

educated, elegant, fastidious,
genteel, gentlemanly, gracious,
ladylike, nice, polished, polite,
inf posh, precise, *derog* pretentious, *derog* prissy, sensitive,
sophisticated, stylish, subtle,
tasteful, *inf* upper-crust,
urbane, well-bred, well brought-
up. *Opp* RUDE. 2 *refined oil*. clarified, distilled, processed, purified, treated. *Opp* CRUDE.

refinement *n* 1 breeding,
inf class, courtesy, cultivation,
delicacy, discernment, discrimination, elegance, finesse,
gentility, graciousness, polish,
derog pretentiousness, sensitivity, sophistication, style,
subtlety, taste, urbanity.
2 *refinements in design*. alteration, change, enhancement,
improvement, modification,
perfection.

reflect *vb* 1 echo, mirror, return,
send back, shine back, throw
back. 2 brood, cerebrate,
inf chew things over, consider,
contemplate, deliberate, meditate, ponder, remind yourself,
reminisce, ruminate. ▷ THINK.
3 *Her success reflects her hard
work*. bear witness to, correspond to, demonstrate, evidence,
exhibit, illustrate, indicate,
match, point to, reveal, show.

reflection *n* 1 echo, image, likeness. 2 *reflection of hard work*.
demonstration, evidence, indication, manifestation, result.
3 *no reflection on you*. aspersion, censure, criticism,
discredit, imputation, reproach,
shame, slur. 4 *time for reflection*. cerebration, cogitation,
contemplation, deliberation,
meditation, pondering, rumination, self-examination, study,
thinking, thought.

reflective *adj* 1 glittering,
lustrous, reflecting, shiny,
silvery. 2 ▷ THOUGHTFUL.

reform *vb* 1 ameliorate, amend,
become better, better, change,
convert, correct, improve, make
better, mend, put right, reconstruct, rectify, remodel, reorganize, save. 2 *reform a system*.
purge, reconstitute, regenerate,
revolutionize.

refrain *vb* refrain from abstain
from, avoid, cease, desist from,
do without, eschew, forbear,
leave off, *inf* quit, renounce,
stop.

refresh *vb* 1 cool, energize,
enliven, fortify, freshen, invigorate, *inf* perk up, quench the
thirst of, reanimate, rejuvenate,
renew, restore, resuscitate,
revitalize, revive, slake (*thirst*).
2 *refresh the memory*. activate,
awaken, jog, remind, prod,
prompt, stimulate.

refreshing *adj* 1 bracing, cool,
enlivening, exhilarating, inspir-
iting, invigorating, restorative,
reviving, stimulating, thirst-
quenching, tingling, tonic.
Opp EXHAUSTING. 2 *a refreshing
change*. different, fresh, interesting, new, novel, original,
unexpected, unfamiliar, unforeseen, unpredictable, welcome.
Opp BORING.

refreshments *n* drinks,
eatables, *inf* eats, *inf* nibbles,
snack. ▷ DRINK, FOOD.

refrigerate *vb* chill, cool, freeze,
ice, keep cold.

refuge *n* asylum, *inf* bolt-hole,
cover, harbour, haven, *inf* hideaway, hideout, *inf* hidey-hole,
hiding-place, protection,
retreat, safety, sanctuary,
security, shelter, stronghold.

refugee n displaced person, émigré, exile, fugitive, outcast, runaway.

refund n rebate, repayment. ● vb give back, pay back, recoup, reimburse, repay, return.

refusal n inf brush-off, denial, disagreement, disapproval, rebuff, rejection, veto. *Opp* ACCEPTANCE.

refuse n detritus, dirt, garbage, junk, litter, rubbish, trash, waste. ● vb baulk at, decline, deny, disallow, inf jib at, inf pass up, rebuff, reject, repudiate, say no to, spurn, turn down, veto, withhold. *Opp* ACCEPT, GRANT.

refute vb counter, discredit, disprove, negate, prove wrong, rebut.

regain vb be reunited with, find, get back, recapture, reclaim, recoup, recover, repossess, retake, retrieve, return to, win back.

regal adj derog haughty, imperial, kingly, lordly, majestic, noble, palatial, derog pompous, princely, queenly, royal, stately. ▷ SPLENDID.

regard n 1 gaze, look, scrutiny, stare. 2 attention, care, concern, consideration, deference, heed, notice, reference, respect, sympathy, thought. 3 admiration, affection, appreciation, approbation, approval, deference, esteem, favour, honour, love, respect, reverence, veneration. ● vb 1 behold, contemplate, eye, gaze at, keep an eye on, look at, note, observe, scrutinize, stare at, view, watch. 2 *regarded me as a liability*. account, consider,

deem, esteem, judge, look upon, perceive, rate, reckon, respect, think of, value, view, weigh up.

regarding prep about, apropos, concerning, connected with, involving, on the subject of, pertaining to, inf re, respecting, with reference to, with regard to.

regardless adj **regardless of** careless about, despite, heedless of, indifferent to, neglectful of, notwithstanding, unconcerned about, unmindful of.

regime n administration, control, discipline, government, leadership, management, order, reign, rule, system.

regiment vb arrange, control, discipline, organize, regulate, systematize.

region n area, country, department, district, division, expanse, land, locality, neighbourhood, part, place, province, quarter, sector, territory, tract, vicinity, zone.

register n archives, catalogue, chronicle, diary, directory, file, index, inventory, journal, ledger, list, record, roll, tally. ● vb 1 enlist, enrol, enter your name, join, sign on. 2 *register a complaint*. catalogue, enter, list, log, make official, minute, present, record, set down, submit, write down. 3 *register emotion*. betray, display, divulge, express, indicate, manifest, reflect, reveal, show. 4 *register in a hotel*. inf check in, sign in. 5 *register what someone says*. keep in mind, make a note of, mark, notice, take account of.

regress vb backslide, degenerate, deteriorate, fall back, go back, move backwards, retreat,

retrogress, revert, slip back.
Opp PROGRESS.

regret n 1 bad conscience, compunction, contrition, guilt, penitence, pricking of conscience, remorse, repentance, self-accusation, self-condemnation, self-reproach, shame. 2 disappointment, grief, sadness, sorrow, sympathy. • vb accuse yourself, bemoan, be regretful, be sad, bewail, deplore, deprecate, feel remorse, grieve (about), lament, mourn, repent (of), reproach yourself, rue, weep (over).

regretful adj apologetic, ashamed, conscience-stricken, contrite, disappointed, guilty, penitent, remorseful, repentant, rueful, sorry. ▷ SAD. Opp UNREPENTANT.

regrettable adj deplorable, disappointing, distressing, lamentable, reprehensible, sad, shameful, undesirable, unfortunate, unhappy, unlucky, unwanted, upsetting, woeful, wrong.

regular adj 1 consistent, constant, equal, even, fixed, measured, ordered, predictable, recurring, repeated, rhythmic, steady, symmetrical, systematic, uniform, unvarying. □ daily, hourly, monthly, weekly, yearly. 2 a regular procedure. accustomed, common, commonplace, conventional, customary, established, everyday, familiar, frequent, habitual, known, normal, official, ordinary, orthodox, prevailing, proper, routine, scheduled, standard, traditional, typical, usual. 3 a regular supporter. dependable, faithful, reliable. Opp IRREGULAR. • n inf faithful, frequenter,

habitué, regular customer, patron.

regulate vb 1 administer, conduct, control, direct, govern, manage, monitor, order, organize, oversee, restrict, supervise. 2 regulate temperature. adjust, alter, balance, change, get right, moderate, modify, set, vary.

regulation n by-law, commandment, decree, dictate, directive, edict, law, order, ordinance, requirement, restriction, rule, ruling, statute.

rehearsal n dress rehearsal, inf dry run, exercise, practice, preparation, inf read-through, inf run-through, inf try-out.

rehearse vb drill, go over, practise, prepare, inf run over, inf run through, try out.

rehearsed adj calculated, practised, pre-arranged, premeditated, prepared, scripted, studied, thought out. Opp IMPROMPTU.

reign n administration, ascendancy, command, empire, government, jurisdiction, kingdom, monarchy, power, rule, sovereignty. • vb be king, be on the throne, be queen, command, govern, have power, hold sway, rule, inf wear the crown.

reincarnation n rebirth, return to life, transmigration.

reinforce vb 1 back up, bolster, buttress, fortify, give strength to, hold up, prop up, stay, stiffen, strengthen, support, toughen. 2 reinforce an army. add to, assist, augment, help, increase the size of, provide reinforcements for, supplement.

reinforcements plur n additional troops, auxiliaries, back-up, help, reserves, support.

reinstate vb recall, rehabilitate, restore, take back, welcome back. Opp DISMISS.

reject vb 1 cast off, discard, discount, dismiss, eliminate, exclude, jettison, inf junk, put aside, scrap, send back, throw away, throw out. 2 reject friends. disown, inf drop, inf give someone the cold shoulder, jilt, rebuff, renounce, repel, repudiate, replace, inf send packing, shun, spurn, turn your back on. 3 reject an invitation. brush aside, decline, refuse, say no to, turn down, veto. Opp ACCEPT, ADOPT.

rejoice vb be happy, celebrate, delight, exult, glory, revel, triumph. Opp GRIEVE.

relapse n degeneration, deterioration, recurrence (of illness), regression, reversion, inf setback, worsening. • vb backslide, degenerate, deteriorate, fall back, have a relapse, lapse, regress, retreat, revert, sink back, slip back, weaken.

relate vb 1 communicate, describe, detail, divulge, impart, make known, narrate, present, recite, recount, rehearse, report, reveal, tell. 2 ally, associate, compare, connect, consider together, coordinate, correlate, couple, join, link. **relate to 1** appertain to, apply to, bear upon, be relevant to, concern, inf go with, pertain to, refer to. **2** relate to other people. be friends with, empathize with, fraternize with, handle, have a relation-

ship with, identify with, socialize with, understand.

related adj affiliated, akin, allied, associated, cognate, comparable, connected, consanguineous, interconnected, interdependent, interrelated, joined, joint, linked, mutual, parallel, reciprocal, relative, similar, twin. ▷ RELEVANT. Opp UNRELATED.

relation n 1 old use kinsman, old use kinswoman, plur kith and kin, member of the family, relative. ▷ FAMILY. **2** relation of a story. ▷ NARRATION.

relationship n 1 affiliation, affinity, association, attachment, bond, closeness, connection, consanguinity, correlation, correspondence, interconnection, interdependence, kinship, link, parallel, pertinence, rapport, ratio, tie, understanding. ▷ SIMILARITY. Opp CONTRAST. **2** affair, inf intrigue, inf liaison, love affair, romance, sexual relations. ▷ FRIENDSHIP.

relative adj ▷ RELATED, RELEVANT. **relative to** commensurate (with), comparative, proportional, proportionate. Opp UNRELATED. • n ▷ RELATION.

relax vb 1 be easy, be relaxed, calm down, cool down, feel at home, inf let go, inf put your feet up, rest, inf slow down, inf take it easy, unbend, unwind. Opp TENSION. **2** relax your vigilance. abate, curb, decrease, diminish, ease off, lessen, loosen, mitigate, moderate, reduce, release, relieve, slacken, soften, temper, inf tone down, unclench, unfasten, weaken. Opp INCREASE.

relaxation n 1 ease, informality, loosening up, relaxing, repose, rest, unwinding. ▷ RECREATION. *Opp* TENSION. 2 abatement, alleviation, diminution, lessening, *inf* let-up, mitigation, moderation, remission, slackening, weakening. *Opp* INCREASE.

relaxed adj derog blasé, calm, carefree, casual, comfortable, contented, cool, cosy, easy-going, *inf* free and easy, friendly, good-humoured, happy, *inf* happy-go-lucky, informal, insouciant, *inf* laid-back, *derog* lax, leisurely, light-hearted, nonchalant, peaceful, reassuring, restful, serene, *derog* slack, tranquil, unconcerned, unhurried, untroubled. *Opp* TENSE.

relay n 1 shift, turn. 2 *live relay*. broadcast, programme, transmission. ● vb broadcast, communicate, pass on, send out, spread, televise, transmit.

release vb 1 acquit, allow out, deliver, discharge, dismiss, emancipate, excuse, exonerate, free, let go, let loose, let off, liberate, loose, pardon, rescue, save, set free, set loose, unchain, unfasten, unfetter, unleash, unshackle, untie. *Opp* DETAIN. 2 fire off, launch, let fly, let off, send off. 3 *release information*. circulate, disseminate, distribute, issue, make available, present, publish, put out, send out, unveil.

relegate vb 1 consign to a lower position, demote, downgrade, put down. 2 banish, dispatch, exile.

relent vb acquiesce, become more lenient, be merciful, capitulate, give in, give way, relax, show pity, soften, weaken, yield.

relentless adj 1 dogged, fierce, hard-hearted, implacable, incessant, inexorable, intransigent, merciless, inexorable, obstinate, pitiless, remorseless, ruthless, uncompromising, unfeeling, unforgiving, unmerciful, unyielding. ▷ CRUEL. 2 unceasing, unrelieved, unstoppable, unyielding. ▷ CONTINUOUS.

relevant adj appertaining, applicable, apposite, appropriate, apropos, apt, connected, essential, fitting, germane, linked, material, pertinent, proper, related, relative, significant, suitable, suited, to the point. *Opp* IRRELEVANT.

reliable adj certain, conscientious, consistent, constant, dependable, devoted, efficient, faithful, honest, infallible, loyal, predictable, proven, punctilious, regular, reputable, responsible, safe, solid, sound, stable, staunch, steady, sure, trusted, trustworthy, trusty, unchanging, unfailing. *Opp* UNRELIABLE.

relic n heirloom, heritage, inheritance, keepsake, memento, remains, reminder, remnant, souvenir, survival, token, vestige.

relief n abatement, aid, alleviation, assistance, assuagement, comfort, cure, deliverance, diversion, ease, help, *inf* let-up, mitigation, palliation, relaxation, release, remedy, remission, respite, rest.

relieve vb abate, alleviate, anaesthetize, assuage, bring relief to, calm, comfort, console, cure, diminish, disburden, disencumber, dull, ease, lessen, lift, lighten, make less, mitigate, moderate, palliate, reduce, relax, release, rescue, soften, soothe, unburden. ▷ HELP. *Opp* INTENSIFY.

religion *n* 1 belief, creed, divinity, doctrine, dogma, *derog* pietism, theology. 2 creed, cult, denomination, faith, persuasion, sect. □ *Buddhism, Christianity, Hinduism, Islam, Judaism, Sikhism, Taoism, Zen.*

religious *adj* 1 devotional, divine, holy, sacramental, sacred, scriptural, theological. *Opp* SECULAR. 2 church-going, committed, dedicated, devout, God-fearing, godly, *derog* pietistic, pious, *derog* religiose, reverent, righteous, saintly, *derog* sanctimonious, spiritual. *Opp* IRRELIGIOUS. 3 *religious wars.* bigoted, doctrinal, fanatical, sectarian, schismatic.

relinquish *vb* concede, give in, hand over, part with, submit, surrender, yield.

relish *n* 1 appetite, delight, enjoyment, enthusiasm, gusto, pleasure, zest. 2 flavour, piquancy, savour, tang, taste. ● *vb* appreciate, delight in, enjoy, like, love, revel in, savour, take pleasure in.

reluctant *adj* averse, disinclined, grudging, hesitant, loath, unenthusiastic, unwilling. *Opp* EAGER.

rely *vb* **rely on** *inf* bank on, count on, depend on, have confidence in, lean on, put your faith in, *inf* swear by, trust.

remain *vb* old use abide, be left, carry on, continue, endure,

keep on, linger, live on, persevere, persist, stay, *inf* stay put, survive, tarry, wait. **remaining** ▷ RESIDUAL.

remainder *n* balance, excess, extra, remnant, residue, residuum, rest, surplus. ▷ REMAINS.

remains *plur n* 1 crumbs, debris, detritus, dregs, fragments, *inf* leftovers, oddments, *inf* odds and ends, offcuts, remainder, remnants, residue, rubble, ruins, scraps, traces, vestiges, wreckage. 2 *historic remains.* heirloom, heritage, inheritance, keepsake, memento, monument, relic, reminder, souvenir, survival. 3 *human remains.* ashes, body, bones, carcass, corpse.

remake *vb* piece together, rebuild, reconstitute, reconstruct, redo. ▷ RENEW.

remark *n* comment, mention, observation, opinion, reflection, statement, thought, utterance, word. ● *vb* 1 assert, comment, declare, mention, note, observe, pass comment, reflect, say, state. 2 heed, mark, notice, observe, perceive, see, take note of.

remarkable *adj* amazing, astonishing, astounding, conspicuous, curious, different, distinguished, exceptional, extraordinary, important, impressive, marvellous, memorable, notable, noteworthy, odd, out-of-the-ordinary, outstanding, peculiar, phenomenal, prominent, signal, significant, singular, special, strange, striking, surprising, *inf* terrific, *inf* tremendous, uncommon, unforgettable, unusual, wonderful. *Opp* ORDINARY.

remedy n inf answer, antidote, corrective, countermeasure, cure, cure-all, drug, elixir, medicament, medication, medicine, nostrum, palliative, panacea, prescription, redress, relief, restorative, solution, therapy, treatment.
● vb alleviate, inf ameliorate, answer, control, correct, counteract, inf fix, heal, help, mend, mitigate, palliate, put right, rectify, redress, relieve, repair, solve, treat. ▷ CURE.

remember vb 1 be mindful of, have a memory of, have in mind, keep in mind, recognize. 2 learn, memorize, retain. 3 remember old times. be nostalgic about, hark back to, recall, recollect, reminisce about, review, summon up, tell stories about, think back to. 4 remember Christmas. celebrate, commemorate, observe. Opp FORGET.

remind vb give a reminder to, jog the memory of, nudge, prompt.

reminder n 1 aide-mémoire, cue, hint, inf memo, memorandum, mnemonic, note, inf nudge, prompt, inf shopping list. 2 heirloom, inheritance, keepsake, memento, relic, souvenir, survival.

reminisce vb be nostalgic, hark back, look back, recall, remember, review, tell stories, think back.

reminiscence n account, anecdote, memoir, memory, recollection, remembrance.

reminiscent adj evocative, nostalgic, recalling, redolent, suggestive.

remiss adj careless, dilatory, forgetful, irresponsible, lax, negligent, slack, thoughtless. Opp CAREFUL.

remit vb 1 remit a debt. cancel, let off, settle. 2 abate, decrease, ease off, lessen, relax, slacken. 3 dispatch, forward, send, transmit. ▷ PAY.

remittance n allowance, fee, payment.

remnants plur n bits, fragments, inf leftovers, oddments, offcuts, residue, scraps, traces, vestiges. ▷ REMAINS.

remodel vb ▷ RENEW.

remorse n bad conscience, compunction, contrition, grief, guilt, mortification, pangs of conscience, penitence, pricking of conscience, regret, repentance, sadness, self-accusation, self-reproach, shame, sorrow.

remorseful adj ashamed, conscience-stricken, contrite, grief-stricken, guilt-ridden, guilty, penitent, regretful, repentant, rueful, sorry. Opp UNREPENTANT.

remorseless adj dogged, implacable, inexorable, intransigent, merciless, obdurate, pitiless, relentless, ruthless, uncompromising, unforgiving, unkind, unmerciful, unremitting. ▷ CRUEL.

remote adj 1 alien, cut off, desolate, distant, far-away, foreign, God-forsaken, hard to find, inaccessible, isolated, lonely, outlying, out of reach, out of the way, secluded, solitary, unfamiliar, unfrequented, inf unget-at-able, unreachable. Opp CLOSE. 2 a remote chance. doubtful, implausible, improbable, negligible, outside,

poor, slender, slight, small,
unlikely. *Opp* SURE. **3** *a remote*
manner. abstracted, aloof, cold,
cool, detached, haughty, preoccupied, reserved, standoffish,
uninvolved, withdrawn.
Opp FRIENDLY.

removal *n* **1** relocation, remov-
ing, taking away, transfer,
transportation. **2** elimination,
eradication, extermination,
liquidation, purge, purging.
▷ KILLING. **3** *removal from a*
job. deposition, dethronement,
dislodgement, dismissal,
displacement, ejection, expulsion, *inf* firing, making redundant, ousting, redundancy,
inf sacking, transference,
unseating. **4** *removal of teeth*.
drawing, extraction, pulling,
taking out, withdrawal.

remove *vb* **1** abolish, abstract,
amputate (*limb*), banish, clear
away, cut off, cut out, delete,
depose, detach, disconnect,
dismiss, dispense with,
displace, dispose of, do away
with, eject, eliminate, eradicate,
erase, evict, excise, exile, expel,
expunge, *inf* fire, *inf* get rid of,
inf kick out, kill, oust, purge,
root out, rub out, *inf* sack, send
away, separate, strike out,
sweep away, take out, throw
out, turn out, undo, unfasten,
uproot, wash off, wipe (*tape-
recording*), wipe out. **2** *remove*
furniture. carry away, convey,
move, take away, transfer,
transport. **3** *remove a tooth*.
draw out, extract, pull out, take
out. **4** *remove clothes*. doff (*a*
hat), peel off, strip off, take
off.

rend *vb* cleave, lacerate, pull
apart, rip, rupture, shred, split,
tear.

render *vb* **1** cede, deliver,
furnish, give, hand over, offer,
present, proffer, provide,
surrender, tender, yield.
2 *render a song*. execute, interpret, perform, play, produce,
sing. **3** *rendered me speechless*.
cause to be, make.

rendezvous *n* appointment,
assignation, date, engagement,
meeting, meeting-place, *old use*
tryst.

renegade *n* apostate, backslider,
defector, deserter, fugitive,
heretic, mutineer, outlaw, rebel,
runaway, traitor, turncoat.

renege *vb* **renege on** abjure,
abrogate, *inf* back out of, break,
default on, fail to keep, go back
on, *sl* rat on, repudiate, *sl* welsh
on.

renew *vb* **1** bring up to date,
inf do up, *inf* give a face-lift to,
improve, mend, modernize,
overhaul, recondition,
reconstitute, recreate, redecorate, redesign, redevelop, redo,
refit, refresh, refurbish, regenerate, reintroduce, rejuvenate,
remake, remodel, renovate,
repaint, repair, replace, replenish, restore, resume, resurrect,
revamp, revitalize, revive,
touch up, transform, update.
2 *renew an activity*. come back
to, pick up again, recommence,
restart, resume, return to.
3 *renew vows*. confirm, re-
affirm, reiterate, repeat, restate.

renounce *vb* **1** abandon, abjure,
abstain from, declare your
opposition to, deny, desert,
discard, disown, eschew, forgo,
forsake, forswear, give up,
reject, repudiate, spurn.
2 *renounce the throne*. abdicate,
inf quit, relinquish, resign,
surrender.

renovate vb ▷ RENEW.

renovation n improvement, modernization, overhaul, reconditioning, redevelopment, refit, refurbishment, renewal, repair, restoration, transformation, updating.

renowned adj celebrated, distinguished, eminent, illustrious, noted, prominent, well-known. ▷ FAMOUS.

rent n 1 fee, hire, instalment, payment, rental. 2 *a rent in a garment.* ▷ SPLIT. • vb charter, farm out, hire, lease, let.

reorganize vb rationalize, rearrange, re-deploy, reshuffle, restructure.

repair vb 1 inf fix, mend, overhaul, patch up, put right, rectify, refit, restore, service. ▷ RENEW. 2 darn, patch, sew up.

repay vb 1 compensate, give back, pay back, recompense, refund, reimburse, remunerate, settle. 2 avenge, get even, inf get your own back, reciprocate, requite, retaliate, return, revenge.

repeal vb abolish, abrogate, annul, cancel, invalidate, nullify, rescind, reverse, revoke.

repeat vb 1 do again, duplicate, redo, rehearse, replay, replicate, reproduce, re-run, show again. 2 echo, quote, recapitulate, re-echo, regurgitate, reiterate, restate, retell, say again.

repel vb 1 check, drive away, fend off, fight off, hold off, inf keep at bay, parry, push away, rebuff, repulse, resist, ward off, withstand. 2 *repel water.* be impermeable to, exclude, keep out, reject.

3 *cruelty repels us.* alienate, be repellent to, disgust, nauseate, offend, inf put off, revolt, sicken, inf turn off. Opp ATTRACT.

repellent adj 1 impermeable, impervious, resistant, unsusceptible. 2 ▷ REPULSIVE.

repent vb bemoan, be repentant about, bewail, feel repentance for, lament, regret, reproach yourself for, rue.

repentance n contrition, guilt, penitence, regret, remorse, self-accusation, self-reproach, shame, sorrow.

repentant adj apologetic, ashamed, conscience-stricken, contrite, grief-stricken, guilt-ridden, guilty, penitent, regretful, remorseful, rueful, sorry. Opp UNREPENTANT.

repertory n collection, repertoire, repository, reserve, stock, store, supply.

repetitive adj boring, incessant, iterative, monotonous, recurrent, repeated, repeating, repetitious, tautologous, tedious, unchanging, unvaried. ▷ CONTINUAL.

replace vb 1 make good, put back, reinstate, restore, return. 2 be a replacement for, come after, follow, oust, succeed, supersede, supplant, take over from, take the place of. ▷ DEPUTIZE. 3 *replace worn parts.* change, renew, substitute.

replacement n inf fill-in, proxy, stand-in, substitute, successor, understudy.

replenish vb fill up, refill, renew, restock, top up.

replete adj inf bursting, crammed, gorged, inf jampacked, overloaded, sated, stuffed. ▷ FULL.

replica n *inf* carbon copy, clone, copy, duplicate, facsimile, imitation, likeness, model, reconstruction, reproduction.

reply n acknowledgement, answer, *inf* come-back, reaction, rejoinder, response, retort, riposte. • *vb* answer, give a reply, react, rejoin, respond. **reply to** ▷ ACKNOWLEDGE, COUNTER.

report n 1 account, announcement, article, communication, communiqué, description, dispatch, narrative, news, record, statement, story, *inf* write-up. 2 backfire, bang, blast, boom, crack, detonation, discharge, explosion, noise. • *vb* 1 announce, broadcast, circulate, communicate, declare, describe, disclose, divulge, document, give an account of, notify, present a report on, proclaim, publish, put out, record, recount, reveal, state, tell. 2 *report for duty*. announce yourself, check in, clock in, introduce yourself, make yourself known, present yourself, sign in. 3 *report someone to the police*. complain about, denounce, inform against, *inf* tell on.

reporter n columnist, commentator, correspondent, journalist, newscaster, newsman, newswoman, newspaperman, newspaperwoman, news presenter, photojournalist.

repose n calm, calmness, comfort, ease, inactivity, peace, peacefulness, poise, quiescence, quiet, quietness, relaxation, respite, rest, serenity, stasis,

stillness, tranquillity. ▷ SLEEP. *Opp* ACTIVITY.

reprehensible adj blameworthy, culpable, deplorable, disgraceful, immoral, objectionable, regrettable, remiss, shameful, unworthy, wicked. ▷ GUILTY. *Opp* INNOCENT.

represent *vb* 1 act out, assume the guise of, be an example of, embody, enact, epitomize, exemplify, exhibit, express, illustrate, impersonate, incarnate, masquerade as, personify, pose as, present, pretend to be, stand for, symbolize, typify. 2 characterize, define, delineate, depict, describe, draw, paint, picture, portray, reflect, show, sketch. 3 act for, speak for, stand up for.

representation n depiction, figure, icon, image, imitation, likeness, model, picture, portrait, portrayal, resemblance, semblance, statue.

representative adj 1 archetypal, average, characteristic, illustrative, normal, typical. *Opp* ABNORMAL. 2 *representative government*. chosen, democratic, elected, elective, popular. *Opp* TOTALITARIAN. • n 1 delegate, deputy, proxy, spokesman, spokeswoman, stand-in, substitute. 2 agent, *inf* rep, salesman, salesperson, saleswoman, *inf* traveller. 3 ambassador, consul, diplomat, emissary, envoy, legate. 4 *Amer* congressman, councillor, Member of Parliament, MP, ombudsman.

repress *vb* 1 control, crush, curb, keep down, limit, oppress, overcome, put down, quell, restrain, subdue, subjugate. 2 *repress emotion*. *inf* bottle up, frustrate, inhibit, stifle, suppress.

repressed *adj* 1 cold, frigid, frustrated, inhibited, neurotic, *inf* prim and proper, tense, unbalanced, undemonstrative, *inf* uptight. *Opp* UNINHIBITED. 2 *repressed emotion. inf* bottled up, hidden, latent, subconscious, suppressed, unconscious, unfulfilled.

repression *n* 1 authoritarianism, censorship, coercion, control, despotism, dictatorship, oppression, restraint, subjugation, totalitarianism, tyranny. 2 *repression of emotion. inf* bottling up, frustration, inhibition, suffocation, suppression.

repressive *adj* authoritarian, autocratic, brutal, coercive, cruel, despotic, dictatorial, fascist, harsh, illiberal, oppressive, restricting, severe, totalitarian, tyrannical, undemocratic, unenlightened. *Opp* LIBERAL.

reprieve *n* amnesty, pardon, postponement, respite, stay of execution. ● *vb* commute a sentence, forgive, let off, pardon, postpone execution, set free, spare.

reprimand *n* admonition, castigation, censure, condemnation, criticism, *inf* dressing-down, *inf* going-over, *inf* lecture, lesson, *inf* rap on the knuckles, rebuke, remonstration, reproach, reproof, scolding, *inf* slap on the wrist, *inf* slating, *inf* talking-to, *inf* telling-off, *inf* ticking-off, upbraiding, *inf* wigging. ● *vb* admonish, berate, blame, *inf* carpet, castigate, censure, chide, condemn, correct, criticize, disapprove of, *inf* dress down, find fault with, *inf* haul over the coals, *inf* lecture, *inf* rap, rate, *inf* read the riot act to, rebuke, reprehend, reproach, reprove, scold, *inf* slate, *inf* take to task, *inf* teach a lesson, *inf* tell off, *inf* tick off, upbraid. *Opp* PRAISE.

reprisal *n* counter-attack, getting even, redress, repayment, retaliation, retribution, revenge, vengeance.

reproach *n* blame, disapproval, disgrace, scorn. ● *vb* censure, criticize, scold, show disapproval of, upbraid. ▷ REPRIMAND. *Opp* PRAISE.

reproachful *adj* admonitory, censorious, condemnatory, critical, disapproving, disparaging, reproving, scornful, withering.

reproduce *vb* 1 copy, counterfeit, duplicate, forge, imitate, mimic, photocopy, print, redo, reissue, reprint, simulate. ▷ REPEAT. 2 beget young, breed, increase, multiply, procreate, produce offspring, propagate, regenerate, spawn.

reproduction *n* 1 breeding, cloning, increase, multiplying, procreation, proliferation, propagation, spawning. 2 *inf* carbon copy, clone, copy, duplicate, facsimile, fake, forgery, imitation, likeness, print, replica.

repudiate *vb* 1 deny, disagree with, dispute, rebuff, refute, reject, scorn, turn down. *Opp* ACKNOWLEDGE. 2 *repudiate an agreement.* abrogate, discard, disown, go back on, recant, renounce, rescind, retract, reverse, revoke.

repugnant adj ▷ REPULSIVE.

repulsive adj abhorrent, abominable, beastly, disagreeable, disgusting, distasteful, distressing, foul, gross, hateful, hideous, loathsome, nasty, nauseating, nauseous, objectionable, obnoxious, odious, offensive, inf off-putting, repellent, repugnant, revolting, inf sick, sickening, unattractive, unpalatable, unpleasant, unsavoury, unsightly, vile. ▷ UGLY. Opp ATTRACTIVE.

reputable adj creditable, dependable, esteemed, famous, good, highly regarded, honourable, honoured, prestigious, reliable, respectable, respected, trustworthy, unimpeachable, inf up-market, well-thought-of, worthy. Opp DISREPUTABLE.

reputation n character, fame, name, prestige, recognition, renown, repute, standing, stature, status.

reputed adj alleged, assumed, believed, considered, deemed, famed, judged, purported, reckoned, regarded, rumoured, said, supposed, thought.

request n appeal, application, call, demand, entreaty, petition, plea, prayer, question, requisition, solicitation, suit, supplication. ● vb adjure, appeal, apply (for), ask, beg, beseech, call for, claim, demand, desire, entreat, implore, importune, invite, petition, pray for, require, requisition, seek, solicit, supplicate.

require vb 1 be missing, be short of, depend on, lack, need, want. 2 require a response. call for, coerce, command, compel, direct, force, insist, instruct,

make, oblige, order, put pressure on. ▷ REQUEST. **required** ▷ REQUISITE.

requirement n condition, demand, essential, necessity, need, precondition, prerequisite, provision, proviso, qualification, Lat sine qua non, stipulation.

requisite adj compulsory, essential, imperative, indispensable, mandatory, necessary, needed, obligatory, prescribed, required, set, stipulated. Opp OPTIONAL.

requisition n application, authorization, demand, mandate, order, request, voucher. ● vb 1 demand, order, inf put in for, request. 2 appropriate, commandeer, confiscate, expropriate, occupy, seize, take over, take possession of.

rescue n deliverance, emancipation, freeing, liberation, recovery, release, relief, salvage. ● vb 1 emancipate, extricate, free, let go, liberate, loose, ransom, release, save, set free. 2 get back, recover, retrieve, salvage.

research n analysis, enquiry, examination, experimentation, exploration, fact-finding, inquiry, investigation, inf probe, scrutiny, searching, study. ● vb inf check out, inf delve into, experiment, investigate, inf probe, search, study.

resemblance n affinity, closeness, coincidence, comparability, comparison, conformity, congruity, correspondence, equivalence, likeness, similarity, similitude.

resemble *vb* approximate to, bear resemblance to, be similar to, compare with, look like, mirror, sound like, *inf* take after.

resent *vb* begrudge, be resentful about, dislike, envy, feel bitter about, grudge, grumble at, object to, *inf* take exception to, *inf* take umbrage at.

resentful *adj* aggrieved, annoyed, begrudging, bitter, disgruntled, displeased, embittered, envious, grudging, hurt, indignant, irked, jaundiced, jealous, malicious, offended, *inf* peeved, *inf* put out, spiteful, unfriendly, ungenerous, upset, vexed, vindictive. ▷ ANGRY.

resentment *n* animosity, bitterness, discontent, envy, grudge, hatred, hurt, ill-will, indignation, irritation, jealousy, malevolence, malice, pique, rancour, spite, unfriendliness, vexation, vindictiveness. ▷ ANGER.

reservation *n* **1** condition, doubt, hedging, hesitation, misgiving, proviso, qualification, qualm, reluctance, reticence, scepticism, scruple. **2** *hotel reservation.* appointment, booking. **3** *a wildlife reservation.* ▷ RESERVE.

reserve *n* **1** cache, fund, hoard, *inf* nest-egg, reservoir, savings, stock, stockpile, store, supply. **2** *inf* back-up, deputy, *plur* reinforcements, replacement, stand-by, *inf* stand-in, substitute, understudy. **3** *a wildlife reserve.* enclave, game park, preserve, protected area, reservation, safari-park, sanctuary. **4** aloofness, caution, modesty, quietness, reluctance, reticence, self-consciousness,

self-effacement, shyness, *derog* stand-offishness, taciturnity, timidity. ● *vb* **1** earmark, hoard, hold back, keep, keep back, preserve, put aside, retain, save, set aside, stockpile, store up. **2** *reserve seats.* *inf* bag, book, order, pay for. **reserved** ▷ RETICENT.

reside *vb* reside in dwell in, inhabit, live in, lodge in, occupy, settle in.

residence *n old use* abode, address, domicile, dwelling, dwelling-place, habitation, home, quarters, seat. ▷ HOUSE.

resident *adj* in residence, living-in, permanent, remaining, staying. ● *n* citizen, denizen, dweller, householder, house-owner, inhabitant, *inf* local, native.

residual *adj* abiding, continuing, left over, outstanding, persisting, remaining, surviving, unconsumed, unused.

resign *vb* abandon, abdicate, *sl* chuck in, forsake, give up, leave, quit, relinquish, renounce, retire, stand down, step down, surrender, vacate. **resigned** ▷ PATIENT. **resign yourself to** ▷ ACCEPT.

resilient *adj* **1** bouncy, elastic, firm, plastic, pliable, rubbery, springy, supple. *Opp* BRITTLE. **2** *a resilient person.* adaptable, buoyant, irrepressible, strong, tough, unstoppable. *Opp* VULNERABLE.

resist *vb* avoid, be resistant to, check, confront, counteract, defy, face up to, hinder, *inf* hold out against, *inf* hold your ground against, impede, inhibit, keep at bay, oppose, prevent, rebuff, refuse, stand

up to, withstand. ▷ FIGHT.
Opp ASSIST, YIELD.

resistant *adj* defiant, hostile,
intransigent, invulnerable,
obstinate, opposed, refractory,
stubborn, uncooperative, unresponsive, unyielding. **resistant
to** against, impervious to,
invulnerable to, opposed to,
proof against, repellent of, unaffected by, unsusceptible to,
unyielding to. *Opp* SUSCEPT-
IBLE.

resolute *adj* adamant, bold,
committed, constant, courageous, decided, decisive, determined, dogged, firm, immovable, immutable, indefatigable,
derog inflexible, *derog* obstinate, persevering, persistent,
pertinacious, relentless,
resolved, single-minded,
staunch, steadfast, strong-
minded, strong-willed,
derog stubborn, tireless,
unbending, undaunted,
unflinching, unshakable,
unswerving, untiring, unwavering. *Opp* IRRESOLUTE.

resolution *n* 1 boldness,
commitment, constancy, determination, devotion, doggedness,
firmness, *derog* obstinacy,
perseverance, persistence,
pertinacity, purposefulness,
resolve, single-mindedness,
staunchness, steadfastness,
derog stubbornness, tenacity,
will-power. ▷ COURAGE.
2 commitment, oath, pledge,
promise, undertaking, vow.
3 *resolution at a meeting*. decision, motion, proposal, proposition, statement. 4 *resolution of
a problem*. answer, denouement, disentangling, resolving,
settlement, solution, sorting
out.

resolve *n* ▷ RESOLUTION.
● *vb* 1 agree, conclude, decide
formally, determine, elect, fix,
make a decision, make up your
mind, opt, pass a resolution,
settle, undertake, vote. 2 *resolve
a problem*. answer, clear up,
disentangle, figure out, settle,
solve, sort out, work out.

resonant *adj* booming, echoing,
full, pulsating, resounding,
reverberant, reverberating,
rich, ringing, sonorous, thunderous, vibrant, vibrating.

resort *n* 1 alternative, course of
action, expedient, option,
recourse, refuge, remedy,
reserve. 2 *a seaside resort*. holiday town, retreat, spa, *old
use* watering-place. ● *vb* **resort
to** 1 adopt, *inf* fall back on,
have recourse to, make use of,
turn to, use. 2 frequent, go to,
inf hang out in, haunt, invade,
patronize, visit.

resound *vb* boom, echo, pulsate,
resonate, reverberate, ring,
rumble, thunder, vibrate.
resounding ▷ RESONANT.

resourceful *adj* clever, creative,
enterprising, imaginative,
ingenious, innovative, inspired,
inventive, original, skilful,
inf smart, talented.
Opp SHIFTLESS.

resources *plur n* 1 assets, capital, funds, possessions, property, reserves, riches, wealth.
▷ MONEY. 2 *natural resources*.
materials, raw materials.

respect *n* 1 admiration, appreciation, awe, consideration,
courtesy, deference, esteem,
homage, honour, liking, love,
politeness, regard, reverence,
tribute, veneration. 2 *perfect in
every respect*. aspect, attribute,

characteristic, detail, element, facet, feature, particular, point, property, quality, trait, way.
● *vb* admire, appreciate, be polite to, defer to, esteem, have high regard for, honour, look up to, pay homage to, revere, reverence, show respect to, think well of, value, venerate. *Opp* DESPISE.

respectable *adj* **1** decent, genteel, honest, honourable, law-abiding, refined, respected, unimpeachable, upright, worthy. **2** *respectable clothes.* chaste, clean, decorous, dignified, modest, presentable, proper, seemly. *Opp* DISREPUTABLE. **3** *a respectable sum.* ▷ CONSIDERABLE.

respectful *adj* admiring, civil, considerate, cordial, courteous, deferential, dutiful, gentlemanly, gracious, humble, lady-like, obliging, polite, proper, reverent, reverential, *derog* servile, subservient, thoughtful, well-mannered. *Opp* DISRESPECTFUL.

respective *adj* individual, own, particular, personal, relevant, separate, several, special, specific.

respite *n* break, *inf* breather, delay, hiatus, holiday, intermission, interruption, interval, *inf* let-up, lull, pause, recess, relaxation, relief, remission, rest, time off, time out, vacation.

resplendent *adj* brilliant, dazzling, glittering, shining, splendid. ▷ BRIGHT.

respond *vb* respond to **1** acknowledge, answer, counter, give a response to, react to, reciprocate, reply to.

2 *respond to need.* ▷ SYMPATHIZE.

response *n* acknowledgement, answer, reply, comeback, counter, counterblast, feedback, reaction, rejoinder, reply, retort, riposte.

responsible *adj* **1** at fault, culpable, guilty, liable, to blame. **2** *a responsible person.* accountable, answerable, concerned, conscientious, creditable, dependable, diligent, dutiful, ethical, honest, in charge, law-abiding, loyal, mature, moral, reliable, sensible, sober, steady, thinking, thoughtful, trustworthy, unselfish. *Opp* IRRESPONSIBLE. **3** *a responsible job.* burdensome, decision-making, executive, *inf* front-line, important, managerial, *inf* top. *Opp* MENIAL.

responsive *adj* alert, alive, aware, impressionable, interested, open, perceptive, receptive, sensitive, sharp, sympathetic, warm-hearted, wide-awake, willing. *Opp* UNINTERESTED.

rest *n* **1** break, *inf* breather, breathing-space, comfort, ease, hiatus, holiday, idleness, inactivity, indolence, interlude, intermission, interval, leisure, *inf* let-up, *inf* lie-down, *inf* loafing, lull, nap, pause, quiet, recess, relaxation, relief, remission, repose, respite, siesta, tea-break, time off, vacation. ▷ SLEEP. **2** base, brace, bracket, holder, prop, stand, support, trestle, tripod. **3** ▷ REMAINDER. ● *vb* **1** be still, doze, have a rest, idle, laze, lie back, lie down, lounge, nod off, *inf* put your feet up, recline, relax, snooze, *inf* take a nap, *inf* take it easy, unwind. ▷ SLEEP. **2** lean, place, position, prop, set, stand, support. **3** *It all rests on the weather.* depend, hang, hinge, rely, turn. **come to rest** ▷ HALT.

restaurant *n* eating-place. □ *bistro, brasserie, buffet, café, cafeteria, canteen, carvery, diner, dining-room, grill, refectory, snack-bar, steak-house.*

restful *adj* calm, calming, comfortable, leisurely, peaceful, quiet, relaxed, relaxing, reposeful, soothing, still, tranquil, undisturbed, unhurried, untroubled. *Opp* EXHAUSTING.

restless *adj* **1** agitated, anxious, edgy, excitable, fidgety, highly-strung, impatient, *inf* jittery, jumpy, nervous, *inf* on tenterhooks, restive, skittish, uneasy, worked up, worried. ▷ ACTIVE. **2** *a restless night.* disturbed, interrupted, sleepless, *inf* tossing and turning, troubled, uncomfortable, unsettled. *Opp* RESTFUL.

restore *vb* **1** bring back, give back, make restitution, put back, reinstate, replace, return. **2** *restore antiques.* clean, *inf* do up, fix, *inf* make good, mend, rebuild, recondition, reconstruct, refurbish, renew, renovate, repair, touch up. **3** *restore good relations.* re-establish, rehabilitate, reinstate, reintroduce, rekindle, revive. **4** *restore to health.* cure, nurse, rejuvenate, resuscitate, revitalize.

restrain *vb* **1** check, control, curb, govern, hold back, inhibit, keep back, keep under control, limit, regulate, rein in, repress, restrict, stifle, stop, strait-jacket, subdue, suppress.

2 arrest, bridle, confine, detain, fetter, handcuff, harness, imprison, incarcerate, jail, *inf* keep under lock and key, lock up, manacle, muzzle, pinion, tie up. **restrained** ▷ CALM, DISCREET.

restrict *vb* circumscribe, confine, control, cramp, delimit, enclose, impede, imprison, inhibit, keep within bounds, limit, regulate, shut. ▷ RESTRAIN. *Opp* FREE.

restriction *n* ban, check, constraint, control, curb, curfew, inhibition, limit, limitation, proviso, qualification, regulation, restraint, rule, stipulation.

result *n* **1** conclusion, consequence, effect, end-product, fruit, issue, outcome, repercussion, sequel, upshot. **2** *result of a trial.* decision, judgement, verdict. **3** *result of a sum.* answer, product, score, total. ● *vb* arise, be produced, come about, develop, emanate, emerge, ensue, eventuate, follow, happen, issue, occur, proceed, spring, stem, take place, turn out. **result in** ▷ CAUSE.

resume *vb* begin again, carry on, continue, *inf* pick up the threads, proceed, recommence, reconvene, re-open, restart.

resumption *n* continuation, recommencement, re-opening, *inf* restart.

resurrect *vb* breathe new life into, bring back, raise (from the dead), reawaken, restore, resuscitate, revitalize, revive. ▷ RENEW.

retain *vb* **1** *inf* hang on to, hold, hold back, keep, keep control of, maintain, preserve, reserve, save. *Opp* LOSE. **2** *retain moisture.* absorb, soak up. **3** *retain facts.* keep in mind, learn, memorize, remember. *Opp* FORGET.

retaliate *vb* avenge yourself, be revenged, counter-attack, exact retribution, *inf* get even, *inf* get your own back, *inf* give tit for tat, hit back, pay back, repay, revenge yourself, seek retribution, *inf* settle a score, strike back, *inf* take an eye for an eye, take revenge, wreak vengeance.

retaliation *n* counter-attack, reprisal, retribution, revenge, vengeance.

retard *vb* check, handicap, hinder, hold back, hold up, impede, obstruct, postpone, put back, set back, slow down. ▷ DELAY. **retarded** ▷ BACKWARD.

reticent *adj* aloof, *derog* antisocial, bashful, cautious, *derog* cold, cool, demure, diffident, discreet, distant, modest, quiet, remote, reserved, restrained, retiring, secretive, self-conscious, self-effacing, shy, silent, *derog* standoffish, taciturn, timid, uncommunicative, unemotional, undemonstrative, unforthcoming, unresponsive, unsociable, withdrawn. *Opp* DEMONSTRATIVE.

retinue *n* attendants, company, entourage, followers, *inf* hangers-on, servants, suite, train.

retire *vb* **1** give up, leave, quit, resign. **2** *retire from society.* become reclusive, cloister yourself, go away, go into retreat, retreat from the world, sequester yourself, withdraw.

3 aestivate, go to bed, hibernate, *sl* hit the hay. ▷ SLEEP.

retort *n* answer, *inf* comeback, rebuttal, rejoinder, reply, response, retaliation, riposte.
● *vb* answer, counter, react, rejoin, reply, respond, retaliate, return.

retract *vb* **1** draw in, pull back, pull in. **2** abandon, cancel, disclaim, disown, forswear, *inf* have second thoughts about, recant, renounce, repeal, repudiate, rescind, reverse, revoke, withdraw.

retreat *n* **1** departure, escape, evacuation, exit, flight, retirement, withdrawal. **2** *a secluded retreat.* asylum, den, haven, *inf* hideaway, hideout, hiding-place, refuge, resort, sanctuary, shelter. ● *vb* **1** back away, back down, climb down, decamp, depart, evacuate, fall back, flee, give ground, go away, leave, move back, pull back, retire, *inf* run away, take flight, *inf* take to your heels, *inf* turn tail, withdraw. **2** *the floods retreated.* ebb, flow back, recede, shrink back. *Opp* ADVANCE.

retribution *n* compensation, *Lat* quid pro quo, recompense, redress, reprisal, retaliation, revenge, *old use* satisfaction, vengeance. *Opp* FORGIVENESS.

retrieve *vb* bring back, come back with, fetch back, find, get back, make up for, recapture, reclaim, recoup, recover, regain, repossess, rescue, restore, return, salvage, save, take back, trace, track down.

retrograde *adj* backward, negative, regressive, retreating, retrogressive, reverse.

446

retrospective adj backward-looking, looking back, looking behind, nostalgic, with hindsight.

return n 1 advent, arrival, homecoming, reappearance, re-entry. 2 return to normality. reestablishment (of), regression, reversion. 3 return of a problem recrudescence, recurrence, re-emergence, repetition. 4 return of stolen goods. replacing, restitution, restoration, retrieval. 5 return on an investment. benefit, earnings, gain, income, interest, proceeds, profit, yield.
● vb 1 backtrack, come back, do a U-turn, double back, go back, reassemble, reconvene, re-enter, regress, retrace your steps, revert, turn back. 2 put back, readdress, repatriate, replace, restore, send back. 3 return money. exchange, give back, refund, reimburse, repay. 4 return a verdict. inf come up with, deliver, give, proffer, report. 5 The problem returned. inf crop up again, happen again, reappear, recur, resurface.

reveal vb announce, bare, betray, bring to light, communicate, confess, declare, denude, dig up, disclose, display, divulge, exhibit, expose, inf give the game away, lay bare, leak, inf let on, inf let out, inf let slip, make known, open, proclaim, produce, publish, show, show up, inf spill the beans about, inf take the wraps off, tell, uncover, undress, unearth, unfold, unmask, unveil. Opp HIDE.

revel n carnival, festival, fête, inf jamboree, inf rave-up, inf spree. ▷ REVELRY.

● vb carouse, celebrate, inf have a spree, have fun, indulge in revelry, inf live it up, make merry, inf paint the town red. **revel in** ▷ ENJOY.

revelation n admission, announcement, communiqué, confession, declaration, disclosure, discovery, exposé, exposure, information, inf leak, news, proclamation, publication, revealing, unmasking, unveiling.

revelry n carousing, celebration, conviviality, debauchery, festivity, fun, gaiety, inf high jinks, jollification, jollity, inf junketing, inf living it up, merrymaking, revelling, revels, roistering, inf spree. ▷ PARTY.

revenge n reprisal, retaliation, retribution, spitefulness, vengeance, vindictiveness.
● vb avenge, repay. **be revenged** ▷ RETALIATE.

revenue n gain, income, interest, money, proceeds, profits, receipts, returns, takings, yield.

reverberate vb boom, echo, pulsate, resonate, resound, ring, rumble, throb, thunder, vibrate.

revere vb admire, adore, adulate, beatify, esteem, feel reverence for, glorify, honour, idolize, pay homage to, praise, respect, reverence, value, venerate, worship. Opp DESPISE.

reverence n admiration, adoration, adulation, awe, deference, devotion, esteem, glorification, homage, honour, idolization, praise, respect, veneration, worship.

reverent adj adoring, awed, awestruck, deferential, devoted, devout, pious, prayerful, religious, respectful, reverential, solemn, worshipful. *Opp* IRREVERENT.

reverie *n inf* brown study, daydream, dream, fantasy, meditation.

reverse *adj* back, back-to-front, backward, contrary, converse, inverse, inverted, opposite, rear. ● *n* 1 antithesis, contrary, converse, opposite. 2 back, rear, underside, verso, wrong side. 3 defeat, difficulty, disaster, failure, mishap, misfortune, problem, reversal, setback, *inf* upset, vicissitude.
● *vb* 1 change, invert, overturn, transpose, turn round, turn upsidedown. 2 *reverse a car.* back, drive backwards, go into reverse. 3 *reverse a decision.* abandon, annul, cancel, countermand, invalidate, negate, nullify, overturn, quash, recant, repeal, rescind, retract, revoke, undo.

review *n* 1 examination, *inf* look back, *inf* post-mortem, reappraisal, reassessment, recapitulation, reconsideration, re-examination, report, retrospective, study, survey. 2 *book review.* appreciation, assessment, commentary, criticism, critique, evaluation, judgement, notice, *inf* write-up.
● *vb* 1 appraise, assess, consider, evaluate, examine, *inf* go over, inspect, reassess, recapitulate, reconsider, re-examine, scrutinize, study, survey, take stock of, *inf* weigh up. 2 *review a book.* criticize, write a review of.

revise *vb* 1 adapt, alter, change, correct, edit, emend, improve, modify, overhaul, *inf* polish up, reconsider, rectify, *inf* redo,

inf rehash, rephrase, revamp, reword, rework, rewrite, update. 2 *revise for exams.* brush up, *inf* cram, learn, study, *inf* swot.

revival *n* advance, progress, quickening, reanimation, reawakening, rebirth, recovery, renaissance, renewal, restoration, resurgence, resurrection, resuscitation, return, revitalization, upsurge.

revive *vb* 1 awaken, come back to life, *inf* come round, *inf* come to, quicken, rally, reawaken, recover, resurrect, rouse, waken. *Opp* RELAPSE. 2 bring back to life, *inf* cheer up, freshen, invigorate, refresh, renew, restore, resuscitate, revitalize, strengthen. *Opp* WEARY.

revolt *n* civil war, coup, coup d'état, insurrection, mutiny, putsch, rebellion, reformation, revolution, rising, *inf* take-over, uprising. ● *vb* 1 disobey, dissent, mutiny, rebel, riot, rise up. 2 appal, disgust, nauseate, offend, outrage, repel, sicken, upset. **revolting** ▷ OFFENSIVE.

revolution *n* 1 ▷ REVOLT. 2 circuit, cycle, gyration, orbit, rotation, spin, turn. 3 change, reorganization, reorientation, shift, transformation, *inf* turnabout, upheaval, *inf* upset, *inf* U-turn.

revolutionary *adj* 1 insurgent, mutinous, rebel, rebellious, seditious, subversive. 2 *revolutionary ideas.* avant-garde, challenging, creative, different, experimental, extremist, innovative, new, novel, progressive, radical, *inf* unheard-of, upsetting. *Opp* CONSERVATIVE.
● *n* anarchist, extremist,

freedom fighter, insurgent, mutineer, rebel, terrorist.

revolve vb circle, go round, gyrate, orbit, pirouette, pivot, reel, rotate, spin, swivel, turn, twirl, wheel, whirl.

revulsion n abhorrence, aversion, disgust, hatred, loathing, nausea, outrage, repugnance.

reward n award, bonus, bounty, compensation, decoration, favour, honour, medal, payment, prize, recompense, remuneration, requital, return, tribute. *Opp* PUNISHMENT.
● vb compensate, decorate, give a reward to, honour, recompense, remunerate, repay. *Opp* PENALIZE, PUNISH. **rewarding** ▷ PROFITABLE, WORTHWHILE.

rhapsodize vb be expansive, effuse, enthuse, *inf* go into raptures.

rhetoric n *derog* bombast, eloquence, expressiveness, *inf* gift of the gab, grandiloquence, magniloquence, oratory, rhetorical language, *derog* speechifying.

rhetorical adj [*most synonyms derog*] artifical, bombastic, florid, *inf* flowery, fustian, grandiloquent, grandiose, high-flown, insincere, oratorical, ornate, pretentious, verbose, wordy.

rhyme n doggerel, jingle, poem. ▷ VERSE.

rhythm n accent, beat, measure, metre, movement, pattern, pulse, stress, tempo, throb, time.

rhythmic adj beating, measured, metrical, predictable, pulsing, regular, repeated, steady, throbbing. *Opp* IRREGULAR.

ribald adj bawdy, coarse, disrespectful, earthy, naughty, racy, rude, scur·ilous, *inf* smutty, vulgar. ▷ OBSCENE.

ribbon n band, braid, line, strip, stripe, tape, trimming. **in ribbons** ▷ RAGGED.

rich adj 1 affluent, *inf* flush, *inf* loaded, moneyed, opulent, plutocratic, prosperous, wealthy, *inf* well-heeled, well-off, well-to-do. *Opp* POOR. 2 *rich furnishings*. costly, elaborate, expensive, lavish, luxurious, precious, priceless, splendid, sumptuous, valuable. 3 *rich land*. fecund, fertile, fruitful, lush, productive. 4 *a rich harvest*. abundant, ample, bountiful, copious, plenteous, plentiful, profuse, prolific, teeming. 5 *rich colours*. deep, full, intense, strong, vibrant, vivid, warm. 6 *rich food*. cloying, creamy, fat, fattening, fatty, full-flavoured, heavy, highly-flavoured, luscious, sumptuous, sweet. **rich person** billionaire, capitalist, millionaire, plutocrat, tycoon.

riches plur n affluence, fortune, means, money, opulence, plenty, possessions, prosperity, resources, wealth.

rickety adj dilapidated, flimsy, frail, insecure, ramshackle, shaky, tottering, tumbledown, unsteady, wobbly. ▷ WEAK.

rid vb clear, deliver (from), free, purge, rescue, save. **get rid of** ▷ DESTROY, REMOVE.

riddle n 1 *inf* brain-teaser, conundrum, enigma, mystery, *inf* poser, problem, puzzle, question. 2 filter, screen, sieve.
● vb 1 filter, screen, sieve, sift, strain. 2 *riddle with holes*.

honeycomb, *inf* pepper, perforate, pierce, puncture.

ride *n* ▷ JOURNEY. ● *vb* 1 *ride a bike*. control, handle, manage, sit on, steer. 2 *ride on a bike*. be carried, free-wheel, pedal. 3 *ride on a horse*. amble, canter, gallop, trot. ▷ TRAVEL.

ridge *n* arête, bank, crest, edge, embankment, escarpment. ▷ HILL.

ridicule *n* badinage, banter, burlesque, caricature, contumely, derision, invective, jeering, jibing, lampoon, laughter, mockery, parody, raillery, *inf* ribbing, sarcasm, satire, scorn, sneers, taunts, teasing. ● *vb* be sarcastic, be satirical about, burlesque, caricature, chaff, deride, gibe at, guy, hold up to ridicule, jeer at, jibe at, joke about, lampoon, laugh at, make fun of, make jokes about, mimic, mock, parody, pillory, *inf* poke fun at, *inf* rib, satirize, scoff at, *inf* send up, sneer at, subject to ridicule, *inf* take the mickey, taunt, tease, travesty.

ridiculous *adj* absurd, amusing, comic, comical, *inf* crazy, *inf* daft, eccentric, farcical, foolish, grotesque, hilarious, illogical, irrational, laughable, ludicrous, mad, nonsensical, preposterous, senseless, silly, unbelievable, unreasonable, weird, *inf* zany. ▷ FUNNY, STUPID. *Opp* SENSIBLE.

rife *adj* abundant, common, endemic, prevalent, widespread.

rift *n* 1 breach, break, chink, cleft, crack, fracture, gap, gulf, opening, split. 2 *a rift between friends*. alienation, conflict, difference, disagreement, disruption, division, opposition, schism, separation.

rig *n* 1 ▷ RIGGING. 2 *oil rig*. platform. 3 [*inf*] *sporting rig*. apparatus, clothes, equipment, gear, kit, outfit, stuff, tackle. ● *vb* **rig out** equip, fit out, kit out, outfit, provision, set up, supply.

rigging *n* rig, tackle. □ *halyards, ropes and pulleys, sails.*

right *adj* 1 decent, ethical, fair, good, honest, honourable, just, law-abiding, lawful, moral, principled, responsible, righteous, right-minded, upright, virtuous. 2 *right answers*. accurate, apposite, appropriate, apt, correct, exact, factual, faultless, fitting, genuine, perfect, precise, proper, sound, suitable, true, truthful, valid, veracious. 3 *the right way*. advantageous, beneficial, best, convenient, good, normal, preferable, preferred, recommended, sensible, usual. 4 *your right side*. right-hand, starboard [= *right facing bow of ship*]. 5 *right wing in politics*. conservative, fascist, reactionary, Tory. *Opp* LEFT, WRONG. ● *n* 1 decency, equity, ethics, fairness, goodness, honesty, integrity, justice, morality, propriety, reason, truth, virtue. 2 *right to free speech*. entitlement, facility, freedom, liberty, prerogative, privilege. 3 *right to give orders*. authority, commission, franchise, licence, position, power, title. ● *vb* 1 amend, correct, make amends for, put right, rectify, redress, remedy, repair, set right. 2 pick up, set upright, stand upright, straighten up.

righteous *adj* blameless, ethical, God-fearing, good, guiltless, *derog* holier-than-thou, honest, just, law-abiding, moral, pure, *derog* sanctimonious, upright, upstanding, virtuous. *Opp* SINFUL.

rightful *adj* authorized, *Lat* bona fide, correct, just, lawful, legal, legitimate, licensed, licit, proper, real, true, valid. *Opp* ILLEGAL.

rigid *adj* 1 adamantine, firm, hard, inelastic, inflexible, set, solid, steely, stiff, strong, unbending, wooden. ▷ OBSTINATE. 2 *rigid discipline.* harsh, intransigent, punctilious, stern, strict, uncompromising, unkind, unrelenting, unyielding. ▷ RIGOROUS. *Opp* FLEXIBLE.

rigorous *adj* 1 conscientious, demanding, exact, exacting, meticulous, painstaking, precise, punctilious, rigid, scrupulous, strict, stringent, structured, thorough, tough, uncompromising, undeviating, unsparing, unswerving. *Opp* LAX. 2 *rigorous climate.* extreme, hard, harsh, inclement, inhospitable, severe, unfriendly, unpleasant. ▷ COLD. *Opp* MILD.

rim *n* brim, brink, circumference, edge, lip, perimeter, periphery.

rind *n* crust, husk, outer layer, peel, skin.

ring *n* 1 annulus, band, bracelet, circle, circlet, collar, corona, eyelet, girdle, halo, hoop, loop, O, ringlet. 2 *boxing ring.* arena, enclosure, rink. 3 *drugs ring.* association, band, gang, mob, organization, syndicate. ▷ GROUP. 4 *the ring of a bell.* boom, buzz, chime, clang, clink, *inf* ding-a-ling, jangle, jingle,

knell, peal, ping, resonance, reverberation, tinkle, tintinnabulation, tolling. 5 *give me a ring sometime.* *inf* bell, *inf* buzz, call, *inf* tinkle. ● *vb* 1 bind, circle, embrace, encircle, enclose, encompass, gird, surround. 2 boom, buzz, chime, clang, clink, jangle, jingle, peal, ping, resonate, resound, reverberate, sound (the knell), tinkle, toll. 3 call, *inf* give a buzz, phone, ring up, telephone.

rinse *vb* bathe, clean, cleanse, drench, flush, sluice, swill, wash.

riot *n* affray, anarchy, brawl, chaos, commotion, demonstration, disorder, disturbance, fracas, fray, hubbub, imbroglio, insurrection, lawlessness, mass protest, mêlée, mutiny, pandemonium, *inf* punch-up, revolt, rioting, riotous behaviour, rising, row, *inf* rumpus, *inf* shindy, strife, tumult, turmoil, unrest, uproar, violence. ● *vb* brawl, create a riot, *inf* go on the rampage, *inf* go wild, mutiny, rampage, rebel, revolt, rise up, run riot, *inf* take to the streets. ▷ FIGHT.

riotous *adj* anarchic, boisterous, chaotic, disorderly, lawless, mutinous, noisy, obstreperous, rampageous, rebellious, rowdy, tumultuous, uncivilized, uncontrollable, undisciplined, ungovernable, unrestrained, unruly, uproarious, violent, wild. *Opp* ORDERLY.

rip *vb* gash, lacerate, pull apart, rend, rupture, shred, slit, split, tear.

ripe *adj* mature, mellow, ready to use.

ripen vb age, become riper, come to maturity, develop, mature, mellow.

ripple n ▷ WAVE. • vb agitate, disturb, make waves, purl, ruffle, stir.

rise n 1 acclivity, ascent, bank, camber, climb, elevation, hill, hump, incline, ramp, ridge, slope. 2 *a rise in prices.* escalation, gain, increase, increment, jump, leap, upsurge, upswing, upturn, upward movement.
• vb 1 arise, ascend, climb, fly up, go up, jump, leap, levitate, lift, lift off, mount, soar, spring, take off. 2 get to your feet, get up, stand up. 3 *prices rise each year.* escalate, grow, increase, spiral. 4 *cliffs rise above us.* loom, stand out, stick up, tower. **rise up** ▷ REBEL.

risk n 1 chance, likelihood, possibility. 2 danger, gamble, hazard, peril, speculation, uncertainty, venture.
• vb 1 chance, dare, endanger, hazard, imperil, jeopardize. 2 *risk money.* gamble, speculate, venture.

risky adj inf dicey, inf hazardous, inf iffy, perilous, precarious, unsafe.
▷ DANGEROUS. Opp SAFE.

ritual n ceremonial, ceremony, custom, formality, liturgy, observance, practice, rite, routine, sacrament, service, set procedure, solemnity, tradition.

rival n adversary, antagonist, challenger, competitor, contender, contestant, enemy, opponent, opposition.
• vb 1 challenge, compete with, contend with, contest, emulate, oppose, struggle with, undercut, vie with. Opp COOPERATE.

2 be as good as, compare with, equal, match, measure up to.

rivalry n antagonism, competition, competitiveness, conflict, contention, feuding, opposition, strife. Opp COOPERATION.

river n brook, rivulet, stream, watercourse, waterway. □ channel, confluence, delta, estuary, lower reaches, mouth, source, tributary, upper reaches.

road n roadway, route, way. □ alley, arterial road, avenue, boulevard, bridle-path, bridle-way, bypass, byway, byroad, cart-track, causeway, clearway, crescent, cul-de-sac, drive, driveway, dual carriageway, Amer freeway, highway, lane, motorway, one-way street, path, pathway, ring road, service road, side-road, side-street, slip-road, street, thoroughfare, towpath, track, trail, trunk road, old use turnpike.

roam vb amble, drift, meander, prowl, ramble, range, rove, saunter, stray, stroll, inf traipse, travel, walk, wander.

roar vb bellow, cry out, growl, howl, shout, snarl, thunder, yell, yowl. ▷ SOUND.

rob vb burgle, inf con, defraud, hold up, loot, inf mug, old use mulct, pick pockets, pilfer from, pillage, plunder, ransack, rifle, steal from. ▷ STEAL.

robber n bandit, brigand, burglar, cat burglar, inf conman, defrauder, embezzler, old use highwayman, housebreaker, looter, inf mugger, pickpocket, pirate, shoplifter, swindler, thief.

robbery n breaking and entering, burglary, inf con, confidence trick, embezzlement, fraud, hijacking, *inf* hold-up, larceny, looting, *inf* mugging, pilfering, pillage, plunder, sacking, *inf* scrumping, shoplifting, stealing, *inf* stick-up, theft, thieving.

robe *n* cloak, dress, frock, gown. □ bathrobe, caftan, cassock, dressing-gown, habit, housecoat, kimono, peignoir, surplice, vestment. ● *vb* ▷ DRESS.

robot *n* android, automated machine, automaton, bionic man, bionic woman, computerized machine, mechanical man.

robust *adj* 1 athletic, brawny, fit, *inf* hale and hearty, hardy, healthy, hearty, muscular, powerful, rugged, sound, strong, sturdy, tough, vigorous. 2 durable, serviceable, strongly-made, well-made. *Opp* WEAK.

rock *n* boulder, crag, ore, outcrop, scree, stone. □ igneous, metamorphic, sedimentary. □ basalt, chalk, clay, flint, gneiss, granite, gravel, lava, limestone, marble, obsidian, pumice, quartz, sandstone, schist, shale, slate, tufa, tuff. ● *vb* 1 lurch, move to and fro, pitch, reel, roll, shake, sway, swing, toss, totter, wobble. 2 ▷ SHOCK.

rocky *adj* 1 barren, inhospitable, pebbly, rough, rugged, stony. 2 ▷ UNSTEADY.

rod *n* bar, baton, cane, dowel, pole, rail, shaft, spoke, staff, stick, strut, wand.

rogue *n* blackguard, charlatan, cheat, *inf* con-man, fraud, *old use* knave, mischief-maker, *inf* quack, rapscallion, rascal, ruffian, scoundrel, swindler,

trickster, villain, wastrel, wretch. ▷ CRIMINAL.

role *n* 1 character, impersonation, lines, part, portrayal. 2 *role in a business.* contribution, duty, function, job, position, post, task.

roll *n* 1 cylinder, drum, reel, scroll, spool, tube. 2 catalogue, directory, index, inventory, list, listing, record, register. ● *vb* 1 go round, gyrate, move round, revolve, rotate, run, somersault, spin, tumble, turn, twirl, whirl. 2 coil, curl, furl, make into a roll, twist, wind, wrap. 3 *roll the lawn.* flatten, level off, level out, smooth. 4 *ship rolled in the storm.* lumber, lurch, pitch, reel, rock, stagger, sway, toss, totter, wallow, welter. **rolling** ▷ WAVY. **roll in, roll up** ▷ ARRIVE.

romance *n* 1 idyll, love story, novel. ▷ WRITING. 2 adventure, colour, excitement, fascination, glamour, mystery. 3 affair, amour, attachment, intrigue, liaison, love affair, relationship.

romantic *adj* 1 colourful, dream-like, exotic, fabulous, fairy-tale, glamorous, idyllic, nostalgic, picturesque. 2 *romantic feelings.* affectionate, amorous, emotional, erotic, loving, passionate, *inf* sexy, *inf* soppy, tender. 3 *romantic fiction.* emotional, escapist, heart-warming, nostalgic, reassuring, sentimental, *derog* sloppy, tender, unrealistic. 4 *romantic ideals.* chimerical, *inf* head in the clouds, idealistic, illusory, impractical, improbable, quixotic, starry-eyed, unworkable, Utopian, visionary. *Opp* REALISTIC.

room n 1 *inf* elbow-room, freedom, latitude, leeway, margin, scope, space, territory. 2 *a room in a house.* apartment, cell, *old use* chamber. □ ante-room, attic, audience chamber, bathroom, bedroom, boudoir, cell, cellar, chapel, classroom, cloakroom, conservatory, corridor, dining-room, dormitory, drawing-room, dressing-room, gallery, guest-room, hall, kitchen, kitchenette, laboratory, landing, larder, laundry, lavatory, library, living-room, loft, lounge, music-room, nursery, office, pantry, parlour, passage, play-room, porch, salon, saloon, scullery, sick-room, sitting-room, spare room, stateroom, store-room, studio, study, toilet, utility room, waiting-room, ward, washroom, WC, workroom, workshop.

roomy *adj* capacious, commodious, large, sizeable, spacious, voluminous. ▷ BIG. *Opp* SMALL.

root n 1 radicle, rhizome, rootlet, tap root, tuber. 2 *the root of a problem.* base, basis, bottom, cause, foundation, fount, origin, seat, source, starting-point.
• vb **root out** ▷ REMOVE.

rope n cable, cord, line, strand, string. □ halyard, hawser, lanyard, lariat, lasso, tether. • vb bind, hitch, lash, moor, tether, tie. ▷ FASTEN.

rot n 1 corrosion, corruption, decay, decomposition, deterioration, disintegration, dry rot, mould, mouldiness, putrefaction, wet rot. 2 *What rot!* ▷ NONSENSE. • vb become rotten, corrode, crumble, decay, decompose, degenerate, deteriorate, disintegrate, fester, go bad, *inf* go off, perish, putrefy, rust, spoil.

rota n list, roster, schedule, time-table.

rotary *adj* gyrating, revolving, rotating, rotatory, spinning, turning, twirling, twisting, whirling.

rotate vb 1 go round, gyrate, have a rotary movement, move round, pirouette, pivot, reel, revolve, roll, spin, swivel, turn, turn anticlockwise, turn clockwise, twiddle, twirl, twist, wheel, whirl. 2 *rotate duties.* alternate, pass round, share out, take in turn, take turns.

rotten *adj* 1 bad, corroded, crumbling, decayed, decaying, decomposed, disintegrating, foul, mouldering, mouldy, *inf* off, overripe, perished, putrid, rusty, smelly, tainted, unfit for consumption, unsound. ▷ SOUND.
2 ▷ IMMORAL.

rough *adj* 1 broken, bumpy, coarse, craggy, irregular, knobbly, jagged, lumpy, pitted, rocky, rugged, rutted, stony, uneven. 2 *rough skin.* bristly, callused, chapped, coarse, hairy, harsh, leathery, ragged, scratchy, shaggy, unshaven, wrinkled. 3 *a rough sea.* agitated, choppy, stormy, tempestuous, turbulent, violent, wild. 4 *a rough voice.* cacophonous, discordant, grating, gruff, harsh, hoarse, husky, rasping, raucous, strident, unmusical, unpleasant. *Opp* SMOOTH. 5 *rough manners, a rough fellow.* badly-behaved, bluff, blunt, brusque, churlish, ill-bred, impolite, loutish, rowdy, rude, surly, *inf* ugly, uncivil, uncivilized, undisciplined, unfriendly. 6 *rough treatment.* brutal, cruel, painful, ruffianly,

thuggish, violent. **7** *rough work.*
amateurish, careless, clumsy,
crude, hasty, imperfect, inept,
inf rough and ready, unfinished, unpolished, unskilful.
8 *a rough estimate.* approximate, general, hasty, imprecise,
inexact, sketchy, vague.
Opp EXACT, GENTLE, SMOOTH.

roughly *adv* about, approximately, around, close to, nearly.

round *adj* **1** [*two-dimensional*]
annular, circular, curved, disc-
shaped, hoop-shaped, orbicular,
ring-shaped. **2** [*three-dimensional*] ball-shaped, bulbous,
cylindrical, globelike, globoid,
globular, orb-shaped, spherical,
spheroid. **3** *a round figure.*
ample, full, plump, rotund,
rounded, well-padded. ▷ FAT.
● *n* bout, contest, game, heat,
stage. ● *vb* skirt, travel round,
turn. **round off** ▷ COMPLETE.
round on ▷ ATTACK. **round
the bend** ▷ MAD. **round the
clock** ▷ CONTINUOUS. **round
up** ▷ ASSEMBLE.

roundabout *adj* circuitous,
circular, devious, indirect,
long, meandering, oblique,
rambling, tortuous, twisting,
winding. *Opp* DIRECT.
● *n* **1** carousel, merry-go-round,
old use whirligig. **2** traffic
island.

round-shouldered *adj* hunch-
backed, humpbacked, stooping.

rouse *vb* **1** arise, arouse,
awaken, call, get up, wake up.
2 *rouse to a frenzy.* agitate,
animate, electrify, excite, galvanize, goad, incite, inflame,
provoke, spur on, stimulate,
stir up, *inf* wind up, work up.

rout *vb* conquer, crush, overpower, overwhelm, put to

flight, *inf* send packing.
▷ DEFEAT.

route *n* course, direction, itinerary, journey, path, road, way.

routine *adj* accustomed,
commonplace, customary,
everyday, familiar, habitual,
normal, ordinary, perfunctory,
planned, run-of-the-mill,
scheduled, uneventful, well-
rehearsed. ● *n* **1** course of
action, custom, *inf* drill, habit,
method, pattern, plan, practice,
procedure, schedule, system,
way. **2** *comedy routine.* act,
number, performance,
programme, set piece.

row *n* **1** [rhyme with *crow*]
chain, column, cordon, file,
line, queue, rank, sequence,
series, string, tier. **2** [rhyme
with *cow*] ado, commotion, fuss,
hubbub, hullabaloo, *inf* racket,
rumpus, tumult, uproar.
▷ NOISE. **3** altercation, argument, controversy, disagreement, dispute, fight, fracas,
inf ructions, *inf* slanging match,
squabble. ▷ QUARREL.
● *vb* **1** [rhyme with *crow*] *row a
boat.* move, propel, scull.
2 [rhyme with *cow*] ▷ QUARREL.

rowdy *adj* badly-behaved, boisterous, disorderly, ill-disciplined, irrepressible, lawless,
obstreperous, riotous, rough,
turbulent, undisciplined,
unruly, violent, wild. ▷ NOISY.
Opp QUIET.

royal *adj* imperial, kingly,
majestic, princely, queenly,
regal, stately. ● *n* [*inf*] member
of royal family. □ consort, Her/
His Majesty, Her/His Royal
Highness, king, monarch,
prince, princess, queen, queen
mother, regent, sovereign.
▷ NOBLE.

rub vb 1 caress, knead, massage, smooth, stroke. 2 abrade, chafe, graze, scrape, wear away. 3 *rub clean*. buff, burnish, polish, scour, scrub, shine, wipe. **rub it in** ▷ EMPHASIZE. **rub out** ▷ ERASE. **rub up the wrong way** ▷ ANNOY.

rubbish n 1 debris, detritus, dregs, dross, filth, flotsam and jetsam, garbage, junk, leavings, *inf* left-overs, litter, lumber, muck, *inf* odds and ends, offal, offcuts, refuse, rejects, rubble, scrap, slops, sweepings, trash, waste. 2 ▷ NONSENSE.

rubble n broken bricks, debris, fragments, remains, ruins, wreckage.

ruddy adj fresh, flushed, glowing, healthy, red, sunburnt.

rude adj 1 abrupt, abusive, bad-mannered, bad-tempered, blasphemous, blunt, boorish, brusque, cheeky, churlish, coarse, common, condescending, contemptuous, discourteous, disparaging, disrespectful, foul, graceless, gross, ignorant, ill-bred, ill-mannered, impertinent, impolite, improper, impudent, in bad taste, inconsiderate, indecent, insolent, insulting, loutish, mocking, naughty, oafish, offensive, offhand, patronizing, peremptory, personal (*remarks*), saucy, scurrilous, shameless, tactless, unchivalrous, uncivil, uncomplimentary, uncouth, ungracious, *old use* unmannerly, unprintable, vulgar. ▷ OBSCENE. Opp POLITE. 2 *rude workmanship*. awkward, basic, bumbling, clumsy, crude, inartistic, primitive, rough, rough-hewn, simple, unpolished, unskilful, unsophisticated,

unsubtle. Opp SOPHISTICATED. **be rude to** ▷ INSULT.

rudeness n abuse, *inf* backchat, bad manners, boorishness, *inf* cheek, churlishness, condescension, contempt, discourtesy, disrespect, ill-breeding, impertinence, impudence, incivility, insolence, insults, oafishness, tactlessness, uncouthness, vulgarity.

rudiments plur n basic principles, basics, elements, essentials, first principles, foundations, fundamentals.

rudimentary adj basic, crude, elementary, embryonic, immature, initial, introductory, preliminary, primitive, provisional, undeveloped. Opp ADVANCED.

ruffian n *inf* brute, bully, desperado, gangster, hoodlum, hooligan, lout, mugger, rogue, scoundrel, thug, *inf* tough, villain, *inf* yob.

ruffle vb 1 agitate, disturb, ripple, stir. 2 *ruffle your hair*. derange, disarrange, dishevel, disorder, *inf* mess up, rumple, tangle, tousle. 3 *ruffle your composure*. annoy, confuse, disconcert, disquiet, fluster, irritate, *inf* nettle, *inf* rattle, *inf* throw, unnerve, unsettle, upset, vex, worry. Opp SMOOTH.

rug n blanket, coverlet, mat, matting.

rugged adj 1 bumpy, craggy, irregular, jagged, pitted, rocky, rough, stony, uneven. 2 *rugged conditions*. arduous, difficult, hard, harsh, onerous, rough, severe, tough. 3 *rugged good looks*. burly, hardy, husky, muscular, robust, rough,

strong, sturdy, ungraceful,
unpolished, weather-beaten.

ruin n bankruptcy, breakdown,
collapse, inf crash, destruction,
downfall, end, failure, fall,
ruination, undoing, wreck.
● vb damage, demolish, destroy
devastate, flatten, overthrow,
shatter, spoil, wreck. **ruins**
debris, havoc, remains, rubble,
wreckage.

ruined adj crumbling, derelict,
dilapidated, fallen down, in
ruins, ramshackle, ruinous,
tumbledown, uninhabitable,
unsafe, wrecked.

ruinous adj 1 apocalyptic,
calamitous, cataclysmic, catastrophic, crushing, destructive,
devastating, dire, disastrous,
fatal, harmful, injurious,
pernicious, shattering.
2 ▷ RUINED.

rule n 1 axiom, code, decree,
plur guidelines, law, ordinance,
practice, precept, principle,
regulation, ruling, statute.
2 administration, ascendancy,
authority, command, control,
domination, dominion, empire,
government, influence, jurisdiction, management, mastery,
oversight, power, regime, reign,
sovereignty, supervision,
supremacy, sway. 3 as a
general rule. convention,
custom, norm, routine, standard. ● vb 1 administer, be the
ruler of, command, control,
direct, dominate, govern, guide,
hold sway, lead, manage,
predominate, reign, run, superintend. 2 adjudicate, decide,
decree, deem, determine, find,
judge, pronounce, resolve. **rule
out** ▷ EXCLUDE.

ruler n administrator, inf Big
Brother, law-maker, leader,

manager. □ autocrat, Caesar,
demagogue, despot, dictator,
doge, emir, emperor, empress,
governor, kaiser, king, lord,
monarch, potentate, president,
prince, princess, queen, rajah,
regent, satrap, sovereign, sultan,
suzerain, triumvirate [= three
ruling jointly], tyrant, tsar, vice-
roy. ▷ CHIEF.

rumour n chat, inf chit-chat,
gossip, hearsay, inf low-down,
news, prattle, report, scandal,
inf tittle-tattle, whisper.

run n 1 canter, dash, gallop, jog,
marathon, race, sprint, trot. 2 a
run in the car. drive, excursion,
jaunt, journey, joyride, ride,
inf spin, trip. 3 run of bad luck.
chain, sequence, series, stretch.
4 chicken run. compound, coop,
enclosure, pen. ● vb 1 bolt,
canter, career, dash, gallop,
hare, hurry, jog, race, rush,
scamper, scoot, scurry, scuttle,
speed, sprint, tear, trot. 2 buses
run hourly. go, operate, ply,
provide a service, travel. 3 car
runs well. behave, function,
perform, work. 4 water runs
downhill. cascade, dribble,
flow, gush, leak, pour, spill,
stream, trickle. 5 Who runs the
country? administer, conduct,
control, direct, govern, look
after, maintain, manage, rule,
supervise. **run across** ▷ MEET.
run after ▷ PURSUE. **run
away** ▷ ESCAPE. **run into**
▷ MEET.

runner n 1 athlete, competitor,
entrant, hurdler, jogger,
participant, sprinter. 2 courier,
dispatch-rider, errand-boy,
errand-girl, messenger.
3 plant sends out runners.
offshoot, shoot, sprout, sucker,
tendril.

runny adj fluid, free-flowing, liquid, running, thin, watery. Opp SOLID, VISCOUS.

rupture n 1 breach, break, burst, cleavage, fracture, puncture, rift, split. 2 rupture between friends. break-up, disunity, schism, separation. 3 [medical] hernia. ● vb break, burst, fracture, part, separate, split.

rural adj agrarian, agricultural, Arcadian, bucolic, countrified, pastoral, rustic, sylvan. Opp URBAN.

rush n 1 bustle, dash, haste, hurry, panic, pressure, race, scramble, speed, turmoil, urgency. 2 rush of water. cataract, flood, gush, spate, surge. 3 rush of people. charge, onslaught, stampede. ● vb bolt, burst, bustle, canter, career, charge, dash, fly, gallop, inf get a move on, haste, hasten, hurry, jog, make haste, move fast, race, run, scamper, inf scoot, scramble, scurry, scuttle, shoot, speed, sprint, stampede, inf step on it, inf tear, trot, inf zoom.

rust vb become rusty, corrode, crumble away, oxidize, rot.

rustic adj 1 ▷ RURAL. 2 rustic simplicity. artless, clumsy, crude, naïve, derog oafish, plain, rough, simple, uncomplicated, uncultured, unpolished, unsophisticated.

rusty adj 1 corroded, oxidized, rotten, tarnished. 2 [inf] My French is rusty. dated, forgotten, out of practice, unused.

rut n 1 channel, furrow, groove, indentation, pothole, track, trough, wheel-mark. 2 in a rut. dead end, habit, pattern, routine, treadmill.

ruthless adj bloodthirsty, brutal, callous, cruel, dangerous, ferocious, fierce, hard, heartless, inexorable, inhuman, merciless, pitiless, relentless, sadistic, unfeeling, unrelenting, unsympathetic, vicious, violent. Opp MERCIFUL.

S

sabotage n disruption, vandalism, wilful damage, wrecking. ● vb cripple, damage, destroy, disable, disrupt, incapacitate, put out of action, inf throw a spanner in the works (of), vandalize, wreck.

sack n 1 bag, pouch. 2 inf the boot, inf the chop, dismissal, firing, redundancy, inf your cards. ● vb 1 inf axe, discharge, dismiss, inf fire, give someone notice, inf give someone the boot, inf give someone the chop, inf give someone the sack, lay off, make redundant. 2 ▷ DESTROY, PLUNDER. **get the sack** be dismissed, be sacked, inf get your cards, get your marching orders, lose your job.

sacred adj blessed, blest, consecrated, dedicated, divine, godly, hallowed, holy, religious, revered, sacrosanct, sanctified, venerable, venerated. Opp SECULAR.

sacrifice n immolation, oblation, offering, propitiation, votive offering. ● vb 1 immolate, kill, offer up, slaughter, yield up. 2 abandon, forfeit, forgo, give up, let go, lose, relinquish, renounce, surrender.

sacrilege n blasphemy, desecration, disrespect, heresy, impiety, irreverence, profanation.

sacrilegious adj atheistic, blasphemous, disrespectful, heretical, impious, irreligious, irreverent, profane, ungodly.
▷ WICKED. Opp REVERENT.

sacrosanct adj inviolable, inviolate, protected, respected, secure, untouchable. ▷ SACRED.

sad adj 1 abject, broken-hearted, careworn, cheerless, crestfallen, dejected, depressed, despondent, disappointed, disconsolate, discontented, discouraged, disgruntled, disheartened, disillusioned, dismal, dispirited, dissatisfied, distressed, doleful, dolorous, inf down, downcast, down-hearted, dreary, forlorn, friendless, funereal, gloomy, glum, grave, grief-stricken, grieving, grim, guilty, heartbroken, inf heavy, heavy-hearted, homesick, hopeless, in low spirits, inf in the doldrums, joyless, lachrymose, lonely, inf long-faced, inf low, lugubrious, melancholy, miserable, moody, moping, morose, mournful, pathetic, penitent, pessimistic, piteous, pitiable, pitiful, plaintive, poignant, regretful, rueful, saddened, serious, sober, sombre, sorrowful, sorry, tearful, troubled, unhappy, unsatisfied, upset, wistful, woebegone, woeful, wretched. 2 *sad news*. calamitous, deplorable, depressing, disastrous, discouraging, dispiriting, distressing, grievous, heartbreaking, heart-rending, lamentable, morbid, moving, painful, regrettable, inf tear-jerking, touching,

tragic, unfortunate, unsatisfactory, unwelcome, upsetting. 3 a *sad state of disrepair*.
▷ UNSATISFACTORY. Opp HAPPY.

sadden vb aggrieve, inf break someone's heart, deject, depress, disappoint, discourage, dishearten, dismay, dispirit, distress, grieve, make sad, upset. Opp CHEER.

sadistic adj barbarous, beastly, brutal, inhuman, monstrous, perverted, pitiless, ruthless, vicious. ▷ CRUEL.

sadness n bleakness, care, dejection, depression, desolation, despair, despondency, disappointment, disillusionment, dissatisfaction, distress, dolour, gloom, glumness, grief, heartbreak, heaviness, homesickness, hopelessness, joylessness, loneliness, melancholy, misery, moping, moroseness, mournfulness, pessimism, poignancy, regret, ruefulness, seriousness, soberness, sombreness, sorrow, tearfulness, trouble, unhappiness, wistfulness, woe.
Opp HAPPINESS.

safe adj 1 defended, foolproof, guarded, immune, impregnable, invulnerable, protected, secured, shielded. ▷ SECURE. Opp VULNERABLE. 2 inf alive and well, inf all right, inf in one piece, intact, sound, undamaged, unharmed, unhurt, uninjured, unscathed, well, whole. 3 *safe drivers*. cautious, circumspect, dependable, reliable, trustworthy. 4 *safe pets*. docile, friendly, harmless, innocuous, tame. 5 *safe to drink*. decontaminated, drinkable, eatable, fit for human consumption, fresh, good, non-poisonous, non-toxic, pasteurized, potable, pure, puri-

459

fied, uncontaminated, unpolluted, wholesome. **6** *safe vehicle.* airworthy, roadworthy, seaworthy, tried and tested. *Opp* DANGEROUS. **make safe** ▷ SECURE. **safe keeping** care, charge, custody, guardianship, keeping, protection.

safeguard *vb* care for, defend, keep safe, look after, protect, shelter, shield.

safety *n* **1** cover, immunity, invulnerability, protection, refuge, sanctuary, security, shelter. **2** *safety of air travel.* dependability, harmlessness, reliability.

sag *vb* be limp, bend, dip, droop, fall, flop, hang down, sink, slump. ▷ DROP.

sail *n* **1** canvas. □ *foresail, gaffsail, jib, lateen sail, lugsail, mainsail, mizzen, spinnaker, spritsail, topsail.* **2** cruise, seapassage, voyage. ▷ JOURNEY.
● *vb* **1** captain, navigate, paddle, pilot, punt, row, skipper, steer. **2** cruise, go sailing, put to sea, set sail, steam. ▷ TRAVEL.

sailor *n* mariner, seafarer, *old use* sea dog, seaman. □ *able seaman, bargee, boatman, boatswain, bosun, captain, cox, coxswain,* plur *crew, deck-hand, helmsman, mate, midshipman, navigator, pilot, rating, rower, skipper, yachtsman, yachtswoman.*

saintly *adj* angelic, blessed, blest, chaste, godly, holy, innocent, moral, pious, pure, religious, righteous, seraphic, sinless, virginal, virtuous. ▷ GOOD. *Opp* SATANIC.

sake *n* account, advantage, behalf, benefit, gain, good, interest, welfare.

salary *n* compensation, earnings, emolument, income, pay, payment, remuneration, stipend, wages.

sale *n* marketing, selling, trade, traffic, transaction, vending. □ *auction, bazaar, closing-down sale, fair, jumble sale, market, rummage sale, spring sale.*

salesperson *n* assistant, auctioneer, representative, salesman, saleswoman, shopboy, shop-girl, shopkeeper.

saliva *n inf* dribble, *inf* spit, spittle, sputum.

sallow *adj* anaemic, bloodless, colourless, etiolated, pale, pallid, pasty, unhealthy, wan, yellowish.

salt *adj* brackish, briny, saline, salted, salty, savoury. *Opp* FRESH.

salubrious *adj* health-giving, healthy, hygienic, invigorating, nice, pleasant, refreshing, sanitary, wholesome. *Opp* UNHEALTHY.

salute *n* acknowledgement, gesture, greeting, salutation, wave. ● *vb* accost, acknowledge, address, greet, hail, honour, pay respects to, recognize. ▷ GESTURE.

salvage *n* **1** reclamation, recovery, rescue, retrieval, salvation, saving. **2** recyclable material, waste. ● *vb* conserve, preserve, reclaim, recover, recycle, redeem, rescue, retrieve, reuse, save, use again.

salvation *n* deliverance, escape, help, preservation, redemption, rescue, saving, way out. *Opp* DAMNATION.

salve *n* balm, cream, demulcent, embrocation, emollient, liniment, lotion, ointment,

unguent. • *vb* alleviate,
appease, assuage, comfort, ease,
mitigate, mollify, soothe.

same *adj* 1 actual, identical, self-
same. 2 *two women wearing the
same jacket.* analogous, comparable, consistent, corresponding,
duplicate, equal, equivalent,
indistinguishable, interchangeable, matching, parallel, similar, synonymous [= *having
same meaning*], twin, unaltered,
unchanged, uniform, unvaried.
Opp DIFFERENT.

sample *n* bit, demonstration,
example, foretaste, free sample,
illustration, indication,
instance, model, pattern, representative piece, selection, snippet, specimen, taste, trailer (*of
film*), trial offer.

• *vb* experience, inspect, take a
sample of, taste, test, try.

sanatorium *n* clinic, convalescent home, hospital, nursing
home, rest-home.

sanctify *vb* beatify, bless, canonize, consecrate, hallow, justify,
purify.

sanctimonious *adj* canting,
holier-than-thou, hypocritical,
insincere, moralizing, pharisaical, pietistic, *sl* pi, pious, self-
righteous, sententious,
inf smarmy, smug, superior,
unctuous.

sanction *n* agreement, approval,
authorization, *inf* blessing,
confirmation, consent, encouragement, endorsement, legaliza-
tion, licence, permission, ratification, support, validation.

• *vb* agree to, allow, approve,
authorize, confirm, consent to,
endorse, *inf* give your blessing
to, give permission for, legalize,
legitimize, licence, permit,
ratify, support, validate.

sanctity *n* divinity, godliness.
grace, holiness, piety, sacredness, saintliness.

sanctuary *n* 1 asylum, haven,
protection, refuge, retreat,
safety, shelter. 2 *wildlife sanctuary.* conservation area, park,
preserve, reservation, reserve.
3 *a holy sanctuary.* chapel,
church, holy of holies, holy
place, sanctum, shrine, temple.

sands *plur n* beach, seaside,
shore, *poet* strand.

sane *adj inf* all there, balanced,
Lat compos mentis, *inf* in your
right mind, level-headed, lucid,
normal, of sound mind,
rational, reasonable, sensible,
sound, stable, well-balanced.
Opp MAD.

sanguine *adj* buoyant, cheerful,
confident, expectant, hopeful,
inf looking on the bright side,
optimistic, positive.
Opp PESSIMISTIC.

sanitary *adj* aseptic, bacteria-
free, clean, disinfected, germ-
free, healthy, hygienic, pure,
salubrious, sterile, sterilized,
uncontaminated, unpolluted,
wholesome. *Opp* UNHEALTHY.

sanitation *n* drainage, drains,
lavatories, sanitary arrangements, sewage disposal, sewers.

sap *n* fluid, life-blood, moisture,
vigour, vitality, vital juices.
• *vb* bleed, drain. ▷ EXHAUST.

sarcasm *n* acerbity, asperity,
contumely, derision, irony,
malice, mockery, ridicule,
satire, scorn.

sarcastic *adj* acerbic, acidulous,
biting, caustic, contemptuous,
cutting, demeaning, derisive,
disparaging, hurtful, ironic,
ironical, mocking, satirical,
scathing, sharp, sneering, spite-

461

ful, taunting, trenchant, venomous, vitriolic, withering, wounding. ▷ HUMOROUS.

sardonic adj bitter, black, cruel, cynical, grim, heartless, malicious, mordant, wry.
▷ HUMOROUS.

sash n band, belt, cummerbund, girdle, waistband.

satanic adj demonic, devilish, diabolical, fiendish, hellish, infernal, Mephistophelian.
▷ WICKED. Opp SAINTLY.

satchel n bag, pouch, school-bag, shoulder-bag.

satellite n 1 moon, planet.
2 man-made satellite. spacecraft, sputnik.

satire n burlesque, caricature, derision, invective, irony, lampoon, mockery, parody, ridicule, satirical comedy, scorn, inf send-up, inf spoof, inf take-off, travesty.
▷ WRITING.

satirical adj critical, derisive, disparaging, disrespectful, ironic, irreverent, mocking, scornful. ▷ HUMOROUS, SARCASTIC.

satirize vb be satirical about, burlesque, caricature, criticize, deride, hold up to ridicule, lampoon, laugh at, make fun of, mimic, mock, parody, pillory, inf send up, inf take off, travesty. ▷ RIDICULE.

satisfaction n comfort, content, contentment, delight, enjoyment, fulfilment, gratification, happiness, joy, pleasure, pride, self-satisfaction.
Opp DISSATISFACTION.

satisfactory adj acceptable, adequate, inf all right, competent, fair, inf good enough, inf not bad, passable, pleasing,

satisfying, sufficient, suitable, tolerable, inf up to scratch.
Opp UNSATISFACTORY.

satisfy vb appease, assuage, comfort, comply with, content, fill, fulfil, gratify, make happy, meet, pacify, placate, please, put an end to, quench, sate, satiate, serve (a need), settle, slake (thirst), solve, supply.
Opp FRUSTRATE. **satisfied**
▷ CONTENT.

saturate vb drench, fill, impregnate, permeate, soak, souse, steep, suffuse, waterlog, wet.

sauce n 1 condiment, gravy, ketchup, relish. 2 ▷ INSOLENCE.

saucepan n cauldron, pan, pot, skillet, stockpot.

savage adj 1 barbarian, barbaric, cannibal, heathen, pagan, primitive, uncivilized, uncultivated, uneducated.
Opp CIVILIZED. 2 savage beasts. feral, fierce, undomesticated, untamed, wild. 3 savage attack. angry, atrocious, barbarous, beastly, bestial, blistering, bloodthirsty, bloody, brutal, callous, cold-blooded, cruel, demonic, diabolical, ferocious, fierce, heartless, inhuman, merciless, murderous, pitiless, ruthless, sadistic, unfeeling, vicious, violent. Opp TAME.
● n barbarian, beast, brute, cannibal, fiend, savage person.
● vb attack, bite, claw, lacerate, maul, mutilate.

save vb 1 be sparing with, collect, conserve, economize, hoard, hold back, hold on to, invest, keep, inf lay aside, inf put by, put in a safe place, reserve, retain, scrape together, set aside, inf stash away, store up, take care of, use wisely.

Opp WASTE. **2** *save from captivity.* bail out, deliver, free, liberate, ransom, redeem, release, rescue, set free. **3** *save from destruction.* recover, retrieve, salvage. **4** *save from danger.* defend, deliver, guard, keep safe, preserve, protect, safeguard, screen, shelter, shield. **5** *saved me from looking a fool.* check, deter, preclude, prevent, spare, stop. *Opp* ABANDON.

saving *n* **1** economizing, frugality, parsimony, prudence, *inf* scrimping and scraping, thrift. **2** cut, discount, economy, reduction. **savings** capital, funds, investments, *inf* nest-egg, reserves, resources, riches, wealth.

saviour *n* **1** champion, defender, deliverer, *inf* friend in need, guardian, liberator, rescuer. **2** [*theological*] Christ, Our Lord, The Messiah, The Redeemer.

savour *n* flavour, piquancy, relish, smell, tang, taste, zest. ● *vb* appreciate, delight in, enjoy, relish, smell, taste.

savoury *adj* appetizing, delicious, flavoursome, piquant, salty. ▷ TASTY. *Opp* SWEET.

saw *n* **1** □ chain-saw, hack-saw, jigsaw, ripsaw. **2** [*old use*] *just an old saw.* ▷ SAYING.
● *vb* ▷ CUT.

say *vb* affirm, allege, announce, answer, articulate, assert, asseverate, aver, *old use* bruit abroad, *inf* come out with, comment, communicate, convey, declare, disclose, divulge, ejaculate, enunciate, exclaim, express, intimate, maintain, mention, mouth, phrase, pronounce, *inf* put it about, read out, recite, rejoin, remark, repeat, reply, report,

respond, retort, reveal, signify, state, suggest, tell, utter. ▷ SPEAK, TALK, TELL.

saying *n* adage, aphorism, apophthegm, axiom, catchphrase, catchword, cliché, dictum, epigram, expression, formula, maxim, motto, phrase, precept, proverb, quotation, remark, *old use* saw, slogan, statement, tag, truism, watchword.

scab *n* clot of blood, crust, sore.

scale *n* **1** dandruff, flake, plate, scurf. **2** *remove scale from teeth.* caking, coating, crust, deposit, encrustation, *inf* fur, plaque, tartar. **3** *the scale on a thermometer.* calibration, gradation, graduation. **4** *the social scale.* hierarchy, ladder, order, ranking, spectrum. **5** *small/large scale.* proportion, ratio. ▷ SIZE. **6** *musical scale.* sequence, series. □ *chromatic scale, diatonic scale, major scale, minor scale.* ● *vb* ascend, clamber up, climb, go up, mount. **scales** balance, weighing-machine.

scamper *vb* dash, frisk, frolic, gambol, hasten, hurry, play, romp, run, rush, scuttle.

scan *vb* **1** check, examine, explore, eye, gaze at, investigate, look at, pore over, scrutinize, search, stare at, study, survey, view, watch. **2** *scan the papers.* flip through, glance at, read quickly, skim, thumb through.

scandal *n* **1** discredit, disgrace, dishonour, disrepute, embarrassment, ignominy, infamy, notoriety, obloquy, outrage, reproach, sensation, shame. **2** calumny, defamation, gossip, innuendo, libel, rumour, slander, slur, *inf* smear, *inf* tittletattle.

scandalize *vb* affront, appal, disgust, horrify, offend, outrage, shock, upset.

scandalous *adj* 1 disgraceful, disgusting, dishonourable, disreputable, ignominious, immodest, immoral, improper, indecent, indecorous, infamous, licentious, notorious, outrageous, shameful, shocking, sinful, sordid, unmentionable, unspeakable, wicked. 2 *a scandalous lie.* calumnious, defamatory, libellous, scurrilous, slanderous, untrue.

scansion *n* metre, prosody, rhythm. ▷ VERSE.

scanty *adj* 1 inadequate, insufficient, meagre, mean, *sl* measly, *inf* mingy, minimal, scant, scarce, *inf* skimpy, sparing, sparse, stingy. ▷ SMALL. *Opp* PLENTIFUL. 2 *scanty clothes.* indecent, revealing, *inf* seethrough, thin.

scapegoat *n* dupe, *sl* fall guy, *inf* front, whipping-boy, victim.

scar *n* blemish, brand, burn, cicatrice, cicatrix, cut, disfigurement, injury, mark, scab, scratch. ▷ WOUND. ● *vb* blemish, brand, burn, damage, deface, disfigure, injure, leave a scar on, mark, scratch, spoil.

scarce *adj inf* few and far between, *inf* hard to come by, *inf* hard to find, inadequate, infrequent, in short supply, insufficient, lacking, meagre, rare, scant, scanty, sparse, *inf* thin on the ground, uncommon, unusual. *Opp* PLENTIFUL.

scarcely *adv* barely, hardly, only just.

scarcity *n* dearth, famine, inadequacy, insufficiency, lack, need, paucity, poverty, rarity, shortage, want. *Opp* PLENTY.

scare *n* alarm, jolt, shock, start. ▷ FRIGHT. ● *vb* 1 alarm, dismay, intimidate, make someone afraid, *inf* make someone jump, menace, panic, shake, shock, startle, terrorize, threaten, unnerve. ▷ FRIGHTEN. *Opp* REASSURE.

scarf *n* headscarf, muffler, shawl, stole.

scary *adj* [*inf*] creepy, eerie, hair-raising, horrible, scaring, unnerving. ▷ FRIGHTENING.

scathing *adj* biting, caustic, critical, humiliating, mordant, satirical, savage, scornful, tart, withering. *Opp* COMPLIMENTARY.

scatter *vb* 1 break up, disband, disintegrate, dispel, disperse, divide, send in all directions, separate. 2 *scatter seeds.* broadcast, disseminate, intersperse, shed, shower, sow, spread, sprinkle, strew, throw about. *Opp* GATHER.

scatterbrained *adj* absentminded, careless, crazy, disorganized, forgetful, frivolous, hare-brained, inattentive, muddled, *inf* not with it, *inf* scatty, thoughtless, unreliable, unsystematic, vague. ▷ SILLY.

scavenge *vb* forage, rummage, scrounge, search.

scenario *n* design, framework, layout, outline, plan, scheme, storyline, structure, summary.

scene *n* 1 area, background, context, locale, locality, location, place, position, setting, site, situation, spot, where-

abouts. 2 *a beautiful scene.*
picture, sight, spectacle.
▷ SCENERY. 3 *scene from a film.*
act, chapter, *inf* clip, episode,
part, section, sequence. 4 *a
nasty scene.* altercation, argument, *inf* carry-on, commotion,
disturbance, furore, fuss, quarrel, row, tantrum, *inf* to-do,
inf upset.

scenery *n* 1 landscape, outlook,
panorama, prospect, scene,
terrain, view, vista. 2 *stage
scenery.* backdrop, flats, set,
setting.

scenic *adj* attractive, beautiful,
breathtaking, grand, impres-
sive, lovely, panoramic, picturesque, pretty, spectacular.

scent *n* 1 aroma, bouquet,
fragrance, nose, odour,
perfume, redolence, smell.
2 after-shave, eau de cologne,
lavender water, perfume. 3 *an
animal's scent.* spoor, track,
trail. ● *vb* ▷ SMELL. **scented**
▷ SMELLING.

sceptic *n* agnostic, cynic,
doubter, *inf* doubting Thomas,
disbeliever, scoffer, unbeliever.
Opp BELIEVER.

sceptical *adj* agnostic, cynical,
disbelieving, distrustful, doubting, dubious, incredulous,
mistrustful, questioning,
scoffing, suspicious, uncertain,
unconvinced, unsure.
Opp CONFIDENT.

scepticism *n* agnosticism, cynicism, disbelief, distrust, doubt,
dubiety, incredulity, lack of
confidence, mistrust, suspicion.
Opp FAITH.

schedule *n* agenda, calendar,
diary, itinerary, list, plan,
programme, register, scheme,
timetable. ● *vb* appoint,

arrange, assign, book, earmark,
fix a time, organize, outline,
plan, programme, time, timetable.

scheme *n* 1 approach, blueprint,
design, draft, idea, method,
plan, procedure, programme,
project, proposal, scenario,
strategy, system. 2 *a dishonest
scheme.* conspiracy, *inf* dodge,
intrigue, machinations,
manoeuvre, plot, *inf* ploy,
inf racket, ruse, stratagem,
subterfuge, tactic. 3 *colour
scheme.* arrangement, design.
● *vb* collude, connive, conspire,
inf cook something up,
inf hatch a plot, intrigue, machinate, manoeuvre, plan, plot.

scholar *n* academic, *inf* egghead,
expert, highbrow, intellectual,
professor, pundit, savant.
▷ PUPIL.

scholarly *adj* 1 academic, bookish, *inf* brainy, *inf* deep,
erudite, highbrow, intellectual,
knowledgeable, learned,
lettered, widely-read.
2 *scholarly treatise.* documented, researched, rigorous, scientific, well-argued, well-
informed.

scholarship *n* 1 academic
achievement, education, erudition, intellectual attainment,
knowledge, learning, research,
schooling, scientific rigour,
wisdom. 2 *a scholarship to
Oxford.* award, bursary, endowment, exhibition, fellowship,
grant.

school *n* 1 educational institution. □ *academy, boarding-
school, coeducational school,
college, comprehensive (school),
first school, grammar school,
high school, infant school,
junior school, kindergarten,*

nursery school, playgroup, preparatory school, primary school, public school, secondary school, seminary. 2 *a school of whales.* shoal. ▷ GROUP.

● *vb* ▷ EDUCATE.

science *n* organized knowledge, systematic study. □ acoustics, aeronautics, agricultural science, anatomy, anthropology, artifical intelligence, astronomy, astrophysics, behavioural science, biochemistry, biology, biophysics, botany, chemistry, climatology, computer science, cybernetics, dietetics, domestic science, dynamics, earth science, ecology, economics, electronics, engineering, entomology, environmental science, food science, genetics, geographical science, geology, geophysics, hydraulics, information technology, life science, linguistics, materials science, mathematics, mechanics, medical science, metallurgy, meteorology, microbiology, mineralogy, ornithology, pathology, pharmacology, physics, physiology, political science, psychology, robotics, sociology, space technology, telecommunications, thermodynamics, toxicology, veterinary science, zoology.

scientific *adj* analytical, methodical, meticulous, orderly, organized, precise, rational, regulated, rigorous, systematic.

scientist *n inf* boffin, researcher, scientific expert, technologist.

scintillating *adj* brilliant, clever, coruscating, dazzling, effervescent, flashing, glittering, lively, sparkling, vivacious, witty. *Opp* DULL.

scoff *vb* 1 belittle, be sarcastic, be scornful, deride, disparage,

gibe, jeer, jibe, laugh, mock, *inf* poke fun, ridicule, sneer, taunt, tease. 2 ▷ EAT.

scold *vb* admonish, berate, blame, *inf* carpet, castigate, censure, chide, criticize, disapprove of, find fault with, *inf* jump down someone's throat, *inf* lecture, *inf* nag, rate, rebuke, reprehend, reprimand, reproach, reprove, *inf* slate, *inf* tell off, *inf* tick off, upbraid.

scoop *n* 1 bailer, ladle, shovel, spoon. 2 *news scoop.* exclusive, inside story, *inf* latest, revelation. ● *vb* dig, excavate, gouge, hollow, scrape, shovel, spoon.

scope *n* 1 ambit, area, breadth, compass, competence, extent, field, limit, range, reach, span, sphere, terms of reference. 2 *scope for expansion.* capacity, chance, *inf* elbow-room, freedom, latitude, leeway, liberty, opportunity, outlet, room, space, spread.

scorch *vb* blacken, brand, burn, char, heat, roast, sear, singe.

score *n* 1 account, amount, count, marks, points, reckoning, result, sum, tally, total. 2 *score on furniture.* cut, groove, incision, line, mark, nick, scrape, scratch, slash. ● *vb* 1 account for, achieve, add up, *inf* chalk up, earn, gain, *inf* knock up, make, tally, win. 2 *score a groove.* cut, engrave, gouge, incise, mark, scrape, scratch, slash. 3 *score music.* orchestrate, write out. **settle a score** ▷ RETALIATE.

scorn *n* contempt, contumely, derision, detestation, disdain, disgust, dislike, dismissal, disparagement, disrespect, jeering, mockery, rejection, ridicule, scoffing, sneering, taunt-

ing. *Opp* ADMIRATION. • *vb* be
scornful about, contemn,
deride, despise, disapprove of,
disdain, dislike, dismiss,
disparage, hate, insult, jeer at,
laugh at, look down on, make
fun of, mock, reject, ridicule,
inf scoff at, sneer at, spurn,
taunt, *inf* turn up your nose at.
Opp ADMIRE.

scornful *adj* condescending,
contemptuous, contumelious,
deprecative, derisive, disdainful, dismissive, disparaging,
disrespectful, haughty, insulting, jeering, mocking, patronizing, sarcastic, satirical, scathing, scoffing, sneering,
inf snide, *inf* snooty, supercilious, superior, taunting, withering. *Opp* RESPECTFUL.

scoundrel *n* blackguard,
blighter, bounder, cad, good-for-
nothing, heel, knave, miscreant, rascal, rogue, ruffian,
scallywag, scamp, villain,
wretch.

scour *vb* 1 abrade, buff up,
burnish, clean, cleanse, polish,
rub, scrape, scrub, shine, wash.
2 *scour the house.* comb, forage
through, hunt through, rake
through, ransack, rummage
through, search, *inf* turn upside
down.

scourge *n* 1 affliction, bane,
curse, evil, misery, misfortune,
plague, torment, woe. 2 ▷ WHIP.
• *vb* beat, belt, flagellate, flog,
horsewhip, lash, whip.

scout *n* lookout, spy.
• *vb* explore, get information,
hunt around, investigate, look
about, reconnoitre, search,
inf snoop, spy.

scowl *vb* frown, glower, grimace,
inf look daggers, lower.

scraggy *adj* bony, emaciated,
gaunt, lanky, lean, scrawny,
skinny, starved, thin, underfed.
Opp PLUMP.

scramble *n* commotion, confusion, *inf* free-for-all, haste,
hurry, mêlée, race, rush, scrimmage, struggle. • *vb* 1 clamber,
climb, crawl, grope, move
awkwardly, scrabble.
2 *scramble for gold.* compete,
contend, dash, fight, hasten,
hurry, jostle, push, run, rush,
scuffle, strive, struggle, tussle,
vie. 3 *scramble a message.*
confuse, jumble, mix up.

scrap *n* 1 atom, bit, crumb, fraction, fragment, grain, hint, iota,
jot, mite, molecule, morsel,
particle, piece, rag, scintilla,
shard, shred, sliver, snippet,
speck, trace. 2 *inf* junk, leavings, litter, odds and ends,
offcuts, refuse, rejects, remains,
remnants, residue, rubbish,
salvage, waste. 3 *a friendly
scrap.* argument, quarrel,
scuffle, *inf* set-to, squabble, tiff,
tussle, wrangle. ▷ FIGHT.
• *vb* 1 abandon, cancel, discard,
inf ditch, drop, give up, jettison,
throw away, write off. 2 *scrap
over trifles.* argue, bicker, flare
up, quarrel, spar, squabble,
tussle, wrangle. ▷ FIGHT.

scrape *n* 1 abrasion, graze,
injury, laceration, scratch,
scuff, wound. 2 *an awkward
scrape.* difficulty, escapade,
inf kettle of fish, piece of
mischief, plight, prank, predicament, trouble. • *vb* 1 abrade,
bark, bruise, damage, graze,
injure, lacerate, scratch, scuff,
skin, wound. 2 *scrape clean.*
clean, file, rasp, rub, scour,
scrub. **scrape together**
▷ COLLECT.

scrappy

scrappy *adj* bitty, careless, disjointed, fragmentary, hurriedly done, imperfect, incomplete, inconclusive, sketchy, slipshod, unfinished, unpolished, unsatisfactory. *Opp* PERFECT.

scratch *n* abrasion, damage, dent, gash, gouge, graze, groove, indentation, injury, laceration, line, mark, score, scoring, scrape, scuff, wound. • *vb* abrade, claw at, cut, damage the surface of, dent, gash, gouge, graze, groove, incise, injure, lacerate, mark, rub, scarify, score, scrape, scuff, wound. **up to scratch** ▷ SATISFACTORY.

scrawl *vb* doodle, scribble, write hurriedly. ▷ WRITE.

scream *n* & *vb* bawl, caterwaul, cry, howl, roar, screech, shout, shriek, squeal, wail, yell, yowl.

screen *n* 1 blind, curtain, divider, partition. 2 camouflage, concealment, cover, disguise, protection, shelter, shield, smokescreen. 3 *sift through a screen.* filter, mesh, riddle, sieve, strainer. • *vb* 1 divide, partition off, subdivide, wall off. 2 camouflage, cloak, conceal, cover, disguise, guard, hide, mask, protect, safeguard, shade, shelter, shield, shroud, veil. 3 *screen employees for security. inf* check out, examine, investigate, process, sift out, vet.

screw *n* 1 bolt, screw-bolt. 2 rotation, spiral, turn, twist. • *vb* rotate, turn, twist. **screw down** ▷ FASTEN. **screw up** ▷ BUNGLE, TWIST.

scribble *vb* ▷ SCRAWL.

scrutinize

scribe *n* amanuensis, clerk, copyist, secretary, transcriber, writer.

script *n* 1 calligraphy, handwriting, penmanship. 2 *script of a play.* libretto, screenplay, text, words.

scripture *n* bible, holy writ, sacred writings, Word of God. □ *Bhagavad-Gita, inf the Good Book, the Gospel, Holy Bible, Koran, Upanishad.*

scrounge *vb* beg, cadge, importune.

scrub *vb* 1 brush, clean, rub, scour, wash. 2 ▷ CANCEL.

scruffy *adj* bedraggled, dirty, dishevelled, disordered, dowdy, frowsy, messy, ragged, scrappy, shabby, slatternly, slovenly, tatty, ungroomed, unkempt, untidy, worn out. *Opp* SMART.

scruple *n* compunction, conscience, doubt, hesitation, misgiving, qualm, reluctance, *inf* second thought. • *vb* [*usu neg*] be reluctant, have a conscience (about), have scruples (about), hesitate, hold back (from), *inf* think twice (about).

scrupulous *adj* 1 careful, cautious, conscientious, diligent, exacting, fastidious, *inf* finicky, meticulous, minute, neat, painstaking, precise, punctilious, rigid, rigorous, strict, systematic, thorough. 2 *scrupulous honesty.* ethical, fair-minded, honest, honourable, just, moral, principled, proper, upright, upstanding. *Opp* UNSCRUPULOUS.

scrutinize *vb* analyse, check, examine, *inf* go over with a toothcomb, inspect, investigate, look closely at, *inf* probe, sift, study.

scrutiny *n* analysis, examination, inspection, investigation, probing, search, study.

sculpture *n* three-dimensional art. □ bas-relief, bronze, bust, carving, caryatid, cast, effigy, figure, figurine, maquette, marble, moulding, plaster cast, relief, statue, statuette.
● *vb* carve, cast, chisel, fashion, form, hew, model, mould, *inf* sculpt, shape.

scum *n* dirt, film, foam, froth, impurities, suds.

scurrilous *adj* abusive, calumnious, coarse, defamatory, derogatory, disparaging, foul, indecent, insulting, libellous, low, obscene, offensive, opprobrious, scabrous, shameful, slanderous, vile, vulgar.

sea *adj* aquatic, marine, maritime, nautical, naval, ocean-going, oceanic, salt-water, seafaring, seagoing.
● *n inf* briny, *poet* deep, lake, *old use* main, ocean.

seal *n* 1 sea-lion, walrus. 2 *royal seal*. badge, coat of arms, crest, emblem, escutcheon, impression, imprint, mark, monogram, sign, stamp, symbol, token. ● *vb* 1 close, fasten, lock, make airtight, make watertight, plug, secure, shut, stick down, stop up. 2 *seal an agreement*. affirm, authenticate, *inf* clinch, conclude, confirm, corroborate, decide, endorse, finalize, guarantee, ratify, settle, sign, validate, verify.

seam *n* 1 join, stitching. 2 *seam of coal*. bed, layer, lode, stratum, thickness, vein.

seamy *adj* disreputable, distasteful, nasty, repulsive, shameful, sordid, squalid, unattractive, unpleasant, unsavoury, unwholesome.

search *n* check, enquiry, examination, hunt, inspection, investigation, look, *inf* probe, pursuit, quest, scrutiny.
● *vb* 1 cast about, explore, ferret about, hunt, investigate, *inf* leave no stone unturned, look, nose about, poke about, prospect, pry, seek. 2 *search suspects*. check, examine, *inf* frisk, inspect, scrutinize. 3 *search a house*. comb, go through, ransack, rifle, rummage through, scour.
searching ▷ INQUISITIVE, THOROUGH.

seaside *n* beach, coast, coastal resort, sands, sea-coast, sea-shore, shore.

season *n* period, phase, time.
● *vb* 1 add seasoning to, flavour, *inf* pep up, salt, spice. 2 *season wood*. age, harden, mature, ripen.

seasonable *adj* appropriate, apt, convenient, favourable, fitting, normal, opportune, propitious, suitable, timely, well-timed.

seasoning *n* additives, condiments, flavouring, zest. □ dressing, herbs, mustard, pepper, relish, salt, sauce, spice, vinegar.

seat *n* 1 place, sitting-place. □ armchair, bench, carver, chair, chaise longue, couch, deck-chair, dining-chair, easy chair, Fr fauteuil, form, pew, pillion, pouffe, reclining chair, rocking-chair, saddle, settee, settle, sofa, squab, stool, throne, window seat. 2 *a country seat*. ▷ RESIDENCE. 3 ▷ BUTTOCKS. **seat yourself** ▷ SIT.

secateurs plur n clippers, cutters, pruning shears.

secluded adj cloistered, concealed, cut off, hidden, inaccessible, isolated, lonely, monastic, inf off the beaten track, private, remote, retired, screened, sequestered, sheltered, shut away, solitary, unfrequented, unvisited. Opp PUBLIC.

seclusion n concealment, hiding, isolation, loneliness, privacy, remoteness, retirement, separation, shelter, solitariness.

second adj added, additional, alternative, another, complementary, duplicate, extra, following, further, later, matching, next, other, repeated, subsequent, twin. ● n 1 flash, instant, inf jiffy, moment, inf tick, inf twinkling, inf wink. 2 second in a fight. assistant, deputy, helper, inf number two, inf right-hand man, right-hand woman, second-in-command, inf stand-in, subordinate, supporter, understudy, vice-. ● vb 1 aid, assist, back, encourage, give approval to, help, promote, side with, sponsor, support. 2 second to another job. move, reassign, relocate, shift, transfer.

secondary adj 1 alternative, ancillary, auxiliary, inf backup, extra, inessential, inferior, lesser, lower, minor, nonessential, reinforcing, reserve, second, second-rate, spare, subordinate, subsidiary, supporting, supportive, supplementary, unimportant. 2 secondary sources. copied, derivative, second-hand, unoriginal.

second-hand adj 1 inf hand-me-down, old, used, worn. Opp NEW. 2 second-hand experience. indirect, secondary, vicarious. Opp DIRECT.

second-rate adj commonplace, indifferent, inferior, low-grade, mediocre, middling, ordinary, poor, second-best, second-class, undistinguished, unexciting, uninspiring.

secret adj 1 clandestine, concealed, covert, disguised, hidden, inf hushed up, inf hush-hush, invisible, private, secluded, shrouded, stealthy, undercover, underground, unknown. ▷ SECRETIVE. 2 secret papers. classified, confidential, inaccessible, intimate, personal, restricted, sensitive, top-secret, undisclosed, unpublished. 3 secret meanings. arcane, cryptic, encoded, esoteric, incomprehensible, mysterious, occult, recondite. 4 secret about his private life. ▷ SECRETIVE. Opp OPEN, PUBLIC.

secretary n amanuensis, clerk, filing-clerk, personal assistant, scribe, shorthand-typist, stenographer, typist, word-processor operator.

secrete vb 1 cloak, conceal, cover up, disguise, enshroud, hide, mask, put away, put into hiding. 2 secrete fluid. discharge, emit, excrete, exude, give off, leak, ooze, produce, release.

secretion n discharge, emission, escape, excretion, leakage, release.

secretive adj close-lipped, enigmatic, furtive, mysterious, quiet, reserved, reticent, secret, shifty, silent, taciturn, tight-lipped, uncommunicative, unforthcoming, withdrawn. *Opp* COMMUNICATIVE.

sect *n* cult, denomination, faction, order, party, persuasion. ▷ GROUP.

sectarian *adj* bigoted, clannish, cliquish, cultic, denominational, dogmatic, exclusive, factional, fanatical, inflexible, narrow, narrow-minded, partial, partisan, prejudiced, rigid, schismatic.

section *n* bit, branch, chapter, compartment, component, department, division, element, fraction, fragment, group, instalment, leg (*of journey*), part, passage, piece, portion, quarter, sample, sector, segment, slice, stage, subdivision, subsection.

sector *n* area, district, division, part, quarter, region, zone. ▷ SECTION.

secular *adj* civil, earthly, lay, material, mundane, non-religious, temporal, terrestrial, worldly. *Opp* RELIGIOUS.

secure *adj* 1 cosy, defended, guarded, immune, impregnable, invulnerable, protected, safe, sheltered, shielded, snug, unharmed, unhurt, unscathed. 2 *secure doors*. bolted, burglar-proof, closed, fast, fastened, fixed, foolproof, immovable, locked, shut, solid, tight, unyielding. 3 *secure faith*. certain, confident, firm, stable, steady, strong, sure, unquestioning. ● *vb* 1 defend, guard, make safe, preserve, protect, shelter, shield. 2 anchor, attach, bolt, close, fix, lock, make fast, screw down, tie down. ▷ FASTEN. 3 *secure a loan*. acquire, be promised,

come by, gain, get, obtain, procure, win.

sedate *adj* calm, collected, composed, controlled, conventional, cool, decorous, deliberate, dignified, equable, even-tempered, formal, grave, imperturbable, level-headed, peaceful, *derog* prim, proper, quiet, sensible, serene, serious, slow, sober, solemn, staid, strait-laced, tranquil, unruffled. *Opp* LIVELY. ● *vb* calm, put to sleep, tranquillize, treat with sedatives.

sedative *adj* anodyne, calming, lenitive, narcotic, relaxing, soothing, soporific, tranquillizing. ● *n* anodyne, barbiturate, calmative, depressant, narcotic, opiate, sleeping-pill, soporific, tranquillizer.

sedentary *adj* desk-bound, immobile, inactive, seated, sitting down. *Opp* ACTIVE.

sediment *n* deposit, dregs, grounds, lees, precipitate, remains, residue, *inf* sludge.

sedition *n* agitation, incitement, insurrection, mutiny, rabble-rousing, revolt, treachery, treason. ▷ REBELLION.

seduce *vb* 1 allure, beguile, charm, corrupt, deceive, decoy, deprave, ensnare, entice, inveigle, lead astray, lure, mislead, tempt. 2 debauch, deflower, dishonour, rape, ravish, *old use* ruin, violate.

seduction *n* 1 allurement, attraction, charm, temptation. 2 rape, ravishing. ▷ SEX.

seductive *adj* alluring, appealing, attractive, bewitching, captivating, charming, coquettish, enchanting, enticing, flirtatious, inviting, irresistible, persuasive, provocative, tantalizing, tempting, *inf* sexy. *Opp* REPULSIVE.

see *vb* 1 behold, catch sight of, descry, discern, discover, distinguish, espy, glimpse, identify, look at, make out, mark, note, notice, observe, perceive, recognize, regard, sight, spot, spy, view, watch, witness. 2 *see what someone means.* appreciate, apprehend, comprehend, fathom, follow, *inf* get the hang of, grasp, know, perceive, realize, take in, understand. 3 *see problems ahead.* anticipate, conceive, envisage, foresee, foretell, imagine, picture, visualize. 4 *see what can be done.* consider, decide, discover, investigate, mull over, reflect on, think about, weigh up. 5 *see a play.* attend, be a spectator at, watch. 6 *seeing him tonight.* court, go out with, *inf* have a date with, meet, socialize with, visit, woo. 7 *see you home.* accompany, conduct, escort. 8 *saw fighting in the war.* endure, experience, go through, suffer, survive, undergo. 9 *Guess who I saw today!* encounter, face, meet, run into, talk to, visit. **see to** ▷ ORGANIZE.

seed *n* 1 egg, embryo, germ, ovule, ovum, semen, spawn, sperm, spore. 2 *seed in fruit.* pip, pit, stone. ● *vb* ▷ SOW.

seek *vb* aim at, apply for, ask for, aspire to, beg for, demand, desire, go after, hope for, hunt for, inquire after, look for, pursue, quest after, request, search for, solicit, strive after, try for, want, wish for.

seem *vb* appear, feel, give an impression of being, have an appearance of being, look, pretend to be, sound.

seep *vb* dribble, drip, exude, flow, leak, ooze, percolate, run, soak, trickle.

seer *n* clairvoyant, fortune-teller, oracle, prophet, prophetess, psychic, sibyl, soothsayer, vaticinator.

seethe *vb* be agitated, be angry, boil, bubble, erupt, foam, froth up, rise, simmer, stew, surge.

segment *n* bit, compartment, department, division, element, fraction, fragment, part, piece, portion, quarter, section, sector, slice, subdivision, subsection, wedge.

segregate *vb* compartmentalize, cut off, exclude, isolate, keep apart, put apart, separate, sequester, set apart, shut out.

segregation *n* 1 apartheid, discrimination. 2 isolation, quarantine, seclusion, separation.

seize *vb* 1 abduct, apprehend, arrest, capture, catch, clutch, *inf* collar, detain, grab, grasp, grip, hold, *inf* nab, pluck, possess, snatch, take, take into custody, take prisoner. 2 *seize a country.* annex, invade. 3 *seize property.* appropriate, commandeer, confiscate, hijack, impound, steal, take away. *Opp* RELEASE. **seize up** ▷ STICK.

seizure *n* 1 abduction, annexation, appropriation, arrest, capture, confiscation, hijacking, invasion, sequestration, theft, usurpation. 2 [*medical*] apoplexy, attack, convulsion, epileptic fit, fit, paroxysm, spasm, stroke.

seldom *adv* infrequently, occasionally, rarely.

select *adj* best, choice, chosen, élite, excellent, exceptional, exclusive, favoured, finest, first-class, first-rate, *inf* hand-picked, preferred, prime, privileged, rare, selected, special, top-quality. *Opp* ORDINARY.

● *vb* appoint, cast (*actor for role*), choose, decide on, elect, nominate, opt for, pick, prefer, settle on, single out, vote for.

selection *n* 1 choice, option, pick, preference. 2 *a selection of goods.* assortment, range, variety. 3 *selection from the classics.* excerpts, extracts, passages, quotations.

selective *adj* careful, *inf* choosy, discerning, discriminating, particular, specialized. *Opp* COMPREHENSIVE, IMPERCEPTIVE.

self-confident *adj* assertive, assured, collected, cool, fearless, independent, outgoing, poised, positive, self-assured, self-possessed, self-reliant, sure of yourself. ▷ BOLD. *Opp* SELF-CONSCIOUS.

self-conscious *adj* awkward, bashful, blushing, coy, diffident, embarrassed, ill at ease, insecure, nervous, reserved, self-effacing, sheepish, shy, uncomfortable, unnatural. ▷ TIMID. *Opp* SELF-CONFIDENT.

self-contained *adj* 1 complete, independent, separate. 2 aloof, cold, reserved, self-reliant, uncommunicative, undemonstrative, unemotional.

self-control *n* calmness, composure, coolness, patience, resolve, restraint, self-command, self-denial, self-discipline, self-possession, self-restraint, will-power.

self-denial *n* abstemiousness, fasting, moderation, self-abnegation, self-sacrifice, temperance, unselfishness. *Opp* SELF-INDULGENCE.

self-employed *adj* freelance, independent.

self-esteem *n* 1 ▷ SELF-RESPECT. 2 arrogance, *inf* big-headedness, conceit, egotism, overconfidence, self-admiration, self-importance, self-love, smugness, vanity.

self-explanatory *adj* apparent, axiomatic, blatant, clear, conspicuous, eye-catching, flagrant, glaring, inescapable, manifest, obvious, patent, plain, recognizable, self-evident, understandable, unmistakable, visible.

self-governing *adj* autonomous, free, independent, sovereign.

self-important *adj* arrogant, bombastic, conceited, grandiloquent, haughty, magisterial, ostentatious, pompous, pontifical, pretentious, self-centred, sententious, smug, *inf* snooty, *inf* stuck-up, supercilious, vainglorious.

self-indulgence *n* extravagance, gluttony, greed, hedonism, pleasure, profligacy, self-gratification. ▷ SELFISHNESS. *Opp* SELF-DENIAL.

self-indulgent *adj* dissipated, epicurean, extravagant, gluttonous, gourmandizing, greedy, hedonistic, immoderate, intemperate, pleasure-loving, profligate, sybaritic. ▷ SELFISH. *Opp* ABSTEMIOUS.

selfish *adj* acquisitive, avaricious, covetous, demanding, egocentric, egotistic, grasping, greedy, inconsiderate, mean, mercenary, miserly, self-absorbed, self-centred, self-indulgent, self-interested, self-seeking, self-serving, *inf* stingy, thoughtless, uncaring, ungenerous, unhelpful, unsympathetic, worldly. *Opp* UNSELFISH.

selfishness *n* acquisitiveness, avarice, covetousness, egotism, greed, meanness, miserliness, niggardliness, possessiveness, self-indulgence, self-interest, self-love, self-regard, *inf* stinginess, thoughtlessness.

self-reliant *adj* autonomous, independent, self-contained, self-sufficient, self-supporting.

self-respect *n Fr* amour propre, dignity, honour, integrity, morale, pride, self-confidence, self-esteem.

self-righteous *adj* complacent, *inf* goody-goody, *inf* holier-than-thou, mealy-mouthed, pharisaical, pietistic, pious, pompous, priggish, proud, sanctimonious, self-important, self-satisfied, sleek, smug, superior, vain.

self-sufficient *adj* autonomous, independent, self-reliant, self-supporting.

self-willed *adj* determined, dogged, forceful, headstrong, inflexible, intractable, intransigent, *inf* mulish, obstinate, *inf* pig-headed, single-minded, *inf* stiff-necked, stubborn, uncontrollable, uncooperative, wilful.

sell *vb* 1 auction, barter, deal in, exchange, give in part-exchange, handle, hawk, *inf* keep, *inf* knock down, offer for sale, peddle, *inf* put under the hammer, retail, sell off, stock, tout, trade, *inf* trade in (*traded in my car*), traffic in,

vend. 2 *sell hard*. advertise, market, merchandise, package, promote, *inf* push.

seller *n* dealer, merchant, stockist, supplier, trader, vendor. □ agent, barrow-boy, broker, old use colporteur, costermonger, old use hawker, market-trader, pedlar, *inf* rep, representative, retailer, salesman, salesperson, saleswoman, shop assistant, shopkeeper, storekeeper, street trader, tradesman, traveller, wholesaler. ▷ SHOP.

seminal *adj* basic, constructive, creative, fertile, formative, imaginative, important, influential, innovative, new, original, primary, productive.

send *vb* 1 address, consign, convey, deliver, direct, dispatch, fax, forward, mail, post, remit, ship, transmit. 2 *send a rocket to the moon*. fire, launch, project, propel, release, shoot. **send away** ▷ DISMISS. **send down** ▷ IMPRISON. **send for** ▷ SUMMON. **send-off** *n* ▷ GOODBYE. **send out** ▷ EMIT. **send round** ▷ CIRCULATE. **send up** ▷ PARODY.

senile *adj* declining, doddery, *inf* in your dotage, old, *derog* past it.

senior *adj* chief, elder, higher, high-ranking, major, older, principal, revered, superior, well-established. *Opp* JUNIOR.

sensation *n* 1 awareness, feeling, perception, sense. 2 *affair caused a sensation*. commotion, excitement, furore, outrage, scandal, stir, thrill.

sensational *adj* 1 blood-curdling, hair-raising, lurid, melodramatic, overwritten, scandal-mongering, shocking,

startling, stimulating, violent.
2 [*inf*] *a sensational result.*
amazing, astonishing, astounding, breathtaking, electrifying, exciting, extraordinary, *inf* fabulous, *inf* fantastic, *inf* great, incredible, marvellous, remarkable, spectacular, spine-tingling, stirring, superb, surprising, thrilling, unbelievable, unexpected, wonderful.

sense *n* **1** awareness, consciousness, faculty, feeling, sensation. □ hearing, sight, smell, taste, touch. **2** brains, cleverness, gumption, intellect, intelligence, intuition, judgement, logic, *inf* nous, perception, reason, reasoning, understanding, wisdom, wit. **3** *the sense of a message.* coherence, connotations, denotation, *inf* drift, gist, import, intelligibility, interpretation, meaning, message, point, purport, significance, signification, substance. ● *vb* be aware (of), detect, discern, divine, feel, guess, *inf* have a hunch, intuit, notice, perceive, *inf* pick up vibes, realize, respond to, suspect, understand. ▷ FEEL, HEAR, SEE, SMELL, TASTE. **make sense of** ▷ UNDERSTAND.

senseless *adj* **1** anaesthetized, asleep, comatose, insensate, insensible, knocked out, numb, *inf* out like a light, stunned, unconscious. **2** absurd, crazy, fatuous, meaningless, pointless, purposeless, silly. ▷ STUPID.

sensible *adj* **1** calm, common-sense, commonsensical, cool, discreet, discriminating, intelligent, judicious, level-headed, logical, prudent, rational, realistic, reasonable, reasoned, sage, sane, serious-minded,

sound, straightforward, thoughtful, wise. *Opp* STUPID. **2** *sensible phenomena.* corporeal, existent, material, palpable, perceptible, physical, real, tangible, visible. **3** *sensible clothes.* comfortable, functional, *inf* no-nonsense, practical, useful. *Opp* FASHIONABLE, IMPRACTICAL. **sensible of** acquainted with, alert to, appreciative of, aware of, cognizant of, in touch with, mindful of, responsive to, *inf* wise to.

sensitive *adj* **1** considerate, perceptive, reactive, receptive, responsive, susceptible, sympathetic, tactful, thoughtful, understanding. **2** *a sensitive temperament.* emotional, hypersensitive, impressionable, temperamental, thin-skinned, touchy, volatile, vulnerable. **3** *sensitive skin.* delicate, fine, fragile, painful, soft, sore, tender. **4** *a sensitive topic.* confidential, controversial, delicate, *inf* tricky, secret. *Opp* INSENSITIVE. **sensitive to** affected by, attuned to, aware of, considerate of, perceptive about, receptive to, responsive to, understanding about.

sensual *adj* animal, bodily, carnal, fleshly, physical, pleasure-loving, self-indulgent, voluptuous, worldly. ▷ SEXY. *Opp* ASCETIC.

sensuous *adj* beautiful, emotional, gratifying, lush, luxurious, rich, richly embellished.

sentence *n* **1** exclamation, question, statement, thought, utterance. **2** decision, judgement, pronouncement, punishment, ruling. ● *vb* condemn, pass judgement on, pronounce sentence on.

sentiment *n* **1** attitude, belief, idea, judgement, opinion, outlook, thought, view. **2** *sentiment of a poem.* emotion, feeling, sensibility.

sentimental *adj* **1** compassionate, emotional, nostalgic, romantic, soft-hearted, sympathetic, tearful, tender, warmhearted, *inf* weepy. **2** [*derog*] gushing, *inf* gushy, indulgent, insincere, maudlin, mawkish, *inf* mushy, overdone, over-emotional, *inf* sloppy, *inf* soppy, *inf* sugary, tearjerking, *inf* treacly, unrealistic, *sl* yucky. Opp CYNICAL.

sentimentality *n* bathos, emotionalism, insincerity, *inf* kitsch, mawkishness, nostalgia, *inf* slush.

sentry *n* guard, lookout, patrol, picket, sentinel, watch, watchman.

separable *adj* detachable, distinguishable, fissile, removable.

separate *adj* apart, autonomous, cloistered, cut off, detached, different, discrete, disjoined, distinct, divided, divorced, fenced off, free-standing, independent, individual, isolated, particular, peculiar, secluded, segregated, separated, shut off, solitary, unattached, unconnected, unrelated, unshared, withdrawn.

● *vb* **1** break up, cut off, detach, disconnect, disengage, disentangle, disjoin, dismember, dissociate, divide, fence off, fragment, hive off, isolate, keep apart, part, pull apart, segregate, sever, split, sunder, take apart, uncouple, unfasten, unhook, unravel, unyoke. **2** *The*

paths separate here. bifurcate, branch, diverge, fork. **3** *separated the grain from the chaff.* abstract, distinguish, filter out, remove, set apart, sift out, winnow. **4** *He separated from his partner.* become estranged, disband, divorce, part company, *inf* split up. Opp COMBINE, UNITE.

separation *n* **1** amputation, cutting off, detachment, disconnection, dismemberment, dissociation, division, fission, fragmentation, parting, rift, severance, splitting. Opp CONNECTION. **2** *separation of partners.* break, *inf* break-up, divorce, estrangement, rift, split. Opp UNION.

septic *adj* diseased, festering, infected, inflamed, poisoned, purulent, putrefying, putrid, suppurating.

sequel *n* consequence, continuation, development, *inf* follow-up, issue, outcome, result, upshot.

sequence *n* **1** arrangement, chain, concatenation, course, cycle, line, order, procession, programme, progression, range, row, run, series, set, string, succession, train. **2** *a sequence from a film.* *inf* clip, episode, excerpt, extract, scene, section.

serene *adj* **1** calm, idyllic, peaceful, placid, pleasing, quiet, restful, still, tranquil, unclouded, undisturbed, unperturbed, unruffled, untroubled. **2** *serene temperament.* collected, composed, contented, cool, easy-going, equable, eventempered, imperturbable, pacific, peaceable, poised, self-possessed, *inf* unflappable. Opp BOISTEROUS, EXCITABLE.

series n 1 arrangement, chain, concatenation, course, cycle, line, order, procession, programme, progression, range, row, run, sequence, set, string, succession, train. 2 *TV series.* mini-series, serial, *inf* soap, soap-opera.

serious adj 1 dignified, grave, grim, humourless, long-faced, pensive, poker-faced, sedate, sober, solemn, sombre, staid, stern, straight-faced, thoughtful, unsmiling. Opp CHEERFUL. 2 *serious discussion.* deep, earnest, heavy, honest, important, intellectual, momentous, profound, significant, sincere, weighty. 3 *serious illness.* acute, appalling, awful, calamitous, critical, dangerous, dreadful, frightful, ghastly, grievous, hideous, horrible, *inf* life-and-death, nasty, severe, shocking, terrible, unfortunate, unpleasant, urgent, violent. Opp TRIVIAL. 4 *serious worker.* careful, committed, conscientious, diligent, hard-working.

sermon n address, discourse, homily, lecture, lesson, talk.

serpentine adj labyrinthine, meandering, roundabout, sinuous, snaking, tortuous, twisting, vermicular, winding. Opp STRAIGHT.

serrated adj cogged, crenellated, denticulate, indented, jagged, notched, saw-like, toothed, zigzag. Opp STRAIGHT.

servant n assistant, attendant, *derog* dogsbody, *inf* domestic, *derog* drudge, helper, *derog* hireling, *derog* menial, *old use* servitor, *inf* skivvy, slave, *old use* vassal. □ au pair, barmaid, barman, batman, *inf* boots, butler, chamber-maid,

inf char, charwoman, chauffeur, chef, cleaner, *old use* coachman, commissionaire, cook, *inf* daily, errand boy, factotum, *derog* flunkey, footman, governess, groom, home help, houseboy, housemaid, housekeeper, kitchenmaid, *derog* lackey, lady-in-waiting, maid, maidservant, majordomo, manservant, nanny, page, parlour-maid, *old use* postilion, *old use* retainer, *plur* retinue, scout, scullery maid, *old use* scullion, *old use* seneschal, slave, steward, stewardess, valet, waiter, waitress.

serve vb 1 aid, accommodate, assist, attend, *inf* be at someone's beck and call, further, help, look after, minister to, wait upon, work for. 2 *serve in the forces.* be employed, do your duty, enlist, fight, sign on. 3 *serve goods.* deal out, distribute, dole out, give out, make available, provide, sell, supply. 4 *serve at table.* carve, *inf* dish up, officiate, wait. 5 *serve a sentence.* complete, endure, go through, pass, spend, survive.

service n 1 aid, assistance, benefit, favour, help, kindness, office. 2 *service of the community.* attendance (on), employment (by), ministering (to), work (for). 3 *a bus service.* business, organization, provision, system, timetable. 4 *give the car a service.* check-over, maintenance, overhaul, repair, servicing. 5 *church service.* ceremony, liturgy, meeting, rite, ritual, worship. □ baptism, christening, communion, compline, evensong, funeral, marriage, Mass, matins, Requiem Mass, vespers. ● vb *service a vehicle.* check, maintain, mend, overhaul, repair, tune.

serviceable *adj* dependable, durable, functional, hard-wearing, lasting, practical, strong, tough, usable.

servile *adj* abject, acquiescent, base, *inf* boot-licking, craven, cringing, deferential, fawning, flattering, grovelling, humble, ingratiating, low, menial, obsequious, slavish, submissive, subservient, sycophantic, *inf* time-serving, toadying, unctuous. *Opp* BOSSY. **be servile** ▷ GROVEL.

serving *n* helping, plateful, portion, ration.

session *n* 1 assembly, conference, discussion, hearing, meeting, sitting. 2 *a session at the baths.* period, term, time.

set *adj* 1 *set price.* advertised, agreed, arranged, defined, definite, fixed, prearranged, predetermined, prepared, scheduled, standard. 2 *set in your ways.* established, invariable, predictable, regular, stable, unchanging, unvarying. ● *n* 1 batch, bunch, category, class, clique, collection, combination, kind, series, sort. ▷ GROUP. 2 *a TV set.* apparatus, receiver. 3 *set for a play.* scene, scenery, setting, stage. ● *vb* 1 arrange, assign, deploy, deposit, dispose, lay, leave, locate, lodge, park, place, plant, *inf* plonk, put, position, rest, set down, set out, settle, situate, stand, station. 2 *set a clock.* adjust, correct, put right, rectify, regulate. 3 *set a post in concrete.* embed, fasten, fix. 4 *set like concrete.* become firm, congeal, *inf* gel, harden, *inf* jell, stiffen, take shape. 5 *set a problem.* ask, express, formu-

late, frame, phrase, pose, present, put forward, suggest, write. 6 *set a target.* allocate, allot, appoint, decide, designate, determine, establish, identify, name, ordain, prescribe, settle. **set about** ▷ ATTACK, BEGIN. **set free** ▷ LIBERATE. **set off** ▷ DEPART, EXPLODE. **set on** ▷ ATTACK. **set on fire** ▷ IGNITE. **set out** ▷ DEPART. **set up** ▷ ESTABLISH.

set-back *n inf* blow, check, complication, defeat, delay, difficulty, disappointment, hindrance, *inf* hitch, hold-up, impediment, misfortune, obstacle, problem, relapse, reverse, snag, upset.

settee *n* chaise longue, couch, sofa.

setting *n* 1 background, context, environment, environs, frame, habitat, locale, location, place, position, site, surroundings. 2 *setting for a play.* backcloth, backdrop, scene, scenery, set.

settle *vb* 1 arrange, conclude, deal with, decide, organize, put in order, straighten out. 2 alight, come to rest, land, light, *inf* make yourself comfortable, *inf* park yourself, pause, rest, roost, sit down. 3 *settle things in place.* assign, deploy, deposit, dispose, lay, locate, lodge, park, place, plant, position, put, rest, set, set down, situate, stand, station. 4 *the dust settled.* calm down, clear, compact, go down, sink, subside. 5 *settle what to do.* agree, choose, decide, establish, fix. 6 *settle differences.* end, negotiate, put an end to, reconcile, resolve, sort out, square. 7 *settle debts.* clear, discharge, pay, pay off. 8 *settle new territ-*

ory. become established in, colonize, immigrate, make your home in, occupy, people, set up home in, stay in.

settlement *n* 1 camp, colony, community, encampment, kibbutz, outpost, post, town, village. 2 agreement, arbitration, arrangement, contract, payment.

settler *n* colonist, frontiersman, immigrant, newcomer, pioneer, squatter.

sever *vb* 1 amputate, break, cut off, detach, disconnect, disjoin, part, remove, separate, split, terminate. ▷ CUT. 2 *sever a relationship.* abandon, break off, discontinue, end, put an end to, suspend, terminate.

several *adj* assorted, certain, different, divers, a few, a handful of, many, miscellaneous, a number of, some, sundry, a variety of, various.

severe *adj* 1 aloof, brutal, cold, cold-hearted, cruel, disapproving, dour, exacting, forbidding, glowering, grave, grim, hard, harsh, inexorable, merciless, obdurate, pitiless, relentless, rigorous, stern, stony, strict, unbending, uncompromising, unkind, unsmiling, unsympathetic, unyielding. 2 *severe illness.* acute, critical, dangerous, drastic, fatal, great, intense, keen, life-threatening, mortal, nasty, serious, sharp, terminal, troublesome. 3 *severe penalties.* draconian, extreme, maximum, oppressive, punitive, stringent. 4 *severe weather.* adverse, bad, inclement, violent, *inf* wicked. ▷ COLD, STORMY. 5 *a severe challenge.* arduous, demanding, difficult, onerous, punishing, taxing, tough. 6 *severe style.*

austere, bare, chaste, plain, simple, spartan, stark, unadorned. *Opp* FRIENDLY, MILD, ORNATE.

sew *vb* baste, darn, hem, mend, repair, stitch, tack.

sewage *n* effluent, waste.

sewer *n* drain, drainage, sanitation, septic tank, soak-away.

sewing *n* dressmaking, embroidery, mending, needlepoint, needlework, tapestry.

sex *n* 1 gender, sexuality. 2 carnal knowledge, coition, coitus, congress, consummation of marriage, copulation, coupling, fornication, *inf* going to bed, incest, intercourse, intimacy, love-making, masturbation, mating, orgasm, perversion, rape, seduction, sexual intercourse, sexual relations, union. **have sex (with)** be intimate (with), consummate marriage, copulate (with), couple (with), fornicate (with), have sexual intercourse (with), make love (to), mate (with), rape, ravish, *sl* screw, seduce, unite (with).

sexism *n inf* chauvinism, discrimination, prejudice.

sexual *adj* 1 genital, procreative, progenitive, reproductive. 2 ▷ SEXY.

sexuality *n* gender. □ *bisexuality, hermaphroditism, heterosexuality, homosexuality.*

sexy *adj* 1 amorous, carnal, concupiscent, erotic, lascivious, lecherous, *derog* lewd, libidinous, *derog* lubricious, lustful, passionate, provocative, *derog* prurient, *inf* randy, seductive, sensual, sexual, *inf* sultry, venereal, voluptuous. 2 attractive, *inf* beddable, desir-

able, *sl* dishy, flirtatious. 3 *sexy books*. aphrodisiac, arousing, pornographic, *sl* raunchy, salacious, *inf* steamy, suggestive, titillating, *inf* torrid.
▷ OBSCENE.

shabby *adj* 1 bedraggled, dilapidated, dingy, dirty, dowdy, drab, faded, frayed, *inf* grubby, mangy, *inf* motheaten, ragged, run-down, *inf* scruffy, seedy, tattered, *inf* tatty, threadbare, unattractive, worn, worn-out. *Opp* SMART. 2 *shabby behaviour*. base, contemptible, despicable, disagreeable, discreditable, dishonest, dishonourable, disreputable, ignoble, *inf* low-down, mean, nasty, shameful, shoddy, unfair, unfriendly, ungenerous, unkind, unworthy. *Opp* HONOURABLE.

shack *n* cabin, hovel, hut, lean-to, shanty, shed.

shade *n* 1 ▷ SHADOW. 2 awning, blind, canopy, covering, curtain, parasol, screen, shelter, shield, umbrella, Venetian blind. 3 *a shade of blue*. colour, hue, intensity, tinge, tint, tone. 4 *shades of meaning*. degree, difference, nicety, nuance, variation. ● *vb* 1 camouflage, conceal, cover, hide, mask, obscure, protect, screen, shield, shroud, veil. 2 *shade with pencil*. black out, block in, cross-hatch, darken, fill in, make dark.

shadow *n* 1 darkness, dimness, dusk, gloom, obscurity, penumbra, semi-darkness, shade, umbra. 2 *The sun casts shadows*. outline, shape, silhouette. 3 *a shadow of doubt*. ▷ HINT. ● *vb* dog, follow, hunt, *inf* keep tabs on, keep watch on, pursue, stalk, *inf* tag onto, tail, track, trail, watch.

shadowy *adj* 1 dark, dim, faint, hazy, ill-defined, indefinite, indistinct, nebulous, obscure, unclear, unrecognizable, vague. ▷ GHOSTLY. 2 ▷ SHADY.

shady *adj* 1 *poet* bosky, cool, dark, dim, dusky, gloomy, leafy, shaded, shadowy, sheltered, sunless. *Opp* SUNNY. 2 *a shady character*. devious, dishonest, disreputable, dubious, *inf* fishy, questionable, shifty, suspicious, unreliable, untrustworthy. *Opp* HONEST.

shaft *n* 1 arrow, column, handle, helve, pillar, pole, post, rod, shank, stanchion, stem, stick, upright. 2 duct, mine, pit, tunnel, well, working. 3 *shaft of light*. beam, gleam, laser, pencil, ray, streak.

shaggy *adj* bushy, dishevelled, fibrous, fleecy, hairy, hirsute, matted, rough, tousled, unkempt, unshorn, untidy, woolly. *Opp* SMOOTH.

shake *vb* 1 convulse, heave, jump, quake, quiver, rattle, rock, shiver, shudder, sway, throb, totter, tremble, vibrate, waver, wobble. 2 *shake your umbrella*. agitate, brandish, flourish, gyrate, jar, jerk, *inf* jiggle, *inf* joggle, jolt, oscillate, sway, swing, twirl, twitch, vibrate, wag, *inf* waggle, wave, *inf* wiggle. 3 *The bad news shook us*. alarm, distress, disturb, frighten, perturb, *inf* rattle, shock, s⁺ rtle, *inf* throw, unnerve, unsettle, upset. ▷ SURPRISE.

shaky *adj* 1 decrepit, dilapidated, feeble, flimsy, frail, insecure, precarious, ramshackle, rickety, rocky, shaking, unreli-

able, unsound, unsteady, weak, wobbly. **2** *a shaky voice.* faltering, quavering, quivering, trembling, tremulous. **3** *a shaky start.* nervous, tentative, uncertain, under-confident, unimpressive, unpromising.
Opp STEADY, STRONG.

shallow *adj* **1** *shallow water.* [There are no apt synonyms for this sense.] **2** *shallow argument.* empty, facile, foolish, frivolous, glib, insincere, puerile, silly, simple, *inf* skin-deep, slight, superficial, trivial, unconvincing, unscholarly, unthinking.
Opp DEEP.

sham *adj* artificial, bogus, counterfeit, ersatz, fake, false, fictitious, fraudulent, imitation, make-believe, mock, *inf* pretend, pretended, simulated, synthetic. ● *n* counterfeit, fake, fiction, fraud, hoax, imitation, make-believe, pretence, *inf* put-up job, simulation. ● *vb* counterfeit, fake, feign, imitate, make believe, pretend, simulate.

shambles *plur n* **1** battlefield, scene of carnage, slaughterhouse. **2** [*inf*] chaos, confusion, devastation, disorder, mess, muddle, *inf* pigsty, *inf* tip.

shame *n* **1** chagrin, degradation, discredit, disgrace, dishonour, distress, embarrassment, guilt, humiliation, ignominy, infamy, loss of face, mortification, obloquy, opprobrium, remorse, stain, stigma, vilification. **2** *a shame to mistreat him so.* outrage, pity, scandal, wickedness. ● *vb* abash, chagrin, chasten, discomfit, disconcert, discountenance, disgrace, embarrass, humble, humiliate, make someone ashamed,

mortify, *inf* put someone in his/her place, *inf* show someone up.

shamefaced *adj* **1** abashed, ashamed, chagrined, *inf* hangdog, humiliated, mortified, penitent, *inf* red-faced, remorseful, repentant, sorry. **2** bashful, coy, embarrassed, modest, self-conscious, sheepish, shy, timid.
Opp SHAMELESS.

shameful *adj* **1** *a shameful crime.* base, contemptible, deplorable, disgraceful, infamous, ignoble, low, mean, outrageous, reprehensible, scandalous, unworthy. ▷ WICKED. **2** *shameful to be found out.* compromising, degrading, demeaning, discreditable, dishonourable, embarrassing, humiliating, ignominious, *sl* infra dig, inglorious, lowering, mortifying, undignified.
Opp HONOURABLE.

shameless *adj* **1** barefaced, bold, brazen, cheeky, cool, defiant, flagrant, hardened, impenitent, impudent, incorrigible, insolent, unabashed, unashamed, unrepentant. **2** *shameless nudity.* frank, honest, immodest, indecorous, improper, open, rude, shocking, unblushing, unconcealed, undisguised, unselfconscious.
Opp SHAMEFACED.

shape *n* **1** body, build, figure, physique, profile, silhouette. **2** *geometrical shape.* configuration, figure, form, format, model, mould, outline, pattern. □ [two-dimensional] *circle, diamond, ellipse, heptagon, hexagon, lozenge, oblong, octagon, oval, parallelogram, pentagon, polygon, quadrant, quadrilateral, rectangle, rhomboid,* *rhombus, ring, semicircle, square, trapezium, trapezoid, triangle.* [three-dimensional] *cone, cube, cylinder, decahedron, hemisphere, hexahedron, octahedron, polyhedron, prism, pyramid, sphere.* ● *vb* adapt, adjust, carve, cast, cut, fashion, form, frame, give shape to, model, mould, *inf* sculpt, sculpture, whittle.

shapeless *adj* 1 amorphous, formless, indeterminate, irregular, nebulous, undefined, unformed, unstructured, vague. 2 *a shapeless figure.* deformed, distorted, *inf* dumpy, flat, misshapen, twisted, unattractive, unshapely. *Opp* SHAPELY.

shapely *adj* attractive, comely, *inf* curvaceous, elegant, good-looking, graceful, neat, trim, *inf* voluptuous, well-proportioned. *Opp* SHAPELESS.

share *n* allocation, allotment, allowance, bit, cut, division, due, fraction, helping, part, percentage, piece, portion, proportion, quota, ration, serving, *sl* whack. ● *vb* 1 allocate, allot, apportion, deal out, distribute, divide, dole out, *inf* go halves or shares (with), halve, partake of, portion out, ration out, share out, split. 2 *share work.* be involved, cooperate, join, participate, take part. **shared** ▷ JOINT.

sharp *adj* 1 acute, arrow-shaped, cutting, fine, jagged, keen, knife-edged, needle-sharp, pointed, razor-sharp, sharpened, spiky, tapering. 2 *sharp bend, drop.* abrupt, acute, angular, hairpin, marked, precipitous, sheer, steep, sudden, surprising, unexpected, vertical. 3 *sharp focus.* clear,

defined, distinct, focused, well-defined. 4 *a sharp storm.* extreme, heavy, intense, serious, severe, sudden, violent. 5 *sharp frost.* biting, bitter, keen, nippy. ▷ COLD. 6 *sharp pain.* acute, excruciating, painful, stabbing, stinging. 7 *sharp rejoinder.* acerbic, acid, acidulous, barbed, biting, caustic, critical, cutting, hurtful, incisive, malicious, mocking, mordant, sarcastic, sardonic, scathing, spiteful, tart, trenchant, unkind, venomous, vitriolic. 8 *sharp mind.* acute, agile, alert, artful, astute, bright, clever, crafty, *inf* cute, discerning, incisive, intelligent, observant, penetrating, perceptive, probing, quick-witted, searching, shrewd, *inf* smart. 9 *sharp eyes.* attentive, eagle-eyed, observant, *inf* peeled (*keep your eyes peeled*), quick, watchful, wide-open. 10 *sharp taste, smell.* acid, acrid, bitter, caustic, hot, piquant, pungent, sour, spicy, tangy, tart. 11 *sharp sound.* clear, detached, ear-splitting, high, high-pitched, penetrating, piercing, shrieking, shrill, staccato, strident. *Opp* BLUNT, DULL, SLIGHT.

sharpen *vb* file, grind, hone, make sharp, strop, whet. *Opp* BLUNT.

sharpener *n* file, grindstone, hone, pencil-sharpener, strop, whetstone.

shatter *vb* blast, break, break up, burst, crack, crush, dash to pieces, demolish, destroy, disintegrate, explode, pulverize, shiver, smash, *inf* smash to smithereens, splinter, shatter, wreck. **shattered** ▷ SURPRISED, WEARY.

sheaf *n* bundle, bunch, file, ream.

shear *vb* clip, strip, trim. ▷ CUT.

sheath *n* casing, covering, scabbard, sleeve.

sheathe *vb* cocoon, cover, encase, enclose, put away, put in a sheath, wrap.

shed *n* hut, hutch, lean-to, outhouse, penthouse, potting-shed, shack, shelter, storehouse. • *vb* abandon, cast off, discard, drop, let fall, moult, pour off, scatter, shower, spill, spread, throw off. **shed light** ▷ SHINE.

sheen *n* brightness, burnish, glaze, gleam, glint, gloss, lustre, patina, polish, radiance, reflection, shimmer, shine.

sheep *n* ewe, lamb, mutton, ram, wether.

sheepish *adj* abashed, ashamed, bashful, coy, docile, embarrassed, guilty, meek, mortified, reticent, self-conscious, self-effacing, shamefaced, shy, timid. *Opp* SHAMELESS.

sheer *adj* **1** absolute, arrant, complete, downright, out-and-out, plain, pure, simple, thoroughgoing, total, unadulterated, unalloyed, unmitigated, unmixed, unqualified, utter. **2** *a sheer cliff*. abrupt, perpendicular, precipitous, steep, vertical. **3** *sheer silk*. diaphanous, filmy, fine, flimsy, gauzy, gossamer, *inf* see-through, thin, translucent, transparent.

sheet *n* **1** bedsheet, duvet cover. **2** *[paper]* folio, leaf, page. **3** *[glass, etc]* pane, panel, plate. **4** *[ice, etc]* blanket, coating, covering, film, lamina, layer, membrane, skin, veneer. **5** *[water]* area, expanse, surface.

shelf *n* ledge, shelving.

shell *n* **1** carapace (*of tortoise*), case, casing, covering, crust, exterior, façade, hull, husk, outside, pod. **2** *fired shells at them.* cartridge, projectile. • *vb* attack with gunfire, barrage, bomb, bombard, fire at, shoot at, strafe.

shellfish *n* bivalve, crustacean, mollusc. □ *barnacle, clam, cockle, conch, crab, crayfish, cuttlefish, limpet, lobster, mussel, oyster, prawn, scallop, shrimp, whelk, winkle.*

shelter *n* **1** asylum, cover, haven, lee, protection, refuge, safety, sanctuary, security. **2** barrier, concealment, cover, fence, hut, roof, screen, shield. **3** *seek shelter for the night.* accommodation, lodging, home, housing, resting-place. ▷ HOUSE. **4** *air-raid shelter.* bunker. • *vb* **1** defend, enclose, guard, keep safe, protect, safeguard, screen, secure, shade, shield. **2** *shelter a runaway.* accommodate, give shelter to, harbour, hide, *inf* put up. **sheltered** ▷ QUIET.

shelve *vb* **1** defer, hold in abeyance, lay aside, postpone, put off, put on ice. **2** ▷ SLOPE.

shield *n* **1** barrier, bulwark, defence, guard, protection, safeguard, screen, shelter. **2** *a warrior's shield.* buckler, *heraldry* escutcheon. • *vb* cover, defend, guard, keep safe, protect, safeguard, screen, shade, shelter.

shift *n* **1** adjustment, alteration, change, move, switch, transfer, transposition. **2** *night shift.* crew, gang, group, period, *inf* stint, team, workforce.

• *vb* adjust, alter, budge, change, displace, reposition, switch, transfer, transpose. ▷ MOVE. **shift for yourself** ▷ MANAGE.

shiftless *adj* idle, indolent, ineffective, inefficient, inept, irresponsible, lazy, unambitious, unenterprising. *Opp* RESOURCEFUL.

shifty *adj* artful, canny, crafty, cunning, deceitful, designing, devious, dishonest, evasive, *inf* foxy, furtive, scheming, secretive, *inf* shady, *inf* slippery, sly, treacherous, tricky, untrustworthy, wily. *Opp* STRAIGHTFORWARD.

shimmer *vb* flicker, glimmer, glisten, ripple. ▷ SHINE.

shine *n* brightness, burnish, coruscation, glaze, gleam, glint, gloss, glow, luminosity, lustre, patina, phosphorescence, polish, radiance, reflection, sheen, shimmer, sparkle, var..ish. • *vb* 1 beam, be luminous, blaze, coruscate, dazzle, emit light, flare, flash, glare, gleam, glint, glisten, glitter, glow, phosphoresce, radiate, reflect, scintillate, shed light, shimmer, sparkle, twinkle. 2 *used to shine at maths.* be brilliant, be clever, do well, excel, *inf* make your mark, stand out. 3 *shine your shoes.* brush, buff up, burnish, clean, polish, rub up. **shining** ▷ BRIGHT, CONSPICUOUS.

shingle *n* 1 gravel, pebbles, stones. 2 *roofing shingle.* tile.

shiny *adj* bright, brilliant, burnished, gleaming, glistening, glossy, glowing, luminous, lustrous, phosphorescent, polished, reflective, rubbed, shimmering, shining, sleek, smooth. *Opp* DULL.

ship *n* boat. ▷ VESSEL. • *vb* carry, *inf* cart, convey, deliver, ferry, freight, move, send, transport.

shirk *vb* avoid, dodge, duck, evade, get out of, neglect, shun. **shirk work** be lazy, malinger, *inf* skive, slack.

shiver *n* flutter, frisson, quiver, rattle, shake, shudder, thrill, tremor, vibration. • *vb* chatter, flap, flutter, quake, quaver, quiver, rattle, shake, shudder, tremble, twitch, vibrate.

shock *n* 1 blow, collision, concussion, impact, jolt, thud. 2 *came as a shock.* *inf* bombshell, surprise, *inf* thunderbolt. 3 *state of shock.* dismay, distress, fright, trauma, upset. • *vb* 1 alarm, amaze, astonish, astound, confound, daze, dismay, distress, dumbfound, frighten, *inf* give someone a turn, jar, jolt, numb, paralyse, petrify, rock, scare, shake, stagger, startle, stun, stupefy, surprise, *inf* throw, traumatize, unnerve. 2 *Sadism shocks us.* appal, disgust, horrify, nauseate, offend, outrage, repel, revolt, scandalize, sicken.

shoddy *adj* 1 cheap, flimsy, *inf* gimcrack, inferior, jerry-built, meretricious, nasty, poor quality, *inf* rubbishy, second-rate, shabby, *sl* tacky, *inf* tatty, tawdry, *inf* trashy. 2 *shoddy work.* careless, messy, negligent, slipshod, *inf* sloppy, slovenly, untidy. *Opp* SUPERIOR.

shoe *n plur* footwear. □ boot, bootee, brogue, clog, espadrille, *inf* flip-flop, galosh, gum-boot, *inf* lace-up, moccasin, plimsoll, *pump, sabot, sandal,* inf *slip-on, slipper, trainer, wader, welling-ton.*

shoemaker *n* bootmaker, cobbler.

shoot *n* branch, bud, new growth, offshoot, sprout, sucker, twig. ● *vb* 1 *shoot a gun.* aim, discharge, fire. 2 *shoot the enemy.* aim at, bombard, fire at, gun down, hit, hunt, kill, inf let fly at, open fire on, inf pick off, shell, snipe at, strafe, inf take pot-shots at. 3 *shoot from your chair.* bolt, dart, dash, fly, hurtle, leap, move quickly, race, run, rush, speed, spring, streak. 4 *plants shoot in the spring.* bud, burgeon, develop, flourish, grow, put out shoots, spring up, sprout.

shop *n* boutique, cash-and-carry, department store, *old use* emporium, establishment, market, outlet, retailer, seller, store, wholesaler. □ baker, betting shop, bookshop, butcher, chandler, chemist, confectioner, couturier, creamery, dairy, delicatessen, draper, fishmonger, florist, garden-centre, greengrocer, grocer, haberdasher, herbalist, hypermarket, ironmonger, jeweller, launderette, minimarket, newsagent, off-licence, outfitter, pawnbroker, pharmacy, post office, poulterer, stationer, supermarket, tailor, take-away, tobacconist, toyshop, video shop, vintner, watchmaker.

shopkeeper *n* dealer, merchant, retailer, salesgirl, salesman, saleswoman, stockist, storekeeper, supplier, trader, tradesman.

shopper *n* buyer, customer, patron.

shopping *n* 1 buying, inf spending-spree. 2 goods, purchases.

shopping-centre *n* arcade, complex, hypermarket, mall, precinct.

shore *n* bank, beach, coast, edge, foreshore, sands, seashore, seaside, shingle, strand. ● *vb* **shore up** ▷ SUPPORT.

short *adj* 1 diminutive, inf dumpy, dwarfish, little, midget, fem petite, derog pint-sized, slight, small, squat, inf stubby, inf stumpy, stunted, tiny, inf wee, undergrown. 2 *a short visit.* brief, cursory, curtailed, ephemeral, fleeting, momentary, passing, quick, short-lived, temporary, transient, transitory. 3 *a short book.* abbreviated, abridged, compact, concise, cut, pocket, shortened, succinct. 4 *in short supply.* deficient, inadequate, insufficient, lacking, limited, low, meagre, scanty, scarce, sparse, wanting. 5 *a short manner.* abrupt, bad-tempered, blunt, brusque, cross, curt, gruff, grumpy, impolite, irritable, laconic, sharp, snappy, taciturn, terse, testy, uncivil, unfriendly, unkind, unsympathetic. *Opp* EXPANSIVE, LONG, PLENTIFUL, TALL. **cut short** ▷ SHORTEN.

shortage *n* absence, dearth, deficiency, deficit, insufficiency, lack, paucity, poverty, scarcity, shortfall, want. *Opp* PLENTY.

shortcoming *n* bad habit, defect, deficiency, drawback, failing, failure, fault, flaw, foible, imperfection, limitation, vice, weakness, weak point.

shorten *vb* abbreviate, abridge, compress, condense, curtail, cut, cut down, cut short, diminish, dock, lop, précis, prune, reduce, shrink, summarize, take up (*clothes*), telescope, trim, truncate. *Opp* LENGTHEN.

shortly *adv old use* anon, before long, by and by, directly, presently, soon.

short-sighted *adj* 1 myopic, near-sighted. 2 unadventurous, unimaginative, without vision.

short-tempered *adj* abrupt, acerbic, brusque, crabby, cross, crusty, curt, gruff, irascible, irritable, peevish, peremptory, shrewish, snappy, testy, touchy, waspish. *Opp* GOOD-TEMPERED.

shot *n* 1 ball, bullet, discharge, missile, pellet, projectile, round, *inf* slug. 2 *heard a shot.* bang, blast, crack, explosion, report. 3 *a first-class shot.* marksman, markswoman, sharpshooter. 4 *give it a shot.* attempt, chance, *inf* crack, effort, endeavour, *inf* go, hit, kick, *inf* stab, stroke, try. 5 *photographic shot.* angle, photograph, picture, scene, sequence, snap, snapshot.

shout *vb* bawl, bellow, *inf* belt, call, cheer, clamour, cry out, exclaim, howl, rant, roar, scream, screech, shriek, talk loudly, vociferate, whoop, yell, yelp, yowl. *Opp* WHISPER.

shove *vb inf* barge, crowd, drive, elbow, hustle, impel, jostle, nudge, press, prod, push, shoulder, thrust.

shovel *vb* clear, dig, scoop, shift.

show *n* 1 drama, performance, play, presentation, production. ▷ ENTERTAINMENT. 2 *flower show.* competition, demonstration, display, exhibition, *inf* expo, exposition, fair,

presentation. 3 *show of strength.* appearance, demonstration, façade, illusion, impression, pose, pretence, threat. 4 *just for show.* affectation, exhibitionism, flamboyance, ostentation, pretentiousness, showing off. • *vb* 1 bare, betray, demonstrate, display, divulge, exhibit, expose, make public, make visible, manifest, open up, present, produce, reveal, uncover. 2 *Let your feelings show.* appear, be seen, be visible, catch the eye, come out, emerge, make an appearance, materialize, *inf* peep through, stand out, stick out. 3 *show the way.* conduct, direct, escort, guide, indicate, lead, point out, steer, usher. 4 *show kindness.* accord, bestow, confer, grant, treat with. 5 *This photo shows us at work.* depict, give a picture of, illustrate, picture, portray, represent, symbolize. 6 *Show me how.* clarify, describe, elucidate, explain, instruct, make clear, teach, tell. 7 *Tests show I was right.* attest, bear out, confirm, corroborate, demonstrate, evince, exemplify, manifest, prove, substantiate, verify, witness. **show off** ▷ BOAST. **show up** ▷ ARRIVE, HUMILIATE.

showdown *n* confrontation, crisis, *inf* decider, decisive encounter, *inf* moment of truth.

shower *n* 1 drizzle, sprinkling. ▷ RAIN. 2 douche, shower-bath. • *vb* 1 deluge, drop, rain, spatter, splash, spray, sprinkle. 2 *shower with gifts.* heap, inundate, load, overwhelm.

show-off *n inf* big-head, boaster, braggart, conceited person, egotist, exhibitionist, *inf* poser, poseur, *inf* showman, swaggerer.

showy *adj* bright, conspicuous, elaborate, fancy, flamboyant, flashy, florid, fussy, garish, gaudy, lavish, *inf* loud, lurid, ornate, ostentatious, *inf* over the top, pretentious, striking, trumpery, vulgar. *Opp* DISCREET.

shred *n* atom, bit, fragment, grain, hint, iota, jot, piece, scintilla, scrap, sliver, snippet, speck, trace. ● *vb* cut to shreds, destroy, grate, rip up, scrap, tear. **shreds** rags, ribbons, strips, tatters.

shrewd *adj* acute, artful, astute, calculating, *inf* canny, clever, crafty, cunning, discerning, discriminating, *inf* foxy, ingenious, intelligent, knowing, observant, perceptive, percipient, perspicacious, quick-witted, sage, sharp, sly, smart, wily, wise. *Opp* STUPID.

shriek *vb* cry, scream, screech, squawk, squeal.

shrill *adj* ear-splitting, high, high-pitched, jarring, penetrating, piercing, piping, screaming, screeching, screechy, sharp, shrieking, strident, treble, whistling. *Opp* GENTLE, SONOROUS.

shrine *n* altar, chapel, holy of holies, holy place, place of worship, reliquary, sanctum, tomb. ▷ CHURCH.

shrink *vb* 1 become smaller, contract, decrease, diminish, dwindle, lessen, make smaller, narrow, reduce, shorten. ▷ SHRIVEL. *Opp* EXPAND. 2 *shrink with fear*. back off, cower, cringe, flinch, hang back, quail, recoil, retire, shy

away, wince, withdraw. *Opp* ADVANCE.

shrivel *vb* become parched, become wizened, dehydrate, desiccate, curl, droop, dry out, dry up, pucker up, wilt, wither, wrinkle. ▷ SHRINK.

shroud *n* blanket, cloak, cloud, cover, mantle, mask, pall, veil, winding-sheet. ● *vb* camouflage, cloak, conceal, cover, disguise, enshroud, envelop, hide, mask, screen, swathe, veil, wrap up.

shrub *n* bush, tree. □ berberis, blackthorn, broom, bryony, buckthorn, buddleia, camellia, daphne, forsythia, gorse, heather, hydrangea, japonica, jasmine, lavender, lilac, myrtle, privet, rhododendron, rosemary, rue, viburnum.

shudder *vb* be horrified, convulse, jerk, quake, quiver, rattle, shake, shiver, squirm, tremble, vibrate.

shuffle *vb* 1 confuse, disorganize, intermix, intersperse, jumble, mix, mix up, rearrange, reorganize. 2 *shuffle along*. drag your feet, scrape, shamble, slide. ▷ WALK.

shun *vb* avoid, disdain, eschew, flee, *inf* give the cold shoulder to, keep clear of, rebuff, reject, shy away from, spurn, steer clear of, turn away from. *Opp* SEEK.

shut *vb* bolt, close, fasten, latch, lock, push to, replace, seal, secure, slam. **shut in** ▷ CONFINE, IMPRISON. **shut off** ▷ ISOLATE. **shut out** ▷ EXCLUDE. **shut up** ▷ CONFINE, IMPRISON, SILENCE.

shutter *n* blind, louvre, screen.

shy *adj* apprehensive, backward, bashful, cautious, chary, coy, diffident, hesitant, inhibited, introverted, modest, *inf* mousy, nervous, reserved, reticent, retiring, self-conscious, self-effacing, sheepish, timid, timorous, underconfident, wary, withdrawn. *Opp* ASSERTIVE, UNINHIBITED. ● *vb* ▷ THROW.

sibling *n* brother, sister, twin. ▷ FAMILY.

sick *adj* 1 afflicted, ailing, bed-ridden, diseased, ill, indisposed, infirm, *inf* laid up, *inf* poorly, *inf* queer, sickly, *inf* under the weather, unhealthy, unwell. ▷ ILL. 2 airsick, bilious, carsick, likely to vomit, nauseated, nauseous, queasy, seasick, squeamish. 3 *sick of rudeness*. annoyed (by), bored (with), disgusted (by), distressed (by), *inf* fed up (with), glutted (with), nauseated (by), sated (with), sickened (by), tired, troubled (by), upset (by), weary. 4 [*inf*] *a sick joke*. ▷ MORBID. **be sick** ▷ VOMIT.

sicken *vb* 1 *inf* catch a bug, fail, fall ill, take sick, weaken. 2 appal, be sickening to, disgust, make someone sick, nauseate, offend, repel, revolt, *inf* turn someone off, *inf* turn someone's stomach. **sickening** ▷ REPULSIVE.

sickly *adj* 1 ailing, anaemic, delicate, drawn, feeble, frail, ill, pale, pallid, *inf* peaky, unhealthy, wan, weak. ▷ ILL. *Opp* HEALTHY. 2 *sickly sentiment*. cloying, maudlin, mawkish, *inf* mushy, nasty, nauseating, obnoxious, *inf* off-putting, syrupy, treacly, unpleasant. *Opp* REFRESHING.

sickness *n* biliousness, nausea, queasiness, vomiting. ▷ ILLNESS.

side *n* 1 *sides of a cube*. elevation, face, facet, flank, surface. 2 *side of the road*. border, boundary, brim, brink, edge, fringe, limit, margin, perimeter, rim, verge. 3 *sides in a debate*. angle, aspect, attitude, perspective, point of view, position, school of thought, slant, standpoint, view, viewpoint. 4 *sides in a quarrel*. army, camp, faction, interest, party, sect, team. ● *vb* **side with** ally with, favour, form an alliance with, *inf* go along with, join up with, partner, prefer, support, team up with. ▷ HELP.

sidestep *vb* avoid, circumvent, dodge, *inf* duck, evade, skirt round.

sidetrack *vb* deflect, distract, divert.

sideways *adj* 1 crabwise, indirect, lateral, oblique. 2 *a sideways glance*. covert, sidelong, sly, *inf* sneaky, unobtrusive.

siege *n* blockade. ● *vb* ▷ BESIEGE.

sieve *n* colander, riddle, screen, strainer. ● *vb* ▷ SIFT.

sift *vb* 1 filter, riddle, screen, separate, sieve, strain. 2 *sift evidence*. analyse, examine, investigate, pick out, review, scrutinize, select, sort out, weed out, winnow.

sigh *n* breath, exhalation, murmur, suspiration. ▷ SOUND.

sight *n* 1 eyesight, seeing, vision, visual perception. 2 *within sight*. field of vision, gaze, range, view, visibility. 3 *a brief sight of it*. glimpse, look. 4 *an impressive sight*. display, exhibition, scene, show, showpiece, spectacle. ● *vb* behold, descry, discern, • distinguish, espy, glimpse, make out, notice, observe, perceive, recognize, see, spot. **catch sight of** ▷ SEE.

sightseer *n* globe-trotter, holiday-maker, tourist, tripper, visitor.

sign *n* 1 augury, forewarning, hint, indication, indicator, intimation, omen, pointer, portent, presage, warning. ▷ SIGNAL. 2 *sign that someone was here.* clue, *inf* giveaway, indication, manifestation, marker, proof, reminder, spoor (*of animal*), suggestion, symptom, token, trace, vestige. 3 *put up a sign.* advertisement, notice, placard, poster, publicity, signboard. 4 *identifying sign.* badge, brand, cipher, device, emblem, flag, hieroglyph, ideogram, ideograph, insignia, logo, mark, monogram, rebus, symbol, trademark. ● *vb* 1 autograph, countersign, endorse, inscribe, write. 2 ▷ SIGNAL. **sign off** ▷ FINISH. **sign on** ▷ ENLIST. **sign over** ▷ TRANSFER.

signal *n* 1 communication, cue, gesticulation, gesture, *inf* go-ahead, indication, motion, sign, signal, *inf* tip-off, token, warning. □ alarm-bell, beacon, bell, burglar-alarm, buzzer, flag, flare, gong, green light, indicator, password, red light, reveille, rocket, semaphore signal, siren, smoke-signal, tocsin, old use *trafficator, traffic-lights, warning-light, whistle, winker.* 2 radio signal. broadcast, emission, output, transmission, waves. ● *vb* beckon, communicate, flag, gesticulate, give or send a signal, indicate, motion, notify, sign, wave. ▷ GESTURE.

signature *n* autograph, endorsement, mark, name.

signet *n* seal, stamp.

significance *n* denotation, force, idea, implication, import, importance, message, point, purport, relevance, sense, signification, usefulness, value, weight. ▷ MEANING.

significant *adj* 1 eloquent, expressive, indicative, informative, knowing, meaningful, pregnant, revealing, suggestive, symbolic, *inf* tell-tale. 2 *significant event.* big, consequential, considerable, historic, important, influential, memorable, newsworthy, noteworthy, relevant, salient, serious, sizeable, valuable, vital, worthwhile. *Opp* INSIGNIFICANT.

signify *vb* 1 announce, be a sign of, betoken, communicate, connote, convey, denote, express, foretell, impart, imply, indicate, intimate, make known, reflect, reveal, signal, suggest, symbolize, tell, transmit. 2 *It doesn't signify.* be significant, count, matter, merit consideration.

signpost *n* finger-post, pointer, road-sign, sign.

silence *n* 1 calm, calmness, hush, noiselessness, peace, quiet, quietness, quietude, soundlessness, stillness, tranquillity. *Opp* NOISE. 2 *Her silence puzzled us.* dumbness, muteness, reticence, speechlessness, taciturnity, uncommunicativeness. ● *vb* 1 gag, hush, keep quiet, make silent, muzzle, repress, shut up, suppress. 2 *silence engine noise.* damp, deaden, muffle, mute, quieten, smother, stifle. **Silence!** Be quiet! Be silent! *inf* Hold your tongue! Hush! Keep quiet! *inf* Pipe down! Shut up! Stop talking!

silent adj 1 hushed, inaudible, muffled, muted, noiseless, quiet, soundless. 2 dumb, laconic, inf mum, reserved, reticent, speechless, taciturn, tight-lipped, tongue-tied, uncommunicative, unforthcoming, voiceless. 3 silent listeners. attentive, rapt, restrained, still. 4 silent agreement. implied, implicit, mute, tacit, understood, unexpressed, unspoken, unuttered. Opp EXPLICIT, NOISY, TALKATIVE. **be silent** keep quiet, inf pipe down, say nothing, inf shut up.

silhouette n contour, form, outline, profile, shadow, shape.

silky adj delicate, fine, glossy, lustrous, satiny, sleek, smooth, soft, velvety.

silly adj 1 absurd, asinine, brainless, childish, crazy, daft, inf dopey, inf dotty, fatuous, feather-brained, feeble-minded, flighty, foolish, old use fond, frivolous, grotesque, inf half-baked, hare-brained, idiotic, ill-advised, illogical, immature, impractical, imprudent, inadvisable, inane, infantile, irrational, inf jokey, laughable, light-hearted, ludicrous, mad, meaningless, mindless, misguided, naïve, nonsensical, playful, pointless, preposterous, ridiculous, scatter-brained, inf scatty, senseless, shallow, simple, simple-minded, simplistic, inf soppy, stupid, thoughtless, unintelligent, unreasonable, unsound, unwise, wild, witless. Opp SERIOUS, WISE. 2 [inf] knocked silly. ▷ UNCONSCIOUS.

silt n alluvium, deposit, mud, ooze, sediment, slime, sludge.

silvan adj arboreal, leafy, tree-covered, wooded.

similar adj akin, alike, analogous, comparable, compatible, congruous, co-ordinating, corresponding, equal, equivalent, harmonious, homogeneous, identical, indistinguishable, like, matching, parallel, related, resembling, the same, toning, twin, uniform, well-matched. Opp DIFFERENT.

similarity n affinity, closeness, congruity, correspondence, equivalence, homogeneity, kinship, likeness, match, parallelism, relationship, resemblance, sameness, similitude, uniformity. Opp DIFFERENCE.

simmer vb boil, bubble, cook, seethe, stew.

simple adj 1 artless, basic, candid, childlike, elementary, frank, fundamental, guileless, homely, honest, humble, ingenuous, innocent, lowly, modest, derog naïve, natural, simple-minded, derog silly, sincere, unaffected, unassuming, unpretentious, unsophisticated. Opp SOPHISTICATED. 2 simple instructions. clear, comprehensible, direct, easy, fool-proof, intelligible, lucid, straightforward, uncomplicated, understandable. Opp COMPLEX. 3 a simple dress. austere, classical, plain, severe, stark, unadorned, unembellished. Opp ORNATE.

simplify vb clarify, explain, make simple, paraphrase, prune, inf put in words of one syllable, streamline, unravel, untangle. Opp COMPLICATE.

simplistic adj [always derog] facile, inadequate, naïve, oversimple, oversimplified, shallow, silly, superficial.

simulate *vb* act, counterfeit, dissimulate, enact, fake, feign, imitate, *inf* mock up, play-act, pretend, reproduce, sham.

simultaneous *adj* coinciding, concurrent, contemporaneous, parallel, synchronized, synchronous.

sin *n* blasphemy, corruption, depravity, desecration, devilry, error, evil, fault, guilt, immorality, impiety, iniquity, irreverence, misdeed, offence, peccadillo, profanation, sacrilege, sinfulness, transgression, *old use* trespass, ungodliness, unrighteousness, vice, wickedness, wrong, wrongdoing.
• *vb* be guilty of sin, blaspheme, do wrong, err, fall from grace, go astray, lapse, misbehave, offend, stray, transgress.

sincere *adj* candid, direct, earnest, frank, genuine, guileless, heartfelt, honest, open, real, serious, simple, *inf* straight, straightforward, true, truthful, unaffected, unfeigned, upright, wholehearted. *Opp* INSINCERE.

sincerity *n* candour, directness, earnestness, frankness, genuineness, honesty, honour, integrity, openness, straightforwardness, trustworthiness, truthfulness, uprightness.

sinewy *adj* brawny, muscular, strapping, tough, wiry.
▷ STRONG.

sinful *adj* bad, blasphemous, corrupt, damnable, depraved, erring, evil, fallen, guilty, immoral, impious, iniquitous, irreligious, irreverent, profane, sacrilegious, ungodly, unholy,

unrighteous, vile, wicked, wrong, wrongful.
Opp RIGHTEOUS.

sing *vb* carol, chant, chirp, chorus, croon, descant, hum, intone, serenade, trill, vocalize, warble, whistle, yodel.

singe *vb* blacken, burn, char, scorch, sear.

singer *n* songster, vocalist.
□ alto, balladeer, baritone, bass, carol-singer, castrato, countertenor, plur *choir*, choirboy, choirgirl, chorister, plur *chorus*, coloratura, contralto, crooner, It *diva*, folk singer, minstrel, opera singer, pop star, precentor, It *prima donna*, soloist, soprano, tenor, treble, troubadour.

single *adj* 1 exclusive, individual, isolated, lone, odd, one, only, personal, separate, singular, sole, solitary, unique, unparalleled. 2 *a single person.* celibate, *inf* free, unattached, unmarried. • *vb* **single out**
▷ CHOOSE.

single-handed *adj* alone, independent, solitary, unaided, unassisted, without help.

single-minded *adj* dedicated, determined, devoted, dogged, *derog* fanatical, *derog* obsessive, persevering, resolute, steadfast, tireless, unswerving, unwavering.

singular *adj* 1 ▷ SINGLE.
2 abnormal, curious, different, distinct, eccentric, exceptional, extraordinary, odd, outstanding, peculiar, rare, remarkable, strange, unusual.
▷ DISTINCTIVE. *Opp* COMMON.

sinister *adj* dark, disquieting, disturbing, evil, forbidding, foreboding, frightening, gloomy, inauspicious, malevolent, malignant, menacing, minatory, ominous, threatening, upsetting. 2 *sinister motives.* bad, corrupt, criminal, dishonest, furtive, illegal, nefarious, questionable, inf shady, suspect, treacherous, unworthy, villainous.

sink n basin, stoup, washbowl.
● vb 1 collapse, decline, descend, diminish, disappear, droop, drop, dwindle, ebb, fade, fail, fall, go down, go lower, plunge, set (*sun sets*), slip down, subside, vanish, weaken. 2 be engulfed, be submerged, founder, go down, go under. 3 *sink a ship.* scupper, scuttle. 4 *sink a borehole.* bore, dig, drill, excavate.

sinner n evil-doer, malefactor, miscreant, offender, reprobate, transgressor, wrongdoer.

sip vb drink, lap, sample, taste.

sit vb 1 be seated, perch, rest, seat (yourself), settle, squat, take a seat, inf take the weight off your feet. 2 *sit for a portrait.* pose. 3 *sit an exam.* be a candidate in, inf go in for, take, write. 4 *Parliament sat for 12 hours.* assemble, be in session, convene, gather, get together, meet.

site n area, campus, ground, location, place, plot, position, setting, situation, spot.
● vb ▷ SITUATE.

sitting-room n drawing-room, living-room, lounge.

situate vb build, establish, found, install, locate, place, position, put, set up, site, station.

situation n 1 area, locale, locality, location, place, position,

setting, site, spot. 2 *an awkward situation.* case, circumstances, condition, inf kettle of fish, plight, position, predicament, state of affairs. 3 *situations vacant.* employment, job, place, position, post.

size n amount, area, bigness, breadth, bulk, capacity, depth, dimensions, extent, gauge, height, immensity, largeness, length, magnitude, mass, measurement, proportions, scale, scope, volume, weight, width.
▷ MEASURE. ● vb size up
▷ ASSESS.

sizeable adj considerable, decent, generous, largish, significant, worthwhile. ▷ BIG.

skate vb glide, skim, slide.

skeleton n bones, frame, framework, structure.

sketch n 1 description, design, diagram, draft, drawing, outline, picture, plan, inf rough, skeleton, vignette. 2 *comic sketch.* performance, playlet, scene, skit, turn. ● vb depict, draw, indicate, outline, portray, represent. sketch out
▷ OUTLINE.

sketchy adj bitty, crude, cursory, hasty, hurried, imperfect, incomplete, inexact, perfunctory, rough, scrappy, undeveloped, unfinished, unpolished. Opp DETAILED, PERFECT.

skid vb aquaplane, glide, go out of control, slide, slip.

skilful adj able, accomplished, adept, adroit, apt, artful, capable, competent, consummate, crafty, cunning, deft, dexterous, experienced, expert, gifted, handy, ingenious, masterful, masterly, practised, professional, proficient, qualified, shrewd, smart, talented, trained, versatile, versed, workmanlike. ▷ CLEVER. Opp UNSKILFUL.

skill n ability, accomplishment, adroitness, aptitude, art, artistry, capability, cleverness, competence, craft, cunning, deftness, dexterity, experience, expertise, facility, flair, gift, handicraft, ingenuity, knack, mastery, professionalism, proficiency, prowess, shrewdness, talent, technique, training, versatility, workmanship.

skilled adj experienced, expert, qualified, trained, versed. ▷ SKILFUL.

skim vb 1 aquaplane, coast, fly, glide, move lightly, plane, sail, skate, ski, skid, slide, slip. 2 skim a book. dip into, leaf through, look through, read quickly, scan, skip, thumb through.

skin n casing, coat, coating, complexion, covering, epidermis, exterior, film, fur, hide, husk, integument, membrane, outside, peel, pelt, rind, shell, surface.
  ● vb excoriate, flay, pare, peel, shell, strip.

skin-deep adj insubstantial, shallow, superficial, trivial, unimportant.

skinny adj bony, emaciated, gaunt, half-starved, lanky, scraggy, wasted. ▷ THIN.

skip vb 1 bound, caper, cavort, dance, frisk, gambol, hop, jump, leap, prance, romp, spring. 2 skip the boring bits. avoid, forget, ignore, leave out, miss out, neglect, omit, overlook, pass over, skim through. 3 skip lessons. be absent from, cut, miss, play truant from.

skirmish n brush, fight, fray, scrimmage, inf set-to, tussle.
  ● vb ▷ FIGHT.

skirt vb avoid, border, bypass, circle, encircle, go round, pass round, inf steer clear of, surround.

skit n burlesque, parody, satire, sketch, spoof, inf take-off.

sky n air, atmosphere, poet blue, poet empyrean, poet firmament, poet heavens, space, stratosphere, poet welkin.

slab n block, chunk, hunk, lump, piece, slice, wedge, inf wodge.

slack adj 1 drooping, limp, loose, sagging, soft. Opp TIGHT. 2 slack attitude. careless, dilatory, disorganized, easy-going, flaccid, idle, inattentive, indolent, lax, lazy, listless, neglectful, negligent, permissive, relaxed, remiss, slothful, unbusinesslike, uncaring, undisciplined. Opp RIGOROUS. 3 slack trade. inactive, quiet, slow, slow-moving, sluggish. Opp BUSY.
  ● vb be lazy, idle, malinger, neglect your duty, shirk, inf skive.

slacken vb 1 ease off, loosen, relax, release. 2 slacken speed. abate, decrease, ease, lessen, lower, moderate, reduce, slow down.

slacker n inf good-for-nothing, idler, lazy person, malingerer, sl skiver, sluggard.

slake vb allay, assuage, cool, ease, quench, relieve, satisfy.

slam vb 1 bang, shut. 2 [inf] ▷ CRITICIZE.

slander n backbiting, calumny, defamation, denigration, insult, libel, lie, misrepresentation, obloquy, scandal, slur, smear, vilification. ● vb blacken the name of, calumniate, defame, denigrate, disparage, libel, malign, misrepresent, slur, smear, spread tales about, tell lies about, traduce, vilify.

slanderous adj abusive, calumnious, cruel, damaging, defamatory, disparaging, false, hurtful, insulting, libellous, lying, malicious, mendacious, scurrilous, untrue, vicious.

slang n argot, cant, jargon.
● vb ▷ INSULT. **slanging match**
▷ QUARREL.

slant n 1 angle, bevel, camber, cant, diagonal, gradient, incline, list, pitch, rake, ramp, slope, tilt. 2 slant on a problem. approach, attitude, perspective, point of view, standpoint, view, viewpoint. 3 slant to the news. bias, distortion, emphasis, imbalance, one-sidedness, prejudice. ● vb 1 be at an angle, be skewed, incline, lean, shelve, slope, tilt. 2 slant the news. bias, colour, distort, prejudice, twist, weight. **slanting**
▷ OBLIQUE.

slap vb smack, spank. ▷ HIT.

slash vb gash, slit. ▷ CUT.

slaughter n bloodshed, butchery, carnage, killing, massacre, murder. ● vb annihilate, butcher, massacre, murder, slay. ▷ KILL.

slaughterhouse n abattoir, shambles.

slave n old use bondslave, drudge, serf, thrall, vassal.
▷ SERVANT. ● vb drudge, exert yourself, grind away, labour, inf sweat, toil, inf work your fingers to the bone. ▷ WORK.

slave-driver n despot, hard taskmaster, tyrant.

slaver vb dribble, drool, foam at the mouth, salivate, slobber, spit.

slavery n bondage, captivity, enslavement, serfdom, servitude, subjugation, thraldom, vassalage. Opp FREEDOM.

slavish adj 1 abject, cringing, fawning, grovelling, humiliating, menial, obsequious, servile, submissive. 2 slavish imitation. close, flattering, strict, sycophantic, unimaginative, unoriginal.
Opp INDEPENDENT.

slay vb assassinate, bump off, butcher, destroy, dispatch, execute, exterminate, inf finish off, martyr, massacre, murder, put down, put to death, slaughter. ▷ KILL.

sleazy adj cheap, contemptible, dirty, disreputable, low-class, mean, mucky, run-down, seedy, slovenly, sordid, squalid, unprepossessing.

sledge n bob-sleigh, sled, sleigh, toboggan.

sleek adj 1 brushed, glossy, graceful, lustrous, shining, shiny, silken, silky, smooth, soft, trim, velvety, well-groomed. Opp UNTIDY. 2 a sleek look. complacent, contented, fawning, self-satisfied, inf slimy, inf smarmy, smug, suave, thriving, unctuous, well-fed.

sleep n inf beauty sleep, catnap, coma, dormancy, doze, inf forty winks, hibernation, sl kip, inf nap, repose, rest, inf shut-eye, siesta, slumber, snooze, torpor, unconsciousness.
● vb aestivate, be sleeping, be

unconscious, catnap, *inf* doss
down, doze, *inf* drop off,
drowse, fall asleep, go to bed,
inf have forty winks, hibernate,
sl kip, *inf* nod off, rest, slumber,
snooze, *inf* take a nap. **sleeping**
▷ ASLEEP.

sleepiness *n* drowsiness, lassitude, lethargy, somnolence,
tiredness, torpor.

sleepless *adj* awake, conscious,
disturbed, insomniac, restless,
inf tossing and turning, wakeful, watchful, wide awake.
Opp ASLEEP.

sleepwalker *n* noctambulist,
somnambulist.

sleepy *adj* 1 comatose, *inf* dopey,
drowsy, heavy, lethargic, ready
to sleep, sluggish, somnolent,
soporific, tired, torpid, weary.
2 *a sleepy village.* boring, dull,
inactive, quiet, restful, slow-
moving, unexciting. *Opp* LIVELY.

slender *adj* 1 fine, graceful, lean,
narrow, slight, svelte, sylphlike, trim. ▷ THIN. 2 *slender
thread.* feeble, fragile, tenuous.
3 *slender means.* inadequate,
meagre, scanty, small. *Opp* FAT,
LARGE.

slice *n* carving, layer, piece,
rasher, shaving, sliver, wedge.
● *vb* carve, shave off. ▷ CUT.

slick *adj* 1 adroit, artful, clever,
cunning, deft, dexterous, efficient, quick, skilful, smart. 2 *a
slick talker.* glib, meretricious,
plausible, *inf* smarmy, smooth,
smug, specious, suave, superficial, *inf* tricky, unctuous,
untrustworthy, urbane, wily.
3 *slick hair.* glossy, oiled, plastered down, shiny, sleek,
smooth.

slide *n* 1 avalanche, landslide,
landslip. 2 *photographic slide.*

transparency. ● *vb* aquaplane,
coast, glide, glissade, plane,
skate, ski, skid, skim, slip,
slither, toboggan.

slight *adj* 1 imperceptible, inadequate, inconsequential, inconsiderable, insignificant, insufficient, little, minor, negligible,
scanty, slim (*chance*), small,
superficial, trifling, trivial,
unimportant. 2 *slight build.*
delicate, effeminate, flimsy,
fragile, frail, petite, sickly, slender, slim, svelte, sylphlike,
thin, tiny, weak. *Opp* BIG.
● *n*, *vb* ▷ INSULT.

slightly *adv* hardly, moderately,
only just, scarcely. *Opp* VERY.

slim *adj* 1 fine, graceful, lean,
narrow, slender, svelte, sylphlike, trim. ▷ THIN. 2 *a slim
chance.* little, negligible,
remote, slight, unlikely.
● *vb* become slimmer, diet, lose
weight, reduce.

slime *n* muck, mucus, mud,
ooze, sludge.

slimy *adj* clammy, greasy,
mucous, muddy, oily, oozy,
inf slippy, slippery, slithery,
inf squidgy, *inf* squishy, wet.

sling *vb* cast, *inf* chuck, fling,
heave, hurl, launch, *inf* let fly,
lob, pelt, pitch, propel, shoot,
shy, throw, toss.

slink *vb* creep, edge, move guilt-
ily, prowl, skulk, slither, sneak,
steal.

slinky *adj* [*inf*] *a slinky dress.*
clinging, close-fitting, graceful,
inf sexy, sinuous, sleek.

slip *n* 1 accident, *inf* bloomer,
blunder, error, fault, *Fr* faux
pas, impropriety, inaccuracy,
indiscretion, lapse, miscalculation, mistake, oversight, *inf* slip
of the pen, slip of the tongue,

inf slip-up. **2** *slip of paper*. note, piece, sheet, strip.

• *vb* **1** aquaplane, coast, glide, glissade, move out of control, skate, ski, skid, skim, slide, slither, stumble, trip.

2 *slipped into the room*. creep, edge, move quietly, slink, sneak, steal. **give someone the slip** ▷ ESCAPE. **let slip** ▷ REVEAL. **slip away, slip the net** ▷ ESCAPE. **slip up** ▷ BLUNDER.

slippery *adj* **1** glassy, greasy, icy, lubricated, oily, slimy, *inf* slippy, slithery, smooth, wet. **2** *a slippery customer*. crafty, cunning, devious, evasive, *inf* hard to pin down, shifty, sly, *inf* smarmy, smooth, sneaky, specious, *inf* tricky, unreliable, untrustworthy, wily.

slipshod *adj* careless, disorganized, lax, messy, slapdash, *inf* sloppy, slovenly, untidy.

slit *n* aperture, breach, break, chink, cleft, crack, cut, fissure, gap, gash, hole, incision, opening, rift, slot, split, tear, vent.

• *vb* cut, gash, slice, split, tear.

slither *vb* creep, glide, *inf* skitter, slide, slink, slip, snake, worm.

sliver *n* chip, flake, shard, shaving, snippet, splinter, strip. ▷ PIECE.

slobber *vb* dribble, drool, salivate, slaver.

slogan *n* battle-cry, catchphrase, catchword, jingle, motto, war-cry, watchword. ▷ SAYING.

slope *n* angle, bank, bevel, camber, cant, gradient, hill, incline, pitch, rake, ramp, scarp, slant, tilt. □ [upwards]

acclivity, ascent, rise. □ [downwards] decline, declivity, descent, dip, drop, fall.

• *vb* ascend, bank, decline, descend, dip, fall, incline, lean, pitch, rise, shelve, slant, tilt, tip. **sloping** ▷ OBLIQUE.

sloppy *adj* **1** liquid, messy, runny, *inf* sloshy, slushy, *inf* splashing about, squelchy, watery, wet. **2** *sloppy work*. careless, dirty, disorganized, lax, messy, slapdash, slipshod, slovenly, unsystematic, untidy. **3** ▷ SENTIMENTAL.

slot *n* **1** aperture, breach, break, channel, chink, cleft, crack, cut, fissure, gap, gash, groove, hole, incision, opening, rift, slit, split, vent. **2** *slot on a schedule*. place, position, space, spot, time.

sloth *n* apathy, idleness, indolence, inertia, laziness, lethargy, sluggishness, torpor.

slouch *vb* droop, hunch, loaf, loll, lounge, sag, shamble, slump, stoop.

slovenly *adj* careless, *inf* couldn't-care-less, disorganized, lax, messy, shoddy, slapdash, slatternly, *inf* sloppy, thoughtless, unmethodical, untidy. *Opp* CAREFUL.

slow *adj* **1** careful, cautious, crawling, dawdling, delayed, deliberate, dilatory, gradual, lagging, late, lazy, leisurely, lingering, loitering, measured, moderate, painstaking, plodding, protracted, slow-moving, sluggardly, sluggish, steady, tardy, torpid, unhurried, unpunctual. **2** *slow learner*. backward, dense, dim, dull, obtuse, *inf* thick. ▷ STUPID. **3** *slow worker*. phlegmatic,

reluctant, unenthusiastic, unwilling. ▷ SLUGGISH.
Opp FAST. • vb **slow down** brake, decelerate, inf ease up, go slower, hold back, reduce speed. **be slow** ▷ DAWDLE, DELAY.

sludge n mire, muck, mud, ooze, precipitate, sediment, silt, slime, slurry, slush.

sluggish adj apathetic, dull, idle, inactive, indolent, inert, lazy, lethargic, lifeless, listless, phlegmatic, slothful, torpid, unresponsive. ▷ SLOW. Opp LIVELY.

sluice vb flush, rinse, swill, wash.

slumber n, vb ▷ SLEEP.

slump n collapse, crash, decline, depression, dip, downturn, drop, fall, falling-off, plunge, recession, trough. Opp BOOM.
• vb 1 collapse, crash, decline, dive, drop, fall off, plummet, plunge, recede, sink, slip, inf take a nosedive, worsen. Opp PROSPER. 2 **slump in a chair.** be limp, collapse, droop, flop, hunch, loll, lounge, sag, slouch, subside.

slur n affront, aspersion, calumny, imputation, innuendo, insinuation, insult, libel, slander, smear, stigma.
• vb garble, lisp, mumble.

slurry n mud, ooze, slime.

sly adj artful, inf canny, inf catty, conniving, crafty, cunning, deceitful, designing, devious, disingenuous, inf foxy, furtive, guileful, insidious, knowing, scheming, secretive, inf shifty, shrewd, inf sneaky, inf snide, stealthy, surreptitious, treacherous, tricky, underhand, wily. Opp CANDID, OPEN.

smack vb pat, slap, spank. ▷ HIT.

small adj 1 inf baby, bantam, compact, concise, cramped, diminutive, inf dinky, dwarf, exiguous, fine, fractional, infinitesimal, lean, lilliputian, little, microscopic, midget, inf mini, miniature, minuscule, minute, narrow, petite, inf pint-sized, inf pocket-sized, inf poky, portable, pygmy, short, slender, slight, inf teeny, thin, tiny, toy, undergrown, undersized, inf wee, inf weeny. 2 **small helpings.** inadequate, insufficient, meagre, mean, inf measly, miserly, modest, niggardly, parsimonious, inf piddling, scanty, skimpy, stingy, ungenerous, unsatisfactory. 3 a **small problem.** inconsequential, insignificant, minor, negligible, nugatory, slim (chance), slight, trifling, trivial, unimportant. Opp BIG. **small arms** ▷ WEAPON.

small-minded adj bigoted, grudging, hidebound, illiberal, intolerant, narrow, narrow-minded, old-fashioned, parochial, petty, prejudiced, rigid, selfish, trivial, unimaginative. ▷ MEAN. Opp BROAD-MINDED.

smart adj 1 acute, adept, artful, astute, bright, clever, crafty, inf cute, discerning, ingenious, intelligent, perceptive, perspicacious, quick, quickwitted, shrewd, sl streetwise. Opp DULL. 2 **smart appearance.** bright, chic, clean, dapper, inf dashing, elegant, fashionable, fresh, modish, inf natty, neat, inf posh, inf snazzy, Fr soigné, spruce, stylish, tidy, trim, well-dressed, well-groomed, well-looked-after. Opp SCRUFFY. 3 a **smart pace.** brisk, inf cracking, fast, forceful, quick, rapid, *inf* rattling, speedy, swift. 4 *a smart blow.* painful, sharp, stinging, vigorous. • *vb* ▷ HURT.

smash *vb* 1 *smash to pieces.* crumple, crush, demolish, destroy, shatter, squash, wreck. ▷ BREAK. 2 *smash into a wall.* bang, bash, batter, bump, collide, crash, hammer, knock, pound, ram, slam, strike, thump, wallop. ▷ HIT.

smear *n* 1 blot, daub, mark, smudge, stain, streak. 2 *a smear on your name.* aspersion, calumny, defamation, imputation, innuendo, insinuation, libel, slander, slur, stigma, vilification. • *vb* 1 dab, daub, plaster, rub, smudge, spread, wipe. 2 *smear a reputation.* attack, besmirch, blacken, calumniate, defame, discredit, libel, malign, slander, stigmatize, tarnish, vilify.

smell *n* odour, redolence. □ [pleasant] *aroma, bouquet, fragrance, incense, nose, perfume, scent.* □ [unpleasant] *fetor, mephitis, miasma,* inf *pong, pungency, reek, stench, stink, whiff.* • *vb* 1 inf *get a whiff of,* scent, sniff. 2 *onions smell.* inf *hum,* inf *pong, reek, stink, whiff.*

smelling *adj* [*Smelling* is usually used in combination: sweet-smelling, etc.] 1 *pleasant-smelling.* aromatic, fragrant, musky, odoriferous, odorous, perfumed, redolent, scented, spicy. 2 *unpleasant-smelling.* fetid, foul, gamy, inf *high,* malodorous, mephitic, miasmic, musty, noisome, inf *off,* sl *pongy,* pungent, putrid, rank, reeking, rotten, smelly, stinking, inf *whiffy. Opp* ODOURLESS.

smelly *adj* ▷ SMELLING.

smile *n, vb* beam, grin, leer, laugh, simper, smirk, sneer.

smoke *n* 1 air pollution, exhaust, fog, fumes, gas, smog, steam, vapour. 2 cigar, cigarette, cheroot, inf *fag,* pipe, tobacco. • *vb* 1 emit smoke, fume, reek, smoulder. 2 *smoke cigars.* inhale, puff at.

smoky *adj* clouded, dirty, foggy, grimy, hazy, sooty. *Opp* CLEAR.

smooth *adj* 1 even, flat, horizontal, level, plane, regular, unbroken, unruffled. 2 *smooth sea.* calm, peaceful, placid, quiet, restful. 3 *a smooth finish.* burnished, glassy, glossy, polished, satiny, shiny, silken, silky, sleek, soft, velvety. 4 *smooth progress.* comfortable, easy, effortless, fluent, steady, uncluttered, uneventful, uninterrupted, unobstructed. 5 *a smooth taste.* agreeable, bland, mellow, mild, pleasant, soft, soothing. 6 *a smooth mixture.* creamy, flowing, runny. 7 *a smooth talker.* convincing, facile, glib, insincere, plausible, polite, self-assured, self-satisfied, slick, smug, sophisticated, suave, untrustworthy, urbane. *Opp* ROUGH. • *vb* buff up, burnish, even out, file, flatten, iron, level, level off, plane, polish, press, roll out, sand down, sandpaper.

smother *vb* 1 asphyxiate, choke, cover, kill, snuff out, stifle, strangle, suffocate, throttle. 2 ▷ SUPPRESS.

smoulder *vb* burn, smoke. **smouldering** ▷ ANGRY.

smudge *vb* blot, blur, dirty, mark, smear, stain, streak.

smug *adj* complacent, conceited, *inf* holier-than-thou, pleased, priggish, self-important, self-righteous, self-satisfied, sleek, superior. Opp HUMBLE.

snack *n* bite, *inf* elevenses, *inf* nibble, refreshments. ▷ MEAL.

snack-bar *n* buffet, café, cafeteria, fast-food restaurant, transport café.

snag *n* catch, complication, difficulty, drawback, hindrance, hitch, impediment, obstacle, obstruction, problem, set-back, *inf* stumbling-block. • *vb* catch, jag, rip, tear.

snake *n* ophidian, serpent. □ *adder, anaconda, boa constrictor, cobra, copperhead, flying-snake, grass snake, mamba, python, rattlesnake, sand snake, sea snake, sidewinder, tree snake, viper.* • *vb* crawl, creep, meander, twist and turn, wander, worm, zigzag. **snaking** ▷ TWISTY.

snap *adj* ▷ SUDDEN. • *vb* 1 break, crack, fracture, give way, part, split. 2 *snap your fingers.* click, crack, pop. 3 *dog snapped at me.* bite, gnash, nip, snatch. 4 *snap orders.* bark, growl, *inf* jump down someone's throat, snarl, speak angrily.

snare *n* ambush, booby-trap, *old use* gin, noose, springe, trap. • *vb* capture, catch, decoy, ensnare, entrap, net, trap.

snarl *vb* 1 bare the teeth, growl. 2 *snarl up rope.* confuse, entangle, jam, knot, tangle, twist.

snatch *vb* 1 catch, clutch, grab, grasp, lay hold of, pluck, seize, take, wrench away, wrest away. 2 abduct, kidnap, remove, steal.

sneak *vb* 1 creep, move stealthily, prowl, skulk, slink, stalk, steal. 2 [*inf*] *sneak on someone.* *sl* grass, inform (against), report, *sl* snitch, *inf* tell tales (about).

sneaking *adj* furtive, half-formed, intuitive, lurking, nagging, *inf* niggling, persistent, private, secret, uncomfortable, unconfessed, undisclosed, unproved, worrying.

sneaky *adj* cheating, contemptible, crafty, deceitful, despicable, devious, dishonest, furtive, *inf* low-down, mean, nasty, shady, *inf* shifty, sly, treacherous, underhand, unorthodox, unscrupulous, untrustworthy. Opp STRAIGHTFORWARD.

sneer *vb* be contemptuous, be scornful, boo, curl your lip, hiss, hoot, jeer, laugh, mock, scoff, sniff. **sneer at** ▷ DENIGRATE, RIDICULE.

sniff *vb* 1 *inf* get a whiff of, scent, smell. 2 ▷ SNIVEL. 3 ▷ SNEER.

snigger *vb* chuckle, giggle, laugh, snicker, titter.

snip *vb* clip, dock, nick, nip. ▷ CUT.

snipe *vb* fire, shoot, *inf* take potshots. **snipe at** ▷ CRITICIZE.

snippet *n* fragment, morsel, particle, scrap, shred, snatch. ▷ PIECE.

snivel *vb* blubber, cry, grizzle, mewl, sob, sniff, sniffle, snuffle, whimper, whine, *inf* whinge. ▷ WEEP.

snobbish *adj* affected, condescending, disdainful, élitist, haughty, highfalutin, *inf* hoity-toity, lofty, lordly, patronizing, pompous, *inf* posh, presumptuous, pretentious, *inf* putting on

snoop

airs, self-important, smug,
inf snooty, *inf* stuck-up, supercilious, superior, *inf* toffee-
nosed. ▷ CONCEITED.
Opp UNPRETENTIOUS.

snoop *vb* be inquisitive, butt in,
do detective work, interfere,
intrude, investigate, meddle,
inf nose about, pry, sneak, spy,
inf stick your nose in.

snooper *n* busybody, detective,
investigator, meddler, sneak,
spy.

snout *n* face, muzzle, nose,
nozzle, proboscis, trunk.

snub *vb* be rude to, brush off,
cold-shoulder, disdain, humiliate, insult, offend, *inf* put someone down, rebuff, reject, scorn,
inf squash.

snuff *vb* extinguish, put out.
snuff it ▷ DIE. **snuff out**
▷ KILL.

snug *adj* 1 comfortable,
inf comfy, cosy, enclosed,
friendly, intimate, protected,
reassuring, relaxed, relaxing,
restful, safe, secure, sheltered,
soft, warm. 2 *a snug fit.* close-
fitting, exact, well-tailored.

soak *vb* bathe, *inf* dunk, drench,
immerse, marinate, penetrate,
permeate, pickle, saturate,
souse, steep, submerge, wet
thoroughly. **soaked, soaking**
▷ WET. **soak up** ▷ ABSORB.

soar *vb* 1 ascend, climb, float,
fly, glide, hang, hover, rise,
tower. 2 *prices soared.* escalate,
increase, rise, rocket, shoot up,
spiral.

sob *vb* blubber, cry, gasp, snivel,
inf sob your heart out, whimper. ▷ WEEP.

sober *adj* 1 calm, clear-headed,
composed, dignified, grave, in
control, level-headed, lucid,

society

peaceful, quiet, rational, sedate,
sensible, serene, serious,
solemn, steady, subdued, tranquil, unexciting. *Opp* SILLY.
2 *sober habits.* abstemious,
moderate, *inf* on the wagon,
restrained, self-controlled,
staid, teetotal, temperate.
Opp DRUNK. 3 *sober dress.*
colourless, drab, dull, plain,
sombre.

sociable *adj* affable, approachable, *old use* clubbable, companionable, convivial, extroverted,
friendly, gregarious, hospitable,
neighbourly, outgoing, warm,
welcoming. ▷ SOCIAL.
Opp UNFRIENDLY, WITHDRAWN.

social *adj* 1 civilized, collaborative, gregarious, organized.
2 *social events.* collective,
communal, community,
general, group, popular, public.
▷ SOCIABLE. *Opp* SOLITARY.
• *n* dance, disco, *inf* do, gathering, *inf* get-together, party,
reception, reunion, soirée.
▷ PARTY.

socialize *vb* associate, be sociable, entertain, fraternize, get
together, *inf* go out together,
join in, keep company, mix,
relate.

society *n* 1 civilization, the
community, culture, the human
family, mankind, nation,
people, the public. 2 *the society
of our friends.* camaraderie,
companionship, company,
fellowship, friendship, togetherness. 3 *a secret society, etc.* academy, alliance, association,
brotherhood, circle, club,
confraternity, fraternity, group,
guild, league, organization,
sisterhood, sodality, sorority,
union.

500

sofa *n* chaise longue, couch, settee, sofa bed. ▷ SEAT.

soft *adj* **1** compressible, crumbly, cushiony, elastic, flabby, flexible, floppy, limp, malleable, mushy, plastic, pliable, pliant, pulpy, spongy, springy, squashable, squashy, squeezable, supple, tender, yielding. **2** *soft ground*. boggy, marshy, muddy, sodden, waterlogged. **3** *a soft bed*. comfortable, cosy. **4** *soft texture*. downy, feathery, fleecy, fluffy, furry, satiny, silky, sleek, smooth, velvety. **5** *soft music*. dim, faint, low, mellifluous, muted, peaceful, quiet, relaxing, restful, soothing, subdued. **6** *soft breeze*. balmy, delicate, gentle, light, mild, pleasant, warm. **7** [*inf*] *a soft option*. easy, undemanding. **8** *soft feelings*. ▷ SOFT-HEARTED. *Opp* HARD, HARSH, VIOLENT.

soften *vb* **1** abate, alleviate, buffer, cushion, deaden, decrease, deflect, diminish, lower, make softer, mellow, mitigate, moderate, muffle, pacify, palliate, quell, quieten, reduce the impact of, subdue, temper, tone down, turn down. **2** dissolve, fluff up, lighten, liquefy, make softer, melt. **3** *soften in attitude*. become softer, concur, ease up, give in, give way, *inf* let up, relax, succumb, weaken, yield. *Opp* HARDEN, INTENSIFY.

soft-hearted *adj* benign, compassionate, conciliatory, easygoing, generous, indulgent, kind-hearted, *derog* lax, lenient, merciful, permissive, sentimental, *inf* soft, sympathetic, tender, tender-hearted, tolerant, understanding. ▷ KIND. *Opp* CRUEL.

soggy *adj* drenched, dripping, heavy (*soil*), saturated, soaked, sodden, *inf* sopping, wet through. ▷ WET. *Opp* DRY.

soil *n* clay, dirt, earth, ground, humus, land, loam, marl, topsoil. ● *vb* befoul, besmirch, blacken, contaminate, defile, dirty, make dirty, muddy, pollute, smear, stain, sully, tarnish.

solace *n* comfort, consolation, reassurance, relief. ● *vb* ▷ CONSOLE.

soldier *n* fighter, fighting man, fighting woman, *old use* man at arms, servicewoman, service-woman, warrior. □ *cadet, cavalryman, centurion, commando, conscript, guardsman, gunner, infantryman, lancer, marine, mercenary, NCO, officer, paratrooper, private, recruit, regular, rifleman, sapper, sentry, trooper,* plur *troops, warrior*. ▷ FIGHTER, RANK. ● *vb* **soldier on** ▷ PERSIST.

sole *adj* exclusive, individual, lone, one, only, single, singular, solitary, unique.

solemn *adj* **1** earnest, gloomy, glum, grave, grim, long-faced, reserved, sedate, serious, sober, sombre, staid, straight-faced, thoughtful, unsmiling. *Opp* CHEERFUL. **2** *a solemn occasion*. august, awe-inspiring, awesome, ceremonial, ceremonious, dignified, ecclesiastical, formal, grand, holy, important, imposing, impressive, liturgical, momentous, pompous, religious, ritualistic, stately. *Opp* FRIVOLOUS.

solicit *vb* appeal for, ask for, beg, entreat, importune, petition, seek.

solicitous *adj* **1** attentive, caring, concerned, considerate, sympathetic. **2** ▷ ANXIOUS.

solid *adj* **1** concrete, hard, impenetrable, impermeable, rigid, unmoving. **2** *a solid crowd.* compact, crowded, dense, jammed, packed. **3** *solid gold.* authentic, genuine, pure, real, unadulterated, unalloyed, unmixed. **4** *a solid hour.* continual, continuous, entire, unbroken, uninterrupted, unrelieved, whole. **5** *solid foundations.* firm, fixed, immovable, robust, sound, stable, steady, stout, strong, sturdy, substantial, unbending, unyielding, well-made. **6** *a solid shape.* cubic, rounded, spherical, thick, three-dimensional. **7** *solid evidence.* authoritative, cogent, coherent, convincing, genuine, incontrovertible, indisputable, irrefutable, provable, proven, real, sound, tangible, weighty. **8** *solid support.* complete, dependable, effective, like-minded, reliable, stalwart, strong, trustworthy, unanimous, undivided, united, unwavering, vigorous. *Opp* FLUID, FRAGMENTARY, WEAK.

solidarity *n* accord, agreement, coherence, cohesion, concord, harmony, like-mindedness, unanimity, unity. *Opp* DISUNITY.

solidify *vb* cake, clot, coagulate, congeal, crystallize, freeze, harden, jell, set, thicken. *Opp* LIQUEFY.

soliloquy *n* monologue, speech.

solitary *adj* **1** alone, anti-social, cloistered, companionless, friendless, isolated, lonely, lonesome, reclusive, unsociable, withdrawn. **2** *a solitary*

survivor. individual, one, only, single, sole. **3** *a solitary place.* desolate, distant, hidden, inaccessible, isolated, out-of-the-way, private, remote, secluded, sequestered, unfrequented, unknown. *Opp* NUMEROUS, PUBLIC, SOCIAL. ● *n* anchorite, hermit, *inf* loner, recluse.

solitude *n* aloneness, friendlessness, isolation, loneliness, privacy, remoteness, retirement, seclusion.

solo *adv* alone, individually, on your own, unaccompanied.

soloist *n* performer, player, singer. ▷ MUSICIAN.

soluble *adj* **1** explicable, manageable, solvable, tractable, understandable. **2** *soluble in water.* dispersing, dissolving, melting. *Opp* INSOLUBLE.

solution *n* **1** answer, clarification, conclusion, denouement, elucidation, explanation, explication, key, outcome, resolution, solving, unravelling, working out. **2** *a chemical solution.* blend, compound, emulsion, infusion, mixture, suspension.

solve *vb* answer, clear up, *inf* crack, decipher, elucidate, explain, explicate, figure out, find the solution to, interpret, puzzle out, resolve, unravel, work out.

solvent *adj* creditworthy, in credit, profitable, reliable, self-supporting, solid, sound, viable. *Opp* BANKRUPT.

sombre *adj* black, bleak, cheerless, dark, dim, dismal, doleful, drab, dreary, dull, funereal, gloomy, grave, grey, joyless, lowering, lugubrious, melancholy, morose, mournful,

serious, sober. ▷ SAD.
Opp CHEERFUL.

somewhat adv fairly, moderately, inf pretty, quite, rather, inf sort of.

song n air, inf ditty, inf hit, lyric, number, tune. □ anthem, aria, ballad, blues, calypso, cantata, canticle, carol, chant, chorus, descant, folk-song, hymn, jingle, Ger lied [plur lieder], lullaby, madrigal, nursery rhyme, plainsong, pop song, psalm, reggae, rock, serenade, shanty, soul, spiritual, wassail.

sonorous adj deep, full, loud, powerful, resonant, resounding, reverberant, rich, ringing. Opp SHRILL.

soon adv old use anon, inf any minute now, before long, inf in a minute, presently, quickly, shortly, straight away.

sooner adv 1 before, earlier. 2 sooner have tea than coffee. preferably, rather.

soot n dirt, grime.

soothe vb allay, appease, assuage, calm, comfort, compose, ease, mollify, pacify, quiet, relieve, salve, settle, still, tranquillize.

soothing adj 1 balmy, balsamic, comforting, demulcent, emollient, healing, lenitive, mild, palliative. 2 soothing music. calming, gentle, peaceful, pleasant, reassuring, relaxing, restful, serene.

sophisticated adj 1 adult, sl cool, cosmopolitan, cultivated, cultured, elegant, fashionable, inf grown-up, mature, polished, inf posh, derog pretentious, refined, stylish, urbane, worldly. Opp UNSOPHISTICATED. 2 sophisticated ideas. advanced,

clever, complex, complicated, elaborate, hard to understand, ingenious, intricate, involved, subtle. Opp PRIMITIVE, SIMPLE.

soporific adj boring, deadening, hypnotic, sedative, sleep-inducing, sleepy, somnolent. Opp LIVELY.

sorcerer n conjuror, enchanter, enchantress, magician, magus, medicine man, necromancer, sorceress, old use warlock, witch, witch-doctor, wizard.

sorcery n black magic, charms, conjuring, diabolism, incantations, magic, inf mumbo-jumbo, necromancy, the occult, spells, voodoo, witchcraft, wizardry.

sordid adj 1 dingy, dirty, disreputable, filthy, foul, miserable, inf mucky, nasty, offensive, polluted, putrid, ramshackle, seamy, seedy, inf sleazy, inf slummy, squalid, ugly, unclean, undignified, unpleasant, unsanitary, wretched. Opp CLEAN. 2 sordid dealings. avaricious, base, corrupt, covetous, degenerate, despicable, dishonourable, ignoble, ignominious, immoral, mean, mercenary, rapacious, selfish, inf shabby, shameful, unethical, unscrupulous. Opp HONOURABLE.

sore adj 1 aching, burning, chafing, delicate, hurting, inflamed, painful, raw, red, sensitive, smarting, stinging, tender. 2 aggrieved, hurt, irked, inf peeved, inf put out, resentful, upset, vexed. ▷ ANNOYED. ● n abrasion, abscess, boil, bruise, burn, carbuncle, gall, gathering, graze, infection, inflammation, injury, laceration, pimple, rawness, redness,

scrape, spot, swelling, ulcer.
▷ WOUND. **make sore** abrade,
burn, bruise, chafe, chap, gall,
graze, hurt, inflame, lacerate,
redden, rub.

sorrow n 1 affliction, anguish,
dejection, depression, desolation, despair, desperation,
despondency, disappointment,
discontent, disgruntlement,
dissatisfaction, distress, dolour,
gloom, glumness, grief, heartache, heartbreak, heaviness,
homesickness, hopelessness,
loneliness, melancholy, misery,
misfortune, mourning, sad feelings, sadness, suffering, tearfulness, tribulation, trouble,
unhappiness, wistfulness, woe,
wretchedness. Opp HAPPINESS.
2 sorrow for wrongdoing. apolo-
gies, guilt, penitence, regret,
remorse, repentance.
● vb agonize, be sorrowful, be
sympathetic, bewail, grieve,
lament, mourn, weep.
Opp REJOICE.

sorrowful adj broken-hearted,
dejected, disconsolate,
distressed, doleful, grief-
stricken, heartbroken, long-
faced, lugubrious, melancholy,
miserable, mournful, regretful,
rueful, saddened, sombre, tearful, unhappy, upset, woebegone,
woeful, wretched. ▷ SAD, SORRY.
Opp HAPPY.

sorry adj 1 apologetic, ashamed,
conscience-stricken, contrite,
guilt-ridden, penitent, regretful,
remorseful, repentant, shamefaced. 2 sorry for the homeless.
compassionate, concerned,
merciful, pitying, sympathetic,
understanding.

sort n 1 brand, category, class,
classification, description,
form, genre, group, kind, make,

mark, nature, quality, set, type,
variety. 2 breed, class, family,
genus, race, species, strain,
stock, variety. ● vb arrange,
assort, catalogue, categorize,
classify, divide, file, grade,
group, order, organize, put in
order, rank, systematize, tidy.
Opp MIX. **sort out** 1 choose,
inf put on one side, segregate,
select, separate, set aside. 2 sort
out a problem. attend to, clear
up, cope with, deal with, find
an answer to, grapple with,
handle, manage, organize, put
right, resolve, solve, straighten
out, tackle.

soul n 1 psyche, spirit.
2 [inf] poor soul! ▷ PERSON.

soulful adj deeply felt, eloquent,
emotional, expressive, fervent,
heartfelt, inspiring, moving,
passionate, profound, sincere,
spiritual, stirring, uplifting,
warm. Opp SOULLESS.

soulless adj cold, inhuman,
insincere, mechanical, perfunctory, routine, spiritless, superficial, trite, unemotional,
unfeeling, uninspiring, unsympathetic. Opp SOULFUL.

sound adj 1 durable, fit, healthy,
hearty, inf in good shape,
robust, secure, solid, strong,
sturdy, tough, undamaged,
uninjured, unscathed, vigorous,
well, whole. 2 sound food. eatable, edible, fit for human
consumption, good, wholesome.
3 sound ideas. balanced, coherent, commonsense, correct,
convincing, judicious, logical,
orthodox, prudent, rational,
reasonable, reasoned, sane,
sensible, well-founded, wise.
4 a sound business. dependable,
established, profitable, recognized, reliable, reputable, safe,

secure, trustworthy, viable.
Opp BAD, WEAK. ● *n* din, noise,
resonance, timbre, tone.
□ [Most of these words can be
used as either *nouns* or *verbs*.]
*bang, bark, bawl, bay, bellow,
blare, blast, bleat, bleep, boo,
boom, bray, buzz, cackle, caw,
chime, chink, chirp, chirrup,
chug, clack, clamour, clang,
clank, clap, clash, clatter, click,
clink, cluck, coo, crack, crackle,
crash, creak, croak, croon, crow,
crunch, cry, drone, echo, explosion, fizz, grate, grizzle, groan,
growl, grunt, gurgle, hiccup,
hiss, honk, hoot, howl, hum,
jabber, jangle, jeer, jingle, lisp,
low, miaow, moan, moo,
murmur, neigh, patter, peal,
ping, pip, plop, pop, purr,
quack, rattle, report, reverberation, ring, roar, rumble, rustle,
scream, screech, shout, shriek,
sigh, sizzle, skirl, slam, slurp,
smack, snap, snarl, sniff, snore,
snort, sob, splutter, squawk,
squeak, squeal, squelch, swish,
throb, thud, thump, thunder,
tick, ting, tinkle, toot, trumpet,
twang, tweet, twitter, wail,
warble, whimper, whine,
whinny, whir, whisk, whiz,
whoop, woof, yap, yell, yelp,
yodel, yowl.* ▷ NOISE.
● *vb* 1 become audible, be
heard, echo, make a noise, resonate, resound, reverberate.
2 *sound a signal.* activate,
cause, create, make, make audible, produce, pronounce, set off,
utter. **sound out** check, examine, inquire into, investigate,
measure, plumb, probe,
research, survey, test, try.

soup *n* broth, consommé, stock.

sour *adj* 1 acid, acidic, acidulous.
bitter, citrus, lemony, pungent,
sharp, tangy, tart, unripe, vinegary. 2 *sour milk.* bad,
curdled, *inf* off, rancid, stale,
turned. 3 *sour remarks.* acerbic,
bad-tempered, bitter, caustic,
cross, crusty, curmudgeonly,
cynical, disaffected, disagreeable, grudging, grumpy, ill-
natured, irritable, jaundiced,
peevish, petulant, snappy, testy,
unpleasant.

source *n* 1 author, begetter,
cause, creator, derivation,
informant, initiator, originator,
root, starting-point. 2 *source of
river.* head, origin, spring,
start, well-head, well-spring.
▷ BEGINNING.

souvenir *n* heirloom, keepsake,
memento, relic, reminder.

sovereign *adj* 1 absolute, all-
powerful, dominant, highest,
royal, supreme, unlimited.
2 *sovereign state.* autonomous,
independent, self-governing.
● *n* emperor, empress, king,
monarch, prince, princess,
queen. ▷ RULER.

sow *vb* broadcast, disseminate,
plant, scatter, seed, spread.

space *adj* extraterrestrial, interplanetary, interstellar, orbiting.
● *n* 1 emptiness, endlessness,
ionosphere, infinity, stratosphere, the universe. 2 *space to
move about. inf* elbow-room,
expanse, freedom, latitude,
leeway, margin, room, scope,
spaciousness. 3 *an empty space.*
area, blank, break, chasm,
concourse, distance, duration,
gap, hiatus, hole, intermission,
interval, lacuna, lapse, opening,
place, spell, stretch, time,
vacuum, wait. ● *vb space things
out.* ▷ ARRANGE.

spacious *adj* ample, broad, capacious, commodious, extensive,

large, open, roomy, sizeable, vast, wide. ▷ BIG. *Opp* SMALL.

span *n* breadth, compass, distance, duration, extent, interval, length, period, reach, scope, stretch, term, width.
• *vb* arch over, bridge, cross, extend across, go over, pass over, reach over, straddle, stretch over, traverse.

spank *vb* slap, slipper, smack. ▷ HIT, PUNISH.

spar *vb* box, exchange blows, scrap, shadow-box. ▷ FIGHT.

spare *adj* 1 additional, auxiliary, extra, free, inessential, in reserve, leftover, odd, remaining, superfluous, supernumerary, supplementary, surplus, unnecessary, unneeded, unused, unwanted. *Opp* NECESSARY. 2 *a spare figure*. ▷ THIN.
• *vb* 1 be merciful to, deliver, forgive, free, have mercy on, let go, let off, liberate, pardon, redeem, release, reprieve, save. 2 *spare money, time, etc.* afford, allow, donate, give, give up, manage, part with, provide, sacrifice. **sparing** ▷ ECONOMICAL, MISERLY.

spark *n* flash, flicker, gleam, glint, scintilla, sparkle.
• *vb* **spark off** ignite, kindle. ▷ PROVOKE.

sparkle *vb* burn, coruscate, flash, flicker, gleam, glint, glitter, reflect, scintillate, shine, spark, twinkle, wink. ▷ LIGHTEN.

sparkling *adj* 1 brilliant, flashing, glinting, glittering, scintillating, shining, shiny, twinkling. ▷ BRIGHT. *Opp* DULL. 2 *sparkling drinks.* aerated, bubbling, bubbly, carbonated, effervescent, fizzy, foaming.

sparse *adj inf* few and far between, inadequate, light, little, meagre, scanty, scarce, scattered, sparing, spread out, thin, *inf* thin on the ground. *Opp* PLENTIFUL.

spartan *adj* abstemious, ascetic, austere, bare, bleak, disciplined, frugal, hard, harsh, plain, rigid, rigorous, severe, simple, stern, strict. *Opp* LUXURIOUS.

spasm *n* attack, contraction, convulsion, eruption, fit, jerk, outburst, paroxysm, seizure, *plur* throes, twitch.

spasmodic *adj inf* by fits and starts, erratic, fitful, intermittent, interrupted, irregular, jerky, occasional, *inf* on and off, periodic, sporadic. *Opp* CONTINUOUS, REGULAR.

spate *n* cataract, flood, flow, gush, inundation, onrush, outpouring, rush, torrent.

spatter *vb* bespatter, besprinkle, daub, pepper, scatter, shower, slop, speckle, splash, splatter, spray, sprinkle.

speak *vb* answer, argue, articulate, ask, communicate, complain, converse, declaim, declare, deliver a speech, discourse, ejaculate, enunciate, exclaim, express yourself, fulminate, harangue, hold a conversation, hold forth, object, *inf* pipe up, plead, pronounce words, read aloud, recite, say something, soliloquize, *inf* speechify, talk, tell, use your voice, utter, verbalize, vocalize, voice. ▷ SAY, TALK. **speak about** ▷ MENTION. **speak to** ▷ ADDRESS. **speak your mind** be honest, say what you think, speak honestly,

speak out, state your opinion,
voice your thoughts.

speaker n lecturer, mouthpiece,
orator, public speaker, spokesperson.

spear n assegai, harpoon, javelin, lance, pike.

special adj 1 different, distinguished, exceptional, extraordinary, important, infrequent, momentous, notable,
noteworthy, odd, inf out-of-the-
ordinary, rare, red-letter (day),
remarkable, significant,
strange, uncommon, unconventional, unorthodox, unusual.
Opp ORDINARY. 2 Petrol has a
special smell. characteristic,
distinctive, idiosyncratic,
memorable, peculiar, singular,
unique, unmistakable. 3 my
special chair. especial, individual, particular, personal. 4 a
special tool for the job. bespoke,
proper, specific, specialized.

specialist n 1 authority,
connoisseur, expert, fancier
(pigeon fancier), master, professional, inf pundit, researcher.
2 [medical] consultant.
▷ MEDICINE.

speciality n inf claim to fame,
expertise, field, forte, genius,
inf line, specialization, special
knowledge, special skill,
strength, strong point, talent.

specialize vb specialize in be a
specialist in, be best at, concentrate on, devote yourself to,
have a reputation for.

specialized adj esoteric, expert,
specialist, unfamiliar.

species n breed, class, genus,
kind, race, sort, type, variety.

specific adj clear-cut, defined,
definite, detailed, exact,
explicit, express, fixed, identi-

fied, individual, itemized,
known, named, particular,
peculiar, precise, predetermined, special, specified,
unequivocal. Opp GENERAL.

specify vb be specific about,
define, denominate, detail,
enumerate, establish, identify,
itemize, list, name, particular-
ize, inf set out, spell out, stipulate.

specimen n exemplar, example,
illustration, instance, model,
pattern, representative, sample.

specious adj casuistic, deceptive, misleading, plausible,
seductive.

speck n bit, crumb, dot, fleck,
grain, mark, mite, old use mote,
particle, speckle, spot, trace.

speckled adj blotchy, brindled,
dappled, dotted, flecked, freckled, mottled, patchy, spattered
(with), spotted, spotty, sprin-
kled (with), stippled.

spectacle n ceremonial, ceremony, colourfulness, display,
exhibition, extravaganza,
grandeur, magnificence, ostentation, pageantry, parade,
pomp, show, sight, spectacular
effects, splendour. **spectacles**
▷ GLASS.

spectacular adj beautiful,
breathtaking, colourful,
dramatic, elaborate, eye-catching, impressive, magnificent,
derog ostentatious, sensational,
showy, splendid, stunning.

spectator n plur audience,
beholder, bystander,
plur crowd, eye-witness, looker-
on, observer, onlooker, passer-
by, viewer, watcher, witness.

spectre n apparition, ghost,
phantom, presentiment, vision,
wraith. ▷ SPIRIT.

spectrum *n* compass, extent, gamut, orbit, range, scope, series, span, spread, sweep, variety.

speculate *vb* 1 conjecture, consider, hypothesize, make guesses, meditate, ponder, reflect, ruminate, surmise, theorize, weigh up, wonder. ▷ THINK. **2** *speculate in shares.* gamble, invest speculatively, *inf* play the market, take a chance, wager.

speculative *adj* 1 abstract, based on guesswork, conjectural, doubtful, *inf* gossipy, hypothetical, notional, suppositional, suppositious, theoretical, unfounded, uninformed, unproven, untested. *Opp* PROVEN. **2** *speculative investments.* *inf* chancy, *inf* dicey, *inf* dodgy, hazardous, *inf* iffy, risky, uncertain, unpredictable, unreliable, unsafe. *Opp* SAFE.

speech *n* 1 articulation, communication, declamation, delivery, diction, elocution, enunciation, expression, pronunciation, speaking, talking, using words, utterance. **2** dialect, idiolect, idiom, jargon, language, parlance, register, tongue. **3** *a public speech.* address, discourse, disquisition, harangue, homily, lecture, oration, paper, presentation, sermon, *inf* spiel, talk, tirade. **4** *speech in a play.* dialogue, lines, monologue, soliloquy.

speechless *adj* dumb, dumbfounded, dumbstruck, inarticulate, *inf* mum, mute, nonplussed, silent, thunderstruck, tongue-tied, voiceless. *Opp* TALKATIVE.

speed *n* 1 pace, rate, tempo, velocity. **2** alacrity, briskness, celerity, dispatch, expeditiousness, fleetness, haste, hurry, quickness, rapidity, speediness, swiftness. ● *vb* 1 *inf* belt, *inf* bolt, *inf* bowl along, canter, career, dash, dart, flash, flit, fly, gallop, *inf* go like the wind, hasten, hurry, hurtle, make haste, move quickly, *inf* nip, *inf* put your foot down, race, run, rush, shoot, sprint, stampede, streak, tear, *inf* zoom. **2** *speed on the road.* break the speed limit, go too fast. **speed up** ▷ ACCELERATE.

speedy *adj* 1 expeditious, fast, *old use* fleet, nimble, quick, rapid, swift. **2** *a speedy exit.* hasty, hurried, immediate, precipitate, prompt, unhesitating. *Opp* SLOW.

spell *n* 1 bewitchment, charm, conjuration, conjuring, enchantment, incantation, magic formula, sorcery, witchcraft, witchery. **2** *the spell of the theatre.* allure, captivation, charm, enthralment, fascination, glamour, magic. **3** *a spell of rain.* interval, period, phase, season. **4** *a spell at the wheel.* session, stint, stretch, term, time, tour of duty, turn, watch. ● *vb* augur, bode, foretell, indicate, mean, portend, presage, signal, signify, suggest. **spell out** ▷ CLARIFY.

spellbound *adj* bewitched, captivated, charmed, enchanted, enthralled, entranced, fascinated, hypnotized, mesmerized, overcome, overpowered, transported.

spend *vb* 1 *inf* blue, consume, *inf* cough up, disburse, expend, exhaust, *inf* fork out, fritter, *inf* get through, invest, *inf* lash out, pay out, *inf* shell out, *inf* splash out, *inf* splurge, squander. **2** *spend time.* devote, fill, occupy, pass, use up, waste.

spendthrift *n inf* big spender, prodigal, profligate, wasteful person, wastrel. *Opp* MISER.

sphere *n* **1** ball, globe, globule, orb, spheroid. **2** *sphere of influence.* area, department, discipline, domain, field, province, range, scope, speciality, subject, territory. **3** *social sphere.* caste, class, domain, milieu, position, rank, society, station, stratum, walk of life.

spherical *adj* ball-shaped, globe-shaped, globular, rotund, round, spheric, spheroidal.

spice *n* **1** flavouring, piquancy, relish, seasoning. □ *allspice, bayleaf, capsicum, cardamom, cassia, cayenne, chilli, cinnamon, cloves, coriander, curry powder, ginger, grains of paradise, juniper, mace, nutmeg, paprika, pepper, pimento, poppy seed, saffron, sesame, turmeric.* **2** *add spice to life.* colour, excitement, gusto, interest, *inf* lift, *inf* pep, sharpness, stimulation, vigour, zest.

spicy *adj* aromatic, fragrant, gingery, highly flavoured, hot, peppery, piquant, pungent, seasoned, spiced, tangy, zestful. *Opp* BLAND.

spike *n* barb, nail, pin, point, projection, prong, skewer, spine, stake, tine. ● *vb* impale, perforate, pierce, skewer, spear, spit, stab, stick.

spill *vb* **1** overturn, slop, splash about, tip over, upset. **2** brim, flow, overflow, run, pour. **3** *lorry spilled its load.* discharge, drop, scatter, shed, tip.

spin *vb* **1** gyrate, pirouette, revolve, rotate, swirl, turn, twirl, twist, wheel, whirl. **2** *head was spinning.* be giddy, reel, suffer vertigo, swim. **spin out** ▷ PROLONG.

spindle *n* axis, axle, pin, rod, shaft.

spine *n* **1** backbone, spinal column, vertebrae. **2** *hedgehog's spines.* barb, bristle, needle, point, prickle, prong, quill, spike, spur, thorn.

spineless *adj* cowardly, craven, faint-hearted, feeble, helpless, irresolute, *inf* lily-livered, pusillanimous, *inf* soft, timid, unheroic, weedy, *inf* wimpish. ▷ WEAK. *Opp* BRAVE.

spiral *adj* cochlear, coiled, corkscrew, turning, whorled. ● *n* coil, curl, helix, screw, whorl. ● *vb* **1** turn, twist. **2** *spiralling prices.* ▷ FALL, RISE.

spire *n* flèche, pinnacle, steeple.

spirit *n* **1** *Lat* anima, breath, mind, psyche, soul. **2** *supernatural spirits.* apparition, *inf* bogy, demon, devil, genie, ghost, ghoul, gremlin, hobgoblin, imp, incubus, nymph, phantasm, phantom, poltergeist, *poet* shade, shadow, spectre, *inf* spook, sprite, sylph, vision, visitant, wraith, zombie. **3** *spirit of a poem.* aim, atmosphere, essence, feeling, heart, intention, meaning, mood, purpose, sense. **4** *fighting spirit.* animation, bravery, cheerfulness, confidence, courage, daring, determination, dynamism, energy, enthusiasm, fire, fortitude, *inf* get-up-and-go, *inf* go, *inf* guts, heroism, liveliness, mettle, morale, motivation, optimism, pluck, resolve, valour, verve, vivacity, will-power, zest. **5** ▷ ALCOHOL.

spirited *adj* active, animated, assertive, brave, brisk, buoyant, courageous, daring, determined, dynamic, energetic, enterprising, enthusiastic, frisky, gallant, *inf* gutsy, intrepid, lively, mettlesome, plucky, positive, resolute, sparkling, sprightly, vigorous, vivacious. *Opp* SPIRITLESS.

spiritless *adj* apathetic, cowardly, defeatist, despondent, dispirited, dull, irresolute, lacklustre, languid, lethargic, lifeless, listless, melancholy, negative, passive, slow, unenterprising, unenthusiastic. *Opp* SPIRITED.

spiritual *adj* devotional, divine, eternal, heavenly, holy, incorporeal, inspired, other-worldly, religious, sacred, unworldly, visionary. *Opp* TEMPORAL.

spit *n* **1** dribble, saliva, spittle, sputum. ● *vb* dribble, expectorate, salivate, splutter. **spit out** ▷ DISCHARGE. **spitting image** ▷ TWIN.

spite *n* animosity, animus, antagonism, *inf* bitchiness, bitterness, *inf* cattiness, gall, grudge, hate, hatred, hostility, ill-feeling, ill will, malevolence, malice, maliciousness, malignity, rancour, resentment, spleen, venom, vindictiveness. ● *vb* ▷ ANNOY.

spiteful *adj* acid, acrimonious, *inf* bitchy, bitter, *inf* catty, cruel, cutting, hateful, hostile, hurtful, ill-natured, invidious, malevolent, malicious, nasty, poisonous, punitive, rancorous, resentful, revengeful, sharp, *inf* snide, sour, unforgiving,

venomous, vicious, vindictive. *Opp* KIND.

splash *vb* **1** bespatter, besprinkle, shower, slop, *inf* slosh, spatter, spill, splatter, spray, sprinkle, squirt, wash. **2** *splash about in water*. bathe, dabble, paddle, wade. **3** *splash news across the front page*. blazon, display, exhibit, flaunt, *inf* plaster, publicize, show, spread. **splash out** ▷ SPEND.

splay *vb* make a V-shape, slant, spread.

splendid *adj* admirable, awe-inspiring, beautiful, brilliant, costly, dazzling, dignified, elegant, fine, first-class, glittering, glorious, gorgeous, grand, great, handsome, imposing, impressive, lavish, luxurious, magnificent, majestic, marvellous, noble, ornate, *derog* ostentatious, palatial, *inf* posh, refulgent, regal, resplendent, rich, royal, *derog* showy, spectacular, *inf* splendiferous, stately, sublime, sumptuous, *inf* super, superb, supreme, wonderful. ▷ EXCELLENT.

splendour *n* beauty, brilliance, ceremony, costliness, display, elegance, *inf* glitter, glory, grandeur, luxury, magnificence, majesty, nobility, ostentation, pomp, pomp and circumstance, refulgence, richness, show, spectacle, stateliness, sumptuousness.

splice *vb* bind, conjoin, entwine, join, knit, marry, tie together, unite.

splinter *n* chip, flake, fragment, shard, shaving, shiver, sliver. ● *vb* chip, crack, fracture, shatter, shiver, smash, split. ▷ BREAK.

split n 1 break, chink, cleavage, cleft, crack, cranny, crevice, fissure, furrow, gash, groove, leak, opening, rent, rift, rip, rupture, slash, slit, tear. 2 breach, dichotomy, difference, dissension, divergence of opinion, division, divorce, estrangement, schism, separation. ▷ QUARREL. ● vb 1 break up, disintegrate, divide, divorce, go separate ways, move apart, separate. 2 *split logs*. burst, chop, cleave, crack, rend, rip apart, rip open, slash, slice, slit, splinter, tear. ▷ CUT. 3 *split profits*. allocate, allot, apportion, distribute, divide, halve, share. 4 *road splits*. bifurcate, branch, diverge, fork. **split on** ▷ INFORM.

spoil vb 1 blight, blot, blotch, bungle, damage, deface, destroy, disfigure, *inf* dish, harm, injure, *inf* make a mess of, mar, *inf* mess up, ruin, stain, undermine, undo, upset, vitiate, worsen, wreck. *Opp* IMPROVE. 2 *food spoiled in the heat*. become useless, curdle, decay, decompose, go bad, *inf* go off, moulder, perish, putrefy, rot, *inf* turn. 3 *spoil children*. coddle, cosset, dote on, indulge, make a fuss of, mollycoddle, over-indulge, pamper.

spoken adj oral, unwritten, verbal, *Lat* viva voce. *Opp* WRITTEN.

spokesperson n mouthpiece, representative, spokesman, spokeswoman.

sponge vb 1 clean, cleanse, mop, rinse, sluice, swill, wash, wipe. 2 [*inf*] *sponge on friends*. be dependent (on), cadge (from), scrounge (from).

spongy adj absorbent, compressible, elastic, giving, porous, soft, springy, yielding. *Opp* SOLID.

sponsor n *inf* angel, backer, benefactor, donor, patron, promoter, supporter. ● vb back, be a sponsor of, finance, fund, help, patronize, promote, subsidize, support, underwrite.

sponsorship n aegis, auspices, backing, benefaction, funding, guarantee, patronage, promotion, support.

spontaneous adj 1 *inf* ad lib, extempore, impromptu, impulsive, *inf* off-the-cuff, unplanned, unpremeditated, unprepared, unrehearsed, voluntary. 2 *a spontaneous reaction*. automatic, instinctive, instinctual, involuntary, mechanical, natural, reflex, unconscious, unconstrained, unforced, unthinking. *Opp* PREMEDITATED.

spooky adj creepy, eerie, frightening, ghostly, haunted, mysterious, scary, uncanny, unearthly, weird.

spool n bobbin, reel.

spoon n dessert-spoon, ladle, table-spoon, teaspoon.

spoon-feed vb cosset, help, indulge, mollycoddle, pamper, spoil.

spoor n footprints, scent, traces, track.

sporadic adj erratic, fitful, intermittent, irregular, occasional, periodic, scattered, separate, unpredictable.

sport n 1 activity, amusement, diversion, enjoyment, entertainment, exercise, fun, games, pastime, play, pleasure, recreation. □ *aerobics, angling, archery, athletics, badminton, base-*

*ball, basketball, billiards, blood
sports, bobsleigh, bowls, boxing,
canoeing, climbing, cricket,
croquet, cross-country, curling,
darts, decathlon, discus, fishing,
football, gliding, golf, gymnastics, hockey, hunting, hurdling,
ice-hockey, javelin, jogging,
keep-fit, lacrosse, marathon,
martial arts, mountaineering,
netball, orienteering, pentathlon,
inf ping-pong, polo, pool, pot-
holing, quoits, racing, rock-
climbing, roller-skating, round-
ers, rowing, Rugby, running,
sailing, shooting, shot, show-
jumping, skating, skiing, skin-
diving, sky-diving, snooker, soccer, squash, street-hockey,
surfing, surf-riding, swimming,
table-tennis, tennis, toboggan-
ing, trampolining, volley-ball,
water-polo, water-skiing, wind-
surfing, winter sports, wrestling,
yachting.* ▷ ATHLETICS, RACE.
2 badinage, banter, humour,
jesting, joking, merriment, raillery, teasing. ● *vb* 1 caper,
cavort, divert yourself, frisk
about, frolic, gambol, lark
about, rollick, romp, skip
about. 2 *sport new clothes.*
display, exhibit, flaunt, show
off, wear.

sporting *adj* considerate, fair,
generous, good-humoured,
honourable, sportsmanlike.

sportive *adj* coltish, frisky,
kittenish, light-hearted, playful,
waggish. ▷ SPRIGHTLY.

sportsperson *n* contestant,
participant, player, sportsman,
sportswoman.

sporty *adj* 1 active, athletic,
energetic, fit, vigorous. 2 *sporty
clothes.* casual, informal,
inf loud, rakish, showy,
inf snazzy.

spot *n* 1 blemish, blot, blotch,
discoloration, dot, fleck, mark,
patch, smudge, speck, speckle,
stain, stigma. 2 *spot on the skin.*
birthmark, boil, freckle,
plur impetigo, mole, naevus,
pimple, pock, pock-mark,
plur rash, sty, whitlow, *sl* zit.
3 *spots of rain.* bead, blob, drop.
4 *spot for a picnic.* locale, locality, location, neighbourhood,
place, point, position, scene,
setting, site, situation. 5 *an
awkward spot.* difficulty,
dilemma, embarrassment,
mess, predicament, quandary,
situation. 6 *spot of bother.* bit,
small amount, *inf* smidgen.
● *vb* 1 blot, discolour, fleck,
mark, mottle, smudge, spatter,
speckle, splash, spray, stain.
2 ▷ SEE.

spotless *adj* 1 clean, fresh,
immaculate, laundered,
unmarked, unspotted, white.
2 *spotless reputation.* blameless,
faultless, flawless, immaculate,
innocent, irreproachable, pure,
unblemished, unsullied, untarnished, *inf* whiter than white.

spotty *adj* blotchy, dappled,
flecked, freckled, mottled,
pimply, pock-marked, pocky,
spattered, speckled, speckly,
inf splodgy, spotted.

spouse *n* better half, *old
use* helpmate, husband, partner,
wife.

spout *n* duct, fountain, gargoyle,
geyser, jet, lip, nozzle, outlet,
rose (*of watering-can*), spray,
waterspout. ● *vb* 1 discharge,
emit, erupt, flow, gush, jet,
pour, shoot, spew, spit, spurt,
squirt, stream. 2 ▷ TALK.

sprawl *vb* 1 flop, lean back, lie,
loll, lounge, recline, relax,
slouch, slump, spread out,

stretch out. 2 be scattered, branch out, spread, straggle.

spray n 1 drizzle, droplets, fountain, mist, shower, splash, sprinkling. 2 *spray of flowers.* arrangement, bouquet, branch, bunch, corsage, posy, sprig. 3 *spray for paint.* aerosol, atomizer, spray-gun, sprinkler, vaporizer. ● vb diffuse, disperse, scatter, shower, spatter, splash, spread in droplets, sprinkle.

spread n 1 broadcasting, broadening, development, diffusion, dispensing, dispersal, dissemination, distribution, expansion, extension, growth, increase, passing on, proliferation, promotion, promulgation. 2 *spread of a bird's wings.* breadth, compass, extent, size, span, stretch, sweep. 3 ▷ MEAL. ● vb 1 arrange, display, lay out, open out, unfold, unfurl, unroll. 2 broaden, enlarge, expand, extend, fan out, get bigger, get longer, get wider, lengthen, *inf* mushroom, proliferate, straggle, widen. 3 *spread news.* advertise, broadcast, circulate, diffuse, dispense, disperse, disseminate, distribute, divulge, give out, make known, pass on, pass round, proclaim, promote, promulgate, publicize, publish, scatter, sow, transmit. 4 *spread butter.* apply, cover a surface with, smear.

spree n *inf* binge, debauch, escapade, *inf* fling, frolic, *inf* orgy, outing, revel. ▷ REVELRY.

sprightly adj active, agile, animated, brisk, *inf* chipper, energetic, jaunty, lively, nimble, *inf* perky, playful, quickmoving, spirited, sportive, spry, vivacious. *Opp* LETHARGIC.

spring n 1 bounce, buoyancy, elasticity, give, liveliness, resilience. 2 *clock spring.* coil, mainspring. 3 *spring of water.* fount, fountain, geyser, source (*of river*), spa, well, well-spring. ● vb bounce, bound, hop, jump, leap, pounce, vault. **spring from** come from, derive from, proceed from, stem from. **spring up** appear, arise, burst forth, come up, develop, emerge, germinate, grow, shoot up, sprout.

springy adj bendy, elastic, flexible, pliable, resilient, spongy, stretchy, supple. *Opp* RIGID.

sprinkle vb drip, dust, pepper, scatter, shower, spatter, splash, spray, strew.

sprint vb dash, *inf* hare, race, speed, *inf* tear. ▷ RUN.

sprout n bud, shoot. ● vb bud, come up, develop, emerge, germinate, grow, shoot up, spring up.

spruce adj clean, dapper, elegant, groomed, *inf* natty, neat, *inf* posh, smart, tidy, trim, well-dressed, well-groomed, *inf* well-turned-out. *Opp* SCRUFFY. ● vb **spruce up** ▷ TIDY.

spur n 1 encouragement, goad, impetus, incentive, incitement, inducement, motivation, motive, prod, prompting, stimulus, urging. 2 *motorway spur.* branch, projection. ● vb animate, egg on, encourage, impel, incite, motivate, pressure, pressurize, prick, prod, prompt, provide an incentive, stimulate, urge.

spurn vb disown, give (someone) the cold shoulder, jilt, rebuff, reject, renounce, repel, repudiate, repulse, shun, snub, turn your back on.

spy n contact, double agent, fifth columnist, *sl* grass, infiltrator, informant, informer, *inf* mole, private detective, secret agent, snooper, stool-pigeon, under-cover agent. ● vb 1 be a spy, be engaged in spying, eavesdrop, gather intelligence, inform, *inf* snoop. 2 ▷ SEE. **spy on** keep under surveillance, *inf* tail, trail, watch.

spying n counter-espionage, detective work, eavesdropping, espionage, intelligence, snooping, surveillance.

squabble vb argue, bicker, clash, *inf* row, wrangle. ▷ QUARREL.

squalid adj 1 dingy, dirty, disgusting, filthy, foul, insalubrious, mean, mucky, nasty, poverty-stricken, repulsive, run-down, *inf* sleazy, slummy, sordid, ugly, uncared-for, unpleasant, wretched. *Opp* CLEAN. 2 *squalid behaviour.* corrupt, degrading, dishonest, dishonourable, disreputable, immoral, scandalous, *inf* shabby, shameful, unethical, unworthy. *Opp* HONOURABLE.

squander vb *inf* blow, *inf* blue, dissipate, *inf* fritter, misuse, spend unwisely, *inf* splurge, use up, waste. *Opp* SAVE.

square adj 1 perpendicular, rectangular, right-angled. 2 *a square deal.* *inf* above-board, decent, equitable, ethical, fair, honest, honourable, proper, *inf* right and proper, *inf* straight. ● n 1 piazza, plaza. 2 [inf] old-fashioned square. bourgeois, conformist, conservative, conventional person, die-hard, *inf* fuddy-duddy, *inf* old fogy, *inf* stick-in-the-

mud, traditionalist. ● vb square an account. ▷ SETTLE. **squared** chequered, criss-crossed, marked in squares.

squash vb 1 compress, crumple, crush, flatten, mangle, mash, pound, press, pulp, smash, stamp on, tamp down, tread on. 2 *squash into a room.* cram, crowd, pack, push, ram, shove, squeeze, stuff, thrust, wedge. 3 *squash an uprising.* control, put down, quash, quell, repress, suppress. 4 *squash with a look.* humiliate, *inf* put down, silence, snub.

squashy adj mashed up, mushy, pulpy, shapeless, soft, spongy, squelchy, yielding. *Opp* FIRM.

squat adj burly, dumpy, plump, podgy, short, stocky, thick, thickset. *Opp* TALL. ● vb crouch, sit.

squeamish adj *inf* choosy, dainty, fastidious, finicky, over-scrupulous, particular, *inf* pernickety, prim, *inf* prissy, prudish, scrupulous.

squeeze vb 1 clasp, compress, crush, embrace, enfold, exert pressure on, flatten, grip, hug, mangle, pinch, press, squash, stamp on, tread on, wring. 2 cram, crowd, pack, push, ram, shove, squash, stuff, tamp, thrust, wedge. **squeeze out** expel, extrude, force out.

squirm vb twist, wriggle, writhe.

squirt vb ejaculate, eject, gush, jet, send out, shoot, spit, spout, splash, spray, spurt.

stab n 1 blow, cut, jab, prick, puncture, thrust, wound, wounding. 2 *stab of pain.* ▷ PAIN. ● vb bayonet, cut, injure, jab, lance, perforate, pierce, puncture, skewer, spike, stick, thrust, transfix, wound. **have a stab at** ▷ TRY.

stability n balance, constancy, durability, equilibrium, firmness, immutability, permanence, reliability, solidity, soundness, steadiness, strength. *Opp* INSTABILITY.

stabilize vb balance, become stable, give stability to, keep upright, make stable, settle. *Opp* UPSET.

stable adj 1 balanced, firm, fixed, solid, sound, steady, strong, sturdy. 2 constant, continuing, durable, established, immutable, lasting, long-lasting, permanent, predictable, resolute, steadfast, unchanging, unwavering. 3 *a stable personality*. balanced, even-tempered, reasonable, sane, sensible. *Opp* UNSTABLE.

stack n 1 accumulation, heap, hill, hoard, mound, mountain, pile, quantity, stock, stockpile, store. 2 chimney, pillar, smokestack. 3 *stack of hay*. *old use* cock, haycock, haystack, rick, stook. ● vb accumulate, amass, assemble, build up, collect, gather, heap, load, mass, pile, *inf* stash away, stockpile.

stadium n amphitheatre, arena, ground, sports-ground.

staff n 1 baton, cane, crook, crosier, flagstaff, pike, pole, rod, sceptre, shaft, stake, standard, stave, stick, token, wand. 2 *staff of a business*. assistants, crew, employees, *old use* hands, personnel, officers, team, workers, workforce. ● vb man, provide with staff, run.

stage n 1 apron, dais, performing area, platform, podium,

proscenium, rostrum. 2 *stage of a journey*. juncture, leg, phase, period, point, time. ● vb arrange, *inf* get up, mount, organize, perform, present, produce, *inf* put on, set up, stage-manage.

stagger vb 1 falter, lurch, pitch, reel, rock, stumble, sway, teeter, totter, walk unsteadily, waver, wobble. 2 *price staggered us*. alarm, amaze, astonish, astound, confuse, dismay, dumbfound, flabbergast, shake, shock, startle, stun, stupefy, surprise, worry.

stagnant adj motionless, sluggish, stale, standing, static, still, without movement. *Opp* MOVING.

stagnate vb achieve nothing, become stale, be stagnant, degenerate, deteriorate, idle, languish, stand still, stay still, vegetate. *Opp* PROGRESS.

stain n 1 blemish, blot, blotch, discoloration, mark, smear, smudge, speck, spot. 2 *a wood stain*. colouring, dye, paint, pigment, tinge, tint, varnish. ● vb 1 blacken, blemish, blot, contaminate, dirty, discolour, make dirty, mark, smudge, soil, tarnish. 2 *stain your reputation*. besmirch, damage, defile, disgrace, shame, spoil, sully, taint. 3 *stain wood*. colour, dye, paint, tinge, tint, varnish.

stair n riser, step, tread. **stairs** escalator, flight of stairs, staircase, stairway, steps.

stake n 1 paling, palisade, pike, pile, pillar, pole, post, rod, sceptre, shaft, spike, standard, stave, stick, upright. 2 *a gambler's stake*. bet, pledge, wager. ● vb 1 fasten, hitch, secure, tether, tie up. 2 *stake a* *claim*. establish, put on record, state. **3** *stake my life on it*. bet, chance, gamble, hazard, risk, venture, wager. **stake out** define, delimit, demarcate, enclose, fence in, mark off, outline.

stale *adj* **1** dry, hard, limp, mouldy, musty, *inf* off, old, *inf* past its best, tasteless. **2** *stale ideas*. banal, clichéd, familiar, hackneyed, old-fashioned, out-of-date, overused, stock, threadbare, *inf* tired, trite, uninteresting, unoriginal, worn out. *Opp* FRESH.

stalemate *n* deadlock, impasse, standstill.

stalk *n* branch, shaft, shoot, stem, trunk, twig. • *vb* **1** chase, dog, follow, haunt, hound, hunt, pursue, shadow, tail, track, trail. **2** *stalk about*. prowl, rove, stride, strut. ▷ WALK.

stall *n* booth, compartment, kiosk, stand, table. • *vb* be obstructive, delay, hang back, haver, hesitate, pause, *inf* play for time, postpone, prevaricate, procrastinate, put off, stonewall, stop, temporize, waste time.

stalwart *adj* courageous, dependable, determined, faithful, indomitable, intrepid, redoubtable, reliable, resolute, robust, staunch, steadfast, sturdy, tough, trustworthy, valiant. ▷ BRAVE, STRONG. *Opp* WEAK.

stamina *n* endurance, energy, *inf* grit, indomitability, resilience, staunchness, staying power, *inf* stickability.

stammer *vb* falter, hesitate, hem and haw, splutter, stumble, stutter. ▷ TALK.

stamp *n* **1** brand, die, hallmark, impression, imprint, print, punch, seal. **2** *stamp of genius*. characteristic, mark, sign. **3** *stamp on a letter*. franking, postage stamp. • *vb* **1** bring down, strike, thump. **2** *stamp a mark*. brand, emboss, engrave, impress, imprint, label, mark, print, punch. **stamp on** ▷ SUPPRESS. **stamp out** ▷ ELIMINATE.

stampede *n* charge, dash, flight, panic, rout, rush, sprint. • *vb* **1** bolt, career, charge, dash, gallop, panic, run, rush, sprint, *inf* take to your heels, tear. **2** *stampede cattle*. frighten, panic, rout, scatter.

stand *n* **1** base, pedestal, rack, support, tripod, trivet. **2** booth, kiosk, stall. **3** grandstand, terraces. • *vb* **1** arise, get to your feet, get up, rise. **2** *Stand it on the floor*. arrange, deposit, erect, locate, place, position, put up, set up, situate, station, upend. **3** *Trees stand along the avenue*. be, be situated, exist. **4** *My offer stands*. be unchanged, continue, remain valid, stay. **5** *Can't stand onions*. abide, bear, endure, put up with, suffer, tolerate, *inf* wear. **stand by** ▷ SUPPORT. **stand for** ▷ SYMBOLIZE. **stand in for** ▷ DEPUTIZE. **stand out** ▷ SHOW. **stand up for** ▷ PROTECT, SUPPORT. **stand up to** ▷ RESIST.

standard *adj* accepted, accustomed, approved, average, basic, classic, common, conventional, customary, definitive, established, everyday, familiar, habitual, normal, official, ordinary, orthodox, popular, prevailing, prevalent, recognized, regular, routine, set, staple (*diet*), stock, traditional, typical, universal, usual. *Opp* UNUSUAL. ● *n* 1 archetype, benchmark, criterion, example, exemplar, gauge, grade, guide, guideline, ideal, level of achievement, measure, measurement, model, paradigm, pattern, requirement, rule, sample, specification, touchstone, yardstick. 2 average, level, mean, norm. 3 *standard of a regiment*. banner, colours, ensign, flag, pennant. 4 *lamp standard*. column, pillar, pole, post, support, upright. **standards** ▷ MORALITY.

standardize *vb* average out, conform to a standard, equalize, homogenize, normalize, regiment, stereotype, systematize.

standoffish *adj* aloof, antisocial, cold, cool, distant, frosty, haughty, remote, reserved, reticent, retiring, secretive, self-conscious, *inf* snooty, taciturn, unapproachable, uncommunicative, unforthcoming, unfriendly, unsociable, withdrawn. *Opp* FRIENDLY.

standpoint *n* angle, attitude, belief, opinion, perspective, point of view, position, stance, vantage point, view, viewpoint.

standstill *n* dead end, deadlock, halt, *inf* hold-up, impasse, jam, stalemate, stop, stoppage.

staple *adj* basic, chief, important, main, principal.
▷ STANDARD.

star *n* 1 celestial body, sun. □ *asteroid, comet, evening star, falling star, lodestar, morning star, nova, shooting star, supernova.* 2 asterisk, pentagram. 3 *TV star*. attraction, big name, celebrity, *It* diva, *inf* draw, idol,

leading lady, leading man, personage, *It* prima donna, starlet, superstar. ▷ PERFORMER.

starchy *adj* aloof, conventional, formal, prim, stiff.
▷ UNFRIENDLY.

stare *vb* gape, *inf* gawp, gaze, glare, goggle, look fixedly, peer. **stare at** contemplate, examine, eye, scrutinize, study, watch.

stark *adj* 1 austere, bare, bleak, depressing, desolate, dreary, gloomy, grim. 2 *stark contrast*. absolute, clear, complete, obvious, perfect, plain, sharp, sheer, thoroughgoing, total, unqualified, utter.

start *n* 1 beginning, birth, commencement, creation, dawn, establishment, founding, fount, inauguration, inception, initiation, institution, introduction, launch, onset, opening, origin, outset, point of departure, setting out, spring, springboard. *Opp* FINISH. 2 *an unfair start*. advantage, edge, headstart, opportunity. 3 *bank-loan gave me a start*. assistance, backing, financing, help, *inf* leg-up, *inf* send-off, sponsorship. 4 *a nasty start*. jump, shock, surprise. ● *vb* 1 depart, embark, *inf* get going, *inf* get under way, *sl* hit the road, *inf* kick off, leave, move off, proceed, set off, set out. 2 *start something*. activate, beget, begin, commence, create, embark on, engender, establish, found, *inf* get cracking on, *inf* get off the ground, *inf* get the ball rolling, give birth to, inaugurate, initiate, instigate, institute, introduce, launch, open, originate, pioneer, set in motion, set up. *Opp* FINISH. 3 *start at sudden noise*. blench, draw back, flinch, jerk, jump, quail, recoil, shy, spring up, twitch, wince. **make someone start** ▷ STARTLE.

startle vb agitate, alarm, catch unawares, disturb, frighten, give you a start, jolt, make you jump, make you start, scare, shake, shock, surprise, take aback, take by surprise, upset. **startling** ▷ SURPRISING.

starvation n deprivation, famine, hunger, malnutrition, undernourishment, want.

starve vb die of starvation, go hungry, go without, perish. **starve yourself** diet, fast, go on hunger strike, refuse food. **starving** ▷ HUNGRY.

state n 1 plur circumstances, condition, fitness, health, mood, inf shape, situation. 2 agitation, excitement, inf flap, panic, plight, predicament, inf tizzy. 3 a sovereign state. land, nation. ▷ COUNTRY. ● vb affirm, announce, assert, asseverate, aver, communicate, declare, express, formulate, proclaim, put into words, report, specify, submit, testify, voice. ▷ SAY, SPEAK, TALK.

stately adj august, dignified, distinguished, elegant, formal, grand, imperial, imposing, impressive, lofty, majestic, noble, pompous, regal, royal, solemn, splendid, striking. Opp INFORMAL. **stately home** ▷ MANSION.

statement n account, affirmation, announcement, annunciation, assertion, bulletin, comment, communication, communiqué, declaration, disclosure, explanation, message, notice, proclamation, proposition, report, testament, testimony, utterance.

statesman n diplomat, politician.

static adj constant, fixed, immobile, immovable, inert, invariable, motionless, passive, stable, stagnant, stationary, steady, still, unchanging, unmoving. Opp MOBILE, VARIABLE.

station n 1 calling, caste, class, degree, employment, level, location, occupation, place, position, post, rank, situation, standing, status. 2 fire station. base, depot, headquarters, office. 3 radio station. channel, company, transmitter, wavelength. 4 railway station. halt, platform, stopping-place, terminus, train station. ● vb assign, garrison, locate, place, position, put, site, situate, spot, stand.

stationary adj at a standstill, at rest, halted, immobile, immovable, motionless, parked, pausing, standing, static, still, stock-still, unmoving. Opp MOVING.

stationery n paper, office supplies, writing materials.

statistics n data, figures, information, numbers.

statue n carving, figure, statuette. ▷ SCULPTURE.

statuesque adj dignified, elegant, imposing, impressive, poised, stately, upright.

stature n 1 build, height, size, tallness. 2 artist of international stature. esteem, greatness, recognition. ▷ STATUS.

status n class, degree, eminence, grade, importance, level, position, prestige, prominence, rank, reputation, significance, standing, station, stature, title.

staunch adj ▷ STEADFAST.

stay n 1 holiday, old use sojourn, stop, stop-over, visit. 2 *stay of execution*. ▷ SUPPORT. ● vb 1 old use bide, carry on, continue, endure, inf hang about, hold out, keep on, last, linger, live on, loiter, persist, remain, survive, old use tarry, wait. 2 *stay in a hotel*. old use abide, be accommodated, be a guest, be housed, board, dwell, live, lodge, reside, settle, old use sojourn, stop, visit. 3 *stay judgement*. ▷ DELAY.

steadfast adj committed, constant, dedicated, dependable, determined, devoted, faithful, firm, loyal, patient, persevering, reliable, resolute, resolved, single-minded, sound, stalwart, staunch, steady, true, trustworthy, trusty, unchanging, unfaltering, unflinching, unswerving, unwavering. ▷ STRONG. Opp UNRELIABLE.

steady adj 1 balanced, confident, fast, firm, immovable, poised, safe, secure, settled, solid, stable, substantial. 2 *a steady flow*. ceaseless, changeless, consistent, constant, continuous, dependable, endless, even, incessant, invariable, never-ending, nonstop, perpetual, persistent, regular, reliable, repeated, rhythmic, inf round-the-clock, unbroken, unchanging, undeviating, unfaltering, unhurried, uniform, uninterrupted, unrelieved, unremitting, unvarying. Opp UNSTEADY. 3 ▷ STEADFAST. ● vb 1 balance, brace, hold steady, keep still, make steady, secure, stabilize, support. 2 *steady your nerves*. calm, control, soothe, tranquillize.

steal vb 1 annex, appropriate, arrogate, burgle, commandeer, confiscate, embezzle, expropriate, inf filch, hijack, inf knock off, inf lift, loot, inf make off with, misappropriate, inf nick, peculate, pick pockets, pilfer, pillage, inf pinch, pirate, plagiarize, plunder, poach, purloin, inf rip you off, rob, seize, shop-lift, inf sneak, inf snitch, inf swipe, take, thieve, usurp, walk off with. 2 *steal quietly upstairs*. creep, move stealthily, slink, slip, sneak, tiptoe.

stealing n robbery, theft, thieving. □ break-in, burglary, embezzlement, fraud, hijacking, housebreaking, larceny, looting, misappropriation, mugging, peculation, pilfering, pillage, piracy, plagiarism, plundering, poaching, purloining, scrumping, shop-lifting.

stealthy adj clandestine, concealed, covert, disguised, furtive, imperceptible, inconspicuous, quiet, secret, secretive, inf shifty, sly, inf sneaky, surreptitious, underhand, unobtrusive. Opp BLATANT.

steam n condensation, haze, mist, smoke, vapour.

steamy adj 1 blurred, clouded, cloudy, fogged over, foggy, hazy, misted over, misty. 2 *a steamy atmosphere*. close, damp, humid, moist, muggy, inf sticky, sultry, sweaty, sweltering. 3 [inf] steamy sex scenes. ▷ SEXY.

steep adj 1 abrupt, bluff, headlong, perpendicular, precipitous, sharp, sheer, sudden, vertical. Opp GRADUAL. 2 *steep prices*. ▷ EXPENSIVE. ● vb ▷ SOAK.

steeple n pinnacle, point, spire.

steer vb be at the wheel, control, direct, drive, guide, navigate, pilot. **steer clear of** ▷ AVOID.

stem n peduncle, shoot, stalk, stock, trunk, twig. ● vb arise, come, derive, develop, emanate, flow, issue, originate, proceed, result, spring, sprout. **2** to stem the flow. ▷ CHECK.

stench n mephitis, inf pong, reek, stink. ▷ SMELL.

step n **1** footfall, footstep, pace, stride, tread. **2** doorstep, rung, stair, tread. **3** a step forward. advance, move, movement, progress, progression. **4** step in a process. action, initiative, manoeuvre, measure, phase, procedure, stage. ● vb put your foot, stamp, stride, trample, tread. ▷ WALK. **steps** ladder, stairs, staircase, stairway, stepladder. **step down** ▷ RESIGN. **step in** ▷ ENTER, INTERVENE. **step on it** ▷ HURRY. **step up** ▷ INCREASE. **take steps** ▷ BEGIN.

stereoscopic adj solid-looking, three-dimensional, inf 3-D.

stereotype n formula, model, pattern, stereotyped idea.

stereotyped adj clichéd, conventional, formalized, hackneyed, predictable, standard, standardized, stock, typecast, unoriginal.

sterile adj **1** arid, barren, childless, dry, fruitless, infertile, lifeless, unfruitful, unproductive. **2** sterile bandage. antiseptic, aseptic, clean, disinfected, germ-free, hygienic, pure, sanitary, sterilized, uncontaminated, uninfected, unpolluted. **3** a sterile attempt. abortive, fruitless, hopeless, pointless, unprofit-

able, useless. Opp FERTILE, FRUITFUL, SEPTIC.

sterilize vb **1** clean, cleanse, decontaminate, depurate, disinfect, fumigate, make sterile, pasteurize, purify. **2** sterilize animals. castrate, caponize, emasculate, geld, neuter, perform a vasectomy on, spay, vasectomize.

stern adj adamant, austere, authoritarian, critical, dour, forbidding, frowning, grim, hard, harsh, inflexible, obdurate, resolute, rigid, rigorous, severe, strict, stringent, tough, unbending, uncompromising, unrelenting, unremitting. ▷ SERIOUS. Opp SOFT-HEARTED. ● n stern of ship. aft, back, rear end.

stew n casserole, goulash, hash, hot-pot, ragout. ● vb boil, braise, casserole, simmer. ▷ COOK.

steward, stewardess ns **1** attendant, waiter. ▷ SERVANT. **2** marshal, officer, official.

stick n branch, stalk, twig. □ bar, baton, cane, club, hockey-stick, pike, pole, rod, staff, stake, walking-stick, wand.
● vb **1** bore, dig, impale, jab, penetrate, pierce, pin, poke, prick, prod, punch, puncture, run through, spear, spike, spit, stab, thrust, transfix. **2** stick with glue. adhere, affix, agglutinate, bind, bond, cement, cling, coagulate, fuse together, glue, gum, paste, solder, weld. ▷ FASTEN. **3** stick in your mind. be fixed, continue, endure, keep on, last, linger, persist, remain, stay. **4** stick in mud. become trapped, get bogged down, seize up, jam, wedge. **5** ▷ TOLERATE. **stick at**

▷ PERSIST. **stick in** ▷ PEN-
ETRATE. **stick out** ▷ PROTRUDE.
stick together ▷ UNITE. **stick
up** ▷ PROTRUDE. **stick up for**
▷ DEFEND. **stick with**
▷ SUPPORT.

sticky *adj* 1 adhesive, glued,
gummed, self-adhesive. 2 *sticky
paint*. gluey, glutinous,
inf gooey, gummy, tacky,
viscous. 3 *sticky weather*.
clammy, close, damp, dank,
humid, moist, muggy, steamy,
sultry, sweaty. Opp DRY.

stiff *adj* 1 compact, dense, firm,
hard, heavy, inelastic, inflexible, rigid, semi-solid, solid,
solidified, thick, tough, unbending, unyielding, viscous. 2 *stiff
joints*. arthritic, immovable,
painful, paralysed, rheumatic,
taut, tight. 3 *a stiff task*. arduous, challenging, difficult,
exacting, exhausting, hard,
laborious, tiring, tough, uphill.
4 *stiff opposition*. determined,
dogged, obstinate, powerful,
resolute, stubborn, unyielding,
vigorous. 5 *a stiff manner*. artificial, awkward, clumsy, cold,
forced, formal, graceless,
haughty, inelegant, laboured,
mannered, pedantic, self-
conscious, standoffish, starchy,
stilted, *inf* stuffy, tense, turgid,
ungainly, unnatural, wooden.
6 *stiff penalties*. cruel, drastic,
excessive, harsh, hurtful,
merciless, pitiless, punishing,
punitive, relentless, rigorous,
severe, strict. 7 *stiff wind*.
brisk, fresh, strong. 8 *stiff
drink*. alcoholic, potent, strong.
Opp EASY, RELAXED, SOFT.

stiffen *vb* become stiff, clot,
coagulate, congeal, dry out,
harden, jell, set, solidify,
thicken, tighten, toughen.

stifle *vb* 1 asphyxiate, choke,
smother, strangle, suffocate,
throttle. 2 *stifle laughter*. check,
control, curb, dampen, deaden,
keep back, muffle, restrain,
suppress, withhold. 3 *stifle free
speech*. crush, destroy, extinguish, kill off, quash, repress,
silence, stamp out, stop.

stigma *n* blot, brand, disgrace,
dishonour, mark, reproach,
shame, slur, stain, taint.

stigmatize *vb* brand, condemn,
defame, denounce, disparage,
label, mark, pillory, slander,
vilify.

still *adj* at rest, calm, even, flat,
hushed, immobile, inert, life-
less, motionless, noiseless,
pacific, peaceful, placid, quiet,
restful, serene, silent, smooth,
soundless, stagnant, static,
stationary, tranquil, unmoving,
unruffled, untroubled, windless.
Opp ACTIVE, NOISY. ● *vb* allay,
appease, assuage, calm, lull,
make still, pacify, quieten,
settle, silence, soothe, subdue,
suppress, tranquillize.
Opp AGITATE.

stimulant *n* anti-depressant,
drug, *inf* pick-me-up, restorative, *inf* reviver, *inf* shot in the
arm, tonic. ▷ STIMULUS.

stimulate *vb* activate, arouse,
awaken, cause, encourage,
excite, fan, fire, foment, galvanize, goad, incite, inflame,
inspire, instigate, invigorate,
kindle, motivate, prick, prompt,
provoke, quicken, rouse, set off,
spur, stir up, titillate, urge,
whet. Opp DISCOURAGE.

stimulating *adj* arousing, challenging, exciting, exhilarating,
inspirational, inspiring, interesting, intoxicating, invigorat-

ing, provocative, provoking, rousing, stirring, thought-provoking, titillating. *Opp* UNINTERESTING.

stimulus *n* challenge, encouragement, fillip, goad, incentive, inducement, inspiration, prompting, provocation, spur, stimulant. *Opp* DISCOURAGEMENT.

sting *n* bite, prick, stab. ▷ PAIN.
• *vb* 1 bite, nip, prick, wound. 2 smart, tingle. ▷ HURT.

stingy *adj* 1 avaricious, cheese-paring, close, close-fisted, covetous, mean, mingy, miserly, niggardly, parsimonious, penny-pinching, tight-fisted, ungenerous. 2 *stingy helpings.* inadequate, insufficient, meagre, *inf* measly, scanty. ▷ SMALL. *Opp* GENEROUS.

stink *n, vb* ▷ SMELL.

stipulate *vb* demand, insist on, make a stipulation, require, specify.

stipulation *n* condition, demand, prerequisite, proviso, requirement, specification.

stir *n* ▷ COMMOTION.
• *vb* 1 agitate, beat, blend, churn, mingle, mix, move about, scramble, whisk. 2 *stir from sleep.* arise, bestir yourself, *inf* get a move on, *inf* get going, get up, move, rise, *inf* show signs of life, *inf* stir your stumps. 3 *stir emotions.* activate, affect, arouse, awaken, challenge, disturb, electrify, excite, exhilarate, fire, impress, inspire, kindle, move, resuscitate, revive, rouse, stimulate, touch, upset.

stirring *adj* affecting, arousing, challenging, dramatic, electrifying, emotional, emotion-

charged, emotive, exciting, exhilarating, heady, impassioned, inspirational, inspiring, interesting, intoxicating, invigorating, moving, provocative, provoking, rousing, spirited, stimulating, thought-provoking, thrilling, titillating, touching. *Opp* UNEXCITING.

stitch *vb* darn, mend, repair, sew, tack.

stock *adj* accustomed, banal, clichéd, common, commonplace, conventional, customary, expected, hackneyed, ordinary, predictable, regular, routine, run-of-the-mill, set, standard, staple, stereotyped, *inf* tired, traditional, trite, unoriginal, usual. *Opp* UNEXPECTED.
• *n* 1 cache, hoard, reserve, reservoir, stockpile, store, supply. 2 *stock of a shop.* commodities, goods, merchandise, range, wares. 3 *farm stock.* animals, beasts, cattle, flocks, herds, livestock. 4 *ancient stock.* ancestry, blood, breed, descent, dynasty, extraction, family, forebears, genealogy, line, lineage, parentage, pedigree. 5 *meat stock.* broth, soup. • *vb* carry, deal in, handle, have available, *inf* keep, keep in stock, market, offer, provide, sell, supply, trade in. **out of stock** sold out, unavailable. **take stock** ▷ REVIEW.

stockade *n* fence, paling, palisade, wall.

stockings *n* nylons, panti-hose, socks, tights.

stockist *n* merchant, retailer, seller, shopkeeper, supplier.

stocky *adj* burly, compact, dumpy, heavy-set, short, solid, squat, stubby, sturdy, thickset. *Opp* THIN.

stodgy *adj* **1** filling, heavy, indigestible, lumpy, soggy, solid, starchy. *Opp* SUCCULENT. **2** *a stodgy lecture.* boring, dull, ponderous, *inf* stuffy, tedious, tiresome, turgid, unexciting, unimaginative, uninteresting. *Opp* LIVELY.

stoical *adj* calm, cool, disciplined, impassive, imperturbable, long-suffering, patient, philosophical, phlegmatic, resigned, stolid, uncomplaining, unemotional, unexcitable, *inf* unflappable. *Opp* EXCITABLE.

stoke *vb* fuel, keep burning, mend, put fuel on, tend.

stole *n* cape, shawl, wrap.

stolid *adj* bovine, dull, heavy, immovable, impassive, lumpish, phlegmatic, unemotional, unexciting, unimaginative, wooden. ▷ STOICAL. *Opp* LIVELY.

stomach *n* abdomen, belly, *inf* guts, *inf* insides, *derog* paunch, *derog* pot, *inf* tummy. ● *vb* ▷ TOLERATE.

stomach-ache *n* colic, *inf* collywobbles, *inf* gripes, *inf* tummyache.

stone *n* **1** boulder, cobble, *plur* gravel, pebble, rock, *plur* scree. ▷ ROCK. **2** block, flagstone, sett, slab. **3** *a memorial stone.* gravestone, headstone, memorial, monolith, obelisk, tablet. **4** *precious stone.* ▷ JEWEL. **5** *stone in fruit.* pip, pit, seed.

stony *adj* **1** pebbly, rocky, rough, shingly. **2** *stony silence.* adamant, chilly, cold, coldhearted, expressionless, frigid, hard, *inf* hard-boiled, heartless, hostile, icy, indifferent, insensitive, merciless, pitiless, steely, stony-hearted, uncaring, unemotional, unfeeling, unfor-

giving, unfriendly, unresponsive, unsympathetic.

stooge *n* butt, dupe, *inf* fall-guy, lackey, puppet.

stoop *vb* **1** bend, bow, crouch, duck, hunch your shoulders, kneel, lean, squat. **2** condescend, degrade yourself, deign, humble yourself, lower yourself, sink.

stop *n* **1** ban, cessation, close, conclusion, end, finish, halt, shut-down, standstill, stoppage, termination. **2** *a stop for refreshments.* break, destination, pause, resting-place, stage, station, stopover, terminus. **3** *a stop at a hotel.* holiday, *old use* sojourn, stay, vacation, visit. ● *vb* **1** break off, call a halt to, cease, conclude, cut off, desist from, discontinue, end, finish, halt, *inf* knock off, leave off, *inf* pack in, pause, quit, refrain from, rest from, suspend, terminate. **2** *stop the flow.* bar, block, check, curb, cut off, delay, frustrate, halt, hamper, hinder, immobilize, impede, intercept, interrupt, *inf* nip in the bud, obstruct, put a stop to, stanch, staunch, stem, suppress, thwart. **3** *stop in a hotel.* be a guest, have a holiday, *old use* sojourn, spend time, stay, visit. **4** *stop a gap.* *inf* bung up, close, fill in, plug, seal. **5** *stop a thief.* arrest, capture, catch, detain, hold, seize. **6** *the rain stopped.* be over, cease, come to an end, finish, peter out. **7** *the bus stopped.* come to rest, draw up, halt, pull up.

stopper *n* bung, cork, plug.

store *n* **1** accumulation, cache, fund, hoard, quantity, reserve, reservoir, stock, stockpile, supply. ▷ STOREHOUSE. 2 *a grocery store*. outlet, retail business, retailers, supermarket. ▷ SHOP. ● *vb* accumulate, aggregate, deposit, hoard, keep, lay by, lay in, lay up, preserve, put away, reserve, save, set aside, *inf* stash away, stockpile, stock up, stow away.

storehouse *n* depository, repository, storage, store, store-room. □ armoury, arsenal, barn, cellar, cold-storage, depot, granary, larder, pantry, safe, silo, stock-room, strong-room, treasury, vault, warehouse.

storey *n* deck, floor, level, stage, tier.

storm *n* 1 disturbance, onslaught, outbreak, outburst, stormy weather, tempest, tumult, turbulence. □ blizzard, cloudburst, cyclone, deluge, dust-storm, electrical storm, gale, hailstorm, hurricane, mistral, monsoon, rainstorm, sandstorm, simoom, sirocco, snowstorm, squall, thunderstorm, tornado, typhoon, whirlwind. 2 *storm of protest*. ▷ CLAMOUR.
● *vb* ▷ ATTACK.

stormy *adj* angry, blustery, choppy, fierce, furious, gusty, raging, rough, squally, tempestuous, thundery, tumultuous, turbulent, vehement, violent, wild, windy. *Opp* CALM.

story *n* 1 account, anecdote, chronicle, fiction, history, narration, narrative, plot, recital, record, scenario, tale, yarn. □ allegory, children's story, crime story, detective story, epic, fable, fairy-tale, fantasy, folk-tale, legend, mystery, myth, novel, parable, romance, saga, science fiction, SF, thriller, inf whodunit.

2 *story in newspaper*. article, dispatch, exclusive, feature, news item, piece, report, scoop. 3 falsehood, *inf* fib, lie, tall story, untruth.

storyteller *n* author, biographer, narrator, raconteur, teller.

stout *adj* 1 *inf* beefy, big, bulky, burly, *inf* chubby, corpulent, fleshy, heavy, *inf* hulking, overweight, plump, portly, solid, stocky, *inf* strapping, thick-set, *inf* tubby, well-built. ▷ FAT. *Opp* THIN. 2 *stout rope*. durable, reliable, robust, sound, strong, sturdy, substantial, thick, tough. 3 *stout fighter*. bold, brave, courageous, fearless, gallant, heroic, intrepid, plucky, resolute, spirited, valiant. *Opp* WEAK.

stove *n* boiler, cooker, fire, furnace, heater, oven, range.

stow *vb* load, pack, put away, *inf* stash away, store.

straggle *vb* be dispersed, be scattered, dangle, dawdle, drift, fall behind, lag, loiter, meander, ramble, scatter, spread out, stray, trail out, trail, wander. **straggling** ▷ DISORGANIZED, LOOSE.

straight *adj* 1 aligned, direct, flat, linear, regular, smooth, true, unbending, undeviating, unswerving. 2 neat, orderly, organized, right, *inf* shipshape, sorted out, spruce, tidy. 3 *a straight sequence*. consecutive, continuous, non-stop, perfect, sustained, unbroken, uninterrupted, unrelieved.
4 ▷ STRAIGHTFORWARD. *Opp* CROOKED, INDIRECT, UNTIDY. **straight away** at once, directly, immediately, instantly, now, without delay.

straighten vb disentangle, make straight, put straight, rearrange, sort out, tidy, unbend, uncurl, unravel, untangle, untwist.

straightforward adj blunt, candid, direct, easy, forthright, frank, genuine, honest, intelligible, lucid, open, plain, simple, sincere, straight, truthful, uncomplicated. Opp DEVIOUS.

strain n 1 anxiety, difficulty, effort, exertion, hardship, pressure, stress, tension, worry. 2 *genetic strain*. ▷ ANCESTRY. • vb 1 haul, heave, make taut, pull, stretch, tighten, tug. 2 *strain to succeed*. attempt, endeavour, exert yourself, labour, make an effort, strive, struggle, toil, try. 3 *strain yourself*. exercise, exhaust, overtax, *inf* push to the limit, stretch, tax, tire out, weaken, wear out, weary. 4 *strain a muscle*. damage, hurt, injure, overwork, pull, rick, sprain, tear, twist, wrench. 5 *strain liquid*. clear, drain, draw off, filter, percolate, purify, riddle, screen, separate, sieve, sift.

strained adj 1 artificial, constrained, distrustful, embarrassed, false, forced, insincere, self-conscious, stiff, tense, uncomfortable, uneasy, unnatural. 2 *strained look*. drawn, tired, weary. 3 *strained interpretation*. far-fetched, incredible, laboured, unlikely, unreasonable. Opp NATURAL, RELAXED.

strainer n colander, filter, riddle, sieve.

strand n fibre, filament, string, thread, wire. • vb 1 abandon, desert, forsake, leave stranded, lose, maroon. 2 *strand a ship*. beach, ground, run aground, wreck. **stranded** ▷ AGROUND, HELPLESS.

strange adj 1 abnormal, astonishing, atypical, bizarre, curious, eerie, exceptional, extraordinary, fantastic, *inf* funny, grotesque, irregular, odd, out-of-the-ordinary, outré, peculiar, quaint, queer, rare, remarkable, singular, surprising, surreal, uncommon, unexpected, unheard-of, unique, unnatural, untypical, unusual. 2 *strange neighbours*. *inf* cranky, eccentric, sinister, unconventional, weird, *inf* zany. 3 *a strange problem*. baffling, bewildering, inexplicable, insoluble, mysterious, mystifying, perplexing, puzzling, unaccountable. 4 *strange places*. alien, exotic, foreign, little-known, off the beaten track, outlandish, out-of-the-way, remote, unexplored, unmapped. 5 *strange experience*. different, fresh, new, novel, unaccustomed, unfamiliar. Opp FAMILIAR, ORDINARY.

strangeness n abnormality, bizarreness, eccentricity, eeriness, extraordinariness, irregularity, mysteriousness, novelty, oddity, oddness, outlandishness, peculiarity, quaintness, queerness, rarity, singularity, unconventionality, unfamiliarity.

stranger n alien, foreigner, guest, newcomer, outsider, visitor.

strangle vb 1 asphyxiate, choke, garotte, smother, stifle, suffocate, throttle. 2 *strangle a cry*. ▷ SUPPRESS.

strangulate vb bind, compress, constrict, squeeze.

strangulation n asphyxiation, garotting, suffocation.

strap n band, belt, strop, tawse, thong, webbing. • vb ▷ FASTEN.

stratagem n artifice, device, inf dodge, manoeuvre, plan, ploy, ruse, scheme, subterfuge, tactic, trick.

strategic adj advantageous, critical, crucial, deliberate, key, planned, politic, tactical, vital.

strategy n approach, design, manoeuvre, method, plan, plot, policy, procedure, programme, inf scenario, scheme, tactics.

stratum n layer, seam, table, thickness, vein.

straw n corn, stalks, stubble.

stray adj 1 abandoned, homeless, lost, roaming, roving, wandering. 2 stray bullets. accidental, casual, chance, haphazard, isolated, lone, occasional, odd, random, single. • vb 1 get lost, get separated, go astray, meander, move about aimlessly, ramble, range, roam, rove, straggle, wander. 2 stray from the point. deviate, digress, diverge, drift, get off the subject, inf go off at a tangent, veer.

streak n 1 band, bar, dash, line, mark, score, smear, stain, stria, striation, strip, stripe, stroke, vein. 2 a selfish streak. component, element, strain, touch, trace. 3 streak of good luck. period, run, series, spate, spell, stretch, time. • vb 1 mark with streaks, smear, smudge, stain, striate. 2 streak past. dart, dash, flash, fly, gallop, hurtle, move at speed, rush, inf scoot, speed, sprint, tear, inf whip, zoom.

streaky adj barred, lined, smeary, smudged, streaked, striated, stripy, veined.

stream n 1 beck, brook, brooklet, burn, channel, freshet, poet rill, river, rivulet, streamlet, watercourse. 2 cascade, cataract, current, deluge, effluence, flood, flow, fountain, gush, jet, outpouring, rush, spate, spurt, surge, tide, torrent. • vb cascade, course, deluge, flood, flow, gush, issue, pour, run, spill, spout, spurt, squirt, surge, well.

streamer n banner, flag, pennant, pennon, ribbon.

streamlined adj 1 aerodynamic, elegant, graceful, hydrodynamic, sleek, smooth. 2 ▷ EFFICIENT.

street n avenue, roadway, terrace. ▷ ROAD.

strength n 1 brawn, capacity, condition, energy, fitness, force, health, might, muscle, power, resilience, robustness, sinew, stamina, stoutness, sturdiness, toughness, vigour. 2 strength of purpose. inf backbone, commitment, courage, determination, firmness, inf grit, perseverance, persistence, resolution, resolve, spirit, tenacity. Opp WEAKNESS.

strengthen vb 1 bolster, boost, brace, build up, buttress, encourage, fortify, harden, hearten, increase, make stronger, prop up, reinforce, stiffen, support, tone up, toughen. 2 strengthen an argument. back up, consolidate, corroborate, enhance, justify, substantiate. Opp WEAKEN.

strenuous adj 1 arduous, backbreaking, burdensome, demanding, difficult, exhausting, gruelling, hard, laborious, punishing, stiff, taxing, tough, uphill. *Opp* EASY. 2 *strenuous efforts.* active, committed, determined, dogged, dynamic, eager, energetic, herculean, indefatigable, laborious, pertinacious, resolute, spirited, strong, tenacious, tireless, unremitting, vigorous, zealous. *Opp* CASUAL.

stress *n* 1 anxiety, difficulty, distress, hardship, pressure, strain, tenseness, tension, trauma, worry. 2 accent, accentuation, beat, emphasis, importance, significance, underlining, urgency, weight.
● *vb* 1 accent, accentuate, assert, draw attention to, emphasize, feature, highlight, insist on, lay stress on, mark, put stress on, repeat, spotlight, underline, underscore.
2 *stressed by work.* burden, distress, overstretch, pressurize, pressure, push to the limit, tax, weigh down.

stressful *adj* anxious, difficult, taxing, tense, tiring, traumatic, worrying. *Opp* RELAXED.

stretch *n* 1 period, spell, stint, term, time, tour of duty. 2 *stretch of country.* area, distance, expanse, length, span, spread, sweep, tract.
● *vb* 1 broaden, crane (*your neck*), dilate, distend, draw out, elongate, enlarge, expand, extend, flatten out, inflate, lengthen, open out, pull out, spread out, swell, tauten, tighten, widen. 2 *stretch into the distance.* be unbroken, continue, disappear, extend, go, reach out, spread. 3 *stretch resources.* overextend, overtax, *inf* push to the limit, strain, tax.

strew *vb* disperse, distribute, scatter, spread, sprinkle.

strict *adj* 1 austere, authoritarian, autocratic, firm, harsh, merciless, *inf* no-nonsense, rigorous, severe, stern, stringent, tyrannical, uncompromising. *Opp* EASYGOING. 2 *strict rules.* absolute, binding, defined, *inf* hard and fast, inflexible, invariable, precise, rigid, stringent, tight, unchangeable. *Opp* FLEXIBLE. 3 *strict truthfulness.* accurate, complete, correct, exact, meticulous, perfect, precise, right, scrupulous.

stride *n* pace, step. ● *vb* ▷ WALK.

strident *adj* clamorous, discordant, grating, harsh, jarring, loud, noisy, raucous, screeching, shrill, unmusical. *Opp* SOFT.

strife *n* 1 animosity, arguing, bickering, competition, conflict, discord, disharmony, dissension, enmity, friction, hostility, quarrelling, rivalry, unfriendliness. ▷ FIGHT. *Opp* COOPERATION.

strike *n* 1 go-slow, industrial action, stoppage, walk-out, withdrawal of labour. 2 assault, attack, bombardment.
● *vb* 1 bang against, bang into, beat, collide with, hammer, impel, knock, rap, run into, smack, smash into, *inf* thump, *inf* whack. ▷ ATTACK, HIT. 2 *strike a match.* ignite, light. 3 *tragedy struck us forcibly.* affect, afflict, *inf* come home to, impress, influence. 4 *clock struck one.* chime, ring, sound. 5 *strike for more pay.* *inf* come out, *inf* down tools, stop work, take industrial action, withdraw labour, work to rule.

6 *strike a flag, tent.* dismantle, lower, pull down, remove, take down.

striking *adj* affecting, amazing, arresting, conspicuous, distinctive, extraordinary, glaring, imposing, impressive, memorable, noticeable, obvious, out-of-the-ordinary, outstanding, prominent, showy, stunning, telling, unmistakable, unusual. *Opp* INCONSPICUOUS.

string *n* 1 cable, cord, fibre, line, rope, twine. 2 chain, file, line, procession, progression, queue, row, sequence, series, stream, succession, train. ● *vb* string together connect, join, line up, link, thread. **stringed instruments** strings. □ *banjo, cello, clavichord, double-bass, inf fiddle, guitar, harp, harpsichord, lute, lyre, piano, sitar, spinet, ukulele, viola, violin, zither.*

stringy *adj* chewy, fibrous, gristly, sinewy, tough. *Opp* TENDER.

strip *n* band, belt, fillet, lath, line, narrow piece, ribbon, shred, slat, sliver, stripe, swathe. ● *vb* 1 bare, clear, decorticate, defoliate, denude, divest, *old use* doff, excoriate, flay, lay bare, peel, remove the covering, remove the paint, remove the skin, skin, uncover. *Opp* COVER. 2 *strip to the waist.* bare yourself, disrobe, expose yourself, get undressed, uncover yourself. *Opp* DRESS. **strip down** ▷ DISMANTLE. **strip off** ▷ UNDRESS.

stripe *n* band, bar, chevron, line, ribbon, streak, striation, strip, stroke, swathe.

striped *adj* banded, barred, lined, streaky, striated, stripy.

strive *vb* attempt, *inf* do your best, endeavour, make an effort, strain, struggle, try. ▷ FIGHT.

stroke *n* 1 action, blow, effort, knock, move, swipe. ▷ HIT. 2 *a stroke of the pen.* flourish, gesture, line, mark, movement, sweep. 3 *[medical]* apoplexy, attack, embolism, fit, seizure, spasm, thrombosis. ● *vb* caress, fondle, massage, pass your hand over, pat, pet, rub, soothe, touch.

stroll *n, vb* amble, meander, saunter, wander. ▷ WALK.

strong *adj* 1 durable, hard, hard-wearing, heavy-duty, impregnable, indestructible, permanent, reinforced, resilient, robust, sound, stout, substantial, thick, unbreakable, well-made. 2 *strong physique.* athletic, *inf* beefy, *inf* brawny, burly, fit, *inf* hale and hearty, hardy, *inf* hefty, *inf* husky, mighty, muscular, powerful, robust, sinewy, stalwart, *inf* strapping, sturdy, tough, well-built, wiry. 3 *strong personality.* assertive, committed, determined, domineering, dynamic, energetic, forceful, independent, reliable, resolute, stalwart, steadfast, *inf* stout, strong-minded, strong-willed, tenacious, vigorous. ▷ STUBBORN. 4 *strong commitment.* active, assiduous, deep-rooted, deep-seated, *derog* doctrinaire, *derog* dogmatic, eager, earnest, enthusiastic, fervent, fierce, firm, genuine, intense, keen, loyal, passionate, positive, rabid, sedulous, staunch, true, vehement, zealous. 5 *strong government.* decisive, dependable, *derog* dictatorial, fearless, *derog* tyrannical,

unswerving, unwavering.
6 *strong measures*. aggressive, draconian, drastic, extreme, harsh, high-handed, ruthless, severe, tough, unflinching, violent. **7** *a strong army*. formidable, invincible, large, numerous, powerful, unconquerable, well-armed, well-equipped, well-trained. **8** *strong colour, light*. bright, brilliant, clear, dazzling, garish, glaring, vivid. **9** *strong taste, smell*. concentrated, highly-flavoured, hot, intense, noticeable, obvious, overpowering, prominent, pronounced, pungent, sharp, spicy, unmistakable. **10** *strong evidence*. clear-cut, cogent, compelling, convincing, evident, influential, persuasive, plain, solid, telling, undisputed. **11** *strong drink*. alcoholic, concentrated, intoxicating, potent, undiluted. *Opp* WEAK.

stronghold *n* bastion, bulwark, castle, citadel, *old use* fastness, fort, fortification, fortress, garrison.

structure *n* **1** arrangement, composition, configuration, constitution, design, form, formation, *inf* make-up, order, organization, plan, shape, system. **2** complex, construction, edifice, erection, fabric, framework, pile, superstructure. ▷ BUILDING. ● *vb* arrange, build, construct, design, form, frame, give structure to, organize, shape, systematize.

struggle *n* **1** challenge, difficulty, effort, endeavour, exertion, labour, problem.
2 ▷ FIGHT. ● *vb* **1** endeavour, exert yourself, labour, make an effort, move violently, strain, strive, toil, try, work hard,

wrestle, wriggle about, writhe about. **2** *struggle through mud*. flail, flounder, stumble, wallow. **3** ▷ FIGHT.

stub *n* butt, end, remains, remnant, stump. ● *vb* ▷ HIT.

stubble *n* **1** stalks, straw. **2** beard, bristles, *inf* five-o'clock shadow, hair, roughness.

stubbly *adj* bristly, prickly, rough, unshaven.

stubborn *adj* defiant, determined, difficult, disobedient, dogged, dogmatic, headstrong, inflexible, intractable, intransigent, mulish, obdurate, obstinate, opinionated, persistent, pertinacious, *inf* pig-headed, recalcitrant, refractory, rigid, self-willed, tenacious, uncompromising, uncooperative, uncontrollable, unmanageable, unreasonable, unyielding, wayward, wilful. *Opp* AMENABLE.

stuck *adj* **1** bogged down, cemented, fast, fastened, firm, fixed, glued, immovable. **2** *stuck on a problem*. baffled, beaten, held up, *inf* stumped, *inf* stymied.

stuck-up *adj* arrogant, *inf* big-headed, bumptious, *inf* cocky, conceited, condescending, *inf* high-and-mighty, patronizing, proud, self-important, snobbish, *inf* snooty, supercilious, *inf* toffee-nosed. *Opp* MODEST.

student *n* apprentice, disciple, learner, postgraduate, pupil, scholar, schoolchild, trainee, undergraduate.

studied *adj* calculated, conscious, contrived, deliberate, intentional, planned, premeditated.

studious *adj* academic, assiduous, attentive, bookish, brainy,

earnest, hard-working, intellectual, scholarly, serious-minded,
thoughtful.

study *vb* **1** analyse, consider,
contemplate, enquire into,
examine, give attention to,
investigate, learn about, look
closely at, peruse, ponder, pore
over, read carefully, research,
scrutinize, survey, think about,
weigh. **2** *study for exams.*
inf cram, learn, *inf* mug up,
read, *inf* swot, work.

stuff *n* **1** ingredients, matter,
substance. **2** fabric, material,
textile. ▷ CLOTH. **3** *all sorts of
stuff.* accoutrements, articles,
belongings, *inf* bits and pieces,
inf clobber, effects, *inf* gear,
impedimenta, junk, objects,
inf paraphernalia, possessions,
inf tackle, things. ● *vb* **1** compress, cram, crowd, force, jam,
pack, press, push, ram, shove,
squeeze, stow, thrust, tuck.
2 *stuff a cushion.* fill, line, pad.
stuff yourself ▷ EAT.

stuffing *n* **1** filling, lining,
padding, quilting, wadding.
2 *stuffing in poultry.* forcemeat,
seasoning.

stuffy *adj* **1** airless, close, fetid,
fuggy, fusty, heavy, humid,
muggy, musty, oppressive,
stale, steamy, stifling, suffocating, sultry, unventilated, warm.
Opp AIRY. **2** [*inf*] *a stuffy old
bore.* boring, conventional,
dreary, dull, formal, humourless, narrow-minded, old-fashioned, pompous, prim, staid,
inf stodgy, strait-laced.
Opp LIVELY.

stumble *vb* **1** blunder, flounder,
lurch, miss your footing, reel,
slip, stagger, totter, trip,
tumble. ▷ WALK. **2** *stumble in
speech.* become tongue-tied,

falter, hesitate, pause, stammer,
stutter.

stumbling-block *n* bar, difficulty, hindrance, hurdle,
impediment, obstacle, snag.

stump *vb* baffle, bewilder,
inf catch out, confound,
confuse, defeat, *inf* flummox,
mystify, outwit, perplex, puzzle,
inf stymie. **stump up** ▷ PAY.

stun *vb* **1** daze, knock out, knock
senseless, make unconscious.
2 amaze, astonish, astound,
bewilder, confound, confuse,
dumbfound, flabbergast, numb,
shock, stagger, stupefy. **stunning** ▷ BEAUTIFUL, STUPEN-
DOUS.

stunt *n inf* dare, exploit, feat,
trick. ● *vb* stunt growth.
▷ CHECK.

stupendous *adj* amazing, colossal, enormous, exceptional,
extraordinary, huge, incredible,
marvellous, miraculous,
notable, phenomenal, prodigious, remarkable,
inf sensational, singular,
special, staggering, stunning,
tremendous, unbelievable,
wonderful. *Opp* ORDINARY.

stupid *adj* [*Most synonyms
derog*] **1** addled, bird-brained,
bone-headed, bovine, brainless,
clueless, cretinous, dense, dim,
doltish, dopey, drippy, dull,
dumb, empty-headed, feather-
brained, feeble-minded, foolish,
gormless, half-witted, idiotic,
ignorant, imbecilic, imperceptive, ineducable, lacking, lumpish, mindless, moronic, naïve,
obtuse, puerile, senseless, silly,
simple, simple-minded, slow,
slow in the uptake, slow-
witted, subnormal, thick, thick-
headed, thick-skulled, thick-
witted, unintelligent, unthink-

ing, unwise, vacuous, weak in the head, witless. **2** *a stupid thing to do.* absurd, asinine, barmy, crack-brained, crass, crazy, fatuous, feeble, futile, half-baked, hare-brained, ill-advised, inane, irrational, irrelevant, irresponsible, laughable, ludicrous, lunatic, mad, nonsensical, pointless, rash, reckless, ridiculous, risible, scatterbrained, thoughtless, unjustifiable. **3** *stupid after a knock on the head.* dazed, in a stupor, semi-conscious, sluggish, stunned, stupefied. Opp INTELLIGENT. **stupid person** ▷ FOOL.

stupidity *n* absurdity, crassness, denseness, dullness, *inf* dumbness, fatuity, fatuousness, folly, foolishness, futility, idiocy, ignorance, imbecility, inanity, lack of intelligence, lunacy, madness, mindlessness, naïvety, pointlessness, recklessness, silliness, slowness, thoughtlessness. Opp INTELLIGENCE.

stupor *n* coma, daze, inertia, lassitude, lethargy, numbness, shock, state of insensibility, torpor, trance, unconsciousness.

sturdy *adj* **1** athletic, brawny, burly, hardy, healthy, hefty, husky, muscular, powerful, robust, stalwart, stocky, *inf* strapping, vigorous, well-built. **2** *sturdy shoes, etc.* durable, solid, sound, substantial, tough, well-made. **3** *sturdy opposition.* determined, firm, indomitable, resolute, staunch, steadfast, uncompromising, vigorous. ▷ STRONG. Opp WEAK.

stutter *vb* stammer, stumble. ▷ TALK.

style *n* **1** dash, elegance, flair, flamboyance, panache, polish, refinement, smartness, sophistication, stylishness, taste. **2** *not my style.* approach, character, custom, habit, idiosyncrasy, manner, method, way. **3** *style in writing.* diction, mode, phraseology, phrasing, register, sentence structure, tenor, tone, wording. **4** *style in clothes.* chic, cut, design, dress sense, fashion, look, mode, pattern, shape, tailoring, type, vogue.

stylish *adj* Fr à la mode, chic, *inf* classy, contemporary, *inf* dapper, elegant, fashionable, modern, modish, *inf* natty, *inf* posh, smart, *inf* snazzy, sophisticated, *inf* trendy, up-to-date. Opp OLD-FASHIONED.

subconscious *adj* deep-rooted, hidden, inner, intuitive, latent, repressed, subliminal, suppressed, unacknowledged, unconscious. Opp CONSCIOUS.

subdue *vb* check, curb, hold back, keep under, moderate, quieten, repress, restrain, suppress, temper. ▷ SUBJUGATE.

subdued *adj* **1** chastened, crestfallen, depressed, downcast, grave, reflective, repressed, restrained, serious, silent, sober, solemn, thoughtful. ▷ SAD. Opp EXCITED. **2** *subdued music.* calm, hushed, low, mellow, muted, peaceful, placid, quiet, soft, soothing, toned down, tranquil, unobtrusive.

subject *adj* **1** captive, dependent, enslaved, oppressed, ruled, subjugated. **2** *subject to interference.* exposed, liable, prone, susceptible, vulnerable. Opp FREE. ● *n* **1** citizen, dependant, national, passport-holder, taxpayer, voter. **2** *subject for* *discussion.* affair, business, issue, matter, point, proposition, question, theme, thesis, topic. 3 *subject of study.* area, branch of knowledge, course, discipline, field. □ *anatomy, archaeology, architecture, art, astronomy, biology, business, chemistry, computing, craft, design, divinity, domestic science, drama economics, education, electronics, engineering, English, environmental science, ethnology, etymology, geography, geology, heraldry, history, languages, Latin, law, linguistics, literature, mathematics, mechanics, medicine, metallurgy, metaphysics, meteorology, music, natural history, oceanography, ornithology, penology, pharmacology, pharmacy, philology, philosophy, photography, physics, physiology, politics, psychology, religious studies, science, scripture, social work, sociology, sport, surveying, technology, theology, topology, zoology.* ● *vb* 1 *subject a thing to scrutiny.* expose, lay open, submit. 2 ▷ SUBJUGATE.

subjective *adj* biased, emotional, *inf* gut (*reaction*), idiosyncratic, individual, instinctive, intuitive, personal, prejudiced, self-centred. *Opp* OBJECTIVE.

subjugate *vb* beat, conquer, control, crush, defeat, dominate, enslave, enthral, *inf* get the better of, master, oppress, overcome, overpower, overrun, put down, quash, quell, subdue, subject, tame, triumph over, vanquish.

sublimate *vb* channel, convert, divert, idealize, purify, redirect, refine.

sublime *adj* ecstatic, elated, elevated, exalted, great, heavenly, high, high-minded, lofty, noble, spiritual, transcendent. *Opp* BASE.

submerge *vb* 1 cover with water, dip, drench, drown, *inf* dunk, engulf, flood, immerse, inundate, overwhelm, soak, swamp. 2 dive, go down, go under, plummet, sink, subside.

submission *n* 1 acquiescence, capitulation, compliance, giving in, surrender, yielding. ▷ SUBMISSIVENESS. 2 contribution, entry, offering, presentation, tender. 3 *a legal submission.* argument, claim, contention, idea, proposal, suggestion, theory.

submissive *adj* accommodating, acquiescent, amenable, biddable, *derog* boot-licking, compliant, deferential, docile, humble, meek, obedient, obsequious, passive, pliant, resigned, servile, slavish, supine, sycophantic, tame, tractable, unassertive, uncomplaining, unresisting, weak, yielding. *Opp* ASSERTIVE.

submissiveness *n* acquiescence, assent, compliance, deference, docility, humility, meekness, obedience, obsequiousness, passivity, resignation, servility, submission, subservience, tameness.

submit *vb* 1 accede, bow, capitulate, concede, give in, *inf* knuckle under, succumb, surrender, yield. 2 *submit a proposal.* advance, enter, give in, hand in, offer, present, proffer, propose, propound, put forward, state, suggest. **submit to** ▷ ACCEPT, OBEY.

subordinate adj inferior, junior, lesser, lower, menial, minor, secondary, subservient, subsidiary. • n aide, assistant, dependant, employee, inferior, junior, menial, inf underling.
▷ SERVANT.

subscribe vb subscribe to 1 contribute to, covenant to, donate to, give to, patronize, sponsor, support. 2 subscribe to a magazine. be a subscriber to, buy regularly, pay a subscription to. 3 subscribe to a view. advocate, agree with, approve of, inf back, believe in, condone, consent to, endorse, inf give your blessing to.

subscriber n patron, regular customer, sponsor, supporter.

subscription n fee, due, payment, regular contribution, remittance.

subsequent adj coming, consequent, ensuing, following, future, later, next, resultant, resulting, succeeding, successive. Opp PREVIOUS.

subside vb 1 abate, calm down, decline, decrease, die down, diminish, dwindle, ebb, fall, go down, lessen, melt away, moderate, quieten, recede, shrink, slacken, wear off. 2 subside into a chair. collapse, descend, lower yourself, settle, sink. Opp RISE.

subsidiary adj additional, ancillary, auxiliary, complementary, contributory, inferior, lesser, minor, secondary, subordinate, supporting.

subsidize vb aid, back, finance, fund, give subsidy to, maintain, promote, sponsor, support, underwrite.

subsidy n aid, backing, financial help, funding, grant, maintenance, sponsorship, subvention, support.

substance n 1 actuality, body, concreteness, corporeality, reality, solidity. 2 chemical, fabric, make-up, material, matter, stuff. 3 substance of an argument. core, essence, gist, import, meaning, significance, subject-matter, theme. 4 [old use] a person of substance.
▷ WEALTH.

substandard adj inf below par, disappointing, inadequate, inferior, poor, shoddy, unworthy.

substantial adj 1 durable, hefty, massive, solid, sound, stout, strong, sturdy, well-built, well-made. 2 big, consequential, considerable, generous, great, large, significant, sizeable, worthwhile. Opp FLIMSY, SMALL.

substitute adj 1 acting, deputy, relief, reserve, stand-by, surrogate, temporary. 2 alternative, ersatz, imitation.
• n alternative, deputy, locum, proxy, relief, replacement, reserve, stand-in, stopgap, substitution, supply, surrogate, understudy. • vb 1 change, exchange, interchange, replace, inf swop, inf switch. 2 substitute for an absentee. act as a substitute, cover, deputize, double, stand in, supplant, take the place of, take over the role of, understudy.

subtle adj 1 delicate, elusive, faint, fine, gentle, mild, slight, unobtrusive. 2 subtle argument. arcane, clever, indirect, ingenious, mysterious, recondite, refined, shrewd, sophisticated,

tactful, understated.
▷ CUNNING. Opp OBVIOUS.

subtract vb debit, deduct,
remove, take away, take off.
Opp ADD.

suburban adj residential, outer,
outlying.

suburbs n fringes, outer areas,
outskirts, residential areas,
suburbia.

subversive adj challenging,
disruptive, insurrectionary,
questioning, radical, seditious,
traitorous, treacherous, treas-
onous, undermining, unsettling. ▷ REVOLUTIONARY.
Opp CONSERVATIVE, ORTHODOX.

subvert vb challenge, corrupt,
destroy, disrupt, overthrow,
overturn, pervert, ruin, undermine, upset, wreck.

subway n tunnel, underpass.

succeed vb 1 accomplish your
objective, inf arrive, be a
success, do well, flourish,
inf get on, inf get to the top,
inf make it, prosper, thrive.
2 be effective, inf catch on,
produce results, work. 3 be
successor to, come after, follow,
inherit from, replace, take over
from. Opp FAIL. **succeeding**
▷ SUBSEQUENT.

success n 1 fame, good fortune,
prosperity, wealth. 2 success of
a plan. accomplishment,
achievement, attainment,
completion, effectiveness,
successful outcome. 3 a great
success. inf hit, inf sensation,
triumph, victory, inf winner.
Opp FAILURE.

successful adj 1 booming, effective, effectual, flourishing, fruitful, lucrative, money-making,
productive, profitable, profit-
making, prosperous, rewarding,

thriving, useful, well-off. 2 best-
selling, celebrated, famed,
famous, high-earning, leading,
popular, top, unbeaten, victorious, well-known, winning.
Opp UNSUCCESSFUL.

succession n chain, flow, line,
procession, progression, run,
sequence, series, string.

successive adj consecutive,
continuous, in succession,
succeeding, unbroken, uninterrupted.

successor n heir, inheritor,
replacement.

succinct adj brief, compact,
concise, condensed, epigrammatic, pithy, short, terse, to the
point. Opp WORDY.

succulent adj fleshy, juicy,
luscious, moist, mouthwatering, palatable, rich.

succumb vb accede, be overcome, capitulate, give in, give
up, give way, submit, surrender, yield. Opp SURVIVE.

suck vb suck up absorb, draw
up, pull up, soak up. **suck up
to** ▷ FLATTER.

sudden adj 1 abrupt, brisk,
hasty, hurried, impetuous,
impulsive, precipitate, quick,
rash, inf snap, swift, unconsidered, unplanned, unpremeditated. Opp SLOW. 2 a sudden
shock. acute, sharp, startling,
surprising, unannounced, unexpected, unforeseeable, unforeseen, unlooked-for.
Opp PREDICTABLE.

suds n bubbles, foam, froth,
lather, soapsuds.

sue vb 1 indict, institute legal
proceedings against, proceed
against, prosecute, summons,
take legal action against. 2 sue
for peace. ▷ ENTREAT.

suffer vb 1 bear, cope with, endure, experience, feel, go through, live through, *inf* put up with, stand, tolerate, undergo, withstand. 2 *suffer from a wound*. ache, agonize, feel pain, hurt, smart. 3 *suffer for a crime*. atone, be punished, make amends, pay.

suffice vb answer, be sufficient, *inf* do, satisfy, serve.

sufficient adj adequate, enough, satisfactory. Opp INSUFFICIENT.

suffocate vb asphyxiate, choke, smother, stifle, stop breathing, strangle, throttle.

sugar n □ brown sugar, cane sugar, caster sugar, demerara, glucose, granulated sugar, icing sugar, lump sugar, molasses, sucrose, sweets, syrup, treacle.
● vb sweeten.

sugary adj 1 glazed, iced, sugared, sweetened. ▷ SWEET. 2 sugary sentiments. cloying, honeyed, sickly. ▷ SENTIMENTAL.

suggest vb 1 advise, advocate, counsel, moot, move, propose, propound, put forward, raise, recommend, urge. 2 call to mind, communicate, hint, imply, indicate, insinuate, intimate, make you think (of), mean, signal.

suggestion n 1 advice, counsel, offer, plan, prompting, proposal, recommendation, urging. 2 breath, hint, idea, indication, intimation, notion, suspicion, touch, trace.

suggestive adj 1 evocative, expressive, indicative, reminiscent, thought-provoking. 2 ▷ INDECENT.

suicidal adj 1 hopeless, *inf* kamikaze, self-destructive. 2 ▷ DESOLATE.

suit n outfit. ▷ CLOTHES.
● vb 1 accommodate, be suitable for, conform to, fill your needs, fit in with, gratify, harmonize with, match, please, satisfy, tally with. Opp DISPLEASE. 2 *That colour suits you.* become, fit, look good on.

suitable adj acceptable, applicable, apposite, appropriate, apt, becoming, befitting, congenial, convenient, correct, decent, decorous, fit, fitting, handy, *old use* meet, opportune, pertinent, proper, relevant, right, satisfactory, seemly, tasteful, timely, well-chosen, well-judged, well-timed. Opp UNSUITABLE.

sulk vb be sullen, brood, mope, pout.

sullen adj 1 anti-social, bad-tempered, brooding, churlish, crabby, cross, disgruntled, dour, glum, grim, grudging, ill-humoured, lugubrious, moody, morose, *inf* out of sorts, petulant, pouting, resentful, silent, sour, stubborn, sulking, sulky, surly, uncommunicative, unforgiving, unfriendly, unhappy, unsociable. ▷ SAD. 2 *a sullen sky*. cheerless, dark, dismal, dull, gloomy, grey, leaden, sombre. Opp CHEERFUL.

sultry adj 1 close, hot, humid, *inf* muggy, oppressive, steamy, stifling, stuffy, warm. Opp COLD. 2 *sultry beauty*. erotic, mysterious, passionate, provocative, seductive, sensual, sexy, voluptuous.

sum n aggregate, amount, number, quantity, reckoning, result, score, tally, total, whole. ● vb **sum up** ▷ SUMMARIZE.

summarize vb abridge, condense, digest, encapsulate, give the gist, make a summary, outline, précis, *inf* recap, recapitulate, reduce, review, shorten, simplify, sum up. *Opp* ELABORATE.

summary *n* abridgement, abstract, condensation, digest, epitome, gist, outline, précis, recapitulation, reduction, résumé, review, summation, summing-up, synopsis.

summery *adj* bright, sunny, tropical, warm. ▷ HOT. *Opp* WINTRY.

summit *n* 1 apex, crown, head, height, peak, pinnacle, point, top. *Opp* BASE. 2 *summit of success*. acme, apogee, climax, culmination, high point, zenith. *Opp* NADIR.

summon *vb* 1 command, demand, invite, order, send for, subpoena. 2 assemble, call, convene, convoke, gather together, muster, rally.

sunbathe *vb* bake, bask, *inf* get a tan, sun yourself, tan.

sunburnt *adj* blistered, bronzed, brown, peeling, tanned, weather-beaten.

sundry *adj* assorted, different, *old use* divers, miscellaneous, mixed, various.

sunken *adj* 1 submerged, underwater, wrecked. 2 *sunken cheeks*. concave, depressed, drawn, hollow, hollowed.

sunless *adj* cheerless, cloudy, dark, dismal, dreary, dull, gloomy, grey, overcast, sombre. *Opp* SUNNY.

sunlight *n* daylight, sun, sunbeams, sunshine.

sunny *adj* 1 bright, clear, cloudless, fair, fine, summery, sunlit, sunshiny, unclouded. *Opp* SUNLESS. 2 ▷ CHEERFUL.

sunrise *n* dawn, day-break.

sunset *n* dusk, evening, gloaming, nightfall, sundown, twilight.

sunshade *n* awning, canopy, parasol.

superannuated *adj* 1 discharged, *inf* pensioned off, *inf* put out to grass, old, retired. 2 discarded, disused, obsolete, thrown out, worn out. ▷ OLD.

superannuation *n* annuity, pension.

superb *adj* admirable, excellent, fine, first-class, first-rate, grand, impressive, marvellous, superior. ▷ SPLENDID. *Opp* INFERIOR.

superficial *adj* 1 cosmetic, external, exterior, on the surface, outward, shallow, skin-deep, slight, surface, unimportant. 2 careless, casual, cursory, desultory, facile, frivolous, hasty, hurried, inattentive, lightweight, *inf* nodding (*acquaintance*), oversimplified, passing, perfunctory, simple-minded, simplistic, sweeping (*generalization*), trivial, unconvincing, uncritical, undiscriminating, unquestioning, unscholarly, unsophisticated. *Opp* ANALYTICAL, DEEP.

superfluous *adj* excess, excessive, extra, needless, redundant, spare, superabundant, surplus, unnecessary, unneeded, unwanted. *Opp* NECESSARY.

superhuman *adj* 1 god-like, herculean, heroic, phenomenal, prodigious. 2 *superhuman powers*. divine, higher, metaphysical, supernatural.

superimpose *vb* overlay, place on top of.

superintend *vb* administer, be in charge of, be the supervisor of, conduct, control, direct, look after, manage, organize, oversee, preside over, run, supervise, watch over.

superior *adj* **1** better, *inf* classier, greater, higher, higher-born, loftier, more important, more impressive, nobler, senior, *inf* up-market. **2** *superior quality.* choice, exclusive, fine, first-class, first-rate, select, top, unrivalled. **3** *superior attitude.* arrogant, condescending, contemptuous, disdainful, élitist, haughty, *inf* high-and-mighty, lofty, paternalistic, patronizing, self-important, smug, snobbish, *inf* snooty, stuck-up, supercilious. *Opp* INFERIOR.

superlative *adj* best, choicest, consummate, excellent, finest, first-rate, incomparable, matchless, peerless, *inf* tip-top, *inf* top-notch, unrivalled, unsurpassed. ▷ SUPREME.

supernatural *adj* abnormal, ghostly, inexplicable, magical, metaphysical, miraculous, mysterious, mystic, occult, other-worldly, paranormal, preternatural, psychic, spiritual, uncanny, unearthly, unnatural, weird.

superstition *n* delusion, illusion, myth, *inf* old wives' tale, superstitious belief.

superstitious *adj* credulous, groundless, illusory, irrational, mythical, traditional, unfounded, unprovable.

supervise *vb* administer, be in charge of, be the supervisor of, conduct, control, direct, govern, invigilate *(an exam),* *inf* keep an eye on, lead, look after, manage, organize, oversee,

preside over, run, superintend, watch over.

supervision *n* administration, conduct, control, direction, government, invigilation, management, organization, oversight, running, surveillance.

supervisor *n* administrator, chief, controller, director, executive, foreman, *inf* gaffer, head, inspector, invigilator, leader, manager, organizer, overseer, superintendent, timekeeper.

supine *adj* **1** face upwards, flat on your back, prostrate, recumbent. *Opp* PRONE. **2** ▷ PASSIVE.

supplant *vb* displace, dispossess, eject, expel, oust, replace, supersede, *inf* step into the shoes of, *inf* topple, unseat.

supple *adj* bending, *inf* bendy, elastic, flexible, flexile, graceful, limber, lithe, plastic, pliable, pliant, resilient, soft. *Opp* RIGID.

supplement *n* **1** additional payment, excess, surcharge. **2** *a newspaper supplement, etc.* addendum, addition, annexe, appendix, codicil, continuation, endpiece, extra, insert, postscript, sequel. ● *vb* add to, augment, boost, complement, extend, reinforce, *inf* top up.

supplementary *adj* accompanying, added, additional, ancillary, auxiliary, complementary, excess, extra, new, supportive

supplication *n* appeal, entreaty, petition, plea, prayer, request, solicitation.

supplier *n* dealer, provider, purveyor, retailer, seller, shopkeeper, vendor, wholesaler.

supply n 1 cache, hoard, quantity, reserve, reservoir, stock, stockpile, store. 2 equipment, food, necessities, provisions, rations, shopping. 3 *a regular supply*. delivery, distribution, provision, provisioning. ● vb cater to, contribute, deliver, distribute, donate, endow, equip, feed, furnish, give, hand over, pass on, produce, provide, purvey, sell, stock.

support n 1 aid, approval, assistance, backing, back-up, bolstering, contribution, cooperation, donation, encouragement, fortifying, friendship, help, interest, loyalty, patronage, protection, reassurance, reinforcement, sponsorship, succour. 2 brace, bracket, buttress, crutch, foundation, frame, pillar, post, prop, sling, stanchion, stay, strut, substructure, trestle, truss, underpinning. 3 *financial support*. expenses, funding, keep, maintenance, subsistence, upkeep. ● vb 1 bear, bolster, buoy up, buttress, carry, give strength to, hold up, keep up, prop up, provide a support for, reinforce, shore up, strengthen, underlie, underpin. 2 *support someone in trouble*. aid, assist, back, be faithful to, champion, comfort, defend, encourage, favour, fight for, give support to, help, rally round, reassure, side with, speak up for, stand by, stand up for, stay with, *inf* stick up for, *inf* stick with, take someone's part. 3 *support a family*. bring up, feed, finance, fund, keep, look after, maintain, nourish, provide for, sustain. 4 *support a charity*. be a supporter of, be interested in, contribute to, espouse (*a cause*),

follow, give to, patronize, pay money to, sponsor, subsidize, work for. 5 *support a point of view*. accept, adhere to, advocate, agree with, allow, approve, argue for, confirm, corroborate, defend, endorse, explain, justify, promote, ratify, substantiate, uphold, validate, verify. Opp SUBVERT, WEAKEN. **support yourself** lean, rest.

supporter n 1 adherent, admirer, advocate, aficionado, apologist, champion, defender, devotee, enthusiast, *inf* fan, fanatic, follower, seconder, upholder, voter. 2 ally, assistant, collaborator, helper, henchman, second.

supportive adj caring, concerned, encouraging, helpful, favourable, heartening, interested, kind, loyal, positive, reassuring, sustaining, sympathetic, understanding. Opp SUBVERSIVE.

suppose vb 1 accept, assume, believe, conclude, conjecture, expect, guess, infer, judge, postulate, presume, presuppose, speculate, surmise, suspect, take for granted, think. 2 daydream, fancy, fantasize, hypothesize, imagine, maintain, postulate, pretend, theorize. **supposed** ▷ HYPOTHETICAL, PUTATIVE. **supposed to** due to, expected to, having a duty to, meant to, required to.

supposition n assumption, belief, conjecture, fancy, guess, *inf* guesstimate, hypothesis, inference, notion, opinion, presumption, speculation, surmise, theory, thought.

suppress vb 1 conquer, *inf* crack down on, crush, end, finish off, halt, overcome, overthrow, put an end to, put down, quash, quell, stamp out, stop, subdue. **2** suppress emotion. bottle up, censor, choke back, conceal, cover up, hide, hush up, keep quiet about, keep secret, muffle, mute, obstruct, prohibit, repress, restrain, silence, smother, stamp on, stifle, strangle.

supremacy *n* ascendancy, dominance, domination, dominion, lead, mastery, predominance, pre-eminence, sovereignty, superiority.

supreme *adj* best, choicest, consummate, crowning, culminating, excellent, finest, first-rate, greatest, highest, incomparable, matchless, outstanding, paramount, peerless, predominant, pre-eminent, prime, principal, superlative, surpassing, *inf* tip-top, top, *inf* top-notch, ultimate, unbeatable, unbeaten, unparalleled, unrivalled, unsurpassable, unsurpassed.

sure *adj* **1** assured, certain, confident, convinced, decided, definite, persuaded, positive. **2** *sure to come.* bound, certain, compelled, obliged, required. **3** *a sure fact.* accurate, clear, convincing, guaranteed, indisputable, inescapable, inevitable, infallible, proven, reliable, true, unchallenged, undeniable, undisputed, undoubted, verifiable. **4** *a sure ally.* dependable, effective, established, faithful, firm, infallible, loyal, reliable, resolute, safe, secure, solid, steadfast, steady, trustworthy, trusty, undeviating, unerring, unfailing, unfaltering, unflinching, unswerving, unwavering. *Opp* UNCERTAIN.

surface *n* **1** coat, coating, covering, crust, exterior, façade, integument, interface, outside, shell, skin, veneer. **2** *cube has six surfaces.* face, facet, plane, side. **3** *a working surface.* bench, table, top, worktop. • *vb* **1** appear, arise, *inf* come to light, come up, *inf* crop up, emerge, materialize, rise, *inf* pop up. **2** coat, cover, laminate, veneer.

surfeit *n* excess, flood, glut, overabundance, overindulgence, oversupply, plethora, superfluity, surplus.

surge *n* burst, gush, increase, onrush, onset, outpouring, rush, upsurge. ▷ WAVE. • *vb* billow, eddy, flow, gush, heave, make waves, move irresistibly, push, roll, rush, stampede, stream, sweep, swirl, well up.

surgery *n* **1** biopsy, operation. **2** *a doctor's surgery.* clinic, consulting room, health centre, infirmary, medical centre, sickbay.

surly *adj* bad-tempered, boorish, cantankerous, churlish, crabby, cross, crotchety, *inf* crusty, curmudgeonly, dyspeptic, gruff, *inf* grumpy, ill-natured, ill-tempered, irascible, miserable, morose, peevish, rough, rude, sulky, sullen, testy, touchy, uncivil, unfriendly, ungracious, unpleasant. *Opp* FRIENDLY.

surmise *vb* assume, believe, conjecture, expect, fancy, gather, guess, hypothesize, imagine, infer, judge, postulate, presume, presuppose, sense, speculate, suppose, suspect, take for granted, think.

surpass vb beat, better, do better than, eclipse, exceed, excel, go beyond, leave behind, *inf* leave standing, outclass, outdistance, outdo, outperform, outshine, outstrip, overshadow, top, transcend, worst.

surplus n balance, excess, extra, glut, oversupply, remainder, residue, superfluity, surfeit.

surprise n 1 alarm, amazement, astonishment, consternation, dismay, incredulity, stupefaction, wonder. 2 *a complete surprise*. blow, *inf* bolt from the blue, *inf* bombshell, *inf* eye-opener, jolt, shock.
● vb 1 alarm, amaze, astonish, astound, disconcert, dismay, dumbfound, flabbergast, nonplus, rock, shock, stagger, startle, stun, stupefy, *inf* take aback, take by surprise, *inf* throw. 2 *surprise someone doing wrong*. capture, catch out, *inf* catch red-handed, come upon, detect, discover, take unawares.

surprised adj alarmed, amazed, astonished, astounded, disconcerted, dismayed, dumbfounded, flabbergasted, incredulous, *inf* knocked for six, nonplussed, *inf* shattered, shocked, speechless, staggered, startled, struck dumb, stunned, taken aback, taken by surprise, *inf* thrown, thunderstruck.

surprising adj alarming, amazing, astonishing, astounding, disconcerting, extraordinary, frightening, incredible, *inf* offputting, shocking, staggering, startling, stunning, sudden, unexpected, unforeseen, unlooked-for, unplanned, unpredictable, upsetting.
Opp PREDICTABLE.

surrender n capitulation, giving in, resignation, submission.
● vb 1 acquiesce, capitulate, *inf* cave in, collapse, concede, fall, *inf* give in, give up, give way, give yourself up, resign, submit, succumb, *inf* throw in the towel, *inf* throw up the sponge, yield. 2 *surrender your ticket*. deliver up, give up, hand over, part with, relinquish. 3 *surrender your rights*. abandon, cede, renounce, waive.

surreptitious adj clandestine, concealed, covert, crafty, disguised, furtive, hidden, private, secret, secretive, shifty, sly, *inf* sneaky, stealthy, underhand. *Opp* BLATANT.

surround vb besiege, beset, cocoon, cordon off, encircle, enclose, encompass, engulf, environ, girdle, hem in, hedge in, ring, skirt, trap, wrap.

surrounding adj adjacent, adjoining, bordering, local, nearby, neighbouring.

surroundings n ambience, area, background, context, environment, location, milieu, neighbourhood, setting, vicinity.

surveillance n check, observation, reconnaissance, scrutiny, supervision, vigilance, watch.

survey n appraisal, assessment, census, count, evaluation, examination, inquiry, inspection, investigation, review, scrutiny, study, triangulation.
● vb 1 appraise, assess, estimate, evaluate, examine, inspect, *inf* look over, review, scrutinize, study, view, weigh up. 2 do a survey of, map out, measure, plan out, plot, reconnoitre, triangulate.

survival n continuance, continued existence, persistence.

survive vb 1 inf bear up, carry on, continue, endure, keep going, last, live, persist, remain. 2 survive disaster. come through, live through, outlast, outlive, pull through, weather, withstand. Opp SUCCUMB.

susceptible adj affected (by), disposed, given, inclined, liable, open, predisposed, prone, responsive, sensitive, vulnerable. Opp RESISTANT.

suspect adj doubtful, dubious, inadequate, questionable, inf shady, suspected, suspicious, unconvincing, unreliable, unsatisfactory, untrustworthy. • vb 1 call into question, disbelieve, distrust, doubt, have suspicions about, mistrust. 2 suspect that she's lying. believe, conjecture, consider, guess, imagine, infer, presume, speculate, suppose, surmise, think.

suspend vb 1 dangle, hang, swing. 2 suspend work. adjourn, break off, defer, delay, discontinue, freeze, hold in abeyance, hold up, interrupt, postpone, put off, inf put on ice, shelve. 3 suspend from duty. debar, dismiss, exclude, expel, lay off, lock out, send down.

suspense n anticipation, anxiety, apprehension, doubt, drama, excitement, expectancy, expectation, insecurity, irresolution, nervousness, not knowing, tension, uncertainty, waiting.

suspicion n 1 apprehension, apprehensiveness, caution, distrust, doubt, dubiety, dubiousness, inf funny feeling, guess, hesitation, inf hunch, impression, misgiving, mistrust, presentiment, qualm, scepticism, uncertainty, wariness. 2 suspicion of a smile. glimmer, hint, inkling, shadow, suggestion, tinge, touch, trace.

suspicious adj 1 apprehensive, inf chary, disbelieving, distrustful, doubtful, dubious, incredulous, in doubt, mistrustful, sceptical, uncertain, unconvinced, uneasy, wary. Opp TRUSTFUL. 2 suspicious character. disreputable, dubious, inf fishy, peculiar, questionable, inf shady, suspect, suspected, unreliable, untrustworthy. Opp TRUSTWORTHY.

sustain vb 1 continue, develop, elongate, extend, keep alive, keep going, keep up, maintain, prolong. 2 ▷ SUPPORT.

sustenance n eatables, edibles, food, foodstuffs, nourishment, nutriment, provender, provisions, rations, old use victuals.

swag n booty, loot, plunder, takings.

swagger vb parade, strut.
▷ WALK.

swallow vb consume, inf down, gulp down, guzzle, ingest, take down. ▷ DRINK, EAT. **swallow up** absorb, assimilate, enclose, enfold, make disappear.
▷ SWAMP.

swamp n bog, fen, marsh, marshland, morass, mud, mudflats, quagmire, quicksand, saltmarsh, old use slough, wetlands. • vb deluge, drench, engulf, envelop, flood, immerse, inundate, overcome, overwhelm, sink, submerge, swallow up.

swampy adj boggy, marshy, muddy, soft, soggy, unstable, waterlogged, wet. *Opp* DRY, FIRM.

swarm n cloud, crowd, hive, horde, host, multitude.
▷ GROUP. ● vb cluster, congregate, crowd, flock, gather, mass, move in a swarm, throng. **swarm up** ▷ CLIMB. **swarm with** ▷ TEEM.

swarthy adj brown, dark, dark-complexioned, dark-skinned, dusky, tanned.

swashbuckling adj adventurous, aggressive, bold, daredevil, daring, dashing, *inf* macho, manly, swaggering. *Opp* TIMID.

sway vb 1 bend, fluctuate, lean from side to side, oscillate, rock, roll, swing, undulate, wave. 2 *sway opinions.* affect, bias, bring round, change (someone's mind), convert, convince, govern, influence, persuade, win over. 3 *sway from a chosen path.* divert, go off course, swerve, veer, waver.

swear vb 1 affirm, asseverate, attest, aver, avow, declare, give your word, insist, pledge, promise, state on oath, take an oath, testify, vouchsafe, vow. 2 blaspheme, curse, execrate, imprecate, use swearwords, utter profanities.

swearword n *inf* bad language, blasphemy, curse, execration, expletive, *inf* four-letter word, imprecation, oath, obscenity, profanity, swearing.

sweat vb 1 *inf* glow, perspire, swelter. 2 ▷ WORK.

sweaty adj clammy, damp, moist, perspiring, sticky, sweating.

sweep vb brush, clean, clear, dust, tidy up. **sweep along**
▷ MOVE. **sweep away**
▷ REMOVE. **sweeping**
▷ GENERAL, SUPERFICIAL.

sweet adj 1 aromatic, fragrant, honeyed, luscious, mellow, perfumed, sweetened, sweet-scented, sweet-smelling. 2 [*derog*] sickly sweet. cloying, saccharine, sentimental, sickening, sickly, sugary, syrupy, treacly. 3 *sweet sounds.* dulcet, euphonious, harmonious, heavenly, mellifluous, melodious, musical, pleasant, silvery, soothing, tuneful. 4 *a sweet nature.* affectionate, amiable, attractive, charming, dear, endearing, engaging, friendly, genial, gentle, gracious, lovable, lovely, nice, pretty, unselfish, winning. *Opp* ACID, BITTER, NASTY, SAVOURY. ● n 1 *inf* afters, dessert, pudding. 2 [*usu plur*] *old use* bon-bons, *Amer* candy, confectionery, *inf* sweeties, *old use* sweetmeats. □ acid drop, barley sugar, boiled sweet, bull's-eye, butterscotch, candy, candyfloss, caramel, chewing-gum, chocolate, fondant, fruit pastille, fudge, humbug, liquorice, lollipop, marshmallow, marzipan, mint, nougat, peppermint, rock, toffee, Turkish delight.

sweeten vb 1 make sweeter, sugar. 2 *sweeten your temper.* appease, assuage, calm, mellow, mollify, pacify, soothe.

sweetener n □ artificial sweetener, honey, saccharine, sugar, sweetening, syrup.

swell vb 1 balloon, become bigger, belly, billow, blow up, bulge, dilate, distend, enlarge, expand, fatten, fill out, grow, increase, inflate, mushroom, puff up, rise. **2** *swell numbers*. augment, boost, build up, extend, increase, make bigger, raise, step up. *Opp* SHRINK.

swelling *n* blister, boil, bulge, bump, distension, enlargement, excrescence, hump, inflammation, knob, lump, node, nodule, prominence, protrusion, protuberance, tumescence, tumour.

sweltering *adj* humid, muggy, oppressive, steamy, sticky, stifling, sultry, torrid, tropical. ▷ HOT.

swerve *vb* career, change direction, deviate, diverge, dodge about, sheer off, swing, take avoiding action, turn aside, veer, wheel.

swift *adj* agile, brisk, expeditious, fast, *old use* fleet, fleetfooted, hasty, hurried, nimble, *inf* nippy, prompt, quick, rapid, speedy, sudden. *Opp* SLOW.

swill *vb* **1** bathe, clean, rinse, sponge down, wash. **2** ▷ DRINK.

swim *vb* bathe, dive in, float, go swimming, have a dip.

swimming-bath *n* baths, leisure-pool, lido, swimmingpool.

swim-suit *n* bathing-costume, bathing-dress, bathing-suit, bikini, swimwear, trunks.

swindle *n* cheat, chicanery, *inf* con, confidence trick, deception, double-dealing, fraud, knavery, *inf* racket, *inf* rip-off, *inf* sharp practice, *inf* swizz, trickery. ● *vb inf* bamboozle, cheat, *inf* con, cozen, deceive, defraud, *inf* diddle, *inf* do, double-cross, dupe, exploit, *inf* fiddle, *inf* fleece, fool, gull, hoax, hoodwink, mulct, *inf* pull

a fast one on you, *inf* rook, *inf* take you for a ride, trick, *inf* welsh (*on a bet*).

swindler *n* charlatan, cheat, cheater, *inf* con man, counterfeiter, double-crosser, extortioner, forger, fraud, hoaxer, impostor, knave, mountebank, quack, racketeer, scoundrel, *inf* shark, trickster, *inf* twister.

swing *n* change, fluctuation, movement, oscillation, shift, variation. ● *vb* **1** be suspended, dangle, flap, fluctuate, hang loose, move from side to side, move to and fro, oscillate, revolve, rock, roll, sway, swivel, turn, twirl, wave about. **2** *swing opinion*. affect, bias, bring round, change (someone's mind), convert, convince, govern, influence, persuade, win over. **3** *support swung to the opposition*. change, move across, shift, transfer, vary. **4** *swing from a path*. deviate, divert, go off course, swerve, veer, waver, zigzag.

swipe *vb* **1** lash out at, strike, swing at. ▷ HIT. **2** ▷ STEAL.

swirl *vb* boil, churn, circulate, curl, eddy, move in circles, seethe, spin, surge, twirl, twist, whirl.

switch *n* circuit-breaker, lightswitch, power-point. ● *vb* change, divert, exchange, redirect, replace, reverse, shift, substitute, *inf* swap, transfer, turn.

swivel *vb* gyrate, pirouette, pivot, revolve, rotate, spin, swing, turn, twirl, wheel.

swoop *vb* descend, dive, drop, fall, fly down, lunge, plunge, pounce. **swoop on** ▷ RAID.

sword n blade, broadsword, cutlass, dagger, foil, kris, rapier, sabre, scimitar.

sycophantic adj flattering, servile, inf smarmy, toadyish, unctuous.

syllabus n course, curriculum, outline, programme of study.

symbol n mark, sign, token. □ badge, brand, character, cipher, coat of arms, crest, emblem, figure, hieroglyph, ideogram, ideograph, image, insignia, letter, logo, logotype, monogram, motif, number, numeral, pictogram, pictograph, trademark.

symbolic adj allegorical, emblematic, figurative, meaningful, metaphorical, representative, significant, suggestive, symptomatic, token (gesture).

symbolize vb be a sign of, betoken, communicate, connote, denote, epitomize, imply, indicate, mean, represent, signify, stand for, suggest.

symmetrical adj balanced, even, proportional, regular. Opp ASYMMETRICAL.

sympathetic adj benevolent, caring, charitable, comforting, compassionate, commiserating, concerned, consoling, empathetic, friendly, humane, interested, kind-hearted, kindly, merciful, pitying, soft-hearted, solicitous, sorry, supportive, tender, tolerant, understanding, warm. Opp UNSYMPATHETIC.

sympathize vb inf be on the same wavelength, be sorry, be sympathetic, comfort, commiserate, condole, console, empathize, feel, grieve, have sympathy, identify (with), mourn, pity, respond, show sympathy, understand.

sympathy n affinity, commiseration, compassion, concern, condolence, consideration, empathy, feeling, fellow-feeling, kindness, mercy, pity, rapport, solicitousness, tenderness, understanding.

symptom n characteristic, evidence, feature, indication, manifestation, mark, marker, sign, warning, warning-sign.

symptomatic adj characteristic, indicative, representative, suggestive, typical.

synthesis n amalgamation, blend, coalescence, combination, composite, compound, fusion, integration, union. Opp ANALYSIS.

synthetic adj artificial, bogus, concocted, counterfeit, ersatz, fabricated, fake, inf made-up, man-made, manufactured, mock, inf phoney, simulated, spurious, unnatural. Opp GENUINE, NATURAL.

syringe n hypodermic, needle.

system n 1 network, organization, inf set-up, structure. 2 approach, arrangement, logic, method, methodology, Lat modus operandi, order, plan, practice, procedure, process, routine, rules, scheme, technique. 3 system of government. constitution, regime. 4 system of knowledge. categorization, classification, code, discipline, philosophy, science, set of principles, theory.

systematic adj according to plan, businesslike, categorized, classified, codified, constitutional, co-ordinated, logical, methodical, neat, ordered, orderly, organized, planned, rational, regimented, routine, scientific, structured, tidy, well-arranged, well-organized, well-rehearsed, well-run. *Opp* UNSYSTEMATIC.

systematize *vb* arrange, catalogue, categorize, classify, codify, make systematic, organize, rationalize, regiment, standardize, tabulate.

T

table *n* 1 bench, board, counter, desk, gate-leg table, kitchen table, worktop. 2 *table of information*. agenda, catalogue, chart, diagram, graph, index, inventory, list, register, schedule, tabulation, timetable. • *vb* bring forward, lay on the table, offer, proffer, propose, submit.

tablet *n* 1 capsule, drop, lozenge, medicine, pastille, pellet, pill. 2 *tablet of soap*. bar, block, chunk, piece, slab. 3 *tablet of stone*. gravestone, headstone, memorial, plaque, plate, tombstone.

taboo *adj* banned, censored, disapproved of, forbidden, interdicted, prohibited, proscribed, unacceptable, unlawful, unmentionable, unnamable. ▷ RUDE. • *n* anathema, ban, curse, interdiction, prohibition, proscription, taboo subject.

tabulate *vb* arrange as a table, catalogue, index, list, pigeonhole, set out in columns, systematize.

tacit *adj* implicit, implied, silent, undeclared, understood, unexpressed, unsaid, unspoken, unvoiced.

taciturn *adj* mute, quiet, reserved, reticent, silent, tight-lipped, uncommunicative, unforthcoming. *Opp* TALKATIVE.

tack *n* 1 drawing-pin, nail, pin, tintack. 2 *the wrong tack*. approach, bearing, course, direction, heading, line, policy, procedure, technique. • *vb* 1 nail, pin. ▷ FASTEN. 2 sew, stitch. 3 *tack in a yacht*. beat against the wind, change course, go about, zigzag. **tack on** ▷ ADD.

tackle *n* 1 accoutrements, apparatus, *inf* clobber, equipment, fittings, gear, implements, kit, outfit, paraphernalia, rig, rigging, tools. 2 *a football tackle*. attack, block, challenge, interception, intervention. • *vb* 1 address (yourself to), apply yourself to, attempt, attend to, combat, *inf* come to grips with, concentrate on, confront, cope with, deal with, engage in, face up to, focus on, get involved in, grapple with, handle, *inf* have a go at, manage, set about, settle down to, sort out, take on, undertake. 2 *tackle an opponent*. attack, challenge, intercept, stop, take on.

tacky *adj* adhesive, gluey, *inf* gooey, gummy, sticky, viscous, wet. *Opp* DRY.

tact *n* adroitness, consideration, delicacy, diplomacy, discernment, discretion, finesse, judgement, perceptiveness, politeness, savoir-faire, sensitivity, tactfulness, thoughtfulness,

understanding. Opp TACTLESS-
NESS.

tactful adj adroit, appropriate,
considerate, courteous, delicate,
diplomatic, discreet, judicious,
perceptive, polite, politic,
sensitive, thoughtful, understanding. Opp TACTLESS.

tactical adj artful, calculated,
clever, deliberate, planned, politic, prudent, shrewd, skilful,
strategic.

tactics n approach, campaign,
course of action, design, device,
manoeuvre, manoeuvring,
plan, ploy, policy, procedure,
ruse, scheme, stratagem, strategy.

tactless adj blundering, blunt,
boorish, bungling, clumsy,
discourteous, gauche, heavy-
handed, hurtful, impolite,
impolitic, inappropriate, inconsiderate, indelicate, indiscreet,
inept, insensitive, maladroit,
misjudged, thoughtless, uncivil,
uncouth, undiplomatic, unkind.
▷ RUDE. Opp TACTFUL.

tactlessness n boorishness,
clumsiness, gaucherie, indelicacy, indiscretion, ineptitude,
insensitivity, lack of diplomacy,
misjudgement, thoughtlessness,
uncouthness. ▷ RUDENESS.
Opp TACT.

tag n 1 docket, label, marker,
name tag, price tag, slip,
sticker, tab, ticket. 2 a Latin
tag. ▷ SAYING. ● vb identify,
label, mark, ticket. **tag along
with** ▷ FOLLOW.

tail n appendage, back, brush (of
fox), buttocks, end, extremity,
rear, rump, scut (of rabbit),
tail-end. ● vb dog, follow, hunt,
pursue, shadow, stalk, track,
trail. **tail off** ▷ DECLINE.

taint vb 1 adulterate, contaminate, defile, dirty, infect,
poison, pollute, soil. 2 taint a
reputation. besmirch, blacken,
blemish, damage, dishonour,
harm, ruin, slander, smear,
spoil, stain, sully, tarnish.

take vb 1 acquire, bring, carry
away, inf cart off, catch, clasp,
clutch, fetch, gain, get, grab,
grasp, grip, hold, pick up,
pluck, remove, secure, seize,
snatch, transfer. 2 take prison-
ers. abduct, arrest, capture,
catch, corner, detain, ensnare,
entrap, secure. 3 take property.
appropriate, get away with,
pocket. ▷ STEAL. 4 take 2 from
4. deduct, eliminate, subtract,
take away. 5 take passengers.
accommodate, carry, contain,
have room for, hold. 6 take a
partner. accompany, conduct,
convey, escort, ferry, guide,
lead, transport. 7 take a taxi.
engage, hire, make use of,
travel by, use. 8 take a subject.
have lessons in, learn about,
read, study. 9 can't take pain.
abide, accept, bear, brook,
endure, receive, inf stand,
inf stomach, suffer, tolerate,
undergo, withstand. 10 take
food, drink. consume, drink,
eat, have, swallow. 11 It takes
courage to own up. necessitate,
need, require, use up. 12 take a
new name. adopt, assume,
choose, select. **take aback**
▷ SURPRISE. **take after**
▷ RESEMBLE. **take against**
▷ DISLIKE. **take back**
▷ WITHDRAW. **take in**
▷ ACCOMMODATE, DECEIVE,
UNDERSTAND. **take life** ▷ KILL.
take off ▷ IMITATE. **take off,
take out** ▷ REMOVE. **take on,
take up** ▷ UNDERTAKE. **take**

over ▷ USURP. **take part**
▷ PARTICIPATE. **take place**
▷ HAPPEN. **take to task**
▷ REPRIMAND. **take up**
▷ BEGIN, OCCUPY.

take-over n amalgamation, combination, incorporation, merger.

takings n earnings, gains, gate, income, proceeds, profits, receipts, revenue.

tale n account, anecdote, chronicle, narration, narrative, relation, report, sl spiel, story, yarn. ▷ WRITING.

talent n ability, accomplishment, aptitude, brilliance, capacity, expertise, facility, faculty, flair, genius, gift, ingenuity, knack, inf know-how, prowess, skill, strength, versatility.

talented adj able, accomplished, artistic, brilliant, distinguished, expert, gifted, inspired, proficient, skilful, skilled, versatile. ▷ CLEVER. Opp UNSKILFUL.

talisman n amulet, charm, fetish, mascot.

talk n 1 baby-talk, inf blarney, chat, inf chin-wag, inf chitchat, confabulation, conference, conversation, dialogue, discourse, discussion, gossip, intercourse, language, palaver, inf powwow, inf tattle, inf tittle-tattle, words. 2 a public talk. address, diatribe, exhortation, harangue, lecture, oration, inf peptalk, presentation, sermon, speech, tirade.

• vb 1 address one another, articulate ideas, commune, communicate, confer, converse, deliver a speech, discourse, discuss, enunciate, exchange views, have a conversation,

inf hold forth, lecture, negotiate, inf pipe up, pontificate, preach, pronounce words, say something, sermonize, speak, tell, use language, use your voice, utter, verbalize, vocalize. □ babble, bawl, bellow, blab, blether, blurt out, breathe, burble, call out, chat, chatter, clamour, croak, cry, drawl, drone, gabble, gas, gibber, gossip, grunt, harp, howl, intone, jabber, jaw, jeer, lisp, maunder, moan, mumble, murmur, mutter, natter, patter, prattle, pray, prate, rabbit on, rant, rasp, rattle on, rave, roar, scream, screech, shout, shriek, slur, snap, snarl, speak in an undertone, splutter, spout, squeal, stammer, stutter, tattle, vociferate, wail, whimper, whine, whinge, whisper, witter, yell. 2 talk French. communicate in, express yourself in, pronounce, speak. 3 get someone to talk. confess, give information, inf grass, inform, inf let on, inf spill the beans, inf squeal, inf tell tales. ▷ SAY, SPEAK. **talk about** ▷ DISCUSS. **talk to** ▷ ADDRESS.

talkative adj articulate, inf chatty, communicative, effusive, eloquent, expansive, garrulous, glib, gossipy, long-winded, loquacious, open, prolix, unstoppable, verbose, vocal, voluble, wordy. Opp TACITURN. **talkative person** chatter-box, sl gas-bag, gossip, sl wind-bag.

tall adj colossal, giant, gigantic, high, lofty, soaring, towering. ▷ BIG. Opp SHORT.

tally n addition, count, reckoning, record, sum, total.

• vb 1 accord, agree, coincide,

concur, correspond, match up,
square. 2 *tally up the bill*. add,
calculate, compute, count,
reckon, total, work out.

tame adj 1 amenable, biddable,
broken in, compliant, disciplined, docile, domesticated,
gentle, manageable, meek, mild,
obedient, safe, subdued,
submissive, tamed, tractable,
trained. 2 *tame animals*.
approachable, bold, fearless,
friendly, sociable, unafraid. 3 *a
tame story*. bland, boring, dull,
feeble, flat, insipid, lifeless,
tedious, unadventurous, unexciting, uninspiring, uninteresting, vapid, *inf* wishy-washy.
Opp EXCITING, WILD. • *vb* break
in, conquer, curb, discipline,
domesticate, house-train,
humble, keep under, make
tame, master, mollify, mute,
quell, repress, subdue, subjugate, suppress, temper, tone
down, train.

tamper *vb* **tamper with** alter,
inf fiddle about with, interfere
with, make adjustments to,
meddle with, tinker with.

tan *n* sunburn, suntan.
• *vb* bronze, brown, burn,
colour, darken, get tanned.

tang *n* acidity, *inf* bite, *inf* edge,
inf nip, piquancy, pungency,
savour, sharpness, spiciness,
zest.

tangible adj actual, concrete,
corporeal, definite, material,
palpable, perceptible, physical,
positive, provable, real, solid,
substantial, tactile, touchable.
Opp INTANGIBLE.

tangle *n* coil, complication,
confusion, jumble, jungle, knot,
labyrinth, mass, maze, mesh,
mess, muddle, scramble, twist,
web. • *vb* 1 complicate, confuse,

entangle, entwine, *inf* foul up,
intertwine, interweave, muddle,
ravel, scramble, *inf* snarl up,
twist. 2 *tangle fish in a net*.
catch, enmesh, ensnare, entrap,
trap. *Opp* DISENTANGLE, FREE.
3 *tangle with criminals*. become
involved with, confront, cross.
tangled ▷ DISHEVELLED, INTRI-
CATE.

tangy adj acid, appetizing,
bitter, fresh, piquant, pungent,
refreshing, sharp, spicy, strong,
tart. *Opp* BLAND.

tank *n* 1 aquarium, basin,
cistern, reservoir. 2 *army tank*.
armoured vehicle.

tanned adj brown, sunburnt,
suntanned, weather-beaten.

tantalize *vb* bait, entice, frustrate, *inf* keep on tenterhooks,
lead on, plague, provoke, taunt,
tease, tempt, titillate, torment.

tap *n* 1 *Amer* faucet, spigot, stop-
cock, valve. 2 knock, rap.
• *vb* knock, rap, strike. ▷ HIT.

tape *n* 1 band, belt, binding,
braid, fillet, ribbon, strip,
stripe. 2 audiotape, cassette,
magnetic tape, tape-recording,
videotape.

taper *n* candle, lighter, spill.
• *vb* attenuate, become
narrower, narrow, thin. **taper
off** ▷ DECLINE.

target *n* 1 aim, ambition, end,
goal, hope, intention, objective,
purpose. 2 *target of attack*. butt,
object, quarry, victim.

tariff *n* 1 charges, menu, price-
list, schedule. 2 *tariff on
imports*. customs, duty, excise,
impost, levy, tax, toll.

tarnish *vb* 1 blacken, corrode,
dirty, discolour, soil, spoil,
stain, taint. 2 *tarnish a reputation*. blemish, blot, calumniate,

defame, denigrate, disgrace, dishonour, mar, ruin, spoil, stain, sully.

tarry vb dawdle, delay, *inf* hang about, hang back, linger, loiter, pause, procrastinate, temporize, wait.

tart adj 1 acid, acidic, acidulous, astringent, biting, citrus, harsh, lemony, piquant, pungent, sharp, sour, tangy. 2 *a tart rejoinder.* ▷ SHARP. Opp BLAND, SWEET. • n 1 flan, pastry, pasty, patty, pie, quiche, tartlet, turnover. 2 ▷ PROSTITUTE.

task n activity, assignment, burden, business, charge, chore, duty, employment, enterprise, errand, imposition, job, mission, requirement, test, undertaking, work. **to take to task** ▷ REPRIMAND.

taste n 1 character, flavour, relish, savour. 2 bit, bite, morsel, mouthful, nibble, piece, sample, titbit. 3 *an acquired taste.* appetite, appreciation, choice, fancy, fondness, inclination, judgement, leaning, liking, partiality, preference. 4 *a person of taste.* breeding, cultivation, culture, discernment, discretion, education, elegance, fashion sense, finesse, good judgement, perception, perceptiveness, polish, refinement, sensitivity, style, tastefulness. • vb nibble, relish, sample, savour, sip, test, try. **in bad taste** ▷ TASTELESS. **in good taste** ▷ TASTEFUL.

tasteful adj aesthetic, artistic, attractive, charming, *Fr* comme il faut, correct, cultivated, decorous, dignified, discerning, discreet, discriminating, elegant, fashionable, in good taste, judicious, *inf* nice, polite, proper, refined, restrained, sensitive, smart, stylish, tactful, well-judged. Opp TASTELESS.

tasteless adj 1 cheap, coarse, crude, *inf* flashy, garish, gaudy, graceless, improper, inartistic, in bad taste, indecorous, indelicate, inelegant, injudicious, in poor taste, *inf* kitsch, *inf* loud, meretricious, ugly, unattractive, uncouth, uncultivated, undiscriminating, unfashionable, unimaginative, unpleasant, unrefined, unseemly, unstylish, vulgar. Opp TASTEFUL. 2 *tasteless food.* bland, characterless, flavourless, insipid, mild, uninteresting, watered-down, watery, weak, *inf* wishy-washy. Opp TASTY.

tasty adj appetizing, delectable, delicious, flavoursome, luscious, *inf* mouth-watering, *inf* nice, palatable, *inf* scrumptious, toothsome, *sl* yummy. □ acid, bitter, creamy, fruity, hot, meaty, peppery, piquant, salty, savoury, sharp, sour, spicy, sugary, sweet, tangy, tart. Opp TASTELESS.

tattered adj frayed, ragged, rent, ripped, shredded, tatty, threadbare, torn, worn out. Opp SMART.

tatters plur n bits, pieces, rags, ribbons, shreds, torn pieces.

tatty adj 1 frayed, old, patched, ragged, ripped, scruffy, shabby, tattered, torn, threadbare, untidy, worn out. 2 ▷ TAWDRY. Opp SMART.

taunt vb annoy, goad, insult, jeer at, reproach, tease, torment. ▷ RIDICULE.

taut adj firm, rigid, stiff, strained, stretched, tense, tight. Opp SLACK.

tautological *adj* long-winded, otiose, pleonastic, prolix, redundant, repetitious, repetitive, superfluous, tautologous, verbose, wordy. *Opp* CONCISE.

tautology *n* duplication, long-windedness, pleonasm, prolixity, repetition, verbiage, verbosity, wordiness.

tavern *n old use* alehouse, bar, hostelry, inn, *inf* local, pub, public house.

tawdry *adj inf* Brummagem, cheap, common, eye-catching, fancy, *inf* flashy, garish, gaudy, inferior, meretricious, poor quality, showy, tasteless, tatty, tinny, vulgar, worthless. *Opp* TASTEFUL.

tax *n* charge, due, duty, imposition, impost, levy, tariff, *old use* tribute. □ *airport tax, community charge, corporation tax, customs, death duty, estate duty, excise, income tax, poll tax, property tax, rates,* old use *tithe, toll, value added tax.* *vb* 1 assess, exact, impose a tax on, levy a tax on. 2 *tax someone's patience.* burden, exhaust, make heavy demands on, overwork, pressure, pressurize, strain, try. ▷ TIRE. **tax with** accuse of, blame for, censure for, charge with, reproach for, reprove for.

taxi *n* cab, *old use* hackney carriage, minicab.

teach *vb* advise, brainwash, coach, counsel, demonstrate to, discipline, drill, edify, educate, enlighten, familiarize with, give lessons in, ground in, impart knowledge to, implant knowledge in, inculcate habits in, indoctrinate, inform, instruct, lecture, school, train, tutor.

teacher *n* adviser, educator, guide. □ *coach, counsellor, demonstrator, don, governess, guru, headteacher, housemaster, housemistress, instructor, lecturer, maharishi, master, mentor, mistress, pedagogue, preacher, preceptor, professor, pundit, schoolmaster, schoolmistress, schoolteacher, trainer, tutor.*

teaching *n* 1 education, guidance, instruction, training. □ *brainwashing, briefing, coaching, computer-aided learning, counselling, demonstration, familiarization, grounding, indoctrination, lecture, lesson, practical, preaching, rote learning, schooling, seminar, tuition, tutorial, work experience, workshop.* 2 *religious teachings.* doctrine, dogma, gospel, precept, principle, tenet.

team *n* club, crew, gang, *inf* line-up, side. ▷ GROUP.

tear *n* 1 [rhymes with *fear*] droplet, tear-drop. [*plur*] *inf* blubbering, crying, sobs, weeping. 2 [rhymes with *bear*] cut, fissure, gap, gash, hole, laceration, opening, rent, rip, slit, split. ● *vb* claw, gash, lacerate, mangle, pierce, pull apart, rend, rip, rive, rupture, scratch, sever, shred, slit, snag, split. **shed tears** ▷ WEEP.

tearful *adj inf* blubbering, crying, emotional, in tears, lachrymose, snivelling, sobbing, weeping, *inf* weepy, wet-cheeked, whimpering. ▷ SAD.

tease *vb inf* aggravate, annoy, badger, bait, chaff, goad, harass, irritate, laugh at, make fun of, mock, *inf* needle, *inf* nettle, pester, plague, provoke, *inf* pull someone's leg, *inf* rib, tantalize, taunt, torment, vex, worry. ▷ RIDICULE.

teasing *n* badinage, banter, chaffing, joking, mockery, provocation, raillery, *inf* ribbing, ridicule, taunts.

technical *adj* 1 complicated, detailed, esoteric, expert, professional, specialized. 2 *technical skill.* engineering, industrial, mechanical, technological, scientific.

technician *n* engineer, mechanic, skilled worker, *plur* technical staff.

technique *n* 1 approach, dodge, knack, manner, means, method, mode, procedure, routine, system, trick, way. 2 *an artist's technique.* art, artistry, cleverness, craft, craftsmanship, expertise, facility, *inf* knowhow, proficiency, skill, talent, workmanship.

technological *adj* advanced, automated, computerized, electronic, scientific.

tedious *adj* banal, boring, dreary, *inf* dry-as-dust, dull, endless, *inf* humdrum, irksome, laborious, long-drawn-out, long-winded, monotonous, prolonged, repetitious, slow, soporific, tiresome, tiring, unexciting, uninteresting, vapid, wearing, wearisome, wearying. *Opp* INTERESTING.

tedium *n* boredom, dreariness, dullness, ennui, long-windedness, monotony, repetitiousness, slowness, tediousness.

teem *vb* 1 abound (in), be alive (with), be full (of), be infested, be overrun (by), *inf* bristle, *inf* crawl, proliferate, seethe, swarm with. 2 ▷ RAIN.

teenager *n* adolescent, boy, girl, juvenile, minor, youngster, youth.

teetotal *adj* abstemious, abstinent, *sl* on the wagon, restrained, self-denying, self-disciplined, temperate.

teetotaller *n* abstainer, non-drinker.

telegram *n* cable, cablegram, fax, telex, wire.

telepathic *adj* clairvoyant, psychic.

telephone *n inf* blower, carphone, handset, phone.
• *vb inf* buzz, call, dial, *inf* give someone a buzz, *inf* give someone a call, *inf* give someone a tinkle, phone, ring, ring up.

telescope *vb* abbreviate, collapse, compress, elide, shorten.

telescopic *adj* adjustable, collapsible, expanding, extending, retractable.

televise *vb* broadcast, relay, send out, transmit.

television *n inf* the box, monitor, receiver, *inf* small screen, *inf* telly, video.

tell *vb* 1 acquaint with, advise, announce, assure, communicate, describe, disclose, divulge, explain, impart, inform, make known, narrate, notify, portray, promise, recite, recount, rehearse, relate, reveal, utter. ▷ SPEAK, TALK. 2 *tell the difference.* calculate, comprehend, decide, discover, discriminate, distinguish, identify, notice, recognize, see. 3 *told me what to do.* command, direct, instruct, order. **tell off** ▷ REPRIMAND.

teller n 1 author, narrator, raconteur, storyteller. 2 *teller in a bank*. bank clerk, cashier.

telling adj considerable, effective, influential, potent, powerful, significant, striking, weighty.

temper n 1 attitude, character, disposition, frame of mind, humour, *inf* make-up, mood, personality, state of mind, temperament. 2 *watch your temper*. anger, churlishness, fit of anger, fury, hot-headedness, ill-humour, irascibility, irritability, *inf* paddy, passion, peevishness, petulance, rage, surliness, tantrum, unpredictability, volatility, *inf* wax, wrath. 3 *keep your temper*. calmness, composure, *sl* cool, coolness, equanimity, sang-froid, self-control, self-possession.
● vb 1 assuage, lessen, mitigate, moderate, modify, modulate, reduce, soften, soothe, tone down. 2 *temper steel*. harden, strengthen, toughen.

temperament n attitude, character, *old use* complexion, disposition, frame of mind, *old use* humour, *inf* make-up, mood, nature, personality, spirit, state of mind, temper.

temperamental adj 1 characteristic, congenital, constitutional, inherent, innate, natural. 2 *temperamental moods*. capricious, changeable, emotional, erratic, excitable, explosive, fickle, highly-strung, impatient, inconsistent, inconstant, irascible, irritable, mercurial, moody, neurotic, passionate, sensitive, touchy, undependable, unpredictable, unreliable, *inf* up and down, variable, volatile.

temperance n abstemiousness, continence, moderation, self-discipline, self-restraint, sobriety, teetotalism.

temperate adj calm, controlled, disciplined, moderate, reasonable, restrained, self-possessed, sensible, sober, stable, steady. Opp EXTREME.

tempest n cyclone, gale, hurricane, tornado, tumult, typhoon, whirlwind. ▷ STORM.

tempestuous adj fierce, furious, tumultuous, turbulent, vehement, violent, wild. ▷ STORMY. Opp CALM.

temple n church, house of god, mosque, pagoda, place of worship, shrine, synagogue.

tempo n beat, pace, rate, rhythm, pulse, speed.

temporal adj earthly, fleshly, impermanent, material, materialistic, mortal, mundane, non-religious, passing, secular, sublunary, terrestrial, transient, transitory, worldly. Opp SPIRITUAL.

temporary adj 1 brief, ephemeral, evanescent, fleeting, fugitive, impermanent, interim, makeshift, momentary, passing, provisional, short, short-lived, short-term, stopgap, transient, transitory. 2 *temporary captain*. acting. Opp PERMANENT.

tempt vb allure, attract, bait, bribe, cajole, captivate, coax, decoy, entice, fascinate, inveigle, lure, offer incentives, persuade, seduce, tantalize, woo. **tempting** ▷ APPETIZING, ATTRACTIVE.

temptation n allure, allurement, appeal, attraction, cajolery, coaxing, draw, enticement, fascination, inducement, lure, persuasion, pull, seduction, snare, wooing.

tenable adj arguable, believable, conceivable, credible, creditable, defendable, defensible, feasible, justifiable, legitimate, logical, plausible, rational, reasonable, sensible, sound, supportable, understandable, viable. *Opp* INDEFENSIBLE.

tenacious adj determined, dogged, firm, intransigent, obdurate, obstinate, persistent, pertinacious, resolute, single-minded, steadfast, strong, stubborn, tight, uncompromising, unfaltering, unshakeable, unswerving, unwavering, unyielding. *Opp* WEAK.

tenant n inhabitant, leaseholder, lessee, lodger, occupant, occupier, resident.

tend vb 1 attend to, care for, cherish, cultivate, guard, keep, *inf* keep an eye on, look after, manage, mind, minister to, mother, protect, supervise, take care of, watch. 2 *tend the sick.* nurse, treat. 3 *tend to fall asleep.* be biased, be disposed, be inclined, be liable, be prone, have a tendency, incline.

tendency n bias, disposition, drift, inclination, instinct, leaning, liability, partiality, penchant, predilection, predisposition, proclivity, proneness, propensity, readiness, susceptibility, trend.

tender adj 1 dainty, delicate, fleshy, fragile, frail, green, immature, soft, succulent, vulnerable, weak, young. 2 *tender meat.* chewable, eatable, edible. 3 *a tender wound.* aching, inflamed, painful, sensitive, smarting, sore. 4 *a tender*

love-song. emotional, heartfelt, moving, poignant, romantic, sentimental, stirring, touching. 5 *tender care.* affectionate, amorous, caring, compassionate, concerned, considerate, fond, gentle, humane, kind, loving, merciful, pitying, soft-hearted, sympathetic, tender-hearted, warm-hearted. *Opp* TOUGH, UNSYMPATHETIC.

tense adj 1 rigid, strained, stretched, taut, tight. 2 *a tense person.* anxious, apprehensive, edgy, excited, fidgety, highly-strung, intense, jittery, jumpy, *inf* keyed-up, nervous, on edge, *inf* on tenterhooks, overwrought, restless, strained, stressed, *inf* strung up, touchy, uneasy, *sl* uptight, worried. 3 *a tense situation.* exciting, fraught, *inf* nail-biting, nerve-racking, stressful, worrying. *Opp* RELAXED.

tension n 1 pull, strain, stretching, tautness, tightness. 2 *the tension of waiting.* anxiety, apprehension, edginess, excitement, nervousness, stress, suspense, unease, worry. *Opp* RELAXATION.

tent n □ bell tent, big-top, frame tent, marquee, ridge tent, tepee, trailer tent, wigwam.

tentative adj cautious, diffident, doubtful, experimental, exploratory, half-hearted, hesitant, inconclusive, indecisive, indefinite, nervous, preliminary, provisional, shy, speculative, timid, uncertain, uncommitted, unsure, *inf* wishy-washy. *Opp* DECISIVE.

tenuous adj attenuated, fine, flimsy, fragile, insubstantial, slender, slight, weak. ▷ THIN. *Opp* STRONG.

tepid adj **1** lukewarm, warm. **2** a tepid response. ▷ APATHETIC.

term n **1** duration, period, season, span, spell, stretch, time. **2** a school term. Amer semester, session. **3** technical terms. appellation, designation, epithet, expression, name, phrase, saying, title, word. **terms 1** conditions, particulars, provisions, provisos, specifications, stipulations. **2** a hotel's terms. charges, fees, prices, rates, schedule, tariff.

terminal adj deadly, fatal, final, incurable, killing, lethal, mortal. ● n **1** keyboard, VDU, work-station. **2** passenger terminal. airport, terminus. **3** electric terminal. connection, connector, coupling.

terminate vb bring to an end, cease, come to an end, discontinue, end, finish, inf pack in, phase out, stop, inf wind up. ▷ END. Opp BEGIN.

terminology n argot, cant, choice of words, jargon, language, nomenclature, phraseology, special terms, technical language, vocabulary.

terminus n destination, last stop, station, terminal, termination.

terrain n country, ground, land, landscape, territory, topography.

terrestrial adj earthly, mundane, ordinary, sublunary.

terrible adj **1** acute, appalling, awful, inf beastly, distressing, dreadful, fearful, fearsome, formidable, frightening, frightful, ghastly, grave, gruesome, harrowing, hideous, horrendous, horrible, horrific, horrifying, insupportable, intolerable, loathsome, nasty, nauseating, outrageous, revolting, shocking, terrific, terrifying, unbearable, vile. **2** ▷ BAD.

terrific adj Terrific may mean causing terror (▷ TERRIBLE). It is more often used informally of anything which is extreme in its own way: a terrific problem ▷ EXTREME; terrific size ▷ BIG; a terrific party ▷ EXCELLENT; a terrific storm ▷ VIOLENT.

terrify vb appal, dismay, horrify, inf make your blood run cold, petrify, shock, terrorize. ▷ FRIGHTEN. **terrified** ▷ FRIGHTENED. **terrifying** ▷ FRIGHTENING.

territory n area, colony, old use demesne, district, domain, dominion, enclave, jurisdiction, land, neighbourhood, precinct, preserve, province, purlieu, region, sector, sphere, state, terrain, tract, zone. ▷ COUNTRY.

terror n alarm, awe, consternation, dismay, dread, fright, inf funk, horror, panic, shock, trepidation. ▷ FEAR.

terrorist n assassin, bomber, desperado, gunman, hijacker.

terrorize vb browbeat, bully, coerce, cow, intimidate, menace, persecute, terrify, threaten, torment, tyrannize. ▷ FRIGHTEN.

terse adj abrupt, brief, brusque, compact, concentrated, concise, crisp, curt, epigrammatic, incisive, laconic, pithy, short, inf short and sweet, inf snappy, succinct, to the point. Opp VERBOSE.

test n analysis, appraisal, assay, assessment, audition, inf check-over, inf check-up, evaluation,

examination, inspection, interrogation, investigation, probation, quiz, screen-test, trial,
inf try-out. ● *vb* analyse,
appraise, assay, assess, audition, check, evaluate, examine,
experiment with, inspect, interrogate, investigate, probe,
inf put someone through their
paces, put to the test, question,
quiz, screen, try out.

testify *vb* affirm, attest, aver,
bear witness, declare, give
evidence, proclaim, state on
oath, swear, vouch, witness.

testimonial *n* character reference, commendation, recommendation, reference.

testimony *n* affidavit, assertion,
declaration, deposition,
evidence, statement, submission.

tether *n* chain, cord, fetter,
halter, lead, leash, painter,
restraint, rope. ● *vb* chain up,
fetter, keep on a tether, leash,
restrain, rope, secure, tie up.
▷ FASTEN.

text *n* 1 argument, content,
contents, matter, subject
matter, wording. 2 *a literary
text.* book, textbook, work.
▷ WRITING. 3 *a text from scripture.* line, motif, passage, quotation, sentence, theme, topic,
verse.

textile *n* fabric, material, stuff.
▷ CLOTH.

texture *n* appearance, composition, consistency, feel, grain,
quality, surface, tactile quality,
touch, weave.

thank *vb* acknowledge, express
thanks, say thank you, show
gratitude.

thankful *adj* appreciative,
contented, glad, grateful, happy,

indebted, pleased, relieved.
Opp UNGRATEFUL.

thankless *adj* bootless, futile,
profitless, unappreciated,
unrecognized, unrewarded,
unrewarding. *Opp* PROFITABLE.

thanks *plur n* acknowledgement,
appreciation, gratefulness, gratitude, recognition, thanksgiving. **thanks to** as a result
of, because of, owing to,
through.

thaw *vb* become liquid, defrost,
de-ice, heat up, melt, soften,
uncongeal, unfreeze, unthaw,
warm up. *Opp* FREEZE.

theatre *n* 1 auditorium, hall,
opera-house, playhouse.
2 acting, dramaturgy, histrionic
arts, show business, thespian
arts. □ *ballet, masque, melodrama, mime, musical, music-
hall, opera, pantomime, play.*
▷ DRAMA, ENTERTAINMENT,
PERFORMANCE.

theatrical *adj* dramatic,
histrionic, thespian. 2 [*derog*] *a
theatrical exit.* affected, artificial, calculated, demonstrative,
exaggerated, forced, *inf* hammy,
melodramatic, ostentatious,
overacted, overdone, *inf* over
the top, pompous, self-
important, showy, stagy,
stilted, unconvincing, unnatural. *Opp* NATURAL.

theft *n* burglary, larceny, pilfering, robbery, thievery.
▷ STEALING.

theme *n* 1 argument, core,
essence, gist, idea, issue,
keynote, matter, point, subject,
text, thesis, thread, topic. 2 *a
musical theme.* air, melody,
motif, subject, tune.

theology *n* divinity, religion,
religious studies.

theoretical adj abstract, academic, conjectural, doctrinaire, hypothetical, ideal, notional, pure (*science*), putative, speculative, supposititious, unproven, untested. *Opp* PRACTICAL, PROVEN.

theorize vb conjecture, form a theory, guess, hypothesize, speculate.

theory n 1 argument, assumption, belief, conjecture, explanation, guess, hypothesis, idea, notion, speculation, supposition, surmise, thesis, view. 2 *theory of a subject*. laws, principles, rules, science. *Opp* PRACTICE.

therapeutic adj beneficial, corrective, curative, healing, healthy, helpful, medicinal, remedial, restorative, salubrious. *Opp* HARMFUL.

therapist n counsellor, healer, physiotherapist, psychoanalyst, psychotherapist.

therapy n cure, healing, remedy, tonic, treatment. □ *chemotherapy, group therapy, hydrotherapy, hypnotherapy, occupational therapy, physiotherapy, psychotherapy, radiotherapy.* ▷ MEDICINE.

therefore adv accordingly, consequently, hence, so, thus.

thesis n 1 argument, assertion, contention, hypothesis, idea, opinion, postulate, premise, premiss, proposition, theory, view. 2 *a research thesis*. disquisition, dissertation, essay, monograph, paper, tract, treatise.

thick adj 1 broad, *inf* bulky, chunky, stout, sturdy, wide. ▷ FAT. 2 *a thick layer*. deep, heavy, substantial, woolly. 3 *a*

thick crowd. compact, dense, impassable, impenetrable, numerous, packed, solid. 4 *thick liquid*. clotted, coagulated, concentrated, condensed, firm, glutinous, heavy, jellied, sticky, stiff, viscid, viscous. 5 *thick growth*. abundant, bushy, luxuriant, plentiful. 6 *thick with visitors*. alive, bristling, *inf* chock-full, choked, covered, crammed, crawling, crowded, filled, full, jammed, swarming, teeming. *Opp* THIN.

thicken vb coagulate, clot, concentrate, condense, congeal, firm up, gel, jell, reduce, solidify, stiffen.

thickness n 1 breadth, density, depth, fatness, viscosity, width. 2 *a thickness of paint, rock*. coating, layer, seam, stratum.

thief n bandit, brigand, burglar, cat-burglar, cutpurse, embezzler, footpad, highwayman, housebreaker, kleptomaniac, looter, mugger, peculator, pickpocket, pilferer, pirate, plagiarist, poacher, purloiner, robber, safe-cracker, shoplifter, stealer, swindler. ▷ CRIMINAL.

thieving adj dishonest, light-fingered, rapacious. ● n ▷ STEALING.

thin adj 1 anorexic, attenuated, bony, cadaverous, emaciated, fine, flat-chested, gangling, gaunt, lanky, lean, narrow, pinched, rangy, scraggy, scrawny, skeletal, skinny, slender, slight, slim, small, spare, spindly, underfed, undernourished, underweight, wiry. *Opp* FAT. 2 *a thin layer*. delicate, diaphanous, filmy, fine, flimsy, gauzy, insubstantial, light, *inf* see-through, shallow, sheer (*silk*), superficial, translucent,

wispy. **3** *a thin crowd.* meagre, scanty, scarce, scattered, sparse. **4** *thin liquid.* dilute, flowing, fluid, runny, sloppy, watery, weak. **5** *thin atmosphere.* rarefied. **6** *a thin excuse.* feeble, implausible, tenuous, transparent, unconvincing. *Opp* DENSE, STRONG, THICK.
• *vb* dilute, water down, weaken. **thin out 1** become less dense, decrease, diminish, disperse. **2** make less dense, prune, reduce, trim, weed out.

thing *n* **1** apparatus, artefact, article, body, contrivance, device, entity, gadget, implement, invention, item, object, utensil. **2** affair, circumstance, deed, event, eventuality, happening, incident, occurrence, phenomenon. **3** *a thing on your mind.* concept, detail, fact, factor, feeling, idea, point, statement, thought. **4** *a thing to be done.* act, action, chore, deed, job, responsibility, task. **5** [*inf*] *a thing about snakes.* aversion, fixation, *inf* hang-up, mania, neurosis, obsession, passion, phobia, preoccupation. **things 1** baggage, belongings, clothing, equipment, *inf* gear, luggage, possessions, *inf* stuff. **2** *How are things?* circumstances, conditions, life.

think *vb* **1** attend, brood, chew things over, cogitate, concentrate, consider, contemplate, day-dream, deliberate, dream, dwell (on), fantasize, give thought (to), meditate, *inf* mull over, muse, ponder, *inf* rack your brains, reason, reflect, remind yourself of, reminisce, ruminate, use your intelligence, work things out, worry. **2** *Do you think it's true?* accept,

admit, assume, be convinced, believe, be under the impression, conclude, deem, estimate, feel, guess, have faith, imagine, judge, presume, reckon, suppose, surmise. **think better of** ▷ RECONSIDER. **thinking** ▷ INTELLIGENT, THOUGHTFUL. **think up** ▷ DEVISE.

thinker *n inf* brain, innovator, intellect, inventor, *inf* mastermind, philosopher, sage, savant, scholar.

thirst *n* **1** drought, dryness, thirstiness. **2** *thirst for knowledge.* appetite, craving, desire, eagerness, hunger, itch, longing, love (of), lust, passion, urge, wish, yearning, *inf* yen.
• *vb* be thirsty, crave, have a thirst, hunger, long, strive (after), wish, yearn. **thirst for** ▷ WANT.

thirsty *adj* **1** arid, dehydrated, dry, *inf* gasping, panting, parched. **2** *thirsty for news.* avid, craving, desirous, eager, greedy, hankering, itching, longing, voracious, yearning.

thorn *n* barb, bristle, needle, prickle, spike, spine.

thorny *adj* **1** barbed, bristly, prickly, scratchy, sharp, spiky, spiny. **2** ▷ DIFFICULT.

thorough *adj* **1** assiduous, attentive, careful, comprehensive, conscientious, deep, detailed, diligent, efficient, exhaustive, extensive, full, *inf* in-depth, methodical, meticulous, minute, observant, orderly, organized, painstaking, particular, penetrating, probing, scrupulous, searching, systematic, thoughtful, watchful. *Opp* SUPERFICIAL. **2** *a thorough rascal.* absolute, arrant, complete, downright, out-and-out, perfect, proper, sheer, thoroughgoing, total, unmitigated, unmixed, unqualified, utter.

thought n 1 inf brainwork, brooding, inf brown study, cerebration, cogitation, concentration, consideration, contemplation, day-dreaming, deliberation, intelligence, introspection, meditation, mental activity, musing, pensiveness, ratiocination, rationality, reason, reasoning, reflection, reverie, rumination, study, thinking, worrying. 2 a clever thought. belief, concept, conception, conclusion, conjecture, conviction, idea, notion, observation, opinion. 3 no thought of gain. aim, design, dream, expectation, hope, intention, objective, plan, prospect, purpose, vision. 4 a kind thought. attention, concern, consideration, kindness, solicitude, thoughtfulness.

thoughtful adj 1 absorbed, abstracted, anxious, attentive, brooding, contemplative, dreamy, grave, introspective, meditative, pensive, philosophical, rapt, reflective, serious, solemn, studious, thinking, wary, watchful, worried. 2 thoughtful work. careful, conscientious, diligent, exhaustive, intelligent, methodical, meticulous, observant, orderly, organized, painstaking, rational, scrupulous, sensible, systematic, thorough. 3 a thoughtful kindness. attentive, caring, compassionate, concerned, considerate, friendly, good-natured, helpful, obliging, public-spirited, solicitous, unselfish. ▷ KIND. Opp THOUGHTLESS.

thoughtless adj 1 absentminded, careless, forgetful, hasty, heedless, ill-considered, impetuous, inadvertent, inattentive, injudicious, irresponsible, mindless, negligent, rash, reckless, inf scatter-brained, unobservant, unthinking. ▷ STUPID. 2 a thoughtless insult. cruel, heartless, impolite, inconsiderate, insensitive, rude, selfish, tactless, uncaring, undiplomatic, unfeeling. ▷ UNKIND. Opp THOUGHTFUL.

thrash vb beat, birch, cane, flay, flog, lash, scourge, whip. ▷ DEFEAT, HIT.

thread n 1 fibre, filament, hair, strand. □ cotton, line, silk, string, thong, twine, wool, yarn. 2 thread of a story. argument, continuity, course, direction, drift, line of thought, plot, story line, tenor, theme. ● vb put on a thread, string together. **thread your way** file, pass, pick your way, wind.

threadbare adj frayed, old, ragged, scruffy, shabby, tattered, tatty, worn, worn-out.

threat n 1 commination, intimidation, menace, warning. 2 threat of rain. danger, forewarning, intimation, omen, portent, presage, risk, warning.

threaten vb 1 browbeat, bully, cow, intimidate, make threats against, menace, pressurize, terrorize. ▷ FRIGHTEN. Opp REASSURE. 2 clouds threaten rain. forebode, foreshadow, forewarn of, give warning of, portend, presage, warn of. 3 the recession threatens jobs. endanger, imperil, jeopardize, put at risk.

threatening adj forbidding, grim, impending, looming,

menacing, minatory, ominous, portentous, sinister, stern, *inf* ugly, unfriendly, worrying. *Opp* SUPPORTIVE.

three *n* triad, trio, triplet, triumvirate.

three-dimensional *adj* in the round, rounded, sculptural, solid, stereoscopic.

threshold *n* **1** doorstep, doorway, entrance, sill. **2** *threshold of a new era.* ▷ BEGINNING.

thrifty *adj* careful, *derog* closefisted, economical, frugal, *derog* mean, *derog* niggardly, parsimonious, provident, prudent, skimping, sparing. *Opp* EXTRAVAGANT.

thrill *n* adventure, *inf* buzz, excitement, frisson, *inf* kick, pleasure, sensation, shiver, suspense, stifle, titillation, tremor. ● *vb* arouse, delight, electrify, excite, galvanize, rouse, stimulate, stir, titillate. **thrilling** ▷ EXCITING.

thriller *n* crime story, detective story, mystery, *inf* whodunit. ▷ WRITING.

thrive *vb* be vigorous, bloom, boom, burgeon, *inf* come on, develop strongly, do well, expand, flourish, grow, increase, *inf* make strides, prosper, succeed. *Opp* DIE. **thriving** ▷ PROSPEROUS, VIGOROUS.

throat *n* gullet, neck, oesophagus, uvula, windpipe.

throaty *adj* deep, gravelly, gruff, guttural, hoarse, husky, rasping, rough, thick.

throb *vb* beat, palpitate, pound, pulsate, pulse, vibrate.

throe *n* convulsion, effort, fit, labour, *plur* labour-pains, pang, paroxysm, spasm. ▷ PAIN.

thrombosis *n* blood-clot, embolism.

throng *n* assembly, crowd, crush, gathering, horde, jam, mass, mob, multitude, swarm. ▷ GROUP.

throttle *vb* asphyxiate, choke, smother, stifle, strangle, suffocate. ▷ KILL.

throw *vb* **1** bowl, *inf* bung, cast, *inf* chuck, fling, heave, hurl, launch, lob, pelt, pitch, propel, put (*the shot*), send, *inf* shy, *inf* sling, toss. **2** *throw light.* cast, project, shed. **3** *throw a rider.* dislodge, floor, shake off, throw down, throw off, unseat, upset. **4** ▷ DISCONCERT. **throw away** ▷ DISCARD. **throw out** ▷ EXPEL. **throw up** ▷ PRODUCE, VOMIT.

throw-away *adj* **1** cheap, disposable. **2** *throw-away remark.* casual, offhand, passing, unimportant.

thrust *vb* butt, drive, elbow, force, impel, jab, lunge, plunge, poke, press, prod, propel, push, ram, send, shoulder, shove, stab, stick, urge.

thug *n* assassin, *inf* bully-boy, delinquent, desperado, gangster, *inf* hoodlum, hooligan, killer, mugger, *inf* rough, ruffian, *inf* tough, troublemaker, vandal, *inf* yob. ▷ CRIMINAL.

thunder *n* clap, crack, peal, roll, rumble. ▷ SOUND.

thunderous *adj* booming, deafening, reverberant, reverberating, roaring, rumbling. ▷ LOUD.

thus *adv* accordingly, consequently, for this reason, hence, so, therefore.

thwart *vb* baffle, baulk, block, check, foil, frustrate, hinder, impede, obstruct, prevent, stand in the way of, stop, stump.

ticket n 1 coupon, pass, permit, token, voucher. 2 price ticket. docket, label, marker, tab, tag.

ticklish adj 1 inf giggly, responsive to tickling, sensitive. 2 a ticklish problem. awkward, delicate, difficult, risky, inf thorny, touchy, tricky.

tide n current, drift, ebb and flow, movement, rise and fall.

tidiness n meticulousness, neatness, order, orderliness, organization, smartness, system. Opp DISORDER.

tidy adj 1 neat, orderly, presentable, shipshape, smart, inf spick and span, spruce, straight, trim, uncluttered, well-groomed, well-kept. 2 tidy habits. businesslike, careful, house-proud, methodical, meticulous, organized, systematic, well-organized. Opp UNTIDY.
 ● vb arrange, clean up, groom, make tidy, neaten, put in order, rearrange, reorganize, set straight, smarten, spruce up, straighten, titivate. Opp MUDDLE.

tie vb 1 bind, chain, do up, hitch, interlace, join, knot, lash, moor, rope, secure, splice, tether, truss up. ⊳ FASTEN. Opp UNTIE. 2 tie in a race. be equal, be level, be neck and neck, draw.

tier n course (of bricks), layer, level, line, order, range, rank, row, stage, storey, stratum, terrace.

tight adj 1 close, fast, firm, fixed, immovable, secure, snug. 2 a tight lid. airtight, close-fitting, hermetic, impermeable, imper-

vious, leak-proof, sealed, waterproof, watertight. 3 tight supervision. harsh, inflexible, precise, rigorous, severe, strict, stringent. 4 tight ropes. rigid, stiff, stretched, taut, tense. 5 a tight space. compact, constricted, crammed, cramped, crowded, dense, inadequate, limited, packed, small.
 6 ⊳ DRUNK. 7 ⊳ MISERLY. Opp FREE, LOOSE.

tighten vb 1 become tighter, clamp down, close, close up, constrict, harden, make tighter, squeeze, stiffen, tense. ⊳ FASTEN. 2 tighten ropes. pull tighter, stretch, tauten. 3 tighten screws. give another turn to, screw up. Opp LOOSEN.

till vb cultivate, dig, farm, plough, work.

tilt vb 1 angle, bank, cant, careen, heel over, incline, keel over, lean, list, slant, slope, tip. 2 tilt with lances. joust, thrust. ⊳ FIGHT.

timber n beam, board, boarding, deal, lath, log, lumber, plank, planking, post, softwood, tree, tree trunk. ⊳ WOOD.

time n 1 date, hour, instant, juncture, moment, occasion, opportunity, point. 2 duration, interval, period, phase, season, semester, session, spell, stretch, term, while. □ aeon, century, day, decade, eternity, fortnight, hour, lifetime, minute, month, second, week, weekend, year. 3 time of Nero. age, days, epoch, era, period. 4 time in music. beat, measure, rhythm, tempo.
 ● vb 1 choose a time for, estimate, fix a time for, judge, organize, plan, schedule, timetable. 2 time a race. clock, measure the time of.

timeless adj ageless, deathless, eternal, everlasting, immortal, immutable, indestructible, permanent, unchanging, undying, unending.

timely adj appropriate, apt, fitting, suitable.

timepiece n □ chronometer, clock, digital clock, digital watch, hourglass, stopwatch, sundial, timer, watch, wristwatch.

timetable n agenda, calendar, curriculum, diary, list, programme, roster, rota, schedule.

timid adj afraid, apprehensive, bashful, chicken-hearted, cowardly, coy, diffident, faint-hearted, fearful, modest, inf mousy, nervous, pusillanimous, reserved, retiring, scared, sheepish, shrinking, shy, spineless, tentative, timorous, unadventurous, unheroic, wimpish. ▷ FRIGHTENED. Opp BOLD.

tingle n 1 itch, itching, pins and needles, prickling, stinging, throb, throbbing, tickle, tickling. 2 a tingle of excitement. quiver, sensation, shiver, thrill. • vb itch, prickle, sting, tickle.

tinker vb dabble, fiddle, fool about, interfere, meddle, inf mess about, inf play about, tamper, try to mend, work amateurishly.

tinny adj cheap, flimsy, inferior, insubstantial, poor-quality, shoddy, tawdry.

tinsel n decoration, glitter, gloss, show, sparkle, tinfoil.

tint n colour, colouring, dye, hue, shade, stain, tincture, tinge, tone, wash.

tiny adj diminutive, dwarf, imperceptible, infinitesimal, insignificant, lilliputian, microscopic, midget, inf mini, miniature, minuscule, minute, negligible, pygmy, inf teeny, unimportant, inf wee, inf weeny. ▷ SMALL. Opp BIG.

tip n 1 apex, cap, crown, end, extremity, ferrule, finial, head, nib, peak, pinnacle, point, sharp end, summit, top, vertex. 2 tip for a waiter. inf baksheesh, gift, gratuity, inducement, money, inf perk, present, reward, service-charge, inf sweetener. 3 useful tips. advice, clue, forecast, hint, information, pointer, prediction, suggestion, tip-off, warning. 4 rubbish tip. dump, rubbish-heap. • vb 1 careen, incline, keel, lean, list, slant, slope, tilt. 2 drop off, dump, empty, pour out, spill, unload, upset. 3 tip a waiter. give a tip to, remunerate, reward. **tip over** ▷ OVERTURN.

tire vb 1 become bored, become tired, flag, grow weary, weaken. 2 debilitate, drain, enervate, exhaust, fatigue, inf finish, sl knacker, make tired, overtire, sap, inf shatter, inf take it out of, tax, wear out, weary. Opp REFRESH. **tired** ▷ WEARY. **tired of** bored with, inf fed up with, impatient with, sick of. **tiring** ▷ EXHAUSTING.

tiredness n drowsiness, exhaustion, fatigue, inertia, jet-lag, lassitude, lethargy, listlessness, sleepiness, weariness.

tireless adj determined, diligent, dogged, dynamic, energetic, hard-working, indefatigable, persistent, pertinacious, resolute, sedulous, unceasing, unfaltering, unflagging, untiring, unwavering, vigorous. *Opp* LAZY.

tiresome *adj* 1 boring, dull, monotonous, tedious, tiring, unexciting, uninteresting, wearisome, wearying. *Opp* EXCITING. 2 *tiresome delays*. annoying, bothersome, distracting, exasperating, inconvenient, infuriating, irksome, irritating, maddening, petty, troublesome, trying, unwelcome, upsetting, vexatious, vexing.

tiring *adj* debilitating, demanding, difficult, exhausting, fatiguing, hard, laborious, strenuous, taxing, wearying. *Opp* REFRESHING.

tissue *n* 1 fabric, material, structure, stuff, substance. 2 *tissue-paper*. □ *lavatory paper, napkin, paper handkerchief, serviette, toilet paper, tracing-paper*.

title *n* 1 caption, heading, headline, inscription, name, rubric. 2 appellation, designation, form of address, office, position, rank, status. □ *Baron, Baroness, Count, Countess, Dame, Doctor, Dr, Duchess, Duke, Earl, Lady, Lord, Marchioness, Marquis, Master, Miss, Mr, Mrs, Ms, Professor, Rev, Reverend, Sir, Viscount, Viscountess.* ▷ RANK, ROYAL. 3 *title to an inheritance*. claim, deed, entitlement, interest, ownership, possession, prerogative, right. ● *vb* call, designate, entitle, give a title to, label, name, tag.

titled *adj* aristocratic, noble, upper class.

titter *vb* chortle, chuckle, giggle, snicker, snigger. ▷ LAUGH.

titular *adj* formal, nominal, official, putative, *inf* so-called, theoretical, token. *Opp* ACTUAL.

toast *vb* 1 brown, grill. ▷ COOK. 2 *toast a guest*. drink a toast to, drink the health of, drink to, honour, pay tribute to, raise your glass to.

tobacco *n* □ *cigar, cigarette, pipe tobacco, plug, snuff*.

together *adv* all at once, at the same time, collectively, concurrently, consecutively, continuously, co-operatively, hand in hand, in chorus, in unison, jointly, shoulder to shoulder, side by side, simultaneously.

toil *n* *inf* donkey work, drudgery, effort, exertion, industry, labour, work. ● *vb* drudge, exert yourself, grind away, *inf* keep at it, labour, *inf* plug away, *inf* slave away, struggle, *inf* sweat. ▷ WORK.

toilet *n* 1 convenience, latrine, lavatory, *sl* loo, *old use* privy, urinal, water closet, WC. 2 [*old use*] *make your toilet*. dressing, grooming, making up, washing.

token *adj* cosmetic, dutiful, emblematic, insincere, nominal, notional, perfunctory, representative, superficial, symbolic. *Opp* GENUINE. ● *n* 1 badge, emblem, evidence, expression, indication, mark, marker, proof, reminder, sign, symbol, testimony. 2 *a token of esteem*. keepsake, memento, reminder, souvenir. 3 *a bus token*. coin, counter, coupon, disc, voucher.

tolerable *adj* 1 acceptable, allowable, bearable, endurable, sufferable, supportable. 2 *tolerable food*. adequate, all right, average, fair, mediocre, middling, *inf* OK, ordinary, passable, satisfactory. *Opp* INTOLERABLE.

tolerance n 1 broad-mindedness, charity, fairness, forbearance, forgiveness, lenience, open-mindedness, openness, patience, permissiveness. 2 *tolerance of others*. acceptance, sufferance, sympathy (towards), toleration, understanding. 3 *tolerance in moving parts*. allowance, clearance, deviation, fluctuation, play, variation.

tolerant adj big-hearted, broad-minded, charitable, easygoing, fair, forbearing, forgiving, generous, indulgent, *derog* lax, lenient, liberal, magnanimous, open-minded, patient, permissive, *derog* soft, sympathetic, understanding, unprejudiced. *Opp* INTOLERANT.

tolerate vb abide, accept, admit, bear, brook, concede, condone, countenance, endure, *inf* lump (*I'll have to lump it!*), make allowances for, permit, *inf* put up with, sanction, *inf* stick, *inf* stand, *inf* stomach, suffer, *inf* take, undergo, *inf* wear, weather.

toll n charge, dues, duty, fee, levy, payment, tariff, tax.
● vb chime, peal, ring, sound, strike.

tomb n burial-chamber, burial-place, catacomb, crypt, grave, gravestone, last resting-place, mausoleum, memorial, monument, sepulchre, tombstone, vault.

tonality n key, tonal centre.

tone n 1 accent, colouring, expression, feel, inflection, intonation, manner, modulation, note, phrasing, pitch, quality, sonority, sound, timbre. 2 *tone of a poem, place.*

air, atmosphere, character, effect, feeling, mood, spirit, style, temper, vein. 3 *colour tone.* colour, hue, shade, tinge, tint, tonality. **tone down** ▷ SOFTEN. **tone in** ▷ HARMONIZE. **tone up** ▷ STRENGTHEN.

tongue n dialect, idiom, language, parlance, patois, speech, talk, vernacular.

tongue-tied adj dumb, dumbfounded, inarticulate, *inf* lost for words, mute, silent, speechless.

tonic n boost, cordial, dietary supplement, fillip, *inf* pick-me-up, refresher, restorative, stimulant.

tool n apparatus, appliance, contraption, contrivance, device, gadget, hardware, implement, instrument, invention, machine, mechanism, utensil, weapon. □ [carpentry] auger, awl, brace and bit, bradawl, chisel, clamp, cramp, drill, file, fretsaw, gimlet, glasspaper, hacksaw, hammer, jigsaw, mallet, pincers, plane, pliers, power-drill, rasp, sander, sandpaper, saw, screw- driver, spokeshave, T-square, vice, wrench. □ [gardening] billhook, dibber, fork, grass-rake, hoe, lawnmower, mattock, pruning knife, pruning shears, rake, roller, scythe, secateurs, shears, sickle, spade, Strimmer, trowel. □ [various] axe, bellows, chainsaw, chopper, clippers, crowbar, cutter, hatchet, jack, ladder, lever, penknife, pick, pickaxe, pitchfork, pocket-knife, scissors, shovel, sledge-hammer, spanner, tape-measure, tongs, tweezers.

tooth n □ canine, eye-tooth, fang, incisor, molar, tusk, wisdom *tooth.* **false teeth** bridge, denture, dentures, plate.

toothed *adj* cogged, crenellated, denticulate, indented, jagged, serrated. *Opp* SMOOTH.

top *adj inf* ace, best, choicest, finest, first, foremost, greatest, highest, incomparable, leading, maximum, most, peerless, pre-eminent, prime, principal, supreme, topmost, unequalled, winning. ● *n* 1 acme, apex, apogee, crest, crown, culmination, head, height, high point, peak, pinnacle, summit, tip, vertex, zenith. 2 *top of a table.* surface. 3 *top of a jar.* cap, cover, covering, lid, stopper. *Opp* BOTTOM. ● *vb* 1 complete, cover, decorate, finish off, garnish, surmount. 2 beat, be higher than, better, cap, exceed, excel, outdo, outstrip, surpass, transcend.

topic *n* issue, matter, point, question, subject, talking-point, text, theme, thesis.

topical *adj* contemporary, current, recent, timely, up-to-date.

topography *n* features, geography, *inf* lie of the land.

topple *vb* 1 bring down, fell, knock down, overturn, throw down, tip over, upset. 2 collapse, fall, overbalance, totter, tumble. 3 *topple a rival.* oust, overthrow, unseat. ▷ DEFEAT.

torch *n* bicycle lamp, brand, electric lamp, flashlight, lamp, *old use* link.

torment *n* affliction, agony, anguish, distress, harassment, misery, ordeal, persecution, plague, scourge, suffering, torture, vexation, woe, worry,

wretchedness. ▷ PAIN.
● *vb* afflict, annoy, bait, be a torment to, bedevil, bother, bully, distress, harass, inflict pain on, intimidate, *inf* nag, persecute, pester, plague, tease, torture, vex, victimize, worry. ▷ HURT.

torpid *adj* apathetic, dormant, dull, inactive, indolent, inert, lackadaisical, languid, lethargic, lifeless, listless, passive, phlegmatic, slothful, slow, slow-moving, sluggish, somnolent, spiritless. *Opp* LIVELY.

torrent *n* cascade, cataract, deluge, downpour, effusion, flood, flow, gush, inundation, outpouring, overflow, rush, spate, stream, tide.

torrential *adj* copious, heavy, relentless, soaking, teeming, violent.

tortuous *adj* bent, circuitous, complicated, contorted, convoluted, corkscrew, crooked, curling, curvy, devious, indirect, involved, labyrinthine, mazy, meandering, roundabout, serpentine, sinuous, turning, twisted, twisting, twisty, wandering, winding, zigzag. *Opp* DIRECT, STRAIGHT.

torture *n* 1 cruelty, degradation, humiliation, inquisition, persecution, punishment, torment. 2 affliction, agony, anguish, distress, misery, pain, plague, scourge, suffering. ● *vb* 1 be cruel to, brainwash, bully, cause pain to, degrade, dehumanize, humiliate, hurt, inflict pain on, intimidate, persecute, rack, torment, victimize. 2 *tortured by doubts.* afflict, agonize, annoy, bedevil, bother, distress, harass, *inf* nag, pester, plague, tease, vex, worry.

toss vb 1 bowl, cast, inf chuck, fling, flip, heave, hurl, lob, pitch, shy, sling, throw. 2 toss about in a storm. bob, dip, flounder, lurch, move restlessly, pitch, plunge, reel, rock, roll, shake, twist and turn, wallow, welter, writhe, yaw.

total adj 1 complete, comprehensive, entire, full, gross, overall, whole. 2 total disaster. absolute, downright, out-and-out, outright, perfect, sheer, thorough, thorough-going, unalloyed, unmitigated, unqualified, utter. ● n aggregate, amount, answer, lot, sum, totality, whole. ● vb 1 add up to, amount to, come to, make. 2 add up, calculate, compute, count, find the sum of, find the total of, reckon up, totalize, inf tot up, work out.

totalitarian adj absolute, arbitrary, authoritarian, autocratic, despotic, dictatorial, fascist, illiberal, one-party, oppressive, tyrannous, undemocratic, unrepresentative.
Opp DEMOCRATIC.

totter vb dodder, falter, reel, rock, stagger, stumble, teeter, topple, tremble, waver, wobble.
▷ WALK.

touch n 1 feeling, texture, touching. 2 brush, caress, contact, dab, pat, stroke, tap. 3 an expert's touch. ability, capability, experience, expertise, facility, feel, flair, gift, knack, manner, sensitivity, skill, style, technique, understanding, way. 4 a touch of salt. bit, dash, drop, hint, intimation, small amount, suggestion, suspicion, taste, tinge, trace. ● vb 1 be in contact with, brush, caress, contact, cuddle, dab, embrace, feel,

finger, fondle, graze, handle, hit, kiss, lean against, manipulate, massage, nuzzle, pat, paw, pet, push, rub, stroke, tap, tickle. 2 touch the emotions. affect, arouse, awaken, concern, disturb, impress, influence, inspire, move, stimulate, stir, upset. 3 touch 100 m.p.h. attain, reach, rise to. 4 I can't touch her skill. be in the same league as, inf come up to, compare with, equal, match, parallel, rival. **touched** ▷ EMOTIONAL, MAD. **touching** ▷ EMOTIONAL. **touch off** ▷ BEGIN, IGNITE. **touch on** ▷ MENTION. **touch up** ▷ IMPROVE.

touchy adj edgy, highly strung, hypersensitive, irascible, irritable, jittery, jumpy, nervous, over-sensitive, peevish, querulous, quick-tempered, sensitive, short-tempered, snappy, temperamental, tense, testy, tetchy, thin-skinned, unpredictable, waspish.

tough adj 1 durable, hard-wearing, indestructible, lasting, rugged, sound, stout, strong, substantial, unbreakable, wellbuilt, well-made. 2 tough physique. inf beefy, brawny, burly, hardy, muscular, robust, stalwart, strong, sturdy. 3 tough opposition. invulnerable, merciless, obdurate, obstinate, resilient, resistant, resolute, ruthless, stiff, stubborn, tenacious, unyielding. 4 a tough taskmaster. cold, cool, inf hardboiled, hardened, inf hardnosed, inhuman, severe, stern, stony, uncaring, unsentimental, unsympathetic. 5 tough meat. chewy, hard, gristly, leathery, rubbery, uneatable. 6 tough work. arduous, demanding, difficult, exacting, exhausting, gruelling, hard, laborious, stiff, strenuous, taxing, troublesome. **7** *a tough problem.* baffling, intractable, *inf* knotty, mystifying, perplexing, puzzling, *inf* thorny. *Opp* EASY, TENDER, WEAK.

toughen *vb* harden, make tougher, reinforce, strengthen.

tour *n* circular tour, drive, excursion, expedition, jaunt, journey, outing, peregrination, ride, trip. ● *vb* do the rounds of, explore, go round, make a tour of, visit. ▷ TRAVEL.

tourist *n* day-tripper, holiday-maker, sightseer, traveller, tripper, visitor.

tournament *n* championship, competition, contest, event, match, meeting, series.

tow *vb* drag, draw, haul, lug, pull, trail, tug.

tower *n* □ belfry, campanile, castle, fort, fortress, keep, minaret, pagoda, skyscraper, spire, steeple, turret. ● *vb* ascend, dominate, loom, rear, rise, soar, stand out, stick up

towering *adj* **1** colossal, gigantic, high, huge, imposing, lofty, mighty, soaring. ▷ TALL. **2** *a towering rage.* extreme, fiery, immoderate, intemperate, intense, mighty, overpowering, passionate, unrestrained, vehement, violent.

town *n* borough, city, community, conurbation, municipality, settlement, township, urban district, village.

toxic *adj* dangerous, deadly, harmful, lethal, noxious, poisonous. *Opp* HARMLESS.

trace *n* **1** clue, evidence, footprint, *inf* give-away, hint,

indication, intimation, mark, remains, sign, spoor, token, track, trail, vestige. **2** ▷ BIT.
● *vb* **1** detect, discover, find, get back, recover, retrieve, seek out, track down. ▷ TRACK.
2 *trace an outline.* copy, draw, go over, make a copy of, mark out, sketch. **kick over the traces** ▷ REBEL.

track *n* **1** footmark, footprint, mark, scent, spoor, trace, trail, wake *(of ship).* **2** *a farm track.* bridle-path, bridleway, cart-track, footpath, path, route, trail, way. ▷ ROAD. **3** *a racing track.* circuit, course, dirt-track, race-track. **4** *railway track.* branch, branch line, line, mineral line, permanent way, rails, railway, route, tramway.
● *vb* chase, dog, follow, hound, hunt, pursue, shadow, stalk, tail, trace, trail. **make tracks** ▷ DEPART. **track down** ▷ TRACE.

trade *n* **1** barter, business, buying and selling, commerce, dealing, exchange, industry, market, marketing, merchandising, trading, traffic, transactions. **2** *a skilled trade.* calling, career, craft, employment, job, *inf* line, occupation, profession, pursuit, work. ● *vb* buy and sell, do business, have dealings, market goods, merchandise, retail, sell, traffic (in). **trade in** ▷ EXCHANGE. **trade on** ▷ EXPLOIT.

trader *n* broker, buyer, dealer, merchant, retailer, roundsman, salesman, seller, shopkeeper, stockist, supplier, tradesman, trafficker *(in illegal goods),* vendor.

tradition *n* **1** convention, custom, habit, institution, prac-

tice, rite, ritual, routine, usage.
2 *popular tradition.* belief, folk-
lore.

traditional *adj* 1 accustomed,
conventional, customary, established, familiar, habitual,
historic, normal, orthodox,
regular, time-honoured, typical,
usual. *Opp* UNCONVENTIONAL.
2 *traditional stories.* folk,
handed down, old, oral, popular, unwritten. *Opp* MODERN.

traffic *n* conveyance, movements, shipping, transport,
transportation. ▷ VEHICLE.
● *vb* ▷ TRADE.

tragedy *n* adversity, affliction,
inf blow, calamity, catastrophe,
disaster, misfortune.
Opp COMEDY.

tragic *adj* 1 appalling, awful,
calamitous, catastrophic,
depressing, dire, disastrous,
dreadful, fatal, fearful, hapless,
ill-fated, ill-omened, ill-starred,
inauspicious, lamentable,
terrible, tragical, unfortunate,
unlucky. 2 *a tragic expression.*
bereft, distressed, funereal,
grief-stricken, hurt, pathetic,
piteous, pitiful, sorrowful,
woeful, wretched. ▷ SAD.
Opp COMIC.

trail *n* 1 evidence, footmarks,
footprints, marks, scent, signs,
spoor, traces, wake (*of ship*).
2 path, pathway, route, track.
▷ ROAD. ● *vb* 1 dangle, drag,
draw, haul, pull, tow. 2 chase,
follow, hunt, pursue, shadow,
stalk, tail, trace, track down.
3 ▷ DAWDLE.

train *n* 1 carriage, coach, diesel,
inf DMU, electric train, express,
intercity, local train, railcar,
steam train, stopping train.
2 *train of servants.* cortège,
entourage, escort, followers,

guard, line, retainers, retinue,
staff, suite. 3 *train of events.*
▷ SEQUENCE. ● *vb* 1 coach, discipline, drill, educate, instruct,
prepare, school, teach, tutor.
2 do exercises, exercise, *inf* get
fit, practise, prepare yourself,
rehearse, *inf* work out. 3 ▷ AIM.

trainee *n* apprentice, beginner,
cadet, learner, *inf* L-driver,
novice, pupil, starter, student,
tiro, unqualified person.

trainer *n* coach, instructor,
teacher, tutor.

trait *n* attribute, characteristic,
feature, idiosyncrasy, peculiarity, property, quality, quirk.

traitor *n* apostate, betrayer,
blackleg, collaborator, defector,
deserter, double-crosser, fifth
columnist, informer, *inf* Judas,
quisling, renegade, turncoat.

tramp *n* 1 hike, march, trek,
trudge, walk. 2 *a homeless
tramp.* beggar, *inf* destitute
person, *inf* dosser, *inf* down and
out, drifter, homeless person,
rover, traveller, vagabond,
vagrant, wanderer.
● *vb* *inf* footslog, hike, march,
plod, stride, toil, traipse, trek,
trudge, *sl* yomp. ▷ WALK.

trample *vb* crush, flatten,
squash, *inf* squish, stamp on,
step on, tread on, walk over.

trance *n* *inf* brown study, day-
dream, daze, dream, ecstasy,
hypnotic state, rapture, reverie,
semi-consciousness, spell,
stupor, unconsciousness.

tranquil *adj* 1 calm, halcyon
(*days*), peaceful, placid, quiet,
restful, serene, still, undisturbed, unruffled. *Opp* STORMY.
2 *a tranquil mood.* collected,
composed, dispassionate,
inf laid-back, sedate, sober,

unemotional, unexcited, untroubled. *Opp* EXCITED.

tranquillizer *n* barbiturate, bromide, narcotic, opiate, sedative.

transaction *n* agreement, bargain, business, contract, deal, negotiation, proceeding.

transcend *vb* beat, exceed, excel, outdo, outstrip, rise above, surpass, top.

transcribe *vb* copy out, render, reproduce, take down, translate, transliterate, write out.

transfer *vb* bring, carry, change, convey, deliver, displace, ferry, hand over, make over, move, pass on, pass over, relocate, remove, second, shift, sign over, take, transplant, transport, transpose.

transform *vb* adapt, alter, change, convert, improve, metamorphose, modify, mutate, permute, rebuild, reconstruct, remodel, revolutionize, transfigure, translate, transmogrify, transmute, turn.

transformation *n* adaptation, alteration, change, conversion, improvement, metamorphosis, modification, mutation, reconstruction, revolution, transfiguration, transition, translation, transmogrification, transmutation, *inf* turn-about.

transgression *n* crime, error, fault, lapse, misdeed, misdemeanour, offence, sin, wickedness, wrongdoing.

transient *adj* brief, ephemeral, evanescent, fleeting, fugitive, impermanent, momentary, passing, *inf* quick, short, shortlived, temporary, transitory. *Opp* PERMANENT.

transit *n* conveyance, journey, movement, moving, passage, progress, shipment, transfer, transportation, travel.

transition *n* alteration, change, change-over, conversion, development, evolution, modification, movement, progress, progression, shift, transformation, transit.

translate *vb* change, convert, decode, elucidate, explain, express, gloss, interpret, make a translation, paraphrase, render, reword, spell out, transcribe. ▷ TRANSFORM.

translation *n* decoding, gloss, interpretation, paraphrase, rendering, transcription, transliteration, version.

translator *n* interpreter, linguist.

transmission *n* 1 broadcasting, communication, diffusion, dissemination, relaying, sending out. 2 *transmission of goods*. carriage, carrying, conveyance, dispatch, sending, shipment, shipping, transfer, transference, transport, transportation.

transmit *vb* 1 convey, dispatch, disseminate, forward, pass on, post, send, transfer, transport. 2 *transmit a message*. broadcast, cable, communicate, emit, fax, phone, radio, relay, telephone, telex, wire. *Opp* RECEIVE.

transparent *adj* 1 clear, crystalline, diaphanous, filmy, gauzy, limpid, pellucid, *inf* seethrough, sheer, translucent. 2 *transparent honesty.* ▷ CANDID.

transplant *vb* displace, move, relocate, reposition, resettle, shift, transfer, uproot.

transport n carrier, conveyance, haulage, removal, shipment, shipping, transportation. □ *aircraft, barge, boat, bus, cablecar, car, chair-lift, coach, cycle, ferry, horse, lorry, Metro, minibus,* old use *omnibus, ship, space-shuttle, taxi, train, tram, van.* □ *air, canal, railway, road, sea, waterways.* ▷ VEHICLE, VESSEL. ● vb 1 bear, carry, convey, fetch, haul, move, remove, send, shift, ship, take, transfer. 2 ▷ DEPORT.

transpose vb change, exchange, interchange, metathesize, move round, rearrange, reverse, substitute, swap, switch, transfer.

transverse adj crosswise, diagonal, oblique.

trap n ambush, booby-trap, deception, gin, mantrap, net, noose, pitfall, ploy, snare, trick. ● vb ambush, arrest, capture, catch, catch out, corner, deceive, dupe, ensnare, entrap, inveigle, net, snare, trick.

trappings plur n accessories, accompaniments, accoutrements, adornments, appointments, decorations, equipment, finery, fittings, furnishings, inf gear, ornaments, paraphernalia, inf things, trimmings.

trash n 1 debris, garbage, junk, litter, refuse, rubbish, sweepings, waste. 2 ▷ NONSENSE.

travel n globe-trotting, moving around, peregrination, touring, tourism, travelling, wandering. □ *cruise, drive, excursion, expedition, exploration, flight, hike, holiday, journey, march, migration, mission, outing, pilgrimage, ramble, ride, safari, sail, sea-passage, tour, trek, trip, visit, voyage, walk.* ● vb inf gad

about, inf gallivant, journey, make a trip, move, proceed, progress, roam, poet rove, voyage, wander. ▷ GO. □ *aviate, circumnavigate (the world), commute, cruise, cycle, drive, emigrate, fly, free-wheel, hike, hitchhike, march, migrate, motor, navigate, paddle, pedal, pilot, punt, ramble, ride, row, sail, shuttle, steam, tour, trek, walk.*

traveller n 1 astronaut, aviator, commuter, cosmonaut, cyclist, driver, flyer, migrant, motorcyclist, motorist, passenger, pedestrian, sailor, voyager, walker. 2 *a company traveller.* inf rep, representative, salesman, saleswoman. 3 *overseas travellers.* explorer, globe-trotter, hiker, hitchhiker, holidaymaker, pilgrim, rambler, stowaway, tourist, tripper, wanderer, wayfarer. 4 *live as travellers.* gypsy, itinerant, nomad, tinker, tramp, vagabond.

travelling adj homeless, itinerant, migrant, migratory, mobile, nomadic, peripatetic, restless, roaming, roving, touring, vagrant, wandering.

treacherous adj 1 deceitful, disloyal, double-crossing, double-dealing, duplicitous, faithless, false, perfidious, sneaky, unfaithful, untrustworthy. 2 *treacherous conditions.* dangerous, deceptive, hazardous, misleading, perilous, risky, shifting, unpredictable, unreliable, unsafe, unstable. *Opp* LOYAL, RELIABLE.

treachery n betrayal, dishonesty, disloyalty, double-dealing, duplicity, faithlessness, infidelity, perfidy, untrustworthiness. ▷ TREASON. *Opp* LOYALTY.

tread *vb* tread on crush, squash underfoot, stamp on, step on, trample, walk on. ▷ WALK

treason *n* betrayal, high treason, mutiny, rebellion, sedition. ▷ TREACHERY.

treasure *n* cache, cash, fortune, gold, hoard, jewels, riches, treasure trove, valuables, wealth. ● *vb* adore, appreciate, cherish, esteem, guard, keep safe, love, prize, rate highly, value, venerate, worship.

treasury *n* bank, exchequer, hoard, repository, storeroom, treasure-house, vault.

treat *n* entertainment, gift, outing, pleasure, surprise. ● *vb* 1 attend to, behave towards, care for, look after, use. 2 *treat a topic*. consider, deal with, discuss, tackle. 3 *treat a patient, wound*. cure, dress, give treatment to, heal, medicate, nurse, prescribe medicine for, tend. 4 *treat food*. process. 5 *treat a friend to dinner*. entertain, give a treat, pay for, provide for, regale.

treatise *n* disquisition, dissertation, essay, monograph, pamphlet, paper, thesis, tract. ▷ WRITING.

treatment *n* 1 care, conduct, dealing (with), handling, management, manipulation, organization, reception, usage, use. 2 *treatment of illness*. cure, first aid, healing, nursing, remedy, therapy. ▷ MEDICINE, THERAPY.

treaty *n* agreement, alliance, armistice, compact, concordat, contract, covenant, convention, *inf* deal, entente, pact, peace, protocol, settlement, truce, understanding.

tree *n* bush, sapling, standard. □ *bonsai, conifer, cordon, deciduous tree, espalier, evergreen, pollard, standard.* □ *ash, banyan, baobab, bay, beech, birch, cacao, cedar, chestnut, cypress, elder, elm, eucalyptus, fir, fruit-tree, gum-tree, hawthorn, hazel, holly, horse-chestnut, larch, lime, maple, oak, olive, palm, pine, plane, poplar, redwood, rowan, sequoia, spruce, sycamore, tamarisk, tulip tree, willow, yew.*

tremble *vb* quail, quake, quaver, quiver, rock, shake, shiver, shudder, vibrate, waver.

tremendous *adj* alarming, appalling, awful, fearful, fearsome, frightening, frightful, horrifying, shocking, startling, terrible, terrific. ▷ BIG, EXCELLENT, REMARKABLE.

tremor *n* 1 agitation, hesitation, quavering, quiver, shaking, trembling, vibration. 2 earthquake, seismic disturbance.

tremulous *adj* 1 agitated, anxious, excited, frightened, jittery, jumpy, nervous, timid, uncertain. *Opp* CALM. 2 quivering, shaking, shivering, trembling, *inf* trembly, vibrating. *Opp* STEADY.

trend *n* 1 bent, bias, direction, drift, inclination, leaning, movement, shift, tendency. 2 *latest trend*. craze, *inf* fad, fashion, mode, *inf* rage, style, *inf* thing, vogue, way.

trendy *adj inf* all the rage, contemporary, fashionable, *inf* in, latest, modern, stylish, up-to-date, voguish. *Opp* OLD-FASHIONED.

trespass *vb* encroach, enter illegally, intrude, invade.

trial n 1 case, court martial, enquiry, examination, hearing, inquisition, judicial proceeding, lawsuit, tribunal. 2 attempt, check, inf fling, go, run, experiment, rehearsal, test, testing, trial run, inf try-out. 3 a sore trial. affliction, burden, difficulty, hardship, nuisance, ordeal, sl pain in the neck, inf pest, problem, tribulation, trouble, worry.

triangular adj three-cornered, three-sided.

tribe n clan, dynasty, family, group, horde, house, nation, pedigree, people, race, stock, strain.

tribute n accolade, appreciation, commendation, compliment, eulogy, glorification, homage, honour, panegyric, praise, recognition, respect, testimony. **pay tribute to** ▷ HONOUR.

trick n 1 illusion, legerdemain, magic, sleight of hand. 2 deceitful trick. cheat, inf con, deceit, deception, fraud, hoax, imposture, joke, inf leg-pull, manoeuvre, ploy, practical joke, prank, pretence, ruse, scheme, stratagem, stunt, subterfuge, swindle, trap, trickery, wile. 3 clever trick. art, craft, device, dodge, expertise, gimmick, knack, inf know-how, secret, skill, technique. 4 a trick of speech. characteristic, habit, idiosyncrasy, mannerism, peculiarity, way. ● vb inf bamboozle, bluff, catch out, cheat, inf con, cozen, deceive, defraud, inf diddle, dupe, fool, hoax, hoodwink, inf kid, mislead, outwit, inf pull your leg, swindle, inf take in.

trickery n bluffing, cheating, chicanery, deceit, deception,

dishonesty, double-dealing, duplicity, fraud, inf funny business, guile, inf hocus-pocus, inf jiggery-pokery, knavery, inf skulduggery, slyness, swindling, trick.

trickle vb dribble, drip, drizzle, drop, exude, flow slowly, leak, ooze, percolate, run, seep. Opp GUSH.

trifle vb behave frivolously, dabble, fiddle, fool about, play about. **trifling** ▷ TRIVIAL.

trill vb sing, twitter, warble, whistle.

trim adj compact, neat, orderly, inf shipshape, smart, spruce, tidy, well-groomed, well-kept, well-ordered. Opp UNTIDY. ● vb 1 clip, crop, cut, dock, pare down, prune, shape, shear, shorten, snip, tidy. 2 ▷ DECORATE.

trip n day out, drive, excursion, expedition, holiday, jaunt, journey, outing, ride, tour, visit, voyage. ● vb 1 blunder, catch your foot, fall, stagger, stumble, totter, tumble. 2 trip along. caper, dance, frisk, gambol, run, skip. **make a trip** ▷ TRAVEL.

trite adj banal, commonplace, ordinary, pedestrian, predictable, uninspired, uninteresting.

triumph n 1 accomplishment, achievement, conquest, coup, inf hit, knockout, masterstroke, inf smash hit, success, victory, inf walk-over, win. 2 return in triumph. celebration, elation, exultation, joy, jubilation, rapture. ● vb be victorious, carry the day, prevail, succeed, take the honours, win. **triumph over** ▷ DEFEAT.

triumphant *adj* **1** conquering, dominant, successful, victorious, winning. *Opp* UNSUCCESSFUL. **2** boastful, *inf* cocky, elated, exultant, gleeful, gloating, immodest, joyful, jubilant, proud, triumphal.

trivial *adj inf* fiddling, *inf* footling, frivolous, inconsequential, inconsiderable, inessential, insignificant, little, meaningless, minor, negligible, paltry, pettifogging, petty, *inf* piddling, *inf* piffling, silly, slight, small, superficial, trifling, trite, unimportant, worthless. *Opp* IMPORTANT.

trophy *n* **1** booty, loot, mementoes, rewards, souvenirs, spoils. **2** *a sporting trophy*. award, cup, laurels, medal, palm, prize.

trouble *n* **1** adversity, affliction, anxiety, burden, difficulty, distress, grief, hardship, illness, inconvenience, misery, misfortune, pain, problem, sadness, sorrow, suffering, trial, tribulation, unhappiness, vexation, worry. **2** *crowd trouble*. bother, commotion, conflict, discontent, discord, disorder, dissatisfaction, disturbance, fighting, fuss, misbehaviour, misconduct, naughtiness, row, strife, turmoil, unpleasantness, unrest, violence. **3** *engine trouble*. breakdown, defect, failure, fault, malfunction. **4** *took the trouble to get it right*. care, concern, effort, exertion, labour, pains, struggle, thought. ● *vb* afflict, agitate, alarm, anguish, annoy, bother, cause trouble to, concern, discommode, distress, disturb, exasperate, grieve, harass, *inf* hassle, hurt, impose on, inconvenience, interfere with,

irk, irritate, molest, nag, pain, perturb, pester, plague, *inf* put out, ruffle, threaten, torment, upset, vex, worry. *Opp* REASSURE. **troubled** ▷ WORRIED.

troublemaker *n Fr* agent provocateur, agitator, criminal, culprit, delinquent, hooligan, malcontent, mischief-maker, offender, rabble-rouser, rascal, ringleader, ruffian, scandalmonger, *inf* stirrer, vandal, wrongdoer.

troublesome *adj* annoying, badly-behaved, bothersome, disobedient, disorderly, distressing, inconvenient, irksome, irritating, naughty, *inf* pestiferous, pestilential, rowdy, tiresome, trying, uncooperative, unruly, upsetting, vexatious, vexing, wearisome, worrisome, worrying. *Opp* HELPFUL.

trousers *n inf* bags, breeches, corduroys, culottes, denims, dungarees, jeans, jodhpurs, *old use* knickerbockers, *inf* Levis, overalls, *Amer* pants, plusfours, shorts, ski-pants, slacks, *Scot* trews, trunks.

truancy *n* absenteeism, desertion, malingering, shirking, *inf* skiving.

truant *n* absentee, deserter, dodger, idler, malingerer, runaway, shirker, *inf* skiver. **play truant** be absent, desert, malinger, *inf* skive, stay away.

truce *n* agreement, armistice, cease-fire, moratorium, pact, peace, suspension of hostilities, treaty.

true *adj* **1** accurate, actual, authentic, confirmed, correct, exact, factual, faithful, faultless, flawless, genuine, literal, proper, real, realistic, right, veracious, verified, veritable. Opp FALSE. 2 *a true friend.* constant, dedicated, dependable, devoted, faithful, firm, honest, honourable, loyal, reliable, responsible, sincere, staunch, steadfast, steady, trustworthy, trusty, upright. 3 *the true owner.* authorized, legal, legitimate, rightful, valid. 4 *true aim.* accurate, exact, perfect, precise, inf spot-on, unerring, unswerving. Opp INACCURATE.

truncheon n baton, club, cudgel, staff, stick.

trunk n 1 bole, shaft, stalk, stem, stock. 2 *a person's trunk.* body, frame, torso. 3 *an elephant's trunk.* nose, proboscis. 4 *a clothes' trunk.* box, case, casket, chest, coffer, crate, locker, suitcase.

trust n 1 assurance, belief, certainty, certitude, confidence, conviction, credence, faith, reliance. 2 *a position of trust.* responsibility, trusteeship.
• vb 1 inf bank on, believe in, be sure of, confide in, count on, depend on, have confidence in, have faith in, inf pin your hopes on, rely on. 2 assume, expect, hope, imagine, presume, suppose, surmise. Opp DOUBT.

trustful adj confiding, credulous, gullible, innocent, trusting, unquestioning, unsuspecting, unsuspicious, unwary. Opp DISTRUSTFUL.

trustworthy adj constant, dependable, ethical, faithful, honest, honourable, inf loyal, moral, on the level, principled, reliable, responsible, inf safe, sensible, sincere, steadfast, steady, straightforward, true,

old use trusty, truthful, upright. Opp DECEITFUL.

truth n 1 facts, reality. Opp LIE. 2 accuracy, authenticity, correctness, exactness, factuality, genuineness, integrity, reliability, truthfulness, validity, veracity, verity. 3 *an accepted truth.* axiom, fact, maxim, truism.

truthful adj accurate, candid, correct, credible, earnest, factual, faithful, forthright, frank, honest, proper, realistic, reliable, right, sincere, inf straight, straightforward, true, trustworthy, valid, veracious, unvarnished. Opp DISHONEST.

try n attempt, inf bash, inf crack, effort, endeavour, experiment, inf go, inf shot, inf stab, test, trial. • vb 1 aim, attempt, endeavour, essay, exert yourself, make an effort, strain, strive, struggle, venture. 2 *try something new.* appraise, inf check out, evaluate, examine, experiment with, inf have a go at, inf have a stab at, investigate, test, try out, undertake.
trying ▷ ANNOYING, TIRESOME.
try someone's patience ▷ ANNOY.

tub n barrel, bath, butt, cask, drum, keg, pot, vat.

tube n capillary, conduit, cylinder, duct, hose, main, pipe, spout, tubing.

tuck n cram, gather, insert, push, put away, shove, stuff. **tuck in** ▷ EAT.

tuft n bunch, clump, cluster, tuffet, tussock.

tug vb drag, draw, haul, heave, jerk, lug, pluck, pull, tow, twitch, wrench, inf yank.

tumble vb 1 collapse, drop, fall, flop, pitch, roll, stumble, topple, trip up. 2 *tumble things into a heap.* disarrange, dump, jumble, mix up, rumple, shove, spill, throw carelessly, toss.

tumbledown adj badly maintained, broken down, crumbling, decrepit, derelict, dilapidated, ramshackle, rickety, ruined, shaky, tottering.

tumult n ado, agitation, chaos, commotion, confusion, disturbance, excitement, ferment, fracas, frenzy, hubbub, hullabaloo, rumpus, storm, tempest, upheaval, uproar, welter.

tumultuous adj agitated, boisterous, confused, excited, frenzied, hectic, passionate, stormy, tempestuous, turbulent, unrestrained, unruly, violent, wild. *Opp* CALM.

tune n air, melody, motif, song, strain, theme. • vb adjust, calibrate, regulate, set, temper.

tuneful adj inf catchy, euphonious, mellifluous, melodic, melodious, musical, pleasant, singable, sweet-sounding. *Opp* TUNELESS.

tuneless adj atonal, boring, cacophonous, discordant, dissonant, harsh, monotonous, unmusical. *Opp* TUNEFUL.

tunnel n burrow, gallery, hole, mine, passage, passageway, shaft, subway, underpass. • vb burrow, dig, excavate, mine, penetrate.

turbulent adj 1 agitated, boisterous, confused, disordered, excited, hectic, passionate, restless, seething, turbid, unrestrained, violent, volatile, wild. 2 *a turbulent crowd.* badly-behaved, disorderly, lawless, obstreper-

ous, riotous, rowdy, undisciplined, unruly. 3 *turbulent weather.* blustery, bumpy, choppy (*sea*), rough, stormy, tempestuous, violent, wild, windy. *Opp* CALM.

turf n grass, grassland, green, lawn, *poet* sward.

turgid adj affected, bombastic, flowery, fulsome, grandiose, high-flown, overblown, pompous, pretentious, stilted, wordy. *Opp* ARTICULATE.

turmoil n inf bedlam, chaos, commotion, confusion, disorder, disturbance, ferment, inf hubbub, inf hullabaloo, pandemonium, riot, row, rumpus, tumult, turbulence, unrest, upheaval, uproar, welter. *Opp* CALM.

turn n 1 circle, coil, curve, cycle, loop, pirouette, revolution, roll, rotation, spin, twirl, twist, whirl. 2 angle, bend, change of direction, corner, deviation, inf dogleg, hairpin bend, junction, loop, meander, reversal, shift, turning-point, inf U-turn, zigzag. 3 *your turn in a game.* chance, inf go, innings, opportunity, shot, stint. 4 *a comic turn.* ▷ PERFORMANCE. 5 *a nasty turn.* ▷ ILLNESS. • vb 1 circle, coil, curl, gyrate, hinge, loop, move in a circle, orbit, pivot, revolve, roll, rotate, spin, spiral, swivel, twirl, twist, whirl, wind, yaw. 2 bend, change direction, corner, deviate, divert, go round a corner, negotiate a corner, steer, swerve, veer, wheel. 3 *turn a pumpkin into a coach.* adapt, alter, change, convert, make, modify, remake, remodel, transfigure, transform. 4 *turn to and fro.* squirm, twist, wriggle,

writhe. **turn aside** ▷ DEVIATE.
turn down ▷ REJECT. **turn
into** ▷ BECOME. **turn off**
▷ DEVIATE, DISCONNECT, REPEL.
turn on ▷ ATTRACT, CONNECT.
turn out ▷ EXPEL, HAPPEN,
PRODUCE. **turn over**
▷ CONSIDER, OVERTURN. **turn
tail** ▷ ESCAPE. **turn up**
▷ ARRIVE, DISCOVER.

turning-point n crisis, crossroads, new direction, revolution, watershed.

turnover n business, cash-flow,
efficiency, output, production,
productivity, profits, revenue,
throughput, yield.

twiddle vb fiddle with, fidget
with, fool with, mess with,
twirl, twist.

twig n branch, offshoot, shoot,
spray, sprig, sprout, stalk,
stem, stick, sucker, tendril.

twilight n dusk, evening, eventide, gloaming, gloom, half-
light, nightfall, sundown,
sunset.

twin adj balancing, corresponding, double, duplicate, identical,
indistinguishable, inf look-
alike, matching, paired, similar, symmetrical. ● n clone,
counterpart, double, duplicate,
inf look-alike, match, pair,
inf spitting image.

twirl vb 1 gyrate, pirouette,
revolve, rotate, spin, turn,
twist, wheel, wind, whirl.
2 twirl an umbrella. brandish,
twiddle, wave.

twist n 1 bend, coil, curl, kink,
knot, loop, tangle, turn, zigzag.
2 a twist to a story. revelation,
surprise ending. ● vb 1 bend,
coil, corkscrew, curl, curve,
loop, revolve, rotate, screw,
spin, spiral, turn, weave, wind,

wreathe, wriggle, writhe,
zigzag. 2 twist ropes. entangle,
entwine, intertwine, interweave, tangle. 3 twist a lid off.
jerk, wrench, wrest. 4 twist out
of shape. buckle, contort, crinkle, crumple, distort, screw up,
warp, wrinkle. 5 twist meaning.
alter, change, falsify, misquote,
misrepresent. **twisted**
▷ CONFUSED, PERVERTED,
TWISTY.

twisty adj bending, bendy,
circuitous, coiled, contorted,
crooked, curving, curvy, inf in
and out, indirect, looped, meandering, misshapen, rambling,
roundabout, serpentine, sinuous, snaking, tortuous, twisted,
twisting, inf twisting and turning, winding, zigzag.
Opp STRAIGHT.

twitch n blink, convulsion, flutter, jerk, jump, spasm, tic,
tremor. ● vb fidget, flutter, jerk,
jump, start, tremble.

two n couple, duet, duo, match,
pair, twosome.

type n 1 category, class, classification, description, designation, form, genre, group, kind,
mark, set, sort, species, variety.
2 He was the very type of evil.
embodiment, epitome, example,
model, pattern, personification,
standard. 3 printed in large
type. characters, font, fount,
lettering, letters, print, printing, typeface.

typical adj 1 characteristic,
distinctive, particular, representative, special. 2 a typical
day. average, conventional,
normal, ordinary, orthodox,
predictable, standard, stock,
unsurprising, usual.
Opp UNUSUAL.

tyrannical *adj* absolute, authoritarian, autocratic, *inf* bossy,
cruel, despotic, dictatorial,
domineering, harsh, high-
handed, illiberal, imperious,
oppressive, overbearing, ruthless, severe, totalitarian, tyrannous, undemocratic, unjust.
Opp DEMOCRATIC, LIBERAL.

tyrant *n* autocrat, despot, dictator, *inf* hard taskmaster,
oppressor, slave-driver.
▷ RULER.

U

ugly *adj* 1 deformed, disfigured,
disgusting, dreadful, frightful,
ghastly, grim, grisly, grotesque,
gruesome, hideous, horrible,
inf horrid, ill-favoured, loathsome, misshapen, monstrous,
nasty, objectionable, odious,
offensive, repellent, repulsive,
revolting, shocking, sickening,
terrible. 2 *ugly furniture*.
displeasing, inartistic, inelegant, plain, tasteless, unattractive, unpleasant, unprepossessing, unsightly. 3 *an ugly mood*.
angry, cross, dangerous, forbidding, hostile, menacing, ominous, sinister, surly, threatening, unfriendly. *Opp* BEAUTIFUL.

ulterior *adj* concealed, covert,
hidden, personal, private,
secondary, secret, undeclared,
underlying, undisclosed, unexpressed. *Opp* OVERT.

ultimate *adj* 1 closing, concluding, eventual, extreme, final,
furthest, last, terminal, terminating. 2 *ultimate truth*. basic,
fundamental, primary, root,
underlying.

umpire *n* adjudicator, arbiter,
arbitrator, judge, linesman,
moderator, official, *inf* ref,
referee.

unable *adj* impotent, incompetent, powerless, unfit, unprepared, unqualified. *Opp* ABLE.

unacceptable *adj* bad, forbidden, illegal, improper, inadequate, inadmissible, inappropriate, inexcusable,
insupportable, intolerable,
invalid, taboo, unsatisfactory,
unsuitable, wrong.
Opp ACCEPTABLE.

unaccompanied *adj* alone,
lone, single-handed, sole, solo,
unaided, unescorted.

unaccountable *adj* ▷ INEXPLIC-
ABLE.

unaccustomed *adj* ▷ STRANGE.

unadventurous *adj* 1 cautious,
cowardly, spiritless, timid,
unimaginative. 2 *an unadventurous life*. cloistered, limited,
protected, sheltered, unexciting. *Opp* ADVENTUROUS.

unalterable *adj* ▷ IMMUTABLE.

unambiguous *adj* ▷ DEFINITE.

unanimous *adj* ▷ UNITED.

unasked *adj* ▷ UNINVITED.

unassuming *adj* ▷ MODEST.

unattached *adj* autonomous,
inf available, free, independent,
separate, single, uncommitted,
unmarried, *inf* unspoken for.

unattractive *adj* characterless,
colourless, displeasing, dull,
inartistic, inelegant, nasty,
objectionable, *inf* off-putting,
plain, repellent, repulsive,
tasteless, uninviting, unpleasant, unprepossessing, un-
sightly. ▷ UGLY. *Opp* ATTRACT-
IVE.

unauthorized adj illegal, illegitimate, illicit, irregular, unapproved, unlawful, unofficial. Opp OFFICIAL.

unavoidable adj certain, compulsory, destined, fated, fixed, ineluctable, inescapable, inevitable, inexorable, mandatory, necessary, obligatory, predetermined, required, sure, unalterable.

unaware adj ▷ IGNORANT.

unbalanced adj 1 asymmetrical, irregular, lopsided, off-centre, shaky, uneven, unstable, wobbly. 2 biased, bigoted, one-sided, partial, partisan, prejudiced, unfair, unjust. 3 unbalanced mind. ▷ MAD.

unbearable adj insufferable, insupportable, intolerable, overpowering, overwhelming, unacceptable, unendurable. Opp TOLERABLE.

unbeatable adj ▷ INVINCIBLE.

unbecoming adj dishonourable, improper, inappropriate, indecorous, indelicate, offensive, tasteless, unattractive, unbefitting, undignified, ungentlemanly, unladylike, unseemly, unsuitable. Opp DECOROUS.

unbelievable adj ▷ INCREDIBLE.

unbelieving adj ▷ INCREDULOUS.

unbend vb 1 straighten, uncurl, untwist. 2 loosen up, relax, rest, unwind.

unbending adj ▷ INFLEXIBLE.

unbiased adj balanced, disinterested, enlightened, even-handed, fair, impartial, independent, just, neutral, non-partisan, objective, open-minded, reasonable, inf straight, unbigoted, undogmatic, unprejudiced. Opp BIASED.

unbreakable adj ▷ INDESTRUCTIBLE.

unbroken adj ▷ CONTINUOUS, WHOLE.

uncalled-for adj ▷ UNNECESSARY.

uncared-for adj ▷ DERELICT.

uncaring adj ▷ CALLOUS.

unceasing adj ▷ CONTINUOUS.

uncertain adj 1 ambiguous, arguable, inf chancy, confusing, conjectural, cryptic, enigmatic, equivocal, hazardous, hazy, inf iffy, imprecise, incalculable, inconclusive, indefinite, indeterminate, problematical, puzzling, questionable, risky, speculative, inf touch and go, unclear, unconvincing, undecided, undetermined, unforeseeable, unknown, unresolved, woolly. 2 uncertain what to believe. agnostic, ambivalent, doubtful, dubious, inf hazy, insecure, inf in two minds, self-questioning, unconvinced, undecided, unsure, vague, wavering. 3 an uncertain climate. changeable, erratic, fitful, inconstant, irregular, precarious, unpredictable, unreliable, unsettled, variable. Opp CERTAIN.

unchanging adj ▷ CONSTANT.

uncharitable adj ▷ UNKIND.

uncivilized adj anarchic, anti-social, backward, barbarian, barbaric, barbarous, brutish, crude, disorganized, illiterate, Philistine, primitive, savage, uncultured, uneducated, unenlightened, unsophisticated, wild. Opp CIVILIZED.

unclean adj ▷ DIRTY.

unclear *adj* ▷ UNCERTAIN.

unclothed *adj* ▷ NAKED.

uncomfortable *adj* 1 bleak, cold, comfortless, cramped, hard, inconvenient, lumpy, painful. 2 *uncomfortable clothes.* formal, restrictive, stiff, tight, tight-fitting. 3 *an uncomfortable silence.* awkward, distressing, embarrassing, nervous, restless, troubled, uneasy, worried. *Opp* COMFORTABLE.

uncommon *adj* ▷ UNUSUAL.

uncommunicative *adj* ▷ TACITURN.

uncomplimentary *adj* censorious, critical, deprecatory, depreciatory, derogatory, disapproving, disparaging, pejorative, scathing, slighting, unfavourable, unflattering. ▷ RUDE. *Opp* COMPLIMENTARY.

uncompromising *adj* ▷ INFLEXIBLE.

unconcealed *adj* ▷ OBVIOUS.

unconditional *adj* absolute, categorical, complete, full, outright, total, unequivocal, unlimited, unqualified, unreserved, unrestricted, wholehearted, *inf* with no strings attached. *Opp* CONDITIONAL.

uncongenial *adj* alien, antipathetic, disagreeable, incompatible, unattractive, unfriendly, unpleasant, unsympathetic. *Opp* CONGENIAL.

unconquerable *adj* ▷ INVINCIBLE.

unconscious *adj* 1 anaesthetized, *inf* blacked-out, comatose, concussed, *inf* dead to the world, insensible, *inf* knocked out, *inf* knocked silly, oblivious, *inf* out for the count, senseless, sleeping. 2 blind, deaf, igno-

rant obvou unaare 3 *unconscious humour.* accidental, inadvertent, unintended, unintentional, unwitting. 4 *an unconscious reaction.* automatic, *sl* gut, impulsive, instinctive, involuntary, reflex, spontaneous, unthinking. 5 *an unconscious desire.* repressed, subconscious, subliminal, suppressed. *Opp* CONSCIOUS.

unconsciousness *n inf* blackout, coma, faint, oblivion, sleep.

uncontrollable *adj* ▷ UNDISCIPLINED.

unconventional *adj* abnormal, atypical, *inf* cranky, eccentric, exotic, futuristic, idiosyncratic, independent, inventive, nonconforming, non-standard, odd, off-beat, original, peculiar, progressive, revolutionary, strange, surprising, unaccustomed, unorthodox, *inf* way-out, wayward, weird, zany. *Opp* CONVENTIONAL.

unconvincing *adj* implausible, improbable, incredible, invalid, spurious, unbelievable, unlikely. *Opp* PERSUASIVE.

uncooperative *adj* lazy, obstructive, recalcitrant, selfish, unhelpful, unwilling. *Opp* COOPERATIVE.

uncover *vb* bare, come across, detect, dig up, disclose, discover, disrobe, exhume, expose, locate, reveal, show, strip, take the wraps off, undress, unearth, unmask, unveil, unwrap. *Opp* COVER.

undamaged *adj* ▷ PERFECT.

undefended *adj* defenceless, exposed, helpless, insecure, unarmed, unfortified, unguarded, unprotected,

vulnerable, weaponless.
Opp SECURE.

undemanding *adj* ▷ EASY.

undemonstrative *adj* ▷ ALOOF.

underclothes *plur n* lingerie, *inf* smalls, underclothing, undergarments, underthings, underwear, *inf* undies. □ *bra, braces, brassière, briefs, cami-knickers, corset, drawers, garter, girdle, knickers, panties, panti-hose, pants, petticoat, slip, suspenders, tights, trunks, underpants, underskirt, vest.*

undercurrent *n* atmosphere, feeling, hint, sense, suggestion, trace, undertone.

underestimate *vb* belittle, depreciate, dismiss, disparage, minimize, miscalculate, misjudge, underrate, under-value. *Opp* EXAGGERATE.

undergo *vb* bear, be subjected to, endure, experience, go through, live through, put up with, *inf* stand, submit yourself to, suffer, withstand.

underground *adj* 1 buried, hidden, subterranean, sunken. 2 clandestine, revolutionary, secret, subversive, unofficial, unrecognized.

undergrowth *n* brush, bushes, ground cover, plants, vegetation.

undermine *vb* burrow under, destroy, dig under, erode, excavate, mine under, ruin, sabotage, sap, subvert, tunnel under, undercut, weaken, wear away.

underprivileged *adj* deprived, destitute, disadvantaged, down-trodden, impoverished, needy, oppressed. ▷ POOR. *Opp* PRIV-ILEGED.

undersea *adj* subaquatic, subma-rine, underwater.

understand *vb* 1 appreciate, apprehend, be conversant with, *inf* catch on, comprehend, *inf* cotton on to, decipher, decode, fathom, figure out, follow, gather, *inf* get, *inf* get to the bottom of, grasp, interpret, know, learn, make out, make sense of, master, perceive, realize, recognize, see, take in, *inf* twig. 2 *understand animals.* be in sympathy with, empa-thize with, sympathize with.

understanding *n* 1 ability, acumen, brains, cleverness, discernment, insight, intellect, intelligence, judgement, pene-tration, perceptiveness, percipi-ence, sense, wisdom. 2 *understanding of a problem.* appreciation, apprehension, awareness, cognition, compre-hension, grasp, knowledge. 3 *understanding between people.* accord, agreement, compassion, consensus, consent, considera-tion, empathy, fellow feeling, harmony, kindness, mutuality, sympathy, tolerance. 4 *a formal understanding.* arrangement, bargain, compact, contract, deal, entente, pact, settlement, treaty.

understate *vb* belittle, *inf* make light of, minimize, *inf* play down, *inf* soft-pedal. *Opp* EXAGGERATE.

undertake *vb* 1 agree, attempt, consent, covenant, guarantee, pledge, promise, try. 2 *undertake a task.* accept responsibility for, address, approach, attend to, begin, commence, commit yourself to, cope with, deal with, embark on, grapple with, handle, manage, tackle, take on, take up.

undertaking n 1 affair, business, enterprise, project, task, venture. 2 agreement, assurance, contract, guarantee, pledge, promise, vow.

undervalue vb belittle, depreciate, dismiss, disparage, minimize, miscalculate, misjudge, underestimate, underrate.

underwater adj subaquatic, submarine, undersea.

undeserved adj unearned, unfair, unjustified, unmerited, unwarranted.

undesirable adj ▷ OBJECTIONABLE.

undisciplined adj anarchic, chaotic, disobedient, disorderly, disorganized, intractable, rebellious, uncontrollable, uncontrolled, ungovernable, unmanageable, unruly, unsystematic, untrained, wild, wilful. Opp OBEDIENT.

undiscriminating adj ▷ IMPERCEPTIVE.

undisguised adj ▷ OBVIOUS.

undistinguished adj ▷ ORDINARY.

undo vb 1 detach, disconnect, disengage, loose, loosen, open, part, separate, unbind, unbuckle, unbutton, unchain, unclasp, unclip, uncouple, unfasten, unfetter, unhook, unleash, unlock, unpick, unpin, unscrew, unseal, unshackle, unstick, untether, untie, unwrap, unzip. 2 undo someone's good work. annul, cancel out, destroy, mar, nullify, quash, reverse, ruin, spoil, undermine, vitiate, wipe out, wreck.

undoubted adj ▷ INDISPUTABLE.

undoubtedly adv certainly, definitely, doubtless, indubitably, of course, surely, undeniably, unquestionably.

undress vb disrobe, divest yourself, inf peel off, shed your clothes, strip off, take off your clothes, uncover yourself. **undressed** ▷ NAKED.

undue adj ▷ EXCESSIVE.

undying adj ▷ ETERNAL.

uneasy adj anxious, apprehensive, awkward, concerned, distressed, distressing, disturbed, edgy, fearful, insecure, jittery, nervous, restive, restless, tense, troubled, uncomfortable, unsettled, upsetting, worried.

uneducated adj ▷ IGNORANT.

unemotional adj apathetic, clinical, cold, cool, dispassionate, frigid, hard-hearted, heartless, impassive, indifferent, objective, unfeeling, unmoved, unresponsive. Opp EMOTIONAL.

unemployed adj jobless, laid off, on the dole, out of work, redundant, inf resting, unwaged. ▷ IDLE.

unendurable adj ▷ UNBEARABLE.

unenthusiastic adj ▷ APATHETIC, UNINTERESTED.

unequal adj 1 different, differing, disparate, dissimilar, uneven, varying. 2 unequal treatment. biased, prejudiced, unjust. 3 an unequal contest. ill-matched, one-sided, unbalanced, uneven, unfair. Opp EQUAL, FAIR.

unequalled adj incomparable, inimitable, matchless, peerless, supreme, surpassing, unmatched, unparalleled, unrivalled, unsurpassed.

unethical adj ▷ IMMORAL.

uneven adj 1 bent, broken, bumpy, crooked, irregular, jagged, jerky, pitted, rough, rutted, undulating, wavy. 2 *an uneven rhythm.* erratic, fitful, fluctuating, inconsistent, spasmodic, unpredictable, variable, varying. 3 *an uneven load.* asymmetrical, lopsided, unsteady. 4 *uneven contest.* ill-matched, one-sided, unbalanced, unequal, unfair. *Opp* EVEN.

uneventful adj ▷ UNEXCITING.

unexciting adj boring, dreary, dry, dull, humdrum, monotonous, predictable, quiet, repetitive, routine, soporific, straightforward, tedious, trite, uneventful, uninspiring, uninteresting, vapid, wearisome. ▷ ORDINARY. *Opp* EXCITING.

unexpected adj accidental, chance, fortuitous, sudden, surprising, unforeseen, unhoped-for, unlooked-for, unplanned, unpredictable, unusual. *Opp* PREDICTABLE.

unfair adj ▷ UNJUST.

unfaithful adj deceitful, disloyal, double-dealing, duplicitous, faithless, false, fickle, inconstant, perfidious, traitorous, treacherous, treasonable, unreliable, untrue, untrustworthy. *Opp* FAITHFUL.

unfaithfulness n 1 duplicity, perfidy, treachery, treason. 2 adultery, infidelity.

unfamiliar adj ▷ STRANGE.

unfashionable adj dated, obsolete, old-fashioned, *inf* out, outmoded, passé, superseded, unstylish. *Opp* FASHIONABLE.

unfasten vb ▷ UNDO.

unfavourable adj 1 adverse, attacking, contrary, critical, disapproving, discouraging, hostile, ill-disposed, inauspicious, negative, opposing, uncomplimentary, unfriendly, unhelpful, unkind, unpromising, unpropitious, unsympathetic. 2 *an unfavourable reputation.* bad, undesirable, unenviable, unsatisfactory. *Opp* FAVOURABLE.

unfeeling adj ▷ CALLOUS.

unfinished adj imperfect, incomplete, rough, sketchy, uncompleted, unpolished. *Opp* PERFECT.

unfit adj 1 ill-equipped, inadequate, incapable, incompetent, unsatisfactory, useless. 2 *unfit for family viewing.* improper, inappropriate, unbecoming, unsuitable, unsuited. 3 *an unfit athlete.* feeble, flabby, out of condition, unhealthy. ▷ ILL. *Opp* FIT.

unflagging adj ▷ TIRELESS.

unflinching adj ▷ RESOLUTE.

unforeseen adj ▷ UNEXPECTED.

unforgettable adj ▷ MEMORABLE.

unforgivable adj inexcusable, mortal (*sin*), reprehensible, shameful, unjustifiable, unpardonable, unwarrantable. *Opp* FORGIVABLE.

unfortunate adj ▷ UNLUCKY.

unfriendly adj aggressive, aloof, antagonistic, antisocial, cold, cool, detached, disagreeable, distant, forbidding, frigid, haughty, hostile, ill-disposed, impersonal, indifferent, inhospitable, menacing, nasty, obnoxious, offensive, remote, reserved, rude, sour, standoffish, *inf* starchy, stern, supercilious, threatening, unapproachable, uncivil, uncongenial, unenthusiastic, unforthcoming, unkind, unneighbourly, unresponsive, unsociable, unsympathetic, unwelcoming. *Opp* FRIENDLY.

ungainly *adj* ▷ AWKWARD.

ungodly *adj* ▷ IRRELIGIOUS.

ungovernable *adj* ▷ UNDISCIPLINED.

ungrateful *adj* displeased, illmannered, rude, selfish, unappreciative, unthankful. *Opp* GRATEFUL.

unhappy *adj* **1** dejected, depressed, dispirited, down, downcast, gloomy, miserable, mournful, sorrowful. ▷ SAD. **2** *unhappy about losing.* badtempered, disaffected, discontented, disgruntled, disillusioned, displeased, dissatisfied, *inf* fed up, *inf* grumpy, morose, sulky, sullen, unsatisfied. **3** *an unhappy choice.* ▷ UNSATISFACTORY.

unhealthy *adj* **1** ailing, debilitated, delicate, diseased, feeble, frail, infected, infirm, *inf* poorly, sick, sickly, suffering, unwell, valetudinary, weak. ▷ ILL. **2** *unhealthy conditions.* deleterious, detrimental, dirty, harmful, insalubrious, insanitary, noxious, polluted, unhygienic, unwholesome. *Opp* HEALTHY.

unheard-of *adj* ▷ UNUSUAL.

unhelpful *adj* disobliging, inconsiderate, negative, slow, uncivil, uncooperative, unwilling. *Opp* HELPFUL.

unhygienic *adj* ▷ UNHEALTHY.

unidentifiable *adj* anonymous, camouflaged, disguised, hidden, undetectable, unidentified, unknown, unrecognizable. *Opp* IDENTIFIABLE.

unidentified *adj* anonymous, incognito, mysterious, nameless, unfamiliar, unknown, unmarked, unnamed, unrecognized, unspecified. *Opp* SPECIFIC.

uniform *adj* consistent, even, homogeneous, identical, indistinguishable, predictable, regular, same, similar, single, standard, unbroken, unvaried, unvarying. *Opp* DIFFERENT. ● *n* costume, livery, outfit.

unify *vb* amalgamate, bring together, coalesce, combine, consolidate, fuse, harmonize, integrate, join, merge, unite, weld together. *Opp* SEPARATE.

unimaginative *adj* banal, boring, clichéd, derivative, dull, hackneyed, inartistic, insensitive, obvious, ordinary, prosaic, stale, trite, ugly, uninspired, uninteresting, unoriginal. *Opp* IMAGINATIVE.

unimportant *adj* ephemeral, forgettable, immaterial, inconsequential, inconsiderable, inessential, insignificant, irrelevant, lightweight, minor, negligible, peripheral, petty, secondary, slight, trifling, trivial, valueless, worthless. ▷ SMALL. *Opp* IMPORTANT.

uninhabitable *adj* condemned, in bad repair, unliveable, unusable. *Opp* HABITABLE.

uninhabited *adj* abandoned, deserted, desolate, empty, tenantless, uncolonized, unoccupied, unpeopled, unpopulated, untenanted, vacant.

uninhibited adj abandoned, candid, casual, easygoing, frank, informal, natural, open, outgoing, outspoken, relaxed, spontaneous, unbridled, unconstrained, unrepressed, unreserved, unrestrained, unselfconscious, wild. Opp REPRESSED.

unintelligent adj ▷ STUPID.

unintelligible adj ▷ INCOMPREHENSIBLE.

unintentional adj accidental, fortuitous, inadvertent, involuntary, unconscious, unintended, unplanned, unwitting. Opp INTENTIONAL.

uninterested adj apathetic, bored, incurious, indifferent, lethargic, passive, phlegmatic, unconcerned, unenthusiastic, uninvolved, unresponsive. Opp INTERESTED.

uninteresting adj boring, dreary, dry, dull, flat, monotonous, obvious, predictable, tedious, unexciting, uninspiring, vapid, wearisome. ▷ ORDINARY. Opp INTERESTING.

uninterrupted adj ▷ CONTINUOUS.

uninvited adj 1 unasked, unbidden, unwelcome. 2 an uninvited comment. gratuitous, unsolicited, voluntary.

uninviting adj ▷ UNATTRACTIVE.

union n 1 alliance, amalgamation, association, coalition, confederation, conjunction, federation, integration, joining together, merger, unanimity, unification, unity. 2 amalgam, blend, combination, combining, compound, fusion, grafting, marrying, mixture, synthesis, welding. 3 marriage, matrimony, partnership, wedlock.

unique adj distinctive, incomparable, lone, inf one-off, peculiar, peerless, inf second to none, single, singular, unequalled, unparalleled, unrepeatable, unrivalled.

unit n component, constituent, element, entity, item, module, part, piece, portion, section, segment, whole.

unite vb ally, amalgamate, associate, blend, bring together, coalesce, collaborate, combine, commingle, confederate, connect, consolidate, conspire, cooperate, couple, federate, fuse, go into partnership, harmonize, incorporate, integrate, interlock, join, join forces, link, link up, marry, merge, mingle, mix, stick together, tie up, unify, weld together. ▷ MARRY. Opp SEPARATE.

united adj agreed, allied, coherent, collective, common, concerted, coordinated, corporate, harmonious, integrated, joint, like-minded, mutual, inf of one mind, shared, inf solid, unanimous, undivided. Opp DISUNITED. **be united** ▷ AGREE.

unity n accord, agreement, coherence, concord, consensus, harmony, integrity, like-mindedness, oneness, rapport, solidarity, unanimity, wholeness. Opp DISUNITY.

universal adj all-embracing, all-round, boundless, common, comprehensive, cosmic, general, global, international, omnipresent, pandemic, prevailing, prevalent, total, ubiquitous, unbounded, unlimited, widespread, worldwide.

universe *n* cosmos, creation, the heavens, *old use* macrocosm.

unjust *adj* biased, bigoted, indefensible, inequitable, one-sided, partial, partisan, prejudiced, undeserved, unfair, unjustified, unlawful, unmerited, unreasonable, unwarranted, wrong, wrongful. *Opp* JUST.

unjustifiable *adj* excessive, immoderate, indefensible, inexcusable, unacceptable, unconscionable, unforgivable, unjust, unreasonable, unwarranted. *Opp* JUSTIFIABLE.

unkind *adj* abrasive, *inf* beastly, callous, caustic, cold-blooded, discourteous, disobliging, hard, hard-hearted, harsh, heartless, hurtful, ill-natured, impolite, inconsiderate, inhuman, inhumane, insensitive, malevolent, malicious, mean, merciless, nasty, pitiless, relentless, rigid, rough, ruthless, sadistic, savage, selfish, severe, sharp, spiteful, stern, tactless, thoughtless, uncaring, uncharitable, unchristian, unfeeling, unfriendly, unpleasant, unsympathetic, unthoughtful, vicious. ▷ ANGRY, CRITICAL, CRUEL. *Opp* KIND.

unknown *adj* 1 anonymous, disguised, incognito, mysterious, nameless, strange, unidentified, unnamed, unrecognized, unspecified. 2 *an unknown country.* alien, foreign, uncharted, undiscovered, unexplored, unfamiliar, unmapped. 3 *an unknown actor.* humble, insignificant, little-known, lowly, obscure, undistinguished, unheard-of, unimportant. *Opp* FAMOUS.

unlawful *adj* ▷ ILLEGAL.

unlikely *adj* 1 dubious, farfetched, implausible, improbable, incredible, suspect, suspicious, *inf* tall (*story*), unbelievable, unconvincing, unthinkable. 2 *an unlikely possibility.* distant, doubtful, faint, *inf* outside, remote, slight. *Opp* LIKELY.

unlimited *adj* ▷ BOUNDLESS.

unload *vb* disburden, discharge, drop off, *inf* dump, empty, offload, take off, unpack. *Opp* LOAD.

unloved *adj* abandoned, discarded, forsaken, hated, loveless, lovelorn, neglected, rejected, spurned, uncared-for, unvalued, unwanted. *Opp* LOVED.

unlucky *adj* 1 accidental, calamitous, chance, disastrous, dreadful, tragic, unfortunate, untimely, unwelcome. 2 *an unlucky person.* *inf* accidentprone, hapless, luckless, unhappy, unsuccessful, wretched. 3 *an unlucky number.* cursed, ill-fated, ill-omened, ill-starred, inauspicious, jinxed, ominous, unfavourable. *Opp* LUCKY.

unmanageable *adj* ▷ UNDISCIPLINED.

unmarried *adj* *inf* available, celibate, *inf* free, single, unwed. **unmarried person** bachelor, celibate, spinster.

unmentionable *adj* ▷ TABOO.

unmistakable *adj* ▷ DEFINITE, OBVIOUS.

unnamed *adj* ▷ UNIDENTIFIED.

unnatural *adj* 1 abnormal, bizarre, eccentric, eerie, extraordinary, fantastic, freak, freakish, inexplicable, magic, magical, odd, outlandish, preternatural, queer, strange,

supernatural, unaccountable, uncanny, unusual, weird.
2 *unnatural feelings.* callous, cold-blooded, cruel, hard-hearted, heartless, inhuman, inhumane, monstrous, perverse, perverted, sadistic, savage, stony-hearted, unfeeling, unkind. **3** *unnatural behaviour.* actorish, affected, bogus, contrived, fake, feigned, forced, insincere, laboured, mannered, *inf* out of character, overdone, *inf* phoney, pretended, *inf* pseudo, *inf* put on, self-conscious, stagey, stiff, stilted, theatrical, uncharacteristic, unspontaneous. **4** *unnatural materials.* artificial, fabricated, imitation, man-made, manufactured, simulated, synthetic. *Opp* NATURAL.

unnecessary *adj* dispensable, excessive, expendable, extra, inessential, needless, non-essential, redundant, supererogatory, superfluous, surplus, uncalled-for, unjustified, un-needed, unwanted, useless. *Opp* NECESSARY.

unobtrusive *adj* ▷ INCONSPICUOUS.

unofficial *adj* friendly, informal, *inf* off the record, private, secret, unauthorized, unconfirmed, undocumented, unlicensed. *Opp* OFFICIAL.

unorthodox *adj* ▷ UNCONVENTIONAL.

unpaid *adj* **1** due, outstanding, owing, payable, unsettled.
2 *unpaid work.* honorary, unremunerative, unsalaried, voluntary.

unpalatable *adj* disgusting, distasteful, inedible, nasty, nauseating, *inf* off, rancid, sickening, sour, tasteless, unaccept-

able, unappetizing, uneatable, unpleasant. *Opp* PALATABLE.

unparalleled *adj* ▷ UNEQUALLED.

unpardonable *adj* ▷ UNFORGIVABLE.

unplanned *adj* ▷ SPONTANEOUS.

unpleasant *adj* abhorrent, abominable, antisocial, appalling, atrocious, awful, bad-tempered, beastly, bitter, coarse, crude, despicable, detestable, diabolical, dirty, disagreeable, disgusting, displeasing, distasteful, dreadful, evil, execrable, fearful, fearsome, filthy, foul, frightful, ghastly, grim, grisly, gruesome, harsh, hateful, *inf* hellish, hideous, horrible, horrid, horrifying, improper, indecent, inhuman, irksome, loathsome, *inf* lousy, malevolent, malicious, mucky, nasty, nauseating, objectionable, obnoxious, odious, offensive, *inf* off-putting, repellent, repugnant, repulsive, revolting, rude, shocking, sickening, sickly, sordid, sour, spiteful, squalid, terrible, ugly, unattractive, uncouth, undesirable, unfriendly, unkind, unpalatable, unsavoury, unwelcome, upsetting, vexing, vicious, vile, vulgar. ▷ BAD. *Opp* PLEASANT.

unpopular *adj* despised, disliked, friendless, hated, ignored, *inf* in bad odour, minority (*interests*), out of favour, rejected, shunned, unfashionable, unloved, unwanted. *Opp* POPULAR.

unpredictable *adj* changeable, surprising, uncertain, unexpected, unforeseeable, variable. *Opp* PREDICTABLE.

unprejudiced *adj* ▷ UNBIASED.

unpremeditated *adj* ▷ SPON-
TANEOUS.

unprepared *adj inf* caught
napping, caught out, ill-equipped, surprised, taken off-guard,
unready. *Opp* READY.

unpretentious *adj* humble,
modest, plain, simple, straightforward, unaffected, unassuming, unostentatious,
unsophisticated. *Opp* PRETEN-
TIOUS.

unproductive *adj* 1 ineffective,
fruitless, futile, pointless,
unprofitable, unrewarding,
useless, valueless, worthless.
2 *an unproductive garden.* arid,
barren, infertile, sterile,
unfruitful. *Opp* PRODUCTIVE.

unprofessional *adj* amateurish,
casual, incompetent, inefficient,
inexpert, lax, negligent, shoddy,
inf sloppy, unethical, unfitting,
unprincipled, unseemly, unskilful, unskilled, unworthy.
Opp PROFESSIONAL.

unprofitable *adj* futile, loss-
making, pointless, uncommer-
cial, uneconomic, ungainful,
unproductive, unremunerative,
unrewarding, worthless.
Opp PROFITABLE.

unprovable *adj* doubtful, inconclusive, questionable, undemon-
strable, unsubstantiated, unver-
ifiable. *Opp* PROVABLE, PROVEN.

unpunctual *adj* behindhand,
belated, delayed, detained, last-
minute, late, overdue, tardy,
unreliable. *Opp* PUNCTUAL.

unravel *vb* disentangle, free,
solve, sort out, straighten out,
undo, untangle.

unreal *adj* chimerical, false,
fanciful, illusory, imaginary,
imagined, make-believe, non-
existent, phantasmal,
inf pretend, *inf* pseudo, sham.
▷ HYPOTHETICAL. *Opp* REAL.

unrealistic *adj* 1 inaccurate,
non-representational, unconvincing, unlifelike, unnatural,
unrecognizable. 2 *unrealistic
ideas.* delusory, fanciful, idealistic, impossible, impracticable,
impractical, over-ambitious,
quixotic, romantic, silly, visionary, unreasonable, unworkable.
3 *unrealistic prices.*
▷ EXCESSIVE. *Opp* REALISTIC.

unreasonable *adj* ▷ IR-
RATIONAL.

unrecognizable *adj* ▷ UNIDEN-
TIFIABLE.

unrelated *adj* 1 different, independent, unconnected, unlike.
2 ▷ IRRELEVANT. *Opp* RELATED.

unreliable *adj* 1 deceptive,
false, flimsy, implausible, inaccurate, misleading, suspect,
unconvincing. 2 *unreliable
friends.* changeable, disreputable, fallible, fickle, inconsistent, irresponsible, treacherous,
undependable, unpredictable,
unsound, unstable, untrustworthy. *Opp* RELIABLE.

unrepentant *adj* brazen,
confirmed, conscienceless,
hardened, impenitent, incorrigible, incurable, inveterate,
irredeemable, shameless,
unapologetic, unashamed,
unblushing, unreformable,
unregenerate. *Opp* REPENTANT.

unripe *adj* green, immature,
sour, unripened. *Opp* RIPE.

unrivalled *adj* ▷ UNEQUALLED.

unruly *adj* ▷ UNDISCIPLINED.

unsafe *adj* ▷ DANGEROUS.

unsatisfactory *adj* defective,
deficient, disappointing,
displeasing, dissatisfying,

faulty, frustrating, imperfect, inadequate, incompetent, inefficient, inferior, insufficient, lacking, not good enough, poor, *inf* sad (*state of affairs*), unacceptable, unhappy, unsatisfying, *inf* wretched. Opp SATISFACTORY.

unscrupulous *adj* amoral, conscienceless, corrupt, *inf* crooked, cunning, dishonest, dishonourable, immoral, improper, self-interested, shameless, *inf* slippery, sly, unconscionable, unethical, untrustworthy. Opp SCRUPULOUS.

unseemly *adj* ▷ UNBECOMING.

unseen *adj* ▷ INVISIBLE.

unselfish *adj* altruistic, caring, charitable, considerate, disinterested, generous, humanitarian, kind, liberal, magnanimous, open-handed, philanthropic, public-spirited, self-effacing, selfless, self-sacrificing, thoughtful, ungrudging, unstinting. Opp SELFISH.

unsightly *adj* ▷ UGLY.

unskilful *adj* amateurish, bungled, clumsy, crude, incompetent, inept, inexpert, maladroit, *inf* rough and ready, shoddy, unprofessional. Opp SKILFUL.

unskilled *adj* inexperienced, unqualified, untrained. Opp SKILLED.

unsociable *adj* ▷ UNFRIENDLY.

unsophisticated *adj* artless, childlike, guileless, ingenuous, innocent, lowbrow, naïve, plain, provincial, simple, simple-minded, straightforward, unaffected, uncomplicated, unostentatious, unpretentious, unrefined, unworldly. Opp SOPHISTICATED.

unsound *adj* ▷ WEAK.

unspeakable *adj* dreadful, indescribable, inexpressible, nameless, unutterable.

unspecified *adj* ▷ UNIDENTIFIED.

unstable *adj* capricious, changeable, fickle, inconsistent, inconstant, mercurial, shifting, unpredictable, unsteady, variable, volatile. Opp STABLE.

unsteady *adj* 1 flimsy, frail, insecure, precarious, rickety, *inf* rocky, shaky, tottering, unbalanced, unsafe, unstable, wobbly. 2 changeable, erratic, inconstant, intermittent, irregular, variable. 3 *an unsteady light*. flickering, fluctuating, quavering, quivering, trembling, tremulous, wavering. Opp STEADY.

unsuccessful *adj* 1 abortive, failed, fruitless, futile, ill-fated, ineffective, ineffectual, loss-making, sterile, unavailing, unlucky, unproductive, unprofitable, unsatisfactory, useless, vain, worthless. 2 *unsuccessful contestants*. beaten, defeated, foiled, hapless, losing, luckless, vanquished. Opp SUCCESSFUL.

unsuitable *adj* ill-chosen, ill-judged, ill-timed, inapposite, inappropriate, incongruous, inept, irrelevant, mistaken, unbefitting, unfitting, unhappy, unsatisfactory, unseasonable, unseemly, untimely. Opp SUITABLE.

unsure *adj* ▷ UNCERTAIN.

unsurpassed *adj* ▷ UNEQUALLED.

unsuspecting *adj* ▷ CREDULOUS.

unsympathetic *adj* apathetic, cool, cold, dispassionate, hard-hearted, heartless, impassive, indifferent, insensitive, neutral, pitiless, reserved, ruthless, stony, stony-hearted, unaffected, uncaring, uncharitable, unconcerned, unfeeling, uninterested, unkind, unmoved, unpitying, unresponsive. Opp SYMPATHETIC.

unsystematic adj anarchic, chaotic, confused, disorderly, disorganized, haphazard, illogical, jumbled, muddled, *inf* shambolic, *inf* sloppy, unmethodical, unplanned, unstructured, untidy. Opp SYSTEMATIC.

unthinkable adj ▷ INCONCEIVABLE.

unthinking adj ▷ THOUGHTLESS.

untidy adj 1 careless, chaotic, cluttered, confused, disorderly, disorganized, haphazard, *inf* higgledy-piggledy, in disarray, jumbled, littered, *inf* messy, muddled, *inf* shambolic, slapdash, *inf* sloppy, slovenly, *inf* topsy-turvy, unsystematic, upside-down. 2 *untidy hair*. bedraggled, blowzy, dishevelled, disordered, rumpled, scruffy, shabby, tangled, tousled, uncared-for, uncombed, ungroomed, unkempt. Opp TIDY.

untie verb cast off (*boat*), disentangle, free, loosen, release, unbind, undo, unfasten, unknot, untether.

untried adj experimental, innovatory, new, novel, unproved, untested. Opp ESTABLISHED.

untroubled adj carefree, peaceful, straightforward, undisturbed, uninterrupted, unruffled.

untrue adj ▷ FALSE.

untrustworthy adj ▷ DISHONEST.

untruthful adj ▷ LYING.

unused adj blank, clean, fresh, intact, mint (*condition*), new, pristine, unopened, untouched, unworn. Opp USED.

unusual adj abnormal, atypical, curious, *inf* different, exceptional, extraordinary, *inf* freakish, *inf* funny, irregular, odd, out of the ordinary, peculiar, queer, rare, remarkable, singular, strange, surprising, uncommon, unconventional, unexpected, unfamiliar, *inf* unheard-of, *inf* unique, unnatural, unorthodox, untypical, unwonted. Opp USUAL.

unutterable adj ▷ INDESCRIBABLE.

unwanted adj ▷ UNNECESSARY.

unwarranted adj ▷ UNJUSTIFIABLE.

unwary adj ▷ CARELESS.

unwavering adj ▷ RESOLUTE.

unwelcome adj disagreeable, unacceptable, undesirable, uninvited, unpopular, unwanted. Opp WELCOME.

unwell adj ▷ ILL.

unwholesome adj ▷ UNHEALTHY.

unwieldy adj awkward, bulky, clumsy, cumbersome, inconvenient, ungainly, unmanageable. Opp HANDY, PORTABLE.

unwilling adj averse, backward, disinclined, grudging, half-hearted, hesitant, ill-disposed, indisposed, lazy, loath, opposed, reluctant, resistant, slow, uncooperative, unenthusiastic, unhelpful. Opp WILLING.

unwise adj *inf* daft, foolhardy, foolish, ill-advised, ill-judged, illogical, imperceptive, impolitic, imprudent, inadvisable, indiscreet, inexperienced, injudicious, irrational, irresponsible, mistaken, obtuse, perverse, rash, reckless, senseless, short-sighted, silly, stupid, thoughtless, unintelligent, unreasonable. *Opp* WISE.

unworldly *adj* ▷ SPIRITUAL.

unworthy *adj* contemptible, despicable, discreditable, dishonourable, disreputable, ignoble, inappropriate, mediocre, second-rate, shameful, substandard, undeserving, unsuitable. *Opp* WORTHY.

unwritten *adj* oral, spoken, verbal, *inf* word-of-mouth. *Opp* WRITTEN.

unyielding *adj* ▷ INFLEXIBLE.

upbringing *n* breeding, bringing-up, care, education, instruction, nurture, raising, rearing, teaching, training.

update *vb* amend, bring up to date, correct, modernize, review, revise.

upgrade *vb* enhance, expand, improve, make better.

upheaval *n* chaos, commotion, confusion, disorder, disruption, disturbance, revolution, *inf* to-do, turmoil.

uphill *adj* arduous, difficult, exhausting, gruelling, hard, laborious, stiff, strenuous, taxing, tough.

uphold *vb* back, champion, defend, endorse, maintain, preserve, protect, stand by, support, sustain.

upkeep *n* care, conservation, keep, maintenance, operation, preservation, running, support.

uplifting *adj* civilizing, edifying, educational, enlightening, ennobling, enriching, human-

izing, improving, spiritual. *Opp* SHAMEFUL.

upper *adj* elevated, higher, raised, superior, upstairs.

uppermost *adj* dominant, highest, loftiest, supreme, top, topmost.

upright *adj* **1** erect, on end, perpendicular, vertical. **2** *an upright judge.* conscientious, fair, good, high-minded, honest, honourable, incorruptible, just, moral, principled, righteous, *inf* straight, true, trustworthy, upstanding, virtuous.
● *n* column, pole, post, vertical.

uproar *n* *inf* bedlam, brawling, chaos, clamour, commotion, confusion, din, disorder, disturbance, furore, *inf* hubbub, *inf* hullabaloo, *inf* a madhouse, noise, outburst, outcry, pandemonium, *inf* racket, riot, row, *inf* ructions, *inf* rumpus, tumult, turbulence, turmoil.

uproot *vb* deracinate, destroy, eliminate, eradicate, extirpate, get rid of, *inf* grub up, pull up, remove, root out, tear up, weed out.

upset *vb* **1** capsize, destabilize, overturn, spill, tip over, topple. **2** *upset a plan.* affect, alter, change, confuse, defeat, disorganize, disrupt, hinder, interfere with, interrupt, jeopardize, overthrow, spoil. **3** *upset feelings.* agitate, alarm, annoy, disconcert, dismay, distress, disturb, excite, fluster, frighten, grieve, irritate, offend, perturb, *inf* rub up the wrong way, ruffle, scare, unnerve, worry.

upside-down *adj* inverted, *inf* topsy-turvy, upturned, wrong way up.

upstart n Fr nouveau riche, social climber, inf yuppie.

up-to-date adj 1 advanced, current, latest, modern, new, present-day, recent. 2 contemporary, inf in, modish, stylish, inf trendy. Opp OLD-FASHIONED.

upward adj ascending, going up, rising, uphill. Opp DOWNWARD.

urban adj built-up, densely populated, metropolitan, suburban. Opp RURAL.

urge n compulsion, craving, desire, drive, eagerness, hunger, impetus, impulse, inclination, instinct, inf itch, longing, pressure, thirst, wish, yearning, inf yen.
● vb accelerate, advise, advocate, appeal to, beg, beseech, inf chivvy, compel, counsel, drive, inf egg on, encourage, entreat, exhort, force, goad, impel, implore, importune, incite, induce, invite, move on, nag, persuade, plead with, press, prod, prompt, propel, push, recommend, solicit, spur, stimulate. Opp DISCOURAGE.

urgent adj 1 acute, compelling, compulsive, dire, essential, exigent, high-priority, immediate, imperative, important, inescapable, instant, necessary, pressing, top-priority, unavoidable. 2 an urgent cry for help. eager, earnest, forceful, importunate, insistent, persistent, persuasive, solicitous.

usable adj acceptable, current, fit to use, functional, functioning, operating, operational, serviceable, valid, working.

use n advantage, application, benefit, employment, function,

necessity, need, inf point, profit, purpose, usefulness, utility, value, worth. ● vb 1 apply, administer, deal with, employ, exercise, exploit, handle, make use of, manage, operate, put to use, utilize, wield, work. 2 consume, drink, eat, exhaust, expend, spend, use up, waste, wear out.

used adj cast-off, inf hand-me-down, second-hand, soiled. Opp UNUSED.

useful adj 1 advantageous, beneficial, constructive, good, helpful, invaluable, positive, profitable, salutary, valuable, worthwhile. 2 a useful tool. convenient, effective, efficient, handy, powerful, practical, productive, utilitarian. 3 a useful player. capable, competent, effectual, proficient, skilful, successful, talented. Opp USELESS.

useless adj 1 fruitless, futile, hopeless, pointless, unavailing, unprofitable, unsuccessful, vain, worthless. 2 inf broken down, inf clapped out, dead, dud, impractical, ineffective, inefficient, unusable. 3 a useless player. incapable, incompetent, ineffectual, lazy, unhelpful, unskilful, unsuccessful, untalented. Opp USEFUL.

usual adj accepted, accustomed, average, common, conventional, customary, everyday, expected, familiar, general, habitual, natural, normal, official, ordinary, orthodox, predictable, prevalent, recognized, regular, routine, standard, stock, traditional, typical, unexceptional, unsurprising, well-known, widespread, wonted. Opp UNUSUAL.

usurp *vb* appropriate, assume, commandeer, seize, steal, take, take over.

utensil *n* appliance, device, gadget, implement, instrument, machine, tool.

utter *vb* articulate, *inf* come out with, express, pronounce, voice. ▷ SPEAK, TALK.

V

vacancy *n* job, opening, place, position, post, situation.

vacant *adj* 1 available, bare, blank, clear, empty, free, hollow, open, unfilled, unused, usable, void. 2 abandoned, deserted, uninhabited, unoccupied, untenanted. 3 *a vacant look.* absent-minded, abstracted, blank, deadpan, dreamy, expressionless, far-away, fatuous, inattentive, vacuous. *Opp* BUSY.

vacate *vb* abandon, depart from, desert, evacuate, get out of, give up, leave, quit, withdraw from.

vacuous *adj* apathetic, blank, empty-headed, expressionless, inane, mindless, uncomprehending, unintelligent, vacant. ▷ STUPID. *Opp* ALERT.

vacuum *n* emptiness, space, void.

vagary *n* caprice, fancy, fluctuation, quirk, uncertainty, unpredictability, *inf* ups and downs, whim.

vagrant *n* beggar, destitute person, *inf* down-and-out, homeless person, itinerant, tramp,

traveller, vagabond, wanderer, wayfarer.

vague *adj* 1 ambiguous, ambivalent, broad, confused, diffuse, equivocal, evasive, general, generalized, imprecise, indefinable, indefinite, inexact, loose, nebulous, uncertain, unclear, undefined, unspecific, unsure, *inf* woolly. 2 amorphous, blurred, dim, hazy, ill-defined, indistinct, misty, shadowy, unrecognizable. 3 absent-minded, careless, disorganized, forgetful, inattentive, scatter-brained, thoughtless. *Opp* DEFINITE.

vain *adj* 1 arrogant, *inf* big-headed, boastful, *inf* cocky, conceited, egotistical, haughty, narcissistic, proud, self-important, self-satisfied, *inf* stuck-up, vainglorious. *Opp* MODEST. 2 *a vain attempt.* abortive, fruitless, futile, ineffective, pointless, senseless, unavailing, unproductive, unrewarding, unsuccessful, useless, worthless. *Opp* SUCCESSFUL.

valiant *adj* bold, brave, courageous, doughty, gallant, heroic, plucky, stalwart, stout-hearted, valorous. *Opp* COWARDLY.

valid *adj* acceptable, allowed, approved, authentic, authorized, *Lat* bona fide, convincing, current, genuine, lawful, legal, legitimate, official, permissible, permitted, proper, ratified, rightful, sound, suitable, usable. *Opp* INVALID.

validate *vb* authenticate, authorize, certify, endorse, legalize, legitimize, make valid, ratify.

valley *n* canyon, chasm, coomb, dale, defile, dell, dingle, glen, gorge, gulch, gully, hollow, pass, ravine, vale.

valour *n* bravery, courage, pluck.

valuable *adj* 1 costly, dear, expensive, generous, irreplaceable, precious, priceless, prized, treasured, valued. 2 *valuable advice*. advantageous, beneficial, constructive, esteemed, helpful, invaluable, positive, profitable, useful, worthwhile. *Opp* WORTHLESS.

value *n* 1 cost, price, worth. 2 advantage, benefit, importance, merit, significance, use, usefulness. ● *vb* 1 assess, estimate the value of, evaluate, price, *inf* put a figure on. 2 appreciate, care for, cherish, esteem, *inf* have a high regard for, *inf* hold dear, love, prize, respect, treasure.

vandal *n* barbarian, delinquent, hooligan, looter, marauder, Philistine, raider, ruffian, savage, thug, trouble-maker.

vanish *vb* clear, clear off, disappear, disperse, dissolve, dwindle, evaporate, fade, go away, melt away, pass. *Opp* APPEAR.

vanity *n* arrogance, *inf* bigheadedness, conceit, egotism, narcissism, pride, self-esteem.

vaporize *vb* dry up, evaporate, turn to vapour.

vapour *n* exhalation, fog, fumes, gas, haze, miasma, mist, smoke, steam.

variable *adj* capricious, changeable, erratic, fickle, fitful, fluctuating, fluid, inconsistent, inconstant, mercurial, mutable, protean, shifting, temperamental, uncertain, unpredictable, unreliable, unstable, unsteady, *inf* up-and-down, vacillating, varying, volatile, wavering. *Opp* INVARIABLE.

variation *n* alteration, change, conversion, deviation, difference, discrepancy, diversification, elaboration, modification, permutation, variant.

variety *n* 1 alteration, change, difference, diversity, unpredictability, variation. 2 array, assortment, blend, collection, combination, jumble, medley, miscellany, mixture, multiplicity. 3 brand, breed, category, class, form, kind, make, sort, species, strain, type.

various *adj* assorted, contrasting, different, differing, dissimilar, diverse, heterogeneous, miscellaneous, mixed, *inf* motley, multifarious, several, sundry, varied, varying. *Opp* SIMILAR.

vary *vb* 1 change, deviate, differ, fluctuate, go up and down, vacillate. 2 *vary your speed*. adapt, adjust, alter, convert, modify, reset, switch, transform, upset. *Opp* STABILIZE.

varied, varying ▷ VARIOUS.

vast *adj* boundless, broad, colossal, enormous, extensive, gigantic, great, huge, immeasurable, immense, infinite, interminable, large, limitless, mammoth, massive, measureless, monumental, never-ending, titanic, tremendous, unbounded, unlimited, voluminous, wide. ▷ BIG. *Opp* SMALL.

vault *n* basement, cavern, cellar, crypt, repository, strongroom, undercroft. ● *vb* bound over, clear, hurdle, jump, leap, leapfrog, spring over.

veer *vb* change direction, dodge, swerve, tack, turn, wheel.

vegetable *adj* growing, organic. ● *n* ▷ artichoke, asparagus, aubergine, bean, beet, beetroot, broad bean, broccoli, Brussels sprout, butter bean, cabbage, carrot, cauliflower, celeriac, celery, chicory, courgette, cress, cucumber, garlic, kale, kohlrabi, leek, lettuce, marrow, mushroom, onion, parsnip, pea, pepper, potato, pumpkin, radish, runner bean, salsify, shallot, spinach, sugar beet, swede, sweetcorn, tomato, turnip, watercress, zucchini.

vegetate *vb* be inactive, do nothing, *inf* go to seed, idle, lose interest, stagnate.

vegetation *n* foliage, greenery, growing things, growth, plants, undergrowth, weeds.

vehement *adj* animated, ardent, eager, enthusiastic, excited, fervent, fierce, forceful, heated, impassioned, intense, passionate, powerful, strong, urgent, vigorous, violent. *Opp* APATHETIC.

vehicle *n* conveyance. ▷ ambulance, *inf* buggy, bulldozer, bus, cab, camper, caravan, carriage, cart, old use charabanc, chariot, coach, dump truck, dustcart, estate car, fire-engine, float, gig, go-kart, hearse, horse-box, jeep, juggernaut, lorry, minibus, minicab, *inf* motor, motor car, old use omnibus, pantechnicon, patrol-car, pick-up, removal van, rickshaw, scooter, sedan-chair, side-car, sledge, snowplough, stage-coach, steam-roller, tank, tanker, taxi, traction-engine, tractor, trailer, tram, transporter, trap, trolley-bus, truck, tumbrel, van, wagon,

sl wheels. ▷ CAR, CYCLE, TRAIN, VESSEL.

veil *vb* camouflage, cloak, conceal, cover, disguise, hide, mask, shroud.

vein *n* 1 artery, blood vessel, capillary. 2 *mineral vein.* bed, course, deposit, line, lode, seam, stratum. 3 ▷ MOOD.

veneer *n* coating, covering, finish, gloss, layer, surface. ● *vb* ▷ COVER.

venerable *adj* aged, ancient, august, dignified, esteemed, estimable, honourable, honoured, old, respectable, respected, revered, reverenced, sedate, venerated, worshipped, worthy of respect.

venerate *vb* adore, esteem, hero-worship, honour, idolize, look up to, pay homage to, respect, revere, reverence, worship.

vengeance *n* reprisal, retaliation, retribution, revenge, *inf* tit for tat.

vengeful *adj* avenging, bitter, rancorous, revengeful, spiteful, unforgiving, vindictive. *Opp* FORGIVING.

venom *n* poison, toxin.

venomous *adj* deadly, lethal, poisonous, toxic.

vent *n* aperture, cut, duct, gap, hole, opening, orifice, outlet, passage, slit, slot, split. ● *vb* articulate, express, give vent to, let go, make known, release, utter, ventilate, voice. ▷ SPEAK.

ventilate *vb* aerate, air, freshen, oxygenate.

venture *n* enterprise, experiment, gamble, risk, speculation, undertaking. ● *vb* 1 bet, chance, dare, gamble, put forward, risk,

speculate, stake, wager.
2 *venture out.* dare to go, risk
going.

venturesome *adj* adventurous,
bold, courageous, daring,
doughty, fearless, intrepid.

venue *n* meeting-place, location,
rendezvous.

verbal *adj* **1** lexical, linguistic.
2 *a verbal message.* oral, said,
spoken, unwritten, vocal, word-
of-mouth. *Opp* WRITTEN.

verbatim *adj* exact, faithful,
literal, precise, word for word.

verbose *adj* diffuse, garrulous,
long-winded, loquacious, prolix,
rambling, repetitious, talkative,
voluble. ▷ WORDY. *Opp* CON-
CISE.

verbosity *n inf* beating about
the bush, circumlocution,
diffuseness, garrulity, long-
windedness, loquacity, periph-
rasis, prolixity, repetition,
verbiage, wordiness.

verdict *n* adjudication, assessment, conclusion, decision,
finding, judgement, opinion,
sentence.

verge *n* bank, boundary, brim,
brink, edge, hard shoulder,
kerb, lip, margin, roadside,
shoulder, side, threshold,
wayside.

verifiable *adj* demonstrable,
provable.

verify *vb* affirm, ascertain, attest
to, authenticate, bear witness
to, check out, confirm, corroborate, demonstrate the truth of,
establish, prove, show the truth
of, substantiate, support,
uphold, validate, vouch for.

verisimilitude *n* authenticity,
realism.

vermin *plur n* parasites, pests.

vernacular *adj* common, everyday, indigenous, local, native,
ordinary, popular, vulgar.

versatile *adj* adaptable, all-
purpose, all-round, flexible,
gifted, multi-purpose, resourceful, skilful, talented.

verse *n* lines, metre, rhyme,
stanza. □ blank verse, Chaucer-
ian stanza, clerihew, couplet,
free verse, haiku, hexameter,
limerick, ottava rima, penta-
meter, quatrain, rhyme royal,
sestina, sonnet, Spenserian
stanza, terza rima, triolet,
triplet, vers libre, villanelle.
▷ POEM.

versed *adj* accomplished,
competent, experienced, expert,
knowledgeable, practised, proficient, skilled, taught, trained.

version *n* **1** account, description,
portrayal, reading, rendition,
report, story. **2** adaptation,
interpretation, paraphrase,
rendering, translation.
3 design, form, kind, mark,
model, style, type, variant.

vertical *adj* erect, perpendicular, precipitous, sheer, upright.
Opp HORIZONTAL.

vertigo *n* dizziness, giddiness,
light-headedness.

very *adv* acutely, enormously,
especially, exceedingly,
extremely, greatly, highly,
inf jolly, most, noticeably,
outstandingly, particularly,
really, remarkably, *inf* terribly,
truly, uncommonly, unusually.

vessel *n* **1** ▷ CONTAINER. **2** bark,
boat, craft, ship. □ aircraft-
carrier, barge, bathysphere,
battleship, brigantine, cabin
cruiser, canoe, catamaran, clip-
per, coaster, collier, coracle,
corvette, cruise-liner, cruiser,

cutter, destroyer, dhow, dinghy, dredger, dugout, ferry, freighter, frigate, galleon, galley, gondola, gunboat, houseboat, hovercraft, hydrofoil, hydroplane, ice-breaker, junk, kayak, ketch, landing-craft, launch, lifeboat, lighter, lightship, liner, long-boat, lugger, man-of-war, merchant ship, minesweeper, motor boat, narrow-boat, oil-tanker, packet-ship, paddle-steamer, pontoon, power-boat, pram, privateer, punt, quinque-reme, raft, rowing-boat, sailing-boat, sampan, schooner, skiff, sloop, smack, speed-boat, steamer, steamship, submarine, tanker, tender, torpedo boat, tramp steamer, trawler, trireme, troopship, tug, warship, whaler, wind-jammer, yacht, yawl.

vet *vb inf* check out, examine, investigate, review, scrutinize.

veteran *adj* experienced, mature, old, practised.
● *n* experienced soldier, ex-serviceman, ex-servicewoman, old hand, old soldier, survivor.

veto *n* ban, block, embargo, prohibition, proscription, refusal, rejection, *inf* thumbs down. ● *vb* ban, bar, blackball, block, disallow, dismiss, forbid, prohibit, proscribe, quash, refuse, reject, rule out, say no to, turn down, vote against. *Opp* APPROVE.

vex *vb inf* aggravate, annoy, bother, displease, exasperate, harass, irritate, provoke, *inf* put out, trouble, upset, worry. ▷ ANGER.

viable *adj* achievable, feasible, operable, possible, practicable, practical, realistic, reasonable, supportable, sustainable, usable, workable. *Opp* IMPRACTICAL.

vibrant *adj* alert, alive, dynamic, electric, energetic, lively, living, pulsating, quivering, resonant, thrilling, throbbing, trembling, vibrating, vivacious. *Opp* LIFELESS.

vibrate *vb* fluctuate, judder, oscillate, pulsate, quake, quiver, rattle, resonate, reverberate, shake, shiver, shudder, throb, tremble, wobble.

vibration *n* juddering, oscillation, pulsation, quivering, rattling, resonance, reverberation, shaking, shivering, shuddering, throbbing, trembling, tremor.

vicarious *adj* delegated, deputed, indirect, second-hand, surrogate.

vice *n* 1 badness, corruption, degeneracy, degradation, depravity, evil, evil-doing, immorality, iniquity, lechery, profligacy, promiscuity, sin, venality, villainy, wickedness, wrongdoing. 2 bad habit, blemish, defect, failing, fault, flaw, foible, imperfection, shortcoming, weakness.

vicinity *n* area, district, environs, locale, locality, neighbourhood, outskirts, precincts, proximity, purlieus, region, sector, territory, zone.

vicious *adj* 1 atrocious, barbaric, barbarous, beastly, bloodthirsty, brutal, callous, cruel, diabolical, fiendish, heinous, hurtful, inhuman, merciless, monstrous, murderous, pitiless, ruthless, sadistic, savage, unfeeling, vile, violent. 2 *a vicious character.* bad, *inf* bitchy, *inf* catty, depraved, evil, heartless, immoral, malicious, mean, perverted, rancorous, sinful, spiteful, venomous, villainous, vindictive, vitriolic, wicked. 3 *vicious animals.* aggressive, bad-tempered, dangerous, ferocious, fierce, snappy, untamed, wild. 4 *a vicious wind.* cutting, nasty, severe, sharp, unpleasant. Opp GENTLE.

vicissitude n alteration, change, flux, instability, mutability, mutation, shift, uncertainty, unpredictability, variability.

victim n 1 casualty, fatality, injured person, patient, sufferer, wounded person. 2 *sacrificial victim.* martyr, offering, prey, sacrifice.

victimize vb bully, cheat, discriminate against, exploit, intimidate, oppress, persecute, inf pick on, prey on, take advantage of, terrorize, torment, treat unfairly, inf use. ▷ CHEAT.

victor n champion, conqueror, prizewinner, winner. Opp LOSER.

victorious adj champion, conquering, first, leading, prevailing, successful, top, top-scoring, triumphant, unbeaten, undefeated, winning. Opp UNSUCCESSFUL.

victory n achievement, conquest, knockout, mastery, success, superiority, supremacy, triumph, inf walk-over, win. Opp DEFEAT.

vie vb compete, contend, strive, struggle.

view n 1 aspect, landscape, outlook, panorama, perspective, picture, prospect, scene, scenery, seascape, spectacle, townscape, vista. 2 angle, look, perspective, sight, vision. 3 *political views.* attitude, belief, conviction, idea, judgement,

notion, opinion, perception, position, thought. ● vb 1 behold, consider, contemplate, examine, eye, gaze at, inspect, observe, perceive, regard, scan, stare at, survey, witness. 2 *view TV.* look at, see, watch.

viewer n plur audience, observer, onlooker, spectator, watcher, witness.

viewpoint n angle, perspective, point of view, position, slant, standpoint.

vigilant adj alert, attentive, awake, careful, circumspect, eagle-eyed, observant, on the watch, on your guard, inf on your toes, sharp, wakeful, wary, watchful, wideawake. Opp NEGLIGENT.

vigorous adj active, alive, animated, brisk, dynamic, energetic, fit, flourishing, forceful, full-blooded, inf full of beans, growing, hale and hearty, healthy, lively, lusty, potent, prosperous, red-blooded, robust, spirited, strenuous, strong, thriving, virile, vital, vivacious, zestful. Opp FEEBLE.

vigour n animation, dynamism, energy, fitness, force, forcefulness, gusto, health, life, liveliness, might, potency, power, robustness, spirit, stamina, strength, verve, inf vim, virility, vitality, vivacity, zeal, zest.

vile adj bad, base, contemptible, degenerate, depraved, despicable, disgusting, evil, execrable, filthy, foul, hateful, horrible, immoral, loathsome, low, nasty, nauseating, obnoxious, odious, offensive, perverted, repellent, repugnant, repulsive, revolting, sickening, sinful, ugly, vicious, wicked.

vilify vb abuse, calumniate, defame, denigrate, deprecate, disparage, revile, *inf* run down, slander, *inf* smear, speak evil of, traduce, vituperate.

villain n blackguard, criminal, evil-doer, malefactor, mischief-maker, miscreant, reprobate, rogue, scoundrel, sinner, wretch. ▷ CRIMINAL.

villainous adj bad, corrupt, criminal, dishonest, evil, sinful, treacherous, vile. ▷ WICKED.

vindictive adj avenging, malicious, nasty, punitive, rancorous, revengeful, spiteful, unforgiving, vengeful, vicious. *Opp* FORGIVING.

vintage adj choice, classic, fine, good, high-quality, mature, mellowed, old, seasoned, venerable.

violate vb 1 breach, break, contravene, defy, disobey, disregard, flout, ignore, infringe, overstep, sin against, transgress. 2 *violate someone's privacy*. abuse, desecrate, disturb, invade, profane. 3 [*of men*] *violate a woman*. assault, attack, debauch, dishonour, force yourself on, rape, ravish.

violation n breach, contravention, defiance, flouting, infringement, invasion, offence (against), transgression.

violent adj 1 acute, damaging, dangerous, destructive, devastating, explosive, ferocious, fierce, forceful, furious, hard, harmful, intense, powerful, rough, ruinous, savage, severe, strong, swingeing, tempestuous, turbulent, uncontrollable, vehement, wild. 2 *violent behaviour.* barbaric, berserk, bloodthirsty, brutal, cruel, desperate, frenzied, headstrong, homicidal, murderous, riotous, rowdy, ruthless, uncontrolled, unruly, vehement, vicious, wild. *Opp* GENTLE.

VIP n celebrity, dignitary, important person.

virile adj *derog* macho, manly, masculine, potent, vigorous.

virtue n 1 decency, fairness, goodness, high-mindedness, honesty, honour, integrity, justice, morality, nobility, principle, rectitude, respectability, righteousness, right-mindedness, sincerity, uprightness, worthiness. 2 advantage, asset, good point, merit, quality, *inf* redeeming feature, strength. 3 *sexual virtue.* abstinence, chastity, honour, innocence, purity, virginity. *Opp* VICE.

virtuoso n expert, genius, maestro, prodigy, showman, *inf* wizard. ▷ MUSICIAN.

virtuous adj blameless, chaste, decent, ethical, exemplary, fair, God-fearing, good, *derog* goody-goody, high-minded, high-principled, honest, honourable, innocent, irreproachable, just, law-abiding, moral, noble, principled, praiseworthy, pure, respectable, right, righteous, right-minded, sincere, *derog* smug, spotless, trustworthy, uncorrupted, unimpeachable, unsullied, upright, virginal, worthy. *Opp* WICKED.

virulent adj 1 dangerous, deadly, lethal, life-threatening, noxious, pernicious, poisonous, toxic, venomous. 2 *virulent abuse.* acrimonious, bitter, hostile, malicious, malign, malignant, mordant, nasty, spiteful, splenetic, vicious, vitriolic.

viscous *adj* gluey, sticky, syrupy, thick, viscid. *Opp* RUNNY.

visible *adj* apparent, clear, conspicuous, detectable, discernible, distinct, evident, manifest, noticeable, observable, obvious, open, perceivable, perceptible, plain, recognizable, unconcealed, undisguised, unmistakable. *Opp* INVISIBLE.

vision *n* 1 eyesight, perception, sight. 2 apparition, chimera, day-dream, delusion, fantasy, ghost, hallucination, illusion, mirage, phantasm, phantom, spectre, spirit, wraith. 3 *a man of vision*. far-sightedness, foresight, imagination, insight, spirituality, understanding.

visionary *adj* dreamy, fanciful, far-sighted, futuristic, idealistic, imaginative, impractical, mystical, prophetic, quixotic, romantic, speculative, transcendental, unrealistic, Utopian. ● *n* dreamer, idealist, mystic, poet, prophet, romantic, seer.

visit *n* 1 call, *old use* sojourn, stay, stop, visitation. 2 day out, excursion, outing, trip. ● *vb* call on, come to see, *inf* descend on, *inf* drop in on, go to see, *inf* look up, make a visit to, pay a call on, *inf* pop in on, stay with. **visit regularly** ▷ HAUNT.

visitor *n* 1 caller, *plur* company, guest. 2 holiday-maker, sightseer, tourist, traveller, tripper. 3 *a visitor from abroad*. alien, foreigner, migrant, visitant.

visor *n* protector, shield, sunshield.

vista *n* landscape, outlook, panorama, prospect, scene, scenery, seascape, view.

visualize *vb* conceive, dream up, envisage, imagine, picture.

vital *adj* 1 alive, animate, animated, dynamic, energetic, exuberant, life-giving, live, lively, living, sparkling, spirited, sprightly, vigorous, vivacious, zestful. *Opp* LIFELESS. 2 *vital information*. compulsory, current, crucial, essential, fundamental, imperative, important, indispensable, mandatory, necessary, needed, relevant, requisite. *Opp* INESSENTIAL.

vitality *n* animation, dynamism, energy, exuberance, *inf* go, life, liveliness, *inf* sparkle, spirit, sprightliness, stamina, strength, vigour, *inf* vim, vivacity, zest.

vitriolic *adj* abusive, acid, biting, bitter, caustic, cruel, destructive, hostile, hurtful, malicious, savage, scathing, vicious, vindictive, virulent.

vituperate *vb* abuse, berate, calumniate, censure, defame, denigrate, deprecate, disparage, reproach, revile, *inf* run down, slander, upbraid, vilify.

vivacious *adj* animated, bubbly, cheerful, ebullient, energetic, high-spirited, light-hearted, lively, merry, positive, spirited, sprightly. *Opp* LETHARGIC.

vivid *adj* 1 bright, brilliant, colourful, dazzling, fresh, *derog* gaudy, gay, glaring, glowing, intense, rich, shining, showy, strong, vibrant. 2 *a vivid description*. clear, detailed, graphic, imaginative, lifelike, lively, memorable, powerful, realistic, striking. *Opp* LIFELESS.

vocabulary *n* 1 diction, lexis, words. 2 dictionary, glossary, lexicon, phrase book, word-list.

vocal *adj* 1 oral, said, spoken, sung, voiced. 2 *vocal in discussion*. communicative, forthcoming, loquacious, outspoken, talkative, vociferous. *Opp* TACITURN.

vocation *n* calling, career, employment, job, life's work, occupation, profession, trade.

vogue *n* craze, fad, fashion, *inf* latest thing, mode, rage, style, taste, trend. **in vogue** ▷ FASHIONABLE.

voice *n* accent, articulation, expression, idiolect, inflexion, intonation, singing, sound, speaking, speech, tone, utterance. ● *vb* ▷ SPEAK.

void *adj* 1 blank, empty, unoccupied, vacant. 2 *a void contract*. annulled, cancelled, inoperative, invalid, not binding, unenforceable, useless. ● *n* blank, emptiness, nothingness, space, vacancy, vacuum.

volatile *adj* 1 explosive, sensitive, unstable. 2 *volatile moods*. changeable, erratic, fickle, flighty, inconstant, lively, mercurial, temperamental, unpredictable, *inf* up and down, variable. *Opp* STABLE.

volley *n* barrage, bombardment, burst, cannonade, fusillade, salvo, shower.

voluble *adj* chatty, fluent, garrulous, glib, loquacious, talkative. ▷ WORDY.

volume *n* 1 *old use* tome. ▷ BOOK. 2 *volume of a container*. aggregate, amount, bulk, capacity, dimensions, mass, measure, quantity, size.

voluminous *adj* ample, billowing, bulky, capacious, cavernous, enormous, extensive, gigantic, great, huge, immense, large, mammoth, massive, roomy, spacious, vast. ▷ BIG. *Opp* SMALL.

voluntary *adj* 1 elective, free, gratuitous, optional, spontaneous, unpaid, willing. *Opp* COMPULSORY. 2 *a voluntary act*. conscious, deliberate, intended, intentional, planned, premeditated, wilful. *Opp* INVOLUNTARY.

volunteer *vb* 1 be willing, offer, propose, put yourself forward. 2 ▷ ENLIST.

voluptuous *adj* 1 hedonistic, luxurious, pleasure-loving, self-indulgent, sensual, sybaritic. 2 *voluptuous figure*. attractive, buxom, *inf* curvaceous, desirable, erotic, sensual, *inf* sexy, shapely, *inf* well-endowed.

vomit *vb* be sick, *inf* bring up, disgorge, *inf* heave up, *inf* puke, regurgitate, retch, *inf* spew up, *inf* throw up.

voracious *adj* avid, eager, fervid, gluttonous, greedy, hungry, insatiable, keen, ravenous, thirsty.

vortex *n* eddy, spiral, whirlpool, whirlwind.

vote *n* ballot, election, plebiscite, poll, referendum, show of hands. ● *vb* ballot, cast your vote. **vote for** choose, elect, nominate, opt for, pick, return, select, settle on.

vouch *vb* **vouch for** answer for, back, certify, endorse, guarantee, speak for, sponsor, support.

voucher *n* coupon, ticket, token.

vow *n* assurance, guarantee, oath, pledge, promise, under-

taking, word of honour.
● *vb* declare, give an assurance,
give your word, guarantee,
pledge, promise, swear, take an
oath.

voyage *n* cruise, journey,
passage. ● *vb* circumnavigate,
cruise, sail. ▷ TRAVEL.

vulgar *adj* 1 churlish, coarse,
common, crude, foul, gross, ill-
bred, impolite, improper, indecent, indecorous, low, offensive,
rude, uncouth, ungentlemanly,
unladylike. ▷ OBSCENE.
Opp POLITE. 2 *vulgar colour
scheme.* crude, gaudy, inartistic,
in bad taste, inelegant, insensitive, lowbrow, plebeian, tasteless, tawdry, unrefined, unsophisticated. *Opp* TASTEFUL.

vulnerable *adj* 1 at risk,
defenceless, exposed, helpless,
unguarded, unprotected, weak,
wide open. 2 easily hurt, sensitive, thin-skinned, touchy.
Opp RESILIENT.

W

wad *n* bundle, lump, mass, pack,
pad, plug, roll.

wadding *n* filling, lining, packing, padding, stuffing.

wade *vb* ford, paddle, splash.
▷ WALK.

waffle *n* evasiveness, padding,
prevarication, prolixity, verbiage, wordiness. ● *vb inf* beat
about the bush, *inf* blather on,
hedge, prattle, prevaricate.

waft *vb* 1 be borne, drift, float,
travel. 2 bear, carry, convey,
puff, transmit, transport.

wag *vb* bob, flap, move to and
fro, nod, oscillate, rock, shake,
sway, undulate, *inf* waggle,
wave, *inf* wiggle.

wage *n* compensation, earnings,
emolument, honorarium,
income, pay, pay packet, recompense, remuneration, reward,
salary, stipend. ● *vb* carry on,
conduct, engage in, fight, prosecute, pursue, undertake.

wager *vb* bet, gamble.

wail *vb* caterwaul, complain,
cry, howl, lament, moan,
shriek, waul, weep, *inf* yowl.

waist *n* middle, waistline.

waistband *n* belt, cummerbund,
girdle.

wait *vb* delay, halt, hesitation,
hiatus, *inf* hold-up, intermission, interval, pause, postponement, rest, stay, stop, stoppage.
● *vb* 1 *old use* bide, delay, halt,
inf hang about, *inf* hang on,
hesitate, hold back, keep still,
linger, mark time, pause,
remain, rest, *inf* sit tight, stand
by, stay, stop, *old use* tarry.
2 *wait at table.* serve.

waive *vb* abandon, cede, disclaim, dispense with, forgo, give
up, relinquish, remit, renounce,
resign, sign away, surrender.

wake *n* 1 funeral, vigil, watch.
2 *wake of a ship.* path, track,
trail, turbulence, wash.
● *vb* 1 arouse, awaken, bring to
life, call, disturb, galvanize,
rouse, stimulate, stir, waken.
2 become conscious, bestir
yourself, *inf* come to life, get
up, rise, *inf* stir, wake up.
wake up to ▷ REALIZE.
waking ▷ CONSCIOUS.

wakeful *adj* alert, awake,
insomniac, *inf* on the qui vive,
restless, sleepless.

walk n 1 bearing, carriage, gait, stride. 2 constitutional, hike, *old use* promenade, ramble, saunter, stroll, traipse, tramp, trek, trudge, *inf* turn. 3 *a paved walk.* aisle, alley, path, pathway, pavement. ● vb 1 be a pedestrian, travel on foot. □ amble, crawl, creep, dodder, *inf* foot-slog, hike, hobble, limp, lope, lurch, march, mince, *sl* mooch, pace, pad, paddle, parade, *old use* perambulate, plod, promenade, prowl, ramble, saunter, scuttle, shamble, shuffle, slink, stagger, stalk, steal, step, *inf* stomp, stride, stroll, strut, stumble, swagger, tiptoe, *inf* toddle, totter, tramp, trample, traipse, tramp, trek, troop, trot, trudge, waddle, wade. 3 *don't walk on the flowers.* stamp, step, trample, tread. **walk away with** ▷ WIN. **walk off with** ▷ STEAL. **walk out** ▷ QUIT. **walk out on** ▷ DESERT.

walker n hiker, pedestrian, rambler.

wall n □ barricade, barrier, bulkhead, bulwark, dam, dike, divider, embankment, fence, fortification, hedge, obstacle, paling, palisade, parapet, partition, rampart, screen, sea-wall, stockade. **wall in** ▷ ENCLOSE.

wallet n notecase, pocketbook, pouch, purse.

wallow vb 1 flounder, lie, pitch about, roll about, stagger about, tumble, wade, welter. 2 *wallow in luxury.* glory, indulge yourself, luxuriate, revel, take delight.

wan adj anaemic, ashen, bloodless, colourless, exhausted, faint, feeble, livid, pale, pallid, pasty, sickly, tired, waxen, worn.

wand n baton, rod, staff, stick.

wander vb 1 drift, go aimlessly, meander, prowl, ramble, range, roam, rove, saunter, stray, stroll, travel about, walk, wind. 2 *wander off course.* curve, deviate, digress, drift, err, go off at a tangent, stray, swerve, turn, twist, veer, zigzag. **wandering** ▷ INATTENTIVE, NOMADIC.

wane vb decline, decrease, dim, diminish, dwindle, ebb, fade, fail, *inf* fall off, grow less, lessen, peter out, shrink, subside, taper off, weaken. *Opp* STRENGTHEN.

want n 1 demand, desire, need, requirement, wish. 2 *a want of ready cash.* absence, lack, need. 3 *war against want.* dearth, famine, hunger, insufficiency, penury, poverty, privation, scarcity, shortage. ● vb 1 aspire to, covet, crave, demand, desire, fancy, hanker after, *inf* have a yen for, hunger for, *inf* itch for, like, long for, miss, pine for, please, prefer, *inf* set your heart on, thirst after, thirst for, wish for, yearn for. 2 *want manners.* be short of, lack, need, require.

war n campaign, conflict, crusade, fighting, hostilities, military action, strife, warfare. □ ambush, assault, attack, battle, blitz, blockade, bombardment, counter-attack, engagement, guerrilla warfare, invasion, manoeuvres, operations, resistance, siege, skirmish. **wage war** ▷ FIGHT.

ward n charge, dependant, minor. ● vb **ward off** avert, beat off, block, chase away, check, deflect, fend off, forestall, parry, push away, repel,

repulse, stave off, thwart, turn
aside.

warder *n* gaoler, guard, jailer,
keeper, prison officer.

warehouse *n* depository, depot,
store, storehouse.

wares *plur n* commodities,
goods, manufactures, merchandise, produce, stock, supplies.

warlike *adj* aggressive, bellicose, belligerent, hawkish,
hostile, militant, militaristic,
pugnacious, warmongering,
warring.

warm *adj* 1 close, hot, lukewarm, subtropical, sultry,
summery, temperate, tepid,
warmish. 2 *warm clothes.* cosy,
thermal, thick, winter, woolly.
3 *a warm welcome.* affable,
affectionate, ardent, cordial,
emotional, enthusiastic,
excited, fervent, friendly,
genial, impassioned, kind,
loving, passionate, sympathetic,
warm-hearted. *Opp* COLD,
UNFRIENDLY. ● *vb* heat, make
warmer, melt, raise the
temperature of, thaw, thaw out.
Opp COOL.

warn *vb* admonish, advise, alert,
caution, counsel, forewarn, give
a warning, give notice, inform,
notify, raise the alarm, remind,
inf tip off.

warning *n* 1 advance notice,
augury, forewarning, hint,
indication, notice, notification,
omen, portent, premonition,
presage, prophecy, reminder,
sign, signal, threat, *inf* tip-off,
inf word to the wise. □ *alarm,
alarm-bell, beacon, bell, fire-
alarm, flashing light, fog-horn,
gong, hooter, red light, siren,
traffic-lights, whistle.* 2 *let off
with a warning.* admonition,

advice, caveat, caution, reprimand.

warp *vb* become deformed, bend,
buckle, contort, curl, curve,
deform, distort, kink, twist.

warrant *n* authority, authorization, certification, document,
entitlement, guarantee, licence,
permit, pledge, sanction,
search-warrant, warranty,
voucher. ● *vb* ▷ JUSTIFY.

wary *adj* alert, apprehensive,
attentive, *inf* cagey, careful,
chary, cautious, circumspect,
distrustful, heedful, observant,
on the lookout, on your guard,
suspicious, vigilant, watchful.
Opp RECKLESS.

wash *n* old use ablutions, bath,
rinse, shampoo, shower.
● *vb* 1 clean, cleanse, flush,
launder, mop, rinse, scrub,
shampoo, sluice, soap down,
sponge down, swab down, swill,
wipe. 2 bath, bathe, *old use*
make your toilet, perform your
ablutions, shower. 3 *The sea
washes against the cliff.* break,
dash, flow, lap, pound, roll,
splash. **wash your hands of**
▷ ABANDON.

washing *n* cleaning, dirty
clothes, laundry, *inf* the wash.

washout *n* débâcle, disappointment, disaster, failure, *inf* flop.

waste *adj* discarded, extra,
superfluous, unprofitable,
unusable, unused, unwanted,
worthless. 2 *waste land.* bare,
barren, derelict, empty, overgrown, run-down, uncared-for,
uncultivated, undeveloped,
unproductive, wild.
● *n* 1 debris, dregs, effluent,
excess, garbage, junk, leavings,
inf left-overs, litter, offcuts,
refuse, remnants, rubbish,

scrap, scraps, trash, unusable material, unwanted material, wastage. 2 extravagance, indulgence, overprovision, prodigality, profligacy, self-indulgence.
• *vb* be wasteful with, dissipate, fritter, misspend, misuse, overprovide, *sl* splurge, squander, use up, use wastefully.
Opp CONSERVE. **waste away** become emaciated, become thin, become weaker, mope, pine, weaken.

wasteful *adj* excessive, expensive, extravagant, improvident, imprudent, lavish, needless, prodigal, profligate, reckless, spendthrift, thriftless, uneconomical, unthrifty.
Opp ECONOMICAL. **wasteful person** ▷ SPENDTHRIFT.

watch *n* chronometer, clock, digital watch, stopwatch, timepiece, timer, wrist-watch.
• *vb* 1 attend, concentrate, contemplate, eye, gaze, heed, keep an eye open for, keep your eyes on, look at, mark, note, observe, pay attention, regard, see, spy on, stare, take notice, view. 2 watch *sheep*. care for, chaperon, defend, guard, keep an eye on, keep watch on, look after, mind, protect, safeguard, shield, superintend, supervise, take charge of, tend. **keep watch** ▷ GUARD. **on the watch** ▷ WATCHFUL. **watch your step** ▷ BEWARE.

watcher *n plur* audience, *inf* looker-on, observer, onlooker, spectator, viewer, witness.

watchful *adj* attentive, eagle-eyed, heedful, observant, *inf* on the lookout, *inf* on the qui vive, on the watch, quick, sharp-

eyed, vigilant. ▷ ALERT.
Opp INATTENTIVE.

watchman *n* caretaker, custodian, guard, lookout, night-watchman, security guard, sentinel, sentry, watch.

water *n* 1 Adam's ale, bath water, brine, distilled water, drinking water, mineral water, rainwater, sea water, spa water, spring water, tap water. 2 lake, lido, ocean, pond, pool, river, sea. ▷ STREAM.
• *vb* damp, dampen, douse, drench, flood, hose, inundate, irrigate, moisten, saturate, soak, souse, spray, sprinkle, wet. **water down** ▷ DILUTE.

waterfall *n* cascade, cataract, chute, rapids, torrent, white water.

waterlogged *adj* full of water, saturated, soaked.

waterproof *adj* damp-proof, impermeable, impervious, water-repellent, water-resistant, watertight, weatherproof.
Opp LEAKY. • *n* cape, groundsheet, *inf* mac, mackintosh, sou'wester.

watertight *adj* hermetic, sealed, sound. ▷ WATERPROOF.

watery *adj* 1 aqueous, bland, characterless, dilute, diluted, fluid, liquid, *inf* runny, *inf* sloppy, tasteless, thin, watered-down, weak, *inf* wishy-washy. 2 watery *eyes*. damp, moist, tear-filled, tearful, *inf* weepy. ▷ WET.

wave *n* 1 billow, breaker, crest, heave, ridge, ripple, roller, surf, swell, tidal wave, undulation, wavelet, *inf* white horse. 2 flourish, gesticulation, gesture, shake, sign, signal. 3 *a wave of enthusiasm.* current, flood, ground swell, outbreak, surge, tide, upsurge. **4** *a new wave*. advance, fashion, tendency, trend. **5** *radio waves*. pulse, vibration. • *vb* **1** billow, brandish, flail about, flap, flourish, fluctuate, flutter, move to and fro, ripple, shake, sway, swing, twirl, undulate, waft, wag, waggle, wiggle, zigzag. **2** gesticulate, gesture, indicate, sign, signal. **wave aside** ▷ DISMISS.

wavelength *n* channel, station, waveband.

waver *vb* *inf* be in two minds, be unsteady, change, falter, flicker, hesitate, quake, quaver, quiver, shake, shiver, shudder, sway, teeter, tergiversate, totter, tremble, vacillate, wobble.

wavy *adj* curling, curly, curving, heaving, rippling, rolling, sinuous, undulating, up and down, winding, zigzag. *Opp* FLAT, STRAIGHT.

way *n* **1** advance, direction, headway, journey, movement, progress, route. ▷ ROAD. **2** distance, length, measurement. **3** *a way to do something*. approach, avenue, course, fashion, knack, manner, means, method, mode, *Lat* modus operandi, path, procedure, process, system, technique. **4** *foreign ways*. custom, fashion, habit, *Lat* modus vivendi, practice, routine, style, tradition. **5** *funny ways*. characteristic, eccentricity, idiosyncrasy, oddity, peculiarity. **6** *in some ways*. aspect, circumstance, detail, feature, particular, respect.

waylay *vb* accost, ambush, await, buttonhole, detain, intercept, lie in wait for, pounce on, surprise. ▷ ATTACK.

wayward *adj* disobedient, headstrong, obstinate, self-willed, stubborn, uncontrollable, uncooperative, wilful. ▷ NAUGHTY. *Opp* COOPERATIVE.

weak *adj* **1** breakable, brittle, decrepit, delicate, feeble, flawed, flimsy, fragile, frail, frangible, inadequate, insubstantial, rickety, shaky, slight, substandard, tender, thin, unsafe, unsound, unsteady, unsubstantial. **2** *weak in health*. anaemic, debilitated, delicate, enervated, exhausted, feeble, flabby, frail, helpless, ill, infirm, listless, *inf* low, *inf* poorly, puny, sickly, slight, thin, tired out, wasted, weakly, *derog* weak. **3** *a weak character*. cowardly, fearful, impotent, indecisive, ineffective, ineffectual, irresolute, poor, powerless, pusillanimous, spineless, timid, timorous, unassertive, weak-minded, wimpish. **4** *a weak position*. defenceless, exposed, unguarded, unprotected, vulnerable. **5** *weak excuses*. hollow, lame, *inf* pathetic, shallow, unbelievable, unconvincing, unsatisfactory. **6** *weak light*. dim, distant, fading, faint, indistinct, pale, poor, unclear, vague. **7** *weak tea*. dilute, diluted, tasteless, thin, watery. *Opp* STRONG.

weaken *vb* **1** debilitate, destroy, dilute, diminish, emasculate, enervate, enfeeble, erode, exhaust, impair, lessen, lower, make weaker, reduce, ruin, sap, soften, thin down, undermine, *inf* water down. **2** abate, become weaker, decline, decrease, dwindle, ebb, fade, flag, give in,

give way, sag, wane, yield.
Opp STRENGTHEN.

weakling *n* coward, *inf* milksop,
inf pushover, *inf* runt, *inf* softie,
weak person, *inf* weed,
inf wimp.

weakness *n* 1 *inf* Achilles' heel,
blemish, defect, error, failing,
fault, flaw, flimsiness, foible,
fragility, frailty, imperfection,
inadequacy, mistake, shortcoming, softness, *inf* weak spot.
2 debility, decrepitude, delicacy, feebleness, impotence,
incapacity, infirmity, lassitude,
vulnerability. ▷ ILLNESS. 3 *a*
weakness for wine. affection,
fancy, fondness, inclination,
liking, partiality, penchant,
predilection, *inf* soft spot, taste.
Opp STRENGTH.

wealth *n* 1 affluence, assets,
capital, fortune, *old use* lucre,
means, opulence, possessions,
property, prosperity, riches, *old
use* substance. ▷ MONEY.
Opp POVERTY. 2 *a wealth of
information.* abundance,
bounty, copiousness, cornucopia, mine, plenty, profusion,
store, treasury. *Opp* SCARCITY.

wealthy *adj* affluent, *inf* flush,
inf loaded, moneyed, opulent,
joc plutocratic, privileged, prosperous, rich, *inf* well-heeled,
well-off, well-to-do. *Opp* POOR.
wealthy person billionaire,
capitalist, millionaire, plutocrat, tycoon.

weapon *n* bomb, gun, missile.
□ airgun, arrow, atom bomb,
ballistic missile, battering-ram,
battleaxe, bayonet, bazooka,
blowpipe, blunderbuss, boomerang, bow and arrow, bren-gun,
cannon, carbine, catapult, clay-
more, cosh, crossbow, CS gas,
cudgel, cutlass, dagger, depth-

charge, dirk, flame-thrower,
foils, grenade, old use halberd,
harpoon, H-bomb, howitzer,
incendiary bomb, javelin, knuck-
leduster, lance, land-mine, laser
beam, longbow, machete,
machine-gun, mine, mortar,
musket, mustard gas, napalm
bomb, pike, pistol, pole-axe,
rapier, revolver, rifle, rocket,
sabre, scimitar, shotgun, inf six-
shooter, sling, spear, sten-gun,
stiletto, sub-machine-gun, sword,
tank, tear-gas, time-bomb, tomahawk, tommy-gun, torpedo,
truncheon, warhead, water-
cannon. **weapons** armaments,
armoury, arms, arsenal, magazine, munitions, ordnance,
weaponry. □ artillery, automatic
weapons, biological weapons,
chemical weapons, firearms,
missiles, nuclear weapons, small
arms, strategic weapons, tactical
weapons.

wear *vb* 1 be dressed in, clothe
yourself in, don, dress in, have
on, present yourself in, put on,
wrap up in. 2 *wear a smile.*
adopt, assume, display, exhibit,
show. 3 *wears the carpet.*
damage, fray, injure, mark,
scuff, wear away, weaken.
4 *wear well.* endure, last,
inf stand the test of time,
survive. **wear away** ▷ ERODE.
wear off ▷ SUBSIDE. **wear out**
▷ WEARY.

wearisome *adj* boring, dreary,
exhausting, monotonous,
repetitive, tedious, tiring,
wearying. ▷ TROUBLESOME.
Opp STIMULATING.

weary *adj* bone-weary, *inf* dead
beat, *inf* dog-tired, *inf* done in,
drawn, drained, drowsy, enervated, exhausted, *inf* fagged,
fatigued, fed up, flagging, foot-

sore, impatient, jaded, *inf* jet-lagged, *sl* knackered, listless, prostrate, *inf* shattered, *inf* sick (of), sleepy, spent, tired out, travel-weary, wearied, *inf* whacked, worn out. *Opp* FRESH, LIVELY. ● *vb* 1 debilitate, drain, enervate, exhaust, fatigue, *inf* finish, make tired, *sl* knacker, overtire, sap, *inf* shatter, *inf* take it out of, tax, tire, wear out. *Opp* REFRESH. 2 become bored, become tired, flag, grow weary, weaken.

weather *n* climate, the elements, meteorological conditions. □ blizzard, breeze, cloud, cyclone, deluge, dew, downpour, drizzle, drought, fog, frost, gale, hail, haze, heatwave, hoar-frost, hurricane, ice, lightning, mist, rain, rainbow, shower, sleet, slush, snow, snowstorm, squall, storm, sunshine, tempest, thaw, thunder, tornado, typhoon, whirlwind, wind. ● *vb* ▷ SURVIVE. **under the weather** ▷ ILL.

weave *vb* 1 braid, criss-cross, entwine, interlace, intertwine, interweave, knit, plait, sew. 2 *weave a story*. compose, create, make, plot, put together. 3 *weave through a crowd*. dodge, make your way, tack, *inf* twist and turn, wind, zigzag.

web *n* criss-cross, lattice, mesh, net, network.

wedding *n* marriage, nuptials, union.

wedge *vb* cram, force, jam, pack, squeeze, stick.

weep *vb* bawl, *inf* blub, blubber, cry, *inf* grizzle, lament, mewl, moan, shed tears, snivel, sob, wail, whimper, whine.

weigh *vb* 1 measure the weight of. 2 *weigh evidence*. assess, consider, contemplate, evaluate, judge, ponder, reflect on, think about, weigh up. 3 *evidence weighed with the jury*. be important, carry weight, *inf* cut ice, count, have weight, matter. **weigh down** ▷ BURDEN. **weigh up** ▷ EVALUATE.

weighing-machine *n* balance, scales, spring-balance, weighbridge.

weight *n* 1 avoirdupois, burden, density, heaviness, load, mass, pressure, strain, tonnage. 2 *My voice has some weight*. authority, credibility, emphasis, force, gravity, importance, power, seriousness, significance, substance, value, worth. ● *vb* ballast, bias, hold down, keep down, load, make heavy, weigh down.

weird *adj* 1 creepy, eerie, ghostly, mysterious, preternatural, scary, *inf* spooky, supernatural, unaccountable, uncanny, unearthly, unnatural. 2 *weird behaviour*. abnormal, bizarre, *inf* cranky, curious, eccentric, *inf* funny, grotesque, odd, outlandish, peculiar, queer, quirky, strange, unconventional, unusual, *inf* way-out, *inf* zany. *Opp* CONVENTIONAL, NATURAL.

welcome *adj* acceptable, accepted, agreeable, appreciated, desirable, gratifying, much-needed, *inf* nice, pleasant, pleasing, pleasurable. *Opp* UNWELCOME. ● *n* greeting, hospitality, reception, salutation. ● *vb* 1 give a welcome to, greet, hail, receive. 2 *They welcome criticism*. accept, appreciate, approve of, delight in, like, want.

weld vb bond, cement, fuse, join, solder, unite. ▷ FASTEN.

welfare n advantage, benefit, felicity, good, happiness, health, interest, prosperity, well-being.

well adj **1** fit, hale, healthy, hearty, inf in fine fettle, lively, robust, sound, strong, thriving, vigorous. **2** All is well. all right, fine, inf OK, satisfactory. ● n fountain, shaft, source, spring, waterhole, well-spring. □ artesian well, borehole, gusher, oasis, oil well, wishing-well.

well-behaved adj cooperative, disciplined, docile, dutiful, good, hard-working, law-abiding, manageable, inf nice, polite, quiet, well-trained. ▷ OBEDIENT. Opp NAUGHTY.

well-bred adj courteous, courtly, cultivated, decorous, genteel, polite, proper, refined, sophisticated, urbane, well-brought-up, well-mannered. Opp RUDE.

well-built adj athletic, big, brawny, burly, hefty, muscular, powerful, stocky, inf strapping, strong, sturdy, upstanding. Opp SMALL.

well-known adj celebrated, eminent, familiar, famous, illustrious, noted, derog notorious, prominent, renowned. Opp UNKNOWN.

well-meaning adj good-natured, obliging, sincere, well-intentioned, well-meant. ▷ KIND. Opp UNKIND.

well-off adj affluent, comfortable, moneyed, prosperous, rich, inf well-heeled, well-to-do. Opp POOR.

well-spoken adj articulate, educated, polite, inf posh, refined, inf upper crust.

wet adj **1** awash, bedraggled, c'ammy, damp, dank, dewy, drenched, dripping, moist, muddy, saturated, sloppy, soaked, soaking, sodden, soggy, sopping, soused, spongy, submerged, waterlogged, watery, wringing. **2** wet weather. drizzly, humid, misty, pouring, rainy, showery, teeming. **3** wet paint. runny, sticky, tacky. ● n dampness, dew, drizzle, humidity, liquid, moisture, rain. ● vb dampen, douse, drench, irrigate, moisten, saturate, soak, spray, sprinkle, steep, water. Opp DRY.

wheel n circle, disc, hoop, ring. □ bogie, castor, cog-wheel, spinning-wheel, steering-wheel. ● vb change direction, circle, gyrate, move in circles, pivot, spin, swerve, swing round, swivel, turn, veer, whirl.

wheeze vb breathe noisily, cough, gasp, pant, puff.

whereabouts n location, neighbourhood, place, position, site, situation, vicinity.

whiff n breath, hint, puff, smell.

whim n caprice, desire, fancy, impulse, quirk, urge.

whine vb complain, cry, inf grizzle, groan, moan, snivel, wail, weep, whimper, inf whinge.

whip n birch, cane, cat, cat-o'-nine-tails, crop, horsewhip, lash, riding-crop, scourge, switch. ● vb **1** beat, birch, cane, flagellate, flog, horsewhip, lash, scourge, inf tan, thrash. ▷ HIT. **2** beat, stir vigorously, whisk.

whirl vb circle, gyrate, pirouette, reel, revolve, rotate, spin, swivel, turn, twirl, twist, wheel.

whirlpool n eddy, maelstrom, swirl, vortex, whirl.

whirlwind n cyclone, hurricane, tornado, typhoon, vortex, waterspout.

whisk n beater, mixer. • vb beat, mix, stir, whip.

whiskers plur n bristles, hairs, moustache.

whisper n 1 murmur, undertone. 2 a whisper of scandal. gossip, hearsay, rumour. • vb breathe, hiss, murmur, mutter. ▷ TALK.

whistle n hooter, pipe, pipes, siren. • vb blow, pipe.

white adj chalky, clean, cream, ivory, milky, off-white, silver, snow-white, snowy, spotless, whitish. ▷ PALE.

whiten vb blanch, bleach, etiolate, fade, lighten, pale.

whole adj coherent, complete, entire, full, healthy, in one piece, intact, integral, integrated, perfect, sound, total, unabbreviated, unabridged, unbroken, uncut, undamaged, undivided, unedited, unexpurgated, unharmed, unhurt, uninjured, unscathed. Opp FRAGMENTARY, INCOMPLETE.

wholesale adj comprehensive, extensive, general, global, indiscriminate, mass, total, universal, widespread. Opp LIMITED.

wholesome adj beneficial, good, healthful, health-giving, healthy, hygienic, nourishing, nutritious, salubrious, sanitary. Opp UNHEALTHY.

wicked adj abominable, inf awful, bad, base, beastly, corrupt, criminal, depraved, diabolical, dissolute, egregious, evil, foul, guilty, heinous, ill-tempered, immoral, impious, incorrigible, indefensible, iniquitous, insupportable, intolerable, irresponsible, lawless, lost (soul), machiavellian, malevolent, malicious, mischievous, murderous, naughty, nefarious, offensive, perverted, rascally, scandalous, shameful, sinful, sinister, spiteful, inf terrible, ungodly, unprincipled, unregenerate, unrighteous, unscrupulous, vicious, vile, villainous, violent, wrong. ▷ IRRELIGIOUS, OBSCENE. Opp MORAL. **wicked person** ▷ VILLAIN.

wickedness n baseness, depravity, enormity, guilt, heinousness, immorality, infamy, iniquity, irresponsibility, old use knavery, malice, misconduct, naughtiness, sin, sinfulness, spite, turpitude, ungodliness, unrighteousness, vileness, villainy, wrong, wrongdoing. ▷ EVIL.

wide adj 1 ample, broad, expansive, extensive, large, panoramic, roomy, spacious, vast, yawning. 2 wide sympathies. all-embracing, broad-minded, catholic, comprehensive, eclectic, encyclopedic, inclusive, wide-ranging. 3 arms open wide. extended, open, outspread, outstretched. 4 a wide shot. off-course, off-target. Opp NARROW.

widen vb augment, broaden, dilate, distend, enlarge, expand, extend, flare, increase, make wider, open out, spread, stretch.

widespread adj common, endemic, extensive, far-reaching, general, global, pervasive, prevalent, rife, universal, wholesale. Opp RARE.

width n beam (of ship), breadth, broadness, calibre (of gun), compass, diameter, distance across, extent, girth, range, scope, span, thickness.

wield vb 1 brandish, flourish, handle, hold, manage, ply, wave. 2 wield power. employ, exercise, exert, have, possess, use.

wild adj 1 wild animals. free, undomesticated, untamed. 2 a wild moor. deserted, desolate, inf God-forsaken, natural, overgrown, remote, rough, rugged, uncultivated, unenclosed, unfarmed, uninhabited, waste. 3 wild behaviour. aggressive, barbaric, barbarous, berserk, boisterous, disorderly, ferocious, fierce, frantic, hysterical, lawless, mad, noisy, obstreperous, on the rampage, out of control, rabid, rash, reckless, riotous, rowdy, savage, uncivilized, uncontrollable, uncontrolled, undisciplined, ungovernable, unmanageable, unrestrained, unruly, uproarious, violent. 4 wild weather. blustery, stormy, tempestuous, turbulent, violent, windy. 5 wild enthusiasm. eager, excited, extravagant, uninhibited, unrestrained. 6 wild notions. crazy, fantastic, impetuous, irrational, silly, unreasonable. 7 a wild guess. inaccurate, random, unthinking. Opp CALM, CULTIVATED, TAME.

wilderness n desert, jungle, waste, wasteland, wilds.

wile n artifice, gambit, inf game, machination, manoeuvre, plot, ploy, ruse, stratagem, subterfuge, trick.

wilful adj 1 calculated, conscious, deliberate, intended, intentional, premeditated, purposeful, voluntary. Opp ACCIDENTAL. 2 a wilful character. inf bloody-minded, determined, dogged, headstrong, immovable, intransigent, obdurate, obstinate, perverse, inf pig-headed, refractory, self-willed, stubborn, uncompromising, unyielding, wayward. Opp AMENABLE.

will n aim, commitment, desire, determination, disposition, inclination, intent, intention, longing, purpose, resolution, resolve, volition, will-power, wish. ● vb 1 command, encourage, force, influence, inspire, persuade, require, wish. 2 will a fortune. bequeath, hand down, leave, pass on, settle on.

willing adj acquiescent, agreeable, amenable, assenting, complaisant, compliant, consenting, content, cooperative, disposed, docile, inf game, happy, helpful, inclined, pleased, prepared, obliging, ready, well-disposed. ▷ EAGER. Opp UNWILLING.

wilt vb become limp, droop, fade, fail, flag, flop, languish, sag, shrivel, weaken, wither. Opp THRIVE.

wily adj artful, astute, canny, clever, crafty, cunning, deceptive, designing, devious, disingenuous, furtive, guileful, ingenious, knowing, scheming, shifty, shrewd, skilful, sly, tricky, underhand. ▷ DISHONEST. Opp STRAIGHTFORWARD.

win vb **1** be the winner, be victorious, carry the day, come first, conquer, overcome, prevail, succeed, triumph. **2** win a prize. achieve, acquire, inf carry off, collect, inf come away with, deserve, earn, gain, get, obtain, inf pick up, receive, secure, inf walk away with. Opp LOSE.

wind n **1** air-current, blast, breath, breeze, current of air, cyclone, draught, gale, gust, hurricane, monsoon, puff, squall, storm, tempest, tornado, whirlwind, poet zephyr. **2** wind in the stomach. flatulence, gas, heartburn. • vb bend, coil, curl, curve, furl, loop, meander, ramble, reel, roll, slew, snake, spiral, turn, twine, twist, inf twist and turn, veer, wreathe, zigzag. **winding** ▷ TORTUOUS. **wind up** ▷ FINISH.

window n □ casement, dormer, double-glazed window, embrasure, fanlight, French window, light, oriel, pane, sash window, skylight, shop window, stained-glass window, windscreen.

windswept adj bare, bleak, desolate, exposed, unprotected. ▷ WINDY.

windy adj blowy, blustery, boisterous, breezy, draughty, fresh, gusty, squally, stormy, tempestuous. ▷ WINDSWEPT. Opp CALM.

wink vb **1** bat (eyelid), blink, flutter. **2** lights winked. flash, flicker, sparkle, twinkle.

winner n inf champ, champion, conquering hero, conqueror, first, medallist, prizewinner, title-holder, victor. Opp LOSER.

winning adj **1** champion, conquering, first, leading,

prevailing, successful, top, top-scoring, triumphant, unbeaten, undefeated, victorious. Opp UNSUCCESSFUL. **2** a winning smile. ▷ ATTRACTIVE.

wintry adj arctic, icy, snowy. ▷ COLD. Opp SUMMERY.

wipe vb brush, clean, cleanse, dry, dust, mop, polish, rub, scour, sponge, swab, wash. **wipe out** ▷ DESTROY.

wire n **1** cable, coaxial cable, flex, lead, wiring. **2** cablegram, telegram. ▷ COMMUNICATION.

wiry adj lean, muscular, sinewy, strong, thin, tough.

wisdom n astuteness, common sense, discernment, discrimination, good sense, insight, judgement, judiciousness, penetration, perceptiveness, perspicacity, prudence, rationality, reason, sagacity, sapience, sense, understanding. ▷ INTELLIGENCE.

wise adj **1** astute, discerning, enlightened, erudite, fair, just, knowledgeable, penetrating, perceptive, perspicacious, philosophical, sagacious, sage, sensible, shrewd, sound, thoughtful, understanding, well-informed. ▷ INTELLIGENT. **2** a wise decision. advisable, appropriate, considered, diplomatic, expedient, informed, judicious, politic, proper, prudent, rational, reasonable, right. Opp UNWISE. **wise person** philosopher, pundit, sage.

wish n aim, ambition, appetite, aspiration, craving, desire, fancy, hankering, hope, inclination, inf itch, keenness, longing, objective, request, urge, want, yearning, inf yen. • vb ask, choose, crave, desire, hope, want, yearn. **wish for** ▷ WANT.

wisp *n* shred, strand, streak.

wispy *adj* flimsy, fragile, gossamer, insubstantial, light, streaky, thin. *Opp* SUBSTANTIAL.

wistful *adj* disconsolate, forlorn, melancholy, mournful, nostalgic, regretful, yearning. ▷ SAD.

wit *n* 1 banter, cleverness, comedy, facetiousness, humour, ingenuity, jokes, puns, quickness, quips, repartee, witticisms, wordplay. ▷ INTELLIGENCE. 2 comedian, comic, humorist, jester, joker, wag.

witch *n* enchantress, gorgon, hag, sibyl, sorceress, *plur* weird sisters.

witchcraft *n* black magic, charms, enchantment, *inf* hocus-pocus, incantation, magic, *inf* mumbo-jumbo, necromancy, the occult, occultism, sorcery, spells, voodoo, witchery, wizardry.

withdraw *vb* 1 abjure, call back, cancel, *inf* go back on, recall, rescind, retract, take away, take back. 2 *withdraw from the fight.* back away, back down, back out, *inf* chicken out, *inf* cry off, draw back, drop out, fall back, move back, pull back, pull out, *inf* quit, recoil, retire, retreat, run away, *inf* scratch, secede, shrink back. ▷ LEAVE. *Opp* ADVANCE, ENTER. 3 *withdraw teeth.* extract, pull out, remove, take out.

withdrawn *adj* bashful, diffident, distant, introverted, private, quiet, reclusive, remote, reserved, retiring, shy, silent, solitary, taciturn, timid, uncommunicative. *Opp* SOCIABLE.

wither *vb* become dry, become limp, dehydrate, desiccate, droop, dry out, dry up, fail, flag, flop, sag, shrink, shrivel, waste away, wilt. *Opp* THRIVE.

withhold *vb* check, conceal, control, hide, hold back, keep back, keep secret, repress, reserve, retain, suppress. *Opp* GIVE.

withstand *vb* bear, brave, confront, cope with, defy, endure, fight, grapple with, hold out against, last out against, oppose, *inf* put up with, resist, stand up to, *inf* stick, survive, take, tolerate, weather (storm). *Opp* SURRENDER.

witness *n* bystander, eyewitness, looker-on, observer, onlooker, spectator, viewer, watcher. ● *vb* attend, behold, be present at, look on, note, notice, observe, see, view, watch. **bear witness** ▷ TESTIFY.

witty *adj* amusing, clever, comic, droll, facetious, funny, humorous, ingenious, intelligent, jocular, quick-witted, sarcastic, sharp-witted, waggish.

wizard *n* enchanter, magician, magus, sorcerer, *old use* warlock, witch-doctor.

wobble *vb* be unsteady, heave, move unsteadily, oscillate, quake, quiver, rock, shake, sway, teeter, totter, tremble, vacillate, vibrate, waver.

wobbly *adj* insecure, loose, rickety, rocky, shaky, teetering, tottering, unbalanced, unsafe, unstable, unsteady. *Opp* STEADY.

woe *n* affliction, anguish, dejection, despair, distress, grief, heartache, melancholy, misery, misfortune, sadness, suffering, trouble, unhappiness, wretchedness. ▷ SORROW. Opp HAPPINESS.

woebegone adj crestfallen, dejected, downhearted, forlorn, gloomy, melancholy, miserable, inf sorry for yourself, woeful, wretched. ▷ SAD. Opp CHEERFUL.

woman n sl bird, bride, old use dame, old use damsel, daughter, dowager, female, girl, girlfriend, derog hag, derog harridan, housewife, hoyden, derog hussy, lady, lass, madam, Madame, maid, old use maiden, matriarch, matron, mistress, mother, derog termagant, derog virago, virgin, widow, wife.

wonder n 1 admiration, amazement, astonishment, awe, bewilderment, curiosity, fascination, respect, reverence, stupefaction, surprise, wonderment. 2 a wonder of science. marvel, miracle, phenomenon, prodigy, inf sensation. ● vb ask yourself, be curious, be inquisitive, conjecture, marvel, ponder, question yourself, speculate. ▷ THINK. **wonder at** ▷ ADMIRE.

wonderful adj amazing, astonishing, astounding, extraordinary, impressive, incredible, marvellous, miraculous, phenomenal, remarkable, surprising, unexpected, old use wondrous. Opp ORDINARY.

woo vb 1 sl chat up, court, make love to. 2 woo custom. attract, bring in, coax, cultivate, persuade, pursue, seek, try to get.

wood n 1 afforestation, coppice, copse, forest, grove, jungle, orchard, plantation, spinney,

thicket, trees, woodland, woods. 2 blockboard, chipboard, deal, planks, plywood, timber. □ balsa, beech, cedar, chestnut, ebony, elm, mahogany, oak, pine, rosewood, sandalwood, sapele, teak, walnut.

wooded adj afforested, poet bosky, forested, silvan, timbered, tree-covered, woody.

wooden adj 1 ligneous, timber, wood. 2 wooden acting. dead, emotionless, expressionless, hard, inflexible, lifeless, rigid, stiff, stilted, unbending, unemotional, unnatural. Opp LIVELY.

woodwind n □ bassoon, clarinet, cor anglais, flute, oboe, piccolo, recorder.

woodwork n carpentry, joinery.

woody adj fibrous, hard, ligneous, tough. ▷ WOODEN.

woolly adj 1 wool, woollen. 2 woolly toy. cuddly, downy, fleecy, furry, fuzzy, hairy, shaggy, soft. 3 woolly ideas. ambiguous, blurry, confused, hazy, ill-defined, indefinite, indistinct, uncertain, unclear, unfocused, vague.

word n 1 expression, name, term. 2 ▷ NEWS. 3 ▷ PROMISE. ● vb articulate, express, phrase. **word for word** ▷ VERBATIM.

wording n choice of words, diction, expression, language, phraseology, phrasing, style, terminology.

wordy adj chatty, diffuse, digressive, discursive, garrulous, long-winded, loquacious, pleonastic, prolix, rambling, repetitious, talkative, unstoppable, verbose, voluble, inf windy. Opp CONCISE.

work n 1 inf donkey-work, drudgery, effort, exertion,

worker *inf* fag, *inf* graft, *inf* grind,
industry, labour, *inf* plod, slav-
ery, *inf* slog, *inf* spadework,
strain, struggle, *inf* sweat, toil,
old use travail. **2** *work to be
done.* assignment, chore,
commission, duty, errand,
homework, housework, job,
mission, project, responsibility,
task, undertaking. **3** *regular
work.* business, calling, career,
employment, job, livelihood,
living, métier, occupation, post,
profession, situation, trade.
● *vb* **1** *inf* beaver away, be busy,
drudge, exert yourself, *inf* fag,
inf grind away, *inf* keep your
nose to the grindstone, labour,
make efforts, navvy, *inf* peg
away, *inf* plug away, *inf* potter
about, *inf* slave, *inf* slog away,
strain, strive, struggle, sweat,
toil, travail. **2** act, be effective,
function, go, operate, perform,
run, succeed, thrive. **3** *work
slaves hard.* drive, exploit,
utilize. **working** ▷ EMPLOYED,
OPERATIONAL. **work out**
▷ CALCULATE. **work up**
▷ DEVELOP, EXCITE.

worker *n* artisan, breadwinner,
coolie, craftsman, employee,
old use hand, labourer,
member of staff, navvy, operative, operator, peasant,
practitioner, servant, slave,
tradesman, wage-earner, working man, working woman,
workman.

workforce *n* employees, staff,
workers.

workmanship *n* art, artistry,
competence, craft, craftsmanship, expertise, handicraft,
handiwork, skill, technique.

workshop *n* factory, mill,
smithy, studio, workroom.

world *n* **1** earth, globe, planet.
2 area, circle, domain, field,
milieu, sphere.

worldly *adj* avaricious, covetous, earthly, fleshly, greedy,
human, material, materialistic,
mundane, physical, profane,
secular, selfish, temporal.
Opp SPIRITUAL.

worm *vb* crawl, creep, slither,
squirm, wriggle, writhe.

worn *adj* **1** frayed, moth-eaten,
old, ragged, *inf* scruffy, shabby,
tattered, *inf* tatty, thin, threadbare, worn-out. **2** ▷ WEARY.

worried *adj* afraid, agitated,
agonized, alarmed, anxious,
apprehensive, bothered,
concerned, distraught,
distressed, disturbed, edgy,
fearful, *inf* fraught, fretful,
guilt-ridden, insecure, nervous,
nervy, neurotic, obsessed (by),
on edge, overwrought,
perplexed, perturbed, solicitous, tense, troubled, uncertain,
uneasy, unhappy, upset, vexed.

worry *n* **1** agitation, anxiety,
apprehension, disquiet,
distress, fear, neurosis, perplexity, perturbation, tension,
unease, uneasiness. **2** affliction, annoyance, bother, burden,
care, concern, misgiving, problem, *plur* trials and tribulations, trouble, vexation.
● *vb* **1** agitate, annoy,
inf badger, bother, depress,
disquiet, distress, disturb, exercise, *inf* hassle, irritate, molest,
nag, perplex, perturb, pester,
plague, tease, threaten,
torment, trouble, upset, vex.
Opp REASSURE. **2** *worry about
money.* agonize, be anxious, be
worried, brood, exercise yourself, feel uneasy, fret.

worsen vb 1 aggravate, exacerbate, heighten, increase, intensify, make worse. 2 *his health worsened.* decline, degenerate, deteriorate, fail, get worse, *inf* go downhill, weaken. Opp IMPROVE.

worship n adoration, adulation, deification, devotion, glorification, homage, idolatry, love, praise, reverence, veneration. • vb admire, adore, adulate, be devoted to, deify, dote on, exalt, extol, glorify, hero-worship, idolize, kneel before, lionize, laud, look up to, love, magnify, pay homage to, praise, pray to, *inf* put on a pedestal, revere, reverence, venerate.

worth n benefit, cost, good, importance, merit, quality, significance, use, usefulness, utility, value. **be worth** be priced at, cost, have a value of.

worthless adj old use bootless, dispensable, disposable, frivolous, futile, *inf* good-for-nothing, hollow, insignificant, meaningless, meretricious, paltry, pointless, poor, *inf* rubbishy, *inf* trashy, trifling, trivial, trumpery, unimportant, unproductive, unprofitable, unusable, useless, vain, valueless. Opp WORTHWHILE.

worthwhile adj advantageous, beneficial, considerable, enriching, fruitful, fulfilling, gainful, gratifying, helpful, important, invaluable, meaningful, noticeable, productive, profitable, remunerative, rewarding, satisfying, significant, sizeable, substantial, useful, valuable. ▷ WORTHY. Opp WORTHLESS.

worthy adj admirable, commendable, creditable, decent, deserving, estimable, good, honest, honourable, laudable, meritorious, praiseworthy, reputable, respectable, worth supporting, worthwhile. Opp UNWORTHY.

wound n damage, hurt, injury, scar, trauma. □ amputation, bite, bruise, burn, contusion, cut, fracture, gash, graze, laceration, lesion, mutilation, puncture, scab, scald, scar, scratch, sore, sprain, stab, sting, strain, weal, welt. • vb cause pain to, damage, harm, hurt, injure, traumatize. □ amputate, bite, blow up, bruise, burn, claw, cut, fracture, gash, gore, graze, hit, impale, knife, lacerate, maim, make sore, mangle, maul, mutilate, scratch, shoot, sprain, strain, stab, sting, torture. Opp HEAL, MEND.

wrap n cape, cloak, mantle, poncho, shawl, stole. • vb bind, bundle up, cloak, cocoon, conceal, cover, do up, encase, enclose, enfold, enshroud, envelop, hide, insulate, lag, muffle, pack, package, shroud, surround, swaddle, swathe, wind.

wreathe vb adorn, decorate, encircle, festoon, intertwine, interweave, twist, weave.

wreck n 1 hulk, shipwreck. ▷ WRECKAGE. 2 *the wreck of all my hopes.* demolition, destruction, devastation, loss, obliteration, overthrow, ruin, termination, undoing. • vb 1 annihilate, break up, crumple, crush, dash to pieces, demolish, destroy, devastate, ruin, shatter, smash, spoil, *inf* write off. 2 *wreck a ship.* capsize, founder, ground, scuttle, sink, shipwreck.

wreckage *n* bits, debris, *inf* flotsam and jetsam, fragments, pieces, remains, rubble, ruins.

wrench *vb* force, jerk, lever, prize, pull, rip, strain, tear, tug, twist, wrest, wring, *inf* yank.

wrestle *vb* grapple, strive, struggle, tussle. ▷ FIGHT.

wretch *n* 1 beggar, down-and-out, miserable person, pauper, unfortunate. 2 ▷ VILLAIN.

wretched *adj* 1 dejected, depressed, dispirited, downhearted, hapless, melancholy, miserable, pathetic, pitiable, pitiful, unfortunate. ▷ SAD. 2 ▷ UNSATISFACTORY.

wriggle *vb* crawl, snake, squirm, twist, waggle, wiggle, wobble, worm, writhe, zigzag.

wring *vb* 1 clasp, compress, crush, grip, press, shake, squeeze, twist, wrench, wrest. 2 coerce, exact, extort, extract, force.

wrinkle *n* corrugation, crease, crinkle, *inf* crow's foot, dimple, fold, furrow, gather, line, pleat, pucker, ridge, ripple.
● *vb* corrugate, crease, crinkle, crumple, fold, furrow, gather, make wrinkles, pleat, pucker up, ridge, ripple, ruck up, rumple, screw up.

wrinkled *adj* corrugated, creased, crinkly, crumpled, furrowed, lined, pleated, ridged, ripply, rumpled, screwed up, shrivelled, undulating, wavy, wizened, wrinkly. *Opp* SMOOTH.

write *vb* be a writer, compile, compose, copy, correspond, doodle, draft, draw up, engrave, indite, inscribe, jot, note, pen, print, put in writing, record, scrawl, scribble, set down, take down, transcribe, type. **write off** ▷ CANCEL, DESTROY.

writer *n* 1 amanuensis, clerk, copyist, *derog* pen-pusher, scribe, secretary, typist. 2 author, bard, composer, *derog* hack, littérateur, wordsmith. □ biographer, columnist, contributor, copy-writer, correspondent, diarist, dramatist, essayist, freelancer, ghost-writer, journalist, leader-writer, librettist, novelist, playwright, poet, reporter, scriptwriter.

writhe *vb* coil, contort, jerk, squirm, struggle, thrash about, thresh about, twist, wriggle.

writing *n* 1 calligraphy, characters, copperplate, cuneiform, handwriting, hieroglyphics, inscription, italics, letters, longhand, notation, penmanship, printing, runes, scrawl, screed, scribble, script, shorthand. 2 authorship, composition, journalism. 3 hard copy, literature, manuscript, opus, printout, text, typescript, work. □ article, autobiography, belles-lettres, biography, comedy, copy-writing, correspondence, crime story, criticism, detective story, diary, dissertation, documentary, drama, editorial, epic, epistle, essay, fable, fairy-tale, fantasy, fiction, folk-tale, history, legal document, legend, letter, libretto, lyric, monograph, mystery, myth, newspaper column, non-fiction, novel, parable, parody, philosophy, play, poem, propaganda, prose, reportage, romance, saga, satire, science fiction, scientific writing, scriptwriting, SF, sketch, story, tale, thesis, thriller, tragedy, tragi-comedy, travel writing, treatise, trilogy,

TV script, verse, inf whodunit, yarn.

written adj documentary, inf in black and white, inscribed, in writing, set down, transcribed, typewritten. Opp SPOKEN.

wrong adj 1 base, blameworthy, corrupt, criminal, crooked, deceitful, dishonest, dishonourable, evil, felonious, illegal, illegitimate, illicit, immoral, iniquitous, irresponsible, mendacious, misleading, naughty, reprehensible, sinful, specious, unethical, unjustifiable, unlawful, unprincipled, unscrupulous, vicious, villainous, wicked, wrong-headed. **2** wrong answers. erroneous, fallacious, false, imprecise, improper, inaccurate, incorrect, inexact, misinformed, mistaken, unfounded, untrue. **3** a wrong decision. curious, ill-advised, ill-considered, ill-judged, impolitic, imprudent, injudicious, misguided, misjudged, unacceptable, unfair, unjust, unsound, unwise, wrongful. **4** go the wrong way. abnormal, contrary, inappropriate, incongruous, inconvenient, misleading, opposite, unconventional, undesirable, unhelpful, unsuitable, worst. **5** Something's wrong. amiss, broken down, defective, faulty, out of order, unusable. Opp RIGHT.
● vb abuse, be unfair to, cheat, damage, do an injustice to, harm, hurt, injure, malign, maltreat, misrepresent, mistreat, traduce, treat unfairly. **do wrong**
▷ MISBEHAVE.

wrongdoer n convict, criminal, crook, culprit, delinquent, evil-doer, law-breaker, malefactor, mischief-maker, miscreant, offender, sinner, transgressor.

wrongdoing n crime, delinquency, disobedience, evil, immorality, indiscipline, iniquity, malpractice, misbehaviour, mischief, naughtiness, offence, s¹ 1, sinfulness, wickedness.

wry adj 1 askew, aslant, awry, bent, contorted, crooked, deformed, distorted, lopsided, twisted, uneven. **2** a wry sense of humour. droll, dry, ironic, mocking, sardonic.

Y

yard n court, courtyard, enclosure, garden, inf quad, quadrangle.

yarn n 1 fibre, strand, thread. **2** account, anecdote, fiction, narrative, story, tale.

yawning adj gaping, open, wide.

yearly adj annual, perennial, regular.

yearn vb ache, feel desire, hanker, have a craving, hunger, itch, long, pine.
▷ WANT.

yellow adj □ chrome yellow, cream, gold, golden, orange, tawny.

yield n 1 crop, harvest, output, produce, product. **2** earnings, gain, income, interest, proceeds, profit, return, revenue. ● vb 1 acquiesce, agree, assent, bow, capitulate, inf cave in, cede, comply, concede, defer, give in, give up, give way, inf knuckle under, submit,

succumb, surrender, *inf* throw
in the towel, *inf* throw up the
sponge. **2** *yield interest.* bear,
earn, generate, pay out,
produce, provide, return,
supply. **yielding** ▷ FLEXIBLE,
SPONGY, SUBMISSIVE.

young *adj* **1** baby, early, growing, immature, new-born,
undeveloped, unfledged, young-
ish. **2** *young people.* adolescent,
juvenile, pubescent, teenage,
underage, youthful. **3** *young for
your age.* babyish, boyish,
callow, childish, girlish,
inf green, immature, inexperienced, infantile, juvenile, naïve,
puerile. ● *n* brood, family,
issue, litter, offspring, progeny.
young creatures bullock, calf,
chick, colt, cub, cygnet, duck-
ling, fawn, foal, gosling, heifer, kid, kitten,
lamb, leveret, nestling, pullet,
puppy, yearling. **young people**
adolescent, baby, boy,
derog brat, child, girl, infant,
juvenile, *inf* kid, lad, lass,
inf nipper, teenager, toddler,
derog urchin, youngster, youth.

youth *n* **1** adolescence, babyhood, boyhood, childhood, girlhood, growing up, immaturity,
infancy, minority, pubescence,
inf salad days, *inf* teens.
2 adolescent, boy, juvenile,
inf kid, *inf* lad, minor, stripling,
teenager, youngster.

youthful *adj* fresh, lively,
sprightly, vigorous, well-
preserved, young-looking.
▷ YOUNG.

Z

zany *adj* absurd, clownish,
crazy, eccentric, idiotic,
inf loony, *inf* mad, madcap,
playful, ridiculous, silly,
sl wacky.

zeal *n derog* bigotry, earnestness,
enthusiasm, fanaticism,
fervour, partisanship.

zealot *n* bigot, extremist, fanatic,
partisan, radical.

zealous *adj* conscientious, diligent, eager, earnest, enthusiastic, fanatical, fervent, keen,
militant, obsessive, partisan,
passionate. *Opp* APATHETIC.

zenith *n* acme, apex, apogee,
climax, height, highest point,
meridian, peak, pinnacle,
summit, top. *Opp* NADIR.

zero *n cricket* duck, *tennis* love,
naught, nil, nothing, nought,
sl zilch. **zero in on** ▷ AIM.

zest *n* appetite, eagerness,
energy, enjoyment, enthusiasm,
exuberance, hunger, interest,
liveliness, pleasure, thirst, zeal.

zigzag *adj* bendy, crooked, *inf* in
and out, indirect, meandering,
serpentine, twisting, winding.
● *vb* bend, curve, meander,
snake, tack, twist, wind.

zone *n* area, belt, district,
domain, locality, neighbourhood, province, quarter, region,
section, sector, sphere, territory, tract, vicinity.

zoo *n* menagerie, safari park,
zoological gardens.

zoom *vb* career, dart, dash,
hurry, hurtle, race, rush, shoot,
speed, *inf* whiz, *inf* zip. ▷ MOVE.